ACCLAIM FOR MARJORIE GARBER'S

Shakespeare After All

"A return to the times when the critic's primary function was as an enthusiast, to open up the glories of the written word for the reader."
—*The New York Times*

"A lifetime of learning has gone into the production of this massive volume. . . . Garber is sensitive to significant details in the language . . . and she gives cogent accounts of historical contexts."
—*The Boston Globe*

"Garber's is the most exhilarating seminar room you'll ever enter."
—*Newsweek*

"A delight. . . . Polished, thoughtful, eminently useful. . . . Not only a wonderful guide to the plays, but just as importantly, it's a guide to the reading of the plays. . . . Garber writes elegantly and insightfully. . . . The reader seeking an informed guide to each play simply cannot do better."
—*The Providence Journal*

"Impossibly full . . . engagingly written. . . . It fills you with gratitude on virtually every page. Here, in a book, is a Shakespearean course for our time."
—*The Buffalo News*

"An absolute joy. . . . Extremely lively and witty. . . . Remarkable. . . . Authoritative."
—*Tucson Citizen*

"Stimulating and informative."
—*The Charlotte Observer*

"Garber keeps her eye on the goal, to illuminate the experience of reading and seeing the plays, and achieves it with quiet efficiency."
—*San Jose Mercury News*

MARJORIE GARBER

Shakespeare After All

Marjorie Garber is William R. Kenan, Jr., Professor of English and American Literature and Language and chair of the Department of Visual and Environmental Studies at Harvard University. She lives in Cambridge and Nantucket, Massachusetts.

ALSO BY MARJORIE GARBER

A Manifesto for Literary Studies

Quotation Marks

Academic Instincts

Sex and Real Estate

Symptoms of Culture

Dog Love

Bisexuality and the Eroticism of Everyday Life

Vested Interests: Cross-Dressing and Cultural Anxiety

Shakespeare's Ghost Writers: Literature as Uncanny Causality

Coming of Age in Shakespeare

Dream in Shakespeare

Shakespeare After All

Shakespeare After All

MARJORIE GARBER

ANCHOR BOOKS
A Division of Random House, Inc.
New York

FIRST ANCHOR BOOKS EDITION, SEPTEMBER 2005

Grateful acknowledgment is made to Harcourt, Inc., for permission to reprint an excerpt from "Marina" from *Collected Poems 1909–1962* by T. S. Eliot. Copyright 1936 by Harcourt, Inc. Copyright © 1964, 1963 by T. S. Eliot.

Excerpt from "Little Gidding" from *Four Quartets* by T. S. Eliot. Copyright 1942 by T. S. Eliot and renewed 1970 by Esme Valerie Eliot. Reprinted by permission of Harcourt, Inc.

The Library of Congress has cataloged the Pantheon edition as follows:
Garber, Marjorie B.
Shakespeare after all / Marjorie Garber.
p. cm.
Includes bibliographical references and index.
1. Shakespeare, William, 1564–1616—Criticism and interpretation—
Handbooks, manuals, etc. I. Title.
PR2976.G368 2004
822.3'3—dc22
2004040063

Anchor ISBN: 0-385-72214-1

Author photograph © Beverly Hall
Book design by Robert C. Olsson

www.anchorbooks.com

Printed in the United States of America
10 9 8 7 6 5 4 3 2

For B. J., the onlie begetter

Indeed all the great Masters have understood that there cannot be great art without the little limited life of the fable, which is always the better the simpler it is, and the rich, far-wandering, many-imaged life of the self-seen world beyond it.

William Butler Yeats, *"Emotion of Multitude"*

CONTENTS

A NOTE ON THE TEXT

THERE ARE MANY excellent modern editions of Shakespeare's plays. In the Suggestions for Further Reading at the end of this book I list several of the best-known, most reliable, and most available recent editions, with the expectation that a reader of this book may already own a copy of the collected works of Shakespeare or individual editions of the plays. The act, scene, and line numbers cited in the chapters that follow refer to *The Norton Shakespeare* (1997), itself based on the text of *The Oxford Shakespeare* (1986), but readers who own or have access to other editions will be able to find the quoted passages without difficulty. Line numbers may vary slightly, since lines of prose will be of differing lengths depending upon the width of the printed page or column. For textual variants and alternative readings from Quarto or Folio texts, readers should consult the textual notes in any good modern edition. When citing the names of characters in the plays, I have occasionally departed from the choices made by the Norton editors, preferring, for example, the more familiar "Brabantio" to "Brabanzio" in *Othello*, "Gratiano" to "Graziano" in *The Merchant of Venice*, "Ancient" Pistol to "Ensign" Pistol in *Henry IV Part 2* and *Henry V*, and "Imogen" to "Innogen" in *Cymbeline*. I have also chosen to quote from the 1623 Folio edition of *King Lear* instead of the *Norton Shakespeare*'s conflated version. All biblical citations, unless noted otherwise, are from the 1599 edition of the Geneva Bible.

Although it is not possible to know with certainty the chronology of composition of the plays—or even, sometimes, of their performance—the sequence given here follows the order suggested by *The Norton Shakespeare* with the exception of a few minor changes. For the convenience of the general reader *Henry VI Part 1* is discussed before *Part 2* and *Part 3*, even though it was written after them. The Norton editors place *The Merry Wives of Windsor* between *Henry IV Part 1* and *Henry IV Part 2*, but I have elected, again for reasons of readerly convenience, to discuss the two history plays in adjacent chapters. In this case the plays in question—*Merry Wives* and *2 Henry IV*—are dated in the same years, so there is no significant disruption of chronology. With *Romeo and Juliet* and *A Midsummer Night's Dream*, two plays thought to have been written in the same time period, I have reversed the *Norton*'s order, choosing to discuss Shakespeare's love tragedy before moving on to his great comic send-up of "tragical" love. Likewise, I discuss *Cymbeline* before *The Winter's Tale*. Modern scholars differ about which of these two plays was written first; each was performed in 1611. But such changes are a matter of editorial discretion and do not affect the argument for a generally historical sequence. Readers should bear in mind that the dating of the plays is in many cases still highly speculative and controversial, and that it is therefore difficult to draw firm conclusions about Shakespeare's development as a playwright from this, or any, order of the plays. The presentation of plays in this volume follows the practice of the Norton, Oxford, and other recent editions in grouping the plays by approximate chronology rather than according to genres like comedy, history, tragedy, and romance, with the intent of allowing the reader to observe the use of images, staging, and language across genres in the course of Shakespeare's theatrical career.

Shakespeare After All

Introduction

EVERY AGE creates its own Shakespeare.

What is often described as the timelessness of Shakespeare, the transcendent qualities for which his plays have been praised around the world and across the centuries, is perhaps better understood as an uncanny timeliness, a capacity to speak directly to circumstances the playwright could not have anticipated or foreseen. Like a portrait whose eyes seem to follow you around the room, engaging your glance from every angle, the plays and their characters seem always to be "modern," always to be "us."

"He was not of an age, but for all time." This was the verdict of Shakespeare's great rival and admirer, the poet and playwright Ben Jonson, in a memorial poem affixed to the First Folio of Shakespeare's plays. "Thou art a monument without a tomb," wrote Jonson,

> And art alive still, while thy book doth live,
> And we have wits to read, and praise to give.

We might compare this passage to Shakespeare's own famous lines in Sonnet 18, the sonnet that begins "Shall I compare thee to a summer's day?" and ends:

> So long as men can breathe or eyes can see,
> So long lives this, and this gives life to thee.

The sonnets have indeed endured, and given life to the beloved addressee, but it is the sonnet that praises him, not the unnamed "fair youth" to whom the sonnet is written, that lives on in our eyes, ears, and memory.

Both "of an age" *and* "for all time," Shakespeare is the defining figure of the English Renaissance, and the most cited and quoted author of every era since. But if we create our own Shakespeare, it is at least as true that the Shakespeare we create is a Shakespeare that has, to a certain extent, created us. The world in which we live and think and philosophize is, to use Ralph Waldo Emerson's word, "Shakspearized."

"I have a smack of Hamlet myself, if I do say so," wrote Samuel Taylor Coleridge. Goethe thought so, too, and so did Sigmund Freud. So, indeed, did the actress Sarah Bernhardt, who, having played the role in a celebrated production in France in 1899, and again in London in 1901, declared that she could not imagine Hamlet as a man.

But perhaps *Hamlet,* a play that from the Romantic era on has been established as the premier Western performance of consciousness, is too obvious a case to make the point. The Macbeths have become emblems of ambition, Othello a figure for jealous love, Lear a paradigm of neglected old age and its unexpected nobilities, Cleopatra a pattern of erotic and powerful womanhood, Prospero in *The Tempest* a model of the artist as philosopher and ruler. Romeo and Juliet are ubiquitous examples of young love, its idealism and excess. But if Shakespeare seems to us in a surprising way so "modern," it's because in a sense his language and his characters have created a lexicon of modernity. This is a book devoted in part to exploring the remarkable omnipresence of Shakespeare in our lives.

King Lear as written and performed in its original historical context was concerned with pressing questions for the seventeenth century, like absolute monarchy, and royal succession and the obligations of vassals. For most citizens of the twenty-first century, "king" is an archaic title, as it emphatically was not for the subjects of James I, under whose patronage Shakespeare's company, the King's Men, performed and prospered. Mid-twentieth-century readers often translated "king" into "father," seeing the drama as one centered on the family rather than the realm. Lear's railing against the heavens has often been understood as existential. At various moments Lear became a sign of male power, of the pathos of aging, even of the end of an actor's career. "King Lear" is a cultural icon, cited by philosophers, legislators, and politicians, as well as literary scholars—and gerontologists and therapists. The character has a cultural life derived from, but also distinct from, the play.

The Merchant of Venice is another powerful example of the translatability of these plays. The first Shylock was a comic butt, who may have appeared in a red fright wig and a false nose, the standard signs of Jewishness on the Elizabethan stage. Shylock was played as a comic figure until the mid-eighteenth century, when the actor Charles Macklin transformed him into a villain. Only in the nineteenth century did Shylock become a sympathetic or a tragic figure, masterfully portrayed by Edmund Kean in a performance that impressed Romantic authors like Coleridge and William Hazlitt. (It was Coleridge who said that Kean had the gift of revealing Shakespeare by flashes of lightning.) The early twentieth century saw empathetic productions of the play in the Yiddish theater, as well as a monstrous Shylock performed in Weimar under the aegis of Nazi Germany. After the Holocaust an anti-Jewish portrayal of this figure seems almost unimaginable—which is not to say that it will not be attempted. The point is that the play has changed, along with the times. *The Merchant of Venice* itself has a history, a kind of cultural biography that has transformed it from its moment of origination. Although we can revisit and understand the context of production and of belief, from the sixteenth century and indeed from the sources that preceded Shakespeare, this play, like all the others, is a living, growing, changing work of art. The role it plays for contemporary readers, audiences, and cultural observers is to a certain extent a reflection of its own history.

The same is true with *Othello*. The question of Othello's particularity as a black man and a Moor has been balanced against a certain desire to see him as a figure of universal humanity. This tendency toward generalization was in part an homage to Shakespeare, seen as a portrayer of universal types, and also a liberal shift away from racial stigmatizing, an attempt to dissociate the play from any tinct of bias. Earlier eras saw all too vividly the hero's color, especially in places, like the United States, where race and inequality had for a long time been issues of national concern. In the later twentieth century, critics have emphasized the context of cultural oppression in the play, while others have wrestled with Othello's tendency to acquiesce with assumptions of his inferiority. Black actors like James Earl Jones and Laurence Fishburne have displaced the blackface portrayals of the past. Productions still sometimes depict the character as consumed with self-doubt, but the heroic Othello has returned to the stage and screen—an Othello often portrayed as culturally identified with blackness and with his titular role as "the Moor of Venice."

One more familiar example, that of *The Tempest,* may serve to reinforce this general observation about the changing and growing nature of the plays, and their place as cultural "shifters," expanding their meanings as they intersect with new audiences and new circumstances in the world. After years as the premier art fable of Shakespearean drama, *The Tempest,* the story of an artist/creator often movingly described as "Shakespeare's farewell to the stage" (although at least one more play would be written and staged by his company before what scholars think may have been his retirement to Stratford), *The Tempest* was reconsidered, in the later twentieth century, as a reflection upon English colonial explorations and "first encounter" narratives of the sixteenth and early seventeenth centuries. This reconsideration was framed in part by responses to colonial and postcolonial issues in the *twentieth* century, the century in which, and from which, critics and performers now regarded the play. Caliban's otherness was now celebrated as difference rather than as cultural immaturity. Prospero's famous concession, "This thing of darkness I / Acknowledge mine," is addressed apparently to Caliban, but—as we will see—the "thing of darkness" is also something Prospero encounters in his own mind and soul. It is important to underscore the fact that postcolonial readings did not render the earlier understandings and resonances of *The Tempest* obsolete. Rather, they augmented, added nuance, questioned verities, such as Prospero's wisdom and ideal mastery, and even toyed with the idea of reversals of power, giving Caliban and his co-conspirators an alternative voice in the play. Aimé Césaire's *Une Tempête* and Roberto Fernández Retamar's *Calibán* both give Shakespeare's *Tempest* full-fledged postcolonial rewritings. The hallmark of a complex work of art is that it can not only endure but also benefit from any number of such strong rereadings. This, indeed, is one appropriate instrumental test of what we have come to call "greatness" in art and literature.

But where did "Shakespeare" stand on these questions? As I will suggest throughout the chapters that follow, the brilliant formal capacities of drama are such that the playwright's voice is many voices. Shakespeare is Prospero, Caliban, Ariel, and the wondering Miranda. He is Othello, Desdemona and Iago, Shylock, Portia and Antonio. One of the tremendous achievements of these remarkable plays is the way one view will always answer another. Desdemona and Emilia debate women's virtue from the "ideal" and "realist" viewpoints. Neither is definitively right. Both are "Shakespeare." No sooner does Ulysses laud the universal value of "degree" and hierarchy than, in the next moment, he argues that the inferior Ajax be substituted for the incomparable Achilles. What is Shakespeare's own view of such political questions? The answer—which is not an answer—lies in his plays. Yet so powerful has been the cultural effect of these plays that readers, critics, actors, and audiences often seek to align their meanings with Shakespeare's biography.

In some eras, including our own, there has been a tendency, indeed a desire, to read the plays as indicators of Shakespeare's mood, life crises, and frame of mind. Thus Thomas Carlyle asked rhetorically, "[H]ow could a man delineate a Hamlet, a Coriolanus, a Macbeth . . . if his own heroic heart had never suffered?"[1] Certain passages in *Hamlet, King Lear,* and *Troilus and Cressida* were once taken as evidence of a certain "sex horror" on the part of the author, and were traced to his ambivalent relationship to his wife. The "last plays," including the sublimely beautiful *Winter's Tale* and *The Tempest*—not to mention *Pericles,* the most popular of Shakespeare's plays in his lifetime—were dismissed out of hand by certain early-twentieth-century commentators like Lytton Strachey as infallible indications of the sad decline of a once-great writer who turned to the genre of romance out of boredom. The political, cultural, and social views of our own era are likewise grafted onto our Shakespeare, who has been, or has become, a keen analyst of power and gender. In essence, and in effect, we cannot resist creating our own Shakespeare. Again, I want to insist that this is a sign of strength in both playwright and critic, not a condition to be deplored or seen through.

The conditions of the stage in Shakespeare's lifetime unquestionably shaped the kinds of plays and characters he produced. No women were permitted to perform on the English public stage. All the female roles in his plays were written for and performed by boy players, skilled adolescent apprentices with high voices that had not yet "cracked," or changed. And yet Shakespeare created classic female characters who have become models of speech and conduct across the centuries, from the "shrew" Katherine to the loving daughters Cordelia and Miranda to Juliet, the modern paradigm of romantic love and longing.

The many cross-dressed roles in the plays took advantage of this material and historical fact, allowing both maleness and femaleness to be bodied forth in performance, and leading, in subsequent centuries, to a particular admiration for the liveliness and initiative of these Shakespearean women. Rosalind, played by a boy actor, cross-dresses as the boy "Ganymede" to enter the Forest of Arden; Portia, played by a boy actor, cross-dresses as the young doctor of laws to enter the courtroom in Venice; Viola, played by a boy actor, cross-dresses as the young man "Cesario" in Illyria; Imogen, played by a boy actor, cross-dresses as the boy "Fidele" in the Welsh hills.

The theaters were closed after 1642 during the Puritan Revolution, and when they reopened, after the restoration of the monarchy with the accession of Charles II in 1660, actresses did appear in female roles. Thomas Coryate, an English traveler in Venice, reported in 1608 that he "saw women acte, a thing that I never saw before—though I have heard that it hath been sometimes used in London—, and they performed it with as good a grace, action, gesture, and whatsoever convenient for a Player, as ever I saw any masculine Actor."[2] Some traditionalists of the time decried the change, claiming that the boys had done a better job of playing women. Female identity on the stage had become—like kingliness, madness, and exoticism—an aesthetically produced effect. The actors were not themselves kings, madmen, Moors, or shepherds, but they were able to portray those archetypes convincingly. This was not a matter of identity but of performance. The advent of actresses, some of them celebrated for their powerful performances of Shakespearean roles, changed forever how female parts—and female dramatic characters—were interpreted and understood.

Certainly the social politics of an era have had an effect upon interpretation. Modern productions of *The Taming of the Shrew* often struggle to absolve Shakespeare of antifeminism, much as productions of *The Merchant of Venice* try to underscore his empathy for Shylock the Jew or productions of *Titus Andronicus* to find some nobility in the villainous Aaron the Moor. Yet the brilliance and capaciousness of Shakespeare's plays are such that almost always the "answer" to such social concerns is located right in the play. Iago would not be as powerful a character as he is if his words did not contain some painful and unwelcome "truth." Prospero's words do not always trump those of his "servants," Caliban and Ariel.

Shakespeare always presents both his ideas and his character types contrapuntally, offering a response and a qualification, another way of looking at things, within the play itself. Despite a concerted attempt to find it, there is no "Shakespearean" point of view, so that claims like "Shakespeare said" or "Shakespeare believed" or "Shakespeare tells us"—claims that sometimes seem to imply an authoritative and consistent philosophical consciousness—can always be exposed by looking at the context of the quotation. Shakespeare's plays do not have a single voice, a lyric "I," or a "focalized" character through whom the audience or reader is tacitly expected to interpret the play. Even in the extreme case of Hamlet's musings, or in the more general case of the dramatic soliloquy, a powerful Shakespearean medium (often, again, excerpted as if it were an embedded lyric poem, a performance piece), the audience is given extensive evidence *within the play* to judge and evaluate the truth claims and ethical assertions that are so eloquently set forth by these charismatic speakers. We should remember that some of the most effective soliloquies, both in Shakespeare and elsewhere in English Renaissance drama, are put in the mouths of, and at the service of, Machiavellian characters: Richard III, Iago, Edmund in *King Lear*. And what they say is seductive, sometimes persuasive, and usually effective, at least in the short term. Yet it is no more—or less—accurate to say that "Shakespeare's philosophy" is that of Edmund than it is to say that his philosophy is that of Hamlet.

THE STAGE AND THE PAGE

There has always been a productive tension between the idea of the play as a poem or a text and the idea of the play as a performance. Some portions of Shakespeare's plays are inaccessible to us because they are made up of spectacles or performances rather than words. Examples include the masque in *The Tempest;* the apparitions in *Macbeth;* the tilt, or challenge, in *Pericles;* the descended god Jupiter in *Cymbeline;* and music throughout the comedies, including the music that is the "food of love" in Orsino's opening speech in *Twelfth Night,* but that has, by the end of the speech, become "not so sweet now as it was before." Battle scenes, like those in the English history plays and in *Antony and Cleopatra,* are also moments of high visual interest and onstage action, important to the tenor and pace of the play, and easy to underestimate (or skip over entirely) if one reads the plays as literature rather than visualizing them as theater.

Since the texts (today we would say "scripts") of stage plays were not generally regarded as "literature," many of the first published versions of the plays are of uncertain authority. In these years before copyright, first introduced in England in 1709, authors did not control the printing of their plays. The printer or bookseller took the profit, and the author sometimes had little or no opportunity to review or affect what was published. The editors of the First Folio of Shakespeare make this very clear in their letter to the readers: "[W]here before you were abused with diverse stolen and surreptitious copies, maimed and deformed by the frauds and stealths of injurious impostors that exposed them: even those are now offered to your view cured, and perfect of their limbs, and . . . absolute in their numbers."

The image of the works of Shakespeare as no longer "maimed" but now "perfect of their limbs" draws an analogy between the body of the text and the human body. "Numbers" are verses, rhythms, and rhymes. Where previous versions had violated Shakespeare's meter and distorted his verse, the Folio will correct it, make it "absolute," or perfect. We should also note that this same letter "to the great variety of readers" made it quite clear that the First Folio was a commercial venture. The disparagement of earlier versions of the plays was conjoined with a direct invitation to buy the Folio, the "perfect" version, published, as the title page declared, "according to the true original copies":

> The fate of all books depends upon your capacities: and not of your heads alone, but of your purses. Well! It is now public, and you will stand for your privileges, we know: to read, and censure. Do it, but buy it first. That doth best commend a book, the stationer says. . . . Judge your sixpence worth, your shillings worth, your five shillings worth at a time, or higher, for you rise to the just rates, and welcome. But whatever you do, buy.

The plays in the First Folio were therefore prepared as works to be read, reread, and judged. "Read him, therefore; and again, and again," urged the editors.

Some of the earlier, "unauthorized" copies have their own liveliness, a freshness that offers a glimpse of the spirit of this emerging and transgressive early modern theater. A good example can be found in the much-maligned First Quarto version of one of Hamlet's most famous speeches:

> To be or not to be—I, there's the point,
> To Die, to sleep, is that all? I, all:
> No, to sleep, to dream, I, mary, there it goes,
> For in that dream of death, when we awake,
> And borne before an everlasting Judge,
> From whence no passenger ever returned,
> The undiscovered country, at whose sight
> The happy smile, and the accursed damned.
> But for this, the joyful hope of this,
> Who'd bear the scorns and flattery of the world,
> Scorned by the right rich, the rich cursed of the poor?
> The widow being oppressed, the orphan wronged,
> The taste of hunger, or a tyrant's reign,
> And thousand more calamities besides,
> To grunt and sweat under this weary life,
> When that he his full quietus make,
> With a bare bodkin, who would this endure,
> But for a hope of something after death?
> Which puzzles the brain, and doth confound the sense,

Which makes us rather bear those evils we have,
Than fly to others that we know not of.
I, that, O this conscience makes cowards of us all. . . .

                    Hamlet, *First Quarto, 3.1.60–81*

Compare this unfamiliar version to the one that has become canonical, the version, based upon the Folio text and the Second Quarto (Q2), that generations of poets, students, and actors have learned by heart:

To be, or not to be; that is the question:
Whether 'tis nobler in the mind to suffer
The slings and arrows of outrageous fortune,
Or to take arms against a sea of troubles,
And, by opposing, end them. To die, to sleep—
No more, and by a sleep to say we end
The heartache and the thousand natural shocks
That flesh is heir to—'tis a consummation
Devoutly to be wished. To die, to sleep.
To sleep, perchance to dream. Ay, there's the rub,
For in that sleep of death what dreams may come
When we have shuffled off this mortal coil
Must give us pause. There's the respect
That makes calamity of so long life,
For who would bear the whips and scorns of time,
Th'oppressor's wrong, the proud man's contumely,
The pangs of disprized love, the law's delay,
The insolence of office, and the spurns
That patient merit of th'unworthy takes,
When he himself might his quietus make
With a bare bodkin? Who would these fardels bear,
To grunt and sweat under a weary life,
But that the dread of something after death,
The undiscovered country from whose bourn
No traveller returns, puzzles the will,
And makes us rather bear those ills we have
Than fly to others that we know not of?
Thus conscience does make cowards of us all,
And thus the native hue of resolution
Is sicklied o'er with the pale cast of thought,
And enterprises of great pith and moment
With this regard their currents turn awry,
And lose the name of action. . . .

                    Hamlet, *First Folio, 3.1.58–90*

Undeniably, the poetry of the second passage is more reflective and more compelling. The "sea of troubles," the ruminative "To sleep, perchance to dream," the "undiscovered country from whose bourn / No traveller returns" (rather than "at whose sight / The happy smile, and the accursed damned")—who could think of doing without them? They are among the cornerstones of our culture. Yet *theatrically* these gorgeous philosophical digressions and rich metaphors slow down the action. The formal "who would," replacing the more colloquial "who'd," is a mark of the transition from spoken to written language. Late-twentieth-century and twenty-first-century directors, influenced in part by developments in the modern theater, have noted the playability of the First Quarto (2,160 lines) as contrasted with the much longer Second Quarto (3,732 lines) and First Folio (ca. 3,500 lines), and experimental productions based upon the First Quarto have been successful with audiences. Every production is an interpretation, and we are used to directors—both in theater and in films—rearranging scenes, shortening speeches, and conflating characters or cutting them altogether. This is part of what directors do as part of their own craft: "fidelity to the text" is balanced with what works on the stage. So it should not come as a surprise, or as a violation of essential verities, that stage directors should have found the First Quarto, in part because of its unfamiliarity, a source of theatrical invigoration.

The very centrality of Shakespeare to modern culture has led to a desire to identify and fix the "real" Shakespeare, both the man and the play-text. But the very nature of plays written for performance as well as the conditions of early modern printing and publication, at a time when the modern concept of copyright was in its nascent form, work against this understandable wish for authenticity. There are three reasonably authoritative versions of *Hamlet* (the First Quarto, Second Quarto, and Folio texts) and two versions of *King Lear,* a Quarto and a Folio text so different from each other that *The Norton Shakespeare,* following the editors of the Oxford edition, prints both. Readers have the opportunity to compare differing versions of speeches, the assignment of particular lines (who speaks the final lines, Edgar or Albany?), and whole sections of the plays that differ crucially from each other. The *King Lear* known to most mid-twentieth-century students and readers was in fact a "conflated" text, assembled by editors. That is to say, confronted with two differing versions of a word, a phrase, a speech, or a speech assignment, the editor chose the one that made the most sense or the one that struck him as the most "Shakespearean." Needless to say, this kind of decision was to a certain extent a self-fulfilling prophecy, creating an idea of "Shakespeare" through editorial decision making. The First Folio version of "To be, or not to be" will doubtless strike most readers and hearers as more "Shakespearean" than the First Quarto's "To be or not to be—I, there's the point." But each is in some way "authentic." And neither, strictly speaking, was written by Shakespeare.

The First Folio was produced by two of Shakespeare's fellow players, John

Heminge and Henry Condell, in 1623, seven years after Shakespeare's death. The plays, like all plays written for the public stage during this period, were conceived as theatrical rather than literary vehicles. Some were not published in any form in Shakespeare's lifetime: the quarto of *Othello,* for example, was not published until 1622, six years after the playwright's death and only a year before the First Folio, from which it differs in hundreds of ways, small and large, from words to passages to punctuation. Certainly, as we have noted, Shakespeare did not see any of his plays through the press in the way that a modern author might. The real process of "editing" Shakespeare's works did not take place until centuries later, with the work of the great eighteenth-century editors from Alexander Pope through Edmond Malone. This is why some Shakespeareans have come to say, in a kind of shorthand, that although he lived and wrote in the late sixteenth and early seventeenth centuries, Shakespeare could almost be called an eighteenth-century author. Many of the textual decisions made in the eighteenth century, where editors "corrected" what seemed to be Shakespearean infelicities or errors based upon their own literary taste, have come down to us today as part of the Shakespeare text. Some of the work of modern editors in the twenty-first century has been to disentangle the often inspired, occasionally idiosyncratic conjectures from the original if sometimes puzzling phrase-ology of the quartos published during Shakespeare's lifetime and the First Folio, printed under the supervision of men who knew him, acted in his plays, and may have collaborated in their production.

Editing practices have changed a great deal since the time of Shakespeare. As noted above, early modern play texts were not regarded in the period as "liter-ary" works of art. This is indeed why Ben Jonson was able to disconcert people by publishing his own plays in 1616 in folio format, with the word "works" on the title page. Plays were not "works"—that elevated term was reserved for seri-ous writing, like sermons and poems. Plays were more like potboilers or comics. Thomas Bodley, the founder of the Bodleian Library, the main research library at the University of Oxford, called them "riff-raff" and "baggage books," and ordained that no plays be shelved in his grand new space: even if "some little profit might be reaped (which God knows is very little) out of some of our play-books, the benefit thereof will nothing near countervail the harm that the scan-dal will bring into the library when it shall be given out that we stuff it full of baggage books. . . ."[3]

The late seventeenth and eighteenth centuries were a period in which Shake-speare, though indisputably "great," was also judged to be a writer wanting in taste, an unfortunate by-product of a barbarous age. His plays, remarkable though they were, could be "improved" by more sophisticated modern writers. Thus Nahum Tate's 1681 version of *King Lear* "improved" the ending by allow-ing Lear's daughter Cordelia to live and to marry Edgar. ("Divine Cordelia, all the gods can witness / How much thy love to Empire I prefer!" Edgar declares at the close.) If this seems idiosyncratic, it was also popular. Tate's was the only version of *Lear* performed well into the nineteenth century, even though it was constantly being worked and reworked by the actors who played the roles. Other plays underwent similar "improvement" in the Restoration period. *The Taming of the Shrew* became John Lacy's *Sauny the Scot* (1667); *Antony and Cleopatra* was transmuted into Dryden's *All for Love; or, The World Well Lost* (1678).

Samuel Johnson, another great eighteenth-century editor, wrote of the task of a "conjectural critic" that

> [o]ut of many readings possible, he must be able to select that which best suits with the state, opinion, and modes of language prevailing in every age, and with his author's particular cast of thought, and turn of expression. Such must be his knowledge, and such his taste. Conjectural criticism demands more than humanity possesses, and he that exercises it with most praise has very frequent need of indulgence.[4]

In other words, the conjectural or emendatory critic was required to make inspired guesses, inserting changes in Shakespeare's text to conform to his own taste and the taste of the age, replacing what the surviving quartos and folios said with what Shakespeare *should* have said—and, it was sometimes claimed, by what he had in fact said, or meant to say. The early-eighteenth-century editor Nicholas Rowe found in the 1685 Fourth Folio version of *The Comedy of Errors* a word he saw was clearly misspelled or misprinted: Lady Adriana, addressing the Duke, describes "Antipholus, my husband, / Whom I made Lord of me, and all I had, / (At your *impotent* Letter)" (5.1.138–140). Rowe recognized that "impotent" must be wrong, since in context Adriana would be explaining that she had taken a husband as a result of the Duke's impotent, or powerless, letters. Thus, realizing that "impotent letters" gave exactly the reverse sense from what must have been intended, Rowe neatly corrected this in his 1709 edition by changing "impotent" to "all-potent." The correct reading, "important letters" (i.e., letters full of import or of importuning), had to be found by going back to the First Folio, not to the Fourth. "Conjecture has all the joy and all the pride of invention, and he that has once started a happy change, is too much delighted to consider what objections may rise against it," observed Doctor Johnson.[5]

Two hundred years later, reputable twentieth-century editors were still defending this practice. "Sometimes an inspired guess gives us with absolute conviction of rightness what Shakespeare must have written, even though we rely on faith and not on concrete evidence," wrote Fredson Bowers in 1966. The attraction, and the lure, was a numinous sense of oneness with the greatest of writers, what seems like a kind of channeling. Thus, pointing to "the old critic Theobald" and his emendation of the "nonsense" phrase "a Table of green fields," in the story of Falstaff's death in *Henry V,* to "a babbl'd of green fields,"

Bowers suggested that Theobald had "what was surely a real meeting of minds with Shakespeare."[6]

Improvement, of course, was in the eye, or rather the ear, of the beholder. Even without conjectural editing or other acts of critical ingenuity, the editors had to select from among the versions offered by various alternative source texts, quarto or folio, with the intention of choosing the most felicitous or most mellifluous option. One celebrated example from *Hamlet* was the rendering of a key adjective in one of the play's most famous speeches, Hamlet's first soliloquy, in act I, scene 2:

> O that this too too _____ flesh would melt,
> Thaw, and resolve itself into a dew. . . .

The First and Second Quartos both give "sallied." The Folio gives "solid." Editors who do not like "solid" have emended "sallied" to "sullied." The modern reader thus has a choice of a word that seems to connote immutable physicality ("too too solid flesh") or a word that carries the sense of corruption, filth, or wear ("too too sullied flesh"). "Sullied," the preference of several modern editors, is not present in any of the original printed texts. Which word did Shakespeare write? Early modern spelling was far from regularized (Shakespeare's own name is spelled in a variety of ways in the period, from Shakespeare to Shakspere, Shaxspere, and Shaxberd). Even if we knew the answer to the question, that would be only one way of determining the preferred reading, since at this point both "solid" and, to a lesser extent, "sullied" have themselves become recognizable cultural phrases with a secondary "authority" born of long usage. To restore "sallied" would be "correct" if one wished to follow the quartos. But "too too sallied flesh" (perhaps flesh that had traveled too long, or gone out to fight too much, in the past?) would have to compete in the Shakespearean marketplace with "sullied" and the popular favorite, "solid." It is not that we have no authentic Shakespeare texts, but rather that we have several. From the beginning, "Shakespeare" was Shakespeares.

Eighteenth-century editors feuded with one another in print, often genially, occasionally acerbically. Like biblical commentary, Shakespeare editing was an additive process, in which rival experts expressed differing opinions by first summarizing the previous debate. After Othello kills Desdemona, Johnson comments: "I am glad that I have ended my revisal of this dreadful scene. It is not to be endured." He describes the death of Cordelia at the end of *King Lear* in very similar terms, commending the "improvement" of Nahum Tate's happier ending, in which, as we have noted, Cordelia lives to marry Edgar:

> In the present case the publick has decided. Cordelia, from the time of Tate, has always retired with victory and felicity. And, if my sensations could add any thing to the general suffrage, I might relate, that I was many

years ago so shocked by Cordelia's death, that I know not whether I ever endured to read again the last scenes of the play till I undertook to revise them as editor.[7]

Johnson saw the plays as concerned above all with ethical behavior. The eloquent 1765 "Preface" to his edition of the plays declared, "Nothing can please many, and please long, but just representations of general nature," and asserted with unparalleled lucid grace that

> Shakespeare is above all writers, at least above all modern writers, the poet of nature; the poet that holds up to his readers a faithful mirrour of manners and of life. His characters are not modified by the customs of particular places . . . by the peculiarities of studies or professions . . . or by the accidents of temporary fashions or temporary opinions; they are the genuine progeny of common humanity, such as the world will always supply, and observation will always find. . . . In the writings of other poets a character is too often an individual; in those of Shakespeare it is commonly a species.[8]

For this reason he thought that Shakespeare's "real power is not shewn in the splendour of particular passages, but by the progress of his fable, and the tenour of his dialogue." It would be an error in judgment to try "to recommend him by select quotations."[9]

But this was not the universal view. The poet Alexander Pope, an early Shakespeare editor whose edition of the plays had appeared almost forty years before Johnson's, had marked the "beauties" of Shakespeare so that readers could find them easily. "Some of the most shining passages are distinguish'd by commas in the margin," he explained in his preface, "and where the beauty lay not in particulars but in the whole, a star is prefix'd to the scene."[10] This practice, of listing "beauties" and "faults," was a common feature of eighteenth-century criticism, and it survives in our modern books of quotations. When applied, as by Pope, to Shakespeare, the listing of "beauties" contributed to a split between regarding the plays as stage vehicles and as poems.

The Reverend William Dodd's popular collection, *The Beauties of Shakespeare: regularly selected from each play, with a general index, digesting them under proper heads,* was published in 1752 and was still available, in pocket-book form, in the early twentieth century. Dodd dispensed with such niceties as the speaker of the lines and the act, scene, and line numbers by which the passage could be found. Instead he organized his book by play, and under each play by heading. The section on *All's Well That Ends Well*—the first in the book, since the order was alphabetical rather than chronological—thus contained selections on "Cowardice," "Honour due to Personal Virtue only not to Birth," "Advice to Young Women," "Life Chequered," and "Excuse for Unreasonable Dislike," among others. Jaques' celebrated set piece in *As You Like It* was easily findable under the title it still carries informally today, "The Seven Ages." The better-known plays were organized more directly with regard to plot—"Lady Percy's Pathetic Speech to Her Husband," "Prince Henry's Modest Defence of Himself," "Lear on the Ingratitude of His Daughters"—so that the speaker and even the context were restored, and major characters like Lear, Antony, and Hamlet could be found in the index among the moral themes. But the focus of the volume, and of its index ("War, miseries of"; "Wisdom, superior to fortune"; "Women, frailty of"), made it clear that this tiny forerunner of *Bartlett's Familiar Quotations* offered the reader, as its compiler explained in his preface, "so large a fund for observation, and so much excellent and refined morality, that no one would have wanted it longer." Dodd, unfortunately, did not profit as fully as perhaps he might have done from this moral compendium of Shakespearean wisdom. Employed as a tutor to the son of Lord Chesterfield, he entertained lavishly and, finding himself in difficulties, rashly forged his patron's signature to a check. Although Chesterfield refused to prosecute, the Lord Mayor of London sent the case to court, and Dodd was found guilty and sentenced to be hanged.

Despite the unhappy end of the Reverend Mr. Dodd, the vogue for "beauties" of Shakespeare flourished, and pointed in two directions: toward Shakespeare as poet, and toward Shakespeare as moral arbiter and guide. Both were in some tension with the idea of Shakespeare as playwright, actor, and man of the theater.

Still, throughout this period, Shakespeare remained a favorite of audiences, and of theater companies. It was the actor David Garrick, celebrated for his performances as Richard III, Macbeth, and Hamlet, who masterminded the Shakespeare Jubilee of 1769—and posed for the statue of Shakespeare. Yet the Jubilee, a three-day festival that in essence re-created Stratford-upon-Avon as "the birthplace of Shakespeare," was a cultural event (as it happens, a failed one) rather than a theatrical venue; the planned activities, many of them spoiled by rain, included pageants, parades, fireworks, and souvenirs celebrating the playwright rather than the plays. On the London stage, and increasingly throughout Europe and America, major actors from Garrick to Kean and Henry Irving produced and starred in versions of the plays. These performances, too, were often regarded as moral and exemplary, as well as interpretative. Poets continued to attend productions (Keats greatly admired Kean), but the divide between page and stage, between the sayable and the playable, continued to widen.

At the beginning of the nineteenth century a Romantic critic like Hazlitt could contend without hesitation that the plays were spoiled by being performed. Romantic writers from Coleridge to Keats engaged with Shakespeare's plays most directly as a mode of poetry. Coleridge, one of the greatest Shakespeare critics of his own or any era, spoke of Shakespeare largely as a "poet," and addressed his remarks to "the readers of Shakespeare." In a series of highly successful lectures for general audiences, he contended that "Shakespeare's characters, from Othello and Macbeth down to Dogberry and the Grave-digger, may be termed ideal realities. They are not the things themselves so much as abstracts of the things which a great mind takes into itself and then naturalizes them to his own conception."[11] Coleridge saw one of the poet's greatest talents as his ability to move beyond the topical, and beyond reflections on historical personages. "In the plays of Shakespeare every man sees himself, without knowing that he does so."[12]

Likewise, although Keats took pleasure in the theater, published reviews, and at one time aspired to be a playwright, his relationship to Shakespeare, expressed in his letters as well as his own poems, was primarily a relation of poet to poet. "Shakespeare led a life of Allegory; his works are the comments on it," he wrote in a letter to his brother and sister-in-law, George and Georgiana Keats.[13] He longed to know in what position Shakespeare sat when he began "To be, or not to be." In fact, whether cited, quoted, or used as a model of the poetic life, Shakespeare appears very frequently in Keats's letters, never more powerfully than in his celebrated notion of negative capability, in which he described his sudden realization, after a debate with a very definite-minded friend, of the essential quality "to form a Man of Achievement especially in Literature and which Shakespeare possessed so enormously—I mean *Negative Capability,* that is when man is capable of being in uncertainties, Mysteries, doubts without any irritable reaching after fact and reason."[14] A poet, especially a "great poet," needs to leave his mind open to ideas and to conflicting realities, and the preeminent model for this was Shakespeare. "The poetical Character" avoids the "egotistical sublime," Keats wrote in another letter. "It has no character. . . . It has as much delight in conceiving an Iago as an Imogen."[15] Iago is here imagined as the arch-villain. Imogen is the heroine of *Cymbeline,* a great favorite of nineteenth-century audiences. This viewpoint is of a piece with Keats's claim that "Shakespeare led a life of Allegory." The plays do not reflect the personal opinions, or the moral or political attitudes, of their author. They are *philosophical,* but they are not necessarily evidence of *Shakespeare's* philosophy. Every character, from Iago to that other great nineteenth-century favorite, Dogberry, is inhabited by the playwright and finds a persona and a voice.

Shakespeare criticism, like all critical interpretation, is, to a certain extent, inevitably contrapuntal. Ideas develop as commentary and argument. Thus, for example, a claim that the plays should be valued for their ethical and moral exemplarity begets a counterclaim that the plays are best regarded as close observations of early modern courts, spy networks, gender relations, and theatrical practice. An interest in historical context will arise to try to qualify some of the universal or transhistorical claims about what is typically, uniquely, or quintessentially human. A study of the emotions or the passions as they were understood in the sixteenth century will disclose something surprising about a play that has become assimilated to modern notions about "human nature."

In the early twentieth century, the focus by influential critics like A. C.

Bradley on "heroes" and Shakespearean tragedy made tacit claims for the pre-eminence of plays like *Hamlet, Othello, Lear,* and *Macbeth,* plays that were not necessarily the most highly valued in Shakespeare's own time or since. The universalizing of these tragic heroes—whose soliloquies produced a sense of interior consciousness rather like Romantic odes and modern lyric poems—inevitably led to a reaction that insisted upon their cultural specificity, upon categories of identity like race and class, gender, ethnicity and religion. Through this lens, as we have seen, Othello's pride and anxiety about race and culture took precedence over his undifferentiated humanness; Shylock's difference from the Christian Venetians was again stressed in critical interpretation and in perfor-mance. Gertrude and Ophelia emerged as major consciousnesses within *Hamlet,* offering other voices and other perspectives to balance the centrality of the title role. In a modern world where "colonialism" became the shorthand name for both sixteenth-century and nineteenth- and twentieth-century political prac-tices, Caliban, long viewed as an allegorical figure ("This thing of darkness I / Acknowledge mine"), seemed to possess, as well, a distinctly nonallegorical political reality. Just as it became possible to imagine that previously laughable impossibility, "*Hamlet* without the prince," so it became possible to see Caliban as a complex, nuanced figure full of pathos, rage, and untapped power.

Shakespeare's plays are living works of art. Their meanings grow and change as they encounter vivid critical and theatrical imaginations. When the great Victorian actor Henry Irving died, the *Times* of London wrote glowingly about his interpretations of Shakespearean characters from Hamlet to Shylock and Coriolanus, many of which were "hotly" debated in the period. Irving's Mac-beth, the paper reported, had been especially controversial: "It seems a little sur-prising now, in a generation which accepts Macbeth as a poet, a 'man of letters manqué,' that such fierce storms should have been raised by the view that he was a moral coward."[16] The idea of Macbeth as a "man of letters manqué" would perhaps surprise some twenty-first-century audiences. Peter Brook's landmark production of *A Midsummer Night's Dream* at the Royal Shakespeare Theatre in 1970 transformed the play, taking what had been a vehicle for gauzy sets and lambent lighting and transforming it into a white space with toys and a trapeze. But before him, Max Reinhardt in Germany had sensed something else about the *Dream,* something dark and dangerous. When Reinhardt came to Hollywood in the years before World War II, he made a film of *A Midsummer Night's Dream,* with Mickey Rooney as Puck and Joe E. Brown as Flute, that told another story about the play. With the advent of film versions, the multi-plicity of interpretations is something every spectator expects. Olivier's *Hamlet,* Kenneth Branagh's *Hamlet,* Franco Zeffirelli and Mel Gibson's *Hamlet* could not be more different, but they are all "Shakespeare's" *Hamlet* (although the Zeffirelli production starring Gibson displayed the name of the director in print larger than that of the playwright). Film versions of *Romeo and Juliet, Much Ado About Nothing,* and *Twelfth Night* are seen by more spectators in an evening than some of Shakespeare's plays were during his lifetime.

If productions have changed readings, criticism and theory have also influenced productions. The 1921 silent film of *Hamlet,* with Danish actress Asta Nielsen in the title role, was based upon the writings of Victorian critic E. P. Vining. Laurence Olivier's *Hamlet,* emphasizing the passionate relationship between Hamlet and his mother, and declaring itself the "tragedy of a man who could not make up his mind," was strongly inflected by the work of Sigmund Freud. Postcolonial readings of *The Tempest* helped shape a number of important productions in the 1990s, while a roster of adaptations, from Bertolt Brecht's *Coriolanus* and Aimé Césaire's *Une Tempête* to films like *O* and *Scotland, PA,* have stretched the boundaries of "Shakespearean" drama. The strength of the plays, the evidence of what we call their "greatness," is their capacity to be reinterpreted, reread, and performed anew in every generation.

BIOGRAPHY AND AUTHORSHIP

William Shakespeare was born in 1564 and died in 1616. His birth date is said to have been April 23—which is also, as it happens, the date of his death, and is, in addition, Saint George's Day, the holiday of England's patron saint. This detail alone gives some idea of the mythic status that Shakespeare seems to have achieved, or which has developed around him. He was brought up in the market town of Stratford-upon-Avon, where his father, John Shakespeare, was a glover, a wool merchant, and the bailiff, or mayor, of the town. His mother's name was Mary Arden. William was one of eight children. Several of his siblings died in childhood, a common occurrence in the period. He was very probably educated at the Stratford grammar school, where he seems to have gotten a good classical education, centering on the study of Latin texts, like Ovid's *Metamorphoses,* Virgil's *Aeneid,* and the plays of Plautus. In his memorial poem for Shakespeare in the First Folio, Ben Jonson says he had "small Latin and less Greek," but this may tell us more about the learned Jonson than it does about Shakespeare.

Most of Shakespeare's plays have sources, although what he borrowed, he transformed. As Walter Savage Landor wrote—in a passage that Emerson quoted in his own essay on quotation—Shakespeare "was more original than his originals. He breathed upon dead bodies and brought them into life."[17] We should bear in mind that the notion of "originality" in this period was quite different from the modern sense of something never seen before, a sense that gained ascendancy in the eighteenth century in works like Edward Young's *Conjectures on Original Composition* (1759). In the Renaissance, the notion of *inventio,* with its etymological root in "finding," referred to the discovery, by search or endeavor, of ideas or images that could be used in rhetoric. Shakespeare's plays draw on classical mythology, historical chronicle (Plutarch's *Parallel Lives* in the 1579 translation by Sir Thomas North; English and Scottish chronicles by Edward Hall, John Stow, and Raphael Holinshed), the writings of his contemporaries (including Elizabethan novels, plays by other authors, and verse), and the Bible. Shakespeare's Bible was usually the 1560 translation known as the Geneva Bible, a version so popular that it went through 122 editions between 1560 and 1611. The Geneva Bible was issued in quarto form, and was thus easy to consult. It was also the first Bible to be fully numbered by chapter and verse. The other Bible Shakespeare is thought perhaps to have used is the Bishops' Bible, published in folio in 1568, but this version never attained the popularity of the Geneva Bible. The so-called King James Bible, commissioned by the monarch, was produced by a team of scholars in 1611, too late to have been Shakespeare's reference text in his earlier plays, although its poetry, and its ubiquity, had a profound effect upon virtually all subsequent English authors.

At the age of eighteen, Will Shakespeare married Anne Hathaway, who was twenty-six years old and already pregnant with their first child, Susanna. This, too, is a not-unusual fact about sixteenth-century life. The themes of pregnancy before marriage, and of precontract, or marriages without official sanction of clergy, recur in a number of his plays, principally in *Measure for Measure.* Shakespeare and his wife also had twins, a boy and a girl, Hamnet and Judith; Hamnet died young, at the age of eleven, in 1596, after Shakespeare had moved to London to pursue his career. Shakespeare was an actor as well as a poet and playwright. He was a shareholder in one of the most successful—and well-managed—companies of his day, working collaboratively with other actors, two of whom, John Heminge and Henry Condell, would survive him and compile the First Folio of his works.

The fact that Shakespeare lived in London for so much of his life, and seems to have moved back to Stratford only at the end, has occasioned a good deal of speculation about his marriage. In his will he left his wife his "second-best bed," a legacy that may or may not suggest a lack of affection. The curiosity of scholars on this point, which has extended, for example, to an argument that the "second-best" bed was the marital bed, the first-best being reserved for guests, is an indication of how very much every piece of Shakespeare history and legend has been mined for what it might reveal about Shakespeare the man. The will emerges as a significant document in the relative absence of other personal evidence. Although there is as much of a "paper trail" for Shakespeare as for many other early modern writers, his subsequent celebrity has been such that readers have sought, and demanded, more.

We do not have personal letters, diaries, or commonplace books written by Shakespeare. This, combined with the sheer volume of the plays and their magnificent language, has led some people to speculate that he could not be their author. Surely, they say, it must have been somebody of a higher social status (like the Earl of Oxford) or a lawyer (like Sir Francis Bacon) or someone who knew the court (Queen Elizabeth herself has been suggested). This so-called Authorship Controversy, a minor wrinkle in Shakespeare studies, has been a persistent object of fascination, in part because it suggests that we might like the plays to transcend individual authorship entirely; it seems we want to make

Shakespeare less like a man, and more like a kind of god. As one early commentator on the controversy asked, how could one person know so many *words*?[18]

Shakespeare has been credited with the invention of thousands of new words in English. In practice many of these new words are actually new grammatical uses for existing words—nouns made into verbs and verbs made into nouns. And of course the survival of the plays, and the celebrity of their author, made Shakespeare the apparent inventor, whether or not he was the real one. When in the late nineteenth century the editors of the new *Oxford English Dictionary* put out a call for "men of letters" to assist them in their task of finding the histories of words, volunteers combed the books on their shelves and in their local libraries, often identifying Shakespeare as the point of origin. Since the dictionary, which was to be organized "on historical principles," was intended to "make a dictionary worthy of the English language," the historical trail often led back to Shakespeare, even in those cases when the scholars privately acknowledged that a less well known author had in fact used a given word first.

The supposed mystery of Shakespeare's life and work—a mystery that was not, as we have noted, more mysterious than many other early modern lives—became itself part of the romance of Shakespeare's reputation. Some writers preferred the absence of detail, which allowed both for speculation and for idealization. "Is it not strange," wrote Ralph Waldo Emerson, "that the transcendent men, Homer, Plato, Shakespeare, confessedly unrivalled, should have questions of identity and of genuineness raised respecting their writings?" Novelist Charles Dickens was delighted at the absence of any Shakespeare biography to speak of. "The life of Shakespeare is a fine mystery," he wrote, "and I tremble every day lest something should turn up."[19] Many other writers have likewise preferred to keep the mystery alive, and doing so has precisely the effect shrewdly observed by Emerson: it renders Shakespeare, or "Shakespeare," transcendent. Rather than being a mere writer with a biography that can be mined for clues to the meaning of his work, Shakespeare remains apart. The spirit of this will (or Will) not-to-know is embodied in Matthew Arnold's sonnet "Shakespeare":

> Others abide our question. Thou art free.
> We ask and ask: Thou smilest and art still,
> Out-topping knowledge. For the loftiest hill
> Who to the stars uncrowns his majesty,
> Planting his steadfast footsteps in the sea,
> Making the heaven of heavens his dwelling-place,
> Spares but the cloudy border of his base
> To the foil'd searching of mortality;
> And thou, who didst the stars and sunbeams know,
> Self-school'd, self-scann'd, self-honour'd, self-secure,

Didst walk on earth unguess'd at. Better so!
All pains the immortal spirit must endure,
   All weakness which impairs, all griefs that bow
   Find their sole speech in that victorious brow.[20]

Despite the persistence of the Authorship Controversy, there seems no significant reason to doubt that Shakespeare of Stratford was the author of the plays. The whole concept of authorship needs to be understood differently in a sixteenth- and seventeenth-century context. Plays were written collaboratively, under pressure of time and the stage, somewhat like film and television scripts today, and there was as yet no system of copyright. As we have said before, whoever published a work was its owner.

THE THEATER IN RENAISSANCE ENGLAND

Residents of early modern England who had never been to "the theater"—that is, to one of the new playhouses being built on the bankside of the Thames—had nevertheless almost surely experienced "theater" in their everyday life. They might be apprentices; or countesses; or courtesans; or great landowners; or bricklayers, like the playwright Ben Jonson; or glovers, like Shakespeare's father; or apple-sellers; or fishwives; or servants; or actors; or knights; or aldermen and their wives. It would not matter what station in life they held (in this time period it would have been called "status" or "rank," "sort" or "kind," rather than social class). All of them—men, women, children, nobles, citizens, laborers—had lived, and were living, in a world rich in theatricality, a world of cultural performance.

They might have observed the Lord Mayor of London in his fur gown and his chain of office parading through the streets. Or they might have seen street jugglers, or mountebanks. Possibly they had been to a cockfight, or a bearbaiting at the Bear Garden. They might well have witnessed a public execution, one of the favorite public spectacles of the age, held on a scaffold—the same word used for the stage. Almost certainly they had been to church—either to the officially sanctioned Church of England, founded by King Henry VIII when he broke away from the Roman Catholic Church over questions of divorce and royal supremacy, or to one of the other Protestant churches then spreading through Europe in the wake of the Reformation, or even to a Catholic service. Despite the Reformation, there remained many Catholics in England, though they were not permitted to hold public office and were sometimes regarded as agents of the Pope. Quite likely, early modern Londoners had seen Queen Elizabeth—if it was before 1603—on one of her progresses, or her successor, King James, enter the city of London amid pageantry, accompanied by throngs of followers, upon his accession to the throne. In short, theatricality—in the public world, the church, the monarchy—would have been all around them, in the very conditions of their lives.

Public playhouses or amphitheaters had been built on the outskirts of the city of London—in the "suburbs," as they were called, or the "Liberties." As its name implies, this was a kind of threshold place, not technically part of the city of London; it was either to the north in the suburbs of Middlesex, beyond the city walls, or to the south, on the bankside of the River Thames, in the area called Southwark—the place where the Globe theater, Shakespeare's theater, was built in 1599. Londoners would have had to travel to get there, by walking across a bridge or, if they could afford it, taking a ferry across the river.

Why were these playhouses—the Rose, the Fortune, the Curtain, the Swan, the Globe—on the outskirts of the city? Because neither the city fathers nor certain religious elements in society wanted them inside. Theater and stage plays were regarded as dangerous, partly because they were so seductive, so exciting, so mesmerizing. But the Lord Mayor of London and the other city officials were also worried about things like the spread of plague—bubonic plague, the incredible scourge of Europe, which killed as much as a sixth of the city population in 1603.

Because the plague was so rampant—and Shakespeare makes constant mention of it, from an early play like *Romeo and Juliet* to a late play like *The Winter's Tale*—large gatherings of people were regarded as occasions for the spread of infection. A theatergoer could wear a mask, or could carry a nosegay of flowers, since bad odors were thought to spread the plague. But when a certain number of deaths from plague were recorded in the city—by statute, under King James, this meant more than thirty in any given week—the theaters were closed down, and the actors and company had to take the show on the road.

Plague, then, was one kind of threat that the theater presented. Another kind of threat that concerned civic officials—and royal ones, too—was the possibility of sedition: critical, subversive references to affairs of state, or to living persons in high places—Queen Elizabeth or, in the plays, King James, or officials from other countries like Holland, France, or Spain. So the theaters could be "infectious" in metaphorical as well as literal ways, spreading new and dangerous ideas, bringing together large numbers of people. These playhouses held thousands of spectators—by modern estimates, Shakespeare's Globe would have held three thousand. An official called the Master of the Revels reviewed in advance any play that spectators might see on the public stage, and suggested necessary cuts or revisions.

Where there were large gatherings of people, there could be riots—so, at least, thought the authorities, the Privy Council and the monarch. And since plays were put on in the afternoon, they were an incitement to idleness. Apprentices and others might be tempted to skip work in order to go to the theater. For all these reasons, civic authorities were suspicious and watchful.

City officials did not like the players and playhouses, and neither did the Puritans, who saw all acting as a kind of falsehood or pretense. Puritans saw the onstage phenomenon of common men playing the parts of kings and princes as a kind of class-jumping, dangerous to social stability. They saw the wearing of rich costumes—sometimes the actual cast-off clothing of real nobles and royals—as a sign of excess and ambition. They saw theatricality, pageantry, and ritual itself as things to be associated with "popery," with the Catholic Church.

Puritan observers had another crucial objection as well. They saw the fact that on the public stage the parts of women were played by boys, by boy actors, as a sign of depravity, temptation, and sin. The Book of Deuteronomy had said that men should not wear the clothing of women, or women the clothing of men: "The woman shall not wear that which pertaineth unto a man, neither shall a man put on a woman's garments: for all that do so *are* abomination unto the LORD thy God" (Deuteronomy 22:5). Yet in these acting companies, boys, acting apprentices, played all the women's parts.

It was only in England that this was the case. On the Italian stage, for example, women played women's parts, and English travelers to Italy sometimes came back marveling that women could play these parts as well as the boys did, as we have seen in the case of Thomas Coryate. Puritan critics, often called "antitheatricalists," saw the presence of these boy players in their gowns and masks and fans as not only wicked but also disturbing and seductive to both male and female spectators. The worry, on the part of both secular and religious critics, was that theatrical representation would cross a boundary—that theater, supposedly mere fantasy, would invade and influence life: political life, social life, erotic life, the life of the mind. This, as city planners ever since Plato's *Republic* had warned, was its irresistible fascination, as well as its danger.

The great new public institution of the theater, then, the birthplace of the greatest drama in the English-speaking world, was located on the margins of the city, and on the margins of society. Fortunately for Shakespeare and his colleagues, both Queen Elizabeth and King James had an interest in the theater. Each of them reveled in theatricality. They understood perfectly the power of theatrical display—after all, *their* costumes and entourages were part of the theatricalization of power. "We princes," said Queen Elizabeth, "are set on stages, in the sight and view of all the world duly observed."[21] King James, in his book on kingship, *Basilicon Doron,* wrote, "a King is as one set on a stage, whose smallest actions and gestures, all the people gazingly doe behold."[22]

Elizabeth, the daughter of Henry VIII, remained unmarried, the perpetual object of adoration and courtship from English noblemen and from foreign royalty, and, increasingly, the focus of anxiety as she aged past childbearing, with no successor in view. King James, who acceded to the throne after Elizabeth's death in 1603, had been crowned James VI of Scotland before he became James I of England. As Elizabeth's cousin and the son of her hated rival, Mary, Queen of Scots (whom Elizabeth had had beheaded), he prudently sought the favor of the childless "Virgin Queen" Elizabeth. James had a wife, and children, and male favorites, all of whom had to be maintained at considerable cost to the state. He took great pleasure in dancing and in masques and extravagant entertainments. He also understood that he was the exemplary viewer, the one for whose kingly gaze all spectacles were performed. Upon his accession to the throne, King James became the patron of Shakespeare's company, formerly known as the Lord Chamberlain's Men, now the King's Men. A scholar who commissioned the "King James" translation of the Bible, he was an expert on witchcraft and was the author of a book on demonology; thus it is not entirely surprising to find Shakespeare writing, in the early years of James's reign, a play about witches and cauldrons and apparitions.

Actors risked being apprehended as "vagabonds" or "masterless men" because they often traveled from town to town, from great house to great house, performing their plays. In the late sixteenth century and even into the seventeeth, when plague closed the playhouses, they necessarily traveled as well. So the new acting companies came under the protection of noble and royal personages, becoming technically the "servants" or "men" of a patron. The companies of the period were thus typically called by the name or title of the patron: "Lord Strange's Men" or "the Lord Admiral's Men."

Shakespeare's company had begun as the Lord Chamberlain's Men, and then became the King's Men. Their chief rival, the company for which in the 1580s and 1590s Christopher Marlowe wrote most of his plays, was the Lord Admiral's Men. These were companies of adult male actors, some of whom, like Shakespeare himself, owned a "share" of the company and thus were called "sharers." The company was a joint-stock company, like those founded to explore the colonies. It also included apprentices and hired actors for smaller parts, about fifteen players in all, with many parts doubled in performance, and extra players added when needed for a larger cast.

The actors performed in repertory, regularly learning new scripts; playing in the afternoons, they presented several different plays a week. The same actors were used, therefore, over and over again, and the parts were tailored to them. Polonius confirms to Hamlet that he himself had once played in the university, a common place for plays in the Elizabethan period. "I did enact Julius Caesar," he boasts. "I was killed i'th' Capitol. / Brutus killed me" (3.2.93–94). To a contemporary audience, this would have been a metatheatrical in-joke. Shakespeare's *Julius Caesar* was written and performed immediately prior to *Hamlet,* and the actor who played Polonius here alludes slyly to his role in that earlier tragedy. The joke becomes all too serious when this character, Polonius, is slain in the play of *Hamlet*—presumably by the same actor who played the character that killed him in *Julius Caesar.*

As the example of *Hamlet* records, the adult companies faced competition from troupes of boy players, like the Boys of Paul's, the Children of the Queen's Revels, and the Children of the Chapel Royal. "The boys do bear it away," reports the First Player in *Hamlet,* explaining why this visiting troupe has come to Denmark—the adult company has fallen out of fashion. (Rosencrantz calls "the boys," less respectfully, "an eyrie of children, little eyases, that cry out on the top of question and are most tyrannically clapped for't.") Often connected with choir schools, the companies of boy actors acted in private theaters like Blackfriars and also at court, performing perhaps one play a week. Around the turn of the seventeenth century there was a real vogue for these child players, who often performed satirical dramas.

Shakespeare's own company seems not to have suffered unduly from competition. In its later years the company was quite prosperous. It leased the private indoor Blackfriars theater, where after 1609 some of the late romances were staged, by torchlight. Its larger public amphitheater, the Globe, had been built on the bankside of the Thames in 1599.

What did the Globe theater look like? It was a many-sided playhouse, built so that it seemed virtually round, and it was open to the sky. There were three levels of seating with admission, depending upon the social status of the spectator and the size of his or her purse. The so-called groundlings stood in the pit (on the "ground"), close to the platform stage; they paid a penny in entrance fee. For a little more money (twopence) they could have seats on a bench in one of the upper galleries. For more money still (about sixpence, a day's pay for a skilled artisan) a patron could sit in one of the "lords' rooms" next to the balcony that overhung the stage. From there the spectators could not see the stage action so well, but they could be seen. At the same time, these early modern "luxury boxes" had, like their modern counterparts, more privacy than the ordinary seats. In broad comparative terms, the atmosphere would have resembled a modern sporting event or rock concert more than, say, a chamber music concert or an opera. Orange-sellers offered refreshment.

In the early modern playhouse, the plays were presented in the afternoon, in natural light, and with very few props, though with lavish costumes. Scenes set in darkness—like the opening scene in *Hamlet* with the sentries, or the opening scene in *Othello* where loud voices wake the sleeping Brabantio, or the gorgeous love scene in Juliet's orchard that has come to be known as the "balcony scene"—were played in full light. What created the sense of darkness and mystery was the language, costumes, and props. Torches, candles, or other visual cues could identify the time as "night," as could costumes (like "nightgowns"). Or, of course, the playwright could indicate the time of day, or night, through words ("this odd-even and dull watch o' th' night"). This was, then, from a playwright's point of view, a theater of deliberate, though sometimes haphazard, illusion. Women were played by boys, kings by commoners; night scenes, staged in the middle of the afternoon, were created by language. The audience was conditioned to hold two contradictory "truths" in mind at once.

The action took place on a stage that was open to the public: There was no front curtain, no proscenium. A platform extended down very close to the crowd. Despite the size of the audience, the scale was intimate. It was the perfect format for the soliloquy, the great innovation of early modern drama—the voiced thought of the actor communicating itself to the audience. The typical playhouse had three levels: There was a main stage, with a little curtained-off section at the back, called by modern scholars "the inner stage" or "discovery space," where, for example, the old counselor Polonius hid behind a curtain to spy on Hamlet and his mother, or where in *The Tempest* the young lovers Ferdinand and Miranda would be "discovered," as the stage direction says, playing chess. This discovery space could be used for tombs and prison cells—as, for example, in *Romeo and Juliet* or in *Measure for Measure.* Two doors at the back of the stage, leading to the "tiring house" (that is, the attiring house, or dressing room), were used for processions. At the beginning of *Richard III* the coffin of the dead King Henry VI would be borne in from one side, set down, and later carried off on the other side. In the great procession of Renaissance kingship in act I of *King Lear,* the King, followed by his sons-in-law, his daughters, and all his retainers, might make his ceremonial entrance from one of these doors, slowly filling the stage with majesty. In *Antony and Cleopatra* the two doors could serve as emblematic entry points for the warring armies of Rome and Egypt.

Other details of the stage increased this sense of microcosm. Above the main stage was a balcony, used for locations like battlements and upper bedchambers. The sentries in *Hamlet,* for example, might stand there, or Richard III when he appears, in a staged Renaissance tableau, "aloft, between two bishops." Juliet would appear there for her famous "balcony scene," and so would Prospero in *The Tempest,* "above, unseen." In the main stage was a kind of trapdoor. When in the first act of *Hamlet* we hear that the Ghost "cries under the stage," we might expect to find him there, or when in *Macbeth* the witches make the apparitions disappear, that is perhaps where the apparitions might go. When the prisoner Barnardine clambers reluctantly from his cell in *Measure for Measure,* he might come from the inner stage or from the trap. To make the emblem even plainer, this lower stage into which the villain falls—or out of which specters emerge—was known as the "hell." The area above the stage, where a little roof kept the rain off, was known as the "heavens." Thus, when Shakespeare's company came to build their theater in 1599 and chose to call it the Globe, they had ready-made for them an entire allegory of the human actor on the stage of life, caught between heaven and hell. "What should such fellows as I do," asks Hamlet, "crawling between heaven and earth?" (3.1.127–128). The terms are much older than Shakespeare—they go back to medieval drama, to the common prop of the "hell-mouth," out of which devils could emerge, and to the familiar figure of the Vice. But Shakespeare capitalizes on them. As soon as his new theater is built, he begins to draw double meanings from its name.

Before the building of the Globe, when Shakespeare's company played in a building called simply the Theater, the word "globe" in his plays refers either to the sun—a "globe of fire"—or else to something round—a fat person, like Falstaff, called by Prince Hal "thou globe of sinful continents" (*2 Henry IV* 2.4.257). But in the plays of 1599 and after, "globe" suddenly begins to mean Earth, and stage, to Shakespeare. Hamlet, as we will see, speaks of remembering the Ghost and his message so long as "memory holds a seat / in this distracted globe" (*Hamlet* 1.5.96–97)—that is, in his mind, in the mad world he inhabits, and in the Globe theater, where the puzzled audience is also "distracted" by Hamlet's amazement and grief. In *Othello* Desdemona's death suggests to the distraught Othello that there should "be now a huge eclipse / Of sun and moon, and that th'affrighted globe / Should yawn at alteration" (5.2.108–110)—in other words, that the terrified world, and the equally terrified audience, should be astonished and appalled. To yawn is to gape, but the notion of a "yawning gulf" recalls images of hell in medieval literature and art. Othello imagines an earthquake as the counterpart of his—and the audience's—personal horror. In *Troilus and Cressida,* in that famous speech in which Ulysses speaks of the necessity of degree and order in the universe, he says that disorder will "make a sop of all this solid globe" (1.3.113)—will melt the earth, and bring the audience to tears and chaos. And Prospero, in his great speech in *The Tempest* dissolving the wedding masque, speaks also of the overwhelming of a globe:

> Our revels now are ended. These our actors,
> As I foretold you, were all spirits, and
> Are melted into air, into thin air;
> And like the baseless fabric of this vision,
> The cloud-capped towers, the gorgeous palaces,
> The solemn temples, the great globe itself,
> Yea, all which it inherit, shall dissolve;
> And, like this insubstantial pageant faded,
> Leave not a rack behind.
>
> The Tempest *4.1.148–156*

A "distracted" globe; a globe that "dissolves"; a globe that becomes a "sop." For a culture that had so recently circumnavigated, and had thus come to believe in, the physical globe, these were warning signs, signs of illusion, instability, and impermanence.

SHAKESPEARE AND CULTURE

Every age creates its own Shakespeare. Another way of saying this is to observe that Shakespeare serves a wide variety of cultural purposes, from political nationalism around the globe to modern-day instruction in "leadership" for business and corporate culture.

Shakespeare is in a way always two playwrights, not one: the playwright of *his* time, the late sixteenth and early seventeenth centuries in England, and the playwright of *our* time, whatever time that is. The playwright of *now.* In America no author is cited as frequently by congressmen, by lawyers, by television personalities—not just by the tiny minority of valiant souls who are English majors. In a world increasingly diverse and complex, Shakespeare is read and performed and discussed all over the globe—from France to Egypt to Romania to Japan to Israel.

Shakespeare as an institution, the cultural veneration of Shakespeare, what is sometimes called "Bardolatry," has existed at least since the middle of the eighteenth century—since the actor David Garrick staged the Shakespeare Jubilee in 1769. Shakespeare's home in Stratford-upon-Avon has been a major tourist site from that time to this. The Globe theater was rebuilt in the 1990s near its original site on the River Thames in the Southwark district of London largely as a result of the zeal of an American actor, Sam Wanamaker. But there are Stratfords—and Globe theaters—from Canada to Connecticut to California, and this should tell us something, too, about the persistent "universality" of Shakespeare.

The enormous box office success of Shakespeare films, both relatively straightforward interpretations and more freewheeling adaptations, and the return of star-laden Shakespeare productions to Broadway suggest that watching Shakespeare is at least as popular as reading him. At the same time, adaptations of the plays into novels, like Jane Smiley's best seller *A Thousand Acres* (a rewriting of *King Lear*), continue to prove that Shakespeare was a brilliant inventor and deployer of *plots* as well as of language. In the realm of popular culture, no less an authority than Aaron Spelling, the creator of numerous prime-time television dramas, has said he could not imagine soap operas without the inspiration of *Hamlet* and *King Lear*.

Shakespeare is part of our common culture: "Shakespeare" is one of the ways we communicate with one another today on issues of cultural seriousness—political, moral, ethical, social. Shakespeare the philosopher, Shakespeare the historian, Shakespeare the therapist, Shakespeare the moralist. This is Shakespeare as cultural shorthand. It is not an exaggeration to say that in the American public sphere only the Bible has the same moral authority.

But what we might call "Shakespeare literacy" has changed a great deal over the years—not always in a single direction. In Britain, eighteenth-century philosophers, economists, and politicians could assume that their readers would understand references to Shakespearean characters, plays, and phrases. In *The Theory of Moral Sentiments* (1759), Adam Smith summoned an example from Shakespeare to reinforce his general point about the special pleasure people take in "the unsocial Passions," that is, negative feelings like hatred and resentment. "We detest Iago," Smith wrote, "as much as we esteem Othello; and delight as much in the punishment of the one, as we are grieved at the distress of the other."[23] Edmund Burke's "Speech on Conciliation with America" (1775) is full of quotes from *Hamlet, Julius Caesar, Othello,* and *Macbeth*.

A conversation between two young men in Jane Austen's novel *Mansfield Park* (1814) gives a good sense of the role Shakespeare was thought to play in national consciousness and cultural education in Austen's day. The lively Henry Crawford, determined to win the affection of the novel's sober-minded heroine, Fanny Price, tries to convince her that there is a serious side to his nature by reading aloud to the assembled company from Shakespeare's *Henry VIII*. Crawford's reading is warmly praised by Fanny's cousin, Edmund Bertram, who plans to be a clergyman and has previously objected to the idea of theatrical performances being staged in his family's home. Edmund has, however, no objection to Shakespeare, at least as read aloud in polite company:

> "That play must be a favourite with you," said he; "You read as if you knew it well."
> "It will be a favourite I believe from this hour," replied Crawford; "—but I do not think I have had a volume of Shakespeare in my hand before, since I was fifteen.—I once saw Henry the 8th acted.—Or I have heard of it from somebody who did—I am not certain which. But Shakespeare one gets acquainted with without knowing how. It is a part of an Englishman's constitution. His thoughts and beauties are so spread abroad that one touches them every where, one is intimate with him by instinct.—No man of any brain can open at a good part in one of his plays, without falling into the flow of his meaning immediately."
> "No doubt one is familiar with Shakespeare in a degree," said Edmund, "from one's earliest years. His celebrated passages are quoted by every body; they are in half the books we open, and we all talk Shakespeare, use his similes, and describe with his descriptions; but this is totally distinct from giving his sense as you gave it. To know him . . . pretty thoroughly is, perhaps, not uncommon; but to read him well aloud, is no every-day talent."[24]

Reading aloud in this era before television was a popular household pastime, and all the men in the Bertram family are said to have some skill in it, but Fanny has to admit to herself that Henry Crawford reads with exceptional flair: "It was truly dramatic. His acting had taught Fanny, what pleasure a play might give." Fanny, who has long objected to the plan for a theater at Mansfield Park, is caught between her pleasure and her moral scruples. The whole scene, in short, is managed with great deftness, and the cultural role of Shakespeare, whether his work is read aloud, performed onstage, understood as an English trait, or used as the equivalent of a secret handshake identifying members of the club, is here subtly and perceptively explored.

I have quoted this exchange at some length because Austen, like Shakespeare, is often cited out of context as if her views coincided with those of one or another of her fictional characters. Thus from the passage above it is not uncommon to quote "Shakespeare one gets acquainted with without knowing how. It is a part of an Englishman's constitution" and "we all talk Shakespeare, use his similes, and describe with his descriptions" as if these were Jane Austen's observations about the place of Shakespeare in English culture. And indeed they may be. But Henry Crawford's casually careless "one" does not in fact reflect any deep knowledge of Shakespeare on his part—he is not sure whether he actually saw *Henry VIII* performed or merely heard about such a performance from an acquaintance. The solemn Edmund sees a great difference between using Shakespeare as a cultural tagline ("we all talk Shakespeare") and understanding "his sense," which—despite Edmund's praise of the performance—Crawford is not so likely to do. Moreover, since the plot of *Mansfield Park* turns in large part on the question of whether a theater is a morally dangerous institution that has no place in a gentleman's home, both the drama and the comic irony of this scene are enhanced by the underlying question of whether Shakespeare is more properly performed or read.

Like both the earnest Edmund and the opportunistic Henry, Samuel Taylor Coleridge saw the cultural utility of Shakespeare as a marker of national pride. "The Englishman who without reverence, a proud and affectionate reverence, can utter the name of William Shakespeare, stands disqualified for the office of critic," he asserted in one of his popular public lectures, defending Shakespeare against the charge made by Voltaire, among others, that Shakespeare was merely a wild genius, lacking understanding and prudence, "a sort of beautiful *lusus naturae,* a delightful monster—wild, indeed, and without taste or judgment, but like the inspired idiots so much venerated in the East, uttering, among the strangest follies, the sublimest truths."[25] The impulse both to claim and to export Shakespeare was allied to other strategies that positioned England as an international power. Thomas Carlyle hailed him as the spirit of English world mastery:

> This King Shakespeare does not he shine, in crowned sovereignty, over us all, as the noblest, gentlest, yet strongest of rallying-signs; *in*destructible; really more valuable in that point of view than any other means or appliance whatsoever? We can fancy him as radiant aloft over all Nations of Englishmen, a thousand years hence. From Paramatta, from New York, wheresoever, under what sort of Parish-Constable soever, English men and women are, they will say to one another: "Yes, this Shakespeare is ours; we produced him, we speak and think by him; we are of one blood and kind with him."[26]

Paramatta, or Parramatta, is near Sydney, Australia. Carlyle's Shakespeare-fancying Englishmen, who "speak and think by him," rule the British colonies, present and former, across the entire globe. A more ironic view, from the perspective of a later and more battle-weary England after World War I, is expressed in Virginia Woolf's novel *Mrs. Dalloway,* where we are told of a shell-shocked young soldier soon to commit suicide, "Septimus was one of the first to volunteer. He went to France to save an England which consisted almost entirely of Shakespeare's plays. . . ."

Yet Shakespeare has not always had this classic or transcendent status, and the increasing expansion or dilation into the realm of politics and popular culture is in a way a return—though, like all returns, it is a return with a difference.

PLANET SHAKESPEARE

In early modern America, as in early modern England, Puritans objected to the theater, and to Shakespeare. "Our greatest Glory, and our greatest Shame," wrote one anonymous seventeenth-century poet. At Harvard in the early years of the eighteenth century, "Shakespeare was an attractive forbidden fruit, and it was fashionable for undergraduates to indulge their appetites. But in the classroom he was never read, and referred to only occasionally in classes in rhetoric."[27]

It was only with the rise of elocution and oratory as academic subjects that Shakespeare became part of the standard curriculum. *McGuffey's Readers,* a classic series of American instructional texts, used set speeches from Shakespeare as exemplary moral lessons. The speeches were characterized by descriptive captions ("Antony Over Caesar's Body," "The Dream of Clarence," "The Remorse of King John") rather than set off by the names of the plays, and the plays themselves were not read in their entirety. It is striking, from a twenty-first-century perspective, to see that *King John* and *Henry VIII,* now seldom taught in college, much less in secondary schools, were especially well represented in these selections. Harvard was founded in 1636, twenty years after the death of Shakespeare, by a man whose family came from Stratford-upon-Avon, and Yale was founded in 1701. But the first Shakespeare courses taught at Harvard and Yale did not appear until the 1870s. Initially used for declamation, and then for the biographical study of the author, Shakespeare's plays were not studied in American schools and colleges as literary works—that is, with students each reading the complete text of a play—until the late nineteenth century.

"Planet Shakespeare" sounds like a postmodern theme park, but in fact it is a fantasy of Ralph Waldo Emerson's. Writing in his journals in the spring of 1864, Emerson lamented the fact that neither Oxford nor Harvard had a "Shakspeare Professorship" to honor the greatest writer in English, although in Florence, during the Renaissance, Boccaccio had been appointed to lecture on Dante. "Shakespeare should be the study of the University," he wrote. For Emerson, Shakespeare was "the chosen closet companion" whose works could be read and consulted, "mythologizing every fact of the common life." In reading the plays, he found the dramatic action engrossing and distracting, and preferred for that reason to start at the end, "for the interest of the story is sadly in the way of poetry. It is safer therefore to read the play backwards." Shakespeare, he thought, was the only topic on which an American could safely converse with an Englishman with whom he was unacquainted. And, citing a phrase from Thomas Gray's ode "The Progress of Poesy," he imagined that from outer space the world we live in would be understood and valued chiefly because it had been the home of Shakespeare: "if Intellect perceives & converses 'in climes beyond the solar road,' they probably call this planet, not Earth, but *Shakespeare*. In teleology, they will come to say, that the final cause of the creation of the earth was Shakespeare."[28]

Ralph Waldo Emerson was one of those Harvard students who read—and absorbed—Shakespeare on their own time. Like Keats, he admired Shakespeare's capacity to efface the personal, so unlike the "egotistical" poetry of the Romantics. "Shakespeare alludes to himself nowhere in his drama," he would subsequently write in a journal entry, and "Shakespeare immortalizes his characters"—not, that is, himself.[29] In the essay "Shakespeare; or, The Poet," in *Representative Men* (1850), Emerson noted the degree to which Shakespeare had created nineteenth-century culture. "Now, literature, philosophy and thought are Shakspearized. His mind is the horizon beyond which, at present, we do not see."[30] Emerson was impatient with the minutiae of biography, voicing skepticism that "the chronicle of parentage, birth, birth-place, schooling, school-mates, earning of money, marriage, publication of books, celebrity, death" could actually answer questions about the genesis, meaning, or power of Shakespeare's writing. Instead, he counseled a closer look at the plays themselves: "Shakspeare is the only biographer of Shakspeare; and even he can tell nothing, except to the Shakspeare in us." Although its perspective may have changed, the contemporary world is still "Shakspearized."

Sigmund Freud, for example, used Shakespearean characters as the models for some of his most influential cases studies and theories about human behavior. In *The Interpretation of Dreams* Freud sees Hamlet's condition as the modern version of the Oedipus complex, making ruminative and conflicted what was transparent in the classical original. Where Sophocles' Oedipus kills his father and marries his mother, Hamlet fantasizes rather than acts. "Some Character-Types Met with in Psycho-Analytic Work" includes a section, "The Exceptions," that uses Richard III as its chief example ("a figure created by the greatest of poets—a figure in whose character to claim to be an exception is closely bound up with and is motivated by the circumstance of congenital disadvantage"),[31] and another section, "Those Wrecked by Success," that instances the Macbeths. "The Theme of the Three Caskets" talks about the motif of choosing death in both *The Merchant of Venice* and *King Lear,* while Freud's masterwork, *The Interpretation of Dreams,* cites examples from *Hamlet, Henry IV Part 1* and *Part 2, Henry VI Part 3, Julius Caesar, King Lear, Macbeth, A Midsummer Night's Dream, Othello, Romeo and Juliet,* and *Timon of Athens.* In his letters Freud compares himself to Hamlet and his beloved daughter Sophie to Lear's daughter Cordelia.

Karl Marx knew Shakespeare so well that many of his allusions are buried seamlessly within his writing. The Romans whom he sees as underlying the French Revolution come straight out of *Julius Caesar*. When he discusses the fetishism of the commodity, he quotes the words of Dogberry, the foolish constable in *Much Ado About Nothing*.[32] He cites Mistress Quickly from *Henry IV Part 1* on the value of commodities.[33] And like Freud, he recurs to the image of Snug the joiner in his lion's costume in *A Midsummer Night's Dream*. For Marx, the image is an index of the sham governance of Louis-Napoléon ("he got together about ten thousand loafers and tatterdemalions to play the people, as Snug the joiner played the Lion").[34] For Freud, the image is an analogy to a lion in a patient's dream, a lion of whom the dreamer was "not afraid," and who turned out to symbolize her husband's boss ("this lion can be compared to the lion in *A Midsummer Night's Dream*, who reveals himself to be Snug the joiner; and all the lions we are not afraid of in our dreams are just like that").[35] Marx's daughter Eleanor wrote that Marx had frequently read aloud to his children when they were growing up: "Shakespeare was our family Bible, and before I was six I knew whole scenes from Shakespeare by heart."[36] In a set of questions posed by two of his daughters in a family parlor game, Marx identified Shakespeare, along with Aeschylus and Goethe, as one of his favorite poets.

Needless to say, it was not only scholars who read Shakespeare and applied what they read to their own daily life and thought. Poets and politicians knew their Shakespeare and cited him freely. Memorization, like reading aloud, was part of the culture in the United States as in England, Germany, and elsewhere in Europe. According to one scholar, Thomas Jefferson thought *King Lear* more likely to instill proper filial sentiments than "all the dry volumes of ethics and divinity that were ever written."[37] Mark Twain wrote that when he was a pilot-apprentice on the Mississippi his pilot-master would recite Shakespeare to him by the hour. "He did not use the book, and did not need to; he knew his Shakespeare as well as Euclid ever knew his multiplication table."[38]

Abraham Lincoln often quoted Shakespeare at length and by heart during the period of the Civil War. Lincoln's favorite Shakespeare play was *Macbeth*, which he found all too apposite as a story of tyranny and murder. Six days before his own assassination, while en route by steamer to Washington from the Confederate capital of Richmond, he read aloud to some friends this passage from act 3, scene 2:

> Duncan is in his grave.
> After life's fitful fever he sleeps well.
> Treason has done his worst. Nor steel nor poison,
> Malice domestic, foreign levy, nothing
> Can touch him further.

Such uncanny associations between Shakespeare and history are not uncommon. John F. Kennedy, like Lincoln, loved Shakespeare and quoted him often in his speeches. After Kennedy was assassinated, his brother Robert addressed the 1964 Democratic National Convention, urging his listeners not only to look back but also to look forward. He said that when he thought of President Kennedy, he thought of what Shakespeare said in *Romeo and Juliet:*

> When he shall die
> Take him and cut him out in little stars,
> And he shall make the face of heaven so fine
> That all the world will be in love with night
> And pay no worship to the garish sun.

Robert Kennedy was quoting Juliet, in the optimistic moment of her love for Romeo and marriage to him, her words an ironic prophecy of the untimely death that lay in store for them both. Robert F. Kennedy himself would be assassinated less than five years later, in 1968. (The eerie uncanniness of his quotation is underscored for those who are familiar with the textual history of this passage. For it was not until the printing of the Fourth Quarto of the play that the text appeared as "When *he* shall die. . . ." The Folio and the Second and Third Quartos of *Romeo and Juliet* all read not "he" but "I.")

President Lyndon Johnson did not quote Shakespeare so much as he was parodied through him, in Barbara Garson's satirical send-up *Macbird* (1966), a broad-brush political allegory that identified Johnson/Macbeth/Macbird as the culprit in the murder of Kennedy/Duncan/Ken O'Dunc. It will not be especially useful to chronicle the disappearance of confident and knowledgeable Shakespeare quotation in public life, except to say that parodies like *Macbird*—and less tendentious Shakespeare "adaptations" like *West Side Story*—began gradually to take over the public space that previously had been occupied by a more direct engagement with Shakespeare's language and the characters and plots of his plays.

Historian Lawrence Levine has ably described the shift of Shakespeare in America from popular culture in the nineteenth century (traveling troupes, Shakespeare speeches as part of vaudeville bills, huge crowds and riots at productions, audiences shouting lines back at the actors) to the "high culture" of twentieth-century repertory companies. Similarly, Graham Holderness, Michael Dobson, and others have well recounted the rise of the "Shakespeare myth" in Britain, and the emergence of Shakespeare as England's "national poet."[39]

As a complement to Emerson's "Shakspearized" literature, philosophy, and thought, we might take note of the way politics, business, and popular culture have been "Shakspearized" in subsequent generations. Consider, for example, the many roles of *Henry V.* In one of his letters, Edmund Burke, the British statesman and political philosopher, expressed his disgust at the comportment of Lord Malmesbury and his failed mission to Paris in 1796, where he was sent to negotiate with the French Directory. "He is placed on a stage, than which no Muse of fire that had ascended the highest heaven of invention, could imagine any thing more awful and august," wrote Burke. "It was hoped, that in this swelling scene . . . he would have stood forth in the form, and in the attitude of a hero. On that day, it was thought he would have assumed the port of Mars."[40] These infolded references to the prologue of Shakespeare's *Henry V*, delivered in the midst of a passionate denunciation, clearly imply that Burke expected his readers to recognize the aptness of these buried quotations. Malmesbury, a failed leader and politician, was no Henry V.

When Laurence Olivier declaimed King Henry's "Crispin Crispian" speech on a radio program called "Into Battle" in 1942, the speech, with its poignant invocation of "We few, we happy few, we band of brothers," became a patriotic call to arms for embattled Britain during World War II. The Olivier production of *Henry V* (1944) followed the broadcast excerpt, with the result that the speech, with its political ardor, was in effect reinserted into the play after its separate life as a work of inspirational motivation.

At the turn of the twenty-first century, executives and CEOs were offered leadership advice from Shakespeare, in the form of a number of books on "the Bard" and "the business stage." Here, too, the hero of Agincourt emerged in a starring role. Other Shakespearean "managers" whose stories were deemed useful for leaders included Richard III, Macbeth, and Coriolanus. The role model for nineteenth-century poets and philosophers, the indecisive, inward-looking Hamlet with his famous propensity for delay, is seldom, or never, invoked.[41]

Andrew Carnegie, the steel magnate, philanthropist, and self-educated founder of a system of free libraries, liked to insert Shakespeare quotations throughout his essays on business, capitalism, and public affairs. In each case the passage is aptly if sometimes surprisingly selected to illustrate a contemporary issue. In his famous article "The Gospel of Wealth" (1889), Carnegie drew on the example of Shylock to suggest that a graduated estate tax might encourage philanthropy in other rich men.

[B]y all means such taxes should be graduated, beginning at nothing upon moderate sums to dependents, and increasing rapidly as the amounts swell, until of the millionaire's hoards, as of Shylock's, at least:

> The other half
> Comes to the privy officer of the state.

This policy would work powerfully to induce the rich man to attend to the administration of wealth during his life, which is the end that society should always have in view, as being by far the most fruitful for the people.

In another essay he cited a famous exchange between Owen Glendower and Hotspur from *Henry IV Part 1* to make a point about the inadequacy of fighting with a volunteer army: "We need a large regular army of trained soldiers. . . . Thirty-eight thousand more men are to be called for the regular army; but it is easy 'to call spirits from the vasty deep'—they may not come." And in "Popular Illusions About Trusts" (1900), Carnegie invoked yet another iconic Shakespearean moment to demonstrate his point: "Already those ghosts of numerous departed trusts which aimed at monopolies have marched across the stage of human affairs, each pointing to its fatal wound, inflicted by that great corrective, competition. Like the ghosts of Macbeth's victims, the line threatens to stretch longer and longer, and also like those phantoms of the brain, they 'come like shadows, so depart.' "[42] Himself born in Dunfermline, Fife, the ancient capital of Scotland, Carnegie had emigrated to the Pittsburgh area as a boy from the land of Macbeth and Macduff (the "Thane of Fife") to make his fortune.

Clearly Carnegie, despite his lack of formal education (or because of it?), had read Shakespeare with attention and care, and brought images from the plays to bear on situations of public policy in ways that were highly pertinent. Twenty-first-century books on Shakespeare and management, however shrewdly and wittily organized, belong instead to the genre of the self-help manual. Henry V, Coriolanus, and Macbeth are examples of successful and unsuccessful leadership, and models to serve as inspiration or warning for modern executives. Like the psychoanalytic case studies such as "Those Wrecked by Success," they take Shakespearean characters seriously as types of persons—in this case, types of leaders.

But the contrast between the Shakespeare of Carnegie, Lincoln, and JFK (the first two, we might emphasize, self-educated readers) and the modern-day "Shakespeare" of public life can best be seen by turning to the way Shakespeare is used in political discourse today.

When a U.S. senator wanted words solemn enough to match the occasion of the September 11, 2001, terrorist attacks on the Pentagon and the World Trade Center, he reached for Shakespeare, declaring, in a moving speech reported in the *Congressional Record,* "Shakespeare wrote, 'Grief hath changed me since you saw me last.' We are all changed. Yesterday changed all of us."[43] While the sentiments of the isolated quotation were perfectly appropriate for the occasion, the context was not. The line came from *The Comedy of Errors,* where it is spoken by an old man long separated by chance from one of his sons, and now, after seven years, brought face-to-face with him. In context the line meant "you do not recognize me because my grief has aged me," and the emotion that brought it forth was joy at reunion, not grief at unimaginable loss. So what the senator had done was to locate, whether by reading through the plays or by consulting an index or a book of quotations, a line from Shakespeare that seemed to describe the feeling he wished to convey, without any particular concern for the play or the dramatic context. Bringing together the idea of "grief" with the name of "Shakespeare" conveys a moral seriousness that may be otherwise difficult to achieve. The literary context has become secondary to the name of the author.

The use of Shakespeare in this way has been increasing. We could call it, perhaps, "decorative" or "enforcing," rather than referential. This is a quite common mode of citation in modern life, and it has its effectiveness. Whether it is "all the world's a stage" or "one touch of nature makes the whole world kin," Shakespearean taglines and Shakespearean "philosophy" or wisdom, dislocated from their dramatic context, often assume a certain weightiness (indeed, a rhetorical ponderousness) that is belied by looking at the dramatic situation. This habit of disembodied quotation tends to make Shakespeare into an all-purpose sage, a single author representing the totality of the world's wisdom. The World Wide Web has made this practice even more common (many Shakespeare Web resources will, in fact, quote—out of context—Othello's "there's magic in the web of it"). The result, as we have noticed, is a certain flattening out of "Shakespeare," for by removing the speech prefixes, and thus the particularity of these utterances, they can be seen to "mean" something quite opposite to what they suggest in context. One classic example is Iago's artful praise of reputation over gain ("Who steals my purse steals trash . . . / . . . But he that filches from me my good name / Robs me of that which not enriches him / And makes me poor indeed"). As readers and audiences of *Othello* know, Iago is here at his most hypocritical, gulling Othello into thinking that his reputation has been sullied by Desdemona's (imagined) infidelity. In fact, Iago himself is constantly asking for money ("put money in thy purse," he enjoins his dupe Roderigo), and cares not at all for "good name." Yet the sentiments so cleverly tweaked by Shakespeare—putting this bromide in the mouth of a most unlikely speaker, one with clear ulterior motives—are completely lost when the passage is quoted out of context as "Shakespeare's" view of the relative importance of morality and profit. Likewise, Polonius's advice to his son Laertes in *Hamlet*, a collection of weary maxims that the early modern period would have recognized as empty commonplaces, is often cited out of context as Shakespeare on thrift ("Neither a borrower nor a lender be"), Shakespeare on decorum ("the apparel often proclaims the man"), and so on. As with Iago, so also with Polonius. He signally fails to follow, or to exemplify, his own counsel.

"Shakespeare," like the Bible or the words of Abraham Lincoln, adds a note of gravitas to ordinary utterance. And it is undeniable that Shakespeare's words are almost always more evocative, and better chosen, than most utterances in contemporary speech. Quotations from the King James Bible, also, as we have seen, a product of those golden years of English prose and poetry, have the same capacity to move hearers and speakers—a resonance lost in more modern and technically more accurate translations. But the way Shakespearean analogues and Shakespeare quotations are used in public life today is very different from the way they functioned in the past, when the world was "Shakspearized" and Shakespeare was part of an Englishman's internal constitution.

When members of the U.S. Congress quote Shakespeare they are invoking his cultural authority, not necessarily his plays. A short list of Shakespearean references in the *Congressional Record* will make this perfectly clear. It is not only that twenty-first-century politicians and lawmakers may not always know their Shakespeare as well as did their predecessors, but also that they do not expect the general public to recognize the context of the references. Citing Shakespeare gives weight and heft to a political statement. Here is an assortment of not-untypical Shakespeare citations read into the official record of the proceedings and debates of the U.S. Congress:

- "William Shakespeare once wrote, 'For in that sleep of death, what dreams may come when we have shuffled off this mortal coil must give us pause.' Hundreds of years before the death tax was even conceived, Shakespeare captured the worries felt by thousands of Americans."[44]
- "In sum, to paraphrase Shakespeare, which is not done very often on the Senate floor, adoption of the amendments will rob California of that which cannot enrich the northwest generators and yet will make California poor, indeed."[45]
- "In Shakespeare's play *Julius Caesar,* the soothsayer warned Caesar to 'beware the Ides of March.' Caesar did not listen and Caesar perished. Today, on this Ides of March, I bring my colleagues fair warning. If we do not pass the Colombia aid package soon, our friends in Colombia could suffer the same fate as Caesar and our own children could be next."[46]
- "Shakespeare wrote, 'What's past is prologue.' And I believe no other phrase can quite describe both the achievements of the Republican Congress and its vision for America's future."[47]
- "The words of William Shakespeare's King Lear are ringing loudly in the ears of many Americans: 'Fool me not to bear it tamely; touch me with noble anger.' The old trusting king had just been grossly betrayed by two of his daughters. Collectively this nation has reason for an anger comparable to that of King Lear. In America the democratic process has just been mugged by the Supreme Court."[48]

In each of these cases Shakespeare plays the role of enforcer or uplifter. The other lawmakers gathered in the chamber, and the constituents at home, are not asked to call to mind the specific circumstances of Hamlet; Iago; the Soothsayer in *Julius Caesar;* Antonio, the usurping Duke of Milan in *The Tempest;* or Lear's reproof to his daughters about their stripping him of attendant knights—to give, in sequence, the sources of these quotations. Instead, Shakespeare is evoked, and invoked, as an eloquent coiner of eloquent phrases. The phrases, floating free of their immediate context, have become "Shakespeare."

The practice of citing "Shakespeare" as a cultural enforcer can sometimes obscure both the irony and the wit of the original. What might once have been called "Bartlett's Familiar Shakespeare," and is now to be found at www.Shakespeare.com, has changed the way Shakespeare intersects with contemporary culture. It is no longer the case that a knowledge of the plays or of the playwright necessarily precedes quotation from them. A phrase like "The lady protests too much, methinks" (in context an observation, ironically spoken by Gertrude, on the overacting of the grieving Player Queen in the play-within-the-play in *Hamlet*) is regularly used, or abused, to mark any perceived disingenuousness or pretended reluctance, even when the person doing the protesting is male. The quote has become a kind of verbal macro, implying a generalized doubt about someone's sincerity—not a specific reference to *Hamlet*, Gertrude, or the way a play can catch the conscience of the king (or queen).

Before we dismiss this as a lamentable sign of the declining importance of the humanities in the higher education of politicians (although that would be a fair assessment), we might note how much these citations are like the "beauties of Shakespeare" of an earlier day. Arguably there has been a further loss of context—neither Pope nor the Reverend Mr. Dodd would have viewed the perfidious Antonio in *The Tempest* as a moral arbiter—but a more charitable view would be that the power of Shakespeare's evocative language "transcends" the immediate context of the plays.

Today Shakespeare is more likely to be a citation, a tagline, an adage, or a slogan. One might draw cautious analogies with the technique known as "sampling" in contemporary popular music, or with the advertising practice called "branding." To give one of the more extreme examples of how this might work in Shakespearean citation, a business columnist discussing the fate of the stealth bomber mused, "B2, or not B2," and knew that he would be taken as educated and not "highbrow" for almost-quoting Hamlet—because Shakespeare belongs to everyone. A variant of this same visual logo appeared in an airline's in-flight magazine, where the ability to select seats electronically was indicated by the query "2B or not 2B, that is the question."

Shakespeare was a popular dramatist long before he was a respectable and respected author. His return to the domain of the popular is a move outward, onto thousands of stages and screens, in hundreds of lands and languages. Those languages include the lexicons (and logos) of politics, business, current events, and advertising, as well as what the Romantic poets—among our best Shakespeare critics—recognized as the language of the heart.

We need not give up any of our Shakespeares in order to encounter new ones on this planet that Emerson thought extraterrestrials would call "not Earth, but *Shakspeare*." The plays are tough, durable, rich, flexible, capacious, and endlessly evocative. They are also provocative, alluring, suggestive, and challenging. They will not break from being bent or reshaped to fit a new context, or a new idea. Every production is an interpretation. That these plays can sustain so many powerful and persuasive interpretations is in fact as close as I can come to explaining the elusive nature of their greatness. To spend a few hours with them is pure pleasure. To spend a lifetime with them is a remarkable privilege.

At the close of many of Shakespeare's plays a figure of nominal authority—typically not the hero or heroine, but rather a survivor or successor—looks on those assembled and invites them to go off together, to discuss what they have seen and heard. "Go hence to have more talk of these sad things"; "All this can I / Truly deliver"; "Myself will straight aboard, and to the state / This heavy act with heavy heart relate"; "Speak what we feel, not what we ought to say"; "So call the field to rest, and let's away / To part the glories of this happy day"; "Lead us from hence where we may leisurely / Each one demand an answer to his part / Performed in this wide gap of time." In practical terms, these are stage-clearing speeches. The Elizabethan and Jacobean playhouse had no front curtain, and all the actors had to leave the stage in order for the play to conclude. But as with everything apparently mechanical in Shakespeare, the gesture inviting the onlookers to "relate" is also magical, reaching across the stage to the audience, across the years to each new generation of spectators and readers. This book takes up that invitation.

The Two Gentlemen of Verona

DRAMATIS PERSONAE

Duke of Milan
Silvia, *his daughter*
Proteus, *a gentleman of Verona*
Launce, *his clownish servant*
Valentine, *a gentleman of Verona*
Speed, *his clownish servant*
Thurio, *a foolish rival to Valentine*
Antonio, *father of Proteus*

Panthino, *his servant*
Julia, *beloved of Proteus*
Lucetta, *her waiting-woman*
Host, *where Julia lodges*
Eglamour, *agent for Silvia in her escape*
Outlaws
Servants, musicians

N THIS EARLY romantic comedy Shakespeare introduces a number of situations that will be expanded or refined in later plays: a love triangle that impels one heroine to take refuge in a friar's cell to escape an unwanted marriage when her lover is banished (*Romeo and Juliet*); a plucky second heroine, dressed as a boy, who is compelled by circumstances to woo another woman on behalf of the man she loves (*Twelfth Night*); a clumsy, inept would-be lover who hires musicians to serenade his lady with a very lovely song (*Cymbeline*); a set of outlaws resident in the woods who decide that a wandering nobleman should be their leader (compare the exiled court in *As You Like It* and the helpful sailors and pirates in *Twelfth Night* and *Pericles*); and an elopement plot involving a rope ladder (*Romeo* again, but also with a glance at *The Merchant of Venice*). Other soon-to-be-familiar Shakespearean elements, like the clown who speaks the truth in his malapropisms, the duke-father who gives the law and also gives (or refuses to give) his daughter's hand in marriage, and the pair of young men who are described as like twins or brothers when young but are individuated—and made rivals—by love, make *The Two Gentlemen of Verona* a harbinger of much that is most pleasurable and intricate in later Shakespearean comedies, tragedies, and romances. Just as it has become a pleasant cliché to describe *Hamlet* as a play "entirely made of quotations," since so many of its lines and phrases have become famous even to those who do not know the play-text, so we might regard *Two Gentlemen* as an anthology of bits and pieces waiting to be crafted into more compelling drama.

But this would be to sell short what is actually, on its own terms, a lively and often funny play, which contains, among its other assets, a genuinely comic early clown and one of the most beautiful lyric songs in all of Shakespeare. *Two Gentlemen* is not concerned with developing characters who possess individual psychology: the wavering affections of a young man forthrightly named Proteus and the glorious banality in love thoughts and lover's behavior that attach to another young man called Valentine should exempt these Shakespearean striplings from any obligation to exhibit complex and nuanced motivations. The play is a kind of love cartoon, with a plethora of dominating fathers (one each for Proteus, Valentine, and the idealized Silvia; only the clownish servant Launce seems to have a mother as a well as a father). Its "psychology" is penetrating enough on the level of general behavior. Two young men, inexperienced in romantic courtship, compete for one woman. One of the men abandons his former love for a new one at least in part because the second lady is the object of his friend's passionate affection. Critics have called this "mimetic desire"— a desire arising in imitation of another's desire. Anyone who has been an adolescent will remember the emotion, and the inexplicable aura that attached to the "popular" girl, or boy, who seemed to be popular because she or he was popular rather than for any identifiable individual characteristics.

Proteus and Valentine are best friends, and as the play begins they are about to be separated. Valentine is embarking on a journey of cultural and political education, of a kind quite typical for a young nobleman of the period. Proteus, though he acknowledges that this is a worthy goal, prefers to stay at home, because he is in love with Julia.

The childhood bond between the two young men is described as a time in which their psychological identifications with each other were so close that they seemed in a way to be versions of the same person. "I knew him as myself," explains Valentine, "for from our infancy / We have conversed, and spent our hours together" (2.4.56–57). From the beginning of Shakespeare's career to the end, with both pairs of male and pairs of female friends, this model of ideal and indivisible youthful friendship is presented as something that will be disrupted by heterosexuality, or, more accurately, by romantic love and a desire to marry. Very similar passages appear in plays like *A Midsummer Night's Dream* (Helena and Hermia, 3.2.199–215), *As You Like It* (Celia and Rosalind, 1.3.67–70), and *The Winter's Tale* (Polixenes and Leontes, 1.2.69–77). In each case what is being described is a paradisal twinship prior to differentiation. It is not a judgment on the quality or intensity of the prior friendship to note that in every case it is superseded by romantic heterosexual love. To the contrary, these early friendships are strongly idealized. But each is seen retrospectively, as something that *was,* once, in the past. In the present case, perhaps the earliest in Shakespeare, both Proteus and Valentine move forward, in the play's terms, toward the pair of marriages promised in the play's final lines. It is not an accident that the very first line of the play, "Cease to persuade, my loving Proteus," announces a sundering of the pair of male friends, or that the motive force for each of the two male characters thenceforth is romantic courtship:

> I rather would entreat thy company
> To see the wonders of the world abroad
> Than, living dully sluggardized at home,
> Wear out thy youth with shapeless idleness.
> But since thou lov'st, love still, and thrive therein—
> Even as I would, when I to love begin.
>
> Two Gentlemen *1.1.5–10*

Early modern scholars have long pointed to the tradition of male-male friendship, sometimes called the Friendship Cult, that was strongly in place in England and in Europe at this time. Spenser has a book subtitled "Of Friendship" in *The Faerie Queene,* and the philosophy of Neoplatonism encouraged the idealization of a passionate friendship of equals, which technically would rank "higher" than the relation of a man and a woman in marriage, since men were higher on the hierarchical scale than women, and ideal relationships, at least in theory, more elevated than carnal ones. More recent scholars of the period have emphasized the fact that such ardent friendships could also be and often were erotic, both in terms of the emotional energy they produced and in the actual physical and sexual relationships between men. Many letters from poets to patrons, and from kings and noblemen to their friends, employ a love rhetoric that seems fully eroticized. Perhaps the most germane example here is that of Shakespeare's own sonnets, which probably date from the same period as *Two Gentlemen.* The sequence begins with passionate love sonnets to an idealized and beautiful fair young man, and then goes on to tell the story of a triangular relationship with a rival poet in which a "dark lady" provokes jealousy and insistent physical desire.

It is extremely useful to bear this background of strong male-male "friendship" in mind, but as the opening passage cited above makes fairly clear, the central design of *The Two Gentlemen of Verona* is in fact focused on a pattern of heterosexual relations. Thus in quick succession we learn of Proteus's love for Julia, Valentine's love for Silvia, Proteus's pursuit of Silvia (whether or not it is motivated largely by Valentine's desire for her), and the reassortment of lovers at the close, in which Proteus, still true to his name, changes his mind again:

Proteus	Inconstancy falls off ere it begins.
	What is in Silvia's face but I may spy
	More fresh in Julia's, with a constant eye?
Valentine	Come, come, a hand from either.
	Let me be blessed to make this happy close.
	'Twere pity two such friends should be long foes.
	[JULIA *and* PROTEUS *join hands*]
Proteus	Bear witness, heaven, I have my wish for ever.
Julia	And I mine.

5.4.111–118

In fact, Proteus's second reversal—returning him to the love for Julia with which the play began—comes at a moment when he and the audience are explicitly reminded of the meaning of his name, something that no one onstage has noted or commented upon. The venturesome Julia, having disguised herself as the boy "Sebastian" and been employed in that guise by Proteus as an emissary to Silvia, presents him, by "mistake," not with the ring Silvia has disdained but with the ring Proteus had earlier given to her. How did you get the ring? he demands:

> Proteus   At my depart
>   I gave this unto Julia.
> Julia   And Julia herself did give it me,
>   And Julia herself hath brought it hither.
>
> *5.4.94–97*

Unmasking herself, and offering an apology for her "immodest raiment," Julia points out with commendable restraint, all things considered, that

> It is the lesser blot, modesty finds,
> Women to change their shapes than men their minds.
>
> *5.4.106–107*

And to this mild reproof Proteus responds as if he had never thought about what it mean to be "Proteus," or protean:

> Proteus   Than men their minds! 'Tis true. O heaven, were man
>   But constant, he were perfect. . . .
>
> *5.4.108–109*

All this is comic, of course. Were Shakespeare's play an allegory, like Spenser's *Faerie Queene,* or a medieval morality play, like *Everyman,* the unmasking of Julia's assumed identity and the unmasking of Proteus's inner nature would be underscored more pointedly. As it is, the dyad of Proteus and Valentine offers a double vision of what such young men typically are like: ardent *and* changeable; selfish *and* optimistic; needlessly, carelessly cruel *and* hoping, always, to be forgiven. The "friends" are types of friendship, but they are also versions of each other, in different moods and modes; the jealousy-substitution-usurpation plot is both characteristic of self-regarding young men of a certain age and class, and—just one plane below the surface of this deliberately superficial play— indicative of the different ways a single individual may behave in different places and different circumstances.

Structurally, this play has a good deal in common with other early Shake-spearean comedies: a stern duke-father; a broken oath; the central theme of losing-oneself-to-find-oneself, here centered on the blithely self-regarding and self-justifying Proteus. "To leave my Julia shall I be forsworn," he declares when he arrives at the Duke's court and determines to win Silvia at any cost, including the cost of his former love and his friendships. "To love fair Silvia, shall I be forsworn; / To wrong my friend I shall be much forsworn. . . . Love bade me swear, and Love bids me forswear" (2.6.1–3, 6). Still, he vacillates:

> I cannot leave to love, and yet I do.
> But there I leave to love where I should love.
> Julia I lose, and Valentine I lose.
> If I keep them I needs must lose myself.
> If I lose them, thus find I by their loss
> For Valentine, myself, for Julia, Silvia.
> I to myself am dearer than a friend,
> For love is still most precious in itself,
> And Silvia—witness heaven that made her fair—
> Shows Julia but a swarthy Ethiope.
> I will forget that Julia is alive,
> Rememb'ring that my love to her is dead,
> And Valentine I'll hold an enemy,
> Aiming at Silvia as a sweeter friend.
> I cannot now prove constant to myself
> Without some treachery used to Valentine.
>
> *2.6.17–32*

As we have noted, Proteus does not fully appreciate, as the audience will, the determinative function of his name (the "changeable one"). His discrimination between the fair Silvia and Julia (the "swarthy Ethiope") is a fair/dark distinction that will recur in a later and better comedy, *A Midsummer Night's Dream,* where Hermia is at one point called an "Ethiope" in contrast to her friend and rival, Helena. (Romeo, however, will praise Juliet's beauty by invoking this exotic image: "It seems she hangs upon the cheek of night / As a rich jewel in an Ethiope's ear—" [*Romeo and Juliet* 1.5.42–43].) This does not mean, of course, that Julia is African, or looks African; "Ethiope" in this context is a deliberate rhetorical overstatement, meant to be comic: Julia may have darker hair, eyes, or brows than the "fair" Silvia, but the two women will be more similar than dissimilar (compare the "dark lady" of Shakespeare's sonnets, also dark-haired, not dark-skinned). And—as in the case of *Dream,* where the rival ladies are described as contrastingly tall and short, as well as fair and dark—the comedic effect here may be heightened if the distinction is not made too great onstage. What is being exhibited here is Proteus's own unreliable judgment, not some "real" difference between Julia and Silvia.

In formal terms, then, this pair of hapless male lovers looks forward to, and

to a certain extent resembles, the indistinguishable Lysander and Demetrius of
A Midsummer Night's Dream. There, too, we are told that one of the young men
once loved woman A but now has metamorphosed into a lover of woman B,
and regards his earlier passion as mere infatuation, puppy love, compared to the
real thing he is sure he now experiences. In *Dream,* as we will see, things get
even more complicated when both men are transformed into lovers of the formerly scorned and jilted lady, leaving her previously complacent rival now suddenly without any suitor at all.

Julia's initial conversation with her waiting-woman Lucetta in act 1, scene 1,
anticipates other playful discussions between Shakespeare's women on the endlessly fascinating topic of falling in love: Portia and Nerissa in *The Merchant
of Venice,* Rosalind and Celia in *As You Like It,* Juliet and her nurse in *Romeo
and Juliet.* In fact, Julia uses the same stratagem Juliet will employ to deceive
the Nurse at the Capulet feast, feigning an interest in two other young men
before inquiring about her true object: "What think'st thou of the fair Sir
Eglamour? . . . What think'st thou of the rich Mercatio? . . . What think'st thou
of the gentle Proteus?" (1.2.9, 12, 14). The teasing, punning conversation about
Proteus's love letter sets an appealing tone of rhetorical camaraderie. But Proteus has been sent by his father to the court, to follow Valentine—"he cannot be
a perfect man, / Not being tried and tutored in the world" (1.3.20–21)—and
together the women determine on a plan for Julia to cross-dress and follow him:

Lucetta	But in what habit will you go along?
Julia	Not like a woman, for I would prevent
	The loose encounters of lascivious men.
	Gentle Lucetta, fit me with such weeds
	As may beseem some well-reputed page.
Lucetta	Why, then, your ladyship must cut your hair.
Julia	No, girl, I'll knit it up in silken strings
	With twenty odd-conceited true-love knots.
	To be fantastic may become a youth
	Of greater time than I shall show to be.
Lucetta	What fashion, madam, shall I make your breeches?
Julia	That fits as well as "Tell me, good my lord,
	What compass will you wear your farthingale?"

2.7.39–51

Lucetta insists that Julia's costume must have a codpiece, the bagged appendage
to the front of the close-fitting hose or breeches worn by men from the fifteenth
to the seventeenth century, and thus a visible onstage signature of maleness.
(The word "cod" in the period meant "bag," "scrotum," "peapod," and "stomach," and it is used by Shakespeare at one time or another in each of these
senses.) This little scene prepares the audience for what had become an attrac-

tive Elizabethan convention in prose and verse romance, the heroine cross-dressed as a male page—a device that Shakespeare would bring to the stage and employ to delightful and purposeful effect in a whole range of subsequent plays, from the great "festive" comedies of his middle period, *The Merchant of Venice*, *As You Like It*, and *Twelfth Night*, to the late romance *Cymbeline*.

But the scene also calls attention to the artifice of gender. The part of Julia, like that of Lucetta, Silvia, and every other Shakespearean woman, would originally have been performed by a boy actor. Since no women were permitted to act in stage plays for the public, the extensive and playful discussion of male and female clothing, and Julia's (perhaps pretended) dismay at the idea of wearing a codpiece ("Out, out, Lucetta. That will be ill-favoured" [54]), will remind the audience that maleness and femaleness are *roles* on the Shakespearean stage. And since the boy actor playing Julia is shortly to assume the role of the page "Sebastian," the discussion of costume also draws attention to the double deception of a boy playing a girl playing a boy. This, incidentally, is one dramatic reason for Julia's swoon in the final scene (5.4) as well as the "blush" noted with interest by the Duke. Since female characters dressed as boys in these plays will look very like "real" boys (especially since they *are* boys), onstage femininity is often marked, in scenes of confrontation or high emotion, by just such a swoon. Rosalind will swoon at a similarly key moment in *As You Like It*, Viola will confess her martial cowardice in *Twelfth Night*, and so on. Proteus's exclamation, "Look to the boy," on seeing his supposed page fall to the ground in a faint, underscores both Julia's disguised female identity (a scant few lines before she reveals it) and Proteus's own persistent and characteristic blindness in failing to recognize the woman he loves. As for the Duke, his observation ("I think the boy hath grace in him. He blushes" [5.4.162]) serves to remind the audience at the very end of the play that the apparently male-male couple onstage is "actually" a man and a woman, Proteus and Julia. For despite the fact that she has revealed her identity to her lover, Julia appears to be dressed like a page at the end of the play. Valentine's response to the Duke, that the page hath "more grace than boy" in him, is received with ducal puzzlement—"What mean you by that saying?"—and we should recall that dukes themselves were, and are, customarily styled "your Grace."

If the turning point of the heterosexual romantic-love plot is the re-recognition by each lover of his or her intended partner, the turning point of the "friendship" plot comes after what seems to be a final rupture. Proteus has perfidiously reported to Silvia's father the Duke her intended elopement with Valentine, thus ensuring that the Duke, who favors another suitor—the dull but apparently wealthy Thurio—will banish Valentine from the city. Silvia, attempting to avoid the marriage with Thurio by seeking the haven of a friar's cell, escapes into a nearby forest, with the help of a loyal knight with the romance name of Eglamour. This is, of course, the very forest where the exiled Valentine has, improbably, been adopted by a bunch of outlaws as their king.

beginning of act 2—before the audience got a chance to see for itself the unparalleled Silvia:

> Valentine   Why, how know you that I am in love?
>
> Speed   Marry, by these special marks: first, you have learned, like Sir
> Proteus, to wreath your arms like a malcontent; to relish a
> love-song, like a robin redbreast; to walk alone, like one that
> had the pestilence; to sigh, like a schoolboy that had lost his
> ABC; to weep, like a young wench that had buried her
> grandam; to fast, like one that takes diet; to watch, like one
> that fears robbing; to speak puling, like a beggar at Hallow-
> mas. You were wont, when you laughed, to crow like a cock;
> when you walked, to walk like one of the lions. When you
> fasted, it was presently after dinner; when you looked sadly, it
> was for want of money. And now you are metamorphosed
> with a mistress, that when I look on you, I can hardly think
> you my master.

> *2.1.15–28*

Similar catalogues of lovers' behavior will appear in later plays: Benedick speaking of Claudio in *Much Ado,* Rosalind speaking of Orlando in *As You Like It,*
Mercutio on Romeo, Polonius (rightly or wrongly) on Hamlet. Elizabethan
miniatures often showed images of the "lover" in such elaborate and signifying disarray, sighing, arms folded. "[Y]ou chid / at Sir Proteus for going
ungartered," Speed reminds him (64–65), and now Valentine is in the same
condition—and loving every minute of it. That Silvia is much wiser about love
than her suitor becomes immediately evident when she enters, and receives
from Valentine a love letter he has written at her direction "[u]nto [a] secret,
nameless friend of yours" (92); it takes the better part of the scene for him to get
the point that the love letter he has written for her to send—and which he
resents out of jealousy—is actually intended for himself. The word "friend,"
incidentally, resounds throughout this scene, as if to open up and complicate
the Valentine-Proteus bond:

> Speed   Why, she hath given you a letter.
>
> Valentine That's the letter I writ to her friend.
>
> Speed   And that letter hath she delivered, and there an end.

> *2.1.142–144*

"Friend" as a word meaning "a lover of the opposite sex" appears with some frequency in Shakespeare's plays in a romantic or erotic connection (for example,
in the mention of Juliet's pregnancy in *Measure for Measure,* "He hath got his
friend with child" [1.4.28]; or in Iago's salacious remark to Othello, "to be naked

with her friend in bed / An hour or more" [*Othello* 4.1.3–4]; or, closer in time to the early *Two Gentlemen,* Berowne's abjuration of masked balls and other love games in *Love's Labour's Lost,* where he pledges to "never come in visor to my friend" [5.2.404]). When in act 2, scene 1, of *Two Gentlemen* the charged term "friend" migrates, casually but insistently, from Valentine's relation with Proteus to Valentine's relation with Silvia, the whole apparatus of "friendship," like the similarly codified and conventionalized apparatus of romantic love, seems deliberately to be placed under scrutiny. The two codes are potentially at odds, and become *actually* and comically at odds, as we have seen, in Valentine's serio-comic volte-face near the end of the play ("All that was mine in Silvia I give thee"). Such an act of generosity would produce chaos and misrule, not ideal friendship or love. And, equally to the point, Silvia would not stand for it.

This conflict is entirely characteristic of Shakespeare, particularly in his early playwriting career, who tends in play after play to explore and explode conventional systems of social practice and belief by setting them at odds with one another, and by supplying them with adherents who apply the rules so strictly that their intrinsic folly and limitation are self-evident. The comedy of a too-strict law can become tragic in an instant, as death threatens to follow upon the enforcement of an edict handed down from above.

We need no further evidence of the fragility of the models of love and friendship in *Two Gentlemen* than the way the "low," or comic, plot of Launce the clown mirrors—and mimicks—that of the eponymous "gentlemen." The play introduces two quite different comic servants: the witty page Speed, always aware of, and frequently obsessed with, wordplay (note his extended riff on mutton, sheep, and "baa"/"bah" in act 1, scene 1), and the hapless Launce, a true Shakespearean clown, who speaks in malapropisms, and whose inadvertent language seems to know more "truth" than he does. When the two meet up at the Duke's court, and Launce mistakes Speed's term of address, "your mastership," for an inquiry about his "master's ship," which is at sea, Speed's comeback establishes the linguistic distance between them: "Well, your old vice still, mistake the word" (3.1.277). Speed and Launce together itemize the qualities of Launce's love, the milkmaid, in a catalogue of virtues and vices that resembles the antiblazon of the greasy kitchen wench Nell in *The Comedy of Errors.* Launce's love has sour breath; she talks in her sleep; she has no teeth; she is "curst," or shrewish; and she is too "liberal," or loose. For each of these vices the optimistic Launce finds a value: a toothless woman will give him all the breadcrusts, a woman too liberal with her favors still cannot be liberal with his money if he has none. The play invites us to contrast this list of highly specific qualities with the incomparable Silvia, whose praise, in the beautiful lyric "Who is Silvia? What is she, / That all our swains commend her?" (4.2.37–38), seems by contrast exceedingly *un*specific and ideal ("Holy, fair, and wise is she," "Is she kind as she is fair?").

But Launce's true passion is not for his ladylove, but for his dog. In fact, his highest praise of the milkmaid is that "[s]he hath more qualities than a water-spaniel" (3.1.267–268). In case the audience is in any danger of missing the point, Shakespeare also has Proteus compare his own love for Silvia to that of a fawning spaniel (4.2.14–15). A dog named Crab, who features largely both in the comic set pieces of the plot and in its "romance" action, is Launce's best friend, and the account of Launce's parting from Crab (probably named for the sour crab apple) is placed by Shakespeare, with his genius for scene-to-scene juxtaposition, right after Proteus's leave-taking from Julia. Proteus and Julia exchange rings (for experienced Shakespeare-watchers a surefire clue to a later recognition scene) and a kiss that points directly ahead to Romeo and Juliet (Julia: "And seal the bargain with a holy kiss" [2.2.7]).

In terms of literary style, we should note that this very early play already demonstrates Shakespeare's superb command of the medium of prose, especially for comic effect. Launce's lengthy description of his leave-taking from the surly, ungrateful Crab, with the improvised puppet-show demonstration of how his parents responded to their son's departure, is a classic outpouring of bathetic emotion, exhibited in soliloquy to the audience:

> I think Crab, my dog, be the sourest-natured dog that lives. My mother weeping, my father wailing, my sister crying, our maid howling, our cat wringing her hands, and all our house in a great perplexity, yet did not this cruel-hearted cur shed one tear. He is a stone, a very pebble-stone, and has no more pity in him than a dog. A Jew would have wept to have seen our parting. Why, my grandam, having no eyes, look you, wept herself blind at my parting. Nay, I'll show you the manner of it. This shoe is my father. No, this left shoe is my father. No, no, this left shoe is my mother. Nay, that cannot be so, neither. Yes, it is so, it is so, it hath the worser sole. This shoe with the hole in it is my mother; and this my father. A vengeance on't, there 'tis. Now, sir, this staff is my sister, for, look you, she is as white as a lily and as small as a wand. This hat is Nan our maid. I am the dog. No, the dog is himself, and I am the dog. O, the dog is me, and I am myself. Ay, so, so. Now come I to my father. "Father, your blessing." Now should not the shoe speak a word for weeping. Now should I kiss my father. Well, he weeps on. Now come I to my mother. O that she could speak now, like a moved woman. Well, I kiss her. Why, there 'tis. Here's my mother's breath up and down. Now come I to my sister. Mark the moan she makes.—Now the dog all this while sheds not a tear nor speaks a word. But see how I lay the dust with my tears.

2.3.4–28

Any aficionado of modern stand-up comedy will recognize this as an opening monologue, and an accomplished one. The whole family, from sister to grandmother to hand-wringing cat, is instantly and powerfully evoked, though none of them ever appears on the stage. The byplay with the shoes is a kind of puppetry (hand puppets were very popular in public entertainments in the period), with the jest about the shoe with the hole in it representing his mother, and the equally broad joke on the malodorous shoe (Launce's own, of course) and the mother's unsweet breath. Launce's swipe at Jews cannot be wished away; here and elsewhere in the plays the social caricature of the hard-hearted or mercenary Jew is casually invoked, with the implication that most in the audience would recognize this characterization and agree with it. His name-sake character in *The Merchant of Venice,* Lancelot Gobbo, shares Launce's views of Jewish nature. Launce's inability to distinguish between himself and the dog ("I am the dog. No, the dog is himself, and I am the dog. O, the dog is me, and I am myself") pokes fun at the identity crises of his master, Proteus ("Julia I lose, and Valentine I lose. / If I keep them I needs must lose myself [2.6.19–20]). As for Crab the dog, he alone is described as unnatural. For the dog was the most proverbial loyal and faithful of companions. "There is not any creature," wrote Edward Topsell in his *History of Four-Footed Beasts,* "more loving to his Master, or more Serviceable . . . than is a Dog."

The bromide that "a man's best friend is his dog" is an ancient one, and early modern authors wrote extensively about the comparison of the two species. Topsell's *History of Four-Footed Beasts,* published in 1607 but based on earlier texts, notably the Swiss naturalist Konrad von Gesner's mid-sixteenth-century *Historiae Animalium,* includes a large section on relations between humans and dogs, and Dr. John Caius's *Of English Dogges* is a translation of Abraham Flem-ing's *De Canibus Britannicis* (1576).

Here is a suggestive passage from a poem by Sir John Davies, the author of more weighty works like *Orchestra* (1596), a poem in praise of dancing and the harmony of the spheres, and *Nosce Teipsum* (*Know Thyself;* 1599), both of which have demonstrable affinities with Shakespeare's early plays. In this early epigram, written probably in the period 1590–1594, he takes "Cineas's" self-description ("Thou saist thou art as weary as a dogge, / As angry, sick, and hun-gry as a dogge") and turns it into a praise of canine nature:

> I will compare thee better to a dogge.
> Thou art as fair and comely as a dogge,
> Thou art as true and honest as a dogge,
> Thou art as kinde and liberall as a dogge,
> Thou art as wise and valiant as a dogge.
>
> *Davies, "In Cineam"*

The Launce-Crab relationship is simultaneously comic and moving. Launce has been instructed by Proteus to give Silvia a lapdog as a present. Caius's trea-tise *Of English Dogges* had emphasized that "[t]hese puppies the smaller they be, the more pleasure they prouoke, as more meete play fellowe for minsing mistrisses to beare in their bosoms, to keepe company withal in their chamber, to succour with sleepe in bed, and nourishe with meate at boourde, to lay in their lappes, and licke their lippes."[1] But Launce somehow loses the elegant lapdog and makes the ultimate sacrifice of offering instead his own pet ("who is," as he explains to the appalled Proteus, "as big as ten of yours, and therefore the gift the greater" [4.4.49–50]). When Crab disgraces himself under the Duke's table ("all the chamber smelled him"; "I, having been acquainted with the smell before, knew it was Crab"), Launce takes both the blame and the whipping, as he has before "sat in the stocks for puddings he hath stolen," and "stood on the pillory for geese he hath killed." How many masters, he asks rhetorically, but with truth, would do this for their servants?

> Nay, I remember the trick you served me when I took my leave of Madam Silvia. Did not I bid thee still mark me, and do as I do? When didst thou see me heave up my leg and make water against a gentlewoman's farthingale? Didst thou ever see me do such a trick?
>
> *4.4.29–33*

Topsell's *History,* expounding on canine deportment, explains that "it is the nature of a Dog when he maketh water, to hold up his leg." What is at stake in this one-sided comic dialogue between voluble clown and silent dog is the nature of "natural" behavior, for men and for dogs, with a mild query, somewhere just below the surface, about which of these various creatures— noblemen, clowns and servants, dogs—are the most admirable, or the least culpable. And of course Launce's generous gesture of giving away his dog, however misplaced and unwelcome, points directly, wittily, and deftly toward Valentine's similar gesture of sacrifice in the next act: "All that was mine in Silvia I give thee." In every way, the Launce-Crab relationship undercuts the self-inflated rhetoric of the two young masters, and all three "couples," each threatened with separation, are reunited at the play's close.

But of course Launce and Crab have exited the scene by the time the Duke arrives to "applaud [Valentine's] spirit" and bestow Silvia's hand upon him. The luckless Thurio, perfectly reasonably, declines to fight for her, since he now realizes that she loves someone else. And the "high," or aristocratic, plot of *Two Gentlemen* culminates in Valentine's closing invitation, as the couples parade offstage, to a single marriage day that will unite both pairs—"our day of marriage shall be yours, / One feast, one house, one mutual happiness" (5.4.169–170). The end of the play is very characteristic of Shakespeare, early and late: those left onstage agree to go off together to discuss what has transpired, leaving the audience to do the same, and to compare its fuller knowledge with the partial awareness that is all that any character in the play possesses. "I'll tell you as we pass along, / That you will wonder what hath fortunèd," Valentine tells the Duke, and adds, "Come, Proteus, 'tis your penance but to hear / The story of your loves discoverèd" (165–168). This invitation to replay the play accomplishes the necessary clearing of the stage. But the blithe confidence of these victorious "two gentlemen" lacks any sense of the real dangers they have passed. The witty wordplay of Lucetta and Julia, and the comic underplot of Launce and Crab, do far more to mitigate the self-satisfied triumph of the lovers than the spurious threats posed by rival lovers, stern fathers, or forest outlaws. The partialness of this sense of plenitude is perfectly "Shakespearean"; any play that ends with so firm a claim to "happiness" is balanced on the edge of the disasters-that-did-not-happen, rewarding its characters for the moment, but cautioning the audience, at the same time, that such perfect satisfaction is indeed a matter of fortune as well as desert, and that its completion, as always, lies offstage.

The Taming of the Shrew

DRAMATIS PERSONAE

IN THE INDUCTION

Christopher Sly, *beggar and tinker*

A Hostess

A Lord

Bartholomew, *his page*

Huntsmen

Servants

Players

IN THE PLAY-WITHIN-THE-PLAY

Baptista Minola, *a gentleman*
   of Padua

Katherine, *his elder daughter*

Bianca, *his younger daughter*

Petruchio, *a gentleman of Verona,*
   suitor of Katherine

Grumio, *his servant*

Curtis, *his servant*

Gremio, *a rich old man of Padua,*
   suitor of Bianca

Hortensio, *another suitor, who*
   disguises himself as Licio, a teacher

Lucentio, *from Pisa, who disguises*
   himself as Cambio, a teacher

Tranio, *his servant*

Biondello, *his servant*

Vincentio, *Lucentio's father*

A Pedant (schoolmaster),
   from Mantua

A Widow

A Tailor

A Haberdasher

An Officer

Servingmen, including
   Nathaniel, Philip, Joseph,
   and Peter

Other servants of Baptista
   and Petruchio

ISCUSSIONS OF THIS play often center on two key dramatic elements: first, the "Induction," or framing device, in which a drunken tinker is led to believe he is a great lord, married to a "lady" (a page boy in disguise), and being entertained by the performance of a play (the *Taming*-play proper, with the courtship of Petruchio and Kate); and second, Kate's so-called obedience speech at the very end of the play (act 5, scene 2), in which the headstrong and independent woman, the supposed shrew of the title, enjoins her fellow wives to "serve, love, and obey" their husbands, and symbolically to "place your hands below your husband's foot."

These two dramatic moments are rightly seen as key to both production and interpretation, and I will take them up in turn. But there are other elements to

the plot that are also worth our careful attention, in part because they reflect—
and anticipate—Shakespeare's continuing interest in certain kinds of interpersonal relationships, like those between apparently compliant and apparently
defiant women, the pleasures and dangers of the "language lesson," and the love
banter of married or engaged couples, a war of words that will resound delightfully through the plays from *Taming* to *Much Ado About Nothing* to the teasing
equality of Hotspur and Lady Percy in *Henry IV Part 1*.

Some larger themes of dream, impersonation, transformation, and disguise,
initiated in the Induction, carry through and unify the entire play. Typically, for
Shakespeare, these have both "high" and "low" versions: the echoes of Ovid's
Metamorphoses will suggest the empowering possibilities of transformation
upward toward the status of a "god" (or a "lord"), while the recasting of roles
throughout the play to facilitate a forbidden courtship (the master disguised as
a tutor; the servant disguised as his master) will suggest the dangerous malleability of social categories. Women and servants—like Sly the tinker in the
Induction—are subsidiary or dependent figures who threaten to become
"high," with topsy-turvy results for the social order. The fact that roles representing these various social ranks were all performed by stage players (all "low"
by early modern standards of status) and that women's roles on the public stage
in England were performed by boy actors underscores the degree to which
social order and hierarchy are both cultural fictions and material realities of life.
It is the inevitable and fruitful tension between these two aspects, the fiction
and the fact, that animates the plot, the comedy, and the cleverness of this play.

The Induction begins with the drunken tinker, Christopher Sly, and the
joke played upon him by a lord who spots Sly asleep in front of an alehouse and
suggests that Sly be conveyed to bed in the best chamber of the Lord's house;
plied with music, sweetmeats, and wine; and surrounded with "wanton pictures," including paintings of the metamorphoses of the gods:

Lord   Persuade him that he hath been lunatic,
        And when he says he is, say that he dreams,
        For he is nothing but a mighty lord.
                    Taming Induction 1.59–61

For the greater amusement of the gathering, a page is instructed to costume
himself as Sly's wife, the noble lady of the house. Sly is to be told that he has
slept and dreamed for fifteen years, that his wife has mourned for his companionship, and that he has now awakened to his right senses. Just as this plan is
being devised, along comes a company of players, much as will later occur in
Hamlet, and these players, already known to the Lord and warmly welcomed by
him, are straightaway employed, like the troupe that arrives in Hamlet's Elsinore, to perform in front of a designated audience. Cautioned that the supposed lord (the transformed Sly) has "never heard a play" and may respond
oddly to what he sees, the players agree to perform a "pleasant comedy," suppos-

edly to soothe the troubled brain of the newly awakened "lord." The stage is set for the play-within-the-play, which will be the entire remaining action of *The Taming of the Shrew*.

The language of dream is everywhere in this little framing scene: the Lord notes that Sly's experience is to be "[e]ven as a flatt'ring dream or worthless fancy" (Induction 1.40), where "fancy" carries the meaning of "fantasy" or "imagination." "Am I a lord, and have I such a lady?" Sly wonders:

> Or do I dream? Or have I dreamed till now?
> I do not sleep. I see, I hear, I speak.
> I smell sweet savours, and I feel soft things.
> Upon my life, I am a lord indeed,
> And not a tinker, nor Christopher Sly.
>
> *Induction 2.66–71*

Bear in mind that both the "real" lord and the false one in this scene are impersonators, one actor playing the part of a nobleman, the other playing the part of a tinker wrongly convinced that he is a nobleman. Neither is "a lord indeed." And although the masquerade of Bartholomew the page as a "lady" leads to some inevitable bawdy byplay (Sly summarily commands that she undress and join him there, and has to be cautioned that having sex too soon will bring on a recurrence of his lunacy), in fact *all* the women's parts in *The Taming of the Shrew* are played—as always in this period on the English public stage—by boy actors. So "Lady" is as fictional a role as "Lord." When in the next scenes of the play proper Kate the "shrew" is described as "too rough," "stark mad or wonderful froward" (1.1.55, 69), the audience might, if it wished, look back at the role of Bartholomew, the manifestly "false" image of femininity. How does a "real" woman behave? Like the outspoken Kate; like her more conventional sister, Bianca, whose "silence . . . mild behaviour and sobriety" (70–71) are praised by her many suitors; or like the simpering and apparently compliant Bartholomew, the page dressed as a lady—a lady who also, we might note, gets "her" way, deftly eluding the clumsy embraces of Sly.

Thus the Induction, the play-before-the-play, introduces and mirrors all the major issues that will preoccupy the actors in the main drama to come. Such an induction was not uncommon for an early modern play; among the most famous examples is the Induction for Thomas Kyd's *Spanish Tragedy*, explicitly recalled in Sly's phrase "Go by, Saint Jeronimy" (Induction 1.7), echoing a tag phrase from that play, "Hieronimo, beware! go by, go by!" (*Spanish Tragedy* 3.12.31), in which a murdered man and the figure of Revenge sit onstage throughout and observe the action. In other popular genres, too, like the fairy tale and the dream vision, a "frame story" was often used to encapsulate the narrative. Thus many medieval dream visions began with someone who falls asleep and dreams the rest of the story. It makes sense, then, that audiences and readers of Shakespeare's play might seek, and find, some correspondences between what happens in the frame (the story of Christopher Sly) and what happens in the "taming" plot.

One important source for the play is George Gascoigne's *Supposes* (1566), the Prologue, or Argument, of which is worth quoting here, to give something of the flavor of the time and of the wordplay:

> I suppose you are assembled here, supposing to reap the fruit of my tra-
> vails: and to be plain, I mean presently to present you with a Comedy
> called Supposes: the very name wherof may peradventure drive into every
> one of your heads a sundry suppose, to suppose the meaning of our sup-
> poses. Some percase will suppose we mean to occupy your ears with
> sophistical handling of subtil suppositions. Some other will suppose we go
> about to dicipher unto you some quaint conceits, which hitherto have
> been only supposed as it were in shadows: and some I see smiling as though
> they supposed we would trouble you with the vain suppose of some wan-
> ton suppose. But understand, this our suppose is nothing else but a mis-
> taking or imagination of one thing for an other. For you shall see the
> master supposed for the servant, the servant for the master: the freeman for
> a slave, and the bondslave for a freeman: the stranger for a well-known
> friend, and the familiar for a stranger.[1]

Many details of Gascoigne's play are borrowed, or altered, by Shakespeare, and the use and adaptation of such source material in the writing of plays was standard practice in the period. Our modern ideas about a writer's "originality"— like the concept of the "author" as having authority over his work—date from the eighteenth century, the era in which copyright law was established, and in which the Shakespeare text as we know it was edited, regularized, and codified in a series of important editions. Since readers and audiences of *The Taming of the Shrew* today are not likely to know Gascoigne's play or to have had a chance to see it performed, it will not be particularly useful here to draw detailed comparisons. The key issue, well underscored in Gascoigne's own Prologue, is that the word "suppose" could have a number of related meanings, from deliberate impersonation to mistake to counterfeits, substitutions, false inferences, guesses, and vain beliefs, and that all of these meanings are deployed in the construction and performance of Shakespeare's play. The play itself is structured, in a fashion that would become increasingly important for the playwright's work, as a series of performances within performances, or plays-within-the-play, from the Induction to the masquerades of Bianca's suitors to Kate's shrewishness to Petruchio's devices. The final, much-debated scene in which Kate delivers her speech about women's obedience is itself a performance, staged—at Petruchio's request and command—for an onstage audience of husbands and fathers, who are watching the responses of their wives and daughters.

In approaching and analyzing the central action of *The Taming of the Shrew*, it may be useful first to summarize the plot in broad terms. Lucentio, a young man from Pisa, arriving in Padua to begin his university studies, comes by accident upon two suitors discussing their courtship of Bianca, a beautiful young woman. Unfortunately, Bianca has an elder sister, Kate, who is as combative and outspoken, or "curst," as Bianca is demure, and their father, Baptista, has made it clear that a husband must be found for Kate before he will grant anyone permission to marry Bianca. Lucentio determines to enter the marriage sweepstakes himself, changing clothes—and places—with his servant, Tranio. Tranio is now "Lucentio," and Lucentio is "Cambio" (literally, the "changed one," or the "one who changes"), a schoolmaster. For Baptista is seeking tutors—a music master and a schoolmaster who can teach poetry and language—for his daughters, and this is the only way to get access to the protected Bianca. Her other two suitors, the young man Hortensio and the older, wealthy Gremio, also develop plans for outwitting the blocking father, Baptista. Hortensio will disguise himself as a music master; Gremio will hire "Cambio" to serve his own purposes—or so he thinks. Thus Tranio, pretending to be Lucentio, will "officially" woo Bianca, asking her father for her hand, while Lucentio, disguised as the humble schoolmaster, will win her love. This "high"/"low" plot enables Shakespeare to introduce two kinds of wordplay that would recur throughout the rest of his dramatic career: the jokes on musical fingering and tuning, and the double-entendre language lesson, both in act 3, scene 1. The language lesson, in which Lucentio whispers his real message to Bianca under cover of the construing of a passage from Latin, will recur to comic effect in plays like *Henry IV Part 1, Henry V,* and *The Merry Wives of Windsor.*

When the supposed Lucentio's courtship requires the assent of his father, the impersonators conscript the elderly Pedant from Mantua who happens to be wandering by, to play "Vincentio of Padua," thereupon, through the inevitable logic of comic discovery, ensuring that the "real" father will shortly enter the action and confront his imitator. We should note that some key comic elements that are instrumental to *The Comedy of Errors* are also present here, in a play that was written at about the same time. The traveling Pedant is told, quite falsely, " 'Tis death for any one in Mantua / To come to Padua" (4.2.82–83); it is this erroneous information that induces him to pretend to be Vincentio. This device, trivial and incidental in *Taming,* is the opening gambit of *The Comedy of Errors,* where it is no joke: Egeon, a Syracusan merchant apprehended in Ephesus without ransom money, faces the apparent certainty of death by beheading at sundown. In *Taming,* the comic confrontation of the two "Vincentios," one on either side of a door (5.1), mirrors a similar encounter between the twin Dromios of *Errors,* each unaware of the other's identity. A third comic—or dramatic—element that the two plays have in common is the link between the Bianca plot and the Kate plot, for in *The Comedy of Errors* Adriana, the wife of Antipholus of Ephesus, is similarly characterized as assertive, "rough," and outspoken, and is paired, and contrasted, with a milder, more compliant and conventional sister, Luciana.

Most people who have read or seen a performance of *The Taming of the*

Shrew will remember it chiefly for the "taming" plot, the courtship—described over the years as everything from passionate to abusive, and ultimately oddly tender—between Petruchio, who "comes to wive it wealthily in Padua" (to quote the hit song from the 1948 Cole Porter musical *Kiss Me, Kate*), and the "shrew" of the title, Baptista's elder daughter, Katherina, also known as Katherine or Kate. The opening salvo between these two well-matched lovers reads to a modern audience like a dialogue almost designed for a latter-day Kate, Katharine Hepburn, in her series of witty romantic comedies with Spencer Tracy. Later bantering lovers in Shakespeare's plays—Beatrice and Benedick in *Much Ado About Nothing,* Hotspur and Lady Percy in *Henry IV Part 1,* and others—owe much to this early and lively pair, although the physical violence of the "taming" story will disappear in subsequent love plays, transmuted into bouts of wit. We might note that Lady Percy, too, is a "Kate," as is the French princess (formally "Catherine") in *Henry V,* whom King Harry woos and wins in plain English fashion ("but a good heart, Kate, is the sun and the moon"):

Petruchio	Good morrow, Kate, for that's your name, I hear.
Katherine	Well have you heard, but something hard of hearing.
	They call me Katherine that do talk of me.
Petruchio	You lie, in faith, for you are called plain Kate,
	And bonny Kate, and sometimes Kate the curst,
	But Kate, the prettiest Kate in Christendom,
	Kate of Kate Hall, my super-dainty Kate—
	For dainties are all cates, and therefore "Kate"—
	Take this of me, Kate of my consolation:
	Hearing thy mildness praised in every town,
	Thy virtues spoke of, and thy beauty sounded—
	Yet not so deeply as to thee belongs—
	Myself am moved to woo thee for my wife.
Katherine	Moved? In good time. Let him that moved you hither
	Re-move you hence. I knew you at the first
	You were a movable.
Petruchio	Why, what's a movable?
Katherine	A joint-stool.
Petruchio	Thou hast hit it. Come, sit on me.
Katherine	Asses are made to bear, and so are you.
Petruchio	Women are made to bear, and so are you.

2.1.180–198

This extended conversation, the first between this high-spirited pair, displays both their wittiness and their uncanny "modernity"—which is to say, the heritage of wrangling courtship that would extend, through Shakespeare and Restoration comedy to the plays and films of the twentieth and twenty-first centuries. A "cate" was a delicacy; a "movable" was a piece of furniture; a "joint-stool" was a three- or four-legged stool, a modest household item of little value (compare the later quip in *King Lear,* "Cry you mercy, I took you for a join-stool" [Quarto 1, 3.6.44], a proverbial joking apology for overlooking someone). As swiftly as one of them introduces a figure, the other turns it to a second, punning use: Petruchio's acceptance of the role of "joint-stool" immediately becomes a sexual invitation ("Come, sit on me") and leads to the double entendre on "bear," to carry burdens (Petruchio is an "ass," a beast of burden, and a fool), and "bear," to have children (Katherine is a woman, and will have to learn a woman's role, both in bearing children and in bearing the weight of a man in the marriage bed). The rest of the scene continues in this heady, exhilarating, and combative spirit, full of stichomythic exchanges (Katherine: "Where did you study all this goodly speech?" Petruchio: "It is extempore, from my mother-wit." Katherine: "A witty mother, witless else her son" [2.1.255–257]), and culminates, characteristically for Shakespeare, in a temporary rejection of wit and wordplay in favor of plain speech:

> Petruchio Thus in plain terms: your father hath consented
> That you shall be my wife, your dowry 'greed on,
> And will you, nill you, I will marry you.
> Now, Kate, I am a husband for your turn,
> For by this light, whereby I see thy beauty—
> Thy beauty that doth make me like thee well—
> Thou must be married to no man but me,
> For I am he am born to tame you, Kate. . . .
>
> *2.1.261–268*

Whatever Kate's, or even Petruchio's, feelings in the matter, the audience will by this time be convinced that what he says is true, and that these two characters not only are well matched but are actually enjoying themselves.

Petruchio's chosen method of "taming," as he has already explained to us, is to "woo her with some spirit" by contradicting everything she says, praising her behavior as if it were just what the occasion demanded:

> Say that she rail, why then I'll tell her plain
> She sings as sweetly as a nightingale.
> Say that she frown, I'll say she looks as clear
> As morning roses newly washed with dew.
> Say she be mute and will not speak a word,
> Then I'll commend her volubility,
> And say she uttereth piercing eloquence.
> If she do bid me pack, I'll give her thanks
> As though she bid me stay by her a week.

> If she deny to wed, I'll crave the day
> When I shall ask the banns, and when be marrièd.
>
> 2.1.168–178

This same logic of erotic contradiction, if we may so term it, persists through-out Petruchio's madcap instant courtship, wedding, and reception of the bride at his house in the country. It is in these scenes at Petruchio's house that Kate, rushed away from the home of her father and sister, experiences the full brunt of the "taming" strategy: hungry, she is denied food when her husband pretends that well-cooked meat is burnt and not worth eating; charmed by the elegant styles presented to her by a haberdasher and a tailor, she is told that the attractive cap and well-fashioned gown are "lewd and filth" and "marred" so that—as a favor to her—her husband will not permit her to have or to wear them. Thus, in their "honest mean habiliments," they set forth again for her father's house and the postponed wedding celebration.

Significantly, Kate's response to this unaccountable and erratic behavior is likened to the experience of sleeping and waking—as one of the servants notes, "she, poor soul, / Knows not which way to stand, to look, to speak, / And sits as one new risen from a dream" (4.1.165–167). Kate's situation is, in fact, analogous to that of the pretended lord Christopher Sly in the Induction, an analogy made more vivid by the presence of Sly and his "lady" on (or above) the stage in many productions. Like Sly, Kate is told the opposite of what she knows or believes to be true. Unlike him, she at first resists. But also unlike him, she will adapt and change as a result of the experience of the play.

By the end of act 4 Kate has caught on to Petruchio's mood and is willing to call the sun the moon, and the moon the sun, according to his whim. Direct contradiction, she sees, is not the way to deal with him:

> be it moon, or sun, or what you please,
> And if you please to call it a rush-candle
> Henceforth I vow it shall be so for me.
>
> 4.6.13–15

"Henceforth" is the key word here; it marks a turning point for both of them. When in the next moment they encounter the old man Vincentio—journeying to Padua to see his son Lucentio—and Petruchio hails him as a beautiful young girl, Kate is quick to follow his lead, greeting Vincentio in similar fashion:

> Young budding virgin, fair, and fresh, and sweet,
> · · · · · · · · · · · · · · · · · ·
> Happ[y] the man whom favourable stars
> Allots thee for his lovely bedfellow.
>
> 4.6.38–42

Again the audience is invited to think of the situation of Christopher Sly, whose page boy "lady" sits beside him to watch this "taming" play. And again Petruchio, having made his point about mastery, returns the world from confusion:

> Why, how now, Kate, I hope thou art not mad.
> This is a man, old, wrinkled, faded, withered,
> And not a maiden as thou sayst he is.
>
> *4.6.43–45*

This marks the beginning of Petruchio and Kate's mutual collaboration; Kate acts as his accomplice and recognizes Vincentio with wit and invention. The arrival of Vincentio signals the intertwining of the two plots, the Kate plot and the Bianca plot, and the resolution awaits characters and audience in the fifth act of the play, when the Pedant playing "Vincentio of Padua" encounters the "right Vincentio," the false and true Lucentios are identified, and the marriage of Bianca and Lucentio is revealed to have taken place earlier without either father's permission.

Two fascinating further reversals follow immediately upon these comic disclosures: first, the married couple of Petruchio and Katherine, suddenly and completely in accord with each other, and left onstage alone to close the scene, constitute themselves as an amused and indulgent audience:

> Katherine   Husband, let's follow to see the end of this ado.
> Petruchio   First kiss me, Kate, and then we will.
>
> *5.1.122–124*

Without emphasis, Kate calls him "love": "Nay, I will give thee a kiss. Now pray thee, love, stay" (129). There is no longer a question of "taming"; this is a marriage, one consummated in couplets as well as quips. Attention now shifts to the unresolved elements of the love plot, and thus to the story of Bianca, who has been joined by a nameless (but wealthy) widow, the new bride of Bianca's failed suitor Hortensio. And here we encounter the second reversal. For it is suddenly far from clear who is the real "shrew" of the play's title—and even who is appointed to do the "taming."

Act 5, scene 2, the climactic scene in which the famous "obedience" speech is delivered, is in fact a love test, a wager about wifely obedience entered upon by characters who believe that the risks and dangers of courtship are past, so that they may now take pleasure in their newly married condition, as masters (and mistresses) of their own lives, no longer beholden to parents or other authority figures. Such premature overconfidence on the part of Shakespearean lovers will show itself toward the close of many of his romantic comedies, including *Love's Labour's Lost, A Midsummer Night's Dream,* and *The Merchant of Venice.* In this case, the three young men, jesting with the father-in-law Baptista, agree upon a

bet as to which one is married to "the veriest shrew." It is Petruchio who proposes the terms, and he does so in response to the idea that his own wife is
without question the worst shrew of the bunch. "Let's each one send unto his
wife," Petruchio proposes, "And he whose wife is most obedient / To come at
first when he doth send for her / Shall win the wager which we will propose"
(5.2.67–70).

Here it may be worth pausing for a moment to reflect on the meanings of
the word "shrew," which meant, in order of historical appearance,

- a wicked, evil-disposed, or malignant man; a mischievous or vexatious
person; a rascal, a villain;
- the Devil;
- a thing of evil nature or influence;
- a person, especially (now only) a woman given to railing or scolding or
other perverse or malignant behavior; frequently, a scolding or turbulent
wife.

These definitions, adapted from the *Oxford English Dictionary*, tell an interesting tale of their own, as "shrew" migrates across the social and gender spectrum
from male to female. (In *The Comedy of Errors*, a play written at about the
same time as *Taming*, the word is used by Antipholus of Ephesus to chastise
a man he thinks is his servant [4.1.51].) But over time "shrew" became increasingly gender-specific, coming to mean a *woman* who scolds or makes trouble.
Especially a *wife* who does so. In some cases "shrew" came to mean just "wife,"
or "woman," not even "troublesome wife." (See, for example, the language-
challenged Sir Andrew Aguecheek speaking to Maria the waiting-gentlewoman
in *Twelfth Night*—"Bless you, fair shrew" [*Twelfth Night* 1.3.39]—where Sir
Andrew manifestly and comically misuses the term.) But this men-only conversation about which new wife is most shrewish deserves, and gets, a quick comeuppance, as the two supposedly compliant wives refuse to obey their husbands'
commands. Bianca sends word through a servant that "she is busy and she cannot come" (*Taming* 5.2.86). Hortensio's wife (the Widow), guessing—with perfect accuracy—that he has "some goodly jest at hand," tells the same messenger
that "[s]he will not come. She bids you come to her" (95–96).

With "cannot" and "will not" ringing across the stage, and a role reversal
("She bids you come to her") having been suggested by the Widow, who has
already had, and perhaps tamed, at least one husband, Petruchio ups the ante,
instructing his servant to go to Kate and "Say I command her come to me"
(100). Before the others have finished chuckling at his folly, Kate is onstage, asking her husband's will, and then dutifully departing, at his request, to round up
the two recalcitrant wives. Lucentio and Hortensio regard this as a "wonder," or
portent. Baptista, the father, declares that "she is changed," and promises a second dowry for this new daughter. Here again is that language of transformation
that has been present in the play since the Sly Induction and Lucentio's choice

of "Cambio" as his name when in disguise. And it is in this context that Kate returns, leading Bianca and the Widow, and delivers, at her husband's charge, her celebrated speech, fulfilling his request that she "tell these headstrong women / What duty they do owe their lords and husbands" (134–135).

Since interpretations of this speech have so greatly colored—or vexed—productions and readings of the play, it may be useful to underscore two points that initially may seem to be at odds with each other: first, that there is a context for this speech not only within Shakespeare's historical time period but, more important, within this play and the constellation of other Shakespearean plays that engage the same issues; and second, that every production is an interpretation, and that plays, like other works of art, are living things that grow and change over time and in response to changing circumstances. The clearest modern example here, and one to which we will come, is the reception and production of a play like *The Merchant of Venice* in the context of twentieth-century European history and the Holocaust. Questions of women's rights, women's independence, and cultural and political feminism arising long after the initial writing and staging of *Taming* will, inevitably, have changed the expectations and responses of audiences—and of actors. (Remember yet again that the first "Kate" was a boy actor, and that women did not play this part, or any parts on the English public stage, until after the start of the Restoration in 1660.) Modern actresses have often delivered Kate's "obedience" speech with a wink, or with a tone of evident irony, attempting to get around its apparent meaning or to reverse (or, in the play's own terms, "tame," or master) that meaning. In my view this is perfectly legitimate, and it increases the power and range of the play. But such an interpretation will need to be prepared for throughout—perhaps through creative links and flashbacks to the Sly Induction and the evident "theatricality" or stagedness of the "taming" plot—since much of the internal evidence in the play points in the other direction, toward a "straight" reading of these lines.

Part of the problem, if it is a problem, is that many modern readers do not want Shakespeare to hold, or to have held, views that are socially or politically incompatible with their own; this is "our Shakespeare," who seems to know us better than we know ourselves, since, in a way, he, or his plays, have made us who and what we are. Thus, to discover, say, any trace of anti-Jewish sentiment or anti-Moorish (antiblack) sentiment in "our Shakespeare" feels like a disappointment, perhaps even a betrayal. I am deliberately avoiding anachronistic terms like "anti-Semitism" and "racism," but there is no doubt that these terms are in the minds of some modern readers and audiences. Likewise, evidence in the plays of "antifeminism" or of a hierarchical social model in which husbands rule and control their wives is not the evidence many contemporary appreciators would prefer to find.

Nonetheless, it is reasonable to follow the evidence, and see where it leads us.

The only other plays in which Shakespeare uses the term "shrew" as a noun in this sense are *Twelfth Night* (where, as we have already noticed, the hapless Sir Andrew comically misuses the word) and *The Comedy of Errors,* a play written at a time close to that of *The Taming of the Shrew* and that contains, as we have seen, many similar scenes, characters, devices, and themes (including the major theme of dream or transformation and the linked conundrum of identity). Although the "shrew" in *The Comedy of Errors* is a male servant, the character clearly and extensively accused of shrewishness in the popular sense (henpecking, railing, nagging) is a wife, the outspoken Adriana, married to Antipholus of Ephesus, and she is reproved for her behavior by a figure of considerable female authority, the Abbess, who will turn out to be her long-lost mother-in-law, the mother of the twin Antipholuses and the wife of the merchant Egeon. Placed in a position of judgment, the Abbess entraps Adriana by inviting her to report whether she has "reprehended" her husband "rough enough," and in public:

Adriana	It was the copy of our conference.
	In bed he slept not for my urging it.
	At board he fed not for my urging it.
	Alone, it was the subject of my theme.
	In company I often glancèd it.
	Still did I tell him it was vile and bad.
Abbess	And thereof came it that the man was mad.
	The venom clamours of a jealous woman
	Poisons more deadly than a mad dog's tooth.
	It seems his sleeps were hindered by thy railing,
	And thereof comes it that his head is light.

Errors 5.1.63–73

And so on and on, through a whole litany of Adriana's faults and upbraidings— all, we might note, in protest of her husband's visits to a courtesan. "Headstrong," a word used explicitly by Petruchio in reference to the need to tame Kate ("And thus I'll curb her mad and headstrong humour" [*Taming* 4.1.190]) and later in his charge to her ("tell these headstrong women / What duty they do owe their lords and husbands" [5.2.134–135]), is a criticism directly leveled at Adriana in *The Comedy of Errors* by her more conventional sister, Luciana ("headstrong liberty is lashed with woe [2.1.15]), in a passage that seems a close counterpart to Kate's "obedience" speech. Here is the unmarried Luciana, making a claim for "men's rights" to her married sister:

Luciana	O, know he is the bridle of your will.
Adriana	There's none but asses will be bridled so.
Luciana	Why, headstrong liberty is lashed with woe.
	There's nothing situate under heaven's eye
	But hath his bound in earth, in sea, in sky.

> The beasts, the fishes, and the wingèd fowls
> Are their males' subjects, and at their controls.
> Man, more divine, the master of all these,
> Lord of the wide world and wild wat'ry seas,
> Indued with intellectual sense and souls,
> Of more pre-eminence than fish and fowls.
> Are masters to their females, and their lords.
> Then let your will attend on their accords.

Adriana This servitude makes you to keep unwed.
Luciana Not this, but troubles of the marriage bed.
Adriana But were you wedded you would bear some sway.
Luciana Ere I learn love, I'll practise to obey.

Errors 2.1.13–29

And here is Kate, addressing her sister, Bianca, and the Widow, who has twice defied Petruchio by asserting her own mastery of the situation over his (Widow: "We will have no telling. . . . She shall not." Petruchio: "I say she shall."):

Katherine Thy husband is thy lord, thy life, thy keeper,
> Thy head, thy sovereign, one that cares for thee,
> And for thy maintenance commits his body
> To painful labour both by sea and land,
> To watch the night in storms, the day in cold,
> Whilst thou liest warm at home, secure and safe,
> And craves no other tribute at thy hands
> But love, fair looks, and true obedience,
> Too little payment for so great a debt.
> Such duty as the subject owes the prince,
> Even such a woman oweth to her husband,
> And when she is froward, peevish, sullen, sour,
> And not obedient to his honest will,
> What is she but a foul contending rebel,
> And graceless traitor to her loving lord?
> I am ashamed that women are so simple
> To offer war when they should kneel for peace,
> Or seek for rule, supremacy, and sway
> When they are bound to serve, love, and obey.

Taming 5.2.150–168

It is difficult to read—much less perform—these lines as ironic, given their similarity to the passages in *The Comedy of Errors* and, more mundanely, given the length and sustained nature of Kate's speech, which extends for more than forty lines, and culminates in the famous injunction to her fellow wives to swallow their pride and show their obedience and subservience:

> Then vail your stomachs, for it is no boot,
> And place your hands below your husband's foot,
> In token of which duty, if he please,
> My hand is ready, may it do him ease.
>
> *5.2.180–184*

We may note that Petruchio does not in fact demand this act of physical humbling, but—quite to the contrary—greets the whole speech, and the whole performance, with an audience member's praise, a tone of easy, familiar equality, and a sexual invitation: "Why, there's a wench! Come on, and kiss me, Kate." A few lines later his stage-clearing lines, "Come, Kate, we'll to bed. / We three are married, but you two are sped" (188–189), leave the two losers of the wager, Lucentio and Hortensio, to speak the final couplet, which demonstrates, as will so often be the case at the end of Shakespeare's plays and especially his comedies, that there is still a discrepancy between what has been learned by those onstage and by the audience in the theater:

> Hortensio   Now go thy ways, thou hast tamed a curst shrew.
> Lucentio   'Tis a wonder, by your leave, she will be tamed so.
>
> *5.2.192–193*

One thing that has surely taken place in the course of the play is that Kate has been awakened into action, and perhaps also into passion, by her breaking away from her father and sister. Cast in the role of "curst shrew" or Ugly Duckling in the household of Baptista, where she is the "bad girl" or bad daughter and Bianca the good daughter, Kate comes alive in her slanging matches with Petruchio. Her final performance is for him, and seems to represent not an abandonment of her earlier independence, but a revised understanding of what freedom means, in sexuality and in marriage. Bianca, whose name means "white," is pure and virginal but is also a blank slate; unrebellious as a child, she becomes, belatedly and at least for a comic moment, a rebellious wife rather than a defiant daughter. The next time Shakespeare uses this name it will be for a courtesan in *Othello,* whose external "whiteness," or purity, is at variance with her profession. The Widow, whose stage type reflects some "common wisdom" about the supposed lustiness of women who remarry after their husbands' deaths, shows the way in this rebellion, and since there is no preparation in the play for her marriage (Hortensio weds her quickly on the rebound from his rejection by Bianca), she can easily offer a model of a marriage of convenience, and profit, rather than of love. Whatever we may think of the sentiments voiced in Kate's "obedience" speech, Petruchio seems at least as appealing a figure as Lucentio (not to mention Hortensio) as a life partner and bed partner.

One pertinent question we might ask is whether the play is "meant" to be experienced from Kate's perspective or from Petruchio's. There is, of course, no way to know Shakespeare's "intention," a will-o'-the-wisp that has led many commentators astray. What is more important here is to remember that stage plays, unlike novels, memoirs, or lyric poems, have no single point of view, and no narrative voice. The play can be entered from many different perspectives—the Widow's as well as Kate's, Lucentio's and Baptista's as well as Petruchio's—so that there is no single "right" point of view. Indeed, it is one of Shakespeare's brilliant gifts as a dramatist to provide, in almost every case, a credible contrary argument, onstage, to what might seem to be a prevailing viewpoint. The "philosophy" of Shakespeare's plays is offered, always, contrapuntally, with opposing ideas placed in explicit juxtaposition. These plays are not constellated around a single hero or heroine; *Taming* is not "Kate's story" or "Petruchio's story" any more than *King Lear* is only the story of an errant and aging king, or *Hamlet* the story of an ambitious, thwarted, and melancholy prince. The "main characters" of the drama are linked to others, always, by analogy, by theme, and by language or image, so that Kate can be grouped with the women, with the daughters, and with her husband, as well as with the sleeping Christopher Sly, likewise caught between "flatt'ring dream" and "worthless fancy." When in the Induction the cross-dressed page tells Sly, "I am your wife in all obedience" (Induction 2.104), the question of wifely obedience is already put in play—especially when the first thing this "wife" does is disobey her "husband's" peremptory command, "Madam, undress you and come now to bed" (113). From this delayed bedding to Petruchio's "Come, Kate, we'll to bed" at the end of act 5, the play will explore key questions of gender, sexuality, language, equality, freedom, duty, and desire.

Editors have frequently noted the degree of "local color" in Christopher Sly's language and references, clearly placing him as a product of Shakespeare's native Warwickshire. This regionalism has sometimes led to a fuller attempt to read the play as reflecting the playwright's biography and personal views. Is the insistence of these early comedies on the character of the shrewish woman or shrewish wife any commentary on Shakespeare's own marriage? James Joyce, for example, has a character in *Ulysses* remark about "shrewridden Shakespeare and henpecked Socrates."[2] As intriguing a question as this may be, it has little importance when it comes to interpreting the plays. The "biographical interpretation" of the plays was once a predominant mode; thus many passages in the great tragedies were taken to reflect a revulsion at women and marriage, occasioned by some disillusioning event in Shakespeare's life, while the late romances were variously seen as evincing a final tranquillity or a bored distancing from the world of the stage and the events of real life. Likewise, some early modern cultural facts of life—like the ambivalent view of the remarried widow, noted above, or the financial dependence of a noblewoman or gentlewoman on her father or husband—have appropriately been taken as guides to the inflection or meaning of the plays. We have seen that the prevailing cultural attitude of female subservience to husbandly authority, as expressed by Saint Paul in his

Titus Andronicus

DRAMATIS PERSONAE

Saturninus, *eldest son of the late Emperor of Rome; later Emperor*
Bassianus, *his brother*
Titus Andronicus, *a Roman nobleman, general against the Goths*
Lucius, *son of Titus*
Quintus, *son of Titus*
Martius, *son of Titus*
Mutius, *son of Titus*
Lavinia, *daughter of Titus*
Young Lucius, *a boy, son of Lucius*
Marcus Andronicus, *a tribune of the people, Titus's brother*
Publius, *his son*
Sempronius, *kinsman of Titus*

Caius, *kinsman of Titus*
Valentine, *kinsman of Titus*
A Captain
Aemilius
Tamora, *Queen of the Goths, later wife of Saturninus*
Alarbus, *her son*
Demetrius, *her son*
Chiron, *her son*
Aaron, *a Moor, her lover*
A Nurse
A Clown
Senators, tribunes, Romans, Goths, soldiers, and attendants

THE PLAYGOERS of Shakespeare's time would have been far more familiar with Roman history and classical mythology than is a modern audience. The examples of the Greeks and the Romans were used as models for history writing, and the popularity of works like Sir Thomas North's translation of Plutarch's *Parallel Lives of the Noble Grecians and Romans* (1579) gave rise to the idea that a third set of lives, those of the English kings and heroes, might be seen as "parallel" to those of the ancients. The depravities of Tarquin and Nero, like the excellences of Caesar, were frequently cited; no book other than the Bible, North suggested, was so important a guide. Politicians and theorists, and the Queen and her counselors, looked to classical Rome as the pattern for the English nation and its nascent imperial power.

The classical myths were well known through readings of Ovid—a basic text in grammar school education—Virgil, and other ancient poets. For Elizabethans, these were not arcane or obscure texts. References to Tereus, Philomela, and Procne, to Dido and Aeneas, would have been part of the common store of knowledge, as is clear from those many moments in Shakespeare's plays when "low" characters joke about mythological figures.

Shakespeare's audience would also know, far better than we, the recent history of the stage, including the popularity of revenge tragedies like Kyd's *Spanish Tragedy* and Marlowe's *Jew of Malta*. Titus's "mad" fantasy that the disguised Tamora is a personified spirit of Revenge would evoke memories of the figure of Revenge in Kyd's highly successful play. The main character of *The Spanish Tragedy*, Hieronimo, loses a son to murder and goes mad in consequence, staging a play to try to trap his enemies; in many ways he is like Shakespeare's Titus, once honored, then disregarded and reviled. The main character of *The Jew of Malta*, Barabas, is a Machiavellian villain with a twisted sense of humor, full of revenge fantasies and bitterly angry against those who condemn him because he is a Jew; in some ways he may be said to resemble and to anticipate Aaron, Shakespeare's witty and vengeful Moor. When Aaron boasts to Titus's son Lucius that he "must talk of murders, rapes, and massacres, / Acts of black night, abominable deeds, / Complots of mischief, treason, villainies" (5.1.63–65), he sounds very much like Marlowe's Barabas.

And the vogue for Seneca, a Roman "closet-dramatist" who wrote for readers or declaimers rather than for the onstage performance of live actors, would have rendered both familiar and appealing the long speeches and broad gestures indicated in Shakespeare's text, which was, of course, designed for performance. Indeed, much of the punning, doubled language about the loss of "hands" in this play of mutilation and maiming addresses not only the instrumental but also the rhetorical loss incurred by those who suffer physical punishment. "How can I grace my talk," wonders Titus, "Wanting a hand to give it action?" (5.2.17–18). Lavinia's horrendous injuries, "her hands cut off and her tongue cut out, and ravished" (stage direction, act 2, scene 4), make it impossible for her to speak or gesture, causing her desperate interrogators to plead with her to "talk in signs" (3.2.12; see also 3.1.121, 143).

So, much that seems strangest or most arcane to us in *Titus Andronicus* would have been well within the cultural reach of a contemporary audience: the story of the heroic and doomed Andronici; the horrific fate of Lavinia; the mutilations and humiliations of her father, Titus; and the cannibal banquet at which Titus gets his belated revenge against Tamora, Queen of the Goths. These appalling spectacles, which uncannily resemble the events of a modern horror film, are not what we are used to thinking of as "Shakespearean." Shakespeare for twenty-first-century readers is a playwright associated with subtle language, architectonic plots, and the precise delineation of character, not with brutal and elemental acts of violence. In particular, the use of what our time has come to call "black humor" or moments of "absurdist" and "existential" comedy may seem out of place in the lexicon of a Shakespeare best known to many readers for his emotional verisimilitude and his psychological acuity. But in the shape, characters, and domestic situations of *Titus*, Shakespeare's earliest tragedy, can be seen not only harbingers of future tragic plots of the family, from *Hamlet* to *King Lear*, but also an extraordinarily powerful story in its own right—one that may serve, in our consideration, as the root or radical form of all Shakespearean tragedy.

Before we turn to the play itself, it may be useful to identify some of these elements, which include the popular Elizabethan theme of madness, feigned or real (an issue that will reappear with full force in the "madness" of the title characters—and of others—in *Hamlet, Othello,* and *King Lear*); the powerful spectacle of a father's grief at the fate of a beloved daughter (which will recur in the Polonius-Ophelia relationship in *Hamlet,* as well as in the anguished scenes of Lear with Cordelia); the general pattern of strong father-daughter and mother-son relations, so heavily fraught in this play (Titus and Lavinia; Tamora and her sons), as in later tragedies (*Coriolanus*) and romances (*The Tempest*); and the emergence at the end of the play of a political solution involving a pragmatic and effective new ruler set over against the heroic sufferings and losses of the immediate tragic past and its titanic figures. As we will see, both at the end of *Titus Andronicus* and at the end of most other Shakespearean tragedies, the audience is left with mixed emotions: the tragic heroes, with their excesses, their eloquence, their errors, and their magnificent suffering, are replaced by figures of lesser emotional scope, though often of far greater practical and political acumen. An invitation to social and cultural healing often closes the play, but even when what is lost is madness or rage, an audience may remember most the grandiosity of those tragic figures who have suffered and died. The renewal and restoration, even the improvement, of the political world of here-and-now cannot fully compensate for their disappearance from the stage.

This is, however, to begin at the end, something I do here quite consciously because *Titus Andronicus* is so often undervalued or misunderstood, regarded as a Shakespearean stepchild rather than a legitimate heir. Even those critics who celebrate the play—and there have been many, especially in recent years—often applaud its exceptionalism in the canon. But to look closely at this play is to see not only Shakespeare in the raw, or Shakespeare in the rough, but Shakespeare very much in command of both his theater and his plot. The word "plot," indeed, will recur throughout the play, from the forged letter accusing Titus's sons of regicide, a letter described by Tamora as a "complot of this timeless tragedy" (2.3.265), to the highly literal "sandy plot" on which the handless Lavinia is invited to inscribe her story with a stick (4.1.68). It is a relatively new term in the drama.

The play begins with a conflict over power, of a kind that will become familiar in other early plays of Shakespeare. Two brothers are competing for the right to be named emperor: one, Saturninus, is the elder and thus has the legal and lineal right to the throne, but he lacks the requisite moderation and judgment. The other, Bassianus, is more fit to rule by temperament and moral qualities, but his claim is less strong in law. The choice between them will fall upon the war hero Titus Andronicus, with whose daughter, Lavinia, Bassianus is in love. All this is sketched by the playwright, with typical economy and skill, in the first sixty lines. It is the kind of scenario we will often find at the beginning of his plays, from *Romeo and Juliet* to *A Midsummer Night's Dream* and

Richard II—two rival factions and a judge whose judgment cannot contain the impending strife.

The entry of Titus, accompanied by his four living sons and the body of a son recently killed by the Goths, disrupts the action for a moment. Here we might think ahead to the two short scenes that precede the entry of King Lear, which similarly turn on the ruler's choice between legal right and personal merit in his sons-in-law Albany and Cornwall, and on a rivalry between Edmund and Edgar, the two sons of the Duke of Gloucester. Titus, it turns out, has lost twenty-one of his twenty-five sons in the war, and he brings with him in triumph to the tomb of his ancestors Tamora the captive Queen of the Goths; her three sons Alarbus, Chiron, and Demetrius; and her lover, Aaron the Moor. Despite Tamora's pleas, the Romans' demand for vengeance will lead to the sacrificial death of her eldest son ("Alarbus' limbs are lopped," reports Titus's son Lucius) in retribution for Titus's loss. Vengeance begets vengeance, and this act will open the way to all the deaths and mutilations to come.

But this is as yet only a foreboding for the future. As Titus is welcomed by his brother Marcus, the tribune, and given the white candidate's robe of office, his power and honor seem assured. He is to "help to set a head on headless Rome" (1.1.186) by choosing the emperor, and he does so, against what the audience clearly perceives as both love and merit, electing the elder brother, Saturninus, and granting his wish to make Lavinia, Bassianus's beloved, his empress. The double-tongued nature of Saturninus, whose name suggests a "saturnine," or sullen, temperament, is evident in his remarks of acknowledgment, which—like everything in this play—contain the seeds of discord and portend ironic reversal:

> Thanks, noble Titus, father of my life.
> How proud I am of thee and of thy gifts
> Rome shall record; and when I do forget
> The least of these unspeakable deserts,
> Romans, forget your fealty to me.
> *Titus 1.1.253–257*

Saturninus *is* proud, but of himself, not of Titus, and he will indeed forget the "deserts" he so artfully calls "unspeakable." We might note here that, at this early point in the play, words like "headless" and "unspeakable" are metaphors, and metaphors only, parts of the ordinary language of imagery with which we ornament our daily conversation. Before long, when the play's action turns to tragedy, these dead or sleeping metaphors will come to grisly life, with famous (or notorious) stage directions like "Enter a Messenger with two heads and a hand" (3.1.233).

The image of the "body politic" familiar from Renaissance political theory is casually invoked in the figure of the emperor as the "head" of Rome. By structuring his tragedy so that their very language turns against his characters, Shakespeare builds not only irony but also reflexiveness into the dramatic action: in this play of multiple revenges, every word, however careless, counts. This story of a long-ago hero and his unimaginable losses is also a story about consequence and consequences: about what follows from misjudgment in high places.

No sooner has Saturninus attained the throne than he casts a lustful eye on Tamora, and pardons her and her remaining sons. But Titus intends for Saturninus (now the Emperor) to marry Lavinia, since he had expressed the wish to do so, and when Bassianus attempts to "bear his betrothed away," assisted by her brother (and Titus's son) Mutius, Titus without hesitation kills his own son for his act of "dishonour" (1.1.290). In a moment Saturninus's feigned respect for Titus turns to scorn, and he defiantly names "lovely Tamora, Queen of Goths" (312) to be his bride and empress. For his part, Titus, increasingly stubborn, refuses to allow Mutius to be buried in the tomb of the Andronici, despite the pleas of his brother Marcus and his own remaining sons. By choosing emperor over kindred, impersonal law over personal affection, Titus has made the kind of error that, in Shakespearean tragedy, is irreversible.

In one of the rapidly accumulating verbal foreshadowings of this play, Saturninus accuses his brother Bassianus of "rape" for marrying Lavinia. Bassianus responds:

> "Rape" call you it, my lord, to seize my own—
> My true betrothèd love, and now my wife?
>
> *1.1.402–403*

Rape (from the Latin *rapina,* abduction, robbery) is abduction by force, not necessarily forced sexual intercourse. But this figure, too, will soon turn appallingly literal, when Tamora's sons Chiron and Demetrius—urged on by the vengeful Aaron—commit their sexual assault on Lavinia. For although Tamora (rightly styled "the subtle Queen of Goths" by Marcus Andronicus) pretends to plead for Titus's sons and for Bassianus, using the language of the body we have seen is endemic to the play ("Titus, I am incorporate in Rome, / A Roman now adopted happily" [1.1.459–460]), she whispers her desire for retribution in Saturninus's eager ear. The stage is set for the playing out of these various fantasies of vengeance, and, as if in a nightmare, the stage itself becomes that "other scene" that literalizes what lies below the surface.

In a shift from court to countryside reminiscent of the landscape of a comedy, the action now moves to a nearby wood, where the newly married couples (Bassianus and Lavinia, Saturninus and Tamora) are to go hunting. But as Aaron tells the lustful Chiron and Demetrius,

> The forest walks are wide and spacious,
> And many unfrequented plots there are,
> Fitted by kind for rape and villainy.
>
> *2.1.115–117*

"Plots" is another doubled word here, signifying both land and scheme: the design of the play is deliberately exposing itself to view. And the objective here is also double: to get rid of Bassianus, and to rape and silence Lavinia.

It is not an accident, nor a heavy-handedness on the part of the playwright, that we find mentions of both "Lucrece" (2.1.109) and "Philomel" (2.3.44) *before* the rape of Lavinia that will so closely mirror the fates of those two classical figures, the one raped by the emperor Tarquin, the other, in a tale told by Ovid, raped by Tereus and, like Lavinia, deprived of her tongue, and thus of the power to tell her story.

The boys are to "revel in Lavinia's treasury" (2.1.132) protected by woods that are "ruthless, dreadful, deaf, and dull" (129) while the villainous Aaron stashes a bag of money under a tree. The two "treasures," her sexuality and his gold, are made analogous, and each is a kind of lure or trap. (The device of the hoard of gold beneath a tree that lures young men to their death can be found, in a powerful form, in Chaucer's "Pardoner's Tale.")

The major feature of this wood is a deep pit, variously described as "this abhorrèd pit" (2.3.98); a "subtle hole . . . / Whose mouth is covered with rude-growing briers" (2.3.198–199); an "unhallowed and bloodstainèd hole" (210); a "den" into which one can "look down" and "see a fearful sight of blood and death" (215–216); a "detested, dark, blood-drinking pit" (224); a "fell devouring receptacle, / As hateful as Cocytus' misty mouth" (the mouth of the river of hell; 235–236); a "gaping hollow" (249); and so on. It does not take a Freudian to see that this feature of the landscape is also an allegorical figure for the female body, and explicitly for a woman's genitals, the *vagina dentata,* or devouring sexual "mouth" of legend. The trapdoor in the middle of the Elizabethan stage would serve admirably. First the two young Goths stab Bassianus and tumble him into the pit ("Drag hence her husband to some secret hole, / And make his dead trunk pillow to our lust" [2.3.129–130]); then Aaron leads Titus's two sons there and watches while one falls in and then pulls in the other:

Quintus   Reach me thy hand, that I may help thee out,
           Or, wanting strength to do thee so much good,
           I may be plucked into the swallowing womb
           Of this deep pit, poor Bassianus' grave.

                                   2.3.237–240

The salient point here is not that Shakespeare was capable of so graphic and nightmarish an image of female sexuality, nor that Freud was not the first to invent Freudianism, but rather that the play—and the stage—opens up to become a living metaphor, a dream landscape all too aptly representing the key events that have just taken place: the marriage of Saturninus and the lustful Tamora, the murder of Bassianus, and the rape of Lavinia. This imaginative use of the stage as a figure for the psyche, a geographical literalization of illicit desire, may hark back in some ways to medieval theater practice and the "hell mouth" of the early stage. It calls to mind as well the technique of a painter like Hieronymus Bosch, whose devils are often glimpsed entering or exiting from monstrous body parts. In any case, the audience of *Titus Andronicus* is put on notice, by the rape of Lavinia and by the "pit," "womb," or "bloodstainèd hole" that swallows up the young Andronici, that we have entered a new kind of theatrical world, one in which imagery, staging, and dramatic action work together to create a visceral effect of lust and horror.

No clearer indication of this new dramatic world could be dreamt of, perhaps, than the spectacle presented by Lavinia after the rape. As they mock her appearance, Tamora's two sons, Chiron and Demetrius, explain the reason for her mutilation:

Demetrius	So, now go tell, an if thy tongue can speak,
	Who 'twas that cut thy tongue and ravished thee.
Chiron	Write down thy mind, bewray thy meaning so,
	An if thy stumps will let thee play the scribe.
Demetrius	See how with signs and tokens she can scrawl.
Chiron [*to* LAVINIA]	Go home, call for sweet water, wash thy hands.
Demetrius	She hath no tongue to call nor hands to wash,
	And so let's leave her to her silent walks.

                                                                  2.4.1–8

Robbed of the means either to speak or to write, Lavinia becomes an object rather than a subject—"this object kills me," says her brother Lucius when he first sees her condition (3.1.64)—an object of pity and terror. Lavinia's appearance becomes the occasion for interpretation and embellished lamentation, until a way is found for her to "speak."

Elsewhere in Shakespeare we will encounter the phenomenon of speechlessness as a sign of the loss—or abdication—of full human capacity, whether in Iago's defiant refusal to speak at the end of *Othello* ("from this time forth I never will speak word") or in the speaking silence of the "infant" Perdita in *The Winter's Tale* (the Latin word *infans* means, literally, "unable to speak"). But in Lavinia's case the violently silenced woman is neither a villain nor an infant. Her silence is more like that of Hero, the wronged bride in *Much Ado About Nothing,* who appears muffled and disguised after her public disgrace, and must be brought back to speech and life by her lover's recantation—or, indeed, like that of Lear's daughter Cordelia, whose self-imposed silence ("What shall Cordelia speak? Love, and be silent") unwittingly precipitates tragedy. In this early tragedy the daughter's silence is forcibly imposed from without, but it has the same structural role, and it signifies a living death.

Her uncle Marcus comes upon her in the wood, and slowly realizes the extent of her injuries:

> Speak, gentle niece, what stern ungentle hands
> Hath lopped and hewed and made thy body bare
> Of her two branches, those sweet ornaments
> Whose circling shadows kings have sought to sleep in,
> And might not gain so great a happiness
> As half thy love. Why dost not speak to me?
> Alas, a crimson river of warm blood,
> Like to a bubbling fountain stirred with wind,
> Doth rise and fall between thy rosèd lips,
> Coming and going with thy honey breath.
> But sure some Tereus hath deflowered thee. . . .

2.4.16–26

Marcus's language is worth pausing over for a moment, because it will give us some clues about the larger play and its strategies. The balance and reversal of "gentle"/"ungentle" in the first line cited here is typical of the Shakespeare of the early period (compare "Thou hadst a Richard, till a Richard kill'd him" in *Richard III* [4.4.33], or "My only love sprung from my only hate!" in *Romeo and Juliet* [1.5.135]), and it suggests something about the rhetoric of revenge and payback that is built into *Titus* at every level. That the "ungentle" hands are those of supposed gentlemen, the sons of Tamora, makes their cruelty worse. The phrase "lopped and hewed" in the next line, which seems a particularly grotesque way of describing Lavinia's injuries, in fact directly echoes what was said about the state execution of Alarbus, Tamora's eldest son, in the very first scene of the play: "Alarbus' limbs are lopped" (1.1.143). The executioners in that case were the sons of Andronicus, so the "lopping" of Lavinia is an explicit act of revenge. The grotesquerie of Marcus's imagery increases as his horror increases, first imagining the (absent) arms of Lavinia embracing a kingly lover, then transmuting the blood from Lavinia's severed tongue into a river, a fountain, and her gory mouth into a sweet-smelling garden, in a dreadful inversion of the conventional language of love poetry. When Marcus supplies the obvious mythological reference ("But sure some Tereus hath deflowered thee"), he brings the barely buried story to the surface, and he will then elaborate on the myth and its applications in ways that look forward to a later scene (4.1) where Lavinia locates her own story in her nephew's copy of Ovid's *Metamorphoses*. Here is Marcus:

> Fair Philomel, why she but lost her tongue
> And in a tedious sampler sewed her mind.
> But, lovely niece, that mean is cut from thee.
> A craftier Tereus, cousin, hast thou met,
> And he hath cut those pretty fingers off
> That could have better sewed than Philomel.

2.4.38–44

And here, several scenes later, is the discovery scene, or the scene of reading or instruction, in which Lavinia "speaks" through literature, and specifically through a schoolboy's books:

Titus	Lucius, what book is that she tosseth so?
Young Lucius	Grandsire, 'tis Ovid's *Metamorphoses*.
	My mother gave it me.
Marcus	For love of her that's gone,
	Perhaps, she culled it from among the rest.
Titus	Soft, so busily she turns the leaves.
	Help her. What would she find? Lavinia, shall I read?
	This is the tragic tale of Philomel,
	And treats of Tereus' treason and his rape,
	And rape, I fear, was root of thy annoy.
Marcus	See, brother, see. Note how she quotes the leaves.
Titus	Lavinia, wert *thou* surprised, sweet girl,
	Ravished and wronged as Philomela was,
	Forced in the ruthless, vast, and gloomy woods?
	See, see. . . .

4.1.41–54

Marcus's sentimental and wrongheaded notion, that Lavinia chooses Ovid as a comfort because she loved the sister-in-law whose book it was, is quickly supplanted by the truth: Lavinia can regain a kind of speech by "quot[ing] the leaves." Reading and then writing are the keys to a recovered humanity, as well as the first steps toward further revenge. It is not an accident, I think, that Young Lucius and his books are the proximate agent here. The recovery of the ancient classics made possible the humanist educational reforms of the Tudor period, and in this dramatic (or melodramatic) instance the classics are seen as explicitly enabling a kind of rebirth for Lavinia, reduced to the state of an "infant" by her attackers. Literature here comes to the rescue, replacing speech with writing, and telling the truth across the ages.

Having indicated the nature of the crime, Lavinia is urged to "give signs," and then to write the names of her rapists in the sand with a staff, using her mouth and stumps to guide it. The stage picture is pitiful and appalling, but its point is more than melodramatic horror. To be able to write this accusation "without the help of any hand at all," as her uncle teaches, is to raise the whole question of speech and writing, acting and gesture, in its most extreme form. What is a play? What is a performance?

The play's obsessive concern with dismemberment and with severed body parts has a political referent, one made overt and misleadingly benign in the opening scene, when Marcus Andronicus, the tribune, speaking on behalf of "the people of Rome," invites his brother Titus to become emperor, "And help to set a head on headless Rome" (1.1.186). With this phrase Marcus invokes the traditional image of the body politic, of which the emperor (or king or queen) was the head, his ministers and dependents the limbs—an image familiar from the language of Italian civic humanism, and omnipresent in the politics and poetry of Shakespeare's time. A fuller expression of this figure will appear in a much later play about Rome, the tragedy *Coriolanus,* where it is turned to almost comic use as a kind of fable or allegory: the senators of Rome are the belly, a belligerent citizen the big toe, and so on. It is typical of *Titus Andronicus,* and indeed of Shakespeare's dramaturgy more generally, that this apparently conventional metaphor will take off, will virtually explode into a nightmare of literalization, once the protagonist makes a bad choice. Titus declines to be emperor, in words that prefigure Lear's abdication from his throne: "A better head her glorious body fits / Than his that shakes for age and feebleness" (187–188). And just as with Lear, where the king's desperate pledges to himself after the division of the kingdom ("I'll not weep"; "let me not be mad") turn all too quickly into the spectacle of a weeping storm and a heath full of madness, so Titus's refusal to be the "head" leads, inexorably, to a set of stage actions in which two of his sons are beheaded, his daughter's hands and tongue are brutally removed, and he himself is tricked into asking Aaron to help him chop off his own hand.

These stage spectacles are gruesome to us, and coming one after another they leave the audience horrified. Even in an Elizabethan age where corporal punishment followed the biblical "eye for an eye," where a thief (or a playwright) might lose his hand, where some criminals had their ears cropped, and others were branded, beheaded, disemboweled, or drawn and quartered, the sequence of events in *Titus* must have seemed excessive: "Enter a Messenger with two heads and a hand," says a stage direction in act 3, scene 1. Only moments before, Titus had been assured by Aaron the Moor that his two sons, imprisoned on the false charge of murdering Bassianus, would be spared by the new emperor Saturninus if "Marcus, Lucius or thyself, old Titus, / Or any one of you, chop off your hand / And send it to the King" (3.1.152–154). A serio-comic scene ensues in which each man strives to be the one to sacrifice his hand, and Titus's stratagem—pretending to yield to them, sending them off to get an axe—puts him squarely in Aaron's power: "Come hither, Aaron. I'll deceive them both. / Lend me thy hand, and I will give thee mine" (185–186). Again the literalizing of language that is conventionally figurative (to lend a hand; to give one's hand) adds to the Grand Guignol quality of the scene, but also to its powerful point: nothing is merely a figure, especially on the stage. Poetry and language are deadly earnest. The mocking return of the heads and the hand appears to drive Titus over the edge of madness, as he sets out—again we might think of Lear and his Fool on the heath—in quest of "Revenge's cave":

> Titus   Come, brother, take a head,
>   And in this hand the other will I bear.

> And Lavinia, thou shalt be employed.
> Bear thou my hand, sweet wench, between thine arms.
>
> *3.1.278–281*

This passage has a complicated textual history. The Folio reads "between thy teeth," and the First Quarto, "between thine arms." The Oxford and Norton editors use the First Quarto as the control text, and thus print "arms" rather than "teeth." But the latter image seems to me the stronger and more horrific, since it transforms Titus's beloved daughter, his "sweet wench," into an animal carrying her father's hand in her mouth. The ill-assorted body parts—decapitated heads in the two elder brothers' hands, a hand in Lavinia's mouth—are a speaking picture of the breakdown of the body politic. As for Lucius, he is not to attend them, but rather, as an "exile," to go to the Goths and raise an army "[t]o be revenged on Rome and Saturnine" (3.1.299). Thus the part of the plot that is about political redemption will also be achieved through ironic reversal: the downfall of Tamora the Goth will come at the hands of her own people.

Lucius's exile from Rome is a characteristic mode for Shakespeare: the young political survivor, exempt from some of the psychological agonies of the middle of the play, returns to impose order from without. We might think here of Duncan's son Malcolm, who flees to England to raise a power against Macbeth; or of young Octavius, who enters the action of *Julius Caesar* at the close to implement a political solution in the name of the murdered Caesar. But we might also notice the way in which the concept of "revenge" has here been split in two. Titus will seek the allegorical *personage* Revenge, and his remaining son and successor Lucius will seek revenge as *instrumentality*. Or, to put it another way, Titus will give himself over to tragedy, and Lucius, to history.

How are we to take this quest for Revenge on the part of Titus? When he first mentions her, he has not yet learned, from Lavinia, the full particulars of her rape. When it becomes clear, through Lavinia's writing in the sand, that "[t]he lustful sons of Tamora" are the "[p]erformers of this heinous bloody deed" (4.1.78–79), he sends his grandson to them with a bundle of weapons, to which he has attached a scroll with a pointed allusion from Horace: *"Integer vitae, scelerisque purus / Non eget Mauri iaculis, nec arcu"* (The man of upright life and free from crime does not need the javelins or bows of the Moor). This famous quotation appeared in the standard grammar school textbook of the period, as Chiron will note. (The play is full of deliberate anachronisms of this kind, allowing a Goth from the time of ancient Rome to know the contents of a 1540 English schoolbook. In a later scene another Goth will "gaze upon a ruined monastery," destroyed in the time of Henry VIII.) But again the technique here is one of conscious literalization, since the "Moor" of Horace's ode is a generalized type of exotic warrior, and the phrase by that time had become a cliché, whereas Aaron the Moor is highly particular, and manifestly neither of "upright life" nor "free from crime." The dead metaphor again comes to life. Indeed, Aaron himself, standing by, gets the point the duller sons miss:

> The old man hath found their guilt,
> And sends the weapons wrapped about with lines
> That wound beyond their feeling to the quick.
> But were our witty Empress well afoot
> She would applaud Andronicus' conceit.
>
> *4.2.26–30*

A version of the same event takes place again in the next scene, when Titus supervises Marcus, Young Lucius, and others as they shoot arrows into the air, and dig with tools into the earth, in a vain search for the gods of justice. Here Shakespeare borrows from a scene from Kyd's *Spanish Tragedy,* where the mad Hieronimo plunges his dagger into the ground and shouts for justice; the line he quotes from Ovid's *Metamorphoses,* "Terras Astraea reliquit" (Astraea [the goddess of Justice] has left the earth), as Jonathan Bate notes, is cited twice, in English, in the same play (*Spanish Tragedy* 3.13.108, 140).[1]

The mutilations, tortures, and assorted horrors of this play had for some years earned it a place among Shakespeare's works somewhere between Elizabethan horror genres and poetic allegory. To take its events "straight"—from the handless, tongueless Lavinia to the ground-up sons of Tamora, baked in a pie and served to their unsuspecting mother—seemed, for a while at least, to strain credulity. Later Shakespearean tragedies, though they contain key moments of unspeakable bodily violation (the blinding of Gloucester in *King Lear;* the massacre of Macduff's wife and children in *Macbeth*), often tend to translate and internalize such physical degradations as metaphors, rendering them metaphysical ("filial ingratitude. / Is it not as this mouth should tear this hand / For lifting food to't?" [*Lear* 3.4.14–16]). But *Titus Andronicus* is in a way the radical—the root—of Shakespearean tragedy, the dreamscape or nightmare world laid out for all to see, not disguised by a retreat into metaphor. The more we learn about the events of twentieth- and twenty-first-century warfare, the less easy it becomes to consign such appalling physical terrors and mutilations to the realm of either a barbaric past or a poetic imagination. Like all Shakespeare plays set in the historical past, *Titus* has three, perhaps four, "times" of reference: ancient Rome, Elizabethan England, the shifting contemporary time of each performance—and the literary "time" of its poetic models, from Ovid and Livy to the Elizabethan revenge tragedies like Kyd's *Spanish Tragedy* and Marlowe's *Tamburlaine.* But in many ways, from its almost Brechtian mode of staging physicality to its unrelenting pileup of horrors, *Titus* is the most modern play of Shakespeare's that we have. What was once regarded as alien is all too recognizable as an unwelcome aspect of "human nature."

The final act, with its monstrous banquet presided over by Titus, dressed "like a cook," presents in quick succession the slaying of Lavinia by her father

("Die, die, Lavinia, and thy shame with thee" [5.3.45]) and the revelation that
Tamora's sons, who "ravished [Lavinia], and cut away her tongue," have received
their just deserts:

> Why, there they are both, bakèd in this pie,
> Whereof their mother daintily hath fed,
> Eating the flesh that she herself hath bred.
>
> *5.3.59–61*

Like the earlier rape and mutilation of Lavinia, this is a fairly direct borrowing
from the tale of Philomela and Procne in Ovid's *Metamorphoses*. There Tereus,
having raped Philomela, the sister of his wife, Procne, cuts out Philomela's
tongue to keep her from accusing him. She manages to communicate the truth
by sewing on a sampler (the myth's version of Lavinia's turning the leaves of
Young Lucius's Ovid), and the two sisters revenge themselves on Tereus by serving up his son Itys, the child of Tereus and Procne, in a pie. "Within your self
your Itys you may find" is Procne's reply to her husband. A personal note: It was
the staging of this scene, in Julie Taymor's film *Titus* (1999), that turned me—
a lifelong meat-eater—against the eating of mammals' flesh.

Titus stabs Tamora; Saturninus, in retaliation, kills Titus; and Titus's son
Lucius responds by killing Saturninus, leaving the stage, and Rome, for a
moment at least, under the rehabilitative rule of the Romans, as the Goths
stand by. From aloft, Marcus Andronicus—Titus's brother, the sole survivor of
that embattled generation—speaks to the citizenry in terms that presage other
moments of Shakespearean reconciliation (as, for example, at the close of
Richard III or *Macbeth*), bringing together the themes of fertile agricultural
nature and the body politic:

> O, let me teach you how to knit again
> This scattered corn into one mutual sheaf,
> These broken limbs again into one body.
>
> *5.3.69–71*

The apparent symmetry here is deceptive, since the scattered grain can be gathered by gleaners as a matter of course, but the reassembling of the body politic is
a task for magical agency, mythic transformation, or digital cinema. The oft-
appearing, sometimes uncannily repeated image of the "hand" (Lavinia's,
Titus's), so important to the plot of dismemberment, now returns as an emblem
of union, as Lucius speaks of "that true hand that fought Rome's quarrel out"
(5.3.101) and Marcus challenges his auditors:

> What say you, Romans?
> Have we done aught amiss, show us wherein,
> And from the place where you behold us pleading

> The poor remainder of Andronici
> Will hand in hand all headlong hurl ourselves
> And on the ragged stones beat forth our souls
> And make a mutual closure of our house.
> Speak, Romans, speak, and if you say we shall,
> Lo, hand in hand, Lucius and I will fall.
>
> *5.3.127–135*

The response of the people is acclaim rather than repudiation, as Marcus is told to "bring our emperor gently in thy hand, / Lucius, our emperor—. . . / The common voice do cry it shall be so" (5.3.137–139).

Marcus had addressed his call to the "people and sons of Rome," and it is the "son," Lucius—Titus's son and Marcus's nephew—and Lucius's own son, Young Lucius, who will inherit for the Andronici. The elder Lucius is a Roman soldier, more comfortable with deeds than words, a far more diplomatic version of Shakespeare's later Roman general, Coriolanus. (Lucius: "Alas, you know, I am no vaunter, I. / My scars can witness, dumb although they are, / That my report is just and full of truth" [5.3.112–114].) But his dramatic role is that of bringer of order, as it is for so many surviving authority figures in the later tragedies, many of them both sons and generals: Malcolm in *Macbeth,* Octavius in *Antony and Cleopatra,* Edgar in *King Lear.*

The ceremonial leave-taking that follows, in which brother, son, and grandson, in turn, kiss the slain body of Titus, has the hallmarks of ritual. The degree to which *Titus Andronicus* is herald to more canonical Shakespearean tragic moments may be detected even in Marcus's words to Young Lucius—"How many thousand times hath these poor lips, / When they were living, warmed themselves on thine!" (5.3.166–167)—which anticipate Hamlet's macabre tribute to the skull of his childhood jester Yorick: "Here hung those lips that I have kissed I know not how oft" (*Hamlet* 5.1.174–175). Yet against this scene of filial piety will be placed, with fine dramatic irony and point, another father-son pairing, that of the Moor Aaron and his son. "Behold the child," declares Marcus.

> Of this was Tamora deliverèd,
> The issue of an irreligious Moor,
> Chief architect and plotter of these woes.
> The villain is alive in Titus' house,
> And as he is to witness, this is true.
>
> *5.3.118–123*

"Architect" and "plotter" were both relatively new terms in Elizabethan English, and they point simultaneously to the invention of buildings, schemes, and fictional narratives. Aaron ("irreligious" because non-Christian, presumably; the word "Moor" in this period also meant "Muslim") is designated as the play's "other" playwright, the one who—like Iago in *Othello,* and Gloucester in *Richard III*—lays plots and snares for the protagonists. His crimes are described as "unspeakable," and when he is at last produced onstage under guard in this final scene, he enters after Young Lucius declares himself unable to speak for weeping. But Aaron, unlike Iago, will not be silenced. Although Lucius ordains for him a mode of torture not recognizably different from the horrors that have gone before—"Set him breast-deep in earth and famish him. / There let him stand, and rave, and cry for food" (5.3.178–179)—he remains volubly defiant. Rightly seeing this entombing as a symbolic enwombing, he voices the unreconstructed creed of the proud Machiavel as man, not child:

> Ah, why should wrath be mute and fury dumb?
> I am no baby, I, that with base prayers
> I should repent the evils I have done.
> Ten thousand worse than ever yet I did
> Would I perform if I might have my will.
> If one good deed in all my life I did
> I do repent it from my very soul.
>
> *5.3.183–189*

Like other Elizabethan Machiavels, Aaron goes to his fate declaring his unchanging resolve. Marlowe's Jew of Malta, Barabas, dangling above a cauldron of boiling oil, dies proclaiming, "[H]ad I but escaped this stratagem, / I would have brought confusion on you all, / Damned Christian dogs, and Turkish infidels" (*Jew of Malta* 5.5.86–88). What is slightly unusual—and dramatically unsettling—is the placement of Aaron's speech of defiance *after* Marcus's and Lucius's remarks on the restoration of Roman governance. The image of Aaron, "breast-deep in earth" and still venting his fury, lingers on after the play is done. It is an oddly Beckett-like image (although it is probably an accident that Samuel Beckett's Winnie, buried up to her neck in earth in the second act of the 1961 play *Happy Days,* is married to a near-silent, often hidden figure called Willie).

The lines on which *Titus Andronicus* will close, Lucius's instructions for the burials of Saturninus, Titus, and Lavinia, include a restorative gesture familiar from other Shakespearean endings—"Some loving friends convey the Emperor hence," he says—but the speech as a whole returns once again to revenge rather than universal forgiveness (compare the Prince in *Romeo and Juliet,* "Some shall be pardoned, and some punishèd" [5.3.307]). Here is Lucius:

> My father and Lavinia shall forthwith
> Be closèd in our household's monument.
> As for that ravenous tiger, Tamora,
> No funeral rite nor man in mourning weed,
> No mournful bell shall ring her burial;

But throw her forth to beasts and birds to prey.
Her life was beastly and devoid of pity,
And being dead, let birds on her take pity.
                                            5.3.192–199

This harsh and retributive conclusion—as editors of the play point out, executed felons were treated in such a fashion in Shakespeare's time, their bodies
exposed on the gates of London—calls for silence rather than mourning. At the
same time it recalls the mythological narrative at the heart of Lavinia's story,
the tale of Philomela, who became the nightingale. Lavinia will have an afterlife; Tamora is to be forgotten and devoured, unless the birds of prey take pity
upon her.

The contrast between the nightingale as an idealized, iconic embodiment of
poetry and the spectacle of the mutilated Lavinia and the truly "Gothic"
Tamora is, we might say, a contrast between lyric and tragedy—or between nar-
rated myth and embodied theater. Whether Lavinia and Tamora are regarded as
two sides of the same female coin (the silenced woman; the demonized woman)
or as aspects of the male psychic and social worlds of which they are a part
(Titus's and Aaron's), they are not only powerful dramatic characters, lingering
in the imagination of playgoers, but also the forerunners of other significant
Shakespearean women, from the anguished Ophelia—who dies in song—to
the defiantly powerful Volumnia and Lady Macbeth.

Henry VI Part 1

DRAMATIS PERSONAE

THE ENGLISH

King Henry VI
Duke of Gloucester, *Lord Protector,*
   uncle of King Henry
Duke of Bedford, *Regent of France*
Duke of Exeter
Bishop of Winchester
   (later Cardinal), uncle of King Henry
Duke of Somerset
Richard Plantagenet, *later*
   Duke of York, and Regent of France
Earl of Warwick
Earl of Salisbury
Earl of Suffolk
Lord Talbot
John Talbot
Edmund Mortimer

Sir William Glasdale
Sir Thomas Gargrave
Sir John Fastolf
Sir William Lucy
Woodville, *Lieutenant of the*
   Tower of London
Mayor of London
Vernon
Basset
A Lawyer
A Legate and ambassadors
Messengers, warders, and keepers
   of the Tower of London,
   servingmen, officers, captains,
   soldiers, heralds, watch

THE FRENCH

Charles, *Dauphin of France*
René, *Duke of Anjou,*
   King of Naples
Margaret, *his daughter*
Duke of Alençon
Bastard of Orléans
Duke of Burgundy,
   uncle of King Henry
General of the French garrison
   at Bordeaux

Countess of Auvergne
Master Gunner of Orléans
A Boy, *his son*
Joan la Pucelle
A Shepherd, *father of Joan*
Porter, French sergeant, French
   sentinels, French scout, French
   herald, the Governor of Paris,
   fiends, and soldiers

HIS EARLY PLAY has sometimes been attributed entirely to Shakespeare, but the consensus of scholars and editors today suggests that it
is more likely a collaborative effort by several playwrights. Such collab-
orations were common in the period—our modern notion of "authorship" is
really an eighteenth-century one, having developed at the same time as copyright law—and in any case a play written in Shakespeare's time would have
"belonged" to the company, not to the writer (and, if published, to the publisher, not the "author"). Nonetheless there has been, and will doubtless continue to be, much pushing and prodding at the text of this play to try to
discover which sections, if any, are authentically Shakespearean.

This is in many ways a romantic, if not a quixotic, quest, and it has at times
served merely as an opportunity to praise some elements (often the ones then
identified as "Shakespeare's") and to denigrate others (which are, by implication, not worthy of "Shakespeare," or not his fault). Thus we can say that
Henry VI Part 1 is a play written collaboratively, but as a work that appeared in
the First Folio, it is also "a play by William Shakespeare." The "Shakespeare"
that we have come to admire, revere, quote, and cite is often in part a composite
author, since his works, even the most greatly honored ones, have been
improved and altered over time by the conjectures of editors trying to make
sense of what may appear to be gaps or errors in the printed text. Since we have
no manuscripts, the printed versions, Quarto and Folio, are all that editors have
to work with. In any case, *1 Henry VI* is a lively, smart, sophisticated, and well-
designed play, full of strong characters and fast-paced action. It plays exceedingly well onstage, and it does not deserve the literary condescension that has
sometimes come its way. Both on its own terms and considered in the context
of Shakespeare's other history plays, it is worth the attention of readers, actors,
and critics.

The popularity of history, or chronicle, plays, a new genre in the sixteenth
century, is arguably tied to an emergent sense of English nationalism and cultural pride. Any story about an earlier monarch could, and would, be taken as
reflecting upon, predicting, or praising the current monarch, or as offering
a potential model or critique of living political figures. The artful placement
of such devices as prophecies, curses, and portents, all safely placed in the
historical/fictional past, could be counted upon to "predict" with unerring
accuracy the events and circumstances of the present day. Shakespeare's present is not our present; yet the enduring nature of the plays published under
his name means that they still carry both theatrical and emotional force.
Indeed, sometimes these history plays provide virtually all the information we
have about what "really happened" in the period, and are our principal source of
the stories of such then-famous figures as Talbot, Gloucester, the cardinal Winchester, and even Joan la Pucelle, our "Joan of Arc."

For Shakespeare and his fellow dramatists there were several sources to consult on English history, including Edward Hall's *Union of the Two Noble and Illustre Fameiles of Lancastre and Yorke* (1548) and Raphael Holinshed's *Chronicles of England, Scotland, and Ireland* (actually the work of several writers and revisers), in the second edition of 1587. Beyond these Tudor chronicles there was as well a long history of fable, rumor, and cultural mythology. Queen Elizabeth herself was the descendant of the "union" that took place after the Wars of the Roses, and the anomaly of her reign—a powerful woman on the throne, but an unmarried woman without an heir—is clearly reflected, and deflected, in the play's models of English (male) heroism and dangerous French (female) opposition and perfidy. The cross-dressed, martial Joan, who defeated both the French Dauphin ("Dolphin" in some editions) and the English Talbot in single combat, is one such antithetical figure; the other is the seductively feminine Margaret of Anjou, the bride of Henry VI, described by the chronicler Hall as "of stomack and corage, more like to a man, then a woman," as "desirous of glory, and covetous of honor, and of reason, pollicye, counsaill, and other giftes and talentes of nature, belongyng to a man, full and flowing," and as a "manly woman" who would come to dominate and govern her simpler husband.[1] Joan is introduced at the beginning of the play, and is exposed as a witch or sorcerer near the close; her power wanes as Margaret's rises. But both are presented as duplicitous threats to English power and manhood. The model for Elizabeth in this play is not a woman, but the "ever-living man of memory / Henry the Fifth," as Sir William Lucy calls him, or the heroic soldier Talbot himself.

In point of fact, the "history" in these plays is often altered or revised from what is reported in the chronicle sources, for reasons either political or aesthetic (or both). Thus, for example, the battle reported in act 1, scene 1, of this play, in which the heroic Talbot is defeated by the French, took place historically *after* Jeanne d'Arc took Orléans, an event here staged in act 1, scenes 7 and 8. Likewise, at another point in the dramatic action, Talbot, anticipating his own death in battle and that of his son, refers to the "scarce-cold" body of King Henry V (4.3.50), whose stately funeral procession had opened the play. But in historical fact thirty-one years elapsed between the death of Henry V and the battle in which the two Talbots lose their lives. The fictive compression of time emphasizes the radical rather than gradual reversal of fortune for England from the power of the previous king. The figure of Mortimer conflates two different "Edmund Mortimers" from English history, one a loyalist to the crown, the other a rebel—the Mortimer who appears in *1 Henry VI*. As for the age of the new king, Henry VI, it seems to fluctuate during the course of the play, from juvenile minority at the beginning to a young man's keen "passion of inflaming love," aroused by Suffolk's description of the beauteous Margaret. The King's historical age in the play has been calculated as progressing from four years old (in 2.5) to ten (at his coronation in Paris, 4.1) and then finally to twenty-two in the scene in which he eagerly (perhaps too eagerly) embraces for the first time the idea of marriage:

> King Henry   Whether it be through force of your report,
> My noble lord of Suffolk, or for that
> My tender youth was never yet attaint
> With any passion of inflaming love,
> I cannot tell; but this I am assured:
> I feel such sharp dissension in my breast,
> Such fierce alarums both of hope and fear,
> As I am sick with working of my thoughts.
>
>   *1 Henry VI 5.7.79–86*

Even without any knowledge of the historical relation between Margaret and Henry and its effect upon the future of English politics, there is plenty of information here of the most disquieting kind for an attentive listener to interpret. In a history play about civil war (the Wars of the Roses) and nation-to-nation combat, words like "dissension" and "alarums" should send clear warning signals. As will happen in play after play when Shakespeare deals with history, the quelling of external war often leads to "internal" war, both political (rivalry, usurpation, and sedition) and psychological. Just at the point where England may seem to have quelled the threat from outside, defeating the French and the manifestly threatening Joan, England's king is "sick" with desire for a French bride he has never met. We are invited to contrast this sudden onset of disabling passion with Henry's indifferent response, only a few scenes earlier, to the prospect of marriage with the Earl of Armagnac's daughter—a marriage that, unlike the union with Margaret, would have brought "a large and sumptuous dowry" (5.1.20):

> Marriage, uncle? Alas, my years are young,
> And fitter is my study and my books
> Than wanton dalliance with a paramour.
> Yet call th'ambassadors,
>   and as you please,
> So let them have their answers every one.
> I shall be well content with any choice
> Tends to God's glory and my country's weal.
>
>   *5.1.21–27*

This passivity, and the young King's acceptance of a "contract" made for political and financial reasons on the advice of his elders, stands in sharp distinction to the emotion he shows in the later scene, where his naïveté ("My tender youth was never yet attaint / With any passion") is coupled with an overdependence on Suffolk and his report. The path is clear and direct from here to the final lines of the scene, and the play—Suffolk's declaration, alone onstage and speaking to himself and to the audience, that

> Margaret shall now be queen and rule the King;
> But I will rule both her, the King, and realm.
>
> *5.7.107–108*

It may seem odd to begin an assessment of *Henry VI Part 1* with the end of the dramatic action rather than the beginning, but it is curiously fitting for this play. The works listed in the First Folio as *The Second Part of Henry the Sixt, with the death of the Good Duke Humfrey,* and *The Third Part of Henry the Sixt, with the death of the Duke of Yorke*—the plays familiarly known to modern theatergoers as *Henry VI Part 2* and *Part 3*—were written, performed, and published in quarto form as a two-part sequence before what was called *The First Part of Henry the Sixt* was written, making *1 Henry VI* what today would be called a "prequel." It has affinities with both the flashback and the movie "trailer," since it fills in the blanks (why was the long civil war that was about to ensue called "the Wars of the Roses"?) and entices the audience with hints of things to come (the pride of Gloucester's wife, mentioned in act 1, scene 1, although she does not appear until *Part 2;* Queen Margaret's relationship with Suffolk, which will prove ruinous both to the King and to the realm).

Parts 2 and *3* appeared in print in 1594 and 1595 as *The First Part of the Contention of the Two Famous Houses of York and Lancaster* and *The True Tragedy of Richard Duke of York and Good King Henry the Sixth.* Two-part sequences of this sort were in vogue (Marlowe's two *Tamburlaine* plays are an example); a three-part sequence would have been a surprising innovation. There is historical evidence, from the obligatory registering or licensing of plays with the Master of the Revels, that what we call *Part 1* was licensed for the stage at a later date. So despite the fact that modern productions and mid-twentieth-century critics have tended to regard it as the first play in a "cycle" or nationalist epic, *1 Henry VI* was very likely written as a freestanding play, although its subject matter and its title in the Folio link it directly with *Part 2* and *Part 3*.

The order has direct and important consequences for an assessment of the play's content and design. For if the play the Folio editors called *The First Part* was written *after* the other two plays had been put on, audiences would be especially attentive to details, hints, and foreshadowings that "predicted" the events—involving many of the same characters—that they had already seen onstage. Suffolk's portentous assertion in the play's final lines, "I will rule both her, the King, and realm," would then promise what had already been performed, both in history and in the theater. And young King Henry's sudden access of willful romantic feeling and sexual desire, after a play in which he largely appears as a child and a cipher, points toward the action of *Part 2* and *Part 3,* and ultimately to the lurking figure of old Queen Margaret in the fourth play in this historical sequence, *Richard III. Richard III,* we should note, begins with a funeral cortège, just as does *1 Henry VI:* in *Richard III* the body is that of Margaret's weak, pious, and ineffectual husband, Henry VI, "poor key-cold figure of a holy king," offering the greatest possible contrast to his father and predecessor, the mythic martial hero Henry V, whose funeral and coffin dominate the stage in the opening moments of *1 Henry VI.*

Yet however independently written these plays—and recent scholars have debated whether it is really appropriate to read them as a sequence, a trilogy (the three *Henry VI* plays) or tetralogy (with *Richard III*), or an effective national epic—they contain, both individually and taken together, patterns of symmetry, echo, inversion, and opposition that demonstrate their powerful effectiveness as dramatic vehicles, and as stage pictures. Indeed, for these early Shakespeare history plays, patterns of action are as important as patterns of language: repeated events, scenes that echo one another with a difference, elements of emblematic staging all carry a considerable weight of meaning.

As the funeral procession files across the stage at the beginning of *1 Henry VI,* the Duke of Bedford's opening lines, which gesture simultaneously at the stage and the world, set the scene:

> Hung be the heavens with black! Yield, day, to night!
> Comets, importing change of times and states,
> Brandish your crystal tresses in the sky,
> And with them scourge the bad revolting stars
> That have consented unto Henry's death—
> King Henry the Fifth, too famous to live long.
> England ne'er lost a king of so much worth.
>
> 1.1.1–7

"Heavens" here is a technical stage term, the Elizabethan word for the wooden roof, often decorated with stars and sun, that protected the actors from the open sky. Both the theater and the world should mourn, Bedford instructs, setting up a series of celestial oppositions (day versus night; crystal comets versus "bad, revolting stars") that foreshadow the many sets of earthly rivals (England and France; male and female; Gloucester and Winchester; Lancaster and York; witchcraft and reason; bastard and legitimate) that will structure the play. As always in Shakespearean drama, key words of the opening scene will resound, thematically as well as verbally, throughout the rest of the dramatic action.

The series of encomiums—spoken in turn by Bedford, Gloucester, Exeter, and Winchester—that praise the dead hero-king first seem to reinforce the doubled sense of pride and loss. ("England ne'er had a king until his time," says Gloucester. "We mourn in black; why mourn we not in blood?" responds

Exeter. "Henry is dead, and never shall revive.") But when the Bishop, later Cardinal of Winchester, invokes the Church, the fateful divisions among these rivals begin to reveal themselves. The fact that Bedford is a heroic old man, and that he mourns a heroic young one ("too famous to live long"), is also striking, since this play, like many of Shakespeare's history plays (and, indeed, comedies) of this period, will stress the difference between virile, impetuous youth and impotent, if sometimes wise, old age.

Gloucester claims that churchmen like Winchester prefer weak rulers to strong ones: "None do you like but an effeminate prince, / Whom like a school-boy you may overawe" (1.1.35–36). "Effeminate" in this context, as often in the period, means not "homosexual" but "feeble, unmanly, enervated" (and thus conventionally "like a woman"). "Effeminate" in other Shakespearean contexts also means "self-indulgent, voluptuous, and excessively devoted to women"; importantly, none of these seems at all appropriate for the boy-king Henry VI—until those telltale final lines we have already noted, when in act 5, responding to Suffolk's description of Margaret of Anjou, the King describes himself as sick, inflamed, and torn by the unaccustomed passions of sudden sexual desire, his own internal civil war. But this question of manliness and unmanliness, together with a parallel question about the proper role of women, will play a central role in the play. Bedford fears lest the death of Henry V leave England a place entirely populated by women:

> Posterity, await for wretched years,
> When, at their mothers' moistened eyes, babes shall suck,
> Our isle be made a marish of salt tears,
> And none but women left to wail the dead.
>
> *1.1.48–51*

In the main action of the play, the threat posed by Joan la Pucelle, who defeats the French Dauphin in single combat in act 1, scene 3, and then, as "a woman clad in armour," does the same to the English hero Talbot in act 1, scene 7, is first juxtaposed to the weakness of both the French and the English rulers, the Dauphin and Henry VI, and then gives way to the power of a different kind of "manly" woman, Margaret.

Joan, known as La Pucelle, the Virgin (or, as her name sometimes appears in the Folio, Joan Puzel), represented the paradox of purity/promiscuity, since "puzel" and "pussel" meant "slatternly woman" or "slut." (A later Shakespearean instance of this same erotic paradox can be found in Hamlet's despairing command to Ophelia, "Get thee to a nunnery," where "nunnery" in the period would connote both convent and brothel. For Ophelia, as for Joan, the question of femininity is posed in terms later made famous by Freud: the only two roles imagined for them are virgin or whore.) The term "La Pucelle" was some-times taken, in the sixteenth century, as Joan's surname. Throughout the play, it is used as the occasion for often derogatory wordplay, like Talbot's "*Pucelle* or pucelle, Dauphin or dog-fish" (1.6.85), with glances at the modern word "puzzle" (one of the alternative spellings for "pucelle"), and even at "pizzle," penis. Joan is the *pucelle* (virgin) who is also a puzzel (slut), and who may have a pizzle (since she dresses and fights like a man).

In fact, Joan's cross-dressing sets up an interesting interplay between the historical and the metatheatrical, since the behavior for which the historical Joan was burned at the stake (wearing the clothes of the "opposite sex") was standard theatrical practice for boy actors playing women on the English stage. Puritans and other critics of the early modern theater in England objected to stage plays because they defied the injunction in Deuteronomy that "the woman shall not wear that which pertaineth unto a man, neither shall a man put on a woman's garment" (Deuteronomy 22:5). Nonetheless, since women were not permitted to perform upon the public stage, male-to-female cross-dressing was central, intrinsic, and normative in the plays of Shakespeare and his contemporaries. The scandal produced by Joan's male costume in the play—and in the historical trial that condemned her—thus revisits both the material facts of life on the stage and the particular resistance manifested by religious opposition. In Joan's case, of course, the transformation is from female to male costume rather than, as with the boy actor, from male to female. Her particular violation of sensibilities had to do not only with a loss of supposed femininity, but also with her assumption of the rights and privileges of a man.

Margaret's "manliness" may seem far less overt and threatening than Joan's. Her outer appearance is repeatedly described as feminine and beautiful. But Suffolk describes her to Henry as possessing a "valiant courage and undaunted spirit, / More than in women commonly is seen" (5.7.70–71), and he also tells us, in an aside, that he confidently expects her to "rule the King." The theatrical juxtaposition in *1 Henry VI* is striking: York enjoins Joan, "Fell banning hag, enchantress, hold thy tongue" (5.4.13), and leads her off to be burned at the stake. No sooner have they left the stage than Suffolk enters "with Margaret in his hand," as the stage direction says, and importunes her to speak; he himself is silenced by her "gorgeous beauty" ("Fain would I woo her, yet I dare not speak" [5.5.21]). The overt danger posed by Joan can be identified, vilified, and, by the end of the play, effectively purged. The more covert danger posed by the conventionally feminine Margaret has more lasting effects. It will linger throughout the entire series of plays, and throughout subsequent English history, till it, too, is finally matched and overcome by the triumphant reign of another martial virgin, the English monarch Elizabeth, a rightful ruler, both feminine and powerful, who is herself both queen and king.

The unifying role of Elizabeth Tudor, the descendant of the "Union of the Two Families of Lancaster and York," the daughter of the mingled white rose and red, is thus itself predicted by this play, which provides negative examples of "bad" manly women as her antitypes. But the type for Elizabeth in this play is, of course, neither Joan nor Margaret, but the two heroic male figures, the dead and much-lamented Henry V (whose "deeds exceed all speech" [1.1.15]) and the character who comes closest to a central persona, the figure who announces himself at the gates of Bordeaux as "English John Talbot." In historical fact, Joan of Arc's life was largely over (she was burned at the stake in 1431) before Talbot came prominently onto the scene (John Talbot, Earl of Shrewsbury, died in 1453), but the play deliberately alters history, artfully intertwining "Joan" scenes and "Talbot" scenes to create a contrasting view of the French and English courts and their values.

It is Talbot who has in this play both the central and the most "rounded" role. His feeling of confusion when bested by Joan ("My thoughts are whirlèd like a potter's wheel. / I know not where I am nor what I do" [1.7.19–20]), his willingness to fight in single combat, his affection for his son, and his loyalty to the King and to England all set him apart. The scenes in which he tries to persuade his namesake son, young John, to flee the battle and his certain death, have great pathos, and they prefigure other loyal fighting pairs of fathers and sons in the later plays (for example, the briefly but powerfully sketched relationship between the old and the young Siward in *Macbeth*, as well as the tragically confused and mistaken fathers and sons soon to appear in *Part 2*). "Come— dally not, be gone," urges the father. John answers:

> Is my name Talbot? And am I your son,
> And shall I fly? O, if you love my mother,
> Dishonour not her honourable name
> To make a bastard and a slave of me.
> The world will say he is not Talbot's blood,
> That basely fled when noble Talbot stood.
>
> *4.5.12–17*

This couplet, rhyming "blood" and "stood," begins a longer passage, all in couplets, in which the son makes his case and the father first resists, and then, with mingled pride and sadness, accepts his son's decision:

Talbot   If we both stay, we both are sure to die.
John   Then let me stay and, father, do you fly.

> *4.5.20–21*

Talbot   Shall all thy mother's hopes lie in one tomb?
John   Ay, rather than I'll shame my mother's womb.
Talbot   Upon my blessing I command thee go.
John   To fight I will, but not to fly the foe.

> *4.5.34–37*

John   Stay, go, do what you will: the like do I,
           For live I will not if my father die.
Talbot   Then here I take my leave of thee, fair son,

Born to eclipse thy life this afternoon.
Come, side by side together live and die,
And soul with soul from France to heaven fly.

                                    4.5.50–55

These extended quotations demonstrate the ways in which an earlier writing style, more rhymed and end-stopped than the familiar blank verse of Shakespeare's later plays, can carry its own considerable burden of expressive emotion. Indeed, the restraint and orderliness of the couplet form seem in a way to mirror the older man's attempt to hold his own emotions in check—as well as the curious and quietly agonized joy with which he accepts his son's profession of nobility and fatality. While there is no doubt that the later plays have a greater range, early works like this one have an extraordinarily fine sense of composition, theatricality, and—when they strive for it—emotional power.

Young John Talbot's emphasis on his own legitimacy ("if you love my mother, / Dishonour not her honourable name / To make a bastard . . . of me") underscores a theme that is central to the construction of the play, where the "bastards" (Joan, who disavows her parents; Joan's fictive "child," which she claims, in desperation, to be carrying at the end of the play; the Bishop/Cardinal of Winchester, the illegitimate son of John of Gaunt, twitted by Gloucester as "[t]hou bastard of my grandfather" [3.1.43]; and England's enemy the Bastard of Orléans, who in this play introduces Joan to the Dauphin of France (in act 1, scene 3), are arrayed against the trueborn. Talbot himself will inveigh against

        The ireful bastard Orléans, that drew blood
        From thee, my boy, and had the maidenhood
        Of thy first fight, I soon encounterèd,
        And interchanging blows, I quickly shed
        Some of his bastard blood. . . .

                                    4.6.16–20

That this emphasis is purposeful seems evident from the fact that the historical Sir John Talbot, too, had an illegitimate son, Henry Talbot, who also died in the same battle. Hall, the principal source here, calls him Talbot's "bastard sonne Henry Talbot,"[2] and lists the two sons, together, as those who died "manfully" alongside their father. By omitting the heroic bastard Henry, the play simplifies the opposition between "legitimate" and "bastard," pointing directly toward the ensuing scenes in which Joan pretends to be pregnant (Richard, Duke of York: "Now heaven forfend—the holy maid with child?" [5.6.65]) and claims in rapid succession the Dauphin, Alençon, and René, King of Naples, as the father of her supposititious child.

Incidentally, Talbot's word "maidenhood," which was not uncommon as a term for being "untried" in experience in general and in battle in particular, could be applied to men as well as to women (Romeo and Juliet will be described as possessing "a pair of stainless maidenhoods"). But the old soldier's choice of this word further stresses the analogy and comparison between his young son and Joan, "the holy maid." Joan herself will later report her battle-field challenge to him: " 'Thou maiden youth, be vanquished by a maid' " (4.7.38). Likewise John Talbot kneels to his father in homage; later Joan will ostentatiously refuse to kneel, as an obedient child should, to the shepherd she now repudiates as her father. The culmination of this comparison can be found in the stage picture at the close of the battle scene, when Talbot dies with his son in his arms: "Now my old arms are young John Talbot's grave" (4.7.32). "See where he lies inhearsèd in the arms / Of the most bloody nurser of his harms" (4.7.45–46), observes the Duke of Burgundy. The instruction to "see" directs the eye, and what the audience sees when it follows this invitation is an all-male Pietà: instead of the Virgin Mary cradling her son, Talbot the "nurser" cradling his.

To an early modern audience, as to a modern or postmodern one, this staging would present an unmistakable and powerful spectacle. In essence, it remakes a Catholic icon into a patriotic English one (we should bear in mind, though, that the historical Talbot, who lived long before the founding of the English Church, would have been as much a Catholic as his French rivals). The discrediting of Joan, and the peculiar scene in which she summons her fiends by "charming spells and periapts," written incantations wrapped about the body, follows immediately upon the death of Talbot, as Joan is explicitly labeled a "witch," a "sorceress," and a "Circe" who bewitches men and transforms them into beasts. As we have seen, Joan's fall is linked dramaturgically as well as the-matically to the rise of Margaret, for as the captured Joan is led off ("Curse, mis-creant, when thou com'st to the stake," says York as he conducts her away [5.4.14–15]), Suffolk enters "with Margaret in his hand" and addresses her in the conventional language of romantic love poetry: "Be what thou wilt, thou art my prisoner" (5.5.1). Thus in the course of just a few scenes Talbot is vanquished by Joan, and Joan is replaced by Margaret of Anjou. The conquest of the English by the French is moved from the battlefield to the court, from open warfare to covert seduction, from "external" war to internal or civil war. And as always in the history plays, the state of the nation is twinned with the state of the monarch. Henry, "perplexed with a thousand cares" as he waits for his "faithful and anointed queen" to cross the seas to England, is already vulnerable. So even in the moment of apparent victory another defeat looms; Suffolk's comparison of himself to the Trojan prince Paris, who tried to kidnap Helen from her hus-band, Menelaus, makes it clear that Margaret herself is a Trojan horse, a treach-erous and dangerous gift.

Henry VI Part 2

DRAMATIS PERSONAE

OF THE KING'S PARTY

King Henry VI
Queen Margaret
William de la Pole, *Marquis, later*
Duke, of Suffolk, the Queen's lover
Duke Humphrey of Gloucester,
the Lord Protector, the King's uncle
Dame Eleanor Cobham,
the Duchess of Gloucester

Cardinal Beaufort, *Bishop of*
Winchester, Gloucester's uncle
and the King's great-uncle
Duke of Buckingham
Duke of Somerset
Old Lord Clifford
Young Clifford, *his son*

OF THE DUKE OF YORK'S PARTY

Duke of York
Edward, *Earl of March,*
son of the Duke
Crookback Richard, *son of the Duke*

Earl of Salisbury
Earl of Warwick, *his son*

THE PETITIONS AND THE COMBAT

Two or three Petitioners
Thomas Horner, *an armourer*
Peter Thump, *his man*
Three neighbours, *who drink*
to Horner

Three Prentices, *who drink*
to Peter

THE CONJURATION

Sir John Hume, *a priest*
John Southwell, *a priest*
Margery Jordan, *a witch*

Roger Bolingbroke, *a conjurer*
Asnath, *a spirit*

THE FALSE MIRACLE

Simon Simpcox
Simpcox's Wife
The Mayor of Saint Albans

Aldermen of Saint Albans
A Beadle of Saint Albans
Townsmen of Saint Albans

ELEANOR'S PENANCE

Gloucester's Servants

Two Sheriffs of London

Sir John Stanley

Herald

THE MURDER OF GLOUCESTER

Two Murderers

Commons

THE MURDER OF SUFFOLK

Captain of a ship

Master of that ship

The Master's Mate

Walter Whitmore

Two Gentlemen

THE CADE REBELLION

Jack Cade, *a Kentishman suborned
   by the Duke of York*

Dick the Butcher, *Cade's follower*

Smith the Weaver, *Cade's follower*

A Sawyer, *Cade's follower*

John, *Cade's follower*

Rebels, *Cade's followers*

Emmanuel, the Clerk of Chatham,
   who dies at the rebels' hands

Sir Humphrey Stafford,
   who dies at the rebels' hands

Stafford's Brother, *who dies at
   the rebels' hands*

Lord Saye, *who dies at the
   rebels' hands*

Lord Scales, *who dies at the
   rebels' hands*

Matthew Gough, *who dies at
   the rebels' hands*

A Sergeant, *who dies at the
   rebels' hands*

Three or four Citizens of London

Alexander Iden, *an esquire of
   Kent, who kills Cade*

OTHERS

Vaux, *a messenger*

A Post

Messengers

A Soldier

Attendants, guards, servants,
   soldiers, falconers

MANY OF Shakespeare's plays contain phrases, lines, and passages that, as we have noted, are popularly quoted out of context, so that the phrases assume a cultural life of their own independent of the play in which they first appeared. Thus Macbeth's "Tomorrow, and tomorrow, and tomorrow" speech is taken as a general lament as well as a specific cry of despair, as is Hamlet's "To be, or not to be." *Hamlet,* unsurprisingly, is a gold mine of such phrases, small and large: "Something is rotten in the state of Denmark," for example, has come to have a cultural frame of reference much wider than its

original context. *Henry VI Part 2* is the source of another such celebrated floating quotation, and whereas citers of the "Tomorrow" and "To be" speeches are
fairly likely to know the context from which they derive, this is less likely for
those who quote, often gleefully, sometimes ruefully, one line from act 4 of
the play: "The first thing we do let's kill all the lawyers" (4.2.68).

The speaker is a minor character called Dick the Butcher, a henchman of the
rebel leader Jack Cade, whose insurrectionary rhetoric and far-fetched claim to
be the true king of England are deliberately juxtaposed in the play to the more
plausible claims of the Lancaster king, Henry VI, and his rival, Richard, Duke
of York. Modern-day lawyers, law students, and plaintiffs have tended to debate
whether Shakespeare did or did not mean to speak ill of the legal profession.
But in context this remark—which may have elicited general laughter in the
Elizabethan playhouse, as it often does in the theater today—addresses a whole
range of topics, from law to literacy, that are central to the design of the play.
Cade's response comically glances at Dick's chosen profession, which also in-
flicts damage on "innocent" animals:

> Nay, that I mean to do. Is this not a lamentable thing that
> of the skin of an innocent lamb should be made parchment?
> That parchment, being scribbled o'er, should undo a man?
> 2 Henry VI 4.2.69–71

The revolutionary movement led by Cade is passionately opposed to literacy
and learning. Told that a clerk "can read and write and cast account," Cade
replies, "O, monstrous!" (77), and his attitude is not a joke. The unlucky clerk
is sent away to be hanged as a traitor: "hang him with his pen and inkhorn
about his neck" (96–97). As scholars and editors note, Shakespeare is here conflating two different insurrections, the Peasants' Revolt of Wat Tyler and Jack
Straw in 1381 and the historical Jack Cade's rebellion of 1450. Tyler's revolt was
strongly antiliteracy, reflecting the belief that the skills of reading and writing
were socially divisive and anti-egalitarian. Holinshed's *Chronicles,* one of Shakespeare's sources, reports that Wat Tyler wanted to insert a passage in a charter
"to put to death all lawyers, escheaters, and other which by any office had to
doo with the law."[1] Cade, on the other hand, is described by Holinshed as a
well-spoken young man, whose campaign was abetted by teachers and schoolmasters. So the dramatist's choice, to emphasize Cade's contempt for lawyers
(and his comically placed compassion for the sheep that produce sheepskin for
the Inns of Court), is presumably not so much a reflection of a biographical bias
(Shakespeare as fancied victim of unscrupulous lawyering) as it is part of a larger
pattern in the play. Here, the Jack Cade rebellion, a classic version of "the world
turned upside down," imagines a world without law, degree or rank, sartorial
distinction, education, writing, or print. All these issues were matters of
anxiety—and excitement—in the humanist early modern period, and all were

actively under debate. It is a measure of how "modern" the early moderns were that these categories of distinction are also, if somewhat differently, modules of society and culture today.

The play embeds the Cade rebellion in a larger structure of civil war, claims and cross-claims, and competing modes of authority, including religion, magic, witchcraft, genealogy, and history. Cade's animadversions about writing and print are dramatically anticipated by the concern of the Protector of England, Humphrey, Duke of Gloucester, the brother of Henry V and in this play— unhistorically—still Protector even though Henry VI had attained his majority some time earlier. The play begins with the terms of the King's marriage to Margaret of Anjou, agreed upon by the Marquis of Suffolk, acting for King Henry. That Suffolk is privately Margaret's lover adds to the tension of the scene, as a letter is read indicating, among other things, that Henry will not only forgo the usual dowry of a royal marriage, but will actually pay, in money and in lands, to take this princess of an obscure kingdom as his queen: "the duchy of Anjou and the county of Maine shall be released and delivered to the King her father, and she sent over of the King of England's own proper cost and charges, without dowry." The credulous and unsuspecting Henry is delighted with his bride's looks and "grace in speech," and he creates his proxy the "first Duke of Suffolk." But Humphrey, Duke of Gloucester, the bulwark of old England and its values, is appalled at these developments and the way they threaten to undo his kingly brother's conquest of France. Significantly, he expresses his dismay in terms of writing, print, and reputation:

> O peers of England, shameful is this league,
> Fatal this marriage, cancelling your fame,
> Blotting your names from books of memory,
> Razing the characters of your renown,
> Defacing monuments of conquered France,
> Undoing all, as all had never been!
>
> *1.1.94–99*

Books, letters ("characters"), and monuments are ways of ensuring fame through history. Without them there is not only anarchy, but also historical forgetfulness and neglect.

Although the title by which the play is today best known, *Henry VI Part 2*— which corresponds to the title that appears in the First Folio as *The Second Part of Henry the Sixt*—suggests that the play is the second in a series, this play and *Henry VI Part 3* were almost certainly written before *Part 1*. The title printed in the Quarto edition, *The First Part of the Contention of the Two Famous Houses of York and Lancaster*, has thus tended to be revived by some recent editors and critics, who often abbreviate it to *The First Part of the Contention*. (The printed title to the Quarto of *Part 3* is *The True Tragedy of Richard Duke of York and*

Good King Henry the Sixth.) If titles mean anything at a time when they seem to
have been rather arbitrarily bestowed, this one directs our attention to (1) the
fact that the dispute, or "contention," is not resolved at the end of the play, and
(2) the importance of "the good Duke Humphrey" and the turning point represented by his death.

Gloucester, "the good Duke Humphrey," is in moral reputation the strongest figure in Henry VI's England. But Gloucester is shortly to be undone by
matters both domestic and political, as his wife, Eleanor, is convicted of dab-
bling in witchcraft, and the insidious Suffolk, leagued with Margaret, successfully schemes to get him out of the way. When this happens, and he finds
himself accused of high treason, he speaks to the guileless King and his guileful
accusers in terms that invoke a different kind of crafted history—that of the
stage play:

> Ah, gracious lord, these days are dangerous.
> Virtue is choked with foul ambition,
> And charity chased hence by rancour's hand.
> Foul subornation is predominant,
> And equity exiled your highness' land.
> I know their complot is to have my life,
> And if my death might make this island happy
> And prove the period of their tyranny,
> I would expend it with all willingness.
> But mine is made the prologue to their play,
> For thousands more that yet suspect no peril
> Will not conclude their plotted tragedy.
>
> *3.1.142–153*

"Complot," "prologue," "play," and "plotted tragedy" all address the question of
writing and performance. Plays in Shakespeare's time (a century and a half later,
of course, than the fictive time in which *2 Henry VI* is set) were written, memorized, performed, and—ultimately—printed. We might compare these lines
with Hamlet's observation that the traveling players are "the abstracts and brief
chronicles of the time" (*Hamlet* 2.2.504). A "complot," defined as "a conspiracy"
or "a design of a covert nature," is clearly related—as Gloucester's subsequent
use of "plotted" indicates—to the world of stage tragedy and play. The crossover
between "complot" and "plot" will, in fact, animate not only the rest of this
play, but the two plays that follow it in historical sequence, *3 Henry VI* and
Richard III, leading up to Richard's famous declaration, at the beginning
of *Richard III,* "Plots have I laid, inductions dangerous. . . ."

The degree to which the play is self-conscious about its own dramatic
nature—what is usually called "metadrama"—is underscored by its structure
and composition, as a series of events unfold, each of which could be called a
staged performance or a play-within-the-play. The marriage of Henry and Mar-

garet with which the play begins could be read as such a "show," since it is a cover for the real relationship between Margaret and Suffolk, and Henry's appreciation of his new bride, as we have already noted, focuses on her skill as a persuasive (and dissembling) performer:

> Her sight did ravish, but her grace in speech,
> Her words yclad with wisdom's majesty,
> Makes me from wond'ring fall to weeping joys,
> Such is the fullness of my heart's content.
>
> *1.1.30–34*

The profoundly unpolitical Henry fails to see that her affection is not for him. Meantime her arrival has triggered latent dissension at court. York, who will claim the crown as rightly his, joins Gloucester in the appeal to written history, in a gesture of acknowledgment of the play's textual sources:

> I never read but England's kings have had
> Large sums of gold and dowries with their wives—
> And our King Henry gives away his own,
> To match with her that brings no vantages.
>
> *1.1.124–127*

A simmering dispute between the Protector, Humphrey, Duke of Gloucester, and Cardinal Henry Beaufort, Bishop of Winchester, flares up, and once Gloucester has left the stage "in a rage" the Cardinal expresses his distrust of the "dangerous Protector," too well liked by "the common people" (1.1.144, 161, 155). The moment the Cardinal departs we hear similar cautionary words about him, with the difference that where as Gloucester, the "good Duke," is too popular with the cheering commons, the "haughty Cardinal" exhibits "insolence . . . more intolerable" than any of the princes in the land (171–173). In fact, everyone in court—the Cardinal, Buckingham, Somerset—would like to be Protector, although the King is of age to rule. Good sense and patriotic values are exhibited by Richard Neville, Earl of Salisbury, and his son the Earl of Warwick, who will acquire in these plays the sobriquet of "King-maker" (accorded him by another Elizabethan dramatist, Samuel Daniel, in his epic poem *The Civil Wars Between the Two Houses of Lancaster and York,* 1595) as he superintends the ascendancy of Henry, then York, then Henry once again. Warwick is introduced to the audience—still in this first expository scene—by his father's words of praise:

> Warwick, my son, the comfort of my age,
> Thy deeds, thy plainness, and thy housekeeping
> Hath won thee greatest favour of the commons,
> Excepting none but good Duke Humphrey.
>
> *1.1.187–190*

When Duke Humphrey is betrayed and murdered in act 3, scene 2, before he can be properly tried for treason—a murder agreed upon together by Suffolk, York, the Cardinal, and others—it is Warwick who will emerge to take his place as the de facto protector of England, without the title, and it is to Warwick that the play will give the all-important last words.

At the close of the first scene, however, we are a long way from the end of this unfolding drama of political reversals and conflict between princes and commons. Instead a telltale soliloquy by Richard, Duke of York, lays out his claims, and his plans:

> A day will come when York shall claim his own,
> And therefore I will take the Nevilles' parts,
> And make a show of love to proud Duke Humphrey,
> And when I spy advantage, claim the crown,
> For that's the golden mark I seek to hit.
> Nor shall proud Lancaster usurp my right,
> Nor hold the sceptre in his childish fist,
> Nor wear the diadem upon his head
> Whose church-like humours fit not for a crown.
> Then, York, be still awhile, till time do serve.
> Watch thou, and wake when others be asleep,
> To pry into the secrets of the state—
> .   .   .   .
> And force perforce I'll make him yield the crown,
> Whose bookish rule hath pulled fair England down.
>
> *1.1.238–258*

York's grievances against King Henry are two: Henry is not the rightful heir, and he is a weak monarch, with "church-like humours" and "bookish rule." Henry is too "bookish," or studious and contemplative; Jack Cade's rebellion, as we have already noted, will mark the other side of this spectrum, condemning anyone who can read and write. York's jibe of "childish" is likewise intentional, given all the foregoing discussion about who should be Protector. As Queen Margaret will ask pointedly of Gloucester in act 1, scene 3, if the King is "old enough" to speak for himself, "what needs your grace / To be Protector . . . ?" But Margaret herself makes the same complaint against Henry that York does, comparing him unfavorably to the dashing Suffolk (William de la Pole), who came to court her on the king's behalf:

> I thought King Henry had resembled thee
> In courage, courtship, and proportion.
> But all his mind is bent to holiness,
> To number Ave-Maries on his beads.

His champions are the prophets and apostles,
His weapons holy saws of sacred writ,
His study is his tilt-yard, and his loves
Are brazen images of canonizèd saints.
I would the college of the cardinals
Would choose him Pope, and carry him to Rome,
And set the triple crown upon his head—
That were a state fit for his holiness.

1.3.57–68

Writing in post-Reformation England, Shakespeare could expect these references to Rome and the Pope, like those to the "imperious churchman" Beaufort, to strike a negative chord with the audience, although of course the historical Henry VI ruled over an England where Catholicism was the unchallenged religion of the king and of his land. In effect, Margaret's portrait of Henry paints him as unmanly, preferring prayer before combat and rule. Holiness, like childishness, is a disability:

My lord of Suffolk, say, is this the guise?
Is this the fashions in the court of England?
Is this the government of Britain's isle,
And this the royalty of Albion's king?

1.3.46–49

From her first arrival, then, Margaret dominates the King. Gloucester's wife, Eleanor Cobham, will combine the two kinds of mastery into one dismissive phrase when she warns Henry against his wife's subversive plans: "Good King, look to't in time! / She'll pamper thee and dandle thee like a baby. / Though in this place most master wear no breeches" (1.3.148–150). In Henry's court the woman wears the pants, or breeches, and the husband, though king in name, is treated like a child. These are themes that will recur in *3 Henry VI,* where Margaret is said to wear the breeches instead of the petticoat. Such terms of infantilization and unmanning will also be deployed, for example, in Lady Macbeth's language and attitude toward her husband. But the question of the strong, ruthless woman married to a husband whose ambition is limited by his scruples is also, strikingly, invoked by Eleanor in her discussion of her own marriage to Gloucester, "the good Duke Humphrey."

The first scene of the play had presented politicians and their ambitious plots. Scene 2 deliberately juxtaposes another, contrasting mode of prediction and prognostication, that of dream. Gloucester has had "troublous dreams this night" in which he saw his Protector's staff of office broken in two ("by whom I have forgot / But, as I think, it was by th' Cardinal" [1.2.26–27]), and on the pieces of the broken wand were impaled the heads of the Dukes of Somerset and Suffolk. The dream is predictive, and like all such dreams in these plays, it comes true: Somerset is killed by York's son Richard at the end of the play, and Suffolk decapitated by his captor, Walter Whitmore, in act 4, scene 1, and his head taken to the mourning Queen. Eleanor underrates and misinterprets her husband's dream ("Tut, this was nothing but an argument / That he that breaks a stick of Gloucester's grove / Shall lose his head for his presumption" [1.2.32–34]) and goes on to tell her own, which, significantly, she describes as a "morning's dream," in contrast to her husband's. A well-attuned contemporary audience would understand the difference, derived from medieval dream lore: Eleanor's is, in effect, a conscious wish, rather than an uncanny prediction. She has "dreamed" that she sat on the throne, and that "Henry and Dame Margaret" came and kneeled to her, and put the crown on her head. For Eleanor wants her husband to be King rather than Protector:

> Put forth thy hand, reach at the glorious gold.
> What, is't too short? I'll lengthen it with mine. . . .
>
> 1.2.11–12

When he demurs, protesting his loyalty to the King, she reacts with dismissive scorn:

> Follow I must; I cannot go before
> While Gloucester bears this base and humble mind.
> Were I a man, a duke, and next of blood,
> I would remove these tedious stumbling blocks
> And smooth my way upon their headless necks.
> And, being a woman, I will not be slack
> To play my part in fortune's pageant.
>
> 1.2.61–67

"Were I a man": As always, it is useful to keep in mind that women's parts on the early modern public stage were played by boys. The "manliness" of these strong female characters, who often dominate their milder men, is given an extra dramatic piquancy by this circumstance. "Pageant" is another theater word from the period, denoting not only a play but often an older, medieval "mystery" play, here to be designed, and cast, by Fortune. "[B]eing a woman," Eleanor has her own plans and plots, and in the next moment she is commissioning her clerk to gather "Margery Jordan, the cunning witch," and "Roger Bolingbroke, the conjuror," who will raise a spirit through necromancy.

The two scenes of prediction, the "dream" scene in act 1, scene 2, and the spectacular ceremony of black magic in act 1, scene 4, reinforce each other as ways of telling the future that are alternative to chronicle history and its plots and complots. They thus stand in important contrast not only to the opening scene but also to the long genealogical account of Edward III and his seven sons, another famous set piece in this play, offered by York in act 2, scene 2, lines 10–52 passim, as justification for his claim to the crown, an explanation that Salisbury has said he longs "to hear . . . out at full," and that Warwick praises for its straightforward clarity ("What plain proceedings is more plain than this?") before he offers his own historical prediction:

> My heart assures me that the Earl of Warwick
> Shall one day make the Duke of York a king.
>
> *2.2.78–79*

But in this play of tempered idealism and persistent political cynicism, York's ringing genealogy is itself countered and balanced by the comic and anarchic claim of lineage offered by the rebel Jack Cade, who begins his declaration with the royal "we" ("We, John Cade, so termed of our supposed father—"):

Cade	My father was a Mortimer—
Butcher [*to his fellows*]	He was an honest man and a good bricklayer.
Cade	My mother a Plantagenet—
Butcher [*to his fellows*]	I knew her well, she was a midwife.
Cade	My wife descended of the Lacys—
Butcher [*to his fellows*]	She was indeed a pedlar's daughter and sold many laces. . . .
Cade	Therefore am I of an honourable house.

> *4.2.34–43*

This point-counterpoint structure, in which every "noble" claim has an "ignoble" equivalent, begins after a while to accomplish exactly what Cade intends: to put in question the legitimacy of authority and rule. But in fact the suggestion that Cade is "John Mortimer," and thus a legitimate heir to the throne, is part of a plan by York to "perceive the commons' mind, / How they affect the house and claim of York" (3.1.375). Alone on the stage, York says:

> I have seduced a headstrong Kentishman,
> John Cade of Ashford,
> To make commotion, as full well he can,
> Under the title of John Mortimer.
> In Ireland I have seen this stubborn Cade
> Oppose himself against a troop of kerns.
>
> .   .   .   .
>
> And in the end, being rescued, I have seen
> Him caper upright like a wild Morisco,
> Shaking the bloody darts as he his bells.
>
> *3.1.356–366*

The invocation of the morris dance, an element of native English folk culture, emphasizes the degree to which there is a developing tension between court and folk, native and "foreign," in this play, as *2 Henry VI* offers a series of scenes that function as striking visual and theatrical spectacles.

The magic ceremonies would surely have been theatrical crowd-pleasers, however forbidden by contemporary religion and law. Gathering at night ("wizards know their times" [1.4.14]), the necromancers make a magic circle and conjure a spirit to appear. This kind of scene, familiar and popular from plays like Robert Greene's *Friar Bacon and Friar Bungay* and Marlowe's *Dr. Faustus,* involves a set of riddling prophecies, each of which comes true—although (as would later be the case in *Richard III* and *Macbeth*) they do so in an unexpected way. A question about the future of the King thus produces a piece of complicated syntax with more than one possible interpretation—"The Duke yet lives that Henry shall depose, / But him outlive, and die a violent death" (1.4.29–30)—where much hinges on whether the person who will outlive his rival is "the Duke" (Richard of York) or "Henry." Suffolk is predicted to die "by water," and he meets his fate at the hands of a man called Walter Whitmore, despite his desperate last-minute attempt to persuade his captor to pronounce his name in the French fashion ("Thy name is Gualtier, being rightly sounded" [4.1.38]) to evade the prophecy. The third prediction, that the Earl of Somerset should "shun castles," turns out to mean not that he should avoid fortresses and fortifications but that he will meet his death, far less grandiosely, "underneath an alehouse' paltry sign, / The Castle in Saint Albans"—although as Richard of Gloucester notes, this does fulfill the prophecy, and thus Somerset "[h]ath made the wizard famous in his death" (5.2.2–3, 4).

But if magic is good for theater, it is dangerous for its practitioners, on the stage and off, and the witch, wizard, and accomplice are all betrayed to the Duke of York and sentenced to death. As for Eleanor, Duchess of Gloucester, she—being of noble birth—is given a lesser punishment: the humiliation of public penance, barefoot and dressed in a white sheet, and then exile from England. (As she says, "I, his forlorn Duchess, / Was made a wonder and a pointing-stock / To every idle rascal follower" [2.4.46–48].) Since Eleanor has been explicitly associated early in the play with sartorial display and extravagant finery, this reversal is devastating both visually and psychologically.

And partnering these scenes of necromancy, or black magic, are scenes that purport to show miracles, the "magic" of pre-Reformation Christian faith, dismissed in Shakespeare's time by Protestant theologians. Thus, deftly situated by the playwright between the episode of the wizard, witch, and Duchess conjuring spirits (1.4) and their trial and condemnation (2.3) is a scene in which the Mayor of Saint Albans produces, to King Henry's excitement, a "blind" man, Simpcox, who has supposedly been restored to sight. The pious—and credulous—King praises God on behalf of "believing souls," but Gloucester is more skeptical. He quickly unmasks the impostor by asking him to identify colors, then pointing out that there is no way, had he been born blind, that he would know the *names* for those colors: "If thou hadst been born blind / Thou mightst as well have known our names as thus / To name the several colors we do wear" (2.1.130–132). Simpcox's supposed lameness is as bogus as his blindness, and when threatened with a whipping, he flees. The fine construction of this scene uses Gloucester's cleverness as the fulcrum; one moment he is triumphant in a scene among the commoners (Cardinal Beaufort: "Duke Humphrey has done a miracle today." Suffolk: "True: made the lame to leap and fly away" [2.1.160–161]), the next downcast and undone as his wife's sorcery is revealed—her "[d]ealing with witches and with conjurors" and "[r]aising up wicked spirits from under ground, / Demanding of King Henry's life and death" (171, 173–174). It is worth noting that Buckingham, who makes this announcement, and the King, who ordains the punishment, do not accuse the practitioners of imposture. Simpcox is a risible fake, and is merely whipped out of town; the necromancers are real, and are burned to death.

Henry VI Part 2 consistently plays these "folk," or common, characters off against the noblemen, to powerful theatrical effect. Thus in another telling episode an armourer, Horner, is accused of treason by his apprentice Peter, who claims he has heard Horner say that Richard, Duke of York, was the rightful king (1.3.28–30). According to the jurisprudence of the time, this dispute is to be settled by single combat. The scene of the fight between "appellant and defendant— / The armourer and his man" (2.3.49–50) is both comic in performance (Horner is drunk, Peter terrified) and serious in outcome (Peter kills Horner, who confesses as he dies; but, as the King notes, it is losing the fight, not making the confession, that proves him treasonous: "by his death we do perceive his guilt" [2.3.102]). The weapons used in this combat are "combat flails," long staffs with sandbags fastened to them, thus more capable of inflicting injury than the agricultural flails used in harvesting, but less immediately deadly than the iron flails used as military weapons in war. The combat scene is a visually successful—and in part amusing—interruption of a play that often tends to be dominated by high-sounding talk. But it also marks a middle ground between the weighty, old-fashioned "two-hand sword" of Gloucester (2.1.50), the traditional weapon of earlier combat, and the "staves" wielded by the lawless rebels. Horner and Peter are "low" characters, not noblemen, but they abide by the rules of combat and of law. Thus they stand in useful contrast to their social "betters," from Suffolk to York to Cardinal Beaufort, who plot against law and against the King.

The murder of Gloucester, his body graphically described by Warwick, marks a turning point in the play's attitude toward the display of violence. Suffolk, who hired the murderers, has pretended shock at the news of the Protector's death. (A little scene showing the remorse of the hired killers—"O that it were to do! What have we done?" [3.2.3]—is typical of Shakespeare, and anticipates similar scenes in other history plays and in *Macbeth*.) But Warwick, hearing rumors "[t]hat good Duke Humphrey traitorously is murdered / By Suffolk and the Cardinal Beaufort's means" [3.2.123–124]), demands, on behalf of the "commons," to see the body, and when it is produced onstage Warwick reads the signs of violent death:

> But see, his face is black and full of blood;
> His eyeballs further out than when he lived,
> Staring full ghastly like a strangled man;
> His hair upreared; his nostrils stretched with struggling;
> His hands abroad displayed, as one that grasped
> And tugged for life and was by strength subdued.
> Look on the sheets. His hair, you see, is sticking;
> His well-proportioned beard made rough and rugged,
> Like to the summer's corn by tempest lodged.
> It cannot be but he was murdered here.
> The least of all these signs were probable.

> *3.2.168–178*

I cite this aversive passage at length because it evokes so vividly the desperate appearance of the murdered man, as if he were visible to the audience in all his deathly disarray. This is a version of a technique I will call the "unscene," often used by Shakespeare to bring to life, by narrative, events that take place offstage. (One ready example is Ophelia's description of Hamlet in her closet, his clothing awry, taking her hand and staring into her eyes like a ghost.) In this case, even though the body is onstage, the audience cannot see these particulars except through Warwick's pungent description.

Suffolk, accused, denies the accusation: "Myself and Beaufort had him in protection, / And we, I hope, sir, are no murderers" (180–181). But Warwick, bolstered by the insistence of the commons—who loudly cry, "Down with Suffolk!"—draws his sword against him, and ultimately, again at the behest of the commons (scornfully characterized by Suffolk as "a sort of tinkers," but championed by Salisbury and Warwick), the King announces that Suffolk will be banished from England. The parting scene between Suffolk and Queen Margaret, the only love scene in the play, is affecting despite their perfidy, and is expressed in terms that will recur powerfully in later Shakespeare, with anticipatory echoes of the banishment of Bolingbroke in *Richard II* and Leontes' pledge of perpetual mourning for the wronged Hermione in *The Winter's Tale*. ("Well could I curse away a winter's night," says Suffolk to the Queen, "Though standing naked on a mountain top, / Where biting cold would never let grass grow, / And think it but a minute spent in sport" [337–340].) But this bittersweet interlude is brought to an end, not only by Suffolk's departure, but by another deathbed scene, this one the agonizing death of Cardinal Beaufort, who "sees" the ghost of Gloucester in his mind:

O, torture me no more—I will confess.
Alive again? Then show me where he is.
I'll give a thousand pound to look upon him.
He hath no eyes! The dust hath blinded them.
Comb down his hair—look, look: it stands upright,
Like lime twigs set to catch my wingèd soul.

3.3.11–16

Here again, as with Warwick's speech about the body of Gloucester, the vivid image is summoned by language; no physical ghost presents itself upon the stage. But with the murder of Gloucester a far greater and more visible violence begins to afflict the play; it is symbolized by the sudden presence onstage of severed heads—heads that are produced not only as evidence of violent death, but also as macabre "actors" in the ensuing scenes.

Decapitated heads were not uncommon stage props in the period, and the actual heads of traitors were displayed at the city gates of London as warnings to potential malefactors. Beheading (literal "capital punishment") was the ordained method for noblemen; persons of lesser rank were hanged, witches and heretics burned to death. (This very rank-conscious play will include a scene [4.8] in which "multitudes" of former rebels appear before the King "with halters about their necks" asking for his pardon.) Other Shakespeare plays have their share of onstage severed heads—notably *Macbeth,* which ends with the display of the "usurper's cursèd head," and *Measure for Measure,* in which the head of one deceased prisoner, Ragusine, is substituted for that of the doomed Claudio. But in *2 Henry VI* the severed heads are not only produced as props, they are made to "perform."

Suffolk, whose family name is de la Pole, is twitted by his pirate captors with puns on "poll" and "pole," as they predict his decapitation: "Thy lips that kissed the Queen shall sweep the ground, / And thou that smiledst at good Duke Humphrey's death / Against the senseless winds shall grin in vain" (4.1.75–77). A third pun, on "pool"—the words would have been pronounced alike— provides a further irony, as his death by "water" is assured: "Ay, kennel, puddle, sink, whose filth and dirt / Troubles the silver spring where England drinks" (71–72). Suffolk's defiance likewise invokes his probable fate: "rather let my head / Stoop to the block . . . / And sooner dance upon a bloody pole" (126–129). His death, marked by the stage direction "Enter Whitmore with [Suffolk's head and] body" leads only a few scenes later to another stage direction, "Enter King [Henry] reading a supplication, Queen [Margaret] with Suffolk's head," and thence to a kind of bizarre return to the rhetoric of love: "Here may his head lie on my throbbing breast, / But where's the body that I should embrace?" (4.4.5–6). Queen Margaret's lamentation on the dead head of her lover is punctuated by an all-too-apt exchange between the King and his Lord Chamberlain and treasurer, Lord Saye:

Queen [*to Suffolk's head*]	Hath this lovely face
	Ruled like a wandering planet over me,
	And could it not enforce them to relent,
	That were unworthy to behold the same?
King	Lord Saye, Jack Cade hath sworn to have thy head.
Saye	Ay, but I hope your highness will have his.

4.4.14–19

Ultimately all these heads will be cut off and displayed. The humiliating punishment ordained for Lord Saye by Jack Cade, who boasts that he will rule *in capite,* or in chief, is that his head, placed on a pole, shall be made to "kiss" the decapitated head of his son-in-law, Sir James Cromer: "with these borne before us instead of maces will we ride through the streets, and at every corner have them kiss" (4.7.142–144). The stage direction "Enter two with the Lord Saye's head and Sir James Cromer's upon two poles" makes this image graphically clear. The "kissing" of Saye and his kinsman thus visually mocks the Queen's desperate cradling of her lover's head. Cade's own head will be struck off after he is slain trying to make his escape through the walled garden of "Alexander Iden, an esquire of Kent" (4.9.40). Iden's name and his garden are mentioned in Hall's chronicle, but the Iden/Eden connection underscores the emblematic theme of England as a walled garden paradise, an association bolstered by Iden's own patriotic rhetoric in the scene. Iden's heroic action, undertaken from his country retreat, is then, again, deftly juxtaposed by the playwright to the martial return of York from Ireland, as the crossover between these two scenes will make clear. Iden declares at the end of act 4 that he will "cut off [Cade's] most ungracious head" and bear it "in triumph to the King" (4.9.79–80). York enters two lines later announcing, "From Ireland thus comes York to claim his right, / And pluck the crown from feeble Henry's head" (5.1.1–2).

The Cade rebellion that breaks out in the fourth act, significantly after the murder of "the good Duke Humphrey," thus speaks directly to numerous themes established in the play. Cade's derogation of "silken-coated slaves" (4.2.115) in favor of the leather aprons of craftsmen and laborers echoes the issues of dress and luxury (in defiance of history, he himself is made a "clothier," perhaps to reinforce this point). Through the medieval period and Queen Elizabeth's day, social legibility was ensured by "sumptuary laws" that prescribed, and proscribed, certain kinds of cloth and ornament for various ranks and degrees, largely restricting imported cloth, gold ornament, and other finery to the highest ranks, while the commons were expected to wear cloth of local manufacture. Cade's comical "knighting" of Dick the Butcher anticipates King Henry's knighting of Alexander Iden. One of Cade's complaints against Lord Saye is that he has allowed young people to learn to read, and has—anachronistically—permitted books to be printed:

Thou has most traitorously corrupted the youth of the realm in erecting a grammar school; and, whereas before, our forefathers had no other books but the score and the tally, thou hast caused printing to be used and, contrary to the King his crown and dignity, thou hast built a paper-mill. It will be proved to thy face that thou hast men about thee that usually talk of a noun and a verb and such abominable words as no Christian ear can endure to hear. . . . Moreover, thou hast put [poor men] in prison, and, because they could not read, thou hast hanged them when indeed only for that cause they have been most worthy to live. . . .

4.7.27–39

Lord Saye's response is a spirited defense of humanist education, beginning with a compliment to the County of Kent attributed to "the commentaries Caesar writ": "Large gifts have I bestowed on learnèd clerks / Because my book preferred me to the King, / And seeing ignorance is the curse of God, / Knowledge the wing wherewith we fly to heaven" (4.7.53, 64–67). But Saye's conclusion, "Unless you be possessed with devilish spirits, / You cannot but forebear to murder me" (4.7.68–69), contains a fatal "unless," and his death seems to exemplify the topsy-turvy lawlessness that has broken out in England as if in response to the corruption, ambition, and rivalry at court. (The mention of "devilish spirits" here recalls Eleanor Cobham and the fall of Gloucester.)

The play closes with York and his sons ascendant, but troubling events in the latter acts and scenes make it clear that the "contention" is far from over. The death of Old Lord Clifford turns his son, Young Clifford, into a spirit of vengeance vowing, "York not our old men spares; / No more will I their babes" (5.3.51–52), and pointing ahead directly to his own slaughter of York's son Rutland in *3 Henry VI*. Warwick's last words, seeming to signal a close to the wars, are here, as always in these history plays, laden with an irony unintended by the speaker but clearly perceptible to an audience:

> Now by my hand, lords, 'twas a glorious day!
> Saint Albans battle won by famous York
> Shall be eternized in all age to come.
> Sound drums and trumpets, and to London all,
> And more such days as these to us befall!

5.5.34–37

Warwick, speaking from within the dramatic frame of the fifteenth century depicted in the play, imagines the "eternizing" as an act of historical memory, borne out in Shakespeare's day by the various chronicle sources—Hall, Holinshed, and others—that tell the story of these events. From the perspective of a theatrical audience or reader in the ever-shifting present that is literature's "now," the act of "eternizing" will be accomplished by Shakespeare's play, and

Henry VI Part 3

DRAMATIS PERSONAE

OF THE KING'S PARTY

King Henry VI
Queen Margaret
Prince Edward, *their son*
Duke of Somerset
Duke of Exeter
Earl of Northumberland
Earl of Westmorland
Lord Clifford

Lord Stafford
Somerville
Henry, *young Earl of Richmond*
A Soldier who has killed
  his father
A Huntsman who guards
  King Edward

THE DIVIDED HOUSE OF NEVILLE

Earl of Warwick, *first of York's
  party, later of Lancaster's*
Marquis of Montague, *his brother,
  of York's party*

Earl of Oxford, *their brother-
  in-law, of Lancaster's party*
Lord Hastings, *their brother-
  in-law, of York's party*

OF THE DUKE OF YORK'S PARTY

Richard Plantagenet, *Duke of York*
Edward, Earl of March, *his son,
  later Duke of York and King
  Edward IV*
Lady Gray, *a widow, later Edward's
  wife and queen*
Earl Rivers, *her brother*
George, *Edward's brother, later
  Duke of Clarence*
Richard, *Edward's brother,
  later Duke of Gloucester*
Earl of Rutland, *Edward's brother*

Rutland's Tutor, *a chaplain*
Sir John Mortimer, *York's uncle*
Sir Hugh Mortimer, *his brother*
Duke of Norfolk
Sir William Stanley
Earl of Pembroke
Sir John Montgomery
A Nobleman
Two Gamekeepers
Three Watchmen, *who guard
  King Edward's tent*
Lieutenant of the Tower

THE FRENCH

King Louis
Lady Bona, *his sister-in-law*

Lord Bourbon, *the French High
  Admiral*

OTHERS

A Soldier who has killed his son   Mayor of York
A Second Soldier who has killed   Aldermen of York
   his father   Soldiers, messengers, and
Mayor of Coventry   attendants

IKE THE OTHER plays in the cluster we now often describe as Shakespeare's "first tetralogy"—*1 Henry VI, 2 Henry VI, 3 Henry VI,* and
Richard III—this play has generally been treated either as one in an
epic series describing the events of the Wars of the Roses and the Tudor succession or as a very early work by a playwright still struggling to find his mature
voice. Both assessments undervalue the strength of *3 Henry VI* as an independent drama of great power and interest. Published in quarto form in 1600 as
The True Tragedie of Richard Duke of York, and Good King Henry the Sixth, the
play features at least two brilliantly memorable characters, Richard of Gloucester and Queen Margaret, at their eloquent and vituperative best, and contains,
in addition, several unusually effective theatrical set pieces: the mocking and
death of York, the murder of the boy Rutland, and Henry VI as the horrified
inadvertent witness to the discoveries of "a Soldier who has killed his father"
and "a Soldier who has killed his son"—a perfect, and perfectly appalling,
emblem of civil war. The quality of the poetry, and especially of the imagery, is
vivid throughout, and the portraits of lasciviousness, malevolence, and ambition in high places are as compelling and recognizable today as they would presumably have been in the early modern period.

It is worth taking a close look at this play as a single work, setting aside for a
moment its place in a larger continuum. When it is not dismissed as "early" or
"historical," it is often regarded as anticipatory of the more assured success of
Richard III, and certainly there is much in *3 Henry VI* that directly prefigures, or
predicts, its successor play. Thus, for example, when Laurence Olivier staged—
and then filmed—his version of *Richard III,* he began it with Richard's great
soliloquy, placed squarely at the center of *3 Henry VI:*

> Why, love forswore me in my mother's womb,
> And, for I should not deal in her soft laws,
> She did corrupt frail nature with some bribe
> To shrink mine arm up like a wither'd shrub,
> To make an envious mountain on my back—
> Where sits deformity to mock my body—
> To shape my legs of an unequal size,
> To disproportion me in every part,
> Like to a chaos, or an unlicked bear whelp

That carries no impression like the dam.
And am I then a man to be beloved?
O, monstrous fault, to harbour such a thought!
Then, since this earth affords no joy to me
But to command, to check, to o'erbear such
As are of better person than myself,
I'll make my heaven to dream upon the crown,
And whiles I live, t'account this world but hell,
Until my misshaped trunk that bears this head
Be round impalèd with a glorious crown.
And yet I know not how to get the crown,
For many lives stand between me and home.
And I—like one lost in a thorny wood,
That rends the thorns and is rent with the thorns,
Seeking a way and straying from the way,
Not knowing how to find the open air,
But toiling desperately to find it out—
Torment myself to catch the English crown.
And from that torment I will free myself,
Or hew my way out with a bloody axe.
Why, I can smile, and murder whiles I smile,
And cry "Content!" to that which grieves my heart,
And wet my cheeks with artificial tears,
And frame my face to all occasions.
I'll drown more sailors than the mermaid shall;
I'll slay more gazers than the basilisk;
I'll play the orator as well as Nestor,
Deceive more slyly than Ulysses could,
And, like a Sinon, take another Troy.
I can add colours to the chameleon,
Change shapes with Proteus for advantages,
And set the murderous Machiavel to school.
Can I do this, and cannot get a crown?
Tut, were it farther off, I'll pluck it down.

                    3 Henry VI 3.2.153–195

This magnificent speech is the self-portrait not only of a ruthless politician but also of an actor, one who can "play the orator," "[d]eceive," weep on command, "frame [his] face to all occasions," and "change shapes" even better than the god of shape-shifting, Proteus. The early modern understanding, or misunderstanding, of the political writings of Niccolò Machiavelli, based upon the Frenchman Innocent Gentillet's *Contre Nicolas Machiavel,* identified Machiavellianism with ruthlessness, amoral duplicity, and atheism. (Machiavelli, himself a republican, had produced for the Medici ruler of Florence a conduct book, *The Prince,* advocating a strategic, self-interested, and unsentimental mode of governance based upon a sober view of human nature.) This portrait of energized evil was, needless to say, immensely attractive to dramatists (and other writers), who were able to put onstage the pleasurable self-congratulation of single-minded ambition. By Shakespeare's time the word "Machiavel" was being used, in plays like Marlowe's *Jew of Malta* and Shakespeare's *3 Henry VI,* as the proud boast of a character who set himself apart from mundane humanity, espousing any tactics for his own gain, scornful of sentimentality and religion. Not only Richard of Gloucester but later Shakespeare characters like Iago in *Othello* and Edmund in *King Lear* trace their lineage to this source, and are often described as Machiavels. A Christian audience might also have seen in this account the stigmata of the Antichrist, as Richard's monstrous birth (prodigious rather than miraculous) is repeatedly associated not only with his quest for the crown but also, three times in two lines, with thorns.

Richard's vivid description of his political and emotional state as like that of "one lost in a thorny wood" seeking a way to get to the "open air" has been described as a birth fantasy, in which the infant, "toiling desperately," ultimately escapes from the womb ("[o]r hew my way out with a bloody axe"). We might, alternatively, note the effective local description of a heavily forested feudal England—or, indeed, the Alexander-like solution that Richard devises, cutting himself free rather than merely seeking a pathway, just as Alexander cut the Gordian knot rather than patiently trying to unravel it. (The man who succeeded in untying the Gordian knot was fated, said an oracle, to rule all of Asia.) Richard does, however, dwell here, and elsewhere in the play, on the narrative of his own birth, and the way his misshapen body has destined him for war and policy rather than courtship ("Why, love forswore me in my mother's womb"). The image of the "unlicked bear whelp / That carries no impression like the dam" was early modern folk belief masquerading as science, the idea that bear cubs, when born, had to be licked into physical shape by their mothers. In an equally evocative soliloquy in act 5, Richard will return to this imagined scene of his birth:

> For I have often heard my mother say
> I came into the world with my legs forward.
>
> . . . .
>
> The midwife wondered and the women cried
> "O, Jesus bless us, he is born with teeth!"—
> And so I was, which plainly signified
> That I should snarl and bite and play the dog.
> 5.6.70–71, 74–77

Again he will therefore forswear love, even brotherly love, as he is about to betray both of his brothers, Edward and Clarence:

> I have no brother, I am like no brother;
> And this word, "love," which graybeards call divine,
> Be resident in men like one another
> And not in me—I am myself alone.
>
> *5.6.81–84*

"I am myself alone" is the triumphant—and despairing—cry of the Machiavel. In an essay titled "Some Character-Types Met with in Psycho-Analytic Work" (1916), Sigmund Freud maintained that Richard exemplified persons he called "exceptions," narcissists who "claim to have special rights in view of the injury the external world has done them," and who "feel that they have not been loved enough." Whether we wish to employ modern psychology to assess Richard as "overcompensating" or not, what is indisputable is that dramatic characters of this kind—self-analytical, self-blinded, and dazzlingly articulate—have a roundedness and depth that we associate with the idea of "psychological realism," or recognizable human complexity. Theatrically this is achieved in part by the device of the soliloquy, of which Richard's two brilliant speeches, in acts 3 and 5, are early and powerful examples. Confiding in the audience, boasting and preening before it, the dramatic speaker discloses not only his plans and intentions ("Clarence, beware; thou kept'st me from the light. . . . I will buzz abroad such prophecies / That Edward shall be fearful of his life" [5.6.85–88]) but also things he does not "mean" to disclose, but which the playwright discloses to us over the head of his character, or behind his (crooked) back.

The story of Richard of Gloucester's prodigious birth, and, indeed, the story of his crooked and misshapen body, was—as we will note again in *Richard III*—a fiction, deriving from the work of political opponents, Tudor propagandists anxious to demonize and delegitimize the Plantagenet claim. It appears in Edward Hall's chronicle history *The Union of the Two Noble and Illustre Famelies of Lancastre and Yorke* (1548) and in Sir Thomas More's *History of King Richard III* (1557), both of which date, of course, from the time of Queen Elizabeth, but no document contemporary with the historical Richard (1452–1485) describes him as crookbacked or deformed, and portrait evidence from the period shows him to look not only well formed but handsome and thoughtful. (Josephine Tey's celebrated mystery novel *The Daughter of Time* explores the narrative of Richard's reputation as a deformed and wicked monster, tracing the myth to the ambitious Tudor heir who would become Henry VII—and who makes a mute cameo appearance in this play as "young Henry, Earl of Richmond," prophetically described by Henry VI as "England's hope" [4.7.67–68].)

Nonetheless, in looking at the design of *3 Henry VI* an audience will be concerned not so much with historical accuracy (the play, in Shakespeare's usual way, takes many liberties with dates, events, and the presence or absence of historical actors in specific places and times, and does not purport to be a chronicle record), but rather with dramatic effect. And here the "misshapen" Richard helps to give the play shapeliness. Richard's legendary "monstrous" appearance is repeatedly cited by many other characters as well as by himself: the inimitable Queen Margaret calls him "that valiant crookback prodigy, / Dickie, your boy" (1.4.76–77) and a "foul misshapen stigmatic" (2.2.136); Clifford addresses him as "crookback" (2.2.96), in response to Richard's taunt of "butcher." Prince Edward (Henry VI's son) will address the three York brothers as "[l]ascivious Edward, and thou, perjured George, / And thou, misshapen Dick" (5.5.34–35) and will—fatally, as it turns out—twit Richard as a "scolding crookback" (30) in the scene in which the three brothers stab young Edward to death in front of his mother, Margaret. And in the play's final scene Richard, once more in an aside to the audience, hints at his plan to undermine the apparent peace established on behalf of his brother, now King Edward IV:

> This shoulder was ordained so thick to heave;
> And heave it shall some weight or break my back.
>
> 5.7.23–24

Elements of all of these passages are revisited at the opening of *Richard III*, in the celebrated and compelling soliloquy that begins "Now is the winter of our discontent." Again the question of "deformity" and the way it "mocks" Richard's body is made the ostensible cause of his malevolence—although, as we will see there, he immediately goes on to prove himself a very apt lover indeed.

But balancing this physically "monstrous" man is a politically "monstrous" woman, the powerful and vituperative Queen Margaret, the wife of Henry VI. Margaret and Richard will be chief adversaries in *Richard III*. In *3 Henry VI* the symmetry of their monstrosity—which is to say, their exceptionalism—is established. Margaret is described twice as an "Amazon." "How ill-beseeming is it in thy sex / To triumph like an Amazonian trull," says York to her as she mocks him with a paper crown (1.4.114–115), and later his son, King Edward IV, hearing that "Henry's queen" is " 'ready to put armour on,' " remarks slightingly, "Belike she minds to play the Amazon" (4.1.100, 103, 104). Margaret is several times described in martial terms, each time with the implication that she is violating the natural law of men's dominance over women: "A woman's general," says Richard with disdain, "what should we fear?" (1.2.68); Edward addresses her with "You that are king, though he [Henry] do wear the crown" (2.2.90); and George, soon to be Duke of Clarence, taunts the dead Clifford, "Where's Captain Margaret to fence you now?" (2.6.75). This inversion of expected hierarchy was seen—in a view bolstered by the opinions of experts from Saint Paul to the Calvinist John Knox (author of *The First Blast of the Trumpet Against the Monstrous Regiment* [i.e., governance] *of Women*, 1558)—to prefigure doom. A further point against Margaret was that the young King Henry VI, infatuated by reports of her, abandoned another marriage plan, with the daughter of the Earl of Armagnac, which would have brought him a rich dowry, and arranged instead to bring Margaret of Anjou to England at his own expense, and "without dowry" (*2 Henry VI* 1.1.58). This concession, another topsy-turvy inversion of the usual order of things, not only prefigures King Henry's submissiveness to his queen's stronger will, but also, strikingly, anticipates a similar moment in *3 Henry VI*, when King Edward chooses the widow Elizabeth Gray as his wife and queen, abruptly sabotaging the diplomatic mission of Warwick to the King of France, in quest of a royal marriage with King Louis's sister-in-law Lady Bona (3.3). Thus the same destructive and uxurious action is performed by both the Lancastrian King Henry (in *1 Henry VI*) and the Plantagenet King Edward (in *3 Henry VI*). In both cases the effect is disastrous. To cap the irony, Margaret is actually present at the French king's court on the occasion of this volte-face, and she quickly turns from defeated petitioner to martial avenger (this is the moment when she announces herself finished with mourning and "ready to put armour on"). In act 5, when Margaret praises the boldness and defiance of her young son, the Prince of Wales, in comparison with his milder father, King Henry, Richard again taunts her with the exchange of roles (and apparel) between wife and husband, noting that if Henry had been stronger "you might still have worn the petticoat / And ne'er have stolen the breech from Lancaster" (5.5.23–24).

The most famous description of Queen Margaret in the play, however, is none of these references, but rather a line borrowed and tweaked by Shakespeare's envious fellow playwright Robert Greene to accuse Shakespeare of plagiarizing the work of his contemporaries. The passage has become celebrated because it is one of the earliest apparent references to Shakespeare as a dramatist. In *Greene's Groatsworth of Wit, Bought with a Million of Repentance*, published after his death in 1592, Greene complained of "an upstart Crow, beautified with our feathers, that with his *Tygers heart wrapt in a Players hyde, supposes he is as well able to bumbast out a blanke verse as the best of you: and being an absolute Johannes fac totum,* is in his owne conceit the onely Shake-scene in a countrie." "Tygers heart wrapt in a Players hyde" deliberately cites, and paraphrases, Richard of York's anguished protest to Queen Margaret about the cold-blooded murder of his young son, Rutland, and her cruel proffer of a handkerchief dipped in the son's blood to wipe the eyes of the grieving father:

> O tiger's heart wrapped in a woman's hide!
> How couldst thou drain the life-blood of the child
> To bid the father wipe his eyes withal,
> And yet be seen to bear a woman's face?
> Women are soft, mild, pitiful, and flexible—
> Thou stern, obdurate, flinty, rough, remorseless.
> Bidd'st thou me rage? Why, now thou hast thy wish.
> Wouldst have me weep? Why, now thou hast thy will.
>
> *1.4.138–145*

It is often said, fairly, that Shakespeare's line about the "tiger's heart" would have had to be well known in order for Greene's jest to be recognizable, and it may be that Greene and other University Wits would have found it bombastic. His use of this quotation, among all those he might have culled from the then-extant plays of Shakespeare, suggests that the play we know as *3 Henry VI* was not only familiar to audiences but particularly associated with the writer Greene dubs, dismissively, "Shake-scene."

But there is more to observe about the passage. In context this is a speech about a "manly" (or monstrous) woman—played, of course, by a boy player—and the way her cruel willingness to murder a child (think "Lady Macbeth") not only renders her unwomanly, but also makes the father (think "Macduff") weep with grief and rage. The person York calls a "false Frenchwoman" (1.4.150) is false in every sense. When York urges that she tell "the heavy story right" (161) to elicit tears from her hearers, and rounds his dying declaration out with "take the crown—and with the crown, my curse" (165), he anticipates the chain of curses and omens that will follow many characters through this play and the next, culminating in Margaret's own uncannily predictive curse in *Richard III*. When Richard of Gloucester is restrained from killing her by his brother King Edward in act 5, he protests, "Why should she live to fill the world with words?" (5.5.43), and that is exactly what the figure of old Queen Margaret will do in the play that bears her chief antagonist's name.

The monstrous Richard and the monstrous Margaret—he constantly compared to a dog, she to a tiger—thus frame the "human" action of *3 Henry VI*, the story of the contention between York and Lancaster, the white rose and the red. The play begins with the Yorkists onstage, with "white roses in their hats," and they are shortly joined by King Henry and his supporters, wearing "red roses in their hats." On the one side are Richard Plantagenet, Duke of York, and his sons Edward, Prince of Wales; George, Duke of Clarence; Richard; and Edmund, Earl of Rutland. Rutland is described and imagined as a "child" here for dramatic effect, although in historical fact he was seventeen years old when he was killed, and nine years older than Richard. On the other side are King Henry, Clifford, Northumberland, and others. Instead of a battle, however, for a moment there is an entente. Henry VI agrees to cede his throne to Richard of York after his death, making York and his sons his heirs—and disinheriting his own son, Edward, Prince of Wales. This does not please Queen Margaret, needless to say—but neither does it please the sons of York, who press their father to claim the throne as his immediate right. The glimmer of a peaceful solution gives way, once again, to mutual slaughter and intrigue. A key figure here is the Earl of Warwick, initially a partisan of York. Known as the "King-maker," the historical Warwick was the richest man in England outside the royal family, and he used his power, as this play shows, first to help depose Henry VI in favor of Edward IV (the eldest son of Richard of York), and then, when the imprudent marriage of "lascivious Edward" to Elizabeth Gray offended him, to briefly restore Henry VI to the throne. Warwick was not only one to change sides in this dispute. George, Duke of Clarence, equally irritated at Edward's marriage, allied himself with Warwick and with Henry by marrying Isabel, one of Warwick's daughters; Warwick's other daughter, Anne Neville, was married to Edward, Prince of Wales. It is Anne who, widowed when the young Prince Edward is killed by the Yorkists at the battle of Tewkesbury, becomes in *Richard III* the fearful wife of Richard of Gloucester.

We might linger for a moment on the theme of the deaths of children, since the "child" theme will recur, powerfully, in *Richard III*. The play's mythological imagery is full of hopeful, ingenious fathers and overreaching sons fated to die young: Daedalus and Icarus, Apollo and Phaëthon. The persistent and consistent Christian language is fully consonant, in a Renaissance reading, with the "moralized" readings of these classical myths as types or anticipations of Christ. In *3 Henry VI,* Richard of York loses Rutland, Margaret loses Edward, and both loudly lament their losses. The rather formal, if sometimes foultongued, Margaret surprises us with a nickname of endearment—"O Ned, sweet Ned—speak to thy mother, boy" (5.5.50)—and anticipates Macduff in claiming (inaccurately, in this case) that the York brothers "have no children" (62). Her words

> But if you ever chance to have a child,
> Look in his youth to have him so cut off. . . .
>
> 5.5.64–65

are a foretaste of her more elaborate curse early in *Richard III*. Prince Edward himself has something of the pertness and imprudent freedom of speech that will characterize the Princes in the Tower, who likewise tease Richard about his appearance, with equally fatal consequences. George rightly calls Edward "too malapert" (5.5.32), and a few lines later "young Edward" is stabbed to death in front of his mother. The name Ned will return only two scenes later as the pet name for King Edward's heir ("Come hither, Bess," Edward says to his queen, "and let me kiss my boy. / Young Ned, . . ." [5.7.15–16]). Both Margaret and Queen Elizabeth will have reason at the beginning of *Richard III* to lament the replication on both sides of the York-Lancaster "contention" of children, and husbands, with familiar names, and the eye-for-an-eye scenario of revenge and civil war will become an "Edward for [an] Edward" when this young Prince, too, is murdered in that play. At the end of *3 Henry VI* this is already glanced at with Richard of Gloucester's aside to the audience ("I'll blast his harvest. . . . / This shoulder was ordained so thick to heave" [5.7.21–23]) and the treasonous kiss he offers in response to Edward's invitation to his brothers to kiss the heir to the throne ("Clarence and Gloucester, love my lovely queen; / And kiss your princely nephew, brothers, both" [26–27]):

Richard   Witness the loving kiss I give the fruit.
           [*He kisses the infant prince*]

[*Aside*] To say the truth, so Judas kissed his master,
And cried "All hail!" whenas he meant all harm.

5.7.32–34

Meantime, waiting silently offstage, is the other heir, Henry, Earl of Richmond, whom Henry VI termed "England's hope," and about whom he had prophesied, with "divining thoughts": "This pretty lad will prove our country's bliss" (4.7.69–70). The upshot, as Shakespeare's original audience would obviously have known, would be a Henry for a Henry, as Henry VII, the "Richmond" of *Richard III* (and the grandfather of Elizabeth I), will fulfill the rest of this King Henry's prophecy:

> His looks are full of peaceful majesty,
> His head by nature framed to wear a crown,
> His hand to wield a sceptre; and himself
> Likely in time to bless a regal throne.

4.7.71–74

Henry VI Part 3 will conclude—as, we might say, it began—with this uneasy balance, one king (Edward) cosseting his namesake and heir, while the other (Henry) points prophetically toward a quite different future. King Henry VI, often called a "holy king" as well as a weak or unresolved one, is in fact quite given to the prophetic mode. His final prophecy is linked, in a way that makes perfect sense for the dynamics of this play, with yet another set of animadversions about the "monstrous" Richard:

King Henry   And thus I prophesy: that many a thousand
               Which now mistrust no parcel of my fear,
               And many an old man's sigh, and many a widow's,
               And many an orphan's water-standing eye—
               Men for their sons', wives for their husbands',
               Orphans for their parents' timeless death—
               Shall rue the hour that ever wast thou born.
               The owl shrieked at thy birth—an evil sign;
               The night-crow cried, aboding luckless time;
               Dogs howled, and hideous tempests shook down trees;
               The raven rooked her on the chimney's top;
               And chatt'ring pies in dismal discord sung.
               Thy mother felt more than a mother's pain,
               And yet brought forth less than a mother's hope—
               To wit, an indigested and deformèd lump,
               Not like the fruit of such a goodly tree.
               Teeth hadst thou in thy head when thou wast born,

> To signify thou cam'st to bite the world;
> And if the rest be true which I have heard
> Thou cam'st—

Richard   I'll hear no more. Die, prophet, in thy speech,
>   *He stabs him*
> For this, amongst the rest, was I ordained.

King Henry   Ay, and for much more slaughter after this.
> O, God forgive my sins, and pardon thee.   *He dies*
>   5.6.37–60

The stylistic contrast here is, deliberately and effectively, as strong as the contrast in character. Henry speaks in balanced periodic phrases reminiscent of the Senecan poetry so popular in the period (Seneca's plays had recently been translated and were read and performed in schools): "many an old man's sigh, and many a widow's, /And many an orphan's water-standing eye—"; "Thy mother felt more than a mother's pain, / And yet brought forth less than a mother's hope." (His excoriating phrase "indigested and deformèd lump" echoes Old Lord Clifford in *2 Henry VI,* "foul indigested lump, / As crooked in thy manners as thy shape" [5.1.155–156]; both are versions of the description of chaos in Ovid's *Metamorphoses,* book 1, lines 7–8.) Richard speaks in energetic bursts, and once he has slain Henry he faces the audience to describe himself as "I that have neither pity, love, nor fear," and to make his exciting and terrifying declaration of independent "Machiavellian" agency: "I am myself alone" (5.6.68, 84). It is not too much of an exaggeration to say that in this phrase a new mode of Shakespearean character is born.

Against the emergence of this "modern" type, both in drama and in persona, there remain, still, the powerful remnants of an older pattern of belief and of theater. As is often noted, King Henry's last words, "O, God forgive my sins, and pardon thee!" are a reminder of Christ's last words on the cross. Richard explicitly describes his "loving kiss" for the son and heir of his brother Edward as a Judas kiss. And one of the play's most powerful early scenes, the mocking and death of Richard's noble father, Richard, Duke of York, in act 1, scene 4, is likewise a clear echo of the mocking of Christ, as Margaret places a paper crown upon his head. We may recall that in the first half of the play's first scene, York and King Henry have come to an agreement to end the fighting: Henry will be King during his lifetime, but at his death York and his heirs will succeed to the crown. "Now York and Lancaster are reconciled," York exults, prematurely (1.1.205), but the second half of the scene produces the wrathful entrance of Queen Margaret with the Prince of Wales, the Queen furious at Henry's plan to disinherit his own son. Exeter's faint hope that he will be able to "reconcile them all" (274), a deliberate echo of York's previous line, is likewise doomed to failure, as in the very next scene the sons of York, led on by Richard, persuade their father that he was wrong to agree to wait until Henry's death to succeed him.

Richard's passionate plea, "How sweet a thing it is to wear a crown, / Within whose circuit is Elysium / And all that poets feign of bliss and joy" (1.2.29–31), is a recognizable citation of a famous phrase from Christopher Marlowe's very successful *Tamburlaine:* "That perfect bliss and sole felicity, / The sweet fruition of an earthly crown." The mock coronation of York on a molehill with a paper crown (a detail Shakespeare would have found in Edward Hall's chronicle, and which he recalls in *Richard III* 1.3) is thus at once the unlooked-for, unhappy "fulfillment" of his sons' wish for a quick coronation, and Margaret's carnivalizing and theatricalizing revenge on her rival: woman over man, paper crown rather than golden crown, a molehill rather than a mountain, the enactment of a scoffing version of the martyrdom of Christ, with the added fact that York suffers as father rather than as son, since his own child, Rutland, has been sacrificed. Holinshed's chronicle version of the scene explicitly notes the Christian parallel: "[T]hey kneeled down afore him (as the Iewes did vnto Christ) in scorne, saeing to him: 'Haile king without rule! haile king without heritage!' . . . And at length, hauing thus scorned him with these and diuerse other the like despitefull words, they stroke off his head, which (as yee haue heard), they presented to the queene."[1]

Shakespeare, as so often, is the admiring anti-Marlowe, as Richard is the admiring anti-Tamburlaine. The idealizing vision of royal rule as "sweet fruition" is never allowed to stand in Shakespeare's plays without a realistic political and moral corrective. And where Tamburlaine signaled his increasing displeasure and impatience by an emblematic display of colored tents as signs to his enemy, first white, then red, then black (clearly indicating his intentions of clemency, warfare, and finally death if they do not surrender), the sign system in *3 Henry VI* is both more subtle and more psychologically insidious. The bravado and festivity of the display of white and red roses with which the play begins, the *apparent* emblems of the Wars of the Roses and thus, more generally, the emblems of civil war, are succeeded in the play's most sublime and painful tableau by the desperate events of discovery witnessed by King Henry in act 2, scene 5: "Enter at one door a Soldier with a dead man [his father] in his arms" (stage direction, line 55), and then "Enter at another door another Soldier with a dead man [his son] in his arms" (stage direction, line 79).

Henry is taking refuge from the battle—from what he calls, finely, "the equal poise of this fell war" (2.5.13). Indeed, his wife, the martial Margaret, and his ruthless chief warrior, Lord Clifford, have asked him to stay out of the way, since, he reflects, "They prosper best of all when I am thence" (18). (Clifford is this play's version of a character like Tybalt or Hotspur, full of energy and drive, impelled by revenge or the sensibility of insult, heedless of political moderation.) Thus unmanned, King Henry wishes himself for a moment unkinged as well, as he takes a seat "on this molehill," thereby recalling to the audience the mocking and death of York at the hands of Margaret. (Shakespeare's contemporary George Peele would write in his play *The Battle of Alcazar* [1594], "King

of a mole-hill had I rather be, / Than the richest subject of a monarchy"
2.2.464–465].)[2] Henry's lengthy reverie on the simple life, beginning "O God!
Methinks it were a happy life / To be no better than a homely swain. / To sit
upon a hill, as I do now; / To carve out dials quaintly, point by point"
(*3 Henry VI* 2.5.21–24), anticipates the similar thoughts of another tempera-
mentally unfit monarch, Richard II, in Shakespeare's later play of that name
(King Henry VI: "So many hours must I tend my flock, / So many hours must
I take my rest, / So many hours must I contemplate, / So many hours must I
sport myself" [31–34]; King Richard II: "I'll give my jewels for a set of beads, /
My gorgeous palace for a hermitage, / My gay apparel for an almsman's gown, /
My figured goblets for a dish of wood, / My sceptre for a palmer's walking staff"
[*Richard II* 3.3.146–150]). But this utopian vision of the life of a shepherd, insu-
lated from the cares of the court if not from the depredations of the weather, is
rudely interrupted by the appalling discovery scenes to which Henry is a silent
and suffering onstage witness. Both the "Soldier who has killed his father" and
the "Soldier who has killed his son" think they have gained spoils of war ("some
store of crowns" and "gold") by vanquishing a foe; importantly, their motives
are local and economic rather than gloriously patriotic. Indeed, as the son
laments, he was impressed into the army by the King, and his father, who served
the Earl of Warwick, was "pressed by his master" to fight on the side of York.
Neither the first soldier nor the second is fighting out of personal conviction or
loyalty. Their exclamations of despair are, again, manifestly and explicitly biblical: "Pardon me, God, I knew not what I did," says the son who has killed his
father, "And pardon, father, for I knew not thee" (*3 Henry VI* 2.5.69–70), while
the anguished father who has killed his son undergoes a similarly agonizing
reversal of expectations: "But let me see: is this our foeman's face? / Ah, no, no,
no—it is mine only son!" (2.5.82–83). The entire scene is a play-within-the-play,
of a kind at which Shakespeare the dramatist excels. The appalled King, an
onstage spectator, comments to himself and to the audience, noting of the dead
son that "[t]he red rose and the white are on his face, / The fatal colours of our
striving houses" (97–98). He sees very clearly in this moment that the civil war
is internal and emotional as well as external and political: "I'll aid thee tear for
tear; / And let our hearts and eyes, like civil war, / Be blind with tears, and
break, o'ercharged with grief" (76–78).

This role of the anguished spectator, unable to intervene or to look away,
feeling—as indeed King Henry should—responsible for the tragedy unfolding on the stage, is one that the playwright will make use of many times in
his subsequent career, creating figures like Edgar in *King Lear* who mediate
between the dramatic characters in the play and the audience in the theater. For
the King to be in this position of impotent spectatorship is a sign, however, of
his limitations as a monarch, as well as of his theatrical and literary debt to
an older, more emblematic and allegorical mode of drama. Even if young
Richmond is "England's hope" in a historical sense, the theater's future clearly

belongs to Richard of Gloucester. His astonishing soliloquies, his refusal of self-pity even as he mimes it for an audience, his energy, and his pleasure in plotting all bode well for audiences, whatever they do for the "England" depicted in the plays. This remarkably well-shaped early play is balanced on his misshapen shoulder, which he will use, as he says in the last scene, to "execute" his plans in both senses, accomplishing them when necessary by murder. The new King, Edward IV, has the last word in *3 Henry VI,* as is customary for surviving or inheriting kings in many of the history plays. Edward, who does not suspect his brother Richard's intentions, is full of hope: in his wife, Elizabeth; in his son, Ned; in the fact that Queen Margaret is being ransomed away to France by her father and seems to be leaving England, and the stage, for the last time. But Edward's final words, offered in the traditional rhyming couplet that clears the stage, contain all that an alert audience needs to anticipate a further reversal:

> Sound drums and trumpets—farewell, sour annoy!
> For here, I hope, begins our lasting joy.
>
> 5.7.45–46

To rhyme "joy" and "annoy" is a small stroke of genius; to insert the vain "I hope" as a qualification of the last line takes away all that the proud assertion seems to claim. Almost any production will balance attention in this scene between "lascivious" King Edward and the determined, political Richard of Gloucester, whose opening soliloquy in *Richard III* takes off so brilliantly from the point where this play will end.

Richard III

DRAMATIS PERSONAE

King Edward IV
Duchess of York, *his mother*
Prince Edward, *the King's son*
Richard, *the young Duke of York,
    the King's son*
George, Duke of Clarence,
    the King's brother
Richard, Duke of Gloucester, *later
    King Richard, the King's brother*
Clarence's Son
Clarence's Daughter
Queen Elizabeth, *King
    Edward's wife*
Anthony Woodeville, Earl Rivers,
    her brother
Marquis of Dorset, *her son*
Lord Gray, *her son*
Sir Thomas Vaughan
Ghost of King Henry VI
Queen Margaret, *his widow*
Ghost of Prince Edward, *his son*
Lady Anne, *Prince Edward's widow*
William, Lord Hastings,
    Lord Chamberlain
Lord Stanley, *Earl of Derby, his friend*
Henry, Earl of Richmond,
    *later King Henry VII, Stanley's
    son-in-law*
Earl of Oxford, *Richmond's follower*
Sir James Blunt, *Richmond's follower*
Sir Walter Herbert, *Richmond's
    follower*

Duke of Buckingham, *Richard
    Gloucester's follower*
Duke of Norfolk, *Richard
    Gloucester's follower*
Sir Richard Ratcliffe, *Richard
    Gloucester's follower*
Sir William Catesby, *Richard
    Gloucester's follower*
Sir James Tyrrell, *Richard
    Gloucester's follower*
Francis, Viscount Lovell
Two Murderers, *Richard
    Gloucester's followers*
A Page, *Richard Gloucester's
    follower*
Cardinal
Bishop of Ely
John, *a priest*
Sir Christopher, *a priest*
Sir Robert Brackenbury,
    *Lieutenant of the Tower
    of London*
Lord Mayor of London
A Scrivener
Hastings, *a pursuivant*
Sheriff
Aldermen and Citizens
Attendants, two bishops,
    messengers, soldiers

HE CULTURAL POWER of Shakespeare is well illustrated in the case of *Richard III*, a play that established its central character as a compelling social and dramatic type, and an unforgettable physical figure. Shakespeare's Richard is the creation of a powerful political as well as dramatic imagination. The historical Richard of Gloucester was not a hunchback, he did not have a withered arm, he was not in all probability born with a full set of teeth, and he was almost certainly not carried for two years in his mother's womb. At least, there is no contemporary evidence to support these allegations. They are all developments of Tudor political culture. But they come down to us in the main not through chronicle history but through theater, and they far surpass the historical "truth" in vividness and persistence.

Shakespeare lived and wrote during the reign of Queen Elizabeth, the granddaughter of Henry Tudor, the Richmond of *Richard III*, who would become Henry VII. A dramatic work about the rightful succession of the Tudors, and the end of the reign of the Plantagenets, necessarily benefited from any account of the last Plantagenet king as a monster unworthy to rule. Thus the usurpation of Henry Tudor became, retrospectively, not only an honorable but also a "legitimate" act, rescuing England from the grasp of an allegedly deformed and scheming tyrant. The historical accounts of Richard's deformity and monstrosity thus date not from his own historical time but from that of Henry VII. The raw material for Shakespeare's Richard can be found in works like Polydore Vergil's *Anglica Historia*, an "official history of England" commissioned by Henry VII, and published in 1555, or Sir Thomas More's *History of Richard III*, posthumously published in 1543, eight years after More was beheaded. More had refused to acquiesce in another interested rewriting of history, the Act of Succession that declared Henry VIII's daughter Mary, by Catherine of Aragon, a bastard and vested the succession of the English crown in Elizabeth, Henry's daughter by Anne Boleyn. More called Richard "little of stature, ill-featured of limb, crook-backed . . . hard-favored of visage," and therefore—as if character followed from physical form—both deceptive and cruel. Portrait evidence from Richard's own period does not bear this out, and many historical chronicles attest to his admirable qualities as a soldier and leader—all elements discernible in the Richard of Shakespeare's *Henry VI Part 2* and *Part 3*. But the chronicles also attest to Richard's ambition and ruthlessness. Tudor accounts of his villainy are not so much made up out of whole cloth as they are embroidered.

Nonetheless, Richard's charm, and especially the charm of Shakespeare's Richard, has been such that whole societies have sprung up to defend him. The Richard III Society was founded in England in 1924, and its American counterpart, Friends of Richard III, Incorporated, included actresses Helen Hayes and Tallulah Bankhead and surrealist painter Salvador Dalí as charter members. Mystery writer Josephine Tey published a novel called *The Daughter of Time*, in which a detective, temporarily hospitalized and bedridden, reopens Richard's case with the help of an eager-beaver researcher, and discovers that the well-known story was largely the product of Henry VII's Tudor propaganda. (The novel's title comes from the proverb "Truth is the daughter of time" [*Temporis filia veritas*], familiar in the sixteenth and seventeenth centuries, and used by Johannes Kepler and Desiderius Erasmus, as well as by Sir Francis Bacon in his *Advancement of Learning*. The novel's publication date, 1951, suggests that Tey may have been thinking of more recent propaganda campaigns, from the Cold War, as well as of the distant Wars of the Roses.)

Shakespeare's Richard III is arguably the first fully realized and psychologically conceived character in his plays. Like the god Proteus, who could change his shape at will, like the chameleon that changes its colors to conceal itself from view—both common images of human shape-shifting in the works of writers like the Italian humanist Pico della Mirandola—Richard is a consummate actor, able, as he exults in *Henry VI Part 3*, to "add colours to the chameleon, / Change shapes with Proteus for advantages, / And set the murderous Machiavel to school" (*3 Henry VI* 3.2.191–193). Like the stage "Machiavel" of Elizabethan drama, patterned after an early modern interpretation of Niccolò Machiavelli's *The Prince*, Richard will often speak to the audience in soliloquy, confiding in us his real plans and thoughts while he pretends to those on the stage that he is loyal, compliant, and benign. The device of the soliloquy is made for such intrinsic doubleness, and functions in Shakespeare either—as here—to allow villains to manifest their hypocrisy or—as in *Hamlet*—to produce the effect of voiced thought, as if the audience were inside the mind of the protagonist. For Richard, both of these effects are often in play. In fact, as we will see, throughout the play Richard speaks in *two* voices, two personae, public and private. It is not until the play's last moments, when he loses his audience and confides his fears and hopes only to himself, that Richard's two voices collapse into one on the field at Bosworth. In order to appreciate the full power of that inward collapse, we should consider first the consummate power of rhetoric and stagecraft that is his as the play begins.

Many Shakespeare plays, as we have already noticed and as we will continue to see, begin with a small scene of secondary characters who set the themes and the tone for the greater events to follow. In *Richard III* the stage belongs, from the first, to Richard, whose great opening soliloquy likewise contains the seeds of all the plot developments to follow. Although the speech is long and familiar, it is useful to look at it in detail, as much for its rhetorical sweep and driving rhythms as for the themes—sun and shadow, war and love, men and women, virtue and villainy, proportion and deformity—that will recur in the scenes that follow:

> Now is the winter of our discontent
> Made glorious summer by this son of York;
> And all the clouds that loured upon our house
> In the deep bosom of the ocean buried.

Now are our brows bound with victorious wreaths,
Our bruisèd arms hung up for monuments,
Our stern alarums changed to merry meetings,
Our dreadful marches to delightful measures.
Grim-visaged war hath smoothed his wrinkled front,
And now—instead of mounting barbèd steeds
To fright the souls of fearful adversaries—
He capers nimbly in a lady's chamber
To the lascivious pleasing of a lute.
But I, that am not shaped for sportive tricks
Nor made to court an amorous looking-glass,
I that am rudely stamped and want love's majesty
To strut before a wanton ambling nymph,
I that am curtailed of this fair proportion,
Cheated of feature by dissembling nature,
Deformed, unfinished, sent before my time
Into this breathing world scarce half made up—
And that so lamely and unfashionable
That dogs bark at me as I halt by them—
Why, I in this weak piping time of peace
Have no delight to pass away the time,
Unless to spy my shadow in the sun
And descant on mine own deformity.
And therefore since I cannot prove a lover
To entertain these fair well-spoken days,
I am determinèd to prove a villain
And hate the idle pleasures of these days.
. . . .
Dive, thoughts, down to my soul: here Clarence comes.
                              Richard III *1.1.1–31, 41*

Notice that the speech begins with a characteristically duplicitous enjambment. Its syntax seems, blamelessly, to say that "the [former] winter of our discontent," when the Plantagenets were defeated and eclipsed by the Lancastrians and by Henry VI, is "now . . . made glorious summer" by the rise of Edward IV, the "son" and "sun" of York. But the blank verse line—"Now is the winter of our discontent"—plays against the syntax to make it clear that "now," still, at the present time in which he is speaking to us, Richard dwells in wintry discontent, even though, or perhaps because, his brother Edward is on the throne. The rhythms of this long speech—forty lines but only five sentences—are insistent, and solipsistic. Richard is the supreme egotist, and his world is all within himself. He speaks rhetoric, rather than simple truth, even to himself. The tripartite division of this speech, with sections beginning "Now" (line 1), "But" (line 14), and "And therefore" (line 28), takes the form of logical argument, although there is nothing logi-cal about it. And this pseudological structure is reinforced by strategically placed cue words of an escalating power: "Now," "Now," "And now," at the beginnings of lines; "But I," "I," "I," and "Why, I," culminating in a "therefore" and in a "proof": "And therefore since I cannot prove . . . I am determinèd to prove. . . ."

We have heard Richard say that he has become a villain, a Machiavel, because he is not made for love: "I, that am not shaped for sportive tricks / Nor made to court an amorous looking-glass, / I that am rudely stamped and want love's majesty / To strut before a wanton ambling nymph." And yet in the very next scene we see him "prove a lover"—the thing he says he cannot do—under the most difficult circumstances possible. He proposes marriage to the widow of a man he has had murdered. He does so in the presence of the corpse of her father-in-law. And his proposal is accepted. The Lady Anne, widow of the slain Edward, Prince of Wales, agrees to marry Richard. The coffin of her father-in-law, the "key-cold figure of a holy king," Henry VI, is onstage throughout the wooing scene. (In some modern productions the "lovers" have perched famil-iarly upon it as if it were a park bench.) The moment Anne leaves the stage Richard exults, again, to himself and to us: "Was ever woman in this humour wooed? / Was ever woman in this humour won? / I'll have her, but I will not keep her long" (1.2.215–217). Later, in act 4, we will see him try to perform this feat again, attempting to convince Edward's widow, Queen Elizabeth, whose two sons he has had put to death in the Tower of London, that he should marry her daughter. In the second case he thinks he has succeeded—"Relenting fool, and shallow, changing woman," he sneers as she leaves him—but in fact he has not, and the contrast between these twinned scenes is a telling index of his decline and fall. Elizabeth's daughter, also named Elizabeth, will instead marry Henry Tudor, the Earl of Richmond, ending the Wars of the Roses and begin-ning the Tudor dynasty. The use of twinned scenes with different outcomes is a favorite structural device for Shakespeare throughout his career. In *Romeo and Juliet* it marks the difference between the "comic" and "tragic" parts of the play, as the Nurse twice haltingly delivers messages to Juliet. In *Richard III* the two scenes of "impossible" wooing show the devolution of Richard's character and self-awareness, as he wins the Lady Anne and then, using the same tactics, fails to win the Lady Elizabeth.

At the time of the wooing of Anne, though, Richard is still in top form—for him—and when he succeeds in this apparently impossible task he gleefully revisits the language of his opening soliloquy:

> My dukedom to a beggarly *denier*,
> I do mistake my person all this while.
> Upon my life she finds, although I cannot,
> Myself to be a marv'lous proper man.
> I'll be at charges for a looking-glass

> And entertain a score or two of tailors
> To study fashions to adorn my body.
> Since I am crept in favor with myself,
> I will maintain it with some little cost.
> But first I'll turn yon fellow [the corpse of Henry VI] in his grave,
> And then return lamenting to my love.
> Shine out, fair sun, till I have bought a glass,
> That I may see my shadow as I pass.
>
> *1.2.238–250*

We have seen and heard both of these images before, the shadow and the looking glass. "I . . . am not . . . made to court an amorous looking-glass," Richard said in his opening soliloquy, and now, "I'll be at charges for a looking-glass"— I will commission a mirror, he jokes, so I can admire my "proper," or handsome, body. In fact he is as improper, as inappropriate, as a lover can be, and not because of his body. Later in the play his mother, the Duchess of York, will call him "one false glass," a distorting and distorted mirror. In the Renaissance the mirror was an emblem of instruction and order. Books of conduct and statecraft bore titles like *A Mirror for Magistrates* (1559), *Mirror of Fools* (*Speculum Stultorum*, ca. 1180), and *Mirror of the World* (1481). A "mirror" was an example. Thus Shakespeare's Henry V will be called the "mirror of all Christian kings" (*Henry V* 2.0.6); Hamlet is described by Ophelia as "[t]he glass of fashion and the mould of form" (*Hamlet* 3.1.152); and Hotspur, in *Henry IV Part 2,* is described by his mourning wife, after his death, as "the glass / Wherein the noble youth did dress themselves" (2.3.21–22). According to the Duchess of York in this play, however, although Richard's two dead brothers were true mirrors of the princely semblance of their father, Richard, Duke of York, the namesake son Richard is a crooked reflection, one who distorts everything he has inherited, and everything he perceives and receives. The mirror is part of his protean capacity for change, and it is also part of his actor's persona, for it is an aspect of Richard's genius that he reflects back upon society the corruption and hypocrisy he finds there. Once again, in the final scenes at Bosworth Field, he will turn the mirror inward, upon himself.

But if Richard is a mirror, he is also, he says, a shadow—"Shine out, fair sun, till I have bought a glass, / That I may see my shadow as I pass." This, too, echoes the opening soliloquy, where Richard remarked that "in this weak piping time of peace" he had "no delight to pass away the time, / Unless to spy [his] shadow in the sun." The sun, as we have already noted, is the emblem of the King of England, so Richard's "shadow in the sun" is his desire to eclipse or overshadow his brother Edward, to chill and darken "this son of York." (Remember, too, that these plays were performed in mid-afternoon, in outdoor theaters, so that the pattern of sun, shadow, and reflection is entirely produced by language, and not—as in Laurence Olivier's film of *Richard III*—by the looming, larger-than-life shadow of Richard, glimpsed in conversation with Edward and with Anne, and again at the spy-hole of Clarence's prison cell.)

So powerful is the cultural reputation of "Richard Crookback" that Sigmund Freud, who often wrote case studies configured around Shakespearean types, published a short piece called "The Exceptions," about patients whose "neuroses were connected with some experience or suffering to which they had been subjected in their earliest childhood, in respect to which they knew themselves to be guiltless, and which they could look upon as an unjust disadvantage imposed upon them." His chief example is Richard III, "a figure created by the greatest of poets—a figure in whose character the claim to be an exception is closely bound up with and is motivated by the circumstance of congenital disadvantage." Just as Freud elsewhere argues that we are all little Oedipuses, so here he claims that in some psychological sense we are all little Richards: "Richard is an enormous magnification of something we find in ourselves as well. We all think we have reason to reproach Nature and our destiny for congenital and infantile disadvantages; we all demand reparation for early wounds to our narcissism, our self love."[1]

But however resonant these character types may be in human life or were, at least, among Freud's patients, it is a mistake, I believe, to attribute the malevolence of Shakespeare's Richard to "congenital and infantile disadvantages." That is *his* claim, to be sure, but the claim functions more as an excuse and as a metaphor than as a convincing interior motivation. As his early speeches make clear, Richard enjoys plotting ("Plots have I laid, inductions dangerous") and fomenting disorder. He is a Machiavel because it amuses him, and because he likes it. He cries "exception" when it suits him, but in fact he is quite pleased with himself. His ancestry here is multiple, for while in history he is descended from Richard of York, in theatrical terms he derives from the Machiavel and the Vice, both of which are types (though perhaps archetypes rather than character types) to which Richard explicitly compares himself in this play. When he quips behind the back of the preciously prattling and doomed Edward, Prince of Wales, he remarks aside to the audience, "Thus like the formal Vice, Iniquity, / I moralize two meanings in one word" (3.1.82–83). The Vice figure of the medieval morality plays—which were still being performed in the north of England in Shakespeare's time—was a comic character, a mischief-making reveler often regarded as the servant of the Devil. He carried a broad flat dagger of lath that made a loud slapping sound, and he was generally a figure of ribald improvisation as well as an inciter to rebellion, disobedience, and sin. We could say very generally that the Machiavel was to the incipient genre of revenge tragedy what the Vice was to the older and increasingly comic morality plays. As we have already seen, Richard shares with the Vice not only his sheer delight in evil and disorder but his comic personality. Certainly up to the moment when he becomes king he is consistently witty, ironic, droll, and self-mocking, as in the passage where he purports suddenly to discover that he is handsome after all—a "marv'lous proper man." As his success with Anne demonstrates, there is also something compellingly seductive and erotic about Richard, and this seductiveness is used with even more power, and more lasting success, upon the audience. Through his soliloquies and through his energy in plotting, Richard seduces the theater audience to such an extent that the stage seems dull, flat, and unprofitable whenever, in the course of this very long play, he is not present. Our post-Romantic sensibility may wish to see pathos in these oppositional figures, but in fact for Shakespeare's Richard self-pity is only a tool, a guise, and a ploy.

Just as Richard names himself "Machiavel" and "Vice," letting the bare bones of theatricality show through his character, so other people in the play also perceive—or reveal—his relation to drama, to magic, and to witchcraft. When he interrupts the funeral procession of Henry VI in the first act, the Lady Anne repeatedly calls him a "devil" and a "fiend." Queen Margaret says he is a "hellhound" and a "poisonous bunch-backed toad" (the toad was from ancient times considered one of the "familiars" of witches). And his own mother, the Duchess of York, will use the same expression: "Thou toad, thou toad, where is thy brother Clarence? / And little Ned Plantagenet his son?" (4.4.145–146). Richard as fiend, as devil, as toad, as Vice, and as Machiavel—these figures from the morality and revenge traditions establish the play's powerful links to earlier drama, at the same time that *Richard III* seems wholly about psychologically persuasive characters, not stereotypes or allegorizations.

Richard's voice in the soliloquies, then, Richard's first voice, is the voice of the Devil, the voice of the Vice. But his second voice, the voice in which he presents himself to the world, is, as we should perhaps expect, the voice of absolute virtue, the voice of Christianity, and the voice of the innocent child. A voice that claims "plainness" as its virtue, rejecting flattery, artifice, and deception. Thus act 1, scene 3, finds Richard strolling with his friend Hastings into the midst of the Queen's relatives, Rivers, Dorset, and Gray, Richard's greatest enemies at court. Richard complains to Hastings that everyone misjudges him, taking his straightforwardness amiss, while they themselves are captive to French manners and preciosity:

> Because I cannot flatter and look fair,
> Smile in men's faces, smooth, deceive, and cog,
> Duck with French nods and apish courtesy,
> I must be held a rancorous enemy.
> Cannot a plain man live and think no harm,
> But thus his simple truth must be abused
> With silken, sly, insinuating jacks?

> *1.3.47–53*

A "plain man." "Simple truth." Richard portrays himself as an innocent in a world of schemers and deceivers—although, in the verbal equivalent of the

Devil revealing his cloven hoof, he cannot quite keep the hissing serpent out of the final line—"silken, sly, insinuating jacks." He is a master of the rhetoric of inadequacy. In the opening soliloquy he averred, "I cannot prove a lover"—and promptly did. Here he says he "cannot flatter and look fair"—yet flattery and compliment come to him as second nature, when he wants them to. Richard's disguise, the role he chooses to play here, is that of a man incapable of disguise, incapable of playing a role.

"I am too childish-foolish for this world," he declares ruefully in the same scene. "I would to God my heart were flint like Edward's, / Or Edward's soft and pitiful like mine. / I am too childish-foolish for this world" (1.3.140–142). Just as the Devil comes clothed in the shape of an angel, so the protean Richard comes cloaked in plainness and innocence—and fools them all. Piously he expresses the hope that God will pardon those who killed his brother Clarence—that is, he himself and the two murderers he sent to do the deed. Rivers congratulates him on his Christian forbearance: "A virtuous and a Christian-like conclusion, / To pray for them that have done scathe to us," and Richard replies half to Rivers and half, aside, to us: "So do I ever—[*speaks to himself*] being well advised: / For had I cursed now, I had cursed myself" (1.3.314–317). Alone upon the stage, he addresses the audience and himself once more in soliloquy, describing his methods, and making us his co-conspirators in crime:

> The secret mischiefs that I set abroach
> I lay unto the grievous charge of others.
>
> . . . .
>
> But then I sigh, and with a piece of scripture
> Tell them that God bids us do good for evil;
> And thus I clothe my naked villainy
> With odd old ends, stol'n forth of Holy Writ,
> And seem a saint when most I play the devil.
>
> *1.3.323–324, 332–336*

He will use the same language to his brother King Edward, when Edward invites him, at the beginning of act 2, to be reconciled to the Queen and her relatives—a language of childhood and innocence, with a characteristic hidden doubleness of meaning:

> I do not know that Englishman alive
> With whom my soul is any jot at odds
> More than the infant that is born tonight.
> I thank my God for my humility.
>
> *2.1.70–74*

A characteristically "humble" remark, this observation rings true because the speaker finds himself as much at odds with "the infant that is born tonight" as with the King, the Queen, the Princes, Clarence, Rivers—in short, anyone and everyone who stands in his way. And yet again, in the council chamber scene in act 3, we hear this same opinion that Richard has foisted upon his friends and associates, the idea that Richard is transparent, innocent, Christian, and pure— a clear window, not a false glass. Hastings, once Richard's greatest friend—until he decides not to support Richard's claim to the throne—is secretly marked by him for the execution block. Richard cannot hide his pleasure at the thought, and smiles upon Hastings when he encounters him, prompting this ill-conceived observation:

> I think there's never a man in Christendom
> Can lesser hide his love or hate than he,
> For by his face straight shall you know his heart.
>
> 3.4.51–53

Like so much in this play, Hastings's error in judgment here is the same one against which King Duncan will later warn in *Macbeth,* ruing his own failure to detect the treachery of the Thane of Cawdor: "There's no art / To find the mind's construction in the face. / He was a gentleman on whom I built / An absolute trust" (1.4.11–14). The naive and gullible Hastings is likewise ripe for betrayal. Moments later Richard will theatrically reenter the chamber to accuse his former friend, now the lover of the King's former mistress, Jane Shore, of conspiring for his death "with devilish plots / Of damnèd witchcraft."

Richard's pretense of Christian forgiveness and charity, which appears to balance Queen Margaret's insistent cry for revenge, is, as we have seen, again and again linked to the idea of innocent childhood. When Buckingham urges him to go after the young Princes and separate them from the Queen's relations, Richard replies, "I, as a child, / Will go by thy direction." His is a malign parody of the biblical injunction "and a little child shall lead them" (Isaiah 11:6), as well as of the instruction of Jesus: "Suffer the little children to come unto me, and forbid them not: for of such is the kingdom of God." But Richard is not Christ but Antichrist. Cloaking himself in the language of infancy and childhood, he perpetrates a massacre of the innocents by calling for the murder of the Princes in the Tower. Like King Herod, who (according to the Gospel of Matthew) ordered the slaying of all the young male children in Bethlehem two years old and younger because it had been prophesied that one of them would become King of the Jews, Richard is removing rivals from his path. This is a comparison that might well have seemed natural to Shakespeare's original audience; King Herod was a favorite character from the old mystery plays, and Shakespeare also mentions a theatrical Herod in *Hamlet.*

But in selecting the image of the child as his rhetorical disguise, Richard also invites another comparison—with the child king Henry VI, crowned at nine months of age, under whose reign England was split by civil war. "Woe to that land that's governed by a child," says one citizen to another (2.3.11), and this choric observation is true whether the "child" is one of the young princes, or Henry, or Richard—the literal or the figurative child. The play stages the comparison and contrast between Richard and Henry at the very beginning of the play, in act 1, scene 2, when the funeral cortege of the "key-cold . . . holy king" is halted, and the unholy, vividly alive and electrically exciting Richard woos and wins a reluctant but fascinated Lady Anne. The encounter is marked by a kind of prodigy, or portent, one of many in this play: the wounds of the dead king open and begin to bleed, as if he is slain again, or as if in silent-speaking protest against the audacity of Richard. (The trope of wounds as speaking mouths was common in the poetry of the period; in a later play Shakespeare will have Antony, in his somewhat histrionic funeral oration, point to "sweet Caesar's wounds, poor poor dumb mouths, / And bid them speak for me" [*Julius Caesar* 3.2.216–217]). Nor is the living king, Edward IV, any more effective or vital. Given over to lust and to his adulterous passion for Mistress Shore, King Edward is both sick and corrupt, and so is his land.

Whether Richard speaks to the audience or to the onstage court and populace, his two voices, ironic and "plain," Machiavellian and childlike, are only part of his actor's repertoire. For it is overwhelmingly clear that Richard *is* an actor:

> Plots have I laid, inductions dangerous,
> By drunken prophecies, libels and dreams
> To set my brother Clarence and the King
> In deadly hate the one against the other.
>
> *1.1.32–35*

He rejoices in his opening soliloquy, and his words "plot" and "induction" have double meanings, theatrical meanings. They are schemes and beginnings, but they are also fictions and dramas. An induction is an acted prologue to a play, an old-fashioned practice by Shakespeare's time, although he includes one in *The Taming of the Shrew. Richard III* is full of the language of plays and playing. Not only do the names of stock characters like the Vice call attention to the play as play, but so also does the recurrence of words like "scene," and "pageant," and "play." Buckingham says he "can counterfeit the deep tragedian" and "play the orator"; Margaret calls Elizabeth a "painted queen," the "flattering index of a direful pageant," and a "queen in jest, only to fill the scene" (3.5.5, 93; 4.4.83, 85, 91). The death of the princes is a "dire induction." We hear repeatedly about "tragedy": Hastings thinks he will live to look on the tragedy of the Queen's relations, and then, ironically, goes to his own tragedy; Queen Elizabeth speaks of a scene of tragic violence; old Queen Margaret hopes events will prove "bitter, black and tragical" for her enemies. This is not merely decorative language, nor only the emerging self-consciousness of a new literary form. *Richard III* calls attention to itself as a play because it raises questions of sincerity, authenticity, dangerous rhetoric, and impersonation that were of deep concern both in the court and in the playhouse. Richard acts, and Richard stages plays. His dramatic instinct, like his instinct for dramatic irony, seems unerring.

And then he loses his audience, and loses control of both kinds of "plots," political and dramaturgical.

That kings should try to stage events and render politics visible as theater is demonstrated by a kind of "control" to Richard's own playmaking, when Edward IV tries ineffectually to reconcile the warring factions within his own court. "Hastings and Rivers," he says, "take each other's hand. / Dissemble not your hatred; swear your love." Rivers, thus scripted, supplies the requisite line, however grudgingly: "And with my hand I seal my true heart's love," to which Hastings replies, as he must, "So thrive I, as I truly swear the like." The King now turns to the Queen, a key participant in this factionalism:

> Madam, yourself is not exempt from this,
> Nor your son Dorset;—Buckingham, nor you.
> You have been factious one against the other.
> Wife, love Lord Hastings, let him kiss your hand—
> And what you do, do it unfeignedly.
>
> *2.1.18–22*

This last instruction is, of course, the unlikeliest to take effect, since this entire tableau is both staged and feigned. "Dorset, embrace him; Hastings, love Lord Marquis." The stage is full of enemies shaking hands, enemies in embraces, enemies kissing one another's hands, a ludicrous scene of multiple Judas kisses, over which the sick King attempts to preside. And into the midst of this farrago comes Richard of Gloucester with the news of Clarence's death to break up this comedy of pretenses and to reveal the hollowness behind these feigned reconciliations. "Who knows not that the gentle Duke is dead?" The stage direction instructs that "They all start," frozen in surprise and consternation. "Who knows not he is dead?" asks Rivers, faintly. "Who knows he is?" But Clarence is dead, needless to say, by Richard's own order, as a result of Richard's own, far more successful play.

From the first, though, Richard has been staging plays. The wooing of Anne is such a play, full of wit and gesture, as Richard offers her a dagger and bears his breast for her to stab him, confessing to the murders of her husband and her father-in-law King Henry, and adding: "But 'twas thy heavenly face that set me on." While there are many pragmatic reasons why Anne would consent to this unwanted marriage—a woman alone at court needs a protector—there is a sense in which she wants to believe in his passion, wants to think of herself as the salvation of a "bad" man who will be converted by the love of a good woman. And he is undeniably exciting—as would later be said of Lord Byron, Richard is "mad, bad, and dangerous to know." Still, the effect of the little play having succeeded, Richard coldly surveys the result and offers his own theatrical review: "Was ever woman in this humour wooed? / Was ever woman in this humour won?"

In the council chamber scene in act 3, Richard manipulates exits and entrances to stage an accusation against his former friend Hastings. First he departs, and then, reentering on cue, brandishes his withered arm and twisted body as a kind of dumb show, supposed evidence of witchcraft practiced upon him:

> See how I am bewitched. Behold, mine arm
> Is like a blasted sapling withered up.
> And this is Edward's wife, that monstrous witch,
> Consorted with that harlot, strumpet Shore,
> That by their witchcraft they have markèd me.
>
> *3.4.68–72*

"If they have done this deed, my noble lord—," Hastings begins, and Richard deliberately mistakes his conditional "if" for skepticism and disbelief: " 'If'? Thou protector of this damnèd strumpet, / Talk'st thou to me of 'ifs'? Thou art a traitor. — / Off with his head" (73–76). As the new lover and "protector" of Jane Shore, Hastings is allegedly her co-conspirator. We may notice the degree to which women are blamed by Richard, at least in public, for his situation. The present queen and the former one, as well as Mistress Shore, are labeled witches, and when he is not accusatory he is dismissive ("Relenting fool, and shallow, changing woman"). Women in his world are conveniences and obstacles, mothers and strumpets. Despite his success in wooing Anne, the contempt he shows for courtship and love in the opening soliloquy ("To strut before a wanton ambling nymph") resurfaces periodically, not as defensive overcompensation but rather as genuine disregard.

In many ways the most striking of Richard's staged plays and contrived scenarios is his attempt to gain the assent of the people of London. At the beginning of act 3, scene 5, he rehearses Buckingham for the all-important role of orator: "Come, cousin, canst thou quake and change thy colour?"—can you be as good a chameleon as I am? "Tut," says Buckingham, "I can counterfeit the deep tragedian, . . . ghastly looks / Are at my service, like enforcèd smiles" (3.5.1, 5–9). Yet despite his avowed theatricality, Buckingham's performance fails. He has stocked his audience with shills, a hired claque of cheering men, but still the response is disappointing. The scene is a characteristic Shakespearean "unscene"; it takes place offstage and is reported to an eager and impatient Richard:

Buckingham	And when my oratory drew toward end,
	I bid them that did love their country's good
	Cry "God save Richard, England's royal king!"
Richard Gloucester	And did they so?

Buckingham	No, so God help me. They spake not a word,
	But, like dumb statues or breathing stones,
	Stared each on other and looked deadly pale—
	Which, when I saw, I reprehended them,
	And asked the Mayor, what meant this wilful
	silence?
	His answer was, the people were not used
	To be spoke to but by the Recorder.
	Then he was urged to tell my tale again:
	"Thus saith the Duke . . . thus hath the Duke
	inferred"—
	But nothing spoke in warrant from himself.
	When he had done, some followers of mine own,
	At lower end of the Hall, hurled up their caps,
	And some ten voices cried "God save King
	Richard!"
	And thus I took the vantage of those few:
	"Thanks, gentle citizens and friends," quoth I;
	"This general applause and cheerful shout
	Argues your wisdoms and your love to Richard"—
	And even here brake off and came away.

3.7.20–41

Buckingham's vivid description incorporates patterns of speech and silence, indirect and direct discourse, "dumb statues" and the speaking Recorder (a person with legal knowledge appointed by the mayor and alderman to "record" the customs of the city, and to offer an oral statement of these as evidence of fact). But it is also a discomfiting account of a broken play, a theatrical stratagem gone awry, as the "some ten voices" of the hired shills, hurling their caps in the air, are transformed by the desperate stage manager Buckingham into "general applause and cheerful shout." This attempt to manipulate the people, second-hand, fails dismally, and it is decided that a different kind of spectacle is needed, one that will feature a silent Richard and a dumb show interpreted by confederates: Richard enters "aloft, between two bishops." The Mayor arrives and is told that Richard cannot be spoken to—he is too deep in his meditations, unlike his lascivious brother Edward: "He is not lolling on a lewd day-bed, / But on his knees in meditation; / Not dallying with a brace of courtesans, / But meditating with two deep divines" (3.7.72–75). This staged appearance, like a modern "photo opportunity," is glossed by interested parties for the benefit of the candidate. "See," says the Mayor, "where his grace stands 'tween two clergymen," and Buckingham is quickly there to interpret the dumb show:

Two props of virtue for a Christian prince,
To stay him from the fall of vanity;

And see, a book of prayer in his hand—
True ornaments to know a holy man.—

3.7.96–99

Costumes and ornaments, a dumb show and a set piece. In this case the props (modern "stage properties") include tame clerics, modeling conspicuous piety and virtue, as Buckingham offers the crown, and Richard refuses it, first with indignation, then with sorrow—Richard the humble, Richard the plain man: "Alas, why would you heap this care on me? / I am unfit for state and majesty" (3.7.194–195). A note of comedy is injected when the citizens accept his refusal at face value and have quickly to be rounded up again. ("Will you enforce me to a world of cares?" Richard says with a fine show of reluctance. "Call them again. I am not made of stone" [3.7.213–214].) And to the people he says, "For God doth know, and you may partly see, / How far I am from the desire of this." "Partly" is the key word; they do indeed see only "partly" how eager he is for the crown and for kingship. But he works his magic here for the first time more in dumbness than in speech; he has to try a little harder, and enlist the aid of more assistants, to achieve his Machiavellian ends.

Form and content always mirror each other in Shakespeare's plays, and this is especially self-evident in plays that take as their subject some version of civil war, from the Wars of the Roses to the feuding Capulets and Montagues. As Richard's mother, the Duchess of York, laments, "domestic broils / . . . themselves the conquerors / [M]ake war upon themselves, brother to brother, / Blood to blood, self against self" (2.4.60–62). For most of this play Richard in effect performs as a double agent, using his two kinds of voice and rhetoric to play one side against another. At the close, the two voices will turn inward during the long night before the battle at Bosworth Field, and the "self against self" described by the Duchess becomes "Richard loves Richard; that is, I am I" (5.5.137). But long before he implodes at Bosworth, we can see that form and content for Richard are, as he insists, versions of each other. Just as he is a chameleon and a Proteus, so the play of which he is protagonist (and, paradoxically, antagonist) is also a shape-shifter, engaging the genres of history, tragedy, and comedy in turn. The play is listed in the Folio among the history plays, but the 1597 Quarto edition calls itself a "Tragedy," and the play is full of embedded "comic" moments, though they are usually in the service of tragedy or of villainy.

With *Richard III*, as with some later Shakespeare plays like *King Lear,* there is a deliberate built-in tension between what could be called medieval views of tragedy and those that are more characteristic of the English Renaissance and of the classical revival in education and culture known as humanism. One powerful medieval view of tragedy was that of Fortune's wheel. Fortune, often pictured as a capricious woman, turns a wheel on which men ride up and down, rather in the manner of a modern carnival Ferris wheel. In visual images the whole cycle of the individual's life is on display: the rising and the falling figures are all versions of the same man, as he—it is usually a "he"—reaches the top and then begins to fall. "Falls of Princes" is, indeed, what many medieval tragedies are called (readers of Chaucer's "Monk's Tale" will find a series of them there, prefaced by the Monk's announcement that he will bewail "in manere of tragedie" those who have fallen from high degree and have no remedy to bring them out of adversity). This popular view is reflected, early in *Richard III*, by Queen Elizabeth, the wife of King Edward, when she says, "I fear our happiness is at the height" (1.3.41). She is afraid that they are at the top of Fortune's wheel, and are about to plummet—a fateful remark, and one that will prove true for all the play's characters, even the skeptical and self-motivated Richard. When Richard becomes King Richard, when he finally attains his goal, he begins at the same time to lose his power. His strength—and we have seen it—comes from the position of antagonist, one who opposes or tears down. But Shakespeare's Richard is temperamentally ill-suited to rule. The minute he becomes King he begins to distrust all about him, and the power of speech and persuasion, so confidently his in the early acts, begins to desert him.

Buckingham, who has been his chief aide, his representative to the people, his trained orator and tragedian, now refuses his direction, pretending that he does not understand the director:

King Richard	Ah, Buckingham, now do I play the touch,
	To try if thou be current gold indeed.
	Young Edward lives. Think now what I would speak.
Buckingham	Say on, my loving lord.
King Richard	Why, Buckingham, I say I would be king.
Buckingham	Why, so you are, my thrice-renownèd liege.
King Richard	Ha? Am I king? 'Tis so. But Edward lives.
Buckingham	True, noble prince.
King Richard	O bitter consequence,
	That Edward still should live "true noble prince."
	Cousin, thou wast not wont to be so dull.
	Shall I be plain? I wish the bastards dead,
	And I would have it suddenly performed.
	What sayst thou now? Speak suddenly, be brief.
Buckingham	Your grace may do your pleasure.
King Richard	Tut, tut, thou art all ice. Thy kindness freezes.
	Say, have I thy consent that they shall die?
Buckingham	Give me some little breath, some pause, dear lord,
	Before I positively speak in this.

4.2.9–26

The actors are revolting against the director. The play is not proceeding as King Richard intends, and Buckingham refuses to take direction.

We have noticed that Richard attempts to manipulate his life and those of others around him, and that at the beginning of the play he seemed entirely successful in his illusion-making. But playing against Richard's assumption that he can control this world through his own will, his own language, and his own protean skill as an actor is another kind of plot, whose spokesperson in this play is old Queen Margaret.

Margaret is a figure who very much resembles old Hamlet, the ghost of Hamlet's father. Although the Margaret of the *Henry VI* plays was a seductive Frenchwoman with a strong instinct for rule and a ruthless talent for managing the King, her hapless husband, in *Richard III* Margaret is reduced to, or transformed into, something like a living ghost, a revenant of things past. Like early modern stage ghosts, the Margaret we meet in this play takes her origins from the tradition of the revenge tragedy and from the plays of Seneca. Although she is not literally dead, she comes from the past and from banishment to deliver a message of unrelenting wrath, anger, and revenge. When the audience first sees her, Margaret is the hidden onstage observer of an argument between Richard and Queen Elizabeth. She is there and not there, a listener and then suddenly, shockingly, a participant, as if summoned into dramatic being by the circumstances that have brought these two Yorkists together, wrangling about the throne—a throne she feels should, in any case, be hers, as the widow of the dead King Henry VI, and the mother of the slain Edward, Prince of Wales. It is at this point that we hear Margaret's curse, a curse that is to become the true plot of this play, despite the plural "plots," inductions, and stratagems so ingeniously devised by Richard:

> Margaret   Can curses pierce the clouds and enter heaven?
> Why then, give way, dull clouds, to my quick curses!
> Though not by war, by surfeit die your king,
> As ours by murder to make him a king.
> [*To* ELIZABETH] Edward thy son, that now is Prince of Wales,
> For Edward my son, that was Prince of Wales,
> Die in his youth by like untimely violence.
> Thyself, a queen, for me that was a queen,
> Outlive thy glory like my wretched self.
> Long mayst thou live—to wail thy children's death,
> And see another, as I see thee now,
> Decked in thy rights, as thou art 'stalled in mine.
> Long die thy happy days before thy death,
> And after many lengthened hours of grief
> Die, neither mother, wife, nor England's queen.—
> Rivers and Dorset, you were standers-by,
> And so wast thou, Lord Hastings, when my son
> Was stabbed with bloody daggers. God I pray him

> That none of you may live his natural age,
> But by some unlooked accident cut off.

Richard   Have done thy charm, thou hateful, withered hag.

Margaret   And leave out thee? Stay, dog, for thou shalt hear me.
> If heaven have any grievous plague in store
> Exceeding those that I can wish upon thee,
> O let them keep it till thy sins be ripe,
> And then hurl down their indignation
> On thee, the troubler of the poor world's peace.
> The worm of conscience still begnaw thy soul.
> Thy friends suspect for traitors while thou liv'st,
> And take deep traitors for thy dearest friends.
> No sleep close up that deadly eye of thine,
> Unless it be while some tormenting dream
> Affrights thee with a hell of ugly devils.

1.3.192–224

Margaret calls herself a prophetess, and she prophesies: that Edward, the young Prince of Wales, will die—and he does; that Elizabeth, now the queen, will lose husband, child, and crown—and she does; that Rivers, Dorset, and Hastings will all die—and they do. Richard, she predicts, will lose the ability to sleep, and sleeplessness is the sign throughout Shakespeare of an uneasy conscience. On the field at Bosworth we find Richard "guiltily awake," tortured by "a torment-ing dream," just as she had foretold. Richard will, she says, take his friends for traitors, and he has Hastings murdered on that charge. She says he will take traitors for his friends, and one by one Buckingham, Stanley, and the Bishop of Ely all desert him to flee to the forces of Richmond. Margaret's curse, in short, is nothing less than the plot of the play—until the coming of Richmond. And over and over again one or another of its victims will remember that curse, as Rivers and Gray do en route to their deaths:

Gray   Now Margaret's curse is fall'n upon our heads.

. . . .

Rivers   Then cursed she Hastings; then cursed she Buckingham;
> Then cursed she Richard. O remember, God,
> To hear her prayer for them as now for us.

3.3.14–18

When Buckingham is captured and brought to the block, we hear his final words: "Thus Margaret's curse falls heavy on my neck. . . . Remember Margaret was a prophetess" (5.1.25–27).

The cadences of Margaret's language deliberately recall the biblical rhythms of *lex talionis,* the law of retaliation, from Exodus (chapter 21) and Deuteron-omy (chapter 25). The famous line from Exodus "eye for eye, tooth for tooth, hand for hand, foot for foot" (21:24) was intended only for magistrates, not for individuals to take the law into their own hands. It aimed, in part, to limit punishment to a just equivalent of the crime (thus avoiding "a life for an eye," etc.), but it was, and is still, often misunderstood as a cry for private vengeance. Margaret's sonorous demand,

> Edward thy son, that now is Prince of Wales,
> For Edward my son, that was Prince of Wales,

emphasizes the degree of similarity and repetition involved in this conflict between Lancaster and York. Hers is, importantly, the language of an older generation and also of an older drama, influenced by the balanced poetic lines of the Roman playwright Seneca, whose plays, newly translated and collected under the title *Tenne Tragedies* in 1581 and part of the school curriculum in Latin, had an enormous influence upon Tudor dramatists. Margaret shares this somewhat stilted, balanced choric diction with the Duchess of York, Richard's mother:

Queen Margaret	I had an Edward, till a Richard killed him;
	I had a husband, till a Richard killed him.
. . . .	
Duchess of York	I had a Richard too, and thou didst kill him;
	I had a Rutland too, thou holpst to kill him.

4.4.40–41, 44–45

This old-style language of prophecy, which carries with it so many biblical references, and underscores the quest for revenge that animates both Margaret and Richard, is also the language of the disempowered elders of this play, a generation that has the relics of magnificence and the memory of dominance but no political power. The language of this impotent generation, a generation of ghosts—a symbol of which is the corpse of the "key-cold" Henry VI—stands in sharp contrast to the energetic, seductive, and volatile language of Richard, a language full of vivid, fresh imagery, of stopping and starting, of surprises in tone, voice, and character. The old generation, and the old generation of revenge plays, is as good as dead. Richard of Gloucester, Richard III, is in fact a new kind of character for Shakespeare, a character with a complex, fully developed, and internally contradictory "personality"—in short, a character conceived in terms recognizable from the standpoint of modern psychology. This, of course, is one reason Freud found him fascinating. Richard is also "modern," or at least appealingly "early modern," in his interest in, and use of, the language of economics, profit and loss, and wager. He wants a "world . . . to bustle in" (1.1.152), and his apparently throwaway line "My dukedom to a beggarly *denier*" (1.2.238), after his successful wooing of Anne, anticipates the more famous and more desperate "bet" in the final scenes, "My kingdom for a horse!" (5.7.13). In both cases what is at stake is more than rhetoric. Richard is a master at parlaying much out of little, beginning over after apparent bankruptcy and defeat. And yet the medieval wheel continues to turn. It is suggestive perhaps to think of such a wheel, behind a scrim, inevitably making its full circle, as on the front stage Richard tries once again to be master of his own fate, his country, and a history that is already written.

Margaret's curse is accompanied in the play by a whole host of omens and portents, prophecies and dreams, all of which come true. Stanley dreams that the boar will raise his helm—that Richard, whose sign is the boar, will have their heads—and Hastings laughs at him, disregarding this as mere superstition. Hastings's own horse stumbles three times as it bears him toward the Tower of London, and again he disregards the omen. And the boar does raise his helm. Richard remembers the prophecy of an Irish bard, that he would not live long after he saw "Richmond" (4.2.108–109). Perhaps the most suggestive passage in the play to set next to Margaret's curse for its predictive force, however, is one that comes from a different lexicon, the language of dream. The powerful speech often described as "Clarence's dream" occurs, like the predictive curse, quite early in the play, and while it does lay out a series of incidents that are about to come true—and that Shakespeare's audience would recognize as part of the legendary history of these characters—this dream differs from Margaret's incantatory railing because it reveals something about Clarence's own conflicted interior thoughts. It is also, not incidentally, a magnificent piece of poetry, one that anticipates Shakespeare's late romances, specifically *Pericles* and *The Tempest,* both plays about shipwreck, death, and loss. Clarence dreams that his brother Richard accidentally knocks him overboard, and that he drowns:

> O Lord! Methought what pain it was to drown,
> What dreadful noise of waters in my ears,
> What sights of ugly death within my eyes.
> Methoughts I saw a thousand fearful wrecks,
> Ten thousand men that fishes gnawed upon,
> Wedges of gold, great ouches, heaps of pearl,
> Inestimable stones, unvalued jewels,
> All scattered in the bottom of the sea.
> Some lay in dead men's skulls; and in those holes
> Where eyes did once inhabit, there were crept—
> As 'twere in scorn of eyes—reflecting gems,
> Which wooed the slimy bottom of the deep
> And mocked the dead bones that lay scattered by.
>
> *1.4.21–33*

In literary-historical terms, this passage describes a visit to the underworld, like that experienced by legendary epic figures like Ulysses and Aeneas. But

Clarence's underworld visit is mock-epic rather than epic, and ends with his inglorious drowning in a butt of malmsey, a cask of wine. This was a famous incident to Shakespeare's contemporaries, and Clarence was often derisorily known as "butt-of-malmsey Clarence." Richard glances jokingly at this fate when he remarks that Clarence may be "new-christened" in the Tower (1.1.50). Readers familiar with Shakespeare's late plays will see the strong similarities, and equally strong differences, between this underwater vision and that described in Ariel's second song in *The Tempest,* where again we find skulls and jewels beneath the sea, but imagined as free from the macabre terror of death that seizes upon Clarence:

> Full fathom five thy father lies.
>   Of his bones are coral made;
> Those are pearls that were his eyes;
>   Nothing of him that doth fade
> But doth suffer a sea-change
> Into something rich and strange.
>   The Tempest *1.2.400–405*

In *The Tempest,* as we will see, even the imagination of death turns out to be a fiction, and the "father" mentioned here, Alonso, King of Naples, will be discovered, alive and well, by the end of the play. But for Clarence no such happy reversal lies in store. The device of the predictive dream that comes true is a common one for the literature of the period, and indeed is prevalent in medieval and early modern theories of dreams and dreaming. Most striking, perhaps, from the point of view of Shakespeare's brilliant dramaturgy, are the hints strewn throughout this passage of Clarence's subconscious awareness that Richard means him harm, even as his conscious mind struggles to insist that Richard must, surely, love him. "Methoughts that I had broken from the Tower," he tells Brackenbury, the Lieutenant of the Tower:

> And was embarked to cross to Burgundy,
> And in my company my brother Gloucester,
> Who from my cabin tempted me to walk
> Upon the hatches. . . .
>   Richard III *1.4.9–13*

"Tempted," which can mean merely "persuaded" or "invited," here has a clear subconscious flavor of devilry. Clarence's dream account of how he came to fall is protective of Richard's motives, making the drowning an accident rather than a clear case of intentional malice:

> As we paced along
> Upon the giddy footing of the hatches,

> Methought that Gloucester stumbled, and in falling
> Struck me—that sought to stay him—overboard. . . .
>
> *1.4.16–19*

So Clarence imagines himself as the would-be hero, trying to save his "falling" brother, whose accidental loss of footing ("Gloucester stumbled") is far removed from a purposeful shove. In Freudian terms we would call this "secondary revision," the editing out of the dream thoughts of unacceptable content, and the replacement of them by a more acceptable narrative. Not "Richard threatens me and wishes me dead," but "Richard needs my help, and would certainly not harm me on purpose." The murderers sent by Richard to the Tower immediately demystify this wishful story:

> Second Murderer You are deceived. Your brother Gloucester hates you.
> Clarence   O no, he loves me, and he holds me dear.
>   Go you to him from me.
> First Murderer   Ay, so we will.
>
> *1.4.220–222*

All this inexorable patterning of dream and omen will culminate on the field at Bosworth, when Richard comes face-to-face with the ghosts of all of those he has had murdered. For these omens, which so closely anticipate modern theories about the split and divided self, are also part of a larger pattern of unnaturalism that stretches from the beginning of the play to the end. A rhythmic interplay of the natural and the unnatural, the healthy and the sick, has been set in place, and in action, from the very beginning of Richard's opening soliloquy, when "winter" is "made summer," battle cries turned to "merry meetings," warlike "marches" to the "delightful measures" of the dance—all to the displeasure of the soldierly, ambitious, and vengeful Richard. Although these changes—summer, sociability, dance—suit a comic world, they are at odds with Richard's spirit, and with the play of history and tragedy in which he is protagonist. With the halting of the funeral cortege of Henry VI, a time-honored sign of "disorder" and unnaturalism manifests itself, for the dead king's wounds begin to bleed:

> Lady Anne   O gentlemen, see, see! Dead Henry's wounds
>   Ope their congealèd mouths and bleed afresh.—
>   Blush, blush, thou lump of foul deformity,
>   For 'tis thy presence that ex-hales this blood
>   From cold and empty veins where no blood dwells.
>   Thy deed, inhuman and unnatural,
>   Provokes this deluge supernatural.
>
> *1.2.55–61*

Shakespeare's Richard, a walking hieroglyph of the unnatural, with his hunch-back, his withered arm, and his limp, produces this disturbance in nature wher-ever he goes. We can see this clearly in the contrast between such scenes and the little scene with the three citizens in act 2, a scene of the kind that is often cut in production but that in fact functions as what I call a "window scene," a scene that sheds a moment of light on the surrounding dramatic situation. The char-acters in this scene are of small importance to the story: they are common rather than noble, they are unnamed, and they appear only here. For precisely those reasons, the audience can trust what they say, since they exist only to speak their choric lines. And what they say is that this is a "giddy world," a "troublous world." All their examples, suggestively, are taken from nature:

> Third Citizen   When clouds are seen, wise men put on their cloaks;
> When great leaves fall, then winter is at hand;
> When the sun sets, who doth not look for night?
>
> *2.3.32–34*

On the one hand, these "natural omens" are simply, and unthreateningly, pre-dictive: clouds produce rain; autumn leads to winter; sunset ushers in night. But all these natural prophecies also cite images that have been associated with Richard since the opening soliloquy: clouds, winter, a darkened sun. The name-less citizens realize what the people of the court cannot, that "full of danger is the Duke of Gloucester" (2.3.27).

By the beginning of the fourth act the disorder Richard has engendered in the state has begun to affect his own situation and his own rule. We have already noted Buckingham's thinly veiled horror at the prospect of murdering the Princes in the Tower. Now, rejected by Buckingham, his chief co-conspirator and a fellow nobleman, Richard turns elsewhere for advice—to his page:

> King Richard   Boy.
> Page   My lord?
> King Richard   Know'st thou not any whom corrupting gold
> Will tempt unto a close exploit of death?
>
> *4.2.33–36*

And so Tyrrel is hired to kill the children, to massacre the innocents. There could hardly be any more evident sign of disorder in Richard's interior world than his seeking political guidance from a page. Some pages were in training to be squires and knights (Sir John Falstaff in the *Henry IV* plays alludes to his ear-lier, slimmer days as a page), but pages were, if well born, still low-ranking among the king's servants. Since the intended murder is of two young princes, presumably of about the same age as the page boy, the dramatic irony is double: a child advises a king, and aids in the assassination of children. Bear in mind that the slaughter of the Princes is, as Buckingham tries to argue, an entirely gratuitous act. Richard has falsely but successfully discredited their birth, and has had himself crowned King of England. All he needs to do now is reign. But it is not in his nature to do so. His nature remains that of an antagonist, and the habit of murdering has taken hold of him. He murders now for the sake of murder:

> I must be married to my brother's daughter,
> Or else my kingdom stands on brittle glass.
> Murder her brothers, and then marry her?
> Uncertain way of gain, but I am in
> So far in blood that sin will pluck on sin.
>
> *4.2.62–66*

This statement, occurring as it does early in the fourth act, is a central pivot point for the play. When we hear lines like these again in Shakespeare they will be spoken by a very similar murderer, and a very similar usurping king: Macbeth.

> I am in blood
> Stepped in so far that, should I wade no more,
> Returning were as tedious as go o'er.
>
> Macbeth *3.4.135–137*

It is also of Macbeth that it is said "Macbeth has murdered sleep," just as Margaret's curse has prophesied for Richard ("No sleep close up that deadly eye of thine, / Unless it be while some tormenting dream / Affrights thee with a hell of ugly devils"). The two plays are comparable in numerous ways, from language to plot. But in *Richard III* there is no Lady Macbeth figure to share the protagonist's growing sense of guilty disaster, and so the entire range of emotions, from (over)confidence to fear to disintegration and then again to bravado, will descend upon Richard. As old Margaret will chortle in her familiar choric voice of revenge,

> So now prosperity begins to mellow
> And drop into the rotten mouth of death.
>
> Richard III *4.4.1–2*

The Latinate word "prosperity," akin to the transactions of the busy, bustling Richard, is here literally surrounded and swallowed up by the open-voweled, open-mouthed personage of death. Notice the verbal sequence from "now" to "mellow" to "drop," "rot," and "mouth," before the short *e* sound of "death" picks up, and undoes, the second syllable of "prosperity." And we might remember as well that a "hell-mouth" was a familiar stage property from the medieval and early modern London stage. The diary of theater manager Philip Henslowe, listing all the properties of the Lord Admiral's Men on March 10, 1598, includes, for example, "Item, i rock, i cage, i tomb, i Hell mouth, . . . i bedstead." Engravings from the period show devils onstage exiting from the gaping mouth, which opens wide, like a door or a cave. Richard, by this conceit, is entering the same gaping maw. Again the image draws upon the notion of Fortune's wheel. Richard's prosperity is now about to drop, like an overripe apple from a tree.

No index of disorder in the play's world is more telling, though, than Richard's increasing loss of control over various modes of language. It is not that he cannot speak—to the last he is charming, splenetic, vehement, and eloquent, by turns—but that his language does not transform others, or himself, as once it did. By the end of the fourth act almost all of Richard's most distinguished allies have left him, by one route or another, via the execution block or the path of defection. Hastings, Buckingham, and Stanley are gone, and Richard is left with a far more motley crew: Sir Richard Ratcliffe; Francis, Viscount Lovell; and Sir William Catesby. (As a political rhyme of the period ran, "The cat, the rat, and Lovell our dog / Ruleth all England under a hog.") It is to Ratcliffe and Catesby that Richard turns, in desperation, when he receives the unwelcome news that Richmond is already in the harbor, and that Buckingham—of all people—is expected to welcome him. The confusion of the scene that follows is most uncharacteristic of the formerly smooth and unflappable Richard:

King Richard	Some light-foot friend post to the Duke of Norfolk.
	Ratcliffe thyself, or Catesby—where is he?
Catesby	Here, my good lord.
King Richard	Catesby, fly to the Duke.
Catesby	I will, my lord, with all convenient haste.
King Richard	Ratcliffe, come hither. Post to Salisbury;
	When thou com'st thither—[*to* CATESBY] dull, unmindful villain,
	Why stay'st thou here and goest not to the Duke?
Catesby	First, mighty liege, tell me your highness' pleasure:
	What from your grace I shall deliver to him?
King Richard	O, true, good Catesby. . . .

4.4.371–380

Ratcliffe	What, may it please you, shall I do at Salisbury?
King Richard	Why, what wouldst thou do there before I go?
Ratcliffe	Your highness told me I should post before.
King Richard	My mind is changed.

4.4.384–387

Nothing could be more unlike the Richard of the earlier acts than this indecision, capped with the uncharacteristic admission "My mind is changed."
Richard, once actor, director, stage manager, and prompter, has lost control, not
only of events, but even of his own plans and his sense of self. If this scene were
not so desperate, it would be farcical. As the forces of Richmond close in upon
him, and his former friends, following the prediction of Margaret's curse, desert
him one by one, Richard is left without a role to play. And this is the condition
in which we find him as the battle lines are drawn on Bosworth Field.

The scene at Bosworth is staged in a way that is deliberately both theatrical
and symmetrical. Two tents, two camps, two would-be kings, each with a legitimate claim to the throne, face each other across the wide expanse of the stage.
The time is night, and we hear that Richmond will nap until dawn, the time
appointed for the battle. Richard, on the other hand, is still consumed with disorder. "I will not sup tonight," he says, asking instead for a bowl of wine. Peaceful sleep will elude him—as it later will Macbeth—but on the darkened stage
there now appears a pageant, a moving procession of ghosts, who will speak in
turn to Richard and to Richmond. These are the ghosts of Richard's victims:
Prince Edward; King Henry; Clarence; Hastings; the murdered Princes in the
Tower; the Queen's relations, Rivers, Gray, and Vaughan; the Lady Anne; and
Buckingham. These shadowy figures are modeled on an aspect of early English
drama, the procession of seven vices and seven virtues in the medieval morality
plays, whispering in the ear of mankind. It is likely that the doors on either side
of the Elizabethan stage would have been useful in staging this procession. In
the opening moments of *Richard III* the same doors would have let in, and let
out, the funeral procession of Henry VI. Now they permit the entrance of the
ghosts, their visits to both camps, and their noiseless exit. In an important sense
the ghosts are entering not only the stage, or the field, but also the mind. These
are psychological prompting, embodied guilt and embodied memory. The in-
between world that is the world of the stage is their perfect venue. And the message of each ghost is the same. To Richard, "Despair and die." To Richmond,
"Live and flourish." Are they real or imaginary? By this point in the play
Richard's world has become so much the world of his mind and thought that it
is difficult to make a distinction between inside and out. As the stage direction
instructs, "Richard starteth up out of a dream." And the dialogue of the two
voices, which in earlier scenes was deployed as a way of fooling others, now
moves inside Richard, and manifests itself as another kind of civil war:

> What do I fear? Myself? There's none else by.
> Richard loves Richard: that is, I am I.
> Is there a murderer here? No. Yes, I am.
> Then fly! What, from myself? Great reason. Why?
> Lest I revenge. Myself upon myself?
> Alack, I love myself. Wherefore? For any good

That I myself have done unto myself?
O no, alas, I rather hate myself
For hateful deeds committed by myself.
I am a villain. Yet I lie: I am not.
Fool, of thyself speak well. —Fool, do not flatter.
My conscience hath a thousand several tongues,
And every tongue brings in a several tale,
And every tale condemns me for a villain.

5.5.136–149

Here the Machiavel meets the Machiavel, the looking glass is finally turned inward. The mellifluousness of the play's opening soliloquy is replaced by a set of short, choppy phrases, lines cut up into two and three pieces—a language of extreme fragmentation. "Is there a murderer here? No. Yes, I am." This tortured language is at the furthest remove from either the balanced rotundity of Queen Margaret's incantations or the energetic originality of Richard's speech in the preceding scenes. Eleven "I's" and nine "myselfs" burden these fourteen lines, and the breakdown of language is the final clue to the breakdown of character. The real war is now staged within Richard, rather than between him and his rival for the throne.

The deliberate symmetry of the scene has a little further to go. Each man delivers an oration to his troops: Richmond's is full of images of order and tranquillity—the "safeguard of your wives," "your children's children"—and Richard's, by contrast, full of contempt and disorder. The enemy, he says, consists of "vagabonds, rascals and runaways, / A scum of Bretons and base lackey peasants," of "stragglers," "beggars," and "poor rats," of "these overweening rags of France" (5.6. 46–47, 57, 59, 61, 58). Where Richmond seeks security, Richard evokes danger: "Shall these enjoy our lands? Lie with our wives? Ravish our daughters?" Both men address the same question, but they do so with opposite imagery and opposite effect, Richmond dwelling on safe wives and safe children, Richard on rape. Now, in the last moments of the play, its images of unnaturalism begin to be countered by a return to nature. Richard is told that the sun does not shine today, that it "disdains to shine"—and the sun, as we have seen, is the emblem of the King of England. In the opening soliloquy "this sun of York" was Richard's brother Edward. Now it is Richard, and he, too, is in eclipse. In a moment of martial heroism fully consistent with his bravery and daring throughout the play, Richard goes to his death crying out his willingness to trade his kingdom—for the moment—for a horse. Ever the speculator and gambler, he dies as he has lived.

It is left to Richmond, soon to be Henry VII, the first Tudor king and the grandfather of the reigning Queen Elizabeth of Shakespeare's time, to restore order to the land. As Richard had spoken in images of disorder and decay, so Richmond will declaim in a language of fruitfulness and plenty. The first time the audience encounters him, he speaks of "summer fields," of "fruitful vines," of the "harvest of perpetual peace." Behind the lively, vivid play of political manipulation is the implacable rhythm of seasonal change and renewal. Richmond speaks of fertility and procreation, as the playwright deliberately balances this new harvest against the "winter of . . . discontent" that was the natural habitat of Richard III. In Richmond's victory at Bosworth we hear once more the voice of unification, reconciliation, and forgiveness, together with a return to hierarchy and order: "Inter their bodies as becomes their births. . . . We will unite the white rose and the red" (5.8.15, 19). And then:

> England hath long been mad, and scarred herself;
> The brother blindly shed the brother's blood;
> The father rashly slaughtered his own son;
> The son, compelled, been butcher to the sire. . . .
>
> 5.8.23–26

These images of civil war within the family recall the horrifying scene in *3 Henry VI* that begins with the harrowing stage directions "Enter at one door a Soldier with a dead man [his father] in his arms" and "Enter at another door another Soldier with a dead man [his son] in his arms." In that play the onstage spectator, transfixed and unable to intercede, was the king himself, Henry VI. But this new King Henry, Henry VII, will, he says, heal the internecine warfare of the past. His marriage to Elizabeth, the daughter of King Edward (and the woman Richard tried and failed to marry himself), will "Enrich the time to come with smooth-faced peace, / With smiling plenty, and fair prosperous days" (5.8.33–34). The sun, the King of England, is back where it, and he, belongs.

The portrait of Richmond we get here is, I think, deliberately faceless, without character and virtually without personality, in distinct contrast to the colorful, seductive, and consistently fascinating Richard. Shakespeare could easily have introduced Richmond earlier, perhaps with a scene showing his preparation in France, but the decision not to do so has a powerful consequence. Richmond appears as an effect, rather than as a person. Almost the last thing Richard says is "I think there be six Richmonds in the field. / Five have I slain today, instead of him" (5.7.11–12). He is speaking of a common battlefield practice, dressing lesser soldiers in the costume of the king in order to protect the true king from harm, a species of camouflage. But notice again the anonymity and ordinariness of Richmond, who cannot be distinguished from the other "Richmonds." It is impossible to imagine Richard being cloned in this way, to find six Richards in the field. In terms of metatheater, the play's self-conscious commentary on itself, this observation also reminds us that the doubling of parts was commonplace in the early modern theater, where the number of actors was limited by the size of the company and the parts were often many.

The part of "Richmond" is a small role, relatively speaking, in the long play of *Richard III,* and both Richard and the audience in the theater might well have encountered the actor playing Richmond earlier in the play in one, two, or even several other guises. Richard's part, by contrast, is enormously long. He can neither be duplicated nor doubled.

Henry Tudor, Earl of Richmond, is a force of nature as much as he is a person in this play. He is order reasserting itself in England, the final turn of Fortune's wheel, defeating anarchy and bringing to Shakespeare's theater the prospect of the glorious reign of the Tudors. Richmond functions here as the redeemer of the fallen land, who rescues it from Margaret's cry for revenge and transforms it, for a moment at least, into an ideal and idealizing vision of reconciliation and peace. He is a Christian ruler who defeats—again, for the moment at least—the energetic anarchy of Antichrist, the devil Richard. And yet Shakespeare, like all good writers, knew that the Devil could not be defeated for all time. This dark, malevolent, menacing shadow of a man will not stay dead in his plays. Like a bad dream, although a tempting one, he recurs, and must be vanquished all over again, in such figures from the tragedies as Iago in *Othello,* and Edmund in *King Lear,* and Macbeth, the dark underside of human nature. At the same time, Richard's thrillingly "modern" quality of reflectiveness and confessionality will recur in more "heroic" characters, such as Prince Hal and Hamlet. Richard's final triumph in this play is in fact explicitly parallel to his triumph in the wooing of the Lady Anne. She knew of his crimes, and yet she was won over—and the same will happen to the audience in the theater. We see all the horrors that come with Richard and his world, indeed we are his confidants, privy from the first to his plots and plans. Yet readers and audiences are perpetually fascinated and spellbound, captivated by the unique personality that is Richard III. No societies have sprung up to defend and lionize Richmond. He wins the crown and the queen, but not the play. This, we might say, is the victory of theater over history. If it is temporary, it is nonetheless, for the moment, both perversely satisfying and aesthetically complete.

The Comedy of Errors

DRAMATIS PERSONAE

Solinus, *Duke of Ephesus*

Egeon, *a merchant of Syracuse,*
father of the Antipholus twins

Antipholus of Ephesus, *twin to*
Antipholus of Syracuse,
son of Egeon

Antipholus of Syracuse, *twin to*
Antipholus of Ephesus,
son of Egeon

Dromio of Ephesus, *twin to*
Dromio of Syracuse, bondman of
Antipholus of Ephesus

Dromio of Syracuse, *twin to*
Dromio of Ephesus, bondman of
Antipholus of Syracuse

Adriana, *wife of Antipholus of*
Ephesus

Luciana, *her sister*

Nell, *Adriana's kitchen-maid*

Angelo, *a goldsmith*

Balthasar, *a merchant*

A Courtesan

Doctor Pinch, *a schoolmaster*
and exorcist

Merchant of Ephesus, *a friend*
of Antipholus of Syracuse

Second Merchant, *Angelo's*
creditor

Emilia, *an abbess at Ephesus*

Jailer, messenger, headsman,
officers, and other attendants

LIKE MANY of Shakespeare's comedies, *The Comedy of Errors* begins with an inflexible law and the human dilemma caused by the law's impersonal enforcement. Because of a history of enmity between Ephesus and Syracuse, the play proposes, the laws of the two cities prohibit travel between them ("To admit no traffic to our adverse towns" [1.1.15]). If any citizen of one is found in the other, he is bound to die, and his goods are to be confiscated, unless he is ransomed with a payment of a thousand marks. So declares the Duke of Ephesus, as he enters the stage with his prisoner, the old man Egeon, a merchant of Syracuse. "I am not partial to infringe our laws," says the Duke, with dispassionate dignity. Indeed, like many Shakespearean dukes in the dark opening scenes of comedies, this Duke *is* the law: his role is to enforce it. "Therefore by law thou art condemned to die," he tells Egeon (1.1.25).

Egeon, for his part, is already reconciled to death, as we learn in the first lines of the play, and again after he hears the Duke's decree. Death is a "comfort" to him: "when your words are done, / My woes end likewise with the evening sun" (1.1.26–27). Why is Egeon so resigned, so half-in-love with death? He explains his life story, at the Duke's invitation, in a characteristic speech of dramatic exposition, setting out all the details of his past in a speech that is over a hundred lines long, and packed with romance, adventure, and tragedy.

Born in Syracuse, happily married, he thrived as a merchant, making increasingly frequent trips to Epidamnum in pursuit of business matters. On one of these trips his pregnant wife joined him, and she soon became a "joyful mother of two goodly sons," identical twins. By chance a poor woman at the same inn gave birth to twin sons on the same night, and Egeon bought them as servants to attend his own children. But when his wife grew eager to return home, and he, although "unwilling," agreed, the family was caught in a shipwreck and sundered by "the always-wind-obeying deep."

This is an early instance of the characteristic Shakespearean storm, an event-in-the-world that had its counterpart in actual sixteenth-century storms, often devastating to the seafaring English nation of travelers, merchants, and explorers—but which is also a recurrent dramatic theme, from this early play through *Othello* and *King Lear* to the play aptly named *The Tempest,* that marks a turmoil both inside and outside the minds and psyches of the major characters. For Egeon and his wife and young family, this storm, which seems to be external and physical, marks and records a sundering of the family, and also a split *within* Egeon, the tale-teller, himself.

Egeon names this turn of events to the Duke—and the listening audience—succinctly: it is *tragedy,* a "tragic instance of our harm."

His wife bound her younger son to one end of a mast, and with him one of the servant-twins, and the husband bound the other son and servant to the other end. But before they could be rescued by approaching ships, their own vessel hit a rock: "Our helpful ship was splitted in the midst" (1.1.103). And like the ship, the family was divided ("this unjust divorce of us," Egeon calls it [104]), to be separated, as he believes, forever. The father, one of the sons, and the son's attendant returned home to Syracuse, while the mother and the other son and attendant were taken up by fishermen and borne away. And when at age eighteen Egeon's remaining son grew "inquisitive" about his lost brother, the son—and servant—departed on a quest to find them. Egeon, left behind, longed for the company of both the known and the unknown son, and he has just spent the last several years journeying in quest of them. Now bereft of family, "[h]apless" in the Duke's terms and "[h]opeless and helpless" in his own (1.1.140, 157), Egeon would die "happy," he says, if he only knew that his children were alive:

> But here must end the story of my life,
> And happy were I in my timely death
> Could all my travels warrant me they live.
>
> Errors *1.1.137–139*

This is a long story, but it is worth telling at length here, because every piece of it will return in some guise in the remainder of the play. Although for Egeon these events constitute a "tragedy," in formal generic terms this set piece is a "romance," a fairy-tale-like adventure of shipwreck, loss, and ultimate rediscovery and reunion—comparable, for example, to the plots of later plays that have been termed romances by critics (*Pericles, The Winter's Tale, The Tempest*) and to the tale of his adventures that Othello tells Desdemona. Like many other inset tales in the plays (we could look ahead not only to *Othello* but also to the Ghost's tale in *Hamlet*) it contains, in little, the mythic story of the play to follow. Again like many other inset tales, Egeon's story contains a number of terms that, in their resonant doubleness, will haunt the rest of the dramatic action: words like "happy" (joyous but also lucky, or accidental, by chance), "travel" (in the period, the same as "travail," suffering or work), and "divorce" (a separation or disunion, but with disquieting echoes of the more specific meaning, a dissolution of marriage—a loaded term since the notorious "divorce" of Queen Elizabeth's father, Henry VIII, from Catherine of Aragon).

Thus, for example, "divorce" in the marital sense will be evoked explicitly by Adriana, the wife of Antipholus of Ephesus, in act 2, when she accuses a man she thinks is her husband of infidelity, and imagines what he would do were the circumstances reversed ("Wouldst thou not . . . from my false hand cut the wedding ring, /And break it with a deep-divorcing vow?" [2.2.134–138]). The man she so accuses is, of course, not her own husband, but his unknown identical twin, Egeon's other son, landed by "hap," or chance, in Ephesus on the same day as the father. The "divorce" of Egeon and his wife by the storm at sea—but also, perhaps, by his confessedly "unwilling" decision to return home—is made parallel to the marital discord of the son he lost all those years ago. Even Adriana's phrase "deep-divorcing" echoes the "always-wind-obeying deep" of the original storm in Egeon's story (1.1.63). Once again—and this will be characteristic of the structure of *The Comedy of Errors*—an event in the physical world corresponds to something within the minds, spirits, and behavior of the dramatic characters, and this correspondence is deftly hinted at from the very beginning. The storm takes place inside these characters as well as around them, despite the fact that they seem to have little "psychology" or inwardness in the sense that we will come to expect from later Shakespeare plays. The depth of this play lies in its surface.

The effect of these predictive phrases and their echoes in the remainder of the play is to a certain extent subliminal, since the audience is soon caught up in the more robust farcical action of mistaken identity, intrigue, and slapstick beatings that make up the larger substance of the play. The hint of tragedy (Egeon's death sentence at sundown) and the tonality of romance give way to a more physical comedy of substitutions and misrecognitions, and it is easy to underestimate the sophistication of the play's devices. I stress this because some readers of this early play have found it too broad and farcical for their taste, though productions and adaptations have capitalized on the fast-paced action and physical rhetoric of substitution to make highly successful stage vehicles and films, from Richard Rodgers and Lorenz Hart's *The Boys from Syracuse* (1938) to Jim Abraham's *Big Business* (1988). For this is a play of "errors" in the etymological as well as the human sense: mistakes, but also wanderings (from the Latin *errare,* "to wander"). Shakespeare's key sources here include two plays by the Roman playwright Plautus, *Menaechmi* and *Amphitruo.* In the first of these, a Merchant of Syracuse explains how he once lost one of his twin sons in Epidamnum, and the action includes a number of elements retained in Shakespeare's play: the mistake of one identical twin for the other, the business with the courtesan, the quarrel with the wife, the piece of jewelry (in *Menaechmi* it is a bracelet rather than a chain), the doctor summoned to attend the supposedly insane husband. Shakespeare complicated this plot by adding a second set of twins, the servant Dromios, to the original pair, in his play named Antipholuses rather than Menaechmuses. From *Amphitruo* Shakespeare took the episode of the dinner served by the wife to the "wrong" brother, and the idea of the two sets of twins, masters and servants. Although Ben Jonson famously referred to Shakespeare's "small Latin and less Greek," scholars have determined that Shakespeare seems to have had a fairly wide acquaintance with the Latin classics, and that texts by Plautus, as well as by the Roman poet Ovid, would have been taught at the Stratford grammar school he attended. They would therefore have been familiar to many with similar grammar school educations; the early modern period's "small Latin and less Greek" was far more Latin and Greek than is commanded by most college graduates today.

One popular edition of Plautus, that of Dionysius Lambinus, published in 1576, marked the "errors" in *Menaechmi* (*"coquus errans," "errat hic senex,"* etc.), as well as in *Amphitruo;* if this was the text that Shakespeare used, it may have contributed to the catchphrase that became the title of his play. An English translation of *Menaechmi,* by William Warner, was published in 1595. In addition to these Latin sources Shakespeare drew on certain passages from the Bible, and especially from the writings of Saint Paul, both in Paul's Epistle to the Ephesians and in the Acts of the Apostles, where Ephesus is seen as a city of magic and witchcraft, where the residents "use curious arts." In moving the action of his own play from Plautus's Epidamnum to Ephesus (a location he would use again for the Temple of Diana in *Pericles*), Shakespeare not only chose a location more familiar—in name—to his audience, but also one that permitted a Christian overlay to this classical story. Ephesus was in ancient times a city dedicated to Artemis, or Diana, the goddess of virginity. The city was a thriving center of commerce, and the Temple of Diana attracted many visitors. With the introduction of Christianity, Ephesus became a newly important locale, linked with major figures in the history of the early Church. The city was celebrated as the site of the death of John the Baptist and of Mary Magdalen—and, according to some accounts, of the Virgin Mary. (Thus the theme of virginity, inherited from the cult of Diana, moved across into the

Christian narrative; as we will see, the two are intermingled in the figure of the Abbess in Shakespeare's play.) Perhaps most important for the Renaissance view of Ephesus, Saint Paul dwelt there for three years, teaching and organizing a new church. Paul's writings, especially in the Acts of the Apostles, indelibly associated Ephesus with magic and witchcraft, cheaters and mountebanks, a fact that accounts for some of its fascination for Renaissance authors. In equally influential passages in chapters 5 and 6 of his Epistle to the Ephesians, Paul stressed the importance of hierarchy within the family, instructing wives to obey their husbands, and servants to obey their masters; these instructions will also be important elements in Shakespeare's play.

As for the essentially comic—yet always potentially dangerous—plot element of identical twins, it was a device of particular interest to Shakespeare as a playwright, and also, perhaps, as a man. Himself the father of twins, Hamnet (who died young) and Judith, he would later place a pair of "identical" male and female twins at the heart of *Twelfth Night,* a comedy about shipwreck, identity, and disguise that has much in common with *The Comedy of Errors.* Many characters in other plays, while not literally twins, use the metaphor of twinship as a sign of their intimate friendship, especially in youth. In at least two such instances, Hermia and Helena in *A Midsummer Night's Dream* and Leontes and Polixenes in *The Winter's Tale,* the very interchangeability of the friends, their vaunted twinship, leads to sexual jealousy and rivalry. This is also the case in *The Comedy of Errors,* where Adriana thinks Antipholus of Syracuse is her husband, Antipholus of Ephesus, and Luce (or Nell) the kitchen wench lavishes her affections on the "wrong" Dromio, the one from Syracuse.

The twin plot, like the storm at sea, contributes at once to the physical comedy and to the psychological or emotional unfolding of the plot. As a key element of farce, mistaken identity leads to comic confrontations, where the audience enjoys its superior knowledge—tipped off by a key differentiating piece of costuming or casting, since if these characters were truly identical to us there would be no delicious suspense at the impending mistake, and no laughter at the discomfiture of those not in the know. But modern audiences are also familiar enough with phrases like "split personality" and "psychological split" to see readily that two onstage characters, who look the same and have the same names, might well be representing twin and conflicting aspects of a single person: the Antipholus who loves his wife, the Antipholus who visits the Courtesan; the Antipholus who is a stranger, the Antipholus who is at "home." The story of sundering and reunion is a typical romance, but it is also a story of self-discovery and self-knowledge, emphasized by the many moments when one of the Antipholuses (or indeed one of the Dromios) declares that he is bewitched or transformed, in search not only of a brother but of what he calls "myself."

The "errors" plot is here slightly different from a variant in the same comedic spirit, the "supposes" plot that animates *The Taming of the Shrew.* The Antipholuses and Dromios are *mistaken* for their twin brothers; they do not deliberately disguise themselves in order to impersonate or deceive. Thus the Duke's pertinent set of questions in the final recognition scene, "which is the natural man, / And which the spirit? Who deciphers them?" (5.1.334–335), points to the notion of haunting or possession, and also to the key role of the audience in reading, or deciphering, identities.

After the frame story of Egeon and the Duke, which sets up the menacing threat of death at sundown if the merchant of Syracuse is not ransomed with a payment of a thousand marks, the scene shifts to a conversation between another traveler from Syracuse and another merchant, this one familiar with the laws of Ephesus. The sum of money needed for Egeon's ransom is described as "a thousand marks," where a "mark" was a common European denomination, but elsewhere in the play money is computed in guilders, ducats, angels, and once—to emphasize a tone of low comedy—sixpence. These "errors" could be signs of authorial carelessness, haste, or indifference, but in fact their effect is to generalize, both in space and time: the play seems both ancient and modern, Roman and English, "then" and "now." Without knowing it, Antipholus of Syracuse has come to the same city as his father, but when the Merchant of Ephesus warns him to conceal his identity, he does not recognize his father's story as his own:

Merchant of Ephesus	Therefore give out you are of Epidamnum,
	Lest that your goods too soon be confiscate.
	This very day a Syracusian merchant
	Is apprehended for arrival here,
	And, not being able to buy out his life,
	According to the statute of the town
	Dies ere the weary sun set in the west.
	There is your money that I had to keep.

1.2.1–8

The sum, it turns out, is the same as that needed to ransom Egeon, a thousand marks. If Antipholus of Syracuse were paying attention, and if he were so minded, he could here bring the play to a happy but premature end by using his thousand marks to ransom his countryman. That he does not is an index not of his mean-spiritedness, but rather of his preoccupation with other matters. His melancholy self-absorption here will prefigure that of Antonio in *The Merchant of Venice*. Agreeing to meet the Merchant of Ephesus at five o'clock—the terminus, as it will develop, for all the play's actions, and presumably the same hour as the "sundown" of the Duke's decree—Antipholus of Syracuse hands over the money to his servant Dromio, and sounds one of the play's major notes of losing and finding: "I will go lose myself, / And wander up and down to view the city" (1.2.30–31).

Losing oneself to find oneself is a frequent and powerful theme in Shakespearean drama, and especially in the comedies. Clearly here it is linked directly
to the "errors" of the title. Antipholus of Syracuse's speech on this topic, which
will be echoed unwittingly later on by Adriana, the wife of the other Antipholus, evokes the ideas of twinship, doubling, problematic identity, sundering by
water, and, indeed, the seriocomic parable of split beings in quest of their other
halves that is told by Aristophanes in Plato's *Symposium*. Here is Antipholus of
Syracuse:

> I to the world am like a drop of water
> That in the ocean seeks another drop,
> Who, falling there to find his fellow forth,
> Unseen, inquisitive, confounds himself.
> So I, to find a mother and a brother,
> In quest of them, unhappy, lose myself.
>
> *1.2.35–40*

The familiar word "unhappy" here connotes both bad feelings (melancholy)
and bad luck (ill hap), again tying together inner sensations and outer plot
developments.

Antipholus's "drop of water" speech, emphasizing his isolation and his
search for a lost brother (and mother), as we noted above, is itself matched and
"twinned" with Adriana's speech in act 2, where she confronts the man she
thinks is her errant husband, but who is actually this same Antipholus:

> How comes it now, my husband, O how comes it
> That thou art then estrangèd from thyself?—
> Thy "self" I call it, being strange to me
> That, undividable, incorporate,
> Am better than thy dear self's better part.
> Ah, do not tear thyself from me;
> For know, my love, as easy mayst thou fall
> A drop of water in the breaking gulf,
> And take unmingled thence that drop again
> Without addition or diminishing,
> As take from me thyself, and not me too.
>
> *2.2.119–129*

Adriana's argument is especially of interest in light of the play's constant emphasis on twins and splitting (What is a *self* ? What does it mean to be *incorporate*,
of the same body with, someone else?) and also of its emphasis on disguise. For
this is a *play*, after all. The performers are actors; they are always impersonating
someone else, always both "estranged from" themselves and "undividable." The
circumstance of losing oneself to find oneself is the ordinary everyday business

of the stage, as well as the highly dramatic and potentially tragic story of a sundered family, a threatened merchant, a fragile marriage. Notice, too, that this Antipholus does not recognize the echo of his own words. The repetition of this image in the two speeches makes the love of a brother and a mother parallel and cognate to romantic and marital love, while the two sons are also "splits" of their father, one "inquisitive" and wishing to travel, the other remaining at home with his wife.

The main plot of the play is comic, although it is framed by Egeon's death sentence and the menace of the advancing day. In one famous production at Stratford-upon-Avon, staged by Theodore Komisarjevsky in 1938, a large clock with moving hands marked the race against time, while in another the place of execution was clearly visible on the front stage from the opening scene to the end of the play. The action takes place in a public street and a market, in front of three "houses," marked as the Phoenix (the home of Antipholus of Ephesus), the Porcupine (the house of the courtesan whom the Ephesian Antipholus visits when he is locked out of his own house by mistake), and a priory, or religious house, where we will encounter the Abbess in the last scene of the play. One end of the street leads to the bay, the other to the city. The comedy of errors, or mistaken identities, leads Adriana to take the wrong man for her husband, and the bachelor Antipholus to fall in love with his supposed wife's sister, Luciana. Antipholus of Syracuse gives money to his Dromio, and then meets up with the *other* Dromio, who, of course, denies all knowledge of the thousand marks supposedly given into his care. Antipholus of Ephesus has commissioned a goldsmith to make him a chain, but the chain is given, by mistake, to Antipholus of Syracuse, who at first rejoices that in this magical town he is given "golden gifts"—but soon begins to believe that he has stumbled into a city of witches and mountebanks.

The Comedy of Errors offers a fascinating roster of female roles, each character in her way a type that will recur in later Shakespeare plays: wife, sister/friend, courtesan, comic servant, abbess. Perhaps unexpectedly, it is the wife who voices the more "feminist" sentiments, her unmarried sister who speaks up for traditional wifely subservience. In the following exchange, provoked by the husband's absence from the midday meal, both women use the key word "liberty," a word that is also essential to the play's other ongoing conversation about domestic authority, the relationship between masters and servants:

Luciana	Good sister, let us dine, and never fret.
	A man is master of his liberty.
	Time is their mistress, and when they see time
	They'll go or come. If so, be patient, sister.
Adriana	Why should their liberty than ours be more?
Luciana	Because their business still lies out o'door.
Adriana	Look when I serve him so, he takes it ill.
Luciana	O, know he is the bridle of your will.

| Adriana | There's none but asses will be bridled so. |
| Luciana | Why, headstrong liberty is lashed with woe. |

2.1.6–15

The other female characters in *The Comedy of Errors* also derive from classic and classical types, and each will participate in a lineage that extends throughout the Shakespearean corpus. The Courtesan, whose role in Plautus's version is much more extensive than the role that Shakespeare gives her, is associated with love for money, and therefore with the wrong bestowal of the golden chain. Like Bianca, the Venetian courtesan in *Othello,* she has, if not the stereotypical "heart of gold," at least a genuine affection for the man who spends his time with her, and she is part of a similar love triangle that exhibits one partner's unreasoned jealousy, as well as the "error" of false clues and mistaken identity. Nell the kitchen servant, who pursues Dromio of Syracuse under the mistaken belief that he is Dromio of Ephesus, is elaborately described in a grotesque mode indebted, on the one hand, to the standard antifeminist literature of the past (see, for example, Chaucer's Wife of Bath's "Prologue") and, on the other, to the genre of the antiblazon.

A blazon was the praise of a beautiful woman, usually through a description of the ideal and idealized features of her face: the eyes like stars, the cheeks like roses, the lips like cherries, and so on, as in many sonnet sequences of the period. The antiblazon, also familiar from Italian as well as from English sources, describes the emphatically *un*ideal and materially real characteristics of a woman, focusing on her body below the neck rather than above it. Dromio of Syracuse compares the parts of Nell's body to the parts of the globe, with comical, often scatological, and disparaging results: her buttocks are like Ireland ("I found it out / by the bogs" [3.2.116–117]); the hard and barren palm of her hand is like Scotland, legendary home of both rocks and misers; her breath like Spain, the land of garlic eaters; her complexion like "America" and "the Indies," full of blemishes ("all o'er embellished with rubies, carbuncles, sapphires"). As for Belgium and the Netherlands, then as now known colloquially as the Low Countries, he "did not look so low." Since the word "country" itself was a familiar homonym for a woman's sexual parts ("I could find out countries in her," says Dromio; compare this with Hamlet's teasing remark to Ophelia as he asks to lie in her lap, "Did you think I meant country matters?"), this "world tour" is a sexual map as well as a sly disquisition on contemporary politics. Poets of the period often made similar extended geographical analogies; one familiar example is John Donne's "Elegy 19: To His Mistress Going to Bed":

> License my roving hands, and let them go
> Before, behind, between, above, below.
> Oh my America! My new-found-land!
> My kingdom, safeliest when with one man mann'd.
> My mine of precious stones! My empery!

How blest am I, in this discovering thee!
To enter in these bonds is to be free. . . .

lines 25–31

Donne's love poem, like Shakespeare's comic prose, uses the contemporary obsession with exploration and discovery to explore, and exploit, the pleasures of the body. (This reference in *The Comedy of Errors* is in fact Shakespeare's only mention of "America," although a similar antiblazon in *Twelfth Night,* this one aimed at the ridicule of a *man,* describes Malvolio's face as smiling like a "map with the augmentation of the Indies.") Donne's poem is homage and praise, not comic undercutting, of course, yet he uses many of the same elements: the mine of precious stones, for example, and the lover's paradox that bondage is freedom. This same paradox, a commonplace in love poetry and also in romantic comedy, will find its insistent literal equivalent, throughout *The Comedy of Errors,* in the itinerary of the golden chain (intended for one Antipholus, given to another, promised to the Courtesan, confused and conflated with the worthless and punitive "rope's end" that Dromio of Ephesus is sent to fetch) and in the language of binding and bondage that animates the entire play, from the bond-servants to the supposedly therapeutic binding of madmen at the hands of Doctor Pinch and the officer. How can one distinguish "good" bondage from "bad" bondage? The various ramifications of this question are all brought together in the play's climactic final scene of revelation, when the metaphorical meets the literal (the "bondman Dromio," having gnawed in two his cords, is now "unbound") and the mysterious Abbess recognizes the bound and apparently doomed old man, Egeon:

Whoever bound him, I will loose his bonds,
And gain a husband by his liberty.

5.1.340–341

The Abbess herself is another good example of an early character type that will persist in various permutations through Shakespeare's dramatic career. Other versions of this figure, the supposed widow, bereft of husband and children and turned to the religious life, will appear in the late romances, principally in the figure of Thaisa in *Pericles* and, with an inventive twist, the "dead" Hermione of *The Winter's Tale;* a variant that might be described as the wife-on-the-shelf is Mariana in *Measure for Measure,* abandoned by her fiancé and living a cloistered life in her "moated grange" until circumstances bring them back together. It is one of the happy commonplaces of dramatic and fictional romance that what has been lost will be found, and that sequestration in a nunnery or religious house is a temporary rather than a permanent refuge for figures who have once had lives and families in the world. In this case the Abbess is permitted to intercede in the argument between Adriana and Luciana, and to assert some sharp observations about jealous wives and wandering husbands.

Typically for Shakespeare, the major themes of the play are all doubly inflected, offering both benign and dangerous possibilities. Thus, for example, the question of dream, wonder, magic, and transformation—the journey to Ephesus as a place of wish fulfillment—has its dark underside in the fear of sorcery, trickery, and loss of control over events. Here is Antipholus of Syracuse at the end of act I, having already been mistaken for his identical twin:

> They say this town is full of cozenage,
> As nimble jugglers that deceive the eye,
> Dark-working sorcerers that change the mind,
> Soul-killing witches that deform the body,
> Disguisèd cheaters, prating mountebanks,
> And many suchlike libertines of sin.
>
> *1.2.97–102*

He had given a purse of gold—the thousand marks—to his servant Dromio, only to then encounter the *other* Dromio, who claims he never had it. By the end of the next act Antipholus of Syracuse has met the woman who thinks he is her husband: "What, was I married to her in my dream? / Or sleep I now, and think I hear all this? / What error drives our eyes and ears amiss?" (2.2.182–184). He has also met her sister, Luciana, with whom he will fall in love. "Are you a god?" he asks Luciana, to her initial consternation. "Would you create me new? / Transform me, then, and to your power I'll yield" (3.2.39–40). His Dromio thinks "[t]his is the fairy land," populated by goblins, elves, and sprites, and asks rhetorically, "I am transformèd, master, am I not?" "I think thou art in mind, and so am I," replies Antipholus of Syracuse, who closes out the scene by posing, once again, the conundrum of dream and nightmare: "Am I in earth, in heaven, or in hell? / Sleeping or waking? Mad or well advised? / Known unto these, and to myself disguised!" (2.2.212–214).

Notice that Antipholus tells Dromio he is transformed "in mind," while Dromio's own attention, typically enough, is redirected to the body: "Nay, master, both in mind and in my shape" (2.2.197). It is characteristic of Shakespearean plots, especially but not exclusively in the comedies, to match sets of aristocrats or nobility with sets of servants or commoners. Typically the "high" characters experience on the level of language and the mind, metaphorically, what the "low" characters experience on the level of the body and literally. The Syracusan Dromio speaks of being transformed into an "ape" (a copy, a fool) and an "ass"; when he encounters a woman of Ephesus who claims him for her own, she is not the lady of the house but the greasy kitchen wench Nell (also called Luce), whose overwhelming physicality is comically described in the most specific and repellent terms. The Duke, at the play's close, will wonder whether all the characters have "drunk of Circe's cup" (5.1.271), alluding to the enchantress of the *Odyssey* who transforms men into swine. The implication, as so frequently in mythological transformations, is that this is a making-literal of an already existing state of affairs: the men, bewitched and seduced, are already behaving "like pigs" when they turn into them literally. So, in Shakespeare's *A Midsummer Night's Dream,* a character who behaves like an ass is transformed into one, developing long ears, a braying voice, and an appetite for sex and for hay.

"Here we wander in illusions," asserts the visiting Antipholus, Antipholus of Syracuse. Despite his sense of "wonder" he is made increasingly uneasy by what is, to him, an uncanny situation: everyone he meets seems already to know his name; they give him money, invitations, and thanks, and he is convinced that he has landed in a place of sorcery from which it is wiser to depart. One constant element of the action is his desire to leave Ephesus—a departure that would, of course, prevent him from coming face-to-face with his twin, his long-lost parents, and, ultimately, his wife-to-be Luciana, the woman who thinks she is his sister-in-law, but whom he has already described, in the play's characteristic language of identity and doubling, as "mine own self's better part" (3.2.61).

If dream, fantasy, and transformation are one end of the continuum, then the other end, the darker end, is nightmare and madness: fantasy and loss of contact with reality. As events in the topsy-turvy world of Ephesus continue to escalate, so does physical violence—the Dromios are beaten—and punishment. Adriana sends for Doctor Pinch, a skeletal quack, to cure the supposed madness of her husband. The treatment ordained for madmen, to be tied up and locked in a dark room (or, as Antipholus of Ephesus feelingly describes it, "in a dark and dankish vault" [5.1.248]), will be used again in Shakespeare's other "twin" comedy, *Twelfth Night,* where it is the self-important Malvolio who is bound and locked away. The imprisonment of the Ephesian Antipholus and Dromio is fleeting—they gnaw their bonds and seem miraculously to reappear "past thought of human reason" (5.1.190)—but the threat posed to them, and to the rule of reason and law, is real enough. Doctor Pinch, a mountebank but also a kind of Renaissance psychiatrist, looks disquietingly like a death's-head (if also like the tall, thin actor John Sincklo in Shakespeare's company, for whom parts like this were written):

> a hungry lean-faced villain,
> A mere anatomy, a mountebank,
> A threadbare juggler, and a fortune-teller,
> A needy, hollow-eyed, sharp-looking wretch,
> A living dead man. . . .
>
> *5.1.238–242*

Like the threat of death hanging over Egeon from the beginning of the play, this "living dead man," with "no face" (245), represents the danger posed to comedy itself, as well as to the specific dramatic characters we encounter. For, as we will see, the threat of death frames all Shakespearean comedy. No character we meet in the course of a play will die, but outside, just beyond the boundary of the stage, death lurks and threatens. Comedy exists in a privileged space, poised between darkness and darkness. Like the other metadramatic threats to the play's existence (the threat of premature foreclosure, if Antipholus of Syracuse were to pay the thousand marks in ransom for his countryman; the threat of premature discovery, if the two Dromios, talking to each other across a barrier, were to come face-to-face), the threat of death, the dread coming of sundown to and for the hapless Egeon, is inextricably tied to the very plot and progress of the play. Everything is scheduled to take place at five o'clock, and the time notes are sounded inexorably: morning, the two o'clock dinner hour, the appointment with the merchant and the goldsmith. Most of Shakespeare's plays pay scant attention to the supposed "unities" of time, place, and action, but in *The Comedy of Errors* all are scrupulously observed. Nothing could be more like a "unity" than a pair of separated twins constantly in danger of meeting each other—unless it is two pairs of twins. And the final "unity" is a family reunion.

One of the great structural clevernesses of this play is that the mode of farce leads the audience to have confidence in its own superior knowledge: we know there are two sets of twins, and we even know which is which. But there is of course one great secret kept from the audience, and from the readers of the First Folio, which contained no list of dramatis personae. The fact that the Abbess is Egeon's wife, and the mother of the two Antipholuses, is revealed for the first time less than a hundred lines before the end of the play. The whole of the long last act is one scene, and it ends in a series of revelations, recognitions, and failures of recognition.

Repeating the gesture of the play's first scene, the Duke proclaims that his prisoner, Egeon, can be ransomed "if any friend will pay the sum." The Duke's own compassion has been stirred, and he is looking to escape the enforcement of the too-harsh law: "He shall not die, so much we tender him." Egeon sees, or thinks he sees, his son of Syracuse in the crowd, and appeals to him for rescue, but is denied: "I never saw my father in my life," says Antipholus of Ephesus. And at this point, so dire a moment for Egeon, the Abbess enters, having taken under her protection at the priory the two men who came to her seeking sanctuary, Antipholus and Dromio of Syracuse. On the stage are all the key players, whom the action and staging have so artfully kept separate. Now the play's language returns to the spirit of wonder that animates the genre of romance. In fact, the pattern of this early comedy anticipates many of the key gestures of the late romances *Pericles, Cymbeline, The Winter's Tale,* and *The Tempest:* the family reunion, the theme of losing and finding, some revelations dramatically anticipated by the audience and others that will come as a surprise to them, and the presence of a wise figure of experience—the Abbess in this play, Paulina in *The Winter's Tale,* Cerimon in *Pericles*—who presides over the theatrical denouement. All are hallmarks of Shakespearean romance.

Although it is based on an old Roman comedy, *The Comedy of Errors* includes among its characters an abbess, who inhabits a priory probably marked with the sign of a cross. Antipholus of Syracuse casually emphasizes his strength of religious feeling by saying, "as I am a Christian, answer me" (1.2.77). We have already observed the importance of Saint Paul and his Letter to the Ephesians, both for the change of scene from Plautus's Epidamnum to Ephesus and for some of the play's sentiments about the relations between husbands and wives, masters and servants. The Christian overlay of this classical story becomes especially important toward the close when the scapegoated Egeon is pardoned by the Duke rather than ransomed according to the letter of the law:

> Antipholus of Ephesus   These ducats pawn I for my father here.
> Duke   It shall not need. Thy father hath his life.
>
>   *5.1.391–392*

The word "nativity," which of course can mean merely "birth," begins to suggest its specifically Christian associations when the Abbess announces the imagistic "rebirth" of her sons (since they have been restored to her); the "gossips' feast" of which she speaks is a christening event for godparents ("gossips"), and the period of thirty-three years she mentions—which many editors have seen as evidence of bad mathematics, in adding up the years since the shipwreck—is the traditional age of Christ at his death, and therefore, according to Thomas Aquinas, the "perfect" age that all mankind would ultimately attain after death:

> Abbess   Thirty-three years have I but gone in travail
>   Of you, my sons, and till this present hour
>   My heavy burden ne'er deliverèd.
>   The Duke, my husband, and my children both,
>   And you the calendars of their nativity,
>   Go to a gossips' feast, and joy with me.
>   After so long grief, such festivity!
>
>   *5.1.402–408*

The comic reunion of the two Dromios, which artfully lowers the tone from high romance at the close, ends on a note of "brotherhood":

> Dromio of Ephesus   We came into the world like brother and brother,
>   And now let's go hand in hand, not one before
>   another.
>
>   *5.1.426–427*

A common gesture at the end of a stage play, the exit on a rhyming couplet, here reconfirms on the level of action the tension—and ultimate harmony—

between "brother" and "another." Facing the audience, claiming their applause, they, too, are emblems of brotherly love, and a living enactment of Saint Paul's Epistle to the Hebrews:

> Let brotherly love continue. . . . Remember them that are in bonds, as bound with them; and them which suffer adversity, as being yourselves also in the body. Marriage is honourable in all. . . .
>
> *Hebrews 13:1–4*

Marriage—or the promise of marriage—is the hallmark of dramatic comedy, bondage often the prelude to freedom. *The Comedy of Errors* maps in clear and recognizable terms a pattern that we will find throughout Shakespeare: losing is finding, confusion the path to sanity; the stern edicts of the law may give way to mercy; and madness and dream offer a path to transformation.

Love's Labour's Lost

DRAMATIS PERSONAE

Ferdinand, *King of Navarre*
Berowne, *lord attending on the King*
Longueville, *lord attending on the King*
Dumaine, *lord attending on the King*
Don Adriano de Armado, *an affected Spanish braggart*
Moth, *his page*
Princess of France
Rosaline, *lady attending on the Princess*
Catherine, *lady attending on the Princess*
Maria, *lady attending on the Princess*
Boyet, *lord attending on the Princess*
Two other Lords, *attending on the Princess*
Costard, *a clown*
Jaquenetta, *a country wench*
Sir Nathaniel, *a curate*
Holofernes, *a schoolmaster*
Anthony Dull, *a constable*
Mercadé, *a messenger*
A Forester

To MODERN AUDIENCES, the title *Love's Labour's Lost* is more familiar than the play, and the characters and events may seem obscure and hard to follow, despite the famous "dancelike" rhythms of repetition, inversion, and cyclicality that mark the pattern of the plot. But this early play contains themes, embedded art forms, social laws, and character types that will recur over and over in later and better-known plays, from the idea of losing oneself to find oneself to the play-within-the-play that mirrors, and mocks, the pretensions of the aristocratic audience on and off the stage. As we will see, the play begins with a law so antisocial that it begs to be violated: young men swear together to avoid women, sex, food, and sleep so as to become wise and famous. Although the play has some resonances with actual historical events, its pleasures for an audience of onlookers or readers come from its astonishing freshness and continuing "modernity"—as so often, Shakespeare seems to have anticipated or shaped the social structures and psyches of modern life. The idea of a group of young men pretending to ignore attractive young women—and actually using this "resistance" as a kind of adolescent courtship—is one that is familiar to parents, teachers, psychologists, young people, and, indeed, to everyone who was once young. This is a characteristic Shakespearean mode, superimposing a "timeless" social observation on a "timely" set of historical references and events.

Much that audiences and readers value and admire in later plays is fully formed, and brilliantly available, here. The witty wordplay of Beatrice and Benedick, another pair of lovers resistant to being seen to be in love, in *Much Ado About Nothing;* the revealing play-within-the-play in *Hamlet* or *A Midsummer Night's Dream;* the clever balance of "low" plot and "high" plot that characterizes *Dream,* and *Henry IV Part 1;* the stark reminders that death frames human comedy and daily pleasures, a theme that will take center stage in a darker comedy like *Measure for Measure*—all of these are anticipated and played out in *Love's Labour's Lost.* It is, in fact, one of the greatest pleasures of reading Shakespeare to be able to find oneself in territory at once familiar and new.

Love's Labour's Lost begins, as do many of Shakespeare's comedies, with an inflexible law that is sure to be challenged. In this case the law is a vow, the pledge of the young King of Navarre and his high-spirited friends to forswear all fleshly temptations in quest of intellectual advancement. "Our court shall be a little academe," the King declares, "[s]till and contemplative in living art." By sequestering themselves away from the desires and appetites of the world for a period of three years, they will, he thinks, assure themselves of "fame" and therefore of a kind of eternal life.

The play's opening lines, sonorous, portentous, and, befitting their speaker, just a little pretentious, tell us what we need to know about both the plan, and the young King and his colleagues:

> King   Let fame, that all hunt after in their lives,
>   Live registered upon our brazen tombs,
>   And then grace us in the disgrace of death
>   When, spite of cormorant devouring time,
>   Th'endeavour of this present breath may buy
>   That honour which shall bate his scythe's keen edge
>   And make us heirs of all eternity.
>   Therefore, brave conquerors—for so you are,
>   That war against your own affections
>   And the huge army of the world's desires—
>   Our late edict shall strongly stand in force.
>   Navarre shall be the wonder of the world.
>   Our court shall be a little academe,
>   Still and contemplative in living art.
>   *Love's Labour's Lost 1.1.1–14*

For all of its majesty—these lines closely resemble phrases in Shakespeare's sonnets, which were written at about the same time as the play—the King's speech fairly bristles with warning signs for an alert audience. "Heirs of all eternity" is vainglorious; warring against one's own affections is always a mistake in Shakespeare's plays; edicts are peremptory and ripe for overturning, as are oaths and vows; and to be "[s]till and contemplative," while a happy idea for a work of art like a statue, is both impossible and undesirable when its constituents are living, breathing, loving, fallible human beings. All of this is established, with superb economy, in the first fourteen lines of the play, as the speech shifts from lofty generality ("Let fame . . .") to personal exhortation ("Therefore, brave conquerors—") and finally to specific instructions that are also necessary theatrical exposition for the audience, naming the others onstage and explaining the compact:

> You three—Berowne, Dumaine, and Longueville—
> Have sworn for three years' term to live with me
> My fellow scholars, and to keep those statutes
> That are recorded in this schedule here.
> Your oaths are passed. . . .
>
> *I.I.I5–I9*

The King ends by underscoring this last point: "Subscribe to your deep oaths, and keep it, too." The insistence is its own strong signal: such oaths cannot, and will not, be kept.

The device of the "little academe," which mirrors actual "Platonic" academies in fashion in the Italy and England of the day, is a characteristic Shakespearean invention, for however amusingly and ingeniously this academy is designed, it sets itself up against basic human needs and wants (love, sex, food, company, even frivolity). The academy plan is a sign that the King and his friends don't fully understand themselves or the nature of human nature, and it is thus, from the beginning, doomed to fail. Indeed, no sooner is this hightoned plan announced than titillating and disquieting news arrives: the Princess of France and her ladies are en route. Unfortunately, the courtiers have sworn never to entertain ladies on their supposedly austere scholarly premises. But immediately a loophole is found: they will meet the Princess in the field, in the open air.

Thus, with characteristic deftness, the playwright establishes the self-blindness of his earnest and lively young protagonists, and their susceptibility both to high-sounding goals (fame after death) and to intrinsic appetites (romance, love-play, and—all too soon—amateur theatricals).

From the beginning, it turns out, the King's aristocratic young friends have had their doubts. As Berowne, the genial critic and cynic among them, observes,

> O, these are barren tasks, too hard to keep—
> Not to see ladies, study, fast, not sleep.
>
> *I.I.47–48*

Furthermore, beyond the personal inconvenience of these various modes of abstinence there lies a deeper hubris, which is readily disclosed in a set of rhyming lines, batted back and forth between Berowne and the King:

Berowne   What is the end of study, let me know?
King   Why, that to know which else we should not know.
Berowne   Things hid and barred, you mean, from common sense.
King   Ay, that is study's god-like recompense.

                                                                                1.1.55–58

The tone is playful, and the rhymes make it more so, but the danger is nonetheless clear, to the audience if not to the play's characters. Though Berowne jauntily concedes ("Come on, then, I will swear to study so / To know the thing I am forbid to know" [1.1.59–60]), the quest for forbidden, "god-like" knowledge is the bane of existence for more serious and substantial Renaissance dramatic figures from Marlowe's Doctor Faustus to Shakespeare's Prospero. "God-like" is itself always a telling sign. From the beginning to the end of his dramatic career Shakespeare insists on the human place of human beings, neither god nor animal.

We learn in an artful scene of exposition that these men and women have already met, offstage, at a time before the play began. Each of the ladies has encountered one of the men, and can sing his praises. ("In Normandy saw I this Longueville. / A man of sovereign parts he is esteemed, / Well fitted in arts, glorious in arms," reports Maria, and Catherine describes "[t]he young Dumaine, a well-accomplished youth, / Of all that virtue love for virtue loved" [2.1.43–45, 56–57]. It is with some justice that the Princess exclaims mildly, "God bless my ladies, are they all in love . . . ?" [2.1.77].) The King and Princess are the ranking couple here, but the play's protagonists, the wittiest and least conventional pair of lovers, are Berowne and Rosaline, who prefigure, in their flying bouts of wordplay, the similarly witty and wonderful Beatrice and Benedick of *Much Ado About Nothing*.

As it turns out, the high-spirited young aristocrats show very little propensity for study. In addition to the schoolmaster Holofernes and his assistant, the curate Nathaniel, they have brought along with them, for amusement rather than edification, a fantastical Spaniard, Don Adriano de Armado (whose last name suggests the English sea victory over Spain in 1588); Armado's cheeky page, the boy Moth (pronounced "Mote," an allusion to his small size); and a down-to-earth clown, or rustic, Costard (the name is that of a species of apple; thus he is "Mr. Apple-Head"). Costard is one of the earliest of Shakespeare's wonderfully pragmatic "wise fools," like Bottom in *A Midsummer Night's Dream*. His earthiness stands in implicit contrast to the lofty theoretical sentiments of the King and his friends. Where the noblemen pretend, at least, to be able to ignore the prompting of desire, Costard, caught by the constable Dull in conversation with the comely dairymaid Jaquenetta in violation of the King's edict, explains: "Such is the simplicity of man to hearken after the flesh" (1.1.211–212) and "Sir, I confess the wench" (266).

Costard's simplicity and directness, and his emphasis on the body and the laws of nature, are explicitly contrasted with the ornate style of Jaquenetta's other suitor, Don Armado. Given Armado's literary propensities, it is perhaps inevitable that he expresses his love not only in a long and ludicrous love letter, written in the exaggerated "euphuistic" style, but also in a verbal exhortation:

> Assist me, some extemporal god of rhyme, for I am sure I shall turn sonnet.
> Devise wit, write pen, for I am for whole volumes, in folio.
>
> *1.2.162–164*

A folio was a large-format book, used for serious works like sermons and histories. When Shakespeare's rival Ben Jonson published his own plays in folio form in 1616, he was roundly criticized for doing so, since plays were regarded as inconsequential and trivial, unsuited for the dignity of a folio. Although Shakespeare's plays were ultimately published in folio form, after his death, the idea of love poetry belonging in a folio is a literary joke here. But far more important to *Love's Labour's Lost* is Armado's rhetorical determination to "turn sonnet," to become the author of, and indeed the walking, talking embodiment of, the standard form of Elizabethan love-longing. For to turn sonnet is the fate not only of the low, or comic, lovers in this play, but also of their supposed betters, the King and his friends. Armado's bombastic request for divine assistance, comic in its overwrought vehemence, also points toward a key theme in *Love's Labour's Lost:* the coming to life of written literary forms upon the stage.

This is a play about young lovers caught with their sonnets down—revealing, both shamefacedly and joyously, that far from obeying the King's stern and life-denying edict, they have already fallen in love, and have the poems to prove it. Don Armado and Costard thus represent the warring sides of the King and his men: preciosity and straightforwardness, decorum and crudeness, literature and life. One by one the shamefaced courtiers come forward, announce the dilemma of being in love against the vows they have sworn, and declaim sonnets they have written to their ladies. The scene unfolds brilliantly, almost itself like a sophisticated verse form, *abcd dcba*. First Berowne appears, soliloquizes about his plight, notes that he has written a sonnet to Rosaline and sent it to her, wishes the others were similarly afflicted, and then moves aside, out of sight, to be followed immediately by the King, Longueville, and Dumaine, each of them with a sonnet in hand. They read their sonnets, then hide, but overhear the next-comer. Once the last sonnet has been read, the accusations begin in reverse order, Dumaine accused by Longueville, Longueville's love unmasked by the King, and finally Berowne, who is able to accuse them of "hypocrisy" only for so long as it takes Jaquenetta and Costard to arrive.

For, in a mistake that is a prime engine of the plot, Berowne has given his sonnet to Costard to deliver to Rosaline, and Armado has given his letter to

Costard to deliver to Jaquenetta, and Costard, of course, has mixed them up
and misdelivered them. The "misdirected letter" is a staple of much stage
comedy from classical times, and it will reappear in other plays of Shakespeare,
from comedies to tragedies. But the point here, nicely made by the error of
the "natural man" Costard, is that the two kinds of love, Berowne's and Armado's, are really the same—just as the two beloveds, the dairymaid and the
highborn lady, are more same than different. In other words, Costard's mistake
is not really a mistake. This is a point for the audience, not the characters, to
appreciate; indeed, Berowne's outrage at this error is one of the many elements
of discrepant awareness—characters failing to see what the audience sees—that
is the functional viewpoint of Shakespearean comedy. Like Berowne, the audience of comedy fancies itself seated above and out of sight as the follies of others
play themselves out for its amusement. Again and again throughout his comedies, it will become clear that Shakespeare permits us this quasi-Olympian
detachment only to precipitate us into a consciousness of our own implication
in folly.

   In an extraordinarily beautiful and rhetorically powerful speech, Berowne
finds a way of rephrasing the vows the lovers have taken, locating the true "academe" inside human love and passion rather than beyond it. Love is the best
tutor, for moral as well as for aesthetic education. Other arts affect the intellect
alone:

> But love, first learnèd in a lady's eyes,
> Lives not alone immurèd in the brain,
> But with the motion of all elements
> Courses as swift as thought in every power,
> And gives to every power a double power
> Above their functions and their offices.
> It adds a precious seeing to the eye—
> A lover's eyes will gaze an eagle blind.
> A lover's ear will hear the lowest sound
> When the suspicious head of theft is stopped.
> . . . .
> And when love speaks, the voice of all the gods
> Make heaven drowsy with the harmony.
> Never durst poet touch a pen to write
> Until his ink were tempered with love's sighs.
> . . . .
> From women's eyes this doctrine I derive.
> They sparkle still the right Promethean fire.
> They are the books, the arts, the academes
> That show, contain, and nourish all the world.
>
> *4.3.301–327*

To keep the oaths they have sworn, "To fast, to study, and to see no woman," is in fact "Flat treason 'gainst the kingly state of youth" (288–289). Therefore:

> Let us once lose our oaths to find ourselves,
> Or else we lose ourselves to keep our oaths.
>
> *4.3.335–336*

This terse and elegant injunction summarizes the action in a single sentence. Marked by the rhetorical figure of chiasmus ("oaths"/"selves"/"selves"/"oaths"), Berowne's lines chart both the emotional experience of the characters and the ins and outs of the plot. In all of Shakespearean comedy there is no clearer statement of the function and purpose of a comic plot, and of its transformative effects. The familiar theme of losing oneself to find oneself resonates throughout *Love's Labour's Lost,* as it has in *The Comedy of Errors.* It is the story of Shakespearean comedy writ little, and we will encounter it again and again, in plays from *A Midsummer Night's Dream* to *The Merchant of Venice* and beyond.

Once they are past their embarrassment, the next task for the King and his friends is to woo their ladies. The device of a masque is seized upon, since it offers merriment and an opportunity for elaborate costume. Thus they trick themselves up as "Muscovites or Russians" and advance toward their chosen ladies in disguise to bestow compliments and pledges of love.

The masque becomes a farrago of failed dramatic effects: the boy Moth has been coached in a speech of prologue, but changes it as he goes along in order for it to match actual events, so that when the ladies turn their backs he edits "ever turned their eyes to mortal views" to "ever turned their backs," and "once to behold" to "not to behold." This is comical in performance, and again pertinent to the theme of the impossible ideal and the approachable real that was established in the King's opening speech. The Princess and ladies pretend that the gentlemen all speak Russian ("If they do speak our language, 'tis our will / That some plain man recount their purposes"), eliciting a set of amusing "translations" from English to English by the intermediary Boyet, a lord who attends the Princess; this device, too, finally collapses of its own weight, as, tired of the tennis match of pseudotranslation ("They say . . ."; "She says . . ."; "Say to her . . ."; "Ask them . . ."; "Tell her . . ."), he drops the pretense and steps out of the middle: "She hears herself." Again the question is one of failed language, the dangers of indirection, and the perils of communication. The men nonetheless emerge convinced that their disguises have been successful. But when the "frozen Muscovites" return, triumphant, in their own clothes and identities, they are discomfited to find that not only was their stratagem transparent, they have been tricked into making love to the wrong women. "Why look you pale?" taunts Rosaline, Berowne's beloved. "Seasick, I think, coming from Muscovy" (5.2.393–394). Here, as throughout the play, the women are far more sophisticated and wise than the men, who seem endearingly puppylike and constantly on the verge of further making fools of themselves.

It is at this point that Berowne delivers another important speech, this one abjuring artifice, whether in costume, rhetoric, poetry, or courtly compliment:

> O, never will I trust to speeches penned,
>   Nor to the motion of a schoolboy's tongue,
> Nor never come in visor to my friend,
>   Nor woo in rhyme, like a blind harper's song.
> Taffeta phrases, silken terms precise,
>   Three-piled hyperboles, spruce affectation,
> Figures pedantical—these summer flies
>   Have blown me full of maggot ostentation.
> I do forswear them, and I here protest,
>   By this white glove—how white the hand, God knows!—
> Henceforth my wooing mind shall be expressed
>   In russet yeas, and honest kersey noes.
> And to begin, wench, so God help me, law!
> My love to thee is sound, sans crack or flaw.

5.2.402–415

"Sans 'sans,' I pray you," remarks the unimpressed Rosaline, noting that Berowne uses the very kind of artifice he purports to forswear by ending his impassioned plea in affected French. Russet and kersey are coarse cloth, to be contrasted with the taffeta and silk of fancy phrases. But we might note that Berowne's artful praise of artlessness is offered in the form of a sonnet (fourteen lines in the "Shakespearean" form, three quatrains and a couplet, the last lines of which seem to parody others' naive country language). As he ruefully acknowledges, he has "a trick / Of the old rage" yet.

When the ladies' deception is disclosed, the men see the extent of their own mistake:

> Berowne   The ladies did change favours, and then we,
>   Following the signs, wooed but the sign of she.
>   Now, to our perjury to add more terror,
>   We are again forsworn, in will and error.

5.2.468–471

The mistaken favors are yet another indication of the superficiality of the men's love choices. The King thinks Rosaline is the Princess ("I knew her by the jewel on her sleeve") and has to be told by his beloved that he has romanced the wrong woman, since Rosaline is wearing his love token, and the Princess wears, instead, a pearl given to Rosaline by Berowne. (Princess: "Pardon me, sir, *this* jewel did she wear, / And Lord Berowne, I thank him, is my dear.") In short, the men have mistaken an outer appearance for an inner reality. If this moral needs further pointing, it receives it from the inadvertently hilarious pageant of the "Nine Worthies," in which the play's lowliest characters, from unlettered swain to literary scholar, take upon themselves the personages of heroes.

For after the rigors of courtship the young people are ready to be entertained, and Armado has been asked by his employer, the King, to provide "some delightful ostentation, or show, or pageant, or antic, or firework" (5.1.94–95). The schoolmaster Holofernes has the perfect topic: a pageant of the "Nine Worthies," nine celebrated heroes from the past, traditionally three each from the Bible, the classics, and romance. This is a common theme for Renaissance court entertainments, but it happens also to match, with unerring and devastating appropriateness, the King's opening panegyric to "fame, that all hunt after in their lives." Since the "Worthies" will be played by Holofernes, Armado, Nathaniel, and Costard (each, for reasons of economy, taking upon himself several parts), with a cameo from Moth as the infant Hercules ("Hercules in minority"), the question of heroism and greatness is ripe for a fall. (Berowne characterizes the cast as "[t]he pedant, the braggart, the hedge-priest, the fool, and the boy" [5.2.536].) The King is reluctant to allow this performance to go on, for fear of embarrassment, though Berowne notes feelingly that it will be good to have "one show worse than the King's and his company" (510). But it falls to the Princess to offer a word of generous acceptance, which resonates beyond the immediate circumstances: "That sport best pleases that doth least know how" (512).

As with the "Pyramus and Thisbe" play in *A Midsummer Night's Dream,* an onstage audience of aristocratic lovers watches a mythological version of their own story, and fails to see the similarity so glaringly evident to the audience in the theater. Costard plays Pompey, whom he calls "the Big," only to be corrected by his noble audience. His acknowledgment, "I made a little fault in 'great,' " is ready-made to be turned back on the ambitions of the King and court. When the hapless country curate, Nathaniel, entrusted with the role of Alexander the Great, stumbles on his lines (deliberately written in old-fashioned twelve-syllable verse, not in "modern" iambic pentameter), he is dismissed, in a classic put-down, as "a marvellous good neighbour, faith, and a very good bowler, but for Alisander—alas, you see how 'tis—a little o'erparted" (5.2.572–574). By structuring his play with "high" and "low" plots that mirror each other, Shakespeare is able to poke fun at the pretenses of the characters in the former and to cede the moral high ground to those in the latter. It is entirely characteristic of him that he should put the most ethically reproving remark of the play into the mouth of the character who is arguably his most ridiculous, Holofernes the pedant. When Holofernes finds himself mocked by the courtly audience in the course of the pageant, he turns to them, and to us, with a sorrowful rebuke: "This is not generous, not gentle, not humble" (5.2.617). A modern audience, like its Shakespearean counterpart, might well feel the sting.

The discomfiture of Nathaniel, and the derisive laughter of most of the onstage audience, cannot quite conceal that these noble "worthies," too, are "a little o'erparted," not up to the heroic "conquering" tasks outlined in their collective quest for fame and the defeat of death. Indeed, death itself will intervene by the end of the play, with the arrival of a messenger who reveals that the King of France, the Princess's father, has died—an announcement that interrupts the pageant and points toward the close of *Love's Labour's Lost*. The announcement itself is brilliantly presented, in this play of words and wordiness, as a necessary failure of language:

> Mercadé   I am sorry, madam, for the news I bring
>   Is heavy in my tongue. The King your father—
> Princess   Dead, for my life.
> Mercadé   Even so. My tale is told.

> 5.2.701–703

Reminders of death, in fact, come thick and fast at the end of *Love's Labour's Lost*. In what would seem to be an otherwise lighthearted moment we hear that the lady Catherine had a sister who died of love. This history is not stressed, as the ladies turn their attention immediately to the pleasures of the present moment, but the shadow of death is there. In the pageant of the "Nine Worthies" poor Holofernes the pedant is called a memento mori, "a death's face in a ring" (601).

The play is thus framed by intimations of mortality. The offstage death of the King of France (a personage already described in the first scene of the play as "decrepit, sick, and bedrid" [1.1.136]) is a hallmark of Shakespearean comedy, for these comedies are consistently bounded by tragedy and loss, just beyond the horizon of the play. Likewise, it is a fact of life—and a law of genre—in Shakespeare's comedies that no character we actually meet in a play will die, though many are threatened. Deaths do occur, but they occur offstage. The reports of such deaths may alter the course of the drama, as they do here. The pageant comes to an abrupt end ("Worthies, away. The scene begins to cloud," says Berowne), the King offers condolences in so high a style that the Princess says she cannot understand him ("Honest plain words best pierce the ear of grief," Berowne comments, having learned his own lesson by way of "sans 'sans' "), and the ladies command their lovers to a "trial" of a year and a day. The pleasure-loving King is to exchange his gaudy academy for "some forlorn and naked hermitage / Remote from all the pleasures of the world" (5.2.777–778), and the wordy Berowne, who has played with language throughout, a man "replete with mocks, / Full of comparisons and wounding flouts," is sentenced by his ladylove Rosaline to "jest a twelvemonth in an hospital" to prove his devotion, visiting "the speechless sick." He protests:

> To move wild laughter in the throat of death?—
> It cannot be, it is impossible.

> 5.2.832–833

But Rosaline's answer is quick and sure: this is the way for Berowne to learn that

> A jest's prosperity lies in the ear
> Of him that hears it, never in the tongue
> Of him that makes it. . . .
>
> *5.2.838–840*

A good lesson for actors as well as lovers.

Although it is conventional to say that comedy ends in marriage, Shakespearean comedy seldom does. Instead it ends in the promise of a marriage, to take place at some time subsequent to the playing time and space of the play, after the lovers have proven themselves worthy. This same pattern occurs again and again, in plays like *Much Ado About Nothing, Twelfth Night,* and *Measure for Measure.* The "truth" of these young lovers' loves is guaranteed in the plot by the fact that each pair has met and been attracted before the play begins, so that the appealing romantic notion of "love at first sight" is buttressed by assurance that these loves are of longer duration. But the errors displayed in the Muscovite scene, the failure of each man to distinguish his real beloved, and the lively scorn with which the men treat lesser characters like Holofernes and Nathaniel, lead on to the deliberate deferral of marriage for a year and a day. "That's too long for a play," Berowne comments feelingly.

The question of nature and what is natural in human life and love has been matched throughout the play by an insistent reminder of the seasonal calendar. Berowne, with his initial objections to the plan of study and abstinence set forth by the King, is compared to an untimely blast of cold air: "Berowne is like an envious sneaping frost, / That bites the first-born infants of the spring" (1.1.100–101). But he responds with a vigorous defense of the natural round:

> Well, say I am! Why should proud summer boast
> Before the birds have any cause to sing?
> Why should I joy in any abortive birth?
> At Christmas I no more desire a rose
> Than wish a snow in May's new-fangled shows,
> But like of each thing that in season grows.
>
> *1.1.102–107*

It is the King's plan that is untimely, because it fails to understand the lively spirits of youth, and the propensities for sex, courtship, and play. In a culture far more seasonally dependent than our own, the pattern of nature is taken as more than a powerful metaphor. The blending here of the cycle of the seasons and the religious calendar, from Christmas to the pagan festival of May, marks the appropriateness of time, change, and even death. The attempt to stop time or to alter the seasons will always be, for Shakespeare, a sign of a resistance to what is human.

And in this extremely well-designed play, the same note of temporality, stressed in the first hundred lines of the play, will be struck again at the close, with the songs of the owl and the cuckoo, or Winter (Hiems) and Spring (Ver). Both songs are delightful, and are frequently anthologized; each emphasizes ambivalence as well as pleasure, pleasure as well as ambivalence. In the spring, when "daisies pied and violets blue" all "paint the meadows with delight," the cuckoo mocks married men with his song, which presages cuckoldry. In the winter, when "icicles hang by the wall," the owl sings his "merry note."

The song of winter, like a Brueghel painting, sketches a domestic scene of common life. "Dick the shepherd blows his nail" against the cold, "Tom bears logs into the hall," "Marian's nose looks red and raw." These are all genre characters, summoned from the observation of everyday life in the country, not the court. None of them, or indeed anyone like them, appears in the play, though they might well be found in the audience among the groundlings. But the refrain line of the song of winter, "While greasy Joan doth keel the pot," does have its echoes earlier in the play. For the audience has heard Berowne, in acknowledging his passion for Rosaline, declare, when he is alone at the end of act 3,

> Well, I will love, write, sigh, pray, sue, groan:
> Some men must love my lady, and some Joan.
>
> *3.1.189–190*

Shortly afterward, in denying to the King and his friends that he was in love, as they were, Berowne had insisted no man had ever seen him "write a thing in rhyme" or heard him "groan for Joan"—only to be discomfited when Jaquenetta arrived bearing his letter, written in rhyme, to Rosaline. "Joan" here means the beloved of the common man, the opposite of "my lady," and would have called to mind the proverbial saying "Joan is as good as my lady." That Shakespeare's play begins with the King, and ends with greasy Joan, will give some sense both of his confident and evocative range of social reference, and of his already remarkable command of the playwright's craft.

This is a play that reads "hard" and plays "easy." What makes *Love's Labour's Lost* difficult going for some readers is the topical humor and the banter and baiting among the "low" characters, many of whom are figures of literary and scholarly pretension—schoolmasters, pedants, curates, fantastics. Its comic and satirical targets include small-minded scholars and braggart soldiers, fond of abstruse quotations, Latin in-jokes, and high-minded smuttiness of a schoolboy kind (jokes on flatulence and erection, on women's anatomy and sexuality). This is a young man's play, full of the love of life, impatient with merely "academic" ideas about beauty and desire. The learned jokers, then, are in part there to be laughed at. When the pedant Holofernes launches into a learned, Latinate critique of the local constable, his sycophantic sidekick, Nathaniel the curate, observes dismissively that Dull "hath never fed of the dainties that are bred in a book. / He hath not eat paper, as it were, he hath not drunk ink" (4.2.21–22). Some of the funniest moments in *Love's Labour's Lost* result from this deliberate "confusion" of genres, when the playwright has his characters speak out loud, as if quite naturally, words and phrases designed for reading with the eye rather than hearing with the ear. It is as if a modern lawyer should talk at dinner about the "party of the first part," or as if a television reporter were to recite out loud the punctuation marks as well as the words in a news story.

Thus Holofernes is harshly critical of Armado for failing to pronounce the *b* in "debt," the *l* in "calf," and the guttural *gh* in "neighbor." There is a long jest about the Princess's archery, in which she is said to be hunting a pricket, or young deer, with many heavy puns on "shooter" and "suitor." Holofernes' poem on the topic exhibits the outmoded literary practice of "hunting the letter," or excessive alliteration ("The preyful Princess pierced and pricked a pretty pleasing pricket" [4.2.52]). But part of the humor here is that "hunting the deer," or "dear," is a commonplace figure in love poetry, with the male lover as the hunter and the lady as the "deer." (See, for example, Sir Thomas Wyatt's contemporary sonnet on Anne Boleyn, which begins, "Whoso list to hunt, I know where is an hind.") In Shakespeare's brilliant cartoon of literariness-come-to-life, not only is the hunt literal, but it is the lady who is the shooter/suitor. In one of the most famous comic incidents of the play, the rustic Costard, given a coin by Armado in payment for the delivery of his letter to Jaquenetta, misunderstands Armado's grandiose "There is remuneration" and thinks "remuneration" is the Latin word for "three-farthings" (3.1.126). Moments later, when Berowne tips him a shilling for the same errand, delivering a letter to a lady, saying "there's thy guerdon," Costard puts together what he has learned: a guerdon is "better than remuneration, elevenpence-farthing better" (3.1.156–157). Holofernes and Nathaniel the curate bandy bad Latin and Greek tags back and forth, speaking to each other as if they were living inside Erasmus's colloquies, and applying these lofty terms to the trivial details of everyday life. The page boy Moth's aside to Costard, "They have been at a great feast of languages and stolen the scraps" (5.1.34–35), is a good-humored indictment not only of the pseudo-learned characters in the play or of their historical Elizabethan models, but of all those who allude to the authority of written texts, including the playwright.

For Shakespeare and his audience many of the classical quotations and grammatical niceties would have been familiar stuff, since the references come from set texts in the grammar school curriculum. These learned fellows, in other words, are not particularly learned, though what they know, and boast of knowing, seems arcane to us. Modern scholars have to a certain extent fallen into the trap, debating whether Holofernes is a figure for the poet Gabriel Harvey, for example, or Armado for pamphleteer and dramatist Thomas Nashe, or whether a throwaway reference to "the school of night" in the Quarto (4.3.251) is related to Sir Walter Ralegh's secret philosophical academy of that name.

Undoubtedly, political, philosophical, and literary disputes were animating the London scene at that time—as they do in every age and place. But the play's virtues and successes are not based upon any such antiquarian lore. In the tension between those who eat paper and drink ink and those who hearken after the flesh, the playwright, in this play as in others, will choose a middle way.

In the theater *Love's Labour's Lost* can be a delight, since it is wonderfully well structured, with two sets of lovers (again, characteristically for Shakespeare, one "high," or aristocratic, the other "low"); superbly funny comic characters who regularly make fools of themselves when they are striving to be serious, and a plot that involves the writing and declaiming of bad poetry (always a hit onstage); a fancy-dress masque in which the French lords pretend to be visitors from exotic Moscow; and a play-within-the-play in which the overawed commoners who do the acting forget their lines, omit necessary punctuation (thus reversing the sense), and generally expose the limits of the theater itself as a place of persuasive illusion and uplifting moral instruction. As we have seen, the play abounds with moments of self-reference, like Berowne's wounded remonstrance after the ladies replace the King's edict with their own:

> Our wooing doth not end like an old play.
> Jack hath not Jill. These ladies' courtesy
> Might well have made our sport a comedy.
>
> *5.2.851–853*

The final stage moment, perhaps fittingly, is given to Don Armado, the King's master of ceremonies and producer of pageants. Pronouncing his benediction after the songs of Spring and Winter, Armado for once abjures a moral: "The words of Mercury are harsh after the songs of Apollo. You that way, we this way" (5.2.903–904). Scholars have puzzled over the meaning of this stage direction, which occurs only in the First Folio edition of the play. Does it mean to separate the ladies from the men, or the audience from the actors, or Armado and his "wench" Jaquenetta from the other onstage pairs of lovers? All of these are possible and plausible. What is worth our noting is that the last figure onstage is a stage manager and director, and that in seeming to choose song over language, he in fact does the reverse.

One of the many remarkable pleasures of Shakespearean comedy, as of Shakespeare's plays in general, is the way each play can be situated simultaneously in the past and in the present, in the time of Shakespeare the Elizabethan playwright and the time of Shakespeare the uncanny commentator on modern life. "You that way, we this way" could be understood as pointing toward the past and the always changing future, regardless of what the playwright—or his fellow actors—may have intended by those enigmatic final words.

Romeo and Juliet

Chorus
Romeo
Montague, *his father*
Montague's Wife
Benvolio, *Montague's nephew*
Abraham, *Montague's servingman*
Balthasar, *Romeo's man*
Juliet
Capulet, *her father*
Capulet's Wife
Tybalt, *her nephew*
His page
Petruchio
Capulet's Cousin
Juliet's Nurse
Peter, *servingman of the Capulets*
Samson, *servingman of the Capulets*

Gregory, *servingman of the Capulets*
Other Servingmen
Musicians
Escalus, *Prince of Verona*
Mercutio, *kinsman of Escalus*
County Paris, *kinsman of Escalus*
Page to Paris
Friar Laurence
Friar John
An Apothecary
Chief Watchman
Other Citizens of the Watch
Masquers, guests, gentlewomen, followers of the Montague and Capulet factions

FROM THE OPENING moments of *The Most Excellent and Lamentable Tragedy of Romeo and Juliet* the audience is made aware that there is something seriously wrong in the play's world. The Chorus who speaks the prologue uses a literary form that was traditional for love poetry, the sonnet. Yet the content of the sonnet, however Petrarchan in its use of verbal oppositions and repetitions, is both political and deeply disquieting:

> Two households, both alike in dignity
>   In fair Verona, where we lay our scene,
> From ancient grudge break to new mutiny,
>   Where civil blood makes civil hands unclean.
>   *Romeo and Juliet 1.1.1–4*

No sooner have we heard this sonnet through, with its literary references to "[a] pair of star-crossed lovers" (1.1.6) and the "two-hours' traffic of our stage" (1.1.12) that will be the actual theatrical playing time, than on the stage appear two pairs of quarreling servants, Samson and Gregory, Abraham and Balthasar, and what had a moment before seemed a pretty piece of poetry erupts into a full-scale civil war on the streets of Verona. Samson makes the rude gesture sometimes known as the "fig of Spain," or as "giving the fig," thrusting his thumb between two closed fingers or into his mouth, an early modern version of an equally rude hand gesture popular today. Notice that the "civil hands" of the sonnet have already become very uncivil, and anatomically explicit, fingers:

> Abraham   Do you bite your thumb at us, sir?
> Samson   I do bite my thumb, sir.
> Abraham   Do you bite your thumb at us, sir? . . .
> Samson   No, sir, I do not bite my thumb at you, sir, but I bite my
>   thumb, sir.
>
> *1.1.39–45*

Obviously, pretty poetry and formal sonnets cannot contain this kind of anarchic energy and disorder. The sonnet prologues that introduce and frame act 1 and act 2 will have disappeared by the beginning of act 3. "Reality" in the form of death and loss overtakes literary artifice, and the play is forced, early on, to acknowledge its own tragic shape, which stylized language cannot contain.

Over and over in the first few acts we encounter lines like this: "Where civil blood makes civil hands unclean"; "My only love sprung from my only hate"; "These violent delights have violent ends"; "Tempering extremity with extreme sweet." These are the building blocks of Petrarchism: antithesis and paradox, once powerfully original, but by the time of the writing of Shakespeare's play already subsiding into the territory of cliché. Love and hate. Delight and violence. Extremity and extreme sweet. Once again, as with the Chorus's opening sonnet, the poetry is pretending that it can control contradiction and disorder. Throughout *Romeo and Juliet* artificiality in language will be a sign of lack of self-knowledge, a failure to acknowledge what is wrong in Verona—all the way to the County Paris's final and futile rhyming speech at Juliet's tomb. This kind of balanced line—"My only love sprung from my only hate"—will also disappear as the play turns the corner toward tragedy, with the fateful death of Mercutio in the third act, the middle of the play and its fulcrum. But disorder is present from the beginning. Even old Capulet, lame and feeble, tries to propel himself into the action:

> Capulet   What noise is this? Give me my long sword, ho!
> Capulet's Wife   A crutch, a crutch—why call you for a sword?
>   *Enter old* MONTAGUE [*with his sword drawn*], *and his* WIFE
> Capulet   My sword, I say. Old Montague is come,
>   And flourishes his blade in spite of me.
>
> *1.1.68–71*

The audience is confronted with the ludicrous spectacle of two old men, vainly flailing long-swords at each other while each is held back by his wife. Age pretending to be youth: "A crutch, a crutch—why call you for a sword?" Lady Capulet is clearly casting doubt on her husband's martial—and perhaps his marital—swordsmanship. In this play as in so many others of the period a capacity to handle one's sword is—hundreds of years before Freud—seen as a sign of manliness. For other examples, consider Falstaff's bawdy joking in *1 Henry IV,* Viola/Cesario's terror at the idea of a swordfight with the equally terrified Sir Andrew Aguecheek in *Twelfth Night,* and Lady Macbeth's scornful "Infirm of purpose! / Give me the daggers."

Moreover, this is not the first fight between these two houses. As Prince Escalus, the voice of law in Verona, declares,

> Three civil brawls bred of an airy word
> By thee, old Capulet, and Montague,
> Have thrice disturbed the quiet of our streets
> And made Verona's ancient citizens
> Cast by their grave-beseeming ornaments
> To wield old partisans in hands as old,
> Cankered with peace, to part your cankered hate.
>
> *1.1.82–88*

Partisans were nine-foot-long spears, but the spear-wielders are also "partisans," factionaries in an ongoing dispute.

Escalus, although in title a prince, occupies a structural place analogous to that of the Duke in plays like *The Comedy of Errors* or *A Midsummer Night's Dream.* He ordains and enforces a law that is inflexible and will lead, potentially, to tragedy. His name, an unusual one for Shakespeare, is surely intended to call to mind the Greek playwright Aeschylus, the author of the *Oresteia,* the story of the fall of the House of Atreus, a warring family's rise and catastrophic fall. The law this Escalus now proclaims is a response to the "[t]hree civil brawls" that have disturbed the city streets: in order to keep peace and order in Verona, public fighting will now be crime punishable by death. Thus *Romeo and Juliet,* like many of Shakespeare's plays, begins with an edict, a stern attempt to create order through an unbending law. As in so many cases, especially in the comedies, this law will lead not to order but to a new and more sweeping kind of disorder. Its repressiveness will backfire, just as the King of Navarre's no-girls-allowed rule backfired in *Love's Labour's Lost.* In *Romeo and Juliet,* however, the stern law and its consequences will lead to tragedy.

Nor is disorder present only in the streets. Both Romeo and Juliet themselves are forced to confront a kind of internal disorder, a failure of self-knowledge, represented in the play by the initial love-pairings: Romeo and Rosaline, Juliet and Paris. Romeo's love for Rosaline, as extravagantly performed in the early moments of the play, is really a kind of parody of Petrarchism, a deliberate onstage caricature of the sonnet-writing, lovesick, moon-struck lover who places his lady on a pedestal, and is really in love either with the idea of love or, even more acutely, with the idea of himself as a lover. Romeo's language makes this clear, as he spouts a "Petrarchan" sonnet that could have been produced by rote:

> Here's much to do with hate, but more with love.
> Why then, O brawling love, O loving hate,
> O anything of nothing first create;
> O heavy lightness, serious vanity,
> Misshapen chaos of well-seeming forms,
> Feather of lead, bright smoke, cold fire, sick health,
> Still-waking sleep, that is not what it is!
>
> *1.1.168–174*

This is the language of Petrarchan formula, empty paradoxes and oxymorons— cold fire, sick health—stale poetic images that say nothing and mean nothing. When Romeo falls in love with Juliet, his language changes, and becomes sharply inventive, witty, and original. It is then that Mercutio will recognize him as "himself" again: "Now art thou sociable, now art thou Romeo, now art thou what thou art by art as well as by nature" (2.3.77–78). The Romeo who moons after Rosaline is hardly sociable. He is not even out brawling with his friends in the streets of Verona, because he has chosen, instead, to wander in the woods alone, "[w]ith tears augmenting the fresh morning's dew, / Adding to clouds more clouds with his deep sighs" (1.1.125–126). All for love of Rosaline. "Thou chidd'st me oft for loving Rosaline," he will later say to Friar Laurence, and the Friar will respond, "For doting, not for loving, pupil mine." "Dote" is an important word, especially for the early Shakespeare; throughout the plays it means to be infatuated, or foolishly in love, or in love with the idea of love. From the same root as the word meaning "to take a nap," "dote" is a term of emotional excess or folly. Romeo dotes on Rosaline; he will behave quite differently when he falls in love with Juliet.

In fact, in this very symmetrically designed play, the difference between doting and loving is a principal reason why we are first shown Romeo infatuated with someone other than Juliet. Doting on Rosaline, Romeo, in the imitable pattern of Petrarchan lovers, is comfortable only in the dark. When dawn comes he "[s]huts up his windows, locks fair daylight out, / And makes himself an artificial night" (1.132–133). Artifice is "art," but it is also make-believe—this is an artificial night for an artificial love. We never learn much about Rosaline. She is glimpsed, once, at the Capulet ball, but she is not a dramatic character in the play: she has no lines, she is all Romeo's projection. Like many a fantasied Petrarchan lady she has "sworn that she will still live chaste" (1.1.210)— that she will die a virgin and without progeny, another dangerous sign in a

Shakespearean world concerned with procreation and fertility. By contrast, Juliet's refusal near the end of the play to be "disposed of" in a sisterhood of holy nuns marks a choice against the nunnery and for marriage and marital love.

Balancing the false pair of Romeo and Rosaline is the equally inappropriate couple of Juliet and Paris, a pairing that is artificial for a different reason. It seems almost as if Juliet has never set eyes on Paris, even though they live in the same town. His proposal is brought to her by her mother, in the form of rhyming couplets that function almost like the portrait borne by an ambassador in a royal marriage by proxy when the parties live in distant countries. Here, of course, the practice is pointless, and therefore comic. The passage is certainly one of the most gloriously artificial of the play, as Lady Capulet describes Paris as a good book, for whom Juliet will be the "cover":

> Read o'er the volume of young Paris' face,
> And find delight writ there with beauty's pen.
> Examine every married lineament,
> And see how one another lends content;
> And what obscured in this fair volume lies
> Find written in the margin of his eyes.
> This precious book of love, this unbound lover,
> To beautify him only lacks a cover.
>
> *1.3.83–90*

Juliet's lukewarm reply, "I'll look to like, if looking liking move," seems perfectly suitable in the face of this rather daunting description, which is not really the description of a person at all.

Romeo and Rosaline, Juliet and Paris. The hackneyed language of Petrarchan clichés, on the one hand, and the ornate, bloodless, and perfectly rhyming couplets of Lady Capulet's favorable book report, on the other. Everything will be shattered when Romeo and Juliet first catch sight of each other. It is important to acknowledge that love at first sight is a common phenomenon in the Shakespearean world, and not something to distrust. Like the famous couples of Dante and Beatrice, Petrarch and Laura, whose glances met and held, so Shakespearean lovers from Romeo and Juliet to Ferdinand and Miranda in *The Tempest* meet, exchange glances, and fall in love. Significantly, in *Romeo and Juliet* they do so in a sonnet, and it is a sonnet that ends sonneteering for the rest of the play:

Romeo   [*to* JULIET, *touching her hand*]
        If I profane with my unworthiest hand
          This holy shrine, the gentler sin is this:
        My lips, two blushing pilgrims, ready stand

	To smooth that rough touch with a tender kiss.
Juliet	Good pilgrim, you do wrong your hand too much,
	Which mannerly devotion shows in this.
	For saints have hands that pilgrims' hands do touch,
	And palm to palm is holy palmers' kiss.
Romeo	Have not saints lips, and holy palmers, too?
Juliet	Ay, pilgrim, lips that they must use in prayer.
Romeo	O then, dear saint, let lips do what hands do:
	They pray; grant thou, lest faith turn to despair.
Juliet	Saints do not move, though grant for prayers' sake.
Romeo	Then move not while my prayer's effect I take.
	[*He kisses her*]

1.5.90–103

Her response when he kisses her is "You kiss by th' book"—a better book, apparently, than Paris's. This is a most unusual sonnet, in that it is spoken by two people, and thus breaks the convention of the love sonnet of the adoring lover who writes of, and to, his beloved because he cannot reach her in person, whether because she is married to someone else, or because she insists (like Rosaline) on remaining chaste, or, as in the case of Petrarch's later sonnets to Laura, because she is dead. *Love's Labour's Lost* offers some especially comic instances of what happens when this convention is broken—when a fretting lover is overheard by his lady as he rehearses or composes his sonnet. In *Romeo and Juliet,* by contrast, we have a sonnet that is mutually composed by the two lovers, and, moreover, a sonnet that *works*. It results in a kiss. The sonnet tradition of unattainable or unrequited love is turned inside out, and the artifice of conventional language goes with it. This is love at first sonnet.

When Romeo first catches sight of Juliet his language seems all at once transformed: "O, she doth teach the torches to burn bright! / It seems she hangs upon the cheek of night / As a rich jewel in an Ethiope's ear— / Beauty too rich for use, for earth too dear" (1.5.41–44). Again and again throughout the play this image of brilliant light against the darkness will appear as the emblem or leitmotif of the two young lovers caught in a tragic pattern. Thus Romeo will say of Juliet's tomb that "her beauty makes / This vault a feasting presence full of light" (5.3.85–86). In the balcony scene he says, "her eye in heaven / Would through the airy region stream so bright / That birds would sing and think it were not night" (2.1.62–64). In this charming hypothetical image is contained the gist of the aubade, or dawn, scene, in which the lovers will debate whether the singer is, as Juliet vainly insists, "the nightingale, and not the lark," the night bird rather than the bird of morning. Is it day, and time to go about the deadly daily business of civil strife, or still what Juliet will call "love-performing night"?

Juliet	Wilt thou be gone? It is not yet near day.
	It was the nightingale, and not the lark,

That pierced the fear-full hollow of thine ear.
Nightly she sings on yon pom'granate tree.
Believe me, love, it was the nightingale.

Romeo   It was the lark, the herald of the morn,
No nightingale. Look, love, what envious streaks
Do lace the severing clouds in yonder east.
Night's candles are burnt out, and jocund day
Stands tiptoe on the misty mountain tops.
I must be gone and live, or stay and die.

Juliet   Yon light is not daylight; I know it, I.

3.5.1–12

The language of light in darkness is not merely decorative; instead it is fraught with danger, even when it seems most benign. Juliet says of Romeo, "when I shall die / Take him and cut him out in little stars, / And he will make the face of heaven so fine / That all the world will be in love with night / And pay no worship to the garish sun" (3.2.21–25). Hers is an innocently violent image, and one that points forward to the play's final lines, when the sun does not dare show its head for shame at what has occurred. The same can be said of what would come to be a very frequent image in the Shakespeare plays of this period, Juliet's comparison of their love to a flash of lightning: "It is too rash, too unadvised, too sudden, / Too like the lightning which doth cease to be / Ere one can say it lightens" (2.1.160–162). Night is the interior world—in this case not spatial but temporal—of *Romeo and Juliet,* a middle world of transformation and dream sharply contrasted to the harsh daylight world of law, civil war, and banishment. Night will be the setting for all the play's crucial private moments, moments of tragedy and love: the masque at Capulet's feast; the balcony scene in the orchard; the aubade scene, after the lovers have spent the night together; and the final night, the final darkness of Romeo's visit to Juliet's tomb, his fight with the County Paris, and his death. This is all the more striking when we recall that plays written for the public theater, like *Romeo and Juliet*—which was first presented at the Curtain, and after 1599 at the Globe—were performed in full daylight, in the middle of the afternoon. The sense of foreboding night and pervasive blackness is conjured up entirely by and through language, with the assistance of a few well-placed props and costumes: a lantern, a candle, a nightdress. Night, that is to say, is a state of theater, and a state of mind.

The play is built on such oppositions (light/darkness) just as it is built on the opposition between realistic prose (the language of the Nurse and some speeches of Mercutio) and formal verse (the sonnet prologues and the rhyming couplets favored by Paris—and by Lady Capulet when she is describing him). The central political fact of the plot, the feud between the Montagues and the Capulets, also furnishes the underlying structural pattern that governs theme, image, and language throughout the play. Opposites feud with one another: night and day, darkness and light—and youth and age.

The daylight world of law is also a world of books and authorities and rigid rules of conduct, and the conflict of generations is a crucial one for *Romeo and Juliet,* related to the familiar pattern of justice versus mercy, law versus grace, a pattern memorably articulated in this play by the Friar as he gathers herbs from his garden: "Two such opposèd kings encamp them still / In man as well as herbs—grace and rude will"(2.2.27–28). We have already seen the rude will of old Capulet, foolishly rushing out into the street to join the brawl, shouting for his long-sword. We will later hear him lay down the law to Juliet, threatening to banish her from his house if she does not marry Paris—a banishment that would exactly parallel the banishment already inflicted on Romeo, and one that carries more than a hint of the wrath of an angry God, or a man who thinks he has the power of an angry God. Her father will banish Juliet to the world of experience, the world of fall and redemption.

Just as the play provides Romeo with Rosaline, and Juliet with Paris, as signs of what they do not yet know about themselves and about love, so also each has an older adviser, whose assistance and hindrance will together demonstrate the limits of "wise counsel." Juliet has her Nurse; Romeo has Friar Laurence. Juliet's Nurse is one of the great comic characters of all literature, and her brilliant and funny colloquial speeches illustrate Shakespeare's mastery over the medium of realistic prose. In the opening scenes of the play the Nurse's earthiness and practicality, as well as her frankness in sexual matters, offer a welcome antidote to the artifice, false idealism, and even prissiness embodied in Lady Capulet's advocacy of Paris. The Nurse swears by her maidenhead—as it was, intact, when she was twelve years old. She is secretly delighted by Mercutio's remark that "the bawdy hand of the dial is now upon the prick of noon," even as she pretends to be insulted by his innuendo. Her sense of insult is itself physical, titillated by innuendo: "Now, afore God, I am so vexed that every part about me quivers." And her long comic narrative about Juliet's fall as a child, a narrative that turns on her late husband's labored sexual quip ("dost thou fall upon thy face? / Thou wilt fall backward when thou hast more wit"), shows her at her most amusingly and inconsequentially garrulous; the point of her anecdote seems to be to prove to Lady Capulet that Juliet is almost fourteen years old, something Lady Capulet has just said to the Nurse (1.3.13). The proper Lady Capulet and the young Juliet of these opening scenes are embarrassed by the Nurse's bawdiness, and they try to hush her ("Enough of this. I pray thee hold thy peace"). The audience is more likely to be pleased by the volubility and sexual frankness of this forthright descendant of the Wife of Bath.

Yet the Nurse is a dangerously static character who does not change in the course of the drama. Like the Friar, she is established as a fixed type, and since she does not grow and change, while Juliet does, we can see at once her charm in a comic world, and her inadequacy for the darker world of tragedy. Like the optical test in which the same color looks different against a light background and a dark one, so the Nurse is framed—and assessed—differently in the two halves of the play. Shakespeare shows this to us in two deliberately parallel scenes, one comic, one tragic, in both of which Juliet tries to get information out of the weary and rambling Nurse. (The device is parallel to the two contrasting wooing scenes in *Richard III,* where Richard's early success with the Lady Anne is not repeated when he tries the same approach a second time—aiming to marry the daughter of his brother Clarence—and his suit is rejected.)

In the case of Juliet and her Nurse, the first of these twin scenes, clearly in the comic mode, comes in act 2. The information Juliet wants is a message from Romeo, and it takes her fifty lines to get it. The Nurse arrives panting and complaining that she is out of breath, to find Juliet fretting about her absence: "How art thou out of breath when thou hast breath / To say to me that thou art out of breath? / The excuse that thou dost make in this delay / Is longer than the tale thou dost excuse. / Is thy news good or bad?" (2.4.31–35). The message, when it is finally delivered, is a happy one, suited to romantic comedy: "hie you hence to Friar Laurence's cell. / There stays a husband to make you a wife" (2.4.67–68). Again the audience has reason to be pleased with the Nurse, and with her eagerness to help in the marriage arrangements—she rushes off to fetch a rope ladder to enable Romeo to climb to the balcony. But the next time this same situation occurs, in act 3, scene 2, the message is instead one of tragedy. Romeo has killed Juliet's cousin Tybalt in a fight, and has been banished. And this time the delay is not comic. It is difficult to get any information at all from the Nurse's confused account. Who is dead? Romeo? Tybalt? Both? Here, too, the Nurse's pragmatism, so attractive in comedy, reveals its radical limitations. She is willing to fetch Romeo for a night of comfort, but the moment he is gone she begins to argue that Juliet should marry Paris: "Romeo / Is banishèd. . . . Then, since the case so stands as now it doth, / I think it best you married with the County. / O, he's a lovely gentleman! / Romeo's a dishclout to him" (3.5.212–219). As she says, all too prophetically, "Your first is dead, or 'twere as good he were" (3.5.224). The Nurse's offhand remark to Juliet early in the play, that she would like to "live to see thee married once," now takes on an uncomfortable ambiguity. She would just as soon see her married twice. This cheerfully amoral realism is wholly inadequate for Juliet's needs, and for the needs of tragedy. The conflict of values here points forward to the conversation in *Othello* between the idealistic Desdemona and the practical Emilia, when Desdemona asks whether Emilia could imagine being unfaithful to her husband "for all the world," and gets a pragmatic reply: "The world's a huge thing. It is a great price for a small vice."

For Juliet, then, the advice of the older generation is useless, and she rejects it, as she ultimately must reject the Nurse. The same pattern appears in the relationship of Romeo and Friar Laurence. When he is dealing with Romeo's feelings for Rosaline, the Friar's advice is good enough (he chides Romeo for doting, not for loving), but when he tries to convince Romeo that banishment is preferable to death, and that the Prince, in commuting his death sentence, has done him a favor, Romeo rejects him just as Juliet has rejected the Nurse: "Thou canst not speak of that thou dost not feel. / Wert thou as young as I,

Juliet thy love, / An hour but married, Tybalt murderèd, ... / Then mightst thou speak, then mightst thou tear thy hair, / And fall upon the ground, as I do now, / Taking the measure of an unmade grave" (3.3.64–70). As always in this play, even throwaway lines uttered in extravagant excess (here Romeo's "Taking the measure of an unmade grave") come back to haunt the dramatic action. The Friar's philosophy is a philosophy of moderation: "These violent delights have violent ends. . . . / Therefore love moderately" (2.5.9–14) and "Wisely and slow. They stumble that run fast" (2.2.94). This is excellent advice in the abstract, but, like the Friar's collection of all-purpose rhyming aphorisms, it is disturbingly set apart from experience; so also with the apparent even-handedness of "The earth, that's nature's mother, is her tomb. / What is her burying grave, that is her womb" (2.2.9–10). The Friar's advice is so "theoretical" that he himself disregards it immediately when faced with the experiential facts of tragedy. He agrees to perform the second wedding; indeed, he agrees to perform the first, and hardly "[w]isely and slow"; he plies Juliet with the sleeping potion, intending to perform a quasi-blasphemous resurrection later; and he himself literally stumbles in the graveyard. Old Capulet, of course, is equally hasty, trying to rush Juliet into an early marriage "this very Thursday." The Friar is all authority and no experience, the Nurse all experience and no authority. Once again the older generation, stuck with its proverbs and its books and its ancient feuds, is inadequate to the tragic world of reality, of love and circumstance. We could think here of old Queen Margaret and the Duchess of York, similarly trapped in stasis, unable to respond to time, history, and change.

The structuring "feuds" of *Romeo and Juliet* come together in a powerful way in the famous balcony scene. The scene is set in part upon the upper stage, the "balcony" to Juliet's private chamber, or bedroom. Romeo, standing below on the main apron stage, unseen by Juliet as the scene begins, thus assumes the classic posture of the Petrarchan lover:

Romeo   But soft, what light through yonder window breaks?
         It is the east, and Juliet is the sun.
         Arise, fair sun, and kill the envious moon,
         Who is already sick and pale with grief
         That thou, her maid, art far more fair than she.

                                    2.1.44–48

Juliet is the sun, not the moon, which is sacred to Diana, the goddess of virginity; it is Rosaline who is said to have "Dian's wit." Juliet has come out on the balcony to be alone. She thinks she is speaking in soliloquy and has no idea that she is being overheard when she questions, to herself, the implications of her lover's name: "[W]herefore art thou Romeo?" "Wherefore" means "why," not "where"; Juliet is not looking for Romeo, but asking why he has a name that means he is her family's enemy:

Juliet   What's Montague? It is nor hand, nor foot,
         Nor arm, nor face, nor any other part
         Belonging to a man. O, be some other name!
         What's in a name? That which we call a rose
         By any other word would smell as sweet.
         So Romeo would, were he not Romeo called,
         Retain that dear perfection that he owes
         Without that title. Romeo, doff thy name,
         And for thy name—which is no part of thee—
         Take all myself.

                                          2.1.82–91

The injunction "lose yourself to find yourself" that we saw operative in a play like *Love's Labour's Lost* is embedded, as well, in Juliet's eloquent, and desperate, wish. Names in this play are, it seems, deliberately symmetrical, like so many other structural elements: the dactylic rhythms of MON-ta-gue and CAP-u-let echo each other, as do the names of RO-me-o and JU-li-et. In terms of prosody there is indeed no difference between "Montague" and "Capulet," yet both are restrictive terms that, in the stubborn and recalcitrant feuding, cry out to be abandoned, superseded, or lost. (Compare, in the Henry VI plays, the opposition between "York" and "Lancaster," where the supervening name of "Tudor" puts a temporary end to another blood feud, settled by a marriage.) Romeo will indeed doff his name—"Henceforth I never will be Romeo"—in order to enter the night world of transformation. Her startled response, when she learns that he is present, is also to "doff" something—her maidenly shame:

         Thou knowest the mask of night is on my face,
         Else would a maiden blush bepaint my cheek
         For that which thou hast heard me speak tonight.
         Fain would I dwell on form, fain, fain deny
         What I have spoke; but farewell, compliment.
         Dost thou love me? . . .

                                          2.1.127–132

The walled orchard, like the biblical enclosed garden, the *hortus conclusus,* was a traditional iconographic emblem of virginity in poetry and art (the Song of Songs; Chaucer's "Knight's Tale"; the Unicorn tapestries). In Juliet's image, quickly picked up by Romeo, it becomes a place of love and risk:

Juliet   The orchard walls are high and hard to climb,
         And the place death, considering who thou art,
         If any of my kinsmen find thee here.
Romeo   With love's light wings did I o'erperch these walls,

> For stony limits cannot hold love out,
> And what love can do, that dares love attempt.
>
> *2.1.105–110*

He is winged Cupid, who comes to his beloved Psyche in the dark. Yet there are dangers in this paradisal garden—in Juliet's lightning image, for example:

> Juliet   I have no joy of this contract tonight.
> It is too rash, too unadvised, too sudden,
> Too like the lightning which doth cease to be
> Ere one can say it lightens. . . .
>
> *2.1.159–162*

And there is a danger in Romeo's impulse to swear, to take a vow, especially when Juliet says, if he must do so, then "swear by thy gracious self, / Which is the god of my idolatry" (2.1.155–156). As always in Shakespeare, to take a human being for a god is an error in judgment—if not a blasphemy—that will have untoward consequences. There is danger in the image of Romeo as a "wanton's bird," a child's plaything, and there is a poignant truth in her reply: when he says, "I would I were thy bird," she answers playfully, "I should kill thee with much cherishing." Here, as throughout the early acts of the play, every utterance has a double meaning, encodes a warning, a foreboding of the tragedy to come. In a way, though, the most ominous or fateful element of this beautiful scene is its verticality. Again and again throughout *Romeo and Juliet* a glance or move upward will prefigure a fall, from the moment when the lovers are both aloft in Juliet's chamber to the end, when they are both lying dead in the tomb. There is a comic anticipation of this up/down pattern in the Nurse's long comic speech on the child Juliet's falling on her face and her husband's joke about women falling backward when they come of age. Romeo falls down in Friar Laurence's cell when he hears that he is banished, and the Nurse, with characteristic double entendre, urges him to stand up and be a man ("For Juliet's sake, rise and stand"). Juliet falls prostrate at the feet of her father, and is likewise told to stand. In the aubade scene, Juliet has a premonition of Romeo's final fate: "Methinks I see thee, now thou art so low, / As one dead in the bottom of a tomb" (3.5.55–56). And in the final scene the Prince says to old Montague, "[T]hou art early up / To see thy son and heir more early down." Up/down. From the stars to the tomb. For the pair of star-crossed lovers who are Romeo and Juliet, this is the play's inexorable pattern, mirrored on the stage in a visual image of ascent and fall.

As this up/down spatial pattern makes clear, the overarching structure of the play, borrowed in part from the language of love poetry, is the confusion between love and death. Expressed in such general terms this sounds like a banality, but the exchange is meticulously worked out at all levels of language and action, cascading perhaps from the familiar Elizabethan pun on "die," which meant both to cease to be and to come to sexual climax. We have already noted the Friar's homily, expressed in a paradoxical couplet whose rhyme-words were themselves a familiar pair:

> The earth, that's nature's mother, is her tomb.
> What is her burying grave, that is her womb. . . .
>
> *2.2.9–10*

And this sentiment is repeated throughout the play. When she first meets Romeo, Juliet sends the Nurse to find out about him, remarking, "If he be marrièd / My grave is like to be my wedding bed" (1.5.131–132). Later, faced with the prospect of a hasty and unwelcome wedding with the County Paris, she tells her parents, "Delay this marriage for a month, a week; / Or if you do not, make the bridal bed / In that dim monument where Tybalt lies" (3.5.199–201). Lady Capulet, confronted with Juliet's refusal, exclaims in exasperation, "I would the fool were married to her grave"—a wish that, ironically, comes true. What begins as a kind of literary cliché, depending on the clichéd rhyme of "womb" and "tomb," takes on an increasing reality as the play progresses, and finally crystallizes when Romeo declares, "Well, Juliet, I will lie with thee tonight." Twice we hear mentioned the curious image of Death as a bridegroom—once from old Capulet, and again from Romeo in the final scene:

> Shall I believe
> That unsubstantial death is amorous,
> And that the lean abhorrèd monster keeps
> Thee here in dark to be his paramour?
> For fear of that I still will stay with thee,
> And never from this pallet of dim night
> Depart again. Here, here will I remain
> With worms that are thy chambermaids. O, here
> Will I set up my everlasting rest,
> And shake the yoke of inauspicious stars
> From this world-wearied flesh. . . .
>
> *5.3.102–112*

The deaths of Romeo and Juliet, like the deaths of many major characters in the other love tragedies, are explicitly what we might call "erotic suicides." Iconographically, their deaths engage traditional symbols of male and female sexuality. Romeo drinks from a cup of poison, and the cup is a time-honored symbol of the female in folklore and mythology. Juliet stabs herself with a dagger, an equally common symbol for the male, and one that is much punned on in the course of the play. Her last words leave little doubt of their double meaning: "O happy dagger, / This is thy sheath! There rust, and let me die." In the final scene of the play the literal events we are shown are those of bodily death, but the sexual "die" pun is vividly present. When Romeo says "Thus with a kiss I die," he follows the practice of many Elizabethan poets in merging the two connotations so that they cannot be prised apart. Which is the metaphor here, sex or death? (We will see the same two ancient props, the cup and the dagger, at the close of *Hamlet,* again confirming that in tragedy love and death are often versions of the same act.)

There is a confusion of love and death, too, in the comic scenes: in all the sexual puns of the servants at the beginning of the play, quarreling about whether to cut off the heads of the maids or their maidenheads, and in the dialogue between the Nurse and her servant Peter, whom she upbraids for not intervening when she feels herself insulted by Mercutio. "And thou," she says to Peter, "must stand by, too, and suffer every knave to use me at his pleasure." "I saw no man use you at his pleasure" is his swift reply. "If I had, my weapon should quickly have been out" (2.3.137–141). Even sex in the daylight world of Verona is equated with violence, rather than with love.

The most tangible sign of this violent disorder is the duel, stemming from the civil war in Verona's streets. If *Romeo and Juliet* were a romantic comedy, like *Love's Labour's Lost,* it would end where it begins, with the masque at old Capulet's, a dance, love at first sight, and a pledge of marriage. But it is a comedy gone wrong, a comedy turned inside out, and Romeo's wondering first sight of Juliet at the feast—"O, she doth teach the torches to burn bright!"—is sharply disrupted by an alien and anarchic force in the person of Tybalt: "This, by his voice, should be a Montague. / Fetch me my rapier, boy" (1.5.51–52). Tybalt is a kind of character we will encounter frequently in Shakespeare's plays in one guise or another, an old-style hero from a world that is almost mythic, primitive, or tribal, a spirit of heroic warfare and revenge. Like Hotspur in *Henry IV Part 1,* like Hector in *Troilus and Cressida,* like King Hamlet, and even like Antony in *Antony and Cleopatra* as described by his Roman admirers, Tybalt is a warrior of the old school, and his method of warfare is single combat, the one-on-one fight intended to defend his honor and the honor of his family: "Now, by the stock and honour of my kin, / To strike him dead I hold it not a sin" (1.5.55–56). Recall that he is saying this at a family party, an "old accustomed feast," in a culture (that of Elizabeth's England as well as Escalus's Verona) that places a high value on hospitality and the host-guest relationship. Even old Capulet, no lover of Montagues, thinks Tybalt's behavior is inappropriate: "I would not for the wealth of all this town / Here in my house do him disparagement" (1.5.66–67). Later echoes of this hospitality theme will come from such diverse speakers as Lady Macbeth, who exclaims, stagily, "What, in our house?" when told about the murder of Duncan for which she and her husband are responsible; and the blinded Duke of Gloucester in *King Lear,* who in his agony reminds his torturers that he is their host, and they are his guests. Figures like Tybalt are representatives of an old order of heroism and revenge—on the one hand, heroic, but on the other, unable to function in a modern world of politics and compromise, the world of *The Prince,* the world of law and language. Such characters never survive in Shakespeare's plays. They all die, as did their historical models, usually, before their time. They are like dinosaurs, heroic beasts unfit for a smaller world of accommodation and grace.

Tybalt fights by single combat, by challenge, by the word, and he is, like others of his character type, a nonverbal man, a man of few words who fights instead of speaking, preferring and valuing war over politics. So that when at the beginning of act 3 Tybalt meets Mercutio, the man of infinite language, infinite fantasy, and infinite imagination, conflict is inevitable:

> Tybalt   Mercutio, thou consort'st with Romeo.
> Mercutio "Consort"? What, dost thou make us minstrels? An thou
>   make minstrels of us, look to hear nothing but discords.
>   [*Touching his rapier*] Here's my fiddlestick; here's that shall
>   make you dance. Zounds—"Consort"!
>
> *3.1.40–44*

Mercutio is almost willing to fight because he doesn't like Tybalt's language. The quarrel is a more intricate one than it may first appear, since "consort" meaning to associate with and "consort" meaning to play or sing together come from different root words, though they were beginning to be combined in the late sixteenth century. Shakespeare uses "consort" in each sense. As for "minstrels," they were by definition artisan-entertainers, originally of a servant class, and in any case far below Mercutio and Tybalt on the social scale. Mercutio's quibble thus pretends to understand Tybalt as offering an insult to his rank—hence the colloquial "Zounds" (God's wounds), underscoring the supposed enormity of Tybalt's flat-footed address, intended merely to assert that Mercutio and Romeo are friends. Needless to say, this is far beyond the baffled Tybalt. For just as Tybalt is a man of the old order, doomed to die because he cannot fit into a new political and social world, so Mercutio is also an alien element in custom-bound Verona, representing for this play the spirit of creative imagination and improvisation.

It is Mercutio—whose name is linked to the quicksilver god Mercury—who tells the story of Queen Mab, the Fairy Queen, who brings to birth all dreams of wish fulfillment, all fantasies. Mab, imagined as a tiny being who can traverse the bodies of sleepers,

> gallops night by night
> Through lovers' brains, and then they dream of love;
> O'er courtiers' knees, that dream on curtsies straight;
> O'er ladies' lips, who straight on kisses dream. . . .
>
> *1.4.71–74*

This logic of sensory association—Mab drives over a soldier's neck and he dreams of cutting throats—seems strikingly modern, in one sense, even as the notion of a mischievous Fairy Queen who tangles the manes of horses in the night links Queen Mab to folk superstition and to the equally tiny fairies in *A Midsummer Night's Dream* (Puck, Peaseblossom, Cobweb, Mustardseed). Most characters in *Romeo and Juliet,* when they speak of dreams, have in mind the older sense of omens and portents. "[M]y mind misgives / Some consequence yet hanging in the stars," says Romeo. But Mercutio is the spokesman for the power of dreams, and even though he gaily dismisses them as "the children of an idle brain, / Begot of nothing but vain fantasy," for him dreaming is an aspect of possibility and change, of identity and expression, related to what a much later era would call "the unconscious." And when he dies, this capacity of transformation through language and imagination dies with him. He is not its agent, but rather its emblem, the sign of that possibility.

We may notice that the duel between Mercutio and Tybalt has again been anticipated, in the play's dramatic structure, by a comic scene that seems at first to be of little consequence. In act 2, scene 3, we see Mercutio engage Romeo in a battle of wits, rejoicing that his friend has become "sociable" once more, recovered from his debilitating infatuation with Rosaline. As the puns and quips fly, Mercutio pretends to be overcome, and finally calls upon a friend to part the combatants: "Come between us, good Benvolio. My wits faints." As was the case with the Nurse's first message, the mood here is playful. But a few hours, and only three scenes, later, when the friends encounter Tybalt, the same scenario results in tragedy. The weapons this time are swords rather than words, and it is Romeo who intervenes, while Mercutio is mortally wounded as a result of his intervention. Romeo's murmured explanation, "I thought all for the best," tellingly reinforces the parallel between this duel and the previous one, for the name of Benvolio, the peacemaker in the duel of words, means "wellwisher"—one who thinks all for the best.

Yet even as Mercutio lies in the street dying, he is still able to joke. Romeo says to him wishfully that "[t]he hurt cannot be much," and receives this devastating reply:

> No, 'tis not so deep as a well, nor so wide as a church door, but 'tis enough. 'Twill serve. Ask for me tomorrow, and you shall find me a grave man. I am peppered, I warrant, for this world. A plague o' both your houses!
>
> *3.1.92–95*

The "plague," of course, does come—in multiple forms. There is an actual plague abroad in the city, an "infectious pestilence" that keeps Friar John from delivering the vital letter that would have prevented misconception and tragedy. And the more metaphorical plague of hatred, civil war, and banishment also spreads through the city, and through the theater. The disease is a mortal one, and its name is tragedy.

With the death of Mercutio, the possibility of containment, and of comedy, dies, too. From this point, from the first scene of the third act, tragedy becomes inevitable. The voice of imagination and moderation and perspective is dead, and we stop laughing. Letters now go undelivered, parents can no longer speak with their children. Tragic disorder has come full force upon the play's world. Tybalt is gone, Mercutio is gone, all by the beginning of the third act, and there is no turning back. Uninstructed by the wiser and more worldly Mercutio, badly counseled by the Friar and the Nurse, Romeo and Juliet are left to fend for themselves in a world whose blackness is no longer tipped with silver. Yet under this pressure they do not fail. They learn, they grow, and they change, so that their deaths are tragic, but not futile.

The most striking instance of such growth in the play is the transformation that Juliet undergoes. When we first encounter her, she is wholly submissive, even passive. She is not yet fourteen, and her life is still dominated by external authority: her father, her mother, and the Nurse who has been with her—at first as her wet nurse—since she was born. One of the quieter poignancies of this rich play is the story of the Nurse's own daughter, Susan, who died young, and offstage, before the beginning of the play. It is a story we have heard before, in *Love's Labour's Lost,* where it was Catherine's sister who had died; we will hear it again, in a fictive version that is nonetheless powerful and haunting, in *Twelfth Night,* when Viola, disguised as the boy Cesario, speaks of the "sister" who pined away for love "like patience on a monument, / Smiling at grief." To call this touch Shakespearean is merely to beg the question of its evocative power, and to comment on the rate of child mortality in the period is largely to miss the point. By inventing these backstories for his characters, Shakespeare as playwright gives the characters enormous depth and reach.

Juliet, asked by her mother what her thoughts are about marriage, says, "It is an honor that I dream not of." Confronted with Lady Capulet's approving book report on Paris, she answers only, "I'll look to like, if looking liking move." She is a daughter rather than a prospective wife. It is therefore striking to see how quickly she changes once she sets eyes on Romeo. Immediately this guileless girl of almost fourteen becomes a clever strategist, decoying the Nurse with false preliminary inquiries so that she can attain her true object, to know Romeo's name:

Juliet	Come hither, Nurse. What is yon gentleman?
Nurse	The son and heir of old Tiberio.
Juliet	What's he that now is going out of door?
Nurse	Marry, that, I think, be young Petruchio.
Juliet	What's he that follows here, that would not dance?
Nurse	I know not.
Juliet	Go ask his name.

And then, aside to us the minute the Nurse bustles off: "If he be marrièd, / My grave is like to be my wedding bed" (1.5.125–132).

Juliet will use the same device later in the play when her mother tries to press her toward a hasty and unwelcome marriage, telling her that "early next Thursday" Paris will make her "a joyful bride":

> Juliet   I pray you, tell my lord and father, madam,
>   I will not marry yet; and when I do, I swear
>   It shall be Romeo—whom you know I hate—
>   Rather than Paris. . . .
>
> *3.5.120–123*

She deceives her mother with Mercutio's weapon, wordplay and double meanings.

Nowhere is Juliet's sudden transition to adulthood clearer than in the balcony scene, where she controls the scene completely, declaring her own love rather than waiting for Romeo's declaration, warning him against false vows and rash love contracts. Twice she leaves the balcony, and twice she returns; her exits and entrances are deliberately theatrical, and when she reappears on the balcony she reappears to the audience as well as to Romeo. Each time we think she has departed—to answer the Nurse's call, the barrier of authority, or to obey her own instinct toward modesty, the barrier of formality—she reappears and she herself summons Romeo back. The iconography will mirror her dominance, as she stands above and speaks to her lover. The next love scene between them in this space, the aubade scene (3.5), will find them both aloft, having spent the night in lovemaking. But between those two scenes comes the marriage itself—fatefully performed, in terms of staging, in Friar Laurence's cell, below, almost surely in the same space that will later be used for Juliet's tomb, visually underscoring the play's relentless twinning of womb and tomb. The stage location of the wedding is thus yet another foreshadowing of the tragic pattern that is about to overtake them. The wedding takes place in the last scene of act 2; in the very next scene, the first scene of act 3, the deaths of Mercutio and Tybalt occur. Again the day world defeats the night world, and the Prince, persuaded of his own generosity in doing so, commutes Romeo's death sentence to banishment. All this while, Juliet has been waiting for another night. When we hear her next, she will speak, again from her chamber balcony, in the voice of sexual impatience and desire. Her great speech begins:

> Gallop apace, you fiery-footed steeds,
> Toward Phoebus' lodging. Such a waggoner
> As Phaëthon would whip you to the west
> And bring in cloudy night immediately.
>
> *3.2.1–4*

It is a magnificent piece of poetry, and is fraught with danger signals at every turn. Juliet wishes the chariot of the sun were drawn by Phaëthon, Apollo's headstrong son, who was too young for such a task. The horses ran away with the chariot, and Phaëthon was scorched by the sun, and drowned in the sea. There is danger, too, in the image of a Romeo dead and cut out in little stars, and in Juliet's final image, almost a brothel image, that she is "sold," but "[n]ot yet enjoyed":

> Juliet   So tedious is this day
> As is the night before some festival
> To an impatient child that hath new robes
> And may not wear them.
>
>   *3.2.28–31*

Juliet's apostrophe to "civil night, / Thou sober-suited matron all in black," urges that night "learn me how to lose a winning match / Played for a pair of stainless maidenhoods." The difference between her word "maidenhoods" here and the coarse joking about "maidenheads" in the early moments of the play marks an acknowledgment of the place of sexual love within a larger philosophical and erotic frame. "Maidenhood" is the time of life during which one is a maiden; "maidenhead" is the condition of being a virgin, often, as in this play, with a direct anatomical reference to the hymen as the mark of a woman's chastity. There is a tragic logic to the Nurse's immediate arrival with her confused report of Tybalt's death and Romeo's banishment, and a tragic knowledge to Juliet's response, in which she effectively doffs her name and is no longer Capulet: "Shall I speak ill of him that is my husband? . . . My husband lives, that Tybalt would have slain; / And Tybalt's dead, that would have slain my husband." The word she fears and hates is not "dead" but "banished":

> Why followed not, when she said "Tybalt's dead,"
> "Thy father," or "thy mother," nay, or both.
> . . . .
> "Romeo is banishèd"—to speak that word
> Is father, mother, Tybalt, Romeo, Juliet,
> All slain, all dead. . . .
>
>   *3.2.118–124*

In no way has Juliet seemed a heartless daughter, yet here she expresses the preference that her parents might die rather than that her husband be banished. This is extreme, yet it is part of a pattern we will see over and over again in Shakespeare's plays, when women in love—Hermia, Desdemona, Miranda, and others—choose their husbands rather than their fathers. Juliet is unusual within Shakespeare in having two living parents on the scene. Juliet chooses womanhood, and sexuality, and love and marriage, and therefore, in the context of this play, she is forced to choose solitude and self-banishment. She spoke in soliloquy, or so she thought, in the balcony scene. Here she rejects her family to choose instead the banished Romeo. When the Nurse advises her to marry Paris, she rejects the Nurse, her confidante in this whole affair, and is then almost completely alone: "O most wicked fiend! . . . Go, counsellor! / Thou and my bosom henceforth shall be twain" (4.1.235–240). Tybalt is gone, and with him pride of kinship; her mother and her father are rejected; the Nurse is sent away. Now only Friar Laurence and his potion lie between Juliet and the absolute solitude of the tomb.

The potion, a mysteriously acting drug that simulates death, is not unfamiliar from other early modern plays, or indeed from the cultural history of the period, when pharmaceutical practice was changing, and poisoning one's rivals was often a way to get ahead in political or erotic life. The presence in this play of the apothecary and his shop full of herbs, minerals, and body fragments balances the more medieval herb garden of Friar Laurence. Within the context of Shakespeare's plays, though, the Friar's plan is an aspect of his own vainglory, an opportunity for him to preside over, and perform, a naturalistic resurrection. We will see such sleeping potions, and such apparent resurrections, in later comedies (for example, in *Cymbeline*), where the rebirth of the sleeping lady signals a change in the status of knowledge and understanding for those about her. But Juliet senses that there will be no such audience or renewed understanding. Symbolically, she sends away her mother and the Nurse, and prepares to swallow the vial of sleeping potion alone:

> Farewell. God knows when we shall meet again.
> I have a faint cold fear thrills through my veins
> That almost freezes up the heat of life.
> I'll call them back again to comfort me.
> Nurse!—What should she do here?
> [*She opens curtains, behind which is seen her bed*]
> My dismal scene I needs must act alone.
>
> 4.3.14–19

Juliet knows she is an actress. The language of "acting" in both senses—stage performance and activity—pervades her speeches, from the references to "love-performing night" and "true love acted" to this "dismal scene." Here it is well to remember that the Elizabethan "actress" who played this part was in fact a male actor, since no women were permitted to perform on the public stage; like "night," evoked in the middle of a London afternoon, womanhood is a powerful and convincing dramatic effect, not merely a naturalistic mimetic reality. Modern culture's paradigmatic heterosexual love story, *Romeo and Juliet*, is a play written for an all-male cast.

The language spoken by Romeo and Juliet themselves is increasingly a powerful, original, and allusive blank verse. By contrast, the characters they have left behind seem to relapse, as tragedy closes in upon them, into an older language of melodrama, the exclamatory periods of Senecan tragedy, a language not unlike that spoken by the lamenting queens in *Richard III:*

Nurse   She's dead, deceased. She's dead, alack the day!
Capulet's Wife Alack the day, she's dead, she's dead, she's dead!
                                                          4.4.50–51

Nurse   O day, O day, O day, O hateful day . . .
                                                          4.4.83

Paris   O love! O life: not life, but love in death.
                                                          4.4.73

Capulet   O child, O child, my soul, and not my child!
                                                          4.4.89

These are lines that would not be out of place in Kyd's *Spanish Tragedy,* where the distraught Hieronimo exclaims about the murder of his son: "O eyes, no eyes, but fountains fraught with tears; / O life, no life, but lively form of death" (*Spanish Tragedy* 3.2.1–2). We may be ready to agree with the Friar, when he intervenes: "Peace, ho, for shame! Confusion's cure lives not / In these confusions." Once again the language of the Capulets, the language of the day world, is a language of formality and artifice, the "form" and "compliment" that Juliet dismisses. (Compare Juliet's famous "Fain would I dwell on form, fain, fain deny / What I have spoke; but farewell, compliment. / Dost thou love me?") To it we can juxtapose the language of love, the language of excess as it is spoken by Romeo and Juliet.

Consider again Romeo's lovely phrases, spoken when he first catches sight of Juliet at the Capulets' masque: "O, she doth teach the torches to burn bright! / It seems she hangs upon the cheek of night" (1.5.41–42). Romeo had complained of Rosaline that she would not "ope her lap to saint-seducing gold. / O, she is rich in beauty, only poor / That when she dies, with beauty dies her store" (1.1.207–209). Juliet's store of love, by contrast, is immeasurable:

Juliet   My bounty is as boundless as the sea,
         My love as deep. The more I give to thee
         The more I have, for both are infinite.
                                                          2.1.175–177

Juliet seems in this to prefigure Shakespeare's ageless and timeless Cleopatra, who will tell her Antony: "There's beggary in the love that can be reckoned" (*Antony and Cleopatra* 1.1.15). For when Juliet arrives at Friar Laurence's cell to be married at the end of act 2 she declares:

> They are but beggars that can count their worth,
> But my true love is grown to such excess
> I cannot sum up some of half my wealth.
>
> 2.5.32–34

By the end of the play, language, too, will have grown to excess, maintaining the force of the mature Shakespearean sound in marked and deliberate contrast to the stilted, formal language of the early acts, and of the Capulets. Paris comes to Juliet's tomb, thinking she is dead, and speaks in lukewarm rhyme, the sestet of a sonnet, ending in a couplet:

> The obsequies that I for thee will keep
> Nightly shall be to strew thy grave and weep.
>
> 5.3.16–17

And then we hear the voice of Romeo:

> The time and my intents are savage-wild,
> More fierce and more inexorable far
> Than empty tigers or the roaring sea.
>
> 5.3.37–39

Is it any wonder that Juliet should prefer him?

The question of excess, worth, and "saint-seducing gold" is more than merely decorative language or thematic counterpoint. Boundlessness versus limitation is a key dialectic for Shakespeare in every sphere (language, politics, mortality, sexual passion, geography, stagecraft, etc.). In *Romeo and Juliet,* which we have seen to be an exceptionally well-crafted play, the material worth of "gold" and its limitations as lucre, ornament, and literal status symbol are measured against another kind of quality, associated with the quicksilver Mercutio and with the element of silver in the play. It is not overstating the case to say that gold versus silver constitutes another of the play's defining feuds, and that the critique of gold leads to the stunning climax/anticlimax of the final scene, in which Capulet and Montague, having apparently learned nothing from their losses, vie to build golden statues, each for the other's dead child.

Silver is mentioned three times in the play. In the orchard during the balcony scene Romeo speaks of the "blessèd moon" that "tips with silver all these fruit-tree tops" (2.1.149–150). In the same scene he hears Juliet call his name and thinks, "How silver-sweet sound lovers' tongues by night, / Like softest music to attending ears!" (2.1.210–211). Later in the play, at the news of Juliet's supposed death, a group of musicians debates the question of why music is said to have a silver sound. All these associations are pleasant, combining love, sweet music, and the moon, protective goddess of virgins and regnant light of the nighttime world of privacy and passion.

By contrast, the play's references to gold are frequently negative and debasing. Rosaline, as we have seen, won't "ope her lap to saint-seducing gold," phrases suggesting that Romeo has thought her favors might be purchased by gifts or trinkets. Lady Capulet's praise of Paris as a book talks about the "golden clasps" that lock in the "golden story," proposing to judge this book by his cover. When Romeo is banished, he protests to Friar Laurence that banishment is a euphemism for death: "Calling death banishèd / Thou cutt'st my head off with a golden axe" (3.3.21–22). Most signally, when Romeo goes to the apothecary's shop he pays for his poison with gold. "There is thy gold—worse poison to men's souls," he says, and "I sell thee poison [i.e., the gold]; thou hast sold me none" (5.1.79–80, 83). This apothecary, a "needy man," a "caitiff wretch," with his striking physical appearance and his shop full of empty boxes and pots and remnants of packthread, is in naturalistic terms a figure of poverty and economic depression—and, according to theater historians, a stock character part for the tall, thin actor John Sincklo. But more powerfully, he is surely an emblematic figure for Death, a walking skeleton, a death's-head: "Meagre were his looks. / Sharp misery had worn him to the bones" (5.1.40–41). When the apothecary hesitates to sell him the poison, Romeo says:

> Art thou so bare and full of wretchedness,
> And fear'st to die? Famine is in thy cheeks,
> Need and oppression starveth in thy eyes,
> Contempt and beggary hangs upon thy back.
>
> *5.1.68–71*

Romeo buys death from Death, and—like the condemned man pardoning his executioner—exonerates him.

When we bear all this in mind, we must, I think, approach with great caution and many reservations the final scheme of reconciliation put forward by the Montagues and the Capulets. In the last scene of the play, missing the point of the tragedy that has robbed them of son and daughter, old Montague and old Capulet propose to build, instead of something living, a pair of golden statues. Montague says:

> For I will raise her statue in pure gold
> That whiles Verona by that name is known
> There shall no figure at such rate be set
> As that of true and faithful Juliet.
>
> *5.3.298–301*

Capulet, competitive to the last, replies:

> As rich shall Romeo's by his lady's lie,
> Poor sacrifices of our enmity.
>
> *5.3.302–303*

"At such rate," "rich," and "poor." At the close of the play, at the end of the tragedy, the final tragedy would seem to be that no one left alive onstage has understood the play. The Friar is repentant but unchanged. Old Montague and old Capulet have translated their losses into material terms, into golden statues. And even the Prince is unenlightened:

> A glooming peace this morning with it brings.
>   The sun for sorrow will not show his head.
> Go hence, to have more talk of these sad things.
>   Some shall be pardoned, and some punishèd;
> For never was a story of more woe
> Than this of Juliet and her Romeo.
>
> *5.3.304–309*

Pardon and punishment are mentioned evenhandedly, and the sorrowing sun may remind us of Juliet's exultant fantasy, that when dead Romeo will be translated into constellations of stars, "[t]hat all the world will be in love with night / And pay no worship to the garish sun" (3.2.24–25).

These witnesses, all remnants of an older world of law, have had the experience and missed the meaning. The task of understanding what has transpired is left to the audience, which is part of the group enjoined by the Prince to "Go hence," out of the theater, "to have more talk of these sad things." In effect there are two audiences, one on and one off the stage. Notice the Prince's word "story." The story to be retold here—as at the end of *Hamlet,* when Horatio is urged to stay alive in order to tell the Prince's story—is the play, with all its twists and turns, its near misses, its soliloquies and sonnets, all elements beyond the experience and the understanding of the sobered Veronese families left onstage. The movement beyond tragedy is left to the spectators. The play, not the golden statues, is the real monument to the love and death and tragedy and triumph of two young "star-crossed" lovers who have become for the modern world the very archetypes and words of love.

A Midsummer Night's Dream

DRAMATIS PERSONAE

Theseus, *Duke of Athens*

Hippolyta, *Queen of the Amazons,
  betrothed to Theseus*

Philostrate, *Master of the Revels
  to Theseus*

Egeus, *father of Hermia*

Hermia, *daughter of Egeus, in love
  with Lysander*

Lysander, *loved by Hermia*

Demetrius, *suitor to Hermia*

Helena, *in love with Demetrius*

Oberon, *King of Fairies*

Titania, *Queen of Fairies*

Robin Goodfellow, *a puck*

Peaseblossom, *a fairy*

Cobweb, *a fairy*

Moth, *a fairy*

Mustardseed, *a fairy*

Peter Quince, *a carpenter*

Nick Bottom, *a weaver*

Francis Flute, *a bellows-mender*

Tom Snout, *a tinker*

Snug, *a joiner*

Robin Starveling, *a tailor*

Attendant lords and fairies

SHAKESPEARE WROTE *A Midsummer Night's Dream* in the same years that he wrote *Romeo and Juliet,* and the two plays have a great deal in common. In a way we could say that *A Midsummer Night's Dream* is *Romeo and Juliet* turned inside out, *Romeo and Juliet* transformed into a comedy. In both plays there are strong central figures of authority who attempt to order the world—the Prince in *Romeo and Juliet;* Theseus, Duke of Athens, in *A Midsummer Night's Dream.* In the two plays there are fathers who want to choose their daughters' husbands—old Capulet wants Juliet to marry Paris, Egeus wants Hermia to marry Demetrius—and in both cases the women refuse, choosing instead other lovers (Romeo, Lysander) and planning to run away with them. In both plays the disobedient or rebellious daughter is threatened with the life of a nun (Friar Laurence says he will "dispose" of Juliet among "a sisterhood of holy nuns"; Hermia is asked to imagine wearing "the livery of a nun, / . . . Chanting faint hymns to the cold fruitless moon"). Both plays strongly emphasize the difference between night, which transforms and changes, and day, which is rigid, inflexible, and associated with law. And both plays use similar images and tropes: the lark that rises at dawn, the nightingale that sings at evening, the lover's stereotypical cry, "Ay, me!" which Mercutio will mock, and Juliet sigh from her balcony. In this play the same cry is heard from Lysander:

> Ay me, for aught that I could ever read,
> Could ever hear by tale or history,
> The course of true love never did run smooth. . . .
>
> Dream *1.1.132–134*

The "tale or history" to which he refers is a strangely familiar one, a tale of star-crossed lovers. It is almost as if Lysander has been watching, or reading, *Romeo and Juliet.* And when he describes the fate of such doomed lovers, Lysander uses an image that appears over and over again in *Romeo and Juliet*—the image of lightning:

> Or if there were a sympathy in choice,
> War, death, or sickness did lay siege to it,
> Making it momentany as a sound,
> Swift as a shadow, short as any dream,
> Brief as the lightning in the collied night,
> That, in a spleen, unfolds both heaven and earth,
> And, ere a man hath power to say "Behold!",
> The jaws of darkness do devour it up.
> So quick bright things come to confusion.
>
> *1.1.141–149*

It *is* the tale of Romeo and Juliet, where Juliet thought their love was "too like the lightning which doth cease to be / Ere one can say it lightens." But this play makes clear from the beginning that its note will not be tragic. The first line of the play announces that the audience is to be among the guests at the most canonical of all events in comedy: a wedding. "Now, fair Hippolyta, our nuptial hour / Draws on apace," says Theseus. If *A Midsummer Night's Dream* begins with a wedding—the standard *conclusion* of comedy—why, we might ask, do we need the play at all? The answer, as always in Shakespeare, is that the participants have something to learn. After reminding Hippolyta that "I wooed thee with my sword, / And won thy love doing thee injuries," Theseus announces:

> But I will wed thee in another key—
> With pomp, with triumph, and with revelling.
>
> *1.1.16–19*

But the transition is not so easy to make. The dangerous hints of force and law brought to mind by the troublesome concept of wooing with a sword reveal something about Theseus and the limits of his understanding, limits that will become more evident as the play goes on. Those limits are immediately confirmed, in fact, by the arrival of Egeus, Hermia's father, who has come to court to ask Theseus to enforce the law:

Egeus   Stand forth Demetrius.—My noble lord,
          This man hath my consent to marry her.—
          Stand forth Lysander.—And, my gracious Duke,
          This hath bewitched the bosom of my child.

     · · · · · · · · · · ·

          I beg the ancient privilege of Athens:
          As she is mine, I may dispose of her,
          Which shall be either to this gentleman
          Or to her death, according to our law. . . .

                         1.1.24–27, 41–44

The Duke, Theseus, immediately interposes, to add enforced chastity to Egeus's more restrictive options: marriage to Demetrius or death. Allying himself with the authoritarian father's request, Theseus mildly challenges Hermia to consult her temperament, since her choices are clear:

          Either to die the death, or to abjure
          For ever the society of men.
          Therefore, fair Hermia, question your desires.
          Know of your youth, examine well your blood,
          Whether, if you yield not to your father's choice,
          You can endure the livery of a nun,
          For aye to be in shady cloister mewed,
          To live a barren sister all your life,
          Chanting faint hymns to the cold fruitless moon.

                         1.1.65–73

Recall that this same Theseus is the man who moments before had spoken blithely of wooing Hippolyta with his sword, and who is about to celebrate his own wedding, one that manifestly accords with his personal choice. The rules and customs for dukes and for daughters in Athens may be very different, but still in the larger logic of this play it appears that both the authoritarian father and the authoritarian duke have a good deal to learn about the way love breaks old rules and makes for new ones.

A Midsummer Night's Dream is a play about a war between the sexes as figured in the dissension between Oberon and Titania (or, indeed, between Theseus and Hippolyta—the parts are often doubled in modern productions). The question is which is to be master, the Fairy King or the Fairy Queen; the Duke of Athens or his bride, the conquered Queen of the Amazons. To set the play into historical perspective it is useful to recall that a Virgin Queen sat on the throne of England, and that Queen Elizabeth, a powerful female ruler who called herself a "prince" in formal proclamations, was celebrated by Edmund Spenser in his epic poem *The Faerie Queene,* the first three books of which had been published in 1590, a few years before Shakespeare's play was written. As a woman on the throne, Elizabeth was an anomaly in a world in which most power inhered in men—fathers, husbands, dukes, kings, judges, teachers. By religious precept and by legal mandate women took second place in the social and political hierarchy and in the family. Elizabeth chose never to marry, although her numerous courtships, with suitors both English and foreign, continued well beyond her childbearing years and were a powerful mode of political negotiation. The elusive prize was to become King of England. The prospect of marriage for Elizabeth and the succession crisis that grew more acute as it became evident that she would not marry underlie and underscore many of the anxieties and fantasies in Shakespeare's play. The Duke marries an Amazon whom he woos with his sword; the Fairy Queen is in love with a braying ass; the Fairy King and Fairy Queen quarrel over the possession of a male protégé, the "changeling boy," who may be either a love object or an heir.

Elizabeth was frequently compared to an Amazon, and indeed the intermittent threat of a world of Amazons, a topsy-turvy world in which women ruled over men, was a nightmare that haunted much writing in the period. Elizabeth may very well have been in the audience at the play's first performance, on the occasion of a noble wedding. Clearly a compliment to her is intended in the description by Oberon of Cupid's arrow, aimed at "a fair vestal, thronèd by the west" (2.1.158). The virgin escaped Cupid's love dart and sailed on, fancy free, toward her serener destiny. Furthermore, Queen Elizabeth is dramatically present in this play in *both* partners to the intended nuptials—not only Hippolyta, the Amazon queen, but also Theseus, the powerful ruling Duke of Athens. Theseus, like the historical Elizabeth I, is a benevolent monarch who goes on progresses among his people, generously responding to their sometimes amateur theatrical performances. In other words, in looking at *A Midsummer Night's Dream* we might bear in mind that it represents a way of coming to terms—aesthetic and dramatic as well as political and social terms—with the tremendous cultural enigma posed by the female ruler: the pressure placed upon the society and the culture by the very fact of Elizabeth's rule. In this context Shakespeare's play might be said to dramatize the tension between the part of Elizabeth that was like Theseus and the part of Elizabeth that was like Hippolyta.

A reader interested in history might wonder how this description of the cloistered life of a virgin ("To live a barren sister all your life, / Chanting faint hymns to the cold fruitless moon") would accord with the public image of Queen Elizabeth. But where virginity or maidenhood disempowers Hermia, remanding her to her father's care or to the care of the Church, virginity empowered Elizabeth, who was, through her unmarried state, able to combine the strengths of the regnant Queen with those of the (hypothetically) marriageable woman. Elizabeth encouraged her ladies-in-waiting to marry, but she early asserted, holding up the coronation ring on her finger, that she herself was England's bride. As she wrote to Parliament in 1563, "though I can think [marriage] best for a private woman, yet do I strive myself to think it is not meet for a Prince"—that is, for herself.[1] The battle of the sexes, as a modern cliché would name it, engaged as combatants everyone but the Queen. Thus in this play Theseus can boast of his military conquest of the Amazon Hippolyta and yet tell Hermia, "To you your father should be as a god," which can be perceived as two types of disempowerment of women, in marriage and in singlehood.

"Am not I Hermia? Are not you Lysander?" This is Hermia's question in the middle of the play, act 3, scene 2, when the play's world is most disordered. It is a necessary question, and a familiar one in the Shakespearean middle world or dreamworld. In *The Comedy of Errors* one of the twin Dromios asks, "Am I Dromio? Am I your man? Am I myself?" King Lear will later offer a poignant version of the same desperate, disoriented query: "Who is it that can tell me who I am?" In *A Midsummer Night's Dream* this is a question that will be asked, in various modes and keys, by Bottom and Titania and by Helena and Demetrius, as the world of the Athenian wood strips them of what they thought were their identities. For it is of course the "wood near Athens" that is this play's interior world. Lysander and Hermia decide to run away, and their path takes them through the wood. In fact, *A Midsummer Night's Dream* presents one of the clearest examples of the characteristic Shakespearean triple pattern: from (1) a world of apparent reality and order, with seeds of disorder, to (2) a middle place, an interior world of transformation, in which things become far more evidently disordered (characters wear costumes, masks, or disguises, or acquire asses' heads; they play unaccustomed roles, higher or lower on the social scale, and are freed by fiction), and then out again into (3) the exterior world, the world of so-called reality—though still onstage—armed with new knowledge, and better prepared to rejoin the ongoing world of social action. This kind of basic triple pattern is consistently present in Shakespeare's plays regardless of their genre; it is not solely a comic mode, but rather represents as fundamental the inside/outside structure of dramaturgy as well as of theme and setting. Needless to say, variations on this structure are as important as adherence to it.

In *A Midsummer Night's Dream* many of these elements—night, illusion and dream, disguise and playing, self-dramatization—are present, but they are combined with a geographical location, the wood near Athens. If the basic rhythm is seen as court/country/court, or civilization/wilderness/civilization, the play invites us to ask a fundamental question: Which is really more civilized? The law that would send Hermia either to a nunnery or to death if she refuses to marry as her father directs? Or the world of change and possibility? For above all, the Athenian wood, like most Shakespearean middle worlds, is a place of transformation. Pursuing Hermia and Lysander, Demetrius is chased into the wood by Helena. Chagrined, he tells her that he is "wood within this wood." "Wood," derived from the Old English word *wod*, means "mad" or "lunatic." He is maddened, and also "wooed" (by Helena), within the wood. But to be wood within the wood is also to become part of the wood, to take on its qualities, to become as transformative and changeable as the wood itself.

The title of the play comes from the concept of "midsummer madness," the idea in folk culture in England (and also in Ireland, Sweden, and elsewhere in medieval Europe) that on Midsummer Eve, June 23, the longest day and shortest night of the year, madness, enchantment, and witchcraft would invade and transform the world. The idea is a very old one; it goes back to agrarian festivals held when spring plowing and planting were over, and harvesttime was far off. The holiday was often celebrated with "somergames"—sports, plays, drinking, and dancing, and witches, fairies, and mischievous sprites were thought to range abroad, playing pranks on livestock and on human beings. This is one reason the critic C. L. Barber dubbed *Dream* a "festive" comedy. Within the design of the play this larger and more anarchic cultural festival—in which the fairies and Puck (Robin Goodfellow) are major actors, but which is to a certain extent invisible to mortal eyes—surrounds and shadows the high-cultural and quintessentially civilizing event of the noble or royal wedding, with its hope of legitimate offspring and political succession.

The transformations in the wood are of two kinds: literal and figurative. Which kind is implemented seems to be a matter of social decorum; a "low" character like Bottom is literally turned into an ass and becomes the object of amusement, horror, or—for Titania—sexual desire, whereas the young aristocrats are transformed more genteelly by the use of language and dramatic action. Helena says she will stick to Demetrius's side like a "spaniel," the most loyal and servile of dogs, but she does not turn into a spaniel on the stage. Whether she turns into a "bitch" is another question, one that raises for our age the shifting borderline between the literal and the figurative. So on the level of the lovers, and the court—what we might call the conscious level of the play— such transformations remain safely metaphorical. Below the level of the conscious, among the artisans and the fairies and spirits, the changes appear physical and corporeal, as in a dream or a cartoon. Yet is Bottom really transformed, or just unmasked and revealed? When he appears onstage with the ass's head, and his friends run away from him, he speaks more truly than he knows: "This is to make an ass of me, to fright me, if they could" (3.1.106–107). He alone does not see that he is physically altered. In other words, he is *already* an ass. The wood world and the fairies un-metaphor these metaphors, literalizing figures of speech, creating an interior space—we could call it the unconscious— where people who act like asses look like asses. "O Bottom, thou art changed," says Snout. "What do I see on thee?" And Bottom replies, "What do you see? You see an ass-head of your own, do you?" (3.1.102–104). Again, what makes the exchange so comic is that he does not know of his own transformation. But the wood functions here as a mirror as well as a lens, reflecting Snout's own folly as well as Bottom's. Bottom with an ass's head is more like himself than before, just as Demetrius, his eyes anointed with the magic love-juice and imagining himself in love with Helena, is more like himself than he was before. The play is careful to tell us that he once did love Helena; this is a return to sanity through the alembic of madness.

Not only are the denizens of the Athenian wood in a process of change, the nature and weather of the wood itself have become disordered. This is a clear case of "sympathetic nature," again played out in a dramatic frame. The ostensible cause is a quarrel between Oberon and Titania for the possession of a little Indian page boy, whose birth is described by Titania in images of rich fertility:

> The fairyland buys not the child of me.
> His mother was a vot'ress of my order,
> And in the spicèd Indian air by night
> Full often hath she gossiped by my side,
> And sat with me on Neptune's yellow sands,
> Marking th'embarkèd traders on the flood,
> When we have laughed to see the sails conceive
> And grow big-bellied with the wanton wind,
> Which she with pretty and with swimming gait
> Following, her womb then rich with my young squire,
> Would imitate, and sail upon the land
> To fetch me trifles, and return again
> As from a voyage, rich with merchandise.
> But she, being mortal, of that boy did die;
> And for her sake do I rear up her boy;
> And for her sake I will not part with him.
>
> *2.1.122–137*

In this beautiful passage we hear again the tonic note of mortality so essential to Shakespearean comedy: "But she, being mortal, of that boy did die." Once again, death frames comedy. A figure mentioned in the play—someone we are told about but never actually meet—dies, offstage, and gives the play a depth, resonance, and chiaroscuro beyond its shimmering surface. We saw this with the lady Catherine's sister in *Love's Labour's Lost,* who—we are told—died of love. We will see it again in the fictional "sister" mentioned by the disguised Viola in *Twelfth Night,* who pined away "like patience on a monument, / Smiling at grief." And we will see it again at the end of this play, in the "Most Cruel Death of Pyramus and Thisbe," where yet again lovers will die for their love. It is the path not taken for characters in these stage comedies. We could say that characters offstage die so that those onstage may live, and learn.

The changeling boy is a key figure in *A Midsummer Night's Dream,* although he has no lines, and in some productions he never even appears. He is the emblem of desire—irrational, unattainable—and in fact of what critic René Girard nicely termed "mimetic desire," the desire for someone else's desire. The person who desires, Girard argues, derives his or her desire from envy or emulation. What someone else possesses, or loves, becomes valuable or desirable because it is already desired. Thus the basic pattern of erotic life is triangular.

Love and envy are part of the same structure. A loves C because B loves C is one possible outcome. But another is A professes love for C because A loves/desires/envies B. Here Titania has the boy, so Oberon wants him. By the end of the play Oberon gets him, taking this young page away from the all-female world of the Fairy Queen, where Titania wants to "crown him with flowers" and keep him as her private attendant, and school him instead as a knight, to "trace the forests wild." A changeling was a child secretly substituted for another in infancy, particularly one supposedly left (or in this case, taken) by fairies. The word "changeling" could also denote, in a looser sense, a fickle or inconstant person. Demetrius and Lysander could also be considered changelings in love. As a rhetorical figure, "the Changeling," according to George Puttenham's important handbook *The Arte of English Poesie* (1589), was an interchange of two elements of a proposition, with the ordinary relations between them reversed, "as he that should say, for tell me troth and lie not, lie me troth and tell not." The technical term for this is "hypallage," from the Greek word for "interchange," and in Quintilian it is equivalent to metonymy. This rhetorical pattern of exchange can be seen to underlie the structure of language and action throughout the play, where at one time or another every character is a changeling, and many utterances—not only Bottom's—seem to mean the opposite of what they say.

In dramatic terms, what is most important about the little Indian changeling is that he is the object of desire. He represents, in effect, the powerful irrationality of desire itself, as well as the element of "change" that afflicts every aspect of the play. In the most local sense, he is the cause of the quarrel that has brought dissension and disorder to fairyland. Significantly, the disorder in the wood takes the same form as the disorder in the court: a loss of fertility, a failure of marriage, and a threat of barrenness. Theseus has threatened Hermia with the nunnery; Titania has left Oberon's bed: "I have forsworn his bed and company." Because the wood world is a literalizing world, a world in which human "asses" look like asses, the barrenness and unnaturalism of Titania's sexual abstinence is transferred to the nature and the weather of the countryside. We might bear in mind that this landscape, though officially "Athens," looks a great deal like Shakespeare's England. The winds have sucked up fogs from the sea, the rivers have overflowed their banks, the corn in the fields is rotted before it is ripe:

> Titania   The nine men's morris is filled up with mud,
>   And the quaint mazes in the wanton green
>   For lack of tread are undistinguishable.
>   The human mortals want their winter cheer.
>   No night is now with hymn or carol blessed.
>   Therefore the moon, the governess of floods,
>   Pale in her anger washes all the air,
>   That rheumatic diseases do abound;

And thorough this distemperature we see
The seasons alter: hoary-headed frosts
Fall in the fresh lap of the crimson rose,
And on old Hiems' thin and icy crown
An odorous chaplet of sweet summer buds
Is, as in mock'ry, set. The spring, the summer,
The childing autumn, angry winter change
Their wonted liveries, and the mazèd world
By their increase now knows not which is which;
And this same progeny of evils comes
From our debate, from our dissension.
We are their parents and original.

2.1.98–117

Unseasonable weather, sickness, and disorder are rampant in the "mazèd world," and the cause is the quarrel between Oberon and Titania, the Fairy King and the Fairy Queen. "We are their parents and original"—the misconduct of these two, like the errors of Adam and Eve, disorder the world around them. A discord in temperament becomes, in the un-metaphored world of the wood, a discord in temperature.

This play presents the audience with three parallel worlds, and three rulers or stage managers who try to dictate action and choice: Theseus, who rules the court world of Athens; Oberon, who rules the fairy world of the wood; and Peter Quince, who rules, or rather tries and fails to rule, the equally disordered world of the "rude mechanicals," or artisans—a world of fiction and of art. Each of these "worlds" is a reflection and refraction of the others, and the point is often made in production through the time-honored custom of the doubling of parts. Shakespeare's company, the Lord Chamberlain's Men, later taken under King James's protection and renamed the King's Men, had around fifteen members. The company also employed apprentices and occasional hireling players for its productions to fill out the cast. But doubling parts was standard practice, and since the playwright wrote plays for the company (and sometimes acted in them), this often led to a kind of dramatic construction that would allow the audience to recognize linkages between and among characters. The limitation became an artistic opportunity. A subliminal connection, sometimes fostered by linguistic or thematic cues, could be made across the story line of the plot.

Bottom comments directly on this when he volunteers to play virtually all the parts in the "Pyramus and Thisbe" play—Thisbe and the Lion as well as Pyramus. The customary practice of doubling onstage thus directly underscores crucial parallels among the play's disparate social and political worlds. If we wanted to think about the device in psychological terms, we could see the nested worlds and doubled characters as representing the conscious (Theseus and the court), the unconscious (Oberon and the fairies), and the world of art, dream, and fantasy (Peter Quince and his "actors"; "Bottom's Dream") that mediates between them. A closer look at these three worlds will demonstrate even more clearly what they have in common, and how they differ.

Theseus's world, the framing outer world of the play, is a political realm that stands for law, and claims to stand as well for reason. In his famous speech in act 5 on the lunatic, the lover, and the poet, a speech often quoted out of context as "Shakespeare on imagination," Theseus in fact disparages the poet, and discounts and criticizes art, because it is not reasonable:

> I never may believe
> These antique fables, nor these fairy toys.
> Lovers and madmen have such seething brains,
> Such shaping fantasies, that apprehend
> More than cool reason ever comprehends.
> The lunatic, the lover, and the poet
> Are of imagination all compact.
> One sees more devils than vast hell can hold:
> That is the madman. The lover, all as frantic,
> Sees Helen's beauty in a brow of Egypt.
> The poet's eye, in a fine frenzy rolling,
> Doth glance from heaven to earth, from earth to heaven,
> And as imagination bodies forth
> The forms of things unknown, the poet's pen
> Turns them to shapes, and gives to airy nothing
> A local habitation and a name.
>
> 5.1.2–17

It is a powerful passage of poetry—but what does it say? That the imagination cannot be trusted. That poets are crazy. That art is an illusion. That lovers and madmen—that is, the characters of this play, afflicted by midsummer madness—are given to unrealistic fantasies that "apprehend / More than cool reason ever comprehends." But let us consider the role of "cool reason" in this play—reason as the opposite of art, or of love. When Lysander, who has been in love with Hermia, has his eyes anointed by Puck with the magic love-juice—from a plant called love-in-idleness (the pansy, also called heartsease)—he is instantly transformed into a lover of Helena, and he justifies this change by attributing it to *reason:* "The will of man is by his reason swayed, / And reason says you are the worthier maid" (2.2.121–122). Bottom, the play's wise fool, has a much sounder view of reason and love. When Titania awakes and sees him with his ass's head, she cries out, "I love thee," and Bottom replies:

> Methinks, mistress, you should have little reason for that. And yet, to say the truth, reason and love keep little company together nowadays. . . .
>
> 3.1.126–128

Reason—and Theseus's defense of it—is constantly being undermined in the course of the play, as, for example, when Theseus deduces, or thinks he deduces, what the lovers are doing in the wood. His benign supposition is that they have come to do him honor and "to observe the rite of May," cutting down branches of the fragrant blossoms. In fact, as we know, they have fled into the wood for purposes variously rebellious, defiant, and carnal. Love keeps little company with reason.

If Theseus's world is based on reason and law and rank and hierarchy and a father's authority—and on slow-moving time ("how slow / This old moon wanes")—Oberon's world, the fairy world, is in many ways its opposite. The fairy world is a world of instantaneous time, in which Puck can circumnavigate the globe in less than an hour ("I'll put a girdle round about the earth / In forty minutes" [2.1.175–176]) in pursuit of love-in-idleness. It is a world of enchantment, magic, music, and mischief, in which Puck is the principal actor and agent, for Puck is to Oberon what Bottom is to Peter Quince. Puck himself, *the* Puck or "Robin Goodfellow," is a quicksilver spirit who personifies transformation:

> Puck   Sometime a horse I'll be, sometime a hound,
> A hog, a headless bear, sometime a fire,
> And neigh, and bark, and grunt, and roar, and burn,
> Like horse, hound, hog, bear, fire, at every turn.
>
> *3.1.96–99*

He is a practical joker who likes to impersonate a three-legged stool and disappear out from under when an old woman tries to sit down. He is mischievous and playful and wryly amused at human folly. His exclamation "Lord, what fools these mortals be!" (3.2.115) has, like so many other lines in this play, taken on an independent life as supposed evidence of "Shakespeare's" ideas about the human condition. Puck, we should note, is not Shakespeare's invention. The word was used, without the capital *P*, as early as 1000 B.C.E. to describe an evil, malicious, or mischievous spirit or demon, and in the time of Chaucer and of William Langland, "the pouke" was associated with the biblical Devil. By the sixteenth and seventeenth centuries, in the works of Spenser, Michael Drayton, Jonson, and especially Shakespeare, Puck, otherwise known as Robin Goodfellow or Hobgoblin, had become a crafty spirit, goblin, or sprite, given to mischievous tricks—and even an epithet for a mischievous child (the part would much later be played on film by the young Mickey Rooney in Max Reinhardt's 1935 version of *A Midsummer Night's Dream*). Puck as imagined by Shakespeare and Spenser blended into English folklore and English country life, as can be seen in his list of favorite tricks.

Throughout the play we will see that not only Puck but also his fellow fairies Oberon and Titania embody distinctly human characteristics carried to extremes: human playfulness, human jealousy, human lust. But at the same time they are, importantly, spirits of imagination. In act 3 Puck warns Oberon that the time in which to reunite the lovers is growing short, since dawn is coming, and when day breaks "ghosts, wand'ring here and there, / Troop home to churchyards" (3.2.382–383). Dejected spirits, ghosts in purgatory, and others out of place and unsettled in the netherworld must hide from the sun. "But," Oberon is quick to remind his lieutenant, "we are spirits of another sort" (3.2.389)—spirits of dream and possibility. Like Mercutio's tiny Queen Mab in *Romeo and Juliet*, they are shaping spirits of imagination, wish fulfillment, and fantasy. They are, in fact, very close to what Theseus dismisses as "airy nothing" in his speech about lunatics, lovers, and poets. The idea that fairies were tiny beings, almost invisible to the naked eye—an idea that the modern age takes for granted—was a relatively new one in the early modern period. In the folklore of Shakespeare's time figures like Puck were well known, but many were considered to be of normal human size. The fairies described by poets like Chaucer and Shakespeare's contemporary Edmund Spenser were sometimes full-size, representing an alternative clan, race, or society rather than a different level of existence (magical, supernatural). Oberon and Titania are fairies, but they are clearly envisaged on a human scale. Their attendants—Cobweb, Moth, Mustardseed—are, just as clearly, imagined as minuscule (although they are played on the stage by human actors). Fairy size and visibility would become a major fascination of the Victorian period (the fascination of which *Peter Pan*'s Tinker Bell, *Alice in Wonderland,* and the *Nutcracker* ballet are direct descendants). The late twentieth century's interest in film animation renewed this fascination and expanded the possibilities for portrayal.

The word "fairy" is related to "fay" or "Fate"; the classical three Fates became, over time, associated with human destiny, and were said to attend and preside over childbirth. By making his fairies diminutive, Shakespeare, like the playwright John Lyly in his *Endimion* (printed 1591), emphasized their relation to the subconscious and the unconscious—which is to say, to human psychology and desire. In *Romeo and Juliet* Queen Mab ("the fairies' midwife," according to Mercutio) visits sleepers and influences their dreams. In *A Midsummer Night's Dream* the fairy world is a place of dream and wish fulfillment, of lust and libido, mirroring the psychologies of the play's human characters, from the courtly aristocrats to the humble craftsmen.

The third set of characters in the play, the working-class artisans, or "rude mechanicals" ("mechanical" has the same meaning as the modern "mechanic"), can be located, imaginatively, at the opposite end of the scale from the fairies, with the human lovers in the middle. The fairies are more intuitive and more elevated, some—like Cobweb and Moth—scarcely corporeal at all, while the mechanicals are "palpable-gross," like their play. Their names denote their crafts: Snug the joiner is a furniture maker ("joiner" is another name for carpenter); Bottom the weaver takes his name, at least in one sense, from a skein used to wind thread or yarn ("a bottom of thread"); Flute is a bellows-mender. Their theatrical ambitions thus hark back in one sense to the old guild plays, though these actors are more like entrepreneurs, seeking preferment from the Duke. That their actorly world is one of somewhat anarchic possibility is made clear by Bottom when, as we have already noticed, he offers to play all the parts. Cast as Pyramus, "a lover that kills himself, most gallant, for love," he is curious about the rest of the dramatis personae, and when Flute, whose high voice may be suggested by his name, seems to hesitate when cast as the lady Thisbe, Bottom leaps into the breach:

Bottom   An I may hide my face, let me play Thisbe too. I'll speak in a monstrous little voice: "Thisne, Thisne!"—"Ah Pyramus, my lover dear, thy Thisbe dear and lady dear."

Quince   No, no, you must play Pyramus; and Flute, you Thisbe. . . .

Bottom   Let me play the lion too. I will roar that I will do any man's heart good to hear me. I will roar that I will make the Duke say, "Let him roar again; let him roar again." . . .

Quince   You can play no part but Pyramus; for Pyramus is a sweet-faced man; a proper man as one shall see in a summer's day; a most lovely, gentlemanlike man. Therefore you must needs play Pyramus.

1.2.43–46, 58–60, 69–72

So Bottom is cast, both in the play and in the play-within-the-play, as the "sweet-faced" lover. Crowned with an ass's head, he will be hailed by the awakening Titania—whose eyes, like those of the mortal lovers, have been anointed so that she falls in love with the first person she sees—with "What angel wakes me from my flowery bed?" Shakespeare's audience would have been aware of dangers barely averted. Oberon's "Wake when some vile thing is near" suggests that Titania could have lighted on a worse love object than the amiable Bottom.

As he progresses from Bottom the weaver to Titania's ass-headed lover to the classical hero Pyramus, Bottom does so with unflagging zeal, equanimity, and enthusiasm, all qualities Theseus and the others might do well to emulate. As so frequently in Shakespearean comedy, the "low" characters and the comic plot point up by contrast the shortcomings of the aristocrats. Just as Costard in *Love's Labour's Lost* is closely in tune with the nature of desire ("Such is the simplicity of man to hearken after the flesh" [1.1.211–212]), so Bottom knows more about love than do the Athenian lovers.

What, after all, are those lovers like? For one thing, they are apparently indistinguishable from one another, despite the fact that the play opens with Egeus's strong insistence that Demetrius is preferable to Lysander. We learn nothing about their financial expectations, and little about their families, except that Lysander has an aunt, of "great revenue." As suitors, they seem equally "eligible." Indeed, Puck cannot tell them apart. Having been instructed to anoint the eyes of an Athenian, he chooses the wrong one, transforms Lysander into a suitor for Helena rather than Hermia, and begins the whole process of comical and dangerous disordering in the wood. In this sense, then, Lysander and Demetrius are somewhat akin to the twin brothers in *The Comedy of Errors*. Distinguishing between them is all-important, but also virtually impossible; in modern productions their costumes are usually color-coded so the audience can tell who is who. The same is true for the women as for the men. Here preferences are even more violently expressed. One moment both men swear their love to Hermia, and the next—breaking an oath—they both swear fealty to Helena, attributing the change to "reason."

In a way highly characteristic of Shakespeare, we get, from the perspective of the distraught Helena, a glimpse backward into the "schooldays' friendship" and "childhood innocence" when the two young women were girls, "sisters," and, effectively, twins:

> We, Hermia, like two artificial gods
> Have with our needles created both one flower,
> Both on one sampler, sitting on one cushion,
> Both warbling of one song, both in one key,
> As if our hands, our sides, voices, and minds
> Had been incorporate. So we grew together,
> Like to a double cherry: seeming parted,
> But yet an union in partition,
> Two lovely berries moulded on one stem.
> So, with two seeming bodies, but one heart . . .
>
> 3.2. 204–213

This idyllic vision of undifferentiated mutuality is ruptured by adolescence, by courtship, and by heterosexual desire. In *A Midsummer Night's Dream* the memory of this moment is already nostalgic. The affecting portrait of the two young girls sewing and singing side by side is spoken from the point of view of loss and betrayal: "Is all the counsel that we two have shared— / The sisters' vows, the hours that we have spent . . . / O, is all quite forgot?" The comic energies of the play will pull in another direction. Differentiated by their male suitors, these heretofore identical young women, whose very names seem twinned, suddenly appear as opposites. Thus one of the funniest moments in the dramatic action occurs in what might fairly be called a catfight between Hermia and Helena in act 3, scene 2, a scene in which the two women compare their physical appearance. Helena, playing the part of the injured innocent, calls Hermia a "puppet," and Hermia, so recently the object of both men's desire, seizes upon this word as an explanation for their otherwise inexplicable desertion:

> Puppet? Why, so! Ay, that way goes the game.
> Now I perceive that she hath made compare

Between our statures; she hath urged her height,
And with her personage, her tall personage,
Her height, forsooth, she hath prevailed with him—
And are you grown so high in his esteem
Because I am so dwarfish and so low?
How low am I, thou painted maypole? Speak,
How low am I? I am not yet so low
But that my nails can reach unto thine eyes.

3.2.290–299

This is a scene worthy of any modern soap opera, and it doubtless has inspired several. Helena has the wit to keep saying the words "low" and "little" throughout the balance of the scene to the baffled and infuriated Hermia. Directors obligingly follow what seem to be clear hints here, casting a tall blonde as Helena and a shorter brunette as Hermia. But surely they are also missing the point, which is that appearances are relative or, as Helena remarks, "Love looks not with the eyes, but with the mind, / And therefore is winged Cupid painted blind" (1.1.234–235). Surely the scene would be even more comical if the difference between the two women were slight or nonexistent.

Another sign of the lack of understanding of love that seems to be a universal condition at the play's beginning is the constant repetition of the sign-word "dote," which we have seen to stand for shallow love, self-love, or the condition of being in love with love rather than with another person. Lysander says that Helena "dotes, / Devoutly dotes, dotes in idolatry / Upon this spotted and inconstant man"—Demetrius, who has inconstantly abandoned her for Hermia. Moments later Lysander will wish her well in the same terms ("Helena, adieu, / As you on him, Demetrius dote on you"), whereas Helena complains of Demetrius's "doting on Hermia's eyes." Oberon, describing the magic love-juice, says it "[w]ill make or man or woman madly dote / Upon the next live creature that it sees," and this power is demonstrated by Titania's instant infatuation with Bottom. "O how I love thee, how I dote on thee!" she cries. Oberon, watching her feed her ass-headed lover with a "bottle," or bundle, of hay, is belatedly seized with compassion. "Her dotage now I do begin to pity," he remarks, and forthwith commands the reversal of the enchantments. Finally Demetrius, awakening in the fourth act, explains to Theseus as best he can why he has returned to Helena: "[M]y love to Hermia, / Melted as the snow, seems to me now / As the remembrance of an idle gaud / Which in my childhood I did dote upon" (4.1.162–165).

Contrast this romantic attitude of worship with the pragmatic, down-to-earth, but equally deluded passion of Titania for Bottom. Again, modern productions have tended to go for warm comedy here, giving Bottom an ass-head that could belong to a stuffed animal or be found in a holiday window display. But falling in love with an animal, and in particular with an ass, has a long history of literary and sexual associations. The Roman writer Apuleius's novel *The Golden Ass,* translated into English in the sixteenth century, tells the story of a man who is mistakenly turned into an ass (he anoints himself with the wrong ointment, having sought to become an owl, the emblem of wisdom) and then is coaxed into a sexual relationship with a highborn lady. At one point his noble lover kisses him tenderly on the nose, rather like Titania. Since the time of the Greeks the ass has been a figure of ignorance and stupidity in fables and proverbs. But Titania's infatuation is also clearly one of the body. It is not Bottom's conversation that attracts the Fairy Queen. Both on the level of carnality and of social inappropriateness this "high"/"low" pairing, queen and donkey, ought to send out danger signals in addition to producing smiles of amusement. And Bottom's hybrid status—he is not an ass but an ass-headed man—links him with the kind of monstrous creature that fascinated and horrified Elizabethans, a sign, as indeed he is, of the human capacity to degenerate into an animal state.

On one end of the scale, then, is Titania's lust for the animal/man Bottom. And on the other side, equally of concern, is the resistance to sexuality and sexual love exhibited by Hermia in the wood. She has run off with her suitor, Lysander, but she sharply rejects his invitation that "one turf" should be a pillow for them both in the wood. "[G]entle friend," she says, "for love and courtesy, / Lie further off, in humane modesty." This seems perfectly in keeping with what a well-brought-up young girl ought to say and to think, but it is in fact the small event that produces major trouble. When Puck comes upon them sleeping separately, he thinks Hermia must be the scorned lady he has been sent to assist, and he denigrates Lysander as a "lack-love" and "kill-courtesy." Hermia's dream, in which she is menaced by a serpent while Lysander sits by "smiling at his cruel prey," suggests that Lysander and the serpent are one and the same, the feared and desired lover split into two fantasy figures, the sexual tempter and the distant observer. But what does he observe? Her desire, or just his own? As in *Romeo and Juliet,* so also in *A Midsummer Night's Dream* the question of women's eroticism is addressed directly in a manner both sophisticated and nuanced. A young woman, sexually inexperienced and sheltered by parental supervision, finds herself on the brink of a dangerous and exciting adventure with her lover. In a similar way, Demetrius has warned Helena not to follow him into the wood, which he explicitly describes to her as a place of wildness and sexual risk.

Taken together, the stories of Titania and Bottom, Hermia and Lysander, Helena and Demetrius—and Thisbe and Pyramus—tell a complicated tale about sexual desire. It is a tale that is complicated even further by the list of women, briefly mentioned by Oberon, who were seduced and abandoned by Theseus long ago, before his engagement to Hippolyta. ("Didst not thou," he says accusingly to Titania, "lead him through the glimmering night / From Perigouna whom he ravishèd, / And make him with fair Aegles break his faith, /

With Ariadne and Antiopa?" [2.1.77–80].) Shakespeare's source here is the "Life of Theseus" in Thomas North's 1579 translation of Plutarch's *Parallel Lives;* "Antiopa" is another name for Hippolyta, the Amazon Queen.

The playwright could easily have omitted this reference to Theseus's infidelities, which seem so out of character. The Theseus described by Oberon in this moment seems anything but the benevolent and mild-mannered Athenian ruler we have come to know. The inclusion casts a somber light over the play, deepening the experience of the more harmless and even comical infidelities of Lysander and Demetrius. Furthermore, for any in the audience who are aware of the second half of this story, the narrative behind the play is even more troubling. The child of the union of Theseus and Hippolyta, according to Plutarch, was the fanatically chaste young man Hippolytus, whose tragic death comes as a result of his stepmother Phaedra's lust for him, and, indirectly, because he chooses to honor Artemis, the goddess of chastity, but not Aphrodite, the goddess of love. The "happy ending" of this play of romantic love is in the theater almost completely satisfying. But with Oberon's caution about progeny in the final moments, and his expressed hope, so soon to be dashed, that the offspring of the newly married pair "[e]ver shall be fortunate" (5.2.36), a mythologically minded spectator may be reminded that closure—in general and in this particular case—can only be achieved by forgetting or ignoring what comes next.

The play thus strikes a careful, though also a playful, balance between "cool reason" and the dangers of the irrational. And those dangers are everywhere. There is freedom in fleeing from a repressive parent and a repressive law, as Hermia does, to follow her lover into the wood; there is freedom and possibility in choosing love and marriage over the nunnery. But there is a parallel danger, as we have seen, in excessive sexuality and desire: in the dream of the snake invading Hermia's little Eden, and in the example of Titania doting blindly on the transformed Bottom. When Titania wakes and calls out amorously to Bottom, we have the word of Puck, the amused bystander, for what transpires: "My mistress with a monster is in love." Or, as Titania herself will later express it, "My Oberon, what visions have I seen! / Methought I was enamoured of an ass" (4.1.72–73). This is dream, too, and these are visions. (How many modern lovers, once they have emerged from infatuation—*in + fatuus,* "folly" or "foolishness"—could adopt Titania's rueful exclamation as their own!)

There is danger, too, in the very ambiguity of the wood. The same attributes that make magic possible also make it dangerous. Around the edges of this enchantment lurks the possibility of real madness, as contrasted with the delicious "midsummer" variety, the state of the lunatic rather than the lover or the poet. (A "lunatic," afflicted with the kind of madness that was governed by the changes of the moon, is not so different, we might think, from John Lyly's Endimion, in love with Cynthia, the goddess of the moon—commonly read as a figure for Queen Elizabeth.) In the world of the wood there is no definition. Hermia and Helena, the scansion of whose names, like "Montague" and "Capulet," suggests that they are in a way interchangeable and indistinguishable, are, as it turns out, all too easily confused and swapped. The result is comedy, but also chaos. It is no more orderly for both men to love Helena than for both to love Hermia. When Puck leads the two Athenian men, Lysander and Demetrius, "up and down, up and down" in the darkness, pretending to be first the one and then the other so that they flail helplessly against the dark and fall down, exhausted though unhurt, they are fighting not only each other's specters but also "Puck," imagination, the dark things of the wood. And they are fighting, too, their own double and divided selves.

Puck makes mistakes, and in so doing he increases, rather than decreases, confusion, as he admits to Oberon:

> Believe me, king of shadows, I mistook.
> Did not you tell me I should know the man
> By the Athenian garments he had on?—
>
> *3.2.348–350*

For Puck, such confusions are a source of pleasure rather than concern:

> And so far blameless proves my enterprise
> That I have 'nointed an Athenian's eyes;
> And so far am I glad it so did sort
> As this their jangling I esteem a sport.
>
> *3.2.351–354*

His pleasure here is spectatorial, like that of the Princess of France in *Love's Labour's Lost* ("There's no such sport as sport by sport o'ethrown" [5.2.152]).

But the human lovers, unlike Puck, have permanent identities in the social world, and they cannot exist forever in a condition that shrouds them in darkness, renders their affections unstable, and leaves them prey to the darker side of the imagination. "Am not I Hermia? And are not you Lysander?" There are questions that need to be asked, but also that need to be answered. The ambiguity of the dream state is a crucial, liminal stage, but for the Athenian lovers and for Bottom it is a stage that must be experienced and then left behind. At the same time, the imprint of this salutary instability, this firsthand encounter with fantasy and folly, will change them.

Characteristically, it is not the Athenian lovers—nor the rather pompous Duke Theseus, despite his bromides about lunatics and lovers—who most directly perceive the dangers of illusion. Instead it is Bottom and his friends, who, like the actors who portray them, are engaged in presenting an entertainment to a wealthy and powerful patron in the hope of preferment. Peter Quince's company is consumed with worry about the indecorousness of their too-realistic play: "Pyramus must draw a sword to kill himself, which the ladies cannot abide." And "to bring in—God shield us—a lion among ladies is a most dreadful thing." In order to avoid the dangers of mimesis, Bottom devises an ingenious set of puncturing deflations:

I have a device to make all well. Write me a prologue, and let the prologue seem to say we will do no harm with our swords, and that Pyramus is not killed indeed; and for the more better assurance, tell them that I, Pyramus, am not Pyramus, but Bottom the weaver. This will put them out of fear.

3.1.15–20

Snout now voices the second concern: "Will not the ladies be afeard of the lion?" In eager emulation he proposes the same solution—"Therefore another prologue must tell he is not a lion"—and is brushed aside by Bottom's fertile imagination, which has moved on to another "device":

Nay, you must name his name, and half his face must be seen through the lion's neck, and he himself must speak through, saying thus or to the same defect: "ladies," or "fair ladies, I would wish you" or "I would request you" or "I would entreat you not to fear, not to tremble. My life for yours. If you think I come hither as a lion, it were pity of my life. No, I am no such thing. I am a man, as other men are"—and there, indeed, let him name his name, and tell them plainly he is Snug the joiner.

3.1.32–40

Role-playing is dangerous, these suggestions imply. The condition of being an actor is a condition akin to the performance of magic. To Bottom, "The Most Lamentable Comedy, and Most Cruel Death of Pyramus and Thisbe," that tedious, brief scene, is so potentially believable that he feels he must break its fiction in order to protect society—and his own self-interest. The dangers of the irrational can be combated only by a safe retreat to reality: "I, Pyramus, am not Pyramus, but Bottom the weaver." "[T]ell them plainly he is Snug the joiner." This is a kind of theatrical unmasking that the twentieth century would associate with Brecht, or with Pirandello.

The antidote to the dangers of the irrational in *A Midsummer Night's Dream* is to be found through the agency of art itself. A series of encapsulated art objects—a "sampler," a "dream," a "tedious brief comedy"—will take experience and translate it into artifice. Near the end of the play, the Athenian lovers puzzle aloud about whether they are awake or asleep. Hermia says, "Methink I see these things with parted eye, / When everything seems double," and Demetrius poses the play's central question:

It seems to me
That yet we sleep, we dream.

4.1.189–190

Who can tell? Which is the sleep, which the waking dream or nightmare? Rescued from this radical ambiguity by the mundane memory of a common occurrence—they have encountered the Duke in the wood—the lovers take this

as reassuring evidence of an external reality: "Why then, we are awake. Let's follow him, / And by the way let us recount our dreams"(4.1.194–195). Safely rele-
gated now to the realm of dreams are all the adventures that have made up the
"real" events (that is, the perceived, performed dramatic action) of the play.
This impulse to retell the events that have transpired is a common one at the
end of Shakespeare's plays. At the end of *Romeo and Juliet* the Prince urges his
subjects: "Go hence, to have more talk of these sad things." Almost always, one
implied form that "more talk" or recounting of dreams will take is the replaying
of the play. But in the case of *A Midsummer Night's Dream,* where the title marks
the indissolubility of what is fictive and what is real, the dream-within-the-
dream occupies a special, privileged place.

Thus a key moment for the play, and an even clearer example of the encapsulated art object, is the dramatic incident celebrated—by its flummoxed
speaker—as "Bottom's Dream":

> God's my life! Stolen hence, and left me asleep?—I have had a most rare
> vision. I have had a dream past the wit of man to say what dream it was.
> Man is but an ass if he go about t'expound this dream. Methought I was—
> there is no man can tell what. Methought I was, and methought I had—
> but man is but a patched fool if he will offer to say what methought I had.
> The eye of man hath not heard, the ear of man hath not seen, man's hand
> is not able to taste, his tongue to conceive, nor his heart to report what my
> dream was. I will get Peter Quince to write a ballet of this dream. It shall be
> called "Bottom's Dream," because it hath no bottom, and I will sing it in
> the latter end of a play, before the Duke.

> *4.1.198–210*

As the audience is well aware, this was no dream. The transformed Bottom, a
hybrid monster with an ass's head, courted and made love to by the Queen of
the Fairies—this has been the comical business of the play, hinting at the folly
of love, and at love's lust. ("[M]ethought I had—" a phrase often accompanied
onstage by a gesture sketching absent asses' ears, could with equal appropriateness indicate prodigious endowment below the waist.) Likewise Bottom's dead
metaphor, "Man is but an ass," leaps startlingly to life, as we see firsthand how
the wood-world and the dreamworld render the cliché in literal terms, and thus
make it allegorical. Bottom is not the only man in the play who is an ass—just
the only one who looks like one. His scrambled bodily syntax—"The eye of
man hath not heard, the ear of man hath not seen, man's hand is not able to
taste, his tongue to conceive, nor his heart to report what my dream was"—is at
once a mangling of a passage from Saint Paul's First Epistle to the Corinthians
and an instance of what has become known in psychology, literature, and lin-
guistics as "synesthesia," the use of metaphors in which terms from one kind of
sense impression are used to describe another: for example, a "loud color." The
transforming poetic power of synesthesia is also present in the play in an utter-

ance like Helena's "Love looks not with the eyes, but with the mind, / And therefore is winged Cupid painted blind." Hearing replaces sight in the wood, as night replaces day, and "dream" replaces apparent reality. ("Blind cupid," according to art historian Erwin Panofsky, was a Neoplatonic emblem of carnal, or profane, love rather than its counterpart, spiritual love.) Later in the play the same confusion will persist, as at the close of the "Pyramus and Thisbe" play the actors ask Theseus whether he would prefer to "hear" a bergamask dance or "see" an epilogue.

Bottom's biblical misquotation may be based on the Geneva Bible edition of 1599, "the Eye hath not seen, and nor ear heard, neither have entered into the heart of man . . ." (1 Corinthians 2:9). In William Tyndale's translation, published in 1525, the "eye hath not seen" lines of the same passage end with the following: "But God hath opened them unto us by his spirit. For the spirit searcheth all things, yea, the bottom of God's secrets." The word "bottom" has a wide variety of meanings in the period, from "a skein to wind thread on" to "the last, fundamental, basic." (In modern usage both "bottom" and "ass" are terms for the rump or posterior, but neither was explicitly current in Shakespeare's day.)

The play's greatest internal fiction is neither Hermia's song and sampler nor "Bottom's Dream," but rather that gloriously flawed artifact, the "Pyramus and Thisbe" play, dubiously offered to Theseus and Hippolyta as entertainment for their wedding celebration:

> Lysander   [*reads*] "A tedious brief scene of young Pyramus
>   And his love Thisbe: very tragical mirth."
> Theseus   "Merry" *and* "tragical"? "Tedious" *and* "brief"?
>   That is, hot ice and wondrous strange snow.
>   How shall we find the concord of this discord?
>
>   *5.1.56–60*

The speaker is—of course—Theseus, ever unwilling, in this play, to trust the products of the imagination or of the poet's pen. "Hot ice" and "strange snow" are familiar oxymorons, standard practice in the "Petrarchan" poetry of the time, and utilized by Romeo at his least imaginative when he fancies himself a lovelorn swain pining for the elusive Rosaline. As for "concord" and "discord," these terms resound throughout the play. Like the lovers' tales when they emerge from the wood, tales Theseus found "more strange than true," the "Pyramus and Thisbe" play, like the larger play that contains it, grows, as Hippolyta says, to "something of great constancy." Like the equally anarchic and inept pageant of the "Nine Worthies" in *Love's Labour's Lost*, this play-within-the-play, performed by social inferiors for their putative betters, confronts the themes, aspirations, and pretensions of the aristocrats and comments on the larger play that contains it.

As presented by Peter Quince and his players, "Pyramus and Thisbe" is nothing less than the countermyth of *A Midsummer Night's Dream*—the thing that did not happen, the tragedy encapsulated within the comedy and reduced to a manageable, bearable, and laughable fiction. For if *A Midsummer Night's Dream* has many points in common with *Romeo and Juliet,* the plot of "Pyramus and Thisbe" *is,* in effect, the plot of *Romeo and Juliet.* A pair of lovers, forbidden by their parents to marry or even meet, come together in the middle of the night at a dark tomb to share their love. The lady, Thisbe, arrives before her lover and is at once forced to flee, chased by a lion and leaving behind her a misleading clue, her mantle. Pyramus, grief-stricken, taking the bloody mantle as the sign that his beloved is dead, draws his sword, stabs himself, and dies. The lady Thisbe then returns and kills herself. It is the story of *Romeo and Juliet.* But it is also the story of *A Midsummer Night's Dream,* the story as it might have been.

Consider the prop, the bloody cloak, or mantle: "Thy mantle good, / What, stained with blood?" Pyramus exclaims in stagy disbelief. As is also the case with a more famous red-stained prop in Shakespeare, Othello's handkerchief embroidered with strawberries, the bloody mantle here, especially when its discovery is greeted by Bottom/Pyramus with the histrionic exclamation that "lion vile hath here deflowered my dear" (5.1.281), suggests a sexual misadventure. Bottom's word "deflowered" is inadvertently apposite; he seems to think it means something more like "ravaged" or "destroyed," but the sexual overtones are clear, whether or not "Pyramus" can hear them. And the threat of sexual violation— as well as the gentler mode of sexual invitation—has been present in the larger play since Demetrius warned Helena not to follow him into the wood, and since Lysander beckoned to Hermia to share a single piece of turf as a pillow. Violation by a "monster," whether the serpent of Hermia's dream or the ass-headed hybrid of Bottom's, has been a constant theme, and we should recall that the lion of the "Pyramus and Thisbe" play, like Bottom, is a hybrid man-and-animal, in this case with the body parts reversed: instead of a man with an ass's head, the actor who plays the "lion's part" opens his costume to reveal that he has the head of a man.

A few observations about the language and spirit of this "lamentable comedy" will serve to demonstrate its sublime capacity to produce both laughter and rueful recognition. The rhyming prologue, for example, is declaimed in such a way as to reverse and undermine everything it appears to be saying. This is a familiar trick of early modern drama: "unpointed," or unpunctuated, letters, open to profound misconstruction because the lack of punctuation leads to basic errors in reading, are central plot devices. But the misconstruction is usually an inset—a letter, prophecy, or other text is presented for interpretation— rather than constituting the very fabric of the play, as here:

Quince [*as Prologue*]   If we offend, it is with our good will.
                    That you should think: we come not to offend

But with good will. To show our simple skill,
  That is the true beginning of our end.
Consider then we come but in despite.
  We do not come as minding to content you,
Our true intent is. All for your delight
  We are not here. That you should here repent
    you
The actors are at hand, and by their show
You shall know all that you are like to know.

5.1.108–117

"We do not come as minding to content you." "[W]e come but in despite." "All for your delight / We are not here." The Prologue itself is in a constant state of metamorphosis and transformation. As Theseus notes, in a phrase that could well stand as a description of the entire midsummer night spent in the woods, "His speech [is] like a tangled chain—nothing impaired, but all disordered."

The playwright is able to use this metadramatic medium, the play-within-the-play, to make gentle mock not only of the Athenian lovers but also of the work of other poets and playwrights, notably the old-fashioned habit of using alliterated words and phrases (Pyramus's "Whereat with blade—with bloody, blameful blade— / He bravely broached his boiling bloody breast") and histrionic "Senecan" apostrophes and exclamations:

O grim-looked night, O night with hue so black,
  O night which ever art when day is not;
O night, O night, alack, alack, alack,
  I fear my Thisbe's promise is forgot.

5.1.168–171

The speaker is, again, the unflappable Bottom, in his element. At the opposite end of the scale of confident performance is the total breakdown of fictiveness that comes with Moonshine's halting account: "All I have to say is to tell you that the lantern is the moon, I the man in the moon, this thorn bush my thorn bush, and this dog my dog." Literalization here replaces literary figure and rhetoric. The truth-telling Starveling as Moonshine anticipates the more profound and pointed literalisms of the gravedigger in *Hamlet* (Hamlet: "Upon what ground?" First Clown: "Why, here in Denmark") and the Porter in *Macbeth*. Likewise, the grieving Thisbe offers an inadvertently anti-Petrarchan description of the dead Pyramus, who here has white lips, a red nose, and yellow cheeks, and eyes "green as leeks," in contrast with more orthodox beauties in poetry, who have red lips, pale skin, dark eyes, and yellow hair—and are women.

The wood near Athens has been full of dangerous serpents and monsters, whether in dreams, in rhetoric (Lysander says he'll shake Hermia from him like a serpent), or in action. A stern parent, Egeus, has compelled the lovers to meet secretly. Dangers are all around them, and the Athenians' escape from danger, back to the world of comedy and marriage, is fortunate but not inevitable. The "Pyramus and Thisbe" play neutralizes and makes manageable all the dangers they could have encountered. And it is a measure of their own limitation that none of the noble spectators can see any connection between the play they are watching and the one they are in. In *A Midsummer Night's Dream* it is Theseus who shows some compassion for the amateur actors and their efforts ("never anything can be amiss / When simpleness and duty tender it"), though Hippolyta, despite her acerbic verdict on the play's quality ("This is the silliest stuff that ever I heard"), will feel great empathy for the plight of Pyramus (5.1.83–84, 207). Both royal spectators are right: the play is silly—but it is true.

Once the play is over, and the stage littered with "dead" bodies, the actors at once leap to their feet and begin to caper about in their bergamask dance. Theseus prudently declines to hear (or, rather, as Bottom offers it, to "see") an epilogue. At the close of the tragedy of Pyramus and Thisbe dance does replace death, comedy replaces tragedy, and, as was the case at the end of *Romeo and Juliet,* no one onstage seems to have fully understood what has taken place. Nor do the characters seem to perceive, or particularly to value, the role of art (including theater, and the play-within-the-play) in drawing off and civilizing the element of tragedy implicit in the human condition. It is left to Puck, the spirit of transformation, imagination, and anarchic mischief, to deliver the final word, as the lovers go to their beds accompanied by songs of fertility and procreation once again:

> If we shadows have offended,
> Think but this, and all is mended:
> That you have but slumbered here,
> While these visions did appear;
> And this weak and idle theme,
> No more yielding but a dream . . .
>
> *Epilogue 1–6*

There was no play—there was only a dream. *A Midsummer Night's Dream* has taken place only in our imaginations. So says Puck, as he sweeps the dirt behind the door, trying to protect the threshold, the *limen,* the boundary between inside and outside, art and life, comedy and what lies beyond its borders.

Puck's epilogue, the "real" epilogue of the play, thus revisits and revises the prologue of "Pyramus and Thisbe," which had begun "If we offend, it is with our good will. / That you should think: we come not to offend / But with good will." Where the mechanicals had been prevented from offering their epilogue, Shakespeare now supplies one, and thus reasserts the playwright's control of the "fourth wall" that is the particular, brilliant province of theater. But as the play has already hinted, what lies beyond is history, tragedy, fable, and loss: the off-spring of Hippolyta and Theseus will be the ill-fated Hippolytus, the erotic obsession of Theseus's second wife, Phaedra, and the beasts in the wood will not always be so gentle as the ass-headed Bottom or the timorous man-headed lion. Moreover, something else lies beyond the threshold, as well, for that threshold, that *limen,* is the boundary between actor and audience, itself marked and breached by the device of the epilogue. "The best in this kind are but shadows," said Theseus, meaning actors and plays, and anticipating Puck's "If we shadows have offended." A play is a fiction, art is an illusion, "no more yielding but a dream." Can we be blamed if we wonder—now that we have been told that *we* are reality—when someone else will wake and recognize that we are only dream? Can we be blamed for looking over our shoulders, and wondering who is watching the play in which we are acting, while we watch, onstage, actors watching actors who play actors performing a play? An actor playing Theseus watches an actor playing Bottom play the part of Pyramus, and feels secure in his own comparative reality. The final ambiguity is the ambiguity of all drama, and of art that always shadows the dream world: "It seems to me / That yet we sleep, we dream."

Richard II

DRAMATIS PERSONAE

King Richard II
The Queen, *his wife*
John of Gaunt, *Duke of Lancaster,*
Richard's uncle
Harry Bolingbroke, *Duke of*
Hereford, John of Gaunt's son,
later King Henry IV
Duchess of Gloucester, *widow of*
Gaunt's and York's brother
Duke of York, *King Richard's uncle*
Duchess of York
Duke of Aumerle, *their son*
Thomas Mowbray, *Duke of Norfolk*
Green, *follower of King Richard*
Bagot, *follower of King Richard*
Bushy, *follower of King Richard*
Percy, Earl of Northumberland,
of Bolingbroke's party
Harry Percy, *his son, of*
Bolingbroke's party
Lord Ross, *of Bolingbroke's party*
Lord Willoughby, *of Bolingbroke's*
party

Earl of Salisbury, *of King*
Richard's party
Bishop of Carlisle, *of King*
Richard's party
Sir Stephen Scrope, *of King*
Richard's party
Lord Berkeley
Lord Fitzwalter
Duke of Surrey
Abbot of Westminster
Sir Piers Exton
Lord Marshal
Heralds
Captain of the Welsh army
Ladies attending the Queen
Gardener
Gardener's men
Exton's men
Keeper of the prison at Pomfret
Groom of King Richard's stable
Lords, soldiers, attendants

WHEN SHAKESPEARE's fellow players John Heminge and Henry Condell collected his plays for the first printed collection of his work after his death, they divided the plays in what is now known as the First Folio into three genres. The proper title of the First Folio of 1623 is *Mr. William Shakespeares Comedies, Histories, & Tragedies,* and under the category of "histories" there appeared, in order of the kings' reigns (not the order of Shakespearean composition), all the plays directly concerned with English history, from *The Life and Death of King John* to *The Life of King Henry the Eight.* Published in quarto form during Shakespeare's lifetime as *The Tragedie of Richard II,* the play we call simply *Richard II* became in the First Folio *The Life & death of Richard the Second.*

Before Shakespeare's time there were few history plays as such written in England—English history was told in verse and prose chronicles, and the "history" with which early English drama was principally concerned was the Bible. But an explosion of history plays appeared on the scene in Elizabethan England, some two hundred of them written between the date of the defeat of the Spanish Armada (1588) and the beginning of the new century. These dates may well be significant, because they coincide with a time when England was highly self-conscious and aware of itself as a political power, proud of its absolute monarch, Queen Elizabeth, and worried about the problem of succession—since the Queen had no children—and that of the ever-present possibility of civil war and usurpation. The Wars of the Roses, from which the Tudor dynasty had emerged, were not so far in the past, and those wars themselves, written about and staged by Shakespeare in his first tetralogy (*Henry VI Part 1, Part 2,* and *Part 3,* and *Richard III*), all looked back to Richard II's reign as the beginning of the end of a certain idea of English unity.

A central fact about history plays is that they can be seen to take place in several time periods at once: the time of the events depicted on the stage, the time of the play's writing and first performance, and, especially for long-lived plays like those of Shakespeare, the time in which a modern company performs the play for a modern audience. In this sense a history play is perpetually "timely"—or, as we like to say, rather misleadingly, it is "timeless." It can readily be juxtaposed to the current events of any time and find new and startling relevance. Shakespeare's tragedies—*Macbeth, King Lear, Hamlet, Othello*—are often staged today to coincide with contemporary political figures and debates. For the early modern period, the history plays carried, if possible, even more menacing resonance and power. Thus, to cite a famous example, when in 1601 Queen Elizabeth's former favorite, Robert Devereaux, the Earl of Essex, decided to foment a rebellion against her and to claim the throne for himself, he paid Shakespeare's company to revive *Richard II,* a play popular several years earlier, in order to put the populace in the mood for a "legitimate" usurpation. Some reports say that Queen Elizabeth, learning of this, observed, "I am Richard the Second, know ye not that?" The Essex rebellion failed, and Essex was beheaded for treason. Elizabeth herself was particularly attuned to this propensity for history to repeat itself, on and off the stage. Her own complicity in the execution of Mary, Queen of Scots, in 1587 was masked by a show of political indifference, like that of Bolingbroke toward Richard in this play. Elizabeth, like Bolingbroke, could tell herself she was "not responsible" for the death of her rival, however convenient that death—accomplished by others—might be for the surviving and reigning monarch.

Throughout the history plays, and pointedly in *Richard II,* there appear figures whose dramatic business it is to predict, to see into the future. If we consider more recent maxims about history, like philosopher George Santayana's "Those who cannot remember the past are condemned to repeat it," or the Holocaust survivors' mindful vow "Never again," we can have some idea of the impact of these English history plays on the Elizabethan audience. History was often written and taught comparatively. Plutarch's *Parallel Lives,* newly translated by Sir Thomas North in 1579, juxtaposed a Greek hero to a Roman (e.g., Demosthenes and Cicero; Alexander and Caesar) so as to bring out the strengths and weaknesses of each. The use of the history play to evaluate and critique the current day followed naturally upon this, and often the images of "then" were (and are) uncannily and instructively similar to "now." For early modern England there was also, as we have noted with respect to medieval and Tudor drama, yet another level of time, for these plays engaged not only ethical and political but also moral and religious themes. There is often, as palpably in *Richard II,* a backdrop of sacred time, biblical time, the Edenic pattern of disobedience and fall, and the promise and expectation of redemption. When in *Henry IV Part 1* Bolingbroke's famously "wild" son, Prince Hal, speaks in soliloquy of "[r]edeeming time when men least think I will," he is, and Shakespeare is, invoking a tacit pattern of Christian salvation, together with the popular story of the prodigal son. In *Richard II* the Edenic note—already describing England as a paradise lost—is struck, as we will see, by the elderly and dying John of Gaunt.

The four plays often called the *Henry IV* plays or the *Henriad—Richard II, Henry IV Part 1* and *Part 2,* and *Henry V*—were not initially designed by the playwright to be considered as a group. *Richard II* was written in 1595, considerably earlier than the others (*Henry IV Part 1* in 1596–1597, *Part 2* in 1597–1598, and *Henry V* in 1598–1599). But the plays do concern themselves with the same cast of characters, and they provide a continuous pattern from one to the next—a pattern of transition, as we will see, from one worldview to another. From the image of a king secure atop an orderly world, ruled only by God and His angels (akin to what the mid-twentieth century, facing its own end-of-world crisis in World War II, called, with a certain longing, the "Tudor myth," the "great chain of being," and the "Elizabethan world picture"), to a recognizably "modern" world of politics, comedy, intrigue, and dynamism. This is a transition, accomplished by language, stage picture, action, and character, from stasis to action; from the sacred to the secular; and, in terms of art, from ceremony and ritual to history and drama.

It is useful, in this context, to imagine what the stage might look like at the opening of *Richard II.* In the center, probably, and on a raised platform, is the throne, also known in the period as the "state" (thus in *Henry IV Part 1* the genial Falstaff, who scorns authority, will joke in the tavern scene that he can play the King: "This chair shall be my state" [*1 Henry IV* 2.5.344]). Seated on the state, the throne, is God's deputy, God's anointed and chosen one, Richard of Bordeaux, King of England. He is almost surely wearing a cross. In any case the stage is probably as Christian as it is English, with John of Gaunt, among other nobles, in attendance. (We may think of Chaucer's knights and monks, prioresses and parsons, as well as rising merchants, artisans, and entrepreneurs.) Richard *is* the government, he *is* the state, he *is* England itself—and he is seated there, in the state chamber of Windsor Castle, to give judgment and to rule, to execute and in fact to personify the great role of medieval kingship, to be a leader and the center of his world. And this, as we are about to see, is just what he cannot do.

There enter to him two men: Thomas Mowbray, Duke of Norfolk, and Harry Bolingbroke, the son of Richard's uncle, John of Gaunt. The scene is ceremonious in the extreme: two supplicants accusing each other before their king, dressed formally, speaking formally, hurling down their gages—their gloves—in the ancient feudal gesture of challenge. These are two challengers prepared to battle to the death. And why? Because they accuse each other of the worst possible crime against the state and the King, high treason. Both men greet the King with formal expressions of honor, wishes for his long life and long reign, as vassals should and must, and they make their formal accusations. And then Richard speaks:

> Wrath-kindled gentlemen, be ruled by me.
> Let's purge this choler without letting blood.
>
> . . . .
>
> Forget, forgive, conclude, and be agreed;
> Our doctors say this is no time to bleed.
>
> Richard II *1.1.152–157*

In other words, let us heal the sickness in the state by accommodation, by forgiveness, by turning the other cheek, not by single combat and trial of arms— "be ruled by me." And the challengers refuse. Richard and John of Gaunt together implore them to throw down the gages they have picked up, to relinquish the challenges they have agreed to, and they refuse. So now once more Richard speaks—England speaks:

> We were not born to sue, but to command;
> Which since we cannot do to make you friends
> Be ready, as your lives shall answer it.
>
> . . . .
>
> Since we cannot atone you, we shall see
> Justice design the victor's chivalry.
>
> *1.1.196–203*

"We were not born to sue, but to command; / Which since we cannot do. . . ." The royal "we" modulates, trails off into the voice of impotence. The enjambed line tells the story, as the word "command" is abruptly undercut in the phrase that follows. "Atone" means to "make as one," to reconcile. But, as we will see, the theme of atonement is larger and more pervasive. Richard's is a king's voice without a king's power, in part because he himself is secretly guilty of the crime of which Mowbray is accused, the murder of Richard's uncle, the Duke of Gloucester, an act of high treason. As John of Gaunt will later say to him, echoing the imagery of sickness and disease that Richard himself has already introduced ("Our doctors say this is no time to bleed"),

> Thy deathbed is no lesser than thy land,
> Wherein thou liest in reputation sick.
>
> 2.1.95–96

As always in these plays, the King is the country, and the state of the kingdom is the state of the King. This figure is a medieval inheritance, and it continues to function throughout Shakespeare. King Richard is not only weak, but sick "in reputation," sick in name.

The gorgeous panoply of the opening scene gives way to an even more formal and more elaborate pageant in the play's third scene, the trial by combat. The stage will probably look much the same. The location has shifted to the lists at Coventry, but still the King is seated on the throne, which is—or ought to be—at the center of the stage, at the symbolic center of the world. An imaginative production might well place the throne awkwardly to one side of the stage rather than in the powerful center, reflecting the actual rather than the ideal conditions of Richard's rule. Mowbray and Bolingbroke appear before the King dressed ceremonially in armor, and their language is equally ceremonial. The ancient terms of challenge and rank are spoken by a marshal, representing the King, and by two heralds, representing the challengers. The stage is full of heraldic costume and device, flags, pennants, and armor, the entire pageantry of the medieval and early modern state. Here names have resonant, echoic meanings:

> Lord Marshal What is thy name? And wherefore com'st thou hither
> Before King Richard in his royal lists?
> Against whom comest thou? And what's thy quarrel?
> Speak like a true knight, so defend thee heaven!
> Bolingbroke Harry of Hereford, Lancaster, and Derby
> Am I, who ready here do stand in arms
> To prove by God's grace and my body's valour
> In lists on Thomas Mowbray, Duke of Norfolk,
> That he is a traitor foul and dangerous
> To God of heaven, King Richard, and to me.
> And as I truly fight, defend me heaven!
>
> 1.3.31–41

The ancient ceremony is performed, and Bolingbroke, still in formal terms, requests of the Lord Marshal permission to take leave of King Richard, a message that is duly transmitted, according to protocol, by the Marshal to the king. Richard's reply foreshadows his own fate: "We will descend and fold him in our arms" (1.3.54).

Not the ceremony now, the formal, correct kiss of homage. Not Bolingbroke on his knees and Richard on his throne. Instead, "We will descend." This is the first of the play's many fateful downward movements, which will bring Richard off the throne, then down to the base court at Flint Castle, and finally, in the deposition scene, down from the kingship to an ignominious death.

Even more tellingly, as the opponents stand ready in the lists, the Marshal having given them their lances, again with appropriately formal language and gesture, as the trumpets sound and the combatants move forward, there is a sudden gesture on the stage, and we hear, once more, the Marshal's voice: "Stay, the King hath thrown his warder down" (1.3.118). A warder is a staff, wand, or baton, a symbol of office. In throwing down the warder Richard abruptly brings the ceremony to a close before it has properly begun. This is a broken ceremony, like his earlier "descent" from the throne, and like that gesture it is a visual prediction of things to come, another fateful downward movement en route to Richard's ultimate surrender of the kingship and the throne to his rival Bolingbroke in the deposition scene (4.1). With this broken ceremony Richard symbolizes, to the audience in the theater as well as to that on the stage, the vulnerability of his idea of kingship: the imagined ideal of a land unified and personified by a king who rules by divine right and divine guidance, a feudal order of which the king is unquestioned sovereign. In *Hamlet* broken ceremonies of this kind will be termed "maimed rites," and this is indeed a maimed rite, the failure of an ideal. In practical terms, too, Richard's gesture is untimely, for in keeping the combatants alive, in saving the life of his cousin Bolingbroke, Richard brings down doom upon himself in a more immediate way, making his own tragedy inevitable with the return and ultimate ascendancy of Bolingbroke, who will become Henry IV.

Instead of death, the punishment Richard ordains for Bolingbroke and for Mowbray is banishment. Mowbray is banished forever—perhaps because he knows the dark truth about the death of Gloucester. Bolingbroke is banished for ten years, a sentence that is then further commuted to six ("such is the breath of kings," remarks Bolingbroke with mingled irony and admiration). In his dialogue with his father, old John of Gaunt, on how to endure this period of banishment, the audience can hear for the first time something of Bolingbroke's nature and personality, which stand in such sharp contrast to Gaunt's, and to Richard's:

John of Gaunt   Teach thy necessity to reason thus;
                 There is no virtue like necessity.
                 Think not the King did banish thee,

But thou the King.

. . . . . .

Go, say I sent thee forth to purchase honour,
And not the King exiled thee.

. . . .

Suppose the singing birds musicians,
The grass whereon thou tread'st the presence strewed,
The flowers fair ladies, and thy steps no more
Than a delightful measure or a dance.

. . . .

Bolingbroke   O, who can hold a fire in his hand
By thinking on the frosty Caucasus,
Or cloy the hungry edge of appetite
By bare imagination of a feast,
Or wallow naked in December snow
By thinking on fantastic summer's heat?
O no, the apprehension of the good
Gives but the greater feeling to the worse.

1.3.256.10–264

Gaunt urges his son to make a world within his own imagination, to ignore uncomfortable reality. Bolingbroke replies that he can do no such thing, and that such ameliorative wishful thinking would increase rather than decrease his suffering. Gaunt here plays a part akin to Mercutio in *Romeo and Juliet,* a play written in the same years. He urges the power of the imagination, of poetry and of transforming language, as a way to deal with things as they are. But Bolingbroke is a realist, not an idealist, a romantic, or a dreamer. He cannot "[s]uppose the singing birds musicians" (any more that Romeo can believe, despite Juliet's urging, that "[i]t was the nightingale, and not the lark" [*Romeo and Juliet* 3.5.2] serenading them on the morning of Romeo's own banishment).

It is no accident that the two court scenes in *Richard II,* the two scenes of combat and confrontation (1.1 and 1.3), are separated in the play's first act by a scene in which John of Gaunt speaks with the Duchess of Gloucester, the widow of his murdered brother—a sad, empty scene in which the older generation is shown to be impotent and powerless, placing its faith in God and in an old world order. Since Richard, Gaunt says, is "God's substitute, / His deputy anointed in his sight" (1.2.37–38), the only challenge to him can come from God, and the only revenge for the murder of Gloucester can be God's. This is the old worldview, and the older generation, the relics of Edward III's seven sons, are weak because they are old, and because the world they live in has changed. They have outlived their time. Gaunt will shortly die, and the Duchess of Gloucester as well, and with them will disappear their vision of a world unquestionably ruled, by divine right, by a Christian king ordained by God.

Banishment is the penalty given to Bolingbroke and Mowbray, a penalty exacted for the sin of civil war. But banishment, while it is a civil penalty, is also one with strong biblical overtones, as Mowbray's parting words make plain: "Farewell, my liege. Now no way can I stray: / Save back to England, all the world's my way" (1.3.199–200). A half century later, John Milton's Adam and Eve, expelled from Eden, would face a similar crisis, and a similar opportunity: "The World was all before them, where to choose" (*Paradise Lost,* book 12, line 644). Bolingbroke, further evoking the burden placed on Adam's progeny in Genesis, will later speak of "[e]ating the bitter bread of banishment," of banishment as labor and exile. And yet what is banished is more than a few individuals from a paradisal England. The fall that takes place is the fall of an ideal. The garden that was England, the enclosed state of medieval hierarchy, is now itself subject to a fall. The point is made neatly and explicitly in the garden scene (3.4), a scene that is, like others we have noticed in Shakespeare's plays, a "window scene," a moment of perception that introduces characters we have not met before and will not meet again, but whose observations and actions comment trenchantly on the play of which they are a part. Just as the garden is a common image for the state, so in Renaissance literature the gardener was often both a king figure and a God figure, and this Gardener rules his little island with an orderliness and care that stands in sharp contrast to that of Richard. As one of the Gardener's men asks, in a question addressed as much to the audience as to the Gardener,

> Why should we, in the compass of a pale,
> Keep law and form and due proportion,
> Showing as in a model our firm estate,
> When our sea-wallèd garden, the whole land,
> Is full of weeds, her fairest flowers choked up,
> Her fruit trees all unpruned, her hedges ruined,
> Her knots disordered, and her wholesome herbs
> Swarming with caterpillars?

> *3.4.41–48*

Among these "caterpillars" are the high-ranking social pests Bolingbroke scornfully labels "[t]he caterpillars of the commonwealth," Richard's sycophantic flatterers, whose names—significantly for this garden scene and the pervasive garden images throughout the plays—are Bushy, Bagot, and Green. The Gardener himself sees the parallel (and contrast) between his garden and King Richard's, and mourns for it: "O, what pity is it / That he hath not so trimmed and dressed his land / As we this garden!" (3.4.56–58). The Queen, overhearing the news of her husband's defeat and capture, addresses the Gardener in terms that show that she, too, sees the analogy, calling him "old Adam's likeness" who predicts, against her wishes and her hopes, "a second fall of cursèd man" (74, 77). The garden scene is a decorative set piece, foreshadowing the much more realistic and "low" inset scenes of commentary in later plays, like the Porter scene in *Macbeth*. The Gardener, although he is a worker, not a nobleman, speaks in verse, not prose, and in fact all of *Richard II* is in verse, underscoring both its celebrated "poetic" qualities and the degree to which some of its characters, at least, resist facing facts about the changing locus of power in England. One of Bolingbroke's first moves when he returns to England will be to court the favor of the common people, a technique developed into an art form—and a way of life—by his charming and calculating son, Prince Hal.

In fact, the garden scene is an echo in dramatic terms, with characters and setting, of an analogy first presented to the audience in poetic and rhetorical terms in this play, most strikingly in John of Gaunt's deathbed speech in act 2, our first image of England as a sea-walled garden now in the condition of a fall. This is one of the great speeches of all early Shakespearean drama, one often— like many such ringing pronouncements in the plays—quoted out of context as pure patriotic praise of the land and its people. But as a full citation of the speech will make plain, the joyous note with which the speech appears to begin soon reveals itself as part of an elegiac lament. John of Gaunt's speech is addressed, significantly, not to his nephew King Richard, who arrives too late to hear it, hoping to find Gaunt already dead, but instead to Gaunt's brother York, the last survivor of the older, ordered world, the world of the sons of Edward III:

John of Gaunt   This royal throne of kings, this sceptred isle,
                   This earth of majesty, this seat of Mars,
                   This other Eden, demi-paradise,
                   This fortress built by nature for herself
                   Against infection and the hand of war,
                   This happy breed of men, this little world,
                   This precious stone set in the silver sea,
                   Which serves it in the office of a wall,
                   Or as a moat defensive to a house
                   Against the envy of less happier lands;
                   This blessèd plot, this earth, this realm, this England,
                   This nurse, this teeming womb of royal kings,
                   Feared by their breed and famous by their birth,
                   Renownèd for their deeds as far from home
                   For Christian service and true chivalry
                   As is the sepulchre, in stubborn Jewry,
                   Of the world's ransom, blessèd Mary's son;
                   This land of such dear souls, this dear dear land,
                   Dear for her reputation through the world,
                   Is now leased out—I die pronouncing it—
                   Like to a tenement or pelting farm.

                                                              2.1.40–60

This is a breathtaking speech in more than one sense, because the whole speech of twenty lines is a single sentence, virtually an apostrophe to the land, that gestures in demonstrative language toward a familiar and beloved object. Significantly, the grammatical subject of the sentence, "this England," appears for the first time halfway through the passage, having been preceded by a long list of metaphors, epithets, and appositives ("This royal throne of kings, this sceptred isle, / This earth of majesty . . ."). What the demonstrative pronoun "this" refers to is not made explicit until ten lines later, and by the logic of Gaunt's speech it does not need to be, because everyone—whether on or off the stage—who hears him speak should know without question what he means. The name fits the thing. The lines of praise, with description after description ("This other Eden," "This precious stone set in the silver sea"), offer recognizable synonyms for the perfect England of Gaunt's memory and imagination. As the Latin phrase *nomen est omen* (the name is the sign) suggests, there is a direct correspondence between the word and what it describes or signifies. England *is* a "royal throne of kings," a "sceptred isle," a "demi-paradise," and anyone who hears those phrases spoken ought to recognize their rightness. And yet, as Gaunt goes on to explain, this vital correspondence—this identity—has been lost. That names and titles once directly signified their objects—a notion of a pre-fallen linguistic world—is one reason why he puns so insistently on his own name and its appropriateness to his condition:

> Old Gaunt indeed, and gaunt in being old.
> Within me grief hath kept a tedious fast,
> And who abstains from meat that is not gaunt?
> For sleeping England long time have I watched.
> Watching breeds leanness, leanness is all gaunt.
> The pleasure that some fathers feed upon
> Is my strict fast: I mean my children's looks.
> And therein fasting, hast thou made me gaunt.
> Gaunt am I for the grave, gaunt as a grave,
> Whose hollow womb inherits naught but bones.

> *2.1.74–83*

Gaunt *is* gaunt; but is the King the king? Again, bearing in mind how close the two plays are in their time of composition, we might notice some similarity between John of Gaunt's flippancy on his deathbed and that of Mercutio ("Ask for me tomorrow, and you shall find me a grave man"). Like the death of Mercutio in *Romeo and Juliet*, the death of John of Gaunt is an epochal event in this play's development, a turning point from which there is no going back.

What dies with John of Gaunt? Nothing less than a vision of the world. The vision of England as a garden, an unfallen earthly paradise. The vision of its king as a ruler by right and not by nature, by title and entitlement rather than by credit and merit. And the vision of England as a redemptive Christian nation, a land whose soldiers are, as Gaunt says, "[r]enownèd for their deeds as far from home / For Christian service and true chivalry / As is the sepulchre, in stubborn Jewry"—that is, in Jerusalem. ("Jewry" is imagined as "stubborn" because it does not accept the truth of Christ as redeemer.) The past is a history of glorious foreign wars, King Edward III's wars against the French and the Crusades against the "infidel," all unifying England and its people against a common enemy without. But the only remnants in this play of that glorious, and gloriously unified, past is the report of the heroic deeds of the banished Mowbray. Mowbray is himself a member of the older order, a hero and a knight, who dies—offstage—on a Crusade fighting against external enemies: pagans, Turks, and Saracens. By contrast, Richard's wars all are civil wars: wars against Ireland; wars against Bolingbroke and the rebels; wars against his own land, which he farms out for money to support his own corruption and mismanagement; and, of course, wars against himself. All these ideals and conventions of belief die with John of Gaunt. Yet perhaps the most significant loss of all is the loss of name, the loss of identity, the imagined one-to-one correspondence between the word and that for which it stands.

Consider the many names by which Bolingbroke is known in the course of the play—Bolingbroke who is this play's shape-shifter, a man of many roles, who seems to progress not only from name to name but also from identity to identity. At the beginning of the play, in that very formal trial scene, he is "Hereford" and "Bolingbroke" and "Derby," and the King's relation, although in a moment of significant ambiguity and irony he says to Mowbray in that first scene that he disclaims "the kindred of the King" —in other words, that he does not seek any special privilege from the fact that he and the King are cousins. His ostensible reason for doing so is to allow Mowbray to challenge him without danger, according to protocol, but for the audience this is a glance toward his later rebellion. When Bolingbroke returns from banishment it is, he says, to seek another name, the name of "Lancaster," and the property that he should rightly have inherited from his father, John of Gaunt, property that Richard has seized. Addressed by Lord Berkeley as "Hereford," he is sharp in his reply:

> My lord, my answer is to "Lancaster,"
> And I am come to seek that name in England,
> And I must find that title in your tongue
> Before I make reply to aught you say.

> *2.3.70–74*

"Lancaster" is his father's name, his father's title, and he will have Bushy and Green put to death for taking over his property, and felling his woods, and above all for removing his coat of arms, his heraldic name, from the windows of his estate. By the end of the play, of course, Bolingbroke will have progressed to yet another identity, that of King Henry IV. Yet all of this concern on his

part for names and naming is policy and politics, instrumental rather than personal. Identity for Bolingbroke is a matter of realpolitik, of what he can do
rather than (only) who he is by birth. It is for this reason that we will see
him seek and get the favor of the common people. In this attitude toward power
and legitimacy he stands in sharp contrast both to Richard and to the supporters of the old order: to his father, Gaunt, who could riddle on his name, even
on his deathbed, because he was secure in his own identity, and to York, who
warns Richard that to disregard the laws of inheritance is to put his own right in
jeopardy:

> Take Hereford's rights away, and take from Time
> His charters and his customary rights:
> Let not tomorrow then ensue today;
> Be not thyself, for how art thou a king
> But by fair sequence and succession?
>
> *2.1.196–200*

York, finding himself addressed by the rebellious Bolingbroke as "My gracious
uncle," snaps back at him, "Tut, tut, grace me no grace, nor uncle me no uncle"
(2.3.86). "Grace," a courtesy title given to a duke or duchess, and "uncle" are
serious names: "I am no traitor's uncle." For York, names and titles are identities, and must not be misused.

But of all those who depend upon the name instead of the thing to bestow
identity, the most evident and striking is Richard himself, who returns constantly, throughout the play, to this belief and to the theory of kingship it
implies. In the middle of the third act, for example, word is brought to him that
his armies have deserted and gone over to Bolingbroke. After a moment of
despair, Richard regains his courage:

> I had forgot myself. Am I not King?
> Awake, thou sluggard majesty, thou sleep'st!
> Is not the King's name forty thousand names?
> Arm, arm, my name! . . .
>
> *3.2.79–82*

Richard throughout the play compares himself to Christ, calling Bushy,
Bagot, and Green, his wavering flatterers, "[t]hree Judases," and labeling those
who show him an outward pity "Pilates" who have delivered him to a "sour
cross" (3.2.128; 4.1.230, 231). In crying out "Arm, arm, my name!" he seems to
see his name as possessing a numinous power, like that depicted in the many
Renaissance paintings of the "Adoration of the Name of Jesus," the crowned
name circled with angels, receiving homage from saints and worshipers. Such
paintings, like the famous work by El Greco also called *The Dream of Philip II*

(1579), took their cue from a key passage in Saint Paul's Epistle to the Philippians: "Wherefore God . . . hath given him a name which is above every name; That at the name of Jesus, every knee should bow, of [things] in heaven, and [things] in earth" (2:9–10). Thus at Flint Castle, in act 3, scene 3, the midpoint of the play, when his downfall is assured, we will hear Richard lament,

> O, that I were as great
> As is my grief, or lesser than my name. . . .
> 3.3.135–136

And in the deposition scene, in act 4, scene 1, he will say that he has "no name, no title," now that he is no longer king. Name and title are, to him, the same. For this reason old York is right to criticize the presumptuous and ambitious Northumberland outside the walls of Flint Castle, when Northumberland prematurely "deposes" the King:

Northumberland	Richard not far from hence hath hid his head.
York	It would beseem the Lord Northumberland
	To say "King Richard". . . .
. . . .	
Northumberland	Your grace mistakes. Only to be brief
	Left I his title out.
York	The time hath been,
	Would you have been so brief with him, he would
	Have been so brief with you to shorten you,
	For taking so the head, your whole head's length.
	3.3.6–14

Not only is the name the title, the name of the king can operate independently of the king. This concept is related to a theory known as "the king's two bodies," well described by the modern scholar Ernst Kantorowicz from period documents like the *Reports* of Edmund Plowden, a law apprentice of the Middle Temple in the time of Queen Elizabeth:

For the King has in him two Bodies, *viz.,* a Body natural, and a Body politic. His Body natural (if it be considered in itself) is a Body mortal, subject to all Infirmities that come by Nature of Accident, to the Imbecility of Infancy or old Age, and to the like Defects that happen to the natural Bodies of other People. But his Body politic is a Body that cannot be seen or handled, consisting of Policy and Government, and constituted for the Direction of the People, and the Management of the public weal, and this Body is utterly void of Infancy, and old Age, and other natural Defects and Imbecilities, which the Body natural is subject to, and for this Cause, what

the King does in his Body politic, cannot be invalidated or frustrated by
any Disability in his natural Body.[1]

Thus, in political terms, the king "never dies," and the name of "king" has a
continuous power: "the Relation is to him as King, he as King never dies, but
the King, in which Name it has relation to him, does ever continue."[2] Yet the
body natural is also a sign. When in this play King Richard departs for Ireland
to supervise his wars there, it is another indication of his own impotence, and of
the sickness in the state, that he leaves old York in command—as York sees
more clearly than Richard does: "Here am I, left to underprop his land, / Who,
weak with age, cannot support myself" (2.2.82–83). Yet as the surviving onstage
voice of the old order, York himself is a fervent believer in the doctrine of "the
king's two bodies," as he explains to the rebellious Bolingbroke:

> Com'st thou because the anointed King is hence?
> Why, foolish boy, the King is left behind,
> And in my loyal bosom lies his power.
>
> *2.3.95–97*

Ultimately, however, the ceremonial body, the loyal bosom of York, is as
powerless as Richard, for without soldiers to support him York surrenders to
Bolingbroke in words that echo Richard's from the opening scene:

> But if I could, by Him that gave me life,
> I would attach you all, and make you stoop
> Unto the sovereign mercy of the King.
> But since I cannot, be it known to you
> I do remain as neuter. . . .
>
> *2.3.154–158*

"Neuter" is our word "neutral," or "neutralized," but the undertone of impotence is there as well. York's "cannot" directly recalls Richard's: "We were not
born to sue, but to command; / Which since we cannot do. . . ."

The theory of "the king's two bodies," the man and the state, raises for York,
for Richard, and for the play key questions about the nature of kingship and the
difference between essence and role. Bolingbroke places faith in persona, or
role, in malleability and self-creation; Richard in essence or identity. Broadly,
this difference between essence and role is the difference in the play between an
old, hieratic view of kingship and a new, early modern notion of monarchy. In
terms of theater it is also the difference between a miracle, or morality, play and
a play of dramatic realism and complexity, the difference between the cycle play
of Christ's passion that Richard thinks he is performing and the Shakespearean
play of politics, history, and metamorphosis in which Bolingbroke is an eager

and complicit actor. Richard's view of kingship is expressed clearly in act 3, upon his return to England:

> King Richard   Not all the water in the rough rude sea
> Can wash the balm from an anointed king.
> The breath of worldly men cannot depose
> The deputy elected by the Lord.
> For every man that Bolingbroke hath pressed
> To lift shrewd steel against our golden crown,
> God for his Richard hath in heavenly pay
> A glorious angel. Then if angels fight,
> Weak men must fall; for heaven still guards the right.
>
> *3.2.50–58*

Anointed as Christ was anointed (Apostles 4:26–27), Richard claims the divine right of kings. God will protect him: "Arm, arm, my name!" As in all of Shakespeare's history plays, the symbol of the English kingship is the sun, with its familiar homonym of "son"—or "Son." Thus in this same speech Richard will appropriate the figure of the sun for himself, to demonstrate rhetorically the inevitability of his triumph:

> know'st thou not
> That when the searching eye of heaven is hid
> Behind the globe, and lights the lower world,
> Then thieves and robbers range abroad unseen
> In murders and in outrage bloody here;
> But when from under this terrestrial ball
> He fires the proud tops of the eastern pines,
> And darts his light through every guilty hole,
> Then murders, treasons, and detested sins,
> The cloak of night being plucked from off their backs,
> Stand bare and naked, trembling at themselves?
> So when this thief, this traitor, Bolingbroke,
> Who all this while hath revelled in the night
> Whilst we were wand'ring in the Antipodes,
> Shall see us rising on our throne, the east,
> His treasons will sit blushing in his face,
> Not able to endure the sight of day,
> But, self-affrighted, tremble at his sin.
>
> *3.2.32–49*

In his view, and in this resounding speech, Richard is the sun, and when he rises, having returned from Ireland (here rather grandly termed "the Antipodes," the ends of the earth), Bolingbroke will be exposed and will recognize his sin.

But Bolingbroke does not think in these theological terms. The kingship is for him a political, not a religious, office until he attains it, when his tune and tone will change. And the image of the king as the sun will itself chart the pattern of Richard's tragedy and fall, as it is transferred in the course of this play from Richard to Bolingbroke. By the end of act 3, scene 2, disbanding his soldiers, Richard has already reversed the image: "Discharge my followers. Let them hence away / From Richard's night to Bolingbroke's fair day" (214–215). Richard is now the night, and Bolingbroke the day—the shift of the sun image from the one man to the other begins to balance in imagistic terms the transfer of the kingship. When Richard appears on the walls of Flint Castle, Bolingbroke will compare him to a sun covered with clouds:

> See, see, King Richard doth himself appear,
> As doth the blushing discontented sun
> From out the fiery portal of the east
> When he perceives the envious clouds are bent
> To dim his glory. . . .
>
> *3.3.61–65*

The stage picture here, with Richard aloft on the battlement of the castle, is remarkably similar to the celebrated balcony scene in *Romeo and Juliet*. Richard is the "sun," rising in the "east," here "blushing" as Juliet felt she should blush at being overheard by Romeo. Bolingbroke stands below, on the main stage, and speaks as he gazes up at the King. In act 3, scene 3, Richard will, like Juliet, invoke the figure of Phaëthon, the ill-fated son of Apollo, who tried to control the horses of the sun. But the culmination of the sun image, and the end of Richard's kingship, will come in the deposition scene, when Richard, lamenting that he has "no name, no title," says,

> O, that I were a mockery king of snow,
> Standing before the sun of Bolingbroke
> To melt myself away in water-drops!
>
> *4.1.250–252*

It is Bolingbroke, now, who is the sun, and the king, while Richard is merely a snowman, a "mockery king of snow." Kingship, like power, like language, can melt away into tears, into air.

In the new world Richard must come to experience and know, names are not magic, *nomen* is not *omen*, the name is not necessarily equal to the thing. When in the course of the deposition scene he is forced to surrender the crown and the kingship it signifies, his speech of reluctant compliance becomes a bitter and bitterly truthful pun. "Are you contented to resign the crown?" asks Bolingbroke, and Richard's reply underscores his own divided self, his own indecision and ambivalence. "Ay, no; no, ay; for I must nothing be" is how editors have tended to print out his answer—"Yes, no; no, yes." But the First Folio (and the Fourth Quarto of the play), following the standard spelling of the time, presents this conundrum of a sentiment as "I, no; no, I; for I must nothing be." "I, no; no, I" is a logical picture in words, a chiasmus and a hieroglyph. We might also translate it with another homonym: "I know no I." "I know no I" makes sense for Richard's own profound experience of loss. He has no selfhood if he is not king. Without the crown, he is nothing.

From the beginning, patterns of ascent and descent, up/down movements, dominate the play both in language and in action. In act 1, scene 3, there is Richard's cousinly "descent" from the throne ("We will descend and fold him in our arms"), bringing him to the level of Bolingbroke and foreshadowing the more dire and tragic descents later in the play. Like the actual deposition, this early descent, though apparently voluntary, is compelled by political circumstances. To this first descent, and the gesture in the trial by combat, when the King throws his warder down, could be added any number of others, both physical and verbal: the breaking of the staff of office by the Earl of Worcester, Richard's steward, who resigns and flees to Bolingbroke; Richard's dramatic, theatrical, and finally ineffectual gesture when he returns from Ireland, weeping to be again in England, and stooping to touch its soil once more ("Dear earth, I do salute thee with my hand, / Though rebels wound thee with their horses' hoofs" [3.2.6–7]); and Richard's descent from the walls of Flint Castle (from the upper stage to the base court below), which he glosses, characteristically, with a cautionary tale ("Down, down I come like glist'ring Phaëthon, / Wanting the manage of unruly jades" [3.3.177–178]).

In the same scene at Flint Castle, as Bolingbroke kneels before him in apparent homage, Richard will say ruefully, "Up, cousin, up. Your heart is up, I know" (3.3.192). In the following scene, the Gardener perceives the struggle between the two claimants, accurately, in the image of a scale:

> Their fortunes both are weighed.
> In your lord's scale is nothing but himself
> And some few vanities that make him light.
> But in the balance of great Bolingbroke,
> Besides himself, are all the English peers,
> And with that odds he weighs King Richard down.
>
> *3.4.85–90*

The figure of the scale will recur, as will all of these images of descent and fall, in the great and tragic deposition scene, when Richard himself removes the crown, throws down the mirror he has commanded to be brought to him, descends the throne, and gives voice once more to the seesaw movement of up and down:

> Conveyers are you all,
> That rise so nimbly by a true king's fall.
>
> *4.1.307–308*

Falls of princes, as we have already noted, were the patterns of medieval tragedy. But in *Richard II,* which is a history play as well as a tragedy, there is more than one diagonal pattern. In fact the design of this play, as of a number of others by Shakespeare, is what might be called "chiastic"—that is, X-shaped. One protagonist rises as another falls. The man who rises in this play is, of course, Bolingbroke, the future Henry IV—as York will acknowledge explicitly at the time of the deposition:

> Ascend his throne, descending now from him,
> And long live Henry, of that name the fourth!
>
> *4.1.102–103*

Bolingbroke's "descent" will be an "ascent"—he will "descend" from Richard in a genealogical sense, becoming his de facto heir. The very idea of descent has been altered to suit the upward ambitions of the new king. While Richard has surrounded himself with favorites and squandered away his inheritance, Bolingbroke has sought and won the favor of the common people, as Richard comments bitterly at the end of act 1:

> Ourself and Bushy, Bagot here, and Green
> Observed his courtship to the common people,
> How he did seem to dive into their hearts
> With humble and familiar courtesy,
> What reverence he did throw away on slaves,
> Wooing poor craftsmen with the craft of smiles
> And patient underbearing of his fortune,
> As 'twere to banish their affects with him.
> Off goes his bonnet to an oysterwench.
> A brace of draymen bid God speed him well,
> And had the tribute of his supple knee
> With "Thanks, my countrymen, my loving friends,"
> As were our England in reversion his,
> And he our subjects' next degree in hope.
>
> *1.4.22–35*

The form of this report is what I call an "unscene," a scene that the audience does not actually see, but that is so vividly described it seems almost to be engraved upon the memory. Often, as here, such scenes contain bits of dialogue and stage gesture, which heighten the illusion that the scene has been witnessed rather than retold. (Film directors frequently obliterate the distinction by casting and performing these as-told-to scenes.) What is accomplished by placing such a scene offstage? In the present case, the relentlessness of the up/down movement is exacerbated by Richard's language: Bolingbroke "did seem to dive into their hearts"; "[o]ff goes his bonnet"; "the tribute of his supple knee." All of these gestures, as Richard so clearly sees, are dips preparatory to a rise.

Bolingbroke senses a change in political realities; henceforth he will take his support where he can get it. And his politicking serves him well when the rebels join with him and he rides, triumphant, into London. York's weeping narrative of the procession into the city, told to his wife, completes the pattern that Richard's account had begun:

York	Then, as I said, the Duke, great Bolingbroke,
	Mounted upon a hot and fiery steed,
	Which his aspiring rider seemed to know,
	With slow and stately pace kept on his course,
	Whilst all tongues cried "God save thee,
	Bolingbroke!"
	You would have thought the very windows spake,
	So many greedy looks of young and old
	Through casements darted their desiring eyes
	Upon his visage, and that all the walls
	With painted imagery had said at once,
	"Jesu preserve thee! Welcome, Bolingbroke!"
	. . . .
Duchess of York	Alack, poor Richard! Where rode he the whilst?
York	As in a theatre the eyes of men,
	After a well-graced actor leaves the stage,
	Are idly bent on him that enters next,
	Thinking his prattle to be tedious,
	Even so, or with much more contempt, men's eyes
	Did scowl on gentle Richard. No man cried "God
	save him!"
	No joyful tongue gave him his welcome home;
	But dust was thrown upon his sacred head,
	Which with such gentle sorrow he shook off,
	His face still combating with tears and smiles,
	The badges of his grief and patience. . . .

5.2.7–33

Once again internal quotations—"No man cried 'God save him!' "; "Whilst all tongues cried 'God save thee, Bolingbroke!' "—emphasize the sense of the offstage scene's reality, while York's description of Bolingbroke as an "aspiring rider" underscores his upward trajectory. The double irony of an actor commenting on the ill fortune of another actor would not be lost on any theater audience. But the point is really that Richard would not acknowledge his performance to be an act, while Bolingbroke, akin to the protean actors we have seen in other history plays, eagerly embraces the public stage.

For Bolingbroke, language is a tool and performance second nature. His success is so complete that he turns the inanimate into animate, and animated, objects: "You would have thought the very windows spake" and the walls had called out "Welcome, Bolingbroke!" Likewise, when Bolingbroke returns from exile, we hear from Northumberland (not an easy conquest, and shortly to be Henry IV's enemy and rival) that talking with him was like eating candy: his "fair discourse hath been as sugar, / Making the hard way sweet and delectable" (2.3.6–7).

Bolingbroke is not a courtier—he is a politician, and his "fair discourse" is not flattery but policy. He wins over the testy Northumberland by his conversation, by the force of his words. But when there is no need for words, Bolingbroke does not use them. When his father asks him why he is silent as he begins his banishment—"O, to what purpose dost thou hoard thy words, / That thou return'st no greeting to thy friends?"—Bolingbroke replies, "I have too few to take my leave of you" (1.3.242–244). In the deposition scene, as Richard progresses from image to image, from ceremony to ceremony, during more than a hundred lines of verse, Bolingbroke says nothing—except to send for a looking glass at Richard's request. "Mark, silent King, the moral of this sport," says Richard (4.1.280). Richard for much of his play is a voluble king, a king of words, although unable to speak the language of command (". . . which since we cannot do . . ."). When, early in the play, Richard repeals four years of Bolingbroke's sentence, Bolingbroke murmurs, "How long a time lies in one little word! / . . . such is the breath of kings" (1.3.206–208). But in fact this king's breath has no such power, and Bolingbroke will return from banishment when it pleases him to do so.

Indeed, all around Richard in the opening scenes of the play language itself seems to be dying. This is a perception, or a phenomenon, related to the dislocation of names from things, the failure of the one-to-one correspondence between ideas and essences in which the King, above all others, continues to believe. Thus Mowbray speaks feelingly of his own banishment in terms of a loss of language: "What is thy sentence then but speechless death?" (1.3.166). His tongue, he says, is jailed in his mouth; the English he has spoken all his life will be useless to him. When John of Gaunt dies we are told that he said . . . nothing.

Northumberland   Nay, nothing: all is said.
His tongue is now a stringless instrument.
Words, life, and all, old Lancaster hath spent.
2.1.149–151

Yet Richard's own language has a strength as well as a weakness, a strength in personal and in tragic terms that is as great as his weakness in political terms. If he is unfit to be an early modern king, he is increasingly a man of reflection and sensibility. Whatever history's verdict on Richard of Bordeaux, poetry's assessment of him is, however reluctantly, admiring. We see in the pairing of Richard II and the man who will become Henry IV an intimation of what will become a familiar Shakespearean contrast, between a complex, even mythic, figure imbued with human flaws and human suffering (like, for example, the heroic and tragic Antony in *Antony and Cleopatra*) and a more pragmatic, practical-minded figure of political and martial accomplishment (like the ruthlessly businesslike Octavius Caesar in that play). In fact we could read the chiastic pattern, the X-shaped pattern of rise and fall, in a slightly different way. Instead of charting the fall of Richard and the rise of Bolingbroke, we could say that both diagonals of the X trace the movement of Richard through the play. As he falls, he rises. As he descends in the political world, he rises in the world of drama, tragedy, poetry. The letter *X*—often used today as a synonym for the unknown, or the profane—was from early times used as an abbreviation for, and thus a symbol of, Christ. The "fortunate fall" is the story of Jesus as well as of Adam and Eve: as they fall, they rise. Whatever Shakespeare's Christian audience might have thought, whatever an audience today thinks of Richard, there is little doubt from the nature of his own language in the play that he himself sees this connection, and believes it. We have heard his impatient speeches ring with words like "Judas" and "Pilate" and "sour cross" when he upbraids his followers for their failures. But his moral dignity begins to assert itself as his suffering increases—as, for example, in York's sad tale of his ride through the streets of London, patient though grieving, "his face still combating with tears and smiles," as if he were Jesus serenely riding to Jerusalem on the back of an ass (Matthew 21:2–11).

Politically Richard is not only inept but corrupt. He has wasted his revenues, farmed out his lands in a way no king can afford to do if he is to keep his throne. He is rightfully accused of harboring favorites, and even if the audience has little affinity for the "wavering commons," whose love, as Bagot says, "lies in their purses," neither are we particularly drawn to Bushy, Bagot, and Green, the caterpillars of the commonwealth. Richard shows nothing but callousness in his plot to seize John of Gaunt's property as soon as he is dead: "Pray God we may make haste and come too late!" (1.4.63). But there is something admirable in his demeanor as he faces the loss of power and title, and begins to realize that he is not a king as the modern world defines a king. Returning from Ireland, stooping to salute the earth with his hand, he is already a denizen of an older and simpler world. In this scene (3.2), we see him move from an assertion of the divine right of kings to an awareness of his own humanity, an awareness that is also a comment on the transforming power of language. The failed king—as is often remarked—becomes a poet, telling the tale of his own downfall. The failed ruler becomes a playwright, writing the tragedy of Richard II:

> King Richard   [*Sitting*] For God's sake, let us sit upon the ground,
> And tell sad stories of the death of kings—
> How some have been deposed, some slain in war,
> Some haunted by the ghosts they have deposed,
> Some poisoned by their wives, some sleeping killed,
> All murdered. For within the hollow crown
> That rounds the mortal temples of a king
> Keeps Death his court; and there the antic sits,
> Scoffing his state and grinning at his pomp,
> Allowing him a breath, a little scene,
> To monarchize, be feared, and kill with looks,
> Infusing him with self and vain conceit,
> As if this flesh which walls about our life
> Were brass impregnable; and humoured thus,
> Comes at the last, and with a little pin
> Bores through his castle wall; and farewell, king.
> Cover your heads, and mock not flesh and blood
> With solemn reverence. Throw away respect,
> Tradition, form, and ceremonious duty,
> For you have but mistook me all this while.
> I live with bread, like you; feel want,
> Taste grief, need friends. Subjected thus,
> How can you say to me I am a king?
>
> *3.2.151–173*

We might remember Juliet's similar rejection of "[t]radition, form, and ceremonious duty," in her case offered in the service of love: "Fain would I dwell on form, . . . but farewell, compliment. / Dost thou love me?" (*Romeo and Juliet* 2.1.130–132). Richard instructs his followers to abandon compliment for a different reason: because he is, after all, a mortal man like them, "subjected"— made a subject—to Death and to human necessity. He, and his play, have moved to the contemplation of a greater stage, and a greater kingdom, a kingdom of mankind in which Death holds court. It is, in short, Richard's humanity that he discovers when he is stripped of the trappings of kingship—death, and hunger, and want, and grief. Significantly, he speaks of the future in terms of telling and retelling ("For God's sake, let us sit upon the ground, / And tell sad stories of the death of kings"—this last line invokes the aforementioned genre concerns between tragedy and history). He will use the same figure later on, in his highly ceremonial leave-taking from the Queen, as if to underscore that these characters do come from a more formal, less dynamic world, a world of words:

> In winter's tedious nights, sit by the fire
> With good old folks, and let them tell thee tales
> Of woeful ages long ago betid;
> And ere thou bid goodnight, to quit their griefs
> Tell thou the lamentable fall of me.
>
> *5.1.40–44*

He has already become a literary object. His metamorphosis is toward tale and myth, rather than toward history and time. As York has pointed out, Richard is an actor, one fallen out of favor with the audience. In the scene at Flint Castle, where he agrees to yield up the crown (3.3), he is overtly and self-consciously an actor. Again the stage is set so that the spectators in the theater see it as a stage within a stage. On the balcony, now representing the walls of Flint Castle, Richard appears, and Bolingbroke describes him—as we have seen—as a sun dimmed by "envious clouds." By the end of the scene the sun will have set, have come down from the walls to the base court, the lower or outer court of the castle, and York, seeing him appear, will speak of him in loving terms: "Yet looks he like a king. . . . Alack, alack for woe / That any harm should stain so fair a show!" (3.3.67-70). By this time Richard's kingship is indeed a "show," and Richard knows it. As he says to Aumerle, York's son: "We do debase ourself, cousin, do we not, / To look so poorly and to speak so fair?" (3.3.126-127). The "base" in "debase" is mirrored in the "base court" to which he is forced to descend, as the play's dramatic action mirrors its language. Richard knows that in the world's terms he is a man who plays a king, in Death's court, and if that is the case, why should he not exchange that role for another, any other—the role, for example, of a Christian penitent remote from power and grandeur:

> What must the King do now? Must he submit?
> The King shall do it. Must he be deposed?
> The King shall be contented. Must he lose
> The name of King? A God's name, let it go.
> I'll give my jewels for a set of beads,
> My gorgeous palace for a hermitage,
> My gay apparel for an almsman's gown,
> My figured goblets for a dish of wood,
> My sceptre for a palmer's walking staff,
> My subjects for a pair of carvèd saints,
> And my large kingdom for a little grave,
> A little, little grave, an obscure grave,
> Or I'll be buried in the King's highway,

> Some way of common trade where subjects' feet
> May hourly trample on their sovereign's head,
> For on my heart they tread now, whilst I live.
>
> *3.3.142–157*

This is role-playing; those are props. Richard's implication is that all life is role-playing, a scepter as much a stage property as a walking staff, a king's robes as much a costume as an almsman's gown. If the king is not God's anointed representative, but only a man chosen by other men, then everything that follows is role-playing. Richard's language here is decorative and self-consciously poetic. His rhetorical questions are directed at himself, but his perception is a central one for all persons, not just for kings or actors. From this moment he is able to move downward toward his fate, still the manager of his own actions and the poet of his own progress:

> Down, down I come like glist'ring Phaëthon,
> Wanting the manage of unruly jades.
> In the base court: base court where kings grow base
> To come at traitors' calls, and do them grace.
> In the base court, come down: down court, down King,
> For night-owls shriek where mounting larks should sing.
>
> *3.3.177–182*

Richard begins the play attempting to speak the language of command, the language at which Bolingbroke is so adept, but his own language moves increasingly in the direction of solipsism and soliloquy, the language of interior dialogue. This is nowhere more clear than in the great deposition scene, in which he resigns his crown and his throne to Bolingbroke. He is summoned by his rival in a spirit that shows Bolingbroke, perhaps designedly, in the least favorable light, as a man of authority but not, at this point, a man of sensibility: "Fetch hither Richard, that in common view / He may surrender. So we shall proceed / Without suspicion" (4.1.146–148). On the heels of these politic and peremptory words, King Richard II enters and speaks:

> Alack, why am I sent for to a king
> Before I have shook off the regal thoughts
> Wherewith I reigned? I hardly yet have learned
> To insinuate, flatter, bow, and bend my knee.
> Give sorrow leave awhile to tutor me
> To this submission. Yet I well remember
> The favours of these men. Were they not mine?
> Did they not sometime cry "All hail!" to me?
> So Judas did to Christ. But He in twelve

Found truth in all but one; I, in twelve thousand, none.
God save the King! Will no man say "Amen"?
Am I both priest and clerk? Well then, Amen.
God save the King, although I be not he;
And yet Amen, if heaven do think him me.

                                                                    4.1.153–166

Strikingly, this is a dialogue of one, in which Richard is, as he says, both priest and clerk, offering both prayer and response. He speaks now literally to himself, even in the public court. There could be no more decisive sign of his isolation, or of his vitality even in adversity. (For a parallel in a play written in the same years, we might recall the isolation of Juliet: "Nurse!—What should she do here? / My dismal scene I needs must act alone" [*Romeo and Juliet* 4.3.18–19].) The deposition scene is for Richard a kind of anticeremony—not an interrupted ceremony, like Richard's throwing down of the warder, but the inversion of a hallowed act, like a Black Mass, the reversal of an act of transubstantiation. He is determined to make it a ceremony, to perform it with props that are sacred objects, to moralize what for Bolingbroke is an effectual transfer of power. For this reason Richard describes the crown as a well into which two buckets dip, an image related to the Gardener's image of the scale:

Richard   That bucket down and full of tears am I,
            Drinking my griefs, whilst you mount up on high.
                                                                    4.1.178–179

The very act of placing two hands on the crown—"Here, cousin, seize the crown"—is theatrical and tellingly ironic, as Richard forces Bolingbroke to perform, in the court, a literal version of the action that has brought them together at this moment. Notice that he makes Bolingbroke both actor and accomplice, staging the scene as a vivid enactment of usurpation and loss. The emblem of two hands on a crown was a palpable sign of civil war, one that will appear again in the early moments of *King Lear,* when the King instructs his elder daughters, "This crownet part between you" (1.1.137). Richard, like the Bishop of Carlisle, who is among his supporters, has indeed prophesied a civil war that will tear England apart, a war that will become one of the central topics of the *Henry IV* plays.

Significantly, in this deposition scene, Richard deposes himself. He will not *be* deposed. The ceremony is his to perform, as Bolingbroke stands silently by. And Richard's divestment of his office is like an infernal litany, a reversal of a sacred act:

Now mark me how I will undo myself.
I give this heavy weight from off my head,

[BOLINGBROKE *accepts the crown*]
And this unwieldy sceptre from my hand,
[BOLINGBROKE *accepts the scepter*]

. . . .

With mine own tears I wash away my balm,
With mine own hands I give away my crown,
With mine own tongue deny my sacred state,
With mine own breath release all duteous oaths.

. . . .

Long mayst thou live in Richard's seat to sit,
And soon lie Richard in an earthy pit.
"God save King Henry," unkinged Richard says,
"And send him many years of sunshine days."

4.1.193–211

At this point the sun image, the emblem of the King of England, has been fully transferred to the new king, Henry IV. We may recall Richard's fervent assertion of the divine right of kings: "Not all the water in the rough rude sea / Can wash the balm from an anointed king." That assertion goes unchallenged. By deposing himself, he retains control over both the ceremony and the scene:

Though some of you, with Pilate, wash your hands,
Showing an outward pity, yet you Pilates
Have here delivered me to my sour cross,
And water cannot wash away your sin.

4.1.229–232

As water cannot remove the balm, or chrism, from an anointed king, so it cannot absolve the traitors of their own wickedness. It is perhaps because of his fear that, in losing his identity as king, he has lost *all* identity, Richard takes the ultimate theatrical step, and asks for a looking glass:

O flatt'ring glass,
Like to my followers in prosperity,
Thou dost beguile me! Was this face the face
That every day under his household roof
Did keep ten thousand men? . . .

4.1.269–273

Was this face the face? The echo of Marlowe's *Doctor Faustus* is effective, and would doubtless have resonated for Shakespeare's audience. Faustus the magician had asked to see the shade of Helen of Troy, and greeted her with the famous lines "Was this the face that launched a thousand ships / And burnt the topless towers of Ilium?" (*Doctor Faustus* 18.99–100). England traced its lineage from the fall of Troy, and one name for London was Troynovant, New Troy. The abduction of Helen brought about the tragic end of a great civilization. Richard, purporting to see powerlessness in the mirror (his face once commanded ten thousand, and now can barely command himself), echoes the fate of another city, and another king. The call for a mirror would also have reminded an early modern audience of the story of Narcissus as told by Ovid in the *Metamorphoses*. And the emblem of the mirror was, as we noticed in an earlier history play, *Richard III*, frequently utilized by writers of books of conduct and statecraft (*A Mirror for Magistrates; Mirror of the World*), since a "mirror" was an example or a model—often the model set by a prince or a king. Thus Henry V will be called "the mirror of all Christian kings" (*Henry V* 2.0.6). Richard is, as he is about to acknowledge, a failed mirror in this regard. In calling for a looking glass he is summoning the resources of history and chronicle, but in breaking that mirror, in throwing down the looking glass, he means to symbolize the breaking off of his contact with the world:

Richard	Mark, silent King, the moral of this sport:
	How soon my sorrow hath destroyed my face.
Bolingbroke	The shadow of your sorrow hath destroyed
	The shadow of your face.

4.1.280–283

The exchange is richly resonant, and, as so often in this play, both men are right—or wrong. Richard's ceremonial theatricality (a shadow is an actor, as well as a hint, a ghost, and an illusion) is undercut by Bolingbroke's resolute realism. But the looking glass, a virtual play-within-the-play in little, is not Richard's final request in this scene:

Richard	I'll beg one boon,
	And then be gone and trouble you no more.
	Shall I obtain it?
Bolingbroke	Name it, fair cousin.
	. . . .
	Yet ask.
Richard	And shall I have?
Bolingbroke	You shall.
Richard	Then give me leave to go.

4.1.292–294, 300–303

The Abbot of Westminster describes this as a "woeful pageant," and it is no less. Richard's enacted deposition is a play, and its chief actor is a man who knows now that all men are actors, that they have their exits as well as their entrances.

The wordplay involved in "give me leave to go" substitutes for the expected boon (a jewel perhaps, or a castle, or some other material emolument) permission to depart the new king's company. (We could say that at this point in his career Richard prefers absence to presents.)

Where Richard does go is to Pomfret (Pontefract) Castle, the place where it will be possible for him finally to confront his insistent questions of identity, and to answer them in a riddling, philosophical fashion. His world has shrunk to a small space, a prison, and the even smaller yet infinitely larger world of his own imagination. Like the poet John Donne, who would write that love "makes one little room an everywhere" ("The Good-Morrow"), wittily punning on *stanza,* the Italian word for "room," so Richard, speaking now in soliloquy without even a silent onstage audience, articulates the power of language to contravene perceived reality. In this, we may note, he is curiously close in spirit to his uncle John of Gaunt, who urged the banished Bolingbroke to "[s]uppose the singing birds musicians, / The grass whereon thou tread'st the presence strewed." Here is Richard:

> I have been studying how I may compare
> This prison where I live unto the world;
> And for because the world is populous,
> And here is not a creature but myself,
> I cannot do it. Yet I'll hammer it out.
>
> 5.5.1–5

From the opening scene's admission that he cannot command ("Which since we cannot do . . ."), he has come to a point where the impossible is possible ("I'll hammer it out"). Abandoning as he must the royal "we," he wields, in one sense at least, more power than before, the power of poetic imagination. Many critics have compared him to the Metaphysical poets of the early seventeenth century (Donne, George Herbert, Henry Vaughan, Thomas Traherne, and others) because of his willingness to hammer out incommensurable and difficult comparisons. He ruminates on scriptural texts, and find them contradictory—how can it be both easy and hard to enter the kingdom of heaven?—and concludes, in a phrase that defines his own method, that these things "do set the faith itself / Against the faith" (5.5.13–14). The audience may recall the consistent question throughout this play of the meaning of the Word and the word, God's word and man's, names and things. But now Richard knows he is only an actor, not a godlike king:

> Thus play I in one person many people,
> And none contented. Sometimes am I king;
> Then treason makes me wish myself a beggar,
> And so I am. Then crushing penury

Persuades me I was better when a king.
Then am I kinged again, and by and by
Think that I am unkinged by Bolingbroke,
And straight am nothing. But whate'er I be,
Nor I, nor any man that but man is,
With nothing shall be pleased till he be eased
With being nothing.

                                            5.5.31–41

From these depths of metaphysical speculation, from these unanswerable questions, he is roused by two visitors with opposite motives: the groom who brings him music, and the murderer, Sir Piers Exton. It is almost as if, at the close of this tragedy of a medieval man caught in an early modern world, those stock figures from medieval drama, a good angel and a bad angel, an angel and a devil, had come to battle for him, and it is reminiscent of the similar splintering of persona into many people, as also seen in Richard's soliloquy the night before Bosworth. And Richard himself battles—his last gesture is action, not language. This man who throughout the play has acted only to suspend action, halting challenges, coming between opponents, throwing down his warder to stop the trial by combat, and in consequence filling his reign—and his stage—with repressed violence, now grabs a sword and kills two of his would-be murderers. Self-awareness and self-doubt have brought him to the condition of active man as well as contemplative man. And with this gesture he crosses the threshold from his world to King Henry's—from poetry to drama, from language to action.

Richard's last words may remind his listeners of the medieval debate concerning body and soul, or of the last, despairing words of Marlowe's Doctor Faustus. But where Faustus saw himself as "damned perpetually" by his ambition and hubristic bargain, crying out, as the clock strikes eleven on his final night, "O I'll leap up to my God! Who pulls me down? . . . Earth, gape! O no, it will not harbour me," Richard II offers an oddly serene and confident vision: "Mount, mount, my soul; thy seat is up on high, / Whilst my gross flesh sinks downward, here to die." This is the final triumph of the metaphor of ascent and descent. The soul rises, the flesh is without significance, for a king who wished to be God's anointed, and whose lamentable tale will live after him. But *is* he a holy king? Is Richard a hero, or a victim, or both? Is he finally just a weak man and a poor king, to be pitied or even despised? How is the audience to judge Richard, and to compare him to the ascendant Bolingbroke? The play seems to invite speculation about its underlying genre. Is it first and foremost a tragedy or a history play, the tragedy of Richard or the first episode in the chronicle of Henry IV?

There was in Elizabethan art a kind of picture known as "perspective," or anamorphosis, a distorted projection so designed that when viewed from a particular point, or reflected in a mirror, it appears regular and correctly proportioned. In *Richard II* Bushy alludes to this art form in such a way as to make it clear that the audience would find it familiar, speaking of "perspectives, which, rightly gazed upon, / Show nothing but confusion; eyed awry, / Distinguish form" (2.2.18–20). One of the most famous examples of this painting practice in the early modern period is Hans Holbein the Younger's 1533 portrait *The Ambassadors,* which depicts two elegantly dressed gentlemen, French ambassadors to the court of the English Henry VIII, surrounded with emblems of wealth and power (globes, astronomical and musical instruments, rich fabrics) and standing on a curiously patterned floor, taken from that of Westminster Abbey. "Eyed awry," the portrait when seen from the right-hand corner discloses that the odd pattern in the floor is a skull. The painting is a memento mori and a *vanitas,* reminding both the sitters and the viewer of the impermanence of life, wealth, and worldly position. Shakespeare's *Richard II* is, I believe, another such "perspective," or anamorphosis. Shakespeare gives his spectators two pictures, each of which looks coherent when viewed from a certain angle, yet when "eyed awry" discloses the disquieting shadow of the other.

One good example of such a distorting "perspective" can be found in the rather odd, almost comic episode at the beginning of act 4, when Aumerle, the son of old York, is accused by Bagot of wishing for Bolingbroke's death, and throws down his gage in challenge. Then Fitzwalter throws his gage down, and Percy his; "another lord," not even named, does so as well, and is joined by Surrey. Poor Aumerle has run out of gloves, and has to borrow one in order to meet this barrage of challenges: "Some honest Christian trust me with a gage" (4.1.74). As critics and directors have often noted, this is a parodic revisitation of the first and third scenes of the play, the formal challenges between Bolingbroke and Mowbray. Now it is Bolingbroke—soon to be King Henry IV—who tries to intervene and to stop the violence, but he is unable to do so because the one man who knows the truth of these accusations, Thomas Mowbray, Duke of Norfolk, is dead, killed on a holy Crusade in Venice. King Henry is thus left with a profoundly secular problem, a problem, yet again, of internal strife, rebellion, and civil war.

The other scenes in which Aumerle appears teeter equally on the verge of farce. In act 5, scenes 2 and 3, he is the object of a tug-of-war between his ancient parents, the Duke and Duchess of York, after which all three rush to King Henry and throw themselves on their knees before him. Even Henry comments that "[o]ur scene is altered from a serious thing, / And now changed to 'The Beggar and the King' " (5.3.77–78). The familiar up/down pattern of the "Richard" part of the play repeats itself in both these scenes, the hurling of the gages and the kneeling family. "Good aunt, stand up," the disconcerted king entreats the elderly Duchess of York. There is in both scenes an element of comedy, a genre that seems always to attach itself to the Henry world, and which will emerge full blown in the tavern scenes in *Henry IV Part 1* and *Part 2.*

But there is also internal strife: son against father, wife against husband. We learn that King Henry is himself at odds with his own "unthrifty son," who will emerge as the Prince Hal of the subsequent history plays. In short, although Bolingbroke, now King Henry, is very different from Richard in personality, he is unavoidably like him in circumstance. And as Richard is responsible for the death of his uncle Gloucester, a murder that hangs like a curse over his entire rule, so Henry, although he wishes it were not so, becomes responsible for the murder of Richard, a curse that will follow him and his son through the next series of plays, as Richard's former enemies use his death as their rallying cry.

The Bishop of Carlisle had warned that usurpation would lead to civil war:

> if you crown him, let me prophesy
> The blood of English shall manure the ground,
> And future ages groan for this foul act.
> . . . .
> O, if you rear this house against this house
> It will the woefullest division prove
> That ever fell upon this cursèd earth!
>
> *4.1.127–138*

Richard is murdered, having himself prophesied dissension, having warned that the ambitions of Northumberland would undermine the state of Bolingbroke. And the murder of Richard lies on Henry's head. The stage picture at the end of the play is extraordinarily significant, because it will be dominated by Richard's coffin, which constitutes the final dramatic irony of the play. As Richard, living, sat on the throne of state in the first scene, so Richard, dead, presents an inescapable memento mori, a reminder of death. In an earlier scene, Sir Piers Exton had mused aloud on words he claimed to have heard from the new king, Henry IV: " 'Have I no friend will rid me of this living fear?' " (5.4.2). Shakespeare's source here, as throughout the play, is Holinshed's *Chronicles of England, Scotland, and Ireland,* in which Holinshed writes:

> [K]ing Henrie, sitting on a daie at his table, sore sighing, said: "Haue I no faithfull freend which will deliuer me of him, whose life will be my death, and whose death will be the preseruation of my life?" This saieng was much noted of them which were present, and especiallie of one called sir Piers of Exton.[3]

There may well be a resonance, too, with Henry II's famous query about Thomas à Becket, Archbishop of Canterbury, in 1170: "Will no man rid me of this meddlesome priest?" Expecting a reward, Exton sets out to kill Richard. In the meantime, however, Henry IV has been trying to bring an end to civil strife. He rewards his supporters and beheads the Oxford traitors, but in a significant gesture of mercy he pardons his old enemy, the Bishop of Carlisle. When in the final scene Exton enters, triumphantly, with Richard's body, all Henry's careful plans are undone.

As a theatrical event, the entry of the coffin might well be monumental and stately, as several men move slowly forward bearing their burden of death. Exton's language, as he offers the body to his sovereign, is redolent with unintended ironies. "Great King," he says, "within this coffin I present / Thy buried fear" (5.6.30–31). The "living fear" of Henry IV's rhetorical exclamation is now safely "buried," Exton suggests. But Henry's "buried fear" is in fact something else entirely, a secret, unrevealed fear of guilt and blood upon his hands, so that the death of Richard creates, rather than lays to rest, a "living fear" that cannot be alleviated. The physical manifestation of the coffin on the stage unburies the buried fear and makes it live.

In vain the new king now turns eagerly to sacred history and to typology, as well as to piety, suggesting a pilgrimage as a remedy for secular failings. In short, Henry turns to the same vocabulary of Christian kingship that had animated, and disabled, Richard II's rule. He declares:

> I'll make a voyage to the Holy Land
> To wash this blood off from my guilty hand.
>
> *5.6.49–50*

But history is not so easily appeased, and in *Henry IV Part 2* the intended journey to Jerusalem ends with the king's death in a palace chamber of that name. Once again, the end of this journey is within, instead of in the outside world, and the double meaning of "Jerusalem" joins all the other ironies of language and intention that complicate these English history plays. This play does not end in timelessness, with apocalypse, or with Richard's soul mounting to heaven. It ends instead in history and in ongoing time, in repetition and reversal. The tragic death of Richard II, an unintended effect, becomes the cause, and the curse, that hangs over the *Henry IV* plays and *Henry V*. The way up is the way down. At this point the audience may begin to glimpse the full force of old York's newly minted genealogy, his tale of success and succession addressed to Bolingbroke, the new Henry IV, as he assumes the kingship and its ambivalent heritage: "Ascend his throne, descending now from him."

King John

DRAMATIS PERSONAE

King John of England
Queen Eleanor, *his mother*
Lady Falconbridge
Philip the Bastard, *later knighted*
  as Sir Richard Plantagenet, her
  illegitimate son by King Richard I
  (Coeur-de-lion)
Robert Falconbridge, *her*
  legitimate son
James Gurney, *her attendant*
Lady Blanche of Spain, *niece of*
  King John
Prince Henry, *son of King John*
Hubert, *a follower of King John*
Earl of Salisbury
Earl of Pembroke
Earl of Essex
Lord Bigot

King Philip of France
Louis the Dauphin, *his son*
Arthur, Duke of Brittaine,
  nephew of King John
Lady Constance, *his mother*
Duke of Austria (Limoges)
Châtillon, *ambassador from*
  France to England
Count Melun
A Citizen of Angers
Cardinal Pandolf, *a legate*
  from the Pope
Peter of Pomfret, *a prophet*
Heralds
Executioners
Messengers
Sheriff
Lords, soldiers, attendants

HAKESPEARE'S *The Life and Death of King John* is a play better known to scholars than to modern theater audiences. Asked about the history of the title character, many might summon up associations with the Magna Carta, the historic document of 1215 by which a reluctant John was compelled to share power with his rebellious barons, laying the groundwork for constitutional liberties. Neither the signing of the document nor any hint of this political event is present in the play, however. Instead *King John* offers a drama of succession and its discontents, including some particularly memorable characters and scenes.

Scholars have debated whether Shakespeare's *King John* is based upon the anonymous play *The Troublesome Reign of John, King of England* (published in 1591) or whether it might have preceded it. In any case, the story of King John would have been well known in the period. John Bale's *Kynge Iohan*, a morality play dating from the time of Henry VIII, offers an allegorical treatment of

English history, appropriating the struggle, conventional from morality plays, within the soul of an individual to depict, instead, the struggle of John's England against Catholic and foreign domination. Holinshed's *Chronicles* tells the story of King John at length, and various modern Shakespeare editors have emphasized the parallels between John and Queen Elizabeth, both struggling to establish their legitimate claims to the throne against the rival interests of the Pope and of other lineal heirs. From the perspective of a reader or a spectator, these historical patterns are significant insofar as they underpin, shadow, and deepen the dramatic conflicts onstage.

The energies of Shakespeare's *King John* have much in common with those of *Titus Andronicus,* an early tragedy with which it shares a propensity for physical violence and the thematics of bodily mutilation. Where, for example, *Titus* seems to return repeatedly to the allusive language of heads and hands (both vividly lopped off, onstage, in that robust Senecan play), *King John* is similarly engaged—one might say obsessed—with the imagery of the eye, a thematic emphasis that culminates in the famous scene (4.1), invented by Shakespeare, in which the citizen Hubert of Angiers threatens, on John's orders, to put out the eyes of Prince Arthur, a rival claimant to the throne. King John's own language, and especially his use of the word "signs," likewise links *John* to *Titus* as well as to another early history play, *Richard III.* Here, for example, is the King's remonstrance to Hubert, after John receives what turns out to be the false news of Arthur's murder (Hubert pretends to have done the deed, and is relieved to learn that John now wishes it undone):

King John	Hadst thou but shook thy head or made a pause
	When I spake darkly what I purposèd,
	Or turned an eye of doubt upon my face,
	As bid me tell my tale in express words,
	Deep shame had struck me dumb, made me break off,
	And those thy fears might have wrought fears in me.
	But thou didst understand me by my signs,
	And didst in signs again parley with sin;
	Yea, without stop, didst let thy heart consent,
	And consequently thy rude hand to act
	The deed which both our tongues held vile to name.
	Out of my sight, and never see me more!

King John 4.2.232–243

The "hands," "tongue," and "signs" of *Titus Andronicus* are here combined with the "eye of doubt" and the command "Out of my sight," echoes of the insistent "eye" language of earlier scenes, and especially of the scene of aborted torture. When Hubert, emboldened, announces, "Young Arthur is alive. This hand of mine / Is yet a maiden and an innocent hand, / Not painted with the crimson spots of blood," and says that he is not, and could not bring himself to be, "butcher of an innocent child" (4.2.252–254, 260), John begs his forgiveness: "Doth Arthur live? . . . my rage was blind, / And foul imaginary eyes of blood / Presented thee more hideous than thou art" (261, 265–267). In this play John's emotional respite is short-lived, however, since Arthur in the next scene leaps to his death from the walls of the castle in which he had been imprisoned. This now-unwelcome death of a former rival, like so many hastily and unwarily wished for in Shakespeare's history plays (e.g., the death of Richard II that blights the reign of Henry IV), will come back to haunt the king.

In dramatic terms the rivalry sets up a series of mother-son pairings unusual in Shakespeare's history plays, which are so often preoccupied with the relationships between fathers and sons. Eleanor and John, Lady Falconbridge and the Bastard, and Constance and Arthur are all juxtaposed in scenes that show the mother's affection, the son's loyalty, and the complex politics of mother love, in a way that will not appear again until the late Roman play *Coriolanus*. The first act opens with the entrance of a king and queen, but the queen—Eleanor—is the king's mother, not his wife. And she is also clearly his political confidante and close adviser. Lady Falconbridge's "dear offense" with King Richard I (Richard Coeur-de-lion, the Lion-Hearted), Eleanor's eldest son and John's brother and predecessor, has produced the Bastard as hero and champion. And Arthur's claim, passionately supported by Constance and by her allies of France and Austria, derives from his father, Geoffrey, Constance's husband and Eleanor's second son. When John's forces capture Arthur (officially styled Duke of Brittaine, but called by John, more dangerously, "Arthur of Britain"), Constance is distraught, and in her distress she delivers what is perhaps the play's most memorable single speech, her lament for "pretty Arthur" and her almost metaphysical praise of grief.

The scene, act 3, scene 4, anticipates the torture scene in act 4, scene 1, and it is important to remember that at this point Arthur is neither dead nor even physically threatened. Yet in performance this is a "mad scene," anticipating Ophelia and Lady Macbeth, as Constance enters with her hair down (the conventional stage sign of the madwoman), and the French King Philip ineffectually commands her, "Bind up those tresses. . . . Bind up your hairs" (3.4.61, 68). Her reply is all too apposite: "I tore them from their bonds, and cried aloud, / 'O that these hands could so redeem my son, / As they have given these hairs their liberty!' " (3.4.70–72). She is convinced that her son will die in captivity: "therefore never, never / Must I behold my pretty Arthur more" (88–89). Although Constance begins the scene with histrionic exclamations, a familiar if powerful combination of macabre charnel house language and the erotics of womb and tomb—"Death, Death, O amiable, lovely Death! / Thou odoriferous stench, sound rottenness! . . . I will kiss thy detestable bones, / And put my eyeballs in thy vaulty brows, / And ring these fingers with thy household worms. . . . Come grin on me, and I will think thou smil'st, / And buss thee as thy wife" (25–26, 29–31, 34–35)—she ultimately modulates her tone, and attains, for a moment, an astonishing sublimity of utterance. When the Cardinal chides her for her excessive grieving, she answers in the same tenor as Macduff: "He talks to me that never had a son" (91). And King Philip's mild reproof, aimed at the emotionalism of women—"You are as fond of grief as of your child" (92)—produces the extraordinary conceit that is, perhaps, the play's most often quoted passage:

> Constance Grief fills the room up of my absent child,
> Lies in his bed, walks up and down with me,
> Puts on his pretty looks, repeats his words,
> Remembers me of all his gracious parts,
> Stuffs out his vacant garments with his form;
> Then have I reason to be fond of grief.
> Fare you well. Had you such a loss as I,
> I could give better comfort than you do.
> [*She unbinds her hair*]
> I will not keep this form upon my head
> When there is such disorder in my wit.
> O Lord, my boy, my Arthur, my fair son,
> My life, my joy, my food, my all the world,
> My widow-comfort, and my sorrow's cure!
>
> *3.4.93–105*

The King, like Horatio confronted with the mad Ophelia, "fear[s] some outrage," and follows her offstage. Arthur's desperate leap to his death comes an act later, and it is greeted with equal ceremony—"O death, made proud with pure and princely beauty!" (4.3.35)—by the nobles who discover the body. But by this time both Constance and Eleanor are dead, the passing of these two enemies and rivals twinned, with acute dramatic irony, in a messenger's report to King John:

> King John O, where hath our intelligence been drunk?
> Where hath it slept? Where is my mother's ear,
> That such an army could be drawn in France,
> And she not hear of it?
> Messenger   My liege, her ear
> Is stopped with dust. The first of April died
> Your noble mother. And as I hear, my lord,
> The Lady Constance in a frenzy died
> Three days before. . . .
>
> *4.2.116–123*

In this exchange John speaks in words very similar to those later to be heard from a scornful Lady Macbeth ("Was the hope drunk / Wherein you dress'd yourself?" [*Macbeth* 1.7.35–36]), only to hear, as Macbeth will hear, of the queen's death offstage. "What! mother dead?" John exclaims, rather bathetically, at the news. The historical Constance died in 1201, three years before Eleanor, but Shakespeare's play brings these mighty opposites together in death. In a play written in the time of Elizabeth and focused on a set of martial, political, and religious conflicts often compared with Elizabeth's own, neither Eleanor nor Constance prevails. Instead, as with Elizabeth, the key question continues to be not who will be the power behind the throne, but who will be the legitimate and powerful ruler. The model remains male (John; his son, Prince Henry; the heroic Bastard). Elizabeth would have seen herself in the line of kings, and not among the female consorts. But the theatrical power of these two strong women is very effective, enlivening the play and deepening its pathos.

Against these titanic women of the older generation, the younger women, exemplified by Blanche of Spain, have little power. Blanche, indeed, finds herself in a situation that will become familiar for brides-to-be in Shakespearean plays, torn between love and filial duty—between her husband, Louis of France, and her uncle, King John of England, as the false peace brokered by her wedding immediately escalates to war:

> Which is the side that I must go withal?
> I am with both, each army hath a hand,
> And in their rage, I having hold of both,
> They whirl asunder and dismember me.
> Husband, I cannot pray that thou mayst win.—
> Uncle, I needs must pray that thou mayst lose.—
> Father, I may not wish the fortune thine.—
> Grandam, I will not wish thy wishes thrive.
> Whoever wins, on that side shall I lose,
> Assurèd loss before the match be played.
>
> *3.1.253–262*

Like Octavia in *Julius Caesar,* caught between her husband, Antony, and her brother, Caesar, Blanche discovers that an arranged marriage cannot so easily reconcile determined foes.

Prophecies, like that of the local seer Peter of Pomfret, are used to reinforce the sense of dramatic fatality. Peter's prediction that John will "deliver up" his crown by Ascension Day (4.2.147–152) comes true, but not in the dire sense in which it is taken, since at the beginning of act 5 John voluntarily surrenders his crown to the papal legate in order to receive it ceremonially back from him, thus reconciling himself with Rome. Peter of Pomfret is dismissed as a "dreamer," like the soothsayer in *Julius Caesar,* and the part he plays is a very small one. In fact, although he is onstage at the time, in act 4, his prophecy is reported by the

Bastard rather than spoken by Peter himself. But this slantwise achievement of a prophetic "truth" against its apparently plain meaning is a device that Shakespeare will use repeatedly in other plays, from *Richard III* (where the prophecy that "G" intends mischief refers not to George, Duke of Clarence, but to Richard, Duke of Gloucester) to *Henry IV Part 2* (where the King dies in a chamber called "Jerusalem," not in the Holy Land, as he had expected) and the several prophecies in *Macbeth*.

The larger design of the play pursues a pattern that would become familiar in later histories and tragedies. A king with a clouded title to the throne tries desperately to reinforce that title by repressing, appeasing, or extinguishing a popular rival. Arthur's name, Arthur of Brittaine, we might note here, would have carried historical resonances with the ancient and legendary King of Britain, as well as with Henry VIII's elder brother, the first Tudor heir, Prince Arthur, who died young. Interested parties on all sides attempt to intervene, with results that are either futile or counterproductive. External war (in the plot of the play, the medieval conflict of England against France; in the context of Shakespeare's own time, England's recently concluded war with Spain) is followed by civil strife, both between rival factions and within the divided mind and consciousness of the king. A heroic and entrepreneurial figure— here, the Bastard Falconbridge—emerges to combine the popular and the "noble," and to offer a spirit of patriotic energy otherwise lacking from the tired court.

The short opening scene establishes the political crisis, a claim by the King of France that "young Arthur" Plantagenet is the rightful ruler of Ireland, Poitou, Anjou, Touraine, and Maine, since he is the son of John's deceased brother Geoffrey. Behind Arthur's claim, as John's mother, Queen Eleanor, makes clear, is the importunacy of Arthur's own mother and Geoffrey's widow, Constance, who now resides at the French court. No sooner is this claim between royal rivals mentioned, however, than it is displaced by a more local dispute of a similar kind: two brothers, Robert and Philip Falconbridge, come before the King to urge their claims on an estate in Northamptonshire. Philip is the elder, but is—or may be—a bastard; Robert is the legitimate son of his father, Sir Robert, knighted by Richard Coeur-de-lion, King John's own elder brother and the former king. In a witty and spirited exchange, Philip discloses that he is actually the son of the crusading King Richard, a fact guessed at by both Eleanor and John ("He hath a trick of Coeur-de-lion's face; / The accent of his tongue affecteth him" [1.1.85–86]; "Mine eye hath well examinèd his parts, / And finds them perfect Richard" [1.1.89–90]) and shortly to be verified by his mother. As the Bastard says to her, genially, "He that perforce robs lions of their hearts / May easily win a woman's" (1.1.268–269). Philip is readily persuaded to accept a knighthood, a military career, and a new name—Sir Richard Plantagenet—rather than the life and inheritance of a local squire. He resigns his claims to the Falconbridge estate and joins the forces of Eleanor and John.

Thus, as the play moves onward, the Bastard is established as a lively, profane, and rounded dramatic character, capable of judiciously bawdy jesting with Queen Eleanor, and adroit, as well, in personable asides to the audience, once the stage is cleared of other characters. His language is deliberately colloquial, full of regionalisms, contractions, and local color ("Well, now can I make any Joan a lady," he congratulates himself with amusement the minute the court withdraws, imagining the homage of the countryside: " 'Good e'en, Sir Richard' " [1.1.184–185]). It is easy, and appropriate, to associate this winning Bastard with the later figure of Edmund, the bastard son of the Duke of Gloucester in *King Lear*—as well as with a character like the bastard Spurio in *The Revenger's Tragedy* (who shares Philip/Richard's arch propensity for using the word "Dad" [*John* 2.1.468]). Critics have also compared him to Shakespeare's Mercutio, Autolycus, Jaques, Touchstone, and even Falstaff. In any case, he is not only a brave soldier but also a witty commentator, a refreshingly deflating cynic. It is worth noting that, unlike any others in this distinguished Shakespearean roster, he not only survives, as Edmund, Mercutio, and Falstaff do not, but also retains central power and influence. Indeed, his ascendancy is such that the play will reward him, at the close, with its final, stirring, and patriotic lines, giving him theatrical pride of place over King John's succeeding son, Prince Henry.

When the action shifts to France, the talk is still of legitimacy and usurpation. The King of France, also named Philip, describes John to Arthur as "thy unnatural uncle" who has usurped the lands bequeathed him by Richard the Lion-Hearted. Arthur is addressed and referred to from the outset as "boy" ("fair boy," "this boy," "poor boy," "green boy"), "child" ("poor child," "this oppressed child"), or "little prince"; he is almost always referred to as "young Arthur," in part to increase the dramatic pathos of his imprisonment and death. In a cruelly effective scene with John, Eleanor, and his mother, Constance, Eleanor calls herself his "grandam" and Constance reacts with a vituperative parody of baby talk ("Give grandam kingdom, and it grandam will / Give it a plum, a cherry, and a fig" [2.1.159, 161–162]). In fact, the historical Arthur, Duke of Brittany, was born in 1187, the same year as the French Dauphin, later Louis VIII, and was regarded as old enough to be married to Blanche of Castile, Eleanor's granddaughter, one year his junior (as Hubert explicitly comments in proposing this political match: "Look upon the years / Of Louis the Dauphin and that lovely maid" [2.1.425–426]). In any case, Arthur is a cat's-paw in this conflict, where the real ambitions lie with France and with the Duke of Austria. The French King Philip's description of him, in diplomatic parlay with England's King John, reads uncannily like Lady Capulet's "book report" praising the County Paris to Juliet:

King Philip   Look here upon thy brother Geoffrey's face.
               These eyes, these brows, were moulded out of his;
               This little abstract doth contain that large

Which died in Geoffrey; and the hand of time
Shall draw this brief into as huge a volume.

2.1.99–103

What becomes again clear, though, in the course of this scene, is how much
of the rivalry is based on antagonism between the two women, Eleanor and
Constance, mother-in-law and daughter-in-law. When Eleanor declares Arthur
a "bastard"—an accusation quickly countered by Constance—she unites the
narratives of "low" and "high," royal politics between England and France, John
and Arthur, and the fortunes of the Bastard Falconbridge. Constance retorts:
"My boy a bastard? By my soul I think / His father never was so true begot. / It
cannot be, an if thou wert his mother" (2.1.129–131). Fittingly, then, it is the Bastard Falconbridge who regularly comments ironically on the ensuing action,
offering a steady counterpoint to both martial and amatory declarations.

The city of Angers declines to choose between the claimants to the throne of
England, while acknowledging that it is England's king to whom it owes fealty.
The armies aligned to fight are described, by the Bastard (Falconbridge), in lan-
guage as powerful as any in Shakespeare:

> O, now doth Death line his dead chaps with steel;
> The swords of soldiers are his teeth, his fangs;
> And now he feasts, mousing the flesh of men
> In undetermined differences of kings.
>
> *2.1.352–355*

The spectators of Angers stand by on the battlements, the Bastard observes,
"[a]s in a theatre, whence they gape and point / At your industrious scenes and
acts of death" (375–376).

Just as battle is to be joined, Hubert a Citizen of Angers proposes instead a
peaceful solution, a marriage instead of a war. It is a solution that would be
tried, both in history and in a number of Shakespeare's plays, from *Henry V* to
Antony and Cleopatra, with mixed success. The ambivalence of the moment is
highlighted by the way it is received, onstage, by the Dauphin, Louis of France,
who is the bridegroom-designate, and the skeptical onlooker the Bastard. For
Louis, the occasion is one that provokes a poetic cliché, "making babies" in the
eye of the beloved, a cliché later made popular in poems like John Donne's "The
Exstasie":

Louis the Dauphin   [I]n her eye I find
A wonder, or a wondrous miracle,
The shadow of myself formed in her eye;

. . . .

I do protest I never loved myself

                    Till now enfixèd I beheld myself
                    Drawn in the flattering table of her eye.
                         [*He*] *whispers with* BLANCHE
Bastard   [*aside*] Drawn in the flattering table of her eye,
                    Hanged in the frowning wrinkle of her brow,
                    And quartered in her heart: he doeth espy
                    Himself love's traitor. . . .

                                        2.1.497–499, 505–508

Figuratively hanged, drawn, and quartered by the Bastard's extended image,
Louis is subjected to a kind of verbal torture, thus comically imitating the discourse of conventional Petrarchan suffering. But Louis's response, as formal as
Paris's (or Juliet's) in *Romeo and Juliet,* betokens difficulties, especially because
what he professes to see in Blanche's eye is his own reflection. Once again this
language of the eye points blindly forward, and will turn tragic at the moment
when Hubert threatens to put out Arthur's eyes with a red-hot poker. There,
too, eyes lock on eyes and speak ("My eyes are out," says Arthur in despair,
"Even with the fierce looks of these bloody men" [4.1.72-73]).

   It is this cease-fire, and with it the end of martial glory, that calls forth from
the Bastard what is probably his most powerful speech, the railing against "commodity." As it turns from honest indignation to even more honest self-interest,
the logic of this satirical jeremiad combines droll social commentary and keen
social critique:

              That smooth-faced gentleman, tickling commodity;
              Commodity, the bias of the world,
              The world who of itself is peisèd well,
              Made to run even upon even ground,
              Till this advantage, this vile-drawing bias,
              This sway of motion, this commodity,
              Makes it take head from all indifferency,
              From all direction, purpose, course, intent;
              And this same bias, this commodity,
              This bawd, this broker, this all-changing word,
              Clapped on the outward eye of fickle France,
              Hath drawn him from his own determined aid,
              From a resolved and honourable war,
              To a most base and vile-concluded peace.
              And why rail I on this commodity?
              But for because he hath not wooed me yet—
              Not that I have the power to clutch my hand
              When his fair angels would salute my palm,
              But for my hand, as unattempted yet,

> Like a poor beggar raileth on the rich.
> Well, whiles I am a beggar I will rail,
> And say there is no sin but to be rich,
> And being rich, my virtue then shall be
> To say there is no vice but beggary.
> Since kings break faith upon commodity,
> Gain, be my lord, for I will worship thee.
>
> *2.1.574–599*

In the event, however, it is not "commodity" (self-interest, profit, gain) but rather the all-too-familiar combination of politics and religion that prevails, for the wedding day is interrupted by a personage whom King John characterizes (quoting Henry VIII on Thomas More) as a "meddling priest." John is positioned as the foe of Roman papal power (in an allegorical political reading he is thus analogous to Queen Elizabeth, as Arthur has been taken for the hapless Mary, Queen of Scots, a rival to Elizabeth's throne). And the voice that forbids the marriage, on the grounds that John will not obey the Pope's orders in appointing a bishop of Canterbury, belongs to Pandolf, a papal legate, here unhistorically elevated to the rank of cardinal. Pandolf's argument, elegantly set forth in a classic passage of "school logic," strict and rigorous ratiocination, displays elements of what the period knew as "equivocation" and strongly anticipates some celebrated passages in *Hamlet* and *Macbeth*:

> For that which thou hast sworn to do amiss
> Is not amiss when it is truly done;
> And being not done where doing tends to ill,
> The truth is then most done not doing it.
> The better act of purposes mistook
> Is to mistake again; though indirect,
> Yet indirection thereby grows direct,
> And falsehood falsehood cures, as fire cools fire
> Within the scorchèd veins of one new burned.
>
> *3.1.196–204*

And:

> Against an oath, the truth. Thou art unsure
> To swear: swear'st only not to be forsworn—
> Else what a mockery should it be to swear!—
> But thou dost swear only to be forsworn,
> And most forsworn to keep what thou dost swear;
> Therefore thy later vows against thy first
> Is in thyself rebellion to thyself,

And better conquest never canst thou make
Than arm thy constant and thy nobler parts
Against these giddy loose suggestions. . . .

3.1.209–218

The second of these passages resonates with many swear/forswear/oath moments in early comedies like *Love's Labour's Lost,* as well as with the constant Shakespearean theme of personal civil war ("rebellion to thyself"). But there is, too, a verbal inkling of a later moment of "good" rebellion in Pandolf's phrase "better conquest never canst thou make"—the anticipation here is to Cornwall's worthy servant in *King Lear,* who tells his master, "better service have I never done you / Than now to bid you hold" (*Lear* 3.7.72–73). Before we dismiss this echo as the merest accident, we might recall the circumstances: Cornwall is in the act of putting out Gloucester's eyes. That Shakespeare should, when writing *Lear,* recall the cadence of his earlier warning, in a play that also threatens torture of an innocent man by blinding, seems a fair instance of subliminal association, if it is not a direct and deliberate reference. Indeed, if we are thinking along these lines, we might compare Arthur's leap to his death in *King John* ("The wall is high, and yet will I leap down. / Good ground, be pitiful, and hurt me not" [4.3.1–2]) to the suicidal "leap" of the blind Gloucester from what he thinks is "Dover cliff"—but is actually flat ground.

I noted above that the dynamic of rivalry between women is palpable in this play almost from the outset. One of Shakespeare's chief sources, Holinshed's *Chronicles,* specifies this as a motive for the conflict:

> Surelie queene Elianor the kings mother was sore against hir nephue Arthur, rather mooued thereto by enuie conceiued against his mother, than vpon any iust occasion giuen in the behalfe of the child, for that she saw, if he were king, how his mother Constance would looke to beare most rule within the realme of England, till hir sonne should come to lawfull age, to gouerne of himselfe. . . .[1]

John's death at the close is, in a way, his most dramatic action. Apparently poisoned by a monk, and burning up with fever, he is carried onstage in a litter-chair. "I am a scribbled form," he tells his son, "drawn with a pen / Upon a parchment, and against this fire / Do I shrink up" (5.7.32–34). The self-conscious evocation of the act of writing, and the vivid image of parchment shrinking as it burns, returns the play to the question of history, and of the chronicles of kings. His lineal successor, Prince Henry, is a young man; the Dauphin of France, the young Prince Louis, has sent offers of peace; and Philip Falconbridge, the bastard son of Richard I, has taken on, in more than one way, the voice of the King. "Now hear our English king," he had declared to Cardinal Pandolf in John's name, "For thus his royalty doth speak in me"

(5.2.128–129). With Henry's succession the Bastard becomes not only *his* champion but also *his* voice, and it is to this powerful and fictitious character that Shakespeare gives the all-important final lines of the play:

Prince Henry	I have a kind of soul that would give thanks,
	And knows not how to do it but with tears.
	[*He weeps*]
Bastard	[*rising*] O, let us pay the time but needful woe,
	Since it hath been beforehand with our griefs.
	This England never did, nor never shall,
	Lie at the proud foot of a conqueror
	But when it first did help to wound itself.
	Now these her princes are come home again,
	Come the three corners of the world in arms
	And we shall shock them. Naught shall make us rue
	If England to itself do rest but true.

5.7.108–118

The son who inherits the kingdom weeps and buries his father. The bastard-patriot-hero rallies the troops for England.

The Merchant of Venice

DRAMATIS PERSONAE

Antonio, *a merchant of Venice*
Bassanio, *his friend and Portia's suitor*
Leonardo, *Bassanio's servant*
Lorenzo, *a friend of Antonio and
  Bassanio*
Gratiano, *a friend of Antonio and
  Bassanio*
Salerio, *a friend of Antonio and
  Bassanio*
Solanio, *a friend of Antonio and
  Bassanio*
Shylock, *a Jew*
Jessica, *his daughter*
Tubal, *a Jew*
Lancelot, *a clown, first Shylock's servant
  and then Bassanio's*

Gobbo, *his father*
Portia, *an heiress*
Nerissa, *her waiting-
  gentlewoman*
Balthasar, *Portia's servant*
Stefano, *Portia's servant*
Prince of Morocco, *Portia's
  suitor*
Prince of Aragon, *Portia's
  suitor*
Duke of Venice
Magnificoes of Venice
A jailer, attendants, and
  servants

IN THE LATE twentieth century and into the twenty-first, *The Merchant of Venice* has become, for reasons historical and political as well as literary and dramatic, the site of very great anxiety—anxiety about religion and religious prejudice, about the play's depiction of Jews and of Christians, and also about the place of sexuality and gender. A play that began its stage career with a comic Shylock in a false nose has become transmuted, over the centuries and especially after the Holocaust, into a drama of pathos, loss, and mutual incomprehension, with Shylock often—though not always—emerging as a tragic figure incongruously caught in the midst of a romantic comedy. The courtroom scene in the fourth act, with the public defeat and discomfiture of Shylock, has often seemed to overshadow the moonlight, music, and "manna" of the events in Belmont that actually end the play. Modern productions often include a type of wordless acknowledgment on the part of Jessica, Shylock's daughter, that she feels some empathy for the father she has so merrily abandoned for her Christian husband, Lorenzo, and often stress, as well, the sense of ambivalence that attends upon Antonio's recovery of his wealth at the hands of Portia, who has married his beloved friend and protégé, Bassanio. As I will try to explain, the ambivalence and ambiguity that emerge from a reading or staging of the play are not a sign of its failure, but rather of its signal success. The play produces upon the audience the effect that it also instates and describes in its characters.

The Merchant of Venice is above all Shakespeare's great play about difference. Shakespeare presents a series of what seem to be clear-cut opposites, but each of those opposites begins, as the play goes on, to seem oddly like, rather than unlike, the other. It seems important, therefore, to begin by laying out some of the great dichotomies in this play, and the way in which Shakespeare addresses them. I say "addresses," rather than "resolves," for—as we will see—this is a play that manages its discomfiting topics by creating dramatic situations that are deliberately and relentlessly discomfiting and uncomfortable. At the same time, on the level of sheer beauty of language and power of dramaturgy, the play is disturbingly appealing, just at those moments when one might wish it to be unappealing. The most magnificent of its speeches are also, in some ways, the most wrongheaded. (I am thinking here, for example, of Portia's eloquent and oft-quoted speech on the "quality of mercy," which, in the context of the trial scene, urges on Shylock a generosity of behavior that Portia herself will ultimately fail to show toward him.)

Christian/Jew; Venice/Belmont; male/female. This play concerns itself with the assertion and undercutting of these absolute polarities, of which the distinction between Christian and Jew (and, in another sense, merchant and Jew) is itself a sign, a marker of difference. In other words, Shakespeare takes advantage of these apparent differences in order to put in question the whole issue of difference. How are others, and otherness, related to oneself? To the notion that one *has* a "self"? When the play talks about Old Testament values as contrasted with those of the New Testament, the Hebrew Bible, and the Christian Bible, and about an apparent dialectic between mercy and justice, what it is discussing is a split in belief that was fundamental to Elizabethan culture, and to the establishment of a new state church, the Church of England, under Elizabeth's father, Henry VIII, who named himself Defender of the Faith. But the play does not rest with a simple opposition. Every "Christian" in this play is put into question, their Christian nature tested. And likewise, it is not Shylock's Jewish religion but rather his own periodically mean-spirited misinterpretation of religious and cultural values that is offered for the audience's observation. Furthermore, as again we will see, it is not so unproblematic as it may at first appear to distinguish between Venice and Belmont, both of which are cultures built on gold. Nor yet is it as easy as one might think to distinguish between men and women. "What, shall we turn to men?" Nerissa will joke when Portia presents her disguise plot. As we have noted, on the public stage in early modern England the roles of women were performed by boy actors, and in *The Merchant of Venice* both of the "women" in the play disguise themselves as young men. (Portia disguises herself as a young male doctor of laws.) Her rival for Bassanio's affections, Antonio, diminished by the loss of his money and power, compares himself to a "wether," a castrated ram. At the end of the play, the news of his mended fortunes comes to him from the young, rich, and powerful woman who has married Bassanio. It is not that there is no difference between women and men, but rather that, throughout the play, each character is constantly threatening, or promising, to turn into the other sex.

The Merchant of Venice was written and performed during a time of religious controversy in England, and against the dark background of the Spanish Inquisition. Moors and Jews were both excluded from Spain, and those who attempted to remain were hunted down. Even converts to Christianity were suspected of treason. As an indication of the inside-outside issues of difference and self-difference in the period, we might note that Tomás de Torquemada, the first grand inquisitor in Spain, the man who persuaded Ferdinand and Isabella to expel all Jews who refused to be baptized, was himself of Jewish descent.

If it is concerned with religious controversy and change, the play is also concerned with changes in social culture and in economic structure. The Merchant of Venice is a play about credit, a play about living and trading on margin, as well as on the margins. The young hero, Bassanio, is recognizable as an upwardly mobile young urbanite. He is in debt, and he sees that the best way of resolving his problems is to get (temporarily) into further debt. His new commodity is Portia, a beautiful heiress, in Belmont. He will invest in his attempt to win her, and in order to do so he will borrow more money from Antonio. This play, in other words, is in many ways about capital, an issue as persistently timely in Shakespeare's day as in the modern era. Many great Elizabethan figures—Sir Philip Sidney, the Earl of Essex, the Earl of Leicester, the Earl of Southampton—were thousands of pounds in debt. Queen Elizabeth herself borrowed large sums from European bankers, and Shakespeare's company borrowed to build both the Theatre and the Globe at very high rates of interest. Venice in this play is the place of capital. What does it produce? Not agricultural products, or manufactured goods, or even—so far as one can learn from the play—works of art, but rather money. And the play registers what might be described as a certain cultural anxiety about a shift in economics, a move toward capitalism and away from the landowning aristocracy, in England as well as ostensibly in Venice and Belmont.

Written in 1596–1598, The Merchant of Venice is one of a group of major comedies of Shakespeare's middle period, sometimes called "great" or "festive" comedies, a group that also includes Much Ado About Nothing, As You Like It, and Twelfth Night. The term "festive" refers not so much to the plays' presumptive joyousness as to their thematic links and plot links to seasonal festivals from May Day to Christmas and Twelfth Night, and it is noteworthy that in each of these plays, especially Merchant, there is much that actively resists joyful celebration. (Both Portia and Antonio are melancholy at the opening of the play; Shylock detests stage plays and music; threats of death and loss predominate through much of the dramatic action; and the ending of the play, at least in most productions, is at the best bittersweet, if not entirely bitter.) Again, this is not uncharacteristic of Shakespearean comedy, which always seems to hold death at bay just outside its borders, and tends to postpone the promised weddings, reunions, and consummations, the hallmarks of traditional stage comedy, to some notional "sixth act" beyond the playing time of the play.

Many of the dominant structural elements of *Merchant* are familiar from other plays, like the (apparent) tension between justice and mercy (a key theme in *The Comedy of Errors*), or the pattern of losing oneself to find oneself, often linked to the question of disguise (as, for example, in *Love's Labour's Lost*). The stern Duke charged with upholding a stern law is a familiar figure from *A Midsummer Night's Dream* and *Romeo and Juliet* (where his title is "Prince," but his task is the same), as well as in *The Comedy of Errors*. "The Duke cannot deny the course of law" is how the sentiment is expressed in *Merchant*—or, as Shylock puts it, "If you deny me, fie upon your law: / There is no force in the decrees of Venice" (4.1.100–101). Venice, as a crossroads of commerce and capital, depends upon the consistency of the rule of law. The concept of the bond, which both enslaves and frees, is another common feature between this play and others. The dark jokes on bonds and bondage in *The Comedy of Errors* are here represented by equally resonant quibbles:

Bassanio	This is the man, this is Antonio,
	To whom I am so infinitely bound.
Portia	You should in all sense be much bound to him,
	For as I hear he was much bound for you.

Merchant 5.1.133–134

Characteristically, Portia in this exchange acts not only as a witty and sympathetic lady and a gracious hostess but also as a literary critic, explicating the many meanings of the word "bound." She will act as a critic also in the great trial scene, dissecting the particularities of Shylock's bond and its loopholes, first in moral, then in technical, law.

Perhaps what strikes an audience first about *The Merchant of Venice* is that its two opening scenes present two melancholy people, people who seem to have everything the riches of the world can afford, and who are, nonetheless, unhappy. "In sooth, I know not why I am so sad," says Antonio to his friends Salerio and Solanio in the first line of the play. The two suggest some reasons: perhaps he is worried about all his merchant ships, which are "tossing on the ocean," full of all his goods and wealth. It is of course Antonio, not Shylock, who is the titular character, the "merchant of Venice." Jews were moneylenders in part because they could not—by law—be merchants, could not sell or exchange real commodities or goods. But it is not money worries, nor love, nor indeed anything Antonio can name that makes him sad. His sadness lacks what T. S. Eliot, speaking of the melancholy Hamlet, would call an "objective correlative," or what we might call an adequate and sufficient cause within the play.

At the same time, in Belmont, in the opening line of the second scene, Portia remarks to her maid, "By my troth, Nerissa, my little body is aweary of this great world" (1.2.1–2). Yet Portia, too, is wealthy—"a lady richly left," in Bassanio's phrase, the sole heiress to her father's fortune. The play thus begins with a strong parallelism between Antonio and Portia, both of whom will emerge, in the course of the drama, as lovers of Bassanio. Modern productions often depict Antonio as a gay man explicitly in love with Bassanio, and thus doomed by the plot to solitude at the end of the play. Both homosocial and homoerotic relationships were common, and commonly noted, in the early modern period, an era in which such highly visible dignitaries as Francis Bacon and King James were known to have male lovers. Shakespeare's sonnets, of course, begin with several passionate poems addressed to a young man.

But Antonio's passion for Bassanio, whether it is carnal, idealized, or both, is not the cause of his melancholy, any more than Portia's "aweary" state is caused by love or its lack. Rather, these two characters, twinned by both their placement in the opening scenes and their roles in what will become an evident if unacknowledged love triangle, are caught in something we might call "ennui."

Why are Antonio and Portia "sad" as the play begins? The word carried more specific gravitas in Shakespeare's period than perhaps it does in our own, deriving as it does from the same word as "satiated" or "sated," having had one's fill. They are rich, they are well attended, and yet their lives seem empty. It may be helpful to cast our minds back to another melancholy figure, Antipholus of Syracuse in *The Comedy of Errors*. Antipholus's melancholy came from his self-absorption, from the constant awareness of self that made him almost oblivious to what was going on in the world around him—oblivious, in particular, to the news that one of his countrymen, a merchant of Syracuse, was condemned to die for lack of money to pay a legal penalty. The doomed Syracusan was his own father, Egeon, and Antipholus of Syracuse needed to rouse himself from accidie, to learn to care about other people and the world around him. This was, for him, the necessary prelude both to rediscovering his lost family, and to falling in love. In the same way, Antonio and Portia have to leave the prison of the self-sufficient self and commit themselves to the world, and to human relationships, friendship, passion, and love.

The common feature of such relationships in this play is risk. In fact, the message of the leaden casket is, in a way, the most crucial theme of the play: "Who chooseth me must give and hazard all he hath" (2.7.9). Giving and hazarding are, in a way, the opposite of Shylock's usury, security, and interest. Antonio begins to lose his melancholy when Bassanio appeals to his friendship and seeks to borrow money from him. Since he does not have the money on hand, he has to borrow it, to go into debt to Shylock. Taking on this debt is what, in an odd way, revitalizes him, giving him a purpose for living, a purpose of love and friendship toward Bassanio. The Antonio we see in the trial scene, ready to give his life in payment of the debt, is strangely happier and more alive than the Antonio of the play's opening lines. And Antonio's willingness to risk is promoted, in part at least, by Bassanio's own risk-taking. Bassanio is again and again in this play characterized as a Jason in quest of a golden fleece, a heroic adventurer in quest of a priceless object. "[M]any Jasons come in quest of her," he says of Portia (1.1.172), and later, when he and Gratiano have voyaged to Belmont and won their ladies, Gratiano will say, "We are the Jasons; we have won the fleece" (3.2.240).

Bassanio, as we have already noticed, is something of a fortune hunter, a common enough mode of personal advancement in the early modern period, and not one that would automatically bring criticism on the quester, if he had personal merit. (Portia makes short work of less worthy suitors, who are equally frank about their interest in her fortune. Petruchio in *The Taming of the Shrew* boasts, famously, that he has "come to wive it wealthily in Padua," and he gets what he came for, while in *Twelfth Night* the hapless Sir Andrew Aguecheek is presented as a spectacularly unworthy candidate for the lady's hand.) But Bassanio loves both the lady and her estate. In the same breath in which he mentions Portia's money he praises her fairness and her "wondrous virtues," the remarkable qualities that, we are given to understand, constitute her real wealth.

Moreover, Bassanio's philosophy is that further debt will be the best way to repair his debt. He has already squandered his own estate, and he now seeks to borrow from Antonio, to take a chance on the choice of the three caskets. The simile he uses, the image of the arrow, is a good example of his practice:

> In my schooldays, when I had lost one shaft,
> I shot his fellow of the selfsame flight
> The selfsame way, with more advisèd watch,
> To find the other forth; and by adventuring both,
> I oft found both.

1.1.140–144

"Adventuring" chimes with the Jason theme again, and the element of adventure—which in Shakespeare's time meant to risk, to dare, to commit to chance—is also part of the choice of the three caskets that awaits Bassanio in Belmont. Like all of Portia's suitors, he must select one of the three caskets—gold, silver, or lead—and if the casket he chooses does not contain her picture, he must resign himself to never marrying, to infertility and the lack of a legitimate heir, the great threat of all Shakespearean comedies. It seems at first as if Portia may be in the same repressive position as Juliet and Hermia (and, indeed, in this play, Jessica), since her father insisted upon choosing her husband for her. She is locked up, so to speak, in her own casket, and caskets, like all containers, are images traditionally associated with women in folklore and mythology. Notice that Portia says, "I am locked in one of them" (3.2.40). In act 1 she complains to Nerissa, "I may neither choose who I would nor refuse who I dislike; so is the will of a living daughter curbed by the will of a dead father" (1.2.20–22). But we may also take note of Nerissa's reply, which is both prompt and pertinent: "the lottery that he hath devised in these three chests of gold, silver, and lead, whereof *who chooses his meaning chooses you,* will no doubt never be chosen by any rightly but one who you shall rightly love" (1.2.25–28; emphasis added). If "who chooses his meaning chooses you," the act of choosing a casket is then an act of interpretation, of textual analysis, not a random game of chance. In fact, the casket choice is a kind of psychological test, at the same time that it resembles, and derives from, patterns of folktales and fairy tales.

In a conversation with Nerissa, Portia demolishes the English, Scottish, Italian, French, and German dandies whom we never get to see; each is described satirically as a caricature of the national "type" (the Scot is a penny-pincher, the German a drunkard, the Englishman, in a description often found in early modern satires, dresses in a hopeless mélange of various national fashions). Collectively they are too cowardly, too silent, or too bibulous to try their luck with the caskets. This is a familiar form of humor, and—especially because an Englishman is included in the category of those beneath contempt—merely shows Portia as participating in a kind of merry raillery at the expense of absent and unappealing suitors. But as the casket choice proceeds, her preference for a husband more like her than different from her emerges. We learn as early as the play's second scene that she had already met Bassanio, "a Venetian, a scholar and a soldier," and, significantly, that she had done so in her "father's time"—that is to say, when her father was still alive and ruling. Thus in some sense Bassanio *is* the father's choice, after all. This déjà-vu phenomenon is a device Shakespeare will use more than once to reinforce the "rightness" of an instant love. In *Merchant* Bassanio is identified by Nerissa as an apt choice in act 1, scene 3, long before the actual drama of the casket choosing, and this permits a pleasurable suspense as the audience sees the "wrong" suitors choose badly, and get what they deserve.

It is possible to see Portia in a historical-allegorical frame as a figure for Queen Elizabeth here—a lady richly left, whose father's dead hand seems to control the choice of a husband. Elizabeth, like Portia, was the target of suitors from many nations as well as a number of wellborn Englishmen, each one imagining himself on the brink of becoming King of England. Portia's problem, like Elizabeth's, is that she will inevitably lose or cede power, rather than gain it, if she marries. Indeed, as we will see, when Portia does choose to marry Bassanio she immediately and explicitly names him the "lord" of her mansion and "master" of her servants, so that he replaces her in the position of rule. After that point, following the exigencies of the plot, Portia's power comes from her male disguise as the young doctor of laws, and she regains her power as a woman only at the very end of the play, when she is able to present Antonio with evidence of his restored wealth, and to give Lorenzo and Jessica title to half of Shylock's estate ("Fair ladies, you drop manna in the way / Of starvèd people" [5.1.293–294]). Acknowledging a husband (one whose name, Bassanio, may derive from the Turkish *bashaw* or *pasha,* grandee or head) is an ambivalent moment for Portia as well as a joyous one, and the ambivalence *for the play* will be only partially repaired and reversed by her triumph in the courtroom scene and her management of the "ring trick" at the close.

In any case, the great scene of the casket choice is wonderful theater. Following the codes of such games of choice in myths and fairy tales, there are three suitors, of which the third and last will be the winner, despite—or because of—the fact that he is an ordinary man rather than a prince. The Prince of Morocco chooses the golden casket, the motto of which is "Who chooseth me shall gain what many men desire" (2.7.5). He chooses, that is, literal wealth, externals rather than internals, what Bassanio will call "ornament," and he wins a death's-head, the traditional reward—at least as far back as Chaucer's "Pardoner's Tale"—for those who seek for gold. The Prince of Morocco is proud—and worse, in this play's terms, he is an alien. His prayer on choosing a casket is "Some god direct my judgment!" (2.7.13). In a play as aggressively "Christian" as this one, his deficiencies are glaringly evident even before he makes his choice. Morocco is part of Mauretania, the home of the Moors, a people of mixed Berber and Arab race, Muslim in religion, and thought (from the medieval period through the seventeenth century) to be mostly black or swarthy. (Othello is Shakespeare's most famous Moor, but there is another noteworthy Moor in *Titus Andronicus,* the villainous and unrepentant Aaron. Both are described explicitly as black). When Portia expresses her relief that Morocco is not to be her husband, she does so in a phrase—"Let all of his complexion choose me so" (2.7.79)—that some editors have hoped to wish away as an unwelcome sign of prejudice on the part of Shakespeare's lively heroine. But although "complexion" can indeed mean "temperament," it is used in this play, by both Portia and the Prince of Morocco himself, to mean "skin color." "Mislike me not for my complexion, / The shadowed livery of the burnished sun" (2.1.1–2), says Morocco, and earlier Portia has said, on learning that he is to be a suitor for her hand, "If he have the condition of a saint and the complexion of a devil, I had rather he shrive me than wive me" (1.2.109–110). Here, then, is an early instance of the crisis of difference and differences within the play. It is not only Christian and Jew, but Muslim and Christian, and black and white, that trouble the emotional texture. And no character, not even the much-admired Portia, is exempt.

The second suitor, the Prince of Aragon, chooses the silver casket. He does so, of course, partly for the fairy-tale suspense and the unfolding sequence of choices. He could hardly choose the gold casket again, since the audience already knows what it contains. The motto of the silver casket is "Who chooseth me shall get as much as he deserves." Thus it reflects not infinite desire, but a concept of equivalence and supposed merit. Aragon, too, is proud, and he chooses the metal, not of traditional literary and mythic value, but of commerce—what Bassanio will call "thou pale and common drudge / 'Tween man and man" (3.2.103–104). What Aragon gets, when the casket is opened, is "[t]he portrait of a blinking idiot" (2.9.53). It could as well be a mirror, a literal reflection of his own acquisitiveness and false sense of merit. In any case, it is another kind of death's-head. The Prince of Aragon is often played as an old man, with silver hair and beard. His title identifies him as Spanish and Catholic. (Aragon had been the homeland of Ferdinand, one of the Catholic monarchs of Spain, who together with his wife, Queen Isabella of Castile, began the Spanish Inquisition, persecuting Jews, Muslims, and Moors in a quest for social and religious purity. The first wife of Elizabeth's father, Henry VIII, and the mother of her Catholic half sister, Queen Mary, was Catherine of Aragon, the youngest surviving child of Ferdinand and Isabella.) Black man, old man; Muslim, Catholic—these two suitors exemplify otherness of a more dangerous, because less risible, kind than that represented by drunken Germans and dandified Frenchmen. The stage is thus set, in terms appropriate at once to drama, politics, and fairy tale, for the entry of the insider, the Venetian suitor, Bassanio.

When it is Bassanio's time to choose, his moment of choice is accompanied by music, one of the characteristic signs of the Belmont world, and an element usually associated in Shakespeare's plays with semimagical, "wonderful" transformation. The music is called for by Portia, and the song, "Tell me where is fancy bred," has sometimes been regarded as a clue to the identity of the correct casket, since its rhyme-words, "bred," "head," and "nourishèd," all rhyme with "lead." Both Portia and the audience, having seen the gold and silver caskets opened, are now aware that the right answer must lie in the third. There is no textual evidence to support this claim of affectionate cheating, and the dramatic arc of the play seems to demand that Bassanio choose the right casket because he is a good analyst rather than an opportunist. His choice is prefaced by a speech on "ornament" that focuses on the deceptiveness of appearances— ornament in law, in religion, in beauty, and in art, all central concerns for this play: "So may the outward shows be least themselves. / The world is still deceived with ornament" (3.2.73–74). "Still" here means "always," as well as "yet." Bassanio's conclusion is that he should choose against ornament, choose inward merit rather than "outward shows," thus apparently setting himself apart from the other suitors, even though Morocco's "Mislike me not for my complexion" would have seemed to point inward rather than outward:

> Therefore, thou gaudy gold,
> Hard food for Midas, I will none of thee.

[*To the silver casket*] Nor none of thee, thou pale and common drudge
'Tween man and man. But thou, thou meagre lead,
Which rather threaten'st than dost promise aught,
Thy paleness moves me more than eloquence,
And here choose I. . . .

                                                3.2.101–107

The choice of the three caskets has been a favorite topic for interpretation by
directors, audiences, and critics. Various "meanings" have been suggested for it,
like the Christian lesson that "the last shall be first" (exemplified in a later play,
King Lear, by the choice of Cordelia, "our last and least," over her showier sisters), or the analogy with choices of three in fairy tales and folktales, where the
third is always the "right" choice, and often, as with Cinderella, the humblest.
One of the most suggestive discussions, one that draws upon these structural
and thematic models, is that of Sigmund Freud, who points out, in his essay
"The Theme of the Three Caskets," that a direct analogy might be made
between the three caskets of gold, silver, and lead and the three daughters
(emblematically "caskets," or containers) in *King Lear.* The third daughter,
Cordelia, is the one who does not reply fulsomely to her father's question about
which daughter loves him most. Instead she counsels herself to "[l]ove, and be
silent," just as Bassanio praises the leaden casket because its plain appearance
moves him "more than eloquence." According to Freud, and, indeed, in accordance with Shakespeare's own symbolic practice in the plays, silence is the sign
of death, so that Bassanio's choice, and the thing the old King Lear refuses to see
that he has to choose, is death.[1] Bassanio clearly does choose the possibility of
death, in promising not to marry if he chooses the wrong casket, and in risking
and hazarding all he has, not only Antonio's money, but his own future life.
Thus, ironically, this choice is congruent with and parallel to the choice of the
two other caskets, in that all the suitors "choose" a symbolic death, but only
Bassanio does so willingly and self-knowledgeably.

Bassanio's choice, his willingness to risk everything in order to gain what
he so ardently wishes, leads immediately and directly to Portia's risk, her gift of
herself:

Portia   Myself and what is mine to you and yours
           Is now converted. But now I was the lord
           Of this fair mansion, master of my servants,
           Queen o'er myself; and even now, but now,
           This house, these servants, and this same myself
           Are yours, my lord's. I give them with this ring,
           Which, when you part from, lose, or give away,
           Let it presage the ruin of your love. . . .

                                                3.2.166–173

Having united the themes of money and love, both so crucial throughout the play, by endowing Bassanio with her love and her fortune, Portia validates and symbolizes this love with a ring. In this instance, we may note, it is the woman who bestows the ring, although in the traditional marriage service in the 1559 Book of Common Prayer, in use in Shakespeare's time, it is the man who "shall give unto the woman a ring," and who pledges, "With this ring I thee wed" and "with all my worldly goods I thee endow." Portia's final warning, that if Bassanio loses the ring or gives it away it will "presage," or predict, the end of his love for her, is easily recognizable as a plot hook for the future, especially when he replies in kind, that "when this ring parts from this finger" it can only be when "Bassanio's dead." His acceptance of her hand, beginning "Madam, you have bereft me of all words. / Only my blood speaks to you in my veins" (3.2.175–176), is one of the most evocative brief love passages in all of Shakespeare. At the same time it (re)aligns Bassanio, however temporarily, with silence, the now-productive silence of the leaden casket. His loquacious and joking friend Gratiano more than makes up for any onstage solemnity, however, announcing that he has wooed and won Portia's waiting-gentlewoman Nerissa: "You saw the mistress, I beheld the maid" (3.2.198).

The ring and the subsequent ring trick are crucial elements in *The Merchant of Venice*. Rings, as unbroken circlets, were traditional female symbols in folklore and mythology. Shylock loses a ring ("my turquoise"), a ring given him by his now-dead wife, Leah, and stolen by his eloping daughter, Jessica, and traded away for a monkey, the emblem of licentiousness. The exchange of rings in the "high," or aristocratic, plot—rings exchanged by Portia with Bassanio and Nerissa with Gratiano—will figure importantly in the final scene, when it is revealed that the two husbands have given away their rings to the "judge," or doctor of laws, and "his clerk," who had requested them as the only recompense for their successful defense of Antonio in the courtroom. For a moment this apparent breach of faith seems to put the marriages in jeopardy. Portia will swear, with a figurative wink at the audience, "I'll have that doctor for my bedfellow," and Nerissa will chime in, "And I his clerk." But since the doctor of laws and clerk were—as the audience knows—Portia and Nerissa in disguise, the rings will turn out to have been given back to their rightful owners, the men's wives and their friends and benefactors. This act of self-denying generosity, in giving away what is most dear, thus parallels in a comic spirit the more somber and potentially dangerous generosity of Antonio, who gives his entire fortune, and more, in order to assist Bassanio.

In the exchange of rings and the ring trick, or comic substitution, Shakespeare's play brings together two Renaissance ideals: marriage and friendship. The doctrines of Renaissance friendship stressed similitude, equality, and reciprocity. Early modern Europe continued to be a largely patriarchal culture, and "friendship" in this sense was thought of as an ideal for male-male relations. Montaigne, Erasmus, and Sir Thomas Elyot, in his *Boke Named the Governour*, all set out ethical expectations about the high ideal of friendship, and such devoted friendships were often portrayed in literature, as, for example, in John Lyly's *Euphues,* Spenser's *Faerie Queene* (especially book 4, subtitled "Of Friendship"), and a number of Shakespeare's plays, notably *The Two Gentlemen of Verona* and *The Merchant of Venice,* as well as *The Two Noble Kinsmen,* coauthored by Shakespeare and John Fletcher. In many cases the rhetoric of friendship became combined or conflated with the rhetoric of romantic love, and the word "friend" took on erotic overtones, whether or not the friends were in fact lovers in the modern, sexual sense of the term. (The word "lover" in this period could also mean "friend," or "well-wisher." Shakespeare's Brutus uses the term in this sense when he says, "I slew my best lover for the good of Rome" [*Julius Caesar* 3.2.41–42].) Gift-giving, authorial dedications, and patronage were among the social and cultural evidences of these relations of sentimental regard. Such ideal and idealized friendship, while frequently encountered or depicted among social equals and age-mates, might also describe reciprocal relations between an older and a younger man, or a patron and a protégé—as in the case of Antonio and Bassanio. With the ring trick at the end of *The Merchant of Venice* Shakespeare brings together these many definitions of Renaissance friendship, establishing the husbands and wives as also mutually indebted and admiring friends.

Typically for Shakespeare, these matters of character, affinity, and desire are woven into the dramatic fabric. The complicated interrelationships of women and men, friendship and love, have their correspondences in the structure and setting of the play. As we have already seen, *The Merchant of Venice* alternates its action between two very different geographical—and psychological—locales, Venice and Belmont. Venice, a city of commerce ruled by a forceful duke, was unable (or unwilling) to alter its laws, because to do so would endanger its vital dealings with other nations. But while Venice is unquestionably a place of law, it is also, importantly, a world of *men,* just as Belmont is a world of *women.*

The Venetian Rialto (the bridge of commercial exchange), the Venetian senate, and the Venetian courtroom are all places in which men are the proper actors: Antonio, Bassanio, and Gratiano; Shylock and Tubal; the Duke himself. In fact, in order to function in the Venetian world women have to costume themselves like men. Jessica has to dress like a boy to escape from Shylock's house, and Portia must transform herself into a doctor of laws, and her maid Nerissa into a clerk, in order that they may become active participants in the Venetian world. Otherwise women are shut in houses, as Shylock orders his doors and windows to be locked against the noise and revelry of society. Even Portia, living and ruling in Belmont but secretly about to enter Bassanio's Venetian courtroom, pretends that in her husband's absence she will seek the safe protection of a monastery (3.4.31–32), where she and Nerissa "[w]ill live as maids and widows" (3.2.309) until their husbands' return. She says to Bassanio:

> First go with me to church and call me wife,
> And then away to Venice to your friend;
> For never shall you lie by Portia's side
> With an unquiet soul. . . .
>
> *3.2.302–305*

Or, we might add, "with an unquiet enjambment," for the "never" here seems for a moment to finish the thought. Briefly, in a rhetorical throwaway that is far from thrown away, the play seems to be facing once more the familiar threat of infertility in a comic world. As in *Romeo and Juliet* and *A Midsummer Night's Dream,* where the nunnery, with the protection of friars and clerics, is seen as a safe space for women, out of the bustling and dangerous world, the monastery in *Merchant* (which is only a notional fiction, mentioned by a Portia already planning her own intervention) exists as an alternative to ongoing life and action—and to the stage and the world of the play. For Portia, like Juliet, is about to play a central and visible role in the events of her play, remanding her husband temporarily to a secondary place.

Portia's disguise as a young man follows a tradition that Shakespeare borrowed from Italian comedy. Gender disguise was a popular feature of prose romance (like Sir Philip Sidney's *Arcadia*) as well as drama. Shakespeare had already put a cross-dressed heroine on the stage in *The Two Gentlemen of Verona,* and similarly disguised "women" (played on the English public stage by boy actors) appear in other comedies of this period, like *As You Like It* and *Twelfth Night*—and again in the late romance *Cymbeline.* In *The Merchant of Venice* gender aligns with geography or locale to a significant degree. For Belmont, where Portia rules in her female persona (although as her father's daughter and heir), is, as we have seen, to a certain extent a feminine world, represented onstage by that set of symbols we have come to recognize as folk symbols and dream symbols for women, principally caskets, or boxes, and rings. Even Jessica brings a casket of ducats with her when she flees from Shylock's house in Venice. Belmont is a place apparently removed from politics, animated by doctrines of love and generosity, a place of beauty and social remove (the name Belmont means "beautiful mountain"), where key scenes take place at night and are accompanied by music. Thus in the play's fifth act Lorenzo and Jessica sit beneath the stars and talk of how their own love compares to that of fabled lovers like Troilus and Cressida, Dido and Aeneas. "I am never merry when I hear sweet music," says Jessica (5.1.68), but her melancholy is a melancholy of emotional response, of deep feeling. It is, in fact, a characteristic Shakespearean response to music, what Cleopatra will call "music, moody food / Of us that trade in love" (*Antony and Cleopatra* 2.5.1–2). When Lorenzo speaks critically of "[t]he man that hath no music in himself, / Nor is not moved with concord of sweet sounds" (5.1.82–83), the man who is therefore "fit for treasons, stratagems, and spoils," he is speaking in part of men like Shylock, who hates music, and revelry, and especially the sound of the bagpipe. (We might compare him in this respect to "that spare Cassius," whom Julius Caesar calls "a great observer" who "loves no plays" and "hears no music" [*Julius Caesar* 1.2.203, 204, 205].) Like Venice, Belmont has its gold and treasure, but the rhetoric of gold there is the language of golden stars moving to the harmony of the spheres, a music said by Neoplatonic philosophers to be inaudible to fallen human ears. "Sit, Jessica," invites Lorenzo,

> Look how the floor of heaven
> Is thick inlaid with patens of bright gold.
> There's not the smallest orb which thou behold'st
> But in his motion like an angel sings,
> Still choiring to the young-eyed cherubins.
> Such harmony is in immortal souls,
> But whilst this muddy vesture of decay
> Doth grossly close it in, we cannot hear it.
>
> 5.1.57–64

Golden stars, and a golden fleece. Belmont is a world ruled by Portia, and there are moments in this play when Portia appears to function like a Muse and like a goddess. Lorenzo praises her "godlike amity" (3.4.3), and when at the end of the play she produces the deed giving Lorenzo and Jessica all of Shylock's property, he will exclaim, "Fair ladies, you drop manna in the way / Of starvèd people" (5.1.293). She alone knows the news that three of Antonio's ships, thought lost, are "richly come to harbour suddenly" (5.1.276), information that even the audience does not possess until she tells us. Portia seems to do miracles, and she can change her shape, transforming herself, like a Proteus or a Puck, into the young doctor of laws, Bellario, who is to perform the Daniel-like task of turning judgment into revelation. If Portia, like Juliet, is shadowed by her father's authority, unlike Juliet, she controls her own destiny. Not only has she outlived her father and his "dead hand," but she also lives in a comic world, a world she can change to suit her own devices. At least to a certain degree.

For the play's charmed circle of inclusion and resolution (and "conversion," a word that describes both Portia's love for Bassanio and Jessica's decision to share the faith of her Christian husband) is also a circle of exclusion. Shakespearean comedy tends to work in terms of inclusion and exclusion, so that very frequently in these plays we will find one character cut off from communication and social interaction at the close of the play, the fact of his isolation (these excluded figures tend to be men) seeming somehow both to underscore the happiness of the "insiders" and to mark the precariousness of joy. Thus in *The Merchant of Venice* Antonio is excluded from the round of married pairs at the close, and modern productions, as we have noted, tend to emphasize his solitude. (A less conflicted figure is the comparable benefactor in *Much Ado,* Don

Pedro, who woos a lady on his friend Claudio's behalf, but evinces less passion in doing so, and discourages his protégé's plan to accompany him on his journey rather than remain at home with his newly wedded wife.) But the principal excluded character in *Merchant,* the character who makes this play, for a modern audience, something other than a comedy, is of course Shylock. And the figure of Shylock rouses deep emotions, not only because his plight seems in some ways to mirror that of Jews in Europe from Shakespeare's time to the present, but also because of the desire on the part of many readers, editors, and actors to protect Shakespeare against the accusation of anti-Semitism. The term is anachronistic for Shakespeare's time (it was coined at the end of the nineteenth century; before that one might speak of anti-Judaic feeling), but the prejudice to which it gives a name is not.

Did Shakespeare scorn and dislike Jews, as do many characters in his play? Was it his intention—whatever he achieved—to caricature a despised race and the religion its members practiced? ("Race," unlike "anti-Semite," *is* a familiar term in early modern writing, describing a tribe, nation, or people regarded as of common stock.) And even if the author was not "anti-Semitic," did he write, wittingly or unwittingly, an anti-Semitic play? These are not questions it is easy or appropriate to sidestep, but nor are they questions that can be answered directly or authoritatively. Writers do not control the interpretations of their works—indeed, as we will see, one major theme of this play is the plenitude and "lewdness" of interpretation—and works of literature and art are living things, which grow and change with time. Whatever *The Merchant of Venice* might be said to "mean," or to connote, today, it is not the same thing as what it might have meant or connoted in the last decade of the sixteenth century, in an England ruled by Queen Elizabeth, an England that had officially banished all Jews for the previous three hundred years. Equally sobering, what *The Merchant of Venice* "meant" when it was produced, with a villainous Shylock, in Nazi-held Weimar in 1944, is not the same as what it has "meant" in post-Holocaust productions in London, Jerusalem, New York, or indeed anywhere in the world.

It is possible that Shakespeare had never seen or known a Jew. Jews had been banned from England since the time of Edward I, who expelled them in 1290, after borrowing heavily from Jewish lenders in previous years to support his wars. There were some Jews in the London of Shakespeare's time, but these were likely to be Spanish or Portuguese Jews who presented themselves in public as Christian converts, attending church services, and practicing their own religion only in secret. In 1594 an unfortunate incident occurred in which a Portuguese Jewish physician, Roderigo Lopez, was accused of having plotted against the life of Queen Elizabeth. Lopez had been the Queen's doctor, and he was tried and executed for supposedly plotting to poison her. A popular society physician— he was known to, and by, Sir Francis Walsingham, the Earl of Leicester (Robert Dudley), the Earl of Essex (Robert Devereux), and the Cecils—Lopez was involved in espionage for the government, and ran afoul of Essex, whose intentions for war against the Spanish Lopez opposed. Feeling against Lopez escalated; we may indeed see him as a scapegoat—both an Iberian and a Jew. He was taken to Tyburn and hanged without a warrant signed by the Queen. In the years following his death characters based on Dr. Lopez appeared in plays by Thomas Dekker and Thomas Middleton, and a revival of Christopher Marlowe's 1589 play *The Jew of Malta,* written well before the Lopez affair, enjoyed a surprisingly long run of fifteen performances. Shakespeare seems to have written his play in the wake of this popular and topical success.

In any event, Shakespeare's Jew was, in a way, a literary rather than a "historical" Jew, borrowed from Marlowe, from the Continental tradition, and from the sensation surrounding the execution of Dr. Lopez. But we do both playwright and play a disservice if we see Shylock as a two-dimensional stereotyped figure who represents an archaic and unpardonable prejudice. Marlowe's Jew, Barabas, comes closer to this model, since he is a gleeful Machiavel who boasts of poisoning wells (an old medieval claim about the Jews) and does manage to poison the inmates of a nunnery. That Jews were traditionally associated with poisoning made the accusation of Lopez more plausible in the public mind. But Shylock's character is, deliberately, more complex. (This does not, incidentally, make him a better dramatic character than Barabas, just a different kind of character.) Actors have played the part of Shylock, a much coveted part, in every spirit from comic butt to fiendish devil to persecuted scapegoat.

But what kind of Shylock can speak to the present day? We should consider a few things that Shylock says, assessing him both as a type and as a character—that is, observing how he resists stereotype and also plays with as well as against it. When Bassanio asks him for a loan, offering his friend Antonio as security, Shylock replies, "Antonio is a good man" (1.3.11). "Have you heard any imputation to the contrary?" Bassanio flashes back at him, and Shylock laughs. "Good" to Bassanio is an ethical term; to Shylock it is financial. Antonio will be "good" for the loan; his expectation of wealth is, as they all believe, sufficient to cover it. Bassanio misunderstands Shylock to be making a judgment about his friend's moral worthiness, but Shylock does not consider such issues when he is dealing with the Christians of Venice. When we hear that Antonio has spat upon Shylock in the past and called him a dog, and that he boasts of being likely to do so again, we may consider Shylock wise to avoid the nice ethical considerations that Bassanio expects. It is this dispute, about whether Shylock intends to lend the money as a friend or—as Antonio insists—as an enemy, that leads to the "merry sport," the pound-of-flesh wager, and an extended exchange on the meaning of the words "kind" and "kindness." Shylock will offer a loan in kind, out of kindness, in order to stress his kinship and kindliness. "The Hebrew will turn Christian; he grows kind" is Antonio's summation when Shylock has left the stage (1.3.174). As we will see, this prediction ironically—and painfully—comes true, although Shylock has, as we will also see shortly, the reverse of this conversion in mind.

Shylock shows a similar limitation even in the magnificent and touching speech that—again taken out of context—has become a classic cry for human rights, and specifically for the humanity of Jews. "I am a Jew," he begins.

> Hath not a Jew eyes? Hath not a Jew hands, organs, dimension, senses, affections, passions; fed with the same food, hurt with the same weapons, subject to the same diseases, healed by the same means, warmed and cooled by the same winter and summer as a Christian is? If you prick us do we not bleed? If you tickle us do we not laugh? If you poison us do we not die? And if you wrong us shall we not revenge? If we are like you in the rest, we will resemble you in that. If a Jew wrong a Christian, what is his humility? Revenge. If a Christian wrong a Jew, what should his sufferance be by Christian example? Why, revenge.
>
> *3.1.49–59*

Characters like Gratiano, proud of their "Christian" example, treat Shylock unpardonably in this play, and make derogatory remarks about Jews in general as well as about Shylock in particular. But what does Shylock's speech tell us about his own character and feelings? This bold and resonant protest, which begins as a moving appeal to general humanity, winds up as a cry for revenge, a cry for the predominant emotion of early Elizabethan tragedy, the emotion that names itself as the opposite of the quality of mercy.

Shylock's attitude toward his daughter Jessica is also indicative of an aspect of his nature. He regards her as a possession, like his jewels and his gold, to be hoarded up and not allowed out of his sight. When Jessica escapes, taking his treasure with her, Shylock's exclamation of distress—as it is mocked by the Venetian hangers-on Salerio and Solanio—conflates and confuses the two aspects of his loss in a way that is both comical and sad:

> "My daughter! O, my ducats! O, my daughter!
> Fled with a Christian! O, my Christian ducats!
> Justice! The law! My ducats and my daughter!"
>
> *2.8.15–17*

In other words, Shylock's Jewishness seems at first glance to be a label that condemns him as a villain, but his character is both more complex and more troubled than any cultural stereotype. If, as S. L. Lee wrote long ago, Shylock exemplifies characteristics "distinctive of his race," including "[s]trong domestic affections," sincere "sympathies with the fortunes of his 'tribe,' and firm faith in the sacredness of its separation from the Gentiles,"[2] he also shows domestic irascibility, possessiveness about both persons and things, and a predilection, however habituated by insults and worse, to try to outwit and best his rivals.

Could Shylock change—and should he? The play is full of examples of conversion. Jessica alludes knowledgeably to Saint Paul's Epistle to the Corinthians, declaring, "I shall be saved by my husband. He hath made me a Christian" (3.5.15–16). (Paul had written, "The unbelieving wife shall be saved by her husband" [1 Corinthians 7:14].) The Duke greets Shylock in the courtroom with an invitation to behave like a gentile and abandon his suit for the pound of flesh: "We all expect a gentle answer, Jew" (4.1.33). The ethics of forced conversion seem deeply questionable to modern minds, but there was a line of thinking that assumed that such conversion was for one's "own good," to save the unbeliever's soul. When the clown Lancelot explains that he has left Shylock's employment for Bassanio's, he, too, echoes Saint Paul, when he says that he is going "to bid [his] old master, the Jew, to sup with [his] new master, the Christian." (Paul had exhorted the Ephesians to "put off . . . the old man . . . and put on the new man" [Ephesians 4:22–24].) Lancelot thinks Bassanio has nicer liveries for his servants, and alleges that the Jew is the "very devil incarnation." He is no moral barometer, and certainly he is no theologian. Bassanio, by contrast, speaks respectfully of Shylock ("Shylock thy master" [2.2.130]). The Lancelot's-eye view, in short, cannot be the voice of *The Merchant of Venice*. It is presented in order to be seen through, however much Lancelot's clowning may have appealed to some tastes then—or in our own time.

According to Shakespeare's play, it is not birth or fate that alone makes Shylock who he is. He has moral and ethical choices. He could put off the old man and put on the new man, he could "return a gentle answer." That he does not do so is not ascribed—by the play—to his Jewish identity. There is a joylessness to Shylock that he shares with other excluded figures in Shakespearean comedy, like Malvolio in *Twelfth Night*, who scolds the revelers for gabbling like tinkers and making an alehouse of his lady's house; or Jaques in *As You Like It*, who avers that he is "for other than for dancing measures"; or the villainous Don John in *Much Ado*, who is so melancholy and "tart" that it gives Beatrice heartburn to look at him. Shylock's villainy, if he has any (and it is less customary than it used to be to acknowledge his shortcomings), derives from his preferring unpleasure to pleasure, the same joylessness that makes Lancelot so happy to leave him. Shylock hates music, he hates masques, he hates anything that has to do with the traditional comic elements of release and renewal. "What, are there masques?" he says to Jessica. "Lock up my doors . . . / stop my house's ears—I mean my casements. / Let not the sound of shallow fopp'ry enter / My sober house" (2.5.27–35). In one sense this is merely sound fatherly protectiveness. But Shylock prefers a house shut off against the world of comedy and love, a house of repression and the narrowest kind of law. And it is this anticomic repression, above all, that is both his downfall and his comeuppance in the great trial scene in act 4. (Again it is useful to compare Shylock to Malvolio—roles often played by the same actor—in order to be able to transcend, for a moment at least, our visceral response to what seems to be Shakespeare's harsh dramatic treatment of a Jew.)

The sequence of the trial scene is superbly structured for maximum theatrical effect. The Duke asks Shylock for mercy—"We all expect a gentle answer, Jew"—and does not get it. Portia, dressed as the young lawyer Bellario, does the same. Her famous speech is part of a legal argument and is not the pretty, quotable, "philosophical" set piece it is often thought to be. The supposed doctor of laws, expatiating on the "strange nature" of the suit, which puts Antonio's life in danger, observes, "Then must the Jew be merciful," and Shylock, ever the literalist, seizes on the optative word "must" and takes it for an order: "On what compulsion must I? Tell me that." Portia's reply sets forth the terms of an old debate about the competing virtues of justice and mercy, one with roots as far back as Seneca. This is a humanist as well as a "Christian" argument:

> The quality of mercy is not strained.
> It droppeth as the gentle rain from heaven
> Upon the place beneath. It is twice blest:
> It blesseth him that gives, and him that takes.
> 'Tis mightiest in the mightiest. It becomes
> The thronèd monarch better than his crown.
> His sceptre shows the force of temporal power,
> The attribute to awe and majesty,
> Wherein doth sit the dread and fear of kings;
> But mercy is above this sceptred sway.
> It is enthronèd in the hearts of kings;
> It is an attribute to God himself,
> And earthly power doth then show likest God's
> When mercy seasons justice. Therefore, Jew,
> Though justice be thy plea, consider this:
> That in the course of justice none of us
> Should see salvation. We do pray for mercy,
> And that same prayer doth teach us all to render
> The deeds of mercy. . . .

4.1.179–197

"Strained" is "constrained," or forced; "seasons," an important word for this play—and for Shakespeare generally—here means "tempers" or "alleviates." But Shylock is unmoved by this eloquent plea, which strikes him, perhaps, as something of a long-winded lecture, wandering from the point. "I crave the law, / The penalty and forfeit of my bond," he says. The word "bond" now begins to resonate, as it will throughout the rest of the scene: "Is it so nominated in the bond?" (4.1.254); "I cannot find it. 'Tis not in the bond" (257). Shylock will provide a scale to weigh the pound of flesh, but not a surgeon to stanch the wound. He will, that is, provide the emblem of justice, the balances, or scales, but not the emblem of mercy. If Saint Paul's celebrated dictum "the letter killeth, but the spirit giveth life" is seen to underpin this tension between Shylock and Portia, justice and mercy, it is all the more pertinent when restored to its context in 2 Corinthians, where Paul distinguishes between the New Testament and the Old Testament. God, he says, has made him and the other apostles "ministers of the new testament; not of the letter, but of the spirit; for the letter killeth, but the spirit giveth life" (2 Corinthians 3:6). By contrast, Moses "put a vail over his face, that the children of Israel could not steadfastly look to the end of that which is abolished," and "until this day remaineth the same vail untaken away in the reading of the old testament, which vail is done away with in Christ" (2 Corinthians 3:13–14). Reading and writing, indeed, are a sign of the old way; Paul tells the Corinthians, "Ye are our epistle written in our hearts, . . . written not with ink, but with the Spirit of the living God; not in tables of stone, but in fleshy tables of the heart" (2 Corinthians 3:2–3). The connection between Paul's "fleshy tables of the heart" and Shylock's "pound of flesh" is both evident and oblique. The irony consists, at least in part, in Shylock's insistence on literalizing what Paul, equally insistently, asserts to be a matter of figure.

Shylock, by this estimate, is a bad reader; he reads the letter, not the spirit. And so Portia is moved to act. (In many modern productions, Antonio lies spread-eagled before them, his hands bound, his body in the traditional posture of the crucifixion.) She pronounces her sentence:

Portia	A pound of that same merchant's flesh is thine.
	The court awards it, and the law doth give it.
Shylock	Most rightful judge!
Portia	And you must cut this flesh from off his breast.
	The law allows it, and the court awards it.
Shylock	Most learnèd judge! A sentence: [*to* ANTONIO] come, prepare.

4.1.294–299

And then begins the reversal of fortunes:

Portia	Tarry a little. There is something else.
	This bond doth give thee here no jot of blood.
	The words expressly are "a pound of flesh."
	Take then thy bond. Take thou thy pound of flesh.
	But in the cutting it, if thou dost shed
	One drop of Christian blood, thy lands and goods
	Are by the laws of Venice confiscate
	Unto the state of Venice. . . .
	. . . .
Shylock	Is that the law?

4.1.300–309

The rest of the scene is a constant series of defeats and humiliations for Shylock, or, to look at it in another way, an escalating series of victories for Portia. Shylock says he will accept Bassanio's offer of thrice the bond, which he had earlier scorned. Portia: "Soft, no haste. He shall have nothing but the penalty." Then Shylock says he will take merely his principal, the amount he lent Antonio. Portia: "He hath refused it in the open court." And finally Portia, an even more literal reader than Shylock, tells him: "The law hath yet another hold on you"—the confiscation of his goods, half to Antonio and half to the state, for the crime of intended homicide; the threat that he will die for this crime; and the forced conversion to Christianity. The scene is devastating, with Shylock first voluble and triumphant, then, with a decisive and dramatic turn, weaker and weaker. Again, some modern productions have tended to underscore the obvious: after the distraught Shylock exits the stage, his voice can be heard chanting the Kaddish, the Hebrew prayer for the dead. What does he mourn? The loss of his daughter, now converted and married to a Christian, thus "dead" to him? Or his own reduced and humbled circumstances: "[Y]ou take my life / When you do take the means whereby I live" (4.1.371–372).

The contrast of this great and heartrending scene with the final act in Belmont is startling, and it is clearly meant to be. Shylock's exclusion from the happy recovery of husbands and wives, ships and money is dictated in part by Elizabethan stereotypes and religious prejudice, in part by his own moral blindness, and in part by the engine of the comic plot. Shylock is what is purged from the play's romantic core of generosity and risk. It is his resistance to release and comic freedom, to masque and music, as much as his claim of faith and cultural heritage that banishes him. And if we leave this play with a disquieting sense of a man cruelly and publicly broken, we also leave it with the image of a triumphant heroine, witty and clever, generous to her friends, eloquent and amusing by turns.

Of all Shakespeare's plays, none perhaps has stirred as much controversy in modern times as *The Merchant of Venice*. Audiences, critics, actors, and directors—to say nothing of students and teachers—are regularly in disagreement as to what values, what ethics, and what opinions the play represents. Has Shakespeare wittingly or unwittingly written a tragedy, of which Shylock is the hero, rather than a romantic comedy? It is worth remembering that Shylock was played as a broadly comic figure until 1741, when Charles Macklin turned him into a villain and a monster. Edmund Kean humanized him in the Romantic period, making him pitiable, so that the critic William Hazlitt could write in 1817 that "he becomes a half-favourite with the philosophical part of the audience, who are disposed to think that Jewish revenge is at least as good as Christian injuries."[3] In 1879, during the Victorian period, Henry Irving played the part of Shylock as high tragedy, and from that time to this the play has been Shylock's play. This is probably not what Shakespeare "intended"—the play has in this case overborne the author and his times.

What should we make of this? And what should we make of the Christians in this problematic play? How Christian are they? Is *The Merchant of Venice* perhaps an ironic glimpse at Christian hypocrisy, rather than an endorsement of Christian behavior? Are Salerio and Solanio, who mock and tease Shylock for his manner of speech, ideal citizens of a Christian Venice? Is Antonio's willingness to spit upon Shylock's traditional costume, his "Jewish gaberdine," something that should give the audience pause? Is Portia a heroine, or a spoiled darling, a bossy self-regarding manipulator who treats Shylock with unwarranted cruelty, despite her fine words about the quality of mercy? Ambivalence is everywhere, at least to a modern audience. Consider, for example, the great romantic love scene between Lorenzo and Jessica, the play's pair of conventional lovers. In act 5, as we have noted, they compare themselves to famous lovers of the past: Troilus and Cressida, Pyramus and Thisbe, Dido and Aeneas. But these examples are all tragic instances: Cressida was unfaithful to Troilus, Aeneas deserted Dido, Pyramus and Thisbe died because of a botched lovers' plot. Do Lorenzo and Jessica know what they are saying, or is the play being ironic about them, too? Lorenzo seems to intend one meaning—we are like other famous and idealized lovers—and to produce another.

From first to last this play is quintessentially about interpretation, about the act of decipherment: the casket choice with its three metals and three mottoes, Shylock's reading of the bond, Portia's recourse to an even more literal interpretation of the contract concerning the pound of flesh. We have noted, too, that puns and wordplay are a crucial element in this multiplication and dissemination of meanings: Shylock and Bassanio differ in their understanding of what it means to say that Antonio is a "good man," the Duke invites Shylock to return a "gentle" (and therefore a "gentile") answer in the courtroom. At the beginning of the play, Antonio offers a homonym to assure Bassanio of his full support: "My purse, my person, my extremest means / Lie all unlocked to your occasions" (1.1.138–139). We will want to recall this image of Antonio "unlocked" later on, since the image makes him rather uncomfortably analogous to the caskets, and to Portia, who was "locked in one of them." The identification of money and self—my purse, my person—is one that is made by several characters throughout the play. When Shylock is told that he is to be stripped of his fortune, he protests, as we have noted, "[Y]ou take my life / When you do take the means whereby I live." Antonio seems almost to echo him, two scenes later, when he learns from Portia that his ships have come back safely: "Sweet lady, you have given me life and living" (5.1.285). *The Merchant of Venice* is in part concerned to establish a way of distinguishing between purse and person, not so much for the receiver—Bassanio has a sincere affection for Antonio—but for the giver. Antonio himself is prone to think of his personal worth to his friend as equivalent to, and defined by, his financial worth. When Jessica flees from Shylock's house, she tosses down a casket full of money to Lorenzo, and in a way this careless toss of what is explicitly called a "casket" is the opposite of—and a cheapening of—the love test that Bassanio will have to endure. For these lovers there is no test: "Here, catch this casket. It is worth the pains," says Jessica as she flings it from her father's window (2.6.33).

The "comic" incident between Lancelot and his blind father, old Gobbo, in which the father feels the back of his son's head and thinks that he has grown a beard, is very like the story of Jacob and Esau in the Bible (Genesis 25–27), specifically the moment when Jacob, the younger son, steals his brother's birthright. Jacob and Esau are twins, although Esau is the firstborn. Esau, a hunter and his father's favorite, is a "hairy man," and Jacob, his mother's favorite, is a "smooth man." One day when Esau comes in from the fields and is famished, Jacob persuades him to trade his birthright for a "mess of pottage." And when Isaac is blind and dying, he calls to Esau to hunt some venison, feed him savory stew, and receive his blessing as the elder son. But when Esau has gone, Jacob's mother, Rebecca, persuades him to kill two young goats, serve them as a stew to Isaac, and cover his hands with the hairy kidskins. In the denouement, Isaac says, "The voice is the voice of Jacob, but the hands are the hands of Esau," and he gives Jacob the blessing. Christian typology, noting that in Genesis 25:23 the Lord had told Rebecca she had in her womb two nations that would struggle against each other, and the elder would serve the younger, read "Jacob" as a figure predicting and representing Christians and "Esau" as a figure predicting and representing Jews. That the elder would serve the younger meant both that the Old Testament would serve the New, by providing "types" that could be fulfilled in Christ, and that the Jewish believers in the Old Testament would be subservient to the Christian believers in the New. "Jacob," as Esau remarks bitterly in Genesis, means "supplanter." Lancelot gleefully leaves the service of his "old master," the Jew, for a new master, the young (and Christian) Bassanio.

The casual cruelty of young Gobbo (the name translates as "hunchback" in Italian, and describes the aged, stooping father as a familiar type on the stage of the commedia dell'arte; Gobbo, or Giobbo, is also the Italian name for the Old Testament Job) seems characteristic of a play in which "comedy" is seldom risible, at least to modern sensibilities. But the son's deception of his "sand-blind" father also ties the Gobbo plot in with the several persistent mentions of Jacob throughout the play. Shylock, explaining why it is legitimate to take interest on a loan, paraphrases Genesis, chapters 30 and 31, telling the story of Jacob's relations with his father-in-law, Laban. Wishing to leave Laban's household, Jacob strikes a bargain with him, agreeing to take with him only the spotted or streaked sheep, goats, and cattle. Ordinarily this would mean that he took away a minority of the livestock, leaving the great majority to Laban. But Jacob devises a certain quasi-magical sign, in the form of stripped tree branches, and holds them up before the ewes when they are at the "work of generation," and the result is a bumper crop of striped and spotted sheep, all of which belong to

Jacob. Shylock contends that this is a justifiable dividend, and calls it a blessing. Antonio, on the other hand, points out that "this was a venture, sir, that Jacob served for" (Jacob as adventurer, as venture capitalist *avant la lettre*), and dismisses the whole argument as some Jewish form of casuistry: "The devil can cite Scripture for his purpose" (1.3.94). This sentiment is often to be heard spoken of, and sometimes by, Shakespeare's Machiavellian characters: Richard III boasts that he gulls his victims "with a piece of scripture" or "odd old ends, stol'n forth of Holy Writ" in order to "seem a saint when most I play the devil" (*Richard III* 1.3.335–336). In effect Antonio accuses Shylock of that besetting sin for so many people in the play, the deliberate misinterpretation of a text. "Was this inserted to make interest good," he demands, scornfully, "Or is your gold and silver ewes and rams?" (1.3.90–91). And Shylock replies, with the quick wit that seems to typify his early responses, "I cannot tell. I make it breed as fast" (1.3.92).

This question, of whether money can or should "breed," was at the center of the usury debates in the period. When in the same scene Antonio acknowledges that he not only has spit on Shylock in the past but is likely to do it again, he justifies his attitude by citing a standard complaint against usury: "for when did friendship take / A breed for barren metal of his friend?" (1.3.128–129). No less an authority than Aristotle had said that money, unlike living things, cannot reproduce. Sir Francis Bacon, writing "Of Usury" a few years after *The Merchant of Venice* was written, would aver, "They say it is against nature for money to beget money," in an essay that begins, "Many have made witty invectives against usury," and continues, wittily, "But few have spoken of usury usefully." It is Bacon, we should recall, who employs the word "judaize" to define the activities of usurers, citing, among the "witty invectives," that "usurers should have orange-tawny bonnets, because they do judaize." (Orange-tawny was a color ordained for people of inferior condition, including Jews; these bonnets are the early modern version of the yellow badges medieval European Jews were made to wear, and the yellow star imposed upon Jews by the Nazis.) In *The Merchant of Venice,* a largely urban and apparently most unpastoral play, the image of the sheep is oddly persistent, and it will culminate in a set of gestures and tableaux that establish Antonio in the courtroom as a sacrificial lamb, a figure of Christ.

There are, in fact, two strands of "sheep" imagery, one classical and one biblical (or, as a later dichotomy would phrase it, one Hellenic and one Hebraic). The story of Jason and the quest for the Golden Fleece, associated with the bold adventuring of Bassanio, is placed over against the story of Jacob, the crafty protocapitalist who made his ewes and rams breed, as Shylock would make his gold and silver breed. At the trial, Antonio, believing himself doomed to pay the pound of flesh, will speak with resignation about his condition: "I am a tainted wether of the flock, / Meetest for death" (4.1.113–114). A "tainted wether" is a sick ram, but the word "wether" was often used to describe a ram that had been castrated, and, when employed as a transferred epithet for a human being, could mean a eunuch. Antonio describes himself here as a sterile and impotent animal, without sexual vitality, without the capacity to breed and reproduce. The word "usury" comes from the same root as "use," a word that in Shakespeare's time could also mean "to have sexual intercourse with." So the question of whether money can breed, of whether it is or should be barren, is related to the question of whether a man without money—a man with empty bags—is a metaphorical castrate.

When Portia and Nerissa decide that they must intervene in the court case in Venice, and Portia explains her plan that they should appear there as a lawyer and his clerk, Nerissa asks, "What, shall we turn to men?" She means, of course, disguise themselves as men. But Portia playfully pretends to understand the phrase "turn to" in a different sense. "Fie, what a question's that," she says. "If thou wert near a lewd interpreter!" (3.4.80–81). Arguably, what this play needs is exactly that: a lewd interpreter. For repeatedly its plot lines cross and recross, combining the themes of money and sexuality.

Antonio is a tainted wether of the flock, but is he the only one? Certainly not. We might recall Portia's unsuccessful suitors, who have come to win a wife and fortune, with the penalty for failure clearly set out: "Never to speak to lady afterward / In way of marriage" (2.1.41–42). With his usual skill in juxtaposition for maximum dramatic effect, Shakespeare inserts between the scene of Morocco's erroneous casket choice (2.7) and Aragon's (2.9) the unsalubrious scene in which the Venetians Solerio and Solanio gleefully recount Shylock's losses and mimic him: " 'My daughter! O, my ducats! O, my daughter!' " This scene, too, speaks to the question of money breeding, since both the daughter and the ducats have been hoarded up by Shylock, precisely against their "use." Salerio and Solanio are convulsed with laughter, in part because of the particularity of Shylock's complaint. For what, specifically, has Jessica taken in her casket?

> ". . . two stones, two rich and precious stones,
> Stol'n by my daughter! Justice! Find the girl!
> She hath the stones upon her, and the ducats!"
>
> 2.8.20–22

"Stones" is the common term from the medieval period through the early eighteenth century for testicles. (Thus the comic double meaning when the Hostess in *Henry V,* at the sickbed of the ailing Falstaff, having felt upward from his feet to check if he is still alive, reports that "all was cold as any stone." There is an unmistakable quibble on Falstaff's "two stones" in *Merry Wives,* and the word occurs elsewhere in this sense in Shakespeare.) Shylock's phrase inadvertently makes Jessica into a phallic woman—"She hath the stones upon her"—a joke that is very clear to the Venetians who ridicule him:

Salerio   Why, all the boys of Venice follow him,
          Crying, "His stones, his daughter, and his ducats!"

2.8.23–24

Jessica thus in effect gelds Shylock twice, taking away his family lineage and his
money, both ways he could "breed." Only two scenes later we will hear this
same irritating pair, Salerio and Solanio, make further fun of Shylock in the
same lewd spirit, when he speaks of Jessica's defection. "My own flesh and blood
to rebel!" he exclaims in anger and distress, and they reply, jokingly, "Out upon
it, old carrion, rebels it at these years?" (3.1.30–31).

Sex and money are twinned and ridiculed by the Venetians when it comes to
Shylock and his losses. But the same combination can be a winning one when
invoked by a Venetian Christian who is part of the play's love plot. Thus when
Gratiano announces his love for Nerissa and asks permission to marry her,
noting that he loves the "maid," or waiting-gentlewoman, as Bassanio loves
the "mistress," Portia, he follows his solemn announcement with a joking proposal for a wager: "We'll play with them the first boy for a thousand ducats"
(3.2.213–214). Nerissa asks if they will make this bet "stake down," meaning with
money on the table, and Gratiano, characteristically, takes her phrase in a
bawdy sense, quipping that they would never win at that sport "stake down."
Gratiano is the play's chief bawdy quibbler, its resident "lewd interpreter." In
act 5, scene 1, when he learns from Portia and Nerissa that they are so cross at
the supposed loss of their rings that they will bar their husbands from the marriage bed ("I'll have that doctor for my bedfellow," says Portia, and Nerissa
adds, "And I his clerk"), he grumbles, "Would he were gelt that had it" and "I'll
mar the young clerk's pen." (A modern production might wish to find some
connection here between the Yiddish word *gelt,* a colloquial term for "money,"
itself derived from an old German term meaning "recompense.") Gratiano's
final lines, the lines that end the play, are a stage-clearing couplet rhyming slang
or symbolic terms for male and female sexual organs:

> Well, while I live I'll fear no other thing
> So sore as keeping safe Nerissa's ring.

5.1.305–306

The symbolic or "high" sense of "ring," a marriage circlet, here combines—with
the help of the double-edged "sore"—with the anatomical or "low." But the
joking bet about the first boy for a thousand ducats is also, and importantly,
another equivalence of children and money. Is this really so different from
Shylock's cry "My daughter! O, my ducats!"?

Barrenness threatens the comic world, as it so often does in Shakespeare's
plays, only to be replaced by marriage and the prospect of children. (We may
notice that in this play of fathers and daughters the hoped-for heir of the next

generation will be male.) But why should Antonio emphasize his own condition as a "tainted wether of the flock"? Why should we associate him with the gelded world of Shylock rather than the gilded world of Portia?

One answer to this is suggested by Portia herself, the play's best reader, when she enters the courtroom in act 4. In she sweeps, dressed like a doctor of laws, in men's legal robes, ostensibly a last-minute substitute for a famous lawyer unavoidably kept from court. The Duke welcomes the newcomer, asking if "he" knows what the issue is, and gets Portia's firm assurance, after which she speaks what is perhaps the most astonishing line in the play:

> Which is the merchant here, and which the Jew?
>
> *4.1.169*

Bear in mind that "Jews" on the Elizabethan stage normally wore bright red wigs and large noses, and that Shylock has already alluded memorably to his customary costume, his "Jewish gaberdine," the long, coarse garment, like a cloak, worn by Jews from the medieval period through the early modern. Whatever Antonio is wearing, he is not wearing a red wig or a gaberdine. Venetian merchants dressed like princes. But it seems Portia cannot tell them apart. Is her question rhetorical, an articulation of the principle of "blind justice"? The confusion often engendered for modern readers by the play's title— which character is "the merchant of Venice"?—is repeated in the courtroom. "Which is the merchant here, and which the Jew?" Antonio is a merchant, but he is also a moneylender. In point of fact, most of the moneylenders in England at the time were Christians, not Jews, since there were not many Jews, and they did not, by and large, have very much money. This indeed is the reason why Bacon could list among his "witty invectives against usury" the idea that usurers should wear orange-tawny hats "because they do judaize." If the usurers were actually Jews, they would already, presumptively, be wearing the hats in the color ordained for them. We know that Antonio has lent out money before—that is what makes Shylock so irritated at him—and at the end of the play, in case we forget, the audience will hear him ask permission to take half of Shylock's money "in use," that is, as an investment, for Lorenzo and Jessica. The two men, Antonio and Shylock, are analogous in a number of other ways, too. They are of the same generation, both are lonely, both are excluded at the close. In any case, Portia's question, "Which is the merchant here, and which the Jew?" should startle the audience into an awareness of the similarities between them. They are not entirely opposites.

I would suggest that Shylock and Antonio are themselves aware of this correspondence between them, perhaps not as consciously as the audience, but intuitively. Not only are they rivals in the lending trade, but Antonio will take over from Shylock, administering his funds for Jessica and Lorenzo, adopting and adapting at least that aspect of the paternal role. And when we look closely at the bond, the loan, Shylock's "merry sport," and what becomes of it in the courtroom scene, we will see other twinning elements, suggesting that in a way Shylock wants to make Antonio his double, his counterpart, putting Antonio in Shylock's place. The bond itself, we should notice, is ostensibly stated in "Christian" terms—that is, Shylock will take no interest if the money is repaid on time. "This is kind I offer," he says (1.3.137). We are more like each other than you think. The other conditions of the bond are also suggestive, in the context of the play's themes of infertility and castration. "[I]n a merry sport, / If you repay me not on such a day," says Shylock,

> let the forfeit
> Be nominated for an equal pound
> Of your fair flesh to be cut off and taken
> In what part of your body pleaseth me.
>
> *1.3.144–147*

When Portia reads the bond in open court, she and Shylock agree that it is the breast that is to be cut. "Nearest the heart," the bond says. But the initial iteration is not so specific: the flesh is "to be cut off and taken / In what part of your body pleaseth me." Is it not possible that Shylock has, at least at first, a different kind of cutting in mind, a cutting that is metaphorical and rhetorical as well as physical? I do not suggest that he wants to castrate Antonio, but rather that he wants, symbolically, to circumcise him. To make him a "Jew." (It was not uncommon for an Elizabethan audience to conflate circumcision with castration.) In other words, he wants to perpetrate a forced conversion. If Antonio pays back the money on time, wins the merry sport, Shylock will act like a Christian and take no interest on the loan. If Antonio fails to pay it back on time, Antonio himself will be made to act like a Jew. This would be a transformation of Antonio into Shylock's double. In the event, of course, the opposite happens. Antonio turns Shylock into *his* double, in some ways at least. Shylock is forced to convert to Christianity. The only enforced "mercy" that is offered him, half his money back, is tendered only on condition that he "presently [that is, immediately] become a Christian." Which is the merchant here, and which the Jew? Modern productions have increasingly experimented with doubling these parts, so that an actor will play, in different productions or different performances, the role of Antonio and also the role of Shylock.

The concept of twinning these two figures may also have some correspondence with the biblical function of the scapegoat. The term "scapegoat" is not used by Shakespeare, but it was very much current in his time, having apparently been invented by the Bible translator William Tyndale around 1530 to convey the literal sense of a Hebrew word used only in chapter 16 of Leviticus. There were *two* goats in the ancient Mosaic ritual. On the Day of Atonement, one of the two goats was chosen by lot to be sent into the wilderness, with the

sins of the people symbolically laid upon it; the other goat was sacrificed to
God. The "scapegoat" was the goat that escaped. In the Christian Bible, the
New Testament, this figure becomes the "Lamb of God, which taketh away the
sins of the world" (John 1:29). By the middle of the seventeenth century
Thomas Hobbes would write in *Leviathan* that in Leviticus 16 "Our Saviour
Christ's sufferings seem to be here figured. . . . He was both the sacrificed goat
and the scape Goat."[4]

Which is the merchant here, and which the Jew? As the trial scene begins,
Antonio is apparently about to be sacrificed. By the end of the scene, Shylock
will be driven out. But even though Antonio is embraced by the Christian community in Venice, and later in Belmont, he remains a little at a distance, a
"tainted wether," dependent on the generosity of Portia, who has married Bassanio and now restores Antonio's wealth.

That the play ends in Belmont is, as we have already noted, something of an
anomaly for Shakespeare, who usually puts his "green" or "golden" worlds in the
middle of the play, returning his characters—or most of them—to the ongoing
world of social and political action. Thus the wood near Athens in *A Midsummer Night's Dream,* the "little academe" of *Love's Labour's Lost,* the Forest of
Arden in *As You Like It* are temporary, alternative spaces, countries of the mind
rather than places on the map. Usually, as we have seen, characters repair to
these middle worlds to refresh themselves, to divest themselves of the trappings
of the external world of law and death. The middle world is like a journey into
the unconscious or the subconscious, where one can play roles, test fantasies,
find oneself—or one's selves. But in *The Merchant of Venice,* the Belmont world
is not, despite its romance name, in the middle of the play, but at the end. It
seems to be not a temporary state but a final alternative possibility, something
like a redeemed world. But is it?

Belmont is presented throughout the play both as the opposite of and as an
alternative to Venice. The first scene of the play—the melancholy of Antonio—
takes place in Venice, the second—the melancholy of Portia—in Belmont. Belmont is still the place ruled by Portia's father's dead hand, and by his will, in two
senses, his legacy and his insistence. It is her father who has invented the casket
choice, and who thus seems to control Portia's own choice of a husband and
"lord" for Belmont. And Belmont, for all its air of grace and bounty, its apparent lack of involvement in the commercial world, is to a certain degree a place
dependent upon wealth, upon, in fact, inherited wealth. Belmont depends
upon gold, the very gold seemingly devalued by the scenes we have just witnessed, by the commerce of Venice—the closeness of Shylock, the vanity of the
Prince of Morocco. Belmont would seem to stand not for gold but for the
"golden rule," and yet, although Portia articulates just such an ethic in her
"quality of mercy" speech, she then goes on to disregard it. In other words, it is
not so simple to separate the worlds of Venice and Belmont. They are mutually
dependent. What, for example, is the place of *guilt* in Belmont? Should Lorenzo

feel guilty that wealth comes to him unearned except by marriage to the daughter of a wealthy and disgraced Jew? Should Jessica feel guilty for having left her father's house, and taken his money with her? Should Portia feel any twinge of guilt, either for the way she treats Shylock or for the way she treats Antonio? The placement of the Belmont world in the fifth act, hanging, so to speak, off the edge of the play, emphasizes Belmont's precariousness and its problematic nature, even as it stresses the possibility of salvation through love, beyond the courtroom and the Rialto.

Gold, silver, and lead. The choice of the three caskets is also a choice offered to the audience of Shakespeare's play. The gold of happy endings, of golden stars and the golden rule and the Golden Fleece, but also of inheritance and rivalry, Belmont with all its idealizing quality and all its undercurrents of disquieting cost. The silver of commerce, of the pale and common drudge 'tween man and man, of the use of usury that makes Bassanio's quest possible, makes possible the commercial world of Venice (and of London). And lead. The lead of the third casket, the choice we all have to learn that we all have to choose. The lead of mortality, the choice of death. Notice that the play opens all three of these caskets, not just the last one, and that it once again discloses similarities, as well as differences, between and among them. "I am locked in one of them," says Portia, but she—and the play—is really locked in all three. In this play of difference the casket choice offered to the audience and the reader is a choice not *between* but *of.* We cannot proceed directly to the leaden casket: choosing it first would not be the right choice. We must open the caskets in turn— Belmont, Venice, poetry, death—in order to assess the value of their contents, choosing their meanings ("who chooses his meaning chooses you").

The ambivalence that an audience feels about this play is something built into the play and emerging from it. If we alternately sympathize with Shylock and criticize him; admire Bassanio's energy and deplore his mercantile motives and his use of other people; bask in the glory of Portia's wit and wisdom, her "godlike amity," and critique her as a woman who will always get her way, regardless of the wishes and the feelings of others—if we feel this ambivalence—it is not because the play fails but because it succeeds.

The Merchant of Venice is a deeply disturbing play, whose interpreters over time have sought to purge it of its most dangerous and disturbing energies. It is a play in which the question of intention, of what Shakespeare may have intended, is relevant but not recoverable, and finally not determinative. Portia the goddess, or Portia the spoiled rich girl, the wealthy heiress? Shylock the noble man of suffering and dignity, or Shylock the small-minded patriarch who prizes spiteful victories? Bassanio the impassioned lover, or Bassanio the fortune-hunter? Comedy or tragedy? The history of the play's interpretations encompasses all of these alternatives, and more. Meaning is disseminated here—it will not be contained. And this is an index of the play's enormous theatrical and emotional power. Much critical and theatrical ingenuity has been

N SHAKESPEARE's history plays, as we have seen, the "history" being staged tends to conflate a number of time periods: the time in which the play is set, the time in which it is written, and the time(s) in which it is performed. *Henry IV Part 1* is an especially engaging example of this phenomenon, since although it is firmly set in a late medieval moment, and clearly describes "real" historical personages as recorded by Holinshed and other English chroniclers, it seems also to describe, with uncanny transhistorical pertinence, the grooming of a modern political candidate for office. From the targeting of particular constituencies to the learning of regional languages and customs, the artful insinuations about "character" and fitness for office, and the prodigal-son trajectory of the wastrel-turned-patriot-and-hero, the story of Prince Harry, or Hal, who will become the legendary Henry V, is a model of the making of a national icon. At once the story of the making of a king and the making of a man, the play juxtaposes Hal to a number of other claimants for historical and dramatic attention: his father, Henry IV; his adoptive father figure, Sir John Falstaff; and his rival, Hotspur (Henry, or Harry, Percy).

Some readers and scholars of the group of plays often called the "second tetralogy," *Richard II, Henry IV Part 1* and *Part 2,* and *Henry V*, have regarded them as a kind of English national epic, even dubbing them the *"Henriad,"* on the model of the *Iliad.* Although *Richard II* was written at a slightly earlier time, and the plays manifestly each stand alone as dramatic and theatrical artifacts, these four plays are bound by some overarching patterns that are useful to notice. There is of course a fundamental historical design, the movement from King Richard's reign to that of Henry V, and the development, in the process, of an image of a newly unified modern England, apparently worlds removed from the feudalism of Richard II and the unproblematic assumption of the divine right of kings. (Here we need to bear in mind that one careful observer of such a pattern would be the then-current monarch, Queen Elizabeth.) Arguably, there is as well a moral structure, one that reaches back once again to the morality plays of English dramatic tradition. *Henry IV Part 1* is readily understood as a play about the contention between vice and virtue for the soul of a prince—between the dissoluteness of Falstaff, "that reverend Vice, that grey Iniquity" (2.5.413), and the militant idealism of Hotspur, "the theme of honour's tongue" (1.1.80). And there is also, equally discernibly, a biblical or archetypal structure, one that traces in these four plays the pattern of human history from the first page of Genesis to the last page of Revelation, from the fall of mankind to the promise of redemption, and from the fall of England to its glorious rebirth.

Much of the imagery of *Richard II*, as we noticed, was concerned with England as a little Eden, a "demi-paradise," and with Richard as a kind of Adam and a kind of Christ, suffering what his queen called "a second fall of cursèd man." By the beginning of *Henry IV Part 1* the tide of public opinion has already reversed itself. Richard's loss is mourned, and Bolingbroke, now King Henry IV, is the villain. Even Hotspur, who with his father, Northumberland, swore allegiance to Bolingbroke's cause, now expresses his fury at the fact that the usurpers chose to "put down Richard, that sweet lovely rose, / And plant this thorn, this canker, Bolingbroke" (1.3.173–174). This is post-fall language. Richard is a rose without thorn, Bolingbroke a thorn without rose, a canker, a cancer, a disease. Yet like most falls in English literature, this will turn out to be a fortunate fall, because after the fall of Adam, as Shakespeare's Christian audience would have believed, came the redemption through Christ, and after the fall of Richard will come the redemption of Prince Hal, "[r]edeeming time," as he says, "when men think least I will" (1.2.195).

In *Richard II* the audience was confronted over and over with soliloquy, with the single voice, a voice that became more and more inward-directed, less and less dramatic, as the play progressed. Richard turned away from the world he was unable to rule and created a second world, a poet's and self-dramatist's world, within his mind. Even the ceremonies he invented and performed were increasingly solipsistic. The language of other characters in the play was also often rhetorical rather than instrumental or dramatic, as in the case of John of Gaunt's speech about "this England." Even the Gardener, a relatively "low" character in terms of social status, spoke like a gentleman, in verse, and not like a common laborer or citizen. When an audience turns from that poetic world to the world of *Henry IV Part 1*, it might well be astonished at the sheer dramatic energy of the play. Prose comes to life, "low" characters come to life, expressing themselves in the characteristic patois of their station, from the baffled Francis in the tavern scene, torn between his duty to his prince and the siren call of commerce (Poins's voice from the next room, demanding beer); to Bardolph, the "Knight of the Burning Lamp," whose red nose (indicating his fondness for drink) shines like a lantern in the dark; to the bawdy hostess, Mistress Quickly, who claims indignantly, "Thou or any man knows where to have me" (3.3.117–118); to the brilliance of Falstaff, "sweet Jack Falstaff, kind Jack Falstaff, true Jack Falstaff, valiant Jack Falstaff, and therefore more valiant being, as he is, old Jack Falstaff" (2.5.433–435)—it is, of course, Falstaff who is speaking. The range of the play is as wide as the early modern world itself, from these vernacular splendors of prose to the high and lofty language of Hotspur; the plastic, subtle language of Hal; the puns and wit of the tavern scene; and the heroics of the battlefield.

The play's design is one that emphasizes correspondences between its various worlds. For example, the play begins with a long speech by Henry IV on the need for national unity, a plea to turn the energies of the state away from civil war and outward, toward holy wars in Jerusalem. Henry's first words, the King's first words in the play, are "So shaken as we are, so wan with care" (1.1.1). He has aged; he and his land are weary, and they long for an end to internal strife. The concept of pilgrimage, which is echoed repeatedly in *Richard II* after the banishment of Mowbray and Bolingbroke, here returns, since Henry had sworn at the end of that play to "make a voyage to the Holy Land." This is what he now proposes—to go to Jerusalem:

> The edge of war, like an ill-sheathèd knife,
> No more shall cut his master. Therefore, friends,
> As far as to the sepulchre of Christ—
> Whose soldier now, under whose blessèd cross
> We are impressèd and engaged to fight—
> Forthwith a power of English shall we levy,
> Whose arms were moulded in their mothers' womb,
> To chase these pagans in those holy fields,
> Over whose acres walked those blessèd feet
> Which fourteen hundred years ago were nailed
> For our advantage on the bitter cross.
>
> 1 Henry IV *1.1.17–27*

Even his language sounds more like Richard's than before—Henry's evocation of the "bitter cross" echoes Richard's "sour cross." But no sooner does King Henry propose this expedition than his lofty plan is interrupted, and indeed abruptly canceled, by the arrival of news about another outbreak of civil war, in Wales and Scotland: "It seems then that the tidings of this broil / Brake off our business for the Holy Land" (1.1.47–48). Seconds after Henry has announced his plan for a pilgrimage he has had to abandon it, to face instead the unwelcome prospect of more civil war at home. Juxtaposed to this scene, the first scene of the play, is a scene (1.2) in the Prince's apartments, where we hear Poins's plan for the robbery of Canterbury pilgrims and traders riding to London, the Gads Hill caper. Henry's kingdom is in fact to be threatened by two rebellions, not one: the lawless rebels led by Hotspur, and the lawless rebels led by Falstaff. The Gads Hill caper is another version of Hotspur's rebellion, another kind of anarchy and robbery; both are the result of the failed kingship of Henry IV and his usurpation of the throne. One group of rebels steals crowns and nobles, that is, coins, the other group is out to steal the crown and win over the nobles. Not only nobles and crowns but also sovereigns and angels were coins in Elizabeth's realm (and we might recall Richard II's conviction that "angels" would fight on his side). The play thus places side by side two groups of rebels, a "high" (aristocratic) group and a "low" (tavern-haunting) group, allowing each to point up the qualities of the other.

Another example of the uncanny dramatic correspondences of *1 Henry IV* emerges from Falstaff's wonderful story about the "buckram men" in act 2. (Buckram, a kind of coarse cloth stiffened with gum or paste, was often used for linings.) Falstaff begins by telling Hal that he was attacked by two men:

Falstaff	Two I am sure I have paid—two rogues in buckram suits. . . . here [where] I lay, and thus I bore my point. Four rogues in buckram let drive at me.
Prince Harry	What, four? Thou saidst but two even now.
Falstaff	Four, Hal, I told thee four.
Poins	Ay, ay, he said four.

2.5.176–183

In a matter of seconds, the four have become seven, then nine, and finally eleven, as the Prince comments, mockingly, "O monstrous! Eleven buckram men grown out of two!" Now, this is a funny story all by itself. It shows something of Falstaff's fertile imagination; his tendency to expand, both in girth and in imagination; his proliferation of disorder; and his facility for lying. But the buckram men also lead right to the moment at the close of the play when we hear that the King "hath many marching in his coats" (5.3.25). This was a common battle strategy, as we have noted in connection with other history plays such as *Richard III:* to protect the king, decoys dressed like him would draw attention away from the real monarch in the field. But in many minds the usurping King Henry was himself only a man dressed as a king, with what the Earl of Douglas calls a "borrowed title." In a line that brings together the prevailing language of false or cracked coinage with that of impersonation, Douglas demands of one of these costumed figures, "What art thou / That counterfeit'st the person of a king?" (5.4.26–27). But the person of whom he makes this demand is the King himself. Henry IV does, in a way, "counterfeit" the person of a king ("person" in this sense is nicely related to *persona,* or mask, as well as to "body"). Falstaff's imaginary men in buckram are the "low" and comic counterparts of the many men marching in the King's coats, and Falstaff's lie is in a way no more a lie than Henry's claim to the crown. Men in costume are men in costume, whether they are encountered in the tavern, on the highway, on the battlefield, or, indeed, on the stage.

Henry IV Part 1 works to a certain extent by this mode of comparison and contrast. The play is full of complex correspondences between its characters, as well as telling juxtapositions between its several dramatic worlds. Thus, for example, the King and Falstaff are similar—both are subversives, rebels, pretenders—and both are elderly examples for Prince Hal. But they are also opposite: the King stands for rule, Falstaff for misrule. The King and Hotspur are similar—they are rivals in the same game, a quest for a crown that belongs, rightly, to neither of them. But they are also antithetical. The King is the emblem of authority, Hotspur the emblem of resistance and rebellion. Hotspur and Falstaff are alike—both are embodiments of anarchy and revolt—and they are also unlike. Hotspur is an idealist, Falstaff a cynical realist. Hotspur is a perfect physical specimen, Falstaff a "tun of man." Falstaff and Hal are alike. Both are jokers, scoffers at the world, companions in crime, and wordmongers. But they are also opposed—Falstaff a figure of age and dissoluteness, Hal a figure of youth and vigor. Falstaff, like Juliet's Nurse, cannot change his nature to adjust to new circumstances, while Hal is manifestly in the process of getting an education. The King and Hal, father and son, are opposed and allied at the same time. And finally, Hotspur and Hal are alike in their youth and their valor, alike in their names—Harry to Harry. But they are unlike in their past history— Hotspur is a hero, Hal an apparent wastrel—and in their degree of practical wisdom—Hotspur is a romantic dreamer, Hal a pragmatic realist. Hotspur, we could say, is a Marlovian hero; Hal is the Shakespearean protagonist par excellence. It is worth noting, in this connection, that the historical Henry Percy (Hotspur) was twenty-eight years older than the historical Prince Hal. Henry Percy was in fact of the same generation as Henry IV, not of his son. But here, as so frequently, Shakespeare changes and fictionalizes history to make a better play. He makes Hal and Hotspur contemporaries, to show how much they are both alike and unlike. "Harry to Harry shall, hot horse to horse, / Meet and ne'er part till one drop down a corpse" (4.1.123–124). The play thrives on this kind of balance and equipoise, as it does on the correspondences between and among its several dramatic worlds.

There are at least four dramatic worlds in *1 Henry IV*, each a vital sphere of influence: the court world ruled by King Henry; the tavern world presided over by Falstaff; the world of the rebels, which is also the world of the countryside and of the feudal lords, dominated by Hotspur; and the world of Wales, a world of magic and music, represented by Owen Glendower. Broadly speaking, these various "worlds" correspond to several of the genres of Shakespearean drama: history, comedy, and romance.

The Wales world is the least stressed but in some ways the most suggestive, because it is presented as both an older world of prophecy and omen, and a world of imagination and transformation, miracles and signs. Wales will frequently for Shakespeare be associated with this kind of magic, partly because Wales was, in Shakespeare's time, as to a certain extent it remains, a little-understood place of bards and folklore, of mountains, valleys, and wilderness. Wales and Welshmen (and indeed, although offstage, wild Welshwomen) will be a major element in *Henry V*, and also in the late romance *Cymbeline*. Shakespeare's Owen Glendower is based on the historical Owain Glyndŵr ("Owen of the Glen of Dee Water"), the last Welshman to hold the title "Prince of Wales." Glyndŵr was a major property owner who studied law in London, married the widow of a judge, and raised a large family. He was involved in a series of struggles for Welsh independence, forming alliances with opponents of Henry IV, including the Percys (this play's Northumberland and Hotspur). He captured Edmund Mortimer, and when the King refused to ransom him, Glyndŵr married Mortimer to one of his own daughters. After 1400, with the support of his followers, he named himself "Prince of Wales" and tried to set up an independent government. I note these historical details in part because they give a very different cast to the figure of Glyndŵr, or Glendower, than the one we get from *Henry IV Part 1:* Shakespeare's Glendower.

The Glendower of this play sees himself as the quintessence of all this magical power, as his dialogue with Hotspur at the beginning of act 3 makes clear:

> Glendower   At my nativity
> The front of heaven was full of fiery shapes,
> Of burning cressets; and at my birth
> The frame and huge foundation of the earth
> Shaked like a coward.
> Hotspur   Why, so it would have done
> At the same season if your mother's cat
> Had but kittened, though yourself had never been born.
> Glendower   I say the earth did shake when I was born.
> Hotspur   And I say the earth was not of my mind
> If you suppose as fearing you it shook.
>
> *3.1.12–21*

And even more strikingly,

> Glendower   I can call spirits from the vasty deep.
> Hotspur   Why so can I, or so can any man;
> But will they come when you do call for them?
>
> *51–53*

The confrontation is framed as one between the bard-magician and the warrior-skeptic, despite the fact that both men are political leaders of their troops. In fact, the Glendower world, with its peaceful music sung in Welsh by Lady Mortimer to her husband, and with its signs and its portents, is a world without power in *Henry IV Part 1.* Wales is a romance world, and this play is not a romance. Politics, the audience will clearly see, has more power than omens and portents. Glendower and his family thus represent both an outmoded way of looking at human events and also another kind of excess.

Yet Hotspur's intolerance of this world leads to Glendower's desertion from the rebellion. We hear that the Welshman is "overruled by prophecies"—that his signs and symbols have told him not to fight—but we are meant to wonder, I think, whether it is not Hotspur's rudeness that has led Glendower to withdraw. Wales and the things it represents are part of the kingdom of Britain. An English king, or one who aspires to be an English king, must strive to include it, just as nonmartial elements, like music, magic, romance, and love, must be included in a vision of a harmonious and capacious land. Hotspur, though he embodies some of these elements, does not value them. Prince Hal—himself officially the Prince of Wales—will, by contrast, both recognize and value them by the time of *Henry V*, in which Wales and Welshmen (as well as love and language-learning) play vital roles.

If Wales is this play's space of poetry and dream, its opposite can be found in the cynical and self-doubting court world of Henry IV. The most arresting aspect of Henry's persona as the audience encounters him in *1 Henry IV* is that the buoyant, optimistic, and ambitious Bolingbroke of *Richard II* is now suddenly old. He laments, using the royal "we," his having had to "doff our easy robes of peace / To crush our old limbs in ungentle steel" (5.1.12–13). His very first words in act 1, "So shaken as we are, so wan with care," seem personal rather than general or public. King Henry is a man weighed down by a double sin, the usurpation of Richard's throne and the subsequent murder of Richard. The language that pursues him throughout the play is the language of costume and counterfeiting—as, for example, when he describes to his son Hal his conquest of the common people. Richard II had offered an account of this same "courtship" (*Richard II* 1.4.23–35). Henry's version, despite its sage advice (monarchs gain stature and mystique by limiting their accessibility to the public), is unintentionally revealing:

> By being seldom seen, I could not stir
> But, like a comet, I was wondered at,
> That men would tell their children "This is he."
> Others would say "Where, which is Bolingbroke?"
> And then I stole all courtesy from heaven,
> And dressed myself in such humility
> That I did pluck allegiance from men's hearts,
> Loud shouts and salutations from their mouths,
> Even in the presence of the crownèd King.
> Thus did I keep my person fresh and new,
> My presence like a robe pontifical—
> Ne'er seen but wondered at. . . .
>
> *3.2.46–57*

This is the language of theft, disguise, and false coining: "I *dressed* myself in such humility"; "I *stole* all courtesy from heaven"; "I *pluck[ed]* allegiance from men's hearts." King Henry's language tells us, as does his sudden old age, that his world is fallen, and that the court world as he has made it must pass away. Hotspur and the other rebels see him as the possessor of a borrowed title, as a man who has not earned his kingship. His realm is divided against itself: England is at odds with Wales, with Scotland, with Ireland. Even his last words in this play will carry an ominous double meaning: "Then this remains, that we divide our power"(5.5.35). Although what he means to suggest is a division of the troops, a divided power is always a weakened power in the larger sense of Shakespearean political rhetoric, and audiences may well remember Richard II's cunning ceremony in the deposition scene in that play: "Here, cousin, seize the crown." The England of Henry IV is a fallen world, a world, we might say, made up too much of politics and plotting, and not enough of fellowship and love.

It is, therefore, the dramatic worlds that remain in *Henry IV Part 1*, Hotspur's and Falstaff's, that will present for Prince Hal the real dichotomy and choice. The King and Owen Glendower both have their effects upon his growth and change, but in the central design of this play it is to Hotspur and to Falstaff that we should look in order to understand the making of the Prince, the nation, and the future.

Hotspur, Henry Percy, is a character who seems to represent everything heroic and valiant. In the play's first scene the King describes him, wistfully, as the ideal son and heir, noting that it

> mak'st me sin
> In envy that my Lord Northumberland
> Should be the father to so blest a son—
> A son who is the very theme of honour's tongue,
> Amongst a grove the very straightest plant,
> Who is sweet Fortune's minion and her pride—
> Whilst I by looking on the praise of him
> See riot and dishonour stain the brow
> Of my young Harry. . . .
>
> *1.1.77–85*

The King expresses the wish that these two "Harrys" were changelings, exchanged at birth in the cradle—that Hotspur, whom he so admires, were his real son, in place of the "unthrifty" wastrel Hal. Honor—the "theme of honour's tongue"—is the virtue that seems to define Hotspur and his values throughout the play. The Scot, Douglas, will call him "the king of honour" (4.1.10). Hotspur expresses his own credo early in the play, in his great speech on honor:

> By heaven, methinks it were an easy leap
> To pluck bright honour from the pale-faced moon,
> Or dive into the bottom of the deep,
> Where fathom-line could never touch the ground,
> And pluck up drownèd honour by the locks,
> So he that doth redeem her thence might wear,
> Without corrival, all her dignities.
>
> *1.3.199–205*

We might notice here the language of "plucking," which was also present in Henry IV's account of his courtship of the commons. The King spoke of plucking allegiance from men's hearts; Hotspur will speak of plucking, or retrieving, "drownèd honour." The only condition Hotspur places upon the quest for honor is that it be his alone. The "easy leap" can be made, but the spoils of honor must be worn "without corrival." He is a quasi-mythic hero of the old style, rather like Tybalt in *Romeo and Juliet,* or like Hector in *Troilus and Cressida.* Like Tybalt he is a fighter rather than a talker. In one of this play's most amusing "unscenes," or descriptions of a vivid scenario that has supposedly occurred offstage, Hotspur describes, with disdain, the deportment of a foppish courtier, a "popinjay" with a "pouncet-box," a pomander or perfume box, who comes to visit him on the battlefield:

> when the fight was done,
> When I was dry with rage and extreme toil,
> Breathless and faint, leaning upon my sword,
> Came there a certain lord, neat and trimly dressed,
> Fresh as a bridegroom. . . .
>
> . . . .
>
> He was perfumèd like a milliner,
> And 'twixt his finger and his thumb he held
> A pouncet-box, which ever and anon
> He gave his nose, and took't away again—
>
> . . . .
>
> . . . and still he smiled and talked;
> And as the soldiers bore dead bodies by,
> He called them untaught knaves, unmannerly
> To bring a slovenly unhandsome corpse
> Betwixt the wind and his nobility.

1.3.29–44

"Like a milliner" is typical Hotspur language; this scion of aristocrats has little regard for lords and nobles who do not behave with real nobility, and he lumps them, uncompromisingly, with the middling commercial classes, in this case with a seller of fancy wares, hats, and women's clothing. In a similar vein he will affectionately chide his wife for swearing like a "comfit-maker's wife" rather than voicing a full-blooded oath as befits the wife of a nobleman. A "comfit-maker" was a purveyor of sweetmeats, again distinctly middling rather than high on the social scale.

Hotspur is a man of action. Like Tybalt he prefers single combat, or "single fight," to massed troops; he would rather have fewer soldiers, so as to increase the glory of the battle. Even his dreams are of war. He seems to belong on horseback—"That roan shall be my throne," he says, not entirely joking. He is a larger-than-life figure who has no use for music, and who quips, with a brusquely appealing tenderness, that his wife must wait her turn for his attention until he has finished with the business of war:

> Love? I love thee not;
> I care not for thee, Kate. This is no world
> To play with maumets and to tilt with lips.
> We must have bloody noses and cracked crowns,
> And pass them current, too. God's me, my horse!
>
> > *2.4.81–85*

"Maumets" are dolls, and "crowns" are, simultaneously, royal diadems, heads, and coins. (A "cracked crown" would no longer function as legal money, though Hotspur wants to "pass them current," or, as we would say, as "currency"; a "cracked crown" would also be an injured or broken head, or a challenged or disputed title to the throne.) "Come, wilt thou see me ride?" he says to his wife. "And when I am a-horseback, I will swear / I love thee infinitely" (2.4.91–93).

It should not surprise us that this epic figure considers it merely a trifle to move a river out of its course. "It shall not wind with such a deep indent," he says to Glendower and the other conspirators, complaining that the ambit of the Trent deprives him of a desirable piece of land. "Not wind?" cries the out-raged Glendower. "It shall, it must; you see it doth" (3.1.103). Nor should we be surprised that Hotspur is so frequently described in terms that are taken from classical mythology, from the world of legendary and epic heroes. "Mars in swaddling-clothes" is what King Henry calls him, and "[t]his infant warrior" (3.2.112–113). Hotspur alone is characterized in these epic, and pagan, terms. Prince Hal, his counterpart, will be described in terms that are insistently bibli-cal and Christian. Hotspur comes from an older world of drama, as well as an older world of history and myth. Like the heroes of Christopher Marlowe's plays, he is an overreacher, a hyperbolist, a mythic figure in some ways too big for life and too uncompromising for the world of mere mortal men. Hotspur's grandiose "if we live, we live to tread on kings" (5.2.85) might well remind a Shakespearean audience that Tamburlaine had literally used a conquered East-ern king as his footstool ("villain, thou that wishest this to me, / Fall prostrate on the low disdainful earth, / And be the footstool of great Tamburlaine" [*1 Tamburlaine* 4.2.12–14]). In George Puttenham's *Arte of English Poesie,* the rhetorical term *hyperbole* is "Englished," or translated into English, as "the over-reacher," a term that served the modern critic Harry Levin as the title of his book on Marlowe and his plays.

There is no better parody of Hotspur than Prince Hal's, in act 2 of *Henry IV Part 1*. It sounds almost as if Hal had been present at the scenes the audience has just witnessed between Hotspur and Kate (Lady Percy):

> I am not yet of Percy's mind, the Hotspur of the North—he that kills me some six or seven dozen of Scots at a breakfast, washes his hands, and says to his wife, "Fie upon this quiet life! I want work."
>
> > *2.5.94–97*

Hotspur is easy to parody, because he, too, is a figure of excess. His impatience with the popinjay on the battlefield is understandable and even comic, but his impatience with language in general, and with rhetoric and persuasion in particular, is more serious and more dangerous. One of Shakespeare's most eloquent speakers, Hotspur has a real distrust of language and its effects, and contempt for politics and compromise. As Worcester counsels him after Hotspur has insulted Glendower and lost the assistance of the Welsh,

> You must needs learn, lord, to amend this fault.
> Though sometimes it show greatness, courage, blood—
> And that's the dearest grace it renders you—
> Yet oftentimes it doth present harsh rage,
> Defect of manners, want of government,
> Pride, haughtiness, opinion, and disdain.
>
> *3.1.176–181*

These, too, are Hotspur. He is heroic and idealistic, but he is no politician. Perhaps his greatest flaw, in this play about redeeming time, is his total disregard of time itself: "Doomsday is near: die all, die merrily" (4.1.135). Life and death are less important than glory, and only glory is timeless. But the play suggests that to value honor above all things is to value honor too highly, above life itself, as Hotspur does even in his dying words:

> O Harry, thou hast robbed me of my youth.
> I better brook the loss of brittle life
> Than those proud titles thou hast won of me.
>
> *5.4.76–78*

This is the same Hotspur who insisted that the only condition of the quest for honor should be that he win and wear its titles "without corrival." So it should not surprise us that Hotspur dies at the close of this play, although all of the others—Henry, Hal, Falstaff—live on. His is the most fragile of creeds, the creed of the epic warrior, and his time is passing in England. The Hotspurs of this world, like the Tybalts, cannot survive, although a world deprived of their spirit and their quixotic idealism is a world less valuable to live in. Hal, like the audience, will learn this, and we will see him try to incorporate something of Hotspur in himself, at the close of this play and increasingly in *Part 2* and in *Henry V*.

So Hotspur rejects time in favor of honor. On the other end of the scale of heroism and idealism, Falstaff rejects time as well, the first time we see him:

Falstaff	Now, Hal, what time of day is it, lad?
Prince Harry	Thou art so fat-witted with drinking of old sack, and unbuttoning thee after supper, and sleeping upon benches

after noon, that thou hast forgotten to demand that truly which thou wouldst truly know. What a devil hast thou to do with the time of the day? Unless hours were cups of sack, and minutes capons, and clocks the tongues of bawds, and dials the signs of leaping-houses, and the blessed sun himself a fair hot wench in flame-coloured taffeta, I see no reason why thou shouldst be so superfluous to demand the time of the day.

1.2.1–10

For Falstaff time is only a dimension of pleasure. His use of it is an aspect of disorder. Timelessness, as we will see, is a capacity of comedy, but history—and history plays—will demand a consciousness of time. We have already noted that beneath the exterior of this supple and lifelike play is the vestige of an older allegorical structure, the battle between vice and virtue for the soul of a prince—a familiar topic for the old moralities. In Falstaff we encounter the early modern equivalent of one of the most popular morality play characters, the Vice—the personified figure of depravity or corruption. In the mumming scene in the tavern in act 2, when Hal and Falstaff take turns playing the parts of "Prince" and "King," Hal, in the role of his father, King Henry, admonishes his "son" to avoid the "old fat man" whom he characterizes as "that reverend Vice, that grey Iniquity, that father Ruffian, that Vanity in years." Like the Vice figure, Falstaff is established as the contrary of everything virtuous and orderly. He himself speaks at one point of hitting the Prince with a dagger of lath (2.5.124), the light wooden sword that was the usual stage prop of the medieval Vice. In other words, the play deliberately points in the direction of this medieval heritage, which forms a kind of moral scaffolding for it.

But if Falstaff is a Vice, he is also a Lord of Misrule, a figure popular in, and after, the time of Henry VIII. An ordinary man temporarily raised to high estate, the Lord of Misrule was a personage chosen to preside over Christmas games and revels in a great man's house, as a kind of anti-lord or anti-king. Part of the topsy-turvy world of carnival, the Lord of Misrule reigned chiefly at night, promoting wild singing and dancing as well as drinking, and his "misrule" provided a temporary safety valve for pent-up social, sexual, and political energies. Such festivals predate the Christian era (one such was the Roman Saturnalia), but they are also closely associated with Christian holidays. Thus, for example, Mardi Gras precedes Lent, and Halloween precedes All Saints' Day. (The word "carnival," from *carnevale*, "farewell to meat," gives a sense of the stakes: first there is a defined period of social anarchy—much eating of meat and drinking of wine—then a return to a more repressive or regulatory order of abstinence and law.) As rebellious subjects, analogous to the political rebels led by Hotspur, Falstaff and the Gads Hill robbers mark this carnival instinct in society, and it is characteristic of Hal's role as both rebel and lawgiver that he pays back the money Poins and Falstaff have stolen from the travelers, turning their theft into play. Yet Falstaff himself literally embodies carnival, misrule, and vice, as he cheerfully admits in the tavern at Eastcheap. His language incorporates both rule and misrule, as can be seen in the speech below, which resembles the comically disordered prologues of the plays-within-the-play in *Love's Labour's Lost* and *A Midsummer Night's Dream*, with the important exception that Falstaff's linguistic undoing is deliberate rather than inadvertent:

> Come, sing me a bawdy song, make me merry. I was as virtuously given as a gentleman need to be: virtuous enough; swore little; diced not— above seven times a week; went to a bawdy house not—above once in a quarter—of an hour; paid money that I borrowed—three or four times; lived well, and in good compass. And now I live out of all order, out of all compass.
>
> 3.3.11–17

Falstaff's huge fat body is a visual metaphor similar to that of Nell, the kitchen wench in *The Comedy of Errors:* he *is* out of all compass, the grotesque physical opposite of the enclosed and classical body of a Hotspur or a Hal. As early as the play's second act both Falstaff and Hal have made the most obvious comparison of all, between Hal's deceased grandfather, John of Gaunt, and the companion the Prince calls "Sir John Paunch" (2.2.58). It is as such a living metaphor that Falstaff lumbers across the stage, constantly wishing to be anything but afoot. Once again Shakespeare makes the balance and dramatic elegance of his play clear, for just as Hotspur is almost unimaginable when not astride a horse ("That roan shall be my throne"), so Falstaff roams the stage, and the play, calling for a horse almost as insistently as Richard III. (Falstaff: "Give me my horse, you rogues, give me my horse, and be hanged!" [2.2.27–28].) When war is declared against the rebels, the Prince finds a commission for Sir John, and of course it is an infantry regiment, a "charge of foot." "I would it had been of horse" is Falstaff's response. Standard pronunciation in Shakespeare's time would have made this a manifestly bawdy homonym, "horse"/"whores." Just as Falstaff walks afoot and wants a horse, is old and pretends to be young— "They hate us youth," he shouts lustily during the Gads Hill robbery (2.2.76)— so he is Hotspur's complementary opposite when it comes to the question of honor. Falstaff, it turns out, is a materialist of sorts, and in the lively internal dialogue he calls his "catechism" he finds that honor has neither sense nor substance:

> [H]onour pricks me on. Yea, but how if honour prick me off when I come on? How then? Can honour set-to a leg? No. Or an arm? No. Or take away the grief of a wound? No. Honour hath no skill in surgery, then? No. What is honour? A word. What is in that word "honour"? What is that "honour"? Air. A trim reckoning! Who hath it? He that died o'Wednesday.

Doth he feel it? No. Doth he hear it? No. 'Tis insensible then? Yea, to the
dead. But will it not live with the living? No. Why? Detraction will not
suffer it. Therefore I'll none of it. Honour is a mere scutcheon. And so
ends my catechism.

5.1.129–139

A catechism is a summary in question-and-answer format, especially one
designed for elementary instruction in the Christian religion. A "scutcheon," or
escutcheon, was an armorial shield bearing a coat of arms, and thus a badge of
family honor. To Falstaff, honor is just the empty sign of something, not a commodity, an agent, or anything actually palpable or useful. Hotspur had sworn to
pluck bright honor from the pale-faced moon; Falstaff will have none of it.
Again, it should be no surprise that Falstaff lives, while Hotspur dies.

Yet the play takes an evenhanded view of Falstaff's qualities. While he is not
the sublime antihero sometimes claimed by his uncritical admirers and adherents ("They hate us youth"), he is an excellent antidote to unrealistic idealism,
as well as (in this play, at least) a diverting and amusing stage presence. For all of
his flaws, he speaks, upon occasion, a crucial and even a painful truth, as when,
for example, he acknowledges that he lives in a fallen world: "Thou knowest
that in the state of innocency Adam fell, and what should poor Jack Falstaff do
in the days of villainy?" (3.3.151–153). Not only do human beings eat and drink
and make love, they also die, and where Hotspur had faced the possibility of
death in battle with a kind of ecstatic joy ("die all, die merrily"), Falstaff, predictably, takes the opposite approach, and recruits for his unit the most ragged
fragments of humanity he can find, first drafting young husbands and men
about to be married, allowing them to buy their way out of army service, and
then, taking his profit, filling his ranks with ragamuffins. "I never did see such
pitiful rascals," says the Prince, and Falstaff replies,

Tut, tut, good enough to toss, food for powder, food for powder. They'll
fill a pit as well as better. Tush, man, mortal men, mortal men.

4.2.58–60

This, too, is a truth about war, a fact that Hotspur has all but forgotten, and
that Hal, as King Henry, will do well to remember. In the same way, one of Falstaff's companions, preparing to set out to rob the travelers at Gads Hill, asks
casually how many there are, and is told there are perhaps nine or ten.
"Zounds," says Falstaff in alarm, "will they not rob *us*?" (2.2.57; emphasis
added). Winners can also be losers, victors can also be victims. King Henry IV,
who was the thief and usurper of the kingdom, is himself on the brink of being
robbed of his crown ("Zounds, will they not rob *us*?"). In many ways Falstaff
provides a necessary antidote to the excessive idealism that is Hotspur, and he
does so by reminding his fellows, and the audience, of the nature of "mortal

men." Yet there is also danger and risk in Falstaff's character. He is not a mis-understood roly-poly Everyman. Rule cannot finally be guided by Misrule, or history and order by appetite and desire.

> Falstaff   Why, Hal, thou knowest as thou art but man I dare, but as thou art prince, I fear thee as I fear the roaring of the lion's whelp.
>
> Prince Harry   And why not as the lion?
>
> Falstaff   The King himself is to be feared as the lion. Dost thou think I'll fear thee as I fear thy father? Nay . . .
>
> *3.3.134–139*

That Falstaff does not fear Hal, when he becomes King, as he feared his father, will ultimately be Falstaff's undoing. Between these two poles, the Hotspur world and the Falstaff world, Hal must find his own position, his own identity. It is a measure of Shakespeare's tremendous power as a dramatist that these two worlds come so vividly to life in this play, and that they offer the audience, as they do the Prince, a choice—as the poet Wallace Stevens remarked in another connection—"not between, but of."

The morality play struggle between vice and virtue can also be understood both in terms that resemble the classical psychomachia, or conflict of the soul, and in terms of modern psychology and psychoanalysis. That is to say, the struggle is situated inside Hal as well as outside him. Hal has elements of Falstaff in his nature and character, and elements of Hotspur, and in a sense the whole play is the working out of this inner conflict, the acknowledgment—rather than the suppression or elimination—of the various aspects of his persona that reflect upon, and learn from, the models he finds around him. As we will see with *Hamlet*, and with Prospero in *The Tempest*, and with many other Shakespearean plays in which the protagonist is trying, as we often say, in an underexamined cliché, to "find himself," the play can be understood both as a "real" set of external individuals and environments (the King, Falstaff, Hotspur and the rebels, the tavern, and so on) and as the projection of these elements *within* Prince Hal upon the stage.

Readers and audiences of Shakespeare's history plays have been aware of Hal as a wastrel and a reveler from the closing moment of *Richard II,* when Boling-broke (recently crowned King Henry) asked, "Can no man tell me of my unthrifty son?" In that play, so preoccupied with the relationship of fathers and sons (Gaunt and Bolingbroke, York and Aumerle, Northumberland and his son, whom we will come to know as Hotspur), Bolingbroke's own son, not even named, is already an icon of bad behavior, carousing in the London taverns with "unrestrained loose companions," robbing travelers in narrow lanes, and defending the honor of whores in the stews, or brothels.

To Shakespeare's contemporaries the reputation of Prince Hal, later to become Henry V, was legendary—the story of his miraculous reformation pre-

Hal, then, is in disguise, performing—like Richard III in the play that bears his name—a role that he can doff at will. Whereas Richard III was a "devil" pretending to be an angel, Hal is a virtuous man pretending to be a madcap and a thief—or is he? Whom is he addressing when he says "I know you all"? Surely it is not only the "loose companions" who have just exited the stage, but also the audience in the theater. We are not only his confidants and confederates but also the objects of his deception and manipulation. The "idleness" of playgoers, as well as the idleness of tavern-dwellers, is a tool for his advantage.

There is a great deal in the language of this famous soliloquy that should be suggestive to attentive readers and listeners. "[H]erein will I imitate the sun": the sun, of course, is the emblem of the king of England. When Hal's father's predecessor, Richard II, was the sun, he was covered up by "envious clouds"— that is, by the rebels and by Bolingbroke, who would become Henry IV. But Hal proposes to "permit the base contagious clouds" (his own reputation as a wastrel) to cover him up, so that he will seem more virtuous and more powerful when he does emerge as himself, as the Prince and as the Prodigal Son. "Imitate" is an actor's—or a writer's—word, from the Latin word for "copy." "If all the world were playing holidays, / To sport would be as tedious as to work": Hal is himself in a condition of holiday, or festival, but unlike Falstaff he knows the limits of carnival and misrule. When war comes, and with it the serious issues of life and death, and he finds Falstaff with a bottle of sack in his pistol case, Hal will ask, impatiently, "What, is it time to jest and dally now?" (5.3.54). His "now," a word of time and timeliness, will interrupt and disrupt the perpetual holiday that is the heedless affect of unthinking Falstaffism. Comedy has its bounds, and outside its boundaries lie war, death—and history.

"So when this loose behavior I throw off / And pay the debt I never promisèd": reckonings, bills due and bills paid, an economic language of debt and payment, will be associated with Prince Hal throughout the play. He pays back the money stolen at Gads Hill. He finds and mocks Falstaff's unpaid bill at the tavern for a great deal of sack and a halfpenny's worth of bread. In fact, the language of debts paid and money responsibly handled works in this play as a healing antidote to the imagery of counterfeiting that pursues Hal's father, Henry IV, the king as usurper, and that Falstaff himself will employ in the battlefield scene in this play, when he "riseth up" from apparent death and ignominiously pretends to have slain the heroic Hotspur: " 'Sblood, 'twas time to counterfeit. . . . Counterfeit? I lie, I am no counterfeit. To die is to be a counterfeit, for he is but the counterfeit of a man who hath not the life of a man. But to counterfeit dying when a man thereby liveth is to be no counterfeit, but the true and perfect image of life indeed" (5.4.111–117). In contrast we have Hal's "I'll so offend to make offence a skill, / Redeeming time when men think least I will."

As we have noticed, both Hotspur and Falstaff are in their different ways oblivious to time, Hotspur because he prefers timeless glory even if it comes only with death, and Falstaff because for him all the year *is* playing holidays; life is one long festival. But Hal is quintessentially a man in and of time. He is a man of good timing, like an actor: he can surprise Falstaff on the road, lead him into more and more monstrous lies in the tavern, and finally put his story of the buckram men down with a "plain tale," a true account. Hal is also a man who knows his time. He will wait for the right moment to reveal himself, to step from behind the clouds and shine like the sun, and like the King's son. Equally important is the fact that he is a man who knows the times, who knows that England is changing, and that the commons as well as the "gentles," and the Welsh and the Scots as well as the English, must be included in any unified nation. In all these ways Prince Hal is a man of time. And yet "[r]edeeming time" is also something else again. The phrase comes from a passage in Saint Paul's Epistle to the Ephesians:

> But fornication, and all uncleanness, or covetousness, let it not be once named among you, as becometh saints; Neither filthiness, nor foolish talk-ing, nor jesting, which are not convenient, but rather giving of thanks. For this ye know, that no whoremonger, nor unclean person, nor covetous man, who is an idolater, hath any inheritance in the kingdom of Christ and of God. . . . Be not ye therefore partakers with them. For ye were sometimes darkness, but now are ye light in the Lord: walk as children of light. . . . See then that ye walk circumspectly, not as fools, but as wise, Redeeming the time, because the days are evil. . . . And be not drunk with wine, wherein is excess; but be filled with the Spirit.
>
> *Ephesians 5:3–18, King James Bible*

Plausibly this passage can be taken as a description both of Hal's former life and loose companions (jesting, drinking, fornicating, coveting) and of his reforma-tion, glittering over his fault. The Prince who was "sometimes darkness" will now bring light, like the sun (and the Son), and redeem time, because the days are evil. Paul writes of redeeming "the time," whereas Hal intends to redeem "time"; the presence or absence of the definite article makes a difference. Hal's mode of redemption must address history and mores ("the time" and "the times") in order to point toward transcendence ("time" as timelessness). Shake-speare's brilliant use of biblical typology allows for this allegorical dimension to Prince Hal's character without ever making him into a cutout or a stereotype. The Pauline injunction, doubtless familiar to an Elizabethan audience, would not overshadow the lively surface action of the play, but would nonetheless stand behind it as a backdrop of biblical prophecy.

From the play's opening moments, then, the audience knows more about Hal than anyone in the play does—more than his father, more than Falstaff. Whether or not we are privy, as Shakespeare's original audience would have been, to the legendary reputation of the wastrel-prince-turned-hero-king, we know that this Prince Hal is on holiday, but that he will return to the everyday, and that when he does so, resuming his "real" identity, the result may well be a holiday for his subjects, a redeemed world. Manifestly the Prince is enjoying himself—only the dourest and most suspicious critic could claim that he is merely "using" his tavern friends—but he does have an ulterior motive, something we might call, in modern parlance, "fieldwork" or, even less appealingly, "ethnography." If the tavern world is fun for Hal, it is also part of his education. And although he studies statecraft and policy with the crafty zeal of the born Machiavellian, we could say that in *1 Henry IV* the chief study for the rising Prince is the study of language. Language, after all, was the problem that so vexed the world of *Richard II*, leaving no middle ground between soliloquy and command, between poetry and law.

Language, or the lack of it, is a problem in this play as well, a problem neatly exemplified in the situation of Mortimer, the son-in-law of Owen Glendower. We learn from Mortimer—himself described as a lineal heir to the throne—that he cannot speak the language of his adoptive land:

> This is the deadly spite that angers me:
> My wife can speak no English, I no Welsh.
> *3.1.188–189*

Yet in a way he loves her precisely because he cannot communicate with her through the ordinary medium of discourse:

> I understand thy kisses, and thou mine,
> And that's a feeling disputation;
> But I will never be a truant, love,
> Till I have learned thy language, for thy tongue
> Makes Welsh as sweet as ditties highly penned,
> Sung by a fair queen in a summer's bower,
> With ravishing division, to her lute.
> *3.1.200–206*

He will never leave her *until* he understands her language. In its present form her speech is more like musical incantation than like part of a verbal exchange or dispute. We may notice that the stage direction tells us "the lady sings a Welsh song," but does not transcribe her song, although in *Henry V* the language lessons of Princess Catherine of France present, with charmingly ribald mispronunciation and malapropism, the tug-of-war of translation between the French language and the English tongue.

The status of the Welsh language was a topical issue in Shakespeare's time. In the 1536 Statute of Union, Queen Elizabeth's father, Henry VIII, prohibited the use of Welsh, claiming that it produced "discord variance debate division murmur and sedition," since the speech of the Welsh people is "nothing like, nor consonant to the natural Mother Tongue within this realm." In Old English the word "Welsh" often seems to have meant "foreign," and this sense of otherness is retained in some of the early modern presentations of the idea of Wales. In *1 Henry IV* Welsh is, consistently, a "foreign" tongue, here approximating song. Even though Mortimer calls his inability to understand his wife a "deadly spite," his infatuation seems tied in part to the elusive nature of her inaccessible words. But a government built largely upon looks, or upon music, cannot survive, and Prince Hal's readiness with languages in the plural stands in deliberate contrast to Mortimer's ambivalent attachment to the mystique of Welsh. The problem of incorporating multiple languages and cultures, including Welsh and Welshmen, into a united England is one that Hal will have to face, as king, in *Henry V.*

In a less literal but equally crucial way, Hotspur illustrates the problem of language, since Hotspur, although a great hero, is too impatient either to speak or to listen. "I, that have not well the gift of tongue," he says of himself (5.2.77), and "I profess not talking" (5.2.91). He criticizes those that speak in "mincing poetry," and he has no time to read letters that are sent to him on the eve of battle. There is in fact an interesting stage history behind the portrayal of Hotspur and his language. In *Part 2* his widow, Lady Percy, speaks of him as having been a model of behavior for every young nobleman. "And speaking thick," she says, "which nature made his blemish, / Became the accents of the valiant" (*2 Henry IV* 2.3.24–25). Modern scholars interpret "speaking thick" as speaking quickly and impetuously, understanding "thick" here as an adverb. (The ardent and equally impetuous Cleopatra burdens twenty messengers with her letters to Antony, and is asked, "Why do you send so thick?" [*Antony and Cleopatra* 1.5.62].) The familiar phrase "thick and fast" gives something of the spirit of Lady Percy's remark. But August Wilhelm von Schlegel, the nineteenth-century German translator of Shakespeare, translated "thick" as *stottern*, which in German means "stutter," and there developed a theatrical tradition of playing Hotspur with a difficulty in speech, the opposite, in fact, of speaking "thick and fast." Michael Redgrave, when he played the part, interpreted "speaking thick" to mean speaking gutturally, with a Northumbrian *r.* Laurence Olivier took "speaking thick" to mean speaking with an impediment, and so his Hotspur was performed, memorably, with the inability to pronounce the letter *w.* Why *w*? The dramatic result was that Hotspur, as he lay dying, was unable to pronounce his own last words:

> O, I could prophesy,
> But that the earthy and cold hand of death
> Lies on my tongue. No, Percy, thou art dust,
> And food for—
>
> 5.4.82–85

The victorious Hal, appropriating the language of Hotspur along with his spirit, completes the thought: "For worms, brave Percy." When Hotspur loses speech, he loses life. And when Hal finishes Hotspur's sentence he takes over, not only the "proud titles" of hero and soldier, and their shared title or name of "Harry," but the basic stuff of human life itself, syntax and communication.

Long before the death of Hotspur, Prince Hal is seen as a student of language. We learn from him in the tavern scene that he has carefully studied the jargon and patois of his companions:

> I have sounded the very bass-string of humility. Sirrah, I am sworn brother to a leash of drawers, and can call them all by their christen names, as "Tom," "Dick," and "Francis." They take it already, upon their salvation, that though I be but Prince of Wales, yet I am the king of courtesy, and tell me flatly I am no proud jack like Falstaff, but a Corinthian, a lad of mettle, a good boy—by the Lord, so they call me; and when I am King of England I shall command all the good lads in Eastcheap. They call drinking deep "dyeing scarlet," and when you breathe in your watering they cry "Hem!" and bid you "Play it off!" To conclude, I am so good a proficient in one quarter of an hour that I can drink with any tinker in his own language during my life.
>
> 2.5.5–17

We may notice that the Prince alters the traditional "Tom, Dick, and Harry," removing his own name from the list and adding that of the hapless "drawer," or tapster, Francis, whom he and Poins will genially torment in the episode that follows. His linguistic accomplishment, though lightly worn, is hardly trivial. In politics today, regional accents breed regional prejudices, as they did in Hal's time, and in Shakespeare's, too. To be able to drink with a tinker "in his own language" allows for a level of communication that will become increasingly important when Prince Hal does, indeed, become King of England. The mastery of many languages and regional dialects plays a vital role in the success of the king called Harry in *Henry V*.

Yet there is another reason as well for Hal's presence in the tavern, and for his role as madcap prince, the companion of the riotous Falstaff and Bardolph—a reason we have already noted in looking at the language of the "I know you all" speech. Prince Hal is not the first princely son to be rebuked for associating with thieves and murderers. In a play that draws strongly on biblical typology, he is both implicitly and explicitly compared to Christ—who defended the woman taken in adultery, who took common fishermen for his disciples, who washed the disciples' feet and urged the rich to sell all they had and give the money to the poor, who dined with publicans and sinners. Hal becomes one of the people, as Christ descended to Earth, to learn about them, to instruct them, and to redeem them. Where Bolingbroke, Hal's father, wooed the common people as a calculated act ("Off goes his bonnet to an oysterwench"), Hal's wooing, though in a sense no less calculated, is much closer to an act of love. Like all the most successful monarchs—including Queen Elizabeth—he is a master of role-playing. Acting gives him the twin tools of control and freedom, and almost from the moment we first see him he is improvising, making plays. It is Poins who talks him into the masquerade of the "buckram men"; he and Hal put on "cases," or suits, of buckram, and the robbers don visors, or masks.

In act 2, scene 5, Hal plays out another little performance with Poins at the expense of the unfortunate tapster Francis, monopolizing his attention (who could be rude to the Prince of Wales?) while an insistent voice (Poins's, of course) calls from the other room for service. Torn between fealty and commerce, Francis is the epitome of the changing times, and his attempt at mollification—"Anon, anon, sir!" (2.5.40)—underscores the central theme of time itself. Hal's playacting continues with the wonderful parody of Hotspur killing six or seven dozen Scots before breakfast. Hal is so intoxicated by this vision that he immediately casts yet another scene: "I prithee call in Falstaff. I'll play Percy, and that damned brawn shall play Dame Mortimer his wife" (99–101). Alas, the Percy play never does get performed, but what the audience gets to see in this great scene is the double play of "The Prince and the King," as Hal and Falstaff alternate these roles to the delight of their onstage spectator, the enraptured Hostess ("O Jesu, this is excellent sport, i'faith" [356]). This performance is yet another version of the "counterfeiting" of social and theatrical personae that has already established itself as a key question for the play. Although the scene is well known, it is useful to look at some passages, since this apparently playful exchange points so unerringly into the sober future:

Prince Harry Do thou stand for my father, and examine me upon the particulars of my life.

Falstaff Shall I? Content. This chair shall be my state, this dagger my sceptre, and this cushion my crown. . . . Harry, I do not only marvel where thou spendest thy time, but also how thou art accompanied. For though the chamomile, the more it is trodden on, the faster it grows, so youth, the more it is wasted, the sooner it wears. That thou art my son I have partly thy mother's word, partly my own opinion, but chiefly a villainous trick of thine eye, and a foolish hanging of thy nether lip, that doth warrant me. . . . This pitch, as ancient writers do report, doth defile. So doth the company thou keepest. . . . And yet there is a virtuous man whom I have often noted in thy company, but I know not his name.

Prince Harry What manner of man, an it like your majesty?

Falstaff A goodly, portly man, i'faith, and a corpulent; of a cheerful look, a pleasing eye, and a most noble carriage; and, as I think, his age some fifty, or, by'r Lady, inclining to three-score. And now I remember me, his name is Falstaff. If that man should be lewdly given, he deceiveth me; for, Harry, I see virtue in his looks. . . . there is virtue in that Falstaff. Him keep with; the rest banish.

2.5.342–345, 364–391

Banishment is a serious issue in this play, as in *Richard II*. And so is the matter of counterfeiting a king, which Falstaff is doing—and of deposing a king, which Hal now does, mandating an exchange of roles:

Prince Harry   Dost thou speak like a king? Do thou stand for me, and I'll play my father.
Falstaff   Depose me.

2.5.394–396

But Falstaff readily agrees to play the Prince—in a way, he does so all the time—and Hal now speaks for the King:

Prince Harry   Swearest thou, ungracious boy? Henceforth ne'er look on me. Thou art violently carried away from grace. There is a devil haunts thee in the likeness of an old fat man; a tun of man is thy companion. Why dost thou converse with that trunk of humours, that bolting-hutch of beastliness, that swollen parcel of dropsies, that huge bombard of sack, that stuffed cloak-bag of guts . . . that reverend Vice, that grey Iniquity, that father Ruffian, that Vanity in Years? Wherein is he good, but to taste sack and drink it? Wherein neat and cleanly, but to carve a capon and eat it? Wherein cunning, but in craft? Wherein crafty, but in villainy? Wherein villainous, but in all things? Wherein worthy, but in nothing?
Falstaff   I would your grace would take me with you. Whom means your grace?
Prince Harry   That villainous, abominable misleader of youth, Falstaff; that old white-bearded Satan.
Falstaff   My lord, the man I know.
Prince Harry   I know thou dost.
Falstaff   But to say I know more harm in him than in myself were to say more than I know. That he is old, the more the pity, his white hairs do witness it. But that he is, saving your reverence, a whoremaster, that I utterly deny. If sack and sugar be a fault, God help the wicked. If to be old and merry be a sin, then many an old host that I know is damned. If to be fat be to be hated, then Pharaoh's lean kine are to be loved.

No, my good lord, banish Peto, banish Bardolph, banish
Poins, but for sweet Jack Falstaff, kind Jack Falstaff, true
Jack Falstaff, valiant Jack Falstaff, and therefore more
valiant being, as he is, old Jack Falstaff,
Banish not him thy Harry's company,
Banish not him thy Harry's company.
Banish plump Jack, and banish all the world.

Prince Harry   I do; I will.

2.5.406–439

These are key words, cold words: "I do; I will." The language of the marriage
ceremony here seems deliberately and ironically to signify an impending
divorce. The play-within-the-play predicts the future, as would be clear to
anyone in the audience who knew either the historical facts or Shakespeare's
unerring way with prophecy. It is an extraordinary moment onstage, poised
between "play" and "reality," between "past," "present," and "future"—all rendered for a split second equally notional and fictional. Hal not only "will" banish Falstaff, as we will see him do at the end of *Part 2*. He also *does* banish him,
in the present tense, from this time forward, despite the apparent amity of their
relationship.

The predictions of the "I know you all" soliloquy are already coming true.
For the spectators in the theater this scene has an enriched significance, because
both sides of this conversation are accurate. Falstaff is in some measure a pleasing old man, merry, fond of drink and of company; but he is also a "devil," a
white-bearded Satan, a "reverend Vice" and "grey Iniquity." Falstaff's mock-
incredulous "Depose me?" marks the boundary of seriousness and jest. (To
"depose" for the Renaissance—as for lawyers and judges today—was to take testimony by questioning, as well as to dethrone, and Falstaff uses the word knowingly, in both of its senses.) Role-playing in *Henry IV Part 1* emphasizes the
flexibility and changeability of roles, their impermanence. There will come a
time when Hal must abandon playing, abandon holiday, to preserve the
unchanging role of "Prince" and then of "King." But that time is not yet. For
the moment, he stashes Falstaff behind the arras, or hanging tapestry, in yet
another little stage play, in order to foil the sheriff who has come to arrest him.
This confrontation between law and play will prefigure much that is to come.

It is the news of war, however, that provides the turning point in *Henry IV
Part 1*, shifting the energies of this scene, and of the play as a whole, from
"comedy" to "history." War is the pivot or threshold here, comparable, for
example, to the death of Mercutio in *Romeo and Juliet*, which signaled the play's
transition from comedy to tragedy—or comparable to the achievement of his
long-sought kingship for Richard III, which transformed him from a gleeful
antagonist to a beleaguered and increasingly desperate protagonist. When
comedy turns into history in this play, timelessness turns into time, and also
into teleology—and genealogy. For with the threat of war comes, at last, the real

onstage confrontation between King and Prince, that confrontation we have
seen so deftly counterfeited by Hal and Falstaff in act 2. So skillfully has this
play been put together that the audience may not have registered this central
absence. But the delay, and the set of substitutions that enable that delay, produce their telling effects. Finally, in the middle of the third act, the King and the
Prince face each other—and the audience—for the first time. It is at this point
that we hear Hal, chastised by his father, speak the line that becomes the pivot
of the ensuing action. "I shall hereafter, my thrice gracious lord, / Be more
myself" (3.2.92–93). Glancing back at "I know you all," this declaration marks
the end of "playing holidays," and the sun/son emerges from behind the clouds.
From this point, too, Hal will move away from Falstaff and toward Hotspur,
finding a version of "myself" between, but also transcending, these two models
and rivals.

    Hotspur, however admirable, is still the rebellious enemy to Henry's—and
to Hal's—kingship, and the Prince's language of defiance against him deliberately engages the mercantile imagery of debt and payment we heard in the act 1,
scene 2, soliloquy. Hal is a secular as well as a Christian prince, and, unlike
Richard II, he is aware of the value of money and capital in a changing world.
Here a modern audience needs again to remind itself of the difference between
the fictive date of the play, the mid-fifteenth century, and the date of its composition and first performance, at the end of the sixteenth century. The economics
of the play are grounded in Shakespeare's own time, rather than in the historical
Hal's, although as with virtually everything in Shakespeare this "period" note
speaks uncannily to our own time as well:

> Percy is but my factor, good my lord,
> To engross up glorious deeds on my behalf;
> And I will call him to so strict account
> That he shall render every glory up,
> Yea, even the slightest worship of his time,
> Or I will tear the reckoning from his heart.
>
> *3.2.147–152*

"Factor," "engross," "account," "render," and "reckoning." This is the language
of economic reality, the language of calculation, the same language—although
not the same tone—that mocked Falstaff's gross imbalance of bread and sack. A
"factor" is an agent; a "reckoning" is a bill. Yet in a passage that just precedes this
one we can hear once more the other side of Hal's emerging character, the side
of typology and Christian redemption, of apocalypse now. As a dramatic character, Prince Hal is both a modern man and a transcendent one:

> I will redeem all this on Percy's head,
> And in the closing of some glorious day

> Be bold to tell you that I am your son;
> When I will wear a garment all of blood,
> And stain my favors in a bloody mask. . . .
>
> *3.2.132–136*

The very excessiveness of the language here should alert us to the possibility of some biblical referent. Hal does not usually talk like this, but the Book of Revelation does, as, for example, when discussing the second coming of the King of Kings: "And he had on [his] vesture and on his thigh a name written, KING OF KINGS, AND LORD OF LORDS" (Revelation 19:16). Shakespeare's Hal is still a dramatic character, still an Englishman, still very much alive and bristling with personality, yet behind him now looms the huge shadow of apocalypse. He has come to save England from Percy, from the rebels, and from vice in any form, as well as from the curse of usurpation that has been the unwanted inheritance of Henry IV.

The vision of Prince Hal presented in the succeeding scenes continues to limn this mythic dimension, a dimension that is never at odds with his dramatic realism or human persuasiveness. Thus, for example, Sir Richard Vernon, one of the rebels, reports to a skeptical Hotspur that he has seen a new Prince Hal, a Hal dressed for battle and prepared for war, a Hal no longer Hal but now "young Harry":

> I saw young Harry with his beaver on,
> His cuishes on his thighs, gallantly armed,
> Rise from the ground like feathered Mercury,
> And vaulted with such ease into his seat
> As if an angel dropped down from the clouds
> To turn and wind a fiery Pegasus,
> And witch the world with noble horsemanship.
>
> *4.1.105–111*

Horsemanship is a skill that has been associated throughout the play with Hotspur. Here the horse in question is Pegasus, the winged horse of Greek myth, the horse of the Muses, emblematic of the sacred king's or hero's journey to heaven. The ancient story tells of Bellerophon's attempt to ride Pegasus to heaven, a hubristic move that drew the anger of the gods; like Icarus and Phaëthon, other presumptuous figures, Bellerophon fell, thwarted in his goal. Hal's heroism here is imagined as unquestioned and successful, like that of "an angel dropped down from the clouds," witching, or bewitching, the world with "noble horsemanship." The comparison with Mercury, the Roman god of eloquence, also described as a god of commerce and gain (the name itself derives from the same root as "merchant" and "merchandise"), is telling. The Roman Mercury was protector of both traders and thieves, an apt ancestor for the

Prince Hal of the Gads Hill caper, and was the conductor of souls to the lower world—an appropriate role for a Hal who is about to offer a premature epitaph for the fallen Falstaff. In Shakespeare's time Mercury (who also appears in the Mercutio of *Romeo and Juliet*) was regarded as a bearer of news, as a guide or conductor, and as both a nimble person and a dextrous thief. In a later play in this sequence, *Henry V,* we will encounter the distinctly mock-heroic paean of the French Dauphin to his horse, offered as a kind of love poem, and clearly to be imagined as a comic pendant to this scene—which is, in form, actually another Shakespearean "unscene," as Vernon reports the quasi-mythic sighting. ("I will not change my horse with any that but treads on four pasterns," carols the Dauphin. "He bounds from the earth as if his entrails were hares—*le cheval volant,* the Pegasus. . . . When I bestride him, I soar, I am a hawk; he trots the air; the earth sings when he touches it," and so on [*Henry V* 3.7.11–16].) But in Vernon's account we encounter Hal, for the first and indeed the last time in this play, described in mythological rather than in Christian terms—a Hal on horse-back, a Hal now frankly heroic. Just as Hotspur was a "Mars in swaddling-clothes," Hal is a "feathered Mercury." At the beginning of act 5 he will acknowledge that he has been a "truant . . . to chivalry" (5.1.94) and will challenge Hotspur to "single fight." Thus even before the final battle he has, in effect, succeeded in taking over the best qualities of Hotspur, just as he had earlier taken over the wit, humor, and practical realism of Falstaff. Symbolically, his victory over Hotspur occurs before they fight.

Indeed, in a modern world, the old mode of "single fight" will never prevail, and no sooner does Hal make his offer than the King withdraws it, citing—as kings will—the vague but compelling rationale of "considerations infinite." The feudal world of *Richard II* is now only a distant memory. But in becoming, as he says, "more myself," Prince Hal has begun to resolve his psychomachia, or struggle of the soul. He has found, we might say, the Hotspur in himself as well as the Falstaff, and now the Vernon, who is given in this play an almost choric role, and observes with truth that "England did never owe so sweet a hope, / So much misconstrued in his wantonness" (5.2.67–68).

The final dramatic resolution of the conflict within Hal, and the emblematic unification of the two poles between which he has been moving, occurs in the splendid double epitaph in the play's final scene at Shrewsbury. Hotspur is dying, slain by Hal—a Harry killed by a Harry—and Hotspur's language here, as so frequently, is lofty, mythic, reaching beyond the common world. Hal speaks in reply a language of pragmatic realism that represents a necessary acknowledgment of mortality (Falstaff's "mortal men, mortal men"):

Hotspur   O Harry, thou hast robbed me of my youth.
             I better brook the loss of brittle life
             Than those proud titles thou hast won of me.
             They wound my thoughts more than thy sword my flesh.

But thoughts, the slaves of life, and life, time's fool,
And time, that takes survey of all the world,
Must have a stop. O, I could prophesy,
But that the earthy and cold hand of death
Lies on my tongue. No, Percy, thou art dust,
And food for—

Prince Harry   For worms, brave Percy.

5.4.76–85

The stage picture here may mirror the dichotomy, for no sooner does Hal bid farewell to Percy than he spies Falstaff stretched out on the ground, apparently dead as well, and we hear the Prince speak in a different voice:

What, old acquaintance! Could not all this flesh
Keep in a little life? Poor Jack, farewell.
I could have better spared a better man.

5.4.101–103

This is the language of charity, the language of inclusion and acceptance, an acknowledgment of the nature of (a) literally fallen man.

Next to Hal's solemn gesture, Falstaff's counterfeit resurrection is already somewhat out of key. *Part 2* will make the linguistic pun explicit, but even here Sir John is a "false staff" (see act 1, scene 2). Although the stage direction tells us that "Falstaff rises up," it is hard to regard his reascension without ambivalence, since—even if we have come to love him—his actions here are troubling. Stabbing the dead body of Hotspur, Falstaff will falsely claim to have conquered him. An audience sufficiently attentive to the nuances of the plot will, albeit perhaps reluctantly, begin at this point to separate itself from the resilient fat knight, as does the Prince. Although Falstaff's power as a dramatic character was, and continues to be, enough to assure him a starring role in productions from the eighteenth century to the present, one that often upstages the more centrist Prince, who is trammeled by considerations of state, office, and history, both audiences and critics are invited by the structure of this play to judge him. The real figure who "rises up" at the end of this play is Prince Hal.

Hal's pardon of Falstaff is one of a series of acts of charity, both heartfelt and strategic, that mark the closing action of the play. Hal lies, willingly, to do Falstaff grace. He pardons the Scottish captain, the Earl of Douglas, behaving in a way more generously than his father, who had prisoners put to death in accordance with the rules of war. The pardon of Douglas is a political act—this Prince of Wales understands that Scotland and Wales are necessary parts of any new nation—but it is also an ethical response. Behind the act of pardon a Christian audience would once more have heard the voice of the Christian Bible, and recognized the pattern of typology from the Sermon on the

Mount: "And forgive us our debts, as we forgive our debtors" (Matthew 6:12, King James Bible). Economic language here merges with the language of redemption.

More than anything else, this play finally challenges the audience to deal with its complicated response to Prince Hal. Is the Hal of *Henry IV Part 1* "good" or "bad," agreeable or disagreeable, fun-loving or calculating? Although it is difficult to find some common ground between Machiavelli and Matthew, Hal occupies precisely this difficult middle ground. An audience infatuated with Eastcheap may be suspicious of his calculation, and feel discomfited, itself too well "known," in his "I know you all" speech. In the second scene of the play he has, through the powerful stage conventions of aside and soliloquy, already made us his confidants and co-conspirators. It seems fair to suspect that we will retain an affection for Falstaff and the others longer, and better, than Hal will once he becomes King. But this is one of the things the play would have us learn about kingship: that it demands a shutting-away of feeling as well as an expression of it. Like Theseus in *A Midsummer Night's Dream*, Prince Escalus in *Romeo and Juliet*, and many others of this type—but more than any of them—a Prince Hal destined to be King must be by his very nature both less and more than a generous-minded audience may wish him to be. The condition of Renaissance—or early modern—kingship is a condition of limitation and loss, as well as of power and possibility. When Hal, finding Falstaff alive after taking him for dead, speaks to him in a suggestive phrase for this play, "Thou art not what thou seem'st," Falstaff replies, "No, that's certain: I am not a double man" (5.4.133–134). Not a double man. Falstaff means "not a ghost or a specter" and "not two men," an allusion to his girth as well as to his apparent rebirth. But Hal, Prince Hal, *is* by role and by nature himself a "double man," a living perspective painting, which takes one form when viewed directly and another when viewed awry. The design of Shakespeare's play—and it is a very brilliant and intricate design, but also a very clear and balanced one—makes this point extremely clear. To acknowledge a conscious as well as an unconscious doubleness, putting the personal and the public man in equipoise and sometimes in conflict, is perhaps the most essential lesson in the education of a prince. It is a lesson that Hal learns here, as well as in the succeeding history plays that tell his story. It is also, as we will see, a vital lesson for another Shakespearean prince, equally gifted in soliloquizing and in the arts of the play-within-the-play: Hamlet, Prince of Denmark.

Henry IV Part 2

DRAMATIS PERSONAE

Rumour, *the Presenter*

Epilogue

King Henry IV

Prince Harry, *later crowned King Henry V, son of King Henry IV*

Prince John of Lancaster, *son of King Henry IV*

Humphrey, Duke of Gloucester, *son of King Henry IV*

Thomas, Duke of Clarence, *son of King Henry IV*

Percy, Earl of Northumberland, *of the rebels' party*

Lady Northumberland

Lady Percy, *their son Hotspur's widow*

Travers, *Northumberland's servant*

Morton, *a bearer of news from Shrewsbury*

Scrope, Archbishop of York

Lord Bardolph, *a rebel against King Henry IV*

Thomas, Lord Mowbray, *the Earl Marshal, a rebel against King Henry IV*

Lord Hastings, *a rebel against King Henry IV*

Sir John Coleville, *a rebel against King Henry IV*

Lord Chief Justice

His Servant

Gower, *a Messenger*

Sir John Falstaff, *an "irregular humorist"*

His Page, *an "irregular humorist"*

Bardolph, *an "irregular humorist"*

Poins, *an "irregular humorist"*

Ancient Pistol, *an "irregular humorist"*

Peto, *an "irregular humorist"*

Mistress Quickly, *hostess of a tavern*

Doll Tearsheet, *a whore*

Snare, *a sergeant*

Fang, *a sergeant*

Neville, Earl of Warwick, *a supporter of King Henry*

Earl of Surrey, *a supporter of King Henry*

Earl of Westmorland, *a supporter of King Henry*

Harcourt, *a supporter of King Henry*

Sir John Blunt, *a supporter of King Henry*

Robert Shallow, *a country justice*

Silence, *a country justice*

Davy, *Shallow's servant*

Ralph Mouldy, *a man levied to fight for King Henry*

Simon Shadow, *a man levied to fight for King Henry*

Thomas Wart, *a man levied to fight for King Henry*

Francis Feeble, *a man levied to fight for King Henry*

Peter Bullcalf, *a man levied to fight for King Henry*

Porter *of Northumberland's*   Messenger
   household   Sneak and other musicians
Drawers   Lord Chief Justice's men,
Beadles   soldiers and attendants
Grooms

ECAUSE THE TITLE of this play so clearly indicates that it is a sequel, and, moreover, a sequel to a play that had by the mid-twentieth century become extremely popular, *The Second Part of Henry the Fourth,* as it was called in both the 1600 Quarto and the First Folio of 1623, has frequently been underestimated by critics, readers, and theater directors. The Quarto title page stressed, presumably for the delectation of interested purchasers, that the play would contain not only the story of the King's death and of the "coronation of Henry the Fifth," but also "the humours of Sir John Falstaff, and swaggering Pistol." Whether critics agreed with the eighteenth-century editor Samuel Johnson that Falstaff "has nothing in him that can be esteemed" or whether, with the Romantic William Hazlitt and his followers, they flatly preferred the fat rogue to Prince Hal, the appeal of Falstaff was so considerable that the two *Henry IV* plays have often been combined as a kind of *"Falstaffiad"*: the best example of this is Orson Welles's 1965 film *Chimes at Midnight.* But the play has much more to offer than a continuation of the Falstaff story. It is brilliantly constructed; it deploys characters and types with remarkable deftness; and its ear for language is unerring, from the "high" (Henry IV's lament on kingship; King Henry V's accession speech), to the "low." Not only does it address some of the established symmetries of *Part 1* (for example, Hal's quest for father figures), but it also powerfully explores what lies beyond them.

In the tavern scene of *Henry IV Part 2,* which in so many ways parallels—and parodies—the tavern scene of *Part 1,* Prince Hal's friend Ned Poins, observing Falstaff with the whore Doll Tearsheet perched on his knee, remarks to the Prince, and to the world at large, "Is it not strange that desire should so many years outlive performance?" (2.4.234–235). This wry comment might well serve as a useful epigraph for this entire play, for in a sense every person, every value, every energy, and every desire, with the sole exception of those belonging to Prince Hal himself, seems in *Part 2* to have outlived its performance. The word "performance" here carries both its core notion of doing or accomplishing (with a specific sexual implication that still attaches to the word today) and the ceremonial or theatrical association that we now regularly link with the stage and with "actors." (The gravedigger in *Hamlet* will parse "to act" and "to perform" in a related way.) What seemed lively, improvised, energetic, and hopeful in *Part 1* now seems enervated, tawdry, and corrupted.

The play begins with the appearance of Rumour, "painted full of tongues"— presumably wearing a garment adorned with tongues, to suggest the ubiquity and multiplicity of rumors in the world, just as in the famous "Rainbow portrait" of Queen Elizabeth (attributed to Isaac Oliver ca. 1600) the Queen would be depicted wearing a cloak adorned with eyes and ears, implying that she sees and hears everything. The goddess Rumor (or Fama) was a memorable figure in Virgil's *Aeneid* (book 4), Ovid's *Metamorphoses* (book 12), and Chaucer's *Hous of Fame*. In Virgil she is "a vast, fearful monster, with a watchful eye miraculously set under every feather which grows on her, and for every one of them a tongue in a mouth which is loud of speech, and an ear ever alert" (*Aeneid,* book 4, lines 180–183).[1] Transformed into a dramatic character, she is not only a striking visual figure but also a useful mode of narration, linking this play to the previous one by reminding the audience of the King's victory at Shrewsbury and the death of Hotspur. The play's Rumour is also, with her many tongues, a reminder of the Tower of Babel, and the chaos it brought to humanity. "Upon my tongues," says Rumour, "continual slanders ride, / The which in every language I pronounce" (Induction 6–7). Once, according to the Book of Genesis, "the whole earth had one language and few words," and men gathered together to build a tower with its top in the heavens. But the Lord, seeing this act of pride and ambition, thwarted their intentions, determining to "confound their language, that they may not understand one another's speech" (Genesis 11:1, 7). The project failed, and confusion came upon the earth. It is a similar kind of confusion that has descended upon England as *Henry IV Part 2* opens, a confusion closely related to the question of language, which, as the medium of political role-playing, was one of Prince Hal's principal areas of study in *Part 1*. Late in *Part 2,* Warwick will make the same point:

> The Prince but studies his companions,
> Like a strange tongue, wherein, to gain the language,
> 'Tis needful that the most immodest word
> Be looked upon and learnt. . . .
>
> 2 Henry IV *4.3.68–71*

But the moral Warwick draws from his figure of speech about the Prince's language lessons is a far harsher one, for once Hal learns the "strange tongue" that is the lingua franca of his low companions, those words—which is to say, those companions—will come to "no further use / But to be known and hated" (4.3.72–73). Warwick's word "known" echoes the opening line of Hal's soliloquy in *Part 1,* "I know you all" (1.2), in which the young Prince outlined this very strategy.

Rumour appears in this play as the principle of disorder in language, the proliferation of false tongues ("Stuffing the ears of men with false reports" [Induction 8]), and, characteristically, Rumour produces a lie: the false report that Hotspur lives, and that Prince Hal is dead. This lie is the pattern and the prefiguration of the larger lie that the play as a whole will have to refute: the lie that Hal is still an incurable wastrel, and that under his kingship order will die. "Let order die!" is the desperate declaration of Northumberland, the father of Hotspur (Harry Percy), when at last he receives the news of his son's death (1.1.154). "The times are wild" (1.1.9), he says—and, according to Rumour, he himself is "crafty-sick," feigning illness to avoid the rebels and the battlefield. In another sense, however, his faked sickness is a real one, though one he himself has not recognized or diagnosed. For virtually everyone in this play is sick. "[W]e are all diseased," says the Archbishop of York, "of which disease / Our late King Richard, being infected, died" (4.1.54–58). The disease that afflicts them is the lingering curse of anarchy and usurpation, of having offended God.

This opening scene, which shows Northumberland receiving first the false rumor of his son's victory and then the true report of his death, gives way to a second scene, in which we encounter Falstaff, whose very name begins to echo the theme of falsehood set in train by Rumour. And Falstaff's first words in this play confirm the diagnosis of rampant and persistent illness, as he inquires about a doctor's report on his urine and then begins to descant on deafness, consumption, old age, and the probability of venereal disease. The whole world of the play is, in effect, sick of a social disease, of which Falstaff becomes, increasingly, the sign and the emblem of disintegration. He is now accompanied everywhere he goes by a tiny page, and he lumbers about the estate very much like Don Armado, the braggart soldier in *Love's Labour's Lost* who was pursued, and taunted, by the tiny and witty Moth. Since we will learn later in the play that Falstaff, "now Sir John," was once "a boy, and page to Thomas Mowbray" (3.2.22), the sense of a falling-off from that heroic generation of warriors is underscored. Mowbray, encountered in the trial-by-combat scene in *Richard II*, was exiled from England and died a hero's death in the Crusades, fighting an external war on behalf of his lost country. Falstaff, by contrast, larger than life and very much in England, is still loudly seeking for a horse, the horse he never got in *Part 1* when Hal provided him with a "charge of foot," or infantry. As scene 2 opens his confederate Bardolph has gone to Smithfield, the site of London's central meat market, to buy a horse for him, and as the play ends we hear Falstaff, galvanized by the news of Hal's succession to the throne, call out, "Let us take any man's horses—the laws of England are at my commandment" (5.3.125–126).

Henry IV Part 1 presented a psychomachia, Prince's Hal's choice between Falstaff and Hotspur as alternative models. In *Part 2*, although Falstaff's status in the world has gone up (he has his sword and buckler borne before him by a page, and wants twenty-two yards of satin for his cloak and breeches), the man is shrunk, or rather swollen, into a mere metaphor of himself. Where in *Part 1* he descanted on the concept of honor, if only to question and reject it, in this play his corresponding long soliloquy is not on honor but on sack. Sack, a white wine imported from Spain and the Canary Islands (compare Sir Toby's "cup of canary" in *Twelfth Night* [1.3.68]), generally designates a sweet wine of the sherry class, despite the fact that "sack" probably derives from *sec,* "dry." In *Part 1* Falstaff talks about "sack and sugar" as the comforting drink of old age (2.5.428–430), so perhaps even a sweet wine is not sweet enough for him. In any case, the change from "honor" to "sack" is a parodic example of material culture, the devolution from principles to potables. The Falstaff of this play is a living emblem of appetite. He is instantly recognizable, even to the rebel knight Coleville, by his huge stomach: "I have a whole school of tongues in this belly of mine, and not a tongue of them all speaks any other word but my name" (4.2.16–18). His belly declares his name as clearly as if he were a character in a modern political cartoon—as, in some measure, he already is. The tavern over which he presides is now frankly a brothel, a bawdy house, inhabited not only by the Hostess, Mistress Quickly, but also by the whore Doll Tearsheet. The whole world of *Part 2* is decaying and darkening. Indeed, Falstaff himself must begin to face the inevitability of death, although he will not believe it. "[W]hen wilt thou leave fighting o'days, and foining o'nights, and begin to patch up thine old body for heaven?" Doll Tearsheet asks him, and he replies, "Peace, good Doll, do not speak like a death's-head, do not bid me remember mine end" (2.4.206–210). His allusion here is to the memento mori tradition, deriving from the medieval period but newly energized in early modern Europe, in which Martin Luther wore a death's-head ring and the poet John Donne would sleep, by choice, next to his own funeral effigy.

Just as Falstaff's belly says *his* name, declaring his identity with a "whole school of tongues," names in general in this play show us a great deal about its shrunken character. Many characters could almost be described, as Lord Bardolph describes the rebel troops, as "the names of men instead of men" (1.3.57). The surnames of the women in the brothel—"Quick-lie," "Tear-sheet"—proclaim their owners' profession, in the style of "humors" associated more frequently with the city comedies of Shakespeare's contemporary Ben Jonson, whose characters rejoice in names like Subtle, Face, Lovewit, Dol Common, Morose, and Epicene. In *Henry IV Part 2* we encounter not only Doll Tearsheet and Mistress Quickly but also sergeants called Fang and Snare, and foolish justices called Shallow and Silence—"Silence" being a very suitable name, as Falstaff notes, for a justice of the peace. Yet Justice Silence is far from silent: when he is drunk he sings ballads. The play seems to be moving, quite deliberately, in the direction of types and humors, not as a way of abandoning dramatic realism, but rather to mark the difference between the worlds of *Part 1* and *Part 2*. Falstaff's ragged army recruits have names like Feeble, Mouldy, Shadow, and Wart, one-dimensional names, although these bravely sorry figures—fine small parts in the play—have some individuality and dignity about them. Even Hotspur's magnificent nickname has become a bathetic pun: "Said he young Harry Percy's spur was cold? / Of Hotspur, 'Coldspur'?" (1.1.49–50). The speaker of these lines is Hotspur's father, Northumberland. And the effect upon the drama of such desperate wordplay is as distressing as it is jarring. As Falstaff enlarges, in a kind of moral dropsy, other characters and values are dwindling to shadows of their former selves.

One way of mapping the decline is to notice how much of this play is written in prose. Almost every scene in verse is followed immediately by a longer one in prose, full of topical humor, bawdy puns, sexual innuendo and braggadocio, and endless discussions of how much things cost. The prose world is swallowing up the world of poetry, just as, in Falstaff's own significantly chosen image, he himself is like a sow who has swallowed up all her litter but one. The gender-crossing here—Falstaff as sow rather than boar—is a small note but, yet again, a significant one. In *Part 1* the most grandiloquent figure of heroic poetry was Hotspur, whose own distrust of courtly language and rhetoric was yet another sign of his idealism, if also of his naïveté. The audience is forcefully reminded of Hotspur's absence, and of the spirit he represented and continues to represent, by Lady Percy's beautiful, evocative speech in act 2, a passage that takes explicit account of what is *absent* from this play:

> He was indeed the glass
> Wherein the noble youth did dress themselves.
> He had no legs that practised not his gait;
> And speaking thick, which nature made his blemish,
> Became the accents of the valiant;
> For those that could speak low and tardily
> Would turn their own perfection to abuse
> To seem like him. So that in speech, in gait,
> In diet, in affections of delight,
> In military rules, humours of blood,
> He was the mark and glass, copy and book,
> That fashioned others. . . .
>
> *2.3.21–32*

A version of this same sentiment will turn up in *Hamlet,* again presented from the perspective of love, nostalgia, and loss: Ophelia's memory of a Hamlet before his present melancholy—which is to say, before the play begins—as "[t]he glass of fashion and the mould of form" (*Hamlet* 3.1.152). The glass, or mirror, as we have noted in connection with earlier plays like *Richard III* and *Richard II,* is the emblem or model for deportment and statecraft. In the deposition scene in *Richard II* the King called for a looking glass and then shattered it, as a sign of his own disintegration and the loss of kingship. In *Henry V* the former Prince Hal will appear, transformed, as "the mirror of all Christian kings" (2.0.6). But in *Henry IV Part 2,* with the death of Hotspur, the mirror of nobility, "the glass / Wherein the noble youth did dress themselves," is lost, and mourned.

Instead of Hotspur, the valiant epic warrior who was "the theme of honour's tongue" in *Part 1,* we now have Ancient Pistol. An Elizabethan pistol was a relatively primitive weapon, likely to go off, without warning, at any time. (The first pistols, or pistolets, in England are described in texts dating from the mid-to-late sixteenth century.) Pistol—whose rank of "ancient" (a rank also held by Iago in *Othello*) is a corruption of "ensign," and means "standard-bearer"—is the embodiment of the "braggart soldier," or *miles gloriosus,* a stock character dating back to Roman times. Where Hotspur was impatient with words, Pistol is all mouth. Even Doll Tearsheet, herself a handy woman with an oath, calls him "the foul-mouthedest rogue in England" (2.4.61). Pistol replaces Hotspur as the spokesman of heroic sentiment, and becomes yet another sign of what is happening in this play's world. We noted in connection with Hotspur's character and language that they closely resembled, and also seemed dryly to comment upon, the actions and speech of Christopher Marlowe's Tamburlaine. Hotspur, like Tamburlaine, is a hyperbolic figure, an "overreacher," too big for the world that contains him. With this model in mind, the audience of *Henry IV Part 2* encounters an Ancient Pistol who constantly spouts jumbled fragments of Marlowe and other Elizabethan playwrights. Thus, for example, Pistol invokes "pack-horses / And hollow pampered jades of Asia" (2.4.140–141) in place of Tamburlaine's great challenge to his enemies, "Holla, ye pamper'd jades of Asia!" (*2 Tamburlaine* 4.3.1), spoken by Marlowe's hero when he has harnessed the Asian kings to his chariot and strikes them with a whip. Taken out of context, spoken by a posturing mock-heroic or antiheroic opportunist like Pistol, Tamburlaine's heroic verbiage becomes merely empty and ludicrous display. The effect is both deliberate and wickedly witty, as Shakespeare once again "sends up" his rival Marlowe even as he records his own admiration for the sounding periods of his verse. By contrast, Pistol's own language, like the weapon that gives him his name, is both explosive and inefficient, a fitting counterpart to "Rumour painted full of tongues." The audience may well have sympathized with Falstaff in *Part 1* and may even be inclined to continue its affection in *Part 2,* but it is not so easy to find a kind word to say about Pistol. Not even the whores have much to say on his behalf—although we will learn at the beginning of *Henry V* that he has married Mistress Quickly, and that he lives on, as such gleefully unprincipled characters often do, even as regimes and circumstances change.

Hotspur is gone, and with him has gone a certain concept of honor. Falstaff, as we have noted, now soliloquizes instead on sack, and in place of honor as a grand political ideal we have the coldhearted and cold-blooded betrayal of the rebels by Prince John, Hal's younger brother, at Gaultres Forest. In one of the most chilling moments in Shakespearean drama, John persuades the rebels that they will be given mercy, watches serenely while their armies disband, and then arrests them for treason and sends them to be executed, concluding sanctimoniously, "God, and not we, hath safely fought today" (4.1.347). (This lofty sentiment, spoken by so cold and antipathetic a character, will be repeated with a difference in *Henry V,* when after the hard-fought battle of Agincourt the King will say gratefully, "God fought for us" [*Henry V* 4.8.114].) Throughout the scene of the betrayal at Gaultres Forest we hear over and over again the word "shallow," which becomes a kind of subliminal watchword for *Henry IV Part 2.* "You are too shallow, Hastings, much too shallow," says Prince John (4.1.276), and "Most shallowly did you these arms commence, / Fondly brought forth, and foolishly sent hence" (4.1.344–345). Shallow actions, shallow motives, and a justice called Shallow replace an idealistic—if unrealistic—world in which Hotspur could imagine diving into "the bottom of the deep" in order to "pluck up drownèd honour by the locks" (*1 Henry IV* 1.3.201, 203).

Thus in every aspect of this play—in language, in honor, in literal illness and crafty sickness—the theme of disease and decay predominates, and the language of disease culminates, as we should expect in Shakespeare, with the sickness of the King, which seems to emerge, full-blown, out of all the metaphors that surround him. John of Gaunt had admonished Richard II, "Thy deathbed is no lesser than thy land / Wherein thou liest in reputation sick" (*Richard II* 2.1.95–96). This figure of speech is now transformed into visible dramatic action, as King Henry IV creeps feebly onto the stage, dressed in his nightgown, at the beginning of act 3, to complain that he is unable to sleep:

> How many thousand of my poorest subjects
> Are at this hour asleep? O sleep, O gentle sleep,
> Nature's soft nurse, how have I frighted thee . . . ?
> . . . .
> Canst thou, O partial sleep, give thy repose
> To the wet sea-boy in an hour so rude,
> And in the calmest and most stillest night,
> With all appliances and means to boot,
> Deny it to a king? Then happy low, lie down.
> Uneasy lies the head that wears a crown.
>
> *3.1.4–6, 26–31*

King Henry's sleeplessness, and the language in which he describes it, may well remind a Shakespearean audience of Richard III, and of the later figure of Macbeth—both, like Henry IV, kings with murder on their conscience, who have in effect "murdered sleep" (*Macbeth* 2.2.40). But Henry here speaks, as well, about the limits and demands of kingship, its responsibilities, and, above all, its loneliness, lessons his son has also begun to suspect, and will have to learn. King Henry's death in act 4 is foretokened by omens, very similar to those that created the topsy-turvy world of *A Midsummer Night's Dream:* the River Thames overflows its banks; the seasons have altered, producing a warm winter and a cold summer; and unnatural monsters are begotten and born. For the figures of authority, Henry IV and the Lord Chief Justice, the future seems to hold an even more severe reversal of order, with the anticipated coming of the "wastrel" Prince Hal to the throne. "O God, I fear all will be overturned" (5.2.19), exclaims the Chief Justice, and King Henry anticipates with dread a time when England will become an antigovernment, a haven for all the thieves and murderers of Europe:

> Have you a ruffian that will swear, drink, dance,
> Revel the night, rob, murder, and commit
> The oldest sins the newest kind of ways?
> Be happy; he will trouble you no more.
> England shall double gild his treble guilt,
> England shall give him office, honour, might;
> For the fifth Harry from curbed licence plucks
> The muzzle of restraint, and the wild dog
> Shall flesh his tooth on every innocent.
>
> *4.3.252–260*

These dire predictions of anarchy, of a world turned upside down in bitter reality, and without prospect of a carnival reversal, derive from the fact that neither the King nor the Chief Justice knows what the audience knows: that Hal is continuing to play a role, and that he will return, transformed, as the prodigal son returned, who had been "as dead" to his father, "was lost, and is found" (Luke 15:24).

Hal, on the other hand, is increasingly aware of his role and of its limitations, as he will later learn firsthand the limits of kingship. He is aware, that is to say, of his humanity. "Doth it not show vilely in me to desire small beer?" he asks Poins in act 2, scene 2. "Small beer" was beer of a weak or inferior quality, and thus referred by extension to trivial matters or persons of little importance. Hal longs for—and faults himself for wanting—both a commoner's drink and common companions to drink with. Hal cannot show sorrow at his father's sickness, although he feels it, because every man would think him, as Poins does, a "most princely hypocrite" (2.2.42). "It would be every man's thought, and thou art a blessed fellow to think as every man thinks," agrees the Prince. "Every man would think me an hypocrite indeed" (2.2.43–44, 46). So although Hal is still *in* the tavern world there is a sense in which he is no longer *of* it. Part of his strength in this play will be to emerge from behind the clouds, to show himself as sun and son.

It is worth noting that in *Henry IV Part 2*, a play deftly designed to be a counterfoil and answer to *Part 1*, the central tavern scene is once again located in act 2, scene 5, and the audience comes upon the Prince and Poins about to perform another play, about to disguise themselves as they did in *Part 1* when they became "buckram men" and robbed Falstaff. But Hal now sees this act of costuming—in this case, as "drawers," tavern waiters or tapsters—as a "low transformation." It is now explicitly intended as a fictive vehicle for him, allowing him to descend into the tavern world. In fact, his entry into the world of Falstaff and company now looks more like a classical "descent into the underworld," undertaken by a hero (Ulysses, for example, or Aeneas) who is on a greater quest. "She's in hell already," says Falstaff of Doll Tearsheet—but she is not the only one. Like Falstaff and the others who inhabit it, the tavern is now a shadow or shade of its former self. Its energy seems to have been sapped. Bawdy jokes on discharging and on "foining," or thrusting, are now the main topic of conversation, and these are terms of *war* that are being trivialized. The tavern world, manifestly unfit for the play's new reality, turns warfare into a dirty joke. Thus it is fitting that Hal's final moment of misrule and holiday in the world of the tavern is interrupted—as was also the case in *Part 1*—by a reminder of war and of the outside world of society and politics. There is a knock at the door, and Peto appears with the news that a dozen constables are searching for Falstaff, who is derelict in his duty, having failed to join his soldiers. Once again Hal sounds a familiar note of temporality: "By heaven, Poins, I feel me much to blame / So idly to profane the precious time" (2.4.330–331). Time, precious time, Hal's own commodity, is running out. The King is dying, and England will be either redeemed or lost.

Again, just as in *Part 1*, the King and the Prince are cleverly kept apart by the playwright until the moment of greatest drama and greatest suspense, which here falls very late—in this case act 4, scene 3, the scene at the King's deathbed, where Hal, thinking that his father is dead, puts the royal crown on his own head. His action, in crowning himself, is the reversal—and the dramatic redemption—of Richard II's deposition ceremony. "With mine own hands I give away my crown," said Richard. Hal, with *his* own hands, takes it back, and thus initiates an upward movement, a movement of kingly ascension, that will continue through, and culminate in, *Henry V*. For the son is virtually from the first aware of things his father had spent a lifetime discovering, including the paradoxical pain of kingship and its human cost:

Prince Harry   Why doth the crown lie there upon his pillow,
Being so troublesome a bedfellow?
O polished perturbation, golden care,
That keep'st the ports of slumber open wide
To many a watchful night! . . .
. . . .
                      O majesty,
When thou dost pinch thy bearer, thou dost sit
Like a rich armour worn in heat of day,
That scald'st with safety. . . .

4.3.151–161

When King Henry IV awakes, accuses his son of covetous usurpation, and then hears his explanation for taking the crown, the effect is very like that achieved by Hal's various masquerades throughout these plays:

> O my son,
> God put it in thy mind to take it hence,
> That thou mightst win the more thy father's love.
>
> *4.3.305–307*

It is not an accident that the topic of greatest concern to both father and son, which dominates the balance of this scene, is that of legitimacy in rule. King Henry IV sees himself as accursed because he is a usurper, and the pattern of the House of Lancaster seems almost as if it might parallel that of the House of Atreus in Greek tragedy, cycle after cycle of vengeance, sin, and retribution. The fear of talionic justice, an eye for an eye, haunts the King and the scene. Thus we hear no fewer than four times in this one fairly brief scene an insistent mention of legal succession. The world's whole strength, says Hal, "shall not force / This lineal honour from me" (4.3.175–176). And later in the scene, speaking of the crown, he says, "Accusing it, I put it on my head, / To try with it . . . / The quarrel of a true inheritor" (293–296). For his part, King Henry, reflecting on the "indirect crook'd ways" he himself came to the crown, points out to Hal that "thou the garland wear'st successively" (312, 329)—that Hal inherits, and does not usurp, the crown. This is a belief that Hal entirely shares:

> My gracious liege,
> You won it, wore it, kept it, gave it me;
> Then plain and right must my possession be.
>
> *4.3.348–350*

The "plainness" and "rightness" of this view may seem less obvious to the audience, but it is true that Hal is not a usurper, and it is also true that he has in some sense set out to earn the crown by merit—a far cry from Richard II's ineffectual claim of divine right—by sending himself to school among the people. He is on his way, dramatically at least, to a representative and human kingship, although it is at the same time a kingship of loneliness and restraint. Both will make themselves felt in *Henry V*.

For King Henry IV, and for the old order, time is rapidly running out, and Henry now knows that he will never make his pilgrimage to the Holy Land. His motives for that pilgrimage have always been complex—his dying advice to Hal is to "busy giddy minds / with foreign quarrels" (4.3.342), to turn the energies of chaos and war outward, toward other lands, avoiding the divisive scourge of civil war, that unnamed sickness that has, throughout this play, threatened to consume the land. There is no question but that Henry's planned pilgrimage and Crusade were in part political, a strategy to dissipate what he calls "inward wars" (3.1.102). But increasingly the pilgrimage to Jerusalem has become a moral or ethical journey as well, an intended voyage of expiation, to free the King of the sin of Richard's murder. The last Englishman named in these plays who had died a heroic death in the Holy Land was Thomas Mowbray, Henry's first opponent at the beginning of *Richard II*. His last opponent, here in *Henry IV Part 2,* is Falstaff, the living embodiment of anarchy, misrule, and dissent within England—Falstaff, who had once been Mowbray's page. King Henry seems to view the voyage to Jerusalem as a kind of spiritual cure, but he dies, ironically, not in the Holy Land but in a chamber called "Jerusalem." The prophecy that told him he would "die in Jerusalem" is fulfilled, but, as always, with a bitter twist. Prophecies in these plays, once made, will always come true—but the meaning of the truth is a kind of riddle, as it was with Richard III (who was told he would die once he "saw Richmond") and as it will be, famously, with Macbeth. Henry's death in the Jerusalem Chamber has some affinities with the death of Moses, who led the Israelites to the mountaintop and glimpsed the Promised Land but could not enter it. It is Hal, and not his father, who will complete the journey, and will attempt to restore the Edenic land of milk and honey.

With the death of the King, the way is clear for Prince Hal to acquire a new father in the final scenes of the play, a father whose symbolic nature, representing the law, will displace both Henry IV and his antitype in Falstaff. This new "father," so named by Hal himself, is the Chief Justice. The Chief Justice, we may recall, had entertained the direst views of the future of England with Hal as its king: "I fear all will be overturned," he said. This view, it appears, is shared at least in part by Prince Hal's brothers, for when he enters in act 5, scene 2, as the new King, Henry V, their faces show something of their fear. To them the King speaks in words that establish England as the land of civility as well as civilization:

> This new and gorgeous garment, majesty,
> Sits not so easy on me as you think.
> Brothers, you mix your sadness with some fear.
> This is the English not the Turkish court;
> Not Amurath an Amurath succeeds,
> But Harry Harry.

> *5.2.44–49*

The allusion is to Amurath of Turkey, a sultan who strangled his brothers when he came to the throne so they would not rival or threaten him. The line, in its rich incantation, serves, I think, as a final rejection of the exoticism and savageness of Marlowe, whose plays resound with the names of pagans and Turks. Henry V's language in this scene becomes the language of kingship, the language of majesty and of transformation, never more powerful than in this amazing speech:

> My father is gone wild into his grave,
> For in his tomb lie my affections;
> And with his spirits sadly I survive
> To mock the expectation of the world,
> To frustrate prophecies, and to raze out
> Rotten opinion, who hath writ me down
> After my seeming. The tide of blood in me
> Hath proudly flowed in vanity till now.
> Now doth it turn, and ebb back to the sea,
> Where it shall mingle with the state of floods,
> And flow henceforth in formal majesty.
>
> *5.2.122–132*

This speech is, structurally and emblematically, the pendant or reply to his "I know you all" soliloquy in *Part 1*. It is not, of course, itself a soliloquy, but rather a formal address to the nation. Hal, now Harry, is no longer a prince in training, or a man in disguise. He will now "raze out / Rotten opinion," which is another way of saying that he will defeat "Rumour painted full of tongues." And the "tide of blood" in him, which will now flow in formal majesty, defeats and reverses all the images of overflowing rivers we have encountered in this play and in its predecessor, including the river that overflowed at the King's death, and the river Hotspur wished to move out of its course. What is perhaps most striking about the new King's address is that he picks up, for the first time, the royal "we," legitimately speaking for England, before returning to the more comfortable and familiar "I," "my," and "Harry":

> Now call we our high court of Parliament.
>
> . . . .
>
> Our coronation done, we will accite,
> As I before remembered, all our state;
> And, God consigning to my good intents,
> No prince nor peer shall have just cause to say,
> "God shorten Harry's happy life one day."
>
> *5.2.133, 140–144*

"Nor prince nor peer." This phrase deliberately includes the Lord Chief Justice, for the new King in this scene chooses, as his inescapable destiny, the law as his father. There is a mastery to the way in which he deals with the Chief Justice while still playing out his old role of the prodigal son who has "wasted his substance in riotous living" (as Saint Luke has it), and who returns to his father—

here a new father—as if from the dead. Curiously but appropriately, the Chief Justice presents his case to the new King in the form of a projected play, a play very like the Hal-Falstaff mumming play of *Henry IV Part 1*:

> Question your royal thoughts, make the case yours,
> Be now the father, and propose a son;
> Hear your own dignity so much profaned,
> See your most dreadful laws so loosely slighted,
> Behold yourself so by a son disdained;
> And then imagine me taking your part,
> And in your power soft silencing your son.
>
> *5.2.90–96*

The King's reply is swift and conclusive: "You shall be as a father to my youth" (5.2.117). In this play, which reduces so many characters to symbols and names, the King now embraces a "father" who is the living symbol of justice, law, and rule.

The audience cannot be entirely surprised—although the irrepressible Falstaff is—that in the next scene this King will reject Misrule. Just as in *Part 1* Hal was measured by his similarity to, and distance from, the apparently antithetical figures of Hotspur and Falstaff, so in *Part 2* Falstaff is juxtaposed on the one hand to the Lord Chief Justice of England and on the other to the elderly, lecherous, and foolish Justice Shallow. Shakespeare points up this comparison by focusing attention on the sum of a thousand pounds, for at the beginning of the play Falstaff tries to borrow that amount from the Chief Justice, and at the end we learn that he has in fact succeeded in getting the loan from Justice Shallow. Falstaff does not grow and change as his world changes, and as Prince Hal changes, and so the play, however regretfully, leaves him behind. The last scene shows him virtually indistinguishable from Shallow, whom he both resembles and despises; they are two self-deluded old men unfit to live in Hal's new world. The Chief Justice has all along been Falstaff's enemy, hunting him from tavern to tavern. Falstaff's receipt of the news of his Hal's succession is therefore a cry of triumph: "[T]he laws of England are at my commandment. Blessed are they that have been my friends, and woe to my Lord Chief Justice" (5.3.125–127). Although he has noticed that his old friend Shallow now closely resembles his own servants, and that the servants are foolish justices like Shallow, Falstaff fails to see that he himself has undergone a similar downward metamorphosis, so that of the two schoolfellows who once heard the chimes at midnight together there is now little to choose between them. So, with Shallow in tow as a morsel of amusement, Falstaff races off to London to greet the new King. But Falstaff, the Lord of Misrule, makes a fatal error, for the king he greets is the wrong one: "God save thy grace, King Hal, my royal Hal! . . . God save thee, my sweet boy!" (5.5.39, 41). What a mistake to make. Hal, and the "boy," are gone. This is King Henry V. Rule, Christian Rule, now sits on the throne.

The moment that follows, although it is inevitable, is nonetheless one of the most devastating in any of Shakespeare's plays, as the young King, with ice in his voice, instructs, "My Lord Chief Justice, speak to that vain man." When Falstaff persists, the King says:

> I know thee not, old man. Fall to thy prayers.
> How ill white hairs become a fool and jester!
> I have long dreamt of such a kind of man,
> So surfeit-swelled, so old, and so profane;
> But being awaked, I do despise my dream.
>
> . . . .
>
> Presume not that I am the thing I was.
>
> 5.5.45–54

"Presume not that I am the thing I was" is the final echo of "I know you all," and indeed of the clipped and chilling "I do; I will" with which a younger Hal responded to Falstaff's "banish plump Jack, and banish all the world." Falstaff, who has throughout these two plays boasted of his youth ("They hate us youth," he half joked in *Part 1*), is now unmasked as an "old man," and as a "fool and jester." Falstaff, together with his fellows, is indeed banished. The punishment that was given to Bolingbroke and Mowbray at the beginning of *Richard II* now comes home. Falstaff himself becomes, in effect, one of the figures excluded from a comic world whose exclusion helps to define and delimit that world. The audience cannot help but feel that this is harsh. Characteristically, it is the cold-blooded Prince John, the betrayer of Gaultres Forest, who most applauds the banishment of Falstaff, and this is, incidentally, a brilliant move on the part of the playwright, who allows us a soupçon of righteous indignation on Falstaff's behalf, while at the same time preparing us to accept the necessity of the new King Henry's action. Misrule must be banished in order for Rule to thrive, for order to live and not to die.

The banishment of Falstaff, the end of this kind of holiday, is part of the essential hardship of being a king. The king's role, as will become even clearer in *Henry V*, is a quintessentially lonely one, and the lack of forgiveness shown to Falstaff is part of the cost of being King.

The Merry Wives of Windsor

DRAMATIS PERSONAE

Mistress Margaret Page, *citizen of Windsor*

Master George Page, *citizen of Windsor*

Anne Page, *their daughter, citizen of Windsor*

William Page, *their son, citizen of Windsor*

Mistress Alice Ford, *citizen of Windsor*

Master Frank Ford, *her husband, citizen of Windsor*

John, *their servant*

Robert, *their servant*

Sir John Falstaff

Bardolph, *Sir John Falstaff's follower*

Pistol, *Sir John Falstaff's follower*

Nim, *Sir John Falstaff's follower*

Robin, *Sir John Falstaff's page*

The Host of the Garter Inn

Sir Hugh Evans, *a Welsh parson*

Doctor Caius, *a French physician*

Mistress Quickly, *his housekeeper*

John Rugby, *his servant*

Master Fenton, *a young gentleman, in love with Anne Page*

Master Abraham Slender

Robert Shallow, *his uncle, a Justice*

Peter Simple, *Slender's servant*

Children of Windsor, *appearing as fairies*

HE MERRY WIVES OF WINDSOR is a lively "citizen comedy" that anticipates, in its spirit, both Restoration drama and the screwball comedy of early-twentieth-century film, combining as it does elements of farce, comic violence, and sophisticated and witty dialogue. The typical characters of citizen comedy are middle-class tradesmen and merchants rather than the kings, nobles, and aristocrats who dominate in most of Shakespeare's more familiar plays, and thus at first glance *Merry Wives* may seem idiosyncratic, playful, and less than profound—not, in short, really "Shakespearean."

The fact that the butt of many of the jokes is Sir John Falstaff, the rotund and orotund friend of Prince Hal from the *Henry IV* plays, has disconcerted some of Falstaff's most uncritical critical admirers, whose demurrals sound upon occasion like Troilus discovering the unhappy truth about Cressida: "This is and is not Cressid." Fans of the "fat knight" have likewise wished to believe that the Sir John of *Merry Wives* is and is not Falstaff. For although he has the same name, the same boon companions (Bardolph, Nim, Pistol, even Mistress

Quickly), the same propensity for theft, for eating and drinking, and for hiding behind an arras when threatened with exposure, those who find his antics and discomfitures in *Merry Wives* undignified tend to echo the Epilogue of *2 Henry IV* in claiming "this is not the man."

But a closer look at both the play and its version of Falstaff will disclose much that is appealingly and recognizably "Shakespearean" and, indeed, Falstaffian. As has been often observed, literary characters have only the reality that the author's language imparts to them—and, in the case of drama, the reality given them by actor, director, staging, and theatrical effect. The Falstaff of *The Merry Wives of Windsor* fancies himself a more irresistible ladies' man, and a better intriguer, than either the audience or the "wives" can find him to be. Yet whatever pathos attaches to the rejected companion of Prince Hal's youth at the end of *2 Henry IV* is in this play replaced by broad comedy, as Falstaff's three attempts at seduction (of the same woman!) have three humiliating outcomes. The first attempt finds him hiding from a jealous husband in a buck-basket full of dirty and malodorous washing, then carried out of the house ignominiously and dumped into a ditch; the second attempt requires him to escape disguised as a fat old woman of the neighborhood, though his masquerade is belied by his beard; and the third finds him wandering around in the woods at night, wearing a self-assumed pair of horns, and claiming by this costume to look like a buck in rut rather than that other traditional wearer of horns, a cuckold.

The "merry wives" of the title are Mistress Page and Mistress Ford. The structure of the play combines a love plot (the courtship of Mistress Anne Page, the daughter of Master and Mistress Page, by three suitors—two unsuitable, though rich, the third a young man she chooses against her parents' will) with a plot of gulling and revenge (the attempts by Sir John Falstaff to arrange assignations with the two married women, who band together to plot his hilarious comeuppance). There is in addition a prevailing emphasis throughout the play on shifting language and verbal style, from dialect (the Welsh parson and schoolmaster Sir Hugh Evans; the French doctor-suitor Caius) to literary and dramatic allusion gone wild (the constant quotations and misquotations of Pistol), to malapropism, double entendre and sexual innuendo (Mistress Quickly, now the housekeeper for Doctor Caius), and grammatical instruction (the Latin language lesson administered by the parson to young William Page). Combined as these elements are with a rich sense of place and time—the text of the play is dense with local color, references to food, flora and fauna, law and medical practice in the period, exploration and discovery, and more—they generate a compelling dramatic energy as well as a lively portrait of late-sixteenth-century England.

The title of the play is indicative of its multiple directions and references. Windsor, known then as now as the site of a royal castle, was also a market town. The presence in the play of a character called the Host of the Garter Inn takes note of the fact that Windsor—and specifically St. George's Chapel—was the place where knights were formally installed into the honorific Order of the Garter. The castle clean-up superintended by "fairies" in the masque at the end of act 5, which cites the Garter motto *Honi soit qui mal y pense* (Evil to him who thinks evil of it), refers to this ceremony, as does the mention of "our radiant Queen" (5.5.43) and "fair knighthood's bending knee" (69). But the Host, who is the landlord of an inn, is, like the Pages, Fords, doctors, and parsons of the play, distinctly a middle-class rather than a knightly figure, and the fact that the play begins with a discussion of "a gentleman born," coats of arms, and the questionable personal nobility of Sir John Falstaff situates it clearly as a play about the habits and inhabitants of Windsor the town, rather than Windsor Castle. As for "merry," a word that has native Old English roots and means "pleasurable" and "delightful" as well as "amusing," "diverting," and "funny," in context it describes the pleasant characters of the "wives," or married women of the play, their physical attractiveness, and the witty way they turn the tables on Falstaff (and on the jealous husband Ford). That Windsor should have "merry wives" brings it again into the world of commerce and trade rather than of royalty and nobility; these are not "merry ladies."

The appellation "merry" is in fact applied to the Host by Justice Shallow and to the "merry knight" Falstaff by the Host—here the word means something like "pleasure-loving" or "fun-loving," and has a distinct holiday cast, meaning the opposite of workaday or ordinary. Although this is not, strictly speaking, a play about a seasonal festival, it has many of the earmarks of "carnival," a world turned upside down: a knight robbed of his dignity and forced to cross-dress; women who get the better of men; a denouement in the woods with an antihero (Falstaff) dressed like an animal (as Mistress Page says to her friend Mistress Ford, "The truth being known, / We'll all present ourselves, dis-horn the spirit, / And mock him home to Windsor" [4.4.62-64]). Falstaff cross-dressed as the "old woman of Brentford" is Shakespeare's only grown man dressed in women's attire, apart from the very different account we get of Antony in love-play with Cleopatra ("I drunk him to his bed, / then put my tires and mantles on him / whilst I wore his sword Philippan" [*Antony and Cleopatra* 2.5.21-23]). Falstaff in a skirt is much more like the later "Dame" of English pantomime, a comic, ungainly cross-dressed figure, hardly a conventional erotic target. Plainly Falstaff feels this as humiliation. The classical model here is Hercules enslaved to Omphale and forced to spin and do other kinds of women's work. The whole play continues in this spirit of carnival festivity, ending, as we have already noted, in a masque of woodland "fairies," played by schoolchildren and the Welsh schoolmaster Evans, as well as in the hunting of the horned would-be lover. The Order of the Garter may have its thematic place in this cluster, too: one story of its founding—since disputed—is that the garter in question belonged to the Countess of Salisbury, who inadvertently dropped it while dancing with King Edward III. The King is said to have retrieved the garter and tied it to his own leg, admonishing those who thought this an act of flirtation,

"*Honi soit qui mal y pense.*" Thus the noble history of the Order would have begun with an act of royal cross-dressing, at the opposite end of the scale from Falstaff's both in dignity and in morality. (Anyone who "thinks evil" of Falstaff's intentions would be perfectly correct to do so.) We might also recall that all women's parts on the public stage were in Shakespeare's time played by men. Thus the "old woman of Brentford" (Falstaff in disguise) would perhaps not look so very different from Mistress Quickly, described as Doctor Caius's " 'oman, or his dry-nurse, or his cook, or his laundry, his washer, and his wringer." Although in *2 Henry IV* and *Henry V* Mistress Quickly is obviously the madam of a brothel, in *Merry Wives* her role is a less mercenary one, though her sexual double entendres and malapropisms are familiar. A couple of examples will serve for many here: Mistress Quickly's mispronunciation of "virtuous" as "fartuous" in her description of "a civil modest wife" (2.2.90) and the substitution of "erection" for "direction" in her comment to Falstaff about Mistress Ford, "She does so take on with her men; they mistook their erection," to which the irrepressible Falstaff replies, ruefully, "So did I mine" (3.5.34–36).

The most familiar story told about *The Merry Wives of Windsor* is that Queen Elizabeth, delighted with the figure of Falstaff in Shakespeare's *Henry IV*, asked the dramatist to write another play, showing "Falstaff in love." This, if true, would further tie the interests of Windsor Castle to the "merry" citizenry of Windsor. No contemporary account of this supposed request is extant, although the title page of the First Quarto edition of the play does refer to its being played before "her Maiestie" the Queen in London (Windsor Castle was not yet, in Shakespeare's time, the principal royal seat). The story is first told in print by John Dennis in 1702— "This Comedy was written at her Command, and by her direction, an she was so eager to see it Acted, that she commanded it to be finished in fourteen days"—but the version most usually cited is that of Nicholas Rowe, the early-eighteenth-century Shakespeare editor:

> She was so well pleas'd with that admirable Character of *Falstaff*, in the two Parts of *Henry* the Fourth, that she commanded him to continue it for one Play more, and to shew him in Love. This is said to be the Occasion of his Writing *The Merry Wives of Windsor*. How well she was obey'd, the Play itself is an admirable Proof.[1]

The question of the play's chronological placement among the various *Henry* plays has been a matter for scholarly debate. It is clear from a tagline concerning the character of Fenton, Anne Page's favored suitor ("he kept company with the wild Prince and Poins" [3.2.61]), that the audience would have been expected to recognize those names from *1 Henry IV*, at least to the point of noticing that "Falstaff" and the others were also familiar. What is less clear is the time period in which the play is supposedly to be set, since despite this reference to an episode in a play chronicling the history of a medieval monarch, much of the action clearly takes place in "contemporary"—that is, late-sixteenth-century—Windsor, with a personage on the throne who is alluded to as "our radiant Queen" (5.5.43). This mixing of time periods—it would be anachronistic to call it anachronism—would probably not have bothered an Elizabethan audience, and it will only slightly perturb Shakespeare purists today. Scholars have also differed in their views about whether *Merry Wives* was written before, after, or at the same time as *Henry IV Part 2*, a play that introduces a quite different "Mistress Quickly" and the figure of Justice Shallow, as well as the bombastic and loquacious Ancient Pistol. But any watcher or reader of a modern sequel to a film, play, or novel will readily acknowledge the way in which characters change—in temperament, appearance, fortunes, and morality—depending upon what actor plays the part, who has written or underwritten the sequel, and how the action fits into the spirit and curiosity of the times. In other words, while it is of historical and editorial interest to situate this play in regard to the other plays of Shakespeare that present characters of similar names and with similar fictional pasts, it is not entirely useful. Though one can compare the figures of *Merry Wives* with their eponymous counterparts in the *Henry IV* plays, *Merry Wives* can and does stand alone, as its popularity through the ages has suggested. In recent years the victory of the "merry wives" over their husbands and suitors, and the relative plenitude of female roles, has made the play especially attractive to theater audiences in England and the United States, and around the world.

The love plot, centering on the desirable Anne Page (called Mistress, like all adult women of her era and social class, whether married or unmarried), pits two very unsuitable suitors against each other in time-honored and familiar Shakespearean fashion. The rattle-brained Slender, the nephew of the equally well-named Justice Shallow, is persuaded to offer himself as Anne's partner in marriage, though he seems to think that he is doing her a favor rather than the other way around. ("Will you, upon good dowry, marry her?" asks Shallow [1.1.200–201], and Slender replies, "I will marry her, sir, at your request" [206].) Her other approved suitor is Doctor Caius, a French physician, whose mangling of the "King's English" is manifestly meant to be comical, and who fares as poorly, and as amusingly, as those other French manglers of the language, Alice and Catherine in *Henry V*. Slender is Anne's father's choice—as she laments in an aside to the audience, "O, what a world of vile ill-favour'd faults / Looks handsome in three hundred pounds a year!" (3.4.31–32)—and Caius is her mother's:

> Slender, though well landed, is an idiot;
> And he my husband best of all affects.
> The Doctor is well money'd, and his friends
> Potent at court; he, none but he, shall have her.
> Though twenty thousand worthier come to crave her.
>
> *Merry Wives* 4.4.83–87

Mistress Quickly sees the quandary (" 'Nay,' said I, 'will you cast away your child on a fool and a physician?' " [3.4.93–94]), though she is in fact an even-handed abettor to all parties. Anne's own choice is the Host's candidate, "young Master Fenton," whom the Host describes in memorable, indeed irresistible, terms:

> He capers, he dances, he has eyes of youth; he writes verses, he speaks holiday, he smells April and May,
>
> 3.2.56–58

In a play in which smells, including the unsavory smell of the buck-basket full of dirty laundry, play a recurrent part, this account of the favored young man makes him seem, indeed, like a breath of fresh air. Page (the father) regards him as too highborn and as a fortune-hunter, and vows that if Fenton marries Anne it will be without a dowry. Indeed all three suitors take aim at her fortune (as, in *Merchant*, a play with far more "romantic" pretensions, the fortune-hunter Bassanio does with Portia, not to mention Petruchio and the other suitors in *Taming*). But Fenton's love scene with Anne in act 3 makes it clear that he has changed in the course of his courtship. Allowing for differences of literary mode, he sounds, in fact, not unlike Bassanio:

> Albeit I will confess thy father's wealth
> Was the first motive that I woo'd thee, Anne,
> Yet, wooing thee, I found thee of more value
> Than stamps in gold or sums in sealèd bags;
> And 'tis the very riches of thyself
> That now I aim at.
>
> 3.4.13–18

This rather conventional love plot, intermingled with some elements of farce, resolves itself in a "holiday" way when, under cover of the fairy masque staged to spook out Falstaff at the close, Page urges Slender to elope with Anne, whom he will supposedly recognize because she is wearing a white dress, and Mistress Page urges the Doctor to do the same, telling him that Anne will be disguised as a fairy in green. The suitors follow these instructions, with predictably catastrophic results: in each case, once they get to church, they find that they have married, or are about to marry, a boy. ("[S]he's a great lubberly boy," laments Slender [5.5.170], and Caius has a similar tale to report: "I ha' married *un garçon*, a boy; *un paysan*, by Gar. A boy!" [186–188].) Fenton, when he appears, makes the argument, again very familiar from Shakespearean "true love" plots, that he and Anne were already bound to each other: "The truth is, she and I, long since contracted, / Are now so sure that nothing can dissolve us" (5.5.220–221). Like Bassanio, who met Portia in her "father's time," Fenton thus has a prior, as well as a stronger, claim.

Although *Merry Wives* differs greatly in tone from a play like *Twelfth Night*, one of Shakespeare's most "aristocratic" comedies, it has a number of significant similarities. The idiotic Slender, propped up as a suitor for Anne Page by Justice Shallow, resembles Sir Andrew Aguecheek, the equally fatuous, though technically "noble," suitor for the hand of the Countess Olivia, in a courtship encouraged by Sir Toby Belch. Both Slender and Aguecheek are rich and witless; neither has a clue as to how to court, or even speak to, a woman. Their names bespeak their natures, in a way that is not uncommon for Shakespearean "low" characters in comedies (e.g., the clown called Costard, or "apple-head," in *Love's Labour's Lost*, or the whore Doll Tearsheet in *2 Henry IV*) but is more familiar in the works of a playwright like Ben Jonson, whose characters have names like Face, Subtle, and Epicene. This is a version of the comedy of "humors," based on the theory, prevalent among some thinkers in the early modern period, that personality traits were governed by predominant bodily substances: the "bilious" person was angry because of too much bile, the "phlegmatic" person dull because of an overabundance of phlegm, the "sanguine" person well-balanced because of the appropriate amount of blood in the system, and so on. (Before we dismiss this as a charmingly antiquated view, we might recall the renewed prominence of genetic and other biological theories in the twenty-first-century assessment of human nature.)

"Slender" in the period meant both slight of build and insignificant or trifling. The word applied, that is, both to the character's appearance and to his (meager) capacities. Slender's rival, equally unsuccessful in his quest for Anne Page's hand, is Doctor Caius, whose final consternation and humiliation ("Be Gar, I'll raise all Windsor" [5.5.190]) when confronted with the fact that he has been duped into "marrying" a boy, matches Malvolio's poignant exit line, "I'll be revenged on the whole pack of you" (*Twelfth Night* 5.1.365). As always in Shakespearean comedy, the calm center of social reunion at the close is guaranteed, and guarded, by the escape of some anarchic energies beyond the bounds of the play.

Another device shared by *Merry Wives* and *Twelfth Night* is the duplicitous and duplicate letter. In *Twelfth Night* the gulling of Malvolio is accomplished by Maria's counterfeiting of Olivia's handwriting. In *Merry Wives* the subterfuge is less subtle, as befits its engineer, Falstaff, who merely sends copies of the same letter to the two women he is trying to seduce, changing the salutation. As Mistress Page observes with amusement to her friend Mistress Ford:

Mistress Page   Letter for letter, but that the name of Page and Ford
                 differs!
                 [*She gives* MISTRESS FORD *her letter*]
                 To thy great comfort in this mystery of ill opinions, here's
                 the twin brother of thy letter. But let thine inherit first, for
                 I protest mine never shall. I warrant he hath a thousand of

> these letters, writ with blank space for different names—
> sure, more, and these are of the second edition. He will
> print them, out of doubt—for he cares not what he puts
> into the press when he would put us two. . . .

Mistress Ford   Why this is the very same: the very hand, the very words.

> *2.1.61–73*

The women's further witty banter on Falstaff's desire to "press" and "board"
them (2.1.79–82) is another incidental link with *Twelfth Night*, where Sir Toby
urges the baffled Sir Andrew to "accost" or "board" Olivia if he can; the term is
an indelicacy, as is evident to the wives, although not to Sir Andrew. The plot of
"revenge" against Falstaff is hatched at this moment, and the word recurs often
as the two women plan their attack.

The main point to be made here is that, as we note many correspondences in
language, character, and scenario between *Merry Wives* and other Shakespeare
plays, the middle-class setting delightfully undercuts emotions and pretensions
that run high and wild in other contexts. In other words, the dramatist is able to
use, and reuse, phrases and occasions to quite different effect because *Merry
Wives* is a "city," or citizen, play. Consider the way the jealousy plot involving
Ford and Falstaff anticipates a far more troubling scene in *Othello*. In *Merry
Wives* Ford is constantly described, by his wife and others, as a jealous husband.
Although he has no reason to suspect his wife, he determines to assume a false
identity, that of Master Brooke, in order to pay Falstaff to test the virtue of Mistress Ford. The words "brook" and "ford" are related, and the stratagem is
probably meant to be comically transparent. Part of the joke here is that Falstaff
has already sent his "love letters" to Mistress Ford and Mistress Page, and he
therefore sees the opportunity to succeed in his seduction plans and get paid by
the husband for taking his pleasure. Thus Ford as Brooke comes to Falstaff
and makes his proposition (which sounds quite a lot like the kind of conversation that takes place between Iago and Roderigo in Shakespeare's great jealous-
husband play, *Othello*):

> There is money. Spend it, spend it; spend more; spend all I have; only give
> me so much of your time in exchange of it as to lay an amiable siege to the
> honesty of this Ford's wife. Use your art of wooing, win her to consent to
> you. If any man may, you may as soon as any.

> *2.2.205–210*

The minute he succeeds in suborning Falstaff and is left alone on the stage, Ford
addresses the audience in a long, passionate rant about cuckoldry:

> Who says this is improvident jealousy? My wife hath sent to him, the hour
> is fixed, the match is made. Would any man have thought this? See the hell

of having a false woman! . . . But "cuckold," "wittol"! "Cuckold"—the
devil himself hath not such a name. Page is an ass, a secure ass. He will
trust his wife, he will not be jealous. . . . God be praised for my jealousy!
Eleven o'clock the hour. I will prevent this, detect my wife, be revenged on
Falstaff, and laugh at Page. I will about it. Better three hours too soon than
a minute too late. God's my life: cuckold, cuckold, cuckold!

2.2.254–274

His speech anticipates similarly passionate—and erroneous—expostulations
from a whole roster of "improvidently" jealous husbands in Shakespeare, not
only Othello but also Posthumus in *Cymbeline* and, most closely, Leontes in
The Winter's Tale. But Ford is a tradesman, not a general or a king, and his
speech—a "wittol" is a complaisant cuckold, a husband who winks at his wife's
indiscretions—is received as comedy rather than as pathos and incipient
tragedy. When he revisits this theme at the end of act 3, again speaking to the
audience in soliloquy, he sounds like a domesticated version of Bottom describing his "dream" of transformation—with the important exception that Bottom's
dream of having had an ass's head was true, and Ford's dream of having cuckold's horns is false (Falstaff has just exited with the inflammatory line "You shall
have her, Master Brooke; Master Brooke, you shall cuckold Ford"):

> Ford   Hum! Ha! Is this a vision? Is this a dream? Do I sleep? Master Ford,
> awake! Awake, Master Ford! There's a hole made in your best coat,
> Master Ford. This 'tis to be married! This 'tis to have linen and
> buck-baskets! Well, I will proclaim myself what I am. . . . Though
> what I am I cannot avoid, yet to be what I would not shall not
> make me tame. If I have horns to make one mad, let the proverb go
> with me: I'll be horn-mad.

3.5.120–130

The two courting plots taken together, the one too "high" (Slender's book of
songs and sonnets, an instruction manual for the clueless wooer) and the other
too "low" (Falstaff's attempts to seduce the wives in duplicate; Ford's willingness to pay for proof of his wife's infidelity), expose the unstable and comical
nature of sexual love. And the three punishments of Falstaff designed by Mistresses Ford and Page are exponential developments, both as stage comedy and
as humiliation and discomfiture, as Falstaff has to escape detection first in a basket of dirty laundry, then dressed as an old woman, and finally is sent to impersonate "Herne the hunter" and meet the women at midnight in the park. The
repentant Ford and Master Page both now join in the plan:

> Page   But let our plot go forward. Let our wives
>   Yet once again, to make us public sport,
>   Appoint a meeting with this old fat fellow,

	Where we may take him, and disgrace him for it.
Ford	There is no better way than that they spoke of.
Page	How? To send him word they'll meet him in the Park
	At midnight? Fie, fie, he'll never come.
Evans	You say he has been thrown in the rivers, and has been
	grievously peaten, as an old 'oman. Methinks there should
	be terrors in him, that he should not come. Methinks his
	flesh is punished; he shall have no desires.
Page	So think I too.
Mistress Ford	Devise but how you'll use him when he comes,
	And let us two devise to bring him thither.
Mistress Page	There is an old tale goes that Herne the hunter,
	Sometime a keeper here in Windsor Forest,
	Doth all the winter time at still midnight
	Walk round about an oak, with great ragg'd horns;
	And there he blasts the trees, and takes the cattle,
	And makes milch-kine yield blood, and shakes a chain
	In a most hideous and dreadful manner.
	You have heard of such a spirit, and well you know
	The superstitious idle-headed eld
	Received and did deliver to our age,
	This tale of Herne the hunter for a truth.
	. . . .
Mistress Ford	Marry this is our device,
	That Falstaff at that oak shall meet with us.

4.4.12–40

Once he is there, and in his horns, they will surprise him with a masque of schoolchildren dressed as fairies, "pinch him sound" for violating their place and time of "fairy revel" in "shape profane," and then "mock him home to Windsor."

The scene unfolds just as they intend and desire. Falstaff appears wearing a buck's head and comparing himself to the king of the gods, who likewise transformed himself for love: "Remember, Jove, thou was a bull for thy Europa; love set on thy horns. O powerful love, that in some respects makes a beast a man; in some other, a man a beast! . . . For me, I am here a Windsor stag, and the fattest, I think, i'th' forest. Send me a cool rut-time, Jove" (5.5.2–5, 11–12). The devolution from mythological being to local beast is itself comic, the more so when the wives arrive, address him as "my deer, my male deer," and are told by the jaunty Falstaff that he can handle both of them at once: "Divide me like a bribed buck, each a haunch. . . . [A]nd my horns I bequeath your husbands" (5.5.14–15, 21–23). The sudden appearance of the "fairies," led by schoolmaster Evans in disguise, Pistol dressed as Hobgoblin (or Puck), and Mistress Quickly as the Fairy Queen, and accompanied by Anne Page, completes the

turnaround, converting the stage to something more like the Athenian wood of
A Midsummer Night's Dream or Prospero's masque of Ceres in *The Tempest*,
as Falstaff, outstretched on the stage, hides his face against the forbidden
sight ("I'll wink and couch: no man their works must eye" [5.5.45]). The "Fairy
Queen's" apostrophe to "Fairies, black, grey, green, and white" is followed by
Pistol/Hobgoblin's invocation:

> Elves, list your names. Silence, you airy toys.
> Cricket, to Windsor chimneys shalt thou leap.
> Where fires thou find'st unraked and hearths unswept,
> There punch the maids as blue as bilberry.
> Our radiant Queen hates sluts and sluttery.
>
> 5.5.39–43

This remarkable masque brings together both Fairy Queens (Elizabeth at
Windsor Castle, and in the audience; Mistress Quickly on the stage) and combines, as well, the evanescent and unearthly with the specific, local, and vernacular (lazy maids, the chimneys in the town of Windsor, the local habitation
and name of such elves and fairies as "Cricket" and, in the next lines, "Bead").
There follow, in quick succession, the ceremonial scouring of the castle in
preparation for the Garter ceremony ("Search Windsor castle, elves, within and
out"), the discovery—by "smell"—of Falstaff at the foot of Herne's Oak ("I
smell a man of middle earth"), his punishment by pinching (a traditional fairy
weapon), and his unmasking:

	[The] fairies run away. FALSTAFF *rises.*
Page	Nay, do not fly; I think we have watched you now.
	Will none but Herne the hunter serve your turn?
Mistress Page	I pray you, come, hold up the jest no higher.
	Now, good Sir John, how like you the Windsor wives?
	. . . .
Ford	[*to* FALSTAFF] Now, sir, who's a cuckold now? . . .
Mistress Ford	Sir John, . . . I will never take you for my love again, but I
	will always count you my deer.
Falstaff	I do begin to perceive that I am made an ass.
	[*He takes off the horns*]

5.5.100–115

From buck-basket to buck to cuckold to deer to ass, Falstaff's trajectory is a
lively devolution. The play will end with the revelations of the marriage plot
(Slender and Caius outwitted and mock-married to "great lubberly boy[s]";
Fenton matched with Anne), and with Mistress Page's invitation to "every
one" to

> go home,
> And laugh this sport o'er by a country fire,
> Sir John and all.
>
> *5.5.217–219*

The last word, though, goes to the formerly jealous Ford, whose neat couplet, ending the play, invokes the stratagem of Portia and Nerissa at the end of *The Merchant of Venice:*

> Let it be so, Sir John.
> To Master Brooke you yet shall hold your word,
> For he tonight shall lie with Mistress Ford.
>
> *5.5.220–222*

It is perhaps worth saying one more thing about the plot of language and languages in *Merry Wives*. At various times in the play, traditionally "English" characters like the Host and Falstaff evince either scorn or anxiety, or a mixture of both, at the way in which their language, elsewhere in the play called the "King's English," is being transformed by the pronunciations of foreigners and the miscues of "low" speakers with high linguistic ambitions. Thus the Host, joking about the inept swordsmanship of the Frenchman Caius, suggests that instead of fighting he should "hack our English" (3.1.67). Page says of Nim, "Here's a fellow frights English out of his wits" (2.1.122–123). And Falstaff finds a double humiliation in being undone by the Welshman Evans, "one that makes fritters of English" (5.5.136). This last comment is close enough to Pistol's scorn of the Welshman Fluellen in *Henry V* to remind us that all the *Henry* plays are very much concerned with language-learning, with the different patois and dialects of "high" and "low," and with the tensions that attend upon trying to unify a nation where Welsh and Scots, Irish and English all speak different varieties of the "same" language. The English lessons of Catherine, the French princess, and the gentlewoman Alice in *Henry V* quickly disclose, as does the comic Latin lesson in *Merry Wives,* that translation is itself a very tricky and dangerous business, often producing inadvertent and risible obscenities. In act 4, scene 1, of this play, when schoolmaster Evans tries to drill young William Page on his Latin, we get jokes on *lapis* meaning "stone" (pebble, but also testicle), the "focative" (rather than vocative) case, and the relation of the word *horum* (whore 'em) to the "genitive case," with an additional double meaning in "case." The Latin lesson in the play is taken fairly directly from the most popular Latin primer of the period, and the jokes, familiar schoolboy jokes in any era, would presumably have been amusing to a humanist audience itself newly interested in ancient as well as modern languages.

Not only was the economic and commercial structure of England undergoing changes (from aristocratic to mercantile, from country to town, from landed estates to commerce and trade), but so, too, was the language (or languages) spoken and written in the court, the towns, the streets—and on the stage. We might say that "translation" in the widest sense is at the heart of this play, whether it is Falstaff's translation from knight to buck and from man to "woman," Ford's translation from jealous man to wiser husband, or Evans's, Caius's, and William Page's earnest efforts to speak and be understood.

Much Ado About Nothing

DRAMATIS PERSONAE

Don Pedro, *Prince of Aragon*

Benedick, *of Padua, a lord, companion of Don Pedro*

Claudio, *of Florence, a lord, companion of Don Pedro*

Balthasar, *attendant on Don Pedro, a singer*

Don John, *the bastard brother of Don Pedro*

Borachio, *follower of Don John*

Conrad, *follower of Don John*

Leonato, *governor of Messina*

Hero, *his daughter*

Beatrice, *an orphan, his niece*

Antonio, *an old man, brother of Leonato*

Margaret, *waiting-gentlewoman attendant on Hero*

Ursula, *waiting-gentlewoman attendant on Hero*

Friar Francis

Dogberry, *the Constable in charge of the Watch*

Verges, *the Headborough, Dogberry's partner*

A Sexton

Watchmen

A Boy, *serving Benedick*

Attendants and messengers

THIS PLAY, with its gaily self-deprecating title, seems virtually to inaugurate a genre. It is the forerunner of Restoration stage comedy, of the eighteenth- and nineteenth-century "comedy of manners," and of what has come to be called "screwball comedy," the bantering, witty, sophisticated romantic plots that emerged in the films of the 1930s and 1940s, which philosopher and critic Stanley Cavell has termed "comedies of remarriage"—comedies like *Bringing Up Baby* (1938), *The Philadelphia Story* (1940), and *Adam's Rib* (1949). Its urbane pair of lovers, Beatrice and Benedick (note that her name means "one who blesses," and his name means "one who is blessed"), anticipate the glib and genteel barbs of the disillusioned pairs who populate stage and screen, waiting, like their Shakespearean forerunners, to be offered a chance to be, for once, unashamedly romantic. But as the play begins, both Beatrice and Benedick hold themselves aloof, apparently, from love, keeping their distance from emotion and from each other, even as they observe, with mingled indulgence and affectionate disdain, the nascent courtship between their closest friends, Claudio, a young soldier, and Hero, Beatrice's cousin.

The interest of *Much Ado* lies as much in its ebullient characters as it does in its plot, but the basic design of the play is worth recounting: Soldiers returning from the wars are greeted by those who have stayed at home, waiting to hear about their exploits, and their safety. The soldiers arrive at the house of Leonato, the governor of Messina, where Leonato resides with his elderly brother Antonio, his daughter Hero, and his niece Beatrice, and are invited to stay for a month as Leonato's guests. The ranking officer of the group, Don Pedro, Prince of Aragon, has a bastard brother, Don John, from whom he has been estranged for reasons the play never specifies, and with whom he has just been reconciled. Don John is a classic malcontent, jealous of Pedro and of those he prefers and admires, especially his protégé Claudio, a young Florentine. Among the returning soldiers is Benedick of Padua, a witty and worldly sophisticate, who appears to have had some previous relationship with Beatrice. Beatrice and Benedick are tense, touchy, and witty with each other, in marked contrast to the conventional romantic pair, the naïve and trusting Hero and the equally naïve Claudio, who is young enough to be described later by Benedick as "my lord Lackbeard" (5.1.182). This is part of a common mode of "flyting," or exchange of insults, in the play: Beatrice calls Benedick "Signor Montanto" (1.1.25) (i.e., "Mr. Thrust-and-parry," or "Duel-man") and "the Prince's jester" (2.1.117), while Benedick in turn dubs her "my dear lady Disdain" (1.1.97) and "my lady Tongue" (2.1.239). With the real wars over, or in abeyance, with few casualties and "none of name," or title (1.1.6), the "kind of merry war" that is described as already in existence between Beatrice and Benedick takes over center stage (and is not concluded until play's end, when Benedick will declare, "Peace! I will stop your mouth"—with a kiss (5.4.96).

The two romantic couples follow very different itineraries in their love: Hero and Claudio are quickly betrothed, though not without a hint of trouble to come, since Don Pedro, undertaking the embassy of proposing for the shy and tongue-tied Claudio at a masked ball, is so visibly successful that Claudio, vulnerable and suggestible, is led to believe falsely that "the Prince woos for himself" (2.1.152). Although this mistake is quickly corrected, it comes back in a more malign and dangerous guise when Claudio is falsely convinced that he has witnessed Hero dallying with another man in her chamber window, and publicly denounces her in the church where they are to wed. ("Give not this rotten orange to your friend," he tells her father [4.1.30].) Hero swoons, is thought to be dead, and is concealed by a sympathetic friar, only to be "resurrected" as a muffled and silent figure, the new bride that a chastened Claudio has agreed to marry, sight unseen, as penance for his apparent murder by slander of the innocent Hero. The false scenario of Hero's supposed dalliance, staged by others at the behest of a Don John jealous of Claudio's success, is revealed by the hapless but surprisingly effective detective work of the play's "low" and comic characters, Dogberry, the master constable, and his equally bumbling colleagues on the night watch.

Meantime, Beatrice and Benedick are gulled by their friends into admitting that the "merry war" between them conceals a depth of love and passion. Abandoning defensive repartee for a private acknowledgment of their mutual affection, they then find themselves embroiled in a minitragedy, as the love match between Hero and Claudio turns into a scene of denunciation and death. At this point, significantly in terms of larger patterns of Shakespearean development, Benedick is called upon to choose between his allegiance to his soldier friends—Don Pedro continues to support Claudio in the belief that Hero has been unfaithful, and that her fate, while tragic, was deserved—and his commitment to Beatrice. A palpable turning point, and one that often elicits gasps from the audience, comes when he offers his services to her in a sincere attempt to assist her in her grief, and is startled by what she asks of him, expressed in a terse, two-word command: "Kill Claudio" (4.1.287). After a moment of reflection, he determines to do her will and challenge Claudio to a duel, even at the cost of alienating Don Pedro. The revelation of the true state of affairs by the man Borachio, who acted the part of Hero's lover at the window, at the behest of Don John, and was unmasked by the bumbling Watch ("What your wisdoms could not discover, these shallow fools have brought to light," he confesses [5.1.217–218]), seems to come too late, as Borachio declares that "the lady is dead upon mine and my master's false accusation." This sets the stage for the final reversal, as the bride Claudio has promised, in penance, to wed sight unseen is unmasked as the "former Hero, Hero that is dead!" (5.4.65), and the apparently incompatible Beatrice and Benedick are revealed to have written love sonnets to each other. Deferring the church wedding till after the end of the play ("let's have a dance ere we are married" [5.4.112–113]), and urging Don Pedro, this play's noble excluded figure, "Prince, thou art sad, get thee a wife, get thee a wife" (5.4.117), Benedick presides over the closing ceremonies onstage. Just as a messenger began the play, bringing news of the soldiers' return, so a messenger ends it, announcing the flight and subsequent capture of Don John, who is also, although for quite different reasons, excluded from the comic summing-up. The play ends with a call to dance—"Strike up, pipers"—the conventional close of comedy, but not one always actually present in a Shakespearean play. The notion of dancing as an emblem of harmony, both human and celestial, had been suggested by such works as Sir John Davies' "Orchestra, or A Poem of Dancing" (1596). In this case, dance offers a festive end to a play that, although formally a comedy, is full of dark moments, and often threatens to veer into tragedy.

Was there a quarrel between Don Pedro and Don John beyond the usual sibling (or legitimate/illegitimate) rivalry? And what did take place between Beatrice and Benedick before the play began? Beatrice herself explains lightly to Don Pedro that Benedick "lent" her his heart for a while, and that she "gave him use for it, a double heart for his single one," his having "won it of [her], with false dice" (2.1.242–244). But, tantalizingly, their shared prehistory is never explained. Another question: Is Don Pedro actually proposing to Beatrice when, in a bantering moment, he offers her his hand in marriage ("Will you have me, lady?" [2.1.285])? Her response is both typical and indicative, tapping into the holiday/working-day dichotomy that underpins so much of Shakespearean comedy, and also into this play's own periodic consciousness of rank and status: "No my lord, unless I might have another for working days. Your grace is too costly to wear every day" (2.1.286–287). Questions like these have no answers—they are puzzles and trailing plot threads, embedded by the playwright, whether deliberately or inadvertently, into the text of the play. They hint at emotions and actions underneath the surface, and indeed this play, with its casual allusions to heartbreak, perpetual spinsterhood, fraternal rivalry, and unrequited love, partners the threatening plot elements (Hero's "death"; Benedick's duel) with a constant subtext of unarticulated pain and loss.

The contrast between two pairs of lovers, one unconventional, resistant, and highly skilled at verbal sparring, the other apparently compliant, conventional, and reticent, had been used with great success by Shakespeare in an earlier play, *The Taming of the Shrew.* In other romantic comedies, from *A Midsummer Night's Dream* to *The Merchant of Venice* and *As You Like It,* the two "high," or aristocratic, pairs are more like than unlike, despite some minor differences (Hermia and Lysander, Helena and Demetrius; Portia and Bassanio, Nerissa and Gratiano; Rosalind and Orlando, Celia and Oliver). But in *Much Ado* the initial emphasis is on dissimilarity. Beatrice and Benedick are perhaps a little older, and in any case more worldly—and more wordy—than the tongue-tied Hero and Claudio.

Benedick, unlike Claudio, is socially sophisticated and sexually experienced, prejudiced not against flirtation and lovemaking but against marriage. The first time the audience encounters him, he takes part in a ribald exchange with Don Pedro and old Leonato, Hero's father, that seems meant to establish his identity as a man attractive to women. Using a conventional form of address, Don Pedro says to Leonato "I think this is your daughter," to which Leonato playfully replies, "Her mother hath many times told me so." The anxiety of paternity often surfaces in Shakespearean banter, and will often—as in *The Winter's Tale*—resurface as a serious matter. But here, in the opening lines of a witty romantic comedy, the emphasis is on a backslapping boys-will-be-boys spirit, as Benedick quips boldly, "Were you in doubt, sir, that you asked her?" and Leonato, in reply, gives as good as he gets: "Signor Benedick, no; for then were you a child." Don Pedro then intervenes to make sure the audience understands what it is being told: "You have it full, Benedick. We may guess by this what you are, being a man" (1.1.89–90).

Beatrice has a trace of lover's melancholy, and indeed there is a hint that she has been led on, in the past, to think that Benedick had some feelings for her. That the pair have met before is established early. Again, this is a kind of Shakespearean commonplace, seeming to underscore their rightness for each other even as the play begins. Berowne, in *Love's Labour's Lost,* like Benedick, is very ready to mock the spectacle of others in love, only to be caught, himself, composing and reading a love sonnet. But in the case of Beatrice and Benedick there has clearly been a sundering or a falling-away, one that has left both players tentative, proud, and perhaps also bruised. They will therefore affect an attitude more like Puck's "Lord, what fools these mortals be!" than make any true demonstration of their feelings—at least until hoodwinked by their friends, who lure each with the tantalizing notion that the other is, in fact, head over heels in love.

Much Ado About Nothing is indeed in many ways Shakespeare's great play about gossip. Everything is overheard, misheard, or constructed on purpose for eavesdropping. If *Taming* is one comparison for this play, another, less benign, is *Othello*, and in fact the three Shakespearean "jealousy" plays, *Much Ado, Othello*, and *The Winter's Tale*, are often, and fruitfully, compared. In this play, as we will see, the "Iago figure" is Don John, the malcontent bastard brother of Don Pedro, the Prince of Aragon. Here, as in the tragedy of *Othello* and the tragicomedy of *The Winter's Tale*, a jealous man thinks he sees his beloved dallying with another man. But in this case the scene has been staged in order to deceive. Claudio is the victim, and his "crime" is a double one. From Don John's point of view he has—like Cassio in *Othello*—stolen away the affection and regard of the military commander, in this case, Don Pedro. The rival whom Don John calls, with magnificent contempt, "the most exquisite Claudio" is—again like Cassio—a Florentine, a resident of one of the most elegant and mannered cities in Italy. "That young start-up hath all the glory of my overthrow," John complains to Borachio (whose name means "the drunken one"). "If I can cross him any way, I bless myself every way" (1.3.52–53).

The pretended indifference of Beatrice and Benedick is juxtaposed to the all-too-susceptible naïveté of Claudio, who declares his inexperience and couples it with self-doubt. Claudio in effect asks himself, Could someone like Hero love me? Isn't it more likely that she is in love with, or in bed with, someone else, someone more impressive, or higher ranking, or sexier? He, too, acknowledges that he had been attracted, at an earlier moment, before the play begins, to the woman who will come to preoccupy his love musings and romantic fantasies:

> I looked upon her with a soldier's eye,
> That liked, but had a rougher task in hand
> Than to drive liking to the name of love.
> But now I am returned, and that war-thoughts
> Have left their places vacant, in their rooms
> Come thronging soft and delicate desires,
> All prompting me how fair young Hero is,
> Saying I liked her ere I went to wars.
>
> Much Ado *1.1.246–253*

War is a key theme here, war and its aftermath. The opening scene in Messina presents a society of women and older men (Leonato, his daughter Hero, and his niece Beatrice) from which the young men had departed to fight—a world, that is, waiting for the return of youth and love. The play thus begins with the onset of peace, with the news that few gentlemen have been lost in the late military action ("and none of name") and that the youthful Claudio fought especially bravely, "beyond the promise of his age, doing in the figure of a lamb the feats of a lion" (1.1.12). Beatrice's apparently offhand inquiry about the health of Benedick ("I pray you, is Signor Montanto returned from the wars, or no?") masks—or rather, reveals—a real anxiety about Benedick's safety and well-being. Shortly we will hear from Leonato that there is a "kind of merry war" between Beatrice and Benedick (1.1.49–50), so that the shift from martial war to merry war marks an explicit turning point. As is so often the case, the skills that were so apropos in war will prove of limited value in peacetime. Benedick and Claudio are established as best friends, most in each other's company, but the contrast between the "pleasant," witty, and entertaining Benedick and the earnest and tongue-tied Claudio is soon to be made evident.

Benedick gives us a (rather unsympathetic) sense of what Claudio was like before he committed the folly of falling in love:

> I do much wonder that one man, seeing how much another man is a fool when he dedicates his behaviours to love, will, after he hath laughed at such shallow follies in others, become the argument of his own scorn by falling in love. And such a man is Claudio. I have known when there was no music with him but the drum and the fife, and now he had rather hear the tabor and the pipe. I have known when he would have walked ten mile afoot to see a good armour, and now will he lie ten nights awake carving the fashion of a new doublet. He was wont to speak plain and to the purpose, like an honest man and a soldier; and now is he turned orthography. His words are a very fantastical banquet, just so many strange dishes. May I be so converted, and see with these eyes? I cannot tell. I think not.
>
> 2.3.8–21

"Converted," to an experienced watcher of Shakespearean comedy, is a clear tip-off, since it will be used by such wholehearted new lovers as Portia, speaking of herself, and Rosalind, speaking of the once-wicked, now reformed and romantic Oliver.

In *Much Ado* conversion becomes one of the dominant themes of the play, underscored by the refrain of Balthasar's song "Sigh no more, ladies, sigh no more": "Converting all your sounds of woe / Into hey nonny, nonny" (2.3.56ff.). Hero will be converted into "another Hero," Margaret converted into Hero, Benedick and Beatrice into lovers, tragedy converted into romance and comedy. Benedick is wrong, of course, to think that he will not so easily "convert" to the condition of a lover, and so indeed is Beatrice, who proclaims her own resistance. As Margaret the waiting-gentlewoman says to her, in a phrase quite similar to Benedick's, "[H]ow you may be converted I know not, but methinks you look with your eyes, as other women do" (3.4.75–77). Indeed, Benedick, who teases Claudio about lacking a manly beard, will soon go for a shave, the better to look like a lover. "[T]he barber's man has been seen with him," reports Claudio, laughing, to Don Pedro and Leonato, "and the old ornament of his cheek hath already stuffed tennis balls" (3.2.37–39). The sudden similarity to the "Lackbeard" Claudio is underscored by Leonato: "Indeed, he looks younger than he did by the loss of a beard" (3.2.40–41).

Beatrice is the wittiest speaker in the play, but there is also a certain pathos in her character, produced not only by the hint of a former relationship with Benedick, but also by the conventionality of Leonato, who tells her she will never get a husband "if thou be so shrewd of thy tongue" (2.1.17), and of Antonio, who says she is "too curst." Their remarks underscore her position as an unmarried woman dependent upon the hospitality of her uncle. This is the same position that Rosalind in *As You Like It* occupies at the court of her uncle, Duke Frederick, but there marriage is not the constant topic of conversation— and, of course, Rosalind manages to make her escape, together with her cousin Celia. In *Much Ado About Nothing* Beatrice and Hero are the young women of the household, and it is expected that they will marry—indeed, that marriage will be their vocation. "Well, niece, I hope to see you one day fitted with a husband," says Leonato, and Beatrice's reply is brisk: "Not till God make men of some other mettle than earth. Would it not grieve a woman to be overmastered with a piece of valiant dust?—to make an account of her life to a clod of wayward marl?" (2.1.50–53). Still, there is a good deal of ambiguity between irreverence and yearning in her request to be shown where the bachelors sit in heaven, and particularly in her exclamation once Claudio and Hero are betrothed: "Good lord, for alliance! Thus goes everyone to the world but I, and I am sunburnt. I may sit in a corner and cry 'Heigh-ho' for a husband' " (2.1.278–280). Hero, not incidentally, is her father's heir, a point inquired after, obliquely, by Claudio when he is thinking of wooing her ("Hath Leonato any son, my lord?" Don Pedro: "No child but Hero. She's his only heir. / Dost thou affect her, Claudio?"[1.1.242–244]). Beatrice is not an heiress. While it would be anachronistic to say that she lives by her wits—and indeed, as we have already seen, her wittiness is the source of unease to the men in her household—her position is more precarious than Hero's. When she says, with however much irony in her tone, "Thus goes everyone to the world but I," we can sense for a moment the limitations that she will confront if she does not marry and leave her uncle's house. This is a sentiment that is, again, worn lightly in the early part of the play. It will return, more vividly and painfully, after the humiliation of Hero, when Beatrice longs to revenge her cousin and must instead enlist Benedick's aid to fight with Claudio: "O God that I were a man! I would eat his heart in the market place" (4.1.303–304). It is worth noting that in other Shakespearean comedies of this period the heroine *does* become a man, at least for a little while.

Portia, Rosalind, and Viola all cross-dress, assuming male costumes and names in order to perform some act of rescue, release, or revenge. But Beatrice has this option only in the wishful form of a condition contrary to fact. *Much Ado About Nothing* is a play that engages topics like male bonding and female disempowerment, for all the powerful figures in Messina are men. There are no mothers, and the marriage of Hero, no matter that it becomes a love match, is initially arranged as a suitable contract undertaken, by proxy, between Leonato, the governor of Messina, and the powerful Prince of Aragon, Don Pedro.

The language that Beatrice and Benedick speak to each other is often prose, not verse—a prose made lively, witty, limber, and now suddenly the natural speech of aristocrats. Their "low" counterparts, the constables Dogberry and Verges and the foolish members of the Watch, will also play with language, far less comfortably, and will often let it play with them. Like other rustic Shakespearean literalists—think of the gravedigger in *Hamlet*—they take figurative language at face value, so that one of the Watch, hearing the courtly phrase "seest thou not what a deformed thief this fashion is?" (3.3.108–109), immediately imagines a desperate character called Deformed, a "vile thief this seven year," and the specter of the imaginary thief Deformed will continue to haunt their later and more serious conversations. Don John's plot almost succeeds because of the failure of transparency in language (the confused verbiage of the Watch so frustrates Leonato that he fails to heed what they say). For Beatrice and Benedick and for Dogberry and the Watch, wordplay and the pitfalls of language will almost lead to disaster, and will tend to hold truth at a distance.

In marked and deliberate contrast to these wordsmiths and wordmongers are the play's taciturn or silent characters. Of these the most obdurate is Don John, who characterizes himself at once as a man "not of many words" as he somewhat grudgingly acknowledges Leonato's hospitality (1.1.127). Beatrice, playfully imagining the perfect male ideal, remarks: "He were an excellent man that were made just in the midway between him [Don John] and Benedick. The one is too like an image and says nothing, and the other too like my lady's eldest son, evermore tattling" (2.1.6–9). Don John's silence is emblematic of his malign reserve—we may think ahead to Iago's "From this time forth I never will speak word" (*Othello* 5.2.310)—but the attractive young lovers, Claudio and Hero, are silent, too, and their silence is potentially dangerous, not (like the scheming Don John's) to others, but to themselves. As we have seen, in the structure of the play they are the conventional, well-bred opposites to the more extravagant Beatrice and Benedick, and whereas Beatrice and Benedick speak all the time, these two can hardly bring themselves to speak at all. It is Don Pedro, not Claudio, who does the wooing, which is what first gives rise to the false notion that it is he, not Claudio, who intends to marry Hero. When the betrothal is announced, neither of the principals can speak, and this gives rise to a charming little scene with, as always, ominous undertones. "His grace hath made the match, and all grace say amen to it," says Leonato, the father (2.1.264–265). A silence ensues, in which Beatrice nudges Claudio—"Speak,

Count, 'tis your cue"—and then Hero—"Speak, cousin" (2.1.266, 271). Finally, after an uncomfortable and risible moment of continued silence, amusing to the audience both on and off the stage, Hero whispers in Claudio's ear. We never hear what she says. "Silence is the perfectest herald of joy" is Claudio's explanation (2.1.267), and this might be true, except that, without language to interpret and intercede, mistakes are made, misinterpretations and false "noting" take place, and tragedy looms behind the scenes. This is a frequent theme in Shakespeare—we can think most obviously about Cordelia's dangerous decision, in that other play about "nothing," to "[l]ove and be silent" (*Lear* 1.1.59–60). While there is no direct relation between the surly taciturnity of Don John and the blushing silence of the young lovers, their *thematic* connection is clear. As so often in Shakespeare, the problem is not one of a wicked external diabolus ex machina but of the exploitation of existing internal weaknesses. Don John is a catalyst, or, perhaps more symbolically, a personification of the problems that are bound to arise between two innocent, inexperienced, and silent lovers in a world that depends upon language.

But if Claudio and Hero must learn to speak for themselves, Beatrice and Benedick have to learn to stop talking—at least once in a while. Don Pedro speculates about what is likely to happen after the trick is played upon them and they overhear their friends gossiping about how each is the secret beloved of the other: "That's the scene that I would see, which will be merely a dumb show" (2.3.193–194). They will be struck dumb, jolted out of their customary prattle. When Claudio finally makes his terrible accusation in the church, and Hero swoons, Benedick will admit: "I am so attired in wonder, / I know not what to say" (4.1.143–144).

This is a major turning point for him, a moment when language—his usual language—will not serve him, or insulate him from painful events. As speech is his and Beatrice's natural condition, so speechlessness—whether from astonishment, horror, or love—is the condition to which they may be converted. Language can always, if temporarily, be stopped by a kiss.

The title phrase has had a celebrity virtually independent of the play itself, but its relevance to the dramatic action and language is far more direct than the phrase might at first suggest. A fuss about a trifle. "Big deal" might be our modern counterpart. But "nothing" in the English Renaissance had a wide range of meanings, all of them specific and pertinent. "Nothing" meant a thing or person not worth mentioning—as Don John will say, with hidden intent, that Hero's misdeeds are "[n]ot to be named, . . . not to be spoke of" (4.1.94), which is literally true, since in fact they don't exist. "Nothing" could mean someone of little worth, like the foolish Watch headed by Dogberry. "Nothing," paradoxically, also could mean "everything" or "all," since its sign was the full or empty circle, and in this play whose most characteristic mode of language is paradox, much ado is indeed made about everything. Perhaps most surprising to a modern audience—though not to an audience that knows its *Hamlet* and *King Lear*—is the fact that "nothing" was a slang term for the female sexual organs.

Hamlet teases Ophelia about the "nothing" that lies "between maids' legs" (3.2.106–108). The association survives in our modern word "naughty," which is now conflated with "noughty." In this play there is indeed much ado about Hero's virginity and her sexuality. She herself is embarrassed by sexual thoughts and sexual jokes, as she acknowledges when Margaret helps her dress for her (ill-fated) wedding day. Her shyness about things sexual makes her vulnerable to suggestion and to a practical joke, staged at the behest of the wicked Don John, that has potentially desperate consequences. As if all these "nothings" were not enough, "nothing" in Shakespeare's time was pronounced, we think, the same as "noting." "Much ado about noting" is certainly an apt description of the play's events, and nonevents. To "note" was to observe or mark carefully, to give heed or attention to (something just about everyone in this play signally fails to do), but also to set down as having a certain good or bad character, to point at or indicate by pointing, to mark or brand with some disgrace or defect, and to stigmatize. All these are things that happen in the course of the play. Don John falsely points out what seems to be Hero's infidelity. Claudio denounces her in the church. She is stigmatized, publicly shamed. It is for this reason that Friar Francis—like the Friar Laurence of *Romeo and Juliet* who wanted to "dispose of" Juliet among a sisterhood of nuns—says that he will "conceal" Hero, if all else fails, "[a]s best befits her wounded reputation, / In some reclusive and religious life, / Out of all eyes, tongues, minds, and injuries" (4.1.240–242). In other words, the Friar will take her to a place where she cannot be "noted," where "Rumour painted full of tongues"—that animated figure of malign gossip from *2 Henry IV*—cannot do her more damage.

Characters talk about "nothing" and "noting" throughout the play. In the first scene Claudio asks Benedick if he has "noted" Leonato's daughter, and Benedick, punning on the various senses of "noted her not," but says he only "looked on her." In the same scene Don Pedro says that if Benedick falls in love despite his vows to do otherwise, he will "prove a notable argument" (1.1.209), which is to say, a public laughingstock. In act 4, when Benedick admits to Beatrice, "I do love nothing in the world so well as you. Is not that strange?" (4.1.266–267), she answers, full of grief about her cousin Hero's humiliation, "As strange as the thing I know not. It were as possible for me to say I loved nothing so well as you, but believe me not, and yet I lie not. I confess nothing nor I deny nothing. I am sorry for my cousin" (4.1.268–271). Leonato, confronted with the self-confessed deceiver Borachio, demands, "Which is the villain? Let me see his eyes, / That when I note another man like him / I may avoid him" (5.1.243–245). The Friar speaks of "noting" Hero's innocence in her face. Don Pedro, convinced—after the public denunciation—that Hero is dead, tells Leonato,

> My heart is sorry for your daughter's death,
> But on my honour she was charged with nothing
> But what was true and very full of proof.
>
> *5.1.105–107*

The enjambed line ("she was charged with nothing / But what was true and very full of proof") is richly ambiguous, allowing for the phrase "charged with nothing" to linger in the ear of the audience, before it is capped by the legal certitude of apparent "truth" and "proof."

Probably the most significant verbal exchange on the topic of "nothing" and "noting," however, occurs fairly early in the play, when Don Pedro and Claudio set out to fool Benedick into thinking that Beatrice is in love with him, another pretense that turns out to be true. Pedro tries to get his attendant Balthasar to sing a song, and Balthasar demurs:

> Note this before my notes:
> There's not a note of mine that's worth the noting.
>
> *2.3.49–50*

Don Pedro seems to be struck—as if for the first time—by the possibility of wordplay here. "Why, these are very crochets that he speaks— / Note notes, forsooth, and nothing! (2.3.51–52). "Crochets" are whims and musical notes. Balthasar is punning on the whole question of whether "noting" is worth "nothing" or something—or, perhaps, everything. Ironically, the song he does sing is about infidelity, with its poignant caution:

> Sigh no more, ladies, sigh no more.
> Men were deceivers ever.
>
> *2.3.56–57*

But the men—Claudio and Don Pedro—do not note the song, which means nothing to them. They hear the sweet melody and do not heed the piquant words. As so often with onstage performances in Shakespeare's plays, whether the "Pyramus and Thisbe" play in *A Midsummer Night's Dream* or the songs of the owl and the cuckoo in *Love's Labour's Lost*, there is a discrepancy between what the offstage audience learns and what the onstage audience thinks it knows. The relevance of the inset performance is lost on the spectators for whom it is most germane.

It is not only the language but also the action of "noting" (noticing, slandering, singing) that dominates the stage for much of the play. Many scenes—and a few "unscenes," or offstage scenes—are constructed so that they embody the structure of overhearing. Thus, for example, Leonato's elderly brother, Antonio, tells Leonato that a servant has overheard Don Pedro and Claudio talking in the orchard, and that Don Pedro said he loved Hero and would propose to her. This is a false rumor, as we learn. Don Pedro will propose to Hero on Claudio's behalf, as a noble go-between. But Claudio, like Antonio, will be all too credulous in believing that "the Prince woos for himself." Meantime, Borachio, the confederate of Don Pedro's malcontent brother Don John, is perfuming a "musty room" (the opposite of a fragrant orchard or garden), where he overhears the truth: Don Pedro will act as an emissary for Claudio. At the revels in Leonato's house, in act 2, scene 1, Claudio himself makes the same error as Antonio's servant. He observes Don Pedro talking to Hero, and is convinced that he himself has been betrayed by his friend.

No sooner is this danger allayed by correct information than a second and more insidious danger replaces it, for Claudio's mistake here—while indicative of his self-doubt as a lover—is inadvertent, whereas the mistake that he and Don Pedro make when they spy upon "Hero" in her chamber window is the result of a deliberate trap for the unwary. Don John has persuaded Borachio to enact an apparent seduction scene, tricking Margaret, Hero's waiting-gentlewoman, into wearing her mistress's clothes. What Claudio and Pedro think they see is the virginal Hero engaged in love-play with another man. It is important to bear in mind that this is an escalating series of errors, or false notings. The first is trivial, the second mortal. As so often in Shakespeare—recall the Nurse's two embassies to Juliet, the first comic, the second tragic, in *Romeo and Juliet*—a structural repetition conditions the response of both character and audience.

When Hero is accused in the church, her own father, Leonato, believes that she is guilty, adducing as evidence what he himself has noted: "[S]he will not add to her damnation / A sin of perjury. She not denies it" (4.1.171–172). Since she does not speak—and Hero very frequently declines to speak—her father thinks he has noted that she is guilty. Hero falls to the floor in a swoon, and again there is false noting: many present, including Claudio and Don Pedro, are convinced that she is dead. This mistake sets up the possibility of Hero's quasi-miraculous "rebirth" in the final scene. And in that scene Hero becomes a literal emblem of "nothing," a mysterious masked and unspeaking figure who could be anyone or no one. Claudio, suffused with guilt for having supposedly murdered his innocent beloved by slander, has agreed to take a new bride on faith. He is told he must marry her sight unseen—she is said to be Antonio's daughter, a figure heretofore unmentioned—without noting or seeing her face-to-face. In a version of the classical tale of Orpheus and Eurydice, but here with a happy ending, the faith of the lover revives his "dead" beloved.

The church scene (4.1) is deftly placed in the play between two scenes involving the foolish constables. In the first of these two scenes, Dogberry and his men, having stumbled on Borachio and his crime, attempt to report to Leonato the plot to defame his daughter Hero, but Leonato is too impatient to listen—he will not "note" them—and the result is that both Leonato and Hero suffer. After the church scene, a long-suffering Sexton gets the truth out of Dogberry, and we learn that Don John has fled, so that the audience begins to see the possibility of a satisfactory resolution.

This potentially tragic scenario of noting and false noting, making something of "nothing," has its counterpart in the comic gulling of those impervious sophisticates Beatrice and Benedick. As is not uncommon in Shakespearean plays about marriage, the interval between betrothal and wedding is regarded as a carnival or play space, in which the time can be whiled away by popular jests and entertainments. (A useful comparison could be made here to *A Midsummer Night's Dream,* and indeed to Shakespeare's other play about the wedding of Theseus and Hippolyta, the late tragicomedy *The Two Noble Kinsmen,* written with John Fletcher.) In this case Beatrice's and Benedick's friends determine to set them up, carefully staging little plays within the play in which each is made to overhear the news that the other is secretly in love. As their friends—and the audience—suspect, this has the immediate effect of making each capitulate to the feelings of love that have heretofore been denied or repressed. Indeed, the comic effect, drawn out in these highly successful scenes, is to make both Beatrice and Benedick exhibit the most extravagant and stereotypical signs of love—the very sentimentality that they have mocked in others. When Claudio and Don Pedro pretend to feel pity for the lovelorn Beatrice, they elicit, as soon as they have left the stage, this magnificent piece of combined sophistry and confession from the abashed—and delighted—Benedick:

> This can be no trick. The conference was sadly borne. They have the truth of this from Hero. They seem to pity the lady. It seems her affections have their full bent. Love me! Why, it must be requited. I hear how I am censured. They say I will bear myself proudly if I perceive the love come from her. They say too that she will rather die than give any sign of affection. I did never think to marry. I must not seem proud. Happy are they that hear their detractions and can put them to mending. They say the lady is fair. 'Tis a truth, I can bear them witness. And virtuous—'tis so, I cannot reprove it. And wise, but for loving me. By my troth, it is no addition to her wit—nor no great argument of her folly, for I will be horribly in love with her. I may chance have some odd quirks and remnants of wit broken on me because I have railed so long against marriage; but doth not the appetite alter? A man loves the meat in his youth that he cannot endure in his age. Shall quips and sentences and these paper bullets of the brain awe a man from the career of his humour? No. The world must be peopled. When I said I would die a bachelor, I did not think I would live till I were married.

2.3.196–215

Benedick's charmingly self-regarding reverie is interrupted by Beatrice, come to fetch him in to dinner, and their subsequent conversation at cross-purposes, in which Benedick attempts to wring amorous meanings from the least promising fragments of dialogue ("Ha! 'Against my will I am sent to bid you come in to dinner.' There's a double meaning in that" [2.3.227–228]), has much of the flavor of Malvolio's reaction to the counterfeit letter in *Twelfth Night,* with the salutary difference that Benedick is ultimately wise enough to laugh at himself. The hyperbolic language here, suggesting that the lady will die of unrequited love, is balanced in the romantic plot between Claudio and Hero by the news of the death of the bride defamed at the altar. Both of the scenes of gulling and overhearing, set as affectionate traps for Beatrice and Benedick, are staged in a garden or orchard, itself the highly conventional setting for love and seduction in literature and myth. As Benedick rushes from the stage, he declares that he will take pity on her, love her, and above all, in a complete and joyful capitulation to stereotype: "I will go get her picture" (2.3.232).

We have seen that Beatrice and Benedick are in fact already in love with each other when their friends decide to provoke them into action by gossiping where they can be overheard. Are Hero and Claudio likewise already prone to the behavior that produces their near-tragedy? Is there anything other than a perfectly natural reticence in speech that renders Claudio and Hero vulnerable to the plot devised against them? Hero, like several other virginal heroines in the plays, begins as a dutiful daughter submissive to, and unquestioning of, her father's will. Leonato tells her that he thinks Don Pedro loves her, and she seems to prepare herself for marriage to the Prince. Then it turns out that Claudio is the actual suitor, and she accepts without question this change in plans for her future, submitting willingly to the new marriage. She is entirely accepting, and relatively passive, especially when compared to the more spirited Beatrice. Equally significantly, she is—again like a number of Shakespearean comic and even tragic daughters—shy and reluctant in sexual matters. When the waiting-gentlewoman Margaret (who will impersonate her in the chamber window, flirting with Borachio) makes the earthy suggestion that Hero will soon be heavier by the weight of a husband, her rebuke is immediate: Margaret should be ashamed to think such thoughts.

As for Claudio, Benedick's "my lord Lackbeard," the young war hero whom we have heard speak of his earlier "liking" for Hero before he was distracted by the "rougher task" of battle, he is not automatically to be faulted for seeking a go-between to speak his words of love, a not uncommon practice in this period of arranged marriages. But it is more problematic, perhaps, that he should offer to leave Messina immediately after the marriage, choosing the company of Don Pedro over that of his new wife:

Don Pedro	I do but stay till your marriage be consummate, and then go I toward Aragon.
Claudio	I'll bring you thither, my lord, if you'll vouchsafe me.
Don Pedro	Nay, that would be as great a soil in the new gloss of your marriage as to show a child his new coat and forbid him to wear it.

3.2.1–6

It is impossible not to hear in these lines an echo of Juliet's great speech of sexual eagerness and desire as she waits for her own wedding night: "So tedious is this day / As is the night before some festival / To an impatient child that hath new robes / And may not wear them" (*Romeo and Juliet* 3.2.28–31). The juxtaposition is telling. Juliet, a virginal bride, is far more articulate in her longing than the young soldier Claudio, whose prince and captain voices the passion that he himself does not express, and may not fully acknowledge. The preference, however brief and ceremonial, for male bonding and homosociality over marriage and the wedding bed is indicative of something about Claudio, about his own degree of self-understanding. His histrionic outburst in the church, where he denounces Hero in full view of the congregation, seems of a piece with his ambivalence and self-doubt. He is still looking at himself through others' eyes. This is, of course, why he is so vulnerable to Don John's suggestion, voiced in a temptation scene that closely prefigures Othello's temptation by Iago, save that in the scene with Claudio, Don Pedro is also present. "[T]he lady is disloyal," Don John announces. "Go but with me tonight, you shall see her chamber window entered, even the night before her wedding day. If you love her then, tomorrow wed her. But it would better fit your honour to change your mind" (3.2.85–86, 93–97). John offers what in *Othello* will be called "ocular proof": trust your eyes, not your heart. And Claudio answers in kind: "If I see anything tonight why I should not marry her, tomorrow, in the congregation where I should wed, there will I shame her" (3.2.103–105). And Don Pedro, who—we might think—should know better, is ready to second the attack: "And as I wooed for thee to obtain her, I will join with thee to disgrace her" (3.2.106–107).

The scene that follows is the most dramatic of the play, and indeed one of the most dramatic in Shakespearean comedy. It begins with the formal language of a marriage ceremony, then quickly falls apart, becoming one of those broken ceremonies or maimed rites that mark key scenes in Shakespeare from the lists at Coventry in *Richard II* ("Stay, the King hath thrown his warder down") to the *Mousetrap* play in *Hamlet* ("The king rises." "Give o'er the play."):

Friar	You come hither, my lord, to marry this lady?
Claudio	No.

4.1.4–6

Although Leonato hastens to try to understand this as a mere syntactical nicety ("To be married to her. Friar, you come to marry her"), the full extent of the reversal is shortly manifest:

Claudio	Will you with free and unconstrainèd soul Give me this maid, your daughter?
Leonato	As freely, son, as God did give her me.
Claudio	And what have I to give you back whose worth May counterpoise this rich and precious gift?
Don Pedro	Nothing, unless you render her again.
Claudio	Sweet Prince, you learn me noble thankfulness. There, Leonato, take her back again.

> Give not this rotten orange to your friend.
> She's but the sign and semblance of her honour.
> Behold, how like a maid she blushes here!
> O, what authority and show of truth
> Can cunning sin cover itself withal!
> Comes not that blood as modest evidence
> To witness simple virtue? Would you not swear,
> All you that see her, that she were a maid,
> By these exterior shows? But she is none.
> She knows the heat of a luxurious bed.
> Her blush is guiltiness, not modesty.
>
> *4.1.22–40*

"This looks not like a nuptial," comments Benedick from his place in the congregation, and Beatrice, as shocked as he, replies, " 'True,' O God!" Now Don Pedro swears that he, too, saw Hero "[t]alk with a ruffian at her chamber window." When Don Pedro refers to "vile encounters" between Hero and the man, Don John hastens to interpose, "[T]hey are / Not to be named, my lord, not to be spoke of" (4.1.93–94). Once again the determinedly reticent Don John speaks of not-speaking, in this case with an Iago-like twist, for these particular encounters cannot be named or described, since they did not in fact take place. Claudio's apostrophe to Hero, which will bring her to the point of swooning, is a striking echo of an earlier moment of rejection and farewell. "O Hero! What a Hero hadst thou been," he says in the church scene,

> If half thy outward graces had been placed
> About thy thoughts and counsels of thy heart!
> But fare thee well, most foul, most fair, farewell.
>
> *4.1.98–101*

But notice that we have heard this too-hasty and ill-informed rejection speech from him before, at the masked ball in act 2—the play's other great moment of onstage theatrical spectacle—when Claudio, wearing a visor that hides his identity, is persuaded that Don Pedro has approached Hero to make her his own wife, rather than as an embassy for his friend. Don John and Borachio plant this idea, and it instantly takes root:

Claudio   'Tis certain so, the Prince woos for himself.
            Friendship is constant in all other things
            Save in the office and affairs of love.
            Therefore all hearts in love use their own tongues.
            Let every eye negotiate for itself,
            And trust no agent; for beauty is a witch

Against whose charm faith melteth into blood.
This is an accident of hourly proof,
Which I mistrusted not. Farewell, therefore, Hero.

2.1.152–160

That all hearts in love should use their own tongues is a lesson he does not learn. In the ball scene he is quickly and hopelessly jealous. Again and again he "notes" wrongly; he makes much ado of nothing. It is interesting to recall that at the masked ball the only men who do not wear visors are Don John and Borachio, the two figures who are already falsifying themselves, without benefit of costume. And Claudio's visor, together with his silence, anticipates the masked figure of the unspeaking Hero in the second, far more subdued and penitent, wedding scene (5.4).

By this time only Claudio and Don Pedro, Hero's accusers, still remain in the dark. After her denunciation and swoon in the church, Friar Francis had led Hero offstage with the mystical injunction "Come, lady, die to live," a phrase that prefigures the resurrection to come. Paradox is the chief rhetorical device of the play, and this resonant phrase is its perfect embodiment. If Claudio does not repent of his errors, the Friar counsels Hero, she will be placed in a nunnery. And how did the Friar know that Hero was in fact innocent? "By noting of the lady." By observing her blushes and her anger. Much ado about noting. But eventually because of the revelations of the bumbling but vigilant watchmen, the others know that she is alive and has been unjustly accused.

The revelation or resurrection scene thus unfolds with the usual element of discrepant awareness: the audience in the theater and most of those onstage are aware that Hero is alive, but her husband-to-be and his best man are not. The fiction is that Claudio will marry the daughter of Antonio. "My brother hath a daughter, / Almost the copy of my child that's dead, / And she alone is heir to both of us," Leonato had said to him. "Give her the right you should have giv'n her cousin, / And so dies my revenge" (5.1.272–276). Now, on the morning of this wedding, Leonato asks, "Are you yet determined / Today to marry with my brother's daughter?" and Claudio replies, "I'll hold my mind, were she an Ethiope" (5.4.36–38). The Friar—the same who presided at the first ceremony—will make this marriage, and Antonio is sent to bring in the bride, who enters, like her attendants, masked. Thus in visual and formal terms this third ceremonial scene will incorporate elements from the previous two, the masked ball and the aborted wedding. And yet the mask is, in this case, almost a shroud, since Hero will revive, in her lover's eyes, from death:

Claudio	Which is the lady I must seize upon?
Antonio	This same is she, and I do give you her.
Claudio	Why then, she's mine. Sweet, let me see your face.
Leonato	No, that you shall not till you take her hand

	Before this Friar and swear to marry her.
Claudio	[*to* HERO] Give me your hand before this holy friar.
	I am your husband if you like of me.
Hero	[*unmasking*] And when I lived I was your other wife;
	And when you loved, you were my other husband.
Claudio	Another Hero!
Hero	Nothing certainer.
	One Hero died defiled, but I do live,
	And surely as I live, I am a maid.
Don Pedro	The former Hero, Hero that is dead!
Leonato	She died, my lord, but whiles her slander lived.
Friar	All this amazement can I qualify.

5.4.53–67

The Friar is prepared to tell the story, to "let wonder seem familiar" (5.4.70). But this remarkable romance moment of resurrection and remarriage, a moving spectacle upon the stage, is not permitted to stand uninterrupted. Instead the play turns back toward the familiar and witty terrain of comedy, as Benedick asks, "[W]hich is Beatrice?" He sees her remove her mask, demands to know if she loves him as his friends had sworn, and thus begins to unravel the second, and far more comic, of the play's deceptions:

Benedick	They swore that you were almost sick for me.
Beatrice	They swore that you were wellnigh dead for me.
Benedick	'Tis no such matter. Then you do not love me?
Beatrice	No, truly, but in friendly recompense.

5.4.80–83

Before these proud and sensitive spirits can back away completely from their previous admissions, their friends produce the ocular proof. Claudio has taken from Benedick "a paper written in his hand, / A halting sonnet of his own pure brain, / Fashioned to Beatrice," and Hero gleefully waves "another, / Writ in my cousin's hand, stol'n from her pocket, / Containing her affection unto Benedick" (5.4.86–90). The tables are now completely turned, as Claudio and Hero act (for the moment) the part of the experienced and settled lovers, and Beatrice and Benedick stand exposed in their pretense. "A miracle!" crows Benedick. "Here's our own hands against our hearts" (5.4.91).

It is not an accident that this final reversal is accomplished by means of writing, which tells the truth about their love while the witty speakers fib and spar. We have been vouchsafed a comical glimpse of Benedick trying to write his love poem: "I cannot show it in rhyme. I have tried. I can find out no rhyme to 'lady' but 'baby,' an innocent rhyme; for 'scorn,' 'horn,' a hard rhyme; for 'school,' 'fool,' a babbling rhyme. Very ominous endings. No, I was not born under a rhyming planet, nor I cannot woo in festival terms" (5.2.30–35). And yet he does. *Much Ado About Nothing* is one of several Shakespeare plays to juxtapose overtly the spoken and the written, and in this play the latter is often called upon to stabilize or interpret the former. The penance Leonato had imposed on Claudio, for his slander of Hero in the sacred precincts of the church, was that he should "labour . . . in sad invention" and hang an epitaph upon Hero's tomb. The epitaph, beginning "Done to death by slanderous tongues," ends with the conventional sentiment that poetry will make the dead live forever: "So the life that died with shame / Lives in death with glorious fame" (5.3.3, 7–8). Dogberry the constable, one of Shakespeare's most effective verbal clowns, the mouthpiece for some of the playwright's best malapropisms, relies on writing to pin down elusive fact, instructing the Sexton to "bring his pen and inkhorn to jail" and interjecting, throughout the important and revealing Sexton scene, instructions for translating words into text, as one by one the "malefactors" are charged with their crime: "Pray write down 'Borachio.' . . . Write down 'Master Gentleman Conrad.' . . . Write down that they hope they serve God. . . . Write down Prince John a villain" (4.2.11–36). The Sexton faithfully transcribes the testimony, or "examination," given by the Watch, and takes it to show to Leonato. It is this written evidence that will convince Leonato of Hero's innocence and John's villainy. Dogberry, left alone onstage with the captured men, who vent their spleen by calling him an ass, is magnificent in his wish that the literate Sexton were still present to record this insult:

> O that he were here to write me down an ass! But masters, remember that I am an ass. Though it be not written down, yet forget not that I am an ass. . . . Bring him away. O that I had been writ down an ass!
>
> *4.2.68–78*

That this is a favor the playwright has done for his character, even in the Sexton's absence, has long been a delight to audiences and readers. The role of Dogberry was originally played by Will Kemp, the same actor who played Bottom in *A Midsummer Night's Dream*, and we might imagine that spectators would make this connection. Dogberry/Kemp had already been "writ down an ass," with equal insouciant triumph, in Shakespeare's earlier play.

In contrast to writing, speech is impossibly slippery and treacherous for Dogberry, who says "suspect" for "respect" ("Does thou not suspect my place? Dost thou not suspect my years?" [4.2.67–68]) and "auspicious" for "suspicious," and who thinks it is a compliment when Leontato calls him and his partner "tedious" ("It pleases your worship to say so, but . . . if I were as tedious as a king I could find it in my heart to bestow it all of your worship" [3.5.17–20]). As he reports the crimes of Don John's men, it is striking that he describes all their offenses as versions of bad speech: "Marry, sir, they have committed false report, moreover they have spoken untruths, secondarily they are

Henry V

DRAMATIS PERSONAE

Chorus

King Harry V of England, *claimant to the French throne*

Duke of Gloucester, *his brother*

Duke of Clarence, *his brother*

Duke of Exeter, *his uncle*

Duke of York

Salisbury

Westmorland

Warwick

Archbishop of Canterbury

Bishop of Ely

Richard, *Earl of Cambridge, a traitor*

Henry, *Lord Scrope of Masham, a traitor*

Thomas Grey, *a traitor*

Pistol, *formerly Falstaff's companion*

Nim, *formerly Falstaff's companion*

Bardolph, *formerly Falstaff's companion*

Boy, *formerly Falstaff's page*

Hostess, *formerly Mistress Quickly, now Pistol's wife*

Captain Gower, *an Englishman*

Captain Fluellen, *a Welshman*

Captain MacMorris, *an Irishman*

Captain Jamy, *a Scot*

Sir Thomas Erpingham

John Bates, *an English soldier*

Alexander Court, *an English soldier*

Michael Williams, *an English soldier*

Herald

King Charles VI of France

Isabel, *his wife and queen*

The Dauphin, *their son and heir*

Catherine, *their daughter*

Alice, *an old gentlewoman*

The Constable of France, *a French nobleman at Agincourt*

Duke of Bourbon, *a French nobleman at Agincourt*

Duke of Orléans, *a French nobleman at Agincourt*

Duke of Berri, *a French nobleman at Agincourt*

Lord Rambures, *a French nobleman at Agincourt*

Lord Grandpré, *a French nobleman at Agincourt*

Duke of Burgundy

Montjoy, *the French Herald*

Governor of Harfleur

French Ambassadors to England

 ACH ACT of *The Life of Henry V* begins with a prologue, and each of these, as we will see, has the paradoxical effect of both bringing the audience closer to the dramatic action and marking the impossibility of conveying the "truth" of that action on the stage. The prologue to the first act is justly famous, both for its high rhetorical style and for its evocative description of the theater-space. A character called the Chorus—variously costumed, in the history of stage productions, in armor, in Elizabethan attire, in a supposedly "timeless" cloak, and as the personification of Time himself—comes forth to introduce the action, and the play:

> O for a muse of fire, that would ascend
> The brightest heaven of invention:
> A kingdom for a stage, princes to act,
> And monarchs to behold the swelling scene.
> Then should the warlike Harry, like himself,
> Assume the port of Mars, and at his heels,
> Leashed in like hounds, should famine, sword, and fire
> Crouch for employment. But pardon, gentles all,
> The flat unraisèd spirits that hath dared
> On this unworthy scaffold to bring forth
> So great an object. Can this cock-pit hold
> The vasty fields of France? Or may we cram
> Within this wooden O the very casques
> That did affright the air at Agincourt?
>
> Henry V *Prologue 1–14*

These are the questions the Prologue puts forth, and the answer, of course, is no. This "cock-pit" *cannot* hold the "vasty fields of France," nor can this "wooden O" contain all the soldiery and armor that fought in the Battle of Agincourt.

"Wooden O," now a celebrated phrase often used as shorthand for Elizabethan playhouses in general and for Shakespeare's Globe in particular, is an apt description of the multisided structures built in the Bankside district along the Thames. The Globe, built in 1599, was a polygon with sixteen sides—essentially round. The Curtain, which may have been the site of the first performances of *Henry V*, was also a round playhouse. A "cock-pit" was originally, as the name implies, a place for the fighting of gamecocks, a popular Elizabethan sport. The buildings constructed for this purpose were sometimes used for the performance of plays, and later the term came to be used as a synonym for "theater." (Our term "orchestra pit," for a space below floor level at the front of a theater, is related to the same word.) What is being emphasized with the use of both terms, "wooden O" and "cock-pit," is the inadequate nature of the theater—any theater—to contain such intractable elements as the "vasty fields of France," where the play's battles will be set, or indeed the majesty of kingship, personated onstage by actors. The "gentles" in the audience, gentlemen and gentlewomen, are requested "[g]ently to hear" the play—that is, to make gracious allowances for its inevitable deficiencies.

This kind of apologia is familiar from the epilogues as well as the internal prologues of other Shakespearean plays. (Puck's Epilogue to *A Midsummer Night's Dream*, for example, begins, "If we shadows have offended, / Think but this and all is mended: / That you have but slumbered here.") But in the case of *Henry V,* where what is at stake is English history and English heroism, the prologues (and indeed the final and deflating Epilogue) are both more numerous and more insistent, reminding the audience at every turn that the play's illusion *is* illusion. We are asked to "[s]uppose within the girdle of these walls / Are now confined two mighty monarchies" (Prologue 19–20) and told: "Think, when we talk of horses, that you see them" (26). And in the prologue to act 5 we are asked to "behold, / In the quick forge and working-house of thought, / How London doth pour out her citizens" (5.0.22–24). The "quick forge and working-house of thought" is the mind. Thus these prologues, rather than increasing the realism and immediacy of the play, instead underscore the fact that it *is* a play. While the topic of *Henry V* is history, its mode of presentation is drama, and dramatic fiction. Yet the apparent deficiency is also an advantage. Another way of understanding the claims and disclaimers of the prologues is to see that they announce the immediacy and currency of "history" for the present day— a theme that will itself be stressed by King Henry V when he comes, on the battlefield in act 4, scene 3, to predict the future reputation of those who will have fought with him that day. History is the reputation of the soldier king and his newly united countrymen. In *Henry IV Part 1* Prince Hal pledged, in his "I know you all" soliloquy, that he would fulfill his hidden promise, "[r]edeeming time when men think least I will." T. S. Eliot, perhaps remembering these lines, wrote powerfully in his *Four Quartets* about the role of the poet in culture, where "Every phrase and every sentence is an end and a beginning, / Every poem an epitaph," and where

> We die with the dying:
> See, they depart, and we go with them.
> We are born with the dead:
> See, they return, and bring us with them.
> The moment of the rose and the moment of the yew-tree
> Are of equal duration. A people without history
> Is not redeemed from time, for history is a pattern
> Of timeless moments. . . .
>
> .   .   .   .
>
> History is now and England.
>
> *T. S. Eliot, "Little Gidding," section 5, lines 15–24*

For Shakespeare, too, and specifically for *Henry V*, history is "now and England" when it is retold, rewritten, or presented on the stage. History in the theater is to be played over and over, and it constitutes the epitaph for those who die in war. The audience is urged, by the use of its imagination, working collaboratively with the author and with the actor, to re-create the world of Henry V and to render his time-bound victory—soon to be lost through the weakness of his son and successor, the child-king Henry VI—timeless in memory and power.

As the play opens, we can observe something of both the achievements and the limitations of King Henry V's new world. For example, the bishops who are urging him to battle against France have rather mercenary motives for doing so, but the King whose "sleeping sword of war" they will awaken is, for them, clearly a redeemed man:

> Consideration like an angel came
> And whipped th'offending Adam out of him,
> Leaving his body as a paradise.
>
> *1.1.29–31*

The King is no longer a wild young prince called Hal, but rather a king who has reclaimed the comfortable name of Harry, a name he shared in *Henry IV Part 1* with Hotspur (Harry Percy), his chief rival. And this King Harry is a man who expressly and deliberately defines himself as a Christian king:

> We are no tyrant, but a Christian king,
> Unto whose grace our passion is as subject
> As is our wretches fettered in our prisons.
>
> *1.2.241–243*

From the royal plural to the disquieting image of a king's passion chained to his grace as a prisoner is chained to his prison, these are indications of necessary self-control and even self-sacrifice. It is in this somber spirit of resolve that the King receives a "tun of treasure" sent him by his opposite number, the Dauphin of France. "What treasure, uncle?" he inquires. "Tennis balls, my liege," is the answer (1.2.258). Why tennis balls? They are a symbol of frivolity, appropriate for the playboy prince the Dauphin still thinks he is confronting when he claims, in act 2, that England is "so idly kinged, / Her sceptre so fantastically borne / By a vain, giddy, shallow, humorous youth, / that fear attacks her not" (2.4.26–28). Tennis is a "French" game, said to have originated in France in the Middle Ages; known as "jeu de paume," it is played on a "court." Several Shakespeare plays of this period mention tennis as an aristocratic entertainment, including *2 Henry IV*, where it becomes the occasion for Prince Hal to joke about Poins's lack of clean linen, and *Much Ado About Nothing*, where we are told that Benedick has shaved his beard so as to appear presentable as Beatrice's lover, and that "the old ornament of his cheek hath already stuffed tennis balls"—apparently an actual practice of the period. But King Henry V's

In marked contrast to Richard II, whose death he mourns and repents, this King will not continue to foster favorites who act against the public weal. Rather, he will put aside private feelings and private friendships to become a public man. Three traitors are found among his retinue, Cambridge, Scrope, and Grey. Henry tests them by suggesting that he might offer mercy to a man who has, we are told, "railed against his person," spoken against the King. When Cambridge, Scrope, and Grey all insist that he respond not with mercy but with justice, he turns this same advice against them: "The mercy that was quick in us but late / By your own counsel is suppressed and killed" (2.2.76–77). This language of suppression and repression will characterize both the King and the play. Richard II had found Judases everywhere, and traitors in both Mow-bray and Bolingbroke, but his own weakness was such that he allowed Boling-broke to live, and to return to England—and Bolingbroke became responsible for Richard's death. Henry V, King Harry, is by contrast unyielding to the trai-tors in his midst, his own Judases: "I will weep for thee, / For this revolt of thine methinks is like / Another fall of man" (2.2.137–139).

Again and again in this play we will hear language and see actions that echo and correct the pattern of *Richard II*. Richard's inward wars become outward wars. Richard's weakness with traitors becomes a necessary and merciless execu-tion of malefactors. Just as *Henry IV Part 2* echoed and balanced *Part 1*, so will *Henry V* repeatedly echo and balance *Richard II*: (1) the King who thought he was Christ ("Arm, arm, my name!"; "you Pilates / Have here delivered me to my sour cross" [*Richard II* 3.2.82; 4.1.230–231]) will be contrasted with the King who followed the example of Christ (eating and drinking with common-ers; going in disguise, as an ordinary man, among his fellows) without self-conscious theatricality; (2) the narcissistic, private, inward-looking moment when Richard II calls for a mirror in the deposition scene, only to dash it to the ground in anger, frustration, and self-disgust, is transmuted into the tri-umphantly public moment when Henry V is described, by the choric voice of the prologue in the play's second act, as "the mirror of all Christian kings" (2.0.6); (3) the pattern of banishment and exclusion, sometimes playful and sometimes dead serious (and sometimes both at once), is continued and expanded; and (4) the new King's stern sense of political necessity has been pre-figured in the previous plays. In *Henry IV Part 1*, in reply to Falstaff's lighthearted "Banish plump Jack, and banish all the world," we heard the chilling mono-syllables of resolute reply: "I do; I will"—a lesson Falstaff did not, and would not, learn. In *Part 2* that ominous promise of kingly self-control became an overt rejection: "I know thee not, old man. Fall to thy prayers" (*2 Henry IV* 5.5.45). In *Henry V* the world of "working days" replaces the "playing holidays" of *1 Henry IV*. Thus, too, the execution of Prince Hal's old tavern companion Bar-dolph, who has robbed a church, is accompanied by a terse admonition: "We would have all such offenders so cut off" (3.6.98). So much for old friendships.

In fact, the whole of yet another old order is dying off in this history play: the old order, or "old disorder," of the tavern world and the world of Misrule.

Corporal Nim, whose name is an Old English word meaning "to steal," warns darkly that "[m]en may sleep, and they may have their throats about them at that time, and some say knives have edges" (2.1.18–20); he is hanged like Bardolph. By the end of the play Mistress Quickly, too, is dead, having succumbed, appropriately in this play about French-English wars, to a "malady of France" (5.1.73)—an English term for venereal disease. Most shocking of all, Falstaff is dead, Falstaff who throughout two entire plays steadfastly asserted his youth, and who seemed to be, in his way, an eternal energy, an eternal spirit. "The King has killed his heart" (2.1.79), says Mistress Quickly, and later she poignantly describes the moment when he ascended to the place she calls "Arthur's bosom," a splendidly "English" malapropism for the biblical phrase "in Abraham's bosom" (Luke 16:22):

> "How now, Sir John?" quoth I. "What, man? Be o' good cheer." So a cried out, "God, God, God," three or four times. Now I, to comfort him, bid him a should not think of God; I hoped there was no need to trouble himself with any such thoughts yet. So a bade me lay more clothes on his feet. I put my hand into the bed, and felt them, and they were as cold as any stone. Then I felt to his knees, and so up'ard, and up'ard, and all was cold as any stone.
>
> *2.3.16–23*

This little Shakespearean "unscene," not witnessed by the audience but reported to us, is both comical and poignant. To feel a man from the knees "up'ard, and up'ard" is, for the Hostess, perhaps the surest test of telling life from death (the pun on "stone," meaning "testicle," underscores the point), and for Falstaff, about whom Poins had jested in *Part 2* that his desire had for so many years outlived performance, it is a fitting, if also fittingly bathetic, final encomium.

What has died with Falstaff? It is useful to compare the death of this Sir John to that of another iconic figure, John of Gaunt, in *Richard II*. The old fat man and the old thin man have a good deal in common. Both deaths signal the passing of an order long in power, the "other Eden" world of John of Gaunt, medieval, feudal, and hierarchical, and the world of Misrule of Sir John Falstaff. The death of Falstaff reported in the second act of *Henry V* is a counterpart, and fallen echo, of that earlier defining moment.

We will again encounter this vision of kingship as a role that necessitates coldness, rigid self-control, and fettered passions in Shakespeare's later plays, where calculating characters like Octavius Caesar prevail over more robustly heroic, if flawed, figures like Julius Caesar and Antony of *Antony and Cleopatra*. But the figures that survive and thrive from this play are the eccentric and aberrant ones: Pistol, Fluellen, even the absent Falstaff. Falstaff seemed to die at the end of *Henry IV Part 1*, but he rose up again with a lie. We are told that he has died early in this play, that the King has killed his heart, and yet again he rose up, in the city comedy *The Merry Wives of Windsor.* So comedy will always do, for it is "timeless" and "boundless"—until it comes face-to-face with death.

Increasingly, however, the new King resembles, not the discredited Falstaff, but his chief competitor in the realm of "honour," Hotspur, the Harry Percy whose ambitious heroism and valor in *Henry IV Part 1* have now become part of *this* Harry's persona and role. As we have seen, the French Dauphin miscalculates fatally in sending the English King his taunting gift of tennis balls. The Dauphin, we learn, has written a sonnet in praise of his horse, and he proudly claims, "[M]y horse is my mistress" (3.7.40). What is this but an enormously funny parody of Hotspur in *Part 1,* who says, half-jokingly, to his wife, "That roan shall be my throne" (*1 Henry IV* 2.4.64)? In King Harry, though, the intrinsic values for which Hotspur stood now find a sudden and appropriate place. We hear him declare, in the final wooing scene with Catherine the French princess, that he is no orator—this same witty wordsmith who has been delighting audiences with his nimble tongue for the length of three plays. "I speak to thee plain soldier," he will tell her (5.2.145–146). And the lady he woos is now, like Hotspur's wife, addressed as "Kate." He is like Hotspur, and also like his more ruthless self, in the words he speaks to his troops at Harfleur:

> Once more unto the breach, dear friends, once more,
> Or close the wall up with our English dead.
>
> 3.1.1–2

And this line, we are clearly given to understand, has become a rallying cry and a public slogan, since Bardolph parodies it in the following scene: "On, on, on, on, on! To the breach, to the breach!" (3.2.1). (During World War II, Laurence Olivier, then in uniform as a lieutenant of the Fleet Air Arm, delivered a number of patriotic addresses that closed with a stirring version of "Once more unto the breach.") But most of all, King Harry is the reincarnation of Hotspur's ambitious and capacious spirit in his wonderful speech in act 4 on the occasion of St. Crispin's Day. This speech, often recited out of context, became so popular in England as a patriotic set piece that it was frequently performed on its own. (Olivier's stirring delivery of it in 1942, on a radio program called "Into Battle," became the genesis for the 1944 film of *Henry V.*) Like Hotspur, King Harry now praises the quest for honor, and he expresses the view, as Hotspur had done on the field at Shrewsbury in *Henry IV Part 1,* that if there are fewer soldiers to fight, more glory will accrue to each:

King Harry   By Jove, I am not covetous for gold,
                Nor care I who doth feed upon my cost;
                It ernes me not if men my garments wear;
                Such outward things dwell not in my desires.
                But if it be a sin to covet honour

I am the most offending soul alive.

. . . .

We would not die in that man's company
That fears his fellowship to die with us.
This day is called the Feast of Crispian.
He that outlives this day and comes safe home
Will stand a-tiptoe when this day is named
And rouse him at the name of Crispian.
He that shall see this day and live t'old age
Will yearly on the vigil feast his neighbours
And say, "Tomorrow is Saint Crispian."
Then will he strip his sleeve and show his scars
And say, "These wounds I had on Crispin's day."
Old men forget; yet all shall be forgot,
But he'll remember, with advantages,
What feats he did that day. Then shall our names,
Familiar in his mouth as household words—
Harry the King, Bedford and Exeter,
Warwick and Talbot, Salisbury and Gloucester—
Be in their flowing cups freshly remembered.
This story shall the good man teach his son,
And Crispin Crispian shall ne'er go by
From this day to the ending of the world
But we in it shall be rememberèd,
We few, we happy few, we band of brothers.
For he today that sheds his blood with me
Shall be my brother; be he ne'er so vile,
This day shall gentle his condition.
And gentlemen in England now abed
Shall think themselves accursed they were not here,
And hold their manhoods cheap whiles any speaks
That fought with us upon Saint Crispin's day.

4.3.24–67

This extraordinary speech returns the play to many of the same themes raised at the beginning by the Prologue: memory, epitaph, and mortality. It proposes a kind of immortality in fame familiar from Shakespeare plays in other genres, like *Love's Labour's Lost*. But in this drama of English history the very existence of the play as a commemorative object confirms the ideology of the King's impassioned claim. Old men will remember us, as the reader and the audience remember. And, moreover, they will remember "with advantages," augmenting, expanding and embroidering upon, the facts of the battle. In this patriotic account of the transmission of feats of heroism, the tales told by veterans to their sons reverse the negative affect of "Rumour painted full of tongues" in *Part 2*, glorifying the "story" each time it is repeated. The issue of "reputation," so vital in *Richard II*, here returns with a positive result. Where King Richard II lay "in reputation sick" on the deathbed of his land, King Henry V confidently predicts that the outcome of this battle "[f]rom this day to the ending of the world" will be "freshly remembered" in annual celebration. Instead of appealing ineffectually to the angels on behalf of a theory of divine right, like Richard ("Arm, arm, my name!"), Henry appeals to a "band of brothers." The "fewness" of "[w]e few" may be a Hotspur trait, but the concept of a band of brothers is pure Hal. His education in the tavern world, his awareness of his own desire for "small beer," common comforts and common company, make him more than a vainglorious Hotspur. He has become the modern king a modern England needs. Whatever the audience may feel about his character, its calculations and self-dramatizations, the fit between this King and his circumstances is carefully crafted by the playwright, who was writing almost two hundred years after the Battle of Agincourt and would have had his own modern monarch, as well as Henry V, clearly in mind.

On the eve of Agincourt, the battle in which, famously, a small group of English noblemen and archers defeated a French army of foot soldiers and knights, the King wanders among troops who are weary, hungry, and despondent. The prologue to act 4 traces this royal progress:

> O now, who will behold
> The royal captain of this ruined band
> Walking from watch to watch, from tent to tent,
> Let him cry, "Praise and glory on his head!"
> For forth he goes and visits all his host,
> Bids them good morrow with a modest smile
> And calls them brothers, friends, and countrymen.
> Upon his royal face there is no note
> How dread an army hath enrounded him;
>
> . . . .
>
> A largess universal, like the sun,
> His liberal eye doth give to everyone,
> Thawing cold fear, that mean and gentle all
> Behold, as may unworthiness define,
> A little touch of Harry in the night.
>
> *4.0.28–47*

The cloak the King borrows is that of the old and faithful knight Sir Thomas Erpingham, and under this cloak—as under the cloak of night—the new King goes out among his subjects. To them he speaks in prose, calling himself "Harry Le Roy" (or *le roi*), a transparent alias of truth and falsehood. In this play about

France and England, French lessons and English lessons, "Le Roy" would have been pronounced to rhyme with "toy," but the audience, unlike Ancient Pistol, would clearly understand the ruse. Not realizing the "gentleman's" true identity, Pistol nonetheless offers up an irrepressible praise of his king:

> The King's a bawcock and a heart-of-gold,
> A lad of life, an imp of fame,
> Of parent good, of fist most valiant.
> I kiss his dirty shoe, and from heartstring
> I love the lovely bully. . . .

4.1.45–49

Like another Shakespearean braggart soldier, Don Armado in *Love's Labour's Lost,* Pistol is given to linguistic extravagance, even at the cost of linguistic accuracy. The common soldiers are less tolerant, and less effusive. They are frightened of dying in battle, and are inclined to think that the King does not understand their position. The disguised King, the king in effect come to earth among his subjects, speaks to them in words that recall, although with far more self-possession and self-knowledge, Richard II's belated and heartbroken discovery of his own mortality. "I live with bread, like you," said Richard, "feel want, / Taste grief, need friends. Subjected thus, / How can you say to me I am a king?" (*Richard II* 3.2.171–173). Here is this King's version, less autocratic but equally lonely, rejoicing in rather than deploring his human condition, as he speaks from his disguise as the Welshman Harry Le Roy:

> I think the King is but a man, as I am. The violet smells to him as it doth to me; the element shows to him as it doth to me. All his senses have but human conditions. His ceremonies laid by, in his nakedness he appears but a man.

4.1.99–102

And again:

> By my troth, I will speak my conscience of the King. I think he would not wish himself anywhere but where he is. . . . Methinks I could not die anywhere so contented as in the King's company, his cause being just and his quarrel honourable.

4.1.113–122

This is a doubled language that he learned from Falstaff in the Eastcheap tavern, where his great mentor likewise spoke of himself in the third person ("A goodly, portly man, i'faith, and a corpulent. . . . And now I remember me, his name is Falstaff. . . . Him keep with; the rest banish" [*1 Henry IV* 2.5.384–391]).

The King is playing a role here, at the same time that he is speaking no more or less than the truth. When his soldiers begin to make dispirited observations, like "I wish he were here alone" or "That's more than we know," the audience can sense Henry's growing feeling of isolation ("His ceremonies laid by, in his nakedness he appears but a man"). Anyone who recalls *Henry IV Part 2* will trace this bittersweet sentiment to the scene at this King's father's deathbed, where the son beheld the dying king asleep beside the glittering crown on his pillow ("Uneasy lies the head that wears a crown" [*2 Henry IV* 3.1.31]). As soon as he is alone onstage, Henry V speaks for the first time in this play in soliloquy, out of the darkness:

> What infinite heartsease
> Must kings neglect that private men enjoy?
> And what have kings that privates have not too,
> Save ceremony, save general ceremony?
> *4.1.218–221*

Ceremony, the trappings of office. Henry's rumination harks back, again, to Richard II, who said as he divested himself of the signs of kingship, "I give this heavy weight from off my head, / And this unwieldy sceptre from my hand. . . . / With mine own tears I wash away my balm, / With mine own hands I give away my crown" (*Richard II* 4.1.194–198). Again, here is Henry V:

> 'Tis not the balm, the sceptre, and the ball,
> The sword, the mace, the crown imperial.
> . . . .
> The throne he sits on, nor the tide of pomp
> That beats upon the high shore of this world—
> No, not all these, thrice-gorgeous ceremony,
> Not all these, laid in bed majestical,
> Can sleep so soundly as the wretched slave
> Who with a body filled and vacant mind
> Gets him to rest, crammed with distressful bread.
> *4.1.242–252*

The mention of bread, the staple food of the poor, sounds a persistent note throughout these history plays. As Richard II had marked his ordinary humanity ("I live with bread, like you"), so the tavern bill in Falstaff's pocket recorded, as Prince Hal noted with amusement in *Henry IV Part 1,* "but one halfpennyworth of bread to [an] intolerable deal of sack" (2.5.492–493). Behind this equation of bread with the ordinary, diurnal, "working day" world, the wages of the common man, stand the words of the Sermon on the Mount, "Give us this day our daily bread" (Matthew 6:11). Henry V, already associated with "small beer," is here also linked with a taste for "daily bread," for the working-day food of working-day men. He comes to the battlefield, cloaked, disguised as Harry Le Roy, to lift the spirits of his troops. Here he fulfills his promise to be a "Christian king" in another sense. Again the play stresses the loneliness as well as the responsibility of rule. His is a task that cannot finally be shared.

It is when the King is in disguise that he finds himself caught up in a quarrel with the soldier Williams. He tells the soldiers he has heard the King say that he will not be ransomed, and Williams contends that this is mere propaganda, a public utterance to make the soldiers fight cheerfully in a dangerous cause, and that the King would certainly consent to be ransomed. "If I live to see it," says the disguised King, "I will never trust his word after." "You'll never trust his word after! Come, 'tis a foolish saying," retorts Williams. Who are you that your trust should matter, one way or the other? And so the quarrel develops, and in fact it develops into a curiously familiar shape:

Williams	How shall I know thee again?
King Harry	Give me any gage of thine, and I will wear it in my bonnet. Then if ever thou darest acknowledge it, I will make it my quarrel.
Williams	Here's my glove. Give me another of thine.

4.1.192–196

For a moment we are back in the world of *Richard II,* with the formal challenge between Mowbray and Bolingbroke, complete with gages, oaths, and the promise of a fight—but in how different a spirit. This conflict is based on a matter of opinion rather than a matter of treason, and it is settled by a gesture of generosity and inclusiveness. "Your majesty came not like yourself" is Williams's defense when the truth is revealed, and the King will fill his glove up with gold coins, with "crowns." Bolingbroke's glove was thrown down to gain a crown. His son, Henry V, fills up his own glove with crowns, and gives it freely to a common soldier as a sign of fellowship.

For the same reason that the stage cannot hold the "vasty fields of France," it cannot hold the entire English army massed against the French. But the play presents a representative sampling of the various constituencies the King will need to meld into a single fighting—and living—force. This is the "colonial" moment for *Henry V,* as act 3, scene 2, introduces four officers speaking in four regional accents: Gower the Englishman, MacMorris the Irishman, Jamy the Scot, and the indomitable Fluellen, the Welshman. Together they present, onstage, a microcosm of the whole nation, a living, speaking map of Britain. (We might compare this scene emblematically to the famous "Ditchley portrait" of Queen Elizabeth, by Marcus Gheeraerts the Younger, in which the Queen, the mistress of her kingdom, stands on a map of England. Painted in

1592, the portrait partakes of the same national spirit as *Henry V*. As always, Shakespeare's "history" plays are concerned as much with current history as with the historical past, and his Henry V is a close relation, as well as an ancestor, of the reigning Queen.)

It is worth noting that the Irish captain, MacMorris, takes great offense when someone refers to his nation as if it were a separate entity. "What ish my nation?" he demands. "Who talks of my nation?" (3.3.62–63). His nation is now a part of King Harry's England. The fallen, fragmented world, divided into England, Ireland, Scotland, Wales, and France, is—for a moment, at least—about to be restored. Needless to say, this is an ideological construction. These subject "nations" all declare themselves eager to be ruled. Unlike Owen Glendower, they do not stand apart from English domination. We may recall the sage advice of Henry IV to his son, that he should "busy giddy minds / With foreign quarrels." The same sentiment is voiced more generously in this play by one of the common soldiers, Bates, who intercedes in a growing quarrel between his fellow soldier, Williams, and the disguised Henry V: "Be friends, you English fools, be friends. We have French quarrels enough" (4.1.206–207).

Civil wars, whether of language or of action, must and do give way to the energies of an external war, a war that is thought of, once again, as a kind of holy war. For when the battle is concluded, and the King hears the lengthy roll call of the French who have perished, he asks for "the number of our English dead" and is given a list miraculous for its brevity:

> King Harry   Edward the Duke of York, the Earl of Suffolk,
> Sir Richard Keighley, Davy Gam Esquire;
> None else of name, and of all other men
> But five-and-twenty. O God, thy arm was here,
> And not to us, but to thy arm alone
> Ascribe we all. When, without stratagem,
> But in plain shock and even play of battle,
> Was ever known so great and little loss,
> On one part and on th'other? Take it God,
> For it is none but thine.
>
> *4.8.97–106*

"God fought for us," says the King, calling for "holy rites" to commemorate the dead. Here an attentive Shakespearean audience might remember the far more cynical words of Prince John at Gaultres Forest as he betrayed the rebels: "God, and not we, hath safely fought today" (*2 Henry IV* 4.1.347). In this assertion, as in so many, Henry V both echoes and redeems the language and the actions of his predecessors.

Among the several army captains, the clear audience favorite is the Welshman, Fluellen, who, with an aplomb worthy of Bottom, declares that he is not ashamed of the King:

By Jeshu, I am our majesty's countryman. I care not who knows it, I will
confess it to all the world. I need not to be ashamed of your majesty,
praised be God, so long as your majesty is an honest man.

4.7.102–105

The King—who is, after all, "Harry of Monmouth" and the former Prince of
Wales—has had his own praise for Fluellen: "Though it appear a little out of
fashion, / There is much care and valour in this Welshman" (4.1.82–83). It is
Fluellen who stresses the King's Welsh ties: "All the water in Wye [a Welsh river]
cannot wash your majesty's Welsh plood out of your pody, I can tell you that"
(4.7.97–98). Here yet again we can note an echo of *Richard II,* the pendant to
this play: "Not all the water in the rough rude sea / Can wash the balm from an
anointed king." But King Harry is anointed by the people, by the Welsh
"plood" in his "pody." The confusion of *p* and *b* is a stage convention associated
with comic Welsh characters from Shakespeare's time to the present, and is also
magnificently on display in Fluellen's learned comparison of his king to a classical model he names as "Alexander the Pig." Fluellen knows his history, and proceeds, as did many Renaissance historians, by the same comparative method
exemplified in Plutarch's *Parallel Lives of the Noble Grecians and Romans,* drawing an extended historical analogy between Henry V and Alexander. When the
King gives Fluellen his "favor"—actually a glove that belongs to the common
soldier Williams—and watches to see how he defends himself against a beating,
it is in one sense the playful spirit of the old Prince Hal that is on display. But in
another sense this gesture is King Harry's acknowledgment that one Welshman
is a good as another.

Fluellen's chief opponent and polar opposite is Ancient Pistol, with whom
he becomes embroiled in a comic controversy in act 5. It is noteworthy that
Henry V, a play that centers on war and soldiery, concludes with two extended
comic scenes. In *1 Henry IV* comedy turned to history; here history turns to
comedy, and indeed to the promise of a marriage between the King of England
and the Princess of France. For a brief but brilliant moment, until the sober
voice of the Epilogue returns the audience to English history and to the losses
sustained by the weak King Henry VI ("[w]hich oft our stage hath shown")
the victory over France achieved at Agincourt is transmuted into rapproche-
ment. This play revisits, in both scenes in the final act, a topic that has been
stressed from *Richard II* through the *Henry IV* plays—the question of language
and its relationship to politics and rule. At issue is not only language-learning
but a respect for the multiplicity of languages, and an awareness—both comic
and serious—of the dangers of translation.

The first of these two scenes features the enforced language instruction of
Pistol, presided over by Fluellen, who is waiting for him with a leek, the onion-
like herb that is the national emblem of the Welsh. To Pistol's astonishment and
horror—and to the corresponding amusement of the audience—he is forced to
eat the leek, bite by bite, while Fluellen stands over him with a club. Pistol: "I

eat and eat. . . . Quiet thy cudgel, thou dost see I eat" (5.1.43–46). It is the English captain, Gower, who correctly interprets this event as a language lesson: "I have seen you gleeking and galling at this gentleman twice or thrice. You thought, because he could not speak English in the native garb, he could not therefore handle an English cudgel" (5.1.66–69). Valor, and not elaborate language or high birth, is now the mark of a gentleman—and of an English soldier. Yet our last glimpse of Pistol shows him, unfazed, swearing to turn bawd and cutpurse, and planning to return to England to make his fortune in the stews. The Pistols of this world cannot be killed in battle because they never go to battle. They represent the irreducible mischief in humankind, a mode of misrule that is not holiday, but rather anarchy and animal energy: "for, lambkins, we will live" (2.2.116).

Nonetheless, Pistol's comically discomfiting language lesson makes a serious political point. Warring populations and incomprehensible languages will divide a people just when the people most need to be united. Somewhere behind the scenes there is a faint whiff of a reference to Babel and Pentecost, the first the biblical moment when a multiplicity of languages divided mankind, and the second the moment when the capacity to speak and understand *all* languages enabled the Apostles to communicate universally ("And how hear we every man in our own tongue . . . ?" [Acts 2:8]). This may be one of the reasons for the presence of the rather comic wooing scene between the French Princess and the English King. Charming in itself, it also completes and concludes the theme of language and languages that has been present throughout all these history plays.

Catherine's language lesson in act 3, scene 4 has also engaged this theme, since even in the apparent safety of the Princess's chamber, danger lurks. The innocent French words *pieds* and *robe,* when rendered in the English tongue, are transformed into the vulgar terms "foot" and "cown" (for "gown"), which bring a blush to a maiden's cheek—and which still have their cognate counterparts in vulgar French and English. The delicious sense of naughtiness marked in Catherine's response is appropriate for her rank and station, and is joined—to the audience's amusement—by a palpable sense of resolve. For the Princess and her gentlewoman Alice, having discerned the danger, bravely decide to pronounce the words. This kind of comic language-learning scene, with the inevitable, and often lewd, mispronunciation or mistranslation of "foreign" words, is used by Shakespeare in several plays, including *Love's Labour's Lost* and *The Merry Wives of Windsor.* Closely akin are other scenes of malapropism in which learned and unlearned speakers find themselves at cross-purposes (for example, Dogberry and the Watch versus the aristocrats in *Much Ado About Nothing,* or even the foolish Sir Andrew Aguecheek in *Twelfth Night,* who despite his wealth and fashionable affectations does not know the meaning of the word *pourquoi*). But in *Henry V* the comical scene between the two Frenchwomen—a nice break after all the scenes at war—is in a way a domesticated version of the linguistic squabbles on the battlefield, and prepares the Princess for her political role as an English queen. Throughout *Henry V,* in fact, the King's continuing quest to speak and be understood is counterpointed by the adventures of Fluellen, on the one hand, and Catherine, on the other, so that it is quite fitting that the final act of the play should be divided between them, the first of these two scenes presenting the humiliation of Pistol, and the second the wooing of Catherine, with the King present and active in both.

King Harry's speeches in the wooing scene are prose, a form he has used, for three plays, on the battlefield or in the tavern but never, until now, at court. His declaration of love is couched, deliberately and significantly, in plain language. He is a "plain king," a "fellow of plain and uncoined constancy," who speaks to her "plain soldier" (5.2.124, 149, 146). "Plain" in this period is a term of art in language and style, in contrast to "curious" and "pointed." "Uncoined," meaning "not fabricated or invented," reverses once more the language of counterfeiting that pursued this King's father. Each word must now mean precisely and only what it says:

> King Harry   For these fellows of infinite tongue, that can rhyme themselves into ladies' favours, they do always reason themselves out again. What! A speaker is but a prater, a rhyme is but a ballad; . . . but a good heart, Kate, is the sun and the moon—or rather the sun and not the moon, for it shines bright and never changes, but keeps his course truly.
>
> *5.2.151–159*

"Kate" is itself the King's deliberate Englishing of the Princess's name, and it may remind the audience not only of Lady Percy (Hotspur's forthright Kate, whom he teased about swearing like a "comfit-maker's wife") but also of Kate/Katherine in *The Taming of the Shrew,* whose bridegroom likewise lectured her about the sun and the moon. In the balance of this final scene the King speaks French as well as English, the Princess English (of a comical sort) as well as French, and the betrothal is celebrated with a kiss in which King Harry finds "more eloquence . . . than in the tongues of the French Council" (5.2.256–258). The play that started out with a narrowly construed, casuistical reading of a Latin phrase—*In terram Salicam mulieres ne succedant,* translated as "No woman shall succeed in Salic land"—concludes, apparently, with the fruitful union of French and English, Welsh and Scot in a single, hopeful nation, united by a political marriage that is also presented as a love match.

And yet that hope is deliberately undercut by the play's Epilogue, which immediately follows the betrothal scene. The Epilogue reminds the audience with brutal directness that after Henry V came his son Henry VI, and that the child king Henry VI had so many conflicting advisers that everything gained by his father's war and marriage was swiftly lost. The Epilogue, in the form of a Shakespearean sonnet, returns the scenario to the playhouse, or rather to the "author" of the play and the "little room" in which his actors have performed:

> Thus far with rough and all-unable pen
>   Our bending author hath pursued the story,
> In little room confining mighty men,
>   Mangling by starts the full course of their glory.
> Small time, but in that small most greatly lived
>   This star of England. Fortune made his sword,
> By which the world's best garden he achieved,
>   And of it left his son imperial lord.
> Henry the Sixth, in infant bands crowned king
>   Of France and England, did this king succeed,
> Whose state so many had the managing
>   That they lost France and made his England bleed,
> Which oft our stage hath shown—and, for their sake,
> In your fair minds let this acceptance take.
>
> *Epilogue 1–14*

The triumph of *Henry V* is only a temporary one, momentary in terms of the scope of history. The history plays in Shakespeare's earlier sequence, "[w]hich oft our stage hath shown," depict in grim detail the consequences of the loss of France, the bleeding of England, and the long agony of the Wars of the Roses. The play the audience has been watching is, as the prologues have insisted, only an illusion, forged in the working-house of thought. The conventional request for applause ("let this acceptance take") returns the power to the audience, where it has always been. What we are asked to approve is a spectacle of victory, and a concept of kingship, that is finally only an idea, precariously achieved and too easily lost.

Julius Caesar

DRAMATIS PERSONAE

Julius Caesar
Calpurnia, *his wife*
Marcus Brutus, *a noble Roman,*
   opposed to Caesar
Portia, *his wife*
Lucius, *his servant*
Caius Cassius, *opposed to Caesar*
Casca, *opposed to Caesar*
Trebonius, *opposed to Caesar*
Decius Brutus, *opposed to Caesar*
Metellus Cimber, *opposed to Caesar*
Cinna, *opposed to Caesar*
Caius Ligarius, *opposed to Caesar*
Mark Antony, *a ruler of Rome*
   after Caesar's death
Octavius Caesar, *a ruler of Rome*
   after Caesar's death
Lepidus, *a ruler of Rome after*
   Caesar's death
Flavius, *a tribune of the people*
Murellus, *a tribune of the people*
Cicero, *a senator*
Publius, *a senator*
Popillius Laena, *a senator*
A Soothsayer

Artemidorus
Cinna the Poet
Pindarus, *Cassius's bondman*
Titinius, *an officer in Cassius's*
   army
Lucillius, *in Brutus's army*
Messala, *in Brutus's army*
Varrus, *in Brutus's army*
Claudio, *in Brutus's army*
Young Cato, *in Brutus's army*
Strato, *in Brutus's army*
Volumnius, *in Brutus's army*
Flavius, *in Brutus's army*
Dardanius, *in Brutus's army*
Clitus, *in Brutus's army*
A Poet
A Ghost of Caesar
A Cobbler
A Carpenter
Other Plebeians
A Messenger
Servants
Senators, soldiers, and
   attendants

OR MANY years *Julius Caesar* was regularly taught in American high schools, often as the first play of Shakespeare assigned. One reason for this may have been the concurrent study of Latin. Caesar's *Gallic Wars*, taught in the sophomore year, would have introduced students to the legendary hero of ancient Rome. Another plausible reason for its favor among educators was that *Julius Caesar* is one of the few Shakespeare plays that contains no sex, not a single bawdy quibble. An equal and opposite relation to adolescent sexuality leads high school teachers today to assign *Romeo and Juliet* instead. Young love and eroticism, especially in a work deemed irreproachably classic—and available, in any case, on the movie screen—are perhaps a more enticing way to introduce the music video generation to Shakespeare than a play concerned, as *Caesar* is, with political rivalry, martial competition, and the disillusionment of ideals.

Julius Caesar is one of Shakespeare's most subtle and sophisticated plays, addressing as it does some of the large and important issues that preoccupy the middle plays from *Henry IV Part 1* onward: the nature of kingship, the relationship of the public to the private self, the limits of reason, and the necessity of coming to terms with the irrational—the world beyond reason—as it presents itself in omens and portents, soothsayers and signs. In addition, this "Roman" play demonstrates clearly the crucial importance of the classical past for the readers and audiences of the English Renaissance. To Shakespeare's original audiences, a play about ancient Rome or ancient Troy was not an escapist document about a faraway world, but something very like the opposite: a powerful lesson in modern—that is to say, current, sixteenth century—ethics and statecraft. The Elizabethan view of history suggested that the Greeks and Romans provided models of conduct, that history taught, and that its lessons could—and should—be learned. Plutarch's *Parallel Lives of the Noble Grecians and Romans,* in the 1579 translation of Sir Thomas North, had an enormous influence on Shakespeare's plays and on the ways Elizabethans looked at their own history as it unfolded. The *"Parallel"* in the title *Parallel Lives* meant that the author provided not only a biography but also a comparison; thus the Greek general Alcibiades is compared with the Roman Coriolanus, and the Greek orator Demosthenes with the Roman Cicero. Plutarch's lives of Brutus, Caesar, and Antony were important sources for Shakespeare.

But the comparative method also implied the possibility of adding a third figure, one from the present day. Caesar, like Queen Elizabeth and her father, Henry VIII, was a monumental monarch, both loved and feared. Like Elizabeth, Caesar was a ruler without an heir of his own body, as Shakespeare's Caesar makes clear in the second scene of the play, when he urges Antony to touch Calpurnia, Caesar's wife, when he races in the Feast of Lupercal, the ancient festival of fruitfulness and fertility: "for our elders say / The barren, touchèd in this holy chase, / Shake off their sterile curse" (1.2.9–11). This episode is not in the Plutarchan source; Shakespeare adds it, to help make his point. Caesar's concern for an heir is one of the things that raise Brutus's fears, lest Caesar intend to found a dynasty, preempting the free choice of the people, and setting up a hereditary monarchy.

To Elizabethan England, as to the Rome of Julius Caesar, one of the most dreaded political consequences was the threat of civil war—a war that is pictured in this play both in the spectacle of triumvirs against conspirators after the death of Caesar, Antony and Octavius against Brutus and Cassius, and also in the informing spectacle of "Brutus, with himself at war" (1.2.48). Brutus is torn by his own conflicting feelings, between his private friendship with Caesar and his public dislike of kingship and dictatorship—of any absolute rule that approaches the condition of godhead. In short, the circumstances of Caesar's death, the conspiracy, and the chaos that descended on Rome after the murder would all have had the most direct and lively interest for Shakespeare's audience. And the topic provided for the dramatist a way of working out some of the political concepts with which he was struggling and coming to terms at the close of *Henry V*. Some early editors faulted Shakespeare for the historical "error" in act 2, scene 1, where a clock strikes. Since there were no striking clocks in ancient Rome, this detail was deemed an anachronism, and so it is, but that does not make it a mistake. The presence of a modern clock in Caesar's Rome abruptly reminds the audience of the double time period in which the play is set. Not only a history of the classical past, it is also a story of the present day. The supposed anachronism of the striking clock abruptly jars the audience from any complacency it may be feeling about the difference between "then" and "now."

The play is called *Julius Caesar*, but we might be justified in wondering why it is not called *Brutus*. Brutus's inner struggle occupies the moral center of the drama, and it is Brutus who names himself "poor Brutus, with himself at war." Like Henry IV, who precedes him in the plays, and Macbeth, who follows him, Brutus suffers from the Shakespearean malady of sleeplessness, an index of moral turmoil and guilt. Like Macbeth, and indeed like Hamlet, he hesitates on the brink of a cataclysmic action:

> Since Cassius first did whet me against Caesar
> I have not slept.
> Between the acting of a dreadful thing
> And the first motion, all the interim is
> Like a phantasma or a hideous dream.
> The genius and the mortal instruments
> Are then in council, and the state of a man,
> Like to a little kingdom, suffers then
> The nature of an insurrection.
>
> Julius Caesar 2.1.61–69

Once again, psychomachia, the struggle for control of a soul, is figured here in an image of civil war. Or, to put the matter slightly differently, the outside has again become the inside, and the inside the outside. Civil war inside the individual is projected outward as civil war in the land: "the state of a man, / Like to a little kingdom"—a microcosm—"suffers then / The nature of an insurrection."

Brutus's sleeplessness is mentioned twice: once here, before the murder is committed, and again on the field at Sardis, where the innocence of the boy Lucius and the army guards, sleeping peacefully through the night, is in sharp contrast to Brutus's wakefulness. It is on the field at Sardis that Brutus will see the ghost of Caesar, as Richard III saw the ghosts of his victims, and as Macbeth will see the ghost of Banquo. When the Ghost replies to Brutus's question about its identity, it will declare itself his mirror, as well as his vengeful victim: "Thy evil spirit, Brutus" (4.2.333). Brutus is more than any other character in this play the "great man" who "falls," and thus he has become, for many readers and audiences, the center of the play's tragic energy. He has by far the largest speaking part, and the play's final epitaph, the traditional summing-up of tragedy, concerns Brutus, not Caesar. The memorial passage, a haunting account of homage and of loss, is spoken by Antony, and it has the powerful force of aphorism:

> This was the noblest Roman of them all.
> All the conspirators save only he
> Did that they did in envy of great Caesar.
> He only in a general honest thought
> And common good to all made one of them.
> His life was gentle, and the elements
> So mixed in him that nature might stand up
> And say to all the world "This was a man."
>
> 5.5.67–74

For a moment, at least, the play's definition of "manhood," or of "humanity," seems to hinge on the values exemplified by Brutus. Yet Brutus is consistently, indeed insistently, revealed as a man whose reason, whose trust in the power of order and discourse in the state, was his downfall. His sense of honor—the word that above all typifies him to the time of his death, and beyond—is unrealistic, in that it is not an accurate gauge of the real world. Brutus chooses a particular soldier to hold the sword for his suicide because, he says to the soldier, "Thy life hath had some smatch of honour in it" (5.5.46). Suicide was regarded by many of the ancient Romans as a noble death, especially when used to preserve one's dignity after a military defeat. Cato Brutus, Cassius, Antony, Varrus, and Otho were among the Roman generals who died in what Antony, in a later play, will call the "high Roman fashion" (*Antony and Cleopatra* 4.16.89). But it is easier in this play's world to die by honor than to live by it, despite Mark Antony's mocking refrain in his funeral oration for Caesar, "Brutus is an honourable man." The very repetition of the phrase, as we will see, begins masterfully to undercut the apparent compliment.

In one sense, then, Brutus stands at the center of this play. And yet there are good reasons for the play to be called not *Brutus* but *Julius Caesar*. One reason is largely formal, or conventional: Caesar is the ruler, and while Shakespeare does from time to time give his plays a title that is the ruler's name, rather than the name of the chief protagonist, as in the *Henry IV* plays (where the main figure is Prince Hal), or in *Cymbeline* (where the British king Cymbeline is a relatively minor character), Julius Caesar is more than this play's murdered king. Julius Caesar is also the topic, and the conundrum, of this play—who or what *is* "Julius Caesar"? This is the question, and the problem, that much of the play and many of its characters seek to answer. "O Julius Caesar, thou art mighty yet," says Brutus near the play's close, looking in despair at the bodies of his allies Cassius and Titinius, both suicides. The spirit of "great Caesar's ghost" is more than, and different from, the physical manifestation of a man. It is this ghost of Caesar—his memory, his myth, and his aura—that presides even over the play's final scenes.

There are, in fact, two Julius Caesars, as Caesar himself repeatedly makes clear. There is the private man whose wife cannot give him an heir; the enfeebled, superstitious, "tirèd Caesar" (1.2.117) whom Cassius had to save from drowning, and bear from the river Tiber as Aeneas bore his father Anchises on his shoulders from Troy; the Caesar who, we are told, shook with fever on the campaign in Spain, and cried out for drink like "a sick girl" (1.2.130). And there is the public Caesar, whom Cassius so resents, this human being who is "now become a god":

> Why, man, he doth bestride the narrow world
> Like a Colossus, and we petty men
> Walk under his huge legs, and peep about
> To find ourselves dishonourable graves.
>
> *1.2.136–139*

(We might notice, here again, the iteration of "honourable"/"dishonourable," so key a theme for this play.)

The dichotomy between the public and private Caesars is underscored, again and again, by Caesar. For example, in the speech in the second scene of the play in which he describes his distrust of the "lean and hungry" Cassius, who "loves no plays" (Shakespeare's audience should take note) and, like Shylock, "hears no music," a man whose mind is entirely bent on politics, Caesar takes pains to distinguish the apparent dangers of such a malcontent from any threat that he himself might feel:

> Such men as he be never at heart's ease
> Whiles they behold a greater than themselves,
> And therefore are they very dangerous.
> I rather tell thee what is to be feared
> Than what I fear, for always I am Caesar.
> Come on my right hand, for this ear is deaf,
> And tell me truly what thou think'st of him.
>
> *1.2.209–215*

"Always I am Caesar"; "this ear is deaf." The difference between bodily infirmity and mythic fame is also a difference in time and timelessness—*always* I am Caesar. And this is a difference that Brutus will signally fail to take into account when he joins the conspiracy. Brutus should not be surprised that Julius Caesar is "mighty *yet,*" since "Julius Caesar" is a concept as well as a person. In the play, the mention of Caesar's deafness, a sign of his age, his weakness, and his unwillingness to listen to other people, is twice balanced by references to people who hear well. In act 1, scene 3, Cassius recognizes Casca by his voice, and is told "Your ear is good"—as we might expect in the highly political Cassius, who keeps his ear to the ground. In act 2, Ligarius, who has entered with a kerchief on his head, says he will "discard" his sickness when Brutus promises him "[a]ny exploit worthy the name of honour," and Brutus says he has such an exploit in hand, "Had you a healthful ear to hear of it" (2.1.316–318). All of these are things that Caesar does not, and will not, hear. But Caesar's deafness is proverbial as well as physical. There was a popular saying that a king's left ear was for flattery and private favors, his right ear for truth and for public concerns. And his deafness is also, in some sense, a matter of political policy. He himself is more persuaded of the existence of the public Caesar than of the private man. One proof of this is that he so regularly refers to himself in the third person, as an institution rather than a man, a practice often followed today by aspiring political candidates in their public utterances:

> Caesar should be a beast without a heart
> If he should stay at home today for fear.
> No, Caesar shall not. Danger knows full well
> That Caesar is more dangerous than he.
> We are two lions littered in one day,
> And I the elder and more terrible.
> And Caesar shall go forth.
>
> *2.2.42–48*

Compare this to Brutus's insistent, almost obsessive use of the word "I," for example, in his reply to Cassius in act 1, scene 2:

> That you do love me I am nothing jealous.
> What you would work me to I have some aim.
> How I have thought of this and of these times
> I shall recount hereafter. For this present,
> I would not, so with love I might entreat you,
> Be any further moved. What you have said
> I will consider. What you have to say
> I will with patience hear. . . .
>
> *1.2.163–170*

"I . . . I . . . I." Subjective, introspective, private. Brutus's interiority makes him judge everyone by his own standards, believe everyone to be as rational and as honorable as he is, and this leads directly to his catastrophe. But Caesar's equally insistent depersonalizing of self has its own risks. "I am constant as the Northern Star," he says to Metellus Cimber and the other conspirators, moments before the murder (3.1.60), as a way of explaining why he refuses to pardon Cimber's brother. "And men are flesh and blood, and apprehensive," he goes on,

> Yet in the number I do know but one
> That unassailable holds on his rank,
> Unshaked of motion; and that I am he
> Let me a little show it even in this—
> That I was constant Cimber should be banished,
> And constant do remain to keep him so.
> . . . .
> Hence! Wilt thou lift up Olympus?
> *3.1.67–74*

The "Northern Star," Olympus, and a great Colossus bestriding the earth. These images of constancy, fixity, and huge majesty, geographical images that seem to suggest Caesar as the pillar of the world, the principle of order, the fulcrum of the universe, all have some truth about them. And when he falls it is indeed as if the North Star, by which sailors chart their courses, has come unfixed, or Mount Olympus has been lifted from its place, plunging the whole world into disorder and confusion.

But the public Caesar is as dangerous to the Caesar of flesh and blood as he is to Publius Cimber. At the beginning of act 3, on his way to the Capitol, where he will be assassinated, Caesar is halted, first by the Soothsayer, who had warned him of the Ides of March, and then by Artemidorus, who knows of the conspiracy and has written him a note of warning. "Hail, Caesar! Read this schedule," says Artemidorus (3.1.3), and Decius Brutus, one of the conspirators, quickly interjects, "Trebonius doth desire you to o'er-read / At your best leisure, this his humble suit" (4–5). "O Caesar, read mine first," Artemidorus importunes him, "for mine's a suit / That touches Caesar nearer" (6–7). And Caesar replies, fatally, "What touches us ourself shall be last served" (8). This rejection of the personal, this refusal to acknowledge a private, flesh-and-blood self with private needs, is Caesar's downfall. The self-awareness he would have shown in reading Artemidorus's scroll is here proved lacking once again. The path lies straight before him to the Capitol.

Nor are human warnings the only kinds of help Caesar is offered, and scorns. The Soothsayer, with his warning of the Ides of March, is brushed aside in the play's second scene: "He is a dreamer. Let us leave him. Pass!" (1.2.26). The play is full of dreams, omens, portents, superstitions, and prophecies, all elements of the powerful irrational. Thunder and lightning fill the sky, a "tempest dropping fire" that Casca says is like "a civil strife in heaven" (1.3.10, 11); the "bird of night," the owl, sits in the marketplace at noon, "[h]ooting and shrieking" (26, 28). "A lioness hath whelpèd in the streets," Calpurnia tells Caesar, "[a]nd graves have yawned and yielded up their dead" (2.2.17–18). Shakespeare would return to this moment in *Hamlet,* a play written shortly after *Julius Caesar:*

> In the most high and palmy state of Rome,
> A little ere the mightiest Julius fell,
> The graves stood tenantless, and the sheeted dead
> Did squeak and gibber in the Roman streets. . . .
>   *Hamlet 1.1.106.6–106.9*

These omens and portents, signs of a world profoundly unnatural, may remind us of Owen Glendower, the superstitious Welshman of *1 Henry IV,* and they prefigure, as well, the sign-filled world of *Macbeth,* where a "falcon, tow'ring in her pride of place" is by a "mousing owl hawked at and killed," and, "a thing most strange and certain," King Duncan's horses, "[t]urned wild in nature" and "ate each other," to the amazement of frightened onlookers (*Macbeth* 2.4.12, 13, 14, 16, 18).

In *Julius Caesar* such signs are either dangerously disregarded, as Caesar disregards the Soothsayer's warning, or else they are misconstrued, misinterpreted. In fact, the pattern of omen and portent in this play is closely allied to a pattern of misconstruction or misreading, a misreading not only of signs in the sky, but also of the basic nature of human beings and their propensity for chaos and disorder. Cicero, commenting on the portents in the sky and in the streets, says to Casca,

> Indeed, it is a strange-disposèd time;
> But men may construe things after their fashion,
> Clean from the purpose of the things themselves.
>   *Julius Caesar 1.3.33–35*

"[M]en may construe things after their fashion"—that is, as they wish, and as in their character. So Caesar does, and so Brutus does, and so Cassius does. "Alas, thou hast misconstrued everything," says Titinius in act 5, scene 3, to the dead body of Cassius, slain by his own hand, after Cassius, watching from afar and seeing Titinius surrounded by soldiers, assumes that they are enemies and not friends, and kills himself. This is a mistake all too easy to make in times of civil war, when the "enemy" looks like a friend and fellow countryman. "Alas, thou hast misconstrued everything" is in a way a fitting epigraph for this entire play.

The most blatant misconstruction in *Julius Caesar,* however, is deliberate rather than inadvertent, caused not by blindness of character (over-public, like this play's Caesar, or over-private, like this play's Brutus) but instead by craft and guile. Thus, for example, Decius Brutus deliberately offers a misinterpretation of Calpurnia's dream. Calpurnia, Caesar's wife, had dreamt she saw the statue of Caesar, which, as Caesar relates her dream, "like a fountain with an hundred spouts / Did run pure blood; and many lusty Romans / Came smiling and did bathe their hands in it" (2.2.77–79). That is, she has dreamt of the impending murder. Her dream is a portent that will come true. But his wife's urgent personal appeal to Caesar to stay home from the Capitol is doomed by Decius Brutus, who assures them both, "This dream is all amiss interpreted. / It was a vision fair and fortunate" (83–85). According to Decius Brutus, the dream is a sign that Romans of the future will come to Caesar for "[r]eviving blood," for inspiration—even for relics, as if he were a Christian saint. And this, too, will come true in the play, and beyond it, as Antony makes a relic of Caesar's robe with its stab wounds, and the triumvirs, Antony, Lepidus, and Octavius, use the name of Julius Caesar as a rallying cry for a power struggle of their own. Signs in Shakespeare's plays are morally neutral. They exist to be interpreted. Macbeth need not interpret the "weird sisters" as inciting him to murder; they merely say he will be King. It is his own subconscious, of which they are a theatrical counterpart, that drives him to kill Duncan and take the throne. So Caesar could heed Calpurnia's dream, and save himself. But this would be to show the very self-knowledge, the very awareness of his own human frailty, that he so conspicuously lacks.

That "men may construe things after their fashion" is a statement closely allied to Cassius's often quoted but frequently misunderstood observation, "The fault, dear Brutus, is not in our stars, / But in ourselves, that we are underlings" (1.2.141–142). The fault in Caesar is that he does not sufficiently recognize his own human vulnerability. The fault in Brutus is that he convinces himself that his own sense of honor and reason, his private code, can be used to govern the state and to justify murder:

> Set honour in one eye and death i'th' other,
> And I will look upon them both indifferently;
> For let the gods so speed me as I love
> The name of honour more than I fear death.
>
> *1.2.88–91*

There is a strong echo of Hotspur in this declaration. Because this is what he so firmly believes, Brutus consistently makes a kind of cosmetic error in interpretation, for once he has convinced himself, in a curiously passive and dispassionate phrase, that "[i]t must be by his death" (2.1.10), he begins to speak of the assassination of Caesar as a *ceremony*—as that is, an aspect of order rather than of disorder and chaos. Consider his argument to Cassius, rejecting the proposal that Mark Antony should also be killed—a rejection that has major implications, for, as Cassius suspects, Antony is able to rally the people around the dead Caesar, and against the conspirators. But Brutus objects to Antony's death because it would look bad. "Our course will seem too bloody," he says, and urges:

> Let's be sacrificers, but not butchers, Caius.
> We all stand up against the spirit of Caesar,
> And in the spirit of men there is no blood.
> O, that we then could come by Caesar's spirit,
> And not dismember Caesar! But, alas,
> Caesar must bleed for it. And, gentle friends,
> Let's kill him boldly, but not wrathfully.
> Let's carve him as a dish fit for the gods,
> Not hew him as a carcass fit for hounds.
> . . . .
> We shall be called purgers, not murderers.
>
> *2.1.162, 166–180*

"[S]acrificers, but not butchers." "[P]urgers, not murderers." The modern political sense of "purge" has overtaken this distinction, and exposed it. Brutus is trying to divide the indivisible, to make murder into something holy. Ceremony in this case is a way of avoiding reality, of sanctifying disorder. When after the murder Antony asks for "reasons" why Caesar had to be killed, Brutus assures him that there are plenty, "[o]r else were this a savage spectacle" (3.1.225)—as if his good reasons made the death of Caesar less savage. We hear the word "ceremony" over and over again in the play. Mark Antony is to "leave no ceremony out" in running the course of the Lupercal; Brutus accuses Cassius of behaving with an "enforcèd ceremony" after the assassination, of being "[a] hot friend cooling" (4.2.21, 19). But ceremony is the shield behind which Brutus hides from himself the unsupportable truth, that what he is doing is murdering his friend.

Furthermore, the minute Caesar is dead, Brutus suggests yet another ceremony, one that brings to literal life, onstage, the events of Calpurnia's dream:

> Stoop, Romans, stoop,
> And let us bathe our hands in Caesar's blood
> Up to the elbows, and besmear our swords;
> Then walk we forth even to the market-place,
> And, waving our red weapons o'er our heads,
> Let's all cry, "peace, freedom, and liberty!"
>
> *3.1.106–111*

This is an extraordinary notion, to dip your hands in the blood of the ruler you have murdered, and, waving them about in the air, cry, "peace, freedom, and liberty!" It is a stunning moment in Shakespeare, one that would be remembered by the principals of the French Revolution, and again by Karl Marx, writing of the French Revolution in *The Eighteenth Brumaire of Louis Bonaparte*. There is a terrible irony in the exchange that follows, where ceremony becomes not only ritual but play:

Cassius	Stoop then, and wash.
	[*They smear their hands with Caesar's blood*]
	How many ages hence
	Shall this our lofty scene be acted over,
	In states unborn, and accents yet unknown!
Brutus	How many times shall Caesar bleed in sport,
	. . . .
Cassius	So oft as that shall be,
	So often shall the knot of us be called
	The men that gave their country liberty.

3.1.112–118

In the immediate context of Shakespeare's play, of course, *England* is the state unborn, and *English* the accent yet unknown. For what Cassius predicts is nothing less than Shakespeare's *Tragedy of Julius Caesar*, the play we are now reading or watching. But the verdict of history would be profoundly different from that so confidently predicted by Cassius. And it is an inherent contradiction, even in a play, to assert as Brutus does that Caesar can "bleed in sport."

In fact, as Cassius and Brutus are soon to learn, they have killed the wrong Caesar. They have killed the private man, the one of flesh and blood. But the public man, the myth, lives on, after his death, and after theirs, and long after Shakespeare's. "Julius Caesar, thou art mighty yet." And this removal of strong rule, the assassination of the rightful ruler, inevitably leads to chaos. We have seen this in Shakespeare's English history plays, where a fear of usurpation and regicide and a distrust of the common people usher in years, even decades, of instability. This was the view from the top, the view of strong monarchy. Certainly, whatever Shakespeare's private political views may have been, the plebeians depicted in this play are no foundation on which to build a stable rule. In the funeral oration scene they cheer first Brutus, then Mark Antony, with equal enthusiasm, although the two speakers are saying completely opposite things. It takes a scant forty-one lines for them to make the circuit from "This Caesar was a tyrant" (3.2.66) to "Caesar has had great wrong" (107). The plebeians are a swayable chorus, a malleable, responsive audience to be played upon by the cleverer actor—and Brutus has too many scruples, too many principles, to think of trying to be clever. With characteristic blindness he brushes aside Cassius's all-too-perceptive fears of Antony's skill as an orator. "You know not what you do," Cassius says and continues,

> Do not consent
> That Antony speak in his funeral.
> Know you much the people may be moved
> By that which he will utter?

And Brutus replies, serenely,

> By your pardon,
> I will myself into the pulpit first,
> And show the reason of our Caesar's death.
>
> *3.1.234–239*

The "reason"—he will reason with a populace derisively addressed by one of the tribunes as "[y]ou blocks, you stones, you worse than senseless things!" (1.1.34). It is Mark Antony who, in the scene that follows, uses ceremony to defeat ceremony, Antony who says to the plebeians—almost as if he has heard the tribune's dismissive taunt—"You are not wood, you are not stones, but men" (3.2.139). Mark Antony is in fact the spirit of misrule in this play, the spirit of chaos and anarchy. "Antony that revels long a-nights" (2.2.116), Caesar calls him. Misrule is the natural consequence of the murder of rule, and Antony's coming to the fore, Antony's assumption of command immediately following Caesar's death, is yet another sign of what is bitterly wrong with the whole notion of the conspiracy. Instead of reason, chaos now runs the state.

Approaching the conspirators, foolishly bathing their hands in Caesar's blood to fulfill Brutus's ill-fated ceremony of "peace, freedom, and liberty," Antony from the first time we see him in action in act 3, scene 1, exposes the folly of that entire view. "Let each man render me his bloody hand," he says, and he names them all, one by one, as with mock ceremony he shakes each bloody hand in turn. Brutus, Cassius, Decius Brutus, Metellus Cimber, Cinna, Casca, Trebonius—it is a roll call of doom. Notice that Antony grasps the hand of Trebonius last. Trebonius, we may recall, had been acting as the decoy in the conspiracy. His job was to lure Antony away, not to stab Caesar. Trebonius's hands, therefore, are clean, at least in a physical sense—they are not "bloody," until Antony takes his hand. For Antony's own hand is already covered with blood from saluting all the others. Antony thus marks Trebonius as one of the bloody-handed conspirators, wiping the blood back onto him, showing that he knows Trebonius was part of the plot, and showing, too, something of the contagion, the transmissibility, of the crime of murder and regicide. "Let each man render me his bloody hand." Whether stained with visible or with invisible blood, they are all guilty, all associated, all marked.

The moment Antony is alone with the body of Caesar, he speaks to it in terms that once again expose Brutus's ceremony for the horrific act it is: "O pardon me, thou bleeding piece of earth, / That I am meek and gentle with these butchers" (3.1.257–258). So much for Brutus's plea to the conspirators, "Let's be sacrificers, but not butchers," let's spare Mark Antony. But Antony's own taste for chaos is also fully expressed here, in a prophecy that he himself will make come true:

> Over thy wounds now do I prophesy—
> . . . .
> A curse shall light upon the limbs of men;
> Domestic fury and fierce civil strife
> Shall cumber all the parts of Italy;
> . . . .
> And Caesar's spirit, ranging for revenge,
> . . . .
> Shall in these confines with a monarch's voice
> Cry "havoc!" and let slip the dogs of war.
>
> *3.1.262–276*

Once anarchy is unloosed, it cannot be controlled, and Antony's final words in the oration scene, when he is once again alone upon the stage, underscore his eagerness for this condition of extreme disorder, total chaos: "Now let it work. Mischief, thou art afoot. / Take thou what course thou wilt" (3.2.248–249).

Antony is a master orator, a skillful manipulator of crowds, and his delight in disorder keeps him from feeling bound, like Brutus, by scruple. His behavior in the oration scene is in striking contrast to that of Brutus. Brutus speaks in prose, he appeals to reason, to the wisdom of the people, and he speaks, sometimes, in riddling syllogisms: "not that I loved Caesar less, but that I loved Rome more" (3.2.20–21); "As he was valiant, I honour him. But as he was ambitious, I slew him" (24–25). Brutus makes the cardinal error of leaving the rostrum before Antony has had a chance to speak, thus allowing his competitor a clear field. Antony enters with the people, he stands among them as he hears Brutus speak, and he is thus identified with the commoners even before he mounts to the rostrum to address them. He speaks in evocative, repetitious poetry, incantatory and easy to follow: "Friends, Romans and countrymen, led me your ears" (here again are those "ears"). Each of his observations is punctuated with a refrain, four times repeated: "But Brutus says he was ambitious, / And Brutus is an honourable man." As we have already noted, the sheer iteration of "honourable" begins to put the appropriateness of that word in question. The rhythmic and repetitious nature of this speech explains in part why Antony's funeral oration is the piece of Shakespeare's poetry many schoolchildren are asked to memorize. This speech is not particularly typical of Shakespeare. Rather, it is designed to show Antony's facility in demagoguery. It is easy to memorize, easy to hear and follow, the perfect kind of language to reach and move the shallow masses. Moreover, once he is finished speaking, Antony, who seemed to come up from the people, goes back down among them again, doing a creditable version of what a modern politician would call "working the crowd." "Shall I descend?" he asks. "Come down," the plebeians answer. "Descend." As he is about to produce his shocking stage prop, Caesar's bloody mantle with its gaping holes, and then the body itself, he addresses the crowd directly: "If you have tears, prepare to shed them now" (3.2.163). And, for his finale, he will read them Caesar's will, leaving money and lands to the people of Rome—as it turns out, *they* are Julius Caesar's heirs. Thus the quest for an heir in the opening scene has an unexpected and "democratic" outcome.

"Now let it work," says Antony, opening the way to "mischief"—calamity or harmful action. And it does work. By the beginning of the play's fourth act the audience witnesses the spectacle of the triumvirs, Antony, Octavius, and Lepidus, joined in a counterconspiracy that is entirely cold and heartless.

Antony	These many, then, shall die; their names are pricked.
Octavius	[*to Lepidus*] Your brother too must die. Consent you, Lepidus?
Lepidus	I do consent.
	. . . . .
	Upon condition Publius shall not live,
	Who is your sister's son, Mark Antony.
Antony	He shall not live. Look, with a spot I damn him.

4.1.1–6

Earlier we saw Metellus Cimber, a conspirator, plead—perhaps not in heartfelt terms—for his brother. Now brother damns brother, uncle damns nephew with a prick of the pen. The death of order has been total, and the destructive energies keep turning in upon themselves. So much for Brutus's humanistic faith in mankind as a rational animal.

In this new situation Antony is suddenly at something of a disadvantage. His predilection for chaos makes him more suited to misrule than to rule. The time has come for the cold precision of Octavius Caesar, who is this play's version of the new political man. "Young Octavius" is what Antony had called him in act 3, scene 1, immediately after the death of Caesar. Tell "young Octavius" not to come to Rome yet—the time is not yet ripe, and he is potentially in danger. But by the beginning of the fifth and final act, it is clear that it is Octavius who is in charge, not Antony, despite Antony's seniority. On the plains at Philippi, Antony, as general, directs Octavius to lead his forces on the left side of the field—and Octavius contradicts him:

Octavius	Upon the right hand, I; keep thou the left.
Antony	Why do you cross me in this exigent?
Octavius	I do not cross you, but I will do so.

5.1.18–20

The tone is strikingly reminiscent of Hal to Falstaff—"I do; I will"—another "boy" to another older reveler. Less than five lines later, almost shockingly yet with a casual tone, Antony calls Octavius "Caesar": "Caesar, we will answer on their charge" (5.1.24). So in one way the play has come full circle. Octavius now describes himself as "another Caesar," avenging the memory of the first, although Octavius is less human, less flesh-and-blood, than Julius Caesar ever was.

It is Octavius, not Antony, who speaks the play's final lines, commending the body of Brutus to "all respects and rites of burial," and this final place of public utterance is one that we have been accustomed to see given to princes or dukes or other ruling figures. As Shakespeare moves into the period of his major tragedies, this ultimate act of homage will assume an increasingly conciliating tone, as an attempt to heal the breaches in governance caused by tragedy, war, misunderstanding, and loss. Yet coming as it does after Antony's moving words on the "noblest Roman of them all," Octavius's final speech has something of an ominous ring:

> Within my tent his bones tonight shall lie,
> Most like a soldier, ordered honourably.
> So call the field to rest, and let's away
> To part the glories of this happy day.
>
> *5.5.77–80*

As always in Shakespeare, the final couplet is a stage-clearing gesture. "Let's away" sweeps the characters offstage, and "part[ing] the glories" will mean both sharing the spoils and ascribing, by means of retold tales, the acts of heroism. The word "happy" here is related to "hap," or luck, as well as to its more modern meaning of pleasure or joy. But how many in the audience, then or now, feel "happy" at this spectacle of suicide and loss? Octavius's final words, in fact, point toward a real and important split in Shakespearean drama between dispassionate ruler and tragic hero, a split that seems never to be mended in the plays. Brutus was human, and according to some he was the best of humanity and he is dead. And Caesar is dead, with all his strengths and all his flaws. Octavius is not dead, but in a sense he is also not alive. He is the sober, calculating, self-controlled new man, the politician, who replaces the ancient mythic hero, replacing Julius Caesar and even Antony, rulers with excesses and blind spots, but also with human energies and human passions. Octavius resembles the Prince Hal of *2 Henry IV*, deliberately cold, conscious of title and role. The differing claims of Brutus and Octavius, on the audience and on the play, create one of the most productive tensions in *Julius Caesar,* for this is a history play as well as a tragedy. And the ending of the play is, therefore, two endings, caught in dialectical conflict. One ending foregrounds Brutus and his tragedy, while the other focuses upon Octavius Caesar and the march of empire. The imperial gesture toward the future, consistent with Elizabethan England's sense of itself as an emerging power, is set up in structural opposition to the ghostly reminder of the weight of the past, figured brilliantly in the ghost of the dead Julius Caesar. The cycle of history and the drama of tragedy can never wholly be reconciled, and this play and its playwright are very much aware of that fact. In Antony's ringing epitaph "This was a man," how can we balance humanistic sympathy and empathy with irony and nostalgia? And if there is nostalgia, for the audience onstage or the audience offstage, is it, inevitably, nostalgia for an ideal past that never was?

In many of Shakespeare's plays, as we have seen, the figure of the mirror, or looking glass, is invoked as a mode of character revelation, or alternatively, as a social or cultural model. *Julius Caesar* offers a more ominous version of the topos of the friend as glass, in the mirroring conversation between Cassius and Brutus early in the play. Cassius is trying to persuade Brutus to join the conspiracy to assassinate Caesar:

> Cassius　Tell me, good Brutus, can you see your face?
> Brutus　No, Cassius, for the eye sees not itself
> 　　　　But by reflection, by some other things.
> Cassius　'Tis just;
> 　　　　And it is very much lamented, Brutus,
> 　　　　That you have no such mirrors as will turn
> 　　　　Your hidden worthiness into your eye,
> 　　　　That you may see your shadow. I have heard
> 　　　　Where many of the best respect in Rome—
> 　　　　Except immortal Caesar—speaking of Brutus,
> 　　　　And groaning underneath this age's yoke,
> 　　　　Have wished that noble Brutus had his eyes.
> Brutus　Into what dangers would you lead me, Cassius,
> 　　　　That you would have me seek into myself
> 　　　　For that which is not in me?
> Cassius　Therefor, good Brutus, be prepared to hear.
> 　　　　And since you know you cannot see yourself
> 　　　　So well as by reflection, I, your glass,
> 　　　　Will modestly discover to yourself
> 　　　　That of yourself which you yet know not of.
> 　　　　　　　　　　　　　　　　　*1.2.53–72*

To anyone familiar with Shakespeare's way with mirrors, a phrase like "I, your glass," is, potentially, a dangerous one. Cassius pretends that he reflects a disinterested truth, when in fact his purpose, as he tells the audience once Brutus has left the stage, is something else—seduction:

> Well, Brutus, thou art noble; yet I see
> Thy honourable mettle may be wrought

From that it is disposed. Therefore it is meet
That noble minds keep ever with their likes;
For who so firm that cannot be seduced?

1.2.302–306

Who indeed? Certainly not Brutus, for Cassius knows just how to set about his task.

The particular kind of political seduction Cassius attempts in the scene in which he elects himself Brutus's "glass" is, significantly, focused on the *name*. Cassius has cleverly invoked the name of another Brutus, Lucius Junius Brutus, who helped to expel the Tarquin emperors and to establish the Roman republic—and whom the Marcus Brutus of this play regards as an ancestor. Lucius Junius "would have brooked / Th'eternal devil to keep his state in Rome / As easily as a king," says Cassius, stressing this early hero's republican sentiments (1.2.160–162). So the similarity in name functions as a kind of mirror. But when Cassius shifts his argument from the past to the present, and from Brutus's namesake and ancestor to his friend and rival, his task is more complex. First he persuades Brutus that Brutus is like Caesar in a crucial way, and then that he differs from him, also crucially. "Brutus and Caesar: what should be in that 'Caesar'? / Why should that name be sounded more than yours?" argues Cassius.

> Write them together: yours is as fair a name.
> Sound them: it doth become the mouth as well.
> Weigh them: it is as heavy. Conjure with 'em:
> "Brutus" will start a spirit as soon as "Caesar."
>
> *1.2.143–148*

"Brutus" and "Caesar." The names have the same number of syllables, the same metrical stress, the same weight. So in this, too, these men are twinned, as, at one point or another, almost everyone in the play wants to equate or compare them. But there is another name that also fits these criteria, the unspoken name of Cassius, which has the same stress pattern and the same number of syllables. "Brutus," "Caesar," "Cassius." Why, implies Cassius, should *I* not stride the narrow world like a Colossus?

The play is at considerable pains, from the first, to demonstrate the resemblance between Brutus and Caesar. In act 2, scene 1, for example, Portia, Brutus's wife, kneels to her husband, imploring him to unburden himself to her. Portia, the daughter of the famous statesman Cato, is a character of considerable nobility and forcefulness in her own right. Later in the play we will be told that she herself has committed suicide by swallowing "fire" (live embers). In act 2, scene 2, another Roman wife kneels to another husband. This time it is Calpurnia, the wife of Caesar, pleading with him to heed her dream, and not to go to the Capitol. The two scenes have diametrically opposite outcomes: Caesar does not yield to his wife, while Brutus does yield to his. But the stage picture draws a clear analogy between the two. Later on, after the assassination, the plebeians will suggest a substitution and a succession: "Let him be Caesar. Caesar's better parts / Shall be crowned in Brutus" (3.2.47–48). Here "Caesar" has already, as we will see, taken on a generic meaning, the name of an office (like "czar" or "kaiser") rather than a man.

"Conjure with 'em: / 'Brutus' will start a spirit as soon as 'Caesar.' " Here Cassius is speaking of magic charms, mystical talismans, things in which he clearly does not believe. For the audience, however, this is a proleptic moment, tinged with dramatic irony. Before the play is over, we will see that the name of "Caesar," unlike that of either Brutus or Cassius, does indeed have the power to start a spirit, as Cassius learns at last: "O Julius Caesar, thou art mighty yet. / Thy spirit walks abroad, and turns our swords / In our own proper entrails" (5.3.93–95). And Brutus will learn the same lesson, when he comes face-to-face with the ghost of Caesar—a ghost who names himself as "[t]hy evil spirit, Brutus" (4.2.333).

The rhetoric of eyesight that begins the mirror passage is suggestive of Brutus's dilemma within the play as a whole. "Brutus, I do observe you now of late," Cassius remarks. "I have not from your eyes that gentleness / And show of love as I was wont to have," he says (1.2.34–36), and Brutus replies, "If I have veiled my look, / I turn the trouble of my countenance / Merely upon myself" (39–41). Neither the self-absorption of these moments nor the forceful urging of Cassius in his self-appointed role as Brutus's "glass" will show Brutus the truth as history and Shakespeare will reflect it, until he reasserts the resemblance between himself and his beloved adversary, slaying himself as he slew Caesar.

We have noticed that the conspirators kill the wrong Caesar, the man and not the myth, and that this mistake, or misconstruction, is related to the question of the name. In this play Julius Caesar has not only two personae or characters, but also two names. Roman names for men had three parts: a praenomen, a nomen, and a cognomen. The praenomen was the personal name, typically used only by the immediate family. The nomen indicated the family to which the individual belonged, and the cognomen was sometimes added to distinguish persons within the family. This cognomen (in other Shakespeare plays it is called an "addition") was a kind of nickname, often appropriate to the first holder, that then became part of the family's tradition. Thus, for example, "Agricola" means "farmer" and "Germanicus" means "German." Women's names originally had only one part, a feminine version of the family name, for instance, "Claudia" from "Claudius." Individuals who were not Roman citizens, including slaves and foreigners, had only one name until they were freed or received citizenship. A man adopted into another family, like the Octavius of this play, assumed the full name of his new father but retained his former nomen, adding "anus" to it. Thus Gaius Octavius became—historically, though not in Shakespeare's play—Gaius Julius Caesar Octavianus.

Caesar's full name is Gaius Julius Caesar, and in this play he is addressed almost uniformly as "Caesar." Only a few intimates call him "Julius," and they do so only after his death (Antony at 3.1.205, Brutus at 4.2.71). All the greater, then, is the conspirators' dismay when they discover that it is "Julius" who lies dead, while "Caesar" lives on. And "Caesar" does so in a double sense, since the vengeful Ghost stalks the battlefield, while a new Caesar, like a new phoenix, rises from the ashes of the old. For the stage is not long empty of a Caesar. In this very well-structured play each act seems to focus on one character: act 1 centers on Cassius, act 2 on Brutus, act 3 on Caesar, act 4 on Antony, and act 5 on Octavius. The play's first mention of Octavius comes immediately after Antony's funeral oration, but, as we have seen, Octavius is repeatedly described as "young," as a "peevish schoolboy," an uninitiated novice. In act 4, scene 2, "young Octavius" is addressed or described that way three times in fewer than seventy lines. But the next scene, beginning the fifth act, starts to limn his transformation from boyhood to manhood, which is manifested explicitly through a change of name. Once he has ordered Antony to take the left side of the field, contradicting Antony's instruction, he is suddenly addressed as "Caesar" not only by Antony but by Brutus—and to himself he is now "another Caesar" (5.1.54). In Shakespeare's source, it is Brutus, not Octavius, who contradicts Antony, and the deliberate change on the playwright's part emphasizes the emergence of this strong, defiant, and unshakable figure near the end of the play.

Wordplay with and about names and naming has been linked in other Shakespearean plays to the question of fitness to rule, since it is tied to the linguistic question of *nomen* and *omen,* the name and the sign. Caesar has no doubt about the fittingness of his own name, and he uses it regularly, as we have seen, in the third person. By Shakespeare's time the word "Caesar" had already become a synonym for "monarch," and it is used that way in two early history plays (*3 Henry VI* 3.1.18; *Richard III* 4.4.273.49). But Caesar, like John of Gaunt in *Richard II,* can also "play so nicely" with names (2.1.84), as he does just before his death at the Capitol, reproaching the men before him for thinking they can alter his will when even his closest friend cannot: "Doth not Brutus bootless kneel?"

But of all the *nomen/omen* instances in *Julius Caesar,* or, indeed, in all of Shakespeare, none is more striking than the episode of Cinna the poet, in act 3. Cinna the poet, a loyal citizen, is on his way to Caesar's funeral, having, as he says, "dreamt" that he "did feast with Caesar" (3.3.1). That he puts credence in dreams allies him with the Soothsayer, with Calpurnia, and with other, largely discounted, characters in the play. As Cinna is walking, he is halted by a gang of angry plebeians, who challenge his allegiance and demand to know his name. Unluckily, he bears the same name as one of the conspirators, and the plebeians, taking the name for the sign, fall upon him and beat him, dragging him offstage, probably to his death.

Third Plebeian	Your name, sir, truly.
Cinna	Truly, my name is Cinna.

First Plebeian	Tear him to pieces! He's a conspirator.
Cinna	I am Cinna the poet, I am Cinna the poet.
Fourth Plebeian	Tear him for his bad verses, tear him for his bad verses.
Cinna	I am not Cinna the conspirator.
Fourth Plebeian	It is no matter, his name's Cinna. Pluck but his name out of his heart, and turn him going.

3.3.25–33

This scene is a vivid emblem of the confusion that has fallen upon Rome. When times are bad for anyone, the poet suggests, they are especially bad for poets. In Shakespeare's own time the censorship of poets, playwrights, and other writers was a fact of life, and imprisonment or corporal punishment was often the fate of offenders. John Stubbs, an English Puritan, had his right hand "cut off with a Cleaver" for writing a pamphlet criticizing the prospect of the Queen's marriage with a French nobleman, Henry, Duke of Anjou. A contemporary account reports that "after his Right hand was cut off," Stubbs "put off his Hat with his Left, and said with a loud voice, 'God save the Queen. . . . ' "[1] In the time of King James, a few years after *Julius Caesar,* the playwrights Ben Jonson, John Marston, and George Chapman were imprisoned for sedition, having written unflatteringly in *Eastward Ho* about Scottish royalty.

Behind this wry Shakespearean observation about the dangers of imaginative writing, in Roman or early modern times, lies another important thematic point. Since the name is no longer directly equivalent to the thing, we act at our peril. For, as we have seen, just as one may beat the wrong Cinna, so one may kill the wrong Caesar. The scene with Cinna the poet thus exemplifies and crystallizes much of what has been taking place in the larger play that contains it. Wrongly regarded by some directors as anecdotal and distracting, the scene is sometimes cut from productions, but it is a key moment in the play, and it has, in fact, a companion piece, or pendant. In act 4, scene 2, a nameless poet (identified only as Poet) tries to intrude upon Cassius and Brutus just as they have patched up their quarrel. This episode, unlike that of Cinna the poet, is not derived from any Plutarchan source. The Poet speaks in doggerel, in mediocre rhyming verse (rather like the comically "bad" verse written by Touchstone in *As You Like It*). "Love and be friends, as two such men should be, / For I have seen more years, I'm sure, than ye" (4.2.183–184). Cassius is amused, and Brutus offended. "What should the wars do with these jigging fools," he says, and they chase him away. Brutus's response is reminiscent of that of Prince Hal, when after the outbreak of war he found Falstaff with a bottle of sack in his pistol case ("What, is it a time to jest and dally now?" [*1 Henry IV* 5.3.54]).

The audience is shortly to learn that Brutus's wife, Portia, is dead, having "swallowed fire" (4.2.208), and in retrospect we can sympathize with his impatience. (His Stoicism prevents any more direct or explicit expression of personal distress.) But we are also, once again, shown what kind of value the world without a Caesar places on poetry, on literature—and that is, no value at all. The plebeians who wish to attack Cinna the conspirator merely change their target, and condemn Cinna the poet for his supposed bad verses rather than his supposed bad actions. One of the ironies of the situation is that none of them, of course, would actually have read any of his poetry.

The material nature of stage plays in Shakespeare's time, and the formal contradiction they present, is that they are written in order to be spoken and performed. Despite its apparent emphasis on battlefield actions and on conflicts in political philosophy, *Julius Caesar,* a play set in ancient Rome centuries before the invention of type or print, is directly concerned with the question of writing and speaking, and with the intrinsic treachery of the written word. Much of the play's action is transacted through the exchange of letters and the reading aloud of documents, and these written artifacts seem to take on lives on their own.

Papers are thrown in at Brutus's window in act 2, scene 1. Although Cinna the conspirator does the throwing, we know that it is Cassius who has written the text. But from Brutus's perspective, the letter he receives has another, and more persuasive, author. As he reads the letter aloud, and tries to interpret it according to his own prior beliefs and hopes, a Shakespearean audience might well think of another such letter recipient, and another hopeful interpreter, the gulled steward, Malvolio, in *Twelfth Night:*

> Brutus "Brutus, thou sleep'st. Awake."
> Such instigations have been often dropped
> Where I have took them up.
> "Shall Rome, et cetera?" Thus must I piece it out:
> Shall Rome stand under one man's awe? What, Rome?
> My ancestors did from the streets of Rome
> The Tarquin drive when he was called a king.
> "Speak, strike, redress." Am I entreated
> To speak and strike? O Rome, I make thee promise,
> If the redress will follow, thou receivest
> Thy full petition at the hand of Brutus.
>
> 2.1.48–58

Notice that Brutus immediately calls to mind his noble namesake, Lucius Junius Brutus, who drove the Tarquins from Rome rather than serve under them. Notice, too, how clever Cassius is to make Brutus believe it is the voice of the people summoning him, not Cassius's voice alone. Brutus was suspicious and a little reluctant when Cassius entreated him in his own person. But here he is entirely persuaded, even inflamed, because the petitioner, in his view, is Rome. "O Rome, I make thee promise, / . . . thou receivest / Thy full petition at the hand of Brutus." Like Malvolio, though in how different a key, Brutus imputes to his letter an author different from the real one, though again their "hands" are alike.

This is a play replete with oratory, full of sounding phrases. Classical rhetori-

cians discriminated three main categories of oratory, each of which uses characteristic devices to persuade. Each has a prominent place, both as topic and as
style, in Shakespeare's plays:

> • Deliberative oratory, used to persuade an audience (such as a legislative
> assembly) to approve or disapprove of matters of public policy, and to act
> accordingly. One good example is the discussion among the clerics at the
> beginning of *Henry V* about the meaning and application of the "Salic
> law."
> • Forensic oratory, used to achieve (for example, at a judicial trial) con-
> demnation or approval of an individual's actions. The courtroom scene in
> *The Merchant of Venice* is a classic instance.
> • Epideictic oratory, or "display rhetoric," used on ceremonial occasions to
> dilate upon the praiseworthiness (or the blameworthiness) of a person or
> persons. Funerals are favorite sites for this kind of discourse. The supposed
> death of Hero in *Much Ado About Nothing* calls forth eulogistic language,
> and a tribute in verse.

Difficulty in communication, mixed and failed messages, disregarded omens,
oblique and inaccessible narratives—all these are part of the texture of *Julius
Caesar,* a play in which characters, despite their episodic eloquence, consistently
fail to make themselves understood. The Soothsayer (literally, "truth-teller")
calls out to Caesar, "Beware the ides of March," a message that seems at once
urgent and transparent, but even after the message is repeated Caesar brushes its
speaker aside: "He is a dreamer. Let us leave him. Pass!" (1.2.19, 26). When Cassius and Brutus are deep in discussion about Caesar's worthiness or unworthi-
ness for power, they are continually distracted by shouts from offstage. They
want to know what is taking place—as does the audience, equally intrigued and
distracted—but the only account they can get of this key "unscene," in which,
apparently, Antony offers Caesar a crown, comes through the crusty narration
of Casca. Cassius says that "he will, after his sour fashion, tell you / What hath
proceeded," and after Casca's report, such as it is, Brutus comments, "What a
blunt fellow is this grown to be!" (1.2.181–182, 289). Neither of them thinks that
Casca is deceitful, and indeed the two take some pleasure in his skeptical irony.
But the all-important questions about the offstage scene—What exactly did
Antony say? How did Caesar actually respond? What was the effect upon the
populace?—go unanswered. This is a scene we do not get to see, and it constitutes crucial, yet unavailable, evidence for Brutus. Even within Casca's narrative
we are offered another example of opaque speech, speech that marks a place of
incomprehension rather than communication:

Cassius   Did Cicero say anything?
Casca   Ay, he spoke Greek.

Cassius	To what effect?
Casca	Nay, an I tell you that, I'll ne'er look you i'th' face again. But those that understood him smiled at one another, and shook their heads. But for mine own part, it was Greek to me.

1.2.273–278

This now-proverbial protestation of failed understanding—"it was Greek to me"—is another in the play's catalogue of oblique, deceptive, co-opted, or untranslatable utterances and messages. Cicero's speech, the speech of a great and revered man, cannot be understood, and therefore has no effect, except upon those few learned listeners, offstage, who smiled, and shook their heads. Since the audience in the theater does not even hear Cicero's words, we are at an even further remove than Casca, displaced from the possibility of understanding.

Is there in *Julius Caesar* any mode of speech that avoids these pitfalls of mis-translation and displacement? Indeed there is, and, as we might expect, it is a mode that is associated with Caesar himself, both living and dead. Like several other plays of Shakespeare, this one makes a key turn from one mode to another at a radical moment in the action. In *Romeo and Juliet* the play appears to begin as a comedy, with a love story, a masqued ball, and an assignation assisted by a comic foil, only to transform itself into tragedy at the moment of Mercutio's death. In *1 Henry IV* the generic split is between comedy and history, and the turning point is the onset of war, as Prince Hal turns upon Falstaff to upbraid him for untimely foolery ("What, is it a time to jest and dally now?"). In *Julius Caesar* there is another such major dividing point, and unsurprisingly it occurs at the moment of the death of Caesar. For both living and dead, Caesar is the only character in the play who speaks the language of performance and command—until the rise in the final act of another Caesar, the new man, Octavius.

In the play's second scene, Julius Caesar tells Antony to be sure to touch Calpurnia in the holy chase of the Lupercal, and Antony replies, "When Caesar says 'Do this,' it is performed" (1.2.12). Antony here describes what a later era would call a "performative speech-act," that is, a phrase that not only *says* some-thing but *does* something. Modern speech-act theory points to legal or ritual utterances like "I now pronounce you husband and wife," or "I dub thee Sir Lancelot," or "I declare the Olympic Games to be open," or the injunction of the officiating priest at a baptism to "name this child." Antony receives Caesar's instruction and takes it as a performative utterance (". . . 'Do this,' it is per-formed"). For Caesar to say it is for it to be done. This is regularly the case when Caesar speaks ("Caesar shall go forth") or indeed when his nephew, heir, and namesake speaks ("I do not cross you," Octavius Caesar said to Antony, "but I will do so"). "Will" and "shall" are Caesar's words, Caesar's language. "Bear my greetings to the senators," he says,

> And tell them that I will not come today.
> Cannot is false, and that I dare not, falser.
> I will not come today. . . .
>
> *2.2.62–64*

"Say he is sick," suggests Calpurnia (2.2.64), and Caesar is irate: "Shall Caesar send a lie? . . . Decius, go tell them Caesar will not come" (65, 68). That "will" and "shall" are the proper language of monarchs and conquerors is established in Marlowe's *Tamburlaine,* where the world-conquering hero, addressing one of his subordinates (and speaking of himself, like Caesar, in the third person), declares "Well said, Theridimas! Speak in that mood, / For will and shall best fitteth Tamburlaine" (*1 Tamburlaine* 3.3.40–41). The grammatical "mood" to which Tamburlaine alludes is the imperative mood of a verb expressing a command, in contrast to the indicative, interrogative, optative, or subjunctive mood, expressing fact, question, wish, or conditionality. Besides the two "Caesars," no one else in Shakespeare's play speaks regularly in these active and performative terms. The Caesars, Julius and Octavius, have less use for suasive rhetoric, since when they say "Do this," it is performed.

The most concrete and iconic image of this imperative verbal determination ("will" and "shall") in the play is, cleverly, Julius Caesar's "will," that is to say both his testament and his volition. The will read out by Antony to the people in act 3, scene 2, is Caesar's final speech act, an act that speaks—like all legal wills—after his death, like his ghost and his memory. The will, the document that bequeaths to each citizen of Rome money, and the free range of Caesar's arbors and orchards, is justly associated by Antony, himself a masterful rhetorician, with the posthumous voice of Caesar:

> Antony   I come not, friends, to steal away your hearts.
>   I am no orator as Brutus is,
>   But, as you know me all, a plain blunt man
>   That love my friend; and that they know full well
>   That gave me public leave to speak of him.
>   For I have neither wit, nor words, nor worth,
>   Action, nor utterance, nor the power of speech,
>   To stir men's blood. I only speak right on.
>   I tell you that which you yourselves do know,
>   Show you sweet Caesar's wounds, poor poor dumb mouths,
>   And bid them speak for me. But were I Brutus,
>   And Brutus Antony, there were an Antony
>   Would ruffle up your spirits, and put a tongue
>   In every wound of Caesar, that should move
>   The stones of Rome to rise and mutiny.
> All   We'll mutiny.
>
> *3.2.207–222*

The plebeians earlier castigated by the tribunes as "[y]ou blocks, you stones, you worse than senseless things" are now as foundational as the "stones of Rome," miraculously moved to mutiny by Antony's words. His professions of incapacity ("I am no orator. . . . I have neither wit, nor words, nor worth . . . . I only speak right on") are conventional self-deprecations, familiar in the history of oratory and of storytelling. The persona of the "plain blunt man" is one we have encountered elsewhere in Shakespeare, notably in Richard III and Henry V, both of whom were at their most eloquent when claiming to be least so. Antony's words, likewise, display the artful pretense of artlessness. The figure of speech that makes Caesar's wounds into speaking mouths is also familiar—one notable Shakespearean instance comes in the opening scene of *Richard III,* when the Lady Anne describes the body of Henry VI ("see! Dead Henry's wounds / Ope their congealèd mouths and bleed afresh" [1.2.55–56]). The figure is fairly common in the period, but here it is made vivid by Antony's creative and grotesque suggestion that true eloquence would "put a tongue / In every wound of Caesar."

In terms of staging, what Antony has effectively produced here is yet another kind of play-within-the-play, in a tragedy that is replete with them:

- The offstage "play" in which Antony apparently offers a crown three times to Caesar, and is refused, and Caesar swoons, a play described by the sour Casca as "mere foolery";
- Brutus's bizarre ceremony of bathing hands in the dead Caesar's blood, a ceremony that required the conspirators to wave their hands and weapons in the air, crying out "peace, freedom, and liberty!";
- Antony's ludicrous and telling spectacle of shaking each murderer's bloody hand;
- The great oration scene that pits Brutus against Antony, reason against passion;
- And the final epitaphs over the dead body of Brutus, who is eulogized as "the noblest Roman of them all."

Each of these is an encapsulated artifact, a play-within-the-play, a version of speech or gesture, and each, in its artfulness, seems strikingly in contrast with the straightforward and even heedless energy of language embodied in the speech acts of Caesar. "Always I am Caesar," he declares, and the force of that "always" continues unabated after the assassination, when it is transmuted into "yet": "Julius Caesar, thou art mighty yet."

Among the many proverbial relics of this play that have taken on afterlives of their own—from "Et tu, Bruté" to "It was Greek to me"—is the exclamation "Great Caesar's ghost" (made popular, and newly immortal, by newspaper editor Perry White in the *Superman* series). No such phrase actually occurs in Shakespeare's play, although both "great Caesar" and "the ghost of Caesar" make important cameo appearances. "Enter the Ghost of Caesar" reads the stage direction in act 4, scene 2, as Brutus, reading in his tent, surrounded by sleeping comrades, sits wakeful despite the lulling effect of song. "[I]s not the leaf turned down / Where I left reading?" he asks—another deliberate anachronism, since the codex book with turning pages had not yet been invented in Roman times. The scene anticipates another "reading" scene in later Shakespeare, when in *Cymbeline* Imogen reads a tale of rape from Ovid's *Metamorphoses* in her bedchamber, and is spied upon, once she is asleep, by the villainous intruder Iachimo ("Mine eyes are weak. / Fold down the leaf where I have left," she tells her waiting-woman [*Cymbeline* 2.2.3–4]). Both scenes take a format from medieval dream visions and put it on the stage. But whereas Imogen and medieval dreamers in works like Chaucer's *Book of the Duchesse* fall asleep and have a version of their dreaming thoughts come true, Brutus, like Hamlet, is visited while awake by a specter of which he has already had tormented thoughts (compare Hamlet's "prophetic soul," which had guessed at the story of *his* play's Ghost):

> Brutus How ill this taper burns! Ha! Who comes here?
> I think it is the weakness of mine eyes
> That shapes this monstrous apparition.
> It comes upon me. Art thou any thing?
> Art thou some god, some angel, or some devil,
> That mak'st my blood cold, and my hair to stare?
> Speak to me what thou art.
> Ghost Thy evil spirit, Brutus.
>
> *4.2.326–333*

What does this ghost look like? Its prototype is mentioned in Shakespeare's source in Plutarch merely as a "ghost that appeared to Brutus." Most Elizabethan ghosts were made to appear with all their wounds upon them—thus, in *Macbeth,* the "blood-baltered" body of Banquo shakes "gory locks" at his terrified murderer. The Ghost in *Hamlet* will appear first "in his habit as he lived," dressed in armor, to Hamlet, Horatio, and the sentries—and will then reappear, by convention in his nightclothes, in the Queen's closet, or private chamber. Since old Hamlet was murdered by poison in the ear, his body would not, in any case, be "blood-baltered" or, like Caesar's, covered with stab wounds. There is no sense from Brutus's response that the Ghost that appears to him— "Thy evil spirit, Brutus"—is torn by wounds. Some modern productions prefer to avoid a visible ghost altogether in favor of a spectral voice, and film versions can, of course, make the Ghost otherworldly and transparent, gliding in and out of the tent, and the scene, while the all-too-mortal Brutus gazes in consternation and horror. But perhaps the Ghost should, in fact, be a banal ghost, affable, unflappable, smiling—not terrifying to the sight, just to the mind. The audience has already seen both the bloody robe of Caesar, and his body ("marred, as you see, by traitors"). In the source, Antony displays the robe but not the body. So a bloody ghost appearing in Brutus's tent might be something of an anticlimax. Brutus calls it a "monstrous apparition," and asks the same kinds of questions Hamlet will ask: "Art thou any thing? / Art thou some god, some angel, or some devil?" North's translation of Plutarch says only that the ghost was "a horrible vision of a man, of a wonderful greatness and dreadful look," and in this context words like "horrible," "wonderful," and "dreadful" are terms of unspeakable spiritual, psychological, and emotional, rather than visual, effect. (Again, compare the *Hamlet* Ghost's "O horrible, O horrible, most horrible!") The Latin root *horrere* means "to bristle or stand on end," as hair does, and as Brutus will explicitly note ("mak'st my blood cold, and my hair to stare")—it is, that is to say, a term that describes the effect on the *spectator*, not the appearance of the *spectre* (the two words are, of course, directly linked, to each other and to sight). In this play of omens and portents, of graves that yawn and yield up their dead, of lions walking in the streets, of shrieking owls and men on fire, how much more marvelous and terrifying is the ordinary than the extraordinary. Brutus finds that the "thing" he killed, and suffers every moment for killing, is in all important ways not dead, indeed, is unable to be slain, and is appearing in his tent to reflect the blame, and the crime, back on his friend ("Thy evil spirit, Brutus"). Freud's notion of the uncanny, the uncertainty as to whether something is alive or dead, is perfectly apt for Brutus's response here, although, as Freud himself would note, the audience, knowing this is a play, may feel no similar frisson of uncertainty.

This question of appearance, and appearances, is more than a director's conundrum. From the beginning to the end of *Julius Caesar* it can be said to haunt the play. In the first scene Flavius the tribune commands his partner, Murellus: "Disrobe the images [of Caesar] / If you do find them decked with ceremonies" (1.1.63–64). In a way, the conspirators try, more violently, to perform this same action, disrobing the image, attempting to prove that the emperor has no clothes, that Caesar is merely a man like other men. In the funeral scene Antony literally holds out the robe of the "disrobed" Caesar. But as the audience has come to see, this is not Caesar.

"Julius Caesar, thou art mighty yet." Although both Octavius and Antony expend their final words on the death of Brutus, Cassius and Brutus die, at the last, still obsessed with Caesar, and still addressing themselves to him. "Caesar, thou art revenged," says Cassius as he takes his own life, "Even with the sword that killed thee" (5.3.44–45). And Brutus, running on his own sword, declares, "Caesar, now be still. / I killed not thee with half so good a will" (5.5.50–51). *Julius Caesar* is as likely to be taught and read today in classes on political theory, business, and "leadership" as in the context of Shakespeare and his literary contemporaries. It both models a version of politics ("Friends, Romans, countrymen") and undermines its own models. As a persistent figure of power and possibility, the Ghost still stalks the plains of Philippi, on the page and the stage, haunting the audience's imagination as it haunted Brutus, and as it haunts *Hamlet*, and will haunt the French Revolution and its aftermath. The play, like its Ghost, speaks pertinently, and often impertinently, to the modern and postmodern condition, to modern history, and to modern politics, rhetoric, and oratory. This is, after all, a play rewritten by Brecht and appropriated by Marx. But its lessons are elusive, and its images refract upon the viewer. There is more in heaven and earth, and in Shakespeare, than is dreamt of in political philosophy.

As You Like It

DRAMATIS PERSONAE

Duke Senior, *living in banishment*
Rosalind, *his daughter, later
	disguised as Ganymede*
Amiens, *a Lord attending on him*
Jaques, *a Lord attending on him*
Two Pages
Duke Frederick
Celia, *his daughter, later disguised
	as Aliena*
Le Beau, *a courtier attending on him*
Charles, *Duke Frederick's wrestler*
Touchstone, *a clown*
Oliver, *eldest son of Sir Rowland
	de Bois*
Jaques, *Oliver's younger brother*
Orlando, *Oliver's younger
	brother*

Adam, *a former servant of Sir
	Rowland*
Denis, *Oliver's servant*
Sir Oliver Martext, *a country
	clergyman*
Corin, *an old shepherd*
Silvius, *a young shepherd, in
	love with Phoebe*
Phoebe, *a shepherdess*
William, *a countryman, in love
	with Audrey*
Audrey, *a goatherd, betrothed to
	Touchstone*
Hymen, *god of marriage*
Lords, pages, and other
	attendants

SHAKESPEARE IS A master at bringing literary conventions to life on the stage, thereby both illustrating them and exposing their pretensions and shortcomings. He does this, for example, with the genre of the sonnet in *Love's Labour's Lost,* where the aristocrats, pretending to scorn women and love, not only write truly bad love poems to their ladies but also take the clichés of the sonnet literally, with devastating comic effect. A similar exposure of literary convention produces the belly laughs of the "Pyramus and Thisbe" play in *A Midsummer Night's Dream,* where the amateur actors, convinced that their play is disturbingly lifelike, seek to puncture its illusion at every turn, while also availing themselves of the high-sounding language of Elizabethan and Senecan tragedy. The mock-heroic description of the lover "Pyramus" by his lady "Thisbe," a hilarious scrambling of the traditional blazon in which Pyramus is described as having a "cherry nose," "yellow cowslip cheeks," and eyes "green as leeks," is a comic send-up of one of the most familiar conventions of love poetry. The unrealistic, idealized description, or "false compare," in such "blazons" had already been satirized in Shakespeare's Sonnet 130 ("My mistress' eyes are nothing like the sun").

In *As You Like It* Shakespeare turns his attention to the pastoral, a literary mode that enjoyed a tremendous vogue in Elizabethan England. Pastoral plays, poems, elegies, and romances, borrowed in part from Italian and also from ancient Greek and Latin models, were a favorite with audiences and readers, high and low on the social scale. The benchmarks here are too many to list, but they include Spenser's *Shepheardes Calender* and his *Faerie Queene* (especially book 6) and the love poetry of Marlowe and Ralegh in the Elizabethan period. Later English pastorals, like the poems of Andrew Marvell and Milton (notably his pastoral elegy "Lycidas") and plays like John Fletcher's *Faithful Shepherdess* and Shakespeare's *Winter's Tale* ensured the continued popularity and influence of the genre. The source of Shakespeare's play was a prose pastoral romance, Thomas Lodge's *Rosalynde, Euphues Golden Legacie,* written in 1586–1587 during the author's voyage to the Canary Islands. *As You Like It* incorporates a number of elements of the colonial voyage into its fantasy paradise.

It is important to emphasize that pastoral was profoundly "literary," rather than descriptive or mimetic, virtually from the start. Theocritus, often described as the first pastoral poet, was not himself a shepherd, but rather was a sophisticated participant in the relatively decadent life of Alexandria in the third century B.C.E. His pastoral writings were nostalgic in the strong sense; they evoked—as pastoral has ever since—the emotion of belatedness and loss. It is, as many critics have remarked, a city art rather than a rural one; shepherds do not write idyllic accounts of the perfect simple lives of shepherds. And it is a way of offering a criticism of contemporary social, political, and religious practice in a "safe" context of coded fiction. As the Elizabethan rhetorician George Puttenham wrote in *The Arte of English Poesie,* the intention of pastoral poetry was "not of purpose to counterfeit or represent the rusticall manner of loves and communication: but under the vaile of homely persons, and in rude speeches to insinuate and glaunce at greater matters, and such as perchance had not been safe to have been disclosed in any other sort. . . ."[1] From its earliest appearance pastoral had been used as a mode of social critique: under the guise of merely talking about shepherds, poets could write critical and satirical accounts of government, politics, and religion (a priest was a "pastor"; his congregation was a "flock"). Virgil's *Ecologues,* which sites the pastoral paradise in Arcadia, is replete not only with praise of poets but also with veiled political references to Julius Caesar and Augustus. A poet was, conventionally, a shepherd, and the tradition of the pastoral elegy extended from ancient Greece through Spenser and Milton to Shelley in the Romantic period, and beyond.

The pastoral tradition was also strong in the visual arts, where Arcadian scenes of shepherds and shepherdesses remained popular for centuries, through eighteenth-century classicism and nineteenth-century romanticism. Nicolas Poussin's famous painting entitled *Et in Arcadia Ego* (ca. 1650–1655), in which a group of shepherds in the paradise of Arcadia come across a tomb, and thus encounter death (the tomb's motto can be read either as "I [Death] am also in Arcadia" or "I [the dead person in the tomb] also formerly lived in Arcadia"), has become a classic visual text about the confrontation of mortality and art.[2]

A good modern analogue to the pastoral convention might be the mythology of the American West and the "Western" in fiction and film. Here the conventions seem ready to hand: the heroes in white hats and bad guys in black hats, the loner, the stranger, the lady saloon- or brothel-keeper with the heart of gold, the showdown at high noon. For more than a century this set of conventions has been employed to tell stories that may have little to do, in a literal sense, with the frontier or the West. The word "cowboy," like the word "shepherd," is readily understood as a metaphor, and it need not have any direct connection with livestock in order to carry familiar connotations of recklessness, wildness, or individuality.

Pastoral in the English Renaissance likewise had its recognizable conventions and associations, as well as its familiar topoi: shepherds who are also poets, writing poems and playing upon pipes; the good old shepherd, poor but eager to give hospitality to strangers and to those in need; the "savage" man or men who lacked courtly upbringing but possessed an innate gentleness and gentility (Tudor and Elizabethan writers, like Edmund Spenser, spelled the word "salvage," emphasizing its roots in the Latin *silva*, "wood"); the beautiful shepherdess; the pastoral elegy, mourning the death of a shepherd or shepherdess who was often also a poet; the pastoral debate, on topics like nature versus nurture, or country versus city, a leisurely rhetorical break from the action in which shepherds discourse learnedly with one another about these philosophical topics. These conventions of the genre, and others, too, were so well known to Shakespeare's audience (as the conventions of the Western are to modern audiences) that the playwright could use, mock, and tease them with the confident expectation that his point would quickly be understood. Thus, for example, when Rosalind and Celia decide to flee the corrupt and dangerous urban court for the simple life in the Forest of Arden, Celia says, "Let's away, / And get our jewels and our wealth together" (1.3.127–128). So much for the simple life.

As You Like It is not only a pastoral play but also a play about the nature of pastoral, and it begins with one of the most convenient devices of the pastoral tradition, the journey or sojourn. Needless to say, this is not exclusively a pastoral device. It is a useful clothesline for plot and character developments in works from the *Odyssey* to *Gulliver's Travels* and beyond. For Renaissance pastoral, though, it links up with the period interest in what we would today call "ethnography," the exploration and experience of strange places and unfamiliar peoples. In the world of *As You Like It*, geography assumes some of the aspects of character, so that the place of the play intersects with the persons of the play in ways that are significant and sometimes surprising. What is the nature of the Forest of Arden?

The play's precursor, Thomas Lodge's prose narrative *Rosalynd,* was set in the ancient French forest of Ardenne. There was a Forest of Arden in Shakespeare's county of Warwickshire, northwest of the Avon River. "Arden," as it happens, was also Shakespeare's mother's maiden name. She was born Mary Arden, the daughter of Robert Arden. So it is arguable that some nostalgia for childhood would double the geographical place with a psychological, or at least a remembered, place of ideal past-ness and fantasy. And the name of "Arden" also nicely incorporates the names of two famous paradises, the classical Arcadia and the biblical Eden. By playing with these spellings, Shakespeare combines all the connotations of the real places with an unlocatability that belongs only to fantasy. It is clear, in any case, that Arden is a repository, and indeed a palimpsest, of earthly paradises from literature, myth, and personal history.

For example, Charles the wrestler, the strongman at the usurping Duke Frederick's court, explains that the true Duke, Duke Senior, has removed with his followers to Arden:

> They say he is already in the forest of Ardenne, and a many merry men with him; and there they live like the old Robin Hood of England. They say many young gentlemen flock to him every day, and fleet the time carelessly, as they did in the golden world.
>
> As You Like It *1.1.99–103*

"A many merry men" and "the old Robin Hood of England" associate this forest with another tradition of the rural outlaw. The "golden world' is the classical world, and "carelessly" here carries its unfallen connotation, "without a care," rather than its fallen one of dangerous heedlessness or recklessness. More literally, Arden *is* an Eden, because the audience can sense, in the play's background before the action begins, an unfallen world in which a major figure was Orlando's father, Sir Rowland de Boys. "De Boys" is the Englishing of the French *de bois* or *du bois,* "of the woods," so the old Sir Rowland becomes a man who united in his own person the court world and the country, another mythic persona who fits an older heroic pattern. Rowland, or Roland, is of course the same name as Orlando (the first is French, the second Italian), that of the great hero of the medieval Charlemagne romances, where the hero's friend and adviser, with whom he once fought in single combat, was named Oliver (Orlando's brother is named Oliver in the play). Orlando—because of his signifying name—is thus in some sense the true heir of Sir Rowland, even though he is the youngest of the three brothers. His story follows the logic of the fairy tale, rather than that of the laws of primogeniture, although more than a hint of political concern about estate inheritance infuses this pastoral story. Orlando is denied his birthright by the eldest brother, Oliver, who keeps him at home, "rustically," without the education or resources of a gentleman. "[A]nd the spirit of my father," Orlando says, "which I think is within me, begins to mutiny against this servitude" (1.1.18–20).

Like so many other characters in this play, Orlando is banished, though banished into the paradisal world rather than from it. He will bring with him that most Edenic of all figures, old Adam, the faithful retainer, who demonstrates— Orlando tells him, and the audience—"[t]he constant service of the antique world" (2.3.58). This is an Adam who is compelled by Oliver's perfidy to wander about in a world he fears is savage, seeking loyalty and sustenance. As he does frequently, Shakespeare here reinforces the allusiveness of his language with a visual allusion, for the image of Adam carried on Orlando's back might well remind a Renaissance audience of Aeneas carrying his father Anchises on his back as they fled the ruins of burning Troy. The part of old Adam is one of the roles alleged to have been played by William Shakespeare, who is also said to have played the Ghost in *Hamlet,* and other older men and father figures from King Henry IV to Menenius.

Arden, then, is a kind of Eden. But Arden is also, even more centrally, Arcady or Arcadia, the traditional shepherd's paradise of pastoral, and, by association, not only a place of rustic contentment but also a place of and for poets. *As You Like It* is in many ways an anthology or collective of pastoral types: Silvius, the archetypal sighing shepherd, hopelessly in love and willing to die for his beloved; Phoebe, the disdainful shepherdess; Corin, the wise old shepherd who offers good advice, which is not taken; William and Audrey, foolish rustics; and a collection of various invisible hermits, magicians, and other pastoral personages who add "atmosphere" and "authenticity" to this droll portrait of a genre in transition—including the hermit who, offstage, converts Duke Frederick to a life of contemplation and persuades him to give up his stolen dukedom. These are all pastoral commonplaces, used in part *as* commonplaces by Shakespeare, just as are the love games and singing contests that take up much of the action in the woods. The most common of all activities of pastoral shepherds in English Renaissance literature was the writing of poetry. "Shepherd" virtually *meant* "poet" when it appeared in a literary context, so that if you were told that so-and-so was a shepherd you would be quite surprised to find that he or she spent a good deal of time tending sheep. Thus it is comic, in a way, that the old shepherd Corin does seem to know something about sheep and their care, and may very well not only live with them but smell like them. By contrast, almost everyone in the Forest of Arden writes poetry. Orlando does, and Touchstone does, and so do the courtiers who have accompanied Duke Frederick to the forest. But even Phoebe writes verses. Shepherdesses do not traditionally write poems; rather, poems are written about them. (Sir Walter Ralegh wrote, sometime before 1600, when it was published, a delightfully cynical reply to Christopher Marlowe's "Passionate Shepherd to His Love" called "The Nymph's Reply to the Shepherd.") Phoebe is no cynic, though; rather, she is hopelessly infatu-

ated with the handsome youth "Ganymede," who is Rosalind in disguise. She
not only writes a love poem to "Ganymede," she also quotes poetry—quotes, in
fact, the poetry of Marlowe, not his love lyric "The Passionate Shepherd" but
his Ovidian poem *Hero and Leander*. Marlowe, who died in 1593, is here himself
addressed as a shepherd:

> Dead shepherd, now I find thy saw of might:
> "Who ever loved, that loved not at first sight?"
>
> 3.5.82–83

A period audience would have known the identity of the "dead shepherd,"
whose name is not mentioned. (Some audience members might also remember
the context of the famous line Phoebe quotes, which is the second half of a
rather more coolly ironic couplet: "Where both deliberate, the love is slight, /
Who ever loved, that loved not at first sight?" [Marlowe, *Hero and Leander*, ses-
tiad 1, lines 175–176].) So Shakespeare presents us with a shepherdess in a
remote and timeless forest who has read and memorized verses from the poetry
of his great contemporary and rival, Christopher Marlowe.

This minor but amusing circumstance is indicative of the way the play will
flaunt, and flout, its pastoral conventions, taking them as a known quantity that
can be tweaked at will. The result is both the reinstatement of those conventions, and the pleasures they provide, and also a comical critique or undercutting of them. As Shakespeare did with the sonnet in *Love's Labour's Lost*, taking
something meant to be read and literalizing it onstage, so he does with a pastoral genre most at home in prose and poetic romance, and in lyric. To give one
other suggestive example: One enduring convention about shepherds was that
they were unfailingly hospitable, unlike their selfish counterparts in the world
of the court. But when Rosalind and Celia ask the old shepherd Corin to assist
them with food and shelter, he refuses. Such generosity is not within his power:
"My master is of churlish disposition / And little recks to find the way to heaven
/ By doing deeds of hospitality" (2.4.75–77).

Furthermore, although so many people write poetry in the Forest of Arden,
much of the poetry they write is disquietingly bad. Orlando's exuberant habit of
hanging his poems on tree branches—"Tongues I'll hang on every tree"—is
itself a caricature of the pastoral tendency to carve the lovers' names on tree
trunks (as Orlando himself exclaims, to an imagined Rosalind, "these trees shall
be my books, / And in their barks my thoughts I'll character" [3.2.5–6]). As
Touchstone the fool will have occasion to observe, "Truly, the tree yields bad
fruit" (3.2.105). This, too, is an Eden joke, and one worn, like so many of the
play's jokes, lightly. Touchstone himself further undercuts any naïve sense the
audience may have cherished about the purity and perfection of pastoral by yet
again taking pastoral practices literally. To him, raising sheep is earning a living
by "the copulation of cattle," since he is required "to be bawd to a bell-wether,

and to betray a she-lamb of a twelve-month to a crooked-pated old cuckoldy ram, out of all reasonable match" (3.2.70–72). This faux-scandalized account of January-and-May marriages among livestock is precisely the kind of comment that punctures the pastoral idyll at the same time that it speaks tellingly of behavior often practiced at court.

The Forest of Arden, then, is a golden world, an Eden, an Arcady, and in some sense a tongue-in-cheek parody of all of these. But what is it like? What is the experience of Arden as its travelers experience it, and as the audience experiences it? Arden has an intriguing range of fauna and flora. There are lions and serpents, oak trees and palm trees—and, at least in a song, if not in "real life," winter weather. In short, the world of Arden is not so much a real "English" forest (although the coast of Cornwall, far from Warwickshire and washed by the Gulf Stream, has its palm trees), but rather a place of imagination and possibility, perhaps one enriched by tales of colonial exploration. In the court Rosalind complains to Celia, "O how full of briers is this working-day world!" (1.3.9–10). In Arden she will say to Orlando, "I am in a holiday humour, and like enough to consent" (4.1.59–60). The opposition of working-day and holiday is a familiar dichotomy: Prince Hal averred in his "I know you all" soliloquy that "[i]f all the year were playing holidays, / To sport would be as tedious as to work" (*1 Henry IV* 1.2.182–183). In *As You Like It* the two states are aligned with geography. As Celia says when the two women, and the reluctant Touchstone, decide to enter the forest, "Now go we in content, / To liberty, and not to banishment" (1.3.131–132). To liberty and not to banishment—expulsion from the court world is liberation into Arden, a liberation signaled, as so often in Shakespearean comedy, by transformation in costume and in name.

In a play in which all names have significance, Rosalind has taken the name of Ganymede, the cupbearer of the gods, a lovely Trojan youth who was carried off by Zeus because of his beauty—a beauty that made him sought after by women as well as by men. The tale of Ganymede was understood as the model of male-male love among the Greeks, and still carried that connotation in the humanist Renaissance, which studied the Greek and Roman classics. Celia, whose own name means "heavenly," adopts the name Aliena, "the lost one," a typical pastoral name, but one also linked to the familiar Shakespearean pattern of losing oneself in order to find oneself. Celia has no political need to leave the court, where her father is the usurping and reigning Duke. But in leaving home to travel with her cousin, beloved friend, and virtual sister Rosalind, she estranges herself from her former life as the Duke's daughter, and is able to find and fall in love with a stranger who turns out to be Oliver, Orlando's brother.

The forest they enter, with its oddly mixed flora and fauna and its mythic associations, is a place of extreme variability. Just as time—in Rosalind's phrase—ambles with some people and trots with others, so Arden changes its nature depending upon the temperament and character of the observer. Arden is a projection of one's own beliefs, dreams, or fears—a psychological mirror of the self. As Touchstone says, tellingly, "Ay, now am I in Ardenne; the more fool I" (2.4.12)—recalling, surely intentionally, "Et in Arcadia ego." Arden is an intensifier, a mirror that magnifies both fantasies and preconceptions. Thus, for example, Duke Senior, the exiled "good" Duke, Rosalind's father, begins act 2 with a resounding speech on the moral value of the simple forest life, free from the "penalty of Adam," the cost of the fall or expulsion from paradise:

> Now, my co-mates and brothers in exile,
> Hath not old custom made this life more sweet
> Than that of painted pomp? Are not these woods
> More free from peril than the envious court?
> Here feel we not the penalty of Adam,
> The seasons' difference, as the icy fang
> And churlish chiding of the winter's wind,
> Which when it bites and blows upon my body
> Even till I shrink with cold, I smile, and say
> "This is no flattery. These are counsellors
> That feelingly persuade me what I am."
> Sweet are the uses of adversity,
> Which, like the toad, ugly and venomous,
> Wears yet a precious jewel in his head;
> And this our life, exempt from public haunt,
> Finds tongues in trees, books in the running brooks,
> Sermons in stones, and good in everything.
>
> *2.1.1–17*

There *are* sermons in the stones and books in the brooks—but only because Duke Senior puts them there, just as Orlando will put tongues in the trees. Duke Senior sees the landscape as a moral exemplum, and it becomes one. The forest itself is a blank canvas, on which he is projecting his own interpretation. And what he sees is that the country is more honest, less duplicitous than the court. "[T]he icy fang /And churlish chiding of the winter's wind, / Which when it bites and blows upon my body / Even till I shrink with cold, I smile, and say, / 'This is no flattery. These are counsellors / That feelingly persuade me what I am.' " These views will, indeed, resurface later in Shakespeare's career in another brilliant play about man and nature, *King Lear*.

The fact that Duke Senior is one of two dukes—one wicked, one virtuous—laying claim to the same dukedom suggests that the underlying structure of the play is in part one of psychological splitting. On one level there are indeed two dukes, and the rightful Duke, whose name declares his seniority, regains his proper place, while his usurping brother, Duke Frederick, is converted in the woods—offstage—by a convenient hermit, and vanishes from the play. On another level there is one duke, with the capacity to behave both badly and well. His usurping repressive nature in the court (where he is "Frederick") is overgone by a change of character in the wood, or fantasy world (where he is "Duke Senior"), and his return to his dukedom is assured by the victory of his better nature, exemplified in part by the good treatment accorded to both Rosalind and Celia. That these two kinds of plots can coexist simultaneously is completely typical of Shakespeare and of the way Shakespearean "character" works; the two kings in *Hamlet,* the idealized dead old Hamlet and the demonized living Claudius, are examples of the same mode of literary and psychological structure. In *As You Like It*—and indeed, if one wished, in *Hamlet*—this doubled plot could be foregrounded by doubling the parts.

So Duke Senior sees the wood as a place of moral simplicity and grace. He comments, in effect, on an issue that has already been debated by Rosalind and Celia, the relationship of nature to fortune. By contrast, we might consider the case of Orlando, who will comment on that other great Renaissance set piece for debate, the relationship of nature to nurture. For Orlando, the forest is also a mirror of his inward state, but his state of mind is, for the moment at least, quite different from that of the Duke. In the opening moments of the play we heard Orlando complain that he was not being given the nurture his nature deserved, he was not being brought up as a gentleman. Lamenting this suppression of his education and prospects by his brother Oliver, Orlando goes to the court and challenges the Duke's champion, Charles the wrestler—Charles who undertakes, at Oliver's secret request, to break Orlando's neck rather than his little finger. But Orlando defeats Charles, in the process winning the love—and the neck chain—of Rosalind, and in doing so he incurs the further wrath of Oliver and is persuaded by old Adam to flee into the forest. In act 2, therefore, we find Orlando and Adam wandering in the woods without food or shelter, and Adam ready to die. But Orlando is resolute in his determination to care for his surrogate father: "If this uncouth forest yield anything savage I will either be food for it or bring it for food to thee" (2.6.4–6).

Uncouth and savage, the forest for Orlando is hardly a paradise. Rather, it is the other side of the Renaissance view of nature, a view a later era would dub "hard pastoral," obdurate and antipathetic. It is in this desperate mood, in the next scene, that Orlando bursts, dagger drawn, into the clearing where the Duke and his men are at supper, shouting "Forbear, and eat no more!" (2.7.88). And what does he find? A group of courtiers sitting under a tree, having their bread and wine, and listening to music. Since Amiens, the singer, had instructed the others to "cover the while" as he sang, they have been busily laying a cloth on the table (the early modern meaning of "cover" in this sense, still extant today in restaurants that specify a "cover charge" for service). Into the midst of this idyll comes Orlando, flourishing his weapon and declaring, "I almost die for food; and let me have it" (2.7.103). The Duke's response is mild: "Sit down and feed, and welcome to our table" (104). "Speak you so gently?" says Orlando, abashed. "Pardon me, I pray you. / I thought that all things had been savage here" (105–106). Orlando, who is in his own phrase "inland bred," or civilized, finds that the wilderness is more civilized than he is. He is the savage here. The courtiers in the woods are the counterparts of those "savage men" (or "salvage men") of traditional pastoral romance, who turn out to be "gentle" after all. In fact, paradoxically, the play's true savage man, or bestial man, is found in the court and not in the wood at all, in the person of Charles the wrestler, far more savage than any of the denizens of Arden.

The mirroring function of the forest is never clearer than it is in the case of Jaques, the melancholy courtier, for whom Arden is a mirror precisely because Jaques so ardently wishes it to be one. Jaques (whose name, as Touchstone notes with amusement, is pronounced the same as "jakes," or privy, so that Touchstone, in a gesture of pretended gentility, calls him "Monsieur What-ye-call't" [3.3.60]), is a faddist, a self-conscious self-dramatizer. His melancholy is itself a pleasant affectation, rather than an emotional affliction. Melancholy was a fashionable Elizabethan complaint, a mark of aesthetic and intellectual refinement, a fact that we should bear in mind when encountering both the comparable melancholic affectation of Orsino at the beginning of *Twelfth Night* and, more disconcertingly, the melancholy of Hamlet. Jaques projects himself, emotionally, into the plight of a wounded deer, and it is noteworthy that this scene (2.1), which seems so vivid, and contains direct quotation, is actually an as-told-to adventure. Jaques' adventures and exploits tend to be told as "unscenes," secondhand. But the image is no less vivid for its mode of narration—the deer with his tears running down his innocent nose into the brook, and Jaques railing at the passing deer in the voice of a satirist: " 'Sweep on, you fat and greasy citizens, / 'Tis just the fashion' " (2.1.55–56). In his scenario the coldhearted deer are citizens, city folk, an inversion of the pastoral convention in which city people become country people. Deer, native residents of the forest, are now as heartless as literature usually portrays their city cousins to be. Jaques associates himself, deliberately, with the stricken deer left out of this social order, as he will equally deliberately separate himself from society at the play's close, claiming, "I am for other than for dancing measures" (5.4.182). He is this play's version of a figure excluded from the comic order.

Jaques' encounter with Orlando in the wood in act 3, scene 2, is even more like a mirror than his self-identification with the stricken deer, because it soon becomes clear that Orlando, no fool (except in romantic matters), is consciously mimicking him:

Jaques   I thank you for your company, but, good faith, I had as lief
            have been myself alone.
Orlando   And so had I. But yet for fashion' sake I thank you too for
            your society.

                                                              3.2.231–234

Their dialogue of mutual indifference concludes with the old joke of the fool in the brook:

Jaques	By my troth, I was seeking for a fool when I found you.
Orlando	He is drowned in the brook. Look but in, and you shall see him.
Jaques	There I shall see mine own figure.
Orlando	Which I take to be either a fool or a cipher.

3.2.261–265

The brook will provide a reflecting pool, the natural attributes of the forest presenting Jaques with a material image of his own folly. (We might compare this to the "portrait of a blinking idiot" contained in the silver casket in *The Merchant of Venice*. Both present the haughty onlooker with an unwelcome image of himself.) "Figure" here can mean either "face" or "number," provoking Orlando's witticism on "either a fool or a cipher." Shakespeare's time was the time of the importation of the "cipher," or "zero," into English mathematical practice, which had previously followed a Roman numeral style that lacked any symbol for this concept. Throughout the plays—notably in *King Lear* and *The Winter's Tale*—the notion of the cipher as a mathematical symbol is used as a powerful metaphor. But it is also no accident that this joke of the fool in the brook also recalls the story of Narcissus, who fell in love with his own image in a pond, and withered away into a flower, because he could not break the spell of his own self-love, his self-absorption. This tale from Ovid's *Metamorphoses*, highly popular in the English Renaissance, seems here to be turned by Orlando upon the self-regarding Jaques, but it contains a timely warning as well for Orlando, on the verge of being more in love with the idea of himself as a lover than with any real, nonfictional Rosalind. *As You Like It* regularly uses the device of the pastoral debate to create unlikely twinnings of this sort. Jaques loves himself; Orlando loves "Rosalind," whoever he thinks that personage might be. Orlando, if he were paying strict attention, might learn more than one lesson from his witty joust with the melancholy Jaques. But any lesson temporarily lost on him is available, still, for the education of the audience.

"[L]et the forest judge," says Touchstone the fool, and it does. Many if not most of the characters in this play are overly concerned with self as they enter the Forest of Arden, and this mirroring forest and these mirroring debates give proportion and balance. Thus the forest socializes. Even the obsessive Orlando, whose only dialogue as he enters the forest is with love poems on trees, is taught to participate in a holiday dialogue of love with the supposed Ganymede— a play-within-the-play that rehearses him, through the supposedly fictional courtship of Ganymede/Rosalind, for the supposedly real courtship of Rosalind in earnest. Only Jaques remains, like the deer weeping into the stream or the fool in the brook, staring, Narcissus-like, at his own reflection. It is fitting that he should seek out the hermit of the wood and remain there, on the other side of the looking glass, at the end of the play, rather than proceeding, as even Touchstone does, toward marriage and the resumption of social life in the world. Like so many of Shakespeare's excluded figures, Jaques will be, at the last, self-excluded.

Of all the mirror scenes in *As You Like It,* the most striking is the one that brings together these two crucial figures, Jaques and Touchstone. Again the scene as the audience experiences it is an "unscene," an event that has taken place offstage and that is told to us, this time by Jaques himself:

> A fool, a fool, I met a fool i'th' forest,
> A motley fool—a miserable world!—
> As I do live by food, I met a fool,
> Who laid him down and basked him in the sun,
> And railed on Lady Fortune in good terms,
> In good set terms, and yet a motley fool.
> "Good morrow, fool," quoth I. "No, sir," quoth he,
> "Call me not fool till heaven hath sent me fortune."
> And then he drew a dial from his poke,
> And looking on it with lack-lustre eye,
> Says very wisely "It is ten o'clock."
> "Thus we may see," quoth he, "how the world wags.
> 'Tis but an hour ago since it was nine,
> And after one hour more 'twill be eleven.
> And so from hour to hour we ripe and ripe,
> And then from hour to hour we rot and rot;
> And thereby hangs a tale." When I did hear
> The motley fool thus moral on the time
> My lungs began to crow like chanticleer,
> That fools should be so deep-contemplative,
> And I did laugh sans intermission
> An hour by his dial. O noble fool,
> A worthy fool—motley's the only wear.
>
> *2.7.12–34*

Jaques has met Touchstone in the forest. But he has met a Touchstone pretending to be Jaques. Railing on Lady Fortune is Jaques' idea of entertainment, not Touchstone's. Drawing a clock or watch from his bag and philosophizing on the time, "so deep-contemplative," the fool is himself a mirror; the joke is on Jaques. "O that I were a fool," concludes Jaques. "I am ambitious for a motley coat" (2.7.42–43). To which the audience might reply, in Rosalind's phrase to Touchstone, "Thou speak'st wiser than thou art ware of" (2.4.50). The whole of the play is constructed on paradoxes of this kind: a fool wiser than a self-styled philosopher, outlaws more gentle than the "inland bred" man; noble savages and savage nobles.

Touchstone is one of the most engaging of Shakespearean fools. At around the time this play was written a new comic actor, Robert Armin, joined Shakespeare's company, the Lord Chamberlain's Men. Armin succeeded Will Kemp, the principal clown of the earlier years, whose comedy was often broad and physical. Kemp, one of the original shareholders, was famous for his dancing, and especially for a performance known as Kemp's Jig. Kemp had originated such Shakespearean rustic roles as Costard in *Love's Labour's Lost,* Launce in *The Two Gentlemen of Verona,* and Bottom in *A Midsummer Night's Dream.* Armin's specialty was wit. Shakespeare created for him the deft and subtle verbal comedy of Feste in *Twelfth Night* and the Fool in *King Lear,* and it is thought that Touchstone, too, may have been a role written with Armin in mind. Certainly he made it successful, and this new kind of clown, more often now called a "fool," became one of the most visible elements in Shakespearean drama, balancing and undercutting the attitudes of the onstage "nobility." Paid or professional fools, of course, had long been members of royal and noble households throughout England and Europe. Richard Tarleton was a favorite in the court of Queen Elizabeth and is sometimes said to have been the model for Hamlet's beloved jester Yorick. Many, though not all, fools, jesters, and harlequins wore motley, a multicolored cloth, as a recognizable badge or costume. Known as "allowed fools" or "licensed fools," because they were permitted to say dangerous things without incurring punishment, such court figures functioned both as inside critics and as safety valves. Touchstone, like Feste and Lear's Fool, is permitted to speak truth to power, and escape unscathed, despite periodic threats of discipline or punishment.

Touchstone the licensed fool is, then, in one sense another aspect of "liberty," and of the fact that Arden leads "[t]o liberty and not to banishment." Like all allowed fools, he is himself a mirror, reflecting and commenting on the life and times around him. His name, Touchstone, means "a stone used to test the purity of gold or silver," and thus more generally a test or criterion by which things are judged. "[L]et the forest judge" is his pronouncement, as is "Ay, now am I in Ardenne; the more fool I." Touchstone is the personal equivalent of the forest, an index of human behavior and a way by which other characters come to confront themselves. Consider his answer to Corin's innocent question "And how like you this shepherd's life, Master Touchstone?"

> Touchstone Truly, shepherd, in respect of itself, it is a good life; but in respect that it is a shepherd's life, it is naught. In respect that it is solitary, I like it very well; but in respect that it is private, it is a very vile life. Now in respect it is in the fields, it pleaseth me well; but in respect it is not in the court, it is tedious. As it is a spare life, look you, it fits my humour well; but as there is no more plenty in it, it goes much against my stomach. Hast any philosophy in thee, shepherd?
>
> 3.2.13–20

In essence, Touchstone defines "philosophy" as seeing both sides of every question, providing suitable language (solitary versus private, in the fields versus not in the court, and so on) in order to bolster each argument. The baffled and outmatched Corin is not his only target. Touchstone will articulate the arguments for and against pastoral, for and against court life, arguments that affect and afflict most characters within the play.

Touchstone is fittingly associated with the issue of time, which will play so central a role in the dialectic of holiday and working-day worlds. We have heard Jaques' description of the fool in the forest, drawing his dial from his poke, and saying very wisely, "It is ten o'clock." When he "morals" on the time, drawing a moral or aphorism from it ("And so from hour to hour we ripe and ripe, / And then from hour to hour we rot and rot; / And thereby hangs a tale"), he speaks both what the play will call "philosophy" and also what it will call "bawdry," since the word "hour" was pronounced like the word "whore." Rotting thus becomes a specific affliction with venereal disease as well as a transcendental memento mori, and his moral "tale" hangs, rhetorically, adjacent to the more anatomical "tail." Orlando will later protest to "Ganymede" (the disguised Rosalind), that "[t]here's no clock in the forest" (3.2.275–276), and she will rebuke him by asserting that "[t]ime travels in divers paces with diverse persons" (282–283).Time in the forest is relative, an aspect of experience and personality. Time ambles with some, and trots with others, and gallops with a thief to the gallows. In fact, Rosalind's catalogue of what time does with whom greatly resembles, although it also differs from, that other time catalogue in *As You Like It,* Jaques' great set piece on the seven ages of man.

Here it is important to remind ourselves that this concept—"All the world's a stage"—was in Shakespeare's time already a cliché. For the post-Shakespearean world of readers this is perhaps its most famous articulation, but when Shakespeare put these words in the mouth of one of his most affected poseurs he was making a deliberate theatrical decision. The eloquence of the speech and the appeal of its primary metaphor does not diminish with the knowledge that this is not a "new" idea for Shakespeare and his colleagues, but rather a very old and indeed a tired one. This is entirely typical of Shakespeare, who does something similar in a number of other plays, putting Ulysses' speech on "degree" in the mouth of a character who will not hesitate to violate social hierarchy for political ends, and setting Hamlet's sublime "What a piece of work is a man!" in the context of a coarse and jesting conversation with Rosencrantz and Guildenstern. Putting the familiar cliché in an unfamiliar context is one way of making it dramatically effective, and this is what the playwright does with Jaques:

> All the world's a stage,
> And all the men and women merely players.
> They have their exits and their entrances,
> And one man in his time plays many parts,

His acts being seven ages. At first the infant,
Mewling and puking in the nurse's arms.
Then the whining schoolboy with his satchel
And shining morning face, creeping like snail
Unwillingly to school. And then the lover,
Sighing like furnace, with a woeful ballad
Made to his mistress' eyebrow. Then the soldier,
Full of strange oaths and bearded like the pard,
Jealous in honour, sudden, and quick in quarrel,
Seeking the bubble reputation
Even in the cannon's mouth. And then the justice,
In fair round belly with good capon lined,
With eyes severe and beard of formal cut,
Full of wise saws and modern instances;
And so he plays his part. The sixth age shifts
Into the lean and slippered pantaloon,
With spectacles on nose and pouch on side,
His youthful hose, well saved, a world too wide
For his shrunk shank, and his big, manly voice,
Turning again toward childish treble, pipes
And whistles in his sound. Last scene of all,
That ends this strange, eventful history,
Is second childishness and mere oblivion,
Sans teeth, sans eyes, sans taste, sans everything.

2.7.138–165

The choice of *seven* for the ages of man was a popular one in Shakespeare's time, although some experts contended that there were three, or four, or six. But seven was the number of the planets, and the virtues and vices, and the liberal arts, and so on. The character types mentioned by Jaques do match up with the planets—the schoolboy is mercurial; the lover, venereal; the soldier, martial; the justice, jovial; the old man, saturnine. More strikingly, in a play so concerned with language and poetry, each "age" is described in terms of speech. The infant mewls; the boy whines; the lover sighs and writes poems; the soldier's speech is full of strange oaths; the justice utters wise saws, or sayings, and modern instances, or examples; the old man's voice turns higher and thinner, as he returns from "manly" maturity back toward childhood. Speech is here a rite of passage marking the ages of man. But what is perhaps most central is again the sense of ongoing time. Like Touchstone's "hour to hour we ripe and ripe," this is time outside the forest, working-day time, time that will lead to death. It is thus in sharp contrast to the relative, subjective, and imaginative time within the forest world, where there is "no clock," and time ambles or gallops as it pleases. Jaques' great set piece is memorable, but like its speaker it has limitations, limitations shrewdly inserted by the playwright—not errors, but rather qualifications. Take, for example, the portrait of the last stage, "[s]ans teeth, sans eyes, sans taste, sans everything." Jaques' speech has been a long one—we can only imagine that he milks it, too, for every bit of satirical drama—and this is in part a device to give Orlando time to go back and fetch the loyal old Adam, as he has said he will do. Thus the speech will be winding to its conclusion as old Adam reenters the stage. And as he does so, in his dignity and self-awareness he gives the lie to everything Jaques has just said about the depredations and mortifications of old age.

Furthermore, as with the other dialogues and dialects of this playfully contrapuntal play (Touchstone and Corin on the merits and demerits of country life; Rosalind and Celia on nature and fortune; Jaques and Orlando on love and solitude), Jaques' portentous "seven ages of man" speech has its amusing and subversive pendant in Touchstone's account of the "seven degrees of the lie":

Touchstone	I did dislike the cut of a certain courtier's beard. He sent me word if I said his beard was not cut well, he was in the mind it was. This is called the Retort Courteous. If I sent him word again it was not well cut, he would send me word he cut it to please himself. This is called the Quip Modest. If again it was not well cut, he disabled my judgement. This is called the Reply Churlish. If again it was not well cut, he would answer I spake not true. This is called the Reproof Valiant. If again it was not well cut, he would say I lie. This is called the Countercheck Quarrelsome. And so to the Lie Circumstantial, and the Lie Direct.
Jaques	And how oft did you say his beard was not well cut?
Touchstone	I durst go no further than the Lie Circumstantial, nor he durst not give me the Lie Direct; and so we measured swords, and parted.

5.4.65–79

Jaques is entertained, if he is not instructed. It is not clear whether he sees this as a parody of his own earlier account, so different—in poetry rather than in prose—and yet so similar, in its scholastic desire to categorize. But Jaques has earlier contributed to this pattern of imitative one-upsmanship, a version of the poetical invective contest known as "flyting." In act 2, scene 5, hearing Amiens, one of the lords attending Duke Senior, sing his song of pastoral retreat, "Under the greenwood tree," Jaques adds a deflating verse of his own. Amiens's song is a conventional picture of pastoral idyll and *otium,* or ease:

> Under the greenwood tree
>   Who loves to lie with me,

> And turn his merry note
> Unto the sweet bird's throat,
> Come hither, come hither, come hither.
> Here shall he see
> No enemy
> But winter and rough weather.

> *2.5.1–8*

Jaques sardonically contributes a verse of antipastoral scorn:

> If it do come to pass
> That any man turn ass,
> Leaving his wealth and ease
> A stubborn will to please,
> Ducdame, ducdame, ducdame.
> Here shall he see
> Gross fools as he,
> An if he will come to me.

> *2.5.44–51*

"Gross fools as he" is the trick of the fool in the brook again, this time directed at others. As for "ducdame," probably coined from Latin *ducere*, "to lead," and thus meaning something like "lead them to me"—all the time Jaques has been singing he has either been lowering his voice or advancing casually toward the other pastoral courtiers, so that they have gathered around him. When Amiens asks, on cue, "What's that 'ducdame'?" Jaques can smartly reply, " 'Tis a Greek invocation to call fools into a circle" (2.5.52–53), gesturing at what he has just in fact done. ("Greek" here is learned misdirection, not Jaques' error.)

The Forest of Arden has many "natures," all of them familiar from debate motifs of the time: Nature and Nurture, Nature and Fortune, Nature and Art. Its strength is in its multiplicity and its liberality, the fact that its fantasy landscape can accommodate both palm trees and winter weather. One key to that multiplicity can be found in the play's title, yet another one of those Shakespearean comic titles that seem to be throwaway lines (like *Much Ado About Nothing*, or like the subtitle of *Twelfth Night—What You Will*). *As You Like It* implies *If wishes really did come true.* It presents a fantasyland, in other words, under the sign of the hypothetical—and the great mistress of the hypothetical in this play is, of course, Rosalind. Her cascade of "if's" and "as's" at the end of the play is indicative of both her power and her alignment with the world of wish and fantasy. Still in disguise as "Ganymede," she will say to Orlando near the play's close, "If you do love Rosalind so near the heart as your gesture cries it out, when your brother marries Aliena shall you marry her" (5.2.55–57), and in the great round-robin—or musical chairs—game of love she stages, the operative word is "if." In this complicated denouement, Silvius is in love with Phoebe, Phoebe thinks she is in love with "Ganymede," Orlando loves Rosalind and cannot find her, and Rosalind herself loves Orlando and is about to reveal it:

> [*To* SILVIUS] I will help you if I can. [*To* PHOEBE] I would love you if I could.—Tomorrow meet me all together. [*To* PHOEBE] I will marry you if ever I marry woman, and I'll be married tomorrow. [*To* ORLANDO] I will satisfy you if ever I satisfy man, and you shall be married tomorrow. [*To* SILVIUS] I will content you if what pleases you contents you, and you shall be married tomorrow. [*To* ORLANDO] As you love Rosalind, meet. [*To* SILVIUS] As you love Phoebe, meet. And as I love no woman, I'll meet.
>
> 5.2.102–110

In the contest to define and acquire love, Rosalind is hardly a disinterested spectator, like Jaques, nor, despite her occasional refreshing candor, is she is a genial cynic and realist like Touchstone. For Rosalind, "as you like it" is part of the essential transforming nature of love, which the play is striving to delimit and discover. Her crescendo of "if's" in the final scenes is a crucial statement about the nature of love, which turns out, unsurprisingly, to be closely linked to the nature of theater and theatrical illusion: "I'll have no father if you be not he. / I'll have no husband if you be not he" (5.4.111–112). Rosalind's "if's" carry over into her epilogue, where she is the very incarnation of *if,* and plays once more on the familiar fact that boy actors played the parts of women on the Elizabethan stage: "If I were a woman I would kiss as many of you as had beards that pleased me, complexions that liked me, and breaths that I defied not" (Epilogue 14–16).

The play is constructed as a series of productive and provocative hypotheses, spaces, places, and persons who present, and represent, possibility, indeed often represent what in grammatical terms would be called "conditions contrary to fact," or, in modern legal terms, "counterfactuals": in setting, the forest that mirrors the personality of the traveler; in character, the fool who does some version of the same, showing Jaques as a melancholy fool in the forest, and Orlando as a bad poet; in language, the play's persistent language of "as" and "if." Other than the pleasurable destabilization of expectations and sureties, is there a functional use for this kind of dramatic world? Does it advance the conscious as well as the unconscious narrative of the play? Does it make anything happen? One possible reply is that, by holding the limits and restrictions of everyday life in suspension, this welter of promising but often contradictory hypotheses offers an environment for the growth of love, as well as for the understanding of the often conflicting, and conflicted, nature of desire. Rosalind, of course, is the central player in this drama.

"I'll prove a busy actor in this play," says Rosalind, echoing the Puck of *A Midsummer Night's Dream,* when she is brought to see what the old shepherd Corin calls the "pageant" of Silvius and Phoebe. In many ways Rosalind is a

Puck figure, intervening in the love matches of others, appearing in the liminal space of the epilogue to break the frame between player and character, between audience and actors. Yet as the play opens she is hardly a liberated figure, except by ill chance. Her father, Duke Senior, has been banished to the Forest of Arden. (Like another usurped duke, Prospero in *The Tempest,* Duke Senior seems to prefer books to politics, if his "sermons in stones" speech is any indication.) Rosalind stays on at the court of her usurping uncle, Duke Frederick, and his daughter, Celia. It is for Celia that she stays, Celia who is her inseparable companion and her closest friend, and the picture the audience first gets of Rosalind and Celia is that of obedient daughters and virtual sisters. When Duke Frederick decides to banish the dangerously popular Rosalind from his court, since "her smoothness, / Her very silence, and her patience / Speak to the people, and they pity her" (1.3.71–73), it is in spite of Celia's protest,

> We still have slept together,
> Rose at an instant, learned, played, eat together,
> And wheresoe'er we went, like Juno's swans
> Still we went coupled and inseparable.
>
> *1.3.67–70*

The word "still" here, twice used, means "always." Celia's vision is a miniparadise, unfallen, timeless. The two young women were "coupled and inseparable," like sisters (Rosalind will use the word directly), twins, or aspects of each other. We may be reminded of a very similar passage in *A Midsummer Night's Dream,* in which Helena remembers an unfallen childhood when she and Hermia sat together on one cushion, sewing on one sampler,

> Both warbling of one song, both in one key,
> As if our hands, our sides, voices and minds
> Had been incorporate.
>
> Dream *3.2.207–209*

In these evocative and nostalgic images the young women are girls, living in a world governed by an older generation. For Rosalind and Celia—as, in a rather different kind of play, for Juliet—banishment is a necessary act of breaking away from the father. More precisely, banishment is the sign of that rupture. We may notice that Rosalind's expulsion by Duke Frederick, while explained by him in clearly political and pragmatic terms, happens virtually simultaneously with the dawn of her love for Orlando. "Is it possible on such a sudden that you should fall into so strong a liking with old Sir Rowland's youngest son?" asks Celia (1.3.22–23), and less than ten lines later the Duke enters, with his eyes "full of anger," to announce Rosalind's banishment. In effect the one event is the other. To fall in love is to leave the father. In this case, since Duke Frederick is Celia's father, not Rosalind's, Rosalind is able to rebel against a "bad" or repressive father at the same time that she goes forward into the Forest of Arden, where her "real," "good," and—importantly—absent father is already living. The reunion of father and daughter at the close, in tandem with Rosalind's engagement to Orlando, is enabled, once again, by this kind of psychological and characterological "splitting" of the father into good and bad, repressive and permissive, present and absent.

Thus when Celia makes her telling remark about going "in content / To liberty and not to banishment" (2.1.131–132), liberty can be taken to include the freedom to desire, and the freedom to fall in love. We may notice that even Oliver, the storybook wicked brother, is liberated, or, again, in his word, "converted," by entering the forest. Oliver immediately passes through danger to love, in a way familiar from the conventions of prose romance. Confronting an Edenic serpent and a crouching lioness, he makes his way to Celia and to what is perhaps the most dramatic—and offstage—case of Shakespearean love at first sight. As Rosalind will explain to Orlando,

> for your brother and my sister no sooner met but they looked; no sooner looked but they loved; no sooner loved but they sighed; no sooner sighed but they asked one another the reason; no sooner knew the reason but they sought the remedy; and in these degrees have they made a pair of stairs to marriage, which they will climb incontinent, or else be incontinent before marriage. They are in the very wrath of love, and they will together. Clubs cannot part them.
>
> As You Like It 5.2.28–36

Her phrase "your brother and my sister" suggests both the twinning and the need for differentiation, and her easy reference to sexual desire ("climb incontinent, or else be incontinent before marriage") incorporates the real physicality of love with the ideal romanticism of Orlando's poeticizing.

These reflections bring us to a key question about the structure of the play's plot, one frequently overlooked because its strategy of delay and deception is, theatrically speaking, what makes the play so delightful. Nonetheless, here is the question: Why doesn't Rosalind reveal her identity to Orlando? Why, long after she has seen that she is safe in the forest—her original, ostensible reason for disguise—does she remain Ganymede rather than Rosalind, a boy rather than a woman? When she laments, theatrically, to Celia, "Alas the day, what shall I do with my doublet and hose!" (3.2.200–201), why might not Celia advise her, in the immortal words of burlesque and striptease, to "take it off"? There are at least two kinds of answers to this question: one might be described as instrumental, practical, and functional, and another as symbolic. The first is conscious, the second unconscious; the first has to do with the realm of human psychology, and the second with fantasy and desire. Let me consider them in turn.

The first answer, then, to the question of why Rosalind remains in disguise is related to the necessity of education in love, not so much for herself as for Orlando. Rosalind seems almost instinctively to comprehend some essential truths about love, which is why she is so effective a stage manager of others' loves, and ultimately of her own. She understands that love is the next thing to folly, that to be a lover is to be a fool, as Touchstone says: "We that are true lovers run into strange capers. But as all is mortal in nature, so is all nature in love mortal in folly" (2.4.47–49). His sentiments are very close to those of Puck, who spoke more dismissively of human love as an occasion for amusement: "Lord, what fools these mortals be!" Rosalind receives Touchstone's pronouncement with approbation: "Thou speak'st wiser than thou art ware of."

By contrast, Orlando is not so immediately wise about love. In fact, when they first meet at the wrestling match he does not speak to Rosalind at all, though he is as smitten as she. "Can I not say 'I thank you'?" he asks himself (1.2.215). And then, when Rosalind has left:

> What passion hangs these weights upon my tongue?
> I cannot speak to her, yet she urged conference.
>
> *1.2.224–225*

As we have seen repeatedly, language is the index of full humanity in Shakespeare. When characters cease to speak, or cannot bring themselves to do so, they seal themselves off from society, whether in contexts that are palpably dangerous (the taciturnity of Don John in *Much Ado;* Iago's ultimate vow of silence in *Othello*) or inadvertently so (the inaudible Hero in *Much Ado;* the muffled Claudio, symbolically "dead" till he unmuffles himself and speaks, in *Measure for Measure*). Orlando's failure of language in love, however adorably adolescent, is in part a sign that he does not yet understand what it is to be a lover. From his tongue-tied inability to speak he progresses to a kind of "literary" love, from silence to writing, hanging his poems on trees in the forest, fulfilling in a comically literal way Duke Senior's prophecy of sermons in stones and books in the running brooks. Orlando: "O Rosalind! These trees shall be my books, / And in their barks my thoughts I'll character" (3.2.5–6). He has no idea, of course, that Rosalind is anywhere nearby to read these poems, much less that Touchstone is, to write parodies of them, imitating "the very false gallop of verses." In fact, Orlando's poetical love is rather solipsistic, though again not without its charm. He is another of Shakespeare's parody Petrarchan lovers (like the Romeo of the opening scenes of *Romeo and Juliet*), writing his fruitless poems because, as he thinks, his lady is unattainable and far away, while in reality she is just on the other side of the tree, picking off the poems as fast as he hangs them up. Orlando needs to be brought into direct contact with Rosalind, to stop thinking of her as some idealized, unreal lady, and instead to recognize her particular qualities of generosity and wit. He needs to speak to her rather than about her.

"Truly, the tree yields bad fruit," says Touchstone, after idly parodying Orlando's poems:

> Wintered garments must be lined,
> So must slender Rosalind.
>
> . . . .
>
> "Sweetest nut hath sourest rind,"
> Such a nut is Rosalind.
> He that sweetest rose will find
> Must find love's prick, and Rosalind.
>
> *3.2.94–101*

The "prick" here is the thorn of a rose ("Rosalind" translates as "lovely rose") but also contemporary slang for "penis." Mercutio had punned on the same word, which could also mean "a point on a dial." Shakespeare's Sonnet 20, "A woman's face with nature's own hand painted," addressed to the "master-mistress of my passion," concludes with a more romantic version of the trope. Having given his beloved the face and heart of a woman, but without woman's changeability and falsehood, "nature as she wrought thee fell a-doting," the poet writes,

> And by addition me of thee defeated
> By adding one thing to my purpose nothing.
> But since she pricked thee out for women's pleasure,
> Mine be thy love, and thy love's use their treasure.
>
> *Sonnet 20, lines 10–14*

For a moment the joke is on the boy-actor-as-Rosalind—but only for a moment, and only with a wink to the audience, before the onstage fiction resumes. Rosalind plucking the "bad fruit" of the tree becomes, instead, a comic version of Eve plucking the fruit of the Tree of Knowledge. Once she knows that Orlando is in the forest, Rosalind will seek to descend from the poetic pedestal on which he has placed her, and engage him instead in a play, a holiday pretense of love, which becomes a freeing rehearsal for love itself—if it is not love indeed.

Here the pragmatic wisdom of her decision to remain in disguise becomes evident, for Orlando is comfortable and at ease with the "boy" Ganymede, not tongue-tied as he was in the court, or pretentious as he is in his poems. Modern parlance calls such relationships by names like "male bonding" and "homosocial" love. However we understand the relationship between Orlando and "Ganymede," or however a director chooses to manage it on stage, the connection with "Ganymede" is a kind of breakthrough for Orlando, in which he becomes his easy, joking self. Rosalind as "Ganymede" undertakes to cure him of love, which, she says, is "merely a madness," even though Orlando protests, "I would not be cured, youth," and the nature of the proposed cure is a play-within-the-play. "I would cure you if you would but call me Rosalind and come every day to my cot, and woo me," she says (3.2.381–382). "With all my heart, good youth," Orlando replies, and the rejoinder is swift: "Nay, you must call me Rosalind" (387–388). The play is cast, the parts are given, yet Orlando does not know that the supposed fiction is truer than what he regards as reality. Rosalind's play will work for and upon him as do all plays-within-the-play in Shakespeare, exposing the follies and limitations of the world of the on-stage spectator—as well as the correlative blind spots of the audience in the theater.

But what about the second reason for Rosalind's remaining as "Ganymede," the reason, or set of reasons, that might be connected to the unconscious, to desire, and to the realm of the symbol? "Ganymede," like the changeling boy in *A Midsummer Night's Dream*, is what we could call a phantasmatic placeholder. He, or she, is that with which people fall in love. And Ganymede—it is time to take him out of quotation marks—has a quite distinct reality within the play, whether or not we call him, as Orlando does, by the name of "Rosalind." Phoebe falls in love with Ganymede, and so perhaps does Orlando—but no one wins Ganymede at the close. After the "holiday humor" of the play, the mar-riages blessed by Hymen, who "peoples every town," are, apparently, somewhat more conventional pairings: Silvius and Phoebe, Touchstone and Audrey, Orlando and Rosalind. When the play presents Rosalind finally as both "Rosa-lind" and a boy actor—a little like Snug the joiner in *A Midsummer Night's Dream,* with his head protruding from the lion's costume—where is Gany-mede? A boy actor playing a woman dressed as a boy, and demanding to be addressed as "Rosalind," Ganymede is necessary to falling in love. We could almost say that Ganymede *is* love in *As You Like It,* or in the world of "as you like it." Phoebe, and Audrey, and Rosalind herself were all played by boy actors on Shakespeare's stage, but the magic of Ganymede is not reducible to the gender conventions of the Elizabethan playhouse. Ganymede is that which escapes—the extra something, or something missing, that is the "overestima-tion of the object" associated with falling in love.

As is usually the case when Shakespeare populates his plays with several pairs of lovers, the characteristics of each pair balance the others. Thus, for example, the overidealized infatuation of Silvius for Phoebe is balanced by what might be called the underidealized, or overly pragmatic, relationship between Touch-stone and Audrey. Each of these eccentric pairs represents an aspect of, and a potential danger for, Rosalind and Orlando—and, indeed, for Celia and Oliver. Silvius is a kind of Orlando to excess, a spirit of pure doting, in love with love as well as with the disdainful Phoebe. He is the typical sighing shepherd of pas-toral, and also the typical love-struck lover. And it is Silvius whom Rosalind first encounters in the forest, pouring out his tale of love to the old man Corin in a sequence that will develop as a dialogue about lovers' amiable vices. The young shepherd–old shepherd dialogue is, again, a staple of pastoral poetry, appearing, for example, in Spenser's *Shepheardes Calender.* But another model for this con-versation, more dramatic and potentially more tragic, is the colloquy in *Romeo and Juliet* between Romeo and Friar Laurence in the friar's cell. There Romeo, like Silvius in *As You Like It,* finally rejects his old counselor as one who has not loved.

> Silvius   How many actions most ridiculous
>   Hast thou been drawn to by thy fantasy?
> Corin   Into a thousand that I have forgotten.
> Silvius   O, thou didst then never love so heartily.
>   If thou remembrest not the slightest folly
>   That ever love did make thee run into,
>   Thou hast not loved.
>   Or if thou hast not sat as I do now,
>   Wearing thy hearer in thy mistress' praise,
>   Thou hast not loved.
>
>   .   .   .   .
>
>   O Phoebe, Phoebe, Phoebe!
>
>   *2.4.25–38*

Rosalind, an unseen spectator to this little dialogue, exclaims feelingly, "Alas, poor shepherd, searching of thy wound, / I have by hard adventure found my own," and is quickly matched, and at the same time undercut, by Touchstone: "And I mine. I remember when I was in love I broke my sword upon a stone and bid him take that for coming a-night to Jane Smile, and I remember the kissing of her batlet, and the cow's dugs that her pretty chopped hands had milked" (2.4.39–45). Here is the whole spectrum of love, from Silvius's romantic excess to Touchstone's cynical realism, with Rosalind, as she will so often find herself, in the middle, sympathetic but not excessive. She knows the follies and pains of love, but she also knows its limits. When Phoebe scorns the adoring and available Silvius in favor of the elusive and unattainable Ganymede, Rosalind will admonish Silvius, " 'Tis not her glass but you that flatters her, / And out of you she sees herself more proper / Than any of her lineaments can show her" (3.5.55–57). Silvius is now a mirror, Phoebe's flattering glass. And as for Phoebe:

> [M]istress, know yourself; down on your knees
> And thank heaven, fasting, for a good man's love;
> For I must tell you friendly in your ear,
> Sell when you can. You are not for all markets.
>
>   *3.5.58–61*

Phoebe is not so far away as she thinks herself from the rams and she-lambs being mated by Corin. Love is a real as well as an ideal commitment. In fact, Rosalind functions throughout the play as the voice of common sense as well as of passion. She has something of Juliet's lyricism, something of Portia's wit and worldly wisdom, and something of Teste's license to be rude. She does not hold herself aloof from love, but can be as eager a participant as she is a judicious critic. When Celia teases her about Orlando, revealing that she has encountered him in the forest, Rosalind's response is immediate and unfeigning, a torrent of questions:

> Alas the day, what shall I do with my doublet and hose! What did he when thou sawest him? What said he? How looked he? Wherein was he? What makes he here? Did he ask for me? Where remains he? How parted he with thee? And when shalt thou see him again? Answer me in one word.
>
> *3.2.200–204*

"Answer me in one word" is the closest Rosalind gets to excess, a desire to cram all the world's responses, all possible information about the beloved Orlando, into a single moment in time. (We may contrast this with Orlando's own initial speechlessness.) Celia can hardly get a word in edgewise. Every time she tries to resume her narrative, Rosalind interrupts her with a question, or a smug lover's observation. Remember that she is—as she playfully laments—dressed in her man's clothes. Every once in a while, therefore, she will interject a reminder about her "real" gender: "Do you not know I am a woman? When I think, I must speak.—Sweet, say on" (3.2.227–228). The play is careful to keep reminding the audience of this circumstance (Rosalind/Ganymede grows faint, for example, at the sight of blood). The purpose is not to emphasize a woman's weakness as contrasted with a man's strength, but rather to keep all the plates spinning in the air (a boy player playing a woman playing a boy playing a woman . . .). And throughout, we hear the clear voice of Rosalind, surprisingly wise in her understanding of love. One moment she will explain—as will Juliet, and later Cleopatra, in their plays—that love is necessarily akin to excess:

> O coz, coz, coz, my pretty little coz, that thou didst know how many fathom deep I am in love. But it cannot be sounded. My affection hath an unknown bottom, like the Bay of Portugal.
>
> *4.1.175–178*

The next moment, tempering Orlando's Petrarchan extravagance, she will take pleasure in deflating him. When Orlando tells Ganymede that he would die for Rosalind, he gets an astringent reply: "Men have died from time to time, and worms have eaten them, but not for love" (4.1.91–92). Like "Sell when you can," this is advice from the working-day, not the holiday, world.

But if Rosalind is Ganymede as much as Ganymede is Rosalind—if the boy actor at the close represents another one of the play's imponderable "if"s—then questions of gender and sexuality will also come under the rubric of "as you like it," and the play emerges as not only a fantasy of genre, a pastoral fantasy, but also a fantasy about gender, a fantasy, that is to say, about the very nature of human desire.

So the love pair of Rosalind and Orlando are framed by the instructive—and amusing—examples of other lovers. On one side is the romantic excess of Silvius and Phoebe, and indeed of Orlando himself. On the other side, offering, as we have noted, a necessary balance, is the carnality of Touchstone: "As the ox hath his bow, sir, the horse his curb, and the falcon her bells, so man hath his desires; and as pigeons bill, so wedlock would be nibbling" (3.3.66–68). In an exchange indicative of the comical cross-purposes with which he and Audrey often speak, he defines "poetry" as a kind of "feigning," or lying, and wishes she were "poetical" for strictly unliterary reasons: "for thou swearest to me thou art honest. Now if thou wert a poet, I might have some hope thou didst feign" (3.3.20–22). So much, Touchstone suggests, for the pretensions of poets. Orlando's penchant for poeticizing has already been noted by Jaques, who at one point takes his leave with the startling and frame-breaking observation, "God b'wi'you an you talk in blank verse" (4.1.28). (Shakespeare here anticipates in *As You Like It* the famous discovery by Monsieur Jourdain in Molière's *Le Bourgeois Gentilhomme* that he has been speaking prose for forty years without knowing it.) Touchstone's genial earthiness—"Come, sweet Audrey, / We must be married, or we must live in bawdry" (3.3.79–80)—calls attention to the importance of sexual desire, at the same time that it marks the dangers of "bawdry." The false marriage by the hedge-priest with the wonderful name Sir Oliver Martext, like the moving but unofficial marriage ceremony between two young "men," Ganymede and Orlando, is succeeded by a cluster of ceremonial unions: Phoebe and Silvius, Celia and Oliver, Rosalind and Orlando. Among this genteel company Touchstone will intrude himself to make a fourth pair: "I press in here, sir, amongst the rest of the country copulatives, to swear, and to forswear" (5.4.52–54).

Poetry is traditionally associated with timelessness, and social life, marriage, and procreation with the world of ongoing time. The wedding song at the end of the play points, significantly, to human as well as seasonal renewal, and to urban as well as country life: " 'Tis Hymen peoples every town." Of all Shakespeare's plays, none has more—or more beautiful—songs, and the five songs in *As You Like It* perform something of the same function as the "Pyramus and Thisbe" play in *A Midsummer Night's Dream,* containing and defusing both emotion and potential tragedy. Amiens sings:

> Blow, blow, thou winter wind,
> Thou art not so unkind
>   As man's ingratitude.
> Thy tooth is not so keen,
> Because thou art not seen,

Although thy breath be rude

. . . .

Freeze, freeze, thou bitter sky,
That dost not bite so nigh
    As benefits forgot.
Though thou the waters warp,
Thy sting is not so sharp
    As friend remembered not.

2.7.174–189

This is a statement of the difference between "nature" and humanity. We have noted that it predicts, in a few simple lines, the plot and major imagery of one of Shakespeare's most profound and powerful tragedies, *King Lear*. But in *As You Like It*, where things can be "as you like it," this song is sung as an entertainment. The wind does not blow while it is sung, nor does the bitter sky freeze, any more than the lion really attacks Thisbe. (And, as Bottom intends to assure his audience, "Pyramus is not killed indeed.") The dangers and the evils of the world are encapsulated in song, and therefore controlled by art. But the play's songs, taken as a series or a cycle, have another function as well, traversing the distance between winter and spring, from the coldness of repression and banishment to the springtime of love, marriage, and a reinvigorated social order. Thus the songs progress from "Under the greenwood tree" ("Here shall he see / No enemy / But winter and rough weather") to "Blow, blow, thou winter wind" to "What shall he have that killed the deer?"— a song about the festivities of hunting that is, at the same time, an explicit, if joking, acknowledgment of human sexuality and the dangers of cuckoldry, here seen as a "natural" crest or heraldic badge, older than any aristocracy:

Take thou no scorn to wear the horn;
It was a crest ere thou wast born.
    Thy father's father wore it,
    And thy father bore it.

4.2.14–17

The lovely song of the fifth act will celebrate the return of spring, love, and marriage:

It was a lover and his lass,
With a hey and a ho, and a hey-nonny-no,
That o'er the green cornfield did pass
In springtime, the only pretty ring-time,
When birds do sing, hey ding-a-ding ding,
Sweet lovers love the spring.

5.4.14–19

Like the more schematic songs of Winter and Spring that end *Love's Labour's Lost,* these songs mark the pattern of cyclical renewal in art, in nature, and in human eroticism and love. The play ends, as we should expect, with a reminder of the working-day world, the world beyond the forest. Duke Senior will regain his lands and his dukedom; Orlando will become the Duke's heir; Oliver and Orlando will take up their roles in the world, the crisis created by primogeniture here having been averted by Orlando's fortunate marriage to a duke's daughter. Jaques alone will remain behind, absenting himself from the rustic revelry of the traditional marriage round: "I am for other than for dancing measures."

And yet, as the play begins to move toward its ending, there comes a crucial moment, the moment when Orlando learns that his brother and Celia have fallen in love and will marry. Now, for the first time, he is dissatisfied with his love games. Now, in a moment that is for him a real rite of passage, he wants the real Rosalind, and a real love. "O," he says to Rosalind/Ganymede, "how bitter a thing it is to look into happiness through another man's eyes." And this exchange follows:

> Rosalind   Why, then, tomorrow I cannot serve your turn for Rosalind?
> Orlando   I can live no longer by thinking.
>
> 5.2.43–45

This is the key phrase, the final turning point for Orlando: "I can live no longer by thinking"—that is, by imagining or fantasizing. In this moment he speaks the magic word, the open sesame, the formula that breaks the spell, returning the play to "reality" —and returning "Rosalind" (the role played by Ganymede) to Rosalind.

For if that is really his wish, says Ganymede, seizing on the moment, it can be fulfilled. "I have since I was three year old conversed with a magician, most profound in his art, but not damnable"—a good magician. And the powers learned from that magician will make it possible to produce the real Rosalind, "human as she is," before his eyes tomorrow, "and without any danger." Orlando is nonplussed. "Speakest thou in sober meanings?" he asks, and Rosalind/Ganymede replies, "By my life, I do, which I tender dearly, though I say I am a magician" (5.2.61–63).

The denouement unfolds in a familiar romance manner, as the Duke begins to note some marks of resemblance between Ganymede and his daughter. Orlando agrees, but explains, with that wrongheaded superiority that Shakespeare often gives to his young lovers and then forgives in them, that "this boy is forest-born, / And hath been tutored in the rudiments / Of many desperate studies by his uncle, / Whom he reports to be a great magician / Obscurèd in the circle of the forest" (5.4.30–34). The magic trick that Rosalind says she will perform is in fact the restoration of reality, producing Rosalind "before his eyes," where she has always been. The magic, that is, is at once the magic of love and the magic of theater. And yet it is well to point out that this unmasking is also a re-masking. Which is the "human" truth—the boy actor or the female character?

That Rosalind is a magician is a point she will make, once again, in her epilogue, one of the most compelling moments of Shakespearean stage management in any of the plays. "My way is to conjure you," she will say, reappearing onstage in her women's clothes. As it never does to try to upstage Shakespeare, we should permit his remarkable character to have the last word here, bearing in mind all the boundaries that she traverses as she does so, standing on the edge of the stage, at the end of the play, poised between playing-space and pit, between actors and audience, between female and male, woman and boy. In a modern all-male version of this play I had the good fortune to witness, the actor playing Rosalind dropped his voice at "if I were a woman." (The effect was very similar to the moment, in a modern production of *The Tempest,* when the actor playing Prospero, delivering *his* epilogue, deliberately lost the amplified power of the microphone, leaving him with a voice that was simply, and only, human.) Here is Rosalind:

> It is not the fashion to see the lady the epilogue; but it is no more unhandsome than to see the lord the prologue. If it be true that good wine needs no bush, 'tis true that a good play needs no epilogue. Yet to good wine they do use good bushes, and good plays prove the better by the help of good epilogues. What a case am I in then, that am neither a good epilogue nor cannot insinuate with you in the behalf of a good play! I am not furnished like a beggar, therefore to beg will not become me. My way is to conjure you; and I'll begin with the women. I charge you, O women, for the love you bear to men, to like as much of this play as please you. And I charge you, O men, for the love you bear to women—as I perceive by your simpering none of you hates them—that between you and the women the play may please. If I were a woman I would kiss as many of you as had beards that pleased me, complexions that liked me, and breaths that I defied not. And I am sure, as many as have good beards, or good faces, or sweet breaths will for my kind offer, when I make curtsy, bid me farewell.
>
> *Epilogue 1–19*

Hamlet

DRAMATIS PERSONAE

Ghost of Hamlet, *the late King of Denmark*
King Claudius, *his brother*
Queen Gertrude of Denmark, *widow of King Hamlet, now wife of Claudius*
Prince Hamlet, *son of King Hamlet and Queen Gertrude*
Polonius, *a lord*
Laertes, *son of Polonius*
Ophelia, *daughter of Polonius*
Reynaldo, *servant of Polonius*
Horatio, *a friend of Prince Hamlet*
Rosencrantz, *a friend of Prince Hamlet*
Guildenstern, *a friend of Prince Hamlet*
Francisco, *a soldier*
Barnardo, *a soldier*
Marcellus, *a soldier*

Valtemand, *a courtier*
Cornelius, *a courtier*
Osric, *a courtier*
Gentlemen, courtiers
A Sailor
Two Clowns, a gravedigger and his companion
A Priest
Fortinbras, *Prince of Norway*
A Captain in his army
Ambassadors from England
Players, who play the parts of the Prologue, Player King, Player Queen, and Lucianus, in *The Mousetrap*
Lords, messengers, attendants, guards, soldiers, followers of Laertes, sailors

WATCHING OR READING *Hamlet* for the first time or the twentieth, an observer cannot help being struck, I think, by how much of the play has passed into our common language. Indeed, as many commentators have observed, the experience of *Hamlet* is almost always that of *recognition*, of recalling, remembering, or identifying some already-known phrase or image. It could be said that in the context of modern culture—global culture as well as Anglophone culture—one never does encounter *Hamlet* "for the first time." Instead the play provides a resonant cultural echo, both forming and reflecting concepts—turns of speech, types of character, philosophical ideas—that seem to preexist any single experience of the play, and at the same time to be disseminated from it.

Nor is it only the great set pieces, the philosophical touchstones, that linger in the imagination: the "To be, or not to be" soliloquy, with its passionate broodings on death and the life hereafter (3.1.58); Hamlet's advice to the players ("Speak the speech, I pray you, as I pronounced it to you—trippingly on the tongue," since "the purpose of playing" is "to hold as 'twere the mirror up to nature" [3.2.1–2, 18–20]); or the calm assurance, voiced in the last act, that the readiness is all, that "[t]here's a divinity that shapes our ends, / Rough-hew them how we will" (5.2.10–11). It is not surprising that we remember these passages, for their beauty and for their profound ideas. They are among the greatest in the English language. But there are other, more particular and private lines that also seem somehow to have become part of our culture, and for less explainable reasons, lines that seem minor, even trivial. Why should we remember "Alas, poor Yorick," or that "[s]omething is rotten in the state of Denmark," or that "there are more things in heaven and earth, Horatio, / Than are dreamt of in your philosophy," or that "[t]he lady protests too much, methinks"? Proper names and specific terms, all—Yorick, Denmark, Horatio, the lady. Yet they are for us something else, something more "universal." When we hear someone say "Alas, poor Yorick," we do not think that he or she is speaking of Hamlet's childhood jester. We know that what is at stake is rather the general case of mortality and the human condition, that reaches but to dust. When we are told that "[s]omething is rotten in the state of Denmark" we do not think first of pollution problems in Scandinavia, but rather of a generally corrupt society or situation, a pervasive decay. That someone, anyone, "protests too much" has become a common way of underscoring her, or his, disingenuousness. Few of those who quote or adapt this line will recall that it refers to the Player Queen in "The Murder of Gonzago," *Hamlet*'s play-within-the-play.

Hamlet is one of the most peculiar, private, and detailed among all of Shakespeare's plays. At first glance it does not seem "universal" at all. Fratricide, an incestuous marriage, a prince who pretends to be mad and contemplates death in a spirit of overwhelming melancholy, a young girl who is in fact driven mad, and who, in her madness, drowns herself. What is it about this odd play, derived from older sources—the twelfth-century legend of Amleth, told by the Danish author known as Saxo the Grammarian, which was later adapted into French by François de Belleforest in 1570, the primary source for the supposed ur-*Hamlet*, or original *Hamlet,* a lost play scholars speculate about—that has mined the play into our consciousness to such a degree? What makes *Hamlet* with its many textual variants, its First or "bad" Quarto, Second Quarto, and Folio texts, the most famous of all English dramas and the most admired and quoted of literary documents?

What we have of the imagined ur-*Hamlet* survives in a fragmentary mention of a pale "ghost who cried so miserably at the Theatre like an oyster wife, *Hamlet, revenge,*" so that "Hamlet, revenge" became a common saying of the period, a kind of tagline or joke, this supposed source itself a kind of ghost, existing only in memory, reconstructed in imagination. And the same might be said of the "bad quarto" of 1601, an early published version that notoriously varies from the text we "know" as *Hamlet*, so that, for example, the play's most famous speech reads, "To be or not to be, I there's the point, / To Die, to sleep, is that all? I all: / No, to sleep, to dream, I mary there it goes. . . ." ("I" in early modern English is another way of spelling "aye"; "mary" is the same word as "marry," an interjection of surprise or indignation.) This First Quarto is now again valued by scholars as a likely account of the play in performance—the text was probably written down from memory by a secondary player—and it has been produced successfully on the modern stage. Moving more quickly than the version remastered by the Folio editors for the printed text and cherished by generations of poets and philosophers for its long passages of ruminative reflection, the "bad quarto," now better described simply as Quarto 1, is yet another example of the ways in which Shakespeare in his time, and Shakespeare on the stage instead of the page, differs from the "Shakespeare" who has become a sage cultural authority.

The play's title, taken from the Second Quarto, *The Tragical History of Hamlet, Prince of Denmark,* indicates that we are dealing with both a personal and a political or dynastic situation, with Hamlet the prince and with Hamlet the man. Ophelia tells us what he was like before the play began, before the events that have festered to produce the rottenness that now is Denmark. Her recollection of this ideal young prince is closely akin to Lady Percy's memory of her heroic husband, Harry Percy, or Hotspur, at the beginning of *Henry IV Part 2,* after she has received news of his death. To Lady Percy, Hotspur "was indeed the glass / Wherein the noble youth did dress themselves" (*2 Henry IV* 2.3.21–22), the mirror or model for a generation. Likewise, Ophelia paints a picture of a Hamlet who was once a cynosure, a brilliant center of attraction:

> The courtier's, soldier's, scholar's, eye, tongue, sword,
> Th'expectancy and rose of the fair state,
> The glass of fashion and the mould of form,
> Th'observed of all observers. . . .
>
> Hamlet *3.1.150–153*

Hamlet bears the same name as his father, the former King, and his play is a private chronicle, the story of a history gone awry, and wrenched into tragedy. He is a public and a private man, and, presumably, the heir to the throne. Why is Hamlet not the new King? He says that his uncle Claudius "[p]opped in between th'election and my hopes" (5.2.66), and it is not enough to say, as footnotes dutifully do, that the Danish monarchy was elected rather than passed down from father to son. "Election" here of course has its older meaning of being chosen by a group of supporters; there were no ballot boxes in medieval Denmark, nor in early modern England. Our modern sense of "acclamation" is appropriate here: we see it in practice in the play both in the people's call "Laertes shall be king" (4.5.104) and in Hamlet's own declaration at the point of death, "I do prophesy th'election lights / On Fortinbras. He has my dying voice" (5.2.297–298).

There is an uneasiness and an ambiguity, then, in the very title of this play, despite its apparent straightforwardness, and this sense of uneasiness and ambiguity is set forth with great effect in an early exchange between Hamlet the father and Hamlet the son. "Remember me," cries the ghost of old Hamlet, and the son Hamlet replies, "Remember thee? / Ay, thou poor ghost, while memory holds a seat / In this distracted globe" (1.5.91, 95–97). What is the "distracted globe" of which he speaks? The primary sense of his metaphor refers to his head, his troubled mind. As long as I have a memory, he says—as long as I live—I will remember you, and what you have told me. But the literal sense of "globe" is not absent here. The world of the play is itself "distracted," maddened, diseased. Old Hamlet has been poisoned, and the poison affects not only the King, but the state. We know from plays like *Richard II* and the *Henry IV* plays, and even from *Julius Caesar,* a play written in the same years as *Hamlet,* that when the king is weak, so too is the kingdom. When there is corruption at the top, the land and its people are likewise corrupted and infected. Thus in this play the madness that Hamlet assumes is a madness already present in the state, for the king is the state. Hamlet's "antic disposition," his feigned temperament of the fool and madman, is an objective correlative for the condition of his country and its rule. The world, or "globe," of *Hamlet* the play is deliberately and insistently paralleled to the mind, or "globe," of Hamlet the man. Thus Hamlet the character wears an "inky cloak"—associated, as we will see, with the many scenes of writing that will be depicted in the course of the play. Gertrude, Hamlet's mother, will call his dark costume his "nightly colour" (1.2.68), and the play's world, too, wears a cloak of night, the darkness in which the sentries stumble over one another at the beginning of the play, and the inner darkness of the "black and grainèd spots" that Gertrude is made to acknowledge in her soul.

The world of the play is in a sense a metaphor for the consciousness of its protagonist, and its characters have relationships with Hamlet the prince that are both realistically personal and allusively psychological. The Ghost is both the shade of Hamlet's father, come to stir him, in traditional Elizabethan and Senecan fashion, to revenge, and also a kind of superego, a conscience-prodder, inseparable from Hamlet himself. We may notice that the Ghost speaks only to Hamlet, and, in the scene in the Queen's closet, or private room, is seen only by him. Gertrude sees "nothing," and thinks she sees all there is to see. Likewise Horatio is unquestionably a "real" character, Hamlet's fellow student at the University of Wittenberg in Germany (significantly, the home, as well, of the legendary Doctor Faustus and the real Martin Luther), but he is also a kind of internal censor, a voice that might almost come out of Hamlet's own mind, screening out unacceptable ideas and memories, confident that ghosts don't exist, and cautioning Hamlet in the last act against considering "too curiously" the question of what happens to the body after death.

There is, then, a strong and deliberate parallelism between the mind of Hamlet and the world of Denmark. But there is also, needless to say, a third important meaning to the phrase "this distracted globe" when uttered in the context of Shakespeare's company's history, for *The Tragical History of Hamlet, Prince of Denmark* was staged in the new Globe theater the company had built in the Bankside district of London, and the "distracted globe" is also the mysterious world of the theater, in which we sit as spectators. Hamlet will speak in his dying moments to the onstage onlookers who are "mutes or audience to this act" (5.2.277), unwitting bystanders, and the audience in the theater, from Shakespeare's time to the present, is part of this group. It is in our memory, as well as in theirs, that the tragedy lives on and the story is retold. We need not point to the omnipresent theatrical metaphors or the infinite sequence of plays-within-the-play to see how Hamlet's story has become, for every audience, its own. Like a series of Russian dolls, nested one inside another, or the infinite regress of a theatrical or pictorial illusion (the man on the trademark Quaker oats box, holding a box on which there is a man holding a box), the plays and fictions of *Hamlet* nest inside one another, until we are no longer sure where to place the boundaries of reality and illusion. Hamlet's story becomes the story of a confrontation with consciousness, and it is this story that becomes the haunting chronicle Horatio must live to retell. In its history, as well as its dramatic structure, *Hamlet* the play has itself become a mirror held up to nature, like the "glass of fashion and the mould of form" that was Hamlet the prince. It is perhaps for this reason that so many critics and philosophers have seen themselves in the character. As Samuel Taylor Coleridge famously remarked, "I have a smack of Hamlet myself, if I may say so."[1]

In suggesting that these three worlds—the world of Hamlet's mind and imagination; the physical, political, and "historical" world of Denmark; and the world of dramatic fiction and play—are parallel to and superimposed upon one another, I am suggesting, also, that the play is about the whole question of boundaries, thresholds, and liminality or border crossing: boundary disputes between Norway and Denmark, boundaries between youth and age, boundaries between reality and imagination, between audience and actor. And these boundaries seem to be constantly shifting. The most inexorable boundary possible would seem to be that between life and death, yet the play opens with the appearance of a ghost, a spirit come from the grave, as well as from the contemporary Elizabethan stage, where such evocative and minatory figures were popular. Even language seems to lose its boundaries. Hamlet says to a startled Horatio, "My father—methinks I see my father" (1.2.183). "O where, my lord?" is the astonished reply (184). "In my mind's eye, Horatio" (184). This is all well and good—the "sighting" is safely metaphorical. But only four lines later, Horatio, this play's man of common sense and ultimate rationality, will say, "My lord, I think I saw him yesternight" (188). And this leap into the world of illusion, this crumbling of the expected boundaries between the real and the fictive or imagined, is an essential part of the play's methods. There is, as Polonius will remark in another connection, method in its madness.

If, of all of Shakespeare's plays, only *Hamlet* had somehow survived, if we had only *Hamlet* to represent his theater and his dramatic achievement, we would still regard Shakespeare as a brilliant playwright, and we would have a very good idea of what the early modern stage looked like and how it worked. For one of the central tropes of *Hamlet* the play (and indeed of Hamlet the prince and player) is what is called "metatheater," or "metadrama," the discussion of theater and playing within a play—the play talking about its own materials, and the self-referential gestures toward the world as a stage (or Globe).

As befits a play about the "purpose of playing" in the widest sense, *Hamlet* provides an excellent guide to the use of the early modern stage, and to the thematic interchangeability of stage and world. At the end of the first act, for example, the Ghost "cries under the stage," commanding, "Swear. . . . Swear. . . . Swear," from the trapdoor leading to the "hell" beneath the stage. And in the graveyard scene in the fifth act, Ophelia's grave is the same open "trap." The symmetry would not have been lost on the spectators. The "heavens" above the stage—a covering, ornamented with suns and stars, that protected the actors from the elements—are explicitly compared by Hamlet to the world outside the theater ("this brave o'erhanging, this majestical roof fretted with golden fire" (2.2.291–292). In this, one of his greatest existential speeches, Hamlet guardedly explains his melancholy mood—the fact that he has "lost all [his] mirth"—to his opportunistic, and ultimately treacherous, schoolfellows Rosencrantz and Guildenstern. Unlike many of the great soliloquies in this play, this famous set piece on "man" is written in prose.

The balcony above the stage would have been used as a guard platform by the sentries in the opening scene, with its startling first line—"Who's there?"—flung out not only at the newcomer, another sentry, but also at the audience. "Who's there?" and then, "Nay, answer me." (Recall that this scene of darkness was played in full light, in the middle of the afternoon, and this scene of bitter cold was played in full warmth, in the middle of the summer.) The two doors behind the stage would have gotten much use, for royal entrances and exits, for Ophelia's comings and goings, for the political scenes with the Norwegian Prince Fortinbras and his army, and, of course, for the "maiméd rites" of the funeral procession for the dead Ophelia. The discovery space behind the stage would have been used for Polonius hiding behind the arras in Gertrude's closet—invading her private space.

In the refitting and revising of the play-within-the-play, *The Mousetrap*, we have a good example of how Renaissance plays were adapted for different occasions, sometimes by a second or third playwright. Hamlet asks whether the players could learn "some dozen or sixteen lines" he will insert, to do the work (the detective work, the cultural work) he needs the play to do, in testing Claudius's guilt. *The Mousetrap* is a dramatic fiction that resembles, very closely, what he thinks happened in "real life"—the murder of the previous King, the good King, Hamlet's father. Later in the play Hamlet once again crucially revises a script, in this case the sealed letter from King Claudius, carried by Rosencrantz and Guildenstern, requesting the King of England to cut off Hamlet's head, and again he will imagine it as a staged action: "Ere I could make a prologue to my brains, / They had begun the play" (5.2.31–32).

Through a clever use of playing and of players, and of the repertoire of this particular traveling company, Hamlet will trap his uncle Claudius into a damning sign of guilt—evidence that he, Claudius, is responsible for the death of Hamlet's father, which made possible his own accession to the throne, and to the Queen. The acting company consists of adult players, described by Polonius as "[t]he best actors in the world, either for tragedy, comedy, history, pastoral, pastorical-comical, historical-pastoral, tragical-historical, tragical-comical-historical-pastoral, scene individable or poem unlimited" (2.2.379–382). They play a wide repertoire, from the tragedies of Seneca to the comedies of Plautus. This list, so pedantically offered, is a deliberate parody of the mixed modes that were beginning to appear on the stage, and the academic, comically Aristotelian desire to classify them.

The play's events will turn in part on the visit of this group of traveling players to Elsinore, in Denmark. Why are the players traveling, rather than playing in a theater in the city? As Hamlet points out, they were better off in the city, in terms of both their reputation and their capacity to turn a profit. But we learn from Rosencrantz and Guildenstern that the fashion for child players, the boy actors performing satires in the private theaters, has driven the adult company out of the city. Hamlet, a self-confessed aficionado of the theater, provides a good brief description of the kinds of actors, and parts, there were in sixteenth-century companies, as well as an ironic commentary on the fictionality of real-life roles: "He that plays the King shall be welcome; his majesty shall have tribute of me. The adventurous Knight shall use his foil and target [sword and shield], the Lover shall not sigh gratis [without payment], . . . the Humorous Man [someone governed by the one of humors, which were thought to influence the emotions, such as anger or melancholy]. . . , the Clown . . . , the Lady . . ." (2.2.308–312). Hamlet has met these players before, and he greets them as old friends. The First Player—the main actor, the star—has grown a beard since he saw him last; the boy who plays female parts (addressed by Hamlet as "my young lady and mistress") has not only grown taller, his voice may soon be changing, rendering him no longer fit for women's roles.

By the time the players arrive, we have already seen in Hamlet a certain tendency to self-dramatization. He thinks in theatrical terms. He moralizes on his mourning clothes as a kind of "show," or external display. He assumes the role of fool or antic, with a disarranged costume to match. Even as late as the grave-yard scene, he will speak bitterly about face-painting and makeup, comparing the skull of Yorick to "a fine lady"—"let her paint an inch think, to this favour she must come"—and he has already said as much to the living Ophelia, an innocent victim, in the scene in which he demonstrates his "madness" to her: "I have heard of your paintings, too, well enough. God hath given you one face, and you make yourselves another. You jig, you amble, you lisp" (3.1.142–144). This is an unflattering account of the behavior of women, but it is also a description of the behavior of professional actors, who paint, and who amble, jig, and lisp onstage. Lisping is often associated in Shakespeare with affectation: Rosalind counsels Jaques, "Look you lisp, and wear strange suits" (*As You Like It* 4.1.29–30), and Berowne mocks an ornate courtier as an "ape of form" who can "lisp" to women and men. The jig, a lively dance—English, Scottish, or Irish— was a common element of performance, especially by clowns and fools, on the stage, and is an aspect of the improvised behavior Hamlet warns the players against in his advice to them.

Hamlet's famous "advice to the players" shows us something of the tension between the relatively naturalistic acting favored by Shakespeare's company— confiding in the audience, the soliloquy as a kind of voiced thought—and the older and more bombastic acting style inherited from the medieval mystery plays, and still favored by some of Shakespeare's contemporaries, like Edward Alleyn, the chief tragedian of the rival company, the Lord Admiral's Men. Here is Hamlet:

> Speak the speech, I pray you, as I pronounced it to you—trippingly on the tongue; but if you mouth it, as many of your players do, I had as lief the town-crier had spoke my lines. Nor do not saw the air too much with your hand, thus, but use all gently; for in the very torrent, tempest, and as I may say the whirlwind of your passion, you must acquire and beget a temper- ance that may give it smoothness. O, it offends me to the soul to hear a robustious, periwig-pated fellow tear a passion to tatters, to very rags, to split the ears of the groundlings, who for the most part are capable of noth- ing but inexplicable dumb shows and noise. I would have such a fellow whipped for o'erdoing Termagant. It out-Herods Herod. Pray you avoid it. . . . Be not too tame, neither; but let your own discretion be your tutor. Suit the action to the word, the word to the action, with this special obser- vance: that you o'erstep not the modesty of nature. For anything so over- done is from the purpose of playing, whose end, both at the first and now, was and is to hold as 'twere the mirror up to nature, to show virtue her own feature, scorn her own image, and the very age and body of the time his form and pressure.
>
> *3.2.1–22*

Hamlet warns against overacting, and bellowing, and strutting, and clowns who improvise to get a laugh, and who distract the spectators from the meaning of the play. This is Hamlet's "advice to the players." What is his advice to himself?

We find it, of course, in the extraordinary soliloquies, the internal monologues, the debates and discussions with himself for which this play is famous—
and justly so. It is to a very great extent the soliloquies that have made the play
the favorite of poets and philosophers, not to mention actors and directors. In
each of the first four acts we find Hamlet either stepping forward or being left
alone to ruminate to himself. "I'll be with you straight," he says. "Go a little
before," or "Now I am alone." And, left alone onstage, with only us for company and confidants, he speaks:

> O that this too too solid flesh would melt,
> Thaw, and resolve itself into a dew,
> Or that the Everlasting had not fixed
> His canon 'gainst self-slaughter! O God, O God,
> How weary, stale, flat, and unprofitable
> Seem to me all the uses of this world!
>
> *1.2.129–134*

In act 2, scene 2, we hear his disparaging comparison of himself to the First
Player, who is only an actor, not a prince, and yet is able to show more grief in a
pretended cause than Hamlet can show in a real one:

> O, what a rogue and peasant slave am I!
> Is it not monstrous that this player here,
> But in a fiction, in a dream of passion,
> Could force his soul so to his whole conceit
> That from her working all his visage wanned,
> Tears in his eyes, distraction in 's aspect,
> A broken voice, and his whole function suiting
> With forms to his conceit? And all for nothing.
> For Hecuba!
> What's Hecuba to him, or he to Hecuba,
> That he should weep for her? What would he do
> Had he the motive and the cue for passion
> That I have? He would drown the stage with tears.
>
> *2.2.527–539*

The soliloquy in the fourth act, Hamlet's rebuke to himself for failing to act in a
good cause, is couched, like the second soliloquy, as a negative self-comparison.
Why can he not be more like Fortinbras, the noble soldier avenging his father's
defeat?

> How all occasions do inform against me
> And spur my dull revenge! What is a man
> If his chief good and market of his time

Be but to sleep and feed?—a beast, no more.
Sure he that made us with such large discourse,
Looking before and after, gave us not
That capability and god-like reason
To fust in us unused. Now whether it be
Bestial oblivion, or some craven scruple
Of thinking too precisely on th'event—
A thought which, quartered, hath but one part wisdom
And ever three parts coward—I do not know
Why yet I live to say "This thing's to do,"
Sith I have cause, and will, and strength, and means,
To do't. Examples gross as earth exhort me.

                                        4.4.9.22–9.36

Fortinbras, by contrast, he calls a "delicate and tender prince" willing to risk everything: "Exposing what is mortal and unsure / To all that fortune, death, and danger dare, / Even for an eggshell." His troops battle over a plot of ground that is not even big enough to bury the dead.

These passages, with their rich imagery and their unerring rhythmic ebb and flow, are among the most moving and complex speeches in our literature. But it is the soliloquy in the third act, "To be, or not to be," that has become the hallmark of interiority and consciousness, the speech that—quoted, parodied, parsed, and pondered—has come to define modernity and modern self-consciousness, the birth, in effect, of the modern subject, of modern subjectivity itself:

To be, or not to be; that is the question:
Whether 'tis nobler in the mind to suffer
The slings and arrows of outrageous fortune,
Or to take arms against a sea of troubles,
And, by opposing, end them. To die, to sleep—
No more, and by a sleep to say we end
The heartache and the thousand natural shocks
That flesh is heir to—'tis a consummation
Devoutly to be wished. To die, to sleep.
To sleep, perchance to dream. Ay, there's the rub,
For in that sleep of death what dreams may come
When we have shuffled off this mortal coil
Must give us pause. . . .

                                        3.1.58–70

The diction—the single string of relentless monosyllables, the repetition of the infinitive "to be"—draws a verbal picture of the anguish of thought. And this almost unbearable moment of full consciousness—*too* full consciousness—is what we think of as the condition and the tragedy of modernity. Actors have tried to find new ways to pronounce this speech. In his film of *Hamlet*, Kenneth Branagh speaks it while looking in a mirror—a three-sided mirror, where the actor, seen in full length, beholds, and displays, many selves, many versions of himself. Which is the real one?

We might compare "To be, or not to be" with a similar kind of construction—say, "To do, or not to do." This is the kind of quandary that afflicts Macbeth, as we'll see. It is given voice in a great speech:

> My thought, whose murder yet is but fantastical,
> Shakes so my single state of man that function
> Is smothered in surmise, and nothing is
> But what is not.
>
> Macbeth *1.3.138–141*

"To do, or not to do" is also the problem that confronts Othello, as he trembles on the brink of a dreadful deed. But although Hamlet likewise contemplates action, contemplates murder, contemplates revenge, it is *being*, not *doing*, that has made this character the mirror that subsequent writers, philosophers, and critics have held up to human nature. Being—and remembering—because the essence of the human animal, and the pain and joy of the human condition, are in this play directly linked to memory. "Remember me," cries the Ghost—and later, when Hamlet is in his mother's closet, "Do not forget." Hamlet reflects:

> Remember thee?
> Ay, thou poor ghost, while memory holds a seat
> In this distracted globe. Remember thee?
> Yea, from the table of my memory
> I'll wipe away all trivial fond records,
> All saws of books, all forms, all pressures past,
> That youth and observation copied there,
> And thy commandment all alone shall live
> Within the book and volume of my brain.
>
> Hamlet *1.5.97–103*

Friedrich Nietzsche saw memory as that which distinguishes human beings from animals. Cattle forget, and so they are happy. Humans remember, and so they suffer. "[I]n the smallest and greatest happiness," he wrote in his essay on history, "there is always one thing that makes it happiness: the power of forgetting."[2] Human beings, both individually and as a people, "must know the right time to forget as well as the right time to remember."[3] And in the same essay Nietzsche also wrote, with a glance, unmistakably, at *Hamlet*, that the past has to be forgotten "if it is not to become the gravedigger of the present."[4] The gravedigger—or the ghost? The ghost of Hamlet's father beckons him toward the past, and toward revenge. Hamlet is a ghost of himself when he appears, "unbraced" and "down-gyvèd," in Ophelia's chamber. Ghosts in Shakespeare hark back to *Richard III* and *Julius Caesar,* and will appear again in *Macbeth* and in *Cymbeline,* but ghostliness is never embodied as powerfully, or as multiply, as in this play, where ultimately everyone is a ghost.

The play begins, as it ends, in silence, with a dumb show, here the appearance of the Ghost. Horatio and the sentries serve as chorus, interpreting as best they can what they have seen. Twice the Ghost appears, each time interrupting the spectators' conversation, and although it seems about to speak it twice stalks off without a word. We cannot know, they cannot know, what to make of this. All of us, on and off the stage, are "mutes or audience" to this act. Briefly but importantly, the Ghost is succeeded by another figure, also costumed in a significant way. "But look," says Horatio, "the morn in russet mantle clad / Walks o'er the dew of yon high eastern hill" (1.1.147–148). It is the sun. The pun on sun/son, sunlight and a father's son, is reinforced in the next scene by Hamlet's wry joke, "I am too much i'th'sun" (1.2.67). But this reassuring glimpse of natural light, vividly costumed to the mind's eye in its "russet mantle," stands in sharp contrast to the darkness that succeeds it, the darkness that is Denmark, where cries for torches, artificial light, will punctuate and bring to a premature end the play-within-the-play in the great central *Mousetrap* scene: "Give me some light. Away" (3.2.247).

The "russet mantle" of the sun, and the "complete steel," the medieval armor of the Ghost, introduce as well the crucial question of costume, in this play whose fundamental themes are all related to the very act of acting. Dumb shows, stage lights, curtains, makeup, and costumes. For now Hamlet makes his appearance, in the "inky cloak" that is to be the first of the three costumes he will wear in this play: his inky cloak; his antic disposition, "unbraced," "down-gyvèd"; and his traveler's sea gown, "scarfed" about him. Again it is useful to imagine the stage as a visual spectacle, glittering with jewels, torches, and liveried attendants. In the center, the King and Queen, splendid in silks and furs; Claudius bejeweled and be-ringed, his head crowned, the very emblem of conspicuous consumption. And to the side, Hamlet, a mute spectator of all this magnificence, startling in black from head to toe. "Good Hamlet, cast thy nightly colour off" (2.1.68). This is the Queen, in quest of domestic peace, almost surely (is she?) unaware of the murder of her former husband by her present one. But Hamlet is quick to remind her that there is more than one kind of costume, and that to seem a mourner is not necessarily to be one, just as to seem a king may also be a fiction:

> Seems, madam? Nay, it *is*. I know not "seems."
> 'Tis not alone my inky cloak, good-mother,
> Nor customary suits of solemn black,

> Nor windy suspiration of forced breath,
> No, nor the fruitful river in the eye,
> Nor the dejected haviour of the visage,
> Together with all form, moods, shows of grief
> That can denote me truly. These indeed "seem,"
> For they are actions that a man might play;
> But I have that within which passeth show—
> These but the trappings and the suits of woe.
>
> *1.2.76–86*

Forms, modes, shapes, trappings. Seem, play, act, show. Fake sighs, and dejected looks. This is the language of acting, and acting is what Hamlet sees all around him—a player king and a player queen, acting at grief, and acting it badly. Claudius out-Heroding Herod, out-Hamleting Hamlet, displaying exactly the kind of excessive, overblown acting against which Hamlet will counsel the visiting players. Herod, a familiar figure from medieval drama, was the theater's image of a bombastic king, but it is also the case that he, like Claudius, married his brother's wife. Hamlet's speech here is in fact a kind of advice to the players, to Claudius and to Gertrude, and it points up the most pernicious kind of illusion, the purpose of which is to cheat and conceal. In a play so consistently attentive to the material details of the stage, such pernicious illusions often take the imagistic form of makeup and face-painting: the unction to "skin and film the ulcerous place" (3.4.138); the "harlot's cheek, beautied with plast'ring art" (3.1.53). And, as Hamlet will say of "my lady" and the skull in the graveyard, "let her paint an inch thick, to this favour she must come" (5.1.179).

In act 1, scene 2, his first appearance in the play, Hamlet is both audience and critic. He sees the performance of Claudius, and in effect he gives it a bad review. It is not convincing. One result of this crucial perception, that all around him people are merely masquerading as mourners, acting grief rather than feeling it, is to make Hamlet reject his own costume. If others can counterfeit grief by merely wearing "the trappings and the suits of woe," what is to become of real grief? Hamlet's mourning clothes have become a "show," despite him, in the politic air of Denmark. He has become unwittingly and unwillingly complicit in Claudius's display. His "customary suits of solemn black" (1.2.78), the appropriate costume for mourning, are compromised and sullied by the other "customs" that have crept into the Danish court. Thus Hamlet will later speak of the "monster custom," of "damnèd custom," and Horatio of the "custom" of the gravedigger's callousness (3.4.151.1; 3.4.36; 5.1.63). But his suit of mourning will become a custom more honored in the breach than in the observance, better abandoned than worn, because wearing it aligns him with Danish hypocrisy. He needs a new costume, a new role, to demonstrate the sincerity of his grief and his anger, and he finds that new costume in the "antic disposition" of madness. The allowed fool, or licensed fool, in a royal or noble household was a paid dependent whose social role was both to amuse and to instruct, cloaking moral lessons in jokes and mumming. Hamlet the prince now becomes his own household fool, and allows himself to speak the truth.

It is thought that when the play was first staged Shakespeare himself played the part of the Ghost. Shakespeare's only son, whose name was Hamnet, died in 1596, and Shakespeare's father, John, died in 1601. The play itself, almost obsessively concerned with the relationships between fathers and sons, seems poised across this barrier. And it is with the Ghost, I think, that one should start in approaching and comprehending the world of the play and the problems of Hamlet. Very often, as we have noted in considering the structure of other plays, Shakespeare uses his opening scenes as a kind of cameo, vignette, or miniature of the larger play that will follow, with characters who play no other role. In *Hamlet* we have what is possibly the greatest of these opening scenes, because it develops a mood and a tone that chill the spectator to the core. The night itself is chilly, and the sentries are nervous. "Who's there?" (1.1.1), Barnardo's opening line, ringing out of the darkness, is a challenge not from the sentry on duty but to him, our first hint that the world of the play is inverted, out of joint. From the point of view of a modern or postmodern production, the flung-out line "Who's there?" seems directed almost primarily at the audience, rather than at any character on the stage. Moreover, the challenger is also a sentry, so that these sentries, instead of repelling invaders, find themselves in the confusion of a civil misunderstanding. The challenge comes not from outside Denmark but from within it. And all of this is established within the first five lines.

"Who's there?" "Nay, answer me. Stand and unfold yourself" (1.1.1–2). Barnardo is told to "unfold" himself, ushering in the cloak-and-costume imagery, and also the imagery of folded paper and writing, which will become so predominant later in the play, and at this point there enter upon the stage the more "major" characters of Horatio and Marcellus. We may expect the audience to share the skepticism and rationalism of Horatio—so far, no boundaries of experience have been broken, and there is something reassuring in the colloquialism of his view of the Ghost: "Tush, tush, 'twill not appear" (1.1.28). This would be more reassuring, however, if the Ghost did not, almost immediately, make his appearance, dwarfing, with his "fair and warlike form," all the others upon the stage.

The stage direction says "Enter the Ghost," but the apparition is not so concretely described by the immediate onlookers. It is instead referred to as "this thing" (1.1.19), "this dreaded sight" (23), an "illusion" (108)—"What, has this thing appeared again tonight?" What else it is remains a question, not an answer, a puzzle that must be solved, and with which even Hamlet will be troubled. Is it "a spirit of health or goblin damned" (1.4.21)? We learn little about it in this first glimpse; it is "like the King that's dead" (1.1.39), it is dressed in armor, and although Horatio asks it again and again to speak, it will not. We may gather from its refusal that this is not the common or garden-variety ghost, which comes to give an omen of the future, or to tell the location of buried treasure—ideas that the bookish Horatio has probably come upon in his studies. "Thou art a scholar—speak to it, Horatio," says Marcellus. Ghosts were traditionally to be addressed in Latin, thus Horatio's studies would fit him for the task. The Ghost disappears at the coming of the dawn that banishes all spirits from walking the earth, and the scene closes with Marcellus's lovely, though fearful, speech:

> It faded on the crowing of the cock.
> Some say that ever 'gainst that season comes
> Wherein our saviour's birth is celebrated
> The bird of dawning singeth all night long;
> And then, they say, no spirit can walk abroad,
> The nights are wholesome, then no planets strike,
> No fairy takes, nor witch hath power to charm,
> So hallowed and so gracious is the time.
>
> 1.1.138–145

Similar beliefs about ghosts were articulated in Shakespeare's great "fairy" play, *A Midsummer Night's Dream,* where Puck warns Oberon:

> My fairy lord, this must be done with haste,
> For night's swift dragons cut the clouds full fast,
> And yonder shines Aurora's harbinger,
> At whose approach ghosts, wand'ring here and there,
> Troop home to churchyards; damnèd spirits all
> That in cross-ways and floods have burial
> Already to their wormy bed are gone,
> For fear lest day should look their shames upon.
> They willfully themselves exiled from light,
> And must for aye consort with black-browed night.
>
> Dream 3.2.379–388

Ghosts of this sort were the spectral counterparts of the "vagabonds" or "masterless men" against whom an Elizabethan statute had been proclaimed in 1597, including among them traveling actors. All these dangerous wanderers were regarded as deleterious to the order and safety of the state. Marcellus's pious pronouncement, the equivalent of crossing oneself against the threat of unimaginable danger from another world, closes the first scene on a note of purity and watchfulness, with the rising of the sun. It is the last we will see of this natural, almost pastoral light, for all that Hamlet will proclaim himself "too much i'th' sun" (1.2.67). For at this point there enters upon the stage, with much pomp and ceremony, the new King, Claudius of Denmark, accompanied by his queen, Gertrude, and the rest of his retinue.

Claudius's opening speech, beginning the play's second scene, offers the greatest possible contrast to the dignified and mysterious silence of the Ghost. His speech is a model of policy, a masterly reduction of language to formal public utterance. Its very first word is the politician's "though"—a conditional hedge:

> Though yet of Hamlet our dear brother's death
> The memory be green, and that it us befitted
> To bear our hearts in grief and our whole kingdom
> To be contracted in one brow of woe,
> Yet so far hath discretion fought with nature
> That we with wisest sorrow think on him
> Together with remembrance of ourselves.
>
> *Hamlet 1.2.1–7*

Claudius's main clause here refers not to "our dear brother" or his death, but to "ourselves," that is, himself—the royal "we." His elegantly turned sentence gestures toward grief but quickly comes back to the real subject, himself, before he reverts to the smooth language of politics:

> Therefore our sometime sister, now our queen,
> Th'imperial jointress to this warlike state,
> Have we as 'twere with a defeated joy,
> With one auspicious and one dropping eye,
> With mirth in funeral and with dirge in marriage,
> In equal scale weighing delight and dole,
> Taken to wife. . . .
>
> *1.2.8–14*

The words flow on, smoothly, decoratively. Yet when we stop to think about it, there is a serious and troublesome peculiarity about the concept of "our sometime sister, now our queen." The audience of Shakespeare's time would certainly have recalled the difficulties that arose when Queen Elizabeth's father, Henry VIII, sought to divorce his first wife, Catherine of Aragon, who had briefly been married to his older brother, Prince Arthur, in 1501. Arthur died six months after the wedding, and in 1509, when he succeeded to the throne on the death of his father, Henry VII, Henry VIII married the Spanish princess. When, in 1533, Henry sought annulment of the marriage in order to marry the pregnant Anne Boleyn, Elizabeth's mother, the grounds for his petition were found in a passage in Leviticus that said that a marriage between a man and his brother's wife was incestuous ("And if a man shall lie with his brother's wife, it is an unclean thing, he has uncovered his brother's nakedness; they shall be child-less" [Leviticus 20:21; see also Leviticus 18:16]). Although Catherine and Henry had a daughter, the future Queen Mary, they had no son, and Henry took this, conveniently, as proof that the biblical injunction had been broken. In any case, an audience in England around 1600 would not have forgotten the critical events that had brought their present monarch, circuitously, to the throne. Twentieth-century criticism concerned with the "incest motif" in *Hamlet*, and influenced by Freud, often singles out the relationship between Hamlet and his mother. But in the sixteenth and seventeenth centuries, Claudius's easy phrase "our sometime sister, now our queen" would have been at least as provocative, and at least as potentially disturbing. Nor is it simple to imagine the other chiastic couplings of his first speech—"a defeated joy," "one auspicious and one dropping eye," "with mirth in funeral and with dirge in marriage"—nor "my cousin Hamlet, and my son" (1.2.64). Meaning runs counter to rhetoric here. We are in part seduced into accepting an association between "mirth" and "dirge," not because the connection between the two is admirable or logical, but because they nearly rhyme. Can everything be right in such a state, where lan-guage contradicts itself so effortlessly, so cosmetically, and where the majesty of the King's public utterance crushes together, almost undetected by his courtly listeners, a comic funeral and a tragic marriage?

The language here has become more than language. It is now part of the play's plot, communicating to the audience in the theater—and to certain lis-teners onstage—something opposite from what we are apparently being told. If we listen closely, and detect the strain that holds "mirth" and "funeral" together, we will sense that there is something wrong as surely as we did when we stood in imagination with the shivering sentries to watch the silent figure of the Ghost, in a kind of dumb show. For the appearance of the Ghost in the first scene *is* a dumb show, a "prologue to the omen coming on," a silent, gesturing apparition that invites or demands interpretation. This is the first of several dumb shows in *Hamlet*. Others, as we'll see, will include Ophelia's account of Hamlet's visit to her chamber, and the literal dumb show that prefaces the crucial *Mousetrap* play in the third act. But in his first appearance the speaking King, Claudius, dis-plays at least as much eloquence as the gesturing Ghost. For the moment, at least, he is in control of language, making it jump through hoops, cease to mean what it should. Hamlet will have much reason to distrust "[w]ords, words, words"—or what Claudius himself, in a humbler moment, will call "my most painted word" (3.1.55). The world in which this kind of Claudius-language governs is a topsy-turvy, inverted world—in the Ghost's phrase, "most foul, strange, and unnatural" (1.5.28). It even approaches blasphemy, when we hear, for example, that every time the King drinks, the cannons will blaze away, and "the King's rouse the heavens shall bruit again, / Re-speaking earthly thunder" (1.2.127–128). Properly, thunder is heavenly, not earthly, but in this figure the King, not the gods, is the origin, and the skies can only "re-speak," or echo, what he says and does. By the time Claudius falls to his knees to plead with those heavens, the split between his language and the meaning it cloaks is already too great. "My words fly up," he will acknowledge, "my thoughts remain below" (3.3.97). The Denmark of this play is a place of inversion and perversion, and there is no greater clue to that fact than the tenor and rhetoric of its language.

This split between words and thought, words and meaning, is essential to the way *Hamlet* works. When the everyday language of human beings cannot be trusted, the only "safe" language is deliberate fiction, plays and lies. The only safe world is the world of the imagination, not the corrupt and uncontrollable world of politics. And all of this Shakespeare sets out for us in the architecture of his first act, as we hear the various voices of characters we have not met before, and learn about them through the plot of language. Thus the third scene of this remarkable first act produces yet another father and another son, this time the old counselor Polonius and his son Laertes, and again, as with Claudius and the reluctant Hamlet, the audience has a chance to hear fatherly advice. Indeed, the whole of the first act is built on the advice of fathers to sons, fathers to children, and it culminates with the awful revelations of Hamlet's father, the Ghost, confirming what we have already begun to suspect: that there *is* something rotten in the state of Denmark.

Polonius's language is not so much the language of policy as it is the language of platitude and homily, the language of aphorism and adage, the language of other people's "wisdom." Many of his bromides can be found in collections of proverbial wisdom from the period, and a good number have found their way into political speeches by U.S. legislators read into the *Congressional Record*. The "wisdom" of Polonius offers perhaps the best instance—other than the utterances of Machiavellian Iago—of words from Shakespeare taken out of context, what I have called "Bartlett's Familiar Shakespeare." Sayings like "Neither a borrower nor a lender be" or "[T]he apparel oft proclaims the man" or "This above all, / To thine own self be true" seem to have a certain moral or ethical force when considered in the abstract, but uttered onstage by a dramatic character who has been interpreted in every mode from hapless wise counselor to doddering old fool, these same words begin to coruscate with inadvertent irony. Certainly Laertes, a man who loves his father, takes Polonius's advice, affectionately, with a grain of salt. Claudius decorated his language with sounding phrases that plastered over and concealed his harsher meanings. Polonius reduces himself to the even more anodyne level of the completely impersonal and banal word. The advice may be wiser than the speaker. Modern quoters cite "Shakespeare" at their peril when they are actually, and recognizably, quoting Shakespearean characters carefully crafted to be at variance with their own language. One of this playwright's most substantial achievements is that, whenever he cites truisms or platitudes, he puts them in the mouths of suspect speakers, something that the "Bartlett's"—or, now, the Internet—approach to quotation entirely fails to acknowledge, with the result that the irony turns back upon the quoter. If every critic and philosopher wants to find a smack of Hamlet in himself, no one wants to "be" Polonius.

Some critics over the years have identified Elizabeth's chief secretary of state, William Cecil, Lord Burghley, who died in 1598, as the original of Polonius in *Hamlet,* while others have pointed to the name Polonius (which replaces "Corambis" in the First Quarto) as a topical reference to a Polish statesman. A famous anecdote details Queen Elizabeth's rhetorical triumph over a long-winded Polish ambassador, whom she harangued, extemporaneously, in Latin, a language in which she had been schooled but which had "lain long in rusting."[5] Certainly, as Joan Landis has noted, references to "Poles" and Poland appear importantly elsewhere in the play.[6] But in assessing the relative cultural visibility of sources and analogues, on the one hand, and vivid dramatic characters, on the other, the ambivalent victory here must surely go to Shakespeare's Polonius, whose persona and name have taken on almost as much currency as that of a figure like Falstaff, whose own origins in a historical figure called Sir John Oldcastle have also been eclipsed by the liveliness of Shakespeare's portrayal.

The family tableau quickly reveals its darker side. Applying his own rather suspicious standards to others, Polonius warns his daughter Ophelia about the untrustworthiness of Hamlet's words—"his vows . . . are brokers" (1.3.127)—and forbids her, significantly, to talk to him in the future: "Lord Hamlet is a prince out of thy star" (2.2.141). Laertes has the same opinion. Hamlet "may not," he advises his sister, "as unvalued persons do / Carve for himself." (1.3.19–20). They warn her against seduction and unchastity, sowing the dramatic seeds for her later breakdown into madness. Indeed, the play repeatedly associates the "rotten" thing that male characters need to be on guard against with women and female sexuality. Hamlet's bitter and despairing instruction to Ophelia, "Get thee to a nunnery" (3.1.122), incorporates the two apparently opposite meanings of the word, for in Elizabethan slang a "nunnery" was a brothel. This fear of the power of women and of their excessive capacity for desire at times produces an almost paranoid level of surveillance, in Polonius's case not only over his daughter, Ophelia (whom he will "loose" to Hamlet in the lobby as if Hamlet were a stallion and Ophelia a mare, as he and Claudius overlook the scene), but also over his son. For no sooner has Laertes departed for Paris than Polonius sends spies after him, instructed to offer up slanderous accusations of Laertes' drinking, swearing, and "drabbing" (visiting whores) to see if they yield similar gossip and confidences. Such a technique, to "by indirections find directions out" and by a "bait of falsehood" catch a "carp of truth," was a not unfamiliar one employed by the Elizabethan spy network, under the direction of Cecil's colleague and successor, Sir Francis Walsingham. Used by a father against his own son, and immediately after the genial imparting of moral advice in the guise of a farewell, this cynical proceeding contrasts both with Claudius's manifest and grandiose duplicity and with the anguished truth-telling between father and son, old Hamlet and young Hamlet, that will occupy the stage in the scene to follow.

For it is at this point in the dramatic action that the Ghost once again appears, as the scene shifts away from the plush and politic court to the stark cold air of the night watch. The play's first act is encapsulated by the Ghost's appearance, in scenes 4 and 5. The questions raised by the initial appearance of the inexplicable and silent Ghost have lingered all this time, and finally, with Hamlet, the spectators in the theater confront "this dreaded sight," this "illusion." Once more it mounts to the stage, and, for the first time, it speaks. To whom does it speak? To Hamlet alone, and to us, insofar as we are, for this moment, part of the "distracted globe" that is Hamlet's consciousness. Horatio had four times asked it to speak, and received nothing but a sign. Now it speaks to Hamlet, and the language of Hamlet the father to Hamlet the son is charged with a special kind of intensity: "I am thy father's spirit" (1.5.9). "I'll call thee Hamlet, / King, father, royal Dane" (1.4.25–26). Here is a different kind of advice from father to son. Yet Hamlet speaks of his "prophetic soul." He has imagined, again in his "mind's eye," the tale of murder that the Ghost will tell. How can we divide the world inside Hamlet's mind from that of the "real world" of Denmark? What is this "illusion," which comes to tell Hamlet what he already half knows? For what does it stand, and why does it stir Hamlet to a feigned, creative madness, an antic disposition—to literally playing the fool?

For a long time scholars have debated the theological and religious implications of the Ghost, a debate well articulated in Eleanor Prosser's *Hamlet and Revenge* and in a number of subsequent studies.[7] The Catholic belief in purgatory was not shared or permitted by the new Protestant sects, and Hamlet's worry about whether this is a "spirit of health or goblin damned" depends, to a certain extent, upon whether or not one could or should believe in a good or "honest" Ghost. Old Hamlet describes himself as "[d]oomed for a certain term to walk the night, / And for the day confined to fast in fires / Till the foul crimes done in days of nature / Are burnt and purged away" (1.5.10–13). Several modes of ghost-belief and ghost-practice intersect here, including the ghosts of classical times that returned to demand proper burial, and the ghosts of earlier English drama—notably Thomas Kyd's *Spanish Tragedy* (written ca. 1587)— that framed their plays with calls for revenge. In terms of the history of early modern drama in English, *Hamlet* is the centerpiece between a relatively early play like *The Spanish Tragedy*, with its Ghost, its play-within-the-play in "sundry languages," and its mad and mourning hero, Hieronimo, and a relatively late play like *The Revenger's Tragedy*, in which the skull of the revenger's dead beloved becomes his apt and unerring device to entrap her seducer, and in which the hero, emblematically named Vindice, is finally hoist by his own petard. This progression from ghost to skull will, as we will see, be indicative of the way *Hamlet* itself progresses from the past to the future.

One significant piece of onstage evidence that we have about the status of the Ghost comes from its own language, a language that is in part a reflection of Hamlet's inner consciousness, telling him what he already suspects and intuits, but is also, and crucially, the voice of a world that has ceased to be. "List, Hamlet, list, O list!" (1.5.22). "Of life, of crown, of queen at once dispatched" (1.5.75). "Unhouseled, dis-appointed, unaneled" (1.5.77). "O horrible, O horrible, most horrible!" (1.5.80). "Adieu, adieu, Hamlet" (1.5.91). Derived in part from contemporary translations of the tragedies of Seneca, this is a language that Shakespeare has already burlesqued in the "Pyramus and Thisbe" play in *A Midsummer Night's Dream*—a play clearly intended by its actors to rival the best and most solemn of ancient classical tragedies. "And thou, O wall, O sweet and lovely wall" (*Dream* 5.1.172). "O grim-looked night, O night with hue so black, / O night which ever art when day is not" (168–169). "And farewell friends, / Thus Thisbe ends. / Adieu, adieu, adieu" (332–334). (This is the rhetorical figure known as the tricolon.) The same triplets and the same repetitions haunt the Ghost's language. The Ghost in *Hamlet* speaks, then, out of a literary and dramatic tradition as well as a personal and private past. His speech is more than medieval autobiography; it is epic drama. The stately majesty of these triplets—"List, Hamlet, list, O list!"—recalls a lost language and a half-forgotten world. Thus old Hamlet emerges in costume, language, and message as the embodiment of lost epic and heroic values, the tutelary spirit of a heroic past. This is as significant for his role in the play as his association with the purgatorial wanderings of the unshrived spirit, for he is a spirit of revenge, first cousin not only to Senecan and Elizabethan ghosts but also to the figure of Patroclus in the *Iliad*. Like Patroclus, he reappears to press his reluctant champion into action in an epic world.

As always in trying to untangle these questions of history, culture, and affect, our best guide will be the play itself, which teaches even as it tests and tempts. Let us ask, then: What we do know about old Hamlet when we first encounter him in act 1? We know, from his first appearance, what he looks like. He appears to the sentries and to Hamlet "[a]rmed at all points exactly, cap-à-pie" (1.2.200), clad again in "complete steel," in armor from head to toe. Not for him the soft silks and furs of the Claudius court, or the carefully "rich, not gaudy" costumes of the worldling Laertes, or the posturings of the popinjay Osric. Polonius is right, despite himself: in this play the apparel does proclaim the man. "Such was the very armour he had on," says Horatio,

> When he th'ambitious Norway combated.
> So frowned he once when in an angry parley
> He smote the sledded Polacks on the ice.
>
> *1.1.59–62*

The armor worn by old Hamlet is the same he wore when he defeated "the ambitious Norway"—and who was Norway but old Fortinbras, the father of the young Fortinbras who will be first Hamlet's rival, and then his chosen successor. The drama seems to be playing itself out, over and over, in a cyclical fashion. Old Fortinbras fights with old Hamlet, young Fortinbras with young Hamlet: the dramatic movement here is one of repetition and reversal. And the defeat of Norway came, significantly, in the epic style, in single combat, man against man, a heroic struggle. Old Hamlet defended his country against invaders from outside, and not, as now—and as we saw in the confusions of the very first scene—from civil strife within. We are meant, I think, to feel the difference between this ancient warrior in full steel, wielding his heavy weapons, and the chosen weapon of the new Denmark—and the new England—the rapier, Laertes' pride. Fencing schools, like theaters, were located by statute in the Liberties, or outskirts of London. The Italian sword master Rocco Bonetti established a school of arms in London in 1576, and in 1590 Vincentio Saviolo arrived, and published in 1595 a two-volume treatise on the *duello,* explaining the use of the rapier and dagger, and setting out rules for "honorable Quarrels." But the rapier, despite its lethal effects (an Elizabethan statute of 1562 ordered that "no man shall . . . wear any sword, rapier, or any weapon . . . passing the length of one yard and half a quarter of blade at the uttermost"),[8] was a weapon of sport and private quarrel, not a weapon of war. The final fencing match between Hamlet and Laertes, staged, at Claudius's behest, ostensibly as a friendly challenge, a scene of public sport, marks a deliberate and forceful contrast with the previous offstage epic combat between the warriors of an earlier generation, in which, as Horatio reported, "our valiant Hamlet"—that is, old Hamlet—"[d]id slay this Fortinbras" and inherit "by a seal'd compact / Well ratified in law and heraldry" all the lands old Fortinbras possessed (1.1.83–88).

What else do we know about old Hamlet as the play begins? The same contrast between old and new, heroic and fallen, manifest in the two kinds of martial combat that frame the play can be discerned in the imagery Hamlet uses to describe his idealized father. He consistently chooses the language of heroic myth, so that, comparing old Hamlet to Claudius, he will say, "So excellent a king, that was to this / Hyperion to a satyr" (1.2.139–140). Later he will offer a similar description to his mother:

> Hyperion's curls, the front of Jove himself,
> An eye like Mars, to threaten or command,
> A station like the herald Mercury
> New lighted on a heaven-kissing hill . . .
>
> 3.4.55–58

These are Titans and Olympian gods, classical and pagan, not Christian. They seem to belong in the world of the first speech that Hamlet urges on the traveling players, the world of vengeful Pyrrhus, and of good grandsire Priam and his loyal wife Hecuba, and the fall of the great kingdom of Troy. We will have more to say about this old play, but even from the first it is important to note that King Hamlet is cast from the same ideal and heroic mold.

Old Hamlet is the voice of an older age of stable values, but his values are ultimately inadmissible in a world not of fathers but of sons. His are the ideals against which the play will measure itself. But it is no accident of theatrical construction that the Ghost drops out of the play, leaving the action in the hands and voices of the new men, the political men, Hamlet, Laertes, and Fortinbras, each of whom is in a way more like Octavius Caesar than like Julius Caesar. Hamlet is often compared to Brutus, since both spend so much of their onstage time ruminating on the human condition, often in passages of incomparable poetry that echo the thoughts and debates of contemporary philosophers. But Hamlet, as we will see once again, is finally an "action hero," not only a philosopher. And his mentors are many, not one: old Hamlet, Claudius, the First Player, Laertes, and Fortinbras, to name just a few.

Yet in another way the Ghost does have a controlling part in the events that follow upon his spectral appearances. "I could," he says to Hamlet, "a tale unfold whose lightest word / Would harrow up thy soul" (1.5.15–16). Notice the recurrence of this word "unfold," from the initial challenge of the opening scene ("Who's there?" "Nay, answer me. Stand and unfold yourself"). The whole play is in some sense a process of unfolding, then folding, and unfolding again. Though he does not tell his tale of purgatory, the Ghost tells another tale, equally mythic, that dominates and pulls together language, imagery, and action in *Hamlet* as a whole. The tale he unfolds is the story of his own death, the answer to the questions we have been asking ourselves since the opening of the play: What happened to old Hamlet? What has caused the sickness in the state? Even the tone of this tale is mythic, otherworldly. It is a kind of inset allegory or emblem, a grim and timeless myth recounted within the tauter, more ornate, Renaissance fabric of the surrounding drama:

> 'Tis given out that, sleeping in mine orchard,
> A serpent stung me. So the whole ear of Denmark
> Is by a forgèd process of my death
> Rankly abused. But know, thou noble youth,
> The serpent that did sting thy father's life
> Now wears his crown.
> . . . .
>   Sleeping within mine orchard,
> My custom always of the afternoon,
> Upon my secure hour thy uncle stole
> With juice of cursèd hebenon in a vial,
> And in the porches of mine ears did pour
> The leperous distilment. . . .

1.5.35–40, 59–64

Let us look for a moment at the anatomy of this fable. It is in structure a kind of Eden myth, taking place in a medieval *hortus conclusus,* an enclosed garden. Old Hamlet, the innocent upholder of ancient values, sleeping in a garden, is set upon by the serpent, Claudius, whose world is motivated by the satanic basic appetites of lust, pride, envy, and the desire for power. This fable has a peculiar and far-reaching resonance. Positioned as it is near the beginning of the play, the story will come to mind again and again as the changes are rung on its basic values. In effect it is this play's riddle, the center of its radiating imaginative energy, a scenario that could also be called its primal scene.

To kill old Hamlet in the garden, with poison in the ears.

The *ears* are everywhere. In the advices of fathers to sons that occupy much of the business of the first act; in the ear of Denmark, which is, in the Ghost's phrase, "abused"; and in the whole process of eavesdropping: Polonius dispatching Reynaldo to spy on Laertes and uncover information on his reputation; Claudius and Polonius behind the arras, or curtain, listening to Hamlet and Ophelia; Claudius sending for Rosencrantz and Guildenstern to eavesdrop on Hamlet's plans; Polonius again behind an arras, eavesdropping on Hamlet and Gertrude, stabbed to death this time for his pains. The words that enter like daggers into Gertude's ears. Hamlet's question "Will the King hear this piece of work?" (3.2.41). "List, Hamlet, list, O list!" cries the Ghost—hear, O hear. And there is a sense in which he himself pours poison into the ear of Hamlet, inflaming him to agony, soul-searching, and revenge.

To kill old Hamlet in the garden, with poison *in the ears.*

Poison—the something rotten in the state of Denmark. The whole chain of disease-and-infection imagery that is the most evident of the play's many verbal themes: "th'impostume of much wealth and peace, / That inward breaks and shows no cause without / Why the man dies" (4.4.9.17–9.19). The contagion that spreads unwholesomely through the night. The ulcers beneath the skin, unhealthily cosmeticked over with lies. The poison, above all, of language—of deceit and unctuous pretense, the language of Claudius in his opening speech, the dangerous poison of words, words, words. The words, often, of poisonous *serpents*—not only Claudius, but Rosencrantz and Guildenstern, whom Hamlet will trust, he says, "as I will adders fanged" (3.4.185.2). Serpents, too, with erotic and sexual connotations, a fall from innocence of a special kind. The imagined corruption even of Ophelia. The final engines of poison in the last scene, the poisoned cup and the poisoned rapier, time-honored sexual symbols, both fatal, and taken together (an emblematic scene also staged at the close of *Romeo and Juliet*). The inevitably victorious serpent who is "my lady Worm," the force of bodily corruption and decay in the graveyard, who reduces to the same indifferent dust the great and the simple, the wicked and the pure. The dust of Alexander stopping a bunghole, of Julius Caesar turned to clay.

To kill old Hamlet in the garden, *with poison in the ears.*

An Edenic garden, a garden of attempted innocence. Adam as the first gardener, in the gravedigger's mordant joke. Gertrude, whose act "takes off the rose / From the fair forehead of an innocent love / And sets a blister there" (3.4.41–43), joining together the themes of infection and the garden. Hamlet, "[t]h'expectancy and rose of the fair state," in Ophelia's phrase (3.1.151). And Ophelia, "rose of May" (4.5.156), whose mad songs are all too apt in their scattering of flowers, and whose watery death, "[w]hen down the weedy trophies and herself / Fell in the weeping brook" (4.7.145–146), seems to bring to life the language of Hamlet's first bitter soliloquy: "Fie on't, ah fie, fie! 'Tis an unweeded garden / That grows to seed" (1.2.135–136). In the tragic action of the play Ophelia becomes a symbolic self-deflowerer, performing ceremonially in her madness what she has been proscribed from doing erotically in her love. All these patterns of intertwined language and action seem to flow from the Ghost's private myth of murder. Like the poison of which he speaks, his tale, with its call to revenge, "Holds such an enmity with blood of man / That swift as quicksilver it courses through / The natural gates and alleys of the body" (1.5.65–67).

The call to revenge is a call to repetition: to do the act again, to do it back, to repay injury with injury. Revenge *is* repetition, and repetition *is* compulsion. As we have noted, the Ghost in *Hamlet* is a close relative to other ghosts that stalked the early modern stage, ghosts in plays by, among others, Seneca and Kyd. The "revenge play" was a popular part of the early modern repertoire, and Shakespeare continually reworked this genre throughout his career, even in as late a play as *The Tempest.* But part of the conundrum of Hamlet is the need to establish some relation between revenge, as a moral dynamic and as a theatrical trope, and forgiveness. When Polonius says he will use the players according to their desert, Hamlet is round in his reply: "God's bodykins, man, much better. Use every man after his desert, and who should scape whipping? Use them after your own honour and dignity" (2.2.508–510). Here is Hamlet's version of the Golden Rule, akin to Portia's courtroom plea on behalf of the "quality of mercy." Those readers who have regarded this complicated play as one that marks a cultural turning point between the endless cycle of revenge and the transformative power of a Christian acceptance ("the readiness is all") have tacitly assimilated it to the dialectic of Old and New Law. Yet as with Portia, so also with Hamlet (and *Hamlet*), the voicing of a religious commonplace is nuanced and undercut by the dramatic context. Hamlet may well wish the players a generous reception, and surely he misses no opportunity to puncture the empty platitudes of Polonius. But he remains a revenger, though a revenger with a conscience and a consciousness. His attraction to revenge and his resistance to it are part of the intellectual tension that makes

Hamlet such an engaged and engaging character. In this play, revenge—like the Ghost—goes underground. Francis Bacon famously wrote that "Revenge is a kind of Wilde Justice; which the more Mans Nature runs to the more ought Law to weed it out. . . . Certainly, in taking *Revenge*, A Man is but even with his Enemy; But in passing it over, he is Superior: For it is a Princes part to Pardon."[9] Whatever Hamlet's own view, though, the tempering of justice with mercy, the exploration of both the political and the ethical expediency of revenge's aftermath in reconciliation and forgiveness, is a principal preoccupation of *Hamlet,* as it is of many of the plays that surround it chronologically—*The Merchant of Venice, Measure for Measure,* and *All's Well That Ends Well.* There is good reason for earlier critics to have considered grouping *Hamlet* with the "problem plays."

The ghost of old Hamlet appears to the audience as a virtuous and positive force, recalling a decaying kingdom to the time of its pride and strength. But the values the Ghost espouses are not so easily recaptured or restored. The serpent has entered the garden, and the Edenic world, like the world of heroic myth, has given way to a world whose keynote is mortality. If Adam was the first gardener, he was also the first to come to dust—to what Hamlet will call the "quintessence of dust," in a speech that closely parallels one of the most famous of all Renaissance humanist documents, Pico della Mirandola's *Oration on the Dignity of Man.* But where Pico celebrated the mutability of mankind, Hamlet regards it with suspicion, even with dread. Here is Pico:

> [U]pon man, at the moment of his creation, God bestowed seeds pregnant with all possibilities, the germs of every form of life. Whichever of these a man shall cultivate, the same will mature and bear fruit in him. If vegetative, he will become a plant; if sensual, he will become brutish; if rational, he will reveal himself a heavenly being; if intellectual, he will be an angel and the son of God. And if, dissatisfied with the lot of all creatures, he should recollect himself into the center of his own unity, he will there, become one spirit with God, in the solitary darkness of the Father, Who is set above all things, himself transcend all creatures. Who then will not look with awe upon this our chameleon, or who, at least, will look with greater admiration on any other being?[10]

And here, by contrast, is Hamlet, framing his words with a vision of a sterile earth on the one hand and an empty human future on the other, so that the passage itself progresses from dust to dust:

> [T]his goodly frame, the earth, seems to me a sterile promontory. This most excellent canopy the air, look you, this brave o'erhanging, this majestical roof fretted with golden fire—why, it appears no other thing to me than a foul and pestilent congregation of vapors. What a piece of work is a man! How noble in reason, how infinite in faculty, in form and moving

how express and admirable, in action how like an angel, in apprehension how like a god—the beauty of the world, the paragon of animals! And yet to me what is this quintessence of dust?

2.2.289–298

In such a world, what is real, and what is illusory? The Ghost is called an "illusion," yet in some sense he is "real." He is seen by several persons, including the trustworthy and unimpressionable Horatio, as well as by the spectators in the theater. He speaks to Hamlet, and what he says seems also "real," if Hamlet's "prophetic soul" is to be trusted, since the news the Ghost imparts is expected news, truth, not fiction. Yet the kind of world the Ghost proposes and remembers is in some sense illusory. It belongs to mortality and to past history, and if Hamlet is to find the "real" for himself he must seek it in a different kind of illusion. That is what we will see him do in the subsequent action of the play. Assuming his "antic disposition"—his mask of modernity, his costume of the fool—Hamlet finds an electric gaiety and release with the players. He is free to act through imagination and through art and improvisation as he cannot do in politics or in the world of decaying Denmark. While the players are only maskers, and their play is fiction, and their passions are but a dream of passion, there is a way in which their brand of intentional illusion is more trustworthy, and more open to Hamlet, than is the way of the Ghost. It is fitting that "the play's the thing" wherein he will seek to catch the conscience of the King.

Many of the questions that have troubled readers of *Hamlet*—and actors seeking the arc of his character—have tended to be about Hamlet's behavior and motivation:

- What has caused him to lose all his "mirth" even before he sees the Ghost?
- Is the emotion that grips him, whatever it is, appropriate to its cause? Or is it, as T. S. Eliot suggested, "emotion in excess of the facts as they appear"? Eliot concluded that, in part because Hamlet's emotion lacks this "objective correlative," the play, despite its many compelling aspects, is "certainly an artistic failure."[11]
- Why does Hamlet feign madness? Or *is* it feigned? Does he change, from first act to last? Why can he kill Claudius in the last act, and not at the beginning of the play?
- Finally, most centrally, why does he delay? Does he doubt the truth of the Ghost's message? Is he too cowardly to kill for revenge? Is he unfit to be a hero? This is what the German poet Goethe thought. Is Hamlet a habitual procrastinator, who shirks all his obligations, including the obligation to revenge? This is what the English Romantic critic and poet Coleridge thought. Is he a prey to melancholy, that fashionable Elizabethan complaint that also grips Antonio in *The Merchant of Venice* and Orsino

in *Twelfth Night?* This is what the Victorian critic A. C. Bradley thought. Or is he perhaps not delaying at all, but acting as swiftly as opportunity presents?

Another Victorian critic, E. P. Vining, suggested that the answer to the problem was that Hamlet was really a woman in disguise, and that this accounted for both "his" reluctance to fight and "his" famous delay.[12] Vining was writing at a time when a good deal of scholarship on gender ambiguity and erotic types was being written, and being read, by such influential figures as Havelock Ellis and Edward Carpenter. In fact, part of what made Vining believe that the "mystery" of Hamlet was his/her gender was precisely the fact that Shakespeare's character seemed to behave in ways that some observers in the late nineteenth century regarded as unmanly. "The question may be asked," he wrote, "whether Shakespeare, having been compelled by the course and exigencies of the drama to gradually modify his original hero into a man with more and more of the feminine element, may not at last have had the thought dawn upon him that this womanly man might be in very deed a woman . . . ?"[13] Vining's speculations were influential in the production of a 1920 German silent film version of *Hamlet,* starring the Danish actress Asta Nielsen. In the film, the Danish throne can be occupied only by a male heir, so the female Hamlet is brought up as a man in order to provide political continuity and avoid the loss of Danish lands to arch-foe Norway. The resulting script produced some highly eroticized scenes with a Horatio who does not know Hamlet's secret, and a deathbed revelation of her true gender. The part of Hamlet has not infrequently been played by actresses, including Sarah Bernhardt in 1899 and, more recently, Diane Venora in 2000. "I cannot see Hamlet as a man," Bernhardt declared, when asked about her characterization. "The things he says, his impulses, his actions entirely indicate to me that he was a woman."

In Shakespeare's own time, not only the Player Queen but also the "real" queen, Gertrude, and Ophelia, too, would have been played by boys, so that these nineteenth- and twentieth-century dislocations in the other direction are not, perhaps, so out of keeping. But what is really worth noting here is the connection, in *Hamlet,* between femaleness and excessive emotion, indeed, between femaleness and excessive desire. Many critics have written well on this question, including Janet Adelman and Jacqueline Rose. Hamlet's own fevered imagination thinks of Gertrude as herself a slave to sexual passion—living "[i]n the rank sweat of an enseamèd bed, / Stewed in corruption, honeying and making love / Over the nasty sty—" (3.4.81–83). He tells her:

> You cannot call it love, for at your age
> The heyday in the blood is tame, it's humble,
> And waits upon the judgment. . . .
>
> *3.4.67–69*

"[F]railty, thy name is woman" is his verdict on his mother's hasty marriage to Claudius a month after her husband's death (1.2.146). Thus some recent criticism has focused on the too easy assumption of Gertrude's "guilt"—on the extraordinary, excessive emotion her son shows in this closet, or private room, this most intimate of spaces, more private than the bedchamber of state into which she has been manipulated into admitting a spy, Polonius—blaming her not only for her new marriage, but also for that of which she has no knowledge, the murder of her former husband. She *is* guilty: of being a woman.

Female sexual desire is, in Hamlet's mind, and therefore in the minds of many influential critics of the play, something out of control. It leads to marriage or to madness—to Ophelia's mad songs, so disturbingly erotic that even Horatio is dismayed. And this depiction of women's emotions as too frail and too powerful, taken together with the sense that Hamlet is preeminently the figure of consciousness, interiority, and thought, has led, in the reception of the play, to an interesting cultural effect: women, from Sarah Bernhardt on, have often aspired to be Hamlet, rather than Gertrude or Ophelia—not because Hamlet is a woman, but because "mankind" is Hamlet.

Perhaps the most celebrated and influential set of answers to the question "Why does Hamlet delay?" was offered by Sigmund Freud and by his English disciple and fellow psychoanalyst Ernest Jones. Freud's theory of the "Oedipus complex" uses the story of Sophocles' Oedipus, who literally kills his father and marries his mother (though in both cases he does so unknowingly), as the manifest and mythic version of what Freud tended to regard as a latent desire, best exemplified in its more modern, and repressed, form in *Hamlet*. In *The Interpretation of Dreams* (1900) he offers a powerful and provocative reading of the Shakespearean character: "Hamlet is able to do anything—except take vengeance on the man who did away with his father and took that father's place with his mother, the man who shows him the repressed wishes of childhood realized."[14] He summarizes his argument about Hamlet in a letter to his friend Wilhelm Fliess: "How does he explain his irresolution in avenging his father by the murder of his uncle . . . ? How better than through the torment he suffers from the obscure memory that he himself had contemplated the same deed against his father out of passion for his mother . . . ?"[15] Claudius has "popp'd in between th'election and [his] hopes," and also between his mother and himself. Then why does Hamlet delay in killing this hated rival, Claudius? Because, Ernest Jones explains in *Hamlet and Oedipus* (1949), Hamlet recognizes that Claudius has in fact done what he, Hamlet, wished in fantasy to do: murdered his father so as to have his mother. Thus, says Jones, Hamlet hesitates. How can he kill Claudius for acting on desires that Hamlet himself has had? This is what Freud terms, in *The Interpretation of Dreams,* the "secular advance of repression in the emotional life of mankind." Freud's hypothesis—which also inspired a famous production and its film version, Laurence Olivier's 1948 *Hamlet*—recognizes a key structural component of Shakespeare's play, the presence of several father figures rather than a single father: the dead (idealized) old Hamlet, a martial warrior; the living, despised Claudius, who is King (and Gertrude's lover) in Hamlet's stead; and Polonius, the father as "wretched, rash, intruding fool," who can be killed by accident or mistake ("Is it the King?" Hamlet asks his mother, having stabbed the hidden intruder behind the arras). As we will continue to see, this technique of "splitting," producing several versions of a character type split into component aspects, is one of the most effective devices of *Hamlet,* and will culminate in Hamlet's dying recognition that all his rivals and friends (Horatio, Laertes, Fortinbras, the First Player) are in some ways aspects of himself.

We have noticed that the play is built on the comparison and contrast of various kinds of illusion: the apparently real illusion of the Ghost, verified by the evidence of Hamlet's eyes and ears, and by the apparent truth of his report; the patently false illusion that is the common language of the Claudius court, ambition and lust hypocritically pretending to be sympathy and mourning; and the deliberately fictive illusion of the players, the part of the play that is about its own materials, acting and playing. As he does so often, the First Clown, the gravedigger, speaks (like all wise fools in Shakespeare) more truly than he knows, when he ties together the several meanings of the word "act." "[A]n act hath three branches," he says, "it is to act, to do, to perform" (5.1.11–12). What is the difference between doing and performing? Why can Hamlet in the early scenes, before his sea voyage to England, "perform"—dramatize—but not "do"—not murder and revenge? Why, instead of running his sword through Claudius in act 1, does he choose instead to follow Polonius's procedure, and "by indirections find directions out"? Why does he arrange the elaborate stratagem of *The Mousetrap* to terrify the King, and fright him, as he says, with false fire?

Hamlet as a play is from the first concerned with playing, and the play offers its spectators not only a series of nested plays, but a series of nested audiences. We watch the sentries watching the Ghost (1.1; 1.4). We watch Claudius and Polonius, the fathers, hidden behind a tapestry curtain, watching Ophelia "loosed" to Hamlet in the lobby (3.1). We watch Polonius, again concealed behind a tapestry, watching Hamlet talking to his mother in her closet (3.4). In the *Mousetrap* scene (3.2), we watch Hamlet watching Claudius watch the Player King and Player Queen. The audience of *Hamlet* never knows, securely, whether it is actor, spectator, or eavedropper. Thus, for example, Claudius's opening speech to his court seems straightforward enough, but it soon becomes clear that he is acting a part, the part of a bereaved brother and loving father. He is, in fact, himself a Player King, a man who is King in fiction, and by usurpation. The King is a thing of nothing, as Hamlet will say, under the guise of his own assumed madness, a "play" of its own. And likewise Gertrude is a Player Queen, hiding from the guilty knowledge she may suspect but prefers not to admit, even to herself. If we are not sure of these deceptions within deceptions, we have the voice of Hamlet in the first court scene to remind the audience that there is an "outside" to such complicit fictions. "Seems, madam? . . . I know not 'seems.' "

In the same way, the scene in the Queen's closet is on one level a moment of agonized truth-telling between mother and son. Yet Hamlet's method is deliberately theatrical, holding up a pair of portraits, and demanding, "Look here upon this picture, and on this, / The counterfeit presentment of two brothers" (3.4.52–53). The "pictures" are probably miniatures, lockets worn as keepsakes. In productions Hamlet often wears his father's portrait on a chain about his neck, while Gertrude wears that of her new husband, Claudius. Hamlet's violent yoking of the two together will thus juxtapose not only the images of the two brothers, but also the heads of Hamlet and Gertrude. Even more startling, of course, is the fate of the other spectator beside ourselves, the hapless Polonius, feeling safely protected behind the arras that conceals him, until the sword of Hamlet runs him through. Polonius thinks he is a spectator. By the time he becomes an actor, he has become a corpse. The confrontation with reality in *Hamlet* often takes this tragic form, and knowledge becomes, almost instantaneously, knowledge of death.

If we look closely we will see that the entire play is structured as a series of scenes each of which is a play-within-the-play. It is no accident that a recognition of the transforming power of fiction and illusion will help Hamlet to objectify his feelings about life, that "fiction" will help him to discover "fact." He is able to move in the course of the play from a melancholy passivity and contemplation, rather like Orsino's in *Twelfth Night*, to something more like action, by attaining a sense of crucial detachment that allows him to think, do, and plan, as well as feel. He is able to move from the soliloquies, which dominate the first four acts—and which are rightly reckoned among the humanistic beauties of the play—to the active verbs of the final act, which contains no soliloquy, perhaps because there is no longer any need for one. The players and the plays function as a therapeutic displacement for Hamlet, providing spaces in which he can work out his own problems. One more citation from Freud, this time not focused on Shakespeare or on Hamlet but on the general case of memory, may help to make this structural point clear: "[H]e cannot escape from this compulsion to repeat; and in the end we understand that this is his way of remembering."[16]

The characteristic Shakespearean triple pattern (court–country–court) always includes a return from the enchanted place, whether that place is called a green world, a second world, a place of "antistructure" or of carnival. The middle place is often identified with imagination, art, wonder, and dream (if the play is a comedy or romance), or with wilderness, danger, and madness (if the play is a tragedy). In almost all cases it brings with it an element of disguise and of (temporary) social leveling. There is always a return from this middle place, at least for most of the characters in the play; but those who return often return transformed. People do not come out of the Forest of Arden, or the Athenian wood, or the "heath" in *King Lear* or *Macbeth* (or the Egypt of *Antony and Cleopatra*) the same as they went in. *Hamlet,* too, contains a structure of journey and return. In fact, it contains two such structures, one before the other. The first is an existential journey into the alternative world of the players, while the second is a literal journey to England (where "the men are as mad as he" [5.1.142–143]).

The scene with the players is prefaced, yet again, by a fragment of a play, this time not a dumb show but a rehearsal in progress, as Polonius instructs Reynaldo how best to spy on Laertes. "Take you, as 'twere, some distant knowledge of him, / As thus: 'I know his father and his friends, / And in part him' " (2.1.13–15). Polonius is both playwright and director, though he occasionally forgets his own lines: "[W]hat was I about to say? By the mass, I was about to say something" (2.1.50–51). The whole scene is yet another evidence of the constant and deceitful playacting in Denmark. Polonius's confidence in his son, loudly voiced to his face, is now exposed as a sham. The father will send a spy to check on his son's behavior. It is this scene that is balanced, with superb effect, by the first news of Hamlet's antic disposition, announced to us through the familiar Shakespearean device of the "unscene," a vivid event that takes place offstage and is reported—in this case by the guileless Ophelia:

> Lord Hamlet, with his doublet all unbraced,
> No hat upon his head, his stockings fouled,
> Ungartered, and down-gyvèd to his ankle,
> Pale as his shirt, his knees knocking each other . . .
>
> 2.1.79–82

Ophelia is a naïve and completely believable witness who brings this offstage scene to vivid life. She is one of the few Shakespearean women who can never break away from the sway of a parent. In her innocent account of Hamlet's appearance in her room we have a vision, not so much of one man's madness as of the madness of the world, the madness of the human condition. In contrast to Polonius's insinuating script, which must be memorized, and his tedious, far from brief, "words, words, words" ("More matter with less art," the exasperated Queen will implore him [2.2.97]), Ophelia's description of the antic Hamlet seems more like another dumb show, a silent apparition:

> He took me by the wrist and held me hard,
> Then goes he to the length of all his arm,
> And with his other hand thus o'er his brow
> He falls to such perusal of my face
> As a would draw it. Long stayed he so.
> At last, a little shaking of mine arm,

> And thrice his head thus waving up and down,
> He raised a sigh so piteous and profound
> As it did seem to shatter all his bulk
> And end his being. That done, he lets me go,
> And, with his head over his shoulder turned,
> He seemed to find his way without his eyes,
> For out o' doors he went without their help,
> And to the last bended their light on me.
>
> 2.1.88–101

In its way this is very like the first mysterious appearance of the Ghost: pale, silent, beckoning, waving his arms, disappearing into darkness. Hamlet has in effect *become* a ghost. And Ophelia's report of his demeanor is enough of an "inexplicable dumb show" to generate misinterpretations. "This is the very ecstasy of love," concludes Polonius. Stereotypical lovers, at least in literature, did indeed sometimes present themselves in this kind of disarray—Rosalind describes such a lover in very similar terms in *As You Like It*—and Claudius is of course eager to agree with this diagnosis. But Gertrude has other suspicions: "I doubt it is no other but the main— / His father's death and our o'erhasty marriage" (2.2.56–57).

Everyone is an actor and a director. Polonius proudly acknowledges that he "played once i'th' university" (3.2.89–90). "I did enact Julius Caesar," he says. "I was killed i'th' capitol" (3.2.93). This is probably Shakespeare's joke about his company, for *Julius Caesar* was written and staged in the same years as *Hamlet,* and the actor who played Polonius could well have been seen by the same audience on another afternoon in the role of Caesar. But there is dramatic irony as well as an in-joke here, for ultimately Polonius will suffer a bathetic version of Caesar's death by stabbing. Polonius casts Hamlet in two of his own plays, the "loosing" of Ophelia in the lobby in act 3, scene 1 (watched, as we have noted, by Claudius and Polonius), and the episode in Gertrude's closet in act 3, scene 4, in which again he positions himself as a hidden spectator. Notice that Shakespeare places these two corrupt and cynical "plays" on either side of Hamlet's *Mousetrap* in act 3, scene 2.

The victim of social actors, Hamlet becomes one. He sees that the world around him is peopled by pretenders, that only those who know they are actors are "real." It is for that reason extremely appropriate for the players to appear, as if on cue. They have been conjured out of Hamlet's own imagination. The syllogism works something like this: Hamlet realizes that he is an actor, and that everyone in Elsinore is playing a role; the players arrive at the court and are announced. And they will disappear the same way, when their job is done. With the arrival of the players, the function of illusion in the play begins to shift. Hamlet begins to use it, and to use the players and their repertoire, to investigate his own society—as well as himself.

Before coming to the great play scene, however, it will be helpful, I think, to say a word about the play, or fragment of a play, that precedes *The Mousetrap*, because that older play is very much part of Hamlet's quest for answers. In act 2, scene 2, he asks the First Player to recite a speech from "Aeneas' tale to Dido," a speech that had apparently impressed him so much that he is able to recite much of it from memory. (Memory, and verbal memorization, are among the knowledge arts of the play, alongside reading and "writing fair," like a secretary or a scribe.) The play is about the fall of Troy, long thought by the English to be the source of their own civilization (one name for London was New Troy, or "Troynovant"). Aeneas, taking refuge with Dido in Carthage after fleeing the burning city, tells her the story of its fall. In *Hamlet* Troy seems very like the way Denmark is said to have been during the reign of old Hamlet—a golden age, brave, heroic, and warlike. "[R]everend Priam," the old Trojan king, seems in some ways to resemble an idealized old Hamlet, but on the other hand the desperate and grieving Hecuba, Priam's wife, running barefoot up and down, is sharply contrasted to Gertrude, who married again so quickly after her husband's death that "[t]he funeral baked meats / Did coldly furnish forth the marriage tables" (1.2.179–180). Pyrrhus, an avenger dressed in black ("he whose sable arms, / Black as his purpose . . ." [2.2.432–433]), first pauses with his sword in the air, and then acts, avenging the death of his father. In short, Troy emerges from this speech, one Hamlet so fondly remembers, as a picture of what might have been, what should have been, an epic ideal. Like Hamlet's parting glance at Ophelia, looking over his shoulder, bending his eyes on her—and like the message from the Ghost, "List, Hamlet, list, O list!"—this is for Hamlet a look backward, at a different kind of world, a lost world. Here at the play's midpoint it is his last glance backward, and it accomplishes something crucial for both the character and the play. Through the players, though fiction, he finds not only emotion—a way of engaging and accessing his own suppressed and unarticulated feelings—but also what he so badly needs and longs for: action. He is ready to catch the conscience of the King—in a play. "Action" and "passion" are two sides of the same coin, here not so much opposites as counterparts of each other.

The play Hamlet chooses to confront and entrap Claudius is very different from the Pyrrhus play, "Aeneas' tale to Dido." The Pyrrhus speech came from a play with familiar epic values—Polonius, not surprisingly, found it classical and boring, not relevant to anything he knew or cared about. But *The Mousetrap*, or, to give it its other name, "The Murder of Gonzago," is a thriller, a modern (which is to say, a Renaissance) melodrama, a play of political intrigue. "The story is extant," says Hamlet, "and writ in choice Italian" (3.2.240). Modern, current (or "extant"), and Italian—all harbingers of audience titillation. Italy, the home of Machiavelli, was often presented in English Renaissance drama as the site of scurrilous intrigue and scandal. A playwright had only to set his play there, as Ben Jonson would do with *Volpone* or John Webster with *The Duchess of Malfi,* he had only to give his characters Italian names, and it would be quite clear to the audience that they were being vouchsafed a glimpse into a world of decadence, sin, and forbidden pleasures—as well as of violence, betrayal, and murder.

In the course of the *Mousetrap* play the spectators first witness a dumb show; then hear a conversation, in rhymed couplets, between Player King and Player Queen; and finally see the entrance of the murderer. Throughout, Hamlet acts as interpreter—a role he will play throughout the larger drama, using his soliloquies and asides as a way of commenting to the offstage audience, just as his interpolations during *The Mousetrap* enlighten and disturb the onstage court. "You are as good as a chorus, my lord" (3.2.224), Ophelia will observe, with characteristic artlessness. Hamlet's glosses are brief and to the point. "This is one Lucianus, nephew to the King," he will explain as the murderer makes his appearance (3.2.223). Why "nephew" and not, as in the real case of Claudius and old Hamlet, "brother"? This is an explanation with an added menace—a glance backward that is also a glance forward. For it is Hamlet himself who is "nephew" to King Claudius. The past murder and the present threat are combined: Claudius has killed Hamlet's father; the "nephew" quietly announces that he will avenge that murder with another. And then "[t]he King rises," calling an end to the performance, yet another broken play, perhaps the most famous and most effectively truncated play-within-the-play in all of Shakespeare, structurally akin to "Pyramus and Thisbe" in *A Midsummer Night's Dream* and the pageant of the "Nine Worthies" in *Love's Labour's Lost,* and to Prospero's masque in *The Tempest.*

But which play has the audience of *Hamlet* been watching? As always, our consciousness is closely knit with Hamlet's, and Hamlet, clearly, has been watching not the stage but the King. The suspense for him is in what Claudius will or will not reveal, not in the outcome of "The Murder of Gonzago"—an outcome he already knows and that, indeed, he may in part have written in those elusive, added "dozen or sixteen lines." Once again Claudius and Gertrude are the Player King and the Player Queen. We have been deceived by our eyes again. The play was in the audience. Claudius and Gertrude are the "guilty creatures sitting at a play" of Hamlet's soliloquy (2.2.566), but they are also the bad actors he criticizes in his advice to the players: "O, there be players that I have seen play, and heard others praise, . . . that neither having the accent of Christians nor the gait of Christian, pagan, nor no man . . ." (3.2.25–29). The King and Queen are audience, but they are also players, players now caught in Hamlet's play, caught in *his* mousetrap. Art now acts on life. The play catches the king. What seems to be a mere fiction or fabrication reveals a key truth.

From this moment, from the play's principal turning point (3.2), Hamlet will himself begin to act, not only in the gravedigger's sense of "perform," but also in his sense of "do." When he next appears, he will act, quickly and without remorse, in his mother's closet, stabbing behind the arras at the intruder he is sure is Claudius, killing Polonius instead:

> Thou wretched, rash, intruding fool, farewell.
> I took thee for thy better.
>
> 3.4.30–31

The sentiment, and the phrase, recall Prince Hal's epitaph on the fallen Falstaff at Shrewsbury. "Poor Jack, farewell. / I could have better spared a better man" (*1 Henry IV* 5.4.102–103). As it turns out, Falstaff is not really dead. But with the indubitably dead Polonius, Hamlet wastes no time on pathos or pity. He does not even "lug the guts into the neighbour room" (3.4.186) until he has spoken with, and shamed, his mother. The body of Polonius lies onstage, a visceral object lesson and memento mori, throughout the rest of the scene—much as did, in earlier history plays, the coffins of dead kings.

Having "acted"—having killed Polonius—Hamlet is sent on the emblematic journey toward England, and on the journey he will act again, more deliberately this time, with Rosencrantz and Guildenstern, another pair of players, who desired to "play upon" him (3.2.335), but whom he now casts in a play of his own. En route to England, he will tell Horatio, he found the sealed commission they carried to the English King, asking for his death:

> Being thus benetted round with villainies—
> Ere I could make a prologue to my brains,
> They had begun the play. . . .
>
> 5.2.30–32

By that point Hamlet is totally in command of the language of playing, as well as of the play his mind conceives. He changes Claudius's script, writing out a commission for the death of Rosencrantz and Guildenstern, signing it with the name of the King, and sealing it with his father's signet ring, now in some sense rightfully his. He becomes what we could well call a ghostwriter, writing his anonymous script in the name of the Ghost, and for the revenge the Ghost has sought. A signet is both a seal and an official "signature." We may notice that Hamlet is also a skilled scribe or scrivener, who does not hold it, "as our statists [politicians] do, / A baseness to write fair" (5.2.34–35), and is thus able to substitute his own handwritten text for that originally supplied and ordained by the King. This act of ghostwriting is structurally parallel to his earlier substitution of the "dozen or sixteen lines" in the *Mousetrap* play, making it more pointed and pertinent to the situation in the Danish court. (Critics' attempts to locate and identify those "dozen or sixteen lines" have made for a diverting wild goose chase across the centuries; see my essay "MacGuffin Shakespeare" for a fuller account of this amusing phenomenon.[17] "Dozen or sixteen," we should note, is a proverbial, not a specific, phrase, meaning "some lines" rather than literally twelve to sixteen, so any amount of creative counting, or accounting, will fail of its object, rather like the "ducdame" joke in *As You Like It,* where the gullible audience is the butt of Jaques' wit.)

What has happened to Hamlet? How has he changed by entering into the world of serious "play"? As we have already seen, he has changed in costume, moving from his "inky cloak" (an earlier intimation of his future career as a writer of substitute lines and commissions) to his madman's disarray before Ophelia, to his third costume, his traveler's sea-gown, potentially an emblem of more existential journeys and voyages as well as of his own, highly specific and enforced, travel from Denmark toward England. Hamlet has also changed in language and the way he deploys it. The witty, punning, self-protective Hamlet of the opening scenes was also a monologuist, a speaker in soliloquies. The *Hamlet* film made by Laurence Olivier established a tradition, much copied, of filming or performing the soliloquies in the play with a voice-over, the actor on screen not moving his lips, so that the effect is one of voiced thought, of an intense and overwhelming consciousness, echoing the Hamlet of the Romantics, as much a "universal" philosopher as an action hero in an early modern revenge tragedy. The major soliloquies, one in each of the first four acts ("O that this too too solid flesh would melt"[1.2.129]; "O, what a rogue and peasant slave am I!" [2.2.527]; "To be, or not to be" [3.1.58]; "How all occasions do inform against me / And spur my dull revenge!" [4.4.9.22–9.23]) are interior monologues, syntactically elaborate, full of self-questioning. The "rogue and peasant slave" soliloquy contains ten questions and nine interpolations, while "To be, or not to be" is almost entirely composed of questions, conditionals, infinitives, and passive constructions: "To be, or not to be"; "To die, to sleep." But by the fifth act, after the voyage to England, there are no more soliloquies. Hamlet now talks to others rather than to himself or to the audience, and his language is suddenly full of active verbs, verbs of "doing":

> Up from my cabin,
> My sea-gown scarfed about me in the dark,
> Groped I to find out them, had my desire,
> Fingered their packet, and in fine withdrew
> To mine own room again, making so bold,
> My fears forgetting manners, to unseal
> Their grand commission. . . .
>
> 5.2.13–19

There he found the "exact command" that, so soon as it was read ("on the supervise"), "no leisure bated / No, not to stay the grinding of the axe / My head should be struck off." In the importunacy of this haste he turns to his own devices, substituting, as we have seen, the names (and thus the heads) of Rosencrantz and Guildenstern for his own. *Hamlet* performs this "head trick" in a way quite similar to that in *Measure for Measure*, a play written in the same years, where the head of the hero, Claudio, is spared by the substitution of the head of "[o]ne Ragusine, a most notorious pirate" (4.3.63), who has just conveniently died of a fever. (The preoccupation with pirates in three plays of this period,

Twelfth Night, Hamlet, and *Measure for Measure,* is worth noting. Pirates were a fact of seagoing life in early modern England and Europe. They are also mentioned by Shylock, a resident of the maritime commercial city of Venice; in some early English history plays; and in the other Shakespeare "sea" plays, *Antony and Cleopatra* and *Pericles.*)

Of all the changes in Hamlet as a dramatic character, though, the most striking is the change in his conception of his own role. From the beginning of the play he has lamented the fact that he is not like other people he admires, and to whom he insistently compares himself. He is not like his father, or Horatio, or Laertes, or Fortinbras—or so he thinks. Two of the four best-known soliloquies take this apparent dissimilarity as their starting-off point. In the "rogue and peasant slave" speech Hamlet compares himself unfavorably to the First Player, who can show strong emotion even in a fictional context, and in "How all occasions do inform against me" he contrasts his slowness in martial revenge with the rapidity and bravery of Fortinbras, the "delicate and tender prince" who leads his troops on a mission of honor, where they "[g]o to their graves like beds" and "fight for a plot / . . . Which is not tomb enough and continent / To hide the slain" (4.4.9.38; 4.4.9.52–9.55). Yet Hamlet is very like both the First Player and Fortinbras, and the progress of the play can be measured in part by the progress of his self-recognition in the models he has heretofore seen as indices of his own failure. In using his father's signet ring, as we have seen, he emblematically becomes both King and "Hamlet the Dane." By the play's last scene he is willing to see correspondences he has long ignored (but which have been evident to the audience):

> But I am very sorry, good Horatio,
> That to Laertes I forgot myself;
> For by the image of my cause I see
> The portraiture of his. . . .
>
>   5.2.76–79

And Fortinbras the soldier, whose name means "strong-arm," ordains for Hamlet, as is most fitting, a soldier's burial.

Hamlet's education in the mutability of roles began with the players, and the First Player's tears, but it ends in the graveyard, with the lesson that all human lives are roles, briefly played. The politician, the courtier, the lawyer, the great buyer of land— "That skull had a tongue in it and could sing once" (5.1.70). The skull of Yorick, the court jester during Hamlet's childhood, is in a way the antitype of the Ghost, material rather than spiritual. But it is also a memento mori, a reminder of death, and thus, like the Ghost, another invitation to "remember." The anatomist Andreas Vesalius, who in 1543 (more than half a century before *Hamlet*) published his great work *De humani corporis fabrica,* the first complete textbook of human anatomy, included among his illustrations one of a human skeleton deep in contemplation of a skull. This, we might say, is

Hamlet avant la lettre, an uncanny anticipation of Shakepeare's play. Skulls were common ornaments in the period, yet the skull of Yorick has a particular local habitation and a name. Hamlet's antic disposition may mirror itself on this first mentor and companion, another surrogate father, now "quite chap-fallen." The graveyard strips human beings to the bare bone, and in this cosmic perspective all roles are equal—"let her paint an inch thick, to this favour she must come." After all the wordiness of others in the play, from Polonius to the foppish courtier Osric to the ruminative Hamlet himself, the gravedigger strips language, like lives, to bare and literal essentials. He does not use metaphor, and he does not respond to it. "Upon what ground?" asks Hamlet, looking for a reason or an explanation, and the reply he receives is, "Why, here in Denmark" (5.1.148–149).

The gravedigger is a literalist, and like so many other clowns in Shakespeare he speaks home truths, even in the apparent guise of malapropism or misunderstanding. "How absolute the knave is!" says Hamlet, with some admiration, to Horatio. "We must speak by the card, or equivocation will undo us" (5.1.126–127). But metaphor is a necessary role for language, and language, as we have seen again and again in these plays, is for Shakespeare the touchstone and index of humanity. So Hamlet, although instructed in the graveyard, will leave it again for the world of roles, for a final choice of identity. "This is I, / Hamlet the Dane," he cries, as—in the Folio's stage direction—he "[l]eaps in the grave" of the dead Ophelia, and then grapples with Laertes for his right to mourn. The image of the two men wrestling in an open grave is itself a stunning and effective visual emblem, while the phrase "Hamlet the Dane" brings together the private and the public, the man and the nation, Hamlet reclaiming as his own the name and the titles with which the bereaved son, much earlier, greeted the ghost of his father: "I'll call thee Hamlet, King, father, royal Dane" (1.4.25–26).

At the play's close the audience is once again presented with the theatrical metaphor of a dumb show. Hamlet's duel with Laertes, undertaken at the behest of King Claudius, is a staged piece of theater that, like all the other plays-within-the-play, goes tragically wrong. The poisoned cup and the poisoned rapier—again, time-honored sexual symbols in literature, art, and myth—are inadvertently exchanged, so that they wreak their harm on unintended victims. The "union" Claudius ostentatiously drops into the cup of wine ("The King shall drink to Hamlet's better breath, / And in the cup an union shall he throw / Richer than that which four successive kings / In Denmark's crown have worn" [5.2.209–212]) is a jewel—a "union" was a pearl of singular beauty and great value. But the word was also used, in Shakespeare's day as it is now, as a synonym for marriage. Whether or not the poison drunk by Gertrude got into the cup by way of the "union," as some critics have maintained ("The Queen carouses to thy fortune, Hamlet," she says gaily, as the appalled Claudius urges, "Gertrude, do not drink," and then remarks, aside, "It is the poisoned cup; it is too late"), it is the union itself in that other sense, the "o'erhasty marriage" of Claudius and Gertrude, that carries and disperses the poison.

By the end of the scene they are all dead or dying. The duel is followed, then, by the order that the bodies be placed "[h]igh on a stage," both playing-space and platform, to serve as a silent example. Even in his dying words Hamlet has addressed, not only the spectators upon the stage, but the audience in the theater—in the *language* of the theater:

> You that look pale and tremble at this chance,
> That are but mutes or audience to this act . . .
>
> *5.2.276–277*

A "mute" is a silent person, and also was, in Shakespeare's time, a silent actor, one who had a nonspeaking role. We are all implicated in the outcome of "this change," of this tragedy.

But Hamlet's final injunction is to his friend Horatio:

> If thou didst ever hold me in thy heart,
> Absent thee from felicity a while,
> And in this harsh world draw thy breath in pain
> To tell my story.
>
> *5.2.288–291*

The story is to be told to Fortinbras, and to the English ambassador, both representatives of the political world. However, the injunction to "tell my story" is also—as we have seen so often at the close of Shakespearean tragedy—an injunction to perform the play. In *Romeo and Juliet, Othello, King Lear, Antony and Cleopatra,* in almost every tragedy Shakespeare wrote, this invitation, to "speak of these sad things," is a way of making tragic events bearable, by retelling them, by placing them at once in the realm of the social and of the aesthetic. It is important to note that Horatio himself cannot really do this. He has not heard the soliloquies, without which the play has a very different quality, far more sensational and inexplicable. "[L]et me speak to th' yet unknowing world," he says,

> How these things came about. So shall you hear
> Of carnal, bloody, and unnatural acts,
> Of accidental judgements, casual slaughters,
> Of deaths put on by cunning and forced cause;
> And, in this upshot, purposes mistook
> Fall'n on th'inventors' heads. All this can I
> Truly deliver.
>
> *5.2.323–329*

This is and is not *Hamlet*.

Twelfth Night

DRAMATIS PERSONAE

Orsino, *Duke of Illyria*
Valentine, *attending on Orsino*
Curio, *attending on Orsino*
First Officer
Second Officer
Viola, *a lady, later disguised as*
    Cesario
A Captain
Sebastian, *Viola's twin brother*
Antonio, *another sea-captain*
Olivia, *a Countess*
Maria, *her waiting-gentlewoman*

Sir Toby Belch, *Olivia's kinsman*
Sir Andrew Aguecheek,
    companion of Sir Toby
Malvolio, *Olivia's steward*
Fabian, *a member of Olivia's*
    household
Feste the clown, *her jester*
A Priest
A Servant of Olivia
Musicians, sailors, lords,
    attendants

HAKESPEARE'S PLAY *Twelfth Night, or What You Will* takes the first half of its title from the English holiday celebrated on the evening before January 6—the Twelfth Day of Christmas, otherwise known as the Feast of the Epiphany. According to Christian tradition, this was the time when the Magi, the three wise men, journeyed from the East to Bethlehem, bearing offerings for the infant Christ (Matthew 2:1–11). The word "epiphany" has a more general modern meaning, denoting a revealing manifestation, a sudden flash of insight, or a sudden recognition of identity. On the biblical Feast of the Epiphany it meant the showing of Christ to the Magi, a manifestation of godhead. In England, Twelfth Night was a feast of misrule, a festival of eating and drinking, during which masques and revels were presented. A large cake with a bean or a coin baked into it was served to the assembled company, and the person whose slice of cake contained the coin became the Christmas King, the Lord of Misrule. *What You Will*, the second half of the play's title, speaks both to this customary season of topsy-turvy revelry and to the space of fantasy and wish fulfillment that was the early modern playhouse. Like *Much Ado About Nothing* and *As You Like It*—and many similarly self-dismissive titles of plays by Shakespeare's contemporaries—this apparently deprecating phrase can come back to bite. If some of the play's characters do find that their fantasies come true, others are punished for daring to have fantasies at all.

Twelfth Night was first presented as a private entertainment at the Middle Temple, a law school in London, in 1602, and the play as we have it shows a number of evidences of its Christian festival origins. The fool in this play, whose name—Feste—suggests the spirit of feasting, is constantly speaking about wise men. In act 1, scene 5, for example, addressing "wit," he observes that while men who think they have wit are often fools, "I that am sure I lack thee may pass for a wise man" (1.5.30). Wise men who crow at fools, in Malvolio's words, are no better than the "fools' zanies," the fools' fools. And the Countess Olivia, the lady of the house and Feste's employer, is the biggest fool of all. Feste undertakes to prove this in a wonderful little piece of fool's patter (to which we might compare Lear's Fool's equally deft demonstration of the "sweet and bitter fool" [First Quarto, 4.127]):

> Festes Good madonna, why mournest thou?
> Olivia Good fool, for my brother's death.
> Feste   I think his soul is in hell, madonna.
> Olivia I know his soul is in heaven, fool.
> Feste   The more fool, madonna, to mourn for your brother's soul,
>   being in heaven. Take away the fool, gentlemen.
>
> Twelfth Night *1.5.57–62*

There is an echo of the Twelfth Night occasion, too, in the name Viola chooses for her disguise, "Cesario," the king. "Cesario" will become the "one self king" (1.1.38) Olivia wishes to rule her, and, unmasked as Viola, "Cesario" will participate with Sebastian in a real epiphany, or discovery, as the two reveal to each other—and to Orsino and Olivia—their real identities as twin brother and sister.

Typically, though not always, Shakespearean comedy encloses a transforming middle world—what Northrop Frye, thinking of the forest plays in particular, called a "green world." There is no forest here, no Belmont world of music and art, no realm of fairies. Instead we have, on the one hand, a world of madness and dream, a relatively familiar world of mistaken identity and playing and disguises, like that found in *The Comedy of Errors* or *Love's Labour's Lost,* and, on the other hand, what amounts to an invasion from without. Instead of the court world going to the forest, as in *A Midsummer Night's Dream* or *As You Like It,* in *Twelfth Night* we have the spectacle of a ship foundering off the coast of Illyria, of a sea world invading a land world. This is the comic pattern of *Much Ado About Nothing,* where outsiders—in that case, soldiers and lovers—come to a fixed place and change it. Indeed, it is the pattern of *The Comedy of Errors,* where all the action takes place in Ephesus. But in *Twelfth Night* the "outsiders" not only bring the comic elements of energy, desire, and fruitfully mistaken identities; they also bring key elements from another literary genre: romance. The world of romance invades the world of comedy.

Romance, the genre of Shakespeare's late plays, was a popular Elizabethan mode. Among its signature elements were shipwrecks, the rediscovery of long-lost brothers and sisters, physical marks of recognition, and rebirths from the sea. A fundamentally narrative genre, which would eventually give rise to the modern novel, romance always turns on epiphany, and on moments of rebirth. These elements, it is worth noting, were also present in the farcical *Comedy of Errors,* the plot of which turns on separated twins, lost and found parents, a shipwreck, and the miracle of rebirth, all with a definite Christian undertone. In *Twelfth Night* Shakespeare returns to this basic pattern, as he will have recourse to it yet again in *The Tempest,* near the end of his career. But in *Twelfth Night* he makes an important change from the earlier *Comedy of Errors* design, by making his "identical" twins of different sexes. By doing this he is able to combine an old theme with a newer one, the theme of rebirth with the theme of sexual love and growth, and the freeing and educative function of erotic ambiguity and sexual disguise. Viola as a boy, though carefully described as high-voiced and clear-complexioned, is able to educate both Orsino and Olivia in love, as Rosalind did Orlando in *As You Like It,* because she is herself in a middle space, in disguise, and in both genders. Once again the fact that boy actors played the roles of women on the public stage meant that a boy played a young woman playing a boy—one reason for the plentiful reminders in this play that "Cesario" is not a man, but a woman in disguise. If the audience were to make the same "mistake" as Orsino and Olivia, there would be no comedy, and no play. But if Orsino and Olivia did not make this crucial error, falling in love with the elusive and delusive "Cesario," they would learn nothing. There would be no romance, and no play.

Although the first scene introduces us to Duke Orsino's court, and to his melancholy passion for the elusive Olivia, the chronology of the play begins—as will the later *Tempest*—with a shipwreck, scattering the survivors and casting them up on the seacoast of Illyria. Viola is separated from her twin brother, Sebastian. She is alone; Sebastian has the company of Antonio, a sea captain who has befriended him. The seacoast is itself a typical romance locale, a border place between the sea and land, and thus a liminal or threshold space. In myth and folklore such border places are often associated with rebirth, at once transformative and traumatic (the myth of Odysseus is a good symptomatic example). And the people who come from the sea in this play seem to differ in temperament from the inhabitants of Illyria. They are active, while the Illyrians are passive. They are innovative, energetic, and daring. Antonio, moved by a desire that is, as he says, "[m]ore sharp than filèd steel," follows Sebastian into the town because of the depth of his friendship—a friendship, like that of another Antonio for the young man Bassanio in *The Merchant of Venice,* that puts him in a position of mortal danger. Orsino is Antonio's sworn enemy. Once, in a sea fight, Antonio did him damage (indeed, Antonio is described by Orsino as a kind of seagoing Hotspur, so valiant "[t]hat very envy and the tongue of loss / Cried fame and honour on him" [5.1.52–53]). Yet Antonio is willing to put himself in jeopardy because of his love for Sebastian. As for Sebastian, he, too, is characterized by energy and daring. "I saw your brother," the sea captain tells Viola, "Most provident in peril, bind himself— / Courage and hope both teaching him the practice— / To a strong mast that lived upon the sea" (1.2.10–13). Thus Sebastian, even before the audience actually encounters him, is associated not only with "courage" and "hope" but also with the Christian image of a "living" mast, to which he is willingly bound. Indeed, when he makes his first onstage appearance in front of Olivia's house, he is preceded by material evidence of his valor: Sir Andrew Aguecheek with a broken head, bruised and beaten, and Sir Toby Belch "halting," or limping (5.1.171, 186).

From the first, though, it is Viola, of all the shipwreck survivors, who has the strongest claim upon the audience's attention. Setting foot upon the land, she is at first in despair about her brother's apparent death: "And what should I do in Illyria? / My brother, he is in Elysium" (1.2.3–4). Even so, her fears immediately join with hope—"Perchance he is not drowned. What think you sailors?"—and her mind turns instantly to action: "Know'st thou this country?" "Who governs here?" "Conceal me what I am" (1.2.4, 19, 22, 49). She quickly decides to dress herself like a boy—indeed, to dress herself like her lost brother—and to seek employment with Orsino:

> I'll serve this duke.
>
> . . . .
>
> for I can sing,
> And speak to him in many sorts of music
> That will allow me very worth his service.
>
> *1.2.51–55*

Song and music are her intended gifts. She seems to know Orsino's affectations and his idiom even before she meets him.

The audience, of course, has already encountered this complicated Duke, himself a willing prey to the fashionable Elizabethan affliction of melancholy. His opening words are the opening words of the play, and as is so often the case with Shakespeare, the sheer beauty of the passage can sometimes overshadow its sense. In this great speech, Orsino calls by turns for music and for silence, seeking pain in his aesthetic pleasure almost if he were a later decadent poet like Algernon Swinburne or Ernest Dowson. His closest Shakespearean kin in this spirit are Cleopatra, herself a notable devotee of excess who speaks of music as the "moody food / Of us that trade in love" (*Antony and Cleopatra* 2.5.1–2), and, curiously, Jessica in *The Merchant of Venice,* who is never merry, she says, when she hears sweet music. Yet Orsino, like Cleopatra, wants more, rather than less, of this complex sensation, replete with sweetness and with loss:

> If music be the food of love, play on,
> Give me excess of it that, surfeiting,

> The appetite may sicken and so die.
> That strain again, it had a dying fall.
> O, it came o'er my ear like the sweet sound
> That breathes upon a bank of violets,
> Stealing and giving odour. Enough, no more,
> 'Tis not so sweet now as it was before.
>   [*Music ceases*]
> O spirit of love, how quick and fresh art thou,
> That, notwithstanding thy capacity
> Receiveth as the sea, naught enters there,
> Of what validity and pitch so e'er,
> But falls into abatement and low price
> Even in a minute! So full of shapes is fancy
> That it alone is high fantastical.
>
>   *1.1.1–15*

Orsino glories in love's melancholy, what Feste will call the "melancholy god." It is at Orsino's request that the fool sings the lambent song "Come away, come away death"—a song he had sung the night before, and that Orsino commends to "Cesario" as "old and plain":

> Feste [*sings*]   Come away, come away death,
>   And in sad cypress let me be laid.
>   Fie away, fie away breath,
>   I am slain by a fair cruel maid.
>
>   *2.4.50–53*

The song, with its explicit mentions of shroud, coffin, grave, and yew tree, is part of a larger culture of memento mori and of *vanitas*—in the midst of life we are in death. Orsino is deeply affected: his critical admirers call him "noble," and certainly there is a wholeheartedness to his commitment to aesthetic melancholia and the erotics of loss. When he offers a coin to the singer ("There's for thy pains"), he is smartly answered ("No pains, sir. I take pleasure in singing, sir" [2.4.66–67]), and though Orsino quickly agrees to "pay thy pleasure, then," it is clear that his own pleasure comes not unmixed with pain.

Orsino's initial passion, although he claims it is for Olivia, is rather for the spectacle of himself in love. "Appetite," "excess," "sicken," "die"—these are his words, and if "dying fall," the sinking down or lowering of a note or voice, is a technical term in music, it also suits his temperament and his occasion. Orsino says that his desires pursue him like hounds, and thus he invokes, for the humanistic Renaissance audience familiar with the Greek and Roman classics, the image of Actaeon, a hunter who caught sight of the goddess Diana bathing and was turned into a stag and torn to pieces by his own hounds. Orsino is passive rather than active, passive in the extreme. He does not even go himself to

Olivia to tell her of his love, but instead sends a go-between. His is the apotheosis of aristocratic indolence and moodiness, the opposite of Viola's energy and activity—just as his constant rhetorical insistence upon expressing his thwarted love is the contrary to her resolve not to speak the love she feels, not to reveal herself.

It is dramatically fitting, then, that Orsino's first expression of love is directed toward Olivia, although, as we have noted, his real passion seems reserved for himself. For what is Olivia's situation? Her waiting-gentlewoman Maria will say that she is "addicted to a melancholy" (2.5.176). One of Orsino's gentlemen describes her routine of daily life with chilling vividness:

> The element itself till seven years' heat
> Shall not behold her face at ample view,
> But like a cloistress she will veilèd walk
> And water once a day her chamber round
> With eye-offending brine—all this to season
> A brother's dead love. . . .
>
> *1.1.25–30*

The "element" is the sky. Olivia will keep her face veiled, will retain the outward signs of mourning, for seven long years, as she performs the daily ritual of walking through her chamber and weeping for her dead brother, like a "cloistress," like a nun. Olivia puts herself in a nunnery of her own devising. She is her own repressive parent, and her mourning for her brother puts her in a condition that is itself a kind of symbolic or emblematic death. Notice the phrase "A brother's dead love"—not "A dead brother's love." What will be seasoned, or cured and kept, is the "dead love." The enclosed room in which she cloisters herself, away from the light of the sun, is not only another emblem of enclosed virginity but also an anticipatory counterpart of the "dark room" to which the supposedly mad Malvolio will be confined near the close of the play. As we have seen elsewhere, to be put in a locked room and bound was a standard "cure" for madness.

Olivia's mourning, "addicted to a melancholy," is thus in complete contrast to the way Viola mourns for the loss of *her* brother, Sebastian. Viola's response to what she believes to be her brother's death is life-affirming rather than life-denying, and is manifested outdoors rather than indoors. The anagrammatic relation of three of the play's principal figures, Olivia, Viola, and Malvolio, underscores the degree to which these characters mirror one another. No attentive Shakespearean audience should be surprised to find that Viola, who does turn away from the self-imposed prison of "[a] brother's dead love" and toward the world, will very shortly find herself in love and wishing for marriage.

Critics have noted the predominance of water imagery in this play, from tears to seawater to urine, from dry hands to dry jests to dry fools. Sir Andrew is impressed by "Cesario's" deliberately flowery phrase "rain odours"—"That youth's a rare courtier; 'rain odours'—well" (3.1.78–79). Feste will close the play by singing his song of life and the passage of time, "When that I was and a little tiny boy," with its refrain "For the rain it raineth every day," where "every day," once again, will replace "holiday" at the end of a comedy. But the difference between "eye-offending brine" and the fertile sea is a difference between self-love and love. Self-love, an aspect of pride, is this play's besetting sin, a sin that provokes the language of sickness that envelops much of the play. Orsino speaks of Olivia's having "purged the air of pestilence," but the pestilence is what we perceive. (Recall that "pestilence" was more than a metaphor in Shakespeare's time, when theaters were periodically closed because of the mounting death toll from the plague.) Orsino's opening speech, as we saw, was full of images of excess, surfeit, and appetite—an appetite that might "sicken and so die." This language of contagion and infection will continue throughout *Twelfth Night,* and will crystallize in the figure of Malvolio, whose name explicitly means "ill-wisher" (just as Romeo's well-intentioned friend Benvolio was a "well-wisher"). Malvolio is the play's paradigm of self-love, as even the self-absorbed Olivia has the wit to see: "O, you are sick of self-love, Malvolio, and taste with a distempered appetite" (1.5.77–78).

The rebellious backstairs world, too, is in a sense a result of Olivia's self-absorption. Preoccupied by her own grief, she has given the rule of the household over to Malvolio, her steward. A household steward was a high-ranking servant who supervised the household, the table, and the realm of domestic expenditure. Malvolio is a joyless, self-styled "Puritan" in a Twelfth Night setting, and, equally important, a class-jumping climber in a play populated by— and initially performed for—aristocrats. Puritans in this period were vociferous in their criticism of the theater and of all "popish" holidays and practices, like Christmas. What Jonas Barish has called their "anti-theatrical prejudice," in his book of that title, manifested in the publication of tracts and pamphlets, drew particular attention to the practice of cross-dressing on the English stage. Not only had the Bible forbidden men to wear women's clothing and women to wear men's clothing, but such onstage performances were held to affect both the wearer and the audience. A man dressed as a woman might, in a kind of Lamarckism *avant la lettre,* become contaminated and "womanish," or effemi-nate; an audience, comprising both men and women, might find the cross-dressed performer erotically attractive, and this might lead in turn to illicit desires in the world outside the theater, and to the practice of sodomy. *Twelfth Night* stages such bisexual gender infatuation unforgettably in the figure of "Cesario," with whom both Olivia and Orsino fall in love. But the play's inter-nal criticism of a kind of "cross-dressing" is limited to, or displaced upon, the pretentious "Puritanism" of Malvolio, who dreams of dressing in a "branched velvet gown," a kind of cloth reserved for nobility, and who is ultimately—and literally—double-crossed, duped into wearing unfashionable and uncomfort-able cross-gartered yellow stockings.

Both Malvolio's social climbing and his repressiveness are all too apposite for Olivia's mood as the play opens. She has chosen him because he is "sad and civil"—that is, serious and well behaved. Under his stewardship ordinary pleasures are repressed to the point where they break out in a spontaneous burst of misrule, like a pestilence or a disease. He prevents the expression of honest emotion, and forces truth underground. Thus, for example, Olivia's dependent uncle, Sir Toby Belch, and his companions, the hapless Sir Andrew and Feste, the fool, are singing a "catch," a round song, called "Hold thy peace." That is to say, they are singing a song about not singing—"Hold thy peace" means "Be quiet," or "Shut up." The fool has what Toby calls a "contagious breath," and they have all caught the disease. Into the midst of this amiable racket comes Malvolio, trailing clouds of disapproval: "My masters, are you mad? Or what are you? Have you no wit, manners, nor honesty, but to gabble like tinkers at this time of night? Do ye make an alehouse of my lady's house . . . ?" (2.3.78–81). We may notice the elements of class pretense here. Tinkers, menders of pots and pans, were held in low repute, and were often identified with vagrants or gypsies. An alehouse was a low or common drinking place. But an alehouse is what Olivia's house has become. Orsino's court world speaks in lofty, often high-sounding poetry. Olivia's household largely speaks in prose. And the element of appetite is insisted upon. As Sir Toby famously rebukes Malvolio, "Dost thou think because thou art virtuous there shall be no more cakes and ale?" (2.3.103–104). Just because you repress human appetites, do you think that appetite itself will cease, that there will no longer be a place, or a need, for release and revelry? The denials of desire in Malvolio's world are more malign versions of the vows of abstinence taken by the lords in *Love's Labour's Lost*. There is danger on both sides—too little rule, or too much.

We might remember that as the play begins Feste, the fool, has returned from an unexplained absence. His absence is unexplained, that is, to the play's characters, but the audience in the theater might suspect some reasons why the spirit of feasting has been away. It is Olivia's fault, and through her it is Malvolio's fault. Feste, it seems, was once a welcome pleasure in the house. The only moment in the play when Feste's name is ever spoken is when he is described as "Feste the jester, . . . a fool that the lady Olivia's father took much delight in" (2.4.11–12). With the death of her father and her brother, Olivia has turned aside from both jest and delight. But Feste is an essential part of life, and when he is denied his part he will retaliate by an excess, a surfeit, of revelry and appetite, making "[a]n alehouse of my lady's house." The world of Sir Toby and Sir Andrew Aguecheek in fact resembles nothing so much as the tavern world of *Henry IV*. Sir Toby, the drunken sot who can say "I hate a drunken rogue," is very like Falstaff. His name, "Belch," identifies him with the comedy of humors; when we hear him say "a plague o' these pickle herring" (1.5.105–106), the remark is accompanied by an appropriately loud and vulgar noise. Sir Andrew—his surname comes from "ague," an illness marked by burning fever and then by shivering; essentially malaria—is very like the madcap Justice Shallow of *Henry IV Part 2,* all skin and bones and sexual ambition. Possibly the same two actors would have played the parts. (This dyad is also reminiscent of the comic pair of Dogberry and Verges in *Much Ado About Nothing.*) The preoccupations of this sector of Olivia's household are the preoccupations of manners and courtesy that were part of aristocratic education—here, of course, sadly devoid of any real merit. Sir Toby has imported Sir Andrew as a rich suitor for his niece Olivia. And what are Andrew's accomplishments? He plays the "viol-de-gamboys"—the viola da gamba, a kind of cello—and he has three thousand ducats a year. (The play periodically teases the audience with mentions of violas and violets, a gentle tribute to its singular heroine.) Although Toby says Andrew speaks three or four languages "word for word without book" (1.3.22–23), Andrew does not know the meaning of the word *pourquoi:*

> What is "Pourquoi"? Do, or not do? I would I had bestowed that time in the tongues that I have in fencing, dancing, and bear-baiting. O, had I but followed the arts!
>
> *1.3.78–80*

"Tongues" and "tongs" were pronounced the same. Sir Andrew is lamenting his lack of linguistic skill, but he could also be heard as wishing he had spent more time at the hairdresser's. Fencing, dancing, and bearbaiting, although all period "entertainments," had divergent social standing. In bearbaiting, a popular sport in Southwark—where the theaters were also located—a bear was tied to a stake and set upon by dogs, to the admiration of the crowd. Dancing might be Sir Andrew's strong suit—he has the "back-trick simply as strong as any man in Illyria." Sir Toby wonders aloud, "Wherefore are these things hid? . . . Why dost thou not go to church in a galliard, and come home in a coranto? My very walk should be a jig. I would not so much as make water but in a cinquepace" (1.3.105–109). The mentions of popular French dances are combined, in Toby's usual way, with off-color puns (a "cinquepace" is a five-step dance, also spelled "sinkapace" in the English of the period, but a "sink" is a cesspool). But, in any case, what would be the value of knowing the meaning of *pourquoi*? In a world of sheer revel, the word "why," the energy of motivation, has no meaning.

That the recourse to nonstop revelry here is a manifest response to Olivia's self-cloistering is made clear by the first words the audience hears Sir Toby speak: "What a plague means my niece to take the death of her brother thus? I am sure care's an enemy to life" (1.3.1–2). He is not wrong to criticize her, as his telltale word "plague" suggests he is doing, but Maria is not wrong, either, to tell Toby in her turn, "you must confine yourself within the modest limits of order" (6–7). The two extremes here, Toby's misrule and Olivia's and Malvolio's excessive rule, are really two sides of the same coin. Both are aimless, fruitless, and preoccupied with sterile formalities, whether those formalities are Olivia's ritual daily round or Sir Andrew's back-trick, performed in a "damned coloured" (the Folio reading) or a "flame-coloured" stocking, to set off his bony legs to advantage.

Appetite for appetite's sake is not only a problem for Toby and company—it is Orsino's problem as well. His appetite is for music, and for the melancholy of love, while theirs is for cakes and ale, but it is all mere appetite, not passion or purpose. All of them lack the element of "*pourquoi.*" There is, then, as much dramatic reason for Viola and Sebastian to enter this jaded world as there was necessity for the court in *As You Like It* to journey to the Forest of Arden, or the foolish philosophers of *Love's Labour's Lost* to be confronted with the reality of the Princess and her ladies. Viola's lively spirit acts as an antidote to the willed passivity of both Olivia and Orsino, and perhaps the best brief expression of what she brings to this play can be found in her advice to Olivia when, as "Cesario," she presents Orsino's offer of love: "what is yours to bestow is not yours to reserve" (1.5.167–168). You may give yourself in love and marriage, but you may not refuse or decline to do so. If you remain in the cloister of your own dead affections, satisfying yourself with appetite, you are, yourself, a usurper. The tone of this advice resembles that of the similarly cross-dressed Rosalind, speaking as "Ganymede" to Phoebe, the "proud disdainful shepherdess": "Sell when you can. You are not for all markets" (*As You Like It* 3.5.61).

Viola's own nature is clearly one that combines the virtues of other resource-ful women in Shakespearean comedy, virtues like generosity and risk-taking. Her bravery is shown in the shipwreck incident and in her resolve to serve Orsino. Her generosity manifests itself in the course of that service, since, in her role as "Cesario," she is asked to woo a woman on behalf of the man she secretly loves. As she says to herself, and to the audience, accepting Orsino's commission,

> I'll do my best
> To woo your lady—[*aside*] yet a barful strife—
> Whoe'er I woo, myself would be his wife.
>
> *1.4.39–41*

Shakespeare has here picked up on a theme he introduced in *As You Like It,* when Rosalind, dressed as the boy "Ganymede," and discovering that her beloved Orlando is in the forest, exclaims, "Alas the day, what shall I do with my doublet and hose!" Viola finds her doublet and hose even more of a problem, since they bewitch the lady, and apparently disqualify her for the love of the gentleman:

> My master loves her dearly,
> . . . .
> And she, mistaken, seems to dote on me.
> What will become of this? . . .
> . . . .

>   O time, thou must untangle this, not I.
>   It is too hard a knot for me t'untie.
>
>   *2.2.31–39*

Viola calls herself a "poor monster" because she is, in effect, a hermaphrodite, a creature of two sexes, a gender hybrid—here a woman dressed as a man. Her plan to serve Orsino since she can "sing, / And speak to him in many sorts of music" is reinforced indirectly but importantly by the fool's song in act 2, scene 3, with its reference to the range of the lover's voice:

>   O mistress mine, where are you roaming
>   O stay and hear, your true love's coming,
>   That can sing both high and low.
>
>   *2.3.35–37*

We should note that Viola's situation is different from that of Shakespeare's other cross-dressed comic heroines, in that she does not meet the man she loves until she is already in her gender disguise. Portia meets and marries Bassanio before she conceives of the plot to rescue him and his benefactor, Antonio, by masquerading as a young doctor of laws. Rosalind meets Orlando in the court, and she ends her play restored to her women's clothing, led forth by the marriage god Hymen. Orlando explicitly recognizes her in this costume ("If there be truth in sight, you are my Rosalind" [*As You Like It* 5.4.108]), and she conducts her frame-breaking and gender-bending epilogue in the voice, guise, and clothing of a "lady," while at the same time reminding the audience of "her" other identity as a boy actor. But when Viola first meets Orsino and falls in love with him, she is already dressed as the boy "Cesario." Orsino notices that there is something feminine about her, and puts it down to "Cesario's" youth, praising his wisdom, which seems more mature than his tender years. The comedy of double meanings, discrepant awareness, and imminent unmasking adds both point and pleasure to the scene:

>   [T]hey shall yet belie thy happy years
>   That say thou art a man. Diana's lip
>   Is not more smooth and rubious; thy small pipe
>   Is as the maiden's organ, shrill and sound,
>   And all is semblative a woman's part.
>
>   *1.4.29–33*

Orsino sees and he does not see. "Cesario" looks and sounds like a woman to him. Apparently in part for that reason ("I know thy constellation is right apt / For this affair" [1.4.34–35]), he sends the young "man" off as an emissary of his love to Olivia. And Olivia, of course, falls instantly for "Cesario" when he comes to present Orsino's suit. She is won over by "Cesario's" bold impertinence: as Viola, dressed as "Cesario," begins to read a formal letter written in praise of the "[m]ost radiant, exquisite, and unmatchable beauty," she breaks off to look around the room and ask which is the lady of the house. The "unmatchable beauty" of Olivia is not—Viola pretends—self-evident. Olivia is won over, as well, by "Cesario's" wit ("Are you a comedian?"—an actor—she asks, feigning irritation, her interest piqued) and by "Cesario's" persistence in asking her to lift her veil of mourning ("[W]e will draw the curtain," she says, "and show you the picture" [1.5.204–205]).

But Olivia is also captivated by something else: by the whole ambiguous and fictionalized person that is "Cesario." Like "Ganymede" in *As You Like It*, "Cesario" has a powerful existence, eloquent, erotic, and elusive, that is not merely equivalent to the charms and power of the female character who portrays him, nor to those of the male actor who originated the role. Olivia, like Orsino, sees something, but mistakes—overrationalizes—what she sees. She quotes to herself, with approval, "Cesario's" claim about "his" social status:

> ["]I am a gentleman." I'll be sworn thou art.
> Thy tongue, thy face, thy limbs, actions, and spirit
> Do give thee five-fold blazon. . . .
>
> *1.5.261–263*

Never mind that in the poetic language of the period a "blazon" was usually the itemized praise of a *woman's* beauty. Olivia sees a category crisis, but assigns it to the wrong category: it is not that "Cesario" is really a woman, but that he is really a gentleman. It is this muddle that leads Viola to describe herself as a "poor monster," both man and woman, and neither. "As I am man, / My state is desperate for my master's love" (2.2.34–35). Dressed as "Cesario" she can never inspire Orsino to love her. "As I am woman, now, alas the day, / What thriftless sighs shall poor Olivia breathe!" (36–37). When Olivia discovers that "Cesario" is a woman, there will be no possible good outcome for her love.

And what does happen to the "knot," or tangle, as Viola/Cesario describes it? Olivia, repeatedly rebuffed by "Cesario" (who tells her that "no woman has, nor never none / Shall mistress be of [my heart] save I alone" [3.1.150–151]), meets Sebastian, Viola's male identical twin, in the nick of time, thinks he is "Cesario" with a change of heart, and rushes him off, before he can change his mind, to exchange vows of betrothal at a nearby chantry. We may find it interesting that the place for this assignation is a chantry, a place where Mass was sung daily for the souls of the dead. Presumably this is where Olivia's brother and perhaps also her father are remembered. In every aspect of this play, from the fool's melancholy song in Orsino's court, "Come away, come away, death," love and death have been intertwined. By siting the betrothal in a locale formerly associated with death and mourning, Olivia—and her play—began to right the balance between them.

As for Orsino and Viola, their courtship is even stranger than that of Olivia and Sebastian. Orsino is first convinced that he loves an unattainable woman, Olivia. Then he finds himself attracted to a boy, though one with a woman's voice and complexion. Here we might want to recall the opening lines of Shakespeare's Sonnet 20:

> A woman's face with nature's own hand painted
> Hast thou, the master-mistress of my passion;
> A woman's gentle heart, but not acquainted
> With shifting change, as is false women's fashion. . . .

(Orsino will have uncomplimentary things of his own to say about women's capacity for steadfastness in love.) Finally Orsino will choose, or settle for, Viola—if and when she can demonstrate, by reappearing to him dressed in her women's clothing, that she really is a woman. "Cesario, come," he says, as they sweep off the stage at the play's end,

> For so you shall be while you are a man;
> But when in other habits you are seen,
> Orsino's mistress, and his fancy's queen.
>
> *5.1.372–375*

"Fancy" is in this period the same word as "fantasy," a contraction of the letters. As with "Tell me where is fancy bred," the song from *The Merchant of Venice,* this term ties love, without apology, to wish fulfillment and to dream. But we never see Viola in her women's clothes again. She says she will send for her "maiden weeds" from the sea captain who has kept them for her, but unlike Rosalind, Viola never gets to reappear as a woman. When the play closes she is still dressed as the boy "Cesario."

This final scene, in which lovers meet and siblings find each other, is both long and wonderful. "Wonder," that predominant emotion of romance, is its major key. The twins, male and female yet "identical," and dressed alike ("For him I imitate," Viola says [3.4.348]), stand and stare at each other. We hear the phenomenon described:

> One face, one voice, one habit, and two persons,
> A natural perspective, that is and is not.
>
> *5.1.208–209*

The speaker is Orsino, and by "perspective" he means the kind of perspective painting that Shakespeare will use as a telling comparison in other plays, like *Richard II* and *Antony and Cleopatra:* a picture constructed so as to produce a fantastic effect, seeming distorted except from one particular point of view, or appearing different from different vantage points. In this case the perspective is produced by nature, not by art. The recognition scene may remind a Shake-spearean audience of the similar recognition scenes in *The Comedy of Errors,* with its two pairs of sundered twins. "Do I stand there? I never had a brother," says Sebastian (5.1.219). He articulates the great, open questions of romance: "[W]hat kin are you to me? / What countryman? What name? What parent-age?" (223–224), questions that will become a familiar part of Shakespeare's later romances, *Pericles, Cymbeline, The Winter's Tale,* and *The Tempest.* "Sebastian was my father," replies Viola. "Such a Sebastian was my brother, too" (225–226). Antonio, confronted with the same puzzling perspective, may be thinking of Plato's *Symposium* and the seriocomic fable told there by Aristophanes, of origi-nal, androgynous double beings, split in half, each half seeking through the world for its proper mate:

> Antonio   How have you made division of yourself?
> An apple cleft in two is not more twin
> Than these two creatures. Which is Sebastian?
>
> *5.1.215–217*

But as the romance mists begin to clear, and the truth dawns on them, the con-venience of this solution may appear a little forced, a little too convenient. Viola undertakes to explain the true situation to her brother:

> If nothing lets to make us happy both
> But this my masculine usurped attire,
> Do not embrace me till each circumstance
> Of place, time, fortune do cohere and jump
> That I am Viola. . . .
>
> *5.1.242–246*

"[W]hich to confirm," she says, she will send forthwith for her "maiden weeds." Sebastian, with assurance, and perhaps with some relief, turns to Olivia and demystifies this mystery:

> So comes it, lady, you have been mistook.
> But nature to her bias drew in that.
> You would have been contracted to a maid,
> Nor are you therein, by my life, deceived,
> You are betrothed both to a maid and man.
>
> *5.1.252–256*

The double nature of all human beings, the fact that men and women all have something "masculine" and something "feminine" about them, is an issue that Shakespeare takes up in several of his sonnets, as well as in scenes like this one in the plays. Viola uses all sides of her "nature" in order to make "Cesario" such a captivating creature, a superbly successful "monster." Olivia and Orsino both fall in love with someone, something, they half recognize and do not know. Something similar to, as well as complementary to, themselves.

Viola points to another aspect of that double nature earlier in the play when, as "Cesario," she tells Orsino the fictive story of her imaginary sister. Orsino has tried to draw a distinction between the intensity of a man's love and that of a woman. He is speaking in the language of male-male Renaissance codes of friendship, of ideal and idealizing love, both between persons of equal age and station, and between a protector and a protégé:

> There is no woman's sides
> Can bide the beating of so strong a passion
> As love doth give my heart; no woman's heart
> So big, to hold so much. They lack retention.
> Alas, their love may be called appetite,
> No motion of the liver, but the palate.
>
> *2.4.91–96*

Viola/Cesario replies by telling the story of her love for him, but casting that story as something that happened between two other people:

Viola   In faith, they are as true of heart as we.
         My father had a daughter loved a man
         As it might be, perhaps, were I a woman
         I should your lordship.
Duke   And what's her history?
Viola   A blank, my lord. She never told her love,
         But let concealment, like a worm i'th' bud,
         Feed on her damask cheek. She pined in thought,
         And with a green and yellow melancholy
         She sat like patience on a monument,
         Smiling at grief. Was not this love indeed?

> *2.4.105–114*

Viola, at least in her persona as "Cesario," is a great storyteller. Orsino's attention is caught by this story, which touches on emotions and sensibilities already established as meaningful to him: melancholy, monuments, and dying of unspoken or unrequited love. "But died thy sister of her love, my boy?" he asks, and the answer is a romance riddle:

> I am all the daughters of my father's house,
> And all the brothers too; and yet I know not.
>
> *2.4.119–120*

The pining away of this imagined sister is another way this comedy, like so many of Shakespeare's, frames itself with death. In a way, the problem of gender, and Viola's problem in her cross-gender disguise, are constantly re-posed throughout the play. One or two. Male or female. The puzzle appears to be on the surface. But Viola's position remains very different from Rosalind's or Portia's. Proposing to her, Orsino refers—playfully, he thinks—to the traditional power relations of marital households and of Petrarchan love:

> And since you called me master for so long,
> Here is my hand. You shall from this time be
> Your master's mistress.
>
> *5.1.313–315*

Olivia, continuing the move toward harmony and household normalization, adopts Viola in a different way, without missing a beat: "A sister, you are she" (5.1.315). But Viola is still dressed as a boy, and the capacity for mistaking remains. In one recent production Orsino reached out his hand in that commanding final gesture—"Cesario, come!"—and tried to clasp the hand of . . . Sebastian, who scooted across the stage to the safe shelter of Olivia's side. They both, after all, will still look "identical." Which is "Cesario"? Is he both of them, or neither?

So the play will end, as comedies do, with marriages. Olivia is to marry Sebastian, the husband ex machina, who appears in the nick of time. Viola will marry Orsino—if she can ever manage to recover her women's clothes. And in the meantime, Sir Toby Belch has married Maria, Olivia's waiting-gentlewoman. But how successful are these resolutions? It is one thing to get the heroine into her doublet and hose, as with Rosalind, or her lawyer's gown, as with Portia, in order to perform a certain piece of work, and then have her return to her own clothes and her own world. It is quite another to get the heroine into male costume, then perplex her with problems relating to her real and assumed gender roles, and finally leave her on the stage, in the last moments of the play, described as her "master's mistress" and dressed as a boy. "Cesario" is a cross-dressed heroine whose name means "little monarch" (from the Latin *caedere,* "to cut"—the same word that survives in the "caesura" of prosody, a breathing place or pause). She, or he, is also another kind of take on the Elizabethan dilemma, the ruler with two bodies, one "natural" and female, the other "political" and ungendered—which is to say, gendered as a universal male.

Before leaving this question of "Cesario's" doubled body and triangulated identity (male, female, fantasy beloved), it will perhaps be useful briefly to take note of the debates about human sexuality and physiology in the early modern Europe of Shakespeare's time. As historian Thomas Laqueur and others have observed, some physicians and philosophers followed Galen in positing what has come in modern parlance to be known as a "one-sex" model. Male and female bodies were, according to this view, versions of the "same" body, except that the male genitals were external and the female sex organs, which had the same shape and the same names for each part, were internal. A notion of body heat made the difference: men had more "vital heat," and so their sex organs were forced outside the body. Women, of a cooler constitution, retained their organs inside. The "two-sex" model, according to this view, was a later development in medical biology, dating from the late seventeenth and early eighteenth centuries, when specific terms for female anatomy began to be invented. The implications of this argument for early modern sexual culture have been taken to be the assertion of a standard "male" body, of which the female was a stage (stories abound in the popular literature of women who "became men" when pushed to feats of physical exertion). Critics of this view cite the midwives and others, writing at the same time as Galen (second century C.E.), who did posit something like the existence of two sexes, rather than one.

Arguably the interest in this fascinating set of debates has as much to do with modern and postmodern fantasies and anxieties about sex and gender as it does with Shakespeare. In his cross-dressing plays and in his sonnets and poems Shakespeare explores these boundaries with great intelligence and wit, as he will do again in the later tragedies with female figures of commanding power, like Lady Macbeth, Cleopatra, and Volumnia. He does not ordinarily address questions of gender and anatomy in the plays, although the well-known Sonnet 20, cited here and in my observations on *As You Like It*, contains his famous line about the "one thing to my purpose nothing." When Shakespeare does have his characters jest and dally about questions of anatomy, he often uses words like "thing," and "nothing," which were popular terms for sexual organs, and could indeed be used in reference to both men and women.

Anxieties about men "turning into" women were amply to be found in Puritan antitheatrical diatribes, where they were often linked, as we have seen, to the watching of stage plays and the seductiveness of gender impersonation. In staging a play that involved a set of male and female twins, identical except for gender, Shakespeare revisits ideas as old as Plato's *Symposium*, situating them deftly between the farce of mistaken identity, as in *The Comedy of Errors*, and the "wonderful" discoveries of prose romance. Insofar as historical and cultural considerations, especially in the history of science and medicine, can be taken to chart the climate of belief and expectation in any literary period, these debates are instructive, and, in their own right, intriguing. Questions of "masculinity" and "femininity" are addressed within *Twelfth Night* as much by signifying behaviors and traits (for example, willingness to fight versus fearfulness in combat, a standard by which poor Sir Andrew is "feminized") as by the physical body—sensibly enough, if the roles were initially designed for a same-sex stage. On such a stage, the distinction between "man" and "boy" might be as important, and as telling, as the distinction between "man" and "woman." As is so often the case with Shakespeare, a playwright whose work seems to "translate" so effectively into each new time period that every era—in many lands and many languages—has claimed him for its own, the plays themselves teach us what we need to know, and they speak, uncannily, through their figures and metaphors, to an underlying "material" substrate that can be located as securely in the reader's time as in the author's.

We might notice, too, the somewhat frantic, even fevered, nature of the comedy in the play: the farcical elements (the parade of injuries to Sir Andrew and Sir Toby inflicted by the manly Sebastian; the duel scene, with Sir Andrew and Viola/Cesario each quaking in fear of the other); the almost sado-masochistic images produced by both Olivia and Orsino in discussing their passions (he devoured by "fell and cruel hounds"; she like a bear tied to the stake); and, most of all, the cruel treatment meted out to Malvolio at the end of the play. It is as if the frenetic nature of the comedy, and its dark undertones—the constant shadow of death that haunts this play, its songs, and its black-dressed characters (Olivia, Malvolio)—and, indeed, the pressure put upon the question of gender identity and gender roles threaten to destabilize the happy endings.

Twelfth Night deals with the complexity of asking—and trying to answer—the question of gender on the English Renaissance stage. But the play is not only about the construction of human gender and sexuality in the "real world"; it is also about how to demonstrate that construction in the theater. This is Shakespeare's last cross-dressing play until 1609. *Twelfth Night* was written and performed in 1601. Queen Elizabeth died in 1603, and the cross-dressed woman disappears from Shakespeare's plays, until the figure of Imogen in the late romance *Cymbeline*. Perhaps this device, well-worn and familiar from prose romance and from other plays and playwrights, had simply exhausted its novelty, for a time. Or perhaps all the changes had been rung—again, for a time—on its fruitful and delightful complications. In later years, when Shakespeare returned to this problem of cross-gender identities, roles, traits, and characters, and their meaning for a society and a stage in transition, he would explore these boundaries in other contexts, like the bearded witches in *Macbeth*, the erotic role-swapping love games of Antony and Cleopatra, and the gender-defying sprites in *The Tempest*.

In the early years of its performance the most crowd-pleasing characters in *Twelfth Night* were Sir Toby, Sir Andrew, and Malvolio. The principal activities that occupy and preoccupy them are eating and drinking, singing and dancing. But theirs is not so much a festival as it is the shadow of a festival—dances without partners, eating and drinking without time or occasion, songs about holding your peace. The catalyst of this little world, its motive force, is resentment of Malvolio, the repressive spirit of self-love and usurping rule. Malvolio, as we have noted, is beset with what a modern observer would see as feelings of insecurity. He is all too clear in demonstrating his awareness of his place as a high-ranking employee in the household and his daydreams of aristocratic elevation.

He dreams of becoming Olivia's husband, and of disciplining Sir Toby as an equal (" 'You must amend your drunkenness' " [2.5.65]), and he takes great anticipatory pleasure in the fact that Olivia calls him "fellow." "[L]et this fellow be looked to," she instructs (3.4.57), and he swoons at the word. "Fellow!— not 'Malvolio,' nor after my degree, but 'fellow' " (70–71). This is another of his characteristic misreadings, for while "fellow" could mean "equal," "peer," or "partner," someone belonging to the same class (or "degree"), it could also denote something like the opposite: a servant or person of humble station, a member of the common people, or a person of little esteem or worth. Olivia does not, presumably, put into her choice of the word anything like the precision that Malvolio extracts from it, but in context her use of "fellow" could hardly be taken by the audience as a sign of equality.

The self-love of Malvolio, like its twin manifestations, that of Olivia and of Orsino, plunges the entire household, if not the entire world of Illyria, into something its inhabitants will constantly identify as "madness." This is a familiar Shakespearean middle state, which we recognize from plays like *The Comedy of Errors* to *Hamlet* and *King Lear*. But what does "madness" mean in *Twelfth Night*? As we might expect, it means different things to different people, and bears upon occasion different names, like "dream" and "wonder."

"My masters, are you mad? Or what are you?" This is Malvolio's reproof to the singing, drinking, and carousing of Sir Toby and his friends. To Malvolio, "madness" here is an aspect of morality, a breach of decorum, akin to bad manners. But it is Malvolio himself who will descend into apparent madness in this play, in part at least because of his own nature, his self-love and self-absorption, which are other forms of "madness," or delusion, for this play. In a way, Malvolio is already mad. He is so wrapped up in his own thoughts and fantasies that when Olivia dispatches him to "return" a ring she claims "Cesario" has given her, it never occurs to him that this is in fact a love token sent by the smitten Olivia to the handsome "Cesario." "She returns this ring to you, sir. You might have saved me my pains to have taken it away yourself," Malvolio says. "Come, sir, you peevishly threw it to her" (2.2.4–7, 11). In fact, when Viola, dressed as "Cesario," first arrives at Olivia's house, Malvolio is so self-absorbed that he fails to notice anything about the stranger's appearance:

Olivia	What kind o' man is he?
Malvolio	Why, of mankind.
Olivia	What manner of man?
Malvolio	Of very ill manner: he'll speak with you, will you or no.
Olivia	Of what personage and years is he?
Malvolio	Not yet old enough for a man, nor young enough for a boy; as a squash is before 'tis a peascod, or a codling when 'tis almost an apple. 'Tis with him in standing water between boy and man. He is very well-favoured, and speaks very shrewishly.

1.5.133–143

Like Orsino, and like Olivia herself, Malvolio sees and yet does not see. The undecidability of the young man's gender becomes transmuted into the liminal question of his age. This comic cross-purposes conversation is one that Shakespeare will use often, to good effect: when Juliet tries to get information from the Nurse, for example, or when Hamlet interrogates the gravedigger. It is perhaps a sign that Olivia is almost finished with her protracted period of mourning that she should show any curiosity about the visitor even before she has seen or met him. But Malvolio remains incurious and dismissive.

To Malvolio the only thing that matters is how people perceive him. It is no wonder that Maria can report seeing him "yonder i' the sun practicing behaviour to his own shadow this half-hour" (2.5.14–15). This is an attitude we have seen more self-mockingly struck by Richard III ("Shine out, fair sun, till I have bought a glass, / That I may see my shadow as I pass" [*Richard III* 1.2.249–250])—Malvolio suffers by the comparison. But "practicing behavior" is what Malvolio does all the time. His attitudizing is a parodic version—and inversion—of the empty-headed passion of Sir Andrew for all the supposed courtly skills of his rank ("O, had I but followed the arts!"). It is for this reason that Malvolio becomes not only, as he is, the one figure who links the two sectors of the household and therefore the two plots, mediating between Olivia and Sir Toby, but also, to his great dismay, the play's object lesson in what it means—in a comedy—to be "mad."

The clever Maria conceives her plan, the only fertile thing to come out of the "low" plot in Illyria. She will disguise her handwriting, counterfeiting Olivia's hand, and "drop in his way some obscure epistles of love" that seem to come from the lady of the house herself. Here, then, is another dangerous twinning, in a play replete with them. Sir Toby is so enthralled that he will swear, "I could marry this wench for this device" (2.5.158)—a pledge that tips the playwright's designing hand, and will come true. "Why, thou has put him in such a dream," Toby says, "that when the image of it leaves him, he must run mad" (168–169).

The scene is perhaps the most glorious comic scene in the play, as Malvolio, bowing and prancing and paying homage to his shadow, comes upon a letter on the ground. The onstage audience, Toby, Andrew, and Fabian, concealing themselves inadequately behind an ornamental shrub ("Get ye all three into the box-tree," commands Maria), provide a noisy commentary, as Malvolio embarks upon his short-lived career as a literary critic, and a would-be aristocrat. (Malvolio unquestionably runs away with the play, in almost any production, in part because of the sheer brilliance of this scene.) Like Shylock—a role often taken, in repertory companies, by the same actor—he is at once a figure of painful amusement and of pathos as he picks up the letter:

By my life, this is my lady's hand. These be her very c's, her u's, and her t's, and thus makes she her great P's. It is in contempt of question her hand.

2.5.77–80

This is guffaw-making stuff, as the prim, puritanical Malvolio spells out, apparently in all innocence, a cluster of forthright words for body parts and bodily actions. Whether the *c, u,* and *t* spell "cut" (apparently sometimes used with indecent innuendo in the period to denote a woman's genitals, and a word already introduced through the name of "Cesario") or are part of the more familiar four-letter word "cunt," they provoke a naïve response from the equally addled Sir Andrew ("Her c's, her u's, and her t's? Why that?" [2.5.81]) that underscores the joke. The moment is, again, comparable to one in *The Merchant of Venice,* when Salerio and Solanio mock Shylock's ostensible confusion of daughter and ducats, and ensure a laugh at his expense. "Great P's" may be, to Malvolio's mind, capital letters, but to a grosser imagination they are floods of urine ("pee" itself was originally a euphemism, the first letter of the ruder word "piss"). As various editors have pointed out, there is in the address of the letter (" 'To the unknown beloved, this, and my good wishes' " [2.5.82–83]) no letter *c* and no capital *P.* In other words, the playwright is having a joke on his character, who sails blithely on, himself magnificently unaware of the hilarity he has provoked in onlookers both onstage and offstage. He is intent only on decoding the letter:

> "Jove knows I love,
>   But who?
> Lips do not move,
>   No man must know."

"No man must know." What follows? The numbers altered [the meter changed].

"No man must know." If this should be thee, Malvolio?

. . . .

"I may command where I adore,
   But silence, like a Lucrece knife
With bloodless stroke my heart doth gore.
   M.O.A.I. doth sway my life."

. . . .

"I may command where I adore." Why, she may command me. I serve her, she is my lady. Why, this is evident to any formal capacity. There is no obstruction in this. And the end—what should that alphabetical position portend? If I could make that resemble something in me. Softly— "M.O.A.I." . . . "M." Malvolio—"M"—why, that begins my name. . . . "M." But then there is no consonancy in the sequel. That suffers under probation. "A" should follow, but "O" does. . . . "M.O.A.I." This simulation is not as the former; and yet to crush this a little, it would bow to me, for every one of these letters are in my name. Soft, here follows prose: "If this fall into thy hand, revolve. In my stars I am above thee, but be not afraid of greatness. Some are born great, some achieve greatness, and some have greatness thrust upon 'em. Thy fates open their hands, let thy blood and spirit embrace them, and to inure thyself to what thou art like to be, cast thy humble slough, and appear fresh. Be opposite with a kinsman, surly with servants. Let thy tongue tang arguments of state; put thyself into the trick of singularity. She thus advises thee that sighs for thee. Remember who commended thy yellow stockings, and wished to see thee ever cross-gartered. I say remember, go to, thou art made if thou desirest to be so; if not, let me see thee a steward still, the fellow of servants, and not worthy to touch Fortune's fingers. Farewell. She that would alter services with thee,

The Fortunate-Unhappy"

2.5.87–139

The sequence of reading and analysis or interpretation is interrupted, at each stage, by further ejaculations of ridicule from Fabian and Toby—again heard by the offstage audience but not by Malvolio. A comparable Shakespearean scene, once more from *The Merchant of Venice,* is the scene of the casket choice, in which two similarly oblivious and self-regarding readers, the Prince of Morocco and the Prince of Aragon, extract from the mottoes of the gold and silver caskets messages that seem to answer to their own desires. "M.O.A.I." is itself a great joke, like "ducdame" in *As You Like It,* that word that Jaques said meant "to call fools into a circle." In this case the willing "fools" have sometimes included editors and literary critics, eager to find a meaning that escapes the duller Malvolio. Thus these initials have been taken, for example, for the first letters of the four elements: Mare, Orbis, Aer, and Ignis.[1] The letter goes on, famously, to command him to wear yellow stockings, cross-gartered—that is, with criss-cross laces going up the entire length of the leg, a dandylike, and most un-Puritan, fashion, and one manifestly *out* of fashion in Illyria and in Olivia's house. (Though it is a fashion Malvolio has affected before, as he dreamily reminisces: "She did commend my yellow stockings of late, she did praise my leg, being cross-gartered" [2.5.145–146].) Only a few lines later, Maria, the actual author of the letter, will make it clear that Olivia was only being polite: "He will come to her in yellow stockings, and 'tis a colour she abhors, and cross-gartered, a fashion she detests" (2.5.173–175).

The letter also instructs him to smile—this steward whom Olivia has chosen because he is "sad and civil." And it includes a passage that has had a Malvolian afterlife of its own, cited and commended as Shakespearean wisdom: "Some are born great, some achieve greatness, and some have greatness thrust upon 'em." Shorn of its period contraction, presumably to make it more serious and, oddly, more "Shakespearean," this phrase appears everywhere, sometimes altered in order to make a deflating witticism. Thus Daniel J. Boorstin writes: "Shakespeare . . . divided great men into three classes: those born great, those who achieve greatness, and those who had greatness thrust upon them. It never occurred to him to mention those who hired public relations experts and press secretaries to make themselves look great."[2] But in its original context it is quite deflating enough, since it is presented as an adage that only a Malvolio would take at face value. Like so many other passages of Shakespearean "wisdom" ("Neither a borrower nor a lender be"; "All the world's a stage"; "Good name in man and woman . . . is the immediate jewel of their souls"), this one is embedded in a context, and given to a speaker—or an "author"—who gives the lie to its easy sentiments. The bromides may well be "true," or even true sans quotation marks. But Shakespeare's plays never produce these familiar maxims without some irony, at least of the dramatic variety.

"Some have greatness thrust upon 'em." There could hardly be a philosophy better suited to Malvolio's self-esteem and his concern about rank. He is to be the Cincinnatus of the pantry, called forth to serve, not his country, but his lady. And, in his dream of social climbing, he will indulge a transgressive fantasy of material entitlement. The sumptuary laws of the period, laws of consumption and expenditure that regulated excess in dress, food, and equipage, were explicit about what persons of any social status could or could not wear. As the Elizabethan statute of 1574 declared:

> The excess of apparel and the superfluity of unnecessary foreign wares thereto belonging now of late years is grown by sufferance to such an extremity that the manifest decay of the whole realm generally is like to follow (by bringing into the realm such superfluities of silks, cloths of gold, silver, and other most vain devices of so great cost for the quantity thereof as of necessity the moneys and treasures of the realm is and must be yearly conveyed out of the same to answer the same excess), but also particularly the wasting and undoing of a great number of young gentlemen, otherwise serviceable, and others seeking by show of apparel to be esteemed gentlemen, who, allured by the vain show of those things, do not only consume themselves, their goods, and lands which their parents left unto them, but also run into such debts and shifts as they cannot live out of danger of laws without attempting unlawful acts.[3]

It is sobering to think how pertinent the observations of this statute still seem today, a good example of why "early modern" is in fact the beginning of what we regard as modern life. Two matters that followed upon the enunciating of such a statute, and not without importance either for Elizabethan culture or for Shakespeare's plays, were the implicit encouragement for people, especially of a lesser "degree," to buy and wear only materials, like wool, produced and marketed in England, and what might be called the fantasy of a legible society, the assignment of dress codes, by rank, status, and degree, to various members of the social world, both men and women. Thus the particulars of such statutes ordinarily began with an overarching "None shall wear" or "None shall wear in his apparel," followed by a list of cloth and other materials appropriate to each rank. The negative way the regulations were posed made the rules of dress and luxuries both a restriction and an entitlement. Thus, for example, the 1574 statute ordained, "None shall wear in his apparel: Any silk of the color of purple, cloth of gold tissued, nor fur of sables, but only the King, Queen, King's mother, children, brethren, and sisters, uncles and aunts; and except dukes, marquises, and earls, who may wear the same in doublets, jerkins, linings of cloaks, gowns, and hose, and those of the Garter, purple in mantles only."

How does this affect *Twelfth Night*, and Malvolio's social-climbing pretensions in particular? His daydream is explicit:

> To be Count Malvolio! . . . There is example for't: the Lady of the Strachey married the yeoman of the wardrobe. . . . Having been three months married to her, sitting in my state— . . . Calling my officers about me, in my branched velvet gown, having come from a day-bed where I have left Olivia sleeping—
>
> *2.5.30–44*

"Branched velvet" is what we would today call "figured velvet," and the Elizabethan statute proscribed the wearing of such rich cloth by anyone except those of high estate: "[v]elvet in gowns, coats, or other uttermost garments" was restricted for the use of "dukes, marquises, earls, and their children; viscounts, barons, and knights . . . persons being of the Privy council," and also "barons' sons, knights, and gentlemen in ordinary office attendant upon her majesty's person, and such as have been employed in embassages to foreign princes." So Malvolio's daydream is presumptuous in every detail. He imagines himself rising from a daybed where he has been sleeping with Olivia (here we might compare the image of "lolling on a lewd day-bed" from *Richard III,* where the phrase clearly implies dissoluteness [3.7.72]). He sees himself wrapped in a branched velvet gown and commanding "officers." And—risibly to an early modern audience—he misunderstands the structure of the English peerage, wrongly anticipating that marriage to a countess would make him a count. (The rank of "count"—originally denoting the feudal lordship over a "county"—was equivalent to the English "earl," below a marquis but above a viscount.) According to the British system of peerage, if Olivia were to marry another peer, or titleholder, she would lose her courtesy title (derived from her father) and gain whatever title she would have as the wife of a peer. Should she marry a commoner, like Malvolio or Sebastian, she would retain her courtesy title, but would substitute her new surname for her maiden name ("the Lady Malvolio"? Is "Malvolio" his first name or his last name?). Her commoner husband would certainly not accede to her father's, or brother's, title. (I am presuming here that Illyria = England, following the custom of other Shakespearean plays. The real or geographical Illyria, a district of the Balkan peninsula which had earlier been under the jurisdiction of the popes and then of the Slavic Dalmatians and Croatians, was conquered in the fourteenth and fifteenth centuries by the

Turks, and did not reappear on European maps until the very end of the seventeenth century. In Shakespeare's time, "Illyria" would have been a place-name without a place.)

In Malvolio's reading and interpretation of the letter, Shakespeare thus provides a classic example of self-delusion, and of literary criticism turned inward upon the speaker, finding him, and him alone, the subject of the literary work. But the audience may find itself wondering whether the playwright is being "unfair," tricking Malvolio into humiliation and madness by this clever strategy, a variant of the play-within-the play. Such a sympathetic accusation, protecting the unwitting character against the too-witty author, would be more convincing if Malvolio had not, in thought, word, and action, already laid the groundwork for his own vainglorious fantasies and ignominious fall. In fact, the whole of Maria's letter is merely a counterpart of his daydreaming thoughts, as he saunters down the garden path toward his unfortunate destiny. (Such a ruse would not work, for example, with Sebastian, or indeed with "Cesario.") We might better see Shakespeare not as resorting to gimmicks, but rather as creating a theatrical counterpart for a psychological state. Malvolio thinks these things, and suddenly a letter falls at his feet proclaiming them to be true. A later era would call this "magical thinking"—a term coined by anthropologists to describe the nonscientific causal reasoning they encountered in other cultures. Magic, of course, was still alive and well in the Renaissance, where it was in many ways a precursor to modern science rather than science's opposite. In magical thinking, an individual may believe that his or her thoughts can influence events. In the realm of character and psychology, as with Malvolio, it becomes a species of wish or of wish fulfillment. And for the theater, such magical thinking becomes a highly effective way of externalizing and dramatizing thought.

In terms of comedy, Maria's letter invites Malvolio to change his costume, to put on what in other plays is a version of disguise. For Viola, as we have seen, disguising herself as "Cesario" is both freeing, in terms of action, and constraining, because she cannot "tell her love." In the main, her costume change does offer her mobility and imaginative space—as is also the case with other Shakespearean disguisers, from the "Muscovites" of *Love's Labour's Lost* to Prince Hal to Portia and Rosalind. But what effect does disguise, or change of costume, have upon Malvolio? It confirms him, emblematically, in his own repression. When he appears before Olivia in act 3, scene 4—ironically, she has sent for him because "[h]e is sad and civil, / And suits well for a servant with my fortunes" (3.4.5–6)—he is wearing his yellow stockings, cross-gartered, and, as Maria noted in an earlier scene, he "does smile his face into more lines than is in the new map with the augmentation of the Indies" (3.2.66–68):

> Malvolio   Sweet lady, ho, ho!
> Olivia   Smil'st thou? I sent for thee upon a sad occasion.

> Malvolio   Sad, lady? I could be sad. This does make some obstruction in
> the blood, this cross-gartering, but what of that?
>
> *3.4.17–20*

Malvolio's costume visibly confirms him in what he is—obstructed, repressed, blocked. We may recall his confident decoding of the counterfeit letter: "Why, this is evident to any formal capacity. There is no obstruction in this." Maria's trick, a clever psychological reading of Malvolio's character, intensifies his own characteristics, and causes "some obstruction" in the blood. "Why, this is very midsummer madness," Olivia will decide (midsummer at Christmas, the world doubly turned upside down). And who can blame her?

Meantime Fabian, seeing Sir Andrew Aguecheeck enter with another letter—a challenge to "Cesario" to fight over the courtship of Olivia, "writ," as Toby had instructed him, "in a martial hand"—announces, "More matter for a May morning." Sir Andrew's challenge is foolish enough, modeled on the same comic principle as the Prologue to the "Pyramus and Thisbe" play in *A Midsummer Night's Dream,* with its false logic, odd syntax, and mispunctuated style. " 'Youth, whatsoever thou art, thou art but a scurvy fellow,' " Sir Toby reads. " 'Wonder not, nor admire not in thy mind why I do call thee so, for I will show you no reason for it' " (3.4.133–134, 136–137). Yet at least Sir Andrew is tempered by a little self-knowledge: "I knew 'twas I, for many do call me fool" (2.5.72). Malvolio's folly, which is to say, his excessive self-esteem, is punished in the play far more harshly than Sir Andrew's. Andrew loses his horse, "grey Capulet," as Fabian and Toby conspire to make each of the hapless combatants think the other is "the most skillful, bloody, and fatal opposite that you could possibly have found in any part of Illyria" (3.4.237–238). But on Sir Toby's orders, Malvolio is taken to a dark room and bound. "Why, we shall make him mad indeed," says Fabian, and Maria responds pragmatically, "The house will be the quieter" (3.4.119–120).

Again Malvolio's onstage fate is emblematic of his character. He will be taken to a dark room and bound. But has he not, in a sense, always been there, bound—as the cross-garters bind him, and as he is bound by his own lack of joy and his repressive censoriousness? Malvolio has the temperament to be an eager Egeus, forbidding a daughter's marriage, or a Duke Frederick, condemning a brother and a niece to banishment. It is his misfortune that he is not born to such heights of tyranny. (Some are born great, some achieve greatness . . .) And so he is taken away and bound in a dark room; it is the perfect material analogue for his mental and emotional condition. The physical prison is the imagistic counterpart of the interior prison he has always inhabited. And here we may think again about Olivia's self-cloistering, her chosen imprisonment, watering "once a day her chamber round / With eye-offending brine."

In the dark prison hole where they place him, Malvolio is visited by the one character in this play capable of judging him, Feste, the fool, who is not part of society, or in this play part of the world of sexuality, marriage, or governance. He is a spirit not only of feasting but also of realism and good sense, and, pre-eminently, of language and language-play. It is of perception that he comes to speak to Malvolio, himself pretending to be Sir Topas the curate:

> Feste   Sayst thou that house is dark?
> Malvolio   As hell, Sir Topas.
> Feste   Why, it hath bay windows transparent as barricadoes, and the
>   clerestories toward the south-north are as lustrous as ebony,
>   and yet complainest thou of obstruction?
> Malvolio   I am not mad, Sir Topas; I say to you this house is dark.
> Feste   Madman, thou errest. I say there is no darkness but ignorance,
>   in which thou art more puzzled than the Egyptians in their fog.
>
> 4.2.30–39

The fool here speaks deliberate nonsense: transparent as barricades; lustrous as ebony; a direction called "south-north." "Egyptians" in this instance are unbe-lievers, another glance at the Twelfth Night occasion, and their "fog" is one of the biblical plagues, continuing the theme of pestilence. But the darkness of ignorance in which Malvolio is trapped is the ignorance of self that has beset him all along. It is the same "obstruction" that bound his legs in their cross-garters, the obstruction he failed to find in the language of Maria's letter. And yet there is something pathetic in Malvolio's situation, something almost cruel and dangerous in the extremes to which his adversaries go. Something of the discomfort an audience feels at the comeuppance of Shylock may well also affect our response to the "baffled" Malvolio. Even Sir Toby senses that things may have gone too far. "I would," he says to Maria, "we were well rid of this knavery. If he may be conveniently delivered, I would he were, for I am now so far in offence with my niece that I cannot pursue with any safety this sport to the upshot" (4.2.60–63).

Toby's "I would we were well rid of this knavery," like Orlando's structurally similar remark in *As You Like It,* "I can no longer live by thinking," rejecting the continued fiction of "Ganymede" as "Rosalind," signals the beginning of the end of the revels. But Malvolio is still unable to be freed, unable to free himself: "Fool, fool, fool, I say. . . . I tell thee I am as well in my wits as any man in Illyria" (4.2.95, 98–99). But in Illyria it seems as if they are all mad, all obsessed with self—which is one definition of madness in this play.

It will take a stranger to Illyria to set them free, and that stranger appears in the very next scene. He is, of course, Sebastian, the active, vital counterpart to Olivia's crop of foolish, passive, posturing suitors, Sir Andrew, Malvolio—and even, perhaps, the admirable but mannered Orsino. No sooner has the audience registered Malvolio's complaints about the darkness of his prison cell than it hears these exultant lines spoken by Sebastian in the next scene:

This is the air, that is the glorious sun.
This pearl she gave me, I do feel't and see't,
And though 'tis wonder that enwraps me thus,
Yet 'tis not madness. . . .

                    4.3.1–4

From enclosure we have moved into the light of the open air. In a play so very much concerned with the four elements, we can see those elements distributed across the dramatic characters. "Are all the people mad?" Sebastian wonders aloud (4.1.24), having met Feste at his most obnoxious and Sir Andrew at his usual level of idiocy. But for Sebastian madness soon acquires a different quality, the alternative and opposite to the stultifying self-blindness of Malvolio's dark room. "Or I am mad, or else this is a dream," he will say (4.1.57) as Olivia sweeps down and—thinking he is "Cesario"—claims him for her lover.

Dream and madness are closely related, but the former, at least in Shakespearean comedy, is allied to wish fulfillment, imagination, and creative possibility, while the latter is associated with mental disorder, repression, and imprisonment. When Viola, masquerading as "Cesario," learned that Sebastian might still be alive, she exclaimed her anticipatory pleasure: "Prove true, imagination, O prove true, / That I, dear brother, be now ta'en for you!" (3.4.340–341). And with the appearance of Sebastian in the fourth act, imagination does prove true. This is, after all, the function of the freeing middle world of Shakespeare's comedies—and, to a certain extent, of all of his plays. But Malvolio, released at last from his physical prison, is still not "delivered," in Olivia's phrase, by the play's end.

"[T]ell me," he asks Olivia in the play's last scene, "Why you have given me such clear lights of favour," and

> Why have you suffered me to be imprisoned,
> Kept in a dark house, visited by the priest,
> And made the most notorious geck and gull
> That e'er invention played on? Tell me why?
>
>   *5.1.324–325, 330–333*

The question is both poignant and pertinent, pointing to the necessary limits of revel, about which Sir Toby was so concerned. We may recall Sir Andrew Aguecheek's inability to comprehend the meaning of the word *pourquoi*. At this point *Twelfth Night* almost moves beyond the bounds of comedy and toward another kind of accountability, another kind of moral inquiry. Yet as the plot is explained, both to the mortified Malvolio and to the court people, Olivia is moved to compassion. With the overt designation of Malvolio as "fool," in context a term of endearment, the exchange is underscored. The play's fool, Feste, "Sir Topas," has been the wise man; the officious and overbearing Malvolio is the fool:

Olivia	[*to* MALVOLIO] Alas, poor fool, how have they baffled thee!
Feste	Why, "Some are born great, some achieve greatness, and some have greatness thrown upon them." I was one, sir, in this interlude, one Sir Topas, sir; but that's all one. . . . [B]ut do you remember, "Madam, why laugh you at such a barren rascal, an you smile not, he's gagged"—and thus the whirligig of time brings in his revenges.
Malvolio	I'll be revenged on the whole pack of you.

5.1.358–365

A "whirligig" is a top, a child's spinning toy. The modern cliché would be "What goes around, comes around." Malvolio's final line, his despairing, humiliated exit—"I'll be revenged on the whole pack of you"—sums up the degree to which he has failed to learn from the experience of the play. Viola and Sebastian confront each other in that moment of "wonder" straight out of romance. But Malvolio, the product of self-love in Illyria, can only stalk away, gathering the tattered remnants of his pride around him. He has learned nothing. He excludes himself from the Christmas miracle, and from the comic circle of accommodation and love. We could say that he elects to be a malcontent, to walk away from the world of comedy, which has treated him so ill, and toward another great Elizabethan genre, the revenge tragedy—the genre of *Hamlet*.

As for Feste, it is impossible to imagine him, like Touchstone, married. He seems less like a person than like a sprite or a spirit of music, as much akin to Puck as he is to Touchstone—and yet he is painfully human. His haunting songs both fill and frame the play. Feste's isolation, the fool's isolation, is finally the real isolation in this play of comedy, wonder, and epiphany. A paid clown knows the limits of clowning. A fool whose element is holiday knows the effort implicit in the final lines of his final song:

> A great while ago the world begun,
>> With hey, ho, the wind and the rain,
> But that's all one, our play is done,
>> And we'll strive to please you every day.

5.1.392–395

To please you "every day," to make every day a holiday, is in some sense the role of drama, and especially of dramatic comedy. The fool stands here in the liminal place of the epilogue, parallel to Puck in his play and Rosalind in hers, appealing across the boundary between actor and audience. But the material conditions of society push insistently in, like the wind and the rain.

The confined and magical world of Shakespearean comedy, with its green world and its rigid dukes and laws made to be broken, its holidays and its transformation, is a crucial part of experience as Shakespeare allegorizes it for his audience, but it is not the whole of that experience. And the growth of exclusion in these plays, the strength of the excluded characters, the disappearance of those marriage dances in which Renaissance poets imitated the harmony of the spheres, indeed, the remanding of the contracted marriages to a time and space outside or after the play, the emergence of the clear, plaintive voice of the fool—all these point toward a new phase in Shakespeare's dramatic development, a broader, more painful, but often a staggeringly beautiful and profound vision of humankind in the midst of a tragic universe. For the next time the audience encounters Feste's final song, that song will be sung to a mad king in the middle of a raging storm, by Lear's nameless and tragic Fool:

> He that has and a little tiny wit,
> With heigh-ho, the wind and the rain,
> Must make content with his fortunes fit,
> Though the rain it raineth every day.
>
> King Lear *3.2.73–76*

Troilus and Cressida

DRAMATIS PERSONAE

TROJANS

Priam, *King of Troy*
Hector, *Priam's son*
Deiphobus, *Priam's son*
Helenus, *a priest, and Priam's son*
Paris, *Priam's son*
Troilus, *Priam's son*
Margareton, *a bastard by King Priam*
Cassandra, *Priam's daughter,*
  a prophetess
Andromache, *wife of Hector*
Aeneas, *a commander*

Antenor, *a commander*
Pandarus, *a lord*
Cressida, *his niece*
Calchas, *her father, who has*
  joined the Greeks
Helen, *wife of Menelaus, now*
  living with Paris
Alexander, *servant of Cressida*
Servants of Troilus, musicians,
  soldiers, attendants

GREEKS

Agamemnon, *Commander-in-Chief*
Menelaus, *his brother*
Nestor
Ulysses
Achilles
Patroclus, *his companion*

Diomedes
Ajax
Thersites
Myrmidons, soldiers of Achilles
Servants of Diomedes, soldiers

ROILUS AND CRESSIDA occupies a curious and slightly anomalous place within the Shakespearean canon. On the title pages of the Quarto of 1609 it is described as a "Historie." But in the First Folio of 1623 it is called *The Tragedie of Troylus and Cressida*. In the Folio the play is not listed in the table of contents (the "Catalogue of the Several Comedies, Histories, and Tragedies contained in this Volume"), and it is placed after the last of the history plays and before the first of the tragedies. In a prefatory letter included in the Quarto it is several times described as a "comedy," a word that in the period might mean merely "a play," but it is twice there explicitly called "comical" in a context that makes the meaning clear. The question of how the play might be best classified, and therefore of how to assess—and perform—it, has preoccupied readers over the years.

Nineteenth-century scholars invented a category they called the "problem play," a term borrowed from the works of dramatists of the time (Ibsen, Shaw, Strindberg, and others) whose plays were thought to engage with ongoing social problems (environmental issues, women's rights, venereal disease, prostitution). To those scholars, some Shakespeare plays seemed similarly preoccupied with issues of morality and public and private behavior; in this category they included not only *Troilus and Cressida* but also *All's Well That Ends Well, Measure for Measure,* and *Hamlet.* These plays were sometimes categorized as "cynical," as questioning the possibility of noble or heroic ideals, and as concerned with the less exalted aspects of sexual desire and social critique. This grouping of "problem plays" allowed for the segregation of these more troubled works from apparently more joyous comedies and allowed a deferral of the "problem" of their genre identification—although *The Merchant of Venice,* for example, became increasingly difficult not to think of as a "problem" comedy rather than a "festive" comedy. Another popular designation was "dark comedy," which, like "problem play," drew attention to the difference between plays like *Troilus and Cressida* and Shakespeare's earlier comic works. Both of these terms were operative through at least the first half of the twentieth century, and were gradually superseded when more and more plays, formerly regarded as "light," began to seem "dark," "problematic," unresolved, erotic, and engaged with early modern social, economic, and political concerns.

In any case, the genre of satire and the tone of cynical disillusionment, about everything from sex to war, detected in *Troilus and Cressida* has led not only scholars but also actors, directors, and readers to think of this play as surprisingly "modern" in its outlook, at the same time that it grounds itself in the action of Western civilization's founding event, the Trojan War. Productions of the play have often stressed its paradigmatic status as a play about the noble folly and futility of war, setting the action in the U.S. Civil War (Union Greeks versus Confederate Trojans) or in a variety of twentieth-century conflicts from World War I to Vietnam and the Persian Gulf. There have also been powerful productions that have conflated historical periods, dressing some soldiers as Greeks, some as Boers, some as Rough Riders or storm troopers, some as modern guerrillas. The effect is to generalize about all warfare, its glories and its ignominies, rather than to present or judge the events of a particular conflict. Often productions seem counterpoised between two celebrated utterances of the irreverent Thersites: his redaction of the Trojan War, "All the argument is a whore and a cuckold," and his judgment on the events of the play, "Lechery, lechery, still wars and lechery! Nothing else holds fashion." The emergence in the play of mercantile language, language of buying, selling, trading, and the marketplace, rivaling and replacing the older language of courtly aristocracy, challenge, and honor, would have had as much resonance for the Elizabethan court and audience as it has pertinence to ancient Greece and Troy. This shift from old to new economic verities, as Ulysses speaks of showing foul wares before fair ones and hoping they will sell, is another mark of "modernity" often seized upon by actors and directors. The commodities traded by Ulysses are *heroes*, Ajax chosen over the more highly valued Achilles; a comparable trade in *women* measures the relative market value of a Helen against that of a Cressida.

In some ways we might say that *Troilus and Cressida*, in its puzzling, irresolute quality; its movement back and forth from comedy to cynicism, love to war; its internal debate between idealistic Trojans and pragmatic Greeks; and its failure to generate any *action* at all until the final scenes, is a play that might almost have been written by Hamlet.

In *Hamlet* the old play from which the First Player declaims with such passion is Aeneas's tale to Dido, the story of the fall of Troy and the death of the Trojan King Priam. Hamlet's response to the recitation—which he had requested—seems to establish both the play and its subject matter as belonging to a lost older order, ancient, formal, and heroic, that bears comparison with the lost reign of his own heroic father, another beloved father-king, likewise murdered. The fall of Troy was, then, a mythic event of considerable power, suggesting the end of a noble and ancient civilization, a lost race of heroes. In fact, the fall of Troy could be associated, as well, with a fall of a different kind, the fall of Adam and Eve, and their expulsion from Eden. It is the action of Paris, the Trojan prince, in seizing Helen from her husband, Menelaus, that is the efficient cause of the war.

With this epic background in mind, from the *Iliad* to the *Aeneid*, it is all the more surprising to find Shakespeare's Greeks quarreling among themselves like peevish schoolboys, and to find Paris and Helen singing away to the accompaniment of a lute. Instead of going out to battle, Achilles and Patroclus improvise comic imitations of the Greek leaders for their own amusement. The audience is confronted with a tremendous loss of idealism, with a debased ideal. The loss is on two levels, political and personal, war and love. There are in fact *two* courtships dramatized in the plot of *Troilus and Cressida*:

- The Greeks woo Achilles, trying to get him out of his bed and onto the battlefield;
- Troilus woos Cressida, trying to get her into bed.

These two courtships, one apparently for war, the other apparently for love, will become, in the course of the play, inextricably intertwined. Both love objects play hard to get. Achilles will lose value if he continues to resist; Cressida will lose value if she consents.

The Trojan heroes are depicted as romantic idealists, putting their faith in the imagination and in outmoded codes like chivalry—codes that the new, fallen world (the world of money, mercenaries, and Myrmidons) will neither justify nor support. The Trojans are emotional, excessive, ruled by passion, dominated by the fact that they have seized Helen and must defend her. Pandarus embodies the residue of these qualities without the moral or ethical theory to sustain them: he is, increasingly, a voice for erotic opportunism, and by the close he has devolved into the patron of "traders in the flesh" and "[b]rethren and sisters of the hold-door trade." The Greeks, on the other hand, appear to be rationalists, or to think of themselves, at least, in that light. Half of them are "brains," like Ulysses, who believes in policy and pragmatism, in high-sounding words, and in tricking people for political gain. The other half are brawn, like the "beef-witted" Ajax, and even Achilles, sullen, sulking gladiators—fighters who refuse to fight out of misplaced pride. Their version of the voyeuristic Pandarus is the scurrilous and foul-mouthed Thersites, who functions like an allowed fool in the Greek camp, giving voice to what the Greeks already think and fear. What has happened to heroic civilization? To the possibility for epic fulfillment and national pride?

What would Shakespeare and his audience have known about the Trojan War, and about Troilus and Cressida?

It is worth recalling that the histories of Britain and Troy were intertwined, and Troy was regarded as the birthplace of the English nation. The early inhabitants of Britain traced their heritage to Brutus, the great-grandson of Aeneas, who had fled the burning city of Troy and journeyed to Rome. (Aeneas's story is told in Virgil's *Aeneid*, the foundation myth of Roman literature.) Brutus, whose followers were called Britons, landed in Alban (Albion, the "white island") in about 1074 B.C.E., and the island became known as Britain. Its principal city was initially named New Troy ("Troia Newydd," or "Troynovant," or "Trinovantum"), and only became Londinium (from "Lud's Town," or "Caer-Ludd") in the first century B.C.E. The story of the Trojan War, and of the Greeks and the Trojans, was thus of considerable interest for its perceived value as part of the longer history of England, as well as because of the humanist recovery of classical texts.

In choosing the story of the Trojan War for his subject, Shakespeare was turning his attention to the great model of heroism in Western culture and Western literature, the model of heroic behavior, the source of archetypal examples of what it meant to be a hero, a king, a statesman. And, equally important, he was writing about the land that was the mythic birthplace of England. Brutus was known as the father of the race of British kings. English literature from Chaucer's time to Shakespeare's repeated this story. John Lydgate's *Troy Book*, commissioned by Henry V, was a monumental poem of some thirty thousand lines, in five books, telling the story to the advantage of the Trojans, especially Troilus and Hector. (Homer, thought Lydgate, was a Greek sympathizer whose praise of Achilles merits particular scorn.) The Trojan War was treated by Shakespeare's contemporaries Edmund Spenser and Michael Drayton. Seven books of George Chapman's translation of Homer's *Iliad* (the same translation about which John Keats would write with a sense of joyful discovery two centuries later) were available by the early years of the seventeenth century.

Furthermore, a quarrel between "Greeks" and "Trojans" would have had more than one meaning for Shakespeare and his time, since the humanists, sixteenth-century educational reformers in the newly emerging universities and schools, chose to employ those names for the two educational factions warring at Oxford. The "Greeks" supported the learning of classical language and literature, while the "Trojans" preferred the old medieval curriculum—and the old social hierarchies. Shakespeare's Trojan War, like the war between the academics and scholars of his day, is concerned with language and representation, and with the construction of selves and the idea of the self.

But we should note that Troilus makes only a cameo appearance in the *Iliad*, and Cressida is never mentioned. Their story was transmitted, instead, through medieval poetry and chivalric romance. The best-known and most influential source here would have been Chaucer's wonderful poem *Troilus and Criseyde*, with its enticingly sexy and morally ambivalent heroine, there memorably described as "slydyng of corage." But Cressida's considerable fame by the time of Shakespeare had also meant that she had endured certain attacks on her character by more "moralistic" critics, including the Scottish poet Robert Henryson in his *Testament of Cresseid*. Shakespeare's Pandarus is more a modern "pander," and less a knightly companion, than the Pandarus of Chaucer's version.

Troilus is the archetypal lover familiar from medieval romance, and from Petrarchan literature. His example is cited over and over again in Shakespeare's comedies. In *The Merchant of Venice*, Lorenzo, talking to Jessica in the moonlight, compares himself romantically to Troilus: "[I]n such a night / Troilus, methinks, mounted the Trojan walls, / And sighed his soul toward the Grecian tents / Where Cressid lay that night" (*Merchant* 5.1.3–6). In *As You Like It*, Rosalind ridicules Troilus as a hopeless romantic idealist, exactly his character in the play that bears his name: "Troilus had his brains dashed out with a Grecian club, yet he did what he could to die before, and he is one of the patterns of love." She adds to this, good-humoredly, her own distinctive and deflating coda: "Men have died from time to time, and worms have eaten them, but not for love" (*As You Like It* 4.1.83–86, 91–92). Even Feste, the fool in *Twelfth Night*, assumes that his audience knows the story of Troilus, Cressida, and Pandarus. Having received one coin as remuneration for his singing, he begs another: "I would play Lord Pandarus of Phrygia, sir, to bring a Cressida to this Troilus" (*Twelfth Night* 3.1.45–46). Troilus and Cressida were for Shakespeare's audience as much a cliché as Romeo and Juliet are for the present day.

Troilus and Cressida begins with a Prologue, played by an actor dressed in armor, ready for battle and speaking in a language of high seriousness:

> In Troy there lies the scene. From isles of Greece
> The princes orgulous, their high blood chafed,
> Have to the port of Athens sent their ships,
> Fraught with the ministers and instruments
> Of cruel war. . . .
>
> Troilus and Cressida *Prologue 1–5*

The word "orgulous," which means "proud," appears in Shakespeare only in this passage, underscoring the formality of the moment, all too soon to be replaced by casual disarray. The task of the Prologue is to tell the whole story of the Trojan War in a few lines, and he succeeds remarkably well: "[T]heir vow is made / To ransack Troy, within whose strong immures / The ravished Helen, Menelaus' queen, / With wanton Paris sleeps—and that's the quarrel." Like other Shakespearean Prologues, notably in *Henry V,* this speaker urges the audience to see what cannot be put on any stage, and to take part in the excitement of the moment:

> Now expectation, tickling skittish spirits
> On one and other side, Trojan and Greek,
> Sets all on hazard. And hither am I come,
> A Prologue armed—but not in confidence
> Of author's pen or actor's voice, but suited
> In like conditions as our argument—
> To tell you, fair beholders, that our play
> Leaps o'er the vaunt and firstlings of those broils,
> Beginning in the middle, starting thence away
> To what may be digested in a play.
>
> *Prologue 20–29*

Following the example of the *Iliad, Troilus and Cressida* will begin in medias res, in the middle of things. Here the "things" are not warlike, as we might expect, but languid and romantic. The "Prologue armed" has no sooner finished his lines than Troilus and Pandarus enter upon the stage, and Troilus delivers his first line to the audience: "Call here my varlet. I'll unarm again" (1.1.1). He will unarm, instead of arm for battle. And the cause is familiar—the civil war inside him, provoked by love:

> Why should I war without the walls of Troy
> That find such cruel battle here within?
>
> *1.1.2–3*

This language of arming and unarming, artfully established from the very beginning of the play, will continue throughout, and will provide the underlying design of a plot that mingles love and war with tragic results for both. In his love-play with Helen, Paris, who has, significantly, stayed behind to dally rather than going into the field, invites her to greet the returning warriors:

> Sweet Helen, I must woo you
> To help unarm our Hector. His stubborn buckles,
> With these your white enchanting fingers touched,
> Shall more obey than to the edge of steel

Or force of Greekish sinews. You shall do more
Than all the island kings: disarm great Hector.

3.1.139–144

In the fourth act, Hector appears armed for battle, intending to meet the Greek champion in single combat, but declines to fight Ajax because they are cousins—as Aeneas notes, Ajax is a "blended knight, half Trojan and half Greek" (4.6.88)—and he would not wish to spill a drop of Trojan blood. Instead Hector accepts an invitation from Ajax to visit the "Grecian tents," and Diomedes seconds the invitation, saying that " great Achilles / Doth long to see unarmed the valiant Hector" (4.7.36–37).

Like so much of the language in the play, this apparently straightforward statement is both double-edged and fateful. In the final battle in act 5, scene 9, Achilles, enraged at the slaying of his beloved Patroclus, comes upon Hector, disarmed from a day of battle, and—rather than fighting him one-on-one—surrounds him with his mercenary Myrmidons. "I am unarmed," says Hector. "Forgo this vantage, Greek" (5.9.9). But Achilles gives the command to strike, and then ties the body of the slain Trojan hero ignominiously to his horse's tail, to drag him along the field. "My half-supped sword, that frankly would have fed, / Pleased with this dainty bait, thus goes to bed," he says (5.9.19–20). Even this coy language, as Achilles sheathes his weapon, distinguishes him from the blunt nobility of Hector, who moments before had declared merely, "Rest, sword: thou hast thy fill of blood and death" (5.9.4). The plot of "unarming," predicted by the language of Troilus ("I'll unarm") and of Paris ("unarm our Hector"), thus comes to its inevitable end with the death of Hector, this play's one unambiguous old-style hero, a champion of the same mettle as old Hamlet, and with the same penchant for single combat as Tybalt and Hotspur, though without their splenetic temper. Hector dies, as he has lived, for glory, and love of country. Significantly, in the last scenes he is in pursuit of a mysterious figure described in the stage directions merely as "one in armour," a Greek whose costume represents the honorable spoils of war:

Hector   Stand, stand, thou Greek! Thou art a goodly mark.
           No? Wilt thou not? I like thy armour well.
           I'll frush it and unlock the rivets all,
           But I'll be master of it.

5.6.27–30

Tellingly, Hector's two scenes with the "one in armour" (5.6 and 5.9) are intercut with brief episodes that display Achilles' unsportsmanlike conduct on the battlefield, instructing the Myrmidons to surround Hector and kill him in "fellest manner" (5.7.6), and the cowardice of Thersites (5.8). Historians of ancient warfare and of sword-fighting point out that prizes like the "goodly armour," taken on the battlefield, are signs of the victor's heroism. But the encounter with the "one in armour," who never speaks, and who is the proximate cause of Hector's own death, has always seemed to me to carry another, more uncanny resonance, as if Hector were coming face-to-face with Death itself—and with his own mortality: "Most putrefièd core [i.e., corpse], so fair without, / Thy goodly armour thus has cost thy life" (5.9.1–2).

Troilus and Cressida thus traces the ambit from the "Prologue armed" to the "one in armour," enclosing within itself another story, the story of the unarming and disarming of heroes. The Prologue, a common soldier, had spoken of his battle gear as "suited / In like conditions as our argument," with the word "argument" connoting both a plot and a quarrel. But we will hear the same word in the voice of the cynical Greek Thersites, who sums up the stakes of the conflict, unforgettably, in a single line: "All the argument is a whore and a cuckold" (2.3.65). To him this is the true, unvarnished story of the Trojan War. Helen is the whore; Menelaus the cuckold. But if this is the "argument" of the war, what is the "argument" of the play? Are these terms equally applicable to Cressida and Troilus, the first of whom betrays the second with Diomedes? The play is well designed both to provide a set of ideals and worldviews in conflict, and to show the way they are undercut by their own excess.

Not surprisingly, this play of resounding speeches and epic heroes has generated a quest for Shakespeare's own "philosophy." Such quests are always doomed to failure, because dramatic structure allows for many characters to express diametrically opposed opinions without a conducting authorial voice. Compelling ideas about humanity, mortality, and society are as likely to be found in the lines assigned to clowns or nameless "gentlemen" as in those assigned to certifiable "tragic heroes." In *Troilus and Cressida* Ulysses speaks, in a passage that has become a famous set piece, about the role of hierarchy and "degree." This classic statement of what has been called, by Arthur O. Lovejoy and others, the "great chain of being" describes a worldview in which the universe was imagined as an ordered cosmos, hierarchically linked to systems above and below, and regulated by a benevolent providence. Although Lovejoy suggested that this conception of the world was one that "most educated men were to accept without question," it is clear from Shakespeare's plays, and indeed from Ulysses' speech and its aftermath, that such a view was both contestable and contested. Nonetheless, and especially when taken out of context and presented as "Shakespeare's" idea rather than Ulysses', this passage has been widely admired. As we will see shortly, it is not entirely clear that even Ulysses subscribes to it, however eloquent his public thoughts on the question.

The setting is a council meeting of Greek leaders, gathered outside Agamemnon's tent early in the play, the third scene of the first act, to discuss the problem of winning the war against the Trojans. Why have they not succeeded? Indeed, why have they been waiting outside the gates of Troy for seven

years, making no progress? Agamemnon suggests that the gods are merely testing them:

> Why then, you princes,
> Do you with cheeks abashed behold our works,
> And call them shames, which are indeed naught else
> But the protractive trials of great Jove
> To find persistive constancy in men?
>
> *1.3.16–20*

Old Nestor has a different view. The issue is not one of suffering patiently, but
of action: "In the reproof of chance / Lies the true proof of men" (1.3.32–33).
This is a time for boldness (the "tiger" rather than the "herd"). The greater the
challenge, the more glorious the victory. Ulysses, graciously acknowledging the
stature of both previous speakers ("Agamemnon, . . . nerve and bone of Greece,
/ Heart of our numbers"; "venerable Nestor, hatched in silver" [1.3.53–55, 64]),
responds:

> Degree being vizarded,
> Th' unworthiest shows as fairly in the masque.
> [   ].[1]
> The heavens themselves, the planets, and this centre
> Observe degree, priority, and place,
> Infixture, course, proportion, season, form,
> Office and custom, in all line of order.
>
> . . . .
>
> But when the planets
> In evil mixture to disorder wander,
> What plagues and what portents, what mutiny?
> What raging of the sea, shaking of earth?
> Commotion in the winds, frights, changes, horrors
> Divert and crack, rend and deracinate
> The unity and married calm of states
> Quite from their fixture. O when degree is shaked,
> Which is the ladder to all high designs,
> Then enterprise is sick. How could communities,
> Degrees in schools, and brotherhoods in cities,
> Peaceful commerce from dividable shores,
> The primogenity and due of birth,
> Prerogative of age, crowns, sceptres, laurels,
> But by degree stand in authentic place?
> Take but degree away, untune that string,
> And hark what discord follows. Each thing meets
> In mere oppugnancy. The bounded waters

Should lift their bosoms higher than the shores
And make a sop of all this solid globe;
Strength should be lord of imbecility,
And the rude son should strike his father dead.
Force should be right—or rather, right and wrong,
Between whose endless jar justice resides,
Should lose their names, and so should justice too.
Then everything includes itself in power,
Power into will, will into appetite;
And appetite, an universal wolf,
So doubly seconded with will and power,
Must make perforce an universal prey,
And last eat up himself. . . .

1.3.82–88, 94–124

This magnificent and stirring speech, masterful in its periods, and in its emphasis, traces the consequences of loss of "degree," which will "make a sop of all this solid globe," rendering the continents and the seas indistinguishable. Here, as in all plays written after the move to the Globe theater, "this . . . globe" is also a gesture at the playhouse and the playgoers. To "make a sop" of the Globe is to reduce the audience to tears. Moral and ethical qualities will "lose their names" and become, like the material earth and sea, impossible to tell apart. As a result—this seems a very familiar set of claims—instead of reason, order, and justice, the world will be governed by power, will, and appetite, and the result will be chaos and cultural cannibalism. The "neglection of degree" produces inevitable, and disastrous, results:

The general's disdained
By him one step below; he, by the next;
That next, by him beneath. So every step,
Exampled by the first pace that is sick
Of his superior, grows to an envious fever
Of pale and bloodless emulation.
And 'tis this fever that keeps Troy on foot,
Not her own sinews. To end a tale of length:
Troy in our weakness lives, not in her strength.

1.3.129–137

It is indeed a "tale of length," but its rhetorical power is undeniable, and the effect on Ulysses' hearers immediate. In brief capitulatory phrases Nestor and Agamemnon concede the truth of his analysis and turn to him for guidance:

Nestor   Most wisely hath Ulysses here discovered
                The fever whereof all our power is sick.

Agamemnon   The nature of the sickness found, Ulysses,
              What is the remedy?

1.3.138–141

And yet Ulysses' plea for order is itself disorderly. His doctrine of "degree" leads him, as the audience will shortly see, to propose a clever scheme to further unsettle "degree." He suggests that the Greeks offer as their champion, to fight the Trojan hero Hector in single combat, not Achilles, their best and most celebrated warrior, but Ajax, the "beef-witted Ajax," earlier described as a hodge-podge of qualities, "as valiant as the lion, churlish as the bear, slow as the elephant—a man into whom nature hath so crowded humours that his valour is crushed into folly, his folly farced with discretion" (1.2.19–22).

The celebrated speech on "degree," in other words, is not Shakespeare's philosophy, nor even really Ulysses' philosophy, but rather a convincing piece of rhetoric that is presented as a truism until, almost immediately in this play, particular events begin to qualify or undermine it. The notion of a hierarchical plan that belongs to God and depends upon the reinforcement of the prevailing social order is attractive absolutist politics, not only in the early seventeenth century but also in all other eras seeking validation for existing power structures or cultural logics. The renewed popularity of this view in both England and the United States in the 1930s and 1940s (the time of Lovejoy's *The Great Chain of Being* and E.M.W. Tillyard's *The Elizabethan World Picture*) speaks both to the intellectual interest of the question and also to its perceived historical urgency. But Ulysses, were he an interview subject rather than a fictional character, would almost surely concede that his resounding speech is political rhetoric and ideology, not disinterested truth.

I stress this point because it has become so common to quote "Shakespeare" out of context, whether in political speeches, journalists' columns, or religious sermons, in support of the quoter's own observations or beliefs. What I call "Bartlett's Familiar Shakespeare," taking phrases and passages as if they were evidence of Shakespeare's own opinions rather than those of his characters, reaches an almost comical nadir when a hypocrite like Iago is quoted on the importance of "[g]ood name in man and woman" (*Othello* 3.3.160), or the voice of a blowhard like Polonius, urging his son, "This above all—to thine own self be true" (*Hamlet* 1.3.78), is thought to be expressing Shakespeare's profound belief.

What is Ulysses' most telling evidence for this disrespect of authority and "degree"? The bad behavior of "[t]he great Achilles, whom opinion crowns / The sinew and the forehand of our host," but who is, Ulysses claims, so puffed up by his own "airy fame" that he "[g]rows dainty of his worth" and spends his time lolling upon "a lazy bed" in his tent with his best friend and lover Patroclus, instead of on the battlefield. The scene reported by Ulysses is another classic Shakespearean "unscene," brought to vivid life, dialogue and all, by an onstage reporter. We have only Ulysses' word for the truth of the scene he describes, and yet the episode, with its sexy and disrespectful playacting, is so vibrant and convincing, "scurrile jests" and all, that it is almost as if we have seen it. What Ulysses describes, with such convincing rhetorical specificity, is in fact a play acted offstage—a play in which Patroclus plays the parts of all the Greek generals, while "[t]he large Achilles, on his pressed bed lolling, / From his deep chest laughs out a loud applause." The lineup is in fact another version of the identity parade in act 1, scene 2, where Pandarus and Cressida watch the Trojan heroes pass over the stage, and an anticipation of the "kissing scene" in act 4, scene 6, in which Ulysses and Troilus secretly observe Cressida's overfamiliar reception by the same Greek generals here impersonated by Patroclus.

Ulysses' account of Patroclus performing for Achilles, at once mocking, dismissive, and indignant, gives a good sense of the theatrical practice of the time. Some of his phrases, like "strutting player," will reappear in other Shakespeare plays, while the archly clever use of "topless" here to describe Agamemnon would, almost inevitably, call to mind Marlowe's famous invocation of Helen in *Doctor Faustus,* "Was this the face that launched a thousand ships, / And burnt the topless towers of Ilium?" Here is Ulysses:

> [W]ith ridiculous and awkward action
> Which, slanderer, he "imitation" calls,
> He pageants us. Sometime, great Agamemnon,
> Thy topless deputation he puts on,
> And, like a strutting player, whose conceit
> Lies in his hamstring and doth think it rich
> To hear the wooden dialogue and sound
> 'Twixt his stretched footing and the scaffoldage,
> Such to-be-pitied and o'er-wrested seeming
> He acts thy greatness in. . . .
>
> . . . .
>   At this fusty stuff
> The large Achilles . . .
>
> . . . .
> Cries "Excellent! 'Tis Agamemnon just.
> Now play me Nestor, hem and stroke thy beard,
> As he being dressed to some oration.
>
> . . . .
>   Now play him me, Patroclus,
> Arming to answer in a night alarm."
> And then forsooth, the faint defects of age
> Must be the scene of mirth: to cough and spit,
> And with a palsy, fumbling on his gorget,

> Shake in and out the rivet. And at this sport
> Sir Valour dies, cries, "O, enough, Patroclus!
> Or give me ribs of steel. I shall split all
> In pleasure of my spleen." . . .
>
> *1.3.149–178*

The quotations here, the mockery of a pompous Agamemnon and a senescent Nestor (contrasted with the admiring description of "venerable Nestor, hatched in silver," offered in his own voice), allow Ulysses both the position of innocent and virtuous bystander and the covert pleasure of discomfiting his onstage audience. But the principal effect of this enormously entertaining scene is to allow Ulysses, as we have said, to put forward a course of action diametrically opposed—at least in the short run—to the idea of order and hierarchy. To foil the rebellious Achilles, and to outfox the Trojans, he proposes that Ajax, rather than Achilles, be sent forth as the Greek champion.

Divert and crack, rend and deracinate. *Troilus and Cressida* is a good place to look for the unsettling of apparently settled certainties like rank and social class. It should not surprise us to find, only a few scenes after Ulysses' resounding speech on "degree," that this speech, the exposition of a familiar and prominent worldview, is now being ruthlessly parodied by the even more cynical character Thersites, encouraged by Ajax to offer his own criticism of the Greek leadership. Nestor reports that, following the bad example of Achilles and Patroclus, "in the imitation of these twain . . . many are infect." He continues:

> Ajax is grown self-willed and bears his head
> In such a rein, in full as proud a place
> As broad Achilles, keeps his tent like him,
> Makes factious feasts, rails on our state of war
> Bold as an oracle, and sets Thersites,
> A slave whose gall coins slanders like a mint,
> To match us in comparisons with dirt,
> To weaken and discredit our exposure.
>
> *1.3.185–195*

Thersites, described in the list of dramatis personae added by the eighteenth-century editor Nicholas Rowe as "a deformed and scurrilous Greek," has his own diagnosis of order in the Greek camp: "Agamemnon commands Achilles, Achilles is my lord, I am Patroclus' knower, and Patroclus is a fool" (2.3.46–48). Achilles, predictably, is amused by this, and asks for an explanation:

> Thersites   Agamemnon is a fool to offer to command Achilles; Achilles is
> a fool to be commanded of Agamemnon; Thersites is a fool
> to serve such a fool; and Patroclus is a fool positive.

Patroclus   Why am I a fool?
Thersites   Make that demand to the Creator. It suffices me thou art.

2.3.56–61

So much for order, hierarchy, and the "great chain of being." Similar Shake-spearean parodies can be found in, among other places, *As You Like It* (Touch-stone's "seven degrees of the lie," a comic send-up of Jaques' "seven ages"); *1 Henry IV* (Prince Hal's comic replay of Hotspur's conversation with his wife); and *Love's Labour's Lost* (Costard's carnal wooing of Jaquenetta, in marked con-trast to the language of Don Armado and the noble sonneteers). The carnival-esque undercutting of perceived pomposity in high places makes for wonderful theater as well as terrific political and cultural counterpoint.

Another of Ulysses' remarkable and resonant speeches, echoing down the ages, will demonstrate a similar point. Ulysses is advising a grumpy Achilles, furi-ous at the way in which "the lubber Ajax" has been lauded in the Greek camp, while Achilles himself, the former hero, is ignored or passed by "strangely." The whole strategem, including the behavior of the apparently indifferent generals, Agamemnon, Nestor, and Menelaus, is of course of Ulysses' own devising, as a way to make Achilles reform his ways and return to battle. Consulted, Ulysses hints broadly at the easy forgetfulness of the times, and, indeed, of Time. The extraordinarily vivid, allegorical, and cartoonlike image of Time, wearing a backpack of things forgotten and welcoming the newcomer "like a fashionable host" while he coldly ushers a previous favorite out the door, is as recogniz-able in a modern world of "celebrity culture" as it was in a world of courts and courtiers. Here is Ulysses to Achilles:

> Time hath, my lord,
> A wallet at his back, wherein he puts
> Alms for oblivion, a great-sized monster
> Of ingratitudes. Those scraps are good deeds past,
> Which are devoured as fast as they are made,
> Forgot as soon as done. Perseverance, dear my lord,
> Keeps honour bright. To have done is to hang
> Quite out of fashion, like a rusty mail
> In monumental mock'ry. . . .
>
> . . . .
>
> For Time is like a fashionable host,
> That slightly shakes his parting guest by th' hand
> And, with his arms outrstretched as he would fly,
> Grasps in the comer. Welcome ever smiles,
> And Farewell goes out sighing. O let not virtue seek
> Remuneration for the thing it was;
> For beauty, wit,

High birth, vigour of bone, desert in service,
Love, friendship, charity, are subjects all
To envious and calumniating time.
One touch of nature makes the whole world kin—
That all with one consent praise new-born gauds,
Though they are made and moulded of things past,
And give to dust that is a little gilt
More laud than gilt o'er-dusted.
The present eye praises the present object.

                              3.3.139–147, 159–174

Although this picture of time and fame is fully recognizable today, the line that often leaps out of this passage is "One touch of nature makes the whole world kin." Often used as if it meant something like "We're all brothers and sisters and should love one another," in context it means quite the opposite. What makes the whole world kin is the flightiness of the human attention span, the persistent preference for the flashy over the solid, the new rather than the enduring. Whether or not this is "true," it is not a reassuring piece of "Shakespearean" philosophy. Nor, we might say, is *Troilus and Cressida*.

Over the course of his career Shakespeare wrote three remarkable plays that linked the names of famous lovers in their titles. One of these, *Romeo and Juliet,* was to become, over the ensuing centuries, the modern paradigm for romantic passion. The other two plays, *Troilus and Cressida* and *Antony and Cleopatra,* put onstage the love stories of "mutual pair[s]"—to use a suggestive phrase from *Antony and Cleopatra*—who were already legendary in Shakespeare's time.

The three love tragedies have much in common. Each moves the story to a progressively wider stage than the last, from Renaissance Verona to ancient Troy to the Rome and Egypt of history and empire. Both *Romeo and Juliet* and *Troilus and Cressida* present pairs of lovers whose love is doomed by circumstances beyond their control. In both cases the lovers are pulled apart by hostile camps—the Montagues and the Capulets, the Greeks and the Trojans; in both cases the woman is torn from her lover by her father's act of will. Old Capulet wants Juliet to marry Paris (a very different "Paris" from the dashing abductor of Helen); Calchas, Cressida's father, who has defected to the Greek camp, insists that she be returned to him, traded as a prisoner of war from the Trojans to the Greeks. Almost as if to emphasize these parallels, Shakespeare provides for Troilus and Cressida, as he did for Romeo and Juliet, an aubade, or dawn love scene, that takes place after the first night the lovers have spent together. In *Troilus and Cressida,* this is act 4, scene 2. As in *Romeo and Juliet,* the young man feels he must go because he hears the singing of the lark—incidentally, a distinctively English, rather than ancient Greek or Italian, bird. As in *Romeo and Juliet,* his beloved pleads with him to stay.

The lovers in *Romeo and Juliet* are young and innocent, caught up in a longstanding family feud. In *Troilus and Cressida* the "feud" is the Trojan War, ongoing for seven years as the play begins, and again the lovers are overwhelmed by larger political concerns; they may be older than Romeo and Juliet, but their passions are as raw, as powerful, and as ungoverned. Antony and Cleopatra are old warhorses in love, and instead of being incidental and accidental bystanders, they are principals in the ongoing "feud," the struggle for control of the Roman Empire. In general structural terms, these plays put the "private" and the "public" worlds in conflict (night/day, love/war, passion/realpolitik), with the lovers, separately and conjointly, caught in the midst of forces they cannot control.

In *Troilus and Cressida* Pandarus begins the play as Troilus's profane, joking companion, less romantic and more pragmatic than he about the sexual spoils of love. In this, as is often noted, he is like Mercutio. But his unique position as Cressida's uncle and confidant also allows him to play a role very like that of Juliet's Nurse, and, like the Nurse, Pandarus seems more amusing in the "comic" part of the play than when the action turns in the direction of tragedy. His bawdy joking with his niece Cressida in the first act, as he tries to persuade her to take an interest in Troilus, prefaces a scene—superbly crafted by the playwright to introduce a lengthy cast of characters—in which the nobility of the Trojan force "pass over the stage" one by one as Pandarus points each out to Cressida. Her question "What sneaking fellow comes yonder?" is clearly a tease to her uncle (the "sneaking fellow" is the long-awaited Troilus), and the moment she is alone she acknowledges to herself, and to the audience, that she has already fallen in love. Later, when Cressida has learned she will be forced to leave Troilus and return to her father, Pandarus takes on, belatedly, the voice of Friar Laurence, vainly counseling Cressida, "Be moderate, be moderate" (4.5.1), while Cressida, like Juliet (and Romeo), refuses moderation: "The grief is fine, full, perfect that I taste" (3).

But if *Troilus and Cressida* looks back toward Shakespeare's idealistic love tragedy, *Romeo and Juliet*, it also looks forward to *Antony and Cleopatra*. As Troilus and Ulysses watch Cressida's flirtatious behavior with Diomedes in the Greek camp, Troilus is confronted with a truth he cannot face or bear. "This is and is not Cressid," he declares in his agony. What he sees is the "same" physical or material person, but not the person he thought he knew, and loved. Antony says something very similar, under comparable circumstances: "[W]hat's her name / since she was Cleopatra?" (3.13.99–100). (Cleopatra later in the scene will also bring together reputation and name: "Since my love is Antony again, I will be Cleopatra" [3.13.189].) In each case the lovers express themselves in a language of boundlessness and excess that comes, at the end, into conflict with the mundane realities of the political and social world. Juliet says, "[M]y true love is grown to such excess / I cannot sum up some of half my wealth" (*Romeo and Juliet* 2.5.33–34). Cleopatra teases, "I'll set a bourn how far to be beloved," and Antony replies, "Then must thou needs find out new heaven, new earth" (1.1.16–17).

In Troilus's case the assertion of love's boundlessness comes, characteristically, in a catalogue of poetic excesses; at the same time that he incarnates the lover of the romance tradition he is detached enough to record the extent of that incarnation. The scene takes place in that classic erotic locale, the orchard; Pandarus has arranged for the lovers to meet there. Cressida appears veiled, and full of foreboding; it is not clear whether her fears are virginal or prophetic, but Troilus seeks to reassure her:

Troilus	O let my lady apprehend no fear. In all Cupid's pageant there is presented no monster.
Cressida	Nor nothing monstrous neither?
Troilus	Nothing but our undertakings, when we vow to weep seas, live in fire, eat rocks, tame tigers, thinking it harder for our mistress to devise imposition enough than for us to undergo any difficulty imposed. This is the monstruosity in love, lady— that the will is infinite and the execution confined; that the desire is boundless and the act a slave to limit.

3.2.69–77

Throughout the early scenes Troilus has expressed himself in romantic and Petrarchan clichés, like the Romeo who dotes upon Rosaline. In fact, the lovers whose language Troilus's most resembles early in the play are the far more self-mocking Rosalind of *As You Like It* and the delightfully preening Berowne of *Love's Labour's Lost*. Both are more self-knowledgeable than Troilus, and both, unlike him, inhabit comic worlds. Here is Troilus:

> O Pandarus! I tell thee, Pandarus,
> When I do tell thee "There my hopes lie drowned,"
> Reply not in how many fathoms deep
> They lie endrenched. I tell thee I am mad
> In Cressid's love. . . .

1.1.45–49

(Compare this to "O coz, coz, coz, my pretty little coz, that thou didst know how many fathom deep I am in love. But it cannot be sounded. My affection hath an unknown bottom, like the Bay of Portugal" [Rosalind to Celia, *As You Like It* 4.1.175–178].) And here is Troilus again:

> O, that her hand,
> In whose comparison all whites are ink
> Writing their own reproach. . . .

1.1.52–54

(Compare this to "I here protest, / By this white glove—how white the hand, God knows!" [Berowne to Rosaline, *Love's Labour's Lost* 5.2.410–411].)

But with the realization of his desires, the sexual encounter that follows act 3, scene 2, Troilus's idealism, troped on literature, collides calamitously with political expediency. In the next scene Calchas will demand the return of Cressida. We may notice that her language in the orchard scene is already, perhaps playfully (or innocently?), ominous. Twice she says to Troilus, "Will you walk in, my lord?"—the traditional invitation of the prostitute to her customer. Shortly thereafter, when it has been decided to swap Cressida to the Greeks at her father's behest, this same invitation, "Please you walk in, my lords?" will be spoken by Paris to the Greeks who have come to fetch her—including Diomedes, who will shortly become her lover.

Her devolution onstage is rapid. In act 4, scene 6, the scene of her arrival at the Greek camp, she is kissed by a whole lineup of Greeks (Agamemnon, Nestor, Achilles, and Patroclus), bandies cuckoldry jokes with Menelaus, and promises the skeptical Ulysses a kiss "[w]hen Helen is a maid again." She and Diomedes are already on friendly terms. "Lady, a word. I'll bring you to your father," he says, but he is clearly already attracted to her and she, perhaps, to him. Before long we will hear Ulysses' categorical dismissal:

> Fie, fie upon her!
> There's language in her eye, her cheek, her lip;
> Nay, her foot speaks. Her wanton spirits look out
> At every joint and motive of her body.
> O these encounterers so glib of tongue,
> That give accosting welcome ere it comes,
> And wide unclasp the tables of their thoughts
> To every ticking reader, set them down
> For sluttish spoils of opportunity
> And daughters of the game.
>
> 4.6.55–64

"Daughters of the game" are prostitutes. Cressida, like Helen, is both a "slut" and a "spoil," a trophy of the war.

The stage is set for Troilus's disenchantment, which is as violent and excessive as his love. If Cressida is the anti-Juliet, so, in these latter scenes, is she the anti-Desdemona. As will happen in *Othello*, the jealous lover contrives to watch his beloved from afar, but in this case she is genuinely unfaithful. Troilus's love token is a sleeve rather than a handkerchief, and it is undeniable that she does, in fact, give it to her new lover, Diomedes. Troilus, watching with Ulysses, is appalled and incredulous. "Let it not be believed, for womanhood!" he cries (5.2.129). This cannot be the woman he loves:

> If beauty have a soul, this is not she.
> If souls guide vows, if vows be sanctimonies,

> If sanctimony be the gods' delight,
> If there be rule in unity itself,
> This is not she. . . .
>
> .   .   .   .   .   .
>
>   This is and is not Cressid.
>   *5.2.138–142, 146*

Troilus's despairing declaration, "This is and is not Cressid," tells the only real "truth" the play has to offer. It is a "truth" as metatheatrical as it is metaphysical; the actor who plays Cressida "is" and "is not" the figure of consummate desire and legendary inconstancy.

Troilus's language here will mirror the fall from idealism to shuddering physicality: "The bounds of heaven are slipped, dissolved, and loosed," and now instead "orts of her love, / The fragments, scraps, the bits and greasy relics / Of her o'er-eaten faith, are bound to Diomed" (5.2.156–160). Diomedes gets the leftovers of love's banquet. Troilus's earlier, beautiful lines of erotic anticipation

> I am giddy. Expectation whirls me round.
> Th'imaginary relish is so sweet
> That it enchants my sense. . . .
>
>   *3.2.16–18*

are now turned to disgust. The prevalence throughout the play of this language of appetite and scraps, on the one hand, and of buying and selling, on the other, informs both the story of Cressida and the story of Achilles. Commerce, the desired object made a commodity in the marketplace, is their common bond.

Shakespeare brilliantly sutures the persistent philosophical—and economic—question of value in this play, underscored by Troilus's famous question "What's aught but as 'tis valued?," to the much more highly charged issue of a woman's worth. For as becomes clear from the outset, Helen is worth a war, the loss of countless lives, and the end of a mode of civilization; Cressida—despite the fact that she is, if Pandarus is to be believed, as beautiful as Helen—is tamely exchanged for a single prisoner.

The play sets up the comparison between Cressida and Helen early on, and frequently returns to it. "An her hair were not somewhat darker than Helen's—well, go to, there were no more comparison between the women," Pandarus says to Troilus, who needs no convincing (1.1.39–41). When Paris's servant speaks of "the mortal Venus, the heart-blood of beauty, love's visible soul," Pandarus replies, with deliberate provocation, "Who, my cousin Cressida?" "No, sir, Helen," says the servant. "Could you not find that out by her attributes?" To which Pandarus retorts, "It should seem, fellow, thou hast not seen the Lady Cressid" (3.1.30–36).

Helen's role as cause of the quarrel, and of the deaths on both sides, is widely recognized. "Helen must needs be fair / When with your blood you daily paint her thus," Troilus rails as the sound of battle disturbs him from his love reverie about Cressida in the opening scene. "I cannot fight upon this argument" (1.1.86–88). The Greek Diomedes will later be devastatingly forthright when asked by Paris who deserves Helen most, him or Menelaus. Their claims to the "whore" are equal, he says. "You are too bitter to your countrywoman," says Paris, mildly under the circumstances, and receives in response Diomedes' angry diatribe:

> She's bitter to her country. Hear me, Paris.
> For every false drop in her bawdy veins
> A Grecian's life hath sunk; for every scruple
> Of her contaminated carrion weight
> A Trojan hath been slain. Since she could speak
> She hath not given so many good words breath
> As, for her, Greeks and Trojans suffered death.
>
> *4.1.70–76*

They all acknowledge this—and they all carry on the war, year after year.

In act 2, scene 2, Priam gathers his sons for a war council, and reports Nestor's ultimatum:

> After so many hours, lives, speeches spent,
> Thus once again says Nestor from the Greeks:
> "Deliver Helen, and all damage else—
> As honour, loss of time, travail, expense,
> Wounds, friends, and what else dear that is consumed
> In hot digestion of this cormorant war—
> Shall be struck off." . . .
>
> *2.2.1–7*

Hector, consulted first, is clear in his own mind: "Let Helen go." He argues:

> If we have lost so many tenths of ours
> To guard a thing not ours—nor worth to us,
> Had it our name, the value of one ten—
> What merit's in that reason which denies
> The yielding of her up?
>
> *2.2.16, 20–24*

Troilus objects that the issue is one of honor; rebuked by Helenus for paying insufficient attention to "reason," he is sharp in his reply:

> You are for dreams and slumbers, brother priest.
> You fur your gloves with "reason." ...
>
> . . . .
>
>   Nay, if we talk of reason,
> Let's shut our gates and sleep. ...
>
>   *2.2.36–37, 45–46*

The center of the debate, though, comes in the subsequent exchange between Hector and Troilus, which functions in a way as the fulcrum of the play:

> Hector   Brother, she is not worth what she doth cost
>   The holding.
> Troilus   What's aught but as 'tis valued?
> Hector   But value dwells not in particular will.
>   It holds his estimate and dignity
>   As well wherein 'tis precious of itself
>   As in the prizer. 'Tis mad idolatry
>   To make the service greater than the god.
>
>   *2.2.50–56*

Troilus's lengthy and passionate response again turns on the question of honor and commitment, and ends with an indictment of the Trojans for their vacillation:

> If you'll avouch 'twas wisdom Paris went—
> As you must needs, for you all cried, "Go, go!";
> If you'll confess he brought home noble prize—
> As you must needs, for you all clapped your hands
> And cried, "Inestimable!"—why do you now
> The issue of your proper wisdoms rate,
> And do a deed that never fortune did:
> Beggar the estimation which you prized
> Richer than sea and land? O theft most base,
> That we have stol'n what we do fear to keep!
>
>   *2.2.83–92*

Again, as with his profession of love to Cressida, Troilus speaks in terms of necessary excess: some things are priceless. Like Antony's "There's beggary in the love that can be reckoned" (*Antony and Cleopatra* 1.1.15), Troilus's argument balances "estimation" and the "inestimable."

The scene is interrupted by the appearance of Cassandra, "our mad sister," who prophesies, as she will more than once in the play, the destruction of Troy that the audience well knows is about to come:

> Cry, Trojans, cry! Ah Helen, and ah woe!
> Cry, cry "Troy burns!" —or else let Helen go.
>
> *2.2.110–111*

But Cassandra's vision has no effect; if anything, it redoubles Troilus's fervor, And when Priam asks Paris, Helen's ravisher and lover, for his thoughts, Paris, too, responds in terms of honor: "I would have the soil of her fair rape / Wiped off in honourable keeping her" (2.2.147–148). To give her back would be to acknowledge that she was not worth taking: "Well may we fight for her whom we know well / The world's large spaces cannot parallel" (160–161).

Diametrically different values are placed on women and their roles: Cassandra, the prophetess, is disregarded and powerless; Cressida is unvalued by the state. Only Helen, "the subject" of the quarrel, has any power at all, and her power is ultimately emblematic. Hector, despite his doubts and reasons, has already decided upon his "resolution to keep Helen still; / For 'tis a cause that hath no mean dependence / Upon our joint and several dignities" (2.2.190–192), and Troilus is quick to congratulate him: "Why, there you touched the life of our design" (193). The shedding of Trojan blood is for "glory," not for anger or sexual desire: "She is a theme of honour and renown" (198).

Helen is a "subject," a "cause," a "theme." Cressida is merely a woman, first overidealized, then devalued, finally dismissed by Ulysses as one of the "daughters of the game"—a typical whore—after she is greeted by the Greek generals and kisses them one by one (4.6.64). From the first, it seems, she is aware of the precariousness of her position, as she resists her uncle's matchmaking, and Troilus's importuning:

> Cressida   Yet hold I off. Women are angels, wooing;
> Things won are done. Joy's soul lies in the doing.
> That she beloved knows naught that knows not this:
> Men price the thing ungained more than it is.
> That she was never yet that ever knew
> Love got so sweet as when desire did sue.
> Therefore this maxim out of love I teach:
> Achievement is command; ungained, beseech.
> Then though my heart's contents firm love doth bear,
> Nothing of that shall from mine eyes appear.
>
> *1.2.264–273*

This prudent advice to maidens to hold off yielding in love so as to keep their suitors eager—a tactic that seemed to work for Anne Boleyn and has long been a favorite maxim of middle-class mothers with marriageable daughters—turns out to be advice that Cressida herself will not heed. Like Juliet on the balcony, announcing her love to Romeo ("Fain would I dwell on form, / . . . but farewell, compliment. / Dost thou love me?"), Cressida will acknowledge the social taboo and her decision to cross it in the name of love:

Cressida	Boldness comes to me now, and brings me heart.
	Prince Troilus, I have loved you night and day
	For many weary months.
Troilus	Why was my Cressid then so hard to win?
Cressida	Hard to seem won; but I was won, my lord,
	With the first glance that ever—pardon me:
	If I confess much, you will play the tyrant.

. . . .

                        See, we fools!
Why have I blabbed? Who shall be true to us,
When we are so unsecret to ourselves?
But though I loved you well, I wooed you not—
And yet, good faith, I wished myself a man,
Or that we women had men's privilege
Of speaking first. . . .

3.2.102–118

As for Cassandra, the unheeded voice of an inevitable and unwanted political and historical future, she has in this play neither the credit of a man nor the seductive appeal of a woman. Troilus dismisses her as a "foolish, dreaming, superstitious girl" (5.3.82). She is grouped, for this play's purposes, with the world of dream and prophecy. When old Priam tries in vain to convince Hector to avoid the fateful battle, he names those who believe in such portents—women (Hector's wife, mother, and sister) and old men:

Thy wife hath dreamt, thy mother hath had visions,
Cassandra doth foresee, and I myself
Am like a prophet suddenly enrapt
To tell thee that this day is ominous.

5.3.65–68

Yet a great part of the powerful dramatic irony of the play derives from the fact that it is not only Cassandra, but also Troilus, Cressida, and Pandarus, who "foresee" so clearly what literature will make of them—and still do not believe. The question of "free will" for fictional dramatic characters is probably a moot point or a topic for scholastic philosophers, but in the case of Troilus and Cressida, whose existence in literature is tied so directly to this story of "truth" and "falsehood," Shakespeare provides for the audience a scenario at once moving and tragic: the spectacle of two characters struggling blindly against their own mythic identities. We know what Troilus and Cressida do not: that their rhetorical flourishes ("As true as Troilus," "As false as Cressid") will come true— have, indeed, already come true.

If the role of love and eroticism is compromised in Troy, the place of romantic excess, what role do such passions play in Greece, home of the absconded Helen and the cuckolded husband Menelaus? Hector's challenge to the Greeks, as Aeneas reports it, is couched explicitly in courtly terms:

> ["]He hath a lady wiser, fairer, truer,
> Than ever Greek did compass in his arms,
> And will tomorrow with his trumpet call
> Midway between your tents and walls of Troy
> To rouse a Grecian that is true in love.
> If any come, Hector shall honour him.
> If none, he'll say in Troy when he retires
> The Grecian dames are sunburnt and not worth
> The splinter of a lance." . . .
>
> *1.3.273–280*

The challenge is well understood in the Greek camp, as Ulysses notes, to be directed specifically at Achilles, the acknowledged Greek champion. But who is Achilles' lady? He has no "Grecian dame." Much later in the play we learn that he does have a "fair love," and that she is a Trojan, a daughter of Queen Hecuba. But in Shakespeare's play this lady remains offstage and unnamed; her dramatic role is merely to send the letter reminding Achilles of an oath he has sworn, an oath that keeps him from fighting Hector even once he has determined to do so (5.1.32–39). It is not his love for the daughter of Hecuba but rather his love for Patroclus that will drive him finally to abandon the courtly code and the rules of war altogether.

The relationship between Achilles and Patroclus, who share a tent and loll on a bed, is both a heroic friendship and an erotic bond. Such noble, idealized, and eroticized friendships between men would have been as recognizable to Elizabethans as they were to Homer, Aeschylus, Plato, Theocritus, Martial, and Lucian, among other classical authors. Thersites, contemptuous of both men, is especially derogatory toward Patroclus, whom he calls "Achilles' male varlet," and his "masculine whore" (5.1.14, 16), as well as "boy," an insult in this warrior context. In the same scene Thersites gives Achilles the letter from Hecuba containing her daughter's love token. It seems clear that both the person Achilles addresses as "[m]y sweet Patroclus" (5.1.32) and the princess he calls "my fair love" have claims upon his passion and affection. But when word comes that Patroclus has been killed in battle, Achilles is grief-stricken and enraged. "Great Achilles," Ulysses reports, "[i]s arming, weeping, cursing, vowing vengeance. / Patroclus' wounds have roused his drowsy blood" (5.5.30–32). Achilles, entering, calls out for Hector, "thou brave boy-queller" (47). Setting aside the vow he has made to Hecuba's daughter, he summons his Myrmidons. Dramatically speaking, it is Patroclus—not Helen, not any woman—for whom he will fight and kill Hector.

The last moments of the play are balanced, in a way that Shakespeare would make his signature, between a powerful public pronouncement of loss, Troilus's moving announcement to the Trojan host of the end of an era ("Hector is dead; there is no more to say" [5.11.22]), and Pandarus's epilogue, addressed to panders of the future, slyly imagined as being in the theater audience and already members of a guild or company of bawds ("Good traders in the flesh, . . . / As many as be here of Pandar's hall" [5.11.31.14–31.15]). Like Pistol in *Henry V*, Pandar, no hero, does not die, but lives to practice his trade in the brothels that surround the Globe playhouse. Troilus, as he departs the stage, bitterly participates in Pandarus's translation into a household word:

> Hence, broker-lackey! [*Strikes him*] Ignominy and shame
> Pursue thy like, and live aye with thy name.
>
> *5.11.31.2–31.3*

By the time Shakespeare came to write *Troilus and Cressida,* the two lovers of his play's title had themselves become notorious bywords: Troilus for his fidelity, Cressida for her unfaithfulness. Evidence for this set of automatic cultural associations in the period can be found in *The Taming of the Shrew,* where Petruchio calls for his "spaniel Troilus" (*Taming* 4.1.131). Spaniels were known for their servile fidelity to their masters (the lovesick Helena in *A Midsummer Night's Dream* tells the indifferent Demetrius, "I am your spaniel" [*Dream* 2.1.203]), and Petruchio, bent on proving to Katherine that he will subdue her will to his, demonstrates on this visit to his ramshackle home the fact that all members of his household are unquestioningly faithful. (Since Troilus the spaniel does not appear in the dramatic action, it is not clear whether the legendary fidelity of the species proves correct in this instance.) So when the two lovers look into the future and see their reputations written there—"As true as Troilus" and "As false as Cressid" (3.2.169, 183)—they are performing an act of "prediction" comparable to that of the prophetic politicians and soothsayers of the history plays, who see unerringly because the imagined historical moment in which they are speaking has already happened before the actual.

In this play, with uncanny effect, characters in fact come right out and *say* their own myths, describing their own transformation into literary fame—and literary cliché. And not only Troilus and Cressida—Pandarus, too, announces his own impending allegorical translation into a household word: if you prove false to one another, he says, let all go-betweens, all bawds, be called Pandars. By Shakespeare's time this was already the case, and the word, lowercased, appears regularly in the plays ("reason panders will" [*Hamlet* 3.4.78]; "Ah, you precious pander! Villain, / Where is thy lady?" [*Cymbeline* 3.5.81–82]; "Camillo was his

help in this, his pander" [*Winter's Tale* 2.1.48]), and in *Much Ado About Nothing*
the urbane Benedick, acknowledging to himself that he has fallen in love,
speaks ruefully of "Troilus the first employer of panders" (5.2.27). Yet within the
fiction of *Troilus and Cressida* none of the dramatic speakers knows that he or
she is already legendary. In fact, both Cressida and Pandarus assume that the
fate they ironically predict will *not* take place: Cressida is sure she will be faithful; Pandarus is convinced that the lovers will prove true. Here are the three:

Troilus	True swains in love shall in the world to come
	Approve their truth by Troilus. When their rhymes,
	Full of protest, of oath and big compare,
	Wants similes, truth tired with iteration—
	"As true as steel, as plantage to the moon,
	As sun to day, as turtle to her mate,
	As iron to adamant, as earth to th' centre"—
	Yet, after all comparisons of truth,
	As truth's authentic author to be cited,
	"As true as Troilus" shall crown up the verse
	And sanctify the numbers.
Cressida	Prophet may you be!
	If I be false, or swerve a hair from truth,
	When time is old and hath forgot itself,
	When water drops have worn the stones of Troy
	And blind oblivion swallowed cities up,
	And mighty states characterless are grated
	To dusty nothing, yet let memory
	From false to false among false maids in love
	Upbraid my falsehood. When they've said, "as false
	As air, as water, wind or sandy earth,
	As fox to lamb, or wolf to heifer's calf,
	Pard to the hind, or stepdame to her son,"
	Yea, let them say, to stick the heart of falsehood,
	"As false as Cressid."
Pandarus	Go to, a bargain made. Seal it, seal it. I'll be the witness. Here I
	hold your hand; here, my cousin's. If ever you prove false one
	to another, since I have taken such pain to bring you together,
	let all pitiful goers-between be called to the world's end after
	my name: call them all panders. Let all constant men be
	Troiluses, all false women Cressids, and all brokers-between
	panders. Say "Amen."

3.2.160–190

The ironic placement of this ceremony could not be better—or worse. No
sooner do the lovers exit for their night together than the scene shifts to the

Greek camp, where Calchas, Cressida's father, proposes a swap: the newly captured Trojan Antenor for Cressida. Calchas, famed in classical literature as a seer, had defected from the Trojan camp because he foresaw Troy's tragic end. Now he addresses the Greek generals, who have tried before on his behalf to engineer an exchange for Cressida. Antenor, whom "Troy holds . . . very dear," seems to provide the perfect opportunity: "Let him be sent, great princes, / And he shall buy my daughter" (3.3.27–28). This example of what anthropologists would term "the traffic in women" is devastating to the love plot, and to the characters' reputations over time. Calchas can see the future of Troy, but not the future of Cressida.

For Cressida herself, struggling not only against the political will of the Greeks and Trojans but also against her character's notorious literary history, there is, alas, no reservoir of personal agency, however much she tries to summon it. Her protest to Pandarus is heartfelt, when she hears his news. "Thou must be gone, wench, thou must be gone. Thou art changed for Antenor. Thou must to thy father, and be gone from Troilus," Pandarus says (4.3.15–17). She answers:

> I will not, uncle. I have forgot my father.
> I know no touch of consanguinity,
> No kin, no love, no blood, no soul, so near me
> As the sweet Troilus. . . .
>
> 4.3.21–24

When word comes to Cressida that she must go to her father in the Greek camp, she asks a question that brings the latent, unspoken and crucial, pun to the surface:

> Cressida   And is it true that I must go from Troy?
> Troilus   A hateful truth.
> Cressida   What, and from Troilus too?
> Troilus   From Troy and Troilus.
>
> 4.5.29–31

But though she intends to tear her hair and scratch her cheeks in grief, and vows to "break my heart / With sounding 'Troilus.' I will not go from Troy" (4.3.33–34), what she has to learn, and what the play has to teach, is that Troy and Troilus, despite the near homonym of their names, are not the same. They name two traditions at odds with each other. One is epic history, the other, romance.

Measure for Measure

DRAMATIS PERSONAE

Vincentio, *the Duke of Vienna*
Angelo, *appointed his deputy*
Escalus, *an old lord, appointed*
   Angelo's secondary
Claudio, *a young gentleman*
Juliet, *betrothed to Claudio*
Isabella, *Claudio's sister, novice to*
   a sisterhood of nuns
Lucio, *a "fantastic"*
Two other such Gentlemen
Froth, *a foolish gentleman*
Mistress Overdone, *a bawd*
Pompey, *her clownish servant*

A Provost
Elbow, *a simple constable*
A Justice
Abhorson, *an executioner*
Barnardine, *a dissolute*
   condemned prisoner
Mariana, *betrothed to Angelo*
A Boy, *attendant on Mariana*
Friar Peter
Francesca, *a nun*
Varrius, *a lord, friend to the*
   Duke
Lords, officers, citizens, servants

MEASURE FOR MEASURE," observed Samuel Taylor Coleridge, "is the single exception to the delightfulness of Shakespeare's plays. It is a hateful work, although Shakespearian throughout. Our feelings of justice are grossly wounded in Angelo's escape. Isabella herself contrives to be unamiable, and Claudio is detestable."[1] In fact, *Measure for Measure* has always been controversial, exciting a great deal of critical and directorial interest, and puzzlement. It has been given unhelpful and unhistorical labels like "problem play" and "dark comedy" to explain, or explain away, some of its peculiarities. The play has been of special interest to scholars and critics concerned with English history and the court, with religion (the title phrase comes from the Gospel according to Matthew; a particularly conflicted character is called Angelo; the plot involves nuns, priests, confession, and vows of chastity), and with the representation of women, feminism, and sexuality. Despite Coleridge's spirited animadversion, the play has had many admirers, and it contains passages of brilliant verse—some borrowed by later writers like T. S. Eliot—and powerful, passionate action. On the hatefulness/delightfulness scale articulated by Coleridge it is surely "dark" rather than "festive," but its dramatic patterns and psychological investigations fit superbly well both in the evolving sequence of Shakespearean "romantic" comedies and in the cluster of agonized and even phobic encounters represented by its chronological neighbors among the tragedies, like *Othello* and *King Lear*.

Recent readings of *Measure for Measure* have tended to begin with King James I, who was on the throne of England and Scotland in 1604, when the play was first performed. The play's all-seeing, all-knowing Duke of Vienna has often been compared to James, an absolutist ruler who believed strongly in the divine right of kings. James was a staunch Protestant, raising the stakes for a play like *Measure,* populated by nuns and friars, religious true believers, and self-deceiving hypocrites. With his kingship, beginning in 1603, James ushered in a much greater bureaucracy and apparatus of state spying than had been in place in the equally watchful but more entrepreneurial government of Elizabeth. Above all, James came to be associated with the idea of power in absence, the keystone and cornerstone of absolutist power. James had strong views on morality; he described himself as the father of his country (and, as we will see in this play, as its mother, too), and he was deeply—a modern world would say, neurotically—involved in keeping track of activities going on in all corners of his kingdom. The motif of the disguised ruler, who conceals his real identity to spy on his subjects, was one that appealed to James and that he occasionally put into practice himself. As Thomas Bilson, Bishop of Winchester, declared in his coronation sermon, since princes "can not be Gods by nature," since they are human beings, "framed of the same metal, and in the same moulde, that others are," then

> It foloweth directly, they are gods by Office; Ruling, Iudging, and Punishing in Gods steede, & so deseruing Gods name here on earth.[2]

The Duke in this play is not literally a figure "of" King James, any more than he is a figure "of" God or "of" Christ; his deployment of what the play calls "power divine" is a delegation of power that devolves upon the good ruler as such a ruler was understood in the period. And the ideals for which such a ruler was to stand were those of reason and ethical judgment. "Judging" was the ruler's and the magistrate's duty; it was that obligation that made him, dangerously, like a god, if not like God.

As often as this Duke has been compared to King James, he has also been compared to Shakespeare, or to a playwright, ordering his cast and bringing about his plot devices, dramatic surprises, and denouements. Here, too, there is a danger of too quickly collapsing a fruitful allusiveness into a wooden, fixed identity. It would be more helpful, both in terms of the play's own freestanding energies and in terms of an understanding of its historical place in time, to observe that *Measure for Measure* is a play about *representation* and about *substitution,* two concepts that are as foundational for the theater as they are for the state. Who represents God? Who represents the King, or the Duke? How does an actor represent a character, or a set of ideas, on the stage? Since a "person" (from the Latin *persona*, an actor's mask is one who impersonates, who represents, then an actor is a person, and a person is an actor. Both "counterfeit"—both represent. This was the view of the philosopher Thomas Hobbes in *Leviathan* (1651):

> [1] A person is he whose words and actions are considered either as his own, or as representing the words and actions of another man, or of any other thing to whom they are attributed, whether truly or by fiction.
>
> [2] When they are considered as his own, then is he called a *natural person;* and when they are considered as representing the words and actions of another, then is he a *feigned* or *artificial person*. . . .
>
> [3] . . . [A] *person* is the same that an *actor* is, both on the stage and in common conversation; and to *personate* is to *act,* or *represent,* himself or another; and he that acteth another is said to bear his person, or act in his name.[3]

Hobbes's chapter "Persons, Authors, and Things Personated" is of relevance for those interested in the role of the stage actor in general and the question of authority in particular, since he is especially concerned with the relationship between an "author" and an "actor," where "author" means someone in authority, and "actor" (or "representer") someone who performs an action on the "author's" behalf or at the "author's" behest. The date of *Leviathan* is half a century after Shakespeare's play was produced, so the relevance of Hobbes here is indirect rather than direct. But just as a much more recent "author," like Sigmund Freud, may be said to have described scenarios that bear pertinently on Shakespeare's characters and plays even though he wrote and thought hundreds of years afterward (using the vocabulary of the "other scene" as the place of the unconscious), so it is useful to take note of the range of ways in which, in the years immediately following the heyday of early modern English drama, words that pertained to the theater, the stage, the king's court, and the judge's courtroom were intertwined and disentangled.

There was a time in critical history when the Duke in *Measure for Measure* was seen as a godlike playwright figure, a precursor to Prospero in *The Tempest,* ordering the lives of all the other characters, making sure that things come out right in the end. The logic of representation or substitution is voiced within the play itself, in the recurrence of words like "deputy" and "substitute," and in a phrase like Angelo's, spoken at the play's close—"your grace, like power divine, / Hath looked upon my passes" (5.1.361–362). "Passes" are trespasses—Angelo is citing the Sermon on the Mount (Matthew 6:9–13; Luke 11:1–4), and he seeks to have his sins forgiven by the person he also calls a "dread lord." Lately the Duke has not had such good press. If he is a playwright, he is often seen as a failed playwright who cannot keep his actors in order—a presciently post-Pirandello playwright whose characters are in search of another author. He is often regarded as something of a meddler or busybody, a ruler who may see himself as godlike, but who is mistaken. Some commentators, wittily noticing that he is the Duke of *Vienna*, have compared him, not without point, to a psychoanalyst, probing motives, reading the unconscious, delving into the past, and messing about with other people's sex lives.

The plot of *Measure for Measure* has also been of special interest to critics and audiences concerned with women's place, or places. The rich and problematic character Isabella, whose desire to enter the nunnery begins the play, receives not one but two sexual propositions: the first from Angelo, who wishes to seduce her; the second from the Duke, who wishes to marry her. In an early scene in *Measure for Measure* we learn that a woman who is a novice in the convent of Saint Clare can either speak to a man or look him in the face, but not both at the same time. This crux—the voice or the gaze, the ears or the eyes, the audience that hears or the spectators who watch—will persist as a point of crisis throughout the play. And we might note also the play's famous and discomfiting ending, in which the Duke proposes to Isabella and she does not respond. The supposed conventions of comedy imply that she will accept him; resistant modern readings and stagings have sometimes shown her hesitating or even rejecting his suit. The gap or space of interpretation has often balanced, or unbalanced, the interpersonal encounters that have gone before. Is this a play that ends, as formally it "should," with four marriages (Claudio and Juliet, Angelo and Mariana, Lucio and Kate Keepdown, the Duke and Isabella)? Or does Isabella's silence destabilize this neat equation, reminding the attentive Shakespearean audience of other, earlier hesitations, like that of Rosaline in *Love's Labour's Lost*, who sends her too-confident lover off for a year to tell jokes in a hospital, to bring smiles to the "speechless sick"?

The scene of the play is laid, as we have noted, in Vienna, a Catholic city in Shakespeare's time and the seat of the Holy Roman Empire, ruled by the Catholic Hapsburgs. England had been officially a Protestant country since the 1534 Act of Supremacy created the King, Henry VIII, instead of the Pope, the Supreme Head of the Church in England. During the period 1536–1539 Henry VIII's troops suppressed the monasteries and despoiled them, often seizing their wealth for the crown. Henry's daughter Mary Tudor, who married the Catholic King Philip II of Spain, briefly returned the country to Catholic rule (1553–1558), burning many Protestant heretics at the stake, but at her death the new Queen, Elizabeth, became Supreme Head of the Church in England. Both Elizabeth and James were staunch Protestants. Elizabeth was less zealous than Mary had been in persecution of those who held opposing beliefs, but she did authorize the occasional pursuit, torture, and execution of "papists." Those not in the religious majority were often prudentially advised to dissimulate. The followers of the "old faith" (Catholicism) were, in the time of Elizabeth and of James, forced to hide their beliefs or—in the words of the Porter in *Macbeth*— to "equivocate" about their faith. To complete this broad and rapid account of Catholic-Protestant tensions in the period, let me note also that it is thought that Shakespeare's father, John, was Catholic, that he was a lifelong recusant who declined to attend church, and that his political and economic fortunes may have suffered as a result.

Vienna is also the supposed locale of the *Mousetrap* play in *Hamlet*, "The Murder of Gonzago." "This play is an image of a murder done in Vienna," Hamlet tells King Claudius (*Hamlet* 3.2.217–218). *Hamlet* itself is a play in which a ghost laments the fact that he has gone to his death without the religious comfort of the last rites of the Church and is thus condemned to wander in purgatory, a play that thus marks the same persistent tension between Protestant and Catholic, "old" and new beliefs.

As *Measure for Measure* opens, Vienna is a city riddled with decay and corruption. Under the rule of Duke Vincentio, laws have been allowed to lapse, morality to slacken, and order (what Ulysses in *Troilus and Cressida* called "degree") to become disorder. As the Duke explains to the Friar in the monastery,

> We have strict statues and most biting laws,
> The needful bits and curbs to headstrong weeds,
> Which for this fourteen years we have let slip;
> Even like an o'ergrown lion in a cave
> That goes not out to prey. . . .
>
> Measure for Measure *1.3.19–23*

Like a father who uses the rod only to threaten his child, and not to punish, the Duke has permitted his laws to be ignored. As a result they are no longer either respected or obeyed:

> so our decrees,
> Dead to infliction, to themselves are dead;
> And Liberty plucks Justice by the nose,
> The baby beats the nurse, and quite athwart
> Goes all decorum.
>
> *3.1.27–31*

This is the same concern about hierarchy and "degree" expressed so strongly in *Troilus and Cressida*—that a debased idea of justice produces loss of "degree" in society. But the Duke's solution to the problem is peculiar. He himself, he says, is too closely associated with this laxness to begin to enforce the laws. Instead he has chosen Lord Angelo to serve as his deputy and enforce them in his absence. "In our remove be thou at full ourself. / Mortality and mercy in Vienna / Live in thy tongue and heart," he tells Angelo (1.1.43–45). But mortality and mercy are the two attributes Angelo conspicuously lacks. He is neither human nor merciful as the play opens and as it unfolds, and it is hard to believe that the Duke does not know this perfectly well. The Duke's absence is not precisely what he says it is, and for two reasons: first, because although officially absent he is actually present onstage in disguise, and second, because by deputizing Angelo he creates a structure for testing him. Angelo is being tested, as Vienna is being tested, by the apparent removal of the Duke, who represents order and law.

The Duke's supposed removal from Vienna invites us to group this play with other Shakespeare plays, like *Much Ado About Nothing,* where a middle world of transformation is created not by a geographical shift (for example, court to country to court, as in *A Midsummer Night's Dream,* or *As You Like It,* or *The Winter's Tale*) but by an internal change in the composition and spirit of the community. In *Much Ado,* as in *Twelfth Night,* new people (soldiers home from the war; shipwreck victims washed ashore in Illyria) arrive to change a relatively static onstage society. In *Measure for Measure* the inner world of the play is realized by subtraction rather than by addition or movement: the inner world is the world of Vienna without the Duke. The Duke leaves, and disorder is revealed, but it was always there. So instead of transformation there is confrontation and discovery. In keeping with this, instead of the wild freedom of the Forest of Arden or the Athenian wood—or, indeed, the nighttime world of *Romeo and Juliet*—there is in this play an inner world that is largely composed of enclosed spaces, spaces that confine and compress (like Hamlet's figure of the nutshell) rather than setting characters free. Claudio's dungeon is an enclosed space, as is Isabella's nunnery, and the Duke's monastery, and Mariana's "moated grange," a farmhouse surrounded by a moat that serves in place of a wall, like the enclosed and walled garden, the *hortus conclusus,* of medieval and biblical tradition. Each is imaginatively a sign of a set of other enclosures: virginity and chastity; brotherhood and obedience; even death, as Claudio makes clear when he imagines death as a physical confinement:

> Ay, but to die, and go we know not where;
> To lie in cold obstruction, and to rot;
> This sensible warm motion to become
> A kneaded clod. . . .

> *3.1.118–121*

As the play progresses all the enclosed spaces wait to be opened. Mariana waits to be freed from the isolation of the moated grange; Claudio, and even the drunken prisoner Barnardine, to be freed from prison; Isabella to be freed from the nunnery to a world of human sexuality, choice, and marriage; Angelo to be freed from the walled prison of the self. But initially Vienna appears as a place without appropriate law, and the very lack of good law locks its central characters into their several and separate, but analogous, prisons.

What is law? What are its limits? On what should it be based? The play's title, as we've noted, comes from a verse in the Gospel according to Matthew: "Judge not, that ye be not judged. For with what judgment ye judge, ye shall be judged, and with what measure ye mete, it shall be measured to you again"

(Matthew 7:1–2). At issue throughout the play is the question of retributive justice, and also the question of the fit judge. The Duke's phrase "[m]ortality and mercy," addressed, with some ironic foreshadowing, to Angelo, balances the power to execute with the correlative power to pardon. The so-called Golden Rule—Do unto others as you would have them do unto you—is an injunction repeatedly pressed upon Angelo, both by Escalus, his second-in-command, and by Isabella, Claudio's sister. Put yourself in Claudio's place, they urge. Imagine yourself facing death for the sin of premarital sex. As Isabella says,

> If he had been as you and you as he,
> You would have slipped like him, but he, like you,
> Would not have been so stern.
>
> *2.2.66–68*

This is a prediction that all too clearly will come true, as Angelo does "slip," propositioning Isabella with the promise of freeing her brother if she will only sleep with him—a promise he has no intention of keeping. The play thus centers on the question of whether judging is possible at all. From what vantage point can one fallible human being judge another, mete out measure for measure? As Hamlet replies to Polonius when Polonius tells him he will treat each player according to "his desert," what the player deserves, "God's bodykins, man, much better. Use every man after his desert, and who should scape whipping? Use them after your own honour and dignity" (*Hamlet* 2.2.508–510). In her first interview with Angelo, in act 2, scene 2, Isabella urges this position of mercy upon him:

> Alas, alas!
> Why, all the souls that were were forfeit once,
> And He that might the vantage best have took
> Found out the remedy. . . .
>
> *2.2.74–77*

But to Angelo laws are not human-centered but absolute, inhuman, unchangeable. There is no such thing as mercy, as he makes clear at the beginning of act 2 in a conversation with Escalus. Angelo insists on rigidity:

> We must not make a scarecrow of the law,
> Setting it up to fear the birds of prey,
> And let it keep one shape till custom make it
> Their perch, and not their terror.
>
> *2.1.1–4*

This is the Duke's point, too—spare the rod and spoil the child. But Escalus, with a temperate wisdom that is often linked in these plays to age and experience, replies, "Ay, but yet / Let us be keen, and rather cut a little / Than fall and bruise to death" (2.1.5-6). Angelo, denying this possibility, speaks a line that can be seen only as "tempting fate"—or as another mode of ironic foreshadowing on the part of the playwright:

> 'Tis one thing to be tempted, Escalus,
> Another thing to fall. . . .
>
> *2.1.17–18*

Angelo—the allegorical name is quite uncommon in Shakespeare—defines himself as a man who is above temptation, as something more than a human being. In refusing to imagine himself as human, and thus "fallen," he falls. In trying to be more than a man, he becomes less. From the very beginning of the play we are given evidence that others regard Angelo as either inhuman or less than human. The Duke says of him that he "scarce confesses / That his blood flows, or that his appetite / Is more to bread than stone" (1.3.51–53). Lucio describes him as "a man whose blood / Is very snow-broth; one who never feels / The wanton stings and motions of the sense, / But doth rebate and blunt his natural edge" (1.4.56–59). Elsewhere we are told that "when he makes water his urine is congealed ice" (3.1.354–355). The Viennese speculate that he was not born of a sexual union between man and woman. And this is the man who is called upon to give judgment—to be "[m]ortality and mercy" in Vienna.

The problem here is a familiar one in Shakespeare, one to which it is perhaps too easy to give the catchall therapeutic label "self-knowledge." Angelo, despite, or because of, his angelic name, is as ignorant of his own mortal nature as his city's laws are of the propensities of human beings. The old counselor Escalus knows this, which is why he appeals to Angelo for leniency. And it is Escalus who provides the crucial description of the Duke that is at the opposite pole from Angelo's self-righteous iciness, when he says that the Duke—then thought to be absent from Vienna—is "[o]ne that, above all other strifes, contended especially to know himself" (3.1.456–457).

The word that above all symbolizes, and betrays, Angelo's situation is a word he uses repeatedly, the word "sense." Listening to Isabella, he finds himself moved for the first time by sexual desire, and aside to the audience he observes, "She speaks, and 'tis such sense / That my sense breeds with it" (2.2.144–145). Lucio has earlier described him as a man who "never feels / The wanton stings and motions of the sense." In these contexts "sense" means "desire," sensuality— his "sense breeds" with her speech. But "sense" can also mean "reason"—good sense—and it is characteristic of Angelo that he should confuse the two. Having denied the senses, he begins to substitute one kind of "sense" for the other, pro-ducing a split, of a kind also present in *Troilus and Cressida*, between reason and passion. It is precisely because Angelo has never accepted the senses that he is vulnerable to the first onslaught of passion. Clinging to external laws and precepts rather than contending "to know himself," he falls. Having fallen, he seeks instant gratification of his newfound sense. At the close of his second interview with Isabella, Angelo charts his own turning point:

> I have begun,
> And now I give my sensual race the rein.
> Fit thy consent to my sharp appetite.
> Lay by all nicety and prolixious blushes
> That banish what they sue for. Redeem thy brother
> By yielding up thy body to my will,
> Or else he must not only die the death,
> But thy unkindness shall his death draw out
> To ling'ring sufferance. Answer me tomorrow,
> Or by the affection that now guides me most,
> I'll prove a tyrant to him. As for you,
> Say what you can, my false o'erweighs your true.
>
> 2.4.159–170

The language of weighing and measuring, of scales of justice, so present throughout the play, now becomes *over*weighing, tipping the balance. The monk becomes the satyr. And Isabella's resounding accusation fulfills itself:

> [M]an, proud man,
> Dressed in a little brief authority,
> Most ignorant of what he's most assured,
>
> . . . .
>
> Plays such fantastic tricks before high heaven
> As makes the angels weep. . . .
>
> 2.2.120–125

As Angelo, the "angel," will weep by the play's end.

The play thus asks the question, What is natural? And how can we contend to know ourselves? A failure to understand this central question has led, in Vienna, to two different but related kinds of excess: excess of liberty and excess of restraint. The two instincts, which are really two sides of the same coin, are exemplified by a brother and a sister, Claudio and Isabella, who, like other pairs of Shakespearean siblings (Sebastian and Viola in *Twelfth Night*, Ophelia and Laertes in *Hamlet*), seem so complementary as to be in a way two aspects of the same person. Excess of liberty has produced the situation with which the play opens: Claudio's sexual relationship with his betrothed, Juliet, and Juliet's pregnancy.

Betrothal in the early modern period was a much more formal and legal status than engagement is today. There were two kinds of spousals, present and future ("I *take you* as my spouse" and "I *will take you* . . ."), and the declaration of vows in the present had a binding force, especially when combined with the two other factors that together with the vow made for a marriage contract: the dowry and sexual consummation. In fact, Claudio's situation with regard to Juliet is very similar to the situation of Angelo and Mariana. Both couples have been engaged but not married, bound by a precontract, lacking only the payment of a dowry. (Shakespeare-biography buffs may here wish to recall that Shakespeare married Anne Hathaway when she was already pregnant, and that the couple's daughter Susanna was born five months later.) The all-knowing Duke assures Mariana that she is married in the eyes of God. Nevertheless, for the sin of sexual knowledge Claudio is committed to prison, and the audience's first sight of him comes when he is being led through the streets as an example, at the command of Angelo. "How now, Claudio!" exclaims a startled Lucio, "Whence comes this restraint?" Claudio's answer is prompt and pertinent:

> From too much liberty, my Lucio, liberty.
> As surfeit is the father of much fast,
> So every scope, by the immoderate use,
> Turns to restraint. Our natures do pursue,
> Like rats that raven down their proper bane,
> A thirsty evil; and when we drink, we die.
>
> *1.2.105–110*

Too much liberty produces restraint. Rats lack the power to regurgitate, so what they swallow they must keep inside them. "Proper" here has a double meaning, both "appropriate" (what they deserve) and "natural" (what they cannot help wanting). Sex is both natural and dangerous, and Claudio's and Juliet's excess has led to restraint—to his imprisonment and the threat of death.

But if Claudio has broken a civil law through liberty, Isabella seems to be breaking a natural law through restraint. She is first encountered as she is entering a nunnery, a destination resisted by other Shakespearean women from the Juliet of *Romeo and Juliet* to Hermia in *A Midsummer Night's Dream*. Moreover, though the order Isabella chooses, the Order of Saint Clare, was proverbially the strictest of all sisterhoods, it is not strict enough for Isabella. She desires, as she says, "more strict restraint." Their privileges are too free for her. The Poor Clares, as they were known, lived by begging, and it is arguable that one of the things Isabella is forced to learn in the course of this play is how to beg—though her begging is not disinterested but anguished and direct, pleading with Angelo for her brother's life.

In fact, as Angelo shrewdly observes, he and Isabella have a great deal in common. They refer to themselves, and are described by others, as saints (another Shakespearean danger signal), and Angelo admits that Isabella's virtue is part of her attraction: "O cunning enemy, that, to catch a saint, / With saints doth bait thy hook!" (2.2.184–185). In other words, it will take a saint to catch a saint. But as unnatural as Angelo may seem, in wishing to enforce archaic laws for their own sake, he is not more unnatural than Isabella, who can proudly proclaim, "More than our brother is our chastity" (2.4.185). In a way, there could be no more excessive statement, no greater acknowledgment that Isabella fails to understand the nature of humanity and the sense of sense. It is no accident that she claims to hear her father's voice in her brother's when Claudio consents to die rather than have her relinquish her virginity to Angelo: "There spake my brother; there my father's grave / Did utter forth a voice" (3.1.84–85). Like Ophelia, Isabella could be said here to be using the return to the role of the obedient daughter as a way to avoid certain crises of adulthood. The conflation and confusion of "father" and "brother" as male authority figures is something that will occur in a number of other Shakespeare plays (in *Twelfth Night*, for example, where Olivia initially is imprisoned by her obedience to a "brother's dead love," or, as noted, in *Hamlet*, where Laertes' advice to Ophelia is identical to Polonius's). In *Measure for Measure*, though, where both "father" and "brother" are also religious forms of address, and where confused epithets like "good father friar" and "good brother father" are used to comic effect, Isabella's recourse to finding the voice from her father's grave in the language of her condemned brother takes on a further resonance. In short, this is yet another one of the many temptations, trials, and tests that abound in the play. As the Duke tests Angelo and Isabella and Lucio, and as Angelo is tested by Isabella's youth, beauty, innocence, and eloquence, so Isabella is tempted by self-love. She is at this stage as securely locked in the nunnery of her own self-regard as her brother is locked in the prison.

There is a peculiar and disquieting, or titillating, side to Isabella's denial of desire, a denial that itself exhibits desire. Her protest of chastity against all assaults has a strong psychosexual tone, one that a modern world would classify as a kind of sadomasochism:

> [W]ere I under the terms of death,
> Th'impression of keen whips I'd wear as rubies,
> And strip myself to death as to a bed
> That longing had been sick for, ere I'd yield
> My body up to shame.

2.4.100–104

This sensual imagery of blood, jewels, and martyrdom is one that in the next generation of English writers will recur in the work of a Catholic lyric poet like Richard Crashaw (1613?–1649; see, for example, his extraordinary "Hymn to the Name and Honor of the Admirable Saint Theresa"). Somewhere behind Isabella's language there may also lurk the language of Proverbs, "Who can find a virtuous woman? Her price is beyond rubies" (Proverbs 31:10), a passage often benignly cited as praise of womanly conduct. In Isabella's imagination the rubies have become drops of blood, and the love-longing becomes an equally passionate longing for death and martyrdom. Isabella's excess, her erotic passion, is arguably far stronger than that of either Juliet or Mariana, the two women who represent a more conventional marital love.

In the context of the play, Isabella stands to learn from her contact with Mariana, who only inhabits her moated grange because, in a world governed by men and by men's laws, she has no choice. The substitution of the one for the other, the so-called bed trick, in which one woman sleeps with a man who thinks she is another woman—Mariana having sex with Angelo when he thinks he is having sex with Isabella—is, in the nature of such things, a metaphor, rendering the two women for a moment interchangeable. It is a lie that tells the truth. *Measure for Measure* is a play that turns on both bed tricks and head tricks, two substitutions: the body of Mariana for that of Isabella in Angelo's bed, the head of the dead prisoner Ragusine for the head of the condemned Claudio. The same event that rescues Mariana from the moated grange will free Isabella from the nunnery.

Saint Paul's views on virginity and marriage as expressed in his First Epistle to the Corinthians are clearly germane here: "[I]f thou marry, thou hast not sinned: and if a virgin marry, she hath not sinned. Nevertheless such shall have trouble in the flesh" (1 Corinthians 7:28). "There is difference between a wife and a virgin. The unmarried woman careth for the things of the Lord, that she may be holy both in body and in spirit; but she that is married careth for the things of the world, how she may please [her] husband" (1 Corinthians 7:34). These citations are from the 1599 edition of the Geneva Bible, almost surely the text Shakespeare would have read, a version whose copious marginal notes by Protestant Reformation scholars, and handy quarto size, made it invaluable to readers. The teaching was that men and women could be saints and abstain from sexuality and marriage, or they could choose marriage and the comforts and "trouble" of the flesh.

So Claudio shows excess of liberty, Isabella shows excess of restraint, and Angelo shows first the one and then the other. What all of them lack, and what the play will seek to supply, is a sense of mortality, desire, and limit. This perspective is given expression—oddly, but for Shakespeare characteristically—not by a noble character or a voice of authority, but by the bawd Pompey, a figure who, like Pandarus and Thersites in *Troilus and Cressida,* remains on the outskirts, commenting on the action. In this play Pompey supplies the place occupied in happier comedies by the clown or fool. He speaks more wisdom than he knows, and his wisest observations are disregarded. In his very name, Pompey, can be seen the fallen condition of the play's world, incorporating as it does the sense of "pomp" as worldly vanity, inevitably doomed (as in the "smiling pomp, nor falls" of Sonnet 124), and the heroic figure of Pompey the Great. For that Pompey, Caesar's noble adversary and one of the "Nine Worthies," is now become Pompey Bum, bawd and tapster. "Troth," says the long-suffering Escalus, "and your bum is the greatest thing about you; so that, in the beastliest sense, you are Pompey the Great" (2.1.194–195). This Pompey is the employee of Mistress Overdone, the brothel-keeper, whose place of business is itself a sign of the decay of morals in Vienna. The brothel is at the opposite pole from Isabella's nunnery, the two locations—on the stage as well as in the play-text—again demarcating excess and restraint, this time in sexual terms: a house of sexual license and a house of religious abstinence. We might note that the two kinds of "nunnery" of Hamlet's bitter taunt are here physically realized upon the same stage.

It is to this most insignificant, and in some ways despicable, character, Pompey, that Shakespeare entrusts his definition of the human condition. We have heard Isabella disparage the presumptuousness of human beings in placing themselves among the angels ("man, proud man, / Dressed in a little brief authority"). We now have Pompey's correspondingly stripped view of the condition of humanity, expressed in a dialogue with Escalus, the play's representative of disinterested justice, who has asked him whether he is not really a bawd, and not just, as he claims, a tapster or bartender. Pompey replies in a single existential line that resonates throughout the play: "Truly, sir, I am a poor fellow that would live" (2.1.199). But how would he live—by being a bawd? Does he think, pursues Escalus, that such a trade is lawful?

Pompey	If the law would allow it, sir.
Escalus	But the law will not allow it, Pompey; nor it shall not be allowed in Vienna.
Pompey	Does your worship mean to geld and spay all the youth of the city?
Escalus	No, Pompey.
Pompey	Truly, sir, in my poor opinion, they will to't then.

2.1.202–208

In Pompey's commonsense view sexual desire is a natural part of life, and a law that seeks to regulate or thwart it, whether the nunnery's laws or the punitive laws of Vienna, cannot be enforced. Such a law is against nature, just as Angelo's self-repression, to "rebate and blunt his natural edge," is against nature—"they will to't." As for humanity, again we have Pompey's word: "Truly, sir, I am a poor fellow that would live." Pompey is the bare, forked animal of this play, unadorned by rank or title, by money or special gifts. He is to *Measure for Measure* what the skull of Yorick was to *Hamlet,* and what Thersites' crabbed vision of the Trojan War ("All the argument is a whore and a cuckold") was to *Troilus and Cressida* (2.3.65)—a sign of basic human instincts and necessities. The play also points forward to *King Lear,* in which Poor Tom, the disguised Edgar, will likewise personate "the thing itself," a "poor, bare, forked animal." In one way, then, this play suggests that human nature is why human beings need laws. The Duke's masking, and his descent—like that of the disguised Henry V—among the people, is in this view a necessary step toward finding laws and codes that work from within and below. But if the play contains a fallen and circumscribed view of sexual desire and the "trade" in bodies and desire, it also contains something like its opposite: an idealizing and powerfully naturalized vision of harmonious lovemaking as a figure for process and productivity.

The voicing of this alternative vision is given over, with a perhaps purposive inappropriateness, to the cynical Lucio, whose wonder at the fulfillment of love breaks through his usually glum view of the world. Arriving at the hostile environment of the nunnery in act 1, scene 4, to tell Isabella that Claudio is in prison, he speaks in the language of nature, culture, and harvest:

> Your brother and his lover have embraced.
> As those that feed grow full, as blossoming time
> That from the seedness the bare fallow brings
> To teeming foison, even so her plenteous womb
> Expresseth his full tilth and husbandry.
>
> *1.4.39–43*

The iconography of female earth and male sower is conventional (woman = nature, man = culture). The image is one of complementarity and fertility. The passage itself is luminously beautiful, and it seems to prefigure certain lyric passages embedded in later tragedies, like *Antony and Cleopatra*. This language of growth (the word appears numerous times in the play) is structurally set over against the language of weights and measures, scales and balances. There is a striking—and highly pertinent—biblical precedent for this imagistic conflict (weights and measures versus natural fecundity; repressive laws versus laws of nature) in the evocative incident, so popular in the Renaissance, called "the parable of the talents," a story that—like the play's title—comes from the Gospel according to Matthew. It is the story of a man who goes on a journey, as Duke Vincentio pretends to do. It begins: "For the Kingdome of heaven is as a man that going into a strange countrey, called his servants, and delivered to them his goods." The man gave to his servants, as stewards in his absence, "talents" according to their abilities. (A "talent" is a certain *weight* of silver.) To one servant he gave five talents; to another, two; and to a third, one talent. Then he departed, and after a long time he returned and summoned his servants, to ask them for an account of what they had done. And the man who had been given five talents, and the man who had been given two talents, showed him that they had made use of and multiplied the talents. Each had doubled them, and he said to each, "It is well done, good servant and faithfull; thou hast been faithful in little, I will make thee ruler over much." But the man to whom he had given one talent had done nothing with that talent but bury it, and he said to his master, "Master, I knewe that thou wast an hard man, which reapest where thou sowedst not, and gatherest where thou strawest no; I was therefore afraide, and went, and hid thy talent in the earth." The master was angry, and took the talent away from the man, calling him evil as well as slothful, telling him that he should have invested the talent so that "at my comming should I have received mine own with vantage," and saying, "For unto every one that hath shall be given, and he shall have abundance; but from him that hath not shall be taken away even that which he hath" (Matthew 25:14–30).

Our modern sense of the word "talent" as meaning "personal or natural gifts" derives from this story. Duke Vincentio is the "lord" or "master" of the parable, and the talents he leaves behind with his stewards are readily identifiable. His appointment of Angelo as his deputy is the giving of a talent, and Angelo, instead of using and profiting from it, buries it. By contrast, Claudio does participate in a pattern of productive growth. His violation of the civil law of Vienna is counterbalanced by the "teeming foison" and "plenteous" fruitfulness so richly described by Lucio. The apparent "falls" of characters from Mariana to Claudio, and ultimately to Angelo, are falls into a condition of humanity.

Of all Shakespeare's comedies, *Measure for Measure,* his last comedy, is the most evidently impatient or uncomfortable with its inherited generic form. It is a comedy that exposes the difficulties, perhaps the impossibilities, of its being a comedy—a comedy that, if it ends in marriage at all, ends only in the forced marriage of Lucio to the "punk," or whore, Kate Keepdown; the precontracted marriage of Claudio and Juliet; the marriage under ducal arrangement of Angelo to Mariana; and the unanswered proposal of Duke Vincentio to Isabella. All throughout Shakespeare's dramatic career the comedies have tried to hold death at bay, to keep death outside their charmed circle. As we have seen, news of death does reach a comic society (thus, for example, in *Love's Labour's Lost,* the lady Catherine has a sister who died long before the play began, and word is brought, toward the end of the play, about the death of the King of France), but no character the audience encounters, no member of the dramatis personae, dies in the course of a Shakespearean comedy. (This is a trait that distinguishes the comedies formally from the so-called tragicomedies, or romances, at the end of Shakespeare's career.) But in *Measure for Measure* we confront the face of death: the head of the prisoner Ragusine substituted for the head of Claudio. We come face-to-face with limit, just as Hamlet does when he stares into the eyeless skull of Yorick and recognizes it as the twin of his own. Thus when the Duke, dressed as a friar, counsels the imprisoned Claudio to "[b]e absolute for death," his words carry weight, even though he himself, as the civil authority in Vienna, has the power to prevent it at any time. He tells Claudio:

> Thou hast nor youth nor age,
> But as it were an after-dinner's sleep,
> Dreaming on both. . . .

3.1.32–34

The idea that "life is a dream" was a poetic and theatrical commonplace. A later Shakespearean duke, the exiled Prospero in *The Tempest*, can tell the audience of his masque that the sudden end of the performance is a model for mortality: "We are such stuff / As dreams are made on, and our little life / Is rounded with a sleep." The Spanish playwright Pedro Calderón de la Barca's play *Life Is a Dream* (1635) would exploit the figure to the full. But for Claudio, locked in his dungeon, his own emblematic hell, a despairing glance into the grave ("[t]o lie in cold obstruction and to rot") is both prefaced with and followed by a distinctly Christian resignation: "To sue to live, I find I seek to die, / And seeking death, find life" (3.1.42–43). For a moment he pleads with Isabella to exchange her body for his (inverting, we could say, the "die" pun that animates so much sexual banter in these plays), but when the Duke intervenes to say that Angelo is only testing Isabella's virtue, Claudio is moved to ask for pardon: "I am so out of love with life that I will sue to be rid of it" (3.1.172–173). With this direct, visceral, and imaginative confrontation with his own death Claudio begins his ascent back to life. His appearance in the play's climactic final scene, muffled and unspeaking, will present him as a dramatic emblem: silent, shrouded, he is Death, a dead man, the dead Claudio, "another prisoner . . . like almost to Claudio," and finally, as we will see, a kind of risen Lazarus.

To this point we have been considering the play as one that formally explores the psychology of repression and denial (characters locked up in their separate enclosed spaces, whether prison, or nunnery, or moated grange; Angelo and Isabella as inadvertent doubles, confined by their own superhuman visions of themselves as saints), and over against those images of repression and denial a counterplot of expansion, fertility, and growth, though one that likewise threatens to overflow its boundaries (Juliet's pregnancy before marriage; the brothels and brothel-keepers that are all we see of the commerce of Vienna). But the play's central and most puzzling character, the Duke, traverses a space that is at once psychological and theological, and how the audience responds to him will determine much about the tone of any production.

If Claudio's dungeon is one pole of the play's dramatic geography, it is easy to see the Duke as occupying the other. "Bring me to hear them speak where I may be concealed," he says to the Provost (3.1.51), and so is able to overhear Isabella's conversation with Claudio in the prison. Whether or not he literally appears aloft—in the play-text Lucio calls him "the old fantastical Duke of dark corners" (4.3.146–147), and he says of himself that he is a "looker-on in Vienna," so perhaps he lurks at the edges of the action—Duke Vincentio does pull strings, like a semidivine puppeteer, or, as is so often observed, like a playwright. He substitutes Mariana for Isabella, and he alone seems to know Mariana's sad and hidden story of shipwreck and loss, the tale of her brother's death at sea and the loss of the money to pay her dowry. He substitutes Barnardine for Claudio, then the dead Ragusine for the obdurately, and comically, life-loving

Barnardine, so that no character encountered in the play is put to death, and even the semblance of tragedy is averted. ("O, death's a great disguiser" [4.2.161], he will observe amiably as he directs that Barnardine's head be substituted for Claudio's.) In fact, from the opening moments onward, the Duke follows a path that is recognizably both theatrical and allegorical, descending to earth in disguise among the people to observe their actions and see which of them will believe in him, becoming simultaneously actor and director:

> I love the people [he says to Escalus],
> But do not like to stage me to their eyes.
> Though it do well, I do not relish well
> Their loud applause and *aves* vehement.
>
> *1.1. 67–70*

These are lines that have often been applied to King James, whose ambivalence about crowds and public appearances was frequently noted.

The Duke's predilection for testing and tempting is almost the only "explanation" we have for some of his more humanly puzzling behavior. Why, for example, does he tell Claudio that he should be "absolute for death" when he knows he can save him? Why does he leave Angelo in charge of the state when he suspects him of weakness and inhumanity? Why, above all, does he tell Isabella that her brother is dead, when Claudio is still alive? Why does he stage the whole final public scene, even bringing Isabella to the point where she kneels and prays for Angelo's life to be spared, even though she believes that he has been the agent of her brother's death? These are all tests and trials—in the case of Isabella, "To make her heavenly comforts of despair / When it is least expected" (4.3.102–103). It is worth noting that Renaissance rulers regularly used horrific public events like executions and torture as ways of producing fear and anxiety in the populace. The beheading of noble and royal persons and the maiming and drawing and quartering of political rivals, religious dissidents, and other public figures for moral crimes and crimes against the state were a mode of social regulation. As numerous scholars have pointed out, one of the most powerful devices at the command of the ruler was the occasional and unpredictable use of clemency. When a ruler intervened at the last moment to pardon a prisoner condemned to die, the public approbation was enormous. James used this power—indeed something like "power divine"—to great effect throughout his reign. Since a "scaffold" was both a stage and a place of execution, the theatricality of these events was intensified. As Sir Walter Ralegh, himself to die in the Tower of London, observed trenchantly in a poem that compared life to a stage play, "Only we die in earnest, that's no jest."

Passing among his subjects, listening and watching, the Duke in his disguise is also hidden by darkness, for again and again in *Measure for Measure* significant scenes and actions take place at night. "Upon the heavy middle of the night" Isabella is to go to Angelo's walled garden and yield up her virginity—as Mariana will do in her stead. And at night, the same crucial night, the Duke goes to the prison and finds a warrant for the execution of Claudio; the Provost imparts this information to Claudio: " 'Tis now dead midnight, and by eight tomorrow / Thou must be made immortal" (4.2.53–54). Night cloaks, blurs distinctions, makes dissimulation possible—and forces the soul to contemplate its unimaginable end. Appropriately then, the play's most lyric moment signals the coming of morning, and also the enlightenment that will unscramble its mysteries:

> Look, th' unfolding star calls up the shepherd. Put not yourself into amazement how these things should be. All difficulties are but easy when they are known. . . . Yet you are amazed; but this shall absolutely resolve you. Come away, it is almost clear dawn.
>
> *4.2.185–191*

The speaker is the Duke himself, still in disguise, but forced to hasten the denouement. The Provost, or jailer, has challenged him in his friar's role, and he now produces letters predicting the Duke's imminent return.

The verbal counterpart of the physical device of disguise is a key word this play shares with *Hamlet,* the word "seeming." When the Duke appoints Angelo as his deputy he observes, "Hence shall we see / If power change purpose, what our seemers be" (1.3.53–54). *Seeming* is complicated for the theater, where everyone is a "seemer"—just as for Hobbes "a person is the same that an actor is." What is the tipping point between impersonation and lying? *Measure for Measure,* like *Hamlet,* engages that problem, philosophically and metatheatrically, at every turn. In act 2, scene 3, the Duke, disguised as a friar, greets the compassionate Provost:

> Duke   Hail to you, Provost!—so I think you are.
> Provost   I am the Provost. What's your will, good friar?
>
> *2.3.1–2*

The Provost is a provost, but the friar is not a friar. What seems to be true is not. This seems trivial enough, but it is a classic Shakespearean setup. For in the next scene Angelo propositions Isabella, and, scandalized, she threatens that she will tell on him:

>   Seeming, seeming!
>   I will proclaim thee, Angelo. . . .
>
> *2.4.150–151*

His retort is quick and cynical—and it has an all-too-familiar ring. It will be a case, he points out, of he said / she said:

> Who will believe thee, Isabel?
> My unsoiled name, th'austereness of my life,
> My vouch against you, and my place i'th' state,
> Will so your accusation overweigh
> That you shall stifle in your own report.
>
> *2.4.154–158*

Scholars of the early modern period often warn against mistaking sixteenth- and seventeenth-century literary texts for modern ones. The term for this is "presentism," and it is thought to be a naïve error, a kind of category mistake. Yet Shakespeare has *made* modernity as much as he has uncannily anticipated it, and an exchange like this could now serve as a textbook case of sexual harassment. Angelo is a powerful, authoritative man of good reputation, a high government officer. Isabella is a novice (we could call her an "intern"), a young woman, without influential friends. She wants his assistance; he wants a sexual quid pro quo. "Who will believe thee, Isabel?"

Angelo's word "overweigh" may remind us of the other time he uses the same term: "[M]y false o'erweighs your true." Both usages point directly at the play's title and the language of weights and measures. Yet by the end of the play the verbal disguise marked by "seeming" will undergo a series of reversals, and the great last scene is a series of unmaskings. Isabella pleads with the Duke "[t]o make the truth appear where it seems hid, / And hide the false seems true" (5.1.66–67). But the Duke's way of doing this begins with more dissimulation. His triumphal progress into the city involves a very public embrace of Angelo, his deputy:

> Give me your hand,
> And let the subject see, to make them know
> That outward courtesies would fain proclaim
> Favours that keep within. . . .
>
> *5.1.13–16*

The gesture of taking the hand of a friend or an enemy is a constant and powerful one on Shakespeare's stage, especially in plays that focus on hidden treachery, like *Julius Caesar* and *King Lear*. In this play, as in those, the public extension of the hand invites the duplicitous subordinate to compound his treason. The outward/inward language here recalls the description of the sacraments as the outward sign of an inward grace. And the word "grace" itself does double duty throughout the play, since it is the proper form of address for a Duke: thus, as we have seen, the repentant Angelo will later observe that "your Grace, like power divine, / hath looked upon my passes" (5.1.361–362). (Compare his words with those of York in *Richard II:* "[G]race me no grace, nor uncle me no uncle. / I am no traitor's uncle" [2.3.86–87].)

One of the most visible onstage theatrical portrayals of the outward/inward split is the commonplace device of disguise. Lucio provides a watchword for it when he quotes the Latin proverb *Cucullus non facit monachum,* "The cowl does not make the monk," or, more broadly, "Don't trust appearances." Characteristically—both for Lucio and for Shakespeare—this commonplace is comically *mis*applied when it is cited (Shakespeare never uses clichés straight, but always puts them in the mouth of an unlikely or ironic speaker). Thus Lucio lashes out at "Friar Lodowick" (the Duke in disguise), declaring that the friar is "honest in nothing but in his clothes" (5.1.259–260)—the one thing in which he is in fact dishonest. Stung by the supposed friar's accusations, Lucio reaches out for him: "Why, you bald-pated lying rascal, you must be hooded, must you? Show your knave's visage. . . . Will't not off?" (5.1.345–347). Here Lucio literalizes the verbal gesture about the cowl and the monk, pulling off the friar's hood to reveal the Duke. Gracelessness produces his Grace.

Stripping and unmasking of this kind is emblematic of the whole play, and becomes visually evident as a stage event in the final scene. Just as Angelo appears to be a kind of Machiavel, saying one thing to his court, another to Isabella and to the audience, so the play is full of symbolic disguises. In the final scene alone the Duke is disguised as a friar, Mariana is veiled, and Claudio is muffled when he is at last produced. Onstage are Angelo, in his everyday "disguise" as a justice, and Isabella in her novice's costume. Only moments before, at the end of the fourth act, Isabella had complained to Mariana against the veiling, disguising, and equivocation that are part of the friar/Duke's plan: "To speak so indirectly I am loath— / I would say the truth, but to accuse him so, / That is your part— yet I am advised to do it, / He says, to veil full purpose" (4.6.1–4). The idea of seeing indirectly in a fallen world so as to be able to glimpse the truth more clearly has its own insistent biblical precedent, notably in Corinthians: "For now we see through a glass, darkly; but then face to face" (1 Corinthians 13:12). This is the same book of the Bible in which Saint Paul offers his influential views on virginity and marriage, and it is fitting that the two Pauline themes should come together in the play's dramatic denouement.

For the mode of the final revelations *is* revelation, and its poetic equivalent, romance. The appearance of Mariana, as a mystery woman swathed in veils, translates the dramatic action into a different key. The Duke, pretending not to recognize her, gives over the judgment of her case to Angelo, who is, of course, her unknowing lover, as well as her faithless fiancé. "First, let her show her face, and after speak," says the Duke, and the audience should at this point recall the strictures of the Order of Saint Clare, which held that a woman could either speak or show her face to a man, but not both. On cue, Mariana refuses:

Mariana	Pardon, my lord, I will not show my face
	Until my husband bid me.
Duke	What, are you married?
Mariana	No, my lord.

Duke	Are you a maid?
Mariana	No, my lord.
Duke	A widow then?
Mariana	Neither, my lord.
Duke	Why, you are nothing then; neither maid, widow, nor wife!

5.1.168–176

Shakespeare's Christian audience would here again recall Saint Paul on marriage, virginity, and widowhood. The irrepressible Lucio offers his own answer to this enigma: she is a "punk," a whore. But Mariana, whose name, Mary, like that of Angelo, the angel, is allegorically significant, has a further riddle to propound:

> My lord, I do confess I ne'er was married,
> And I confess besides, I am no maid.
> I have known my husband, yet my husband
> Knows not that ever he knew me.

5.1.182–185

Whether expressed in the form of Freud's tendentious dichotomy of "woman" in the male imagination as either virgin or whore, or via Mariana's deliberately mystifying negations (not a maid, not a wife, not a widow), this puzzling account is presented as a conundrum. Again, a Christian audience would have a ready analogue in the concept of a virgin mother. But the main effect is that of a riddle, a form that will recur in later Shakespearean romances like *Pericles* and *Cymbeline*. This riddle is visual as well as aural or textual, an undecipherable human figure on the stage.

If the veiled Mariana can be said to represent the mystery of woman, the muffled Claudio represents the mystery of death. He stands there, silent, his face covered as hers is, and although the audience knows that Claudio is not dead, this news is not shared by those who love him: his sister, Isabella, his fiancée, Juliet. Once again, as with the unmasking of Mariana, the questions asked have a mysterious timbre that seems almost to come from the world of romance:

Duke	What muffled fellow's that?
Provost	This is another prisoner that I saved,
	Who should have died when Claudio lost his head,
	As like almost to Claudio as himself.

5.1.480–483

Claudio stands revealed, although in this scene he never speaks. Again we can look to the Gospels for a story behind the story, in this case the story of Lazarus, who died and was restored to life. Lazarus had two sisters, Mary and Martha, who went to Jesus and told him their brother was dead. They went to the cave where the grave of Lazarus was; he had been dead four days. Jesus prayed, and cried "with a loud voice, Lazarus, come forth. And he that was dead came forth, bound hand and foot with graveclothes: and his face was bound about with a napkin. Jesus saith unto them, Loose him, and let him go" (John 11:43–44). The stage picture here, with the two anxious women awaiting the return of their lost beloved, is immediately evocative. Claudio is restored from death to life, from the dungeon to marriage and paternity, from the ultimate restraint to the ultimate—though lawful—liberty.

The play's long last scene has offered numerous problems for readers, audience, actors, and directors. In it the Duke attempts to assert control, and though he has some successes, he also has some signal failures. The scene begins with his triumphal "return" to a city he has never left. In rapid succession he reveals the secret of the bed trick (Angelo has slept with Mariana, his betrothed wife, not with Isabella, whom he sought to ravish), announces Claudio's apparent death, sends Mariana and Angelo offstage for a hasty marriage ceremony, brings them back onstage, condemns Angelo to death, provokes Mariana to plead with Isabella to join her in asking for Angelo's pardon, and finally, at long, long last, unmuffling the disguised Claudio, demonstrates that he is alive. At this point he proposes marriage, not once but twice, to Isabella. Why does he break off his first proposal in the middle? Gesturing to the unmuffled figure, he says to her:

> If he be like your brother, for his sake
> Is he pardoned; and for your lovely sake
> Give me your hand, and say you will be mine.
> He is my brother too. But fitter time for that.
>
> *5.1.484–487*

At this point the Duke turns away and begins to do ducal business in an almost manic spirit, addressing governing and judging remarks to Angelo, Lucio, Escalus, the Provost, and anyone else he can find onstage. Only at the very close does he turn once more to Isabella and renew his proposal:

> Dear Isabel,
> I have a motion much imports your good,
> Whereto, if you'll a willing ear incline,
> What's mine is yours, and what is yours is mine.
>
> *5.1.527–530*

What makes him break off and then renew his suit? Remember that this is indeed a very long scene, at the end of which a husband is reunited with his wife, who has believed him dead. But Juliet, the wife, enters upon the scene very late, and does not speak. The reunion is staged, not between husband and wife, but between brother and sister. It is Isabella who is presented with the miraculously living man—"If he be like your brother. . . . He is my brother too." We might conjecture that the Duke has to repeat his proposal because on the first instance Isabella is not listening, but is instead rapt in contemplation of the brother so unexpectedly and miraculously restored to her.

The relationship of Isabella and Claudio is overdetermined, and in its own way excessive. It is Isabella who glancingly mentions the loaded topic of incest when she is pleading with Claudio to die like a man rather than force her to sleep with Angelo: "Is't not a kind of incest to take life / From thine own sister's shame?" (3.1.140–141). We have noted that she conflates her father and her brother in hearing the father's (censoring) voice when Claudio asserts his decision to die: "There spake my brother; there my father's grave / Did utter forth a voice" (3.1.84–85). The father's voice, as so often, says "no": no, Isabella does not have to swap her chastity for her brother's life. We have seen, too, that brothers and fathers are regularly confused with one another by those who try to address the clergy by their official titles: thus the foolish constable Elbow, one of Shakespeare's classic malapropists, greets the Duke, dressed as a friar, with "Bless you, good father friar," to which the Duke jauntily replies, "And you, good brother father." Isabella is free to idealize her brother and his love for her, which is both unreserved and unsexual. How can the Duke compete?

Isabella's reply to the marriage proposal is not given in the text. Directors have therefore had to work out some way of indicating what she does and does not do with this odd invitation from a ruler who has previously denied that the "dribbling dart of love" can ever "pierce [his] complete bosom" (1.3.2, 3). In recent years it has become common to question the Duke's omniscience and power—after all, he fails to get the prisoner Barnardine to consent to die, in one of the play's most darkly comic scenes, and thus almost scuttles his own plan. Whether vainglorious or bumbling, this Duke has often been set up as a figure who is emphatically not a version of "power divine," whatever he or his acolytes may believe. For this reason, and for the same reasons modern directors and audiences try to envisage a less-than-compliant Katherina in *The Taming of the Shrew*, contemporary stagings of *Measure for Measure* often open up the ending rather than closing it down. Sometimes Isabella turns away when the Duke offers his hand, leaving him standing alone, rather foolishly, on the stage (the analogue here is Portia's gift to Antonio of his returned argosies, also staged as an ambivalent moment, since he would rather have Bassanio than a thousand ships loaded with treasure). But this, too, is a decided choice, a choice of refusal rather than acceptance. One dramatic solution that appealed to me was offered at the Stratford (Ontario) Festival some years ago. After the proposal, and the Duke's final exchange with Lucio, everyone but Isabella left the stage. She alone remained, dressed in her white novice's robe. Slowly she reached up to remove her headdress, and then shook her hair free. Instantly her novice's robe was converted to a wedding gown, and she smiled at the audience, indicating, perhaps, her readiness to leave the convent, even though she had not yet accepted the Duke. What was particularly effective about this moment was that it directed attention to the figure of Isabella, making *Measure for Measure* her play as well as, or more than, the Duke's. Whether or not this interpretation-via-stage-action is persuasive to any individual reader or audience member, it should remind us of how much "Shakespeare" is in the action and gesture of the play rather than its language. This is very clear with musical insets (the masque in *The Tempest;* the songs in the comedies and romances; the marvels and portents that attend witches and soothsayers). But it is also true of more "ordinary" moments, which render uncertain and unknowable any final decision about dramatic meaning.

Readers interested in history may wish to observe that the name Isabella is the Spanish equivalent of Elizabeth, and that this Jacobean account of a virgin's choices and suasive power has a certain double-edged resonance. One fantasmic outcome of a reading like this is to see the romance at the end as an iconographic rendering of James's final victory, the deceased Elizabeth's capitulation to the new King's hand and to his will.

But the finest energies of *Measure for Measure* are not so much comic or historical as they are allied with tragedy and romance, with the fact of mortality and the mystery of revelation. If this play is a "comedy," it is not so because it ends in several uneasy marriages, nor because comic figures like Elbow and Barnardine emerge from it as minor heroes of a satisfyingly amusing Shakespearean kind, but rather in the general sense in which Sir Walter Ralegh uses the term in his little poem "On the Life of Man." Ralegh had long been Queen Elizabeth's favorite, but he fell out of favor when he seduced one of her attendants. He was imprisoned by James I for thirteen years on a charge of treason, released, reimprisoned, and finally beheaded. His poem offers a bleak analogy between life ("this short Comedy") with its presumed "happy ending" in heaven and the elements of the theater ("tyring houses" are dressing rooms, "music of division" is melodic descant as contrasted with plainsong). It is well to recall that, as Ralegh astringently notes, the play goes on, even though the individual characters, players, and "actors" in both senses—Hobbes's "Persons, Authors, and Things Personated"—may die:

> What is our life? A play of passion.
> Our mirth the music of division.
> Our mothers' wombs the tyring houses be,
> Where we are drest for this short Comedy.
> Heaven the judicious sharp spectator is,

That sits and marks still who doth act amiss,
Our graves that hide us from the searching sun,
Are like drawn curtains when the play is done.
Thus march we playing to our latest rest,
Only we die in earnest, that's no jest.[4]

Othello

DRAMATIS PERSONAE

Othello, *the Moor of Venice*
Desdemona, *his wife*
Michael Cassio, *his lieutenant*
Bianca, *a courtesan, in love
    with Cassio*
Iago, *the Moor's ancient*
Emilia, *Iago's wife*
A Clown, *a servant of Othello*
The Duke of Venice
Brabantio, *Desdemona's father, a
    senator of Venice*
Gratiano, *Brabantio's brother*

Lodovico, *kinsman of
    Brabantio*
Senators of Venice
Roderigo, *a Venetian gentleman,
    in love with Desdemona*
Montano, *Governor of Cyprus*
A Herald
A Messenger
Attendants, officers, sailors,
    gentlemen of Cyprus,
    musicians

ODERN SCHOLARS sometimes tend to think of race, class, and gender as distinctively contemporary modes of analysis, categories that reflect our own concerns, identities, and anxieties. But the plays of Shakespeare, produced in a period now often described as "early modern England," are themselves strikingly "modern" in this as in other respects. To an extraordinary degree, Shakespeare's plays, from *Titus Andronicus* to *The Tempest,* exhibit and record tensions around and within these categories. And never more than in *Othello*.

Race, class, and gender become crisis points when they categorize something, or someone, as *different,* and also as out of place: out of place, of course, from the point of view of traditional society. A black man marries a white woman, and is chosen by the nation to lead it in time of peril. A soldier, ambitious for preferment, sees his place given to another—given, in fact, to a courtly, educated snob who believes in rank, believes that "the lieutenant is to be saved before the ancient" (2.3.95–96). A woman asserts herself, making her own choice in marriage against her father's will, speaking out in public on civic matters, then daring to contradict her husband's view and offering him advice. These are all signs of transgression, calling boundaries into question. Anxiety, tension, hatred, and desire develop in part out of this sense of destabilization and displacement, out of the divisions and comparisons that are produced by categories like race, class, and gender. And never more so than in *Othello*.

Shakespeare's time—like ours—was one of great historical changes and social anomalies. There were black men and women living in London, some of whom owned property, paid taxes, and went to church; but the slave trade between the West Indies and Africa had already begun. Women of all social ranks claimed the right to education, to financial and other modes of independence—even the right to wear pants in public. Nascent capitalism and the growth of towns and cities had begun to threaten the hereditary aristocrats and landowners with a vision of a different society. *Othello* is not reducible to a political tract, but its richness records and responds to a world in crisis, a crisis figured in part through emergent categories like race, class, gender—and sexuality.

Like so many of Shakespeare's plays—*A Midsummer Night's Dream, As You Like It, Antony and Cleopatra,* and *King Lear*—*Othello* provides us with a geographical shift in the middle of the play, the movement from a civilized place to a wild one, from a locale of order and law to a place of passion and confusion. And as is the case with the central dramatic action in *Measure for Measure,* this play, too, offers us a glimpse of what happens when extremes of reason that deny passion are confronted with extremes of passion that deny reason or logic. The two geographical poles here are Venice and Cyprus: city and wilderness, civilization and anarchy, order and disorder.

Venice appears to be the place of urbanity and civilization, Cyprus the borderland where anything can happen, a place of wildness, passion, and rebellion. The name Cyprus comes from one of the names of the goddess Venus: Kypris—the lady of Cyprus, for whom that island was supposedly named. And the story of Venus (in Greek, Aphrodite) underlies the plot of *Othello.* Venus had a husband, the lame blacksmith god Vulcan (in Greek, Hephaistos), and she also had a lover, the war god Mars (Ares). Vulcan, the artist, the artisan, the blacksmith, jealous of her love affair with a soldier-hero, created a subtle net of gold mesh, and one day when Venus and Mars were together Vulcan sprang his trap, caught the lovers in his net, and held them up to be ridiculed by all the other gods. *Othello* as a play is a kind of dramatic reworking of this tale of Mars, Venus, and Vulcan—a tale that would have been familiar to Shakespeare's audience. Iago is the Vulcan figure, a tortured looker-on; Othello himself the war hero, in this case—significantly—not the adulterous lover but the husband. Yet Iago contrives to expose and ridicule the relationship between Othello and Desdemona, as Vulcan exposed and ridiculed Mars and Venus. We might notice, for example, that in the play Iago is frequently associated with images of nets and snares (one Renaissance term for snares is "toils"). Othello, arriving at Cyprus, greets his wife Desdemona as "my fair warrior," and Venus was thought to be not only the beautiful goddess of love but also a protectress of sailors and a war goddess—a conception of her that seems to have derived from Cyprus itself. In short, the apparent opposites, Venice and Cyprus, are also deeply implicated in each other.

Venice and Cyprus. Venice and Venus. Law and passion. Or, perhaps, Venice—which contains within itself a concealed, suppressed version of

Cyprus—or Venus. Venice *is* Cyprus, Cyprus is Venice masked—not so much its opposite as its hidden self.

Yet Venice presents itself initially as the place of light and reason, the archetype of a Renaissance city, ruled by a Duke who seems to exemplify all of its emblematic qualities, and this vision is clearly limned in the play's third scene. Although it is the middle of the night, a disorderly time, the Duke and Senators are met in a brightly lighted council chamber, light here symbolizing, as it does throughout the play and throughout Shakespeare, a search for control and order. The chamber is full of people, but rather than milling about they are apparently ranged in an orderly way at a central table. And most strikingly, their procedures are so reasonable and logical that they see right through intended deception. A sailor reports that the enemy Turks are heading for Rhodes, rather than Cyprus, but the Duke and the Senators reject his report:

> This cannot be
> By no assay of reason—'tis a pageant
> To keep us in false gaze.
> Othello *1.3.18–20*

To the Turks, the play's chief exterior emblems of disorder, Cyprus is more valuable than Rhodes, so the Duke concludes that, whatever appearances may suggest, they are actually aiming for Cyprus, and so, of course, it proves. No sooner does he assert confidently that the Turk is "not for Rhodes" than a messenger arrives with more news: the Turks are now openly making for Cyprus. Reason has prevailed, has seen through fiction and deceit.

The phrase "false gaze" is a significant one for the play as a whole, and is, typically for Shakespeare, here inserted, as if casually and unimportantly, in an early dramatic interchange among secondary characters. But throughout the rest of *Othello* the audience will see, again and again, other staged "pageants," produced like this one to delude the onlooker, to "keep us in false gaze."

For there is, as the play will quickly demonstrate, a radical limitation to the confidence in reason. The wildness of the border place that is Cyprus, buffeted by unimaginable winds and storms, populated by an unstable people, an island on the very outer limits of civilization—this alternative to Venetian reason and smug self-confidence is predicted in the play long before Othello's army lands literally at Cyprus in act 2. The Cyprus element begins to show itself from the very beginning of the play, in the startling and superbly dramatic—and frightening—opening scene outside Brabantio's Venetian palace. In this scene, as will quickly become clear, "Cyprus" is already in Venice. And with the human anarchy of the Cyprus world, we can see, as well, the limits of Venice.

Othello begins, like *Hamlet,* in darkness, with a whispered conversation between Iago and Roderigo. Something both shocking and surprising has apparently occurred, though it is hard for the moment to know what it is. Roderigo suspects Iago has known all along: "Tush, never tell me!" (1.1.1). But

Iago protests that he had no idea: "If ever I did dream of such a matter, abhor me" (1.1.5). What is this shocking circumstance that has brought about a meeting in the dark of night? It is simply the news of a marriage. The traditional end of comedy, marriage here becomes the beginning of tragedy.

For this is the marriage of "black" Othello, the Moor, and "fair" Desdemona, Brabantio's daughter. And it is under Brabantio's ornate Venetian window that Iago and Roderigo now huddle and make themselves that most terrifying of all human disruptions of order: a voice crying out in the night. "Awake, what ho, Brabantio, thieves, thieves, thieves! / Look to your house, your daughter, and your bags" (1.1.79–80). On the upper stage, peering out of his palace window, Brabantio appears, puzzled and annoyed but not yet really frightened: "What is the reason of this terrible summons? / What is the matter here?" (82–83). And more pointedly: "What tell'st thou me of robbing? This is Venice. / My house is not a grange" (108–109). The wishfully confident surety of his language tells all: this is Venice, home of order and "reason," not a grange, a farmhouse, a barnyard. Nothing nocturnal and animal, bestial and wild, can happen here. But no sooner does he make this confident assertion than the air is split with images of animals and bestial sexuality: "Even now, now, very now, an old black ram / Is tupping your white ewe" (88–89). "[Y]ou'll have your daughter covered with a Barbary horse, you'll have your nephews neigh to you, you'll have coursers for cousins and jennets for germans" (112–115). The voice is, of course, that of Iago, who will speak throughout the play in animal language, who will plant in Othello's mind, indelibly, the image of Desdemona and Cassio "as prime as goats, as hot as monkeys," and who will summon as well that other bestial presence, jealousy, the green-eyed monster. "What profane wretch are you?" demands the senator Brabantio, in a tone that may waver between imperiousness and doubt. And the answer comes back strongly, the stronger for its anonymity, emerging out of the darkness: "I am one, sir, that comes to tell you your daughter and the Moor are now making the beast with two backs" (117–118). And again: "[Y]our fair daughter, / At this odd-even and dull watch o' th' night, / [is] Transported . . . / To the gross clasps of a lascivious Moor" (123–127).

Iago speaks, under the cloak of night, from a moral, as well as a literal, darkness. He cannot be seen; his voice and Roderigo's come to Brabantio as out of some cosmic mist, and the whole scene has the immediacy and terrifying persuasiveness of nightmare. "Give me a taper!" cries Brabantio. "This accident is not unlike my dream. . . . Light, I say, light!" (1.1.142–144). "Accident" here means "occurrence," "incident," "event": Brabantio has already imagined or dreamt this scene, the spectacle of his daughter and Othello in bed. The outcry in the street comes as a confirmation of the inner thoughts he has not acknowledged to himself, thoughts that were censored or blocked by the "reason" that is Venice. And so he calls for light. As the play unfolds, this dichotomy of light and darkness will mirror the dichotomy of Venice and Cyprus. The anarchic scene at Cyprus in act 2, scene 3, where Cassio's drunkenness, provoked by Iago, leads to public clamor and the awakening of Othello and Desdemona, is structurally identical to this opening scene: a loud noise in the night, the call for silence ("Silence that dreadful bell"), and a cry for light. And the scenario will repeat itself a third time, for in act 5, scene 1, the wounding of Cassio and the murder of Roderigo take place in darkness, and the cry will again go out for light. In all of these scenes Iago pretends to be the light-bringer, providing order and clarity, although he is in fact the source of chaos. There is an allusive glance here at the name of Lucifer, literally the "light-bringer," a name for the rebel archangel often used in the early modern period as synonymous with Satan or the Devil. Iago brings light in order to enforce darkness.

Venice and Cyprus. Light and darkness. Black and white.

European languages have loaded the term "blackness" with negativity, in keeping with the privileging of "light" as reason and goodness. This negative valence has spilled over into racial stereotypes; even if it does not originate in them, it overdetermines them. The process continued, indeed escalated, beyond the time of Shakespeare, so that we find, for example, in Richard Steele and Joseph Addison's *Spectator* number 459 of 1712 the phrase "[t]he Blackness and Deformity of Vice," described as part of "the Christian System." The issue is unavoidable in Shakespeare's *Titus Andronicus,* where Aaron the Moor is repeatedly associated with amorality and lust. Much is made in this play of Othello's blackness, as physical description and supposed moral symbol. Sociohistorical discussions about whether Moors were "black" or "tawny" and whether Shakespeare or his sources are conflating northern with southern Africa have their local interest, to be sure, but the play is unambiguous in putting the word "black," as a complex epithet, in the mouth of Iago, and also in the mouth of the self-doubting Othello. "[A]n old black ram," Iago calls him, and we will shortly hear Othello himself muse, "Haply for I am black, /And have not those soft parts of conversation / That chamberers have; or for I am declined / Into the vale of years" (3.3.267–270). Yet Othello is resented by Iago and Roderigo not so much because he is "black" as because he is a stranger in homogenous Venice. He is, as Roderigo calls him, "an extravagant and wheeling stranger / Of here and everywhere" (1.1.137–138), a soldier of fortune.

Here then is the key dramatic point, one typically Shakespearean, at the same time establishing and critiquing a stereotype: Othello *looks* black, but it is Iago who becomes the pole of moral negativity (conventionally, "blackness") in the play. On the other end of this scale, the play presents in emblematic form both false and true images of "whiteness," since the name of the courtesan, or whore, Bianca means "white," or "the white one." Thus we have "black Othello," and *really* (i.e., inwardly, morally) black Iago. "White" Bianca, and *really* (i.e., inwardly, morally) white Desdemona. "Black" and "white" here again demarcate a prevailing cultural, linguistic, and symbolic code, mapped onto conventional (Christian) notions of sin and virtue. Although, as the philosopher Stanley Cavell has noted, Desdemona's name includes the word "demon" (Cavell also observes that there is a "hell" in the middle of "Othello"), she herself is constantly associated, throughout the play, with images of whiteness and purity: wedding sheets; a handkerchief; skin whiter than snow, and "smooth as monumental alabaster." It is this purity of spirit that Othello mistakes for sin, just as he mistakes Iago's malevolence for honesty. The "honest" (that is, chaste and virtuous) Desdemona is accused of dishonesty; the dishonest Iago (insincere, deceitful, lacking in candor and public spirit) is labeled "honest" over and over again in line after line. "My friend, thy husband, honest, honest Iago" (5.2.161), insists Othello to Emilia when Iago's perfidy is unmasked, his frantic repetition of the word "honest" an attempt to prove through a kind of magical arithmetic what cannot be found in the evidence before him. The word "honesty," as has often been noticed, becomes for the play a pivot of meaning, an emblem of its many false assumptions. When Othello demands what he calls "ocular proof," visible proof, of Desdemona's faithlessness, he is asking for exactly this kind of deception, and needless to say he gets it.

The play thus has a strong substructure that links it to the psychomachia, the struggle between two forces, a "good angel" and a "bad angel," for a man's soul. This is a familiar Shakespearean pattern, which we have often encountered in the history plays, like *Richard III* and *Henry IV,* where it was explicitly linked to its medieval origins in the so-called moralities. In *Henry IV,* the story of Prince Hal, the contest was between Falstaff and King Henry IV; in *Othello* a very similar contest pits Iago on one side and Desdemona on the other, the two contending for the possession, in the sense of property or ownership and also that of magical or demonic enchantment, of Othello. Iago is in many ways a more sophisticated version of the medieval Vice, that stock character (also explicitly invoked in connection with Richard III and with Falstaff) who was a figure of consummate evil and anarchy, whose purpose was to coax the hero into sin. But another way of understanding this same dramatic situation—a tug-of-war with Othello at its center—is to see both Iago and Desdemona as reflecting aspects of Othello's own mind. In this case the psychomachia (literally, "struggle of the soul") is taking place *within* him, and the contest he undergoes is a struggle of conflicting impulses, creative or sexual, anarchic or destructive. Because this is a play, and functions on several levels at once, we need not necessarily choose between the notions of interior and exterior struggle: Iago and Desdemona are real dramatic characters, not hallucinations, although the roles they play are inevitably inflected by Othello's own fantasies, not only about them, but also about himself.

So who is Othello? We have noted that Roderigo, an insular Venetian, calls him "an extravagant and wheeling stranger / Of here and everywhere," and it is plain that Brabantio's distrust of him comes, in part, from the fact that he does not really fit into the Venetian world. He is a soldier rather than a statesman or a courtier. He is not native to Venice, but comes instead, presumably, from northern Africa, where Mauritania (the place of origin of the "Moors") was located (on the other side of Morocco from where the country Mauritania now lies). From the medieval period through to the seventeenth century Moors were thought to be black or swarthy, and from the sixteenth century to the nine-teenth the term "blackamoor" was used as a synonym for black-skinned African, Ethiopian, Negro, or any dark-skinned person (thus, for example, from Sir Walter Ralegh's *History of the World:* "The Negro's, which we call the Blacke-Mores"). Equally important, Moors were conventionally Muslims, not Chris-tians. Arguably, Othello's status as a former non-Christian is as important to the play as his status as a former non-Venetian.

One clue to Othello's personality, a personality upon which much of the dramatic action will turn, is his decision before the play begins to appoint Cassio—rather than Iago—as his lieutenant. For Cassio is everything that Othello thinks he himself is not. (We may notice that a "lieutenant"—from the French *lieu,* "place," and *tenant,* "holding"—is one who holds, or takes, the place of another. The specific military usage, as the officer next in rank to the captain, obviously obtains here, but the more literal sense is ironically that which Othello comes to fear, and Iago to desire.) Cassio is a Florentine, and Florence was for the English Renaissance a center of culture and courtship. Cas-sio is a "great arithmetician," as Iago complains, that is, a theoretical (or "desk") soldier, a scholar rather than a man of action. Othello admires the courtly Cas-sio, with his easy good looks and elegant manners, and is all too ready to believe that he could win away Desdemona, could take his captain's place in her bed. We are thus given an indication, before we ever meet Othello, that he is a man who perceives a limitation in himself, a man who doubts his social, though not his martial, abilities. When the audience first catches a glimpse of him, Othello is clearly in control, roused by Iago in act 1, scene 2; but, significantly, the figure of speech through which we first hear him describe himself is one of dammed-up energy, of repression, wildness under control:

> For know, Iago,
> But that I love the gentle Desdemona
> I would not my unhousèd free condition
> Put unto circumscription and confine
> For the seas' worth.
>
> *1.2.24–28*

Love confines him rather than sets him free. "[C]ircumscription and confine" describes a condition of withholding under pressure, and this circumscription will at last burst; in a related image in the middle of the play Othello will speak of his passions as being "[l]ike to the Pontic Sea, / Whose icy current and com-pulsive course / Ne'er knows retiring ebb" (3.3.456–458). A compelling phrase like "compulsive course," although apparently applied only to the Pontic Sea, also known as the Black Sea, is readily applicable to the speaker as well as to the natural world. Othello's course of action and reaction is as "compulsive" as any tidal swell.

There is perhaps an excess of control and rationality in the Othello of the early scenes. Interrupted on his wedding night by a troop of armed men, he says only, mildly, "Keep up your bright swords, for the dew will rust 'em" (1.2.60). The actor James Earl Jones once remarked that Othello was the only Shakespearean warrior we never see in a fight, and indeed throughout the play Othello avoids swordplay, or loses his sword, or urges others to put their weapons away. It has become commonplace, in *Romeo and Juliet* and elsewhere in Shakespeare, to compare marital and martial swordsmanship, male prowess in the bed and on the battlefield (in several plays the equation is explicitly made in the text). And although there is some bawdy joking in *Othello* (in conversations between Iago and Cassio; Cassio and Bianca; Emilia and Desdemona), Othello himself never participates in it. The dimension in which skill in swordplay and skill in love-play are compared and contrasted in this play is that of oblique imagery and implied action: Othello's self-doubts are indeed those of the lover, not the soldier, but he does not see the two roles as mutually displacing or substitutive. The bitter sexual joke is not his: it is, instead, on him.

The main accusation against Othello in the opening scenes is that he has used some kind of black magic to bewitch Desdemona and win her affections. Thus Brabantio lashes out at him: "O thou foul thief, where hast thou stowed my daughter? / Damned as thou art, thou hast enchanted her" (1.2.63–64). It must be witchcraft—what else could lead Desdemona to stray so far from parental and civic expectations, to fall in love with a stranger and a black man? As Brabantio insists in his complaint to the Duke,

> A maiden never bold,
> Of spirit so still and quiet that her motion
> Blushed at herself—and she in spite of nature,
> Of years, of country, credit, everything,
> To fall in love with what she feared to look on!
>
> *1.3.94–98*

To the father, witchcraft is the only plausible explanation. But Othello, with a quiet dignity, and the same soldier's reticence he had shown in the previous scene, preempts the forthcoming accusation:

> Rude am I in my speech,
> And little blessed with the soft phrase of peace,
> . . . .
> And little of this great world can I speak
> More than pertains to feats of broils and battle.
> And therefore little shall I grace my cause

In speaking for myself. Yet, by your gracious patience,
I will a round unvarnished tale deliver
Of my whole course of love, what drugs, what charms,
What conjuration and what mighty magic—
For such proceeding I am charged withal—
I won his daughter.

1.3.81–94

What is Othello's witchcraft? Language—the source of "charm" (from the Latin *carmen*, "song") and magic. A "round unvarnished tale." Despite his Antony-like protestation, "Rude am I in my speech" (compare "I am no orator as Brutus was" [*Julius Caesar* 3.2.208]), Othello has enchanted Desdemona with his story of himself. In fact, Othello's language throughout the play is so resoundingly beautiful that generations of critics, following G. Wilson Knight, have called it "the Othello music." The story of his courtship, as he relates it, is both charming and domestic, though it casts Desdemona in a conventional gender role, as admiring onlooker, that will incorporate its own dangers:

> Her father loved me, oft invited me,
> Still questioned me the story of my life
>
> .   .   .   .
>
> Wherein I spoke of most disastrous chances,
> Of moving accidents by flood and field,
> Of hair-breadth scapes i'th' imminent deadly breach,
> Of being taken by the insolent foe
> And sold to slavery, of my redemption thence,
> And portance in my traveller's history,
> Wherein of antres vast and deserts idle,
> Rough quarries, rocks, and hills whose heads touch heaven,
> It was my hint to speak. Such was my process,
> And of the cannibals that each other eat,
> The Anthropophagi, and men whose heads
> Do grow beneath their shoulders. These things to hear
> Would Desdemona seriously incline,
> But still the house affairs would draw her thence,
> Which ever as she could with haste dispatch
> She'd come again, and with a greedy ear
> Devour up my discourse. . . .
>
> .   .   .   .
>
>   My story being done,
> She gave me for my pains a world of kisses.
> She swore, in faith 'twas strange, 'twas passing strange,
> 'Twas pitiful, 'twas wondrous pitiful.

She wished she had not heard it, yet she wished
That heaven had made her such a man. She thankèd me,
And bade me, if I had a friend that loved her,
I should but teach him how to tell my story,
And that would woo her. Upon this hint I spake.
She loved me for the dangers I had passed,
And I loved her that she did pity them.
This only is the witchcraft I have used.

1.3.128–168

Othello's is a spellbinding story, out of the tradition of romance and epic, complete with monsters, deserts, caves, and cannibals, with the added appeal that it is "true." Indeed the magical language works upon the Duke as it worked upon Desdemona: "I think," he says, "this tale would win my daughter, too." As we will see, it is only when Othello loses language, loses this capacity to enchant through speech, that he loses the vestiges of "civilization," which his speech here clearly praises and exemplifies, and that his tragedy begins. Yet there is something very curious about this tale of courtship. "She loved me for the dangers I had passed, / And I loved her that she did pity them." This is a public, not a personal, perception. She loved me for what I *did;* I loved her because she admired me. As he will over and over again, Othello here confuses the personal with the public, the outer with the inner man. His own defensiveness, which coexists with his pride ("Rude am in my speech"; "Haply for I am black, / And have not those soft parts of conversation / That chamberers have") causes him to misunderstand, radically and tragically, the nature of love in general and Desdemona's love for him in particular. For when Desdemona appears, as she does in the very next moment, it becomes quite plain that this is not how she would describe their courtship.

Desdemona's actions and language may remind us of all the other Shakespearean women who face what seems to them to be a choice between father and lover: Juliet, Rosalind, Cressida, Isabella, Ophelia. Of them all, she is perhaps the most forthright and unambiguous:

Brabantio   Come hither, gentle mistress.
            Do you perceive in all this noble company
            Where most you owe obedience?
Desdemona   My noble father,
            I do perceive here a divided duty.
            To you I am bound for life and education.
            My life and education both do learn me
            How to respect you. You are the lord of duty,
            I am hitherto your daughter. But here's my husband,
            And so much duty as my mother showed

> To you, preferring you before her father,
> So much I challenge that I may profess
> Due to the Moor my lord.
>
> *1.3.177–188*

There is no hesitation here, no doubt or artificial coyness. Where Othello speaks of something like hero worship, Desdemona speaks of love, and of a love that is frankly sexual as well as romantic. They had been interrupted on their wedding night, and now the Duke proposes to send Othello to Cyprus to quell the Turks, leaving Desdemona behind. Othello is willing to go: "The tyrant custom, most grave senators, / Hath made the flinty and steel couch of war / My thrice-driven bed of down." But Desdemona is resolute and determined to be with him, and her speech proclaims a love that will give the lie to any dependence upon mere appearances, upon "ocular proof":

> That I did love the Moor to live with him,
> My downright violence and storm of fortunes
> May trumpet to the world. My heart's subdued
> Even to the very quality of my lord.
> I saw Othello's visage in his mind,
> And to his honours and his valiant parts
> Did I my soul and fortunes consecrate;
> So that, dear lords, if I be left behind,
> A moth of peace, and he go to the war,
> The rites for why I love him are bereft me,
> And I a heavy interim shall support
> By his dear absence. Let me go with him.
>
> *1.3.247–258*

Her eloquent certainty may remind us of Juliet's speech of love-longing for Romeo ("Gallop apace, you fiery-footed steeds, / Towards Phoebus' lodging" [*Romeo and Juliet* 3.2.1–2]). Desdemona is from the first open, generous, sure of herself—unlike Othello. There is no self-doubt here.

In the council chamber scene, and at several key points thereafter, Desdemona will present herself as a social actor in the context of an otherwise man-to-man negotiation: here, and again when she tries to intervene on the side of Cassio, and indeed in the original offstage scene of wooing, when she paused in her housework to overhear and ultimately to participate in the conversation between Othello and her father. Othello's notions of womanhood are, it appears, more conventional than Desdemona's. He prefers a posture of obedience and admiration ("She loved me for the dangers I had passed"), a woman who "knows her place" and does not overstep it; yet as Iago will be quick to observe on the first opportune occasion, "She did deceive her father, marrying you" (3.3.210). Desdemona's outspokenness in the council chamber scene is welcome to her husband, but it is a harbinger of trouble ahead. She had told him she wished that "heaven had made her such a man," but he does not want her to act like a man in the political sphere.

Furthermore, her erotic frankness poses its own dangers. Othello is quick to declare that his own motives for wishing her companionship at Cyprus are not carnal: "I therefor beg it not / To please the palate of my appetite, / Nor to comply with heat—the young affects / In me defunct" (1.3.260–263). Once again we hear from Othello a denial of appetite and personal desire, a denial of the private man. Whether he is protesting too much against a perceived stereotype of the sexually appetitive black man, or merely declaring his own imperviousness to overweening passion, his assertion here draws a line: I am too old and too controlled to be driven by "young affects." Here it is a boast, but how soon the coin will flip the other way, and he will be convinced that Desdemona could indeed be unfaithful to him, "for I am declined / Into the vale of years." A failure to reconcile public and private feelings leaves him with no space for self-knowledge. The clearest danger signal here is his willingness to deny and postpone sexual love; it is as if, in proving himself a civilized man, worthy of the title of Venetian, he has to prove that he is more than a man, that he must compensate for his own ordinary humanity. Othello seems to project a need to be seen as superhuman, and is driven, as a consequence, into a situation of uncontrollable and destructive passion. With his mythical exploits against cannibals and monsters, his heroic status as the only man who can defend Venice in a time of crisis, Othello never takes the time to see himself as a man.

Significantly, at the end of the first act, the act that centers on Othello's marriage, the only ensuing pregnancy is that of Iago's plot against him: "I ha't. It is ingendered. Hell and night / Must bring this monstrous birth to the world's light" (1.3.385–386). These are the last lines of the act, and again they come out of the darkness, as in scene after scene Iago remains onstage and speaks to the audience in soliloquy, plotting his devices, gulling Roderigo and playing on his lusts. For Roderigo is Othello's opposite in terms of sexual passion—incontinently lustful, willing to do anything and spend any sum in order to enjoy Desdemona's body. The first act, then, opens in darkness and closes in darkness, its brief glimpse of Venetian order and reason a prelude to tragedy.

As if to mirror the impending doom, the next act opens with a storm. Venice was a maritime power, like England, and storms at sea were a common and often catastrophic fact of life. But a Shakespearean storm always has an emotional resonance far beyond the historical or meteorological, whether it is the storm in *Twelfth Night* that brings Viola and Sebastian to Illyria, the storm in *The Tempest* that will bring the shipwrecked Neapolitans to Prospero's island, the storm of omens and portents that disturbed the landscape in *Julius Caesar,* or the thunder and lightning that assail both Lear and Macbeth. Our modern colloquial term "brainstorm" gives some sense of the ease with which this figure can be seen as an interior as well as an exterior event, as, indeed, does Desdemona's use of the phrase "storm of fortunes" in describing her love for Othello to the Duke. The storm in *Othello* is a counterpart of the pervasive sea language we have already noticed: the "seas' worth" Othello would not, ordinarily, trade for his freedom; the Pontic Sea that is as icy and compulsive as his jealous rage; and, in the final scene of the play, the lines "Here is my journey's end, here is my butt / And very sea-mark of my utmost sail." In all these instances it is the language of interior journey as well as exterior storm.

Consider Othello's greeting to his bride when he lands at Cyprus. "O my fair warrior!" he says. This is affectionate and charming, but the oxymoron, the hint of an Amazonian Desdemona, will shortly usher in the unwelcome language of civil war. There is a faintly ominous ring to his glad welcome to the end of storm, "If it were now to die, / 'Twere now to be most happy" (2.1.186–187), for, ironically, this will be the last truly happy moment either of them will enjoy. The omnipresent pun on "die," always operative in Shakespeare's love tragedies, is especially so in *Othello,* where sexual consummation is deferred in the interest of war and civic duty, and where the lovers will ultimately die together on a bed fitted with their wedding sheets.

Moreover, the journey to the wild fastnesses of Cyprus is, we quickly learn, entirely futile: "News, friends: our wars are done, the Turks are drowned" (2.1.199). There is no job here for Othello the soldier. His forte is waging external wars against an acknowledged enemy, in this case the barbarous, pagan Turk. But the end of these external wars means, as it does all too often in Shakespeare, the beginning of internal war, civil war: first, the drunken brawling of Cassio and the troops, stage-managed by Iago, and second, the war that ensues within Othello himself, as Iago's monstrous birth comes to light and reveals itself as the monster jealousy. For Iago, serpent and tempter, is hard at work. Othello's wars are done, but Iago's are just beginning.

Once again the time is night, Iago's natural element, and once again Othello and Desdemona withdraw to their marriage bed, for their marriage is as yet unconsummated. As Iago points out with a leer, it is early in the evening, not yet ten o'clock. "Come, my dear love, / The purchase made, the fruits are to ensue. / The profit's yet to come 'tween me and you" (2.3.8–10). The mercantile language here is Othello's. The withdrawal of the married lovers allows Iago a clear shot at Cassio. Cassio is, as Iago complains, fastidiously courteous, kissing ladies' hands and apologizing to their husbands for doing so. He is both patronizing and condescending (boasting that "[t]he lieutenant is to be saved before the ancient"); and above all, he is a bad drinker, whose own eloquence deserts him for drunken mumbling ("Fore God, an excellent song. . . . Fore God, this is a more exquisite song than the other"), like some Florentine version of Sir Toby Belch. Yet Cassio, though he has his weaknesses and character flaws, does not number lust for Desdemona among them, and Iago fails in his tempter's dialogue, one of the few comic moments in this relentlessly tragic play:

Iago [speaking of Othello's early bedtime, with a wink]	He hath not yet made wanton the night with her, and she is sport for Jove.
Cassio	She's a most exquisite lady.
Iago	And I'll warrant her full of game.
Cassio	Indeed, she's a most fresh and delicate creature.
Iago	What an eye she has! Methinks it sounds a parley to provocation.
Cassio	An inviting eye, and yet, methinks, right modest.
Iago	And when she speaks, is it not an alarum to love?
Cassio	She is indeed perfection.
Iago [giving up]	Well, happiness to their sheets.

2.3.15–25

He has failed in his attempt to compromise Cassio directly, and—like Milton's Satan—he will have to resort instead to trickery, to "other proofs."

"[H]appiness to their sheets." This second mention of the wedding sheets will not be the last, and they will emerge in the second half of the play as a powerful emblem of Othello's fall. "Strangle her in her bed, even the bed she hath contaminated," Iago will suggest, and Othello will eagerly concur: "Good, good, the justice of it pleases" (4.1.197–199). But Iago's plot is still in the process of building, and the second night provides him with a scenario very like that of the first night, in Venice, in which to work his designs. Again Roderigo is a willing assistant; again a hue and cry goes up, out of the darkness, the noise and confused shouts, and—this is terrifically effective in the theater—a great bell begins to toll. Once again, Othello's marriage rites—the rites for which Desdemona says she loves him—are interrupted, and Othello storms onto the stage:

> From whence ariseth this?
> Are we turned Turks, and to ourselves do that
> Which heaven hath forbid the Ottomites?
> . . . .
> Silence that dreadful bell— . . .
> . . . .
> What, in a town of war
> Yet wild, the people's hearts brimful of fear,
> To manage private and domestic quarrel
> In night, and on the court and guard of safety!
> 'Tis monstrous. . . .

2.3.152–158, 196–200

Once again, the private and domestic are monstrous to him:

Othello   Honest Iago, that looks dead with grieving,
            Speak. Who began this? On thy love I charge thee.
Iago   I do not know. Friends all but now, even now,
            In quarter and in terms like bride and groom
            Devesting them for bed. . . .

                                            2.3.160–164

"[B]ut now, even now"—this is an echo, detectable to the audience but not to
Othello, of Iago's urgent statement to Brabantio in the opening scene: "Even
now, now, very now, an old black ram / Is tupping your white ewe." And of
course the scene is the same, as Iago goes on insinuate by the use of an astonishingly familiar and insulting simile: the soldiers were "[i]n quarter and in terms
like bride and groom / Devesting them for bed." The actual bride and groom,
Desdemona and Othello, were presumably doing just that when the bell began
to toll. Was the old black ram tupping the white ewe? Or has Iago contrived to
arrange that they are once again prevented from consummating their marriage?
As always, though, the personal note seems to evade Othello. Even when Desdemona appears he returns to the language of the "fair warrior" and the "flinty
and steel couch of war": "Come, Desdemona. 'Tis the soldier's life / To have
their balmy slumbers waked with strife" (2.3.241–242).
    Othello's problem in the opening acts of the play is fundamentally a refusal
to acknowledge the private nature of his own passion and his own person. Ultimately he will blame Desdemona for inciting that passion in him. His energies
are concentrated on the public self, on protecting that elusive entity that Cassio
also seeks desperately to protect: "Reputation, reputation, reputation—O, I ha'
lost my reputation! I ha' lost the immortal part of myself, and what remains is
bestial!" (2.3.246–248). The speaker is Cassio, but it could easily be the Othello
of the late acts. Iago's trenchant reply marks the difference between him and
Cassio coldly and clearly: "As I am an honest man, I had thought you had
received some bodily wound." Why bother with a trifle like reputation? "As I
am an honest man." The hollow refrain of "honest" here echoes throughout the
scene, as Iago's honesty is mentioned four times in a hundred lines. The refrac-
tions of this word mark out the territories of the play, for "honesty" in the
period has a variety of meanings depending upon subject and context: it can
stand for respectability, moral virtue, female chastity, freedom from disgrace.
And "honest," as an epithet meaning "worthy," might be used "in a patronizing
way to an inferior," according to *The Oxford English Dictionary* (definition 1.c).
Cassio's "honest Iago" is thus conceivably as much a social put-down as a term
of praise. That one man's or woman's "honesty" is not the same as another's is a
complex and contestatory truth that lies at the heart of *Othello*—and of Othello.
    It is Othello's very refusal to regard the personal, to trust his own feelings,
that gives Iago the opportunity he seeks, allowing him to divide the world into
those who work "by wit" and those who work "by witchcraft." "Thou know'st
we work by wit and not by witchcraft," he reminds an impatient Roderigo,

"[a]nd wit depends on dilatory time" (2.3.345–346). In the broad structure of the play, "wit" is associated with Iago, with Venetian politics, with wordplay and doubleness, with plots and plotting, and with maleness; "witchcraft," with Africa (Othello the Moor; the Egyptian charmer who gave his mother the fatal handkerchief), with magic, charms, and enchantment, and with women (the charmer; Othello's mother; Desdemona). "Wit and witchcraft" is another way of saying "reason and passion," or even "Venice and Cyprus." And Desdemona's appeal to Othello on the grounds of the personal—of friendship for Cassio—however touching, is ultimately doomed. "Why, this is not a boon," she says. " 'Tis as I should entreat you wear your gloves, / Or feed on nourishing dishes, or keep you warm" (3.3.77–79). She asks Othello to be a private person, to grant leeway to a friend who came with him when he wooed her. But rather like Julius Caesar, who brushed away the warning of the Soothsayer because it pertained to him personally, as an individual rather than as a public man ("What touches us ourself shall be last served" [*Julius Caesar* 3.1.8]), Othello distrusts the personal, and takes refuge in the public self.

Yet, as we have noticed, the play is a domestic tragedy, a simple plot with no subplot, no shift of focus away from the major characters, no "comic relief" except for the venal and Vice-like Iago. *Othello* differs from the other great Shakespearean tragedies in that it does not provide a sympathetic onstage confidant for the audience. In *Hamlet* there is Horatio; in *King Lear,* Edmund; in *Antony and Cleopatra,* Enobarbus; in *Macbeth,* Lennox, Macduff, and the Scottish doctor. All these voice the dismay we feel, and even try to intercede—as if for us—in the dramatic action. But no one onstage in *Othello* sees the tragedy unfolding in time to stop it; by the time Emilia does so, and Lodovico, in the final scenes, things have gone too far. Our only onstage confidant is Iago, who repeatedly makes us complicit in his designs, by addressing us in asides and soliloquies. Many stories are told of audience members in the theater over the centuries who have risen from their seats and shouted the truth at an unhearing Othello, that Desdemona is chaste, that Iago is his enemy, not his friend. But the play is cunningly constructed to keep us out of earshot, unable to insist, like the Duke and Senators in the third scene of the play, that what Othello sees is a "pageant" to keep him in "false gaze." Until the last act, no one on the stage—except Iago—knows what the audience in the theater knows. So Othello will say,

> Excellent wretch! Perdition catch my soul
> But I do love thee, and when I love thee not,
> Chaos is come again.
>
> *3.3.91–93*

This is characteristic Othello hyperbole, and it will come true. Perdition will catch his soul; chaos will indeed come again. Desdemona is the play's principle of order, and the magic of love is the only defense against witchcraft and against mere wit. Othello's loss of faith in Desdemona, like Troilus's loss of faith in Cressida, and Hamlet's in Ophelia and Gertrude, will be irreversible in tragic and dramatic terms, so that for a moment black *is* white, day *is* night, and they are all "turned Turks."

Thomas Rymer's notorious account of *Othello,* in his *Short View of Tragedy* (1693), set out a number of commonsense objections to its plot and tone. For Rymer, writing almost a century after Shakespeare, the play seemed both exaggerated and trivial, not elegant or important. It is worth reviewing some of his objections, both because they are memorably expressed and because some critics, like T. S. Eliot, have been inclined to think that they have never been "cogently" refuted. For other critics, including many in the last decades of the twentieth century, Rymer's arguments about blackamoors, women, and farce, turned inside out, have been the basis of a renewed scholarly and historical approach to the play. Here is Rymer:

> First, this may be a caution to all Maidens of Quality how, without their Parents' consent, they run away with Black-amoors. . . .
>   Secondly, this may be a warning to all good wives that they look well to their linen.
>   Thirdly, this may be a lesson to Husbands, that before their Jealousie be Tragical, the proofs may be Mathematical. . . .

> So much ado, so much stress, so much passion and repetition about an Handkerchief! Why was this not call'd the *Tragedy of the Handkerchief*? . . . Had it been *Desdemona's* Garter, the Sagacious Moor might have smelt a Rat: but the Handkerchief is so remote a trifle, no Booby, on this side *Mauritania,* cou'd make any consequence from it.
>   We may learn here, that a Woman never loses her Tongue, even tho' after she is stifl'd. . . .

> There is in this Play, some burlesk, some humour, and ramble of Comical Wit, some shew, and some *Mimickery* to divert the spectators: but the tragical part is, plainly none other, than a Bloody Farce, without salt or savour.[1]

To this point we have been considering the play from the point of view of its protagonist, Othello, the noble Moor of Venice. But nothing that happens in this play, from the beginning to the end, the opening nightmare to the final tragic scene of murder and suicide, would have happened without Iago. Othello has his flaws—he lacks confidence in himself as a private man, a Venetian, and, perhaps, a lover—and Desdemona, compared to an "entire and perfect chrysolite" (the topaz, emblematic stone of chastity), is perhaps flawed in being too flawless for the world of tragedy, and the Jacobean world. But it is Iago, always behind the scenes, putting words into Roderigo's mouth, insinuating, dropping a clue here and a handkerchief there, who is the play's malign and conscienceless stage manager. Who is he, and what are his motives? Why does he set out so relentlessly to ruin Othello and everything he stands for?

Although his name, like Roderigo's, is Spanish, and may reflect lingering English-Spanish political tensions, Iago is explicitly identified within the play as a Venetian—in fact, in his own mind, as the only true Venetian, since Othello is a Moor, an adventurer, and a stranger, and Cassio an upstart Florentine with fancy manners and a supercilious tone. Like Othello, Iago is jealous of Cassio's courtly ways: "He hath a daily beauty in his life / That makes me ugly" (5.1.19–20). Iago has, then, a social grievance against both these foreigners, who outrank him and command him in his home city and his home army. But he claims as well more specific motives. In the first scene of the play he claims that he hates Othello because Othello has made Cassio his lieutenant, Iago only his "ancient," or ensign, his flag-bearer. At the end of the first act he claims that he hates Othello because "it is thought abroad that 'twixt my sheets / He has done my office" (1.3.369–370)—that Othello has slept with Emilia. In the next scene he claims that he himself now lusts to possess Desdemona in retaliation for the fact that, as he puts it, "the lusty Moor / Hath leaped into my seat" (2.1.282–283). And he claims that Cassio, too, has slept with Emilia: "For I fear Cassio with my nightcap, too" (294). So the motives he brings forth are sexual jealousy, political envy, and reputation. Yet none of these seems convincing. Iago is not a man who—like Othello or Cassio—cares about external reputation. When Roderigo rhapsodizes about Desdemona's "blessed condition," he is quick to reply: "Blessed fig's end! The wine she drinks is made of grapes" (2.1.243). He does not seem overly possessive of the pragmatic and practical Emilia. And although his anger at loss of preferment is real, it does not seem entirely adequate to explain his actions. In fact, his motivations seem deliberately crafted, another Iagoan artifice, something made up after the fact to explain the unexplainable, which is, plainly and simply, "I hate the Moor." This is what the English poet and critic Samuel Taylor Coleridge famously called Iago's "motiveless malignity," a splendid phrase that we may use to describe the degree, as well as the source, of his destructive passion. Iago is the limit case of hatred; however true or false his reasons, the emotion he feels is in excess of them. Indeed, here is a better place for T. S. Eliot's phrase "emotion in excess of the facts as they appear" than *Hamlet,* whose hero's malaise Eliot described as lacking an adequate "objective correlative." The point of Iago's character would seem to be partly in that very excess, that lack of adequation. As we will see, he is not only a figure of hatred and resistance, but also a figure of desire.

Iago is in part the medieval Vice, with his sly humor and his constant attempts to win over the soul of the hero for hell. And he is in part a related medieval and Renaissance dramatic character, the so-called parasite, derived from classical drama, who lives off another, toadies to him, and flatters him for whatever he can get. The great exemplar of this in early modern English drama is the figure of Mosca ("the fly") in Ben Jonson's *Volpone*, who serves his master and finally turns the table so that his master serves him. This is what parasites do, and it is what Iago does. Iago is also, at times, explicitly and recognizably satanic, as Othello indicates in that pitiful moment at the close of the play when he is confronted with the fact that Iago has tricked him into murdering the woman who loved him above everything in the world: "I look down toward his feet, but that's a fable. / If that thou beest a devil I cannot kill thee" (5.2.292–293). Iago has no cloven hoof to show that he is a "demi-devil." As Adam and Eve also discovered, one of the most dangerous things about the Devil is that he can come in such a flattering disguise.

Hate for hate's sake. Motiveless malignity. Iago is successful precisely because he has no second dimension, no doubt, no compassion. From the start he is all action, and he is everywhere. Flattering Othello, and then Roderigo. Shouting out of the darkness, and calling for light. Yet notice that in fact he does nothing himself. Cassio, made drunk by Iago, causes disorder among the troops. Roderigo, goaded by Iago, rouses Brabantio and wounds Cassio. Othello, crazed and maddened by Iago, kills Desdemona. Iago has suggested all of this, but he performs none of it. Even the handkerchief is found by Emilia, not by Iago. He is a voice in the dark, living proof that words have enormous power, even though over and over we hear characters in the play deny this. "[W]ords are words," says Brabantio. "I never yet did hear / That the bruised heart was piercèd through the ear" (1.3.217–218). Iago's words poison everyone who hears them, from Brabantio to Othello. He uses, pertinently, the image of poison in the ear, which played such a crucial and literal part in the death of old Hamlet. And Iago's use of language is worthy of examination. For just as we noticed that he never really *does* anything, but instead moves other people to do things, so he never really *says* anything, but uses language instead to insinuate, to imply, to pull out of people's imaginations the dark things that are already there. Thus Brabantio *recognized* the image Iago shouted to him from the darkness ("This accident is not unlike my dream"). He had already imagined Othello and Desdemona in bed. What Iago did for him, and what he will do for Othello, is not to invent but to confirm his victim's negative fantasies. His skill is that of a mind reader as much as it is that of a provocateur.

It is a mark of Shakespeare's habitually brilliant dramatic construction that this one quick, immediate example involving a secondary character (Iago brings Brabantio's fearful "dream" to life) becomes the template for the major action, the duping of Othello with his own fantasies as bait. For this is Iago's practice and his strategy: again and again he leads Othello to express his own suspicions, suspicions he has already had, for which Iago's trumped-up "evidence" comes as both unwelcome and entirely convincing "confirmation." One of the play's most effective and most devastating plays-within-the-play functions in exactly this manner, while demonstrating once more the way a "pageant" can keep unwary onlookers "in false gaze." In act 3, scene 3, Cassio comes to Desdemona to ask her help in getting Othello's pardon. Their conversation is brief and formal, and it ends with Cassio's thanks and unhappy departure. At a distance, Othello and Iago appear on the scene, too far away to hear, and Iago, the opportunist, makes of Cassio's chastened exit a dumb show that he can interpret. "Ha! I like not that," he says, as if to himself. Instantly Othello's attention is caught: "What dost thou say?"

Iago	Nothing, my lord. Or if, I know not what.
Othello	Was not that Cassio parted from my wife?
Iago	Cassio, my lord? No, sure, I cannot think it,
	That he would steal away so guilty-like
	Seeing you coming.
Othello	I do believe 'twas he.

3.3.34–40

"That he would steal away so guilty-like." This is crime by suggestion, the more plausible because it appears to begin with a generous denial: Iago saw "nothing"; he "cannot think" that it was Cassio.

The same kind of insinuation is achieved through Iago's constant function in the play as *echo*. For as with the many echo poems popular in the period (and like the echo song in John Webster's *Duchess of Malfi*), when Iago echoes Othello, he turns the meaning of the word against itself. A good example occurs in the same scene, as Iago casually asks whether Cassio knew early on that Othello was in love with Desdemona:

Othello	O, yes, and went between us very oft.
Iago	Indeed?
Othello	Indeed? Ay, indeed. Discern'st thou aught in that?
	Is he not honest?
Iago	Honest, my lord?
Othello	Honest? Ay, honest.
Iago	My lord, for aught I know.
Othello	What dost thou think?
Iago	Think, my lord?
Othello	"Think, my lord?" By heaven, thou echo'st me
	As if there were some monster in thy thought
	Too hideous to be shown! . . .

3.3.102–112

The monster, the green-eyed monster, is in Othello's thought as much as it is in Iago's. Otherwise Iago's insinuations would have no effect. This is one reason it is possible to maintain that Iago is inside as well as outside Othello. Put another way, he is the devil Othello deserves. The same kind of temptation directed at the sexually confident Cassio would have no effect.

Iago as echo remembers Brabantio's warning, as the wedded couple leaves for Cyprus, and reproduces it at the first opportune time. Brabantio had cautioned, somewhat bitterly, "Look to her, Moor, if thou hast eyes to see. / She has deceived her father, and may thee" (1.3.291–292). Iago, repeating this, sows doubt: "She did deceive her father, marrying you, / And when she seemed to shake and fear your looks / She loved them most" (3.3.210–212). What is implied, and what is left unsaid? Desdemona is deceitful, and unfaithful. The proof of her love, averred in open court, now becomes evidence of her propensity for infidelity.

My favorite Iagan echo, though, is the one that is so universally quoted out of context to demonstrate "Shakespeare's" views on reputation. From *Bartlett's Familiar Quotations* to the daily newspaper, this passage is evinced as a wise bromide that embodies Shakespeare's philosophy. Whether or not the opinion expressed in the passage below was "Shakespeare's" it is impossible to say. The ideas were commonplaces in his time, so that what this clever playwright does is to torque the bromide by putting it in the mouth of an unlikely or untrustworthy speaker. Iago is a gleeful hypocrite who has already dismissed Cassio's lament for his lost reputation ("I thought you had received some bodily wound"). In conversation with Othello, though, he takes the opposite tack, and proffers one of the best-known passages in the play:

> Good name in man and woman, dear my lord,
> Is the immediate jewel of their souls.
> Who steals my purse steals trash; 'tis something, nothing;
> 'Twas mine, 'tis his, and has been slave to thousands.
> But he that filches from me my good name
> Robs me of that which not enriches him
> And makes me poor indeed.
>
> *3.3.160–166*

This is the same Iago who urged Roderigo, "[P]ut money in thy purse." But in talking about good name, about reputation, he aims unerringly at Othello's weak spot, his public reputation, what we would today, in the language of icons and publicity, call his "image." How powerful this is as a motive is demonstrated appallingly in Othello's own great speech in this scene, where he prospectively abdicates from public life and soldiering because of Desdemona's supposed infidelity. What troubles him most about it, tellingly, is that other people will know about his cuckolding:

> I had been happy if the general camp,
> Pioneers and all, had tasted her sweet body,
> So I had nothing known. O, now for ever

> Farewell the tranquil mind, farewell content,
> Farewell the pluměd troops, and the big wars
> That makes ambition virtue! O, farewell,
> Farewell the neighing steed and the shrill trump,
> The spirit-stirring drum, th'ear-piercing fife,
> The royal banner, and all quality,
> Pride, pomp, and circumstance of glorious war!
> And O, you mortal engines whose rude throats
> Th'immortal Jove's dread clamours counterfeit,
> Farewell! Othello's occupation's gone.
>
> *3.3.350–362*

If we decapitate this speech, removing the first two and a half lines, and begin with "O, now for ever," we get Shakespearean grandeur at full spate, round and resounding, a soldier's heartfelt reminiscence of what he loved about war. But what the speech as a whole says is something rather different: that since his wife is, as he believes, unfaithful, his professional identity is lost. The private and the public are here completely, and confusedly, intertwined. Furthermore, he would rather that every common soldier in the camp had slept with her and kept it a secret, than that she had had a single affair with his officer-friend, and that the affair had come to his notice. It is Othello's shame, not Desdemona's, that he speaks of so feelingly here.

It should come as no surprise that only two lines later we hear him address Iago: "Villain, be sure thou prove my love a whore. / Be sure of it. Give me the ocular proof" (3.3.364–365). We have already heard Desdemona say she "saw Othello's visage in his mind," not in the color of his skin. Now Othello, as if he did not comprehend the duplicity of the "ocular," asks for something he can see. Iago is carefully and calculatingly obtuse:

> [H]ow satisfied, my lord?
> Would you, the supervisor, grossly gape on,
> Behold her topped?
> . . . .
> It were a tedious difficulty, I think,
> To bring them to that prospect. . . .
> . . . .
> Where's satisfaction?
> It is impossible you should see this,
> Were they as prime as goats, as hot as monkeys.
>
> *3.3.399–408*

"Supervisor" and "prospect" are both words that pertain to vision. Does Othello really want to watch? Again, Iago speaks deliberately. I am not sure, he says, that I can show them to you in bed together. The reason he cannot, of course, is that they have not been in bed together. But Othello is led to read between the lines, to read the "truth" that is not there.

And so Iago goes on to invent "proofs," to invent, above all, what he describes as Cassio's dream, in which he claims to have shared a bed with Cassio and heard him betray the fact of the affair:

> I lay with Cassio lately,
> . . . .
> In sleep I heard him say "Sweet Desdemona,
> Let us be wary, let us hide our loves,"
> And then, sir, would he grip and wring my hand,
> Cry "O, sweet creature!," then kiss me hard,
> As if he plucked up kisses by the roots
> That grew upon my lips, lay his leg o'er my thigh,
> And sigh, and kiss, and then cry "Cursèd fate,
> That gave thee to the Moor!"
>
> 3.3.418, 423–430

Othello's response is characteristic—"O monstrous, monstrous!"—and Iago's likewise: "Nay, this was but his dream." Once again Iago chooses the posture of exculpation—Cassio didn't mean it—leaving Othello, like a naïve Freudian, to conclude that the dream told the truth. But of course there was no dream. Whose homoerotic fantasy is this? Soldiers did share beds as a matter of course, especially in battlefield conditions. But the intensity of the scene, with its literal quotation of words that were never spoken, its anatomical specificity ("lay his leg o'er my thigh"), and the highly particularized nature of the male-male kiss— these are all inventions. For whom? For Othello, or for Iago?

All of a sudden we hear of "other" proofs: "[T]his may help to thicken other proofs / That do demonstrate thinly" (3.3.435–436); "If it [the handkerchief] be that, or any that was hers, / It speaks against her with the other proofs" (445–446). What other proofs? There are none. But Othello has demanded proof, has demanded it in legal language, a language that looks ahead to his tragic speech in the final act, "It is the cause, it is the cause, my soul." By claiming that there are other proofs, Iago increases the persuasive power of what are really no proofs at all. As he himself asserts, aside to the audience,

> Trifles light as air
> Are to the jealous confirmations strong
> As proofs of holy writ. . . .
>
> 3.3.326–328

Unavoidably, ineluctably, these proofs, piled on top of one another, all assembled so quickly and devastatingly in a single scene, act 3, scene 3, lead to a devil's bargain and the selling of a soul, as Othello and Iago kneel together and swear revenge on the woman her husband now calls a "fair devil." White is black. False is true. "[L]et her live," suggests Iago, again the devil's advocate, leaving Othello to make the stern decision: she must die. "Now art thou my lieutenant," he says to Iago, and Iago answers, with a terrifying finality, "I am your own for ever."

The scene, with its two kneeling soldiers, is the parody of a marriage, another displacement of sex and death. This is the only marriage scene we see, and in it Iago displaces the bride, Desdemona, as well as the lieutenant, Cassio. Iago's complicated wish, compounded of love and hatred, is to be the person closest to Othello. His resentment of both Desdemona and Cassio is voiced from the first. By the terms of his plot he has achieved this double goal in a single gesture. The bargain is struck, and, in a sense, the tragedy is already complete.

And what are Iago's proofs? Two pieces of evidence: a handkerchief, and a conversation overheard. First, the handkerchief. A white handkerchief, spotted with strawberries. Othello tells the story of the handkerchief more than once, and the details differ in each telling. In one version it is a gift from his mother, woven by an Egyptian charmer, and said to have the power of guaranteeing love: "There's magic in the web of it." In another version it has been given by Othello's father to his mother. (These variations suggest that Othello's storytelling abilities are even more sophisticated—and dangerous—than previously thought.) Othello, characteristically, takes the thing, the sign, for the intangible fact of Desdemona's love, and when he fears she has lost the handkerchief he is certain he has lost her love. The handkerchief, properly a private love token, now becomes, again characteristically, a public spectacle. The white handkerchief marked with red becomes—because Othello makes it so—another version of the white wedding sheets that are so often mentioned in the play. The red embroidery becomes the emblem of the blood of her virginity, and Othello is now convinced that Cassio has had them both. In a most serious and tragic sense he hangs out his dirty linen in public. For him the handkerchief *is* the wedding sheets, and the wedding sheets therefore become a shroud. Deferred sexual consummation, and again deferred sexual consummation—Othello the hero, the patient, public man, wedded to his "occupation" as general and governor, willing to leave the marriage bed at the city's command to instill order in the populace—and now he finds, or thinks he finds, his wedding sheets are already stained by someone else's love. A short step leads to the second piece of ocular proof, the play-within-the-play so artfully staged by Iago, in which Iago and Cassio joke about Bianca, the courtesan, and Othello, again placed so that he can see but cannot hear, thinks they are joking about his wife. He misinterprets this dumb show, as Iago means him to do—for what he sees, after all, is the telltale handkerchief, given by Cassio to Bianca to "take the work out," to copy the design.

From the very beginning, Othello, whose tale would have won the Duke's daughter, has denied his own eloquence: "Rude am I in my speech, / And little blessed with the soft phrase of peace" (1.3.81–82); "Haply for I am black, / And have not those soft parts of conversation / That chamberers have" (3.3.267–269). Generations of audiences and critics have responded to his stirring language, but the breakdown of Othello's speech follows the loss of his faith in Desdemona. Iago's manipulation of language through subtraction—insinuation, artful echo, pause, and silence—ultimately outlasts and outwits the grand speeches and resounding periods. Once again it is Iago who lures Othello to this state, and the turning point, fittingly, is the utterance of the ambiguous word "lie":

Othello	What hath he said?
Iago	Faith, that he did—I know not what he did.
Othello	What, what?
Iago	Lie—
Othello	With her?
Iago	With her, on her, what you will.
Othello	Lie with her? Lie on her? We say "lie on her" when they belie her. Lie with her? 'Swounds, that's fulsome! Handkerchief—confessions—handkerchief. To confess and be hanged for his labour. First to be hanged, and then to confess! . . . It is not words that shakes me thus. Pish! Noses, ears, and lips! Is't possible? Confess? Handkerchief? O devil!

4.1.32–41

Othello says, "It is not words that shakes me thus"—yet it is only words that do, Iago's words.

Loss of language here, as elsewhere in Shakespeare, is emblematic of loss of humanity. Othello's decline into incoherence, fragments of sentences about fragments of bodies, is a sign of his temporary abandonment of human codes and qualities. The "fit" into which he falls, sometimes called "an epilepsy," and associated not only with linguistic loss of control but also with sexual orgasm, the "little death," marks the disintegration of the iron discipline he tried to enforce upon his own desires, his own sense of himself as soldier, general, diplomat, Venetian hero, and husband. The magic web of language has become for him a snare. Yet his magnificent language will return, at full throttle, in the final scenes of the play, during and especially after the murder. It is Iago who chooses the path of silence, and the ultimate, willed, dehumanization that accompanies it. "From this time forth," he will declare at the end of the play, "I never will speak word" (5.2.310). He will retreat into the archetype from which he grew, a "demi-devil," a Vice. We saw in a play like *Measure for Measure* that silence onstage is an emblem of death, as the muffled and unspeaking Claudio is dead—until he recovers to speech. Iago chooses this living death; he chooses against humanity. And yet he cannot be killed.

Iago is the "bad angel," and Desdemona the "good." The power of Desdemona's extraordinary character is such that she, too, bursts through archetype. She is ripped from the play's apparently "comic" beginnings in courtship and marriage. A "maiden never bold," according to her father, she becomes bold, like Juliet, when she sees her husband and reaches out to him. She is "one entire and perfect chrysolite," and yet she is no Isabella—she articulates passion and desire, and she speaks out, finally to her own cost—she is an articulate and ardent woman who intervenes in the world of politics and policy conventionally reserved for men. Othello, even in his jealous agony, praises her skills as a seamstress and a musician, skills possessed by some of the most noteworthy Shakespearean women. And as if for emphasis, the play presents her framed by two women who reflect the very things she is not: Bianca, the courtesan; Emilia, the obedient and pragmatic wife. Bianca is the whore Desdemona is accused of being, yet she is in love with Cassio, who treats her lightly. Emilia, Iago's wife, is a realist and a literalist, like Hamlet's gravedigger, or Macbeth's Porter. Like them, she sees things not for what they could be, but for what they are. Desdemona asks her, in tones of incredulity, whether she could imagine that a woman might be unfaithful to her husband, and Emilia's reply has the frank, down-to-earth tone of Pompey the bawd in *Measure for Measure:*

| Desdemona | Wouldst thou do such a deed for all the world? |
| Emilia | The world's a huge thing. It is a great price for a small vice. |

4.3.66–68

In this small exchange lies a huge conflict of cultures. Emilia in Desdemona's place would see no difficulties. But Desdemona's goodness, and belief in the goodness of others, is her death warrant.

The death scene itself is framed in legalisms. Othello has sought "proof" ("Villain, be sure thou prove my love a whore"). When he comes to her bedside he speaks of "the cause," as if submitting his case to a heavenly—or infernal—judge:

> It is the cause, it is the cause, my soul.
> Let me not name it to you, you chaste stars.
> It is the cause. Yet I'll not shed her blood,
> Nor scar that whiter skin of hers than snow,
> And smooth as monumental alabaster.
> Yet she must die, else she'll betray more men.
> Put out the light, and then put out the light.
> If I quench thee, thou flaming minister,

> I can again thy former light restore
> Should I repent me; but once put out thy light,
> Thou cunning'st pattern of excelling nature,
> I know not where is that Promethean heat
> That can thy light relume. When I have plucked the rose
> I cannot give it vital growth again.
> It needs must wither. I'll smell thee on the tree.

> 5.2.1–15

In dramatic action as well as in language the play has been seeking light all this time, from the moment in the first scene when Brabantio called for light, and in scene after scene, shrouded in darkness, when the call went up for "lights, lights." Here Othello compares Desdemona's life to the candle he holds in his hand, prefiguring later moments in other tragedies (Macbeth's "brief candle" speech; Lady Macbeth's desperate command to have light by her continually). Yet even here, shrouded in the mocking whiteness of her wedding sheets, Desdemona's purity and generosity make themselves manifest. Othello smothers her, and yet she speaks. He has closed the bed-curtains, making of the marriage bed and deathbed another inner stage, and from behind the curtains, as if from death itself, Desdemona speaks: "O, falsely, falsely murdered! . . . A guiltless death I die" (5.2.126, 132). When Emilia asks "who hath done this deed," Desdemona's answer is exculpatory and enigmatic: "Nobody, I myself. Farewell. / Commend me to my kind lord" (5.2.132–133). Her recovery to speech, which has been so insistently equated with humanity, is itself brief, but essential. She speaks from the brink of the grave, as Iago refuses speech. He is dead, even as he lives; she alive, even as she dies.

As for Othello, at the close of the play surrounded by horrified spectators who represent the return of Venetian law, he speaks to them, and through them to the audience in the theater. Like Hamlet at the close of his tragedy, he speaks finally to us, his first words like the restraining arm of Coleridge's Ancient Mariner, enforcing attention even on the unwilling:

> Soft you, a word or two before you go.
> I have done the state some service, and they know't.
> No more of that. I pray you, in your letters,
> When you shall these unlucky deeds relate,
> Speak of me as I am. Nothing extenuate,
> Nor set down aught in malice. Then must you speak
> Of one that loved not wisely but too well,
> Of one not easily jealous but, being wrought,
> Perplexed in the extreme; of one whose hand,
> Like the base Indian [or base Judean], threw a pearl away
> Richer than all his tribe; of one whose subdued eyes,

Albeit unusèd to the melting mood,
Drops tears as fast at the Arabian trees
Their medicinable gum. Set you down this,
And say besides that in Aleppo once,
Where a malignant and a turbaned Turk
Beat a Venetian and traduced the state,
I took by the throat the circumcisèd dog
And smote him thus.

5.2.347–365

Othello kills Othello. He is both Turk and Venetian, as he has been all along, and he dies in the act of describing a noble public gesture, the killing of a public enemy, in front of Venetian ambassadors who are public men themselves. The famous textual crux, "base Indian" (the Quarto reading) or "base Judean" (the Folio reading), is produced by the fact that the capital letters for modern *I* and *J* were the same, and that the letter *n* could look like the letter *u* (the piece of type—*u* or *n*—could also be inserted upside down within the frame). Like many textual ambiguities in Shakespeare, this one, however accidental, is salutary, for it has produced competing readings of great power. If the image is that of the "base Indian," the context is New World exploration and discovery, the "savage" man who does not know the value of the jewel he finds. If the phrase is read as "base Judean," the figure invoked is that of Judas Iscariot. The "pearl of great price" (Matthew 13: 44–52) he throws away, "richer than all his tribe," is the Kingdom of Heaven.

Othello wants to be remembered for his private sins and for his public virtue. His appeal is finally to the civilizing power of language: "a word or two before you go"; "[w]hen you shall these unlucky deeds relate"; "[s]peak of me as I am"; "[t]hen must you speak." As at the end of *Hamlet* and indeed throughout Shakespearean tragedy, retelling becomes the tragic hero's only path to redemption. The request to retell is an injunction to replay the play, to speak of Othello again and again, to learn from tragic drama as we learn from history, by taking its example seriously as a model of conduct.

Samuel Johnson, the great eighteenth-century lexicographer, biographer, essayist, and editor of Shakespeare, wrote at the conclusion of his edition of *Othello:* "I am glad that I have ended my revisal of this dreadful scene; it is not to be endured."[2] As was the case in *Romeo and Juliet,* womb becomes tomb, wedding becomes funeral, marriage bed becomes deathbed. But Johnson's response is a sign of the scene's power. It *is* to be endured—that is its purpose. "Look on the tragic loading of this bed," says Lodovico, the Duke's emissary, to Iago. "This is thy work." In the final scene the audience in the theater is offered its chance to measure the tragic work of two competing dramatists, Iago and Shakespeare. Throughout the play Iago had made us his unwitting and unwilling co-conspirators, presuming on our silence. Now, through Othello's plea,

"Speak of me as I am," the audience can be said to find its own role in the drama. Language, refused by Iago, regained by Desdemona, becomes at last the joint instrument of actor, playwright, and spectators. By gazing upon the final tableau, the tragic loading of the bed, and by replaying, remembering, and even editing the play, the silent audience can find its voice.

All's Well That Ends Well

DRAMATIS PERSONAE

The Dowager Countess
  of Roussillion
Bertram, *Count of Roussillion,*
  her son
Helena, *an orphan, attending*
  on the Countess
Lavatch, *a Clown, the Countess's*
  servant
Reynaldo, *the Countess's steward*
Paroles, *Bertram's companion*
The King of France
Lafew, *an old lord*

First Lord Dumaine
Second Lord Dumaine, *brother*
  to First Lord
Interpreter, *a French soldier*
A Gentleman Austringer
The Duke of Florence
Widow Capulet
Diana, *her daughter*
Mariana, *friend of the Widow*
Lords, attendants, soldiers,
  citizens

WHO CANNOT be crushed with a plot?" laments the braggart soldier Paroles in *All's Well That Ends Well,* after a staged capture by his comrades results in his cowardly (and comical) willingness to betray them, and then in his exposure and discomfiture (4.3.302). The scenario is reminiscent of Falstaff's similar fiction-making in the tavern in Eastcheap in *1 Henry IV,* although the wordy and well-named Paroles is a lesser figure (in all senses: less corpulent and less original and memorable). His combination of dismay and pique also closely resembles that of Malvolio, similarly gulled by unsympathetic peers and a clever plot ("I'll be revenged on the whole pack of you" [*Twelfth Night* 5.1.365]). But we might well take Paroles' complaint about being crushed with a plot as a key phrase for the whole of *All's Well,* a play that is constructed like an elaborate mechanism and goes off with a bang in the powerful final scene. For the alternative to being "crushed" is to have the plot work out to your advantage, despite all indications to the contrary—in effect, to have all end well. This is what happens to, and for, the play's heroine, a young woman equipped with patience, ingenuity, and good sense, as well as a strong passion for an especially unlikable hero.

Classed for much of the twentieth century with the so-called problem plays or "dark comedies," *All's Well* has not enjoyed, recently, the easy popularity with audiences of livelier and more romantic comedies, such as *Twelfth Night* and *As*

You Like It. Yet it contains not one but two roles that would make an actress's career (and have). Both Helena and the Countess are brilliant, complicated, strong women who, finding themselves in impossible situations, emerge not only whole but triumphant. Helena is at least as ingenious as Rosalind, a much more crowd-pleasing heroine. And if Bertram seems like a cad compared to the smitten Orlando, he is not more so than *Much Ado About Nothing*'s Claudio. The real "problem" here may be the mother. Although other comedies present single fathers with power over their children (Leonato in *Much Ado,* Duke Senior in *As You Like It*), *All's Well* is, in a way, the comic counterpart of *Coriolanus,* a tragedy that has encountered a wide range of responses because of its powerful mother, Volumnia, and its curiously immature war-hero son, Coriolanus. *All's Well That Ends Well* has both an authoritative mother and a clever, strong-willed heroine. If it "ends well" for them and less well for Bertram, perhaps it is simply because the play validates their wishes, not his.

It is striking how often the phrase "all's well that ends well," or some variant of it, actually appears in the text. Many of Shakespeare's plays have similar bromides for their titles, like *As You Like It,* or *Twelfth Night, or What You Will,* or the original title of the play—*All Is True*—listed in the Folio as *The Life of King Henry the Eight.* This was a commonplace practice for plays in the period: Thomas Heywood's *If You Know Not Me, You Know Nobody* is one example. But despite one great scene in *As You Like It* that turns on the multiple use of the words "as" and "if," no other Shakespeare play dallies with its name in the insistent way that *All's Well* does. In the fourth act Helena, the plucky heroine, cautions another young woman that she may "suffer" briefly in order to assist her friend but that things will improve:

> All's well that ends well; still the fine's the crown.
> Whate'er the course, the end is the renown.
>
> *All's Well 4.4.35–36*

Shortly thereafter, encountering a setback, Helena reiterates the point: "All's well that ends well yet" (5.1.27). After the many reversals and revelations in the play's last scene, the King of France, inviting the usual offstage explanations of plot details ("Of that . . . more leisure shall express"), uses the same phrase in his closing couplet,

> All yet seems well; and if it end so meet,
> The bitter past, more welcome is the sweet.
>
> *5.3.329–330*

Then, for good measure, he repeats the phrase one more time in the Epilogue that immediately follows, turning the notion of "ending well" from the denouement of the plot to the audience's applause for the play:

The King's a beggar now the play is done.
All is well ended if this suit be won:
That you express content. . . .

. . . .

Ours be your patience then, and yours our parts:
Your gentle hands lend us, and take our hearts.

Epilogue 1–6

It is unusual for a play by Shakespeare to contain so many internal references to its own title, suggesting a certain self-consciousness about its identity as a fiction, and focusing attention upon the expectation both of interim suffering and of a happy outcome. Almost like Troilus and Cressida reciting their own future myths ("[a]s true as Troilus," "[a]s false as Cressid"), the repeated internal assurances that all's well that ends well condition the audience to expect a satisfactory romance resolution, and permit the playwright to describe fairy-tale events, corrupt and even detestable characters, figures (like the Widow) who seem to emerge from the quite different genre of city comedy, and frank scenarios of sexual seduction, and to keep all of these comfortably under control until the disclosures of the last scene. They lighten the "problems" of this "problem play."

All's Well is generally regarded as an early Jacobean play, probably written in the period between *Hamlet* and *Measure for Measure,* with both of which it has obvious thematic and tonal affinities: the deaths of fathers and the circumstances of a court in mourning; meditations on virginity; clowns, fools, and knaves with downright views about human life, venality, and sex. As G. K. Hunter points out in the 1959 Arden edition of *All's Well,* both *Hamlet* and *All's Well* begin with plans for the education of a brash young courtier in Paris (Laertes, Bertram) and address the question of stepparents. *All's Well* and *Measure for Measure* are even more closely bound, by their use of the bed trick, their climactic scenes of "rebirth" and restoration, and their inclusion of extensive discussions of virginity (Helena, Isabella) and a pregnant woman (Helena, Juliet) in the plot. The element of female disguise in these two plays is managed through the bed-trick substitution, rather than, as in the earlier "festive" comedies of the Elizabethan period, through the cross-dressing of the heroine. Both *Measure for Measure* and *All's Well* include as plot devices elements of Catholic religious practice (Isabella as a novice in the Order of Saint Clare; Helena as a pilgrim bound for the shrine of "Saint Jaques le Grand").

Some dilemmas that face the heroines of the "festive" comedies also confront Helena: her mourning for her dead father and her resourceful decision to act on her own by going to the King's court to cure him may remind audiences of three other orphaned daughters—the mourning Olivia and the resourceful Viola of *Twelfth Night,* or the empowered Portia of *The Merchant of Venice.* (In *Merchant* Portia and Nerissa play a ring trick that allows them to *pretend* to have played a bed trick.) The apparent death of Helena and her "miraculous" reappearance is a device used both in *Measure for Measure* (where it is a young man, Claudio, who is supposed dead and then reborn) and in *Much Ado About Nothing* (in which the slandered Hero is said to have died, and her repentant lover, another Claudio, agrees, as will Bertram in *All's Well*, to marry a "new" wife who will turn out to be the former one). But the denouements of these two mature and complicated "comedies" also involve some elements that would become more familiar in the later romances, especially the question of the reunion of husband and wife, the wonder-working doctor, and, again, the key themes of "rebirth" and of succession.

In *All's Well That Ends Well*, Helena, the daughter of a celebrated physician, Gérard de Narbonne, has been living under the protection of the Countess of Rossillion since her father's death. Helena is secretly in love with the Countess's son, Bertram, who has just succeeded to the title at the death of *his* father. Bertram is about to take leave of his mother and join the court of the King of France, accompanied by Lafew, an old and loyal lord and counselor. The King, who is by law now Bertram's "father" (Bertram, still a minor, is his ward), is suffering from a life-threatening ailment, and has "abandoned his physicians." The play thus begins with many mentions of death and dying, and also with some hope for the future.

The Countess's first words, the play's opening line, set the tone: "In delivering my son from me I bury a second husband" (1.1.1–2). From the first, childbirth and death are intermingled, as they will be at the denouement, when Bertram discovers that the wife he has rejected, and whose death has been announced, is not only alive but pregnant with his child: "Dead though she be she feels her young one kick. / So there's my riddle; one that's dead is quick" (5.3.299–300).

It is characteristic of other Shakespearean genres like history and tragedy to emphasize a discrepancy between the generations, whether by underscoring the impotence of the aging elders (*Richard II*, *King Lear*) or by stressing the natural rebelliousness of the young (*Romeo and Juliet*, *Henry IV Part 1*). But one of the things that makes *All's Well* a curious kind of comedy is its insistence on this age gap. The play begins with a king whose infirmities are not only acknowledged but clinically described, and his female counterpart, the Countess, wields sway over her son, Bertram, in a way that deprives him of much agency. If he were more likable, and she less elegant and majestic, it would be easy not only to see his side but also to take it.

Helena's profound sadness, upon hearing of Bertram's departure for the King's court, motivates her to follow him. She determines to go to the court, cure the King with the help of the medical knowledge she has inherited from her father, and ask as her reward that she be married to Bertram. All unfolds as she intends, but the proud and callow Bertram spurns her as too lowborn for him, and even when motivated to go through with the marriage (since to reject it would lose him the care and regard of the King), he swears that he "will not bed her" (2.3.254).

Bertram's concern with social status and his disdain for the idea of marriage with a doctor's daughter seem more culpable in our time than it would have been in his. We are told that Helena's father was a famous doctor, but doctors in general in early modern England were "middling," competing for social and professional status and for the patronage of the elite. And marriage, as we have seen in virtually every play by Shakespeare, was a social and cultural institution, binding family to family, house to house, country to country. Shakespeare's lovers appeal to us as much as they do in part because they seem to have the energy of their own passions; they choose partners with eager single-mindedness, and pursue their loves until, with good fortune (and a smiling playwright), they end in the promise of marriage. From Romeo and Juliet to Rosalind and Orlando, these lovers commit themselves to the fulfillment of individual choice, often against the strong resistance of their families. Although we should note that, without exception, these marriages, however emotionally transgressive in the short run (a Montague loves a Capulet; Portia seeks to outwit her father's test of the caskets), wind up pairing social equals. Even—or especially—in the late romances, when a prince falls in love with a shepherdess or with a young woman shipwrecked on an island, by the play's end we are assured that the shepherdess is a princess in her own right, and that the shipwreck victim is a duke's daughter, and that both are heirs of wealth as well as power. Poor Bertram, then, that we should judge him so harshly for not wanting to marry the clever girl from the "middling" classes whom his mother has chosen for him. Yet the play does not go out of its way to make him a charmer.

In one of several letters that help to mobilize the plot, Bertram writes to Helena listing the impossible conditions upon which he would regard himself as really married to her:

> "When thou canst *get the ring upon my finger, which never shall come off,* and *show me a child begotten of thy body that I am father to,* then call me husband; but in such a 'then' I write a 'never.' "
>
> 3.2.55–58 *[emphasis added]*

He then flees to Florence to fight in the wars. Helena leaves the French court and becomes a pilgrim, heading for the shrine of Saint Jaques (presumably in Santiago de Compostela, Spain), but passing through Florence on her way (somewhat in defiance of ordinary geography). There she meets a widow who lets rooms, and who has encountered Bertram.

Through a series of stratagems involving the Widow and her daughter Diana—whom Bertram desires and attempts to seduce—Helena contrives the famous bed trick, replacing Diana in bed and becoming pregnant with Bertram's child. But the King, the Countess, Bertram, and Lafew all believe that Helena is dead. The final scene, closely akin to a similar set of unmufflings and revelations in *Measure for Measure,* includes the evidence of two rings exchanged by Helena and Bertram (like the ring trick at the end of *The Merchant of Venice,* or the ring and bracelet that signify similarly as love and identity tokens in *Cymbeline*), a riddling conversation of misdirection and misprision between the King and Diana (like the riddle of Mariana's status as maid, widow, or wife in *Measure for Measure*), and a reconciliation between the repentant Bertram and the patient Helena. The King then effectively takes steps to begin the play all over again, by promising to the virginal Diana, if she can prove her story, a dowry and her choice of a husband—just as he had done for Helena.

Shakespeare's main source here was a story told in Boccaccio's *Decameron* (the ninth novel of the third day), probably as mediated through the English translation by William Painter in his *Palace of Pleasure* (1566, 1567, and 1575). Some details are altered, some added, as was the playwright's usual practice with sources. The Helena-Bertram plot is augmented by the addition of the strong figure of the Countess, Bertram's mother, who adores Helena and already treats her as a daughter; by the good old counselor Lafew, again a figure of virtue and steadfastness; and, on the other side, by Paroles, described forthrightly by Helena before his first appearance as "a notorious liar," "a great way fool," and "solely a coward" (1.1.95–96) and by Lafew as an idle dandy, a man whose "soul . . . is his clothes" (2.5.40). In contrast to his "follower" Paroles, even Bertram might be thought to have a few good points, although few critics have admired him unreservedly, despite his "archèd brows, his hawking eye, [and] his curls" (1.1.89; the description is the love-struck Helena's). William Hazlitt, who found the play as a whole "one of the most pleasing of our author's comedies," offered a balanced assessment of Bertram's "willful stubbornness and youthful petulance" in his *Characters of Shakespeare's Plays.*

The play is often compared to a fairy tale, and with good reason. It follows the general pattern of what is sometimes called the "Loathly Lady" story, familiar from Chaucer's "Wife of Bath's Tale." A woman despised by a haughty knight (in Chaucer, because she is old and ugly; in *All's Well,* because she is not a nobleman's daughter) knows the answer to a crucial, lifesaving question. Once she has provided the answer, she gets to choose her husband. (In Chaucer, the young knight, known for his aggressive behavior toward women, must learn "what women most desire" in order to save his own life; in *All's Well,* the life-and-death issue is the illness of the King, for which Helena provides the cure.) The husband first despises and rejects his wife, but soon learns that he is wrong to do so. Once he accepts her as she is, the lady is transformed, and she fulfills his fantasies as well as her desire. The Countess's doubts about Helena's chances of success in curing the King—"How shall they credit / A poor unlearnèd virgin . . . ?" (1.3.225–226)—are echoed by the King himself, but they are deftly refuted by Helena in terms that both revisit the theme of virginity and anticipate the bed trick:

King	Upon thy certainty and confidence
	What dar'st thou venture?
Helena	Tax of impudence,
	A strumpet's boldness, a divulgèd shame;
	Traduced by odious ballads, my maiden's name
	Seared otherwise . . .

2.1.168–172

The King affects to hear a stronger voice within hers—"Methinks in thee some blessèd spirit doth speak, / His powerful sound within an organ weak" (2.1.174–175)—and whether this is the voice of her father (as Isabella in *Measure for Measure* claimed to hear her father's voice in her brother's) or that of heaven, it clearly does the trick. Shortly, in one of those reporting scenes that would become a Shakespearean specialty in the late romances, we hear Lafew, Paroles, and Bertram discussing the cure of the supposedly incurable king:

Lafew	They say miracles are past, and we have our philosophical persons to make modern and familiar things supernatural and causeless. Hence is it that we make trifles of terrors, ensconcing ourselves into seeming knowledge when we should submit ourselves to an unknown fear.
Paroles	Why, 'tis the rarest argument of wonder that hath shot out in our latter times.
Bertram	And so 'tis.

2.3.1–8

The same language of "wonder," that fundamental emotion of the mode of romance, had informed Lafew's initial conversation with the King, introducing "Doctor She," the miracle-working Helena:

Lafew	I have spoke
	With one that in her sex, her years, profession,
	Wisdom and constancy, hath amazed me more
	Than I dare blame my weakness. . . .
	. . . .
King	Bring in the admiration, that we with thee
	May spend our wonder too, or take off thine
	By wond'ring how thou took'st it.

2.1.80–83, 86–88

But to Bertram and Paroles the identity of the wonder worker is itself astonishing ("[I]s not this Helen?") and the ceremony of husband-choosing that follows her triumphal entry with the cured and newly powerful King a cause for consternation.

It is worth pausing for a moment on the stage management of the scene, bearing in mind that Bertram regards himself as too exalted in birth to marry a humble physician's daughter, even if the knowledge at her command is life-bestowing. Shakespeare situates the loyal Lafew onstage as a spectator, where he can see but not hear. Helena addresses herself to four nameless "lords" one by one, and each expresses an eager willingness to be her choice in marriage. But Helena, of course, has another lover in view. Helena turns each of them down, while Lafew mistakes what he is seeing for their rejection of her ("Do all they deny her? An they were sons of mine I'd have them whipped" [2.3.82–83]), setting the stage for Bertram's indignant refusal:

> I know her well:
> She had her breeding at my father's charge.
> A poor physician's daughter, my wife? Disdain
> Rather corrupt me ever.
>
> *2.3.109–112*

The King's vigorous reply speaks directly to the questions of moral and ethical worth, rank, and social distinction:

> 'Tis only title thou disdain'st in her, the which
> I can build up. Strange is it that our bloods,
> Of colour, weight, and heat, poured all together,
> Would quite confound distinction, yet stands off
> In differences so mighty. . . .
>
> *2.3.113–117*

He intends to supply both "title" and a generous dowry: "Virtue and she / Is her own dower; honour and wealth from me" (2.3.139–140). But Bertram refuses point-blank: "I cannot love her, nor will strive to do't" (141).

Critics have differed as to their assessment of Bertram's response, some finding him churlish, others, like Samuel Taylor Coleridge, expressing empathy:

I cannot agree with the solemn abuse which the critics have poured out upon Bertram in *All's Well That Ends Well*. He was a young nobleman in feudal times, just bursting into manhood, with all the feelings of pride of birth and appetite for pleasure and liberty natural to such a character so circumstanced. Of course he had never regarded Helena otherwise than as a dependant in the family. . . . Bertram had surely good reason to look upon the king's forcing him to marry Helena as a very tyrannical act. Indeed, it must be confessed that her character is not very delicate, and it required all Shakespeare's consummate skill to interest us for her.

Coleridge, Table Talk

The heatedness of this response suggests that Coleridge is doing what teachers often warn their students against, and what, contrariwise, directors hope that audiences will do—that is to say, he is "identifying" with a dramatic character. (His own unhappy marriage had been motivated by a utopian scheme invented—and later abandoned—by the poet Robert Southey; Coleridge married the sister of Southey's fiancée.)

To what extent is it just, in terms of Shakespeare's play, to say that Bertram's resistance is based upon overfamiliarity? "I know her well," Bertram responds to the King. The question of a quasi-incestuous relationship is never mentioned, either by him or by Helena, and such domestic arrangements, of persons unrelated by blood but brought up together in near proximity, were common rather than uncommon in early modern England. Coleridge's word "dependant" implies a retainer, attendant, subordinate, or servant, a character more like Lucy Snow or Jane Eyre than like the daughter of a famous physician, however "low" physicians might have ranked on the feudal social scale. Helena is a "gentlewoman" (the word is applied to her twice in the first thirty-five lines) who has been "bequeathed to [the Countess's] over-looking" (1.1.34–35). But Helena is not exciting, or exotic, or even romantic to Bertram, who seeks adventure, sexual provocation, and an exogamous relationship. They may not be brother and sister, but they are mothered by the same woman. Bertram seeks to escape his mother by not marrying the bride she chooses for him. And he is undeniably a social snob, although the term had not been invented in his time. But the process of estrangement and reconciliation followed in the course of the play, where Bertram first disdains Helena and then ultimately pleads to have her reinstated as his wife ("I'll love her dearly, ever ever dearly" [5.3.313]), may represent more than a lesson learned or a change of heart.

The theme of reclamation from the dead itself appears twice, first with the dying King and then with the supposedly dead Helena. Like the bemused Claudio in *Much Ado About Nothing,* who also rejected his wife-to-be and then "lost" her to apparent death, Bertram is offered a second chance in the form of an arranged marriage to another lady—in this case Lafew's daughter Maudlin, who has not been mentioned previously and does not appear in the play. The scene, indeed, has as much in common with *The Winter's Tale* as it does with either *Much Ado* or *Measure for Measure.* "I am not a day of season," observes the King in the climactic final scene,

> For thou mayst see a sunshine and a hail
> In me at once.
>
> 5.3.33–35

He does not know whether to be happy or sad. Mourning the supposedly dead Helena ("Praising what is lost / Makes the remembrance dear" [5.3.19–20]), and gladdened at the news that Bertram, now repentant and obedient, has agreed to an arranged marriage with Lafew's daughter, the King is captive to mixed emotions. His remark about sunshine and hail anticipates a key moment in *King Lear* when (in the Quarto text of the play) the anonymous First Gentleman reports that Cordelia's smiles and tears were like "[s]unshine and rain at once."

Both the poetry and the dramaturgy of this last act seem to gain in pace and power as the events drive toward a conclusion. Bertram's acknowledgment of his "warped" viewpoint and "scornful perspective" comes as close to elegance as this odd character can attain:

> Thence it came
> That she whom all men praised and whom myself,
> Since I have lost, have loved, was in mine eye
> The dust that did offend it.
>
> 5.3.53–56

And the King's response is in a similar key:

> Our rash faults
> Make trivial price of serious things we have,
> Not knowing them until we know their grave.
> Oft our displeasures, to ourselves unjust,
> Destroy our friends and after weep their dust.
>
> 5.3.61–65

His subsequent change of tone and topic—"Be this sweet Helen's knell, and now forget her. / Send forth your amorous token for fair Maudlin" (5.3.68–69)—anticipates Paulina's artful stage management of the statue scene in *The Winter's Tale,* with the crucial difference that Paulina knows the "dead" Hermione is still alive. The emotional turmoil of this long scene in *All's Well* depends to a certain extent upon the King's ignorance of what the audience knows. His later lament, "I am wrapped in dismal thinkings" (129), maintains the sense of dramatic tension, holding off the comic conclusion and replacing it, however briefly, with further forebodings.

Lafew, the father of the "fair Maudlin" (and from the outset of the play Helena's great champion), begins the unraveling process, by asking Bertram for

> a favour from you
> To sparkle in the spirits of my daughter,
> That she may quickly come.
>
> 5.3.75–77

The ring that Bertram tenders is, as Lafew immediately recognizes, the former property of "Helen that's dead":

> Such a ring as this,
> The last that ere I took her leave at court,
> I saw upon her finger.
>
> *5.3.79–81*

Bertram's quick denial gets him into deeper trouble, for the ring originally belonged to the King, who says:

> This ring was mine, and when I gave it Helen
> I bade her, if her fortunes ever stood
> Necessitied to help, that by this token
> I would relieve her. . . .
>
> *5.3.84–87*

"Confess 'twas hers," the King demands,

> and by what rough enforcement
> You got it from her. She called the saints to surety
> That she would never put it from her finger
> Unless she gave it to yourself in bed,
> Where you have never come. . . .
>
> *5.3.108–112*

A baffled Bertram, who has no idea the woman he spent the night with in Florence was Helena, is led off by guards, echoing the King's lines with his defiance:

> If you shall prove
> This ring was ever hers, you shall as easy
> Prove that I husbanded her bed in Florence,
> Where yet she never was.
>
> *5.3.125–128*

Diana now appears, claiming that she is a "poor maid" and Bertram her "seducer," and demanding that "Count Rossillion" marry her, since he is now a widower. Seconded by her mother, the Widow, she confronts him—"Ask him upon his oath if he does think / He had not my virginity" (5.3.186–187)—only to have him dismiss and revile her as "a common gamester to the camp" (190) whom he "boarded . . . i' th' wanton way of youth" (213). Audiences and readers may again be called upon to suspend their judgment (why does Helena want to marry this lout?) as his language, so recently idealistic and romantic, now turns sharply mercantile:

> Her inf'nite cunning with her modern grace
> Subdued me to her rate. She got the ring,
> And I had that which any inferior might
> At market price have bought.
>
> *5.3.218–221*

The ring precipitates the next twist in the plot, since Diana's riddling answer to the King's questions about its provenance produces royal displeasure:

King   Where did you buy it? Or who gave it you?
Diana   It was not given me, nor I did not buy it.
King   Who lent it you?
Diana   It was not lent me neither.
King   Where did you find it then?
Diana   I found it not.
King   If it were yours by none of all these ways,
          How could you give it him?
Diana   I never gave it him.
          . . . .
King   This ring was mine. I gave it his first wife.
Diana   It might be yours or hers for aught I know.
King   [*to attendants*] Take her away, I do not like her now.
          To prison with her. . . .
                              5.3.267–273, 276–279

Here is where *All's Well* most closely resembles *Measure for Measure*, Shakespeare's other bed-trick play. In *Measure for Measure* it is Mariana, the betrothed and abandoned spouse of the deputy Angelo, who substitutes for the virginal Isabella in Angelo's bed. In *All's Well*—where again names are significant—it is Helena who sleeps secretly with her own husband, while Diana (true to her mythological namesake) remains a virgin.

Diana   By Jove, if ever I knew man 'twas you.
King   Wherefore hast thou accused him all this while?
Diana   Because he's guilty, and he is not guilty.
          He knows I am no maid, and he'll swear to't;
          I'll swear I am a maid, and he knows not.
          Great King, I am no strumpet; by my life,
          I am either maid or else this old man's wife.
                              5.3.284–290

(The "old man" to whom she refers is Lafew.) This is too difficult for the King to understand—if he were a quicker study he would have figured out the real story long ago—and it takes the visible production of Helena onstage, in concert with Diana's "riddle," to explain the real state of affairs:

> Diana   He knows himself my bed he hath defiled,
> And at that time he got his wife with child.
> Dead though she be she feels her young one kick.
> So there's my riddle; one that's dead is quick.
> And now behold the meaning.
>
> *5.3.297–301*

Helena's entrance, on cue, bearing Bertram's own riddling challenge to her (" 'When from my finger you can get this ring / And are by me with child . . .' ") proves that his condition-contrary-to-fact has been trumped by her stratagem, and by the King's.

In the Countess's household there is a clown, Lavatch, whose jests and requests early on anticipate some of the play's darker themes. In a part written for Robert Armin, who played the more complex fools of Shakespeare's middle years (replacing the more broadly comic Will Kemp), Lavatch sings a song about Helen of Troy and recites another snatch of verse about marriage and cuckoldry, and thus encapsulates both Bertram's story and Paroles'. Lavatch's desire to marry "Isbel the woman" because he is "driven on by the flesh" may remind audiences of the similarly cheerful and carnal fool Touchstone in *As You Like It*. ("Isbel" is a nicely down-market version of the far more formal, and far more virginal, Isabella, immortalized in Shakespeare's *Measure for Measure*.)

How does the riddling love plot cohere with the much broader comedy of Lavatch and the downfall of the "jackanapes / With scarfs," the posturing Paroles (3.5.84–85)? In a general sense Bertram's adventures and Paroles' are both concerned with honor and dishonor, and with the loss of the material embodiments of honor: a woman's virginity (in the love plot) and the regimental drum (in the comic plot of Paroles and the soldiers). Whether or not the morphological analogy between drum and hymen (both are membranes stretched across cylindrical openings) would have been noted by an early modern audience, the symbolic role of each is fairly clear, and is emphasized by their juxtaposition in *All's Well*. Both become issues in act 3, where we learn from the Widow that Bertram seeks to "[c]orrupt the tender honour of a maid," her daughter Diana (3.5.69), and only a few lines later that Paroles, returning from battle, is melancholy and "shrewdly vexed" because he has lost "our drum" (87). Is the theft of virginity like the theft of a drum?

The plot against Paroles, hatched by two French lords to prove to Bertram that Paroles is, as one of them puts it, "a most notable coward, an infinite and endless liar, an hourly promise-breaker, the owner of no one good quality worthy of your lordship's entertainment" (3.6.10–12), is to "let him fetch off his drum, which you hear him so confidently undertake to do" (17–18). They will pretend to be enemies, "bind and hoodwink" him, and see whether they can persuade him to betray Bertram and "deliver all the intelligence in his power against you" (26–27). The lords regard this as a joke: "O for the love of laughter hinder not the honour of his design; let him fetch off his drum" (36–38). But the resonant word "honour" attaches repeatedly to both the exploit and the drum itself, described by Bertram to Paroles, in deliberately inflated terms, as "this instrument of honour" (57–58). Both before and after the drum scene the word "honour" is used to describe Diana's virginity, for which she will likewise hoodwink Bertram into bargaining in the episode of the ring trick and the bed trick:

Diana	Give me that ring.
Bertram	I'll lend it thee, my dear, but have no power
	To give it from me.
Diana	· Will you not, my lord?
Bertram	It is an honour 'longing to our house,
	Bequeathèd down from many ancestors,
	Which were the greatest obloquy i' th' world
	In me to lose.
Diana	Mine honour's such a ring.
	My chastity's the jewel of our house,
	Bequeathèd down from many ancestors,
	Which were the greatest obloquy i' th' world
	In me to lose. . . .
	. . . . . .
Bertram	Here, take my ring.
	My house, mine honour, yea my life be thine,
	And I'll be bid by thee.

4.2.40–54

Her detailed instructions to him—he is to remain with her only an hour in bed, and not speak to her; she will put another ring on his finger and thus perform a ceremony of betrothal—are described by Bertram as promising "a heaven on earth," but when she is left alone on the stage she makes clear her intentions to "cozen him that would unjustly win" (4.2.77).

In a conversation between the two French lords, the onstage audience, the planned seduction is again juxtaposed to the trick to be played upon Paroles, whom Bertram now describes as a "counterfeit model" who "deceived me like a double-meaning prophesier" (4.3.95–96). Bertram seems completely oblivious of the fact that words like "counterfeit," "deceived," and, indeed, "double-meaning prophesier" might be applicable to himself in his dealings with Diana. But as we have noted, Diana is herself adept at double meanings, and her riddling language, which is to culminate in the final revelation scene, begins as soon as she has struck her bargain: "He had sworn to marry me / When his wife's dead; therefore I'll lie with him / When I am buried" (4.2.72–74). Although these lines represent an early modern commonplace, they are uncannily reminiscent of that other young "Capulet" woman, Juliet ("If he be marrièd / My grave is like to be my wedding bed").

The two hoodwinking scenes (Bertram in the dark with a woman he thinks is Diana; Paroles "muffled"—that is, blindfolded—thinking he has been captured by the enemy) are thus set up to read or interpret each other. Paroles' hooding scene is rendered more comic, and also more pertinent, by the fact that this posturing captain, Bertram's "devoted friend" and a "manifold linguist" (4.3.223–224) whose name means "words," is immediately and completely at a loss for words, since his captors speak a made-up language, which is "translated" by a soldier playing the role of "interpreter." *"Porto tartarossa,"* says the Second Lord Dumaine, and the Interpreter translates, "He calls for the tortures." *"Boblibindo chicurmurco"* is explained as a command to answer the "general's" questions. Paroles does so with alacrity, and sells out his friends, offering military information, slandering the two French lords, and revealing not only the story of the seduction but his letter to Diana urging her to ask Bertram for money in exchange for her favors, and cautioning, "He ne'er pays after-debts, take it before." Shakespeare has used this comedy of interpretation before, notably in the masque of the "Muscovites" in *Love's Labour's Lost,* where the joke is that the "translator" is translating lines from English to English. Clearly, however, the anxiety—and pleasure—of multiple (and changing) languages and meanings was a matter of fascination for Renaissance humanists, diplomats, and writers. Kyd's *Spanish Tragedy,* one of the most celebrated of Elizabethan dramas, ends with a play in "sundry languages" through which the revenge plot is fulfilled:

> Hieronimo   Each one of us must act his part
> In unknown languages;
> That it may breed the more variety:
> As you, my lord, in Latin, I in Greek,
> You in Italian. . . .
> . . . . . .
> Balthazar   But this will be a mere confusion,
> And hardly shall we all be understood . . .
> *Kyd,* Spanish Tragedy *4.1.171–175, 179–180*

As in the *Spanish Tragedy,* so in *All's Well,* a surplus of words breeds "confusion" as often as communication.

In the upshot, Paroles, despite his fine scarves and fine words, dwindles to the comic version of King Lear's "thing itself," fundamental mankind:

Paroles   Simply the thing I am
          Shall make me live.

4.3.310–311

We might compare this to the bawd Pompey's "Truly, sir, I am a poor fellow that would live" in *Measure for Measure,* but Paroles' affinity with Shakespeare's other braggart soldiers is equally strong. His high-sounding apostrophe "Rust, sword; cool, blushes" directly recalls the equally ludicrous sonnet-writing soldier Don Armado ("Adieu, valor; rust, rapier; be still, drum: for your manager is in love" [*Love's Labour's Lost* 1.2.160–161]). And his determination to thrive at any cost—"Paroles live / Safest in shame; being fooled, by fool'ry thrive. / There's place and means for every man alive" (4.3.314–316)—links him with Ancient Pistol, departing from the wars to find a dishonest livelihood at home:

> from my weary limbs
> Honour is cudgelled. Well, bawd I'll turn,
> And something lean to cutpurse of quick hand.
> To England will I steal, and there I'll steal.

Henry V 5.1.75–78

"Simply the thing I am / Shall make me live" is a bleak maxim, but one that we encounter not infrequently in Shakespeare's plays, and we must admit, however grudgingly, that there is an admirable energy in these elemental characters, who—like their more glorious fellows—never die. At the end of the final scene Lafew leads Paroles off the stage, promising to "make sport" with him, and cautioning him, "Let thy curtsies alone, they are scurvy ones" (5.3.319–320).

But if Paroles does not "end well," the play does. As we have seen, *All's Well* concludes with an epilogue, spoken by the King to the audience, much in the spirit of the other comic epilogues in Shakespeare's plays, from Puck's in *A Midsummer Night's Dream* and Rosalind's in *As You Like It* to Prospero's in *The Tempest.* Beginning "The King's a beggar," the epilogue invokes, by implication, the old ballad of "King Cophetua and the Beggar Maid," a story of "high"/"low" courtship cited numerous times in Shakespeare's plays (*Love's Labours Lost* 4.1; *Romeo and Juliet* 2.1; *2 Henry IV* 5.3), and it concludes with a request for the "gentle hands" of the audience—that is to say, their applause. "Ours be your patience then and yours our parts," says the King (Epilogue, line 5). The play that began with a dying King whose case had been abandoned by his physicians, and with a stage full of characters dressed in mourning, thus ends with a topsy-turvy reversal in which kingly condescension, a willing descent to the level of the audience, mirrors the multiple comic options of the close: a living, healthy, and joyful King and Countess; a husband and wife united and expecting an heir; and a poor virgin (Diana) rewarded with a rich dowry and her choice of a husband. As the play prepares for its own reenactment, "day exceeding day," audience and actors, like king and beggar maid, will exchange places, just as the haughty Bertram becomes a beggar when confronted with his restored wife, Helena. Whatever our estimation of the callow but promising Bertram and the astonishingly patient Helena, both the genre of fairy tale and the history of noble marriage suggest that ending well—at least onstage—may be the best medicine.

Timon of Athens

DRAMATIS PERSONAE

Timon of Athens
A Poet
A Painter
A Jeweller
A Merchant
A Mercer
Lucilius, *one of Timon's servants*
An Old Athenian
Lords and Senators of Athens
Ventidius, *one of Timon's false friends*
Alcibiades, *an Athenian captain*
Apemantus, *a churlish philosopher*
One dressed as Cupid in the masque
Ladies dressed as Amazons in the masque
Flavius, *Timon's steward*
Flaminius, *Timon's servant*
Servilius, *Timon's servant*
Other Servants of Timon
A Fool
A Page
Caphis, *a servant to Timon's creditors*

Isidore's Servant, *a servant to Timon's creditors*
Two of Varro's Servants, *servants to Timon's creditors*
Lucullus, *a flattering lord*
Lucius, *a flattering lord*
Sempronius, *a flattering lord*
Lucullus's Servant
Lucius's Servant
Three Strangers, *one called Hostillius*
Titus's Servant, *another servant to Timon's creditors*
Hortensius's Servant, *another servant to Timon's creditors*
Philotus's Servant, *another servant to Timon's creditors*
Phrynia, *a whore with Alcibiades*
Timandra, *a whore with Alcibiades*
The banditti, Thieves
Soldier of Alcibiades' army
Messengers, attendants, soldiers

THE LIFE OF TIMON OF ATHENS is Shakespeare's remarkable play about philanthropy and misanthropy. Among those many Shakespeare plays that have been discovered, by audiences in every generation, to be in uncanny conversation with their present-day concerns, *Timon,* with its luxury-loving lords living on credit, influence, loans, and gifts, is possibly the most pertinent to modern and postmodern life. Yet for a variety of reasons this play is comparatively unknown outside of Shakespearean circles. The text is difficult, at times, and made more so by a number of interpretive "cruxes" about which editorial scholars have disagreed, making even the basic language of the play seem inaccessible, prior to the question of meaning. Timon himself, surnamed in history "the Misanthrope," is in the course of the unfolding action initially bland and ultimately aversive. Despite the brief appearance of two literally gold-digging whores accompanying Alcibiades into exile, there is no conventional love plot to divert attention from the prevailing climate of flattery and greed; and the "churlish philosopher" Apemantus, the truth-telling wise fool of the play, is, with his imprecations and curses, at best an acquired taste. So far as we know, the play was never staged in Shakespeare's lifetime.

Nonetheless, *Timon* is a superb piece of writing, characterization, and theater, and it deserves more recognition. The play is divided into two parts, the first of which shows Timon to be extraordinarily generous, giving gifts, money, entertainments, and banquets to a variety of noble dependents, described in the First Folio's list of "Actors' Names" as "Flattering Lords." In the second half of the play, once Timon has lost his money—he tries to call upon those to whom he has given gifts and support in the past, and is turned away with an amusingly diverse array of (im)plausible excuses—he flees Athens, takes up residence in a cave, digs in the earth and with bitter irony discovers gold, and flings the gold at visitors unwise enough to call upon him.

Critics interested in history do not have to look far to find models for wealthy patrons, sycophantic flatterers, and mutual disenchantment in the Jacobean (or the Elizabethan) court. One early-twentieth-century scholar suggested an equivalence between Timon and the Earl of Essex, and between Ventidius and Sir Francis Bacon, reading the play as a political allegory of patronage and betrayal. However likely or unlikely any such specific historical identification might be (and this reading has not fared well among subsequent scholars), it seems to me, as always, that the power of the play comes from its transhistorical resonances rather than from any Jacobean references. If *Timon* is timeless, it is because it is always timely. The brilliance of the play is the way in which its self-serving and hypocritical flatterers resemble those of every economic and social era.

The Timon story was well known in classical times, and also in early modern England, where scholars have found references in the works of many of Shakespeare's contemporaries (including the playwrights John Lyly, Thomas Nashe, Robert Greene, Thomas Lodge, Thomas Dekker, and John Marston). Both Greene and Dekker refer to "Timonists," indicating that the equivalence Timon = misanthrope must have been widely accepted; otherwise the term could not have been understood.

In Sir Thomas North's 1579 translation of Plutarch's *Parallel Lives,* the version Shakespeare would have read, Timon is twice called "Timon Misanthropos," the appellation Misanthropos used as an "addition" or surname, just as "Coriolanus" ("the conqueror of Corioles") is used for Caius Martius. Shakespeare's principal source for *Timon of Athens* would have been Plutarch's "Life of Marcus Antonius," where the Timon story is told with great emphasis on what in the play is the second half of the narrative: Timon's self-banishment, his odd affinity for Apemantus ("because he was much like of his nature and conditions"), his affection for the "bold and insolent" Alcibiades (whom Timon said he liked because he knew that "one day he would do great mischief unto the Athenians"), Timon's invitation to the Athenian lords to come and hang themselves on his fig tree, and the two epitaphs said to be written on his tomb, one composed by Timon, the other by the poet Callimachus. Shakespeare includes both of these epitaphs, virtually word for word, in his text, although, as many commentators have observed, they contradict each other: the first instructing the passerby, "Seek not my name," the second declaring, "Here lie I, Timon."

Indeed, the name Timon was so strongly associated with this devolution into rage and general hatred that he became a *type,* as is clear in a passage from Montaigne's *Essays,* where (in the John Florio translation of 1603) we hear of

> Timon, surnamed the hater of all mankinde. For looke what a man hateth, the same thing he takes to hart. Timon wisht all evill might light on us: He was passionate in desiring our ruine. He shunned and loathed our conversation as dangerous and wicked, and of a depraved nature.
>
> *Michel de Montaigne, "Of Democritus and Heraclitus"*

Montaigne thought Timon was a captive of his own emotions; he closes his assessment of philosophers who "laugh" or "weepe" at the spectacle of humanity by expressing the view that "[o]ur owne condition is as ridiculous as risible, as much to be laught at as able to laugh."

Francis Bacon's essay "Of Goodness, and Goodness in Nature" brings together the key words "philanthropy" and "misanthropy" by defining goodness as what "the Grecians call *philanthropia,*" calling it "of all virtues and dignities of mind . . . the greatest" and expressing his conviction that "without it man is a busy, mischievous, wretched thing." But even *philanthropia,* this "habit so excellent," is prone to error, and Bacon's list of the possible errors of the philanthrope, the benevolent lover of mankind, reads like a primer of good advice for Timon: "Seek the good of other men, but be not in bondage to their faces or fancies; for that is but facility or softness; which taketh an honest mind prisoner. Neither give thou Aesop's cock a gem, who would be better pleased and happier if he had had a barley-corn." In Aesop's fable "The Cock and the Pearl" a rooster unearths a pearl in the farmyard, but would prefer something to eat, however humble: " 'You may be a treasure,' quoth Master Cock, 'to men that prize you, but for me I would rather have a single barley-corn than a peck of pearls.' " In the same way Shakespeare's Timon will come to prefer a root dug from the earth to unwanted and corrupting gold, once he has seen through the "faces or fancies" of his flatterers. (There is probably a trace memory here, too, of the Sermon on the Mount—"Give not that which is holy unto the dogs, neither cast ye your pearls before swine" [Matthew 7:6].)

For Bacon the disposition to goodness in some men is matched, in others, by a "natural malignity," whether through crossness, difficulty, envy, or "mere mischief." This sounds like a good description of Shakespeare's Iago (we might compare "natural malignity" with Coleridge's famous phrase "motiveless malignity"), but the canonical example Bacon gives, the personage who personifies misanthropy, is, once again, Timon of Athens. Thus Bacon writes of "*misanthropi* that make it their practice to bring men to the bough, and yet never a tree for the purpose of their gardens, as Timon had." The reference is to the well-known incident in the Timon story told by Plutarch, in which Timon invites Athenians, "if any of you be desperate," to hang themselves on the fig tree in his garden. Shakespeare dramatizes this event in act 5, scene 1, of his play.

The general effect of this story is thus to turn Timon, as we have seen from the word "Timonist," into a kind of allegory of misanthropy. A striking comparison from a narrative poem of the period is the incident, described by Edmund Spenser in the third book of *The Faerie Queene,* of the transformation of a tormented character called Malbecco into an emblem of jealousy:

> Yet can he never dye, but dying liues,
>> And doth himself with sorrow new sustaine,
>> That death and life attonce vnto him giues,
>> And painefull pleasure turnes to pleasing paine.
>> There dwels he euer, miserable swaine,
>> Hatefull both to him selfe, and euery wight;
>> Where he through priuy griefe, and horrour vaine,
>> Is woxen so deform'd, that he has quight
> Forgot he was a man, and Gealousie is hight.
>
> *Spenser,* The Faerie Queene, *book 3, canto 10, stanza 60*

This is a version of the general pattern of metamorphosis that, following Ovid (and indeed Homer's Circe), details the upward or downward conversion of a human being into a flower, jewel, beast, or constellation. It is also the same kind of transformation into archetype that took place with Pandarus in *Troilus and Cressida.* Timon's story, like that of Pandarus, would have been familiar to Shakespeare's audiences, whose interest would presumably therefore lie in *how,* rather than *whether,* the expected change would take place.

The transformation is explicitly performed in act 4 of Shakespeare's play, when the self-exiled Timon encounters the self-exiled Alcibiades:

Alcibiades	What art thou there? Speak.
Timon	A beast, as thou art. . . .
	. . . .
Alcibiades	What is thy name? Is man so hateful to thee
	That art thyself a man?
Timon	I am Misanthropos, and hate mankind.

Timon 4.3.48–53

In the course of historical transmission the name Timon becomes the equivalent of "Misanthrope"—a living contradiction, as Alcibiades observes.

It is a measure of the acuteness and acerbity of *Timon of Athens* that it begins with one of those familiar Shakespearean scenes of exposition-via-secondary-character, but instead of lords, servants, or soldiers the commenting onlookers here are artists and artisans: a poet, a painter, a jeweler, and a merchant. Each, of course, regards Timon as a patron. The Painter and the Poet are particularly vain and empty, the Poet full of false modesty ("A thing slipped idly from me" is how he describes his current piece of verse, dedicated, as the Painter observes, "To the great lord" [1.1.19–20]), while the Painter displays his work to the vapid approbation of his colleague: "What a mental power / This eye shoots forth! How big imagination / Moves in this lip! To th' dumbness of the gesture / One might interpret" (31–34). The Painter is as archly modest as his friend, pressing him for more ("is't good?"), and receives the benison of a further banality: "Artificial strife / Lives in these touches livelier than life" (36, 37–38). But as self-absorbed as these creative personages are made to seem, they are accurate enough when it comes to assessing favor and fickleness in Timon's followers. Although all follow him now, "his lobbies fill with tendance, / Rain sacrificial whisperings in his ear, / Make sacred even his stirrup" (81–83), the minute his luck changes they will desert him.

On the heels of this dire prophecy Timon enters and, as the stage direction says, "address[es] himself courteously to every suitor." He is the personification of assured elegance and modest attentiveness, a generous patron whose flaw, if he can be seen to have one, is that he seems invested in his own persona as a source of endless bounty. The first to need his assistance is a messenger from Ventidius, whose debts have landed him in prison. Not only will Timon "pay the debt and free him," he also sends for Ventidius to give him further aid: " 'Tis not enough to help the feeble up, / But to support him after" (1.1.105, 109–110). The next man Timon helps is Lucilius, who wants to marry but is not wealthy enough to satisfy his lady's father. Again Timon is ready to help, offering to double the dowry. Needless to say, these will be among the first to deny him when he comes to them for succor.

From the first it is clear that Timon is not only generous but liberal. When Ventidius tries to repay him, he insists that the money was a gift, not a loan. The first scene ends with the sight of guests en route to "Lord Timon's feast," and the feast itself, including a masque of Cupid and another of Amazon ladies, features the influential men of Athens displaying "much adoring of Timon" (stage direction, act 1, scene 2) as they give and receive yet more gifts. Cautionary notes punctuate this event: first, the invective of Apemantus, who scorns the feast, warns the host, and reflects to himself, "[W]hat a number of men eats Timon, and he sees 'em not!" (1.2.38–39), and second, the dismay of Flavius, Timon's loyal steward, a figure often compared to Kent in *King Lear*, who sees his master's folly and is powerless to stop him:

Flavius [*aside*]   What will this come to?
                     He commands us to provide and give great gifts,
                     And all out of an empty coffer;
                     Nor will he know his purse, or yield me this:
                     To show him what a beggar his heart is,
                     Being of no power to make his wishes good.
                     His promises fly so beyond his state
                     That what he speaks is all in debt, he owes
                     For every word. He is so kind that he now
                     Pays interest for 't. . . .

                                                                    1.2.187–195

When the steward finally succeeds in convincing Timon that all his money has
run out—act 2, scene 2, begins with a particularly vivid portrait of a man of
business tearing his hair out at the profligacy of his noble client: "No care, no
stop; so senseless of expense / That he will neither know how to maintain it /
Nor cease his flow of riot" (2.2.1–3)—Timon is serenely confident. "I am
wealthy in my friends," he asserts (179). All he will need to do is ask them for
their assistance. As was the case in *Lear*, however, the answer to his appeals is
"no"—however cleverly disguised the reply. First he sends to the Senators for
help. "They answer in a joint and corporate voice," the steward reports,

                 That now they are at fall, want treasure, cannot
                 Do what they would, are sorry, you are honourable,
                 But yet they could have wished—they know not—
                 Something hath been amiss—a noble nature
                 May catch a wrench—would all were well—'tis pity. . . .

In short, with fine and empty words, "They froze me into silence" (2.2.199–207).
But Timon is unfazed: "These old fellows / Have their ingratitude in them
hereditary" (208–209). Flavius and the servants will have better luck if they try
younger men, specifically those who have received beneficent and timely gifts
from him, like Ventidius, whom he rescued from debtors' prison, and whose
father has just died and left him a great estate. The second act ends, finely, on
this happy expectation, which everything in the audience's dramatic sense, even
without knowledge of the historical Timon, will lead them to expect to fail.

    And fail it does, spectacularly. The "busyness" of these rich men and their
oblivious self-absorption have something of the spirit of Ben Jonson's comedies, just as the whole story of a good rich man surrounded by pretentious
climbers has something in common with Jonson's great country-house poem,
"To Penshurst." The first three scenes of the third act present three men, all
recently—and in our sight onstage—given lavish gifts by Timon, each turning away Timon's embassy with excuses that are simultaneously comic and

painful. Lucullus, hearing that one of Timon's men is at the door, expects yet another gift—"I dreamt of a silver basin and ewer tonight" (3.1.6–7)—and addresses the messenger in flirtatious terms: "And what hast thou there under thy cloak, pretty Flaminius?" (12–13). Told it is "nothing but an empty box," which Timon hopes he'll fill with money, Lucullus instantly turns prig and scold: "Many a time and often I ha' dined with him and told him on't, and come again to supper to him of purpose to have him spend less" (21–23). Business is business: "[T]his is no time to lend money, especially upon bare friendship without security" (37–38). Lucullus tries to offer Flaminius a tip, or a bribe, to go away: "Here's three solidares. . . . [W]ink at me, and say thou saw'st me not" (39–40).

The next encounter, with Lucius, is brilliantly conceived to show the quick-wittedness that accompanies a complete lack of moral fiber. First Lucius expresses incredulity at the gossip about Timon ("He cannot want for money" [3.2.7]), then surprise at the news that Lucullus denied to help him ("Denied that honourable man? . . . I should ne'er have denied his occasion" [15, 19–20]). Then, when approached himself, he expresses disingenuous regret about "[h]ow unluckily it happened" that he has managed not to have the funds on hand to help his friend: "[T]ell him this from me: I count it one of my greatest afflictions, say, that I cannot pleasure such an honourable gentleman" (42, 49–51). What makes the scene both more amusing and more pointed is the fact that Lucius, like Lucullus before him, has misperceived Timon's emissary as someone who is bringing gifts, not seeking them:

Servilius   May it please your honour, my lord hath sent—
Lucius   Ha! What has he sent? I am so much endeared to that lord,
            he's ever sending. How shall I thank him, think'st thou? And
            what has he sent now?
Servilius   He's only sent his present occasion now, my lord, requesting
            your lordship to supply his instant use with so many talents.

                                                        3.2.26–32

As for the third ungrateful friend, Sempronius, his response is equally devastating and equally funny. This part of the play is Shakespeare at his social-satirical best. Why bother me? Sempronius begins by asking of Timon's servant. Others have benefited from Timon's lavishness, like Lucius, Lucullus, and Ventidius. "All these / Owe their estates unto him" (3.3.2–5). Told that Timon has asked them, and that all three have "denied him" (the echo of Christ and Peter cannot be completely accidental), Sempronius immediately mounts his high horse and demands to know why he is being approached only now: "Must I be his last refuge?" (11). If Timon had just asked him first, he says, he would happily have sent him three times what he is requesting. "And does he think so backwardly of me now / That I'll requite it last? No" (18–19). "No" is of course the point here. These lords are experts at getting to no, by whatever route necessary. The rest of the act turns sharply colder as the creditors gather, presenting their bills to the steward and Timon, who have no money to pay them. Like Lear, Timon is ill-used by those to whom he has been generous. He has also, it seems clear, been unwise, not only in his choice of "friends" but in his management of money. His generosity—like that of many patrons and philanthropists, of whatever era—has become not only a way of life but a self-definition and a self-justification. It is not entirely surprising that Timon, bereft of money and grateful hangers-on, should dwindle into a railing caricature, and then into a pair of epitaphs.

The four major characters of the play—Timon, Apemantus, Alcibiades, and the steward, Flavius—are compared and contrasted with one another in various ways. Like Timon, whom he counts as a friend, Alcibiades finds himself at odds with Athens, though for political and pragmatic rather than ethical reasons. In act 3 he pleads with the Senators for clemency for an unnamed friend, in an oration that has been compared to Portia's and Isabella's eloquent pleas for mercy. The Senators, as befits their structural role as well as their nature, insist repeatedly, "We are for law; he dies" (3.6.85). In the upshot, when Alcibiades persists in his suit, they banish him from the city, incurring his wrath in return: "Banish me? / Banish your dotage, banish usury, / That makes the senate ugly" (96–98). This intemperate rejoinder has something of Coriolanus in it ("I banish you" [*Coriolanus* 3.3.127]), and indeed the "Life of Alcibiades" was partnered in Plutarch's *Parallel Lives of the Noble Grecians and Romans* with the "Life of Coriolanus." Each man, being banished, led an army against his own city. But Alcibiades is far more politic and judicious than Coriolanus, and less a suffering "tragic hero." He occupies the position in this play that is held in other tragedies by the political man who closes out the action: Octavius Caesar in *Antony and Cleopatra,* Aufidius in *Coriolanus,* Fortinbras in *Hamlet,* Richmond in *Richard III,* even Malcolm and Edgar in the final scenes of *Macbeth* and *King Lear,* respectively. Such a man, that is to say, is always ultimately a rationalist, even a compromiser when it suits his circumstances. Like Octavius and Aufidius, Alcibiades is not a tragic character—he will avoid suffering, rather than endure it, if he can. He not only survives the play, but speaks its last, conventional lines of mourning and recovery:

> Dead
> Is noble Timon, of whose memory
> Hereafter more. Bring me into your city,
> And I will use the olive with my sword,
> Make war breed peace, make peace stint war, make each
> Prescribe to other as each other's leech.
> Let our drums strike.

5.5.84–90

Flavius, the steward, tries repeatedly to warn Timon against his fair-weather friends, who, like the elder daughters of King Lear, flatter him to his face and take his gifts, but turn against him, full of self-righteousness and self-justification, the minute he requires something of them. Once Timon has turned misanthrope and taken refuge in his cave, the steward will join him, declaring his fidelity to his master in a way that again recalls Kent's fidelity to Lear:

> Flavius   I'll follow and enquire him out.
>   I'll ever serve his mind, with my best will.
>   Whilst I have gold I'll be his steward still.
>
> *4.2.49–51*

Timon, unlike Lear, remains resolute in his distaste for mankind, despite a variety of overtures (Alcibiades wants him to fight against Athens; the Senators want him to defend it). Ultimately he writes his own epitaph, which is declaimed, with suitable solemnity, by Alcibiades to the Athenian Senators as they make their peace at the end of the play.

As for Apemantus, he, too, is a familiar Shakespearean type, closely akin to "philosophical" or skeptical commentators like Thersites in *Troilus and Cressida,* Jaques in *As You Like It,* and even Mercutio in *Romeo and Juliet.* Identified as a "churlish philosopher," Apemantus is often called a "dog" in the text; thus he is linked with the philosophical school of the Cynics (literally "doglike, currish," although the name came from that of the Athenian gymnasium, Cynosarges, where this philosophy was taught). The omnipresence of dog imagery and dog language in this play (Painter to Apemantus: "You're a dog" [1.1.203]; Apemantus: "Thy mother's of my generation" [1.1.204]; Page to Apemantus: "Thou wast whelped a dog, and thou shalt famish a dog's death" [2.2.81–82]; Timon to Apemantus: "I had rather be a beggar's dog than Apemantus" [4.3.349]), plus the frequent use of words like "bites," "fangs," etc. (the examples are too numerous to mention), is not only thematic, indicating a general tone of carnivorous destruction, nor merely an allusion to the Cynics, but also allegorical in the same veiled though ultimately discernible way that the name of Timon is allegorical. As the play's tragic hero is a "man-hater," so the fool is a "dog." In fact, the many canine references applied to Apemantus the Cynic, starting as they do so early in the play, function as a kind of model or "control" for the emergence of Timon, within the dramatic action, as a one-dimensional symbol of the qualities historians had already attached to him.

The design of the play is marked by telling repetitions: two banquets, two encounters with the Poet and the Painter, two sets of occasions on which Timon deals with his flattering friends. In each case the second event undoes any hope or optimism engendered by the first.

The first banquet is a sumptuous feast, its splendor resisted only by Ape-

mantus, who sits alone at a separate table, and sees through the shallowness of
the occasion:

> I scorn thy meat. 'Twould choke me, for I should ne'er flatter thee. O you
> gods, what a number of men eats Timon, and he sees 'em not! It grieves me
> to see so many dip their meat in one man's blood.
>
> *1.2.37–40*

A masque and gifts given by the host to his guests complete the magnanimity of
the occasion, which is marked by Timon's unfailing courtesy and openhanded-
ness. The second banquet, arranged after his requests for aid have been ingenu-
ously rejected by his self-serving "friends," is quite the reverse. Cautioned by his
steward that he does not have enough money left "to furnish out / A moderate
table" (3.5.11–12), Timon determines, nonetheless, that he will "once more feast
the rascals" (9). The blindly flattered flatterers, now assuring one another that
they would have come to Timon's assistance—"I am sorry when he sent to borrow of me that my provision was out" (3.7.13–14)—and that it is clear now he
was only testing them, sit down to the "noble feast" they confidently expect,
only to have the dishes uncovered to reveal nothing but warm water and stones.
"Uncover, dogs, and lap" (3.7.77) is Timon's memorable invocation. His railing
against the "knot of mouth-friends" begins here in earnest, as they stumble out
of the banquet hall, leaving behind their caps and gowns:

> Most smiling, smooth, detested parasites,
> Courteous destroyers, affable wolves, meek bears,
> You fools of fortune, trencher-friends, time's flies,
> Cap-and-knee slaves, vapours, and minute-jacks!
>
> *3.7.86–89*

In the next scene, the beginning of the fourth act, Timon has left Athens
and, outside its walls, addresses the audience in a lengthy soliloquy of invective
ending in a prayer: "[G]rant, as Timon grows, his hate may grow / To the whole
race of mankind, high and low. / Amen" (4.1.39–41). Since the entire railing
speech is an apostrophe of topsy-turvy instructions, and since Timon is alone
on the stage, the recipients of his contempt are the spectators in the theater:

>   Matrons, turn incontinent!
> Obedience fail in children! Slaves and fools,
> Pluck the grave wrinkled senate from the bench
> And minister in their steads!
> . . . .
>   Maid, to thy master's bed!
> Thy mistress is o'th' brothel. Son of sixteen,

Pluck the lined crutch from thy old limping sire;
With it beat out his brains!

                              4.1.3–6, 13–15

As the speech continues, the personal turns general, and the spirit of Lear railing against the storm is joined with the tone of Ulysses' speech on "degree" (in *Troilus and Cressida*):

> Piety and fear,
> Religion to the gods, peace, justice, truth,
> Domestic awe, night rest, and neighbourhood,
> Instruction, manners, mysteries, and trades,
> Degrees, observances, customs, and laws,
> Decline to your confounding contraries,
> And let confusion live!

                              Timon 4.1.15–21

Timon's two chief encounters with Apemantus mark both the difference between these two characters and their points of intersection. At the feast in act 1 Apemantus, sitting apart, offers a grace that ends, prophetically, "Rich men sin, and I eat root" (1.2.70). As we will see, the opposition between "root" and "rich," or, more specifically, between "root" and "gold," will provide a chief imagistic narrative within the play.

Both gold and roots are products of the earth uncovered by digging. "Gold" in its various senses is omnipresent in Shakespeare, although the use perhaps the most closely analogous to that in *Timon of Athens* comes in *Romeo and Juliet,* which begins with the mention of a woman who will not "ope her lap / To saint-seducing gold," moves on to an apothecary shop where gold and poison are equated, and ends with the extravagant and empty gesture of two gold statues raised in memory of the dead lovers. In folktales and fairy tales, and as, for example, in Chaucer's "Pardoner's Tale," those who seek gold—especially buried or hidden gold—often find death instead. (It is perhaps worth noting that the other well-known "digging scene" in Shakespeare takes place in a graveyard, in *Hamlet.*) The cautionary tale of King Midas, who asked for the gift of turning everything he touched to gold and therefore almost starved to death, was told vividly in Ovid's *Metamorphoses.* Once he has left the city, Timon, digging for roots for sustenance, in a deeply ironic moment discovers gold, the last thing he wants:

> What is here?
> Gold? Yellow, glittering, precious gold?
> No, gods, I am no idle votarist:
> Roots, you clear heavens. . . .

. . . .

This yellow slave
Will knit and break religions, bless th'accursed,
Make the hoar leprosy adored, place thieves,
And give them title, knee, and approbation. . . .

4.3.25–28, 31–37

It is here that he sounds his most Lear-like, railing twice against "ingrateful man" (4.3.188, 194), invoking "tigers, dragons, wolves, and bears" and "new monsters" (189, 190).

To his cave will come, in steady succession, whores, bandits, and the Poet and the Painter, all hungry for the gold that cannot nourish them. ("Believe't that we'll do anything for gold," say Alcibiades' mistresses [4.3.149].) Timon will keep digging until he finds the "one poor root" he seeks for food. The word "root" is surprisingly omnipresent in the play, from the scene of the first feast, where Apemantus mentions it twice, to the digging scene (4.3), where Timon digs passionately in the earth, longing aloud (five times) for roots to eat. Unlike "gold," this is not a Shakespearean commonplace; "root" appears more times in *Timon* than in any other play, and other uses tend to refer more metaphorically to history or to family trees. In the digging scene the two terms come emphatically together, as Timon, eating a root, is asked by Apemantus what news he would like borne back to Athens:

Timon	Tell them there I have gold. Look, so I have.
Apemantus	Here is no use for gold.
Timon	The best and truest,
	For here it sleeps and does no hirèd harm.

4.3.290–292

It may be that this "root" symbolism is related in some way not only to the common theme of digging (and the opposition of humble and exalted, nature and artifice) but also to the hanging tree of the Timon story. In any case, it is Timon himself who will wind up "entomb'd" at the end of the play.

When Timon, digging for sustenance, finds gold instead, he offers a rueful panegyric:

O, thou sweet king-killer, and dear divorce
'Twixt natural son and sire; thou bright defiler
Of Hymen's purest bed; thou valiant Mars;
Thou ever young, fresh, loved, and delicate wooer,
Whose blush doth thaw the consecrated snow
That lies on Dian's lap; thou visible god,
That sold'rest close impossibilities

And mak'st them kiss, that speak'st with every tongue
To every purpose; O thou touch of hearts:
Think thy slave man rebels, and by thy virtue
Set them into confounding odds, that beasts
May have the world in empire.

                                                        4.3.374–384

Apemantus's pledge, "I'll say thou'st gold. / Thou wilt be thronged to shortly" (4.3.386–387), immediately comes true, as a group of outlaws, or "banditti," comes to try to steal it. "Where should he have this gold?" asks one (4.3.392). "It is noised he hath a mass of treasure," another replies (396). These are lower-class versions of the Senators and suitors who swarmed around Timon in the beginning of the play, but they are more direct and, oddly, more honorable: "We are not thieves, but men that much do want" (408). Timon tries to persuade them that nature possesses sufficient bounty: "Behold, the earth hath roots. / Within this mile break forth a hundred springs" (410–411). When they protest, "We cannot live on grass, on berries, water, / As beasts and birds and fishes" (415–416), he faces them down with the same charge of cannibalism that Apemantus had leveled at the lordly flatterers in the court. "[W]hat a number of men eats Timon, and he sees 'em not!" Apemantus had said, scorning the meat at the feast, and now Timon echoes him to the bandits, noting that they are not content to eat even the birds, beasts, and fishes, much less the roots and berries: "You must eat men" (418).

Timon sees clearly, as should audience, that the bandits are less venal and less self-deceiving than the rich men: "Yet thanks I must you con / That you are thieves professed, that you work not / In holier shapes" (4.3.418–420). And when he gives them gold, together with a ringing lecture about how "[e]ach thing's a thief," from the laws to the sun, moon, and earth, concluding, "Steal no less for this I give you, / And gold confound you howsoe'er. Amen" (441–442), they contemplate the same kind of conversion as the one effected by the eloquent virgin Marina among the brothel-goers in *Pericles*. "He's almost charmed me from my profession," says one, and another says, "I'll believe him as an enemy, and give over my trade" (443, 447–448). Although at least one editor prefers to regard these declarations as ironic ("Shakespeare can hardly have wanted at this stage of the play to give a repentant thief the last word"),[1] it seems to me that the contrast between the dishonest, self-blinded noble thieves of the first half of the play and the self-aware and threadbare bandits of the fourth act makes a key point.

No sooner do they exit than the loyal steward, Flavius, enters, seeking his master as Kent sought Lear in the storm:

Flavius   O you gods!
              Is yon despised and ruinous man my lord,

Full of decay and failing? O monument
And wonder of good deeds evilly bestowed!

4.3.451–454

Timon's recognition of the steward as "[o]ne honest man," and his ironic recognition that the one honest man in the world is a steward, who manages the money and estates of another, moves naturally—once he has sent Flavius away, rejecting his company and comfort—into the second embassy of the Poet and the Painter, again come in search of "gold" from their former patron ("[o]ur late noble master"), and ironically addressed by Timon as "honest men" over and over again, eight times in thirty lines. Again the satire against patronage is savage. This time, instead of actual works of art, these workmen come bearing nothing but promises. They have learned that "intent" always looks better than the product itself.

Ultimately *Timon* is a play not only about philanthropy and misanthropy, but also about the use and abuse of patronage. The word "patron" derives ultimately from the same word as "father" (Latin *pater*), and originally it denoted someone who stood to others in a relationship analogous to that of a father— that is, as a protector and defender. (Our word "pattern," for an exemplar or model, is related to this; thus Lear says he will be the "pattern of all patience.") The classical use of *patronus,* "patron," in Roman antiquity influenced the sense, common in the early seventeenth century, of a patron as one who accepted the dedication of a book, and led to our modern concept of a "patron of the arts." One contrast between *King Lear* and *Timon of Athens* is that the paternal-patron Lear and the arts-patron Timon, although they are addressed in very similar "ingrateful" terms by those who benefit from their generosity, are seen from a modern perspective to be owed something different by daughters and by protégés. Thus sentiments that sound both heartless and tragic when spoken by Goneril and Regan in *King Lear* take on, in *Timon,* a discomfiting air of satirical comedy in the mouths of the flattering lords Lucius, Lucullus, and Sempronius.

The epistle dedicatory to the First Folio of Shakespeare's plays, addressed by Shakespeare's friends and colleagues John Heminge and Henry Condell to the Earls of Pembroke and Montgomery, observes with customary praise, "There is a great difference, whether any book choose his patrons, or find them: This hath done both." Their purpose, Heminge and Condell say, is "only to keep the memory of so worthy a friend, and fellow, alive, as was our Shakespeare, by humble offer of his plays, to your most noble patronage." Heminge and Condell invoke as well the older sense of the patron as paternal protector, referring to the plays, significantly, as "orphans" left behind by the death of their author-father: "We have but collected them, and done an office to the dead, to procure his orphans, guardians, without ambition either of self-profit, or fame." It is a matter of some small interest, perhaps, that at this moment in the history of the English language the word "patron" was, in the spirit of nascent capitalism, being extended to what we would today call "customers" or "clients," so that Ben Jonson's Volpone, disguised as a mountebank, or charlatan, addresses a crowd of potential purchasers as "most noble gentlemen, and my worthy patrons!" (*Volpone* 2.1.32). By the time of *Timon,* the word was thus in use to describe both a noble benefactor and a mercantile consumer. The First Folio, with its separate invocation to "the great variety of readers" to "buy it first. . . . whatever you do, buy," is poised at the moment of this dichotomy, with two prefatory letters, one addressed to noble patrons, the other to potential purchasers ("the fate of all books depends upon your capacities, and not of your heads alone, but of your purses"). Something of the same tension, and the same anxiety, can be found in *Timon.*

Timon's epitaph, significantly, cannot be read by the simple soldier who first discovers it, presumably because the inscription is in another language (either Latin, the language of many early modern tomb inscriptions, or Greek). The Soldier therefore determines to take the "character," or writing, in a wax impression, and bring it to Alcibiades, "[a]n aged interpreter, though young in days" (5.4.6). Thus the stage is set for the play's final moments, in which the Senators ask clemency from Alcibiades and his troops; he answers in tones of mild and equitable justice—"Those enemies of Timon's and mine own / Whom you yourselves shall set out for reproof / Fall, and no more" (5.5.56–58)—and he reads aloud, to the audience of Senators on the city walls and patrons in the theater, Timon's angry two-part epitaphs: "Seek not my name" (5.6.73); "Here lie I, Timon" (75). It is Alcibiades, the "[n]oble and young" captain (5.6.13), who has the final words, Alcibiades who has custody of Timon's story and his reputation, "of whose memory / Hereafter more." He is, at the last, both pattern and patron, replacing—as we see so often at the ends of Shakespeare's tragedies— something like greatness with something like efficiency.

King Lear

DRAMATIS PERSONAE

Lear, *King of Britain*
Goneril, *Lear's eldest daughter*
Duke of Albany, *her husband*
Regan, *Lear's second daughter*
Duke of Cornwall, *her husband*
Cordelia, *Lear's youngest daughter*
King of France, *suitor of Cordelia*
Duke of Burgundy, *suitor of Cordelia*
Earl of Kent, *later disguised as Caius*
Earl of Gloucester
Edgar, *elder son of Gloucester, later disguised as Tom o' Bedlam*

Edmund, *bastard son of Gloucester*
Old Man, *Gloucester's tenant*
Curan, *Gloucester's retainer*
Lear's Fool
Oswald, *Goneril's steward*
A Servant of Cornwall
A Knight
A Herald
A Captain
Gentlemen, servants, soldiers, attendants, messengers

ING LEAR has often, and rightly, been regarded as a sublime account of the human condition. Words like "timeless" and "universal," so often used as virtual synonyms for "Shakespeare," here find a fitting place. In the twentieth century in particular the celebrity of the play soared. After the emergence of existentialism in philosophy, *Lear's* ruminations on "being" and "nothing" seemed uncannily apt. The plays of Samuel Beckett—especially *Endgame* and *Waiting for Godot*—seemed to rewrite *King Lear* in a new idiom, and critical books like Maynard Mack's *"King Lear" in Our Time* and Jan Kott's *Shakespeare Our Contemporary* stressed the way the play voiced the despair and hope of a modern era. Yet this extraordinary play, in part a poignant and disaffected family drama, in part the political story of Britain's union and disunion, bears as well explicit markers of the time in which it was written, and the time in which it was set. As we have seen with other Shakespeare plays that engage chronicle history, these three crucial time periods—the time the play depicts, the time of its composition, and the time in which it is performed or read—will always intersect.

That a play depicting the dismemberment of ancient Britain by the willful act of the old King Leir should have relevance to the stage of King James's time is far from surprising. Shakespeare's play was written around 1605, and in the period 1604–1607 James VI and I, King of Scotland and of England, was attempting to persuade Parliament to approve of the union of Scotland and

England into one nation. It was James who first used the term "Great Britain" to describe the unity of the Celtic and Saxon lands (England, Scotland, and Wales). In his accession speech to Parliament on March 19, 1603, James had compared the union of Lancaster and York achieved by his ancestor Henry VII to the even more important "union of two ancient and famous kingdoms, which is the other inward peace annexed to my person." His language concerning civil and external war, and the remarkable metaphor of marriage and divorce that concludes this passage, are closely relevant to the dramatic action of *King Lear*. "Although outward peace be a great blessing," James wrote in "On the Union of the Kingdoms of Scotland and England,"

> yet it is far inferior to peace within, as civil wars are more cruel and unnatural than wars abroad. And therefore [a] great blessing that God has with my person sent unto you, is peace within, and that in a double form. First, by my descent, lineally out of the loins of Henry VII, is reunited and confirmed in me the union of the two princely roses of the two houses of Lancaster and York, whereof that King of happy memory was the first uniter, as he was also the first ground-layer of the other peace. . . .
>
> But the union of these two princely houses is nothing comparable to the union of two ancient and famous kingdoms, which is the other inward peace annexed to my person. . . . Has not God first united these two kingdoms, both in language, religion, and similitude of manners? Yes, has he not made us all one island, compassed with one sea, and of itself by nature so indivisible, as almost those that were borderers themselves on the late borders, cannot distinguish nor know or discern their own limits? These two Countries being separated neither by sea, nor great river, mountain, nor other strength of nature . . .
>
> And now in the end and fullness of time united, the right and title of both in my person, alike lineally descended of both the Crowns, whereby it is now become like a little world within itself, being entrenched and fortified round about with a natural, and yet admirable strong pond or ditch, whereby all the former fears of this nation are now quite cut off. The other part of the island being ever before now, not only the place of landing to all strangers that were to make invasion here, but likewise moved by the enemies of the State, by untimely incursions, to make enforced diversion from their conquests, for defending themselves at home, and keeping sure their back door, as then it was called; which was the greatest hindrance and let that ever my predecessors of the nation had in disturbing them from their many famous and glorious conquests abroad. What God has conjoined then, let no man separate. . . .

In his speeches James regularly referred to the misfortunes that had brought *dis*union on early Britain—that is, the Britain of King Leir. James's scheme of union would repair this ancient breach, correct this old mistake. Shakespeare's play thus has a direct and pertinent topicality to the political issues of his day, a topicality few in his contemporary audiences could miss, although many viewers today will need to be reminded of this historical context. Likewise, the figure of Edgar, disguised as "Poor Tom," the madman, or "Bedlam beggar" (from the Hospital of Saint Mary at Bethlehem in London that was used to house the insane), was an example of the kinds of "masterless men" who roamed Britain's towns and forests at this time, vagabond, often homeless and out of work, men whose very existence was viewed by the monarch as a threat to civil order and authority. Queen Elizabeth's "Homily Against Disobedience and Willful Rebellion" (1570), which she ordained to be proclaimed in the churches, had cautioned explicitly against the marauding of masterless men.

King Lear focuses at once on patriarchy and paternity, on the interaction between the role of the king and the role of the father. For Shakespeare's time the idea of fatherhood was central to notions of governance, and the Bible taught, in the imagery of Saint Paul, that the structure of the family household should take the same form as the political structure. Thus the relationship of parents and children, fathers and daughters, and fathers and sons dominates the action. (We may notice that King Lear has no queen, nor the Duke of Gloucester a duchess.) For twentieth- and twenty-first-century readers and viewers living in nonmonarchical cultures, the notion of kingship may function as a metaphor, so that Lear is viewed primarily as a father, the head of a household, the father of daughters, his kingship receding into a notional world of fairy tale and nightmare.

One further prefatory observation is necessary before we turn to the plot and language of *King Lear*. As a result of textual investigations at the end of the twentieth century, many recent Shakespeare editors have concluded that there are *two* extant viable versions of the play, *The History of King Lear*, published in quarto form in 1608, which is considered to be the play as Shakespeare first wrote it, and *The Tragedy of King Lear*, published in the First Folio (1623), with revisions so substantial as to make it, in effect, a different play. Among the many differences between these versions are the presence in the Quarto of the mock trial scene in which the mad Lear rails at his "counselors," the Fool and "Poor Tom"; the presence in the Quarto, only, of the "[s]unshine and rain at once" passage; and the famous final lines, "We that are young . . . ," which are given to Edgar in the Folio and to Lear's son-in-law Albany in the Quarto. In previous editions, until quite recently, editors followed a long-standing practice of blending the two texts, as is done with other plays where there are both quarto and folio versions, choosing the "best" readings for each line and scene. Contemporary editorial decisions are more radical, in attempting to restore (or "un-edit") the texts as they would have been known to readers and actors of Shakespeare's time. The problem for modern readers and acting companies is that many people "know" a version of *Lear* that, while it may not accord with the most advanced editorial decision making, nonetheless includes things that we are very reluctant to omit or to change, however "impure" the result from a scholarly perspective. In my observations on *King Lear* I will continue to include all scenes and passages that have become customarily associated with the play over the years, using the Folio as my primary source and indicating, when appropriate, for interested readers, when a scene appears only in the Quarto. My general philosophy about Shakespeare's plays—as will already, I hope, be clear—is that they are living works of art that grow and change over time, not museum pieces that must only be preserved in some imagined state of purity (or petrification). Every production is an interpretation; world events and brilliant individual performances alike have shaped and changed these plays, so that they are "Shakespearean" in their protean life, not restricted to some imagined (and unrecapturable) terrain of Shakespeare's "intention" or control. A final note on the Quarto/Folio question for *Lear* will underscore the issues with which I began, since the Quarto text calls itself a "history," and the Folio, a "tragedy." Plainly, as we have already seen, *King Lear* is both, and the elements of history intersect with the elements of tragedy to produce what the poet William Butler Yeats finely called an "emotion of multitude."

The play begins by instantiating a vision of social order. A trumpet is sounded, and a coronet is borne into the state chamber, and then there follow, in order of rank and precedence, the powers of the state: King Lear; his sons-in-law, the Dukes of Albany and Cornwall; and his daughters, in the order of their ages. ("Albany" is the ancient and literary name of Scotland; "Cornwall," of the southwest of England. Together these sons-in-law demarcate the Britain Lear is shortly to dismember.) Elaborate, ornate, imperial—as a madder and a wiser Lear will later declare, "Robes and furred gowns hide all"—the scene before us is one of opulent magnificence and insistent order. It is a scene, above all, of "accommodated man," of humanity surrounded with wealth and power, robes and furs, warmth, food, and attendants—the radical opposite of the vision the play's third act will supply, when Lear will tell the naked and tattered "Poor Tom,"

> [T]hou art the thing itself. Unaccommodated man is no more but such a
> poor, bare, forked animal as thou art.
>
> Lear 3.4.95–97

Unaccommodated man, and accommodated man. As the play begins the audience is confronted with kingly power in all its majesty, mankind apparently accommodated with everything it can imagine or desire. At the center of this world is the King. And yet, when the King begins to speak, we are at once made uneasy, if we are listening closely: "Meantime we shall express our darker purpose" (1.1.34). In a play in which one of the central images will be sight and blindness, this is already a warning signal. What is the King's darker purpose? Nothing less than the division of the kingdom, the willful creation of disorder:

> Know that we have divided
> In three our kingdom, and 'tis our fast intent
> To shake all cares and business from our age,
> Conferring them on younger strengths while we
> Unburdened crawl toward death. . . .
>
> *1.1.35–39*

But this is contrary to everything that we know about kingship. It is clear not only from the precepts and practice of Elizabeth and James but also from every Shakespearean example that the ideal for rulers demands unity, not division, a single king, a strong ruler, and one who is prepared to choose a public life over a private one. Whether the king is Henry V or Julius Caesar, this principle holds: that the king should understand that the obligation is to hold together the state and unify its people. Yet here we have a king who intends to violate every single one of these proven precepts—who will attempt the physically and regally impossible, inviting his elder daughters, "this crownet part between you" (1.1.137), and who will also seek to escape the inescapable burden of mortality, to "[u]nburdened crawl toward death," as if he had regressed to the posture and position of a child.

Moreover, the entire scene has the quality of a fairy tale, and indeed of a well-rehearsed fairy tale: the king, the three daughters (two older and cruel, the youngest loyal, pure, and misunderstood)—there are no surprises here. We know and expect that the elder daughters will be wicked flatterers, the youngest their victim. Their joint business will be the division of the kingdom.

This is a purposeful fall, a fall by choice. The map is already present, the lands partitioned, awaiting the completion of the ritual as the king has designed and planned it. Lear is testing what should need no test: the quality of nature and what is "natural." The whole play that follows will deal with this vexed question, of nature and of the "natural child." What *is* a "natural child"? Is nature what Alfred, Lord Tennyson, would call "Nature, red in tooth and claw," the nature of pelican daughters, dog-hearted daughters, cannibals, and competitors? Or is nature a state akin to grace, a pattern of plenitude and order, like the lands the Lear of this opening scene has in his keeping: "With shadowy forests and with champaigns riched, / With plenteous rivers and wide-skirted meads" (1.1.62–63). Nature as the kingly emblem of fertility, order, harvest, and grace. Which?

Lear   Tell me, my daughters—
> Since now we will divest us both of rule,
> Interest of territory, cares of state—
> Which of you shall we say doth love us most,
> That we our largest bounty may extend
> Where nature doth with merit challenge? . . .
>
> *1.1.46–51*

This is hubris, overweening pride, and presumptuousness, not only a violation of Lear's responsibilities as King and man, but also a tampering with the bonds of nature, as his youngest daughter, Cordelia, well knows. And the replies of the two elder daughters, Goneril and Regan, to this love test have a rehearsed quality, a smooth deceptive flow. The whole scene is stylized and formal, until Cordelia breaks its frame. Goneril's answer is apparently unequivocal:

> Sir, I love you more than words can wield the matter;
> Dearer than eyesight, space, and liberty . . .
>
> *1.1.53–54*

Eyesight, space, and liberty—all key themes in the play, all elements of which Lear and his fellow sufferer Gloucester will be bereft by the play's end.

> A love that makes breath poor and speech unable.
>
> *1.1.58*

And Regan adds,

> I am made of that self mettle as my sister,
> And prize me at her worth. In my true heart
> I find she names my very deed of love—
> Only she comes too short . . .
>
> *1.1.67–70*

Notice "prize," "worth," "deed"—all economic terms, which should alert us to the true nature of the elder daughters' thoughts. Words, these sisters say, cannot express their feelings. "I am alone felicitate / In your dear highness' love," Regan concludes (1.1.73–74).

Having expended words in saying that they have no words, the sisters receive their segments of the dismembered kingdom. Then it is Cordelia's turn to speak:

Lear	Now our joy,
	Although our last and least . . .
	. . . .
	what can you say to draw
	A third more opulent than your sisters? Speak.
Cordelia	Nothing, my lord.
Lear	Nothing?
Cordelia	Nothing.
Lear	Nothing will come from nothing. Speak again.
Cordelia	Unhappy that I am, I cannot heave

according to her bond will distinguish Cordelia's language, and her silence, throughout the play. Like Hamlet in the court of Claudius, dismayed by the falseness of ceremony and the role-playing all around him, Cordelia refuses to play the game, refuses to involve herself in playacting and willful deception. While Hamlet makes use of theatricality as a trap, Cordelia occupies what might be called the vanishing point of theatricality. We may think that Cordelia's rigidity here is too pure a gesture, that she could bend, could compromise—but she, like her sisters, is her father's daughter, stubborn and proud. Her motive in this moment seems plainly to disclaim artifice, to assert, again, something that in her understanding needs no assertion: the true and natural relationship between parent and child. But once disrupted, this "bond" is not restored until tragedy has overtaken both Lear and Gloucester.

Cordelia's rhetoric of silence will continue throughout the play, and will reach what is perhaps its most striking point when she herself becomes a condition of nature, at the point in act 4 (scene 17 in the Quarto text) when, beholding the ruined King, she will appear, in the words of an anonymous gentleman onlooker, like "[s]unshine and rain at once," split between smiles and tears, incapable of speech because of her love and pity. But we will also see the tragic limitations of her silence, the capacity of silence to be radically misunderstood, and the way in which Cordelia overcomes it and returns to speech.

At this point in the play, however, Cordelia's silence is an antidote to the unfeeling hypocrisy of Goneril and Regan, the "glib and oily art" of their glozing speech. Silence, enacted on the stage, also resists the Machiavellian two-facedness of Edmund, that master rhetorician. When Lear in the latter part of the play is reduced to strings of repetitions ("Howl, howl, howl, howl!" as he discovers Cordelia's dead body; or "Kill, kill, kill, kill, kill!"; or, closest to the theme of "nothing," "Never, never, never, never, never"), we experience another version of the rhetoric of silence, the acknowledgment of the unutterable, the literally unspeakable. Like the syntactical breakdown of Othello's language in the scene of his swooning fit (*Othello* 4.1), Lear's repeated iterations of the same word over and over again, without subject or object, and without any rhetorical gesture of control, mark the very limit of language as communication.

From the first scene on, other characters will seek to evade the prevailing duplicity of language in yet another way, by disguising their voices. Thus Kent becomes the country man "Caius," whose plainness of speech is so irritating to the Duke of Cornwall, and who puts on a mockingly courtly language to try to expose the follies of flattery and verbal "accommodation" ("Sir, in good faith, in sincere verity, / Under th'allowance of your great aspect," and so on [2.2.98–99]). The servile language he mocks resembles that of Osric, the foppish courtier in *Hamlet,* whose words were so fashionably contorted they required translation. In a similar way Edgar, eschewing the ornate duplicities of the court, becomes not only "Poor Tom," the "Bedlam beggar" with his nonsensical jingles and visions of fiends ("Poor Tuelygod, Poor Tom" [2.2.177]), but also the rustic with the strange dialect who pretends to rescue the blind

Gloucester at the bottom of Dover "cliff." Gloucester almost recognizes his disguised son by his voice—"Methinks thy voice is altered"; "Methinks you're better spoken" (4.5.7, 10)—and is hastily corrected by Edgar: "You're much deceived. In nothing am I changed / But in my garments" (9–10). Since Gloucester is blind, he cannot see that Edgar's garments, alone, remain unchanged throughout the scene.

The dark side of the rhetoric of silence, the language of limitation and the limitation of language, is that great yawning chasm of "nothing" that pervades the play, emanating from the remarkable and encyclopedic first scene. "Nothing will come of nothing" is Lear's threat, based on his interpretation of Cordelia's silence. And "Nothing will come of nothing" will become Lear's own living epitaph in the acts and scenes to come. "Nothing"—the opposite of "everything," of "accommodation."

"They told me I was everything; 'tis a lie, I am not ague-proof," says Lear near the close of his tragedy (4.5.102). Both Lear and Gloucester will make the mistake of taking themselves for everything. Both are tortured by that haunting word "nothing" until they *become* nothing. Later in the first act Lear's Fool will ask his master, "Can you make no use of nothing, nuncle?" and will be told, "Why no, boy. Nothing can be made of nothing" (1.4.116–118). But nothing is what Lear has left himself, in divesting himself of kingdom and power. As the Fool points out, referring to the new Arabic numbers that were replacing Roman numerals, and the innovation of the nought, the figure zero, from the Arabic word "cipher," meaning "empty," "Now thou art an O without a figure. I am better than thou art, now. I am a fool; thou art nothing" (1.4.158–159).

When he pretends to protect his father by theatrically "concealing" a piece of paper, the bastard Edmund claims that he is reading "nothing," which is true, since what he has in his hand is a false letter he himself has fabricated to implicate his legitimate brother, Edgar. But Gloucester, like Lear, will fall into the trap. "The quality of nothing hath not such need to hide itself," he objects (1.2.33–34). The paper must be *something*. And so Gloucester makes something of it, getting from Edmund the "auricular assurance" (86) that so closely resembles Iago's equally deceiving "ocular proof" in Othello—evidence, in fact, of nothing at all. Gloucester ironically praises his son's behavior as that of a "[l]oyal and natural boy" (2.1.83). Gloucester means "according to nature," but a "natural" son (from the Latin *filius naturalis* and Middle French *fils naturel*) was an illegitimate child, born outside of marriage. Shortly we will see the legitimate son, Edgar, stripped of his rightful place and forced for safety's sake to change his identity into that of the beggar "Poor Tom," declare, "Edgar I nothing am" (2.2.178). We could read this as "I am not Edgar" but also "As Edgar, I am nothing." The play moves remorselessly from its first scene of "everything" (accommodation, luxury, comfort, and security) toward a clear-eyed and scarifying contemplation of "nothing." And the immediate cause is Lear's own lack of self-knowledge.

At the close of the opening scene the audience hears Goneril and Regan, who have flattered their father grossly throughout the public ceremony of the love test, now speak of him privately as a senile fool. "You see how full of changes his age is," says Goneril, and Regan is quick to agree: " 'Tis the infirmity of his age; yet he hath ever but slenderly known himself" (1.1.284, 288–289). She is not entirely wrong, if Lear can commit the action with which he opens the play, the irreversible action that calls down his tragedy upon him: "Only we shall retain / The name and all th'addition to a king" (1.1.133–134). To retain "only the name," the title without the power, is of course impossible. Kent, the loyal friend and vassal, is to Lear in this play what Horatio is to Hamlet, what Banquo is to Macbeth—an index of normality, a foil for the excesses of the tragic hero. Kent calls the abdication folly, and the rejection of Cordelia madness, and he addresses, directly and firmly, the question of retaining "only the name":

> Royal Lear,
> Whom I have ever honoured as my king,
> Loved as my father, as my master followed,
> As my great patron thought on in my prayers—
>
> *1.1.137–140*

"Royal Lear," "king," "father," "master," "patron"—these are the necessary social roles and costumes of accommodated man, and Lear rejects them all, earning Kent's blunt anger. "Be Kent unmannerly / When Lear is mad. What wouldst thou do, old man?" and, "To plainness honour's bound / When majesty falls to folly" (1.1.143–144, 146–147). Thus once again in this great opening scene we hear a note that will be sounded repeatedly. Lear is already mad here, although not yet in the sense of the frantic disorientation that will overtake him by the third act. He is metaphorically, though not yet literally, mad. And he is no longer King, patron, royal Lear. Instead he has become simply—and impotently—an "old man." The same pointed reduction will take place again at the end of act 2, when Gloucester refers to Lear with customary respect as "the King"—"The King is in high rage" (2.2.459)—and Cornwall and Regan dismiss him merely as the "old man" (453, 459). For in stripping himself of these necessary roles, the powerful trappings of kingship, Lear also strips himself of dignity, fear, respect—and friends. "Out of my sight!" he rails at Kent, and Kent, again prophetically, answers, "See better, Lear" (1.1.155–156). Lear's moral blindness is as absolute in this opening scene as Gloucester's physical blindness will be later in the play, and Lear divests himself not only of his kingdom, his daughter Cordelia, and his roles as King and father, but also of those other crucial roles as master and patron, for he divests himself of Kent. The faithful Earl of Kent is banished, his banishment ordained to take place on the sixth day, with a resonance of the banishment of Adam from Eden. He departs with: "Thus Kent, O princes, bids you all adieu; / He'll shape his old course in a country new"

(1.1.183–184). Like Celia in *As You Like It* going forth into the Forest of Arden ("Thus go we in content / To liberty and not to banishment"), or Coriolanus defiantly rejecting Rome ("I banish *you*" [emphasis added]), Kent claims the comparative liberty of exile, when oppression and injustice inhabit the court: "Freedom lives hence, and banishment is here" (1.1.178). With the division of the kingdom and the rejection of Cordelia and Kent, Lear's Britain undergoes a fall. (Kent returns immediately in the disguise of a common man, doffing his exalted rank. "How now, what art thou?" the King will demand of him, and he will respond simply, "A man, sir" [1.4.9–10].)

All appearance of order and rank has disappeared. That great emblematic procession that trailed across the stage—king, nobles, daughters, dependents— is broken up, disrupted. Such a procession, a visual icon of royal power, would have been clearly recognizable to Shakespeare's audience as the sign of contemporary—early modern—sequence and succession, however situated the events of the play might be in the history of early Britain. The sumptuous trappings of civilization are revealed as fictive coverings, and the play's innate primitivism, which goes even further back than Norman or Celtic Britain, begins to reveal itself. This is not, after all, a civilized world. It is a world of monsters, cannibals, and heraldic conflict. "Come not between the dragon and his wrath," Lear commanded Kent as Kent tried to intervene on behalf of Cordelia (1.1.120). Lear is both the dragon, the sign of Britain from Norman times onward, and the wrathful king—a king who thinks he has the power of an angry god. No sooner does he say this than the play is flooded with images of unnatural monsters, monsters that feed upon themselves and their young:

> The barbarous Scythian,
> Or he that makes his generation messes
> To gorge his appetite . . .
>
> *1.1.114–116*

> Ingratitude, thou marble-hearted fiend,
> More hideous when thou show'st thee in a child
> Than the sea-monster—
>
> *1.4.220–222*

> How sharper than a serpent's tooth it is
> To have a thankless child. . . .
>
> *1.4.251–252*

> Humanity must perforce prey on itself,
> Like monsters of the deep.
>
> *Quarto, 16.48–49*

Lear and others now begin to speak of pelican daughters; of tigers, not daughters; of dog-hearted daughters; of sharp-toothed unkindness, like a vulture; of nails that flay a wolfish visage. A whole cluster of monsters is summoned up, in effect, by Lear's initial action in dividing his kingdom, and in wishing to do what no human being and certainly no king can do: to unburdened crawl toward death.

This marvelous, panoramic opening scene, then, poses almost all the issues and introduces almost all the images that will serve to focus the play. Yet the Lear plot is only one of the two major plots that intertwine in *King Lear*. What we have been calling the "opening scene" is framed by two episodes that involve the key figures of Gloucester and his bastard son Edmund. The play is designed with a very clear symmetry: two old men, each with a loyal child he mistakenly considers disloyal (Cordelia and Edgar), and disloyal children or a child he at first thinks loyal and natural (Goneril, Regan, and Edmund). In fact, one Restoration editor, Nahum Tate, dissatisfied with the tragic ending of the play, rewrote it to conclude with a marriage between Cordelia and Edgar. And lest we think this a curious aberration of those times, we should note that the Tate version of the play, "reviv'd with alterations," to quote his title page, held the stage from 1681 to 1838, as the "improv'd" version of *King Lear*, correcting the barbarisms of Jacobean times.

The symmetries provided by these two plots, the Lear plot and the Gloucester plot, are not merely dynastic or structural. Lear, whose error is a mental error, the error of misjudgment in dismembering his kingdom, is punished in the play by a mental affliction, madness. Gloucester, whose sin is a physical sin, lechery, is punished in the play by a physical affliction, blindness. As Edgar says bitterly to Edmund, "The dark and vicious place where thee he got / Cost him his eyes" (5.3.162–163). The blinding of Gloucester is also, of course, a literal evocation of this imagined justness of punishment, an eye for an eye. The manifold mythic and literary associations of blindness, from Oedipus to Freud, link that condition with sexual knowledge, with castration, and with "insight." (As Gloucester will observe ruefully, underscoring the paradox, "I stumbled when I saw.")

The play presents two different paradigms of biblical suffering, juxtaposed and paralleled. Lear is a Job-like character, a man who has everything (family, wealth, honor) and loses everything. The mock trial in scene 13 (in the Quarto only) restages the story of Job and his comforters, here played by the tragically inadequate figures of the Fool and "Poor Tom." We hear Lear, like Job, quest perpetually for patience: "You heavens, give me that patience, patience I need" (2.2.437); "I will be the pattern of all patience. / I will say nothing" (3.2.36–37); "I can be patient, I can stay with Regan, / I and my hundred knights" (2.2.395–396); "I'll not endure it" (1.3.5)—and then, two acts later, "Pour on, I will endure" (3.4.18). But if Lear is a Job, quick to anger and quick to rail against heaven, Gloucester is a more passive and accepting Christian sufferer, a man who is willing to believe that ripeness is all, that men must endure their going hence, even as their coming hither. As if to emphasize the degree of his abnegation, Gloucester begins to speak of the "kind gods" from the moment his eyes are put out.

The latter part of *King Lear* places an increasingly heavy emphasis on this emblematic Christian theme in language and in staging. Cordelia is arguably the real "Christ figure" in the play, speaking of her "father's business" and making her final appearance in a gender-reversed Pietà, held in the arms of a grieving Lear. Some productions of the play have also emphasized Edgar's evident Christ-like qualities; in Peter Brook's film (1971) Edgar is stabbed in the side with a spear as he cries out at the spectacle of death ("O thou side-piercing sight!"). Yet as with all Shakespearean evocations of allegory, whether religious, mythological, or political, the Christian undertones and overtones in *Lear* work best when they are allowed to augment the dramatic action rather than displace it. The power of *King Lear* and its place in our cultural imaginary depend above all, at least for a modern audience, upon its depiction of a human story of love, suffering, and loss.

The gods mentioned in this play are as various as the mythological strains that underpin it. The first mentions are of pagan gods; Lear swears by Apollo and appeals to "the thunder-bearer" and to "high-judging Jove" (2.2.392, 393). In 1606 Parliament passed "An Act to Restrain Abuses of Players"; it stipulated that "no person or persons . . . in any stage play, interlude, show, maygame, or pageant" might "jestingly or profanely speak or use the holy name of God or of Christ Jesus, or of the Holy Ghost or of the Trinity." Thus, swearing by the name of the Christian God on the stage was forbidden by law. Nonetheless the play moves inexorably toward the contemplation of a Christian solution. The pagan gods become at various times kind gods, clearest gods, just gods—or, in one of the play's most famously despairing lines, gods as "wanton boys."

In fact, what we have in *King Lear* are not only two modes of suffering and two kinds of godhead but also two conceptions of tragedy that are cited explicitly and made to play against each other. Familiar from earlier Shakespearean history plays, and notably from *Richard III,* these two modes can be described, in shorthand terms, as cyclical and linear, or as "medieval" and "early modern." As we have often noticed, one popular pattern for tragedy, as exemplified in the kinds of medieval literary works called "falls of princes," was that of the wheel of Fortune. Life was imagined—and often depicted in woodcuts and engravings—as a great wheel. Each man's and each woman's life reached a point of greatest height, greatest prosperity, from which he or she would, ultimately, fall.

We hear a great deal about this kind of tragedy in *King Lear.* The disguised Edgar speaks of what it is like to be "at the worst," at the bottom of Fortune's wheel, only to find that, since he can *say* he is at the bottom, he is not yet really there. (He is in fact immediately confronted with the spectacle of his blinded father, and is moved to observe, "I am worse than e'er I was" [4.1.26]. This is another clear example in the play of the rhetoric of silence, the unutterability of extremes in emotion.) Likewise the disguised Kent, finding himself ignobly placed in the stocks—a punishment that angers his master, Lear, because it is an insult, a disregard of rank—resigns himself to the necessity of patience: "Fortune, good night; / Smile once more; turn thy wheel" (2.2.157–158). Lear's Fool, too, believes in this kind of cycle. He sees that his own prospects are dependent upon the vagaries and vicissitudes of Fortune: "Let go thy hold when a great wheel runs down a hill, lest it break thy neck with following; but the great one that goes upward, let him draw thee after" (2.2.238–240). And as he lies dying at the end of the play even the bastard Edmund, who had cynically observed, "The younger rises when the old doth fall" (3.3.22), accepts with fatality his reversal of fortune: "The wheel is come full circle. I am here" (5.3.164).

This notion of Fortune's wheel is omnipresent in the play, but it is consistently in tension with another pattern, one often associated with Christianity, but also with tragedy in its classical form: the idea of the fortunate fall. "The gods throw incense on our sacrifices"; individual human suffering and human loss are only aspects of the quest for a larger knowledge of the nature of humanity and mortality. Thus the idea of exemplary sacrifice—Christ died for the sins of mankind—is sutured to the dramatic action, at the same time that it is naturalized and humanized. Both Lear and Gloucester "die" in the play—indeed, each dies not once but twice, and each is "reborn." Gloucester believes that he has leapt from Dover "cliff" and has been miraculously preserved to life; Lear in the fourth act dies out of his madness and into fresh garments, out of the grave and into the world again. When they die a second time—when they die on the stage "for real," so to speak—is the second (literal) "death" likely to be any more final than the first (symbolic) one? The play itself is "reborn" (today we often say "revived") each time it is performed. One of the functions of Jacobean tragedy is to take this exemplary and educative form: to present us with great figures who die for sins and mistakes that could be ours, and whose tragedies take place so that ours will not, or need not. Literary tragedy is in this formal sense a scapegoat, substitute, or safety valve. Its cultural value is not only aesthetic but also ameliorative and apotropaic, warding off danger.

But the tragedy of *King Lear* begins at the other end of the scale, not with the supernatural but with the natural. As we have seen, Cordelia's claim of a natural "bond" between parent and child is juxtaposed to an image of the "natural" in its most anarchic and destructive form, in the person of Edmund, the natural, or bastard, son of the Duke of Gloucester. Edmund's villainy is not equated with his bastardy, although the range of meanings of "natural" offers an effective amplification of the serious rumination on the nature of "nature" throughout the play. Philip Falconbridge, the "Bastard" in *King John,* is that play's martial and patriotic center, far more heroic than his conservative (and "legitimate") brother, Robert. The great speech on "bastardy" and baseness should rather be compared to Richard of Gloucester's comparably energetic speech on "deformity" at the beginning of *Richard III*. In both cases the Machiavellian speaker seduces the audience, using his supposed deficiency as both a rhetorical excuse for aberrancy and a gauntlet thrown down daringly to challenge the status quo. Edmund is a close relation of Iago and of Richard III in his contempt for what he regards as passive sentimentalism. Like them he is a Machiavel and a Vice figure, a character who draws strength from his own contrariness. Not for him the old-fashioned view that "our stars" govern our behavior: "I should have been what I am had the maidenliest star in the firmament twinkled on my bastardizing" (1.2.119–121). He revels in disorder, takes pleasure in anarchy. In the early part of the play, when all around him other characters either begin to doubt their own identities or feel it prudent to conceal them, Edmund alone is never doubtful. His masterful manifesto is addressed to Nature, the goddess he elects as the patroness of natural children, the children of disorder:

> Thou, nature, art my goddess. To thy law
> My services are bound. Wherefore should I
> Stand in the plague of custom and permit
> The curiosity of nations to deprive me
> For that I am some twelve or fourteen moonshines
> Lag of a brother? Why "bastard"? Wherefore "base,"
> When my dimensions are as well compact,
> My mind as generous, and my shape as true
> As honest madam's issue? Why brand they us
> With "base," with "baseness, bastardy—base, base"—
> Who in the lusty stealth of nature take
> More composition and fierce quality
> Than doth within a dull, stale, tirèd bed
> Go to th' creating a whole tribe of fops
> Got 'tween a sleep and wake? Well then,
> Legitimate Edgar, I must have your land.
> Our father's love is to the bastard Edmund
> As to th' legitimate. Fine word, "legitimate."
> Well, my legitimate, if this letter speed
> And my invention thrive, Edmund the base
> Shall to th' legitimate. I grow, I prosper.
> Now gods, stand up for bastards!

1.2.1–22

The language of energetic and entrepreneurial "prosperity" ("I grow, I prosper") seems to counter, and to replace, the repressive economics of Lear's love test ("deeds," "worth," etc.). It is almost as if Lear's rejection of the "true" daughter, Cordelia, has brought forth this outburst, so that prosperity now resides not among the orderly processes of rule and kingship but instead in a celebration of the anarchy of sex and law. The next invocation to Nature we hear will be Lear's curse called down upon Goneril: "Into her womb convey sterility" (1.4.240).

Nature goes from pure fecundity to agent of barrenness, and we might notice here how very quickly it is that Lear, too, falls. Even within that emblematic first scene his fall from love to wrath is astonishingly swift, and the conference of the disaffected daughters afterward confirms the audience's misgivings. By the end of the first act the King is nothing but an "Idle old man, / That still would manage those authorities / That he hath given away!" (Quarto, 3.16–18)—at least in Goneril's view. Lear is now for the first time joined onstage by his Fool. It is no accident that the Fool appears just at the moment when Lear has begun to act like a fool. We will see shortly the degree to which this sublime Fool acts as a mirror for the King. Lear's self-stripping, of lands, of friends, of his treasured daughter, is now converted into a stripping *by* his elder daughters, so that he is, for the first time in the play (and, again, quite early), reduced to a tragic quest for self—all the more tragic because it is performed as a piece of unbecoming foolery, a piece of mumming, what Goneril calls one of his "new pranks":

> Does any here know me? This is not Lear.
> Does Lear walk thus, speak thus? Where are his eyes?
> . . . .
>   [H]a, waking? 'Tis not so.
> Who is it that can tell me who I am?
>
> *1.4.191–195*

"Lear's shadow," replies the Fool. Eyes, speaking, and waking are all familiar and indicative themes, and from this point the play will proliferate not only images of this kind but also insistent questions of identity. Goneril, the resistant audience to this poignant scene, is determined to strip her father of half his attendant knights, and it is this issue that calls down upon her his curse, delivered at the end of act 1. Again, this must seem early to us, in view of the pattern of the usual tragic fall. Here is Lear:

> Hear, nature; hear, dear goddess, hear:
> Suspend thy purpose if thou didst intend
> To make this creature fruitful.
> Into her womb convey sterility.
> Dry up in her the organs of increase,
> And from her derogate body never spring
> A babe to honour her. . . .
>
> *1.4.237–243*

Lear wishes upon his eldest daughter a fate that will leave her not only without a child but also without an heir. Since she has inherited part of his kingdom, this is a wish that, if granted, would bring to an end the rule he has granted her. One of the many connotations of the word "nothing" in this period was a slang reference to the female sexual organs (compare Hamlet's lines on the "no thing" that lies "between maids' legs" [*Hamlet* 3.2.109, 107]). Thus Lear's intemperate words to Cordelia ("Nothing will come of nothing") are now transposed into his physical curse upon Goneril—that nothing (no child) should come of her "no thing."

We will hear a similar curse, self-inflicted, spoken in the voice of Lady Macbeth when she assures her fainthearted husband that she is resolute for murder; it is a call for sterility and lack of fruitfulness. The character of Goneril is a strong sketch for Lady Macbeth: ruthless, ambitious, purposeful, and thwarted, married to a man—the Duke of Albany—whom she considers weak and womanish. Maleness and femaleness are in the succeeding scenes made into warring factions: the daughters become "unnatural hags," anticipating the *Macbeth* witches, and the King fears lest the feminine aspects of his own persona emerge to betray him ("women's weapons, water-drops," "this mother," *"Histerica passio"*). Lear's "nature" here is not wholly unlike Edmund's—a destructive goddess, earthy, chthonic, dark, and contrary to order.

Yet Lear holds on to some hope. Perhaps Goneril is the only wicked child. Perhaps Regan will be loyal and natural. No: Regan and her husband, the Duke of Cornwall, will not even speak to Lear, although he now claims the privileges of title he impatiently waived with Kent: "The King would speak with Cornwall; the dear father / Would with his daughter speak" (2.2.266–267). And what is Regan's view, when at last he gains an audience?

> O sir, you are old.
> Nature in you stands on the very verge
> Of his confine. You should be ruled and led. . . .
> *2.2.311–313*

As the blind Gloucester will be ruled and led. Once again the desperate Lear is driven to mummery, to acting out, as he kneels and plays out, to Regan, the scene he has refused to act in front of Goneril:

> Ask her forgiveness?
> Do you but mark how this becomes the house?
> [*Kneeling*] "Dear daughter, I confess that I am old.
> Age is unnecessary. On my knees I beg
> That you'll vouchsafe me raiment, bed, and food."
> *2.2.317–321*

"Age is unnecessary." The issue of necessity is growing on Lear, rivaling for the first time the commonplaces of luxury and privilege. But Regan is unmoved by his distress. She is angry rather than sympathetic at his curse upon her sister,

and the inexorable, remorseless stripping of Lear continues. We may acknowledge, parenthetically, the likelihood that Lear's knights are riotous, as the daughters claim; that Lear fails to keep them in order; that having abdicated his
authority he has given his daughters some faint justification for their complaints. This will make his situation more poignant rather than less. If he does
need their succor, their refusal is all the more heartless.

Goneril would let him keep only fifty knights. Therefore, he says,

> I can be patient, I can stay with Regan,
> I and my hundred knights.
>
> *2.2.395–396*

"Not altogether so," says Regan. In fact, not so at all:

> What, fifty followers?
> Is it not well? What should you need of more . . . ?
> . . . .
> I entreat you
> To bring but five and twenty. . . .
>
> *2.2.402–403, 412–413*

But Lear has not yet learned his lesson. He is still mathematical, still legalistic,
and he turns back to Goneril (it is a truly terrible scene):

> Thy fifty yet doth double five and twenty,
> And thou art twice her love.
>
> *2.2.425–426*

"[T]hou art twice her love"—as if love could be quantified, and as if the ritual
love test of the opening scene could retain any purpose and value. Yet still the
sisters chip away at his retinue:

> Goneril   Hear me, my lord.
> What need you five and twenty, ten, or five,
> To follow in a house where twice so many
> Have a command to tend you?
> Regan   What need one?
>
> *2.2.426–429*

Lear's reply, one of the great speeches in this great play, shows how quickly,
and how low, he has fallen in these first two acts:

> O, reason not the need! Our basest beggars
> Are in the poorest thing superfluous.

> Allow not nature more than nature needs,
> Man's life is cheap as beast's. Thou art a lady.
> If only to go warm were gorgeous,
> Why, nature needs not what thou, gorgeous, wear'st,
> Which scarcely keeps thee warm. But for true need—
> You heavens, give me that patience, patience I need.
> You see me here, you gods, a poor old man,
> As full of grief as age, wretchèd in both.
> If it be you that stirs these daughters' hearts
> Against their father, fool me not so much
> To bear it tamely. Touch me with noble anger,
> And let not women's weapons, water-drops,
> Stain my man's cheeks. No, you unnatural hags,
> I will have such revenges on you both
> That all the world shall—I will do such things—
> What they are, yet I know not; but they shall be
> The terrors of the earth. You think I'll weep.
> No, I'll not weep. . . .

2.2.430–449

"I'll not weep." Like Macduff, Lear thinks of weeping, the show of emotion, as a woman's weakness. His cry is still the old cry of revenge. But in a brilliant moment of Shakespearean stagecraft the stage direction takes over from him, and shows Lear, and the audience, once again the limits of language ("And let not women's weapons, water-drops . . ."):

> No, I'll not weep. I have full cause of weeping,
>   *Storm and tempest*
> But this heart shall break into a hundred thousand flaws
> Or ere I'll weep.—O Fool, I shall go mad!

2.2.449–451

Eyes and weeping, tears, have been with us since Cordelia cautioned her sisters, in that crucial first scene, that she was leaving them with "washed eyes"— her eyes cleansed by weeping, able to see more because they wept. Now Lear, crying out that he will not weep, sees the storm and tempest weep for him, and beseeching the gods to fool him not, calls out in the same breath for his Fool. And the tempest begins in earnest. This is stagecraft of the highest order—here the inner man has come together with the world he inhabits. The King is in high rage, and the storm rages about him. There is no difference between Lear and his tempest, it is within him and without him; he is its cause. He is now ready, and the audience is now ready, for the third act of his tragedy, perhaps the single most extraordinary act of any Shakespearean play.

We have seen that *King Lear* proceeds by analogy and comparison. Lear is compared to Gloucester, Edmund to Goneril and Regan, Goneril and Regan to Cordelia, Edgar to Edmund, and so on. Situations seem to fan out and become general. In the same way, the play draws dramatic strength from juxtaposition of scene to scene, phrase to phrase, to form a kind of node of meaning, a fulcrum. For example, in act 2, scene 2, the audience sees the spectacle of Kent in the stocks, demoted from his accustomed rank, concealing his real identity, and Kent speaks of the extremity of his position. "Nothing almost sees miracles / But misery," he says. "Fortune, good night; / Smile once more; turn thy wheel." The very next thing the audience sees and hears, in act 2, scene 3, is Edgar, newly disguised, also forced to abandon his identity and his rank, also mistreated, also at what he then imagines will be his lowest point, his "worst"—' although both Edgar and Kent will learn again and again that there is worse to come. The play's design thus presents two low points, two stripped, denuded men, two disguises and two confinements; and a dramatic effect is achieved by juxtaposition.

A similar effect develops in the structure of act 3, Lear's remarkable confrontation with nature and with human nature. At the end of act 2 we heard dire warnings of the storm that is about to come. After Lear's proud and pitiful boast, "No, I'll not weep," and the immediately ensuing "Storm and tempest," the act closes with Cornwall's ironically prudent advice to Gloucester, who has expressed his desire to go out to succor the distraught King. "Shut up your doors, my lord," Cornwall says. " 'Tis a wild night. / My Regan counsels well. Come out o'th' storm" (2.2.472–473). Once again, with artful juxtaposition, the next exchange we hear is in a way an answer to this—an answer, this time, by contrast rather than similitude. "Who's there, besides foul weather?" asks the disguised Kent, and a gentleman replies, "One minded like the weather, / Most unquietly" (3.1.1–3). Weather has become something that cannot be shut out. We onlookers cannot "come out of the storm," for it is all around us, and within us, as it is all around Lear and within him. "This tempest in my mind," he will call it. The human condition in the play is now the equivalent of "foul weather," and is, like the loyal gentleman, "minded like the weather, / Most unquietly."

This is a kind of dramatic point it is easy to miss when a play is divided into discrete acts for performance. In a modern production an interval or intermission might separate Kent's remarks in act 3, scene 1, from Cornwall's in act 2, scene 2. But in Shakespeare's time the plays would have been performed straight through, without a break. In the case of *King Lear,* the inexorability of deprivation and suffering increases the dramatic tension to a point where we in the audience—like Edgar, like Kent—can hardly bear what we see before our eyes. Act 3 (in the Folio) begins in the open air with a scene of generosity and charity that stands in brutal opposition to the isolated scenes that are shortly to come. Kent and the gentleman meet and speak of the King's exposure to the elements—of how he "tears his white hair, / Which the impetuous blasts, with eyeless rage, / Catch in their fury and make nothing of" (Quarto, 8.6–8). "[E]yeless rage"; "nothing." And we hear of how he "[s]trives in his little world of man to outstorm / The to-and-fro conflicting wind and rain" (Quarto, 8.9–10). Lear is now a microcosm, a "little world of man." What confronts us, the spectators in the theater, is the inner agony of a man's soul played out as if it were some immense and tragic metaphor writ large upon the landscape, so that we can see it and share it.

At this point the King who was the emblem of all earthly comforts is exposed to the elements. The place in which he finds himself is an articulated metaphor, the counterpart of his state of mind, on the one hand, and of his fallen status in polity and society, on the other. Since the early eighteenth century editors have situated these scenes on a heath, an open space of land. (As the critic Henry Turner notes, neither the Folio nor the Quarto specifies a "heath,"[1] although that designation, aligning the scene with a windswept wasteland familiar in British topography, and possibly with the also wild and eerie heath in *Macbeth*, has by now become conventional.) As if to underscore the inner nature of the storm, Lear himself disclaims any real physical discomfort: "I am cold myself," he admits, but

> This tempest in my mind
> Doth from my senses take all feeling else
> Save what beats there. . . .
>
> *3.4.12–14*

And:

> In such a night
> To shut me out? Pour on, I will endure.
> In such a night as this! . . .
>
> *3.4.17–19*

The play picks up a familiar Shakespearean topos, the journey from civilization to a place of wilderness and apparent unreason—a pattern often used in the comedies and also, as many critics have noted, in the genre of pastoral. Lear's heath is no Forest of Arden. It is a place of transformation and change, but the change it produces is a stripping away, not an augmentation of magical powers, love, agency, or wit. The heath is a reversal of the condition of "civilization," a version of Hobbesian nature, the nature of a life that is "nasty, brutish, and short"—a place in which the only dynamics that count are those of will and power. This is Lear's "little world of man," not only a philosophical microcosm but also a psychological landscape.

It is important to bear in mind, though, that at the beginning of act 3 Lear himself does not see this larger and more "transcendent" picture. He is still the

King—stripped though he may be of daughters, knights, land, and power. As he enters his own "landscape of the mind," the one thought *in* his mind is that he can control it. He will try to invoke and direct Nature ("Hear, nature . . ."). Nature, with a small or a large N, is for him not yet a metaphor of his condition, but rather an instrument of his wrath, something he can use:

> Blow, winds, and crack your cheeks! Rage, blow,
> You cataracts and hurricanoes, spout
> Till you have drenched our steeples, drowned the cocks!
> You sulph'rous and thought-executing fires,
> Vaunt-couriers of oak-cleaving thunderbolts,
> Singe my white head; and thou all-shaking thunder,
> Strike flat the thick rotundity o'th' world,
> Crack nature's moulds, all germens spill at once
> That makes ingrateful man.
>
> *3.2.1–9*

Lear is here demanding—commanding—the destruction of the world. "Germens" are seeds (compare "germination"); to spill the germens that make up the interior of the earth, to crack the molds, is to destroy life and all its possibilities. "Rumble thy bellyful; spit, fire; spout, rain," Lear continues.

> Here I stand your slave,
> A poor, infirm, weak and despised old man,
> But yet I call you servile ministers,
> That will with two pernicious daughters join
>   . . . 'gainst a head
> So old and white as this. O, ho, 'tis foul!
>
> *3.2.14, 18–23*

We may notice how Lear seems to age, onstage, in his own self-description. The rain and wind are false flatterers, who have deserted and weakened him to flock to the side of Goneril and Regan. And yet he feels himself still the King, bereft of power that should rightly still be his. Lear is now victim rather than victor; acted upon, not actor or director; no longer the center of the court, the kingdom, or the world. In a way this is the consummate Shakespearean metaphor, an individual confronting his own radical limitations—or, to use Lear's word, his own "necessities." That resonant word "need" has echoed throughout the play ("What need you five and twenty?"; "What need one?"; "O, reason not the need!"; "But for true need— / You heavens, give me that patience, patience I need"). Now, in extremis, he finds necessity suddenly not in a roster of one hundred knights, not in power or rich clothing, but in a bale of straw:

> Where is this straw, my fellow?
> The art of our necessities is strange,
> And can make vile things precious. . . .
>
> *3.2.68–70*

Among the "vile things" he will come to value and to cherish are people as well as straw.

The storm scene is a learning experience for Lear and for his audiences, as it was for his time. The optimism of the sixteenth-century humanists, as expressed in Pico della Mirandola's *Oration on the Dignity of Man,* placing man so confidently just below the angels, is frayed or lost here, at the beginning of a new, perhaps more skeptical, century. Human beings are vile things that necessity—need, not luxury—makes precious. The "heath" and the storm, then, are effectively understood—and performed—as projections of Lear's mental situation upon a larger screen, at once nature and theater.

But King Lear is not completely alone in the storm, although he speaks, at first, with no apparent concern for anyone but himself: "I am a man / More sinned against than sinning" (3.2.58–59). With him is his Fool. It is for the Fool, and not for himself, that Lear seeks the comforting haven of necessary straw. And who, or what, is Lear's Fool? Who is this most evocative of all Shakespearean clowns and motleys? Above all, perhaps, the Fool, both in his professional position as "allowed fool" in the court and in his specific role in Shakespeare's play, is an aspect of Lear himself. Repeatedly in earlier acts the Fool has artfully and poignantly demonstrated that the King is a fool, just as Feste, his comic prototype in *Twelfth Night,* proved the Countess to be a fool. Thus this Fool will say to the King:

> That lord that counselled thee
> To give away thy land,
> Come, place him here by me;
> Do thou for him stand.
> The sweet and bitter fool
> Will presently appear,
> The one in motley here,
> The other found out there.

Lear   Dost thou call me fool, boy?

Fool   All thy other titles thou hast given away. That thou wast born with.

Kent   This is not altogether fool, my lord.

> *Quarto, 4.123–134*

The Fool is a mirror, as the wasteland and the storm are mirrors, reflecting back at Lear his own concealed image. He is in this sense all too truly "Lear's shadow": at once a reflected image; a delusive semblance or vain object of pursuit; a symbol, prefiguration, foreshadowing, or type; an attenuated remnant, a form from which the substance has departed; a spectral form, a phantom; a parasite or toady; a companion whom a guest brings without invitation; even, in the most modern, and anachronistic connotation, a spy or detective who follows a person in order to keep watch on his movements (*OED*). The professional duty of the "licensed fool" in the period was to say things that were otherwise forbidden, to reveal painful, humbling, and comic truths—in short, to do that which a later age would call speaking truth to power. The role of the fool was to reflect and epitomize the folly of the world around him, and in essence to draw it off, or neutralize it. Thus the Fool gives Kent—disguised as "Caius"—advice about following only a master whose fortunes are on the rise, and this exchange follows:

> Kent   Where learned you this, Fool?
> Fool   Not i'th' stocks, fool.
>
> *2.2.252–253*

Which is the fool, which the sensible man? Or, as Lear will put it, alluding to a familiar game for children, "change places, and handy-dandy, which is the justice, which is the thief?" (4.5.144–145). Handy-dandy: Guess which hand holds the prize. The fool speaks often in handy-dandy, in inversions, reversals, and conundrums. He exemplifies, in part, the aspect of King Lear that has turned its back on his own kingly nature, the Lear who cut his crown in half and gave its meat away.

We have noticed that the Fool appears in the play only at the point when Lear has begun to act like a fool. The fool of the play's opening scenes is the mad Lear before he is mad. As one of the King's knights tells us, speaking of the banishment of Cordelia from the court, "Since my young lady's going into France, sir, the fool hath much pined away" (1.4.62–63). A disputed stage tradition holds that the parts of the Fool and Cordelia were played by the same boy actor. She departs and he appears; when he leaves ("And I'll go to bed at noon" [3.6.39]), she shortly reappears by Lear's side. Lear's final, agonized observation, "And my poor fool is hanged," although it refers to Cordelia, may, according to this view, have evoked as well associations with the *other* fool so dear to the King. Some critics have found this theory more like fictive poetic justice than like stage-historical fact, suggesting that instead of a boy player the celebrated comic actor Robert Armin would have played the Fool's part. But the Fool/Cordelia argument, whatever its historical merits or demerits, points to a linguistic commonality (both are Lear's fools) and to a common social role of comfort and rebuke.

The Fool of this play is also related to the fool of biblical tradition as described by Saint Paul in a passage from 1 Corinthians that can as well be applied to the figure of Bottom in *A Midsummer Night's Dream:* "But God hath chosen the foolish things of the world to confound the wise; and God hath chosen the weak things of the world to confound the things which are mighty; / And base things of the world, and things which are depised, hath God chosen, yea, and things which are not, to bring to nought things that are" (1 Corinthians 1:27–28). Foolish things, weak things, base things, things which are despised, things which are not. Lear's own folly; his weakness, and Gloucester's; Edmund's baseness and the baseness of Goneril and Regan; things which are despised (Lear and "Poor Tom"); things which are not (madness, and nothing; "an O without a figure"; "This is not Lear") bring to nought things that are. The Fool is this kind of holy fool, and he exemplifies the biblical paradox that underlies so much of the play. For Lear, throughout the earlier acts obsessed with rank, obsessed with order and precedence, infuriated because his "man," the disguised Kent, was humiliated in the stocks, though not yet concluding that stocking is an indignity to any man—this same Lear will say to his Fool (in the Folio text of the play), "In, boy; go first." The Fool is to precede the King into the hovel, into the shelter, away from the storm. The passage that lies behind this is the celebrated line from the Gospel according to Saint Matthew: "many [that are] first shall be last; and the last [shall be] first" (Matthew 19:30). Again the verse comes alive in dramatic action: the first shall be last (Lear the King, Gloucester the Duke, the briefly triumphant evil daughters and Edmund); the last shall be first (Cordelia, "our last and least"; Edgar; the Fool).

But if Lear's Fool is this kind of biblical fool, he is also the biblical fool of the Psalms, and especially of Psalm 14: "The fool hath said in his heart, [There is] no God. They are corrupt, they have done abominable works, [there is] none that doeth good." In a play that has so much to say about sex and bastardy and illicit lust, the Fool is the principal taunting voice of corrupt sexuality: "Marry, here's grace and a codpiece—that's a wise man and a fool" (3.2.39–40). A fool's costume often included an exaggerated codpiece, as if to emphasize that a man could be governed either by his mind and judgment or by his body and its desires. It is Lear's Fool who evokes the image of the "cockney" and the live eels she put in her pie; suppressing these unruly phallic symbols, she "knapped 'em o'th' coxcombs with a stick, and cried 'Down, wantons, down!' " (2.2.287–288). Edgar as "Poor Tom" will speak of doing the deed of darkness, of Pillicock on Pillicock Hill; Gloucester and Lear will return, over and over again, to images of sex and lechery. But it is the Fool who above all gives wry voice to this aspect of the human animal, the "natural man."

In the iconography of the medieval and early modern periods the Fool was often to be found in company with Death, as in Hans Holbein's "The Idiot Fool" in his *Dance of Death* series. Sometimes the fool *is* Death in disguise, a skull wearing the traditional cap and bells that were part of the costume of the court jester; at other times he mocks Death or is heedless of him. In *Richard II* Death is explicitly an "antic," or fool, in King Richard's despairing account:

"For within the hollow crown / That rounds the mortal temples of a king / Keeps Death his court; and there the antic sits, / Scoffing his state and grinning at his pomp" (*Richard II* 3.2.156–159). Bearing in mind this very consistent association, we can see Lear's Fool as the death he carries with him, an unacknowledged, and sometimes unwitting, memento mori for a king.

And yet at the same time the Fool, precisely because he is, in extremis, the representative of the body and of self-preservation, becomes the voice of common sense and practical wisdom. His response to the storm, to the tempest that Lear will locate in his own mind, is to urge the King to avoid it, to come out of the storm—which is to say, to avoid self-confrontation: not to look inside himself, at his failures and his pretensions and his tragic hubris. To avoid having the tragic experience at all. "Good nuncle, in, ask thy daughters blessing. Here's a night pities neither wise men nor fools" (3.2.11–12). But Lear is a wiser fool than this, and he chooses to brave the elements, the neutral, not unkind, rain and thunder, rather than to turn back, a craven and defeated man, to the safety of the house. This is, after all, what makes him a tragic figure and a hero—that he confronts and chooses the tragic experience. He asks the question "Who is it that can tell me who I am?" and he answers it with Kent's answer, "A man, sir."

In short, the Fool is a figure of infinite value in the court world, where he reminds Lear by wit and gesture, indeed by his very existence, of Lear's own potential for folly. But when the play moves from a chronicle of royal folly and paternal misjudgment to a parable of the human condition, the Fool's own radical limitation is shown. And when Lear is finally convinced that he himself is a fool, the character called Fool disappears from the play, uttering his final, riddling words (found only in the Folio text): "And I'll go to bed at noon." "I'll go to bed at noon" was a proverbial phrase, meaning "I'll play the fool, too." And Jack-go-to-bed-at-noon was the folk name for the flower purple goat's-beard, or salsify, which closes at midday. The Fool will leave in the middle of the play ("at noon"). He is no longer needed. He has done his job of mirroring the folly that is in every man, and particularly in Lear. There is no more he can do. His place is taken for the rest of the play by Cordelia, who represents not contempt for mankind's limitations but hope for redemption; allegorically, if the Fool is a codpiece, Cordelia—as we have noted from her name—is the heart. Whether or not the same actor played both parts, the larger "part" played by this most intimate companion and closest confidant can be seen to be of a piece. When Lear cries out at the death of Cordelia "And my poor fool is hanged," the word "fool" takes on its conventional meaning as "child," but the resonance of that other "poor fool" (as well as of "Poor Tom") remains.

The Fool, then, is part of Lear's learning process on the heath, in the storm, and I think it is useful to look at the entirety of the third act as a tightly knit sequence that functions as a learning process at the same time that it exhibits onstage Lear's interior world of self-knowledge, what he called his "little world of man." The Fool is with him from the first, and from the first the Fool has realized that Lear has been a fool: in dividing his kingdom; in rejecting his beloved daughter Cordelia; even in failing to heed that instinct that had made him "more affect"—that is, prefer—the Duke of Albany to the Duke of Cornwall.

But the King and the Fool are not alone for long. The Fool urges Lear to go in, and provokes him with another song, another riddle, so that Lear, clinging to the last bits of his sanity, is moved to speak out against the forces that assail him:

> No, I will be the pattern of all patience.
> I will say nothing.
>
> *3.2.36–37*

As if drawn forth from the recesses of his inner consciousness, there now appears onstage, in this dreamlike, ever nightmarish scene, the play's pattern of all patience, Kent, whose anger was real but whose loyalty and patience were greater; who sought to serve authority and therefore returned in disguise to serve his king, even going with good grace to the stocks in that service. The sudden appearance of Kent/Caius upon the heath sets the expectation that underlies everything that is to take place in this great third act, everything that makes up its dramatic pattern, because that pattern is the logic of psychological generation, things called up by the mind. We could imagine the storm scenes as one vast, articulated soliloquy in which no one actually appears but King Lear—and aspects of his own persona given life by his words. This would be a cinematic way of performing these scenes, or a ghostly one, true to the spirit of the events and their placement.

First his mind summons the Fool, and then the ever-patient Kent. Now, moved by the storm's fierceness, Lear's mind begins to ruminate on those sufferers he has never before imagined, sufferers who are *always* out in storms like these. Strikingly, he speaks not *of* them but *to* them, addressing them directly in their absence, in a speech that is part apostrophe and part invocation:

> Poor naked wretches, wheresoe'er you are,
> That bide the pelting of this pitiless storm,
> How shall your houseless heads and unfed sides,
> Your looped and windowed raggedness, defend you
> From seasons such as these? O, I have ta'en
> Too little care of this. Take physic, pomp,
> Expose thyself to feel what wretches feel,
> That thou mayst shake the superflux to them
> And show the heavens more just.
>
> *3.4.28–36*

It is clear from the last line that Lear still believes he can control the elements, the world outside him, as well as the world inside him. It will take his immersion in madness to convince him that he can do neither, and that the heavens may *not* be just. But this invocation to the poor naked wretches with their "looped and windowed raggedness" (an unsurpassable description of tattered clothing and bony limbs) conjures its own living visual metaphor, a human equivalent of the barren wasteland itself. The naked Edgar, dressed in rags, pricked with nails and sticks, is summoned symbolically by Lear's words, and now appears from within the hovel where he has been hiding. Lear, looking at this stripped, barren piece of humanity, has only one question, only one thought: "Didst thou give all to thy two daughters, / And art thou come to this? . . . Couldst thou save nothing? Wouldst thou give 'em all?" (3.4.47–48, 60). "He hath no daughters, sir," Kent intercedes gently, rationality correcting madness. But Lear knows better. He has recognized in "Poor Tom" a living emblem of his own condition. This could happen only in the inner world of the storm. It is madness, but madness with method in it.

Moments before, Lear had spoken of shaking the "superflux" to wretches such as these. It is a word the play's audience has heard before, in his "reason not the need" speech ("Our basest beggars / Are in the poorest thing superfluous"), and we will hear it again in the heartfelt cry of the blinded Gloucester, questing for justice: "Heavens deal so still. / Let the superfluous and lust-dieted man . . . feel your power quickly. / So distribution should undo excess, / And each man have enough" (4.1.60–65). But the King's concern with superflux and caretaking ("O, I have ta'en / Too little care of this") soon shifts to an identification with the "thing" that is "Poor Tom." We have three terms now, not two: "everything," "nothing," and "the thing itself." Lear tells the disguised Edgar,

[T]hou art the thing itself. Unaccommodated man is no more but such a poor, bare, forked animal as thou art. Off, off, you lendings! Come, unbutton here.

3.4.95–98

In the midst of the storm Lear begins to tear off his clothes, to "unbutton," as he will finally be able to do in the play's last scene—there, significantly, with a prayer, not a command ("Pray you, undo this button"). But in penetrating to the identity of "the thing itself," Lear—like Hamlet regarding the skull of Yorick—faces the heart of his own mystery. This "thing" is humanity—the king as well as the beggar, a poor, bare, forked animal. The language of stripping we have encountered from the play's first moments here reaches its culmination, and will carry us through until that time, in a very different mood, when the King will awaken from sleep, in fresh garments, in the fourth act of the play. Lear's encounter with "Poor Tom" is a central recognition scene, one different from but not really secondary to that stunning recognition scene between Lear and Cordelia in act 4. Here one man looks at another and sees himself. Lear looks at "Poor Tom" and sees Lear. At this point in the play, are they two distinct characters? Are they two different people? It is the power, the aesthetic of theatrical representation, of *the play itself*—like "the thing itself"—that renders this matter of identity and fictive representation, if not an unaskable, at least an unanswerable question. Nowhere in literature is allegory more effectively naturalized. (Lear's recognition of "Poor Tom" as "the thing itself," a "thing" that is also an estranged version of himself, points forward to Prospero in *The Tempest*, who will say of his rebellious servant, the enslaved monster Caliban, "This thing of darkness I / Acknowledge mine.")

So Lear evokes first Kent, and with him, the virtue of patience; and then Edgar, and the recognition of barren, stripped humanity. The Fool, whose only comment on the latest manifestation is " 'Tis a naughty night to swim in," now begins to wish for creature comforts, for warmth and rest, like the practical fool he has become. "Now a little fire in a wild field were like an old lecher's heart—a small spark, all the rest on 's body cold" (3.4.99–101). From this fanciful simile of inappropriate sexual desire comes the next spectral manifestation, for immediately the Fool calls out, "Look, here comes a walking fire." This animate will-o'-the-wisp is the Duke of Gloucester, coming with a torch to seek his king and guest. Gloucester has already been established in the play as the "old lecher," the sporting begetter of the bastard Edmund. Now he has come, bearing a little fire in the darkness, to offer fealty and hospitality if he can.

Gloucester and Edgar (the latter still, of course, disguised as "Poor Tom") both see mirrors of their own condition in Lear, even as he finds mirrors in them. Gloucester says, "Our flesh and blood, my lord, is grown so vile / That it doth hate what gets it" (3.4.129–130). For his part, Edgar, masking his language as well as his person from his father by uttering incomprehensible shrieks of madness, spells, riddles, and the names of fiends, finds a cognate lesson in Lear. "He childed as I fathered," he remarks, aside, to the audience (Quarto, 13.99). This is one of those moments in *King Lear* that open up toward the sublime, as the speakers' generalizations on human nature begin to approach the condition of aphorism. It is for perceptions like these, and not for its commentary on seventeenth-century monarchy or the plight of early modern mendicants, that the play is regarded as one of Shakespeare's most magnificent achievements.

Edgar now begins to assume a necessary mediating role in the play, a role he will retain as the tragedy deepens, as events become even more unbearable, even more unspeakable. Edgar as onlooker, as onstage audience and as our confidant, offers a point of perspective from which the audience in the theater can watch and share the appalling proceedings before us. For with the arrival of Gloucester, the storm's transformation is almost over, and Lear is mad.

Over and over again we heard him cry out against the onset of madness: "O, let me not be mad, not mad, sweet heaven!" (1.5.41); "Keep me in temper. I would not be mad" (42); "I prithee, daughter, do not make me mad" (2.2.383); "O Fool, I shall go mad!" (451). In the very first scene of the play we heard Kent say, "Be Kent unmannerly / When Lear is mad," and now Gloucester says to the disguised Kent, "Thou sayst the King grows mad; I'll tell thee, friend, / I am almost mad myself" (3.4.148–149). So is Edgar. So are we. In fact, Lear's madness now becomes itself an emblem, a touchstone, for the madness that afflicts so many others in the play. And this madness is a condition we have seen before in Shakespeare. Hamlet feigned madness (or was it feigned?). And what of Othello? And Ophelia? And (shortly) Lady Macbeth? What is this disease of madness, and what is its function in drama?

Most evidently, and perhaps most importantly, madness permits the maddened victim to speak the truth, like a licensed fool, and be *dis*believed. A madman or madwoman is a sublime version of a fool—in the confines of theater. He or she can echo the prevailing madness of the world, speaking through the onstage audience to an audience in the theater, asserting, proclaiming, or establishing contestatory and unwelcome "truths" about the human condition:

> Lear   They told me I was everything; 'tis a lie, I am not ague-proof.
>
> *4.5.102*

> Gloucester   O, let me kiss that hand!
> Lear   Let me wipe it first; it smells of mortality.
>
> *4.5.125–126*

> Lear   When we are born, we cry that we are come
>   To this great stage of fools.
>
> *4.5.172–173*

As Edgar, ever the audience's eyes and ears onstage, remarks,

> [*aside*] O, matter and impertinency mixed—
>   Reason in madness!
>
> *4.5.164–165*

Edgar is the spokesman for (as he says in the play's last lines in the Folio text) "[w]e that are young." For the survivors, for those who must go on. And Edgar cannot believe, or bear, what he sees.

The King's madness is also a forum for social criticism, a final indictment of a handy-dandy world. In the latter part of act 3 the mad King stages a trial (this trial scene appears only in the Quarto, as scene 13). The scene is part ironic truth, part social satire, and part the final unmasking of "justice," as always limited and inadequate. From this moment the play will move deliberately toward the hope for mercy as contrasted with justice. The trial judges are to be "Poor Tom"—the "robèd man of justice," naked and hunted—and the Fool, his "yoke-fellow of equity," whose only equity is that all men are fools. The prisoners on trial are joint-stools, and the scene onstage is heartrending. A king without a throne rails at joint-stools, real or imagined, without occupants. There is a bitter little joke embedded in this scenario, since the phrase "Cry you mercy, I took you for a joint-stool" appears often in the period as a proverbial expression of disparagement. When in the course of the trial scene in *King Lear* the Fool offers this very phrase as an insult to (the absent) Goneril, he is speaking, in literal fact, to a piece of furniture, thus reversing the usual gesture, in which a wooden "person" is called a thing. (A comic version of this familiar insult can be found in *The Taming of the Shrew* [2.1.196].) The Fool thus offers his backhanded apology to a stool ("Sorry, I took you for a stool"), and his mordant wit may recall the puncturing critique of other Shakespearean literalists, like the gravedigger in *Hamlet* ("Upon what ground?" Hamlet demands of him, and he replies, "Why, here in Denmark"). But the scene is rawly painful, and Edgar weeps as Lear had wept (Edgar: "My tears begin to take his part so much / They mar my counterfeiting" [3.6.17–18]). The storm now inhabits and afflicts them all. "Sir," says Kent, "where is the patience now / That you so oft have boasted to retain?" (3.6.15–16). But the King is mad, and the Fool of practical wisdom departs the play.

As if at a lull in the storm, we hear now that "Oppressèd nature sleeps" (Quarto, 13.86). Notice that it is not the King but "[o]ppressèd nature" that is the figure here. The inner and outer worlds of the play, and of the title character, have collapsed into one another, even as the characters of this third act have echoed and exemplified not only themselves but also parts of Lear. In fact, the madness now rages not only on the heath or in the wilderness but also in the court. For—and this is crucial for the dramaturgy of the central act—act 3 is structured so that indoor scenes set in "civilized" courtly spaces intercut the scenes of the King and the storm. Scenes 3, 5, and 7 of the act, scenes between Edmund and Gloucester; Edmund and Cornwall; and Edmund, Cornwall, Regan, and Goneril are full of the language of inversion: "I like not this unnatural dealing"; "Most savage and unnatural"; "The younger rises when the old doth fall." And, perhaps most strikingly, Cornwall's chilling remark to Edmund: "[T]hou shalt find a dearer father in my love" (3.5.21–22).

In every one of those scenes we *hear* about the unnatural; on the heath, in the storm, we *see* it in action. Edmund's two betrayals—of Edgar and of Gloucester, scene 3 and scene 5—are even more unnatural than the scenes of madness and nakedness we have been witnessing. And these two modes of presentation, metaphoric and literal, will come together in the act's final scene, the scene of the blinding of Gloucester, another scene whose subject is "justice" ("an eye for an eye"), juxtaposed to Lear's mock trial. Technically, dramaturgically, it is extremely difficult for Shakespeare to keep building this act upward, toward climax after emotional climax: the storm, the King's outbursts, his madness, Edgar's tears, "[o]ppressèd nature sleeps." And yet this scene sustains rather than breaks the image and horror. The event it portrays—the onstage blinding of a helpless man—is itself dreadful, and it is almost always unbearable to watch, the audience "blinded" by horror and disgust, tempted to close its eyes against the violation. But what increases the horror even further is the banality of the setting, a domestic interior.

Twice Gloucester reminds his torturers that this is *his* house: "You are my guests"; "I am your host." Their behavior abuses the canons of hospitality, so vital for a culture, and a landscape, in which houses are separated from one another by swaths of unfriendly and depopulated terrain. (We will see a similar violation, and a similar disregard, in the murder of King Duncan when he is the houseguest of the Macbeths.) Like the King thrust out of his own kingdom, Gloucester is thrust from his own home, after being tortured there. Using a figure of speech that has been present throughout the play, Gloucester has told Regan that he sent the King to Dover

> Because I would not see thy cruel nails
> Pluck out his poor old eyes. . . .
>
> *3.7.54–55*

He vows to see "[t]he wingèd vengeance overtake such children." Once again, the "safely" figurative becomes the appallingly literal. "See't shalt thou never," Regan replies—and they pluck out his eyes.

Two significant things take place in this appalling scene. The first is the attempted rescue of Gloucester by Cornwall's servant, who gives his master a fatal wound but is instantly killed himself. This nameless servant provides not only a model of hospitality and decency but also an example of a *good* rebellion against nature and social order, a moral and healthy rebellion against a father figure, very like Cordelia's rebellion against her father, Lear. "I have served you ever since I was a child," the servant says to Cornwall. "But better service have I never done you / Than now to bid you hold" (3.7.71–73). Cordelia and Kent made much the same appeal in the love test of the opening scene. Here a servant not only holds to it, but dies for it.

The second event of significance occurs at the moment of Gloucester's torture, when blinding becomes enlightenment. Like Clarence in *Richard III,* Gloucester calls out for the person he thinks will save him, in this case his son Edmund, and is told, succinctly, "Thou call'st on him that hates thee" (3.7.86). "O, my follies!" he cries. "Then Edgar was abused. / Kind gods, forgive me that, and prosper him!" (3.7.89–90). These "[k]ind gods," plural and unspecified, are evoked at the moment of maximum pain and suffering. We might also notice Gloucester's word "follies"; he now knows that he, too, has been a fool.

In the third act of *King Lear,* Lear's moment of madness is also his moment of sanity: "See better, Lear." Gloucester's moment of blindness is also his moment of insight: "I am almost mad myself"; "I stumbled when I saw." The metaphors of acts 1 and 2—madness, blindness, storm and rage, fools and folly, and the omnipresent metaphor of "nothing"—are all performed on the stage in act 3, translated simultaneously into action and emblem. With "washed eyes,"

like Cordelia and Edgar, the spectators in the theater have seen these figures come to life on the stage. We have seen it happen, and we have seen it
survived, as the suffering audience has also survived it. What is truly remarkable
is that the play can continue to build from this achievement, this recognition,
so that the succeeding scenes grow even richer in power, and more acutely
painful.

With a superbly ironic juxtaposition, characteristic of the design of this play
throughout, the next act opens with Edgar, still disguised as "Poor Tom," convinced that he, like the audience, has now endured "the worst":

> To be worst,
> The low'st and most dejected thing of fortune,
> Stands still in esperance, lives not in fear.
> The lamentable change is from the best;
> The worst returns to laughter. . . .
>
> *4.1.2–6*

If he finds himself at the bottom of Fortune's wheel, he has at least the
advantage of knowing where he is. No unexpected reversal can throw him
lower. Hope ("esperance") is thus kindled by a sense of having lived through
the most difficult moments: "The worst returns to laughter." No sooner has he
spoken these words, however, than he sees before him the spectacle of Gloucester, blind and halting, led by an Old Man: "But who comes here? / My father,
parti-eyed?" (4.1.9–10). Gloucester is poorly led in a literal sense, since his guide
is a poor old man of the country, not a nobleman. But he is also a living emblem
of that poor leading that has brought him, like Lear, to the devastation of
the heath/wasteland in the first place. "O sir, you are old," said Regan to her
father, the King. "You should be ruled and led." The handy-dandy world in
which children lead parents ("The younger rises when the old doth fall") is now
in full view. Gloucester was led by Edmund's lies, by his "auricular assurance";
Lear, by his own obstinacy and that of his daughters. And Gloucester, a walking emblem of this interior blindness, cries out for his true son: "O dear son
Edgar, . . . Might I but live to see thee in my touch / I'd say I had eyes again"
(4.1.21–24). Now Edgar is confronted with a kind of tragedy more immediate
and personal than ever before, and he begins to realize, and to convey to the
audience, his sense that the essence of tragedy may lie not in spectacle but in
identification:

> O gods! Who is't can say "I am at the worst"?
> I am worse than e'er I was.
>
> . . . .
>
> And worse I may be yet. The worst is not
> So long as we can say "This is the worst."
>
> *4.1.25–26, 28–29*

"So long as we can *say* 'This is the worst.' " Again <u>the rhetoric of silence</u> <u>marks the limits of human endurance</u>. As always in Shakespeare, where language is the index of full humanity, speech and communication are bounded by the unutterable and inexpressible. To control language, to produce even a sentence as despairing as "This is the worst," is to know that something more can be endured: "worse I may be yet." Thus there was a crucial difference, in her reply to Lear, between Cordelia's saying "nothing" and saying nothing.

Edgar's response is crucial to an understanding of his role, for as we have already seen, he is the appalled spectator to sights that appall us, the go-between who mediates between actors and audience. And he will be our final link, in the play's final lines (in the Folio edition), to the spectacle that is the tragedy of *King Lear*. As he watches what is perhaps the play's ultimate icon of tragic inconsequence, the encounter on the fields near Dover of the mad King and the blind Duke, Edgar again gives voice to what many spectators in the theater—or readers of the play—may be thinking and feeling:

> I would not take this from report; it is,
> And my heart breaks at it.
>
> *4.5.134–135*

This sentiment is close to the heart of the tragic experience, and it has led generations of writers, critics, and audiences to wonder whether there is any redemption in *King Lear,* anything beyond suffering but endurance, and more suffering.

For Shakespeare as playwright—rather than, say, philosopher or theologian—the challenge was both technical and metaphysical. How does the playwright move beyond the ultimate tragic confrontation, past the moment when a trusted dramatic character says that he has seen "the worst" and then realizes that "worse I may be yet"? After the heartrending meeting of blind man and madman, where can the play go, and how can it take the audience with it?

Shakespeare achieves this further growth, and is able to make his play move even beyond the unspeakable moments of tragedy, by a deliberate recourse to two other dramatic modes he has at his command: comedy and romance. He turns to romance, because it is the mode of transformation and rebirth, and comedy because it is a built-in safety valve for tragic emotions, just as we sometimes laugh uncontrollably when confronted with news that is shocking or traumatic. Both in comedy and in romance there is also the possibility of a saving estrangement, making "victims" appear ultimately invulnerable. The cat in the cartoon does not show signs of pain when he falls off the roof or crashes through the windowpane. Comedians Buster Keaton and Harold Lloyd, faced with impossible adversity, emerge unscathed.

One small but significant example of this kind of "escapist" comic behavior comes in the fifth act, when Albany, Goneril's husband, solicits Edmund on behalf of his own wife, ironically contradicting her sister Regan's claim. "If you will marry," he says to his sister-in-law, "make your loves to me. / My lady is bespoke" (5.3.81–82). *Goneril* is engaged to Edmund, says Albany. I know I am a cuckold, or that she would like to make me one. To this unexpected sign of liveliness in a husband she has clearly dismissed as tamely inconsequential Goneril replies, "An interlude!" (82). An interlude was a comic play, old-fashioned, broad in its humor—a good modern translation of her riposte would be "What a farce!"

For a more extended and moving example of how the mode of comedy functions to adjust the tension of a scene in a tragedy, consider the adventures of the disguised Edgar and the blinded Gloucester on Dover "cliff"—in some ways a paradigm of the way the play depicts the barren condition of the universe:

> There is a cliff [says Gloucester] whose high and bending head
> Looks fearfully in the confinèd deep.
> Bring me but to the very brim of it
> And I'll repair the misery thou dost bear
> With something rich about me. From that place
> I shall no leading need.

4.1.67–72

Notice how the language of this passage subtly anthropomorphizes the cliff. Its "head," high and bending, "[l]ooks" on the water of the English Channel as he himself can no longer do. The disguised Edgar, remembered by his blind father only as "the naked fellow" he met before, in the stormy night, takes his arm and leads him not to the cliff top but to a flat field near Dover. And here is played out a scene that constantly and perilously approaches the condition of comedy or farce. A later era would coin the term "black comedy" for this kind of tonal dissonance, but the Dover "cliff" scene is more pathos than satire:

Gloucester	When shall I come to th' top of that same hill?
Edgar	You do climb up it now. Look how we labour.
Gloucester	Methinks the ground is even.
Edgar	Horrible steep. Hark, do you hear the sea?
Gloucester	No, truly.
Edgar	Why, then your other senses grow imperfect By your eyes' anguish.

> . . . .
> Give me your hand. You are now within a foot
> Of th'extreme verge. For all beneath the moon
> Would I not leap upright.

4.5.1–6, 25–27

The entire scene takes place, we need to recall, on a perfectly level piece of stage. The blind man teeters on the edge of what he imagines to be a hellish drop. It is an extremely risky moment in the theater. And then he jumps, and falls. What keeps this jump, this fall from level ground to level ground, from being wholly and broadly comic? The scene is grotesque—it is, in a way, a mere pratfall. How does it manage to avoid the ridiculous? How is the audience prevented from laughing at this spectacle? What gives it dramatic significance, and makes it work?

The answer lies at least partly in the effectiveness of Edgar's language as he conjures up the image of the infinite distance below, an image that emphasizes everything the play has been saying to this point about human insignificance:

> Come on, sir, here's the place. Stand still. How fearful
> And dizzy 'tis to cast one's eyes so low!
> The crows and choughs that wing the midway air
> Show scarce so gross as beetles. Halfway down
> Hangs one that gathers samphire, dreadful trade!
> Methinks he seems no bigger than his head.
> The fishermen that walk upon the beach
> Appear like mice, and yon tall anchoring barque
> Diminished to her cock, her cock a buoy
> Almost too small for sight. . . .
>
> 4.5.11–20

Here a human being is seen through the wrong end of a telescope: tiny, puny, insignificant and futile, clinging to a cliff for survival and for sustenance. This essential tragicomic moment, a jump from nowhere to nowhere, from flat ground to flat ground, is rendered—instead of being slapstick—very close to sublime. In a sense the cliff is real, and it stretches below us all.

So, too, Gloucester's salvation is real, though not in the sense in which he understands it. In yet another one of his many voices, Edgar greets the blind man as if he had fallen from a great height and is now, miraculously, alive at the bottom of the cliff:

> Hadst thou been aught but gossamer, feathers, air,
> So many fathom down precipitating
> Thou'dst shivered like an egg. But thou dost breathe,
> Hast heavy substance, bleed'st not, speak'st, art sound.
> . . . .
> Thy life's a miracle. Speak yet again.
>
> 4.5.49–52, 55

Like so many others in the play, this scene is a variant of a resurrection ("Thy life's a miracle"), and a resurrection in which once again the sign of being alive is language ("Speak yet again"; "thou . . . speak'st, art sound"). In short, language in this scene continues to shift away from the literal and specific toward the general and the metaphorical. Gloucester's physical fall leads to a spiritual rise, not only a symbolic resurrection but, equally important, a lifting of his spirits. Just as Gloucester arrived at psychological insight through physical blindness, now we find that he has subliminally associated Edgar with "Poor Tom" (though he will not know they are the same person until the instant of his death):

> I'th' last night's storm I such a fellow saw,
> Which made me think a man a worm. My son
> Came then into my mind. . . .
>
> 4.1.33–35

At this point, too, Edgar begins to address Gloucester as "father," using the term in its general sense of "honored old man": "Well pray you, father"; "Sit you down, father"; "Come, father, I'll bestow you with a friend." The complimentary address has its roots in family feeling: to call a stranger "father" is to treat him with the respect and affection due one's own parent. In bringing together, yet again, the metaphorical and the literal, Edgar is able to employ both usages, one enabling him to keep his disguise (to Gloucester), and the other enabling him to cast it aside (to us).

The scene at Dover "cliff," then, is an essentially comic device turned to the service of tragedy, a mistake that is not a mistake, a fall that is not inglorious and ludicrous but glorious and lifesaving. ("Give me your hand. You are now within a foot / Of th'extreme verge.") The episode averts the pitfalls of comedy not only through its suggestive language, which grows ever stronger in the direction of archetype and symbol ("man" and "father" and "son"), but also because of a more specific and emblematic archetype, the story of the blind man Jesus restored to sight, from the Gospel according to Mark:

> And he took the blind man by the hand, and led him out of the town; and when he had spit on his eyes, and put his hands upon him, he asked him if he saw ought. And he looked up, and said, I see men as trees, walking. After that he put his hands again upon his eyes, and made him look up: and he was restored, and saw every man clearly.
>
> Mark 8:23–25

"Look up," says Edgar. "Do but look up"—and Gloucester is restored, not magically to sight, but to an interior vision of the truth. More than once in this act Edgar's language reminds us that he is not only a spectator but also a sufferer. "O thou side-piercing sight!" he cries when he sees the mad King crowned with flowers, and Shakespeare's audience would be invited to think not only of heartache but also of Christ's side pierced by the soldier's spear.

But perhaps even more important for *King Lear* as a whole than these Christological associations is the key gesture of the Dover "cliff" scene, a gesture we have seen before and will see again in this play, the gesture implicit in Edgar's gentle invitation, "Give me your hand," as when Jesus took the hand of the blind man and led him to sight. The taking and losing of hands has been an insistently meaningful gesture in this play since the opening scene, when Burgundy refused to take Cordelia by the hand without her father's promised dowry—a hand not taken, a broken bond. Another bond was broken when Edmund forged Edgar's "hand," his handwriting, in the letter given to Gloucester, and thereby robbed him of his birthright. The theft of Edgar's birthright by his brother Edmund might well remind a Bible-reading audience of the story of Jacob and Esau, a story that also involves the substitution of one "hand" for another. Jacob deceived his blind father, Isaac, and stole his elder brother's birthright by covering his hands with hairy kidskins, and the blind Isaac said to him, "The voice [is] the voice of Jacob, but the hands [are] the hands of Esau," and he gave him his blessing (Genesis 27:22, 27). In the same way, Lear is appalled by the unholy bond between his elder daughters, who have joined against him: "O Regan, will you take her by the hand?" (2.2.359). We find images of hands putting eyes out; of "filial ingratitude. / Is it not as this mouth should tear this hand / For lifting food to't?" (3.4.14–16); of Edmund as more convenient for Regan's hand than for Goneril's; of bloody hands, and hands in plackets. At the same time we also see repeated over and over again this loving gesture of the clasped hand of friendship, and the healing act of laying on of hands. "Give me your hand," says the gentleman to Kent as they part in the storm to look for Lear (3.1.29). "Give me thy hand," says Kent to the frightened Fool as he encounters "Poor Tom"—"Give me thy hand. Who's there?" (3.4.40).

No fewer than three times in one scene (4.5), Edgar says to the blind Gloucester, "Give me your hand"—at the beginning of the scene and at the end (lines 25, 216, and 277). Cordelia seeks Lear's hands in benediction (4.6.51), but Lear is not sure these are his hands (48). The most poignant of all the play's interchanges about the hand comes, of course, in that terrible scene that Edgar "would not take . . . from report," but must believe because he witnessed it, the meeting of the blind Gloucester and the mad Lear, the latter dressed in wildflowers, on the fields near Dover:

| Gloucester | O, let me kiss that hand! |
| Lear | Let me wipe it first; it smells of mortality. |

4.5.125–126

The hand here becomes the emblem of humanity, of the bare human condition, and of the need for touch, contact, kinship, and love. A play that began with a scene about the taking of Cordelia's hand in marriage culminates in this terrible act of homage and humility. Once again, in act 5, scene 2, we will hear Edgar urge Gloucester, "Give me thy hand," as he hastens him from the battle that Lear's forces have lost. But the tragic emblem of the hand as naked mortal bond is most acute in this meeting on Dover field, from which Lear, that "ruined piece of nature," the "natural fool of fortune," exits running, and from which Gloucester is led away by Edgar's hand once again.

We have said that the play progresses by pairings, by analogies and juxtapositions. The relationship between Gloucester and Edgar, father and son, is clearly constructed in a way parallel to the relationship between Lear and Cordelia, father and daughter. In the play's final acts Cordelia begins, like Edgar, to speak in a language that Shakespeare's Christian audience would associate with the Bible and specifically with the life of Jesus (for Cordelia, like Edgar and the Fool, as previously mentioned, is at moments in this play an avatar of Christ). "O dear father, / It is thy business that I go about" (4.3.23–24), she cries out while he sleeps, echoing Christ's words to Mary and Joseph: "How is it that ye sought me? wist ye not that I must be about my Father's business?" (Luke 2:49). But where the unbearable tragedy of Gloucester resolved itself, in a dramatic shift of genres, into a scene that was almost black comedy and grotesque, the scene on Dover "cliff," the play's treatment of Cordelia and Lear turns another way to escape the crushing burden of tragedy. That way, the path of romance, fantasy, poetry, and dream will be the path of the future for Shakespearean dramaturgy, and will manifest itself in the brilliant achievement of several of his last plays, from *Pericles* (which resembles *Lear* in many ways) to *The Tempest*.

The Quarto text, the *Historie of King Lear,* contains one of the loveliest manifestations of this kind of poetry, the lyric passage in which a gentleman reports to Kent about Cordelia's grief. (The passage is omitted from the Folio, perhaps because it was thought to slow down the action.) The gentleman says:

> Patience and sorrow strove
> Who should express her goodliest. You have seen
> Sunshine and rain at once; her smiles and tears
> Were like, a better way. Those happy smilets
> That played on her ripe lip seemed not to know
> What guests were in her eyes, which parted thence
> As pearls from diamonds dropped. In brief,
> Sorrow would be a rarity most beloved
> If all could so become it.
>
> *Quarto, 17.17–24*

Cordelia cried out once or twice, he tells Kent, and "shook / The holy water from her heavenly eyes," and "then away she started / To deal with grief alone." Importantly, this scene is reported to us, rather than shown us. It belongs in the category of what I have been calling Shakespearean "unscenes." (Another scene of this kind will take place in the fifth act of *The Winter's Tale,* when the offstage reunion of a father and his long-lost daughter will be disclosed, in short bursts of information, by a group of courtiers.) By having the scene of Cordelia's grief reported rather than shown, Shakespeare makes possible descriptions such as that of her tears falling from her eyes like "pearls from diamonds dropped," so she becomes virtually an art object, made of precious and eternal jewels. Since the speaker is an anonymous gentleman with no defined character—he exists only to deliver this speech—the picture that he draws is convincing and moving, without any personality or attitude to get in the way. A speech like this becomes a lyric emblem removed from dramatic tension, creating a moment of powerful contemplation.

The most striking single image in this passage is the description of Cordelia's passionately mixed feelings: her smiles and tears were like "[s]unshine and rain at once." We will hear a very similar phrase later, in Edgar's description of the death of Gloucester, who is likewise torn by conflicting emotions: "his flawed heart— / . . . 'Twixt two extremes of passion, joy and grief, / Burst smilingly" (5.3.187–190). Cordelia's "[s]unshine and rain at once" make her into an aspect of the weather, an aspect of nature, like the King in the storm. But where he is a "ruined piece of nature," Cordelia is nature as redemptive sign. For what happens in nature when sunshine and rain appear at once is a rainbow, the emblem of God's covenant with Noah that "the waters shall no more become a flood to destroy all flesh" (Genesis 9:15). Cordelia does not live to see such a new world, but the compelling description of her condition as like sunshine and rain at once paves the way not only for a new kind of Shakespearean drama—the romances—but also for whatever promise, or covenant, is held out for the spectators of this play.

The language of romance and transformation is powerfully present in the scene of Lear's awakening, act 4, scene 7, the scene that follows what has seemed to be the tragic nadir, the meeting of the two old men on the field near Dover. The King is now asleep—that healing sleep denied to kings afflicted by conscience, from Richard III to Macbeth—but his is no ordinary slumber. "In the heaviness of sleep / We put fresh garments on him," says the doctor who attends this ceremony of transformation (4.6.19–20). Lear is a "child-changèd father" (14), both changed by his children and changed into a child. His early wish to "[u]nburdened crawl toward death" is a sign of his ambivalence. We could say that he desired to be mothered by his daughters, only to discover that, like the fabled pelican, these "pelican daughters" feed on blood and may kill their "young." (On the other hand, the "Pelican in Piety," the image of the pelican piercing her breast to feed her children, was also a symbol of Jesus. Like so many images in *King Lear*, this one cuts both ways, and presents itself in both a fallen and a redeemed version in the play.) This is Lear's "resurrection scene," as the aftermath of Gloucester's fall from Dover "cliff" was his. Again the ministrant is a loving child, who seeks the father's hand in benediction. The King's awakening is accompanied not only by fresh garments but also by music, which becomes, as we will see, a traditional ceremonial feature of scenes of "rebirth" in the romances. (In this way the scene looks ahead to the awakening of Thaisa from her coffin in *Pericles;* the awakening of the supposedly dead "Fidele"—the disguised Imogen—in *Cymbeline;* and the statue scene in *The Winter's Tale*.)

This scenario, the extraordinarily powerful and moving reconciliation between parent and child, is absolutely central to the dramaturgy of late Shakespearean drama. Yet Lear at first thinks he is in hell, among the damned:

> You do me wrong to take me out o'th' grave.
> Thou art a soul in bliss, but I am bound
> Upon a wheel of fire, that mine own tears
> Do scald like molten lead.

4.6.38–41

As the recognition scene unfolds, however, hope begins to arise in him: perhaps he is alive, perhaps there is something better to come. The poignancy of this moment is extreme, and we may notice that it is, in many ways, a restaging of the love test in the play's opening scene. It begins, however, not with the King's majesty, but with his humanity, and his desire, contrary to every rule of order and precedence, to humble himself before his daughter:

Lear	I know not what to say.
	I will not swear these are my hands. Let's see:
	I feel this pin prick. Would I were assured
	Of my condition.
Cordelia [*kneeling*]	O look upon me, sir,
	And hold your hands in benediction o'er me.
	You must not kneel.
Lear	Pray, do not mock.
	I am a very foolish, fond old man,
	Fourscore and upward,
	Not an hour more or less; and to deal plainly,
	I fear I am not in my perfect mind.
	Methinks I should know you, and know this man;
	Yet I am doubtful, for I am mainly ignorant
	What place this is; and all the skill I have
	Remembers not these garments; nor I know not
	Where I did lodge last night. Do not laugh at me,
	For as I am a man, I think this lady
	To be my child, Cordelia.
Cordelia	And so I am, I am.
Lear	Be your tears wet? Yes, faith. I pray, weep not.
	If you have poison for me, I will drink it.
	I know you do not love me; for your sisters
	Have, as I do remember, done me wrong.
	You have some cause; they have not.
Cordelia	No cause, no cause.

4.6.47–68

In contrast to the opening scene, it is Lear who now knows not what to say. He now kneels, he now emphasizes his basic and unadorned humanity: "I feel this pin prick"; "I am a very foolish, fond old man." The exchange is heavily weighted with negatives: "I am doubtful"; "I am mainly ignorant"; "the skill I have / Remembers *not* these garments; *nor* I know *not* where I did lodge"; "Do *not* laugh at me"; "I know you do *not* love me." In effect, Lear asks the same question he demanded of her long ago: Do you love me? And once again Cordelia asserts, as she did then, the natural bond of parent and child toward which the play has, all the time, been leading. But she, too, has learned something, and now she is not silent. Crucially, she speaks, and in speaking avoids the ambiguity or supposed equivocation that has led to misunderstanding—and to tragedy. "No cause, no cause." Her affirmation itself comes as a negative. <u>Something *can* come of nothing</u>. Love is not a matter of pretty speeches, nor of "cause," that legal word to which Othello clings, so desperately and futilely, at the end of his tragedy ("It is the cause, it is the cause, my soul" [5.2.1]). Love is a bond that transcends both rhetoric and the law, but it requires expression and communication, voiced or unvoiced. The fourth act of the play closes on this redemptive vision, and even the agonizing events to come cannot render this scene anything but central to the lessons of the play.

Yet in a Shakespearean universe there is no such thing as an abdicated king. The play has experimented with comedy and with romance, but it must return to history and to tragedy, and tragedy is remorseless. It allows no mistakes, and permits no reversals. And Lear has made his mistake. Now we hear him plead with Cordelia to seclude herself with him, away from the world. Her instinct is confrontation, his, retirement:

Cordelia	Shall we not see these daughters and these sisters?
Lear	No, no, no, no. Come, let's away to prison.
	We two alone will sing like birds i'th' cage.
	When thou dost ask me blessing, I'll kneel down
	And ask of thee forgiveness; so we'll live,
	And pray, and sing, and tell old tales. . . .

5.3.7–12

His proposal is that they retreat into a world of art, spectatorship, romance, and ritual, reliving and restaging their reunion:

Upon such sacrifices, my Cordelia,
The gods themselves throw incense.

5.3.20

But Lear's fantasy here is not really far from those other places of retirement from the world figured in Shakespeare plays as nunneries, monasteries, and "little academes." Retreat from the public arena, from governance and power, for this King is tantamount to a symbolic death, and as we have already seen in our discussion of the Fool, in many ways *King Lear* is a play about the acceptance of death.

The play has all along been a process of interlocking plots, cross-relation-ships: the Lear plot and the Gloucester plot, the mad King and the blind Duke, two old men and their faithless and faithful children. The final scene offers yet another kind of interlocking, presenting two playwrights and actor-managers seeking to occupy the same stage. The competing texts might be called "The Play of Edmund" and "The Play of Edgar," or "The Play of Time" and "The Play of Timelessness." For the plays of Edmund and Edgar are already plotted, already in rehearsal. They are plays that embrace opposite philosophies.

Edmund's play is a power play, a play of power exercised. Like all of Shake-speare's uncompromising realists (Iago and Richard III, Prince Hal and Octa-vius Caesar), Edmund is a believer in *now,* and in personal power and influence. His instructions to his captain could well be Prince Hal's:

> Edmund   Know thou this: that men
> Are as the time is. To be tender-minded
> Does not become a sword. . . .
>
> *5.3.30–32*

His campaign is ruthless. He hardly cares which of the two sisters kills the other to get him. To him, as to the other Machiavels (Iago, Richard, arguably even Hal), women are a political asset rather than a sexual or emotional goal. It is Edmund who jokes mordantly on his deathbed—and theirs—using the familiar "die" pun: "all three / Now marry in an instant." Edmund's design is simple enough. No sooner has Lear spoken of going with Cordelia peacefully to prison, like birds in a cage, than Edmund sends a letter, a written text, com-manding their execution. His script requires that they be killed before any of the others have time to protest; he will then take power and become the king. But he reckons without that medieval view of tragedy in which, oddly, he believes more than anyone else in *King Lear;* his modernity is also his fatalism. And he will accept, finally, the verdict of retribution: "The wheel is come full circle. I am here." This is Edmund's play; in tune with the Renaissance tragedy of intrigue, a play of politics and of psychology, of men "as the time is."

But what is Edgar's play? We could say it is the play of apocalypse, of timelessness—an apocalypse played out, yet again, naturalistically rather than supernaturally. Once again, in yet another disguise, Edgar appears onstage, and presents himself to the Duke of Albany, the ranking political figure in the court. " 'If any man of quality or degree within the lists of the army will maintain upon Edmund, supposed Earl of Gloucester, that he is a manifold traitor, let him appear by the third sound of the trumpet' " (5.3.102–105). And the trumpet

sounds three times. At the last sound of the trumpet there appears a masked figure with no name and no face, declaring, "Know, my name is lost" (111). Like
Hamlet, and like so many heroes of biblical and medieval saga, he has come to
reclaim his name ("My name is Edgar, and thy father's son"). At the close of
the play, as we will see, Edgar is able to reclaim not only his place but also his
rightful style of speech, when he appears to challenge his brother Edmund to
combat. "[T]hy tongue some say of breeding breathes" (5.3.133), Edmund will
declare, accepting the challenge from this anonymous champion as coming
from a man of rank, and thus a worthy opponent.

Once again there is a biblical shadow to the scene that cannot be ignored:
the sounding of the trumpet on the day of resurrection. "We shall not all sleep,"
writes Saint Paul, "but we shall all be changed, In a moment, in the twinkling of
an eye, at the last trump: for the trumpet shall sound, and the dead shall be
raised incorruptible, and we shall be changed" (1 Corinthians 15:51–52). Two
passages from the Book of Revelation are also highly relevant: the mention of "a
white horse; and he that sat upon him was called Faithful and True; . . . and he
had a name written, that no man knew, except he himself" (Revelation
19:11–12), and the revelation itself, "I . . . heard behind me a great voice, as of a
trumpet, saying, I am Alpha and Omega, the First and the Last" (Revelation
1:10–11). The first and the last—echoing "the last shall be first," a principal text
for the action and logic of this play.

"Let's exchange charity," says Edgar to Edmund, who now lies dying (5.3.156).
("[W]e shall all be changed.") And even Edmund is moved now for the first time
to speak of good: "Some good I mean to do / Despite of mine own nature"
(217–218). Nature, the reigning goddess of the play's first four acts, is in part vanquished in act 5, in favor of something like grace—or so it seems. And then with
a characteristic reversal comes that dramatic stage picture, the inverted Pietà, the
father, King Lear, holding his dead daughter Cordelia in his arms. Once again we
hear the language of apocalypse: "Is this the promised end?" "Or image of that
horror?" "Fall and cease." The horrified spectators, Kent and the others, ask
whether they are witnessing the end of the world, or only a bitter anticipation of
that final catastrophe. As Kent says, "All's cheerless, dark, and deadly."

Lear has lost Cordelia, and Cordelia is all he has of the human bond that
makes life possible. Now he in his turn acknowledges the loss of language, the
loss of breath, and pleads for his own final stripping toward the grave:

> Why should a dog, a horse, a rat have life,
> And thou no breath at all? Thou'lt come no more.
> Never, never, never, never, never.
> [*To Kent*] Pray you, undo this button. Thank you, sir.
>
> *5.3.281–284*

Edgar calls on him, as he called on Gloucester, to "[l]ook up, my lord," and
Kent cries out,

> O, let him pass. He hates him
> That would upon the rack of this tough world
> Stretch him out longer.
>
> *5.3.288–290*

The image is that of torture, the rack a common implement for the stretching of the body from wrists to ankles. We may note that the rack was an instrument of fifteenth-through-seventeenth-century punitive practice, not of the supposedly more barbarous early Britain of the historical King Leir. Kent calls for the body to "pass" from one world to the next, a common phrase still in use as a "polite" euphemism for dying. But the word "pass" here also carries the sense of "password." Kent asks that the gate be opened, and the King permitted to go through.

The principals are all dead now: Cordelia and her sisters; Edmund; Gloucester and Lear. Kent, still faithful to "authority," speaks in the metaphor of the tragic journey that has been familiar since *Hamlet:*

> I have a journey, sir, shortly to go:
> My master calls me; I must not say no.
>
> *5.3.296–297*

At the last, as he has been all along, Edgar is our representative on the great stage of fools. The Quarto, as we have noted, gives the final lines of the play to the Duke of Albany, the surviving son-in-law of the King. Fittingly, if we want to press the point at all, this is the version titled the *Historie*—rather than the *Tragedie*—of King Lear; the heir speaks for history, the hero for tragedy. The Folio version presents Edgar as the speaker, and the speech itself, like Edgar, addresses the onstage and offstage audiences at once:

> The weight of this sad time we must obey,
> Speak what we feel, not what we ought to say.
> The oldest hath borne most. We that are young
> Shall never see so much, nor live so long.
>
> *5.3.298–301*

Order has been restored. "We that are young"—the *we* here means all audiences, at any time, not just the survivors of the Lear court, or the spectators of Jacobean England. "We" must "[s]peak what we feel," like Cordelia, and Kent, and the Fool—not just what we "ought to say." "We" shall never see so much as the blind Gloucester saw, nor live so long as these characters live, beyond their onstage deaths, in the play that tells their story.

Lear himself is greater at the close of the play than at the beginning. His growth from error to acknowledgment of his poor, stripped nature, to repentance and a humble kneeling before Cordelia, is an upward progression as well as a downward one. He is greater on his knees than on his throne. Cordelia, too, grows and changes from act 1 to act 4, as we see from the two scenes in which she is asked to answer her father, to account for unaccountable love. Her death, which resembles the deaths of Desdemona and Duncan, deaths that extinguish impossible purity, is as the play presents it something to learn from as well as to mourn.

We are left, each of us, with Kent's question and with Edgar's. Is this the promised end, or image of that horror? Is it a vision so unbearable as to hold out no hope for the future? Or is it, deliberately, an *image:* a copy, likeness, picture, shadow, similitude—an imitation in the strong Aristotelian sense—a symbol, an emblem, a sign? In essence, is there any redemption in this play of love, power, deception, and loss, of "ripeness is all"? The play poses this question, but will not answer it. The question remains open; it is not foreclosed, even in the direction of nihilism. Ultimately it is the same question Lear asked of Cordelia. Every production seeks its own response, according to the bond of theater.

Macbeth

DRAMATIS PERSONAE

King Duncan of Scotland
Malcolm, *King Duncan's son*
Donalbain, *King Duncan's son*
A Captain in Duncan's army
Macbeth, *Thane of Glamis, later Thane of Cawdor, then King of Scotland*
A Porter at Macbeth's castle
Three Murderers attending on Macbeth
Seyton, *servant of Macbeth*
Lady Macbeth, *Macbeth's wife*
A Doctor of Physic, *attending on Lady Macbeth*
A Waiting-Gentlewoman, *attending on Lady Macbeth*
Banquo, *a Scottish Thane*
Fleance, *his son*
Macduff, *Thane of Fife*
Lady Macduff, *his wife*
Macduff's Son
Lennox, *a Scottish Thane*

Ross, *a Scottish Thane*
Angus, *a Scottish Thane*
Caithness, *a Scottish Thane*
Menteith, *a Scottish Thane*
Siward, *Earl of Northumberland*
Young Siward, *his son*
An English Doctor
Hecate, *Queen of the Witches*
Six Witches
Three Apparitions, *one an armed head, one a bloody child, one a child crowned*
A Spirit Like a Cat
Other Spirits
An Old Man
A Messenger
Murderers
Servants
A show of eight kings; Lords and Thanes, attendants, soldiers, drummers

THE TRAGEDY OF MACBETH is the great Shakespearean play of stage superstition and uncanniness. It has always been considered by actors to be an unlucky play. Many will refuse to wear costumes that have appeared in productions of it; most, once they are acclimated to the mores of the theater world, will not mention the play's title, or the names of any of its characters, onstage or in the wings or dressing rooms. They call it, instead, "The Scottish Play." Its protagonist is "the Thane"; his wife, "the Queen." Accidents have befallen many casts and productions around the world since the play was first performed: *real* murders committed onstage, fires, falling scenery. One actress playing Lady Macbeth decided that the sleepwalking scene would be more realistic if she closed her eyes; she walked straight off the stage and fell into the orchestra pit, seriously injuring herself. Popular histories like Richard Huggett's *Supernatural on Stage* and classic mystery novels like Ngaio Marsh's *Light Thickens* bear witness to both the "facts" and the superstitions about the play. Why should this be? Does it have anything to do with the play Shakespeare wrote, or is it merely anecdotal lore, extrinsic to a legitimate consideration of the characters and the drama?

The play is about transgression and witches, unleashed powers that have, as theatrical events unfold, already crossed the threshold into the supposedly safe space of the stage. Any idea the audience may have had that events onstage would act as a safety valve, a buffer, or a social astringent, drawing out the poison, making things happen onstage so that they do not have to happen offstage, in our "real" world and lives, has already been challenged in a Shakespearean context by the unintended murder of Polonius in *Hamlet*. Safely stowed, as he thought, on the other side of the arras, or curtain, and thus situated as "spectator" rather than participant or combatant, Polonius is stabbed by a nervous Hamlet when he breaks the code of silence that is enjoined on audience members. He cries out, Hamlet thinks he may be "the King," and the watcher and auditor becomes actor and victim.

This border crossing takes many forms in Shakespearean drama, some of them ameliorative rather than (or as well as) dangerous. The epilogues of certain plays—*As You Like It, The Tempest, Henry V*—reach across the boundaries of the stage to engage the audience in the theater as empowering actors, co-conspirators, or forces of cultural memory. In *Macbeth,* though, the border crossing comes, significantly, at the beginning and throughout the play as well as at its close. And this is no conventional "induction," like the opening of *The Taming of the Shrew* or the first scene of Thomas Kyd's *Spanish Tragedy,* settling a frame audience on the stage to observe and comment on the ensuing action.

Macbeth begins with witches. Before the inception of the play proper, before the audience is introduced to the title character or any of the Scottish nobility or soldiery, the stage is overtaken by creatures from another world. But who are these "witches," as they are usually called? Are they male? Female? Real or imaginary? Benevolent or wicked? Are they, indeed, supernatural, or are they merely old Scottish ladies with a curious rhyming dialect of speech? Critics from Shakespeare's time to ours have debated whether they are "English," "Scottish," or "Continental" witches—this last category, as we will see, conventionally regarded as the most malevolent, powerful, and dangerous. In fact, only once in the actual spoken text of the play is one of them called a witch, and that is in an account of an offstage moment—the rude refusal of a sailor's wife to share her chestnuts: " 'Aroint thee, witch,' the rump-fed runnion cries" (1.3.5). This injudicious act calls down a curse upon the woman's husband, the "pilot" of a ship rather than of a state.

Usually, however, the witches in *Macbeth* are called not "witches" but "weird sisters." *Wyrd* is the Old English word for "fate," and these are, in a way, classical witches as well as Scottish or Celtic ones, Fates as well as Norns. The Three Fates of Greek mythology were said to spin, apportion, and cut the thread of man's life. But the *Macbeth* witches are not merely mythological beings, nor merely historical targets of vilification and superstition: on the stage, and on the page, they have a persuasive psychological reality of their own.

In part the play owes its witches to King James I, first James VI of Scotland and then, succeeding Queen Elizabeth I, king of both countries. James, since 1603 the protector of Shakespeare's company (renamed in his honor the King's Men), was a scholar of witches and witchcraft, the author of a book called *Dae-monologie* (1597). The play was performed in front of him and probably at his request, and the presence of witches in the play, as well as the Scottish locale and (adjusted) Scottish history, acknowledges his interests and underscores his power. James's *Daemonologie* is one of several key texts on witches and their craft that would have influenced the contemporary view. The earlier *Malleus Malefi-carum,* or *The Hammer of Witches* (1484), was, in effect, a professional manual for witch-hunting, while Reginald Scot's *The Discoverie of Witchcraft* (1584) offered an exposé of witch-hunters, claiming that witchcraft did not exist. (The word "discovery," here as in "discovery space," for the area at the rear of the stage, means "exposure" or "revelation." It survives today in legal discourse, where "discovery" pertains to the pretrial interrogation of witnesses in search of salient facts.) Continental witches, according to these various accounts, engaged in practices like cannibalism, the ritual murder of infants, and perverse sexual relations with demons (all activities, we might note in anticipation, that will be displaced onto the "real" figure of Lady Macbeth). These witches were said to fly, to hold witches' Sabbaths, and to be seriously malign and powerful. Local English and Scottish witches, by contrast, had less reach. They were often described as retaliatory, exacting retribution for wrongdoing. Their activities were part of a folk culture of superstition and mysterious agency, regional rather than national, pagan rather than Christian—and, at least to a certain extent, female rather than male.

There is another dimension to James I's relationship to powerful or empow-ered women of which it may be useful to take brief note here, since we will return to it when we come to an extended discussion of Lady Macbeth. James was the son of Mary, Queen of Scots, who was imprisoned in England for nearly twenty years and then executed, in 1587, for her supposed complicity in a plot to assassinate Queen Elizabeth. James, the son of one of these queens and the designated heir of the other, made only a perfunctory protest at Mary's exe-cution. Somewhere behind the dominant figure of King James, whose image is everywhere in *Macbeth,* lie the shadows of these strong female figures, "moth-ers" and queens, with their inescapable aura and their evident power over his life, his fate, and his future.

In any case, although Shakespeare and his contemporaries were surely cognizant of James's interest in witches (an interest that appears in other published works by him, as well as the *Daemonologie*), once it was decided to write a play about Macbeth the playwright was able to manipulate its details about witchcraft in the service not only of politics, but also of dramatic action and character. What Shakespeare did with the weird sisters was make them into an emblematic state of mind—again, the onstage and unmetaphored counterpart of the ambiguous and powerful Lady Macbeth. Are the "witches" inside or outside Macbeth? Are they part of his consciousness, prompting him to ambition or murder—or are they some external supernatural force? The nature of theater does not require an either/or answer to this question; the success of Shakespeare's play is in producing *both* of these effects, alternately and concurrently. The witches are both inside and outside the mind of the protagonist. They tell him what he has already been thinking, just as Iago's vivid animal imagery told Brabantio what he had already been thinking about Desdemona and Othello in bed. If the witches are causative, it is not because they tell Macbeth what to do—or, in fact, because they *tell* him anything—but because, like Iago, they allow him to interpret things as he wants to see them. They are "real" in the sense that they are visible and audible onstage, unlike, for example, the dagger that he sees before him, "[t]he handle toward my hand," or the voice that cries " 'Macbeth shall sleep no more' " (2.2.41). Modern stage directors and filmmakers often use special effects to produce these illusions for the audience in a manifest form: a dagger tied to an invisible filament descends from the flies; an amplified voice booms, seemingly from nowhere. But the stage "reality" of the witches is clearly coded, by the play, as of a different order. Unlike the voice and the dagger, the witches are seen, heard, spoken to, and vouched for by another onstage witness, Banquo, who provides very much the same kind of independent assurance as does Horatio, in *Hamlet,* who sees the ghost of Hamlet's father. Both Horatio and Banquo play a crucial role in establishing a link of verisimilitude with the audience. They are—in the play's terms—ordinary people like ourselves. They are the confidants and companions of the tragic hero. And what they confess to seeing and hearing, we may believe also. (To these we might contrast the situation in *Othello,* where no one onstage represents the audience's view, and the phantasmatic "proofs" of Iago go uncontested, until too late.) The witches are "real" in a dramatic sense—they are visible and audible onstage—and their placement on the borders of the play suggests that they are potentially out there still, ready to whisper into other susceptible ears.

The witches' landscape, the blasted heath, is, typically for Shakespeare, a geographical counterpart of their characters: a wasteland, windswept, empty, unfruitful, uninhabited, inhuman. It is to this wasteland that Macbeth will choose to venture after his first "accidental" meeting with them on the heath. They are a state of mind, and their heath is a country of the mind. Thus the appearance of the witches is structurally analogous to the other shocking and otherworldly events at the beginnings of the great tragedies: the appearance of

the ghost of old Hamlet, and what we might call "Brabantio'
nighttime arrival, in *Othello,* of Iago and Roderigo under his win
obscene images. Again, as there, we have a scene of darkness, and
inexplicable appearance, a voice or voices that utter prophecies, w
ers themselves remain shrouded in mists and mysteries. And the witches disap
pear, like old Hamlet and like Iago, as soon as their tantalizing and tempting
statements are made. "Stay, you imperfect speakers," cries Macbeth (1.3.68),
using "imperfect" in the sense of "unfinished." They hint, they speak in riddles, and they leave their hearers to decipher answers to the riddles they propose. Plainly these witches are not causes; Banquo, who has heard that his
sons will be kings, does not immediately go off to commit murder to fulfill
the prophecy, but Macbeth does. In fact, like all omens and portents in
Shakespeare, the witches exist to be interpreted. They are the essence of ambiguity, ambiguous not only in their speech but in their gender: "You should be
women, / And yet your beards forbid me to interpret / That you are so"
(1.3.43–45). It is Banquo who speaks here, and his word "interpret" is a telling
one. If only Macbeth had felt similarly forbidden to interpret. They "should be
women," yet they are bearded. Furthermore, they are neither wholly of the air
nor of the earth, but rather a combination of these dark elements: "The earth
hath bubbles, as the water has, / And these are of them" (1.3.77–78). Most strikingly, they speak in "charms," or magic riddles, and their language is dominated
by what in the play is called "equivocation": "th'equivocation of the fiend, /
That lies like truth" (5.5.41–42).

The word "equivocation" was much in use in the period, since it was a technical term used to describe the "mental reservation" by which Jesuits, often suspected of treason because of their Catholic faith, could tell untruths or partial
truths under interrogation without breaking their word to God. One of the historical events shadowing *Macbeth* was the so-called Gunpowder Plot, a conspiracy of English Roman Catholics to blow up Parliament, King James, his
wife, and his eldest son on November 5, 1605, in protest against the King's
refusal to grant further religious toleration. The plot was discovered in time; the
conspirators were killed while resisting arrest, or later tried and executed. The
plot exacerbated the already bad relations between English Protestants and
Catholics, and led to rigorous enforcement of legislation requiring attendance
at Anglican church services.

"[T]h'equivocation of the fiend, / That lies like truth" Macbeth will call it,
when he realizes near the close of the play that he has misinterpreted the
witches' apparitions. Equivocation is closely akin to ambiguity, as well as to
indecisiveness, an unwillingness to commit oneself either way. "[D]rink," says
the Porter, "may be said to be an equivocator with lechery," since "it provokes
and unprovokes: it provokes the desire but it takes away the performance"
(2.3.28–29, 27–28). The Porter belongs to that category of truth-telling realists
that also includes Emilia (in *Othello*), Pompey (in *Measure for Measure*), and the

...vedigger (in *Hamlet*). Like them—and like the "wise fools" (Bottom, Costard, Dogberry) who preceded them—the Porter speaks truth. In fact, the only other appearance of the word "equivocation" in Shakespeare, outside of this play, comes in the graveyard scene in *Hamlet*, where Hamlet warns Horatio, "We must speak by the card"—that is, literally—"or equivocation will undo us" (5.1.126–127). Equivocation: ambiguity, the dangerous double meanings of language. Macbeth, we will see, is an equivocator in all things: a man who is split in two directions, who commits murder to become King, and suffers every moment once he is King.

"Fair is foul, and foul is fair," say the witches. In their world, nonhuman and antihuman, everything is equivocal—literally double-voiced. And Macbeth—whose mind encompasses these witches, so that they reflect his own appetite, his own uncensored wish fulfillment—declares, the first time we see him, in his very first words, "So foul and fair a day I have not seen" (1.3.36). So foul *and* fair. His mind is already in a condition to receive the witches and their tempting message. His echo of them is unconscious, but it is there.

"Double, double, toil and trouble," the witches chant. The word "double," too, is a sign of equivocation, of the fatal split in Macbeth, appearing again and again throughout the play, eleven times in all, always in negative contexts: Duncan is at Macbeth's castle in *double* trust, yet Macbeth will murder him; Macduff, according to the witches' apparition, seems to pose no threat, yet Macbeth will make assurance *double* sure, and kill him; Lady Macbeth, called by Duncan "our honoured hostess," who can scarcely wait till nightfall brings the death of her royal guest, tells him that "[a]ll our service / In every point twice done, and then done double" is not enough for so worthy a king (1.6.14–15). Doubleness is everywhere, and the "toil" of which the witches speak is both a trouble and a snare. As he mulls the message of the witches he has just heard, Macbeth performs and enacts the very equivocation he will later rue:

> This supernatural soliciting
> Cannot be ill, cannot be good. If ill,
> Why hath it given me earnest of success
> Commencing in a truth? I am Thane of Cawdor.
> If good, why do I yield to that suggestion
> Whose horrid image doth unfix my hair
> And make my seated heart knock at my ribs
> Against the use of nature? Present fears
> Are less than horrible imaginings.
> My thought, whose murder yet is but fantastical,
> Shakes so my single state of man that function
> Is smothered in surmise, and nothing is
> But what is not.
>
> Macbeth *1.3.129–141*

His "single state of man" has already become doubleness, divided against itself, and equivocation will undo him. Nothing is but what is not.

When we first hear of Macbeth, before we ever meet him, he seems to be in a single state, a state of heroism—fighting, as is characteristic of Shakespeare's tragic protagonists at the outset of their journeys, an external war. "[B]rave Macbeth" he is called, and the message of his heroism is brought to the King's camp by a captain. The whole scene (1.2) deserves our close notice, because in some sense it is the first real scene of the play, and it begins with a question so startling that the question itself seems to present a dumb show: "What bloody man is that?" These are Duncan's first words, the King's first words. A man covered in blood, who seems to foreshadow all the bloody language to come in this play. (As Lady Macbeth will later muse, brokenly, in the sleepwalking scene, "who would have thought the old man to have had so much blood in him?" [5.1.33–34].) The "bloody man" in the second scene of the play is literally a soldier, figuratively the dead Duncan, and ultimately also Macbeth himself, "in blood / Stepped in so far," unable to wash it from his hand.

To Duncan this bleeding Captain arrives with his tale of rebellion and treason:

> Doubtful it stood,
> As two spent swimmers that do cling together
> And choke their art. . . .
>
> *1.2.7–9*

This is one of my favorite Shakespearean images, evoking as it does a vivid picture (we see the exhausted swimmers clearly, though they are nowhere in the cast of characters) and pointing forward to a moment when the two Macbeths, likewise "[d]oubtful" and exhausted, doom each other and pull each other down. The image is itself a powerful diagram of doubleness, and the loss of power that comes with doubleness. The Captain's report tells the tale of a victory over treason, and no sooner is it heard than Ross appears to announce another traitor: the Thane of Cawdor. By the scene's end this wartime traitor, whose sins are in plain sight, will be replaced as both Thane and treasonous subject: "What he hath lost, noble Macbeth hath won." Lost—and won. Foul—and fair. We have already heard the witches speak of "[w]hen the battle's lost and won," as if it does not matter who wins and who loses. Here at the beginning of the play a new cycle has begun. One traitorous Thane of Cawdor replaces another. Heroism in war becomes ambition in peace, and the King of Scotland appoints, unwittingly, his own murderer, his own usurper, to a place of highest trust.

Duncan is a crucial figure for this play: all the drama swirls around him. And Shakespeare's Duncan differs importantly from his source in the historical chronicles. Where Holinshed's Duncan is a weak king, succeeded by a powerful and fair-minded Macbeth who reigns for ten years, Shakespeare makes his king nobler and more virtuous, the usurper more precipitate and vile in his designs, the action much quicker, the outcome more definitive, the King's death more disastrous. Duncan is for this play the opposite of the witches and of Lady Macbeth—he is a benevolent figure of order and trust, evoked regularly and insistently in images of light and of fertility associated with the land. When he invests Macbeth with his new office he does so in a phrase, offered evenhand-edly to Macbeth and to Banquo, that links them directly with nature:

> Welcome hither.
> I have begun to plant thee, and will labour
> To make thee full of growing. . . .
>
> *1.4.27–29*

Banquo, as a loyal subject, responds in a similar figure:

> There if I grow
> The harvest is your own.
>
> *1.4.32–33*

Duncan speaks of his "plenteous joys, / Wanton in fullness." Banquo had earlier asked the witches, "If you can look into the seeds of time / And say which grain will grow and which will not, / Speak then to me." We hear continually about "the seed of Banquo," his fruitfulness, his children. Banquo was thought to be an ancestor of King James, so that in Shakespeare's time it would have been true to say that Banquo's "seed" still ruled the land. By contrast, Macbeth is barren, without issue; "[h]e has no children," as Macduff will say bitterly (4.3.217), lamenting the impossibility of retribution. Duncan's son Malcolm will inherit from his father the same language of plantation and harvest, speaking in the play's last scene of "[w]hat's more to do / Which would be planted newly with the time." This is not merely decorative language; despite the growth of cities like London and Edinburgh, England and Scotland were at the time still largely open land—forests and fields, pasturage and farm. The political clock was tick-ing in the direction of nationalism, the unification of Scotland and England, Christian teleology and absolute monarchy. But the ideology of seasonal cycle is embedded at the center of the play. In a way, the more pointedly national and eschatological the plot, the more essential was the counterpoint of planting and harvesting. As we will see, the tension between cycle and line (even literally, in Banquo's and James's "line" of kings) maps the structure of the play at every point from first to last.

We have seen this same gesture toward fertility and seasonal-cyclical renewal at the close of other Shakespearean plays about kingship. Thus Richmond (who will become Henry VII, Queen Elizabeth's grandfather) speaks in similar terms about plenty and harvest at the end of *Richard III,* a play that *Macbeth* echoes and resembles in many ways. But Duncan is linked with growth more insistently than any other Shakespearean king. When he arrives at Macbeth's castle, which is to be his doom, he speaks in a language that is almost pastoral, and is answered in the same spirit by Banquo:

> King Duncan This castle hath a pleasant seat. The air
> Nimbly and sweetly recommends itself
> Unto our gentle senses.
> Banquo This guest of summer,
> The temple-haunting martlet, does approve
> By his loved mansionry that the heavens' breath
> Smells wooingly here. No jutty, frieze,
> Buttress, nor coign of vantage but this bird
> Hath made his pendant bed and procreant cradle;
> Where they most breed and haunt I have observed
> The air is delicate.
>
> *1.6.1–9*

"Nimbly and sweetly"; "pendant bed and procreant cradle"; "breed and haunt." These are images of birth, spring, and provident nature. But "haunting" in the sense of customary habitation will become, insidiously, "haunting" in the sense of ghostly presence. And the "temple-haunting martlet," the pious and fertile bird, will shortly be exchanged in the play's economy of images for the raven, invoked by Lady Macbeth, and the crow, another black bird and bird of night, called up by Macbeth:

> Light thickens, and the crow
> Makes wing to th' rooky wood.
> Good things of day begin to droop and drowse,
> Whiles night's black agents to their preys do rouse.
>
> *3.2.51–54*

Duncan is linked with light, day, and stars; Macbeth, with darkness, night, and a "brief candle." The pattern is elegant, pervasive, and cumulatively powerful, these language clusters offering an almost subliminal imagistic counterpoint to the ongoing dramatic action, as if the play's unconscious were pushing events forward beyond, as well as through, the conscious agency of the protagonists. Thus we have Duncan's public pronouncement, conferring the title of Thane of Cawdor upon Macbeth and proclaiming that "signs of nobleness, like stars, shall shine / On all deservers." Moments later Macbeth, aside, speaks the underside of the same figure: "Stars, hide your fires, / Let not light see my black and deep desires" (1.4.50–51). Duncan wants the stars to shine, Macbeth commands them to hide. In a moment the audience will hear Lady Macbeth call for blackness:

> Come, thick night,
> And pall thee in the dunnest smoke of hell,
> That my keen knife see not the wound it makes,
> Nor heaven peep through the blanket of the dark
> To cry, "Hold, hold!"
>
> *1.5.48–52*

With the death of Duncan, in the poignant little "window scene" between Ross and an Old Man reporting the state of popular opinion, we will hear that "[b]y th' clock 'tis day, / And yet dark night strangles the travelling lamp. . . . / That darkness does the face of earth entomb / When living light should kiss it" (2.4.6–7, 8–9). We hear also that Duncan's horses, "a thing most strange and certain— / . . . Turned wild in nature" and "ate each other" (2.4.14–16, 19). Night replaces day, nature turns against itself in cannibalistic excess, and the apparition scene with the witches ends, famously, with two great images of the paradoxical and unnatural: a man not born of woman, and a moving grove.

There is a way in which, as I have noted, the unwitting and ultimately dangerous innocence of Duncan resembles the innocence of Desdemona in *Othello*. Both characters are naïve, optimistic, and trusting, and both are murdered. I mention this because it is an important point about Shakespearean structure: in historical terms, in terms of literary source or genre, in terms of gender and cultural power, these two figures (a "real" Scottish king; the "fictional" daughter of a Venetian nobleman) have little or nothing in common. Shakespeare changes his "source" here, as he does so often in the history plays, to make *his* Duncan more virtuous, and more heedless, than the Duncan of the historical chronicles. To read this play as a play about Scottish, or even about English, politics will take us only so far. To see what is so powerfully, eloquently, and immediately *Shakespearean* about it we need to ask different questions, questions about formal structure and role. Duncan—Shakespeare's Duncan—is too innocent for his world, and he is murdered. His credulousness and faith in human nature cannot survive in a world in which wit and witchcraft are represented by Lady Macbeth and the "weird sisters," the two forces edging Macbeth toward his fatal action. This is evident as early as the play's fourth scene, when Duncan expresses surprise that the previous Thane of Cawdor could have been disloyal: "There's no art / To find the mind's construction in the face. / He was a gentleman on whom I built / An absolute trust" (1.4.11–14). But the lesson to be learned, if there is one, eludes the King, since he promptly repeats his error, building an "absolute trust" on the new Thane of Cawdor, who is, of course, Macbeth. Duncan wants to "find the mind's construction in the face," but Macbeth has resolved that "[f]alse face must hide what the false heart doth know"

(1.7.82). "False face" here includes the wearing of visors and disguises; Macbeth's usurpation and murder are conceived throughout the play as an equivocation expressed in and through the language of dress.

Here the reader and critic—if not, significantly, the audience—encounter the celebrated notion of ill-fitting clothing as an "imagistic motif" in *Macbeth*. The phrase is that of Cleanth Brooks, a powerful reader of poetry associated with the literary critical school of the 1940s and 1950s known as New Criticism. Like many critics, including Shakespeare critics, of his time, Brooks analyzed the language of the plays as if they were poems—which, of course, they are. Shakespeare scholars and critics like Caroline Spurgeon (*Shakespeare's Imagery,* 1935) and Wolfgang Clemen (*The Development of Shakespeare's Imagery,* 1951) charted patterns of imagery within and across the plays, suggesting a kind of subliminal theme or subtext of images, governed not by the conscious choices of individual characters but by an underlying dynamic, a kind of imagistic unconscious, that undercut as often as it supported the aims and agency of the dramatic speakers. Thus, to summarize such an argument about clothing imagery briefly, Macbeth begins with clothing that fits him, and moves rapidly, in the course of this relatively short play, toward descriptions of increasing sartorial grotesqueness. His

> The Thane of Cawdor lives. Why do you dress me
> In borrowed robes?
>
> *1.3.106–107*

spoken to the witches at the beginning of the play turns quickly into Banquo's

> New honours come upon him,
> Like our strange garments, cleave not to their mould
> But with the aid of use.
>
> *1.3.143–145*

Time will make these "strange garments" fit, if Macbeth will only be patient, and for a moment he seems inclined to wait for events to unfold, until he is goaded by his wife into untimely action:

> Macbeth   We will proceed no further in this business.
>   He hath honoured me of late, and I have bought
>   Golden opinions from all sorts of people,
>   Which would be worn now in their newest gloss,
>   Not cast aside so soon.
> Lady Macbeth   Was the hope drunk
>   Wherein you dressed yourself?
>
> *1.7.31–36*

By the end of the first act Macbeth is firmly committed to disguise, making—as he will later say—"our faces visors to our hearts, / Disguising what they are" (3.2.35–36). From this point the language of clothing is continually associated with Macbeth and his usurpation: Macduff fears "[l]est our old robes sit easier than our new" (2.4.39)—that is, lest Macbeth's rule be less fit than Duncan's. And in act 5, on the field near Dunsinane, two Scottish noblemen, Caithness and Angus, perceiving Macbeth's imminent downfall, will speak of him in clothing images more exaggerated than any before: "He cannot buckle his distempered cause / Within the belt of rule," says one, and the other replies,

> Now does he feel his title
> Hang loose about him, like a giant's robe
> Upon a dwarfish thief.
>
> 5.2.15–16, 20–22

Thus in the plot of clothing imagery, uncontrollable by Macbeth, controlled only by the playwright and the play, Macbeth has shrunk and withered beneath the borrowed robes, become a caricature of a king: the image is sharply visual, even though it may not be mirrored by actual "borrowed robes" upon the stage.

Yet we should pause here to remember that actors' clothing was indeed often "borrowed," some items the relics of the wardrobes of "real" noblemen and courtiers. In a culture like that of early modern England, where the notion of sumptuary laws still obtained, "ill-fitting" clothing was not only that which was a size too big or small, but also that which pertained to a rank inappropriate for the wearer. The sumptuary laws ordained proper clothing, fabrics, and ornaments for each rank, and—as in a comedy like *Twelfth Night*—some of the class-jumping activities of would-be noblemen, like Malvolio, were held up to ridicule precisely because those who practiced them aspired to a sartorial level above their actual station. The idea was one of a legible society, in which you were what you wore: a version of "uniform" was ordained for each rank, with an added economic impetus, since low-status persons were asked to wear clothing of native materials (English wool), whereas aristocrats and noblemen could wear imported fabrics and lace. Actors occupied a very low social station. Technically they were servants, the "King's Men" or the "Lord Chamberlain's Men," a subterfuge to get around the fact that, if not employed by a nobleman, they were "masterless men" and thus subject to a law designed to curb the roaming of "vandals" and troublemakers across the English countryside. (Acting companies traveled, especially in the summer months and when London was beset by plague.)

The plot of clothing imagery in *Macbeth* speaks to a number of cultural anxieties, current and historical, about both the legibility of social rank and the legitimacy of rule. It is not merely decorative; if it influences the "poetry" of the play, it does so at the level of action, motivation, psychology, and design. Above all, it signifies another level of subliminal control, like the plot of the witches, of which Macbeth and Lady Macbeth are only imperfectly aware, and which constitutes a counterplot to their intentions and desires. Whether the ill-fitting-clothing plot was in practice doubly subversive—whether it suggested, as in an earlier history play like *Richard III* or *Henry V,* that even "real" kings were men in costume—is a question that lingers at the borders of the play.

As with the clothing imagery, so with the "weird sisters": they function by indirection and insinuation. The witches never directly suggest a course of action, nor do they tell Macbeth to murder Duncan. It is his own "horrible imaginings" and his wife's prompting that move him in the direction of action. For Macbeth, as for Othello, the play becomes a psychomachia, an internal tug-of-war between, on the one hand, the loyalty of a subject, the gratitude of a recently honored vassal, and the duties of a host and, on the other, "[v]aulting ambition which o'erleaps itself / And falls on th'other" (1.7.27–28). As was the case with Othello, so, too, with Macbeth: the nature of his language charts the pattern of his inner struggle. But in this case the murder comes not at the end of the play, but near its beginning. The play becomes an examination not of whether he will do the deed, but of what the deed will do to him.

Just as he shrinks from the happy and hesitant wearer of borrowed robes to a dwarfish thief enfolded in a costume meant for a giant, so Macbeth will move from sensitivity to insensitivity. From his first interior agony and moral doubt he will move downward toward a condition in which he feels and senses nothing at all, where he has supped full with horrors, has forgotten the taste of fears, cannot be moved by the death of his wife, and fittingly becomes at the last no longer a man but a rare monster painted upon a pole: a caricature of a tyrant. This is the downward slope, the tragic pattern of Macbeth's fall, and it parallels the exaggerated unfolding of the clothing imagery, from fit to unfit. But it begins in equivocation, in moral ambiguity and interior battle.

The demonstrated equi-vocation, equal-voicing, of "[t]his supernatural so-liciting" that "cannot be ill, cannot be good," balancing moral and immoral possibilities as if they were somehow perfectly equal, becomes a tone at once more emotionally fraught and more wishfully hypothetical as Duncan approaches the castle:

> Macbeth   If it were done when 'tis done, then 'twere well
> It were done quickly. If th'assassination
> Could trammel up the consequence, and catch
> With his surcease success: that but this blow
> Might be the be-all and the end-all, here,
> But here upon this bank and shoal of time,
> We'd jump the life to come. . . .
>
>   *1.7.1–7*

Macbeth sounds here a little like Hamlet, in his mediation on self-slaughter. *If* there were no consequences, action would be easy. But in these "[w]e still have judgement here," says Macbeth. "This even-handed justice / Commends th'ingredience of our poisoned chalice / To our own lips" (1.7.7–8, 10–12). But what is most striking about Macbeth's ruminations is their involuted and convoluted style. "If it were done [completed and past] when 'tis done [performed]"; "catch / With his surcease success." Syntax, double meaning, and deceptive near-rhymes are battling inside him. Now, bolstered by Lady Macbeth's mingled encouragement and scorn, he finds himself waiting for her signal, the bell—that tolling symbol out of *Othello*—and he speaks in the same troubled and contorted language when confronted with a terrifying vision. As I have noted above, filmmakers and theater directors occasionally try to "dramatize" this vision by presenting an actual dagger to the audience's eyes; this takes pressure off the actor, but it also places the audience's-eye view squarely within the consciousness of Macbeth, whereas the play itself is brilliantly careful in the way it offers a variety of competing points of view:

> Macbeth   Is this a dagger which I see before me,
>   The handle toward my hand? Come, let me clutch thee.
>   I have thee not, and yet I see thee still.
>   Art thou not, fatal vision, sensible
>   To feeling as to sight? Or art thou but
>   A dagger of the mind, a false creation
>   Proceeding from the heat-oppressèd brain?
>   I see thee yet, in form as palpable
>   As this which now I draw.
>   Thou marshall'st me the way that I was going.
>
>   . . . .
>
>   I see thee still,
>   And on thy blade and dudgeon gouts of blood,
>   Which was not so before. There's no such thing.
>   It is the bloody business which informs
>   Thus to mine eyes. . . .
>
>   *2.1.33–49*

"Is this . . . ?"; "I have thee not, . . . I see thee still"; "There's no such thing." Internal debate and dialectic, as the invisible dagger turns bloody before his eyes. It is at this point that Macbeth approaches the dread word "murder," which he has all this time been avoiding. His "horrible imaginings" in act 1 produced a murder that was "but fantastical." Now the fantasy is about to merge with reality, and "murder" is mentioned for only the second time in the play. We may notice how hard he tries to avoid the word, to avoid putting a verb to the noun, an action to the idea:

> Now o'er the one-half world
> Nature seems dead, and wicked dreams abuse

The curtained sleep. Witchcraft celebrates
Pale Hecate's offerings, and withered murder,
Alarumed by his sentinel the wolf,
Whose howl's his watch, thus with his stealthy pace,
With Tarquin's ravishing strides, towards his design
Moves like a ghost. . . .

> *2.1.49–56*

Macbeth displaces the agency from himself onto a personified "murder," who resembles one of the witches ("withered"). Subordinate clause after subordinate clause postpones and retards the move to the verb "Moves"; three lines of verse are interposed between "murder" and "Moves." Language here mirrors Macbeth's own doubt and delay; he cannot say the deed, which is tantamount to not doing the deed—and then the bell rings, and the suspense is over:

I go, and it is done. The bell invites me.
Hear it not, Duncan; for it is a knell
That summons thee to heaven or to hell.

> *2.1.62–64*

The reference to Tarquin, above ("With Tarquin's ravishing strides"), is worth our pausing over for a moment, not only because it suggests affinities with Shakespeare's poem *The Rape of Lucrece* but because, as some critics have noticed, it obliquely "feminizes" King Duncan. Lucrece, or Lucretia, was a virtuous wife, whose husband's praise of her led men of the court of the Roman Emperor Tarquinius Superbus to find her especially desirable. The Emperor's nephew, Tarquinius Sextus, stole upon her and raped her, and Lucretia killed herself out of shame. The Roman historian Livy says Tarquin was "inflamed by her purity and beauty," and the story was widely known in the Renaissance, and used by numerous poets. If Macbeth is the Tarquin figure here, Duncan becomes the Lucrece-like rape victim, murdered offstage, and emblematizing a death of ideal purity. (Holinshed's *Chronicles* describes King Duncan as perhaps too "soft and gentle of nature" and says the rebels regarded him as "a faint-hearted milksop.") In a play in which conventionally "male" and "female" qualities are often deliberately displaced, where witches who "should be women" have beards, and Macbeth commends his wife to "[b]ring forth men children only" in accordance with her manly spirit, this further displacement, the slightly indecorous recasting of the story of Lucrece with Duncan in the title role, continues the sense of unease. Nothing is but what is not.

Macbeth's language before the murder, then, is knotty, contorted, difficult to follow and to unscramble syntactically. But a striking change comes over his diction the minute the murder is accomplished: it becomes fragmented, disoriented, and disordered, the words dropping singly, like stones down a well, and echoing as they fall:

Lady Macbeth	Did not you speak?
Macbeth	When?
Lady Macbeth	Now.
Macbeth	As I descended?
Lady Macbeth	Ay.
Macbeth	Hark!—Who lies 'i'th' second chamber?
Lady Macbeth	Donalbain.
Macbeth	[*looking at his hands*] This is a sorry sight.

2.2.15–18

Strikingly now, Macbeth begins to worry about things he could *not* say:

Macbeth	One cried "God bless us" and "Amen" the other,
	As they had seen me with these hangman's hands.
	List'ning their fear I could not say "Amen"
	When they did say "God bless us."
Lady Macbeth	Consider it not so deeply.
Macbeth	But wherefore could I not pronounce "Amen"?
	I had most need of blessing, and "Amen"
	Stuck in my throat.

2.2.24–31

Yet again we encounter, in this character compact of language, a loss of control over speech—not a deliberately postponed conclusion now ("murder . . . Moves"), but a failure to be able to speak, to finish a thought. Macbeth has himself become one of those "imperfect speakers," unfinished and enigmatic:

> Methought I heard a voice cry "Sleep no more,
> Macbeth does murder sleep"—the innocent sleep,
> Sleep that knits up the ravelled sleave of care,
> The death of each day's life, sore labour's bath,
> Balm of hurt minds, great nature's second course,
> Chief nourisher in life's feast—

2.2.33–38

Somewhat to our relief, Lady Macbeth impatiently interrupts this catalogue that threatens to go on forever. "What do you mean?" she asks, and "Who was it that thus cried?" At this point in the play she, unlike her husband, is untouched by horror. Her crisis will come later, and be even more terrible. But at this point, anticipating her own sleepwalking (and hand-washing) scene, she says, dismissively, "A little water clears us of this deed." For Macbeth, though, the horror is already fully present from the moment of the murder, and the curse upon him is sleeplessness, disorder in the world of human nature, the same disease that afflicted Henry IV, and Richard III, and other kings guilty of murder—as well as Brutus when he was contemplating the murder of Caesar.

The murder of Duncan is discovered when Macduff and Lennox knock at the gate of the castle, asking to see their king. The knocking at the gate is itself, on a stage, particularly hollow and horrible, and the Porter, who jokes about being "porter of hell-gate," marks and guards a threshold to nightmare. Like the dangerously permeable border between witches and soldiers, like the literally transgressive boundary between actors and audience, or onstage and offstage, so this gateway is also dramatically and thematically established as a place of crisis. "Up, up, and see / The great doom's image," cries Macduff. "As from your graves rise up, and walk like sprites / To countenance this horror." They are all in a living nightmare, the image of the Last Judgment, the earth's final catastrophe. The characteristic central event of a Shakespearean tragedy is a kind of stripping or divestment, and Macbeth, as we have seen, is now stripped of language, and of sleep, by his horror at his own action. So it is particularly fitting, in the following scene, to find him stripped of clothing as well. Dressed as he is in nightclothes, without weapons or armor, he receives the "news" that is no news to him, and cloaks himself, once more, in borrowed robes, the borrowed robes of language.

Lady Macbeth's response, a superb failure of emphasis—"What, in our house?"—calls semicomic attention to the gross violation of the central value of hospitality, and her almost surely spurious faint is a stratagem of distraction rather than a sign of female frailty. When Macbeth speaks blithely and pictorially of his supposed discovery of Duncan's body, describing that body almost as if it were a work of art—"Here lay Duncan, / His silver skin laced with his golden blood"—we can recall her scornful pun at the time of the murder:

> Infirm of purpose!
> Give me the daggers. . . .
> . . . .
> I'll gild the faces of the grooms withal,
> For it must seem their guilt.
>
> 2.2.50–51, 54–55

Guilt is internal; gilt, external—another equivocation. Macbeth's image of Duncan's golden blood suggests that the internal struggle has been replaced by a "false face." His language takes on a deceptive ornateness, markedly different from the involuted contortion of his earlier equivocation, and also from the naked blankness of his first shock and horror. His sudden, politic volubility—"Had I but died an hour before this chance / I had lived a blessèd time, for from this instant / There's nothing serious in mortality" (2.3.87–89)—is truer than he perhaps intends, and the sudden silence of the real mourners, Duncan's sons, marks their temporary loss of power and his ascendancy. From this point will come the murder of Banquo, and the attempted murder of his innocent son, Fleance, and the inexcusable and brutal murder of Lady Macduff and her children, until Macbeth has nothing left, finally, of the emotion that had filled him with fear. When Banquo, alone on the stage, says ruefully at the beginning of act 3, "Thou hast it now: King, Cawdor, Glamis, all / As the weird women promised; and I fear / Thou played'st most foully for't," the moment will mark both Macbeth's ascendancy and his decline.

The terrible language of equivocation reenters the play as a sign of moral failure, and it does so, significantly, at the play's midpoint, act 3, scene 4. The time is equivocal, too, the night "[a]lmost at odds with morning, which is which." Macbeth's situation, like his language, recalls that of Richard III:

> Macbeth   I am in blood
>   Stepped in so far that, should I wade no more,
>   Returning were as tedious as go o'er.
>
>   *3.4.135–137*

"Tedious": weary, disagreeable, tiresome, exhausting. The tragic and the tedious are, in a way, as much "at odds" as morning and night. Macbeth is in a sense already beyond human emotion, and these centrally placed lines act as a fulcrum, a watershed, a split. Like the equivocator described by the Porter, "that could swear in both the scales against either scale, who committed treason enough for God's sake, yet could not equivocate to heaven," Macbeth is well along the primrose path to the everlasting bonfire.

Like *Richard II, Macbeth* has a chiastic, or X-shaped, structure, charting at once the upward and downward trajectories of its two protagonists. As Macbeth moves downward toward inhumanity and loss of affect, Lady Macbeth moves upward, toward feeling and horror. At the beginning of the play it is Macbeth who hears voices, sees visions: the dagger before him, coated with blood; the voice that cries "Sleep no more"; the ghost of Banquo. Lady Macbeth sees and hears nothing. Like Iago, she has no interior dimension in which to feel this emotional tug-of-war, this battle of the soul. But by the play's close it is Lady Macbeth who has the most terrible vision, presented to us like a play-within-the-play: the vision of a bloody hand that cannot be cleansed. And this exchange of qualities takes place between Macbeth and his wife, two characters whom Freud would use as case studies for "disunited parts of a single psychical individuality" in "Some Character-Types Met with in Psycho-Analytical Work." Yet in the opening scenes we see in Lady Macbeth none of this frailty. We see instead rigidity, resolution, and the rejection of a restricted notion of a woman's place. Lady Macbeth is the strongest character in the play. From the first moment we see her she is resolute, apparently without moral reservation, and devastatingly scornful of her husband's inner struggles, which she equates with unmanliness. The opposite of "man" in this case can be either "child" or "woman." Thus we hear her say,

                                    Yet do I fear thy nature.
                It is too full o'th' milk of human kindness
                To catch the nearest way. . . .

                . . . .

                                            What thou wouldst highly,
                That wouldst thou holily; wouldst not play false,
                And yet wouldst wrongly win. . . .

                                                        1.5.14–20

And later, even more scornfully,

                                                Infirm of purpose!
                        Give me the daggers. . . .

                                            2.2.50–51

Lady Macbeth will take the daggers from her husband and return to the
scene of the crime to finish the task of implicating the grooms in Duncan's murder. In fact, as she repeatedly makes clear, she sees herself as the stronger, the
dominant, the more conventionally "masculine" of the two. I think we can say
with justice that those unisex witches, with their women's forms and their con-
fusingly masculine beards, are, among other things, dream images, metaphors,
for Lady Macbeth herself: physically a woman but, as she claims, mentally and
spiritually a man. It's well to remember at points like these that the actor playing
Lady Macbeth, like the actor playing the far more "feminine" Lady Macduff,
would have been male. Gender on the early modern public stage was performed
rather than "natural." Like darkness, which sometimes needed to be invoked by
language—or props, such as onstage candles and lanterns—in the middle of an
outdoor afternoon performance, gender difference, femaleness, was an achieved
effect rather than a mirror of reality. And this is very germane to the question of
Macbeth's manliness, which his wife so regularly challenges. Neither manliness
nor womanliness can be taken for granted in a world, and on a stage, where gender is by definition an act.

Lady Macbeth's language from the outset troubles this boundary between
proper and improper femaleness or femininity. In two famous speeches early in
the play she undoes the conventions about the naturalness of maternal feeling:

                            Come, you spirits
                That tend on mortal thoughts, unsex me here,
                And fill me from the crown to the toe top-full
                Of direst cruelty. Make thick my blood . . .

                . . . .

                            Come to my woman's breasts,
                And take my milk for gall, you murd'ring ministers.

                                            1.5.38–46

And, yet again,

> I have given suck, and know
> How tender 'tis to love the babe that milks me.
> I would, while it was smiling in my face,
> Have plucked my nipple from his boneless gums
> And dashed the brains out, had I so sworn
> As you have done to this.
>
> 1.7.54–59

A famous essay of 1933 that critiques the concept of character and reality in drama mockingly asks in its title, "How Many Children Had Lady Macbeth?" The question, as posed by the critic L. C. Knights, seems to suggest that such curiosity is extratextual: we cannot answer it, and should not try, since there is no evidence within the play to tell us. Yet Lady Macbeth's evocation of lactation and nursing, at odds with Macduff's later statement about Macbeth, "He has no children," does have a point within the play. It contrasts her with the paragon of onstage motherhood, Lady Macduff, and it associates her with the "unnatural," since her emotions run so counter to the maternal, and her cry to be "unsexed" is itself contrary to physical nature. Most of all, though, it suggests the displacement or replacement of what is conventionally called "maternal instinct." For in place of offspring Lady Macbeth has her husband, whom she alternately taunts and cossets as a "baby" or a child. Thus, as we have seen, she says he is too full of "the milk of human kindness" to take the nearest way to the throne—murder.

Macbeth responds to this continuing challenge by speaking continually, almost obsessively, about infants and children. In his fearful weighing of conscience before the murder he speaks of "pity, like a naked new-born babe, / Striding the blast, or heaven's cherubin, horsed / Upon the sightless couriers of the air" (1.7.21–23). Faced with the specter of Banquo's ghost, the uncomfortable spectacle of Banquo at a banquet planned without him, Macbeth explains his terror of the ghost as fear of the uncanny and the supernatural. He would not be afraid of a bear, a tiger, or an armed rhinoceros, he insists. "If trembling I inhabit then, protest me / The baby of a girl" (3.4.104–105). In contrast to this is his praise of Lady Macbeth: "Bring forth men-children only, / For thy undaunted mettle should compose / Nothing but males" (1.7.72–74). For her part, Lady Macbeth has kept up a constant barrage: "When you durst do it, then you were a man" (1.7.49). The unspoken "it" is the murder of the King. "Infirm of purpose! / Give me the daggers"; " 'Tis the eye of childhood / That fears a painted devil" (2.2.50–51, 52–53). Her slurs upon his manhood are most evident in the banquet scene. "Are you a man?" she asks, and again, "O, these flaws and starts . . . would well become / A woman's story at a winter's fire / Authorized by her grandam" (3.4.57, 62–65), and, yet again, "What, quite unmanned in folly?" (72). All these scathing remarks are asides, to him, to herself, and to the audience, as the splendidly impervious Lady Macbeth of the first several acts carries on the serious business of being "our honoured hostess," explaining to her guests that Macbeth's errant behavior is a physical affliction that should be overlooked—"My lord is often thus"— rather like Iago explaining that Othello often has fits, and should not be judged by them.

Under this verbal assault, half attack and half flirtatious insinuation—for the part of Lady Macbeth is often conceived not as "unwomanly" and cold, but as torridly seductive, Macbeth and Lady Macbeth tied together by erotic as well as political passions—Macbeth can perhaps hardly be blamed for his moral blankness. The ghost of Banquo exits the stage, and Macbeth feels only relief at being again intact: "Why so, being gone, / I am a man again" (3.4.106–107). In act 2, scene 4, there was something inadvertently revealing about his call to "briefly put on manly readiness" when the murder was discovered. In context this means "put on our swords" and other warlike apparatus, to do battle with the (supposed) assassins. But the recurrence of "manly"/"man," together with the ambiguous or equivocal "briefly" (swiftly; for a short duration), tells, as is usual for this play, a double tale.

Desdemona saw in herself a divided duty, felt herself torn between the claims of father and husband, but she unhesitatingly chose Othello over Brabantio. Cressida tried to choose Troilus, but was forced, both by circumstances and by certain aspects of her own character, to return to her father instead. The choice of husband or father, as we have noted, is a recurrent dilemma for Shakespearean women, and it marks not only a space of psychological sundering and individuation for these women (Hermia, Juliet, and Ophelia among them), but also something structural about the plays. In the case of Lady Macbeth, the "choice" is positioned in a slightly oblique and allusive way, but is still powerfully present. The only moment in the early part of the play when she shows any responsiveness to human frailty and pathos comes when she reports her response to the spectacle of the sleeping Duncan: "Had he not resembled / My father as he slept, I had done't" (2.2.12–13). She is unable to murder a "father," though she inspires her husband to try. But Macbeth himself, called a child and taunted as a child, she hounds to murder and to death—his and hers.

The theme of killing the father, whether parricide or regicide, is everywhere in *Macbeth*. Parents killed by children, and also children killed by parents. The play presents, as an emblem of the *socially* unnatural, a pair of fictive parricides. The first is the murder of Duncan. Lady Macbeth can't kill Duncan because he resembles her father, but Duncan's own sons, Malcolm and Donalbain, are quickly suspected of the crime. Here we should note that in the political texture of the play the threat posed by Malcolm to Macbeth's ambitions comes only when Malcolm's father creates him Prince of Cumberland, and thus heir apparent to the throne. Succession of the eldest son was not automatic or assured; this is why Macbeth becomes so agitated at the designation of an official heir, who stands in the way of his own ambitions and of the witches' prophecy. Now Macduff reports that, in the wake of the murder, Malcolm and Donalbain, King Duncan's two sons, "Are stol'n away and fled, which puts upon them / Suspicion of the deed" (2.4.26–27). Reduced to the silence of real grief, these sons, like Hamlet, refuse to play the game of false mourning ordained by the man who is both their father's murderer and his successor. Like Hamlet, Malcolm flees to England.

The second fictive parricide is the murder of Banquo, again by Macbeth, and again the word is given out that the son is to blame. Lennox, who of course believes not a word of it, reports the rumor to another lord: "the right valiant Banquo walked too late, / Whom you may say, if 't please you, Fleance killed, / For Fleance fled: men must not walk too late" (3.6.5–7). Parricide is the ultimate dynastic as well as familial horror. This is the fiction spread by the Macbeth court: that a man can be killed by his own flesh and blood.

For it is this word, "blood," in all its forms, that haunts *Macbeth*. Macbeth addresses the King's sons in so ornate a fashion that his announcement seems to require a gloss or interpretation:

> Macbeth   The spring, the head, the fountain of your blood
>   Is stopped, the very source of it is stopped.
> Macduff   Your royal father's murdered.
>
> 2.3.95–97

Moments later, we hear Donalbain to Malcolm, brother to brother: "Where we are / There's daggers in men's smiles. The nea'er in blood, / The nearer bloody" (2.3.135–137). The bitter pun tells all. Where some have "blood" in the sense of family, issue, children, and lineage, others—like the "childless" Macbeth and Lady Macbeth—have blood in the sense of bloodshed, ultimate disorder rather than orderly sequence, death rather than life, the end of a line rather than a line without end. Blood "issues" from wounds in this play from that first emblematic appearance of the bleeding Captain, the "bloody man," on the battlefield.

Macbeth is prospectively haunted by signs of blood, even before the murder, as "gouts of blood," signs of the "bloody business" at hand, appear on the spectral dagger. Once the murder is done, Lady Macbeth tells him to "wash this filthy witness from [his] hand" and says, "A little water clears us of this deed." But Macbeth can neither wash nor smear the faces of the grooms with blood:

> Will all great Neptune's ocean wash this blood
> Clean from my hand? No, this my hand will rather
> The multitudinous seas incarnadine,
> Making the green one red.
>
> 2.2.58–61

In this dazzling image, evoked twice, first in Latinate polysyllables ("The multitudinous seas incarnadine") and then in monosyllabic native speech ("the green one red") in a way that prefigures the poetry of Milton, Macbeth states the condition of his own engulfment. Rather than being cleansed, his bloody hand will infect and color the world. At this point his situation is still one of pathos and despair. But by the third act, determined now on the murder of Banquo, Macbeth has detached the bloody hand from himself and made it an instrument of infernal darkness:

> Come, seeling night,
> Scarf up the tender eye of pitiful day,
> And with thy bloody and invisible hand
> Cancel and tear to pieces that great bond
> Which keeps me pale. . . .
>
> *3.2.47–51*

With the coming of Banquo's ghost we find Macbeth almost resigned to this inevitable idea of blood: "It will have blood, they say. Blood will have blood." By the middle of the play the fear of blood spilled, of blood on his own hands, has deteriorated into this abstraction of horror. Blood is now a river in which he wades, "[s]tepped in so far," not a sea in which he might wash. The bloody hands have become an abstract concept—"these hangman's hands"—and Macbeth moves downward toward the spectacle of the painted monster on the pole.

But not so Lady Macbeth. Where Macbeth leaves off the language of blood, she picks it up. Where Macbeth forgets to worry about his bloody hands, which will the "multitudinous seas incarnadine," Lady Macbeth becomes for the first time obsessed with her own "filthy witness." Gilt has turned to guilt, and with the guilt and the blood she catches, as well, Macbeth's sleeplessness, so that the audience finds her at the beginning of act 5 wandering, like the ghost of old Hamlet, three nights in her chamber. "Out, damned spot; out, I say. . . . Yet who would have thought the old man to have had so much blood in him? . . . Here's the smell of the blood still. All the perfumes of Arabia will not sweeten this little hand" (5.1.30–34, 42–43). Her feverish and poignant hand-washing, onstage, has several powerful effects: reminding the audience of Macbeth's futile hand-washing gestures immediately after the murder; indicating for the first time an interior dimension of feeling—we could call it conscience—in the previously obdurate Lady Macbeth; and evoking not only Shakespeare's earlier play *Julius Caesar,* but also the biblical scene of hand-washing in which Pontius Pilate attempts to wash his hands of the blood of Christ (Matthew 27:24).

Duncan's principal symbols were light and fertility. In the sleepwalking scene these are reversed, so that we have not fertile blood, progeny, but spilt blood, death; not day but night; not sleep but wakefulness; not natural light but artificial light. Banquo had said of a starless night sky, "There's husbandry in heaven, / Their candles are all out" (2.1.4–5). By contrast Lady Macbeth "has light by her continually. 'Tis her command" (5.1.19–20). She cannot bear the darkness. Shortly we will hear her husband compare human life to a "brief candle," echoing Othello's "Put out the light, and then put out the light." This is the light that Lady Macbeth clutches as she moves restlessly through the night, confessing to her horrified onstage audience, the Doctor and the waiting-gentlewoman, truths we already know, but which will be brought home to us anew by their visible horror. This is another dramatic function of the play-within-the-play: it enables the audience in the theater to participate in an emotion that prior knowledge would otherwise have dulled or diminished. The characters onstage are shocked; in response, we are shocked all over again. As the Doctor says, "I think, but dare not speak," just as Malcolm and Donalbain did not dare to speak, just as the offstage audience, by convention, is mute.

Lady Macbeth's doctor is, as well, part of another overarching pattern in this brilliantly designed play, for he is one of two doctors in *Macbeth,* and the other doctor serves the English court. Written and performed for a king whose political project was to unify Scotland and England, Shakespeare's play increasingly undertakes to distinguish between the two landscapes and polities. As the play progresses, England begins to appear as a redemptive land different from both the barren heath of the witches and the unnatural, blood-drenched Scotland of the usurping Macbeth. If Duncan is an Edenic figure who projects his own innocence onto others and is thus vulnerable to attack, England's king, Edward the Confessor, is a patently holy personage who cures evil. In historical fact, he was the first to cure a disease described as the "king's evil," scrofula (swollen glands in the neck). "[A]t his touch," says the English Doctor, "Such sanctity hath Heaven given his hand, / They presently amend" (4.3.144–146). "Presently" means "immediately," right away; the sick are instantly cured by the royal touch. (This practice of curing the king's evil by the laying on of hands continued for centuries. James did it; Charles II was said to have touched ninety-two thousand persons; the last person supposedly "touched" in England was Samuel Johnson, the great Shakespeare editor and dictionary maker, touched by Queen Anne in 1712, when he was only thirty months old.) By framing his play about medieval Scotland with a mention of the healing touch of the English king, the playwright is able to underscore a crucial opposition. Macbeth's bloody hand brings death; Edward's holy hand brings life and health. Scotland is a land diseased and sick, needing a physic to purge it. "Bleed, bleed, poor country!" cries Macduff, and Malcolm adds: "[E]ach new day a gash / Is added to her wounds."

In the fifth act of the play the language of disease is everywhere. Macbeth asks the Scottish doctor to "cast the water of my land" and "purge it." Lady Macbeth is ill, and her husband demands, impatiently, "Canst thou not minister to a mind diseased . . . ?" (5.3.42). But the "king's evil" that afflicts Macbeth is not so easily cured, because he is himself the sickness in the state, the disease that must be purged. And the physicians to whom he takes his questions and requests are finally not doctors, but witches, brewing their own infernal medicines—once again, the literal counterparts of the metaphorical poison administered by Lady Macbeth ("Hie thee hither, / That I may pour my spirits in thine ear" [1.5.23–24]).

When Macbeth comes to the witches' cave, where fire burns and cauldron bubbles, he is a figure very like Marlowe's Doctor Faustus, seeking forbidden knowledge and demanding answers to the secrets of the future. "How now, you secret, black, and midnight hags," he salutes them imperiously. "What is't you do?" And they reply, "A deed without a name." That Macbeth wants to know its name is part of his vaulting ambition. "Seek to know no more," they caution, and his reply is "I will be satisfied. Deny me this, / And an eternal curse fall on you!" (4.1.119–121). This is a familiar sin, wishing to know a sacred name that cannot be pronounced. And the curse falls—the curse has in fact already fallen—on Macbeth.

This remarkable scene recalls another preoccupation of the court of James I, for not only was James a descendant of Banquo and a scholar of witchcraft, he was also, with the rest of the royal family, an aficionado of the contemporary art form known as the court masque. These aristocratic entertainments included elements of dance and spectacle, and often turned on a contrast between the antimasque, representing disorder, and the masque proper, emblematic of renewed order. Ben Jonson's *Pleasure Reconciled to Virtue* (1618) featured an antimasque of pygmies and a masque of knights; the same author's *The Masque of Queens* (1609) presented an antimasque of witches and other Vice characters, and a second masque of the audience, nobility that would banish the witches. The principal actors and dancers in the masque proper were often noble or royal personages; James's wife, Queen Anne, and his son Prince Henry were frequent participants. At the end of the masque came the dance known as the revels, in which (noble) actors and (noble) audience danced together in an image of harmony, breaking down the barriers of "fiction" and "reality." The King himself, when in the audience, was a key figure, seated on a raised platform known as "the state," his viewpoint always the dominant axis. We should recall, too, that the play *Macbeth* was presented in front of James and his brother-in-law, King Christian IV of Denmark (Queen Anne's brother). The embedded antimasque of witches, singing songs and chanting spells and recipes as they dance around the cauldron, ushers in the element of spectacle so central to the structure of the masque, in this case the three apparitions: the armed head, the bloody child, and the child crowned, with a tree in his hand. Each apparition, though it seems to connote disorder and thus to confirm Macbeth's designs, ultimately will be revealed as an aspect of order. Macbeth, trapped by the apparitions' riddles, fails to comprehend their messages, and the final demonstration, the show of eight kings and Banquo, the last king carrying a mirror or magic glass, brings the spectacle out to the audience, reflecting the face of King James as the lineal successor of Banquo's blood. This mirror trick performs a kind of visual "revels," uniting onstage and offstage performers. (Notice that the line is all-male, and does not include James's mother, Mary, Queen of Scots.)

In one way, then, the final scene of the witches, ending in a dance described as an "antic round," is a fragment of, or a quotation from, a court masque, a pattern predicting order. In another, however, it is closely tied to the central tension between good blood and bad blood, lineage and murder. Consider again the nature of the three apparitions that constitute the magic spectacle. The armed head is Macbeth's bloody head, which will be cut off by Macduff and offered in the final scene to Malcolm: "Behold where stands / Th'usurper's cursèd head" (5.11.20–21). The bloody child is Macduff, untimely ripped from his mother's womb. And the crowned child with a tree in his hand is Malcolm, Duncan's elder son—soon to be the new King—at whose instruction the soldiers hew down branches and bring Birnam Wood, a "moving grove," to Dunsinane. In fact, these images of apparent unnaturalism turn out to be natural after all, symbols of health rather than sickness, temporary and necessary inversions of nature brought about so that order may be restored. But in them we have, as well, a visual summary of both kinds of "blood." The images of children that clustered at the play's beginning return here in a different form, and these fruitful "men-children," Malcolm and Macduff, are figures that defeat and replace the tragic images of slaughtered infants, including the horrific murder of Macduff's "pretty chickens and their dam" (4.3.219). The play suggests that we have been witnessing a kind of massacre of the innocents, like the slaughter by Herod of all the newborn boys in Bethlehem to prevent one of them from becoming the Messiah (Matthew 2:1–18). Macbeth, likewise fearing for his throne, tries to bring about the murders of the men-children Malcolm and Donalbain, and of Banquo's son Fleance. But the crowned child, Malcolm, the Prince of Cumberland, survives and rules. As if to give further support to this victory of the child, the play presents near its close two more brief images of heroic children, both slaughtered, but in a noble cause: Lady Macduff's unfortunate son, who dies trying to protect his mother, and Young Siward, whose father welcomes his death in battle as a "fair death" that makes the son "God's soldier." These are yet more slaughtered innocents, and their deaths can be traced back, in the teleology of unfolding dramatic action, to Lady Macbeth's opening boast that she would have "dashed the brains out" of her nursing infant to fulfill a vow of single-minded ambition.

But if some children die, others survive. One reason Malcolm survives is that he both resembles his father, Duncan, and differs crucially from him. Duncan—Shakespeare's Duncan, if not history's—was innocent and unwary, willing to find the mind's construction in the face. Malcolm will be cagier, more watchful, like Prince Hal in the *Henry IV* plays. In the scene that presents his supposed confession of sins to Macduff (4.3), Malcolm tests his listener, showing a "false face" not to deceive but to adjudicate and to prove. His claims of lechery and avarice are false, but they serve a purpose, showing a young king more capable of perceiving evil than his father was—or, indeed, than is Macduff, whose response to the quick reversals of the scene is surely one of the most bathetic in Shakespeare: "Such welcome and unwelcome things at once / 'Tis hard to reconcile" (4.3.139–140). The scene is crucial for the play, even if its tone is sometimes awkward. Malcolm will be a better king than Duncan, at least according to the ground rules of early modern statecraft.

How does *Macbeth* resolve its central problem of evil and of the nature of ambition? The play presents the audience and reader with not one but two final visions, in a way that we have come to see as characteristic of the playwright. There is a final catastrophe for the tragic hero, and a redemptive and unifying moment for the new King and his court, with audience emotion torn between the options of character and state. Lady Macbeth, tortured by nightmares, follows, ironically, her doctor's advice, and ministers to herself: her death is a suicide, but she has, in a sense, died long before. Indeed, the sleepwalking scene is another version of a "ghost" scene, the restless and tortured spirit vainly seeking repose.

And what of Macbeth? Perhaps significantly, in this remarkable play, Macbeth's final attendant is an officer by the name of Seyton. The editor of the Arden *Macbeth*, Kenneth Muir, gives a quotation from a work of genealogy to establish that the Seytons were hereditary armor bearers to the Kings of Scotland, so that there is "a peculiar fitness in the choice of this name," and then comments, in his own voice, "One critic suggests wildly that Shakespeare intended a quibble on *Satan*."[1] Muir thus is able to equivocate between the tame and the wild, the "peculiar fitness" of "Seyton," and what Muir implies is the arrant unsuitability of "Satan," without naming the critic who had the temerity to make such a proposal. Yet by citing and derogating the temerity of this anonymous critic, he can have things both ways; if the suggestion were really so "wild," he need not have mentioned it at all. And—although I am not his anonymous critic—I find myself very tempted by the "Satan" reading, which re-links the play's last moments with the morality play tradition out of which it clearly comes, and provides, were it to be considered seriously, yet another specter for Macbeth to (mis)interpret. In any case, the calls for Seyton precede and bracket one of the play's great set pieces:

> Macbeth   Seyton!—I am sick at heart
> When I behold—Seyton, I say!—This push
> Will cheer me ever or disseat me now.
> I have lived long enough. My way of life
> Is fall'n into the sere, the yellow leaf,
> And that which should accompany old age,
> As honour, love, obedience, troops of friends,
> I must not look to have but in their stead
> Curses, not loud but deep, mouth-honour, breath,
> Which the poor heart would fain deny and dare not.
> Seyton!

5.3.20–30

Like "Othello's occupation's gone," this is a soldier's lament for the ordinary pleasures of company and fellowship. Life for Macbeth has ceased to hold either sensation or meaning. His wife dies because of too much feeling, he because of too little. And his famous speech on time, "Tomorrow, and tomorrow, and tomorrow," is a rejection of time, a rejection of history and of the learning experience of either life or art:

> Life's but a walking shadow, a poor player
> That struts and frets his hour upon the stage,
> And then is heard no more. It is a tale
> Told by an idiot, full of sound and fury,
> Signifying nothing.
>
> 5.5.23–27

Hamlet had asked Horatio, "in this harsh world draw thy breath in pain / To tell my story." Othello requested that his horrified audience "[s]peak of me as I am." Macbeth alone rejects the tale, and its recuperative powers. For him the image of the world as a stage is not redemptive but a sham and a delusion. We are only actors, and bad actors, who, in Hamlet's phrase, "out-Herod Herod," and the patterns we make on earth are finally meaningless, signifying nothing. "Nothing," that resounding term from *King Lear,* marks the space of the zero and the cipher. Macbeth, whose borrowed robes—his actor's costume—have become "a giant's robe / Upon a dwarfish thief," now sees himself as the miscast victim of a play he never wrote and never understood. His final downward metamorphosis is, fittingly, into a dumb show for others:

> Macduff   We'll have thee as our rarer monsters are,
> Painted upon a pole, and underwrit
> "Here may you see the tyrant."
>
> 5.10.25–27

Yet Macbeth's despairing perception of nihilism in the world around him is, ironically, one thing that shows him to be profoundly human. Like Richard III, he is gallant in his final warlike spirit, doomed and joyous.

The play does not reject this tragic vision of walking shadows and poor players, but rather leaves them with us as a necessary antidote to the smug confidence that all the world's a stage; that acting, disguise, and transformation are saving activities; that theater is a redemptive force. But the play's real recuperation, its real recovery, comes only partly through Macbeth's personal confrontation with mortality and ending, and partly through Malcolm's public assurance of order and continuity. In his final speech, so parallel in its way to Edgar's in *King Lear,* or indeed to Richmond's in *Richard III,* Malcolm regains the Duncan language that has for so long been absent from the play, the language of fer-

tility: "What's more to do / Which would be planted newly with the time."
Time for him is not an ending or a meaningless jumble of syllables, but a new
beginning, a part of redemptive history. Macbeth has been turned imaginatively
into a dumb show, a monster, literally a demonstration or warning, the "show
and gaze o'th' time." That is to say, although his tale may have signified nothing
to him, it signifies volumes to us.

For Malcolm, however, another kind of transformation is also at hand—
a political one. "My thanes and kinsmen," he says. "Henceforth be earls, the
first that ever Scotland / In such an honour named" (5.11.28–30). Henceforth be
earls. There are to be no more thanes, and thus there will be no more destructive cycle, one treasonous Thane of Cawdor replacing another, and so on, ad
infinitum. This is the pattern of cycle, and of an unredeemed history, tomorrow
and tomorrow and tomorrow. But for Malcolm's world, and for that of King
James, cycle is to be replaced by transcendence, by "the grace of Grace." Thanes
become earls. Scotland becomes part of England, as James achieves the union of
Scotland and England with his ascension to the English throne in 1603
(although the union was not formalized until the legislative Act of Union of
1707). The fallen land becomes the land of the holy king who cures and saves.

It is a pleasing and redemptive vision, one that finds its emblematic counterpart in the play in that magic glass, held up in the show of eight kings, reflecting
King James and his descendants to the end of time. And yet the play will not let
us rest with this comforting vision, despite the sense of victory on the battlefield
and in the court. In Roman Polanski's 1971 film, produced in the wake of the
senseless slaughter of Polanski's wife, actress Sharon Tate—then eight months
pregnant—by the Charles Manson gang in 1969, the play ends with a bitter
return to cycle, as Duncan's second son, Donalbain, seeks out the witches and
their prophetic instruction. It is all about to begin again.

At the last, I think, we cannot help but hear again the knocking of the
damned soul at hell's gate. For *Macbeth,* whatever else it is, remains the sublimest and most "modern" of morality plays. And to the redemptive vision of
Malcolm we need continually to oppose the treadmill language of Macbeth—
the speaker like Sisyphus rolling his stone patiently to the top of the hill, only to
have it roll down again, eternally; like Ixion bound to his wheel of fire, revolving
in hell, eternally—the treadmill language of the damned and living soul who is
Macbeth, his life sentence (at once opinion, judgment, utterance, and aphorism) meted out syllable by syllable:

> Tomorrow, and tomorrow, and tomorrow
> Creeps in this petty pace from day to day
> To the last syllable of recorded time,
> And all our yesterdays have lighted fools
> The way to dusty death. . . .

5.5.18–22

Antony and Cleopatra

DRAMATIS PERSONAE

Mark Antony (Marcus Antonius), *triumvir of Rome*

Demetrius, *friend and follower of Antony*

Philo, *friend and follower of Antony*

Domitius Enobarbus, *friend and follower of Antony*

Ventidius, *friend and follower of Antony*

Silius, *friend and follower of Antony*

Eros, *friend and follower of Antony*

Camidius, *friend and follower of Antony*

Scarus, *friend and follower of Antony*

Decretas, *friend and follower of Antony*

Octavius Caesar, *triumvir of Rome*

Octavia, *his sister*

Maecenas, *friend and follower of Caesar*

Agrippa, *friend and follower of Caesar*

Taurus, *friend and follower of Caesar*

Dolabella, *friend and follower of Caesar*

Thidias, *friend and follower of Caesar*

Gallus, *friend and follower of Caesar*

Proculeius, *friend and follower of Caesar*

Lepidus, *triumvir of Rome*

Sextus Pompey (Pompeius)

Menecrates, *friend of Pompey*

Menas, *friend of Pompey*

Varrius, *friend of Pompey*

Cleopatra, *Queen of Egypt*

Charmian, *attending on Cleopatra*

Iras, *attending on Cleopatra*

Alexas, *attending on Cleopatra*

Mardian, *a eunuch, attending on Cleopatra*

Diomed, *attending on Cleopatra*

Seleucus, *attending on Cleopatra*

A Soothsayer

An Ambassador

Messengers

A Boy who sings

A Sentry and men of his Watch

Men of the Guard

An Egyptian

A Clown

Servants

Soldiers

Eunuchs, attendants, captains, soldiers, servants

TWENTY-FIRST-CENTURY scholars have tended to prefer the term "early modern" for the period in which Shakespeare wrote, rather than the earlier label "Renaissance." (Other contenders over the years have included "Tudor/Stuart" and "Elizabethan-Jacobean" or simply "Elizabethan," as in E. K. Chambers's masterwork *The Elizabethan Stage.*) "Early modern" suggests that what is depicted anticipates our present time. "Renaissance," a term borrowed from history and art history and often used to describe fifteenth- and sixteenth-century Italy and Northern Europe rather than seventeenth-century Britain, has variously been seen as historically and geographically inexact, as implying an unfairly "dark" view of the Middle Ages. Yet the sixteenth and seventeenth centuries in England, Scotland, and Wales *were* times of intellectual "rebirth," as literary historians have always recognized. The rediscovery of the classics—often literally rediscovered after years of being "lost"—and a new emphasis on the models provided by earlier moments of civilization and empire led to a focus, in the school curriculum, on Greek and Roman mythology, poetry, and history writing. The curriculum of the Stratford grammar school where Shakespeare studied included Ovid's *Metamorphoses,* William Lily's *Grammatica Latina,* and *Aesop's Fables,* and even some moral philosophy (Cicero) and Roman classics (Sallust).

Ben Jonson's gentle observation in his memorial poem "My Beloved, the Author, Mr. William Shakespeare," affixed to the First Folio, famously alluded to Shakespeare's "small Latin, and less Greek," but all such things are comparative. Shakespeare's knowledge of classical languages was "small" compared to that of Jonson, a self-taught polymath (and the son of a bricklayer). But Shakespeare knew far more Greek and Latin than most readers do today, and he was educated in what we now call "the classics." Queen Elizabeth and King James both knew Latin—Elizabeth once famously harangued an impertinent Polish ambassador, extemporaneously, in that language, observing complacently after the fact that she was glad to have had a chance to use her Latin, which had "long lain rusting." James wrote *Basilicon Doron* and *The True Lawe of Free Monarchies* and presented himself, in iconography and rhetoric, as the inheritor of Roman greatness.

Plutarch's *Parallel Lives of the Noble Grecians and Romans,* newly translated by Sir Thomas North and published in 1579, provided a model—widely utilized in contemporary histories—of example and comparison. Placing ancient rulers and generals side by side, a Greek and a Roman (Theseus with Romulus, Pericles with Fabius, Alcibiades with Coriolanus), Plutarch's *Parallel Lives* suggested a way of reading history that did, indeed, look backward and forward at once. The implication for the eras of Elizabeth and James was clear: England (or, in James's time, Britain) was the third term, the next major Western civilization, and its heroes could and should be seen as the natural inheritors of the patterns discerned by Plutarch. History taught, and it also warned; the stories of yesterday's heroes were models for conduct, statecraft, and martial prowess, but were also lessons about pride, vainglory, and the fleetingness of fame. Plutarch's "Life of Antony" is one of Shakespeare's chief sources here, along with Plutarch's "Of Isis and Osiris" and Virgil's *Aeneid.*

When we approach Shakespeare's magnificent baroque creation *Antony and*

Cleopatra, perhaps the first question that arises is one of genre. Is it a tragedy, the tragedy of Antony, or is it the greatest and most excessive of Shakespeare's history plays? "I and my sword will earn our chronicle" (3.13.178), Antony tells Cleopatra: I will make our place in history through my heroism on the battlefield. But is the play about the end of the old order in Rome, and the coming of the new? Is it about a young, political Octavius Caesar who resembles Prince Hal in his cold calculation? Or is it about Antony and Cleopatra as they appear in the play's last acts, transformed into quasi-mythological beings who transcend time and space? Is this play, that is to say, about Egypt and eternity? Egypt and art? Or about Rome and time? Rome and history? What is the relationship between love and war, and love and order, in *Antony and Cleopatra?*

The question is vital to an audience's experience of the play, and a director's approach to it, although needless to say there is no single answer. How we view the play's values will determine how we view Antony, who stands at its center. Is he a failed hero, or a successful myth? The first act of *Antony and Cleopatra* lays out the conundrum clearly, since it offers a number of views of Antony, all persuasive, and each different from the next. The brief opening scene presents two Roman soldiers discussing what has happened to their general. These are insignificant characters in themselves, and the scene, like so many opening scenes in Shakespeare, gives us what is in fact the common view, the ordinary person's view, of what has recently transpired. And what do the soldiers tell us? That "this dotage of our General's / O'erflows the measure" (1.1.1–2). That Antony "dotes," and that his "dotage"—a word that can mean both infatuation and the foolishness of old age—is related to excess, to overflowing, like that of the Nile, the symbol of Egypt, a river that notoriously overflows its banks. The word "dote" in Shakespeare, as we have had occasion to notice in the romantic comedies, describes a kind of being-in-love-with-love that is usually superseded by a more adult and considered passion. The soldiers note, laughing behind their hands, that this former hero, who once "glowed like plated Mars" in his armor, is now become "the bellows and the fan / To cool a gipsy's lust" (1.1.4, 9). At the outset, then, there is excess and there is paradox. A bellows blows cool air to increase the heat of the fire. And of the fabled "four elements" (earth, water, air, and fire), the last three are Cleopatra's, just as the earth is Antony's. "[Y]ou shall see in him / The triple pillar of the world transformed / Into a strumpet's fool" (1.1.11–13). The jest on "trumpet"/"strumpet," used with ironic effectiveness in *Othello,* is also basic to these soldiers' account of what has happened to their leader. Antony is a has-been, a general who has shirked his duty and abandoned his men, as he himself will shortly acknowledge:

> These strong Egyptian fetters I must break,
> Or lose myself in dotage.
>   *Antony and Cleopatra 1.2.105–106*

This is Caesar's view of Antony as well. Octavius Caesar, fretting in Rome, feels the need of Antony's heroic strength to defeat the threat of Pompey, and offers a heartfelt apostrophe to the absent general: "Antony, / Leave thy lascivious wassails," your drunken and besotted toasts. Once you were a hero, Caesar recalls, and endured famine:

> Thou didst drink
> The stale of horses, and the gilded puddle
> Which beasts would cough at. Thy palate then did deign
> The roughest berry on the rudest hedge.
> Yea, like the stag when snow the pasture sheets,
> The barks of trees thou browsed. On the Alps
> It is reported thou didst eat strange flesh,
> Which some did die to look on; and all this—
> It wounds thine honour that I speak it now—
> Was borne so like a soldier that thy cheek
> So much as lanked not.
>
> *1.4.55–56, 61–71*

Antony is a heroic, historical figure—a man of epic abilities, a representative of the old order of giants, a man who could regain his place in history as a "triple pillar of the world," but who has at the present moment lost himself in dotage, sex, and infatuation. This is the Roman view.

But the view from Egypt is very different, as we should expect. Cleopatra's first description of Antony is deliberately juxtaposed to the view we have just heard espoused by Caesar. In Cleopatra's eyes Antony is not historical, but mythic; not merely heroic, but also Olympian and godlike. She speculates on his whereabouts to one of her ladies, speaking, as is frequently her way, with a frank erotic appreciation:

> O, Charmian,
> Where think'st thou he is now? Stands he or sits he?
> Or does he walk? Or is he on his horse?
> O happy horse, to bear the weight of Antony!
> Do bravely, horse, for wot'st thou whom thou mov'st?—
> The demi-Atlas of this earth, the arm
> And burgonet of men. . . .
>
> *1.5.18–24*

As Antony endorsed the Roman assessment of his behavior, so also he allies himself with the Egyptian account. The first time the audience sees him he rejects, out of hand, the whole Roman Empire and all of politics and nationhood, in favor of timeless love in Egypt:

> Let Rome in Tiber melt, and the wide arch
> Of the ranged empire fall. Here is my space.
> Kingdoms are clay. Our dungy earth alike
> Feeds beast as man. The nobleness of life
> Is to do thus; when such a mutual pair
> And such a twain can do't . . .
>
> *1.1.35–40*

Here is my space. Rome is nothing, and will disappear. Love is everything. "The nobleness of life / Is to do thus." True love *is* excess, and is not to be bounded. (This is a sentiment we heard well expressed by Juliet.) "There's beggary in the love that can be reckoned," says Antony (1.1.15), and when Cleopatra teases him, proposing a target or boundary for his passion—"I'll set a bourn how far to be beloved"—his answer is instant and uncompromising: "Then must thou needs find out new heaven, new earth" (16, 17).

Caesar sees Antony as a figure pointing backward, once glorious, now faded, losing his place in history, and Antony fears that this may be true. Cleopatra sees him as a transcendent being, pointing eternally forward, a kind of metamorphosed deity, and thus a crowning success, and Antony when he is with her shares this view as well. In short, the opening of the play presents Antony in a familiar situation for the Shakespearean tragic hero, a psychomachia or struggle of the soul, between the part of him that is Roman and the part of him that is Egyptian. Rome and Egypt. *The Tragedy of Antony and Cleopatra* is built on a contrast of antithetical places very similar to that of Greece and Troy in *Troilus and Cressida*. (The three love tragedies whose titles link the names of star-crossed lovers, *Romeo and Juliet*, *Troilus and Cressida*, *Antony and Cleopatra*, have a great deal in common thematically: each expands the personal onto a larger stage of history and myth.) Troilus's speech on the "monstruosity in love," which is "that the will is infinite and the execution confined; that the desire is boundless and the act a slave to limit," is a useful gloss and forerunner to this play. Will and desire, infinity and boundlessness are all part of the world of Egypt, while terms like "execution," "confinement," "limitation," and "action" are all associated, to some degree, with the politics of the Roman world.

In the Rome of *Antony and Cleopatra* one Caesar has succeeded another, one Pompey another Pompey. This Rome is a place of time and history, of realpolitik, business, and war. "He was disposed to mirth," says Cleopatra of Antony, "but on the sudden / A Roman thought hath struck him" (1.2.72–73). A "Roman thought" is a serious thought, as well as a thought of Rome. This Rome is governed by a man who embodies all of its virtues and all of its shortcomings, Octavius Caesar, a man who has in the play no personal life, no vices; who does not like to drink wine because it brings out the irrational and emotional side of men. "Our graver business / Frowns at this levity," he observes censoriously in the great and comic drinking scene (2.7.115–116). The Caesar of this play has no visible wife. His loving attentions are centered on that apparently most pure and Roman of affections, the love of a sister, Octavia. Later Octavia will become Antony's wife, in a transaction that has all the romance of a merger between two large corporations, which is essentially what it is. The proxy marriage—not uncommon for royalty in Shakespeare's time—is sealed by a handshake between Antony and Caesar. Octavia is not present, nor is she consulted. And Antony is all business, all policy, when in Rome: "[T]hough I make this marriage for my peace, / I'th' East my pleasure lies" (2.3.37–38).

But if Caesar is tender to his sister, he is ruthless in politics and war. He will arrange, for example, to have those soldiers who have deserted from Antony's forces fight in the front lines of the Roman army, "[t]hat Antony may seem to spend his fury / Upon himself" (4.6.9–10). And at the end of the play he cold-bloodedly tries to deceive Cleopatra into surrendering, because he wants the political benefit of bringing her in triumph back to Rome. Caesar is the spirit of Rome in this play: puritanical, efficient, bloodless. And Octavia, his sister and near-namesake, is the spirit of Roman womanhood. "Octavia is of a holy, cold, and still conversation," says Enobarbus (2.6.120). "Conversation" in this context means disposition, mode or course of life—what a wife for Antony! (It also means "sex," which is even more apropos.) "He married but his occasion here," but "[h]e will to his Egyptian dish again" (127, 123). His "occasion": the marriage is a business opportunity. Enobarbus knows his master, even if his master does not know himself.

The play deliberately contrasts Octavia with Antony's former wife, the heroic Fulvia, an alternative model for the Roman matron, who leads an army into battle ("Fulvia thy wife came first into the field" [1.2.78]) and whose death makes this new marriage possible, even though Antony is still enchanted with Cleopatra. Octavia's mildness and obedience, as we will see, are no match for Cleopatra, nor, indeed, for Antony. She exemplifies the virtue of compromise, but she (like Cressida, and like Blanche of Castile in *King John*) finds that no middle way is possible:

> Husband win, win brother
> Prays and destroys the prayer; no midway
> 'Twixt these extremes at all.
>
> *3.4.18–20*

On the one hand, then, is Rome, and the "holy, cold, and still" Octavia. And on the other, the antithesis of these, the burgeoning land of Egypt and its queen, who is everything Octavia is not. Egypt is a place of enormous, teeming fertility, the contrary of the relatively staid and sexless Octavius and Octavia. Its chief geographical emblem is the fertile Nile:

> The higher Nilus swells
> The more it promises; as it ebbs, the seedsman

> Upon the slime and ooze scatters his grain,
> And shortly comes to harvest.
>
> *2.7.19–22*

Like the river, the Queen teems with life:

> She made great Caesar lay his sword to bed.
> He ploughed her, and she cropped.
>
> *2.2.233–234*

The joke is sexual and biblical: Caesar's sword is made into a ploughshare. The "great Caesar," of course, is not Octavius but Julius. Cleopatra is the mother of Cesarion, by Julius Caesar. She is "the serpent of old Nile," at once wily temptress and genius loci, an Egyptian spirit of place. Repeatedly, Egypt is imaged and established as a place of excess, of boundlessness in desire and will, a place in which night replaces morning, so that, as Enobarbus—that detached and excellent witness—says, "we did sleep day out of countenance, and made the night light with drinking" (2.2.184–185). Egypt is also a place of music, that transforming art of romance, music that in this play, as so often in Shakespeare, breeds melancholy: "music, moody food / Of us that trade in love" (2.5.1–2). In fact, Cleopatra, casting about for recreation when Antony is away, demonstrates at once the nature of Egyptian life and its changeability. First she calls for billiards and shouts, "Let's to billiards," then, "We'll to th' river. There, / My music playing far off" (2.5.3, 10–11). At the river she will fish, or, as she says, "I will betray / Tawny-finned fishes" (11–12), for the betrayal is as much a part of the sport as the angling. These are the entertainments of Egypt: sex, food, appetite, music, drinking, betrayal—and performance. Performances in which Cleopatra and Antony change places and costumes, male and female: "[I] put my tires and mantles on him whilst / I wore his sword Philippan" (2.5.22–23); "tires and mantles" are headdresses and scarves. The sword, with or without Freud, is the sign of male adult prowess, as was clear as well in the image of Caesar "ploughing" Cleopatra with his sword (though we should remember here also the example of the Roman warrior wife Fulvia).

The gender games of Egypt are among Cleopatra's favorites, but so is that game of betrayal. She is willful, contrary, and in every sense provocative. Thus she delights in sending false messages to see how they are received:

> If you find him sad,
> Say I am dancing; if in mirth, report
> That I am sudden sick. Quick, and return.
>
> *1.3.3–5*

As is so often the case in Shakespearean dramatic construction, this apparently negligible foible will come back, later in the play, with far more serious and tragic consequences. For when Cleopatra sends the message that she is dead, she provokes Antony's suicide. But at the beginning of the play her charm is evident, and its politically disastrous effects are not yet brought to the fore. She captivates many in the audience as she captivates Antony. Her own nature is one of antithesis, paradox, opposites, and opposition. (For years I deployed a Shakespeare litmus test in my Harvard lecture course, polling the students as to whether they thought of themselves as Romans or as Egyptians. Not surprisingly, the "Roman" years coincided with relatively conservative upswings in U.S. politics, while the "Egyptian" years were, by and large, liberal.)

Of all the activities typical of Shakespeare's Egypt, though, one of the most striking in the early part of the play is that of fortune-telling. The Soothsayer is an Egyptian. In this Caesar's Rome no such fantasy is tolerated; in Rome the future is told by armies and policy, by Machiavellian manipulation and deception, and by artful shows of strength. In Egypt, by contrast, the future is just another entertainment, another game—a game in the form of a riddle that, like the riddle of the Sphinx, can be misinterpreted. "You shall outlive the lady whom you serve," says the Soothsayer to Charmian and Iras, Cleopatra's ladies (1.2.27). And Charmian says, "O, excellent! I love long life better than figs"(28). Figs are often associated with fecundity and fertility, and sometimes with lust and sex. In "Of Isis and Osiris" Plutarch writes: "The fig leaf is interpreted as drinking and motion and is supposed to represent the male sexual organ"— which, of course, it often covers in statuary. Again, Charmian's casual comment prefigures a more ominous moment late in the play, when the Clown, or rustic, comes to Cleopatra with a poisonous serpent in a basket of figs. The two elements, long life and sexuality, are part of the burgeoning texture of Egypt. But Charmian is wrong to interpret the Soothsayer's message as a harbinger of long life. She will outlive her lady by a few moments only, and her lady, Cleopatra, will die an untimely death.

The Soothsayer will also speak to Antony when both of them come to the hostile climate of Rome. Again his warning is serious, and again it is disregarded:

Antony	Say to me
	Whose fortunes shall rise higher: Caesar's or mine?
Soothsayer	Caesar's. Therefore, O Antony, stay not by his side.
	Thy daemon, that thy spirit which keeps thee, is
	Noble, courageous, high, unmatchable,
	Where Caesar's is not. But near him thy angel
	Becomes afeard, as being o'erpowered. Therefore
	Make space enough between you.

2.3.14–21

Like all quasi-magical or prophetic figures in these plays—the witches in *Macbeth,* for example, or the Fool in *Lear*—the Soothsayer may be understood as existing both as an independent character (he has lines; an actor plays the role) and as an aspect of Antony's conscience and consciousness, here warning him of dangers he partly comprehends but also resists. "Make space enough between you." But when Rome comes to Egypt, when the Egypt and Rome in Antony cannot any longer be disentangled, there is no space. ("[T]hough I make this marriage for my peace, / I'th' East my pleasure lies.")

All the attributes of Egypt are also attributes of its queen: fertility, excess, playing, omens, sex, and appetite. Consider some of the names Cleopatra is given, and gives herself, in the course of the play. She is a "witch," says Antony when he is betrayed by her, but she is also an "enchanting queen." She is Thetis, the mother of that greatest warrior of all, Achilles; she brought him his armor, as Cleopatra buckles Antony into his. She is his "great fairy," a Fairy Queen, powerful and dangerous; she is Isis, the Egyptian goddess of the moon, and earth, and the Nile, and sexual generation, a goddess who appears in mythology always surrounded by snakes. She is Antony's "grave charm," and "thou spell"— both functions of language, as well as of beauty and sexuality—one who bewitches by magic.

The play is full of magic that seems to have Cleopatra as its source, magic that overpowers Antony in Roman eyes, robbing him of his reputation and his name, that most powerful and primitive of all magical properties. "[H]is name, / That magical word of war," Ventidius calls it (3.1.30–31). But increasingly Antony comes to doubt the rightness of names. "I am / Antony yet," he will assert defensively, and "what's her name / Since she was Cleopatra?" (3.13.92–93, 98–99), in a passage behind which we can hear Troilus's cry of despairing unbelief: "This is and is not Cressid." In many parts of the world in the early modern period, as in some places still today, to know someone's real name was to have some measure of control over him or her. Thus the pattern of the losing and finding of names ("This is I, / Hamlet the Dane" [*Hamlet* 5.1.241–242]; "My name is Edgar, and thy father's son" [*Lear* 5.3.164]) often accompanies moments of extreme danger, heroism, and self-realization in Shakespeare's plays. In this play, Antony's quest is to find out what "Antony" means to Rome, to history, and by implication to the generations that will come long after him, including the Shakespearean audience, then and now. Antony is Antony, but the name of Cleopatra, as we have seen, is many names. "[W]rinkled deep in time," she is somehow both ageless and timeless, apparently as beautiful now as when she was "[a] morsel for a monarch"—and that monarch was Julius Caesar, the uncle and adoptive father of Octavius.

Of all the descriptions of Cleopatra in the play, none is so powerful or so justly famous as Enobarbus's compelling picture of her first meeting with Antony "upon the river of Cydnus." In Shakespeare's source, Plutarch's "Life of Antony," there is no direct model for the confidant figure Enobarbus, who fits into the Shakespearean mode of Horatio and Banquo. In Plutarch, we find one Domitius surnamed Aenobarbus, or "red-beard," who accompanied Antony on military campaigns, and another Domitius (without a surname) who deserted him. Shakespeare conflates these two figures and names his character Enobarbus. Of greater importance for the evolution of this dramatic character is the fact that Shakespeare gives to him a speech—the "Cydnus" speech—that in the "Life of Antony" is the words of Plutarch himself. Instead of the omniscient voice of the historian-chronicler, there is the highly critical voice of the loyal soldier skeptical about Cleopatra, cynical about her power over his master, and finally entrapped in the tragedy that overtakes them all. And yet Enobarbus is, albeit unwillingly, dazzled by the spectacle, and by the woman, even as he disapproves of her effect upon Antony. This astonishing passage presents Cleopatra as a paradox of nature and a work of art. It describes an event from the past, a scene that took place, therefore, "offstage," and its lyric potential can be compared to that of the "[s]unshine and rain at once" passage in *King Lear*. This, too, is an "unscene," unseen by the spectators in the theater except in the mind's eye. By contrast, the Cleopatra we see onstage is deliberately "human"—often comic, domestic, playful, sometimes petty and cruel (as she is, for example, with the unfortunate messenger who brings her the news of Antony's marriage). That Cleopatra is flawed, and can be shown to us. But the Cleopatra of legend, the Cleopatra who has ensnared king after king, generation after generation, is a creature of poetry and myth rather than of drama, and so we are offered Enobarbus's admiring and ruefully accepting vision. (Modern readers may have encountered this speech first in its satiric rewriting in *The Waste Land*, by T. S. Eliot.) What is so striking about Enobarbus's speech, though, is its complete lack of irony, despite the speaker's resistance:

Enobarbus	The barge she sat in, like a burnished throne
	Burned on the water. The poop was beaten gold;
	Purple the sails, and so perfumèd that
	The winds were love-sick with them.The oars were silver,
	Which to the tune of flutes kept stroke, and made
	The water which they beat to follow faster,
	As amorous of their strokes. For her own person,
	It beggared all description. She did lie
	In her pavilion—cloth of gold, of tissue—
	O'er-picturing that Venus where we see
	The fancy outwork nature. On each side her
	Stood pretty dimpled boys, like smiling Cupids,
	With divers-coloured fans whose wind did seem
	To glow the delicate cheeks which they did cool,
	And what they undid did.
Agrippa	O, rare for Antony!
Enobarbus	Her gentlewomen, like the Nereides,
	So many mermaids, tended her i'th' eyes,

And made their bends adornings. At the helm
A seeming mermaid steers. The silken tackle
Swell with the touches of those flower-soft hands
That yarely frame the office. From the barge
A strange invisible perfume hits the sense
Of the adjacent wharfs. The city cast
Her people out upon her, and Antony,
Enthroned i'th' market-place, did sit alone,
Whistling to th'air, which but for vacancy
Had gone to gaze on Cleopatra too,
And made a gap in nature.

                                                    2.2.197–224

Cleopatra here is described in her element—or rather, in all her elements: fire, air, earth, and water. As we have noted, Antony's element is that of what the play calls "dungy earth"—so that when he decides later to fight Caesar on the sea rather than the land he is ingloriously defeated, and the land is "ashamed to bear [him]" (3.11.2). Above all, Enobarbus's glittering description is of a natural work of art. Winds lovesick for the purple sails; silver oars whose strokes on the water are sexual, and desired; the fans of the boys, like the bellows mentioned in the opening scene, seeming to heat and cool at once ("what they undid did"). Cleopatra herself is a Venus surrounded by Cupids. Even the air, we are told, wishes to violate its cardinal rule, the rule that "nature abhors a vacuum," so that it, too, may go "to gaze on Cleopatra," herself the ultimate exception to all rules. And yet this object of consummate art is, in the next breath, described by the same Enobarbus in terms of her shortcomings. In fact, her shortcomings are part of the paradox that makes her irresistible:

Enobarbus   I saw her once
        Hop forty paces through the public street,
        And having lost her breath, she spoke and panted,
        That she did make defect perfection,
        And, breathless, pour breath forth.
Maecenas   Now Antony
        Must leave her utterly.
Enobarbus   Never. He will not.
        Age cannot wither her, nor custom stale
        Her infinite variety. Other women cloy
        The appetites they feed, but she makes hungry
        Where most she satisfies. For vilest things
        Become themselves in her, that the holy priests
        Bless her when she is riggish.

                                                    2.2.234–245

She makes hungry where most she satisfies. Cleopatra is more than a woman, she is sexual appetite itself, she is beauty and charm. Even the priests regard her carnal desire as holy. And at the same time, Cleopatra is human weakness, pettiness, and frailty, "hopping" in undignified steps through the public street, panting with loss of breath. Her humanity, like her pettiness and her changeability, somehow increases rather than decreases her astonishing erotic power. She is paradox and contradiction, the incarnation of desire—fire, water, and air, dazzling a man of earth.

Enobarbus praises her as "[o]'er-picturing . . . Venus," and it is worth underscoring this evocation of Venus, since it is central to the iconography of Cleopatra throughout the play. (To "overpicture" is to represent in excess of reality; in Enobarbus's eyes Cleopatra is even more magnificent than the Roman goddess of love and beauty.) The story of Venus and Mars, the love goddess and the war god, is everywhere in *Antony and Cleopatra,* as, indeed, it was in *Othello.* From the opening moments of the play the audience has heard Antony compared to Mars. Philo—a soldier whose name means "love" in Greek—laments the fact that Antony's "goodly eyes, / That o'er the files and musters of the war / Have glowed like plated Mars" (that is, Mars in armor) (1.1.2–4) are now solely bent on Cleopatra. Enobarbus himself makes the comparison: "If Caesar move him" (i.e., provokes him), he says,

> Let Antony look over Caesar's head
> And speak as loud as Mars. . . .
>
> *2.2.4–6*

Cleopatra, outraged at the news of Antony's marriage to Octavia, is torn by her own conflicting feelings, and she describes her lover as what was known in the period as a perspective painting or an anamorphosis (a picture that could be "read" differently from different viewing points, like Holbein's celebrated portrait *The Ambassadors,* whose ornate floor design concealed a skull):

> Let him for ever go—let him not, Charmian;
> Though he be painted one way like a Gorgon,
> The other way's a Mars. . . .
>
> *2.5.116–118*

The story of Mars and Venus, the story of a war god enslaved by a love goddess, was a popular subject for Renaissance painters. Images of Venus or Cupid toying with the discarded armor of Mars, while the god of war sleeps, sated with sexual pleasure, are common in the period. When Antony calls Cleopatra "the armourer of my heart," and has her buckle on his armor for the ill-fated fight with Caesar, in which she will betray him, an early modern audience might well think of this famous scenario of unmanning by love. More specifically, Shakespeare's audiences might also call to mind Helen's unbuckling of Hector in *Troilus and Cressida:* one nonpareil woman buckles, the other unbuckles, but both disarm the heroes they tend.

Associations with Mars and Venus would also "explain" another of the characteristic play activities of the Egyptian world, the exchange of gender roles and adornments. In a way, this is characteristic Egyptian inversion—night for day, love for war, timelessness for time, immortality for mortality—but it is also a behavior in the world of love that is at odds with the usual conventions of war and politics. Thus Caesar's contemptuous account of Antony's life in Egypt includes a glance at what a Roman thinks is "unmanliness":

> [H]e fishes, drinks, and wastes
> The lamps of night in revel; is not more manlike
> Than Cleopatra, nor the queen of Ptolemy
> More womanly than he. . . .
>
> *1.4.4–7*

On the other hand, Cleopatra herself, as we have seen, tenderly remembers such scenes of cross-dressed costume and play:

> Ere the ninth hour, I drunk him to his bed,
> Then put my tires and mantles on him whilst
> I wore his sword Philippan.
>
> *2.5.21–23*

The rough soldier Enobarbus is alarmed by this tendency on Antony's part, this power of Egypt to make the hero effeminate, subjugated to a woman. At the beginning of the play he cautions the ladies in waiting, "Hush, here comes Antony," and Charmian corrects him: "Not he, the Queen" (1.2.68).

It is a telling theatrical moment: from the first, in the formal procession of state, the woman displaces the man. Enobarbus protests against Antony's decision to fight by sea and not by land; he is rightly dubious about Cleopatra's decision to attend the battle, and, indeed, to "appear there like a man" (as it was said, after the fact, that Queen Elizabeth had done at Tilbury at the time of the defeat of the Spanish Armada, costumed like "an androgynous martial maiden"). Enobarbus complains to Cleopatra that rumor says "an eunuch, and your maids / Manage this war," and in fact Antony is increasingly to be found in conversation with Mardian, Cleopatra's attendant eunuch. At one point Mardian speaks wistfully of his own desires, for in Egypt even a eunuch has longings. "Indeed?" says Cleopatra, always alert to erotic possibilities. And Mardian answers,

> Not in deed, madam, for I can do nothing
> But what indeed is honest to be done.

> Yet have I fierce affections, and think
> What Venus did with Mars.
>
> *1.5.15–18*

He hardly has far to look, since Venus and Mars are constantly before him. But Antony is, as we have seen, a Mars whose powers of war are sapped by his enslavement in love, by his ceding of armor, command, and judgment to Cleopatra-Venus. It is to Mardian, late in the play, that Antony will lament angrily,

> O thy vile lady,
> She has robbed me of my sword!
>
> *4.15.22–23*

From such a hero, a line like this, spoken to a eunuch, can hardly fail to carry the obvious sexual implication. Cleopatra has "unmanned" Antony, as Venus unmanned Mars.

But the story of Mars and Venus is only one of the mythological tales and stories suggested by this play, which itself ultimately aspires to the condition of myth. To many in the Renaissance audience the story of Antony's heroism, his capacity to do the impossible, as Caesar so enviously catalogues it—to live on berries and tree bark, to drink from noxious puddles, to do wonders on the field of battle—would have called to mind the exploits of that premier hero Hercules—half man, half god, the son of Jove. And Antony is repeatedly associated with Hercules throughout the play. Cleopatra mockingly calls him a "Herculean Roman" when she teases him about his love for Fulvia. He traces his descent from Alcides, another name for Hercules. One of his loyal soldiers swears by Hercules as Antony rejects his advice to fly by land. And in a mood of self-dramatization Antony complains that Cleopatra is a shirt of Nessus to him. (The shirt of Nessus was given to Hercules' bride by a centaur who desired her. In all innocence, she presented the shirt to Hercules, expecting that it would increase his love for her and inflame his passion, but instead it poisoned him and caused his death.) Most poignantly, the play's spectators become witnesses to a scene (4.3) in which the spirit of Hercules—Antony's tutelary spirit—departs. Much as in the opening moment of *Hamlet,* the scene is set at night, and there are confused soldiers on watch and a rumor of some apparition. A noise of "hautboys" (oboes, from the French words for "high" and "wood") is heard under the stage, and one soldier observes,

> 'Tis the god Hercules, whom Antony loved,
> Now leaves him.
>
> *4.3.13–14*

Hercules was sometimes imagined as a buffoon as well as a hero, because at one point in his "labors" he became enslaved to Omphale, Queen of Lydia, and was forced to dress like a woman and do women's work. Here the analogy is clear: both heroes made captive to powerful Eastern queens, emasculated in the public view. Equally pertinent was the famous "choice of Hercules" between Pleasure and Virtue, understood by Renaissance readers as a lesson in self-determination. Ben Jonson's masque *Pleasure Reconciled to Virtue* (1618) would later bring together the two classical criteria for poetry, that it delight and instruct, but Hercules' choice was to be for the one or the other, and he, unlike his descendant Antony, chose Virtue. For Antony the choice is between Octavia, the "piece of virtue," and Cleopatra, where "[i']th' East my pleasure lies." Finally for him there is no question. Between Rome and Egypt, between the Roman and the Egyptian in himself, he chooses, or acknowledges, Egypt, the world of desire, imagination, and art.

A Jacobean audience for this play would have been mindful both of James I's complicated relations with powerful and seductive regal women—his mother Mary, Queen of Scots; his predecessor, Queen Elizabeth—and also of the strongly held views among many political and religious thinkers of the time that women should not rule over men. (The audience would also have been re-minded that it was really with men that James exercised his Egyptian side.)

The presence of women on the thrones of Europe in the sixteenth and seventeenth centuries had raised concerns among those who thought it was contrary to nature, to God's law, and to political expediency. Scottish religious reformer John Knox's *First Blast of the Trumpet Against the Monstrous Regiment of Women* insisted that scripture and classical history proved that women could not and should not rule. ("I affirm the empire of a woman to be a thing repug-nant to nature," he wrote, citing the view expressed in Aristotle's *Politics* and in other ancient sources that "wheresoever women bear dominion, there the peo-ple must needs be disordered . . . and finally, in the end, they must needs come to confusion and ruin.")[1] In particular, men governed by women reversed the proper order of nature. Tertullian, Augustine, Paul, Jerome, and others are all cited to emphasize the abomination of husbands being ruled by wives. Lest his readers think he is speaking only of married women, Knox insists, with Saint Ambrose, that "from [every] woman, be she married or unmarried, is all authority taken to execute any office that appertains to man."[2]

How does the play invite us to view Antony's choice? Are his soldiers right when they gossip about him at the beginning of the play—is this "dotage," the infatuation of an old soldier for a bewitching siren? What is the nature of the claim he makes when he tells Cleopatra that one tear equals all that is won and lost, when he assures her that one kiss repays him for her treachery, when—as John Dryden would put it when he rewrote and retitled the play in 1678— Antony trades "all for love"? Folly, or heroism? The crux of the play is embodied in this paradox, the essential paradox of Cleopatra's nature.

As we have seen, the play deliberately charts a pattern based upon the four elements of classical and Renaissance lore: earth, water, air, and fire. It moves inexorably away from "dungy earth" toward the quicksilver elements of magic and change:

> By the fire
> That quickens Nilus' slime, I go from hence
> Thy soldier-servant, making peace or war
> As thou affects.

> *1.3.68–71*

This is Antony's pledge to Cleopatra as he leaves for Rome, in the early moments of the play. Later, on the battlefield, he wishes he could include all four elements in his warfare against Caesar:

> Their preparation is today by sea;
> We please them not by land.
> . . . .
> I would they'd fight i'th' fire or i'th' air;
> We'd fight there too. . . .

> *4.11.1–2, 3–4*

But the key to Antony's nature and his struggle is clearly the vision of Cleopatra on the river Cydnus, the woman whom everything becomes, whom air, and water, and fire alike adorn; a woman of contradiction and paradox whom the mortal Antony is constantly seeking to know and to possess. This Cleopatra, who is Antony's Venus, is also his muse, a condition of language as well as of nature and art. This "mutual pair" is also in a way an emblem of metaphor, in the way that they come to define each other. As Cleopatra will say, "[S]ince my lord / Is Antony again, I will be Cleopatra" (3.13.188–189). When in the comic drinking scene Lepidus asks Antony, "What manner o' thing is your crocodile?" (2.7.38), Antony's riddling reply describes not only the symbolic animal of Egypt but the ineffable quality of his love:

> It is shaped, sir, like itself, and it is as broad as it hath breadth. It is just so high as it is, and moves with its own organs. It lives by that which nourisheth it, and the elements once out of it, it transmigrates.

> *2.7.39–42*

The Shakespeare who could write knowingly about "the mournful crocodile" in *Henry VI Part 2* is fully aware of the capacity of this changeable being to seduce and delude.

One of the unusual things about this play is the way in which its amorous stakes are mirrored in the oddness of its structure, its sprawling dramatic shape. It is not usual to find notations in these plays like "act 3, scene 12" or "act 4, scene 14." The act and scene divisions are in the main the contributions of eighteenth-century editors, rather than of Shakespeare or his company, but they are indicative, nonetheless, of changes in location and of the number of times the stage is cleared. The play as a whole is stretched, elongated, until it approximates in size and grandeur the epic and mythic events it contains—events, as we have seen, that span the globe from Rome to Egypt, and encompass the four elements. This is a more demonstrably epic structure than we have encountered before in Shakespeare, and the epic scope is matched by an "epic" content, since among the literary and mythic forebears of Antony and Cleopatra themselves we should also count Aeneas and Dido, the key figures in what was, for Shakespeare's England, the most celebrated epic of them all, Virgil's *Aeneid.*

Aeneas is the legendary hero, the soldier, the man chosen by the gods to found Rome as the successor state to Troy—a Rome that would become the home of "universal peace," the Pax Romana, under his descendant Augustus (Shakespeare's Octavius Caesar). Rome would become, in British lore, the cradle of another great empire and epic civilization, that of Elizabethan and Jacobean England. Aeneas was also, famously, the lover of Dido, Queen of Carthage, and thus another powerful Eastern queen, like Cleopatra (and the Lydian Omphale, who enslaved Hercules). Aeneas's love affair with Dido was stage-managed by his mother, Venus, as a way of providing him safety and succor. Cupid, replacing Aeneas's son Ascanius, won his way into Dido's heart and inflamed her with passion for the Trojan refugee Aeneas.

At a key point in *Antony and Cleopatra* Antony, speaking fondly of a time when he and Cleopatra will wander hand in hand through Elysium, boasts that "Dido and her Aeneas shall want troops, / And all the haunt be ours" (4.15.53–54). Spirits from the underworld will follow them, and desert those earlier, legendary lovers. But Dido and "her" Aeneas may not be together in Elysium, since Aeneas deserted her, and deserted passionate love, to go on to Rome to marry Lavinia and to take up his responsibilities as the founder of the new city. Dido committed suicide on a burning funeral pyre. *"Hic amor, haec patria,"* Aeneas declares, in Virgil's poem: There is my love, there is my country—in Rome. The marriage to Lavinia is a political marriage of convenience, similar to Antony's marriage to Octavia. But for Antony, from the beginning, "Here is my space"—here in Egypt. And the marriage to Octavia is abandoned in favor of Egypt and art, and timelessness, and a legendary love with Cleopatra. So Shakespeare's play presents both epic and anti-epic content, at times deliberately turning away from history and politics toward poetry, romance, fantasy, and desire.

The baseline of historical time, however, is clearly established by Octavius. "The time of universal peace is near," he declares, ". . . the three-nooked world / Shall bear the olive freely" (4.6.5–6). This Caesar is the "Caesar Augustus" of the Christian gospels, and the time of Augustus was also the time when Christ was born in Bethlehem. The play moves toward this anticipation of what Christian

England would have regarded as universal order in history, in time. But these considerations of order, government, and peace are subjugated in the course of the play to the evolution of the two larger-than-life mythic heroes in its title. The play's odd and unusual shape, then, is not only effective but also significant. It is a structural counterpart of the issues and figures it presents, and particular moments, like the raising of Antony to Cleopatra's monument in act 4, have about them a decidedly baroque sensibility, producing a stage picture reminiscent of the glorious twisted figures in Baroque crucifixion and deposition scenes such as those by Caravaggio. The visual image is potentially Christian in its iconography; it is also erotic and sensual. In the monument scene Cleopatra again bears Antony's weight, as she has gloried in doing from the play's earliest moments.

In fact, the use of the stage is effectively made to mirror this split in the play's historical and mythic designs, placing the baroque and eroticized narrative of Antony and Cleopatra against the regularized Renaissance grid of order and symmetry that the play associates with Octavius Caesar. Consider, for example, the use of the double entrance, the two doors located on either side of the rear stage. In *Antony and Cleopatra* these two doors are used to display the two forces in tension with each other, so that we find stage directions like "Enter Pompey at one door, with drum and trumpet; at another, Caesar, Lepidus, and Antony." Or "Enter Agrippa at one door, Enobarbus at another." Caesar's man at one door, Antony's man at the other. The two doors not only show opposition, they also suggest balance. The battle scenes, too, switch from Caesar's camp to Antony's, from one part of the plain to another, and scenes in Rome are intercut with scenes in Egypt. A rhythm of thesis and antithesis is developed, with no synthesis in sight.

Under the leadership of Octavius Caesar, the Roman political world seeks to resist fragmentation, and to impose order: from three parts of the world, to two, to one. In the opening scene Philo had spoken of Antony as the "triple pillar of the world," one of the triumvirs, sharing equal power with Lepidus and Octavius. By the time of act 2, scene 7, the wonderful drinking scene, Lepidus is carried off the stage by a servant, as Enobarbus quips, "There's a strong fellow. . . . A bears the third part of the world" (2.7.83–85). But a triple division is unmanageable, disorderly: "[t]hese three world sharers, these competitors," Menas calls the triumvirs. (The unmanageable three-part division of a world seems to haunt Shakespeare's political plays. It appears signally in *1 Henry IV* and again in *King Lear*.) And so the third part of the world, Lepidus, is done away with, "the poor third is up, till death enlarge his confine" (3.5.10–11). At this point, as Enobarbus points out with customary skepticism,

> [W]orld, thou hast a pair of chops, no more,
> And throw between them all the food thou hast,
> They'll grind the one the other. . . .

3.5.12–14

Octavius and Antony are like a pair of jaws ("chops"), devouring the world between them, and wearing each other down as well.

The play thus narrows to its central split, its central conflict: two doors, two nations, two forces, two philosophies, two generals. Once again the impulses of the rivals are exactly contrary. It is reported to Caesar that Antony has staged a public scene in Egypt, during the course of which, "enthroned" in the marketplace, he gave away portions of his kingdom: Egypt, lower Syria, Cyprus, and Lydia to Cleopatra, other lands to his sons Alexander and Ptolemy. Antony's impulse here, and always, is generosity. We will later see him send, in this same spirit, a box of treasure after the deserting Enobarbus. So Antony gives, Antony disperses, in a gesture as fertile in its own way as the nature of Cleopatra and the overflowing Nile. By contrast, Octavius engrosses up, collects, unifies, and consolidates (as James I would do, and as Prince Hal had done, and Lear, fatally, had not). He wants to make of a dispersed and divided kingdom a single empire with a single ruler: himself. At the end of the play, in his moving lament on the death of Antony, he makes this impulse toward ruthless unity clear once again: "O Antony, / . . . We could not stall together / In the whole world" (5.1.35, 39–40). The world was not large enough to contain them both. This is the view of realpolitik, and thus the literally correct political view in terms of contemporary statecraft. Pragmatically, Rome is better off under Caesar than under Antony. The taxes will be collected; the chariots will run on time.

But at some cost. Efficiency and order—from three parts of the world to two; from two, one—displace passion and generosity. The system displaces the individual. Lepidus tries to reconcile the two forces, Antony and Caesar, and is ridiculed by both sides as a flatterer:

Agrippa	'Tis a noble Lepidus.
Enobarbus	A very fine one. O, how he loves Caesar!
Agrippa	Nay, but how dearly he adores Mark Antony!
. . . .	
Enobarbus	Spake you of Caesar? How, the nonpareil?
Agrippa	O Antony, O thou Arabian bird!

3.2.6–8, 11–12

The whole exchange is drenched in irony, and Lepidus is killed, ground between those two remorseless chops. Octavia in her turn attempts compromise, trying to reconcile her husband and her brother, and she, like so many Shakespearean women before her confronted with this impossible choice, is defeated by it.

Octavius Caesar's political ambition is relentless. Octavius gathers, and Antony disperses. The last half of the play is a continual series of desertions from Antony's camp, as his loyal soldiers reluctantly leave him, one by one, culminating in the agonizing desertion of Enobarbus. As we have already noted, Enobarbus serves for Antony the same dramatic function as Horatio did for

Hamlet, Banquo for Macbeth, and Kent for Lear. All are confidants and advisers, "sane" men rather than madmen, rational realists rather than tragic heroes. Enobarbus deserts from Antony's camp, and in doing so he breaks his own heart. He cannot live in the cold cynicism of Octavius's world.

In one sense, then, there is a real and absolute conflict of philosophies between Rome and Egypt, Octavius and Antony. Their enmity is necessary and unavoidable, and is mirrored in the conflict between the concept of a Renaissance or early modern history play, the play of Rome, and the baroque play of Egypt, which incorporates elements of tragedy, comedy, and romance. And yet it is not sufficient to say that Octavius Caesar is a faceless politician, that the conflict is one of ideology and statecraft, politics and policy. To look at Caesar this way is to disregard a set of highly personal feelings and attitudes that are crucial to the play's design. The competition between Caesar and Antony can as readily be seen in generational terms as in ideological ones—as a battle between youth and age, the old order challenged by the new. This generational debate is one of the most familiar, and most dramatically powerful, in Shakespeare, whether it takes place in the English history plays, in *Romeo and Juliet,* in *Troilus and Cressida,* or in political tragedies like *King Lear* and *Macbeth.* The most passionate rivalry in *Antony and Cleopatra* has its seat in the feelings of Octavius Caesar.

It is important to bear in mind that this is Octavius Caesar, not Julius. The play explicitly posits an older generation of heroes, titans, or giants of the past, from which Octavius is excluded, and of which Antony is the last living representative. Antony is a hero in a world that has grown too efficient to contain and comprehend heroes, a world that has become merely political. Octavius's tone, as he speaks early in the play about Antony's heroic feats as a soldier, and especially his acts of personal deprivation and endurance, is a tone of wonder and disbelief. It is a tone familiar to modern audiences that look back upon the sacrifices and heroism of earlier eras (of pioneers, polar expeditions, the "Greatest Generation"). Antony is a heroic figure who thus closely parallels, in the Shakespearean pantheon of heroes, old-style champions like Hamlet's father, and Hector, and Hotspur, and Tybalt. As with all these figures, his preferred style of combat is "single fight," the one-on-one duel to the death. Hector wishes to fight Achilles in single combat, but is surrounded and ambushed by the Myrmidons; old Hamlet defeated old Fortinbras in single combat before the play *Hamlet* begins; Hotspur confronts Prince Hal face-to-face. So Antony wishes to meet Octavius, but this is not this Caesar's way. In fact, Enobarbus, who frequently speaks aside to himself—and to the audience—much as Edgar did in *King Lear,* is aghast to think that Antony imagines such a confrontation is possible. His tone here is, as so often, both heavily ironic and tinged with sadness:

Enobarbus [*aside*]   Yes, like enough, high-battled Caesar will
                       Unstate his happiness and be staged to th' show

> Against a sworder! . . .
>
> . . . .
>
>   Caesar, thou hast subdued
> His judgement, too.
>
>   *3.13.28–30, 35–36*

"Like enough" is our modern "A likely story!" Even the idea of such a challenge is wholly inappropriate to the world in which Antony and Cleopatra find themselves. For Cleopatra also insists that single combat is the best way. They are like a pair of splendid dinosaurs, who have outlasted the world for which they were made. They have outlasted Julius Caesar, and old Pompey, Gnaeus Pompey. But is this not, in a way, precisely the point? Antony is not a realist in his demand for a "single fight" against Caesar—but is the world, yet, so securely Caesar's? Caesar's own problem is that he is haunted by the past, haunted by a world too great, a canvas too large, for him fully to dominate or comprehend it. He is haunted by the myth of the past. And he is surrounded by its living revenants.

Consider what we know about Cleopatra, her age, her beauty, her charm. Fairly early in the play comes the comic scene with the messenger, in which we see Cleopatra relentlessly quizzing him about Octavia and her defects. Once he realizes that she wants to hear only unflattering reports, he is eager to oblige: Octavia is "[d]ull of tongue, and dwarfish," and she is a widow, not a young virgin. But at this point the messenger goes too far. Seeking to add specificity to this unfavorable account, he volunteers his estimate of her age: "And I do think she's thirty" (3.3.28). Now, in strict historical terms, the Cleopatra of history was twenty-nine years old at the time of these events. But Shakespeare's Cleopatra is a woman of the world, a woman of experience—and, in modern terms, a "diva." Although we hear repeatedly about her past conquests, she never seems to grow any older. She is timeless, but she is not young. As he has done in many other plays when dealing with historical and chronicle material, the playwright artfully alters history to accord with his dramatic purposes. Thus the Cleopatra of this play is "wrinkled deep in time" and a "serpent of old Nile." "Age cannot wither her." She talks about "[m]y salad days, / When I was green in judgement"—when she was in love with Julius Caesar (1.5.72–73). (It is tempting, though unhistorical, to think of her as the original "Caesar salad." Alas, that Caesar was a Mexican restauranteur of the 1920s.) Antony, in an angry mood, condemns her (also in culinary terms) for her past:

> I found you as a morsel cold upon
> Dead Caesar's trencher; nay, you were a fragment
> Of Gnaeus Pompey's, besides what hotter hours
> Unregistered in vulgar fame you have
> Luxuriously picked out.
>
>   *3.13.117–121*

Dead Caesar, and Gnaeus Pompey. These, rather than Octavius, are Antony's near contemporaries. He is a little younger than they, but older by far than their sons, and he belongs to the remarkable world those heroes inhabited. Not only has Antony challenged Octavius to single combat, he has also proposed that the combat take place "at Pharsalia, / Where Caesar fought with Pompey" (3.7.31–32). And this Caesar and Pompey are old Caesar, old Pompey, Julius Caesar and Pompey the Great. The remembered scene is an epic contest between two world-shakers. But the new Caesar and the new Pompey, Octavius Caesar and Sextus Pompeius, are, by contrast, mere politicians, faint echoes of their fathers' grandeur. This is again a familiar pattern to observers of modern politics, where great men's sons often embark upon political careers based upon their famous surnames rather than their innate gifts.

The younger Pompey's anger at Antony is expressed, significantly, in terms of dynastic rather than martial rivalry: "O Antony, / You have my father's house" (2.7.122–123). You live where he lived, you have displaced him—and me. In a way, *Antony and Cleopatra* is, along with *Coriolanus,* the most Oedipal of Shakespeare's plays, full of submerged and smouldering love and resentment, expressed toward Antony, the father figure, the reminder and rebuker of sons. The contest is clearly defined. Young Pompey, and most of all young Caesar, feel not only political rivalry but also sexual jealousy against Antony, who possesses the love of the ageless and timeless Cleopatra, the woman who was mistress to each of their fathers. Time has them all in thrall—except for Cleopatra. She herself seems as desirable as ever.

The play speaks, then, repeatedly about the youth of Caesar and the age of Antony. Antony himself resents the passing of his heyday, and the fact that he can be bested by a boy. As he watches Cleopatra flirt with a mere messenger, as he is compelled to send his sons' schoolmaster—the lowest of emissaries—as his representative to Caesar, he feels a sense of mortality, change, and loss. He is shamed that he must "[t]o the young man send humble treaties" (3.11.62); he declares, "To the boy Caesar send this grizzled head" (3.13.16); and later he cries out in rage, "The witch shall die. / To the young Roman boy she hath sold me" (4.13.47–48). In another mood, exulting after a victory at Alexandria, he preens before Cleopatra:

> My nightingale,
> We have beat them to their beds. What, girl, though grey
> Do something mingle with our younger brown, yet ha' we
> A brain that nourishes our nerves, and can
> Get goal for goal of youth. . . .
>
> *4.9.18–22*

To him in this moment she is, affectionately, a "girl." Antony is already approaching the eternal world beyond ordinary time that will be indisputably his only after death.

And what of Caesar? Caesar in his quiet way is moved by an equally strong passion, angry at being treated like a child:

> He calls me boy, and chides as he had power
> To beat me out of Egypt. My messenger
> He hath whipped with rods, dares me to personal combat,
> Caesar to Antony. Let the old ruffian know
> I have many other ways to die; meantime,
> Laugh at his challenge.
>
> 4.1.1–6

Whipping with rods was a punishment for children. The invitation to personal combat, "Caesar to Antony," calls to mind for the audience, inevitably, that other Caesar, "great Caesar," the lover of Cleopatra.

Sexual and Oedipal jealousy may underlie Caesar's excessive demonstration of pique and insult when Octavia, his sister, returns to him with a small train in attendance. The small train, the audience has learned, is her own idea, since she wrongly believes that she can make peace between Antony and Caesar, her husband and her brother. (Her misplaced optimism here recalls not only the situation of Blanche in *King John,* but also that of Desdemona, disastrously convinced that she can intercede with Othello on behalf of Cassio.) But to Caesar the small retinue is a mortal insult that slights him directly. It is Octavius, not Octavia, who feels ill-used. Consider, too, his zealous concern to satisfy all Cleopatra's desires, to win her from Antony by false promises of honor and consideration, to take her captive and lead her in triumph through the streets of Rome. She will be *his* Cleopatra then, not Julius Caesar's, and not Antony's. The triangular relation of these three, Octavius, Antony, and Cleopatra, is as highly charged as the doomed triad of Othello, Cassio, and Desdemona. It is Antony as much as Cleopatra who occupies Caesar's imagination, Antony whom he wishes to marry to his sister, a sister whose name so closely resembles his own. At the marriage ceremony, as we have seen, it is the brother who stands in for the sister, so that Antony marries her by proxy, but takes the hand of Octavius on the stage. It is Antony who has his father's mistress, and his father's epic greatness, and it is this same Antony who calls him "boy."

Octavius's determination is to humiliate a hero, to bring a legend to its end, since he cannot rival it. Again we might be reminded of the complicated web of love and hatred that bound Iago to Othello. With the death of Antony in the fourth act, it seems as if Octavius may indeed have succeeded. "I am dying, Egypt, dying," Antony declares, and his "dying" here recalls for the audience all those many times when he "died" with her in the double sense so common in these plays, and in the love poetry of the period. Yet in this scene (4.16) Antony dies in a mortal, not an erotic, sense, and he does so as the result of a false message from Cleopatra, the dark outcome of the play's earlier comic scenes with messengers and their messages. Recall that she had used such false messages as a kind of flirtation, a love game ("If you find him sad, / Say I am dancing; if in mirth, report / That I am sudden sick"). But the false message she sends of her own death brings the game to an end, destroys the re-creation of Egypt, and Antony runs to death, as he says, like a bridegroom to his bed:

> Unarm, Eros. The long day's task is done,
> And we must sleep.
>
> *4.15.35–36*

This self-epitaph is remarkably similar to the words that Iras will speak to Cleopatra in act 5: "Finish, good lady. The bright day is done, / And we are for the dark" (5.2.188–189). To Cleopatra the death of Antony is nothing less than the end of the world, for they—these astonishing lovers—are each other's world. As Cleopatra says when he dies in her arms,

> The crown o'th' earth doth melt. My lord!
> O, withered is the garland of the war.
> The soldier's pole is fall'n. Young boys and girls
> Are level now with men. The odds is gone,
> And there is nothing left remarkable
> Beneath the visiting moon.
>
> *4.16.65–70*

"Young boys and girls / Are level now with men." Octavius seems to have won, the "boy" seems to have scored his victory over the "old ruffian." But this is to speak far too soon. For the death of Antony in the fourth act leaves the fifth act entirely to Cleopatra, and the fifth act will become the playing space for transformation, metamorphosis, and myth, a space in which the mortal becomes the immortal.

Dolabella, one of Octavius's soldiers, is sent to guard the Queen. And it is with Dolabella that Cleopatra has a conversation that provides, in effect, the apotheosis for Antony. Notice that this is not a soliloquy, any more than Enobarbus's description of Cleopatra on the Cydnus was a soliloquy. In both cases the great vision of one speaker is interrupted, periodically, by the skeptical interjections of another, and the result is a sharper picture of transformed and transformative greatness. Notice, too, that this conversation begins, once more, by invoking "boys" and "women," conventionally unreliable sources:

Cleopatra	You laugh when boys or women tell their dreams;
	Is't not your trick?
Dolabella	I understand not, madam.
Cleopatra	I dreamt there was an Emperor Antony.

                    O, such another sleep, that I might see
                    But such another man!
Dolabella   If it might please ye—
Cleopatra   His face was as the heav'ns, and therein stuck
                    A sun and moon, which kept their course and lighted
                    The little O o'th' earth.
Dolabella   Most sovereign creature—
Cleopatra   His legs bestrid the ocean; his reared arm
                    Crested the world. His voice was propertied
                    As all the tunèd spheres, and that to friends;
                    But when he meant to quail and shake the orb,
                    He was as rattling thunder. For his bounty,
                    There was no winter in't; an autumn 'twas,
                    That grew the more by reaping. His delights
                    Were dolphin-like; they showed his back above
                    The element they lived in. In his livery
                    Walked crowns and crownets. Realms and islands were
                    As plates dropped from his pocket.
Dolabella   Cleopatra—
Cleopatra   Think you there was, or might be, such a man
                    As this I dreamt of?
Dolabella   Gentle madam, no.
Cleopatra   You lie, up to the hearing of the gods.
                    But if there be, or ever were one such,
                    It's past the size of dreaming. Nature wants stuff
                    To vie strange forms with fancy; yet t'imagine
                    An Antony were nature's piece 'gainst fancy,
                    Condemning shadows quite.

                                              5.2.73–99

In Cleopatra's vision Antony becomes a god, a tutelary spirit. Like a Colossus he bestrides the ocean, like Cleopatra herself he is infinitely fertile, infinitely generous ("For his bounty, / There was no winter in't; an autumn 'twas, / That grew the more by reaping").

"Think you there was, or might be, such a man / As this I dreamt of?" "Gentle madam, no." "No" is the answer of Rome, the answer of realism and politics. But Cleopatra knows better. She knows that the reality of Antony is more remarkable than what the imagination can conceive. Like Cleopatra herself in Enobarbus's description ("O'er-picturing that Venus where we see / The fancy outwork nature"), he puts fantasy ("fancy") at odds with nature. In Cleopatra's vision, Antony is reborn, and he takes his place as a kind of constellation in the sky, a tutelary emblem of love. This is an astonishing lyric moment in the play, the true pendant to Enobarbus's description of the two lovers' first meeting on the Cydnus. Tellingly, as she prepares for her own death, Cleopatra will choose to relive that moment: "I am again for Cydnus / To meet Mark Antony" (5.2.224–225).

And yet in this truly extraordinary play there are more twists and turns to come. For the image of Antony as a natural work of art that defeats all art, as a man who transcends all dreams dreamt by mere boys or women, is closely followed by Cleopatra's own rueful, and doubtless prophetic, vision of what would happen to her if she returned as a captive to Rome. There she would be made a spectacle. There she, and her waiting-women, would be impersonated on a public stage, the pleasant Egyptian art of playacting turned to deadly ridicule in Rome (or in Jacobean England):

> The quick comedians
> Extemporally will stage us, and present
> Our Alexandrian revels. Antony
> Shall be brought drunken forth, and I shall see
> Some squeaking Cleopatra boy my greatness
> I'th' posture of a whore.
>
> *5.2.212–217*

This would be the greatest indignity of all, for Cleopatra, the woman of women, the Venus, the Muse, the Dido, the serpent of old Nile, to be acted on the stage by a boy—a boy like the insolent and ambitious "boy Caesar." A boy Caesar who has, in some sense, wished to play Antony to her Cleopatra, perhaps even Cleopatra to his Antony.

But of course on the Jacobean stage Cleopatra would have been played by a boy. Like Juliet, Cressida, Rosalind, Cordelia, Desdemona, Lady Macbeth, and indeed every female character in Shakespeare who has come to stand in modern literary culture as some essential avatar of womanhood, Cleopatra was originally played by a boy actor, an accomplished stylist of femininity. Shakespeare's company contained no women, and no women were permitted to appear on the public stage. In the first performances of this play, a boy would have played the part of Cleopatra, and spoken, feelingly, her passionate lines about the "squeaking Cleopatra" who would "boy"—and thus, she seems to say, parody or caricature—her "greatness" on the stage in a foreign land. We may recall the love games of Egypt, the carefree and erotic playacting in which Cleopatra exchanged clothing with Antony ("[I] put my tires and mantles on him. . . . / I wore his sword Philippan"). Once again in a major Shakespearean tragedy we have a moment onstage that takes a huge dramaturgical risk, like the leap of Gloucester from Dover "cliff" in *King Lear,* where the actor "fell" not from a height, but from flat ground to flat ground. In this case the risk is, if possible, even more acute. Could we not, as a good Jacobean audience, see through the web of fictions, and say to ourselves, "It *is* a boy"? Would the "boy my greatness" speech not provoke precisely the frame-breaking ridicule that Cleopatra here expressly says she fears?

The magic of the moment is such that—in most productions, at least, unless they are calculated to go against the grain—we never come near such a feeling of theatrical disillusionment. The fictive character of Cleopatra is so strong that she defeats mere "reality," if that is what we should call it—the fact that in Shakespeare's time she was acted by a boy, and that in *any* time the audience is seeing some version of what she predicts they will see in Caesar's Rome: a play that shows Antony a drunk, Cleopatra a whore. Rather, this theatrical moment is a brilliant demonstration of what Cleopatra has just said to Dolabella about Antony, that the reality is greater than what is merely imagined. But here it is the fiction, the legend, the *character* who is "real." Cleopatra is more enduring as a character than any actor or actress who portrays her, and this is her fullest and most conclusive transcendence.

The play now partners this apotheosis with a series of gestures that bring her out of time and into legend:

> I have nothing
> Of woman in me. Now from head to foot
> I am marble-constant. . . .
>
> 5.2.234–236

Cleopatra has not rejected her womanhood, like the Lady Macbeth of "unsex me here." She has instead gone beyond it, become "marble-constant," a steadfast work of art. It is at this point that the Clown enters, with his "pretty worm / Of Nilus," the asp, carried in a basket of figs. As we have already noticed, the basket of figs is a sign of fertility. The snake adds sex and death, and summons the image, for a Judeo-Christian audience, of seduction in Eden. This Clown is a close relation of other sublimely comic and serious Shakespearean low figures, with their unintentionally meaningful malapropisms and clear-eyed acceptance of human foibles: Costard in *Love's Labour's Lost,* the gravedigger (First Clown) in *Hamlet,* the Porter in *Macbeth.* Like them he speaks in unconscious truths, his observations more telling than he knows. Thus he can say of the poisonous snake he delivers to the Queen,

> I would not be the party that should desire you to touch him, for his biting is immortal; those that do die of it do seldom or never recover.
>
> 5.2.240–243

"[H]is biting is immortal." The Clown means "mortal," deadly—but he is righter than he realizes. He brings the worm of Nilus, representative of water, in a basket of figs, the emblem of the earth, to a queen who is now all fire and air, all transmigration and transcendence. Given Cleopatra's consummate erotic nature, the snake is also, of course, a sexual symbol. "Yes, forsooth," the Clown says. "I wish you joy o'th' worm" (5.2.270).

Performance and playing are now for Cleopatra wholly merged with reality:

> Give me my robe. Put on my crown. I have
> Immortal longings in me. . . .
>
> *5.2.271–272*

She arrays herself as she once dressed for her meeting with Antony on the Cydnus, appropriating all symbolic roles at once, actress and goddess, mother, lover, and Muse. Nursing the asp at her breast as she had nursed the children of her fertility, defeating in this perversely expressive gesture of nurture and death the "boy" Octavius, adopted son of her earlier lover, she turns to address the snake as deliverer:

> With thy sharp teeth this knot intrinsicate
> Of life at once untie. . . .
>
> *5.2.295–296*

"Intrinsicate" is both intricate and intrinsic. The man who could untie the Gordian knot was fated, said legend, to rule all of Asia. Alexander trumped the legend by cutting the knot with his sword. But the world that Cleopatra comes to rule, when she unties the knot intrinsicate of life, is even wider and more inclusive than "Asia," than Rome and Egypt, for it is the world of imagination, play, and art.

Yet this is a "history" play, as well as a tragedy. The story it tells is true in chronicle as well as mythic terms, and the play belongs to time as well as to timelessness, to the Plutarchan lesson about rule (and women) as well as to the Shakespearean vision of what fiction can do to mere fact, when deployed with such transgressive mastery. Predictably it is Caesar, the instrument of order, who has the last word in the play—Caesar, who has sent "[t]oo slow a messenger," and who himself arrives too late on the scene. As Caesar contemplates the spectacle of the dead Cleopatra, he comes to perceive that he is viewing the ultimate paradox, the death of a principle of life. Here is his epitaph for the lovers who have eluded him in death as in life:

> No grave upon the earth shall clip in it
> A pair so famous. High events as these
> Strike those that make them, and their story is
> No less in pity than his glory which
> Brought them to be lamented. . . .
>
> *5.2.349–353*

Although it begins as the tragedy of Antony, the play is transformed, by its close, into the tragedy of Antony and Cleopatra, giving equal weight to each of its titanic titular heroes, and blending history and tragedy into a sublime transumptive genre. His glory is history. Their story is legend. Pity, that quintessentially tragic emotion, evoked by catharsis in Aristotle's account, is what is produced here by the "[h]igh events" in the life, love, and death of Antony and Cleopatra. Once again, it is the play, the work of art, that "clips" or clasps them, that is both the grave they transcend and the monument that keeps the legendary lovers alive to the present day. Cleopatra's death manifestly enacts that same sexual pun on "dying" that has been performed, as well as cited, throughout the play ("I am dying, Egypt, dying"; "I wish you joy o'th' worm"). As she stages her own death as a return to the moment that brought the lovers together for the first time—"I am again for Cydnus / To meet Mark Antony"—she defeats death, onstage and offstage, with her "immortal longings." For both Antony and Cleopatra, the play's last acts are a dying into life, a dying into legend. Metaphor—two things becoming one—is their metaphor.

Octavius Caesar's final, moving lines—spoken, as is usual at the close of Shakespearean tragedy, by the political survivor—are at once an attempt at control and an acknowledgment of his limits. As the Roman vanquisher of female power and "effeminizing" passion—passion that inflames a man to love—he has, for the moment, restored a kind of order to both stage and world. As a historical actor, the Augustus Caesar (or Caesar Augustus) of Roman and of Christian history, he has a major role to play. Yet the play that presents him is not, finally, content with history. Octavius is locked in time, in space, and in mortality. But for Cleopatra, the quintessence of paradox, the end is the beginning, the play waits only to begin itself once more, and always, as poetry begins itself again and always. This is as clear to the spectators on the stage as it is to readers and audiences across the centuries:

> [S]he looks like sleep,
> As she would catch another Antony
> In her strong toil of grace.
>
> 5.2.336–338

Significantly, in the second half of the play, Antony's chief attendant, whom he will ask to assist him in running on his sword, is not Enobarbus but a soldier by the name of Eros. The name of the soldier is found in Shakespeare's source in Plutarch, but Plutarch does not comment on its uncanny aptness; Shakespeare takes this apparent happenstance and makes it into a dramatic commentary, having his Antony call on "Eros" repeatedly in the scene in which he urges Eros to help him with his suicide (much as Macbeth, in a similar doubled context, called on his attendant "Seyton"). When Eros, unwilling to kill his master, instead runs on his own sword, Antony learns the lesson from his death, and from the supposed death of Cleopatra that has provoked this high drama:

Thrice nobler than myself,
Thou teachest me, O valiant Eros, what
I should and thou couldst not. My queen and Eros
Have by their brave instruction got upon me
A nobleness in record. But I will be
A bridegroom in my death, and run into't
As to a lover's bed. Come then, and, Eros,
Thy master dies thy scholar. . . .

4.15.95–102

Pericles

DRAMATIS PERSONAE

John Gower, *the Presenter*
Antiochus, *King of Antioch*
His Daughter
Thaliart, *a villain*
Pericles, *Prince of Tyre*
Helicanus, *a grave counsellor of Tyre*
Aeschines, *a grave counsellor of Tyre*
Marina, *Pericles' daughter*
Cleon, *Governor of Tarsus*
Dionyza, *his wife*
Leonine, *a murderer*
King Simonides, *of Pentapolis*
Thaisa, *his daughter*
Three Fishermen, *his subjects*
Five Princes, *suitors of Thaisa*

A Marshal
Lychorida, *Thaisa's nurse*
A ship Master
Cerimon, *a physician of Ephesus*
Philemon, *his servant*
Lysimachus, *Governor of
  Mytilene*
A Bawd
A Pander
Boult, *servant to Bawd and
  Pander*
Diana, *goddess of chastity*
Lords, ladies, pages, messengers,
  sailors, pirates, knights,
  gentlemen

HAKESPEARE'S JACOBEAN rival Ben Jonson had scant respect for *Pericles, Prince of Tyre,* and he resented its enormous popular success. He called it a "mouldy tale," not worth telling—by which he likely meant that it was both archaic and improbable. Jonson, the author of *The Alchemist, Volpone,* and other moral comedies, had little use for fairy tale and romance. And it is very easy to ridicule romance and fairy tale if you have no use for them.

A romance is a story of adventure, often involving a hero who suffers a disaster and then extreme privation, defeating overwhelming odds to emerge triumphant. Such romances were popular in the Greek Hellenistic period and in medieval and early modern Europe. Othello's tale of "scapes i'th' imminent deadly breach," which so enchanted Desdemona, is a good example of the extreme, often baroque shape of the romances of Shakespeare's day. While the label "romance" was not applied categorically to Shakespeare's late plays until the nineteenth century, the genre was a familiar and popular one. Some modern audiences—like some early modern ones—have found these plays deficient in realism, but, as we will see, what they actually do is shift the "real" to a different plane, one more aligned to dream, fantasy, and psychology, while retaining, at the same time, a topical relationship to historical events in Shakespeare's day.

Consider the case of Shakespeare's Pericles: a man who woos a wicked, incestuous princess, solves a riddle, and flees her land—and who just happens to be shipwrecked on the shore of another land, where there is another princess choosing a husband; a man who has no armor to fight in the princess's tournament until there washes up onshore the very suit of armor, now rusted, once given him by his father; a man who is involved in a shipwreck and a storm at sea, and who therefore loses his new wife and parks his infant daughter with a supposedly friendly neighboring king and queen; a man who then neglects to visit his beloved daughter for a period of fourteen years, in the course of which the supposedly friendly king and queen attempt to murder her, and she is stolen away by pirates, sold to a brothel-keeper, and begins to convert the brothel's clientele to chastity. Consider that this same man is finally reunited with both daughter and wife under the most improbable circumstances, including a doctor with miraculous powers and a personal visit, with instructions, from the goddess Diana.

If we consider all this, we will realize that dramatic romance, or, as it was then known, tragicomedy, cannot and ought not be judged exclusively by its realism or its social commentary. Romance speaks about society by speaking about poetry, art, dream, and transcendence—and about the quest of the individual, as human being and as art-maker, for identity and for eternity. In fact, Jacobean audiences loved *Pericles.* It was one of Shakespeare's most popular plays, reprinted no fewer than five times in under thirty years. It was the first of his plays to be revived at the time of the Restoration, when theaters, closed by the Puritan Cromwell, were opened again—and women began for the first time to act upon the public stage. It became popular again in the early twentieth century, when fairy-tale improbabilities caught the public fancy and the play's poetry began to catch the enthusiastic ear of critics; and it is popular again today.

Tragicomedy was an admired dramatic mode in the early years of the seventeenth century, one successfully practiced by Shakespeare's contemporaries, and notably by Francis Beaumont and John Fletcher. Plays of this kind usually combined, as the name implies, elements of tragedy (serious diction, characters of high birth, and desperate events like shipwrecks and wars) and of comedy ("low" characters, bawdy jesting, songs, festivals, and love at first sight). The word "tragicomedy" dates from Roman times, and was first used by the Roman dramatist Plautus, for whom the new genre meant, in part, that "high" characters and "low" ones changed places and swapped dignity for indignity: gods and men, masters and slaves. In Shakespeare's time there was some tension between neoclassical taste, which deplored the mixing of genres, and the emergent popularity of no-holds-barred tragicomedy. (This is another reason why Jonson, a committed classicist, would have found *Pericles* unappealing.) Modern readers of Shakespeare, conditioned by their admiration for his tragedies, with their metaphorical and metaphysical language and the psychological suffering of their heroes, will sometimes criticize *Pericles* as a startling departure from the master's true métier. There have been readers, like Lytton Strachey, who saw these plays as signs of Shakespearean dotage, a falling-off from greatness. But the admirers of the late plays are numerous—many critics have regarded them as the apogee of Shakespeare's achievement—and the case for their evocative poetry and astonishing theatrical brilliance is strong.

It will help, I think, to remember that these are stage plays, designed for performance, and that their elements of spectacle and wonder are—like twenty-first-century "special effects" in films—in themselves appealing to theatrical audiences, however much they lose by being transferred to the medium of print. Indeed, many contemporary visual forms for storytelling, like cartoons and animation, have their analogies with the allegorical style of romance, from Spenser's *Faerie Queene* to dramatic romance. The terms used to describe Shakespeare's late style ("romances," "late plays," "last plays") all postdate his own categories. In the First Folio, compiled by two members of his company after the playwright's death, *The Tempest* and *The Winter's Tale* are listed among the comedies, and *Cymbeline* is among the tragedies. But *Pericles* is not included in the First Folio, and this adds to the complications of its reception. The only text we have for it is a quarto, not regarded as an authorized or very reliable copy, and the literary quality of the text varies considerably from scene to scene.

Theatrical taste, like taste in all the other arts, changes with circumstances, with fashion, and over time, so it should not be surprising to find a preeminent playwright like Shakespeare able to write convincingly in many modes. Again it may be useful to invoke a comparison with film, a medium in which, it is often said, Shakespeare would have excelled had it existed in his time (and for which *Pericles,* with its many exotic changes of scenery, seems to be ideally suited). We accept with equanimity the fact that a twentieth-century director like Steven Spielberg can create both *E.T. the Extraterrestrial* and *Schindler's List,* or that Roman Polanski can make compelling films as apparently different—and also as similar—as *Macbeth, Tess,* and *The Pianist. Pericles* is as "Shakespearean" as *Hamlet* or *Lear,* and indeed, as we will see, it has many correspondences with them. What we need to do is to expand our notion of what "Shakespearean" might mean when we use it to describe a play. And, perhaps, to diminish our notion of what "Shakespearean" means when it is applied, as it often is today, indiscriminately in the public press to denote a "human tragedy."

Readers of Shakespeare's later plays often find it jarring to make the transition from the great tragedies, with their wealth of psychological detail and richness of character. Figures like Hamlet, Macbeth, and Othello seem to invite the audience into the inner workings of their minds, through devices like the soliloquy and through the elaborate deployment of metaphor. And yet *Pericles* also deals with psychological richness and density, as it deals with politics and hierarchy and power, although it does so using a different language and different codes, on the level of cultural fantasy and cultural desire. The romances enact patterns of desire and loss and fear and passion and hatred and ambition, just like the tragedies, but they do so as if they were happening inside our own imaginations, rather than inside the minds of Shakespeare's introspective and ruminative heroes. In my reading of the third act of *King Lear* I suggested that the characters who appear onstage, one by one, are concretizations, or projections, of aspects of Lear's emotional or mental state in the storm. *Macbeth* begins, as we noted, with the vivid image of a civil war like "two spent swimmers that do cling together / And choke their art." In *Antony and Cleopatra,* hearing the music of oboes playing beneath the stage, a soldier observes, " 'Tis the god Hercules, whom Antony loved, / Now leaves him." In *Macbeth* and *Antony and Cleopatra* these remain figures of speech, just as in *Othello* the "green-eyed monster," jealousy, remains a figure of speech: no swimmer, no god Hercules, no monster is listed among the dramatis personae. But in romance, it is as if such figures do come to life upon the stage, not in metaphor but in actuality. This is one reason it is possible to see the dramatic action of each of the last plays as taking the form of a dream: in this case Pericles' dream, or Marina's, in which monsters come to life, and impossible reunions, like wishes, come true.

Of equal concern to editors and readers has been the question of authorship. It seems clear from internal evidence that most of the first two acts of *Pericles* were written by someone else, probably George Wilkins, the author of the novel *The Painfull Aduentures of Pericles, Prince of Tyre,* published a year before the quarto of *Pericles,* and a freelance playwright some of whose plays had been performed by Shakespeare's company, the King's Men. (Wilkins's novel cannot have been the source for the play that we have, since its title page declares it to be "The true History of the Play of *Pericles,* as it was lately presented by the worthy and ancient Poet *Iohn Gower*." The novel, that is, depends for its timeliness on the success of the play, or of a play on the same topic.) As we have noted, plays in this period were often written collaboratively, much as film scripts are today. Nevertheless, *Pericles* contains a number of tropes familiar from the Shakespearean corpus: the idea of the isolated middle world; the conjunction of nature, which exists in and through time, with jewels and art, which are by convention "timeless"; and the great central issue of the family reunion, which is so crucial in the tragedies and romances, and above all the reunion of parent and child (Hamlet and old Hamlet; Cordelia and Lear; Coriolanus and Volumnia; Cymbeline and his lost sons; Leontes, Hermione, and Perdita in *The Winter's Tale*). In *Pericles* we have the reunion of a long-separated husband and wife, Pericles and Thaisa (the kind of event that was formative for one of Shakespeare's earliest plays, *The Comedy of Errors*). But that reunion is, as it were, deliberately subordinated to the reunion of father and daughter, Pericles and Marina. (Shakespeare himself, as we have noted, was the father of two daughters, and much in these late plays seems to be presented from the vantage point of the elder, parental generation, rather than, as in earlier plays, that of the young lovers.) The third, fourth, and fifth sections, or acts, of the play, those generally considered by scholars to be written in whole or in large part by Shakespeare, contain a number of verbal anticipations of phrases and scenes in his other romance plays (*Cymbeline, The Winter's Tale,* and *The Tempest*), as well as echoes of lines from *Macbeth* and *Antony and Cleopatra,* both written at about the same time as *Pericles.* The brothel scenes are surely by Shakespeare, and they resemble moments in *Measure for Measure.*

If Shakespeare took over the play-text of *Pericles* and made it his own, he did so with certain formal limitations or inheritances. He inherited the central Greek romance story of Pericles, or Apollonius of Tyre, a story that had already been told by John Gower (see below); by Chaucer in the introduction to his "Man of Law's Tale"; by Laurence Twine in a novel called *The Patterne of Painfull Adventures,* written at the end of the sixteenth century; by George Wilkins in *The Painfull Aduentures of Pericles, Prince of Tyre,* a novel that plagiarizes whole sections from Twine; and by Sir Philip Sidney. (The "Pyrocles" of Sidney's *Arcadia* can be understood to be Pericles.) And Shakespeare also inherited the figure of Gower, who speaks as Prologue for each section of the play, and who is probably in part responsible for Ben Jonson's dismissal of the play as a "mouldy tale." John Gower (1330?–1408) was a poet who told the story of Pericles in his major work, the *Confessio Amantis.* The prologues spoken by the character of Gower are written in an archaic English—"killen" for "kill," "spoken" for "speak," "eyne" for "eyes"—and in a four-foot rather than a five-foot verse line. Jonson, who famously declared about Spenser's similar archaisms in the *Shepheardes Calender* that "Spenser writ no language," would presumably have had a similar impatience with Shakespeare's Gower. Each new section of *Pericles* begins with this "medieval" poet speaking a "medieval" language in a "medieval" verse form (octosyllabic couplets, the verse form of *Confessio Amantis*). And in the following sections (the quarto was not divided into acts, so the act divisions are perforce provided by modern editors) each begins, as well, with a dumb show, another old-fashioned device, a kind of visual riddle to be deciphered first by Gower onstage and then by the audience offstage. (We might recall that Hamlet's *Mousetrap* play began with a dumb show, which it fell to Hamlet himself to interpret for King Claudius's court.)

Yet the figure of Gower is far from being simply a liability, a relic from an outmoded style of drama. For one thing, his presence and his language stress the archaism of the play as a whole, and this is valuable in naturalizing unlikely events and extreme coincidences. Such coincidences, which are part of the world of romance and fairy tale, are easier to accept if the audience is continually reminded that what it is watching is an old story, an ancient song, a deliberate and self-conscious fiction. So Gower functions as a signal to the spectators that they may suspend their disbelief. The acute unrealism of most of the play is framed by Gower's interpolations, by his reminders that the audience is helping to imagine his story and bring it to life. (It is by the same token no accident that the most jarring moments in *Pericles* are the brothel scenes, which are *too* realistic, given their closely observed language and their bawdy wit, for romance, or for the Gower frame.)

Repeatedly at the end of his prologues Gower reminds us of the inadequacies of *telling*—just as do the prologues in *Henry V.* By stressing the fictionality of the events he is describing, by emphasizing the degree to which they are products of poetic imagination, he brings his audience into the process of creation. In a sense, the play can be understood as having the structure of a dream or a dream vision, one as improbable as that which Pericles calls *his* dream: the reappearance of his lost child. Gower points toward the allegorical structure that lies at the heart of fairy tales, the basic pattern of human life expressed in mythic terms: growing up, leaving one's parents, seeking an identity and a name, temptation and testing in the world, sexual maturity, the begetting of a new generation. Yet even as he conveys the audience to an imaginary land of fairy tale that is also a map of its own desires, Gower insists upon the way *telling* must be replaced by *showing*, lyric and narrative replaced by spectacle and drama:

> And what ensues in this fell storm
> Shall for itself itself perform;
> I nill relate; action may
> Conveniently the rest convey.
> Pericles *10.53–56*

Action, rather than mere words, is necessary, and "[s]hall for itself itself perform." The final rhymes ("may"/"convey"), a traditional verbal sign for ending a scene or clearing the stage, move the play from narrative to performance, and this formal issue becomes a theme within the play proper, as well—as, for example, when Helicanus, the old counselor, is about to explain Pericles' problem to Lysimachus, the governor, in scene 21. "Sit, sir," he says. "I will recount it. / But see, I am prevented" (21.51–52). Prevented, that is, by the arrival of Marina, who will discover Pericles' story for herself in a much more dramatic, even "miraculous" fashion, as she cures him of his melancholy, tells him her name, and, in exchange, learns his name and his story.

There is, then, both value and charm to the Gower frame, even though Shakespeare might not have chosen it, and does not employ it in the other last romances. Not only does the frame-narrator device focus attention on mode (allegorical fairy tale rather than mimetic "realism") and form (showing versus telling), it also offers a kind of unity and control in this peripatetic and picaresque play, "set dispersedly" in various Mediterranean countries. In gleeful defiance of what some humanist theorists understood to be the classical dramatic "unities" (time, place, and action), scenes in *Pericles* take place in Antioch,

Tyre, Tarsus, Pentapolis, Mytilene, and Ephesus, and the events span not a few hours (as in *The Comedy of Errors* or *A Midsummer Night's Dream*), or even a few days or weeks, but rather the enormous period of fourteen years. Why violate the "unity of time" so overtly? Because the structure of Shakespearean dramatic romance demands it, since that structure depends upon the growth and maturation of a second generation, one old enough, by play's end, to marry. As for the third "unity," the "unity of action" specified in Aristotle's *Poetics*—it is, as we have already seen, present in *Pericles* in the extreme. For the actions that make up the play are all repeated. Loss of a parent, loss of a child, shipwreck, privation, suffering, rebirth, and reconciliation: each of the three main characters—Pericles, Thaisa, and Marina—undergoes a version of these events, all to be knit together at the close.

Shakespeare in fact almost always mixes his genres, even from his earliest plays. A typical romance pattern is embedded in *Othello,* in the hero's description of the way he told the story of his adventures to an admiring Desdemona:

> Wherein I spoke of most disastrous chances,
> Of moving accidents by flood and field,
> Of hair-breadth scapes i'th' imminent deadly breach,
> Of being taken by the insolent foe
> And sold to slavery, of my redemption thence,
> And portance in my traveller's history,
> Wherein of antres vast and deserts idle,
> Rough quarries, rocks, and hills whose heads touch heaven,
> It was my hint to speak. Such was my process,
> And of the cannibals that each other eat,
> The Anthropophagi, and men whose heads
> Do grow beneath their shoulders. . . .
>
> *Othello 1.3.133–144*

In *Pericles,* the human is typically mingled with the superhuman, with gods, giants, witches, sorcerers, monsters—figures that populate the imaginative mind of humankind and may stand, upon occasion, for parents, enemies, rivals, and other "blocking figures." Romance is the pattern that underlies both psychology and myth: the quest hero, who stands at its center, who undertakes an adventure to prove himself, and to find his own secret name. This sequence is familiar to us from the story of King Arthur and the knights of the Round Table, from *Parzival,* from *Hamlet,* and from *Coriolanus*—and it is omnipresent in *Pericles.*

In order to find himself, the quester in a romance must ask the proper question, which often presents itself in the form of a riddle, like the Sphinx's riddle. The sign of his success in human terms will be marriage; in political terms, kingship or rule; and in both, fertility: for the family, the birth of a child or children, the provision of an heir; for the land, the coming of spring and harvest after a long period of drought, waste, or winter. Thus romance will often cross over into the terrain of comedy (love, sex, and marriage) as well as history (succession, rule, and plenty). Pericles brings corn—fertility—to the starving and dying land of Tarsus, the kingdom of Cleon and Dionyza, and he also brings to them a version of human fertility in the person of his infant daughter, Marina. But the king and queen of this determined wasteland attempt to kill Marina, to kill the child who emblematizes the springtime and the harvest of the land, and they are themselves killed as a result. In myths the freeing of the land and the self is often visualized as the slaying of a dragon. In Shakespeare the "dragons" tend to be monstrous human beings, naturalized dragons who prevent maturity and fertility: in *Pericles,* the wicked, incestuous Antiochus and the cruel queen Dionyza, both struck by lightning, and the bawds and their customers in the Mytilene brothel, converted to virtue by Marina ("Shall's go hear the vestals sing?" "I am out of the road of rutting for ever" [19.7, 8–9]).

In essence, a romance is a season myth or maturation myth expressed in human terms: as Northrop Frye and others have noted, the hero is linked to spring, to dawn, to fertility, to youth, and to order, while the enemy—the antitype of the hero—is a figure of repression, winter, sterility, darkness, and old age. Often, at least in fairy tales, this antitype is linked to the parental generation, and the story becomes that of a child's (necessary) rebellion against his or her parents, a struggle in the direction of independence, autonomy, and power. The psychology of Carl Jung presumes, in many ways, the cultural ubiquity of such a pattern. The fourteen-year gap at the center of *Pericles,* like the similar gap of sixteen years between acts 3 and 4 of *The Winter's Tale,* thus marks the cycle of events, and the redeeming function of the second generation. The plays of romance are cyclical—they celebrate the recurrence of events: here, the marriage of Pericles to Thaisa, and then, a generation later, the marriage of Marina to Lysimachus. In Shakespearean romance the apparently awkward gap of time allows for the infant to come to maturity.

Romance, myth, ritual, and dream are closely allied to one another, as anthropologists and psychologists have often observed. In *The Interpretation of Dreams* Sigmund Freud outlined a fundamental schema for analysis, based upon his reading of fiction and folktales:

> The Emperor and Empress (or the King and Queen) as a rule really represent the dreamer's parents; and a Prince or Princess represents the dreamer herself or himself. . . . Boxes, cases, chests, cupboards, and ovens represent the uterus, and also hollow objects, ships, and vessels of all kinds. . . . To represent castration symbolically, the dream-work makes use of baldness, hair-cutting, falling out of teeth and decapitation.[1]

If we consider the dramatic events of *Pericles* in relation to the passage just quoted from *The Interpretation of Dreams,* we can see how much of archetypal romance or folktale is built into the play's structure. Fertility and sterility are everywhere in the plot, on the surface (the wasteland theme, the threat of incest, the loss of the king's heir) as well as in the subtext and the details:

- Decapitation. The play opens with a dumb show, the display of severed heads on the walls of Antioch. These are the heads of suitors who failed to answer the incest riddle of King Antiochus and his daughter. For their failure—a failure of knowledge, or a failure of courage—the suitors were decapitated. Instead of marriage, death is their reward.
- Hair-cutting. When Pericles is convinced that his daughter is lost, he allows his hair and beard to grow long, a conventional sign of mourning in many cultures. Pledging that he will cut his hair on Marina's wedding day, he goes unshorn until he is reunited with wife and daughter.
- Boxes, chests, and vessels. Marina is born at sea, on her father's ship; in the same storm her mother, Thaisa, dies, we are told, and her body is placed in a casket, "a chest . . . caulked and bitumed." In this casket of sweet perfumes and spices the supposedly dead Thaisa will be buried, and from it she will be reborn.

It is important to emphasize here that Freud did not go into the consulting room with a checklist; his famous couch was not a Procrustean bed of symptomatology. He derived this catalogue of cultural symbols from his study of the Greek and Roman classics, of mythology, of folklore, and, indeed, of the plays of Shakespeare—and he was then fascinated to see these symbols and symbol clusters reappear in the dreams and fantasies of his patients. The *clusters* of symbols, their repetition and density, not the appearance of one isolated sign, make for significance. Why would these symbols reappear in the dreams of middle-class people in Vienna, Freud's city? Because they, too, were brought up in a culture influenced by these same literary texts and forms. And what relevance can Freud have to Shakespeare, since he lived so long afterward? Freud read Shakespeare with great attention and interest. He wrote about *Macbeth* and *King Lear* and *Richard III* and *The Merchant of Venice* and, most famously, about *Hamlet*. Freud himself is an allegorist and a mythographer, who used Shakespeare's characters as case studies for his observation of what he came to believe was human nature. It is not, that is to say, so much that Shakespeare is "Freudian" as that Freud was a Shakespearean. (Freud's late interest in the Shakespeare Authorship Controversy—he was a belated convert to the Oxford camp—suggests that his notion of the family romance, the child's fantasy that he is not his parents' offspring but the scion of a noble house, could be applied to Freud's own literary and imaginative parentage.)

We could, of course, as well turn to history as to myth for these symbols, since the walls of London were themselves adorned with the severed heads of traitors, and the sea and its storms represented, for sea-walled England, a constant source of danger, and of treasure and prize. What is arguably most effective about the way Shakespeare builds the imagery and action of his plays is the multiplicity of resonances that can be perceived in every line. A historicist reading of *Pericles* would take note of its celebration of the family as a political concept—a concept that glorifies King James and the Stuart royal family, seen as a fertile, "natural" family after the reign of a sterile, "unnatural" Virgin Queen, as the site of authority. The bad family structure of the incestuous Antiochus and his nameless daughter is displaced and replaced through the reunion of the good father and daughter, Pericles and Marina, and the reunion of the good husband and wife, Pericles and Thaisa. When Pericles is reunited with his wife, he also sets up a dynastic inheritance, allowing his daughter Marina and her husband, Lysimachus, to rule in Tyre, while he and Thaisa rule over Pentapolis, Thaisa's dead father's kingdom. (Followers of the Shakespeare biography trail may wish to note that by this time, in 1609, Shakespeare's daughter Susanna had married and had produced a daughter, the playwright's grandchild.) The play is relevant, in part, to the Jacobean court, and the intended political marriages of the King's son Henry (who would die young) and daughter Elizabeth (who would shortly marry), just as the first two acts of the play can be seen to be concerned with one of James's favorite topics, the question of what makes a good ruler. But it is important, I think, to underscore the generic elements of fantasy and archetype in *Pericles*. As always, the historical material enriches our understanding of the play's context and indwelling allegories. But the tone of this play is clearly one of fable and archetype.

The opening scenes of the play offer a series of pairs of fathers and daughters, kings and queens, brief adventures that set the stage for the major conflicts to come. At Antioch Pericles encounters King Antiochus and his nameless daughter (her lack of a name underscoring the need for Marina, later on, to find the meaning of her own name and birth). Following heroic precedent, Pericles successfully interprets the riddle that has stumped other suitors, only to find, to his horror, that the answer is "incest"—an unlawful relation between parent and child. Antiochus treats him with exaggerated courtesy, "glozing," as he says, once he realizes that Pericles knows the answer to the riddle, and Pericles flees for his life, resigning his kingly duties to the old man Helicanus. Pericles is fleeing the anger of Antiochus, but he is also, by the logic of romance, seeking himself. When he approaches Tarsus, the home of Cleon and Dionyza, he brings not conquest, as they fear, but corn to feed the people of their wasted land.

Much of the play's action takes place on the sea, and among the treasures yielded up is the child Marina, whose name means "woman of the sea." Other archetypal romances often turn on the figure of a child born from the water—as in the case of Moses, who is placed in a reed basket and sent off through the bulrushes, adopted by a foster parent (Pharaoh's daughter), and named Moses because, Pharaoh's daughter says, "I drew him forth from the water." Moses will slay his own dragon, in the form of the wicked Pharaoh, and will receive a message on a mountaintop. In Greek mythology the hero Perseus is also put to sea in a casket, and also slays a dragon, the Gorgon Medusa. He rescues a king's daughter, Andromeda, from another dragon (a sea monster) and marries her, and he, too, is brought back to his place of origin by coincidence, and fate, to die. In *The Odyssey* Odysseus is symbolically *re*born from the sea when he comes, naked, to the shore near the island of the Phaeacians, magically conveyed there by a long cord in the form of a goddess's veil.

Marina's birth is the central, and literal, "birth from the sea" in *Pericles,* but it is not the only one. Thaisa, as we have noted, is reborn from her casket after being rescued from the sea, then reborn a second time when she is reunited with Pericles. And Pericles himself seems to undergo a symbolic pattern of birth in scene 5, a scene that begins with his emergence from the water. The stage direction announces, "Enter Pericles wet."

This scene, with its witty, joking, and moralizing fishermen who compare the whales eating little fish to powerful men swallowing the powerless, may remind the audience of other mordant Shakespearean clowns, like the gravedigger in *Hamlet* and the Porter in *Macbeth.* They are particularly close, perhaps, to a Clown soon to appear, the wonderful shepherd's son in *The Winter's Tale.* Pericles' language, when he emerges from the sea, is resoundingly the language of romance, of loss of name and commitment to adventure:

> What I have been, I have forgot to know,
> But what I am, want teaches me to think on:
> A man thronged up with cold. . . .
>
> *5.106–108*

This Lear-like sentiment—"[a] man thronged up with cold"—is one of many phrases that link the suffering of Pericles with that of King Lear. Earlier in the same scene, Pericles cried out at the wind, rain, and thunder to abate:

> Yet cease your ire, you angry stars of heaven!
>
> .   .   .   .
>
> Let it suffice the greatness of your powers
> To have bereft a prince of all his fortunes,
> And, having thrown him from your wat'ry grave,
> Here to have death in peace is all he'll crave.
>
> *5.41, 48–51*

The conventional "wat'ry grave" marks the sea in this scene as womb and tomb, for after the near-death experience in his ill-fated wooing of Antiochus's daughter, Pericles' emergence from the sea is clearly a new beginning. Impressing the fishermen with his humility, his lack of pride (in the face of a sea and storm that treat all men equally regardless of rank), he enlists their aid in the next stage of his quest, the courtship of another king's daughter, Thaisa. He will have a second chance at the same scenario, a chance to apply the lessons he has learned in the initial courtship of what psychoanalysis would call a "bad object." Thaisa, by contrast, will turn out to be the quintessence of the "good object," an ideal as princess, wife, and mother.

Coincidentally—though not surprisingly for the world of romance—the fishermen's nets produce a rusty suit of armor that once belonged to Pericles' father. The logic of romance is often that of psychological generation, in which something thought or imagined becomes "realized" in the plot. Thus in Spenser's *Fairie Queene* a knight who thinks despairing thoughts may encounter a character called Despair, or, when distracted from the nonpareil lady Una, will meet, and be attracted by, her malign near-double, Duessa. In other words, the state of mind of the character can almost magically produce "real" effects in the plot. So it is that Pericles, musing on his situation, in effect wishes his father back into existence:

> To beg of you, kind friends, this coat of worth,
> For it was sometime target to a king.
>
> 5.171–172

In fact, what we have here is the first of the play's father-child reunions. Pericles puts on his father's armor, and becomes a hero like his father—something Hamlet might have done, if the romance elements in *Hamlet* had been further emphasized in the plot. The armor is rusty, a detail that allows Pericles to appear in disguise, as a common man, what the spectators at the tournament will call the "mean knight," the shabby knight. His inside is more valuable than his outside. (But rust also implies disuse; these heroic attributes have lain rusting, and need to be revitalized.) As King Simonides, Thaisa's father, will point out, "Opinion's but a fool, that makes us scan / The outward habit for the inward man" (6.59–60). As with telling and showing, actions here speak louder than appearances. Pericles fights well in this armor, and dances well, too, so he is able to win the hand of Thaisa.

The relationship between Simonides and his daughter Thaisa is everything that the relationship of Antiochus and his daughter is not: filial, lawful, sociable. Here, too, is a contest for a princess's hand, and Pericles will win this one as well. Yet he must undergo a further test. He is still in disguise, his rank unknown. As Antiochus had pretended friendship, and in fact planned to kill him, Simonides does the opposite: he pretends to be stern and to oppose the marriage, while actually welcoming it. Prospero in *The Tempest* will do the same, testing the suitor's ardor, constancy, and faith. The contrast between Antiochus and Simonides is another inside/outside dichotomy, appearances belied by reality.

Significantly, Pericles shows his excellence not only in feats of arms but in the arts. He dances best of all the knights, and he is, as Simonides tells him, "music's master." These are romance traits he will pass on to his daughter Marina, just as Thaisa, described as "a fair day in summer; wondrous fair," will pass on to her daughter the seasonal quality of spring and the primal romance emotion of "wonder."

At the time of the writing of *Pericles* there was a revival at court of the old tradition of the tilt, the encounter between two armed men on horseback, so this medieval tradition had a fresh and fashionable quality onstage, and allowed, as well, a certain element of pageantry and mystery, with the devices, or emblems, of the knights functioning as another kind of riddle. The rusty armor Pericles inherits from his father is also probably related to the "whole armour of God" described by Saint Paul in a famous passage in Ephesians (6:13)—the armor to be assumed by a Christian knight. It represents the faith and virtue of the untried knight about to begin his quest.

What is perhaps most important to note is that these early scenes set forth the raw material for what Shakespeare will make of this fable: a tale of rebirth, transformation, and reconciliation. The relationships between the two fathers and daughters (Antiochus and his daughter; Simonides and Thaisa) are used as foils for the central recognition scene between Pericles and Marina in scene 21. And the trials and sufferings of the romance quest hero Pericles, reborn from the sea, forced to leave his own country, appearing nameless and unknown in Pentapolis to win the love of the chief lady of the land by the strength of his inner qualities—all of these will be repeated, in a language incomparably pure, beautiful, and evocative, in the adventures of Marina, which occupy the last three sections of the play. Marina undergoes the same process as her father: reborn, unknown, making a great marriage by means of her inner qualities. The quest hero becomes a quest heroine, born in a tempest and at sea, and given over to the care of a false parent, a stepmother (Dionyza) who seeks her death.

As in all romances, Marina has an innocent childhood that resembles a prefallen state. We first see her strewing spring flowers from a basket onto the grave of her nurse Lychorida. And yet she, too, inhabits Pericles' storm:

> Ay me, poor maid,
> Born in a tempest when my mother died,
> This world to me is but a ceaseless storm
> Whirring me from my friends.
>
> *15.69–72*

Marina is at the start too trusting, falling first into the hands of the hired murderer Leonine (his name, which means "lionlike," establishes him as a stock romance monster-man) and then into the hands of pirates. Both threats thus come from liminal beings, who occupy boundary places between human and animal, sea and land, lawful and lawless.

Marina's exemplary purity and eloquence are such that she is not ravished by

the pirates, and though she winds up in a brothel she not only remains chaste
but, as we have noted, begins to convert the customers to the path of virtue.
Before long she is giving lessons in the town—"I can sing, weave, sew and
dance," she tells her captors' servant. As Gower reports in scene 20, the prologue to scene 21, she is a paragon, an almost supernatural woman, with an air
of the domestic, who is the counterpart of the heroic knight of romance:

> She sings like one immortal, and she dances
> As goddess-like to her admirèd lays.
> Deep clerks she dumbs, and with her nee'le composes
> Nature's own shape, of bud, bird, branch, or berry,
> That e'en her art sisters the natural roses.

> *20.3–7*

Like Hermia and Helena in *A Midsummer Night's Dream*, Marina is a creator
whose arts rival those of Nature. Fittingly, the final stage in the fulfillment of
her romantic quest will be the retelling of her own tale to the unknown figure
who is discovered to be her father, Pericles. The tale retold is the romantic
quester's final task, like—once again—the task of a knight of the Round Table.
Marina stands at this play's imaginative center, as the doer of magical deeds, the
performer of resurrections, bringing both father and mother back to life—like
the spring and the sea, with which she is linked by name and spirit.

As we have already had occasion to note, one of the kinds of "sources" at
work in *Pericles* is the set of Shakespearean plays and characters that preceded it.
The romances often seem to cite earlier plays, and Pericles, a character legendary for his suffering and forbearance, is especially close to King Lear. Like
Lear, for example, Pericles is plagued throughout the play with the need for
patience. "Patience, good sir, do not assist the storm," cautions Lychorida, the
nurse, pleading with him, in the midst of tempest and shipwreck, not to weep
out his grief. Just in this way Lear cried out, "You think I'll weep. / No, I'll
not weep," as the storm wept for him. But the storm in *Pericles* is as much a
ritual event as it is a psychological one; it marks a passage, and it will later be
internalized in Marina's image of her life as a "ceaseless storm / Whirring
me from my friends." For it is Marina's birth that comes out of the storm, as
Lychorida enters with an infant in her arms, and tells the weeping Pericles,
"Here is a thing too young for such a place, / . . . Take in your arms this piece /
Of your dead queen" (11.15, 17–18). A *thing* too young for such a place. This
piece of your dead queen. This is a kind of expression that gestures toward
symbolism rather than psychology, a language allied to ritual, to magic spell, to
epiphany, to miracle, and to incantation. And Pericles' farewell to Thaisa approaches pure lyricism; his descriptions are poetic but not metaphorical. Signally, in this picture of the world undersea, although there is sadness, there is no
visceral horror of death:

> A terrible childbed hast thou had, my dear,
> No light, no fire. Th'unfriendly elements
> Forgot thee utterly; nor have I time
> To give thee hallowed to thy grave, but straight
> Must cast thee, scarcely coffined, in the ooze,
> Where, for a monument upon thy bones
> And aye-remaining lamps, the belching whale
> And humming water must o'erwhelm thy corpse,
> Lying with simple shells. . . .
>
> *11.55–63*

"Ooze" is a word that recurs only in the late romances, and in *Antony and Cleopatra* and *Coriolanus*. It is a word John Keats would pick up from Shakespeare, and use, notably, in the ode "To Autumn." (Herman Melville, likewise, would use it tellingly in *Billy Budd.*) Pericles' vision of Thaisa's resting place is surprisingly lively—the "belching whale," the "humming water"—and pure. This same concatenation of peaceful images will recur in *The Tempest* in Ariel's song to Ferdinand about Ferdinand's supposedly dead father ("Those are pearls that were his eyes"). We might compare the vivid fear of mortality in the under-sea scenario of "Clarence's dream" in an early play like *Richard III*—and note that in both *Pericles* and *The Tempest* the mourned and beloved person beneath the waves is, in fact, not dead. Indeed Thaisa, buried among jewels, herself a jewel, is already on her way to revival and resurrection. She will wash ashore at Ephesus (where it was thought that Mary went to live after Christ's resurrection, and where the legendary "Seven Sleepers" fell asleep in a cave and awakened, years later, to find that the Roman Empire had become Christian).

Saint Paul wrote of the Ephesians that they "used curious arts" (Acts of the Apostles 19:19), or magic, so Shakespeare's audience would not have been surprised to find at Ephesus just such a natural magician, the doctor Cerimon, who will preside over the reawakening of Thaisa. Cerimon may be seen as a figure poised between the physicians of *Macbeth* and *King Lear,* who knew that to cure the body you also had to cure the mind and soul, and the more perfected and magical figure of Prospero in *The Tempest.* He calls first for music, which accompanies all romance transformations and rebirths in Shakespeare, including that of King Lear: "The music there! I pray you give her air" (12.88–89). And then:

> Gentlemen,
> This queen will live. Nature awakes, a warmth
> Breathes out of her. She hath not been entranced
> Above five hours. See how she 'gins to blow
> Into life's flow'r again.
> . . . .

> She is alive. Behold,
> Her eyelids, cases to those heav'nly jewels
> Which Pericles hath lost,
> Begin to part their fringes of bright gold.
> The diamonds of a most praisèd water
> Doth appear to make the world twice rich. —Live,
> And make us weep to hear your fate, fair creature,
> Rare as you seem to be.
> > *She moves*

> > 12.89–93, 95–102

Thaisa is brought to life. What transpires in this passage is characteristic of the romances at their purest and best. Thaisa is a flower, but also a jewel and a work of art ("fringes of bright gold"; "diamonds of a most praisèd water"). The image of the jewel links husband, wife, and child, as Pericles emerges from the water rejoicing that "spite of all the rapture of the sea / This jewel holds his building on my arm" (5.188–189). Marina's chastity is described as a jewel, Pericles is compared as "diamond to glass." In this central scene of the awakening of Thaisa, the natural and mutable are transformed into the precious and immutable. And the words that accompany this ceremony (conducted by a healer called Cerimon) are themselves the key words of romance:

> The heavens
> Through you increase our wonder, and set up
> Your fame for ever.
>
> .   .   .   .   .   .
> Is not this strange?
> > Most rare.

> > 12.93–95, 104

"[R]are," "strange," "wonder." Modern life has dulled the difference among these superlatives of emotion, rendering "wonderful," "marvelous," "terrific," "fantastic," "fabulous," "spectacular," and the now-conventional "awesome" as tame and indistinguishable terms. But they once carried quite specific, and quite different, associations: "marvelous"—having to do with the prodigious, the supernatural, the unbelievable; "fantastic"—unreal, imaginary; "fabulous"—fabled, fictive; "terrific"—causing terror, dreadful, frightful; and "wonderful"—producing wonder, amazement, and astonishment. Wonder is the emotion that greets a marvel or a prodigy. It was the chief object of the Jacobean court masque, intended to produce a spectacle so imposing that it would generate a kind of catharsis of the imagination—a recognition not of human suffering, but of superhuman possibility and beauty. Wonder in this sense is what is felt and expressed in all the key scenes of *Pericles*.

Thaisa, awakening, speaks in a language we are beginning to recognize as the idiom of romance:

> O dear Diana,
> Where am I? Where's my lord? What world is this?
>
> *12.102–103*

These lines, at once question and declaration, offer both a description of the paradoxes of romance and an acceptance of them. Questions in these last plays play a crucially important role, akin to that of riddles, conundrums, and prophecies. And here indeed we can see what Shakespeare as playwright and craftsman has done with that unpromising, rather tedious, but dangerous riddle with which the play of *Pericles* began:

> He's father, son, and husband mild;
> I mother, wife, and yet his child.
>
> *1.111–112*

Pericles solved the riddle, and although we may not find it particularly difficult to do so, all those severed heads of failed suitors remind us that, by comparison, he is a good analyst and a good quester. But by the midpoint of the play the riddle of Antiochus has become the harbinger of riddles far more taxing—Thaisa's "Where am I? Where's my lord? What world is this?" and, very soon, Pericles' own version of this quester's question, addressed to his unknown daughter:

> Pericles   [W]hat countrywoman?
>   Here of these shores?
> Marina   No, nor of any shores,
>   Yet I was mortally brought forth, and am
>   No other than I seem.
>
> *21.90–93*

She is human, not supernatural, she assures him. We might be reminded of the riddles in *Macbeth* that seem likewise contrary to nature, the man not born of woman and the moving grove. Or of the riddle represented by Mariana in *Measure for Measure*, "neither maid, widow, nor wife." The impossible must be possible, if one can only find one's way to the truth.

In the center of the play we suddenly find Pericles and Thaisa each inhabiting a wasteland: bereft of wife or husband, bereft of child. Each performs an act of self-abnegation. Thaisa, like the Abbess in the early *Comedy of Errors*, elects a religious life and becomes a priestess of Diana, the goddess of chastity. Pericles goes into mourning, refusing to cut his hair or beard, and refusing, as well, to say a word. "He will not speak," says Helicanus. He is "[a] man who for this three months hath not spoken / To anyone" (21.26, 18–19). From what we have seen about the choice of silence in other plays, it is clear that by this refusal Pericles is turning away from life toward a kind of imitative and emblematic death. The man who brought corn and fertility to Tarsus is now himself an infertile king, a sick king in a wasteland, lost in melancholy. In fact, even Marina, the creative spirit who will cure these ills, finds herself temporarily locked into a corrupt and fallen world of brothels, panders, and bawds.

The seasonal energies that animate all of the romances are very close to the surface here. For the pattern that emerges is a familiar mythic story, the classical tale of Ceres and Proserpina, the myth of the lost daughter and the lost harvest. Proserpina, or Persephone, was the daughter of Ceres, or Demeter, the goddess of corn, grain, and harvest. She was stolen away one day by Pluto, god of the underworld, who took her to make her his queen. And Ceres mourned the loss of her daughter, and the crops failed, so that winter came to the land, until Jupiter, king of the gods, promised that he would restore Proserpina to her mother—provided that she had not eaten anything in the underworld. But Proserpina had eaten a few pomegranate seeds, and so for four months of the year—as many months as seeds—she was forced to return to Pluto's kingdom beneath the earth, and her mother mourned. When Proserpina returned each year, so did spring, and then summer and harvest. The story is thus one of life, death, and rebirth, and also of original sin, like the story of Adam and Eve in Eden, where eating forbidden fruit likewise causes a fall.

In *Pericles,* as in *The Winter's Tale,* the Proserpina myth is presented in a very straightforward, poetic, dramatic form. The audience's first sight of Marina as a grown woman comes as she is strewing flowers on her nurse's grave:

> I will rob Tellus of her weed
> To strew thy grave with flow'rs. The yellows, blues,
> The purple violets and marigolds
> Shall as a carpet hang upon thy tomb
> While summer days doth last. . . .
>
> *15.65–69*

In the midst of this pious act she is set upon by the murderer Leonine, and is saved from death only by a band of pirates who bear her off to a more metaphorical hell in the brothel. It is not until Marina is returned to her mother at the play's close that Pericles consents to cut his hair and beard, and that Thaisa relinquishes her chaste priesthood for a return to marriage.

It is in this context that we are presented with the most spellbinding scene in a play full of transfixing moments, the recognition scene between Pericles and Marina: the mourning, wasted father and the virtuous daughter whose art "sisters the natural roses," whose songs are immortal, who dances like a goddess. In a play full of resonances with *Lear,* there is a clear analogy with the reunion scene between King Lear and Cordelia. Music surrounds and invests the restoration of parent to child, child to parent. The recognition is focused upon a riddle, and this riddle, too, will be an "incest" riddle of sorts, marking a fruitful yet lawful relation between father and daughter. Almost immediately Pericles begins to speak to this unknown young woman in metaphors of childbirth. The image he chooses, like James I's famous self-description as a "loving nourishfather," makes the King of Tyre both mother and father at once:

> I am great with woe, and shall deliver weeping.
> My dearest wife was like this maid, and such
> My daughter might have been. My queen's square brows,
> Her stature to an inch, as wand-like straight,
> As silver-voiced, her eyes as jewel-like,
> And cased as richly, in pace another Juno,
> Who starves the ears she feeds, and makes them hungry
> The more she gives them speech. . . .

> *21.94–101*

The echo of Enobarbus's praise of Cleopatra ("she makes hungry / Where most she satisfies" [*Antony and Cleopatra* 2.2.242–243]) purges that phrase of its manifest erotic content, transforming the hunger into a desire for words and song.

Pericles has already half guessed the answer to the riddle of the young woman's birth ("Here of these shores?" "No, nor of any shores" [21.91]). She is the daughter of his wife, and born at sea. The language of jewel and case recalls his lamentation over the supposedly dead body of Thaisa, now figuratively reborn in this young woman (and perhaps mirrored in the casting, if the same boy player performed the roles of the young Thaisa and the adult Marina). The recognition is not fulfilled in a flash, but rather takes its time, moving from revelation to revelation, and in this way approaches the very form of dream and waking, again like the awakening of Lear and his recognition of Cordelia: gradual, puzzling, hard to believe, and finally, true. Throughout the scene Pericles remains the questioner, and each question elicits a fragment of the truth— a truth the audience already knows, but whose effect on Pericles is all-important to the pattern of the play:

Pericles　　　　　　　　　　What were thy friends?
　　　　　　How lost thou them? Thy name, my most kind virgin?

　　　　　　．　．　．　．　．　．　．　．

Marina　　My name, sir, is Marina.

　　　　．　．　．　．　．　．　．

Pericles　　　　　　　　　How, a king's daughter,
　　　　　　And called Marina?

. . . . . .

                    But are you flesh and blood?
              Have you a working pulse and are no fairy?
              Motion as well? Speak on. Where were you born,
              And wherefore called Marina?
Marina   Called Marina
              For I was born at sea.

                                   21.127–128, 130, 137–138, 140–144

As the questions and answers mount—"Where were you bred?"; "How came you in these parts?"; "At sea? What mother?"—Pericles, yet again like Lear, feels his joy so great that he needs to check to see that he is awake, and alive. "Give me a gash, put me to present pain," he says to Helicanus, "Lest this great sea of joys rushing upon me / O'erbear the shores of my mortality / And drown me with their sweetness!" (21.178–181). It is now his turn to propound a riddle, Marina's turn to try to answer it. And his riddle is, again and most explicitly, an "incest" riddle:

              Thou that begett'st him that did thee beget . . .
                                   21.182

This famous riddling pronouncement, one of the play's most vivid phrases, explicitly rewrites the Antiochan riddle with which *Pericles* began, purging it of sin and crime, rendering the connection between father and daughter allegorical and poetic rather than carnal. In his famous dedication to the sonnets, Shakespeare called his patron "the onlie begetter" of the poems his book contained. It is perhaps fitting that Pericles in this great recognition scene should speak, similarly, of Marina, the play's muse, singer, and poet, in such similar terms. And viewed from the point of view of metatext, the play's relation to its sources, "Thou that begett'st him that did thee beget" is also a powerful description of the literary engagement of Renaissance writers with the classical past, and the way in which that past is reproduced in new, romance forms.

Marina now takes the role of quester and questioner: "First, sir, I pray, / What is your title?" Pericles: "I am Pericles / Of Tyre. But tell me now my drowned queen's name." With the familiar Shakespearean gesture of child kneeling to parent, Marina kneels to her father and completes the last part of the catechism, the last part of her quest:

                        Is it no more
              To be your daughter than to say my mother's name?
              Thaisa was my mother, who did end
              The minute I began.

                                   21.195–198

The recognition is complete, the reunion and the ritual finished, and Pericles, yet again like Lear, calls for fresh garments, the lineaments of rebirth. To the sound of heavenly music, we are in effect confronted with a dream within a dream, the epiphany of Diana come to earth, onstage, to send husband and child to Ephesus.

To modern audiences this device may offer delight or consternation. Diana is a dea ex machina, a goddess "from the machine," dropping from the sky. (The Shakespearean stage, borrowing this technology from the popular court masques, would have used a contrivance rather like a winch.) In function, the wonderful figure of Diana merely replaces the more humdrum device of the messenger with a letter, or the omen or portent deciphered by a seer. Here, too, there are opportunities for creative doubling of parts, since Thaisa is a priestess of Diana, and may be imagined as coming herself to fetch her family home. The descended god is never wholly at home in Shakespearean drama, which always takes as its model the human rather than the superhuman. But the Diana episode is both moving and appropriate, and it takes the action where it needs to go—to Ephesus, the place of magic and rebirth.

It is a risky proposition to build *two* recognition scenes into the denouement of a dramatic romance. In the later plays Shakespeare will manage this tricky double epiphany in a variety of ways, including moving one of the scenes offstage. But in *Pericles* both scenes are staged. Astonishingly, the second one—the reunion of husband and wife, Pericles and Thaisa—does not come off as an anticlimax. This scene is, designedly, much briefer, the recognition more abrupt. Pericles speaks once, Thaisa swoons, and Cerimon tells her story. But there falls to Thaisa, as if in recompense for this condensed account, the play's final and perhaps most glorious riddle, a single line so full of mythic expressiveness that it seems to sum up the entirety of the foregoing action:

> O my lord [says Thaisa, waking],
> Are you not Pericles? Like him you spake,
> Like him you are. Did you not name a tempest,
> A birth and death?
>
> *22.51–54*

The simplicity and evocativeness of this bare but eloquent formula are difficult to describe. It is the whole plot of the play. Even more, it is the whole pattern and myth of romance. The evenhanded phrase—"[a] birth and death"— reemphasizes the natural cycle, and leads, as if inevitably, to Pericles' joyful invitation:

> O come, be buried
> A second time within these arms.
>
> *22.65–66*

There is no fear of death here, and in fact there has never really been a fear of death in *Pericles*. Instead this limpidly beautiful play offers metamorphosis, self-discovery, and discovery of the human bond:

> Take in your arms
> This piece of your dead queen.
>
> *11.17–18*

> O come, be buried
> A second time within these arms.
>
> *22.65–66*

> Did you not name a tempest,
> A birth and death?
>
> *22.53–54*

The greatest discovery here is perhaps the place of the human being—humankind—within the cycle even as he or she (Pericles, Thaisa, Marina) transcends it. Cycle and permanence, flower and jewel mark the consonance of time and timelessness in these evocative poetic plays. It has always seemed to me fitting that T. S. Eliot, the poet of *The Waste Land,* should have chosen to write a poem on this play, and to call it "Marina"—a poem that is, so powerfully, *all* riddle, *all* question:

> What seas what shores what grey rocks and what islands
> What water lapping the bow
> And scent of pine and the woodthrush singing through the fog
> What images return
> O my daughter.
>
> . . . . .
>
> By this grace dissolved in place
>
> . . . .
>
> This form, this face, this life
> Living to live in a world of time beyond me; let me
> Resign my life for this life, my speech for that unspoken,
> The awakened, lips parted, the hope, the new ships.
>
> What seas what shores what granite islands towards my timbers
> And woodthrush calling through the fog
> My daughter.
>
> *T. S. Eliot, "Marina"*

Coriolanus

Caius Martius, *later surnamed Coriolanus, patrician of Rome*

Menenius Agrippa, *patrician of Rome*

Titus Lartius, *patrician of Rome, a general*

Cominius, *patrician of Rome, a general*

Volumnia, *Coriolanus's mother*

Virgilia, *his wife*

Young Martius, *his son*

Valeria, *a chaste lady of Rome*

Sicinius Velutus, *a tribune of the Roman people*

Junius Brutus, *a tribune of the Roman people*

Citizens of Rome

Soldiers in the Roman army

Tullus Aufidius, *general of the Volscian army*

His Lieutenant

His Servingmen

Conspirators with Aufidius

Volscian Lords

Volscian Citizens

Soldiers in the Volscian army

Adrian, *a Volscian*

Nicanor, *a Roman*

A Roman Herald

Messengers

Aediles

A gentlewoman, an usher, Roman and Volscian senators and nobles, captains in the Roman army, officers, lictors

THE RHYTHM of the university calendar has more than once required that class lectures on *Coriolanus* coincide with Election Day in the United States. Since the play reads today as, among many other things, a brilliant primer on the grooming of a candidate for high public office—complete with handlers, coaches, strategists, and the stage mother to end all stage mothers, the magnificent Volumnia—this timing has permitted some lively discussions on the uncanny modernity of Shakespeare's play. Whenever we speak of Shakespeare as anticipating issues and character types in the eras that came after him, we should remind ourselves that the plays, and the high regard for Shakespeare in the centuries following his death, have *created* these "modern" types as much as they have paralleled or predicted them. Thus, for example, when a political columnist in a major newspaper, describing a war hero entering politics, writes of "the Coriolanus role-shift problem" (peremptory orders may "sound crisp in a busy commander" but "unduly imperious in a candidate for office in a democracy"),[1] he is describing both the way a general resembles a Shakespearean hero and the way Shakespeare has shaped our ideas of military and cultural heroism.

The play is set in the early years of Rome, and a modern audience will experience *The Tragedy of Coriolanus* with the triple perspective it has learned to expect from Shakespeare's account of history: the play's events and characters intersect with (1) the context of Roman history, and of the play's source in Plutarch's *Lives,* the time of the dramatic action; (2) the events and historical figures of Shakespeare's day, the time of the play's composition; and (3) the present—always shifting—historical moment, the time of the current staging or reading. The interplay among these various levels can produce some of the most effective, and most poignant, moments in a production. Like all Shakespearean plays, *Coriolanus* tells several different kinds of stories at once, depending upon which set of characters and issues is placed in the foreground. In this play the various levels are exceptionally clear, and exceptionally evenhanded, which is one reason why the play has been so successfully staged and appropriated across the political spectrum.

One reading might concentrate on Coriolanus, or Caius Martius, himself, the lone aristocrat, the heroic individual; another might take up the narrative of the common people, the hungry, disempowered "voices"; a third might emphasize the roles of the women in the play, or the family group constellated by the three "V's" (the mother Volumnia, the wife Virgilia, the friend Valeria) and the boy Young Martius, Coriolanus's son. If, for example, we emphasize the character of Coriolanus, we might produce a reading about the nobility of tragedy, about the Aristotelian pattern of the rise and fall of a great man, and, coincidentally but not accidentally, about the upholding of Roman ideals, and the self-made man who is author of himself and of his tragedy. T. S. Eliot regarded *Coriolanus* as Shakespeare's "most assured" dramatic success, and a chancellor of England praised the hero's "Tory virtues." A focus on the common people (plebeians, citizens), on the other hand, would draw attention to issues of class and politics, and to the material need for corn (grain) and for power. Although the general Cominius is the one who says "I shall lack voice," it is actually the people who do so, despite the fact that they are referred to metonymically as "voices" throughout. Bertolt Brecht admired *Coriolanus* from a political perspective far removed from that of T. S. Eliot (or Edmund Burke, who also cited Shakespeare's hero with approval). Brecht's adaptation stressed the historical and economic location of the play, situated between feudalism and nascent capitalism. Similarly, a close examination of the place of women in the play, or a production that placed the issue at its center, would raise questions not only of social roles and marginalization but also of psychology and psychoanalysis. Volumnia has refused to ever treat her son like a child, sending him out to war at an early age, and she emphasizes her own values of manhood; he reacts by seeking her approval, overestimating her power, and both anxiously courting her favor and curtly rejecting it. The extended childhood in which this grown man finds himself will culminate in his exposure as a "boy" and his subsequent downfall.

Thus Aristotelian tragic readings, class and materialist analyses, and psychoanalytic interpretations—to give just a few examples out of a host of possibilities—can readily coexist, one or the other taking precedence as the reader's, actor's, director's, or teacher's focus changes. None is intrinsically "wrong" or "right" (though in practice some are more convincing than others), and the play-text does not privilege one point of view over another, though any single interpretation may do so. What has been especially striking about productions and citations of this play is the way it has been appropriated, consistently over the years, as a commentary on a current political situation, and on issues of morality, ethics, social responsibility, and individual virtue in politics.

Coriolanus's powerful mother, Volumnia, clearly dominates her dutiful son, who is free and independent on the battlefield but subservient to Volumnia in all private and political concerns. In the Victorian era, itself governed by a powerful queen, Volumnia was praised by such a major Shakespearean critic as F. J. Furnivall, who wrote that "from mothers like Volumnia came the men who conquered the known world, and have left their mark for ever on the nations of Europe. . . . no grander, nobler woman, was ever created by Shakespeare's art."[2] Late-twentieth-century productions of the play in Britain underscored, less flatteringly, the overbearing Volumnia's similarity to Prime Minister Margaret Thatcher.

In an analogous fashion the corn riots of Coriolanus's own time, 491 B.C.E., feelingly described by Plutarch and cited within the play as a chief complaint of the people, were paralleled, during the reigns of Queen Elizabeth I and King James I, by corn riots in Oxfordshire (1557) and the Midlands (1607). The displacement of tillage by pasture (the grazing of sheep and cows rather than the planting of crops) and the enclosure of common land (its acquisition or co-optation by aristocrats and landowners) created food shortages across the country. The tension between high and low was exacerbated by fashion, since the starched ruffs of the aristocrats were maintained by the use of cornstarch. Rather than feeding the people, the corn that was grown thus often contributed to the elegance of courtiers. In recent productions a contemporary dimension of the historical corn riots in Coriolanus has been evoked through topical allusions to contemporary food shortages, global famine, or Farm Aid concerts. Such transhistorical topicalities are a mark of virtually all Shakespeare productions these days, but it is worth emphasizing the sense in which Coriolanus is repeatedly discovered as a trenchant and unexpected commentary on the modern political and social scene, whether by poets like Eliot (in his "Coriolan"), playwrights like Brecht, journalists, political commentators, or directors.

It may be useful in approaching Coriolanus to recall the last words of Octavius in Antony and Cleopatra, in which the new Caesar spoke his elegy for the larger-than-life mythic lovers, and pointed, in effect, toward two different kinds of drama, declaring that "their story is / No less in pity than his glory which / Brought them to be lamented." *Pity* is an essential Aristotelian element of tragedy, and *glory* is the fundamental attribute of the heroic history play. The play thus concludes by offering the audience a bifocal choice of sympathies, points of view, and genres. In *Coriolanus,* as in *Julius Caesar,* Shakespeare's other well-known "Roman play," the audience is offered a similar, double-barreled choice, a choice, as Coriolanus himself observes in a flash of insight in the fifth act, between a "happy victory" for Rome and a "mortal" (human and tragic) outcome for its hero. The play ends in death and in victory, in the ambush and murder of a man whose final flaw was his first yielding to human feelings, who was safe so long as he regarded himself as a monster without kin or a lonely dragon in his fen. Shockingly, yet somehow fittingly, it is only at the moment when Coriolanus acknowledges himself as a member of the human race, as a man with human ties—mother, wife, child, friends—that he becomes really vulnerable. For this act of simple human recognition he is murdered. It is as if he had to become human so that he could die. At the same time the play ends in victory for the Roman cause, the Romans reconciled now with the Volscians so that the city is saved.

The play is, then, among other things, a tragedy of context—the story of a man whose nature, as Menenius says, "is too noble for the world" (3.1.255). The last words we hear are Tullus Aufidius's assurance that Coriolanus "shall have a noble memory" (5.6.154), while a Volscian lord praises him as "the most noble corpse that ever herald / Did follow to his urn" (143–144). This is a suitably honorific sentiment—but what good, in the jostling, pragmatic world of politicians and plebeians, is a "noble corpse"? Would it not be better to be a less noble living man? In act 3 Coriolanus himself answers this hypothetical question with a resounding no. He exhorts the Roman senators, those who "prefer / A noble life before a long" (3.1.155–156), to reject the tribunes of the people and their importunate demands for food and power—and he is expelled from the city as a traitor. His mother, the superb and overpowering Volumnia, the voice of Rome in this play, takes the opposite view, urging her son to mildness, suggesting that he use his brain and not his heart: "You might have been enough the man you are / With striving less to be so" and "I would have had you put your power well on / Before you had worn it out" (3.2.19–20, 16–17). The canny, political Aufidius, who is in some ways the Octavius to Coriolanus's Antony, the realist to his idealist, the modern man to his epic hero, speculates about whether it is "pride," or "defect of judgement," or stubborn "nature" that makes Coriolanus the way he is. Plainly all three elements characterize Coriolanus's actions and decisions, and they are all, in the play, quintessential "Roman" traits. But in order to come to some understanding of Coriolanus's nature and the structure of his rise and fall we have first, I think, to look at his context and environment and see how he measures himself against it.

The Rome of *Antony and Cleopatra* was a busy and confident political metropolis, bustling with intrigue and calculation. The time of Augustus Caesar, as we noted, was also the time of the birth of Christ. By contrast, the Rome of *Coriolanus,* some five hundred years earlier, seems to be more like a small town in the midst of Italy (or England), populated by a wavering multitude of poor citizens on the one hand and a crew of old men and generals on the other. The opening stage direction is explicit and indicative: "Enter a Company of mutinous citizens with staves, clubs, and other weapons." This Rome is not the sophisticated home of the mature Antony and the cagy Octavius, nor yet the city of Brutus's ruminative honor and the younger Mark Antony's funeral oration for Julius Caesar. This is instead a Rome that shows us a power vacuum and the manipulations of the up-and-coming new men, the two tribunes, rising agitators and politicos, trying to craft a power base out of citizens armed with crude weapons instead of thoughts.

Strikingly, the citizens in the play are described as "voices." This use of "voice," which in the period could mean both "the right or privilege of speaking or voting" and "that which is generally or commonly said," rumor or report, is a central trope for *Coriolanus,* both the play and the hero of its title. "I shall lack voice," says the eloquent Cominius, in self-deprecating formulaic language, as he launches into his compelling speech in praise of Coriolanus's war deeds. The people's "voices," meaning "votes," is what Coriolanus the candidate stands in the marketplace awkwardly—and angrily—seeking. He himself does "lack voice," in the sense that he is completely devoid of artifice or social grace. "[C]ould he not speak 'em fair?" asks the old counselor Menenius in desperation once Coriolanus has boiled over into intemperate imprecation (3.1.261). Perhaps most centrally, "voices" is a classic metonymy, the use of the part for the whole, an important figure of speech used over and over again in the play, as a rhetorical device but also unmetaphored or re-literalized—as in Menenius's celebrated set piece, the fable of the belly.

The fable of the belly belongs to a familiar genre in political rhetoric, the story of the "body politic." The king or ruler is the head; the other ranks of society and polity are represented, in this allegorical construction, by limbs and organs working in concert to create a healthy body. Such allegorical fables, images of the body politic used as guides for the proper relationship of governor and governed, go back as far as Livy, the Roman historian, and not only were popular but were highly useful to theorists of Italian civic humanism in the sixteenth century. In Shakespeare's time Edward Forset's *Comparative Discourse of the Bodies Natural and Politique* (1606) is a leading example. Livy's *History of Rome* is the direct source of Shakespeare's account, and its version of Menenius's belly fable is very similar—except that Shakespeare has added dramatic details (the interruption of the angry First Citizen, called by Menenius "the great toe of this assembly") and, most tellingly, humorous and animate characteristics ("For look you, I may make the belly smile / As well as speak").

A comparison between Livy's version and Shakespeare's will be instructive. Livy describes Menenius as "an eloquent individual, and one well liked by the *plebs,* as he had been born one of them," and reports:

On being admitted to the camp he is said merely to have related the following apologue, in the quaint and uncouth style of that age: In the days when man's members did not all agree amongst themselves, as is now the case, but had each its own ideas and a voice of its own, the other parts thought it unfair that they should have the worry and the trouble and the labour of providing everything for the belly, while the belly remained quietly in their midst with nothing to do but to enjoy the good things which they bestowed upon it; they therefore conspired together that the hands should carry no food to the mouth, nor the mouth accept anything that was given it, nor the teeth grind up what they received. While they sought in this angry spirit to starve the belly into submission, the members themselves and the whole body were reduced to the utmost weakness. Hence it had become clear that even the belly had no idle task to perform, and was no more nourished than it nourished the rest, by giving out to all parts of the body that by which we live and thrive, when it has been divided equally amongst the veins and is enriched with digested food—that is, the blood. Drawing a parallel from this to show how like was the internal dissension of the bodily members to the anger of the plebs against the Fathers, he prevailed upon the minds of his hearers.

Livy, History of Rome, 2.32³

Here is Shakespeare's dramatic rendering of the same passage, only slightly altered, but very different in effect and tone:

Menenius	There was a time when all the body's members,
	Rebelled against the belly, thus accused it:
	That only like a gulf it did remain
	I'th' midst o'th' body, idle and unactive,
	Still cupboarding the viand, never bearing
	Like labour with the rest; where th'other instruments
	Did see and hear, devise, instruct, walk, feel,
	And, mutually participate, did minister
	Unto the appetite and affection common
	Of the whole body. The belly answered—
First Citizen	Well, sir, what answer made the belly?
Menenius	Sir, I shall tell you. With a kind of smile,
	Which ne'er came from the lungs, but even thus—
	For look you, I may make the belly smile
	As well as speak—it tauntingly replied
	To th' discontented members, the mutinous parts
	That envied his receipt; even so most fitly
	As you malign our senators for that
	They are not such as you.

. . . .

First Citizen	The former agents, if they did complain,
	What could the belly answer?
Menenius	I will tell you,
	If you'll bestow a small of what you have little—
	Patience—a while, you'st hear the belly's answer.
First Citizen	You're long about it.
Menenius	Note me this, good friend:
	Your most grave belly was deliberate,
	Not rash like his accusers, and thus answered:
	"True is it, my incorporate friends," quoth he,
	"That I receive the general food at first
	Which you do live upon, and fit it is,
	Because I am the storehouse and the shop
	Of the whole body. . . .

. . . .

	And though that all at once"—
	You my good friends, this says the belly, mark me—
First Citizen	Ay, sir, well, well.
Menenius	"Though all at once cannot
	See what I do deliver out to each,
	Yet I can make my audit up that all
	From me do back receive the flour of all
	And leave me but the bran." What say you to't?

. . . .

| | The senators of Rome are this good belly, |
| | And you the mutinous members. . . . |

Coriolanus 1.1.85–103, 112–123, 129–135, 137–138

Livy's Menenius tells a good story—echoes of this same passage can be found in *King Lear*, another play written in the same period that is deeply concerned with mutinies in the body politic ("Is it not as this mouth should tear this hand / For lifting food to't?" [*Lear* 3.4.16–17]).

But Shakespeare's masterful Menenius is at once funny, deft, and pointed. His artful use of colloquialisms ("cupboarding the viand"), dialect ("look you," a stereotypical Welsh usage), and direct address ("You my good friends, this says the belly, mark me") demonstrates in action what Livy asserts about Menenius's affinity for speaking with the common people (here labeled English-sounding "citizens" rather than Roman *"plebs"*). The fable of the belly unfolds as something like a cross between an animated cartoon and a stand-up comedy routine, ending in a sonorous blank verse utterance that is also a "gotcha" punch line ("The senators of Rome are this good belly, / And you the mutinous members").

In effect, Menenius is able to disarm his onstage hearers, gently drawing them into his tale, prodding them verbally ("mark me"; "What say you to't?"), soothing them with language, and amusing them with his apparently harmless story of the talking and smiling belly—until the noble soldier Caius Martius, who will later be surnamed Coriolanus, arrives and undoes all his patron's work with a single ill-tempered curse. To the greeting "Hail, noble Martius!" he snaps back, "Thanks. —What's the matter, you dissentious rogues, / That, rubbing the poor itch of your opinion, / Make yourselves scabs?" (1.1.152–154). The First Citizen's reply makes it clear that this is not an extraordinary but rather an ordinary exchange: "We have ever your good word." So much for Menenius's attempt to soothe festering wounds and disagreements with words, with a pretty tale.

Yet Menenius's fable is central to the play in many ways. It suggests and introduces the language of fragmentation, of dismembering and body parts, that will continue throughout as an emblem of the diseased condition of Rome. Not only are the senators a belly and the First Citizen a "great toe," but we also hear that the tribunes of the people are "[t]he tongues o'th' common mouth" (3.1.23), and Coriolanus will accuse them of failing to restrain their charges: "You being their mouths, why rule you not their teeth?" (38). "The noble tribunes are the people's mouths," says one citizen, "[a]nd we their hands" (3.1.271–272). The tribunes, for their part, return the compliment, describing Coriolanus as a diseased limb, a foot that once did noble service but is now gangrened and must be cut away for the health of the rest of the body. Menenius laments that in Coriolanus emblematic body parts are scrambled: "His heart's his mouth. / What his breast forges, that his tongue must vent" (257–258). Coriolanus will later address the citizens as "you fragments"—and he himself will be summarily fragmented, banished from Rome.

The fable of the belly establishes the immediate source of the citizens' dissatisfaction: corn, the demand for food so ridiculed by Coriolanus. Everywhere in the play this political and economic issue turns up as an image, as part of the play's verbal texture. Grain and harvest are key images throughout Shakespeare. The England of his time was, after all, a largely agricultural nation; the same verbal patterns can be found in Renaissance translations of the Bible. At the end of *Macbeth*, Malcolm speaks of "[w]hat's more to do / Which would be planted newly with the time." Richmond (crowned King Henry VII) at the close of *Richard III* speaks of "smiling plenty, and fair prosperous days." The characters in *King Lear* talk continually of seeds, and "germens," and harvest. But in *Coriolanus* the patricians are the grain, the plebeians musty chaff, and Coriolanus himself is the harvester. His mother, Volumnia, calls him a "harvest-man," sent out "to mow / Or all or lose his hire (1.3.33–34), but the harvest of which she speaks is dead bodies. Coriolanus himself will lament that "we ourselves have ploughed for, sowed, and scattered" (3.1.75) the seeds of sedition by permitting power to the common people. In fact, he is not only harvester but grim reaper, refusing to sort flour from bran, grain from chaff (5.1.24–32).

The play's attitude toward various social stations and ranks—patricians, plebeians, tribunes, consuls, generals—is so deftly managed that, as we have noted, the play is capable of being produced successfully from both "the right" and "the left," even though a partisan reading would necessarily be a reductive one. The citizens, whether Romans or Volscians, are portrayed as self-regarding, self-righteous, and vacillating, however just their claims. The moment war with the Volscians is announced, for example, the angry Roman mob steals away, ignoring Martius's ironic suggestion that "[t]he Volscians have much corn" and that war with them would solve the complaint of famine. Facing the city of Corioles, the common soldiers flee from the field of battle, leaving Martius to fight alone. They are interested only in looting and in spoils. Not only are they cowardly, they are also changeable. First they give Martius their voices, or votes, to be consul, and then, guided by the canny tribunes, they withdraw their support. Again with the tribunes' urging they succeed in banishing him from the city, and almost in throwing him from the Tarpeian rock to his death. But when the bad news comes that Martius, now surnamed Coriolanus, is arming against Rome, against them, the citizens change their tune: "When I said 'banish him' I said 'twas pity." "And so did I." "And so did I, and to say the truth so did very many of us" (4.6.149–151). Even in Antium, in the house of the general Aufidius, the mob is fickle and volatile. When Coriolanus arrives there in his mean disguise the servants shoo him out because he seems to be a poor man and no gentleman. But the moment Aufidius embraces and recognizes him, they take it all back: "I knew by his face that there was something in him," one servingman gushes. "He is simply the rarest man i'th' world" (4.5.159–160). At the end of the play, Coriolanus enters marching for the first time *with* the commoners, surrounded by his former enemies—and the people turn against him in the course of the scene and shout for his murder.

In this play the citizens are described as dogs, rabbits, curs, geese, crows pecking at eagles, and a common herd. Aufidius, by contrast, is for Coriolanus a noble quarry, "a lion / That I am proud to hunt." These animal similes will persist throughout the play, making a kind of subliminal beast fable. Coriolanus himself is at times described as a lamb, hunted and destroyed by the wolf (the emblem of Rome, who suckled Romulus and Remus—a she-wolf personified in this play by the dominating and patriotic Volumnia). Coriolanus resents appearing before the people in his "womanish toge" (2.3.105), a complex phrase alluding to the white *(candida)* toga worn by political aspirants—the source of the word "candidate." The Bible warned against false prophets who came like wolves in sheep's clothing (Matthew 7:15). Coriolanus, as we will see, regards such politicking among the commons as an unworthy lie. So he is lamb and wolf at once, the play's animal subtexts binding together without strain the layered codes of ancient fable, Roman mythological history, and Christian allegory. He is also, by inference, a "butterfly," like the one we are told his son tears to pieces—"whether his fall enraged him, or how 'twas, he did so set his teeth and tear it!" Virgilia's praise of her passionately destructive son invokes the sign-word for his father: "Indeed, la, 'tis a noble child" (1.3.59–60, 63). Like father, like son—nobility is closely allied to love and destruction.

But of all the animals in this animal-filled play to which Coriolanus is compared and compares himself, the most striking of all is the dragon. In act 5 Menenius says of him, "There is differency between a grub and a butterfly, yet your butterfly was a grub. This Martius is grown from man to dragon" (5.4.9–11). But the "dragon" term has been chosen by Coriolanus long before, as he is banished from Rome:

> I go alone,
> Like to a lonely dragon that his fen
> Makes feared and talked of more than seen. . . .
>
> 4.1.30–32

A lonely dragon—a heroic, belated, socially isolated survival of another world.

Coriolanus is neither commoner nor political senator. He is often spoken about, seldom speaking. Lartius says of him early in the play that he has been a soldier "[e]ven to Cato's wish" (1.5.28), that he adheres to the old Roman virtues. Like Antony (and Hector, and Hotspur, and Tybalt), he chooses to fight by single combat, alone. "O' me alone," he cries to the people, "make you a sword of me?" (1.7.76). And at the close of the play, so poignantly and pitifully, we hear his final suicidal boast to the Volscians that he alone conquered their city, the city of Corioles, the city whose name he now bears as a trophy attached to his own: "Alone I did it" (5.6.117). Like the innocent he is, he does not realize, in the heat of his anger and despair, that to brag of having taken their city is the surest way to bring on his own death. In this moment he is indeed a lamb going to the slaughter, and his innocence of the world has structural affinities with other doomed Shakespearean "innocents," like Desdemona and Duncan, whose trust in other people led to their downfall. Coriolanus trusts a code, not an individual, but his trust is similarly misplaced and outdated. He is purer than the world that contains him, a lonely dragon, the repository—for all his faults and flaws—of a lost set of Roman virtues.

We learn from Aufidius that he and Martius have sworn that if they meet in single combat they will fight until "one can do no more" (1.2.36). But Aufidius is at heart a politician, and he ultimately backs away from single combat in a way that emphasizes, by contrast, Martius's own uncompromising valor. In act 1, scene 9, the two men fight on the field of battle, but at the last minute other Volscians come to Aufidius's aid. Initially Aufidius condemns their "[o]fficious" interference, but by the end of the first act he has abandoned the idea of fighting "[t]rue sword to sword": "I'll potch [thrust] at him some way / Or wrath or craft may get him" (1.11.15–16). The vernacular word "potch" is a good emblem of the lowering of ideals and expectations. In the second half of the play we see Aufidius openly scheming to take advantage of Coriolanus's pride and weakness. Like

Hotspur, who called out "die all, die merrily" as he went into battle, Coriolanus prefers a noble life before a long. Yet Hotspur's heroics were coupled with an articulate and witty passion for his wife. Coriolanus, though married and a father, regards himself, with wounded and defensive pride, as alone. More than almost any other Shakespearean hero, he aims at a status that is less like that of a man and more like that of a dragon, a god, or a machine—someone, or something, in other words, that does not feel.

In this play that is so directly about language and the ability to speak (or not to speak), the audience fittingly hears of Coriolanus's transformation into a god, and into a force of nature, in the speech by the general Cominius before the Senate, a speech that begins with the rhetorical gesture of incapacity "I shall lack voice":

> I shall lack voice; the deeds of Coriolanus
> Should not be uttered feebly. . . .
>
> . . . .
>
> The man I speak of cannot in the world
> Be singly counterpoised. At sixteen years,
> When Tarquin made a head for Rome, he fought
> Beyond the mark of others. Our then dictator,
> Whom with all praise I point at, saw him fight
> When with his Amazonian chin he drove
> The bristled lips before him. . . .
>
> . . . .
>
>   In that day's feats,
> When he might act the woman in the scene,
> He proved best man i'th' field, and for his meed
> Was brow-bound with the oak. His pupil age
> Man-entered thus, he waxèd like a sea,
> And in the brunt of seventeen battles since
> He lurched all swords of the garland. . . .
>   His sword, death's stamp,
> Where it did mark, it took. From face to foot
> He was a thing of blood, whose every motion
> Was timed with dying cries. Alone he entered
> The mortal gate of th' city. . . .
>
> . . . .
>
> And with a sudden reinforcement struck
> Corioles like a planet. . . .
>
>   *2.2.78–110*

Cominius is a master orator, as effective in his resounding public style as Menenius was in the more folksy prose narrative of the belly fable. His "I shall lack voice" recalls Mark Antony's "I am no orator as Brutus is" and offers a similarly deceptive platform of low expectations. The "profession of incapacity" is of course a familiar rhetorical trope, used by politicians, as well as poets, from ancient times. Under Cominius's skillful manipulation Coriolanus turns, before our eyes—or ears—from a boy so young he is almost a woman, with a beardless "Amazonian" chin, fighting men with "bristled lips," to a hero whose brows are bound with garlands of oak, the traditional emblem of military honor (compare today's "oak-leaf clusters" in bronze or silver, awarded to U.S. soldiers for extraordinary heroism and gallantry in battle). The next permutation transforms Coriolanus into a sea, a natural and irresistible force, and by the end of the speech he will have become an entire planet, invading and destroying the city of Corioles.

But in the midst of these rhetorical descriptions of powerful nature is one comparison of the hero that is at once more ambiguous and more disturbing: "He was a thing of blood, whose every motion / Was timed with dying cries." The Roman hero becomes a *thing*, one mechanically motivated, like a ticking clock or a bomb. This is a movement away from human ties, a movement that is at the root of Coriolanus's political troubles, making him, like Othello, both a superb soldier and a particularly innocent and naïve private man. A thing. When, banished from the Rome and the mother that have given him his identity, Coriolanus goes in noble pique to join forces with the enemy, the Volscian troops under Aufidius, this language of things, of gods and machines, increases ominously:

Cominius	He is their god. He leads them like a thing
	Made by some other deity than nature.

4.6.94–95

Menenius	When he walks, he moves like an engine, and the ground
	shrinks before his treading. . . . He sits in his state as a thing
	made for Alexander. . . . He wants nothing of a god but eternity and a heaven to throne in.

5.4.15–20

Cominius	"Coriolanus"
	He would not answer to, forbade all names.
	He was a kind of nothing, titleless.

5.1.11–13

"[A] kind of nothing." For Coriolanus, this transformation to a god or a thing is something his banishment has forced upon him, and something that, like a hurt child, rejected by Mother Rome, he welcomes as protective coloration, a benign numbness. He speaks with ironic and juvenile pleasure about getting back at the Romans, and, in the last act, about his own rejection of Menenius—a man who "[l]oved me above the measure of a father, / Nay, godded me indeed" (5.3.10–11). And he boasts with equal spite, and equally transparent pain, that he has no social or genealogical connection to the world: "Wife, mother, child, I know not" (5.2.78). He says he will henceforth decline to yield to filial instinct, "but stand / As if a man were author of himself / And knew no other kin" (5.3.35–37). As if a man were his own maker: a god, a thing, an automaton—anything but a man.

This propensity to reject or displace family and personal ties, in favor of the presumed larger purposes and less fraught emotional commitments to warfare and heroism, produces in *Coriolanus* the play a striking and persistent line of imagery that allies its martial heroes with what has been called "male bonding" or "homosocial" behavior—in this case the identification of the love object with the military commander or military rival. Thus Martius on the battlefield, early in the play, exclaims his pleasure at reunion with his general, Cominius:

> O, let me clip ye
> In arms as sound as when I wooed, in heart
> As merry as when our nuptial day was done,
> And tapers burned to bedward!
>
> *1.7.29–32*

We seldom hear him speak with similar intimacy to his temperate and loyal Roman wife, who bears the patriotic name of Virgilia. To a certain extent this erotic language for war is conventional as well as powerfully evocative: in *Antony and Cleopatra* the soldier Antony, a formidable lover, pledges that he will go to death as eagerly as a bridegroom to his bed. But in *Coriolanus* it is something more, since it is precisely the erotic tug-of-war, between private love and public fame, that is missing, replaced by a double code of honor. The use of the word "arms" here is particularly striking, since it is only in English, not in Latin, that this pun on the martial and the marital is feasible. The Latin *arma* means "battle gear," as in the opening line of Virgil's *Aeneid*, *"Arma virumque cano"* (Of arms and the man I sing). The Teutonic "arm," or *earm*, denotes the body part, and traces to the Latin word for "shoulder," but the sublime cleverness of "let me clip [clasp] ye / In arms as sound as when I wooed" is distinctively Shakespearean, and it offers a superb example of the playwright's accomplishment, in combining—at a crucial moment in the history of the language—the strands of native and classical inheritance.

In the early battle Coriolanus embraces a fellow warrior as soundly and as merrily as his wedded wife. By the fourth act, now estranged from Rome and his family, he finds himself addressed by Aufidius in similar, yet more expansive, terms:

> Let me twine
> Mine arms about that body whereagainst
> My grainèd ash an hundred times hath broke,
> And scarred the moon with splinters.
>
> [*He embraces* CORIOLANUS]
>
>   Here I clip
> The anvil of my sword, and do contest
> As hotly and as nobly with thy love
> As ever in ambitious strength I did
> Contend against thy valour. Know thou first,
> I loved the maid I married; never man
> Sighed truer breath. But that I see thee here,
> Thou noble thing, more dances my rapt heart
> Than when I first my wedded mistress saw
> Bestride my threshold. . . .
>
> *4.5.105–117*

Aufidius feels more passion for this "noble thing" than he did for his bride on their wedding night. Once more, this is rhetoric, not sexual invitation. Yet the line between them is a thin one, as Aufidius's servants note, perceiving the way their master flirts with his guest at the dinner table: "Our general himself makes a mistress of him, . . . and turns up the white o'th' eye to his discourse" (4.5.193–195). The deepest passions of generals are for their colleagues, and perhaps even for their enemies. To see this performed and articulated in *Coriolanus* is to have further light shed on the complex erotics of *Othello*.

Coriolanus is a complicated dramatic character, the more so because he seems to have uncanny ahistorical similarities with embedded social types of a much later era, like the products of late-nineteenth- and early-twentieth-century British public schools: he is repressed; devoted to authority; committed to male bonding, fellowship, risk, and danger; slightly overpunctilious; impatient or condescending toward perceived social inferiors; awkward and even unhappy in situations that require small talk, gracious manners, accommodation, compromise, and a show of feeling. Brought up by that remarkable woman Volumnia, who is a cross between political matriarch and stage mother (Rose Kennedy and Mama Rose in the musical *Gypsy*), Coriolanus has also been effectively analyzed through the lens of Freudian theory; as Volumnia herself will say, "There's no man in the world / More bound to's mother" (5.3.159–160).

We have the mother's word, early in the play, concerning her ambitions for her son: "To a cruel war I sent him, from where he returned his brows bound with oak" (1.3.12–13). It is her hope that he will come back with bloody wounds, visible signs of prowess: "His bloody brow / With his mailed hand then wiping, / forth he goes, / Like to a harvest-man that's tasked to mow / Or all or lose his hire" (31–34). At the articulation of this unusual maternal fantasy, the wife, Virgilia, blenches: "His bloody brow! O Jupiter, no blood!" (35)—but who, after all, is listening to Virgilia?

Volumnia, who is the terror of the tribunes, terrorizes Coriolanus's wife, too. Like her son, she is a surprisingly "modern" type as well as a recognizable classic and classical figure: the ambitious mother behind a successful son (who may wind up consulting an even more successful analyst). At the same time, as we have already noted, Volumnia has been praised as a grand and noble figure who shaped one of the "men who conquered the known world." Certainly her press has been more favorable in some eras than in others. What is indubitable is that she is a fabulous dramatic *character,* a part to die for. Her Shakespearean sisters are Lady Macbeth and Goneril, her pallid descendant the wicked queen (and wicked stepmother) in *Cymbeline.* Lady Macbeth's children, missing from the plot, mentioned only in passing ("I have given suck . . ."), are rhetorically sacrificed in favor of her husband-child's ambition; Goneril's womb is cursed by her angry father, who wishes for her nothing but sterility; and Cymbeline's nameless queen has a clownish and loutish son for whom she, too, is overwhelmingly ambitious. Volumnia has the right son, and the right opportunity, to make him great, and to destroy him.

It is also worth noticing that once again in a Shakespearean play we have an absent parent, in this case the father, his place ineffectually filled by Menenius, himself largely under Volumnia's sway. "Is he not wounded? He was wont to come home wounded," he asks after the battle of Corioles. Again the wife, Virgilia, is appalled—"O, no, no, no!"—and again she is overridden by Volumnia: "O, he is wounded, I thank the gods for't! . . . There will be large cicatrices [scars] to show the people" (2.1.107, 108, 133–134). Menenius and Volumnia tabulate that Coriolanus has twenty-seven wounds, a hero's collection, and on parts of the body—the shoulder and the left arm—readily visible for a candidate dressed in a toga.

In plays from *Romeo and Juliet* to *Othello* and *King Lear* we have traced the fortunes of self-confident young women who rebelled against their fathers, and sometimes paid a price for doing so. In *Coriolanus* the dyad is not father-daughter but mother-son, and the consequences of obedience, rebellion, and reunion in this case are equally significant. Volumnia urges her son to display his wounds to the people in the marketplace, and he retorts stubbornly: "I will not do't" (3.2.120). Eleven lines later he yields to her will: "Mother, I am going to the market-place" (3.2.131). Mother, I am going. In the play's last act we will hear a tragic echo of this scene, when Coriolanus vows again "I will not" (5.3.21)—and does. In a very serious sense his banishment from Rome is a rite of passage, an opportunity to leave the stifling home city, and his mother, and Menenius, an opportunity he finally does not take. Instead he reinstates the filial bond, reconciling himself to his mother in one of those striking scenes of child-parent reunion, like that of Lear and Cordelia, that seem so close to the center of the Jacobean Shakespeare.

In this single act, act 5, as we will see, Coriolanus simultaneously gains and loses. He gains humanity, and he loses life. He ceases to be the automaton, the soulless engine, the little god, and he becomes at once a fuller human being and a doomed one. His own words are full of self-knowledge and self-exposure as he consents to Volumnia's request:

> O mother, mother!
> What have you done? Behold, the heavens do ope,
> . . . .
> You have won a happy victory to Rome;
> But for your son, believe it, O believe it,
> Most dangerously you have with him prevailed,
> If not most mortal to him. . . .
>
> *5.3.183–190*

The word "mortal" here carries, very strongly, both of its core meanings: Volumnia's victory is most human, and most deadly, for her son. This is the paradox of tragedy, that to be human is to suffer, and that to be aloof from suffering is to turn one's back on humanity, and to be merely a thing, a tin god. For Coriolanus this is an acknowledgment of the doom he knows will come. It is the tragic choice, the choice of tragedy, of pity rather than glory, in Octavius's terms. Or as Aufidius the politician puts it, congratulating himself on Coriolanus's impolitic act of principle, "I am glad thou hast set thy mercy and thy honour / At difference in thee. Out of that I'll work / Myself a former fortune" (5.3.201–203). "[M]ercy" and "honour" are other words for pity and glory. Coriolanus's choice will make him a tragic figure, and not merely a Roman hero—a man, and not merely a god.

Whatever else it may be said to be "about"—whether history, politics, heroism, or manhood—*Coriolanus* is also, very centrally, a play about language. Again and again in *Coriolanus* the hero is urged to use his eloquence to win over the common people to his cause—and again and again his language fails. His first entry onto the stage is marked in just this way by a failure of language, a curse on those "dissentious rogues," those "scabs," the people. His plea for their "voices" in act 2 likewise fails:

> Your voices! For your voices I have fought,
> Watched for your voices, for your voices bear
> Of wounds two dozen odd. . . .
>   for your voices, have
> Done many things, some less, some more. Your voices!
>
> *2.3.116–120*

Menenius, the old counselor, prides himself not only on his suasive narrative skills but also on his use of language as a safety valve: "What I think, I utter, and spend my malice in my breath" (2.1.48–49). In fact, for this old man, who lacks physical strength, personal magnetism, and sexual vitality, language *is* power. And when Coriolanus fails in his dramatized confrontation with the people, Menenius in irritation asks, "[C]ould he not speak 'em fair?" Could he not tell the people what they wanted and expected to hear, play his part? Language for Menenius is manipulation, obfuscation, compromise, and politics. Language is also politics for Cominius, Coriolanus's fellow general, elder, and sponsor ("the deeds of Coriolanus / Should not be uttered feebly"). But no sooner does the audience hear the eloquent Menenius, the eloquent Cominius, than their politic language is interrupted by the plain speech, and often the insolent boorishness, of Coriolanus. "I cannot," he says, "bring / My tongue to such a pace." He cannot beg, he cannot ask, for favor.

Volumnia urges him to take part in what is essentially a stage play before the people, and Coriolanus argues that acting is dishonest. He distrusts fiction and playing, and he finds the role of actor both dishonorable and difficult: "I had rather have my wounds to heal again / Than hear say how I got them" (2.2.65–66). He prefers wounds to words: "When blows have made me stay I fled from words" (67). He has not yet made his peace with language, and as always in Shakespeare language is the index of humanity. When Volumnia comes to her son with what she regards as a harmless little scenario, her proposal that he display his worthiness and manliness to the people, she conveys to him a violation of every rule and law of honesty to which he has heretofore been trained:

> If it be honour in your wars to seem
> The same you are not, which for your best ends
> You adopt your policy, how is it less or worse
> That it shall hold companionship in peace
> With honour, as in war . . . ?

> *3.2.47–51*

Since you are so ready to deceive in war, why not in peace? If in action, why not in language? But the apparently innocuous suggestion here is deeply shocking to the innocent and unworldly Coriolanus.

From this point in the play, from the third act onward, Coriolanus behaves almost as if he were a man in a dream—or a nightmare—walking through a scenario he can hardly understand, and certainly cannot justify. Look at the elaborate stage directions he gets from Volumnia as she presses him to display himself in the marketplace:

> I prithee now, my son,
> [*She takes his bonnet*]
> Go to them with this bonnet in thy hand,
> And thus far having stretched it—here be with them—

> Thy knee bussing the stones—for in such business
> Action is eloquence, and the eyes of th' ignorant
> More learnèd than the ears—waving thy head,
>
> . . . .
>
>   say to them
> Thou art their soldier. . . .
>
> . . . .
>
> Go, and be ruled, although I know thou hadst rather
> Follow thine enemy in a fiery gulf
> Than flatter him in a bower.
>
>   *3.2.72–82, 90–92*

In short, he is to kneel to them, bare and bow his head, and apologize because he lacks the language to speak to them glozingly and seductively, like a politician. "Must I with my base tongue give to my noble heart / A lie that it must bear?" he asks (3.2.100–101). Must he perform a part? The simple answer of the politicians, Volumnia, Menenius, and Cominius, foster parents and campaign managers, is yes. "Come, come, we'll prompt you," says Cominius, and Volumnia teases him with the promise of the most elusive reward of all, a mother's approval: "To have my praise for this, perform a part / Thou hast not done before" (3.2.106, 109–110). Nothing could be further from his nature, or from his capability. Furthermore, since the tribunes, predictably, are also in rehearsal (3.3), preparing to goad Coriolanus into self-betraying speech, it is no surprise to find that all the prompting in the world cannot prevent him from exploding the moment they provoke him with a carefully chosen epithet, the word "traitor." "How, traitor? . . . The fires i'th' lowest hell fold in the people!" (3.3.69, 71). Menenius sees the disaster but is helpless to stop it—"Is this the promise that you made your mother?"—and Coriolanus replies by rejecting the entire concept of language as power: "I would not buy / Their mercy at the price of one fair word" (3.3.90, 94–95).

When Coriolanus rejects politics-as-usual, the commoners reject him, and banish him from the city. His response is characteristic: "I banish you. . . . There is a world elsewhere" (3.3.127, 139). Banishment in Shakespeare is always highly fraught, whether it is Romeo's banishment from Verona or Bolingbroke's banishment from England, but for Coriolanus the experience is especially destabilizing. (Unlike those other cases, where the banished character temporarily departs from the play, here the play's action follows the banished hero.) His "I banish you" is a gesture of alienation, not only from Rome but also from the world of human interaction and language.

Forced to this point, rather like Hamlet, who similarly distrusts the playacting he sees around him at court, Coriolanus embraces the role of actor, presenting himself in rags at Aufidius's door, but only in order to remove his costume and show himself as himself: "Rather say I play / The man I am"

(3.2.13–14). This is a richly ambiguous choice of words, since for the speaker it means something like "I disdain artifice" but to the knowledgeable listener it also suggests that "man," adulthood and manliness, is a role. In the play's denouement his playing at manhood will be further unmasked when Aufidius cunningly taunts him with the name of "boy." However, among the enemy Volscians, Coriolanus can counterfeit manhood only in the one way he knows—by counterfeiting godhood, and by inspiring in his fellow men an allegiance tantamount to religious awe. His soldiers, in Antium, take him as their grace before meat and their thanks at end. He is a magical personage, a talisman, a living emblem of transcendence. But in making himself into an emblem of godhead and war, Coriolanus has indeed become the antithesis of humanity, the opposite of a man, and once again this rejection of the human is signaled in the play by a rejection of language.

Having taken over the forces of the Volscians, threatening now his own city of Rome—threatening, in Shakespearean terms, something like civil war—Coriolanus is approached by a series of petitioners who plead with him for mercy. To every one of these except the last he denies not only mercy but speech. Cominius is the first emissary, and he finds nothing except a machine:

> I kneeled before him;
> 'Twas very faintly he said "Rise," dismissed me
> Thus with his speechless hand. What he would do
> He sent in writing after me. . . .
>
> *5.1.65–68*

No speech, no human communication—"his speechless hand," and a letter of instruction or command, sent after the fact. The denial of speech is the denial of presence, and of emotion. Menenius is next, and to Menenius and his wordy petition Coriolanus makes the same reply. "O, my son, my son" (5.2.68) is Menenius's opening gambit, and he makes an appeal rather like that of Falstaff to the new King Henry V, the former Prince Hal. I am your real father, I made you what you are, fools have blocked my access to you. And like Falstaff, Menenius gets a dismissive reply: "Away!" Once more Coriolanus offers, instead, a written communication: "Yet, for I loved thee, / Take this along. I writ it for thy sake, / And would have sent it" (85–87). But there is to be no conversation, no voice, no speech: "Another word, Menenius, / I will not hear thee speak" (88). He will neither speak nor hear.

This is indeed the posture of godhead, the attitude of something either above or below the merely human, and it might well be his salvation and his escape if he were willing to spend his life in exile from humanity as well as from Rome. But the third emissary, of course, is his mother, Volumnia, accompanied by his wife, his son, and their friend Valeria. To Volumnia's urgent demand "Why dost not speak?" he has, at last, no answer but to extend his hand and reaffirm the filial bond. Clearly and directly the whole play leads up to this mesmerizing moment onstage, when son kneels to mother, mother kneels to son, and all the family kneels as well, until, in what is perhaps Shakespeare's most poignant stage direction,

[He] holds her by the hand, silent

Earlier, much earlier, Coriolanus had addressed his wife as "[m]y gracious silence," confirming the sense that silence is a key and valued Roman attribute, not the denial of language but a kind of language that transcends speech. Here, in act 5, scene 3, he holds his mother by the hand, silent, and forges again a bond that is at once his salvation and his destruction, his "most mortal" contact with kinship and the human race. The reaching out of the hand, so vital a gesture in *King Lear,* again in *Coriolanus* becomes a gesture of humanization. From this point he will again begin to speak.

In order to approach the majesty of this theatrical moment, and to appreciate the truly stunning effect of the scene onstage, it is useful to bear in mind another aspect of the question of language and silence that is also vital for the play: the matter of names and naming. The question of the proper name, linked in drama to the crucial question of identity and identification—Who am I?—is one that this play asks again and again. Early on, we are offered a kind of control for this concept, much as in *Macbeth* the presence of the "good mother," Lady Macduff, served as a control for the "bad mother" (or non-mother), Lady Macbeth. Here the control is a briefly mentioned character by the name of Censorinus. "And nobly named so," says a tribune, "twice being censor" (2.3.233). The man was fittingly named Censorinus, since he became a censor. As we have seen in other plays, notably in *Richard II,* it is a matter of whether or not the name fits the role.

But what of Coriolanus? What is his true name, the name he merits and deserves either in the play's form as a history or in its form as a tragedy? Martius is one of his names. Caius Martius is what he is called as the play opens. But almost immediately he gains a new name, the surname, or "addition," of Coriolanus, the conqueror of the city of Corioles. After the battle he refuses to accept any spoils or reward, except for two honorable gifts from the general Cominius—the general's own horse, and a title:

> Cominius   [F]rom this time,
> For what he did before Corioles, call him,
> With all th'applause and clamour of the host,
> Martius Caius Coriolanus. Bear th'addition
> Nobly ever!

> *1.10.61–65*

"Addition," meaning a role to be proud of, a title, rank, or public name, a "style" of address, is a familiar term from *Othello, King Lear, Macbeth,* and *Hamlet.* In a play about Rome it is a cognomen, an additional name or epithet (as in the name Scipio Aemilianus Africanus). Thus to his first two names, "Martius Caius," is now added the surname Coriolanus. From what the play has already demonstrated about the man, it will come as no surprise when this honor turns out to be his undoing. But no sooner has he been awarded this honorific surname than we have a chance to see what names mean and do not mean to Martius Caius. Like any war hero, he has a particular request to make of his general, and the boon he requests is that a poor man of Corioles who once gave him shelter be freed. "O, well begged!" say the generals, and "Martius, his name?" But Martius has forgotten his name. "By Jupiter, forgot!" Names have no significance for him—he fails to understand the magic in a name, just as he will fail to appreciate the danger implicit in his own. Did the poor man of Corioles die because Martius had forgotten his name?

In the fourth act, when he is banished from Rome, Coriolanus undergoes a process of stripping similar to that experienced by major characters in other Shakespearean tragedies. Once a man who had everything—mother, wife, child, public honors, even, briefly, the consulate—he swiftly becomes, like Lear, a man without anything; like Edgar, a man in costume, in disguise. And like the disguised Edgar, he has no name. Arriving at the home of his former enemy, he is greeted by Aufidius, himself called "[t]he second name of men," with an insistent catechism of identity: "Whence com'st thou? What wouldst thou? Thy name? / Why speak'st not? Speak, man. What's thy name?" (4.5.52–53). When Coriolanus unmuffles himself, he finds that he is still unrecognizable:

Coriolanus   [*unmuffling his head*]   If, Tullus,
              Not yet thou know'st me, . . .

· · · · · · · · · · ·
                                necessity
              Commands me name myself.
Aufidius   What is thy name?
Coriolanus   A name unmusical to the Volscians' ears
              And harsh in sound to thine.
Aufidius   Say, what's thy name?
              Thou hast a grim appearance, and thy face
              Bears a command in't. . . .
                                What's thy name?
Coriolanus   Prepare thy brow to frown. Know'st thou me yet?
Aufidius   I know thee not. Thy name?
Coriolanus   My name is Caius Martius, who hath done
              To thee particularly, and to all the Volsces,
              Great hurt and mischief. Thereto witness may
              My surname Coriolanus. The painful service,
              The extreme dangers, and the drops of blood

Shed for my thankless country, are requited
But with that surname. . . .

. . . .

Only that name remains.

4.5.53–72

He is now just a living surname—"Only that name remains." It has obliterated all the other names—no wife, no mother, no kin—leaving the name Coriolanus as legend. The surname has become the man, a magic word, said at grace before the soldiers' meal. Even his mother, Volumnia, in her final plea to him, recognizes that the public role and the public name have displaced the personal: "To his surname 'Coriolanus' 'longs more pride / Than pity to our prayers" (5.3.171–172).

Thus by the time Cominius comes to plead with him, and is turned away, Coriolanus has been established as a man explicitly without a name, without a human identity, rejecting, by this time, even the surname. "Yet one time did he call me by my name," Cominius reports,

I urged our old acquaintance and the drops
That we have bled together. "Coriolanus"
He would not answer to, forbade all names.
He was a kind of nothing, titleless,
Till he had forged himself a name o'th' fire
Of burning Rome.

5.1.9–15

The logic here is unassailable, and devastating. What kind of cognomen could be given to the Roman conqueror of Rome? It would be a political oxymoron, a pointed self-contradiction.

Characteristically, with his usual charming obtuseness, Menenius pleads from the other extreme, claiming exactly the kind of name that Coriolanus has forbidden—"thy old father, Menenius"—and referring to him as "my son Coriolanus" (5.2.67, 62). These are names that have been long rejected, long abandoned as too painful and too vulnerable. As if to underscore the point, Shakespeare provides a comic tableau in which Menenius boasts to the Volscian watchmen about the power of his own name: "My name hath touched your ears; it is Menenius." "Be it so," replies the First Watchman, "go back. The virtue of your name / Is not here passable" (5.2.13–15). "Menenius" is not a password or watchword. After his embassy is rejected, the Watch has its revenge, addressing him with elephantine irony: "Now, sir, is your name Menenius?" and " 'Tis a spell, you see, of much power."

Yet when the plea comes from his mother, Coriolanus will reverse himself. Her argument, significantly, is not based initially on kinship, but explicitly—

like son, like mother—on name and reputation. She picks up the conundrum introduced by Cominius—What kind of name could be awarded to the Roman who defeats his home city?—and offers an answer from history:

> [I]f thou conquer Rome, the benefit
> Which thou shalt thereby reap is such a name
> Whose repetition will be dogged with curses,
> Whose chronicle thus writ: "The man was noble,
> But with his last attempt he wiped it out,
> Destroyed his country, and his name remains
> To th' ensuing age abhorred." . . .
>
> *5.3.143–149*

His new addition as conqueror of Rome will be one that makes his name abhorred, hated in later times. Artfully she leads her son from this vision of the future to the true name she wishes instead to provide for him, the name that will be the hallmark and password of his destruction. "Speak to me, son. / . . . Why dost not speak? / . . . Daughter, speak you, / . . . Speak thou, boy. / . . . There's no man in the world / More bound to's mother" (5.3.149, 154, 156, 157, 159–160). She, using only kinship terms and not names, urges speech, and then, encountering only stubborn (and defensive) silence, she chooses gesture:

> Down, ladies. Let us shame him with our knees.
>
> . . . .
>
> This fellow had a Volscian to his mother.
> His wife is in Corioles, and his child
> Like him by chance. —Yet give us our dispatch.
> I am hushed until our city be afire,
> And then I'll speak a little.
>
> *5.3.170, 179–183*

It is this rebuke, and this invitation, that leads him to hold her "by the hand, silent," and seal his own doom. His name has been Caius Martius, and Coriolanus. He has been a man of no name, a figure out of romance, wandering in ragged clothes, incognito, seeking to find himself. But the self he finally finds, the name he finally accepts, is not the surname Coriolanus, but the name of a man bound to his mother. The name of a tragic hero whose time has come.

Aufidius, envious and politic, presides over this final stripping, which will leave the hero nameless in yet another sense, taking away from him all the additions, the names and titles and roles, that have cushioned and protected him from the world:

Aufidius	[T]ell the traitor in the highest degree
	He hath abused your powers.
Coriolanus	Traitor? How now?
Aufidius	Ay, traitor, Martius.
Coriolanus	Martius?
Aufidius	Ay, Martius, Caius Martius. Dost thou think
	I'll grace thee with that robbery, thy stol'n name,
	"Coriolanus," in Corioles?

5.6.85–92

It is probably safe to say that this is a nicety that has escaped Coriolanus, the idea that his nickname might give offense to those whose city he had conquered. But far worse—the worst—is yet to come:

Aufidius	[A]t his nurse's tears [he tells the
	Roman commoners]
	He whined and roared away your victory.
	. . . .
Coriolanus	Hear'st thou, Mars?
Aufidius	Name not the god, thou boy of tears.

5.6.99–100, 102–103

Not Mars's man, Martius, but "boy"—his first name and his final name, a name so truly given and so wounding in spirit that Coriolanus can do nothing but repeat it in disbelief. " 'Boy'? O slave!"

Coriolanus	"Boy"! False hound,
	If you have writ your annals true, 'tis there,
	That, like an eagle in a dove-cote, I
	Fluttered your Volscians in Corioles.
	Alone I did it. "Boy"!

5.6.105, 113–117

The traditional belief in many cultures, that when you know someone's real name you have power over them, is enacted here in this drama, this tragedy of the name. In reaffirming the filial bond, in giving in to his mother's plea, and to the voice(s) of Rome in her voice, Caius Martius Coriolanus finds his fate, his name, and his death. For the death that overtakes him resembles the *sparagmos* of ancient Greek tragedy, the ritual tearing to pieces of the tragic hero, the sacrificial victim. "Tear him to pieces! Do it presently!" (that is, right away) cry the people, and the conspirators set upon him and kill him. The literal dismemberment of his body fulfills and completes the verbal imagery of fragmented body parts that began with the fable of the belly and has continued throughout the play. Around him men now begin to speak of his tale, his annals, his chronicle, his fame, and his noble memory—the record of his public achievements that is equivalent in Shakespeare to the action and events of the play itself. It is arguable that his most signal achievement is that he has marched in with the people, recognizing, for a brief moment, his identity with collective humanity. But with the death of Coriolanus, the "boy of tears," something else dies as well, for in bringing together the two key concepts of name and silence, Coriolanus—both the man and the play—has knotted together two central strands of Shakespearean tragedy.

Over and over again in these plays we have seen one common gesture, the gesture of reaching, as if across an abyss, from one world to another, in affirmation—against all costs—of a human bond of pain and love. Desdemona, murdered by Othello and hidden behind the bed curtains, speaks out of the silence of death, and speaks in words of love: "Commend me to my kind lord." Antony, fooled and betrayed into taking his own life, is hauled up to the monument of Cleopatra, and he dies with words to his lover: "I am dying, Egypt, dying." Cordelia, expelled from her father's kingdom because of her own loving silence, hears him reach out to her from something very like death—"You do me wrong to take me out o'th' grave"—and Cordelia, too, rejects the idea of guilt, blame, or recrimination: "No cause, no cause." In *Coriolanus* we are offered that magical and tragic and transcendent moment between mother and son, in which he "holds her by the hand, silent," and once again the silence tells all.

In a way, all of Shakespeare's tragic heroes are in search of names—in search of their own hidden names, which will also be their deaths. They seek reputation, public name, but ultimately they all seek private names as well. "This is I, / Hamlet the Dane," cries Hamlet as he leaps into the grave. "What is thy name?" Macbeth is asked on the battlefield at Dunsinane, and he replies, "Thou'lt be afraid to hear it. / . . . My name's Macbeth." "Only we shall retain / The name and all th'addition to a king," says Lear, and then: "This is not Lear. / . . . Who is it that can tell me who I am?" Othello laments that "Othello's occupation's gone," speaking of himself in the third person, as a public man, and then, at the end of his play: "Speak of me as I am. / . . . Then must you speak / Of one that loved not wisely but too well." Speak of me as I am; pronounce my name. The rest, as Hamlet says, is silence.

At the close of each of these plays, the audience is left with the political men, the Octaviuses and Aufidiuses, the Horatios and Lodovicos and Malcolms, in a shrunken and impoverished world, a world from which a great name, a great power, has gone. "The death of Antony," says Octavius Caesar, "[i]s not a single doom; in that name lay / A moiety of the world" (5.1.17–19). We are left, that is, in the world we have always lived in, a world in which, oddly, tragedy is a kind of luxury, an indulgence and a catharsis or purgation—something that happens *for* us so that it does not have to happen *to* us. That Shakespeare as playwright understood that function of tragedy is very clear from the "Pyramus and Thisbe" play he provides for the amusement of the Theseus court in *A Midsummer Night's Dream*.

This is what they accomplish for us, all these tragic figures with their titanic strengths and their titanic weaknesses—pride, stubbornness, vanity, and ambition on the one side, and on the other side radical insecurity, self-doubt, lack of self-knowledge, a fear of being merely human, of the bare, forked animal, of the boy of tears. It is through these figures, and these passages, that we discover that which above all Shakespearean tragedy has to offer us, for the radical question that was posed by tragedy is always the riddle of the Sphinx, the riddle that was posed to Oedipus, and that, by his answering it, sealed both his doom and his greatness: "What goes on four legs in the morning, on two at noon, on three in the evening?" The answer to the riddle, and the name behind all these names, is the name of mankind, the name, as Coriolanus says, "most mortal" to us. What Shakespeare accomplishes so brilliantly in *Coriolanus* is to make his bluntest, least self-reflective, and most heedless tragic hero live the riddle—and then solve it.

Cymbeline

DRAMATIS PERSONAE

Cymbeline, *King of Britain*
Princess Imogen, *his daughter, later*
  disguised as a boy named Fidele
Guiderius, *known as Polydore,*
  Cymbeline's son, stolen by Belarius
Arviragus, *known as Cadwal,*
  Cymbeline's son, stolen by Belarius
Queen, *Cymbeline's wife, Imogen's*
  stepmother
Lord Cloten, *her son*
Belarius, *a banished lord, calling*
  himself Morgan
Cornelius, *a physician*
Helen, *a lady attending on Imogen*
Two Lords attending on Cloten
Two Gentlemen
Two British Captains
Two Jailers
Posthumus Leonatus, *a poor*
  gentleman, Imogen's husband
Pisanio, *his servant*
Filario, *a friend of Posthumus*
Iachimo, *an Italian,*
  Filario's friend

A Frenchman, *Filario's friend*
A Dutchman, *Filario's friend*
A Spaniard, *Filario's friend*
Caius Lucius, *ambassador*
  from Rome, later General
  of the Roman forces
Two Roman Senators
Roman Tribunes
A Roman Captain
Philharmonus, a Soothsayer
Jupiter
Ghost of Sicilius Leonatus,
  father of Posthumus
Ghost of the Mother
  of Posthumus
Ghosts of the Brothers of
  Posthumus
Lords attending on Cymbeline,
  ladies attending on the
  Queen, musicians attending
  on Cloten, messengers,
  soldiers

ART HISTORY, part romance, part revenge tragedy, and part satire, incorporating pastoral themes and lyric songs of an unusual beauty, *Cymbeline, King of Britain* is a curious play, presenting one of Shakespeare's most complicated and hard-to-summarize plots. A quick glance at its twists and turns reveals how close complexity can come to absurdity.

Many of this play's improbabilities come from Shakespeare's use of the conventions of the romantic genre, which we have already seen well illustrated in an early play, *The Comedy of Errors,* in which a shipwreck sunders a family that is then humorously and coincidentally reunited by the end of the play.

Under the influence of his cruel and dominating queen, King Cymbeline of Britain refuses to pay tribute to the Romans and opposes his daughter Imogen's marriage to the virtuous gentleman Posthumus Leonatus, who had been brought up at court after the death of his parents. The Queen, his second wife, has a son of her own, the oafish Cloten, whom she wishes to marry to Imogen, and thus make him the King's heir. Many years ago Cymbeline's two young sons were stolen away from court by Belarius, a once-beloved, unjustly banished courtier. Although Cymbeline does not know they are alive, the sons are living in a cave in Wales with their adoptive father, now called Morgan. At court, things go from bad to worse. Posthumus, married to Imogen, is banished by the King. He goes to Rome, where he engages in a conversation with several other men about female chastity and the purity of their wives. He is lured into betting on Imogen's fidelity, with the result that the cynical villain Iachimo, bound for Britain, sets out to seduce her and win the wager. He wins by subterfuge, hiding himself in a trunk in her bedroom, stealing her bracelet—a gift from Posthumus—and convincing Posthumus that he has slept with her. Enraged, Posthumus tries to instigate her murder, but his servant Pisanio allows Imogen to escape in boy's clothes, as "Fidele." In Wales she encounters her lost brothers, Guiderius, now called Polydore, and Arviragus, now called Cadwal. In the ensuing action, Guiderius slays Cloten, who is dressed in Posthumus's clothes. Imogen/Fidele, who has taken a poisoned drug—made by the Queen—under the false belief that it is a restorative, is presumed dead and is buried beside the headless body she takes to be that of her husband. She awakes and flees, and eventually, as "Fidele," enlists on the side of the Romans as a page to the general Lucius. Posthumus joins the British army as a common soldier, and he and the King's "Welsh" sons perform feats of valor on the battlefield. In the end, the identities and histories of all parties are revealed, to universal rejoicing; Cymbeline is reunited with his children; and peace is made between Britain and Rome. In the course of this hectic dramatic action—one editor counted twenty-four separate reversals and recognitions in the final scene—the play also offers a visitation from a descended god, a soothsayer with a riddling prophecy, and two of the most beautiful of Shakespeare's songs, "Hark, hark, the lark" and "Fear no more the heat o' th' sun."

The play takes its name from that of the semi-legendary king, Cymbeline, or Kymbeline (the historical Cunobelinus), who ruled Britain at the time of the birth of Christ. Most characters in *Cymbeline* seem to be indebted, in style and behavior, to the modes of romance or fairy tale: the evil Queen, who will be a literal "wicked stepmother" to the virtuous and ill-used princess, Imogen; the dastardly villain Iachimo, whose roots are in Renaissance Italian intrigue; the faithful but disillusioned courtier who has fled the court and its corruption, and now makes his home in the hills of Wales. But the play is, manifestly, also a history, a narrative of ancient Britain and ancient Rome.

The flatness of some of the romance characterizations—the ways in which these dramatic characters move through their landscapes like dream figures emblematic of psychological or moral states—seems at times tonally at odds with the historical content. Some literary critics at the beginning of the twentieth century were inclined to dismiss the play as the work of a has-been, a washed-up playwright with nothing left to say, a Shakespeare so tired of the theater that he was, as Lytton Strachey famously remarked, "half bored to death." It then became conventional to describe the play as an "experiment" (however at odds that view might be with the "has-been" argument), a mixed-mode play following a Jacobean fashion for such things. Latterly the period term "tragicomedy" has been resurrected, replacing—as we saw also with *Pericles*—categories and labels such as "last plays," "late plays," and "dramatic romance." One oddity of the play's classification is that it was listed among the tragedies in the First Folio, and was given the running title *The Tragedie of Cymbeline*. Yet the events of the play are "happy" ones by almost any standard of fiction: the cartoonish evil queen and her son are killed, the villain confesses his perjury and repents, the lost children are found and restored to their father and to the land.

There is nothing wrong with calling *Cymbeline* an experiment, unless by that we mean to undercut its standing as a play worth reading, staging, remembering, and discussing. For this is a play that tackles, and to a large extent solves, an intriguing set of problems about the relationship between political stories and psychological stories, between the state or polity and the subject, and between the political fiction and the dream.

Cymbeline can usefully be considered a myth of national origin, a play at once historical and romancelike by its very nature and purpose. How did Britain come to be? What kind of a nation was it? Who were its forebears, its originators, its founding fathers and mothers? If we look back over the other plays Shakespeare had been writing in these years, *King Lear* and *Macbeth* among them, it seems clear that this question of origin and futurity was a preoccupation of the period. (It also turns up with some frequency as a topic in court masques, one of King James's favorite modes of entertainment.) *Cymbeline* as a foundation myth culminates in the revelation that the spirit of the founder lives on in the present monarch, James I, who—like King Cymbeline—was celebrated as a peacemaker, and who regarded himself, famously, as the heir to the Roman tradition, as well as the successor to the legendary Brutus, the first ruler of Britain. (Geoffrey of Monmouth's *History of the Kings of Britain* begins with Brutus and names Leir and Cordelia in the list of legendary kings and queens; Cymbeline, "chief of the Catevellauni," is followed in Geoffrey's list by Guiderius and then by Arviragus.) This is a play about the way the British and Roman heritages come together in Cymbeline—and, by implication, in James. Thus it follows a pattern familiar from the other English history plays, situating itself in three time periods at once: its historical setting (ancient Britain), its time of writing and initial performance (James I's Britain), and the time in which it is read, produced, and discussed ("today," that all-purpose shifter).

Like King Cymbeline, James had two sons and a daughter, and it is worth recalling that the question of the royal family as a political structure and a model of the state was one of James's chief concerns as monarch. The presence of heirs supported the idea of an orderly succession, of course, but part of the tension in this play is between the role of king as *pater familias*, head of the household, and his role as patriarch, head of the state. As a husband and a father Cymbeline is weak and doting; he is willing to marry off his beloved daughter, Imogen, to the wicked (and nameless) Queen's son, his stepson, the oafish Cloten. But the play corrects this paternalistic error by supplying a better husband, Posthumus Leonatus, and a whole group of surrogate fathers, not only the ghosts of Posthumus's own father and family, but also the archpatriarch, Jupiter, the king (and father) of the gods. Cymbeline at the beginning of his play is neither a good father nor a good king, but by the end he has come to closely resemble James: he is statesmanlike; he pays tribute where tribute is due; and he is, as James proclaimed himself to be, a "loving nourish-father," both father and mother to his children and to his land.

One issue at stake at the beginning of *Cymbeline,* as it was at the beginning of *Pericles,* is the father's—and king's—right to choose his daughter's husband. The play raises questions related to patriarchy, to absolute monarchy, and to dynastic politics, and it addresses them in a context of romance, dream, and fantasy that helps to craft a solution that is a critique of tyranny. *King Lear* begins with, among other things, Lear's refusal to pay Cordelia's dowry to the Duke of Burgundy ("her price is fallen"); the King of France takes her without a marriage portion. In *Antony and Cleopatra* Octavia is the unhappy pawn in a negotiation between Octavius Caesar and Antony. In *Cymbeline* Imogen not only marries the man she loves, but discovers that he is the ideal political mate. The realization of the fantasy of personal choice becomes the establishment of political orthodoxy.

Yet if *Cymbeline* is a foundation myth, it is also a family romance, embodying the fantasy of being freed from one's family and discovering that one is a member of a family of higher standing. Often, in fairy tales or pastoral romances, the orphaned or adopted child is discovered to be a prince or princess—or a wizard, to recall Harry Potter, the most recent family romance. The term "family romance" was coined by Freud, and it covers a wide variety of instances, from megalomania to daydreaming; but as a literary and mythological trope it far predates modern psychology and reaches back to the earliest times of storytelling. In this play the young male hero, Posthumus Leonatus, is—as his name implies—born after his father's death, then reunited with father and mother in a dream in which his father declares that Jupiter should have been Posthumus's foster father and shielded him from harm. The two sons of King Cymbeline are also caught up in a pattern of family romance, since the man they think is their father, the Welsh countryman "Morgan," is actually the courtier Belarius, who stole them away from their real father, the King. Thus, while Guiderius and Arviragus are living out a true family romance in Freud's sense, Posthumus lives out a family romance *fantasy*. Bearing in mind the Christological background of the play, we might note that the pattern of Christ on earth is another version of family romance, with Joseph the earthly foster father to a man who would be revealed as the Son of God. The family romance is, in essence, the personal or psychological equivalent of the foundation myth or myth of national origin. Both ask, and try to answer, fundamental questions of identity, individual and cultural: Who am I? Who are we? How did I, or we, get to be who and what we are? As so frequently in Shakespeare, the political reading and the psychological reading are not only analogous, but intertwined.

Whatever the mode, the dramaturgy of *Cymbeline* is hardly a complete break from Shakespearean practice. Elements of this kind of romance have appeared in the tragedies. We have seen, for example, the awakening of Lear, dressed in fresh garments, to the accompaniment of music; the seasonal, mythic, and elemental associations that surround Antony and Cleopatra; and Hamlet's rejection of the false father Claudius for the greater and lost father, old Hamlet, his journey to England, and his reclaiming of his lost name. Many of the great comedies of the Elizabethan period, such as *A Midsummer Night's Dream* and *As You Like It*, were preoccupied with questions of pastoral, of city and country. The acquisition of the small indoor Blackfriars theater in 1608, and the interest of the Jacobean court in the theatrical form of the masque, with its visual pyrotechnics, machines, and "wonder," may have spurred Shakespeare's—or his company's—interest in this kind of theatricality, which seems to a modern audience closer to dream and to the logic of the unconscious than to mimesis, the imitation of speech and action in the real world.

The language of characters in *Cymbeline* is occasionally recognizable as the highly compressed, highly emotive and metaphorical language familiar from the tragedies—as, for example, in Posthumus's Othello-like tirade on the infidelities of women, at the end of act 2. Misled by Iachimo, Posthumus believes, wrongly, that his wife, Imogen, has been unfaithful to him, and he complains that her chaste reluctance must have been a sham:

> O vengeance, vengeance!
> Me of my lawful pleasure she restrained,
> And prayed me oft forbearance; did it with
> A pudency so rosy the sweet view on't
> Might well have warmed old Saturn; that I thought her
> As chaste as unsunned snow. O all the devils!
>
> *Cymbeline 2.5.8–13*

This is the heightened diction of revenge tragedy, in the hyberbolic spirit of such contemporary Jacobean revengers as Vindice in Middleton's *Revenger's Tragedy*. Imogen's "False to his bed? What is it to be false?" (3.4.39) hits a similar high note of tragedy, as, indeed, does much of the language of the villainous

Iachimo, particularly in the scene (1.6) in which he tries to tempt Imogen by telling her that Posthumus has been false to her. But on the other hand, we occasionally hear, in *Cymbeline,* the language of pure romance, as, for example, in the wondering response of a British lord to the story of the unlikely way Belarius and his sons (in actuality, the sons of the King) inspired the Britons to victory:

> This was strange chance:
> A narrow lane, an old man, and two boys.
>
> *5.5.51–52*

Here the whole design of the action is expressed in a single phrase, very close in mythic tone to Thaisa's exclamation, in *Pericles,* "Did you not name a tempest? / A birth and death?"

Cymbeline resembles a tragedy not only in the fact that it contains some tragic speech patterns, but also because its plot fulfills and makes explicit a precept implicit in Shakespearean tragedy, the idea of resurrection, regeneration, and rebirth. Cymbeline himself is another king raised to high estate, who falls, through error (here the same uxorious error as Adam's, putting himself under a woman's thrall). His daughter, Imogen, fleeing the court disguised as the boy "Fidele," takes a sleeping potion that—like Juliet's—counterfeits death; she is twice reborn, once to her discoverers in the cave (who turn out to be her natural brothers, the King's stolen sons), and again to her father and her husband in the court. The sons, too, are restored, and thus effectively reborn, to their father, who responds: "O, what am I? A mother to the birth of three?" (5.6.369–370). But as a dramatic character, Cymbeline gets off to a slow start, in part, perhaps, because of this persistent problem of genre. In a narrative romance, like Spenser's *Faerie Queene,* characters are symbolic and can remain in that mode. They represent Error, or Despair, or the True Church. And their symbolic nature, their one-dimensionalism, is something the reader can accept. This is not true of all characters in narrative romance, of course, but even the most rounded, like Spenser's knights of Holiness (Redcrosse), Temperance (Guyon), and Chastity (Britomart), retain an emblematic basis. A schematic and therefore slightly parodic account of this can be gleaned from a footnote to a teaching edition of *The Faerie Queene:*

> Una . . . , representing Truth, in particular the true faith of Redcrosse. In this context, the "lowly Asse" is a symbol of humility. . . . The dwarf may represent common sense, or practical understanding.[1]

This is a useful gloss for a reading of the text, but if we were to try to imagine the scenario as a play—not a hieratic medieval play but a play designed for the commercial early modern theater—we might encounter difficulties. A set of allegorical equivalences like these tends to produce something more like a cartoon character than a recognizable human individual: Superman, Batman, Spider-man, Wonder Woman. (Each of these, we might note, has a "human" other, like Superman's Clark Kent.) Shakespeare's personae, however linked they might be to familiar allegorical personages and types (the Vice, the Machiavel), had to be characters first and symbols second, with voices and motives that are sufficiently mimetic to sustain an audience's engagement. In *Cymbeline* Shakespeare addresses this issue directly. The playwright's task is to blend dramatic action and tension with romance modes and themes.

The play's spectators thus find themselves in a world full of historical anachronism. The Britons of *Cymbeline* are ancient Britons, some living in Luds Town (London), some in the forests and caves of Wales, but the Romans seem simultaneously to be living in the time of Augustus Caesar and that of early modern Italy. Iachimo is presented as a devious and scheming Italian, akin to the characters in Ben Jonson's *Volpone* or Webster's *Duchess of Malfi*. Lucius, the Roman general, is equally clearly a figure who might appear in *Antony and Cleopatra* or *Coriolanus*. In his *Poetics* Aristotle had written that one should prefer a convincing impossibility to an unconvincing possibility (*Poetics,* chapter 25), and that is what this conjunction of time periods in *Cymbeline* produces, once we suspend our disbelief. The play's dramatic universe is thus able to encompass both the basic subject of Shakespeare's history plays (the "matter of Britain," the "matter of Rome") and also the relationship between Renaissance England and Renaissance Italy that is a major feature both of his comedies and of his tragedies.

The play's characters exhibit the same range of possibility and impossibility, or mimetic persuasiveness and emblematic association. Cymbeline, as we have said, is in the opening scenes a doddering and ineffectual dupe, henpecked by his awful queen, and not immediately worthy of tragic identification. The Queen is a stock figure who would become familiar in later fairy tales: the wicked stepmother, like Dionyza in *Pericles*. Her dominance over the weak King, far less emotionally convincing than, say, Lady Macbeth's dominance over Macbeth, or Volumnia's over Coriolanus, is a "given" in the play's world rather than a gradually perceived psychological effect. Thus both Imogen and the doctor, Cornelius, immediately tell the audience that the Queen is a liar and a fraud. "O dissembling courtesy!" says Imogen (1.1.85), and Cornelius says, simply, "I do not like her" (1.5.33). Among the Queen's favorite recreational activities is the brewing of poison, which she uses to end the lives of innocent cats and dogs. (Women, and especially mothers, in the late romances of Shakespeare tend to be either alive and wicked, or good and dead; in this play the good dead women include Belarius's wife, Euriphile; Cymbeline's first queen; and Posthumus's mother.)

Cloten, the Queen's own son, is as unappealing as she, although he is as foolish as she is shrewd and shrewish. In the opening scenes of the play he is accompanied by two lords, one of whom flatters him to his face while the other mocks him, behind his back, to the audience. This is an example of Shakespeare's astonishing and economical facility with framing character, especially in the vein of dramatic satire. Thus when Cloten boasts that one of his fencing opponents could not stand up to him, the Second Lord is right there to tell him, and us, "No, but he fled forward still, toward your face" (1.2.13–14). As Cymbeline's stepson, Cloten is a parodic quest hero, structurally to be compared both to the King's real sons and to Posthumus. When we hear of Posthumus in the first scene that his outside exactly matches his inside, that "[s]o fair an outward and such stuff within" distinguishes no other man at court (1.1.23), we are able much later in the play to witness, in Cloten, a wonderful parody of the quest hero's climactic self-revelation. Dressed in Posthumus's clothes, flourishing his sword at the King's son Guiderius, whom he mistakes for a mere rustic mountaineer, he shouts, "Thou villain base, / Know'st me not by my clothes?" and "Thou injurious thief, / Hear but my name and tremble" (4.2.82–83, 88–89). These are the classic tokens of recognition. (Compare Hamlet's "This is I, / Hamlet the Dane," or, in *Macbeth,* Edgar's "My name is Edgar, and thy father's son," or even the romance ending of *Twelfth Night,* where Sebastian and Viola name each other, and Viola's lover Orsino requests that he might see her in her own clothes, her "women's weeds.") Yet the clothes Cloten wears in this scene are not his own, and his name, despite the fact that it belongs to a "historical" character found in Holinshed's *Chronicles,* related to the Middle English *clott* (lump, or block of wood), is hardly one to produce fear in its hearers. (Guiderius, who beheads him, will shortly speak of sending "Cloten's clotpoll" down the stream [4.2.185], and the word "clotpoll"—literally, "blockhead"—also appears in *Troilus and Cressida.*)

But if Cloten is a travesty of Posthumus, the hero, he is also a parodic version of a familiar pastoral and romance character, the "noble savage," the man who, lacking nurture, has an innate nobility that does not need to be taught. Described memorably by Montaigne, and later to be taken up by Rousseau and other Enlightenment authors, such figures (like Spenser's "salvage nation" and "salvage knight") were regarded as having "natural" manners and graces, uncorrupted by the venality of court or city life. "There is nothing savage or barbarous about those peoples, but that every man calls barbarous anything he is not accustomed to," wrote Montaigne in his essay "On Cannibals." "They are still ruled by natural laws, only slightly corrupted by ours. They are in such a state of purity that I am sometimes saddened by the thought that we did not discover them earlier." Montaigne's famous conclusion was that it was more barbarous to tear a living body apart through torture or to burn a man alive, as was often done by the Inquisition, than it was to eat him dead. The real barbarians were the Europeans, not the "cannibals" of the New World.[2]

Cloten is not a noble savage but the opposite, a savage noble. Despite his courtly opportunities, he remains a boor, and as such he is the contrary of the King's sons, brought up in rustic Wales, but with the natural manners of the (ideal) court and nobility. Animated by lust and appetite, spiteful, scornful, and ambitious, Cloten is the man his mother wants to put at the head of the British state. His death is like the death of a beast or monster as much as like that of a man. In a way, this unlikable character points toward a figure at once less human and more engaging, the music-loving monster Caliban in *The Tempest*. Cloten, who lacks Caliban's excuse, since he is fully human and presumably was brought up at court, is far coarser and more profane, joking of penetration, fingers, and tongues even as he commissions, in act 2, scene 3, the performance of that utterly lovely lyric and aubade "Hark, hark, the lark." In direct contrast to Cloten, and soon to demonstrate themselves as literally noble savages, are the King's sons, Guiderius and Arviragus, who now live in a cave and bear the Welsh names Polydore and Cadwal. Their adoptive father, Belarius, who stole them from the court, calls himself Morgan.

Belarius is a development of a classical pastoral type, or rather the combination of two familiar types, often linked in literature: the old man who once lived in the corrupt court and has now elected to dwell in the purity and innocence of the countryside, and the shepherd father who steals or adopts a changeling child not his own—a child who, inevitably in romance, and usually in pastoral, turns out to be of royal blood. The sons, Guiderius and Arviragus, exhibit their noble qualities despite the humble surroundings in which they live, although they are unaware of their own history, as Belarius observes, to himself and to the audience, the first time we meet them:

> How hard it is to hide the sparks of nature!
> These boys know little they are sons to th' King,
> Nor Cymbeline dreams that they are alive.
> They think they are mine, and though trained up thus meanly
> I'th' cave wherein they bow, their thoughts do hit
> The roofs of palaces, and nature prompts them
> In simple and low things to prince it much
> Beyond the trick of others. . . .

> 3.3.79–86

When Imogen encounters them in act 4, by that time disguised as the page boy "Fidele," she shares the surprise evinced by Orlando in *As You Like It* when he bursts into the Forest of Arden, dagger drawn, to find a highly civilized scene. Like Orlando, Imogen is astonished to find that forest dwellers can have manners:

> These are kind creatures. Gods, what lies I have heard!
> Our courtiers say all's savage but at court.

> 4.2.32–33

There is an embedded irony here, since the "kind creatures" of the cave do originate in the court (as Orlando's singing, table-laying savages are actually

Duke Senior's "co-mates and brothers in exile"). Thus the world of romance (and "family romance") is able, as usual, to have things both ways, so that noble savages turn out not to be real "savages," but in fact nobly born. Earlier, when she first met the boys, Imogen had made the same point made by Belarius. Here is Imogen:

> Great men
> That had a court no bigger than this cave,
>
> . . . .
>
> Could not outpeer these twain.
>
> *3.7.79–84*

As is fairly common for pairs of sons in literary romance, the two boys are temperamental and emblematic opposites: Guiderius exemplifies the active ideal, and Arviragus the contemplative. The contrasting values of the active and the contemplative life had been an important subject of philosophical debate since the time of Aristotle. Commentators like Philo, Origen, Augustine, Gregory, and Thomas Aquinas all expressed views on the topic, which became a commonplace Renaissance theme. (A painting by Paolo Veronese is titled *A Nobleman Between the Active and the Contemplative Life,* and—like Hercules' choice between Pleasure and Virtue, or the Neoplatonic debate between Sacred and Profane Love—this dyad was often represented in pictorial as well as literary form.) Guiderius, the elder son (and Cymbeline's heir), is the "best woodman," the best hunter, and therefore the master of the feast. He will preside over the ritual of preparing the game, a ritual deliberately described in archaic, folkloric terms. It is Guiderius who taunts and then kills Cloten, the false, usurping heir arrayed against the true, disguised heir. His decapitation of Cloten, the removing of "Cloten's clotpoll," is in romance terms the slaying of a monster or dragon, at the same time that it resembles moments of resolution in the tragedies (Macduff holding up the head of Macbeth; the disguised Edgar defeating his rival Edmund). From this defining moment of achieved adulthood Guiderius will move forward, insisting upon leaving the safety of the (womblike) cave and joining, instead, the forces waging war.

The second son, Arviragus, is quieter, more inward and tenderhearted. He is especially fond of music, praising the "angel-like" singing of the boy "Fidele." Arviragus performs what is perhaps the most touching domestic gesture of the entire play. Thinking that Imogen/Fidele is only asleep, he takes off his shoes so as not to make noise: "I thought he slept, and put / My clouted brogues from off my feet, whose rudeness / Answered my steps too loud" (4.2.214–216). At this point neither the audience in the theater nor that on the stage knows that she is alive.

So vital and vibrant are these figures of the Welsh world that next to them the inhabitants of the court world never seem to come fully to life. Iachimo begins strongly, as an Italianate villain of the most satisfactorily corrupt and lustful kind, but he quickly disappears from the play, and when he resurfaces in the last act it is cravenly to confess his sins and beg forgiveness. As for Posthumus, he, too, is largely absent from the play's radical actions. He is described in his absence in superlative terms, from the play's first scene onward, in a familiar Shakespearean scenario: the comments of onlookers describe the hero before he comes upon the stage, just as the Roman soldiers set the scene for Antony, or as Kent and Gloucester discuss King Lear. In this case it is gentlemen of the court who give us the general view of Posthumus. He

> is a creature such
> As, to seek through the regions of the earth
> For one his like, there would be something failing
> In him that should compare. . . .
>
> *1.1.19–22*

> lived in court—
> Which rare it is to do—most praised, most loved;
> A sample to the youngest. . . .
>
> *1.1.46–48*

"Sample" here is "example": Posthumus was a model of good behavior. Notice again he "lived in court— / Which rare it is to do—most praised." In the first moments of the play the court of Cymbeline is already being exposed as a corrupting and fallen influence, and the way is being paved for the ameliorative and invigorating influence of the King's soon-to-be-found sons.

But though the banished Posthumus is described in these elevated terms, not only by the anonymous gentlemen of the first scene but also by his wife, Imogen, and by his man Pisanio, the theater audience never really sees him in action until the deliberately schematic battle of the fifth act. He dreams, he sleeps, he ponders a riddle but "fails to decipher" it. In fact, except for his martial heroism in the climactic battle, when (disguised as a Briton soldier) he joins forces with Belarius and the sons against the Roman army, Posthumus's only visible action is to agree to the wager with Iachimo that tests Imogen's chastity. It is a swaggering, boys-will-be-boys wager (based on a well-known episode in *The Decameron* of Boccaccio, and on a sixteenth-century pamphlet called "Frederyke of Jennen") that leads to separation and loss, and almost to tragedy. From an actor's point of view, Posthumus is a fairly thankless role.

Imogen, on the other hand, is a brilliant part, and it justly became a favorite of actresses and audiences in succeeding centuries. Shakespeare's first crossdressed woman since Viola, and the first and only woman disguised as a boy in one of his Jacobean plays, Imogen resembles both the inventive, disguised heroines of the comedies (Rosalind, Viola, Portia) and also the virtuous and muse-like Marina, a quintessential figure of the romance genre. Like Marina, Imogen is described repeatedly in images of divinity. She is "[m]ore goddess-like than wife-like" (3.2.8), she sings "angel-like," and Belarius says of her, when he encounters her disguised as the boy "Fidele,"

> By Jupiter, an angel—or, if not,
> An earthly paragon. Behold divineness
> No elder than a boy.
>
> *3.6.42–44*

Although Shakespeare never permits the comparison of a human being to a god or goddess to go unchallenged (male rulers, in particular, are cut down to size if they or their followers make this category error), the young women of the last romances come closest to this elusive state. Posthumus, though he "sits 'mongst men like a descended god" (1.6.170), is soon seen doubting his lady's fidelity and sending off messages commanding that she be put to death. But Imogen, described as being like a goddess and an angel (with the usual Shakespearean qualification "or, if not, / An earthly paragon"), is, like Marina, closely associated with art and art making. She sings, and in her cookery she cuts roots into decorative characters (that is, both figures and letters of the alphabet). But where the typical romance heroine is often a fairly passive figure, who is adored ("Admired Miranda!") and who inspires wonder and poetry, Imogen is engagingly active, putting on a riding costume, racing on horseback to Milford Haven on the Welsh coast for her rendezvous with Posthumus, then enlisting as a page in the Roman army once she believes she has lost both her husband and her friends. Imogen, like Rosalind in *As You Like It*, was in Shakespeare's time a boy actor playing a woman who disguises herself as a boy. She is "read" by her Welsh rescuers (who will turn out to be her natural siblings) as somehow both male and female, in a way that is again reminiscent of Rosalind's encounters with Orlando:

> Guiderius   Were you a woman, youth,
>   I should woo hard but be your groom in honesty,
>   Ay, bid for you as I'd buy.
> Arviragus   I'll make't my comfort
>   He is a man, I'll love him as my brother.
>
>   . . . .
>   Be sprightly, for you fall 'mongst friends.
> Imogen   'Mongst friends
>   If brothers. [*Aside*] Would it had been so that they
>   Had been my father's sons. . . .
>
>   . . . .
>   Pardon me, gods,

> I'd change my sex to be companion with them,
> Since Leonatus' false.
>
> *3.6.66–74, 84–86*

Since Arviragus is also, in the plot, a young man, the play takes some pains to emphasize his difference from Imogen, a "woman" (played by a boy) impersonating a boy. When later he speaks, in a lovely passage of verse, about the flowers he will strew on "Fidele's" grave, Guiderius interrupts him impatiently: "Prithee, have done, / And do not play in wench-like words with that / Which is so serious" (4.2.230–232). The "wench-like words" may have reminded a Shakespearean audience that such extended flower passages are often spoken by female characters in the tragedies and romances (Ophelia, Marina, Perdita), but the phrase also marks the difference between the "male" Arviragus and the "female" Imogen/Fidele, as does the immediately following mention of the changing voice of a young man ("our voices / Have got the mannish crack" [236–237]); compare the teasing endured by the boy actor advised by Hamlet to pray that his voice, "like a piece of / uncurrent gold, be not cracked within the ring" (*Hamlet* 2.2.410–411).

Another flower passage, the dirge Guiderius sings for Imogen/Fidele, "Fear no more the heat o'th' sun," culminates in the haunting lines

> Golden lads and girls all must,
> As chimney-sweepers, come to dust.
>
> *4.2.263–264*

"Golden lad" and "chimney-sweeper" were folk names for the dandelion, so this resonant passage, which seems to comment on early promise and loss and the hardships of the working world, is also an embedded nature fable with the implication of rebirth (the "dust" of the dandelion is the seed head that scatters).

Given the unfamiliarity of many modern readers and audiences with *Cymbeline,* it is important to emphasize the degree to which the play—and especially its heroine—was admired in past years. Imogen has been played by such stage luminaries as Sarah Siddons, Helen Faucit, Ellen Terry, and Peggy Ashcroft. Nineteenth-century novelists rhapsodized about her, citing her over and over as a female paragon: Sir Walter Scott in *The Heart of Midlothian,* William Makepeace Thackeray in *Pendennis,* Anthony Trollope in *Barchester Towers* and *The Last Chronicle of Barset,* George Eliot in *Middlemarch.* When Oscar Wilde came to write *The Picture of Dorian Gray,* he had Dorian go to the theater and fall in love with an actress, Sybil Vane, whose three signature parts are Juliet, Rosalind, and Imogen. The nineteenth century's adoration of Imogen may be summed up by Algernon Swinburne's comments in *A Study of Shakespeare* (1880):

The very crown and flower of all her father's daughters, —I do not speak here of her human father, but her divine, —woman above all Shakespeare's women is Imogen. As in Cleopatra we found the incarnate sex, the woman everlasting, so in Imogen we find half-glorified already the immortal godhead of womanhood. I would fain have some honey in my words at parting. . . . and I am, therefore, something more than fain to close my book upon the name of the woman best beloved in all the world of song and all the tide of time: upon the name of Shakespeare's Imogen.[3]

Swinburne's final emphasis, "upon the name of Shakespeare's Imogen," will help to explain why I do not follow the Norton and Oxford editors in changing the character's name back to the historical "Innogen," the name of the wife of Brut, or Brutus, the legendary king of Britain. Innogen is mentioned in Holinshed's *Chronicles,* one of Shakespeare's sources; in book 1, canto 10, of Spenser's *Faerie Queene;* and in Drayton's *Polyolbion* (1612), and the name makes a fascinating shadow appearance in the dramatis personae for *Much Ado About Nothing* in Nicholas Rowe's 1709 edition of Shakespeare's plays. (Rowe listed "Innogen, *Wife to Leonato,*" but no such character appears in *Much Ado,* and the entry was dropped by the editor Lewis Theobald in 1733.) Some editors have speculated that the First Folio's use of "Imogen" throughout may be a misprint, but the name has by this time taken on a life and character of its own. I think that instead of attempting to rewrite literary history (by, for example, inserting footnotes in editions of Swinburne and *Middlemarch* to explain the discrepancy between a restored "Innogen" and a Victorian "Imogen"), we should consider the plays of Shakespeare to be living artifacts with their own significant pasts. Since both the Folio and the Victorians write "Imogen," "Innogen" seems to me a historicist affectation. (Likewise with "Iachimo," which *The Norton Shakespeare* modernizes to "Giacomo." In act 2 an angry Posthumus rails against "yellow Iachimo" [2.5.14], which is likely to be alliterative, and I am not aware of any editorial inclination to respell or repronounce the name of the better-known Iago.)

Imogen/Fidele's double identity as woman and boy, Briton and Roman, resurfaces in the climactic political scene of the play (5.6), a scene not unlike the revelation scene in *Twelfth Night* in the way it manages the surprising disclosure of gender and the discomfiture of the supposed boy's male patron. Imogen, after waking in Wales to find what she thought was the body of her dead husband, has fled to join the Roman army. Her patron is the defeated Roman general Lucius, who asks as his one boon from Cymbeline that the life of his page boy ("a Briton born") be spared:

> Never master had
> A page so kind, so duteous, diligent,

So tender over his occasions, true,
So feat, so nurse-like. . . .

5.6.85–88

In true romance fashion, Cymbeline finds that something in the "boy" jogs his memory: "I have surely seen him. / His favour is familiar to me" (5.6.92–93). Indeed he finds, as he says to the "boy," "I love thee more and more," and he urges "Fidele" to make any request. Imogen replies in the language of riddling disclosure that these scenes so often provoke. The man she looks at, she tells the King, is "no more kin to me / Than I am to your highness, who, being born your vassal, / Am something nearer" (112–114). Belarius, looking on, thinks he recognizes the true identity of the page: "Is not this the boy revived from death?" he asks, aside, and Arviragus replies, again in tones that evoke the recognition scene in *Twelfth Night,* "One sand another / Not more resembles that sweet rosy lad / Who died, and was Fidele. What think you?" "The same dead thing alive," concurs the more matter-of-fact and less poetic Guiderius (120–123). But Pisanio sees a different truth: "It is my mistress. / Since she is living, let the time run on / To good or bad" (127–129). The revelations now come thick and fast. "Fidele" demands to know how Iachimo got the diamond on his finger. Iachimo confesses the whole story of the boasting contest, including the incident of his spying in her bedchamber. Posthumus, suddenly revealed as present, declares his identity ("I am Posthumus, / That killed thy daughter" [217–218]), bursts into a panegyric for his "dead" wife ("O Imogen! / My queen, my life, my wife, O Imogen, / Imogen, Imogen!" [225–227]), is interrupted by the page, whom he does not (of course) recognize, strikes her, and is corrected by the percipient and faithful Pisanio ("O my lord Posthumus, / You ne'er killed Imogen till now" [230–231]). The denouements in the final scene also include the story of Cloten's ignominious death, the Queen's perfidy in the making and distribution of poison, the true identities of the sons and their Welsh "father," Posthumus's heroism when he was disguised as a soldier in the war, and, of course, the meaning of the Soothsayer's riddle.

This variegated cast of characters, some seeming to derive from chronicle history, some from pastoral or romance, others, by their depth of rhetorical spleen, from tragedy, is brought together in a plot and a set of landscapes that reflect this mixture of genres. Myths are the dreams produced by a culture. As was the case with *Pericles* and *The Winter's Tale,* and will be the case with *The Tempest,* classical mythology becomes for this play a mediating deep structure, enabling the playwright to link lyric and dramatic, pagan and Christian, "Renaissance" and "early modern." In turning away from mimesis, from the direct imitation of a human action, toward epiphany and transcendence, Shakespeare was also turning toward creation myths and stories of metamorphosis— stories that, like those in Ovid's *Metamorphoses,* were much more widely read and recognized in his own time than they are in ours.

The settings of *Cymbeline* range from Britain and Rome, familiar loci from the history plays, to a "green world" of magic, music, caves, and hills that is the world of Wales. In earlier Shakespeare plays, "Wales" was associated with figures like the mystical chieftain Owen Glendower (Owain Glyndŵr), the last Welshman to claim the title of Prince of Wales, and with music, magic, poetry, and the Welsh language. By the time of *Cymbeline* Wales could serve as a romantic backdrop, with suitably masquelike topographical features (caves and mountains), for a story of adventure, loss, and rebirth. As with the wilderness settings of the earlier comedies, this Welsh terrain seems to provide a space for what the anthropologist Victor Turner called "antistructure," the salutary and temporary breakdown of hierarchies and identities. It is in "Wales" that a princess can pass herself off as a page boy, and an alternative family of "father," "sons," and their (now dead) "mother," Euriphile, can constitute itself against the real but foolish and fallible royal family. The action of the play, as we have already seen, will involve the recognition by the court world of its (redeemed) identities in the world of Wales, and the reintegration of the two worlds as one by the play's close.

As with other Shakespearean romances (and indeed with late tragedies like *Macbeth* and *Antony and Cleopatra*), the logic of the seasonal cycle is deliberately played off against the pattern of historical and Christian redemption. Posthumus is of a "crescent note"—"in 's spring became a harvest" (1.1.46). Imogen says of her parting from him that before she could give him a parting kiss "comes in my father, / And, like the tyrannous breathing of the north, / Shakes all our buds from growing" (1.3.36–38)—her father is the north wind, and Posthumus is the spring. When husband and wife are reunited at the end of the play, Posthumus takes her in his arms and says, in a magnificent image, "Hang there like fruit, my soul, / Till the tree die" (5.6.263–264). The play has need of these insistent images of fertility, since Cymbeline, like Pericles, presides over a wasteland. His queen reverses the pattern of healthy nature by taking flowers and turning them into poison. First his two sons, and then his daughter, Imogen, are lost, so that he is without an heir. Belarius, explaining his change of fortune, explains that he was falsely accused of treason, and was summarily banished from the court. In the past, says Belarius, "Cymbeline loved me." He recalls:

> Then was I as a tree
> Whose boughs did bend with fruit; but in one night
> A storm or robbery, call it what you will,
> Shook down my mellow hangings, nay, my leaves,
> And left me bare to weather.
>
> *3.3.58, 60–64*

The image is a familiar one, similar, as editors have observed, to a passage in *Timon of Athens* (4.3.259 ff.), but also to Macbeth's "the sere, the yellow leaf" and indeed to the famous "yellow leaves, or none, or few" lines from Sonnet 73. By any estimate, natural or biblical, this is a "fall," and the consequent pattern of loss and renewal is acted out on every level of the play, including, significantly, that of riddle and prophecy.

Posthumus's dream, with its vision of Jupiter and of his own father and ancestors, produces as well a scroll that declares:

> "Whenas a lion's whelp shall, to himself unknown, without seeking find, and be embraced by a piece of tender air; and when from a stately cedar shall be lopped branches which, being dead many years, shall after revive, be jointed to the old stock, and freshly grow; then shall Posthumus end his miseries, Britain be fortunate, and flourish in peace and plenty."
>
> 5.5.232–237

Since Posthumus's other name is Leonatus (born of a lion), the riddle seems at first easy to decipher, although the Soothsayer who unravels it is forced into the realm of questionable etymology. (Imogen, as a *mulier*—"wife" in Latin—is said also to be *mollis aer*—"gentle air"—an etymology suggested by a number of early Christian writers.) The "stately cedar" is identified as the King himself:

> Soothsayer   The lofty cedar, royal Cymbeline,
>   Personates thee, and thy lopped branches point
>   Thy two sons forth, who, by Belarius stol'n,
>   For many years thought dead, are now revived,
>   To the majestic cedar joined, whose issue
>   Promises Britain peace and plenty.
>
> 5.6.453–458

Where for Imogen and for Belarius the image of the fruitful or barren tree was a metaphorical description of their own conditions and states of mind, much in the spirit of figurative language in the tragedies, the prophecy or riddle is at once "flatter" and more pictorial, a verbal emblem or rebus. The rebus (literally "by things," from the Latin *res,* "thing") may be a particularly useful model here. The word entered English at the beginning of the seventeenth century. William Camden's *Remains Concerning Britain* notes, in speaking of people's admiration of poesies, that "they which lackt wit to express their conceit in speech, did use to depaint it out (as it were) in pictures, which they called *Rebus.*"[4]

This "enigmatical representation of a name, word, or phrase by figures, pictures, arrangement of letters, etc." (*OED*) was related to the pictorial emblem, another popular mode in the period. It is when this kind of static visual puzzle is translated into *dramatic* terms, however, that its relationship to the events and language of romance becomes striking.

One of the most intriguing things about the way *Cymbeline* unfolds as a poetic plot is how metaphor is transformed into onstage reality. In looking at *Pericles* we noticed that some kinds of language typical of romance seemed to be largely devoid of the intricate, psychologically revealing metaphors and figures of speech so magnificently deployed in the tragedies (Lear's "Ingratitude, thou marble-hearted fiend"; Othello's "one entire and perfect chrysolite"). What happens to these metaphors when they no longer appear as ruminations by a dramatic character? As in a dream, or an animated film, they come to life on the stage. In effect, they change status, moving from *images* to *props* (theatrical properties). In *Cymbeline* in particular this translation of rhetorical language into material elements in the action—and on the stage—has a powerful cumulative effect.

Consider, for example, the image of the jewel, as predominant in *Cymbeline* as it was in *Pericles*. To Imogen, Posthumus is "this jewel in the world" (1.1.92), and she claims to her father that in marrying him she has added "a lustre" to the British throne (1.1.144). Cloten, contending that she should instead marry *him,* insists, somewhat ironically, that she should choose a husband from among the nobility, and that she "must not foil / The precious note of [the crown] with a base slave" (2.3.115–117). The word "foil," from the word for "leaf" (and "page"), had come to mean a thin leaf of metal placed under a precious stone to set off its brilliance (the frequent use of the word in literary criticism to mean "comparison figure to the hero" comes from this sense of visual enhancement) or, more directly, a setting for a jewel (as in *Richard II,* "Esteem as foil wherein thou art to set / The precious jewel of thy home return" [*Richard II* 1.3.255–256]). Cloten, using "foil" as a verb, probably intends another sense, to "foul," or trample underfoot, although the double sense is clearly present.

But where in *Othello* or *Lear* the jewel was used as a simile to point to the purity of the heroine (Desdemona as a chrysolite, or topaz, emblematic stone of chastity; Cordelia's tears "[a]s pearls from diamonds dropped"), in *Cymbeline* the image almost immediately *realizes itself,* or, as we say, "comes to life," in the form of an object. Scarcely twenty lines after she calls Posthumus a jewel, Imogen gives him a diamond ring "which," she says, "was my mother's," and then he gives her a bracelet. Both pieces of jewelry, as circlets, are signs of unbroken purity, and thus by mythological and literary convention equated with sexual chastity. We do not need to know anything about such conventions to make this connection in *Cymbeline,* however, because Iachimo does it for us, when in Rome he challenges Posthumus to wager his diamond against Imogen's chastity and faithfulness: "If I come off and leave her in such honour as you have trust in, she your jewel, this your jewel, and my gold are yours" (1.4.134–135). His phrase "she your jewel, this your jewel" may serve as a shorthand description of the technique of the play.

A similar pattern occurs with the most familiar stage item of all, the garment or costume. Imogen tells Cloten scornfully—and carelessly—that to her Posthumus's "meanest garment" is far more dear than Cloten and his professed love (2.4.128). Again, of course, she means this as a figure of speech, and as a simple insult. Before long, in this dark fairy tale of a play, Cloten has acquired a garment belonging to Posthumus and worn it into the woods, there intending to ravish Imogen and then to kill her. When he is himself slain by Guiderius, Imogen will awaken next to the headless corpse dressed in her husband's clothes, and believe herself a widow.

We hear repeatedly from Belarius that the King's sons exhibit qualities of nobility. Although they live in a cave, where they are daily constrained to stoop, and thus to remember their humble situation, "their thoughts do hit / The roofs of palaces." The description is metaphorical and psychological: the young men aspire to heroism or greatness. But when Belarius sends them out hunting, he also has them act out, physically, the difference between his status and theirs:

> Now for our mountain sport. Up to yon hill,
> Your legs are young; I'll tread these flats. . . .
>
> *3.3.10–11*

Again the action of the play becomes an emblem of its subject. Likewise, the early figurative description of Posthumus's perfection ("He sits 'mongst men like a descended god") seems almost to predict and to elicit the later stage action, when a real "descended god," Jupiter, comes to instruct him (5.5).

This exchange between metaphor and stage "reality" or materiality is linked with one of the central themes of this play, and of the romances considered as a group, and that is the pervasive theme of "seeming," of taking the outside for the inside, as Imogen did when she misread the body of Cloten, dressed in Posthumus's clothes, for Posthumus. The strong sense of "seeming" here includes not only the familiar, and sometimes flabby, dyad of appearance and reality, but also timely and more particular issues like theft, counterfeiting, and other modes of deception and displacement. Cymbeline thought the Queen was "like her seeming," he says (5.6.65), because she was beautiful and because she flattered him. Both her looks and her words deceived. Cloten and Cymbeline both learn not to take the rustic appearance of Guiderius at face value; Cloten is killed by the young man he dismisses as a "rustic mountaineer," and Cymbeline will ultimately recognize him as his long-lost son and heir.

"Seeming" is a word that has a largely negative valence in the tragedies and "problem plays." We have already noticed Hamlet's "Seems, madam? Nay, it is. I know not 'seems' " (*Hamlet* 1.2.76) and Isabella's "Seeming, seeming! / I will proclaim thee, Angelo" (*Measure for Measure* 2.4.150–151). In *Cymbeline* and in romance more generally, "seeming" is often connected with the experience of wonder and revelation, as, for example, when the awakening Imogen, finding herself untimely buried in the rustic graveyard, exclaims,

The dream's here still. Even when I wake it is
Without me as within me; not imagined, felt.
4.2.308–309

So "seeming" has two opposing theatrical connotations: dream, fantasy, and wonder on the one hand, and deception, guile, pretense, and trickery on the other. A major underlying issue in *Cymbeline* is the question of how to distinguish between them, and this is accomplished by acts of reading and interpretation, including the deciphering of riddles, dreams, prophecies, and signs.

Many editors and scholars have commented upon the apparent disjointedness of this play. But might what seems disunified on one level not have another logic that ties it together? If, instead of seeking the play's meaning from the plot, one seeks it instead in a logic of repetition, layering, and dream, there is a surprising unity in the persistence of

- the image of boxes and trunks;
- the question of sacrifice;
- the loss, and later recovery, of children by parents; and
- the adoption, and later loss, of children by parents.

The most vivid onstage moment in the play is the scene in which Iachimo hides in Imogen's bedchamber, secreting himself into a convenient trunk. In an earlier scene (1.6), having failed to seduce Imogen through an outright lie, his claim that Posthumus has been false to her, Iachimo proceeds in good satanic fashion to try a different kind of temptation. Having failed to appeal to her lack of faith, he smoothly switches his approach (somewhat in defiance of psychological realism) and convinces her that he has merely been joking, and was testing her to confirm his sense of her virtue. Imogen, won over, now agrees to assist him by storing a trunk that he claims contains jewels and "plate" bought as presents for the emperor. Declaring herself willing to "pawn mine honour" for their safety, and thus equating the jewels with her chastity, she decides to put the trunk in her bedroom, where both are presumed safe. The stage is set for that astonishing scene (2.2) in which Iachimo conceals himself in the trunk, emerges once Imogen is asleep, and takes notes on the appearance of the room and of her body. The scene is thus one of double voyeurism: for Iachimo, and for the audience in the theater.

Imogen retires to bed, then sits up reading until she falls asleep. The book she reads, we discover, must be Ovid's *Metamorphoses,* a major reference point for all of Shakespeare's late romances, since it describes the transformations of men, women, nymphs, and gods into animals, flowers, and stars, thus rendering the cyclical permanent, and the mortal, eternal.

The particular story Imogen has been reading is "[t]he tale of Tereus," the story of how Philomela was raped by her brother-in-law Tereus. He cuts out her tongue to keep her from telling what has happened to her, but she manages to communicate the truth through the weaving of a tapestry—the production of a truth-telling work of art. Philomela was transformed into the nightingale, who sings her sad tale over and over. The myth, of course, had been used by Shakespeare as a major model for the plot of *Titus Andronicus*. In a way we could say that Imogen's reading experience describes a version of what happens in the scene once she falls asleep. A man she does not desire invades her room and violates her. Iachimo does not actually rape her, but he does violate her privacy and her nakedness, and he also takes away with him the bracelet that was Posthumus's gift, a sign of love and of marital fidelity.

Iachimo compares his silence, as he steals toward her, to that of Tarquin, evoking the story of the rape of Lucrece already told by Shakespeare in the poem of that title. The scenario of the two "rapes" is similar, for in each case a husband boasts of his wife's virtue and inadvertently inflames the desire of her attacker. Subsequently we learn that the walls of the room are adorned with images of Cleopatra at the Cydnus, when she first met Mark Antony, and also of Diana bathing. Both recall narratives of men beholding consummate female beauty. Diana, the virgin goddess of the hunt, was accidentally spied upon by the hunter Actaeon, and, as Ovid tells the story, Actaeon was turned by her into a stag, hunted down by his own hounds, and finally transformed into a flower. Iachimo is clearly an Actaeon figure here, spying on Imogen, later hunted, finally pardoned.

But the emergence of Iachimo from the trunk in Imogen's chamber is also an image of sexual knowledge, and perhaps even of unconscious desire. Imogen, we should recall, was reading the story of Philomela's rape as she fell asleep. She has been propositioned by Iachimo, and the events that unfold in her bedroom, as she lies asleep on the bed, take the form of a kind of dream, following the pattern of medieval dream visions (which, like Chaucer's *Book of the Duchesse*, often begin with a similar scene of reading). When Iachimo emerges from the trunk and removes her bracelet, he speaks in the language of inside and outside, or "seeming": "[T]his will witness outwardly, / As strongly as the conscience does within" (2.2.35–36). And when he notes intimate details of her body he chortles to himself: "This secret / Will force him think I have picked the lock and ta'en / The treasure of her honour" (2.2.40–42). The "treasure of her honour" is again made equivalent to the treasure in the trunk. The picked lock was a familiar if vulgar image of stolen chastity, as in *Much Ado About Nothing*. (The image is based upon the mechanics of insertion; today locks and keys are still described as "female" and "male" hardware.) The trunk itself is directly compared to Imogen's chastity, or "honour"; supposed to be locked, it is unlawfully entered by Iachimo. When we are told the precise point in the story where Imogen stopped reading—"Here the leaf's turned down / Where Philomel gave up" (2.2.45–46)—the rape scene seems complete. Iachimo/

Tereus, mixing his myths and his metaphors, has approached the bed of Imogen/ Philomela and violated her, taking the sign of her honor, the bracelet.

Thus far, the scenario invites a straightforward psychoanalytic reading: box or trunk corresponds to womb, honor, chastity; both are penetrated and invaded by Iachimo. Especially because the scene presents a literal onstage sleeper, it seems possible to interpret this as a "rape fantasy," whether we interpret the night scene of visitation as an unconscious wish or fear on Imogen's part, as a projective fantasy of Iachimo's, or as a dream scene that belongs to the play rather than to any dramatic character (in effect, the audience's fantasy rather than that of either Imogen or her attacker). But if we view the same scene from the point of view of mythology rather than of psychoanalysis, we find a slightly different and equally suggestive story.

Imogen has agreed to accept a box that is supposed to contain precious things, like jewels and "plate," but that instead contains Iachimo, a figure of guile and lust. The delectable box that contains evil is familiar from the story of Pandora, another peerless beauty, who opened a box (in some versions, a jar) and let out all the sins and diseases of the world, leaving in the bottom of the box only hope. (It is fascinating to note that Pandora's name, which means "many gifts," is the same as Polydore, the "Welsh" name given to the King's son Guiderius.) If we take this mythological view of the scene in Imogen's bedchamber, we can see the relationship of that scene to others in the play that also involve boxes and containers. The Queen also has a box or casket, and since containers in myths and fairy tales are "female" symbols, we should not be surprised that both women in this romance-inflected play are associated with them. The Queen's box, however, is morphologically similar to that of Iachimo: it looks good and contains evil (in this case, the poison or sleeping potion). Pisanio, innocently persuading Imogen to take the box, says,

> My noble mistress,
> Here is a box. I had it from the Queen.
> What's in't is precious.
>
> *3.4.187–189*

Again a container, supposed to enclose something miraculous and beneficial, is opened in the presence of Imogen, and again what is in it almost destroys her.

Two promising boxes, each containing a kind of poison. To the boxes we could now add the cave in which the King's two young sons are brought up. A cave, too, is an enclosure or container, and a frequent symbol in fairy stories and dreams. Certainly the boys are born, or reborn, from this cave, whether we want to call it a "womb" or not. Their foster mother, the dead and mourned Euriphile (literally "good-love"), is everything their stepmother, the living, wicked Queen, is not. So the two boxes encountered in the court, which "seem" beautiful and are deadly (like the Queen herself), are in a way the opposite of the humble cave, which looks unpromising and brings forth unexpected treasure. As Belarius says of the King's sons,

> 'Tis wonder
> That an invisible instinct should frame them
> To royalty unlearned, honour untaught,
> Civility not seen from other, valour
> That wildly grows in them, but yields a crop
> As if it had been sowed. . . .
>
> *4.2.177–182*

The story of Pandora is linked in classical mythology to the figure of Prometheus. Prometheus was the wisest of the Titans; his name means "forethought." He was often regarded as the intercessor for mankind with the Olympian gods, and as its benefactor. In particular, as Renaissance writers often noted, Prometheus was said to have stolen fire from the heavens and given it to man. The king of the gods, Zeus (the Roman Jupiter), gave Pandora, the first woman, to Prometheus's less savvy brother, Epimetheus ("afterthought"), and it was Epimetheus who incautiously allowed the beautiful Pandora to open the fateful box. Prometheus and Epimetheus were literally the "creators" of mankind, fashioning men out of clay, and then—through Prometheus's intrepid act—endowing them with the gift of fire that made them superior to all other animals. For Renaissance mythographers Prometheus was an emblem of Providence. For Christians he was also a "type" of Christ, since his punishment for his generosity to man was to be chained to a rock and pecked by eagles. Iconographically this punishment seemed to writers and artists from Lucian onward to resemble the crucifixion. (Much later, Ralph Waldo Emerson would write, "Prometheus is the Jesus of the old mythology.")

And it was Prometheus who, in another of his contests of wits with Jupiter, negotiated the terms of sacrifice. He took an ox and divided it into two bundles. In one he put the bones, invitingly wrapped up in a package of fat and skin. In the other he put the meat, the flesh and entrails, but hid them in the ox's stomach. Jupiter, given his choice of bundles, unhesitatingly took the bundle of fat, and was infuriated to find that it contained nothing but bones. The bargain was kept, however. From that time human beings were able to keep the best part of the meat for themselves, and to sacrifice only the bones, skin, and fat. So again Prometheus can be seen to have aided mankind in developing civilization. The device here is the same kind of outside/inside contrast, or "seeming," that pervades this play.

The theme of sacrifice is in fact surprisingly pervasive in *Cymbeline*. In a comic early scene, the obnoxious Cloten is advised to change his shirt, since his sweaty exercise has made him "reek as a sacrifice" (1.2.2). (The sly digs at him continue into act 2, when, after he disingenuously laments that he could not duel with a lower-born opponent—"Would he had been one of my rank"—the Second Lord quips, aside to us, "To have smelled like a fool" [2.1.13–15].) The play ends with an invitation from the King, in gratitude for the return of his children and the coming of peace with Rome:

> Let's quit this ground,
> And smoke the temple with our sacrifices.
> *5.6.398–399*

> Laud we the gods,
> And let our crookèd smokes climb to their nostrils
> From our blest altars. Publish we this peace
> To all our subjects. . . .
> *5.6.476–479*

Cloten, the false son, is a noble-dressed sacrifice without inner value. The lost sons, in mean country attire, have within them the "sparks of greatness." When they are returned to their father, they are replaced on the sacrificial altar, as Abraham replaced Isaac, by an acceptable sacrifice of gratitude.

Moreover, this question of sacrifice, and its relationship both to the pattern of "seeming" and to that of parents and children, also connects in a useful and satisfying way with another question the play invites us to ask: that of the relevance of Cymbeline and his story to Shakespeare and his time. As Spenser and others made clear in their own writing, Cymbeline was perhaps best known as the British king at the time of the birth of Christ:

> Next him Tenantius reigned, then Kimbeline;
> What time th'eternall Lord in fleshly slime
> Enwombed was, from wretched Adam's line
> To purge away the guilt of sinfull crime.
> *Spenser,* The Faerie Queene,
> *book 2, canto 10, stanza 50*

The reign of Cymbeline is a crucial moment, a crossroads in British history and in Christian history. Recognition of the historical specificity only hinted at obliquely in the text may help to explain why the "right" answer appears to be for the King of Britain to pay tribute to Rome. His queen had urged him to assert national independence. But there is biblical precedent. Christ is born in Bethlehem because of a command given by the emperor: "And it came to pass in those days, that there went out a decree from Caesar Augustus, that all the world should be taxed" (Luke 2:1.1). Later, when the Pharisees, hoping to trick him, ask of Jesus, "Is it lawful to give tribute to Caesar, or not?" he answers, "Render therefore unto Caesar the things which be Caesar's, and unto God the things which be God's" (Luke 20:22, 25). Likewise Saint Paul writes, in Romans, "Render . . . tribute to whom tribute is due" (Romans 13:7).

We are not told of these Christian associations explicitly in the play. No messenger arrives to announce a miraculous birth. But the call to sacrifice and the promise of "peace / To all our subjects" suggest that the end of *Cymbeline* is millennial and transcendent. The Pax Romana is at hand. James I described himself as a Roman king, and declared that he ruled, and that kings should rule, in the Roman style of the gods. The conjunction of the historical king, Cymbeline, and the then-reigning king, James, might well have suggested that this new, improved king could preside over a new Pax Romana. Myth, history, and religion here come close together, each providing its own version of allegory. As the Jupiter of this play descends to declare, " Whom best I love, I cross, to make my gift, / The more delayed, delighted" (5.5.195–196).

Cymbeline is full of mythological detail and of Christian references and intimations, yet its spirit remains that of tragicomedy and romance. All the rebirths and regeneration of the play are part of this pattern. There is the apparent rebirth of Imogen, who had been laid out as a tragic sacrifice on the ground, and who woke to a transformed world where dream and reality are one: "Without me as within me; not imagined, felt" (4.2.309). A stylized but parallel rebirth is suggested in the situation of Posthumus, whose name implies his "fatherless" state, but who offers himself as a sacrifice in an image of creation as craftsmanship and stamping. "For Imogen's dear life take mine, and though / 'Tis not so dear, yet 'tis a life; you coined it" (5.5.116–117). Posthumus then falls asleep and is visited by his mother, father, and brothers in a dream vision, achieving his own version of the family reunion.

For an absolute monarchy like that of King James, there is, potentially, little difference between history and fantasy, politics and power, since the one can be made to be at the service of the other. For a playwright this conjunction can also be fruitful, as Shakespeare demonstrates through the figure of Imogen. Awakening in Wales from her poisoned sleep to find what she thinks is the body of her dead husband beside her, and noticing the flowers strewn on their grave, she says,

> These flowers are like the pleasures of the world,
> This bloody man the care on't. . . .
>
> *4.2.298–299*

The flowers are the flowers of romance and fantasy, the blood is the blood of tragedy and history.

The Winter's Tale

DRAMATIS PERSONAE

Leontes, *King of Sicilia*
Hermione, *his wife*
Mamillius, *his son*
Perdita, *his daughter*
Camillo, *a Lord at Leontes' court*
Antigonus, *a Lord at Leontes' court*
Cleomenes, *a Lord at Leontes' court*
Dion, *a Lord at Leontes' court*
Paulina, *Antigonus's wife*
Emilia, *a lady attending on Hermione*
A Jailer
A Mariner
Other Lords and Gentlemen, Ladies,
   Officers, and Servants at Leontes'
   court
Polixenes, *King of Bohemia*

Florizel, *his son, in love with*
   Perdita; known as Doricles
Archidamus, *a Bohemian Lord*
Autolycus, *a rogue, once in the*
   service of Florizel
Old Shepherd
Clown, *his son*
Mopsa, *a shepherdess*
Dorcas, *a shepherdess*
Servant of the Old Shepherd
Other Shepherds and
   Shepherdesses
Twelve countrymen disguised as
   satyrs
Time, *as chorus*

*T*HE *WINTER'S TALE* was first performed in 1611, and was then re-played, at the request of King James, in 1612 and again in 1613. Those years were eventful ones for the Stuart royal family. In 1612 the King's eldest son, Prince Henry, died. As Prince of Wales, Henry had been enormously popular, and he had become, in effect, the King's rival in the hearts of the people as well as his heir. In the following year James's daughter, Princess Elizabeth, was married to Frederick, the Elector Palatine; performances of both *The Winter's Tale* and *The Tempest* were arranged as part of the wedding celebration. Frederick accepted the crown of Bohemia in 1619, and Elizabeth became Queen of Bohemia, but shortly thereafter Frederick lost not only Bohemia but also his hereditary status, and Elizabeth, known to history as the Winter Queen, followed her husband into exile.

We may note that both of these events—the death of the King's son; the marriage of the daughter, who became Queen of Bohemia—took place after the writing of Shakespeare's play, and neither can have had any effect whatever upon the plot. The play's chief source was Robert Greene's prose romance *Pan-*

dosto, published in 1588, a text that Shakespeare followed closely in almost all details of his plot. I mention them here only because a post facto knowledge of these historical details does imbue the play with an uncanny topicality.

The play's author had also lost a son, and had married off a daughter. Hamnet Shakespeare died at age eleven in 1596. Susanna married Dr. John Hall in 1607. Yet there is no specifc reason to read the play as in any way "autobiographical," except in the sense that all artistic work is part of the autobiography of its creator. The resonances of *The Winter's Tale*—a very great play—are poetic and mythic, political and ethical, not narrowly historical or personal. If the shadow of the absolute monarch lies behind the quick anger of Leontes and his imperious dismissal of the truth of the Delphic oracle, it is present as a trace, not as a reference. But the cumulative effect of *The Winter's Tale* is echoic, a kind of rhythmic mise en abyme, a hall of mirrors in which stories are told and retold, in which they bisect and intersect. It begins in conversation, and it ends in transformation.

Like a number of other Shakespeare plays, *The Winter's Tale* begins with a brief conversation that seems to take place half offstage and half on, so that the audience is invited to feel itself a privileged spectator, in effect eavesdropping on a private conversation before the public spectacle is put on show. This is a clever dramaturgical device, drawing us into the action and allowing us to consider the immediately succeeding episode, in this case the second half of the first scene, with a more careful and critical eye. The opening stage conversation takes place between two apparently secondary characters: Camillo, a Sicilian, and Archidamus, a Bohemian. The Bohemian court has been in Sicilia for nine months—such extended state visits were not unusual in the period—and Archidamus speaks of the return visit that is apparently planned for "this coming summer." The seasonal and cyclical framework of the play is already visible here.

When they come, says Archidamus, they will see a "great difference betwixt our Bohemia and your Sicilia," and indeed this difference will establish itself from the outset. For, from the point of view of the audience, Sicilia appears to be all court and Bohemia all country. Sicilia is inhabited by lords and ladies, kings, queens, princes, and courtiers, while the citizens of Bohemia, when we meet them, will be shepherds and shepherdesses, clowns, and other rustics. Even King Polixenes will appear in disguise as a shepherd to spy upon his populace, and the "royalty" of Bohemia will be seen in the mock reign of Perdita, the apparently humble mistress of the sheepshearing feast, dressed like Flora, the goddess of flowers. The disclosure of Perdita's true identity and royal birth, a delightful convention of the romance tradition, will also emphasize the degree to which Bohemia is the dream self or fantasy other of Sicilia, just as, in earlier Shakespeare plays, the Forest of Arden is the middle place of the repressive Duke's court in *As You Like It,* or Cyprus the wild underside of the supposedly civilized world of Othello's Venice.

Sicilia appears to be a court removed from the countryside, while Bohemia, famously, and in defiance of ordinary geography, is given a "seacoast." (Ingenious critics have consulted old maps to demonstrate that Bohemia once did have a seacoast, but the phrase "the seacoast of Bohemia" has entered the language as an equivalent of "never-never land," a place of Utopian possibility.) Sicilia is a place of formality and rank, Bohemia—as we encounter it—a place where there are no "gentlemen born." Archidamus is uneasy about how the urbane courtier Camillo will respond to his less-imposing homeland, and proposes, jokingly, "We will give you sleepy drinks," to befuddle your mind, tranquilize your imagination, and soften your judgment. With Shakespeare's consistently shrewd management of dramatic irony, these notional "sleepy drinks," here dreamily benign, will shortly reappear, not in Bohemia but in Sicilia, in Leontes' bitter image in act 2, scene 1, of the "knowledge" of infidelity as a cup poisoned by a spider.

Camillo's courtly response to his guest comes in a speech of necessary exposition, explaining the long relationship of the two kings. Its language is slightly oblique, but it offers the audience not only an explanation but also an implicit warning:

> Sicilia cannot show himself over-kind to Bohemia. They were trained together in their childhoods, and there rooted betwixt them then such an affection which cannot choose but branch now. Since their more mature dignities and royal necessities made separation of their society, their encounters—though not personal—hath been royally attorneyed with interchange of gifts, letters, loving embassies, that they have seemed to be together, though absent; shook hands as over a vast; and embraced as it were from the ends of opposed winds. The heavens continue their loves.
>
> The Winter's Tale *1.1.18–27*

The elegant negativity of the opening ("cannot show himself over-kind") foreshadows a reversal, as does the pious wish of the close ("The heavens continue their loves"), which seems, in a Shakespearean universe, as much a dare as a hope (compare, for example, Othello's equally fateful "If it were now to die / 'Twere now to be most happy"). Translated from the obfuscating language of diplomacy, as politic then as now, this speech reports that the two kings were once childhood friends, but that their respective royal obligations have separated them, so that they have been in touch only through intermediaries: "they have seemed to be together, though absent; shook hands as over a vast; and embraced as it were from the ends of opposed winds." "Seemed," "as it were," "absent," "over a vast," "the ends of opposed winds." These are ominous signs cloaked in optimistic language, and Camillo's compliments presage a "branching" between the two kings that is as much a split as a flourishing, or growth, and that culminates, as we will shortly see, in the image of the cuckold's horns branching from King Leontes' head. A further and even more ominous note of dramatic foreshadowing is offered in the courtiers' offhand references to

Leontes' son, the young prince Mamillius, described as a "gentleman of the greatest promise" who "makes old hearts fresh." As Archidamus remarks wryly, "If the King had no son," the two kings would "desire to live on crutches till he had one" (1.1.39–40). This apparent throwaway line, a condition contrary to fact—"If the King had no son"—will shortly, and tragically, become true. As the audience enters the court of Leontes, King of Sicilia, it enters forewarned, if it has been listening closely. Tragedy—or tragicomedy—lies ahead.

The "winter's tale" of this play's title is both literal and proverbial. The phrase meant something like "fairy tale," or a diverting entertainment, largely for the amusement of women, children, and the old. A mid-sixteenth-century author wrote of "old wives fables and winter tales" (John Olde, *Walther's Antichrist,* translation 1556) as if they were versions of the same, and Lady Macbeth belittles her husband's lack of resolution by observing scornfully that "these flaws and starts, / . . . would well become / A woman's story at a winter fire" (3.4.62–64). The teller of the winter's tale within *The Winter's Tale* is the boy Mamillius, the ill-fated young Prince. His mother, Hermione, urges him to tell a merry tale, but he replies, with the pertness we have come to associate with Shakespearean children, "A sad tale's best for winter. I have one / Of sprites and goblins" (2.1.27–28). Most of the tale is whispered into his mother's ear, but it begins, significantly, "There was a man— / Dwelt by a churchyard." So, we may say, all men—and women—do, living their lives in the neighborhood of death. And if stories and sad tales distance the imminence of death, if fiction removes the constant and direct fear of mortality, still we might remember that it is Mamillius, the teller of the winter's tale, who is the first to die. "If the King had no son"—the hypothetical prophecy comes unexpectedly true, and the world of Sicilia is not prepared to comprehend it.

But where does Sicilia go wrong? What clues are we given in the opening court scene (1.2) that man dwells by a churchyard, and that thus the tale will be, in part, a sad one? Most of our clues come, I think, from the dangerous ignorance of the kings themselves. Polixenes, the King of Bohemia, has been a visitor in Sicilia for nine months ("[n]ine changes of the wat'ry star"), and all this time he has left his throne "[w]ithout a burden" (1.2.1, 3). Even lacking the explicit evidence of *King Lear,* in which a monarch declared his hope to "[u]nburdened crawl toward death" by relinquishing his office, we know by now that no king in Shakespeare can do this of his own volition. It is his role, as King and man, to bear the burden of rank and responsibility. When Polixenes suddenly decides it is time to return home, and Leontes presses the Queen, Hermione, to urge him to stay, she elicits from him an account of the two kings in childhood that is far more circumstantial than Camillo's, and that speaks directly to the impossible idea of leaving one's throne without a burden. Here is Polixenes on the subject of the kings' youth (note that in any "realistic" play he would presumably have imparted this information long before; its iteration here is for the audience in the theater, not the audience on the stage):

> We were, fair Queen,
> Two lads that thought there was no more behind
> But such a day tomorrow as today,
> And to be boy eternal.
>
>   *1.2.63–66*

To be "boy eternal": never to age, always to be a child. This is an Eden world he projects, a world out of time, and Time, as we will see, is an important component of this play, so important that he appears later on as a speaking character. Polixenes continues:

> We were as twinned lambs, that did frisk i'th' sun,
> And bleat the one at th'other. What we changed
> Was innocence for innocence. We knew not
> The doctrine of ill-doing, nor dreamed
> That any did. Had we pursued that life,
> And our weak spirits ne'er been higher reared
> With stronger blood, we should have answered heaven
> Boldly, "Not guilty," the imposition cleared
> Hereditary ours.
>
>   *1.2.69–77*

In his view, the unfallen innocence of the boys, until it was changed by the onset of "stronger blood," qualified them to disclaim original sin, the hereditary imposition of the guilt of all mankind. "By this," says Hermione softly, "we gather / You have tripped since." "Tripped" is a muted, child's word for a fall, but a fall nonetheless. And on what does Polixenes base his fall? Why, on women. On sex and desire, the "stronger blood" of sexual maturity and adulthood:

> O my most sacred lady,
> Temptations have since then been born to's; for
> In those unfledged days was my wife a girl.
> Your precious self had not yet crossed the eyes
> Of my young playfellow.
>
>   *1.2.78–82*

Temptations, innocence, lambs, and "boy eternal"—the associations here are simultaneously seasonal and Christian. And in both contexts Polixenes seems to question the very nature of mortal man, who lives by the churchyard.

It will be left, in this romance as in others of Shakespeare's late period, for the second generation to prove all too literally what these two kings fail to understand. For the instantaneous jealousy of Leontes seems to associate him, too, with this eagerness to blame women and adulthood for all their problems, and to wish instead to be "boy eternal." We have seen in other plays, like *Coriolanus,* that to be always a "boy" is to resist facing the world. In the second generation of *The Winter's Tale* the two sons, Mamillius and Florizel, are twinned just like their fathers; in the fifth act Paulina, Antigonus's wife, encountering Florizel for the first time, exclaims:

> Had our prince,
> Jewel of children, seen this hour, he had paired
> Well with this lord. There was not full a month
> Between their births.
>
> 5.1. 115–118

But Mamillius, "[j]ewel of children," of course does not live to see this hour. His name, "Mamillius" (which may derive from another romance tale of Robert Greene, *Mamillia*), suggests the mother's breast, and thus infancy and dependency, though this royal child, like others of his period, was apparently given into the care of a wet nurse, since his father declares angrily to Hermione, "I am glad you did not nurse him." In an appropriately natural phrase we are told that after the accusation of Hermione, Mamillius "straight declined, [he] drooped," while his "twin," Florizel, whose names suggests flowering and harvest, lives to confront his father, reject his status as a dependent child, and choose a wife.

The two poles of action and development, twinned but also opposed, are focused in this play (as in so many of Shakespeare's) through a set of double-edged words, words that function as swing terms, or serious puns, key words for dramatic action. "Blood" is one such term, denoting violence, strong emotion, and death, on the one hand, and lineage, kinship, and family on the other— just as in Camillo's opening speech to "branch" was both to split apart and to grow. Other polar words chart this same crucial opposition, which begins in the first scenes and continues throughout the play: "dear," which means both "costly" and "beloved"; "issue," which means both "result," or causal outcome, and "progeny," or children; and, most reflexively in terms of the dramatic form itself, the word "play," which comes in rapid succession to stand for (1) innocent child's play, (2) tempting, seductive sexual play, and (3) acting and impersonation—disguised, deceptive play. Thus Leontes, rent by sudden and unreasoning sexual jealousy, says to his son, Mamillius:

> Go play, boy, play. Thy mother plays, and I
> Play too; but so disgraced a part, whose issue
> Will hiss me to my grave. . . .
>
> 1.2.188–190

Here are two kinds of issue, and three kinds of play, as well as a sibilant ("issue . . . hiss me") that seems almost to ally the jealous Leontes with a serpent.

("S is a most easy and gentle letter," wrote Shakespeare's contemporary Ben Jonson, "and softly hisseth against the teeth.") It is interesting to note that the entities most usually described as "hissing," in the early modern period as also today, are devils, serpents, and audiences.

Certainly readers and spectators are quick to notice the extreme rapidity with which Leontes falls into his jealousy—a fall so rapid that it seems sharply stylized, at the same time that its emotional intensity is very real. To generations of Shakespeare-watchers the jealous Leontes has called to mind the jealous Othello, equally convinced of his wife's infidelity on little evidence except his own propensity for self-comparison and self-doubt.

Iago's "Trifles light as air / Are to the jealous confirmations strong / As proofs of holy writ" become, in *The Winter's Tale*, Leontes' certainty that the oracle at Delphos will provide "a greater confirmation" of Hermione's guilt. Nor is Othello the only Shakespearean model here. When Leontes speaks of the supposed adulterers "paddling palms and pinching fingers" (1.2.117) he sounds very like Hamlet, pleading with his mother not to let the "bloat King," Claudius, "[p]inch wanton" on her cheek or "paddl[e]" in her neck "with his damned fingers" (*Hamlet* 3.4.166–169). Similarly, Leontes' impassioned speech on "nothing" (1.2.286–298) sounds like King Lear's. As in a pencil sketch by an old master—just a few strokes, but what suggestive strokes—the character of Leontes emerges from these ghosts and echoes of earlier Shakespearean tragic sufferers, Othello and Hamlet and Lear. Leontes' language in the first act reflects his relationship to tragedy. It is turgid, highly compressed, metaphorical, full of exclamations and self-interruptions, and, in consequence, sometimes hard to follow: "Too hot, too hot: / To mingle friendship farre is mingling bloods" (1.2.110–111), and "Inch-thick, knee-deep, o'er head and ears a forked one! (187), and this sour little fable:

> [M]any a man there is, even at this present,
> Now, while I speak this, holds his wife by th'arm,
> That little thinks she has been sluiced in's absence,
> And his pond fished by his next neighbour, by
> Sir Smile, his neighbour. . . .
>
> *1.2.193–197*

It is Leontes who coins the vivid image of the spider in the cup, an image that, again, may call to mind other poisoned cups, like the one in *Hamlet,* which in dramatic context become associated with the idea of a poisoned female sexuality:

> There may be in the cup
> A spider steeped, and one may drink, depart,
> And yet partake no venom, for his knowledge
> Is not infected; but if one present

> Th'abhorred ingredient to his eyes, make known
> How he hath drunk, he cracks his gorge, his sides,
> With violent hefts. I have drunk, and seen the spider.
>
> 2.1.41–47

"I have drunk, and seen the spider." But of course it is Leontes who has in effect invented the spider, and dropped it in the cup. Here again there is an instructive comparison with Othello, at the moment when he feels the public humiliation of his supposed cuckoldry:

> I had been happy if the general camp,
> Pioneers and all, had tasted her sweet body,
> So I had nothing known. . . .
>
> Othello 3.3.350–352

Leontes feels that his *knowledge* has been "infected," and infection almost immediately becomes a dominant metaphor for his entire course, spreading as always from the king to his subjects. From a scene of apparent health and order, then, we pass rapidly to infection and disease. "There is a sickness / Which puts some of us in distemper," says Camillo to Polixenes, "but / I cannot name th' disease" (1.2.384–386). "A sickness caught of me, and yet I well?" Polixenes asks (398), and when he learns of the King's suspicion, he cries:

> O, then my best blood turn
> To an infected jelly, . . .
> .   .   .   .
>   my approach be shunned,
> Nay hated, too, worse than the great'st infection
> That e'er was heard or read.
>
> 1.2.418–424

Natural words, like "grow," ordinarily associated with health, are now used instead to describe sickness. Leontes' wintry imagination even recalls the months of his courtship with Hermione as "[t]hree crabbèd months" that "had soured themselves to death" (1.2.104). Once again in a Shakespearean kingdom we are to have a wasteland, a sick king bereft of wife and of children, and the play's initial counsellor figure, Camillo (who follows in the pattern of doctors like Cerimon in *Pericles* and Cornelius in *Cymbeline*), will flee the country, leaving the art of healing to a wonder-worker of a different order, Paulina.

Of all Leontes' tortured exclamations, though, perhaps the most startling is the outburst in which he claims evidence of Hermione's transgression:

> Is whispering nothing?
> Is leaning cheek to cheek? Is meeting noses?

> Kissing with inside lip? Stopping the career
> Of laughter with a sigh—a note infallible
> Of breaking honesty. Horsing foot on foot?
> Skulking in corners? Wishing clocks more swift,
> Hours minutes, noon midnight? And all eyes
> Blind with the pin and web but theirs, theirs only,
> That would unseen be wicked? Is this nothing?
> Why, then, the world and all that's in't is nothing,
> The covering sky is nothing, Bohemia nothing,
> My wife is nothing, nor nothing have these nothings
> If this be nothing.
>
> *1.2.287–298*

The manifest irony here is that all these things *are* nothing. They have no sig-nificance, and represent only Leontes' own projection ("[s]kulking," "[w]ish-ing"). But just as Leontes "saw" a spider in the cup because he put it there, poisoning his own imagination, so he makes something of these rhetorically conjured nothings. In a way he borrows a technique from Polixenes, who had spoken of himself as a zero. Polixenes' word for "zero" is "cipher"; the context here is a phrase of compliment for the warm hospitality he has—heretofore—received in Sicilia, and his figure of speech imagines that a numeral followed by a zero (10; 1,000; 10,000) makes something of nothing:

> And therefore, like a cipher,
> Yet standing in rich place, I multiply
> With one "We thank you" many thousands more.
>
> *1.2.6–8*

Leontes, like the master of binary fictions that he is, multiplies his one convic-tion of Hermione's infidelity by a thousand nothings, a thousand pieces of "evi-dence" that are evidence of nothing at all. In doing so, moreover, he does something else as well: he creates a universe that is entirely solipsistic. He denies the reality of the world, the reality of the stage ("The covering sky is nothing, Bohemia nothing, / . . . If this be nothing"). He thus creates a mental world of total egoism, total self-involvement, in which there is "nothing" left but Leontes himself: no external objects, no systems of value or communication are permit-ted to stand. The King withdraws into a mental prison of his own "diseased opinion," next to which the physical prison to which he sends his wife, Hermione, is an oasis of light and health.

In fact, as if to prove this, the pregnant Queen, who "rounds apace," herself therefore a living emblem of fertility and growth, descends into the prison and almost immediately gives birth to her child. The imagistic equivalent between womb and prison is confirmed by Paulina, who argues to the King that "[t]his child was prisoner to the womb" and is therefore freed by nature when she is born (2.2.62–64), and also by Hermione, who is said to have addressed the infant as "My poor prisoner" and declared "I am innocent as you" (2.2.31–32). A double point is being made here. On the one hand, a literal prison is no prison at all when it is compared to mental bondage (another commonplace of the period; see the Richard Lovelace poem "To Althea, from Prison," which begins "Stone walls do not a prison make / Nor iron bars a cage," or the "servitude" of Ferdinand to Prospero and Miranda in *The Tempest*). On the other hand, we are all prisoners of the mortal condition, the condition of *blood* in all its senses. The play's antidote to this imprisonment is embodied in the word "grace," associated throughout the play with Hermione and asserted by her strongly as she goes off to the prison, directing her ladies not to weep: "This action I now go on / Is for my better grace" (2.1.123–124). Much later in the play a repentant Leontes will recall that "she was as tender / As infancy and grace" (5.3.26–27).

By contrast, Leontes is associated with wrath, jealousy, and punitive justice, and thus, in these early acts, with death rather than life. He (in company with Brutus, Macbeth, Richard III, and others) suffers from the Shakespearean symptom of a diseased conscience, sleeplessness. When Paulina attempts to cure him by reconciling him not directly with the Queen, but instead with the newborn child, she announces as she enters with the child in her arms, "I come to bring him sleep." In this scene she claims the role of doctor directly: "I / Do come with words as medicinal as true, / Honest as either" (2.3.33, 36–38). And yet in a way she hopes to cure him not with words but with silence:

> The silence often of pure innocence
> Persuades when speaking fails.
>
> *2.2.43–44*

The word "infant" comes from the Latin *infans,* meaning "unable to speak." The newborn child is speechless, and Paulina argues that the absence of language here connotes innocence.

But as so often in Shakespeare, this argument fails; as was the case with Cordelia ("Love and be silent"), communication among human beings requires more: silence, subject to interpretation, is insufficiently eloquent to plead the case. This is one reason why silence occupies the two extreme poles of Shakespearean dramaturgy. It characterizes both those who refuse humanity, like Iago, and those who transcend it, like the "statue" of Hermione in this play's final scene, and like all those characters, in this play and other romances, who are struck dumb by "wonder" or "amazement." Leontes *should* be struck this way by the innocent Perdita, who resembles him—as Paulina is quick to point out, reading her legitimacy in her face ("Although the print be little, the whole matter / And copy of the father: eye, nose, lip" [2.3.99–100])—but he is not, and he commands that she be killed. Perdita, whose name means "the lost one," is first ordered to be burnt, and then, in a travesty of "mercy," the sentence is mitigated; now she is to be exposed to the elements in some deserted place. As he takes up the child, Antigonus, Paulina's husband, interjects an explicit note of Christian symbolism in a single sentence: "I'll pawn the little blood which I have left / To save the innocent" (2.3.166–167).

Leontes' enslavement to his own prison of the mind has brought down disease and sterility upon the landscape, sleeplessness and solipsism upon himself. The winter movement of the play, the weight almost of tragedy, threatens to move beyond the reversible limits of romance.

It is particularly striking, therefore, that at this point in the play there occurs one of what I have been calling "window scenes"—scenes that open up, for a brief moment, a new world of insight. The scene I have in mind is the first scene of act 3, and the event is the return of the King's emissaries from the oracle of Apollo. Here is what these emissaries say when they return to Sicilia:

> Cleomenes The climate's delicate, the air most sweet;
> Fertile the isle, the temple much surpassing
> The common praise it bears.
>
> . . . .
>
> Dion   O, the sacrifice—
> How ceremonious, solemn, and unearthly
> It was i'th' off'ring!
> Cleomenes   But of all, the burst
> And the ear-deaf'ning voice o' th' oracle,
> Kin to Jove's thunder, so surprised my sense
> That I was nothing.
>
> *3.1.1–11*

In this short description we are offered a complete reversal of the conditions of Sicilia and its king: a delicate, sweet climate instead of infection; a fertile island, rather than a sterile land; a ceremonious and solemn sacrifice, symbolically made, rather than the unnatural and perverse sacrifice of the newborn child. Most of all, we hear Cleomenes' wonder at the voice of the oracle, which was so overwhelming that, in his own phrase, "I was nothing." Leontes had reduced all the world outside himself to nothing—the sky, Bohemia, his wife. Cleomenes does the opposite, feeling himself rendered insignificant by the voice of the god. Fittingly, Apollo is the god not only of poetry and music—both of which are key elements in the latter part of the play—but also of healing. And the messengers, racing along the road with their sealed prophecy, another romance riddle, close out the scene with a pious wish: "Go. Fresh horses! / And gracious be the issue."

> Leontes   Break up the seals, and read.
> Officer [*reads*] Hermione is chaste, Polixenes blameless, Camillo a true
>   subject, Leontes a jealous tyrant, his innocent babe truly

begotten, and the King shall live without an heir if that
which is lost be not found.

3.2.130–134

But Leontes, of course, denies the oracle, denies, in effect, holy writ: "There
is no truth at all i'th' oracle. / . . . This is mere falsehood." And on the utterance
of this blasphemy, word arrives immediately of young Mamillius's death; Queen
Hermione faints and is reported dead herself; and the stricken King gives himself over to a pattern of fruitless ritual, a daily visitation of their single grave. He
is apparently condemned to perpetual winter, as Paulina points out starkly: ten
thousand years of naked fasting on a barren hillside in winter will not move the
gods his way. The tragic winter movement of the play is closed, and the situation seems without hope.

It is at this point that Shakespeare deftly and imaginatively transfers our concerns from Sicilia to Bohemia, allowing the audience to follow along in what is
apparently the one unfinished aspect of the tale, the fate of the child Perdita, the
King's daughter. Perdita, as we have seen, is in the custody of Antigonus, the
courtier husband of Paulina, and Antigonus is in his own mind bent upon a noble
action. Just as his wife's name designedly invokes the figure of Saint Paul, so
Antigonus's name suggests Antigone, the elder daughter of Oedipus, who, to bury
her brother, defied King Creon's decree, was condemned to death, and killed herself before the repentant Creon could reverse his decree. Antigonus, too, will die.
Is there any justice, any literary or human justification, for his death? If Mamillius's death can be regarded as a reminder of the existence of evil and death in the
world, an innocent death confirming the unaccountability of loss, why is a second
death dramatically necessary? Isn't one symbolic sacrifice to mortality enough?

Perhaps it is. But Antigonus is also culpable, in a way that Mamillius is not.
In the play he is most directly compared to Camillo, another of the King's
courtiers. But whereas Camillo refuses to carry out Leontes' mad command,
and flees, Antigonus consents to do so, and is killed. In the action and dramatic
logic of *The Winter's Tale,* Camillo then "replaces" Antigonus as Paulina's husband at the close. The character is redeemed, so to speak, by the change. (The
two parts may originally have been doubled in performance, and often are cast
in this way in modern productions.) This is a good example of the difference
between romance characters and tragic ones, where tragedy is irreversible: Antigonus's death, "tragic" in local terms, is subsumed, dramatically, into a bittersweet ending in which Paulina does recover a husband, and is included in the
cluster of celebratory "reunions" at the close.

In addition to his blind obedience to Leontes, Antigonus betrays another
flaw: he seems to believe that Hermione may indeed have committed adultery,
since as he lays down the child he says, "this being indeed the issue / Of King
Polixenes." For this lack of faith, too, we may perhaps imagine that he is punished. And yet the manner of his punishment is of particular interest, for it is

thematically linked—and linked in spectacular fashion—to the basic cyclical structure of the play.

"Exit, pursued by a bear" announces what is, arguably, the most famous of all Shakespearean stage directions. This is testament, surely, to the Jacobean love of spectacle, evidenced by the Bear Garden on the bank of the Thames, and the popular pastime of watching bearbaiting (a favorite with Henry VIII and Elizabeth I). But the bear of *The Winter's Tale* is also linked to the landscape and practice of romance. Antigonus had been warned that the coast of Bohemia harbored "creatures / Of prey." And, more to the point, the bear is an animal of special interest—as contrasted, say, with the exotic elephant or zebra—because bears are associated with a particular natural pattern: they hibernate, passing the winter in a state of torpor, and then reawaken in the spring. Thus they offer a pattern of death and rebirth, even of resurrection: several ancient Greek cults worshiped bear gods, believing that the bear died and was reborn.

The embedded tragedy of Antigonus's death is mitigated somewhat, in the context of *The Winter's Tale,* by the way it is described. For this is another Shakespearean "unscene," unseen by the audience, reported in this case by an interested—and agitated—spectator:

Clown	I would you did but see how it chafes, how it rages, how it takes up the shore. But that's not to the point. O, the most piteous cry of the poor souls! Sometimes to see 'em, and not to see 'em; now the ship boring the moon with her mainmast, and anon swallowed with yeast and froth, as you'd thrust a cork into a hogshead. And then, for the land-service, to see how the bear tore out his shoulder-bone, and how he cried to me for help, and said his name was Antigonus, a nobleman! But to make an end of the ship—to see how the sea flap-dragoned it! But first, how the poor souls roared, and the sea mocked them, and how the poor gentleman roared, and the bear mocked him, both roaring louder than the sea or weather.
Old Shepherd	Name of mercy, when was this, boy?
Clown	Now, now. I have not winked since I saw these sights. The men are not yet cold under water, nor the bear half dined on the gentleman. He's at it now.

3.3.83–98

The lovely elegance of "dined" here contributes, oddly enough, to our sense of distancing in this remarkable report. It is a report of not one but two tragedies, and yet the atmosphere of Bohemia and the simple and compassionate tone of the Old Shepherd and the Clown conspire to make it seem not immediate tragedy, but far-off romance, shipwreck, and loss.

The bear's victim cried out for help, and said his name was Antigonus, a nobleman. What difference did his name and rank make to the bear? There is no such thing as rank in the Bohemia to which the audience is now introduced, despite the political existence of a king and prince—both of whom will shortly appear in humble disguise. There is no visible court, no corrupted world of "civilization"; all that we see of Bohemia is seacoast and shore and nature, the radicals of existence. As the seasons are cyclical, so life and death are cyclical; as Mamillius is a flower who droops and declines, so the infant Perdita is laid down by Antigonus with the words "Blossom, speed thee well." And as the Clown is compassionate witness to an emblem of loss, so his father, the Old Shepherd, becomes beneficiary to something found, something he compares to the riches that surround it, and identifies as fairy gold: Perdita, the lost child of romance. At this still point in the play, between losing and finding, between tragedy and epiphany, the Old Shepherd speaks lines that offer, in their balance and their tone of calm acceptance, the underlying fable of the play:

> Now bless thyself. Thou metst with things dying, I with things new-born.
>
> *3.3.104–105*

This is the fable that underlies the winter's tale we were never allowed to hear, the tale that begins "There was a man— /. . . Dwelt by a churchyard." As Old Shepherd and Clown together prepare to bury the dead, and nurture the living, and all the while turn tragedy into romance by feeling its story, the turn toward spring and rebirth is almost at hand.

In marked contrast to the Bohemian engagement with time as a cycle, the world of Sicilia has reduced itself, by the midpoint of the play, to a condition of stasis. Time there is not only linear, but one-directional and futile. Leontes, in Paulina's words, will not be helped even by the prayers of

> [a] thousand knees,
> Ten thousand years together, naked, fasting,
> Upon a barren mountain, and still winter
> In storm perpetual. . . .
>
> *3.2.208–211*

We may notice how even the cadence and phrasing here are static, still, perpetual, and locked, like Leontes' jealous fantasy, in impossible hyperbole. Leontes condemns himself to the fruitless and empty ritual of a daily visit to the graves of his queen and son:

> Upon them shall
> The causes of their death appear, unto

> Our shame perpetual. Once a day I'll visit
> This chapel where they lie, and tears shed there
> Shall be my recreation. . . .
>
> *3.2.234–238*

Here again is that word "perpetual," denoting not redemptive life but eternal death.

The Queen, Hermione, is of course only *thought* to be dead; she chooses to withdraw into obscurity, out of life and its rhythms. In this she is rather like Thaisa and those other mothers in Shakespeare's plays who, losing their husbands and children, seclude themselves in religious sanctuaries as abbesses or nuns. Yet Leontes' word "recreation" (comfort or consolation) embeds within it the notion of re-creation, and the audience will come to know Hermione as a statue, an artifact that is re-created, through patience and faith, back into the cycle of life and time once again.

At the end of act 3, however, these latent revivals are far from evident, and the barrenness of time in Sicilia appears in marked contrast with the liveliness of time on the seacoast of Bohemia, where perpetuity is achieved not by transcendence but by repetition—not by becoming an art object, whether a statue or a winter's tale, but by subsuming oneself into the cycle of nature. In a particularly beautiful passage Florizel describes the peculiar quality of time in Bohemia, which is at once fleeting and permanent. He is praising his beloved Perdita and describing his joy in even her most insignificant actions:

> What you do
> Still betters what is done. When you speak, sweet,
> I'd have you do it ever; when you sing,
> I'd have you buy and sell so, so give alms,
> Pray so; and for the ord'ring of your affairs,
> To sing them too. When you do dance, I wish you
> A wave o'th' sea, that you might ever do
> Nothing but that, move still, still so,
> And own no other function. Each your doing,
> So singular in each particular,
> Crowns what you are doing in the present deeds,
> That all your acts are queens.
>
> *4.4.135–146*

Being and becoming here fold into each other; waves, like the flowers that live and die in Perdita's garden, each in its appointed season, are not immortal or eternal, except by the illusion of repetition, each new wave appearing as a re-incarnation of the last. The word "still" ("move still, still so") carries the double meaning of "unmoving" and "always," so that the lovely paradox of "move still" encapsulates the meaning of the whole image, and contrasts sharply with Paulina's picture of "still winter / In storm perpetual."

Time in its various guises—barren time, fruitful time, redemptive time—is clearly a central topic for *The Winter's Tale,* and the concept is emblematized, and brought to life, in the figure of Time, the Chorus who introduces act 4. This ancient figure of Father Time with his hourglass represents a survival from older literature, rather like Gower, the narrator of *Pericles.* And like Gower, Time is in a way necessary, or at least useful, as a device to smooth over the rough spots left by a gap of sixteen years between acts 3 and 4. (The audience might well be reminded of that "vast," or wasteland, evoked in the play's opening conversation between Camillo and Archidamus.)

Shakespeare the playwright here returns to the awkward device, used in *Pericles,* of bisecting his play with a major gap in time. By now it is clear that the pattern of Shakespearean romance requires a mature second generation, a marriage, and a redemptive union—hence the need for many years to pass between the original act of disruption and the final consensus. But the intrusion of the figure of Time, we might contend, draws attention to this gap rather than naturalizes it. Why then does Shakespeare choose to employ it?

Time speaks of himself as "I that please some, try all; both joy and terror / Of good and bad; that makes and unfolds error." He says, "[I]t is in my power / To o'erthrow law, and in one self-born hour / To plant and o'erwhelm custom" (4.1.1–2, 7–9). He speaks of "my tale" and "my scene," and he tells us, "I mentionèd a son o'th' King's," when so far as we know he has not, since we have never seen or heard from him before. And he finishes his speech by describing "th'argument of Time," and by offering an apologia to the audience in advance, hoping that we will like what is to come. It does not take much to see that this is the voice of a playwright talking, an artist introducing and describing a work of art. His phrase "joy and terror" is close enough to Aristotle to suggest the dimensions and requirements of drama. Time boasts that he can break rules ("o'erthrow law" and "overwhelm custom"), rules like the so-called dramatic unities, of time, place, and action, which the play does break, extravagantly, as it unfolds over time and space. Time is a craftsman, an artist, and a maker, as we will see again much later on, when the statue of Hermione is revealed, and is seen to be lined with age. "Hermione was not so much wrinkled, nothing / So agèd as this seems," exclaims Leontes, who remembers her as a young woman. And Paulina replies, "So much the more our carver's excellence" (5.3.27–28, 30). "[O]ur carver" is here both Time and Shakespeare. The presence of Time, the Chorus, is not nearly as intrusive or distracting as may first appear; the play is framed by time, and is in effect itself a kind of hourglass, waiting to be turned once more, and to begin anew.

No sooner does the audience encounter Time, his glass and his scythe, than we are introduced to another figure who seems both to be in and of time and also to transcend it. That figure is Autolycus, the trickster, peddler, cheat, and self-described "snapper-up of unconsidered trifles" (4.3.25–26)—a character who is thus, plausibly, a counter-creator, another fiction-maker, player, and playwright. Camillo and Polixenes, conferring on the whereabouts of Prince Florizel, determine that he has been seen in the neighborhood of a certain shepherd's cottage, and decide to investigate the matter for themselves. In order to enter the true world of Bohemia, in which the shepherd and not Polixenes is king, they doff the appurtenances of rank and disguise themselves as elderly countrymen. The Bohemia world is a version of "carnival," the low become high, the hierarchy of order and power inverted, a potentially subversive challenge from below to the sometimes repressive ideology of order. As with Falstaff and Prince Hal in the *Henry IV* plays, disguise allows the infiltration of the alternative society, and the social logic of the world turned upside down pervades much of Bohemia, knowingly and not. So we will find Perdita dressed as a "Queen of the Feast" to shepherds, and Polixenes trapped in his country costume, a king forced into the position of a commoner.

"We must disguise ourselves," Polixenes declares, in the familiar rallying cry of those entering Shakespearean middle worlds. The phrase serves as a magic word, parole, or open sesame, for no sooner does he say this than he and Camillo are confronted with the embodiment of the concept of disguise, Autolycus. Indeed, Autolycus seems in a way to be all role, no essence. It is difficult to isolate his "true" nature out of the mass of fictions; in act 4 he presents himself as, in rapid sequence, a robbed man (who himself robs the Clown), a peddler with a pack of (worthless) finery and bawdy ballads, and a courtier supposedly in the service of King Polixenes. Autolycus is the play's resident artist and genius loci, spirit of place. His name reveals his link with the classical trickster Autolycus, one of the master thieves of Greek tradition, and a son of the quicksilver god Hermes, or Mercury. Looking back across the Shakespearean spectrum, we see he has some formal and structural connections with Puck in *A Midsummer Night's Dream* and with the aptly named Mercutio in *Romeo and Juliet,* as well as with a host of thieves and rogues; and in a way he looks forward to the idealized and more benign figure of Ariel in *The Tempest.* But Autolycus differs crucially from Puck and Ariel because he is human, a rascal as well as a wonder-worker.

In his role as nature spirit and Bohemian genius loci, Autolycus is most certainly a harbinger of the seasons, as his first song, though characteristically bawdy, nonetheless declares:

> When daffodils begin to peer,
>> With heigh, the doxy over the dale,
> Why then comes in the sweet o'the year,
>> For the red blood reigns in the winter's pale.

4.3.1–4

Daffodils—and doxies, or prostitutes. The red blood of desire is the same blood of lineage and incipient violence that was present in the Leontes court. With the second verse, and the mention of "[t]he white sheet bleaching on the hedge," we begin to see Autolycus not only as peddler and singer, but also as something like the spirit of springtime itself. Pulling sheets off hedges becomes a poetic and prosaic way of describing not only a common peddler's theft, but also the melting of snow in the spring. Even the lark, the redemptive bird that rises in the morning in the English countryside, becomes "summer songs for me and my aunts / While we lie tumbling in the hay." The servant who rushes into the feast of sheepshearing to announce that a singing peddler is at the door is eager to stress the chasteness of his tunes—apparently in contrast to the language of those offered by the usual run of peddlers. "He has the prettiest love songs for maids, so without bawdry, which is strange, with such delicate burdens of dildos and fadings, 'Jump her, and thump her'" (4.4.191–194). There is characteristic misspeaking in this comic scene: dildos were then, as they are now, penile sex toys; "with a fading" refers to a popular song "of an indecent character" (*OED*); and "jump her" meant then just what it means today, to have sex with her. But Autolycus's talents are not, apparently, restricted to the inculcation of virtue; there is magic in his web. As the same servant reports, "why, he sings 'em over as they were gods or goddesses. You would think a smock were a she-angel, he so chants to the sleeve-hand and the work about the square on't" (4.4.205–207). As he chants, he enchants, making the smocks and sleeves come to life. Charming in itself, this embedded detail also, we might note, points straight ahead to the statue scene, where, again, the apparently inanimate will be summoned to life by a powerful natural magician.

Why does the play need and welcome a contrary spirit like Autolycus? As with his simpler forebears in the comedies, like Lucio in *Measure for Measure,* Autolycus will be excluded from the play's summing-up. In fact, he goes out of his way to stress those aspects of his character that render him an outlaw to society. Responding in act 5 to the offstage reunion between Perdita and her father, he comments wryly, "Now, had I not the dash of my former life in me, would preferment drop on my head." (Here we may, if we like, hear an echo of Edmund, dying, in *King Lear:* "Some good I mean to do, / Despite of mine own nature" [5.3.217–218].) But Autolycus is true to character and true to type, and when he has effected his transformations and discoveries, he disappears, absenting himself from the final reunions and revelations. Yet what he has contributed has been essential.

I noted above that Autolycus springs into being the moment that disguise is mentioned, and that he seems a counterpart not only of the (downscale) disguises of Camillo and Polixenes, but also of the (upscale) "unusual weeds" of Perdita, who is costumed as Flora, the goddess of blossoming plants. (Remember Antigonus's benediction, "Blossom, speed thee well.") "Weeds" is a common period term for clothing (we still speak of "widow's weeds"), but it is also associated, in Jacobean times as today, with the garden, and Florizel confirms this seasonal association, declaring that she is "no shepherdess, but Flora / Peering in April's front" (4.4.2–3).

Yet as lovely as the courtship of Florizel and Perdita seems to be, and as strongly as it evokes the patterns of Ovidian myth, there still seems to be an important dimension missing from the quality of their love. As Florizel says, emphasizing the Ovidian link to metamorphosis,

> The gods themselves,
> Humbling their deities to love, have taken
> The shapes of beasts upon them. Jupiter
> Became a bull, and bellowed; the green Neptune
> A ram, and bleated; and the fire-robed god,
> Golden Apollo, a poor humble swain,
> As I seem now. . . .
>
> *4.4.25–31*

These are all details of myths of seduction and metamorphosis, gods pursuing nymphs for love. But Florizel chooses to distance himself from the erotic aspect of courtship:

> Their transformations
> Were never for a piece of beauty rarer,
> Nor in a way so chaste, since my desires
> Run not before mine honour, nor my lusts
> Burn hotter than my faith.
>
> *4.4.31–34*

An insistent theme in the late Shakespeare, the determination to embrace chastity and lawful marriage rather than sexual license, is here rather unusually voiced, not by a watchful father (Simonides, Prospero) but by the young lovers themselves. Florizel, despite his flowering name, insists upon it, and Perdita in her ceremony of flower giving (so reminiscent, in a different tonality, of Ophelia's similar gesture in *Hamlet*) evokes chastity and unchastity at every turn. Thus to Camillo she offers "[t]he marigold, that goes to bed wi'th' sun, / And with him rises, weeping" (4.4.105–106), and to the shepherdesses, whose "virgin branches" yet bear their "maidenheads growing," she gives "pale primroses, / That die unmarried ere they can behold / Bright Phoebus in his strength—a malady / Most incident to maids" (122–125). In other words, Perdita's bestowal of flowers, however symbolically connected to sexual "deflowering" (again, a common term in the period), is, like Florizel's language, infused with awareness of her virgin status. She is mistress of the Old Shepherd's house, not yet of her husband's.

It is at this point, significantly, that Autolycus bounds onto the scene, bringing with him among his wares "tawdry-laces," "poking sticks" (for the propping of collars and the pleating of ruffs), and the ballad of the woman who "was turned into a cold fish for she would not exchange flesh with one that loved her." "The ballad," as he says, "is very pitiful, and as true" (4.4.268–270). The anarchic energy he brings to the sheepshearing feast is ameliorative, erotic, and sexual as well as antihierarchical and chaotic. The ballads that make up his most attractive stock are a popular "news" medium as well as a popular mythology (notice how the "cold fish" story is structured like an Ovidian transformation). And when the shepherdess Mopsa announces, "I love a ballad in print, alife, for then we are sure they are true" (251–252), the playwright allows himself to mock both the emergent culture of print and publicity and the claim for poetic "truth."

The long and celebrated sheepshearing scene, act 4, scene 4, is focused on that mainstay of pastoral, the debate—a format we saw both employed and gently mocked in Shakespeare's other major pastoral play, *As You Like It*. In this case the debate takes a very familiar form, that of "Nature and Art"—which is the greater, which the lesser? But, again with the characteristic Shakespearean twist, this most conventional of conventions is undercut from within, for each of the two debaters winds up arguing *against* his or her own interest. Perdita, who thinks she is a lowborn shepherdess and wants to marry a young man who is a king's son, argues for social purity, for not marrying out of one's proper rank, while Polixenes, a king disguised as a countryman in order to detect and foil this misalliance, speaks blithely of marrying "a gentler scion to the wildest stock":

Perdita	Sir, the year growing ancient,
	Not yet on summer's death, nor on the birth
	Of trembling winter, the fairest flowers o'th' season
	Are our carnations and streaked gillyvors,
	Which some call nature's bastards. Of that kind
	Our rustic garden's barren, and I care not
	To get slips of them.
Polixenes	Wherefore, gentle maiden,
	Do you neglect them?
Perdita	For I have heard it said
	There is an art which in their piedness shares
	With great creating nature.
Polixenes	Say there be,
	Yet nature is made better by no mean
	But nature makes that mean. So over that art
	Which you say adds to nature is an art
	That nature makes. You see, sweet maid, we marry
	A gentler scion to the wildest stock,
	And make conceive a bark of baser kind
	By bud of nobler race. This is an art
	Which does mend nature—change it rather; but
	The art itself is nature.

4.4.79–97

Perdita's distrust of art runs deep; she is uncomfortable in her "unusual weeds," her costume of Flora, and later, when Camillo urges her to practice further deceit—dressing Florizel in Autolycus's clothes "as if / The scene you play were mine," she resists: "I see the play so lies / That I must bear a part" (4.4.581–582, 638–639). She is sensitive to the way costume can change not only appearance but temperament and character. Earlier, primping shyly in her new gown, she had claimed, "Sure this robe of mine / Does change my disposition," and she associates the performance with that of a local seasonal festival: "Methinks I play as I have seen them do / In Whitsun pastorals" (4.4.134–135, 133–134).

Whitsun (Whitsunday) was an English springtime festival, seven weeks after Easter, for which masquerading was a central part of the celebration. The figures of Robin Hood and Maid Marian were among the key players. A "king" and "queen" were appointed, and this "May-game," as it was also known, became intermittently the target of clerical protest. But this paganized festival has its roots in a Christian holy day, Pentecost, when the Holy Spirit is said to have entered the Apostles, and they were able to speak "with other tongues" (Acts 2:4) and thus to go forth and preach Christ's ministry throughout the world. In essence, Pentecost is a reversal of the fall wrought by the Tower of Babel in Genesis (11:1–9), when the Lord "confused the language" of impious men seeking to build a tower to heaven, rendering them unable to communicate with one another, and frustrating their design. By contrast, Pentecost took many languages and in effect made them one, by giving the Apostles the ability to speak and understand them all.

This transformation mirrors a pattern that lies close to the center of *The Winter's Tale*, as we have already seen, in the etymology of the word "infant" from the Latin for "unable to speak." Perdita as an infant could not move and persuade her father, as Paulina had hoped. (Paulina's name, as we have noted, links her with the Apostle Paul, whose story is likewise told in the Book of Acts.) Now, sixteen years later, an articulate if unpracticed Perdita will learn to speak and to play her part. As Leontes' servant will report to him when—following Camillo's plan—the young couple, Florizel and Perdita, seek refuge in Sicilia from Polixenes' wrath, "when she has obtained your eye," she will "have your tongue too" (5.1.105–106).

For the sheepshearing scene, which seems almost to enact a minicycle of the seasons—beginning in harvest and succumbing to a wintry blast of paternal anger—now gives way to another journey over water, bringing Camillo home, and Perdita, too, though she does not know it. The fifth act of *The Winter's Tale*, masterful in its architecture and capacious in its mythmaking, in effect stages the family reunion three times, in three successive scenes, one seasonal or cyclical, the second narrative or reported, and the third ekphrastic or apocalyptic, the statue come to life. Underlying them all is the one Ovidian myth that—beyond all others—informs the play: the story of Proserpina, the daughter of Ceres, the harvest goddess, who was stolen away by the god Pluto, or Dis, taken to the underworld, and then permitted to return to the earth for eight months of the year. Because she had eaten four seeds of the pomegranate, Proserpina was required to remain in Pluto's kingdom for the four months that become winter. Upon her return, her mother rejoiced, and the earth bloomed again. Perdita had acknowledged this story in the course of the sheepshearing scene: "O Proserpina, / For the flowers now that, frighted, thou letst fall / From Dis's wagon!" (4.4.116–118).

When she and Florizel appear at Leontes' court in act 5, Perdita is described by an admiring servant as "the most peerless piece of earth, I think, / That e'er the sun shown bright on" (5.1.93–94). As the couple stand, in the King's phrase, "begetting wonder," Leontes, who of course does not recognize his daughter, greets them in a language that is correspondingly seasonal and "natural": "Welcome hither, / As is the spring to th'earth!" (150–151). Here the myth fairly bursts forth from the play. In what may be a vestigial memory of an older nature myth, Leontes briefly thinks of marrying this paragon himself, echoing the incest motif we have seen proposed, and set aside, in *Pericles*. It may be of some interest that stagings of the play have sometimes, perhaps unwittingly, reinvigorated this disruptive moment on the path to reunion by doubling the parts of the young Hermione of acts 1 and 2 and her grown daughter of the later acts. In any case, Leontes quickly reverses himself, pledging to be of service to the young pair.

In the second scene of this final act, a further wonder is revealed, a wonder so surprising and unbelievable that it is twice compared to an "old tale"—the truth of which the audience has been long aware—that Perdita is the King's lost child. The fact that we are indeed aware of this may be one reason why the revelation takes place offstage. For to the spectators in the theater this is old news, while to the courtiers who report their amazement, it is powerfully new. The technique is the same as that used in Lady Macbeth's sleepwalking scene, where the horror of the onstage spectators, the Doctor and the Waiting-Gentlewoman, renews the audience's sense of anguish at a murder whose perpetrator and method we have already seen for ourselves. In *Pericles* we were witness to two parallel reunions, of parent and child and of husband and wife; in *The Winter's Tale* Shakespeare refines his technique, subordinating the offstage meeting of father and daughter, preparing the way for an even more astounding scene. Thus we are in effect backstage with the courtiers; each new lord who arrives adds a piece of the puzzle. The language of the First Gentleman seems to echo the prevailing theme of Whitsun, or Pentecost: "There was speech in their dumbness, language in their very gesture. They looked as they had heard of a world ransomed, or one destroyed" (5.2.11–13). But it is the Third Gentleman whose report is of the greatest interest. Describing Perdita's response to the story of her mother's death, he says, "[S]he did, with an 'Alas,' I would fain say bleed tears; for I am sure my heart wept blood. Who was most marble there changed colour. Some swooned, all sorrowed" (5.2.78–82). Once again, a figure of speech is about to become reality. The gentleman's phrase—"Who was most marble there changed colour"—serves as a hint and a preparation for the literal turning of marble into color with the awakening of Hermione. (Classical statues were originally painted, but much Renaissance statuary, imitating the condition of marble pieces discovered after centuries had passed, was monochromatic.)

As for the third scene, it is difficult to know what to say. Though he may have matched the gradualism, the suspense, and the enchantment of this scene elsewhere, surely Shakespeare never surpassed it. The presiding genius of this scene is neither Time (who in a way governed the first scene, the seasonal myth) nor Autolycus (who was present onstage in the second, underscoring and sharpening the account), but the final artist and wonder-worker of the play, Paulina. The scene is set in her home, which is described as both a chapel and a gallery. The visitors are led through the other exhibits, in the first of Paulina's delaying maneuvers, and then at last they are set before the statue, and Paulina draws the curtain. "Prepare," she says, "[t]o see the life as lively mocked as ever / Still sleep mocked death" (5.3.18–20). Silent they stand in front of it, lost in wonder. Leontes notes the statue's wrinkles, and is reminded of the carver's excellence in imagining what Hermione would have looked like had she lived. Perdita kneels to kiss the statue's hand, and is asked to hold off, to show patience: "the colour's / Not dry." Leontes urges Paulina not to close the curtain, and she cautions—revealing another clue to an offstage audience that is not yet in on her secret—"No longer shall you gaze on't, lest your fancy / May think anon it moves." Slowly, deliberately, the spell is woven: "Would you not deem it breathed, and that those veins / Did verily bear blood?" and "The very life seems warm upon her lip," and, especially, echoing the ambivalently allusive reference to "our carver":

Leontes   [M]ethinks
          There is an air comes from her. What fine chisel
          Could ever yet cut breath? . . .

                                        5.3.77–79

As Leontes moves to kiss her, and is gently checked by Paulina—"Shall I draw the curtain?"—the action turns double, aimed at both onstage and offstage audiences at once. "It is required / You do awake your faith," declares Paulina, to Hermione's family and to the spectators in the theater, and then:

          Music; awake her; strike!
          [*Music*]
[*To* HERMIONE] 'Tis time. Descend. Be stone no more. Approach.
Strike all that look upon with marvel. Come,
I'll fill your grave up. Stir. Nay, come away.
Bequeath to death your numbness, for from him

Dear life redeems you.
[*To* LEONTES]   You perceive she stirs.

5.3.98–103

In this moment Paulina is a true descendant of her namesake, the Apostle Paul, who spoke to the Ephesians and the Romans of awakening out of sleep to redemption, and to the Corinthians of the natural body and the spiritual body, the earthly and the heavenly. "Behold, I shew you a mystery; We shall not all sleep, but we shall all be changed" (1 Corinthians 15:51). Yet if Paulina is herself Pauline, and the scene a visibly Christian one, transforming the diurnal and cyclical into the redemptive, so, too, is she here evoking a recognizably mythic and Ovidian scene, for we are very close, at this moment, to the myth of Pygmalion, the King of Cyprus, and a sculptor. Pygmalion, shocked at the vices of earthly women, made an ivory statue and fell in love with it. He kissed it and touched it, praying to Venus for a lover like his ivory girl. Venus answered his prayer, bringing the statue to life, and giving her to Pygmalion. The couple married, and in nine months Pygmalion's wife gave birth to a girl (*Metamorphoses,* book 10). Thus the story of Pygmalion foreshadows the story of Leontes, whose wife became a statue for a time, and whose daughter, reunited with her parents, brings the narrative to a close worthy of dramatic romance. *The Winter's Tale* charts the union of the myth of Proserpina and Pygmalion, the story of natural cycle and the story of art and desire.

The Proserpina story concludes with the reunion of a mother and daughter, and we might note that at the end of the play there is a triad of women— Hermione, Perdita, and Paulina—who seem closely bound to one another. Although after the revelation to her husband that she is alive—"If this be magic, let it be an art / Lawful as eating," cries Leontes—Hermione "hangs about his neck," her first public words in sixteen years are spoken not to the husband but to her daughter, for whose sake, she says, encouraged by the oracle, she has "preserved" herself to see her child again. The set of three marriages or remarriages with which the play ends (Leontes and Hermione; Perdita and Florizel; Paulina and Camillo) is thus matched by a shift from the autocratic, wrathful, and almost tragic male rule of the King to the collective and collaborative female "magic" of the women, who have sustained one another and their secret to see the oracle fulfilled.

There is, moreover, one additional pattern that lies beneath the surface and calls for our attention, a pattern both more basic and more metadramatic, since it speaks to the very condition of the play as a theatrical event. As we have noted, when Paulina says "It is required / You do awake your faith," she is speaking to the offstage audience as well as to the members of Leontes' and Polixenes' courts. Generations of scholars, directors, actors, and audiences have recognized that the astonishing phenomenon with which this play closes, the statue that comes to life, is a strong and apt figure for the transformative power of drama in general and of Shakespearean drama in particular. Evoking the audience's aid—as in other plays, like *As You Like It* and *The Tempest,* the chief actor will do in the epilogue—Paulina re-creates art as life, and life as art. The statue "is" the play. Just as the shepherdesses who listened to (and bought from) Autolycus loved a ballad in print, "for then we know they are true," the statue of Hermione is the extraordinary emblem of Shakespearean craftsmanship—a blend of nature and of art, awakened by the faith of the Shakespearean audience, the same power that centuries later Coleridge would call the "willing suspension of disbelief," but here dramatized and set before our eyes. The statue comes to life, as the play comes to life, as Shakespeare's dramatic universe in all its complexity and variety comes to life upon the stage, crafted in part by Time, the Chorus; in part by Autolycus, the errant spirit of fertility, the snapper-up of unconsidered trifles; in part by Paulina, with her biblical name and her quasi-magical powers. As the couples depart the stage to discuss what they have seen and heard—"Hastily lead away," commands Leontes—the debate of Nature and Art is restaged as the age-old problem of dramatic "reality," where Polixenes' phrase may prevail. The art itself is nature.

The Tempest

DRAMATIS PERSONAE

Prospero, *the rightful Duke of Milan*

Miranda, *his daughter*

Antonio, *his brother, the usurping Duke of Milan*

Alonso, *King of Naples*

Sebastian, *his brother*

Ferdinand, *Alonso's son*

Gonzalo, *an honest old counsellor of Naples*

Adrian, *a lord*

Francisco, *a lord*

Ariel, *an airy spirit attendant upon Prospero*

Caliban, *a savage and deformed native of the island, Prospero's slave*

Trinculo, *Alonso's jester*

Stephano, *Alonso's drunken butler*

The Master of a ship

Boatswain

Mariners

Spirits

THE MASQUE
Spirits appearing as:

Iris

Ceres

Juno

Nymphs, reapers

SHAKESPEARE'S POWERFUL late romance *The Tempest* has been addressed by modern critics from two important perspectives: as a fable of art and creation, and as a colonialist allegory. These readings very much depend on one's conception of European man's place in the universe, and on whether a figure like Prospero stands for all mankind or for one side of a conflict.

The first interpretation, following upon the ideas of Renaissance humanism and the place of the artist/playwright/magician, offers a story of mankind at the center of the universe, of "man" as creator and authority. Such a reading is, by its nature, at once aesthetic, philosophical, and skeptical. Prospero is man-the-artist, or man-the-scholar: Ariel and Caliban represent his ethereal and material selves—the one airy, imaginative, and swift; the second earthy, gross, and appetitive. Prospero has often been seen as a figure for the artist as creator—as Shakespeare's stand-in, so to speak, or Shakespeare's self-conception, an artist figure unifying the world around him by his "so potent art." By his magic, his *good* magic, or what has been described as *white* (or benevolent) magic, he subdues anarchic figures around him, like Caliban and his mother, Sycorax, the previous ruler of the island, who is also a magician (often thought of as a practitioner of *black,* or malevolent, magic). Prospero's magic books enable him as well to thwart the incipient revolts of both high and low conspirators, and to exact a species of revenge against those who usurped his dukedom and set him adrift on the sea—for *The Tempest* is one of Shakespeare's most compelling "revenge tragedies," turned, at the last moment, toward forgiveness.

But there is something troubling about this idealized picture of a Renaissance man accommodated with arts and crafts, dominance and power, in a little world, a little island, that he takes and makes his own. Many critical observers, especially in the later twentieth century, have seen Prospero as a colonizer of alien territory *not* his own, a European master who comes to an island in the New World, displaces its native ruler, enslaves its indigenous population (in this case emblematized by Caliban), and makes its rightful inhabitants work for him and his family as servants, fetching wood and water, while he and his daughter enjoy all the amenities of the temperate climate and the fertile land. The tensions between the aesthetic and the political lie at the heart of the play.

First staged in 1611, with King James present in the audience, *The Tempest* was subsequently performed as part of the marriage celebration for his daughter, the Princess Elizabeth, whom the King was about to "lose" to her husband, Frederick, the Elector Palatine—just as Prospero "loses" his daughter, Miranda, as he tells Alonso, King of Naples, "in this last tempest," to Ferdinand, the King's son. So the political and social context, the timeliness, of the play may have been evident from the beginning.

Although it takes the form of an extended scene of instruction between Prospero and Miranda, father and daughter, the play is fundamentally built on the continuous contrast between Prospero's two servants, Ariel and Caliban, mind and body, imagination and desire or lust. If Ariel is imagination personified, surely Caliban is something like libido (sexual desire) or id (basic human drives). If one thing is clear on Prospero's island, it is that, for all his anarchic and disruptive qualities, Caliban is *necessary*—like the body itself. "We cannot miss him," says Prospero (meaning, "We cannot do without him"). "He does make our fire, / Fetch in our wood, and serves in offices / That profit us" (1.2.314–316). Later in the play, after Caliban foils the conspiracy against his life, Prospero will say ruefully of him, "This thing of darkness I / Acknowledge mine" (5.1.278–279). What Prospero acknowledges in this phrase is not only responsibility (Caliban is my slave), but also identity (Caliban, the "thing of darkness," is part of me).

In one way we might say that *The Tempest* is macrocosmic: Caliban is a spirit of earth and water, Ariel a spirit of fire and air, and together they are elements harnessed by Prospero, here a kind of magician and wonder-worker closely allied to Renaissance science. Together these figures give us a picture of the world. In another way we could say that *The Tempest* is microcosmic, its structural design a mirror of the human psyche: Caliban, who is necessary and burdensome, the libido, the id, a "thing of darkness" who must be acknowledged; Ariel the spirit of imagination incarnate, who cannot be possessed forever, and therefore must be allowed to depart in freedom. And in yet a third way the play's design illustrates the basic doctrines of Renaissance humanist philosophy. Mankind is a creature a little lower than the angels, caught between the bestial and the celestial, a creature of infinite possibilities. In all of these patterns Prospero stands between the poles marked out by Ariel and Caliban.

The second kind of interpretation, the colonial or postcolonial narrative, follows upon early modern voyages of exploration and discovery, "first contact," and the encounters with, and exploitation of, indigenous peoples in the New World. In this interpretive context *The Tempest* is not idealizing, aesthetic, and "timeless," but rather topical, contextual, "political," and in dialogue with the times. Yet manifestly this dichotomy will break down, both in literary analysis and in performance. It is perfectly possible for a play about a mage, artist, and father to be, at the same time, a play about a colonial governor, since Prospero himself is, or was, the Duke of Milan. His neglect of his ducal responsibilities ("rapt in secret studies," he allowed his brother to scheme against him) led first to his usurpation and exile, then to his establishment of an alternative government on the island, displacing and enslaving the native inhabitant Caliban, whose mother, Sycorax, had ruled there before Prospero's arrival and who, as Caliban says, "first was mine own king" (1.2.345).

Caliban's name is a variant of "cannibal" (deriving from "Carib," a fierce nation of the West Indies), and Shakespeare's play owes much to Montaigne's essay "Of Cannibals" (1580), which draws trenchant and unflattering comparisons between the supposedly civilized Europeans and the native islanders. "There is nothing savage or barbarous about those peoples, but that every man calls barbarous anything he is not accustomed to," Montaigne writes. Despite the nakedness and unfamiliar ways of these tribes, contemporary European societies "surpass them in every kind of barbarism," like treachery, disloyalty, tyranny, and cruelty, which "are everyday vices in us." As for cannibalism itself, there is "more barbarity in lacerating by rack and torture a body still fully able to feel things, in roasting him little by little . . . than in roasting and eating him after his death."[1]

Colonialist readings have gained force in the last fifty years by analogy with the historical events of postcolonialism, whether in South Asia, Africa, or the Caribbean, but they are also entirely pertinent to Shakespeare's own time. During the years when *The Tempest* was written and first performed, Europe, and England in particular, was in the heyday of the period of colonial exploration. Sir Walter Ralegh is one important and charismatic figure who went from the Elizabethan court to the New World, and in his account, *The Discovery of the Large, Rich, and Beautiful Empire of Guiana* (1596), he describes encounters with native populations of just this kind. Captain John Smith set out with the Virginia colonists in 1606, and his *General History of Virginia, New England, and the Summer Isles* (1624) is another key source for this period, documenting the encounter of Englishmen (for which we may read Prospero's Italians/Europeans) with a native culture and climate in the New World.

There are moments in the play that clearly evoke the local historical context: as, for example, when Trinculo, the drunken jester, stumbling over the recumbent form of Caliban, imagines a fast way to make money, by exhibiting him back in the Old World for a fee:

> Were I in England now, as once I was, and had but this fish painted, not a holiday-fool there but would give a piece of silver. There would this monster make a man. Any strange beast there makes a man. When they will not give a doit to relieve a lame beggar, they will lay out ten to see a dead Indian.
>
> The Tempest 2.2.26–31

"Were I in England" is Shakespeare's typical sly wit—an in-joke for the English audience, like the scene in which the gravedigger in *Hamlet* remarks that no one in England would detect Hamlet's infirmity: "There the men are as mad as he" (5.1.142–143).

Many of the twentieth-century rewritings of *The Tempest* are inspired by New World concerns, and even are written from the point of view of the oppressed. The Uruguayan philosopher and critic José Enrique Rodó wrote his *Ariel* in 1900, calling upon Latin America to retain cultural values unsullied by the materialism of the United States; in 1913 he published *El Mirador de Próspero* (Prospero's Balcony). Martinican playwright Aimé Césaire published the first version of his *Une Tempête,* a radical adaptation of Shakespeare's play, in 1968, and the Cuban revolutionary intellectual Roberto Fernández Retamar wrote his *Calibán* in 1971. The story of *The Tempest* has intersected, repeatedly and always interestingly, with other "political" and colonial moments, through and beyond the postcolonial period of the mid-twentieth century. In many revisionist readings, Caliban becomes a more central and sympathetic figure. In some productions, dating as early as the turn of the last century, he is a loner and a misunderstood "hero," dispossessed of his birthright by the invading Europeans. From W. H. Auden's poem *The Sea and the Mirror* (1944) to Césaire's *Une Tempête,* an adaptation explicitly made "for a Black theater," to films as diverse as *Forbidden Planet* (1956) and *Prospero's Books* (1991), *The Tempest* has retained its power and fascination.

But is Prospero's enchanted island in the Old World or the New World? The play's indebtedness to many New World texts is evident in its descriptions: the storm in the "still-vexed Bermudas"; the native inhabitants, often associated by critics with American Indians; the echoes of Jamestown and the early Virginia tracts, as well as of Montaigne's influential account of New World natives. In literal geographical terms, however, the island must be located in the Mediterranean Sea, not far from the coast of Africa. The King and court party are returning from the wedding of Claribel to an African in Tunis, and Sycorax hails from Algiers ("Argier"). Scholars have also begun to remind us that an even closer island, one actually within the "British isles," was famed for the wildness of its inhabitants, linking Ireland as yet another colonial space evoked by the play's suggestively rich and elusive landscape. That *all* of these associations seem germane is now virtually taken for granted.

What is most magical about the isle, however, is that in being many places at once, geographically, culturally, and mythographically hybrid, it eludes location and becomes a space for poetry, and for dream. It is not found on any map. Prospero's enchanted island, while drawn from real explorations and published accounts, is ultimately a country of the mind. And this is made clear by the very structure of the play, which starts out in medias res, in clamor, in shipwreck, and in darkness.

As *The Tempest* begins, the audience finds itself in the middle of a storm at sea. All around is confusion: "A tempestuous noise of thunder and lightning heard." Voices cry out, seemingly from nowhere, in disconnected fragments that recall other Shakespearean storms, and other romances.

> Boatswain   Keep your cabins; you do assist the storm.
> Gonzalo   Nay, good, be patient.
>
> *1.1.12–14*

These lines might have come from the shipwreck scene in *Pericles,* where the nurse Lychorida urges the King in very similar words: "Patience, good sir, do not assist the storm."

"What care these roarers for the name of king?" cries the Boatswain in despair. This is an echo of the storm in *The Winter's Tale,* in which the nobleman Antigonus was torn to pieces by the bear. Those waves, too, "roared," with no regard for such cultural niceties as rank and status. This present tempest, the tempest in the play that bears that name, is thus somehow the quintessential storm, the "perfect" storm, distilled of all the Shakespearean tempests we have weathered before, from *Othello* and *King Lear* to the romances. Indeed, this scene is often played in total darkness, emphasizing the confusion and disorder.

And yet in a moment the audience will discover that the tempest that has whirled about us was not a tempest at all, but a piece of art. We find ourselves, in fact, in a position very close to that of Miranda, Prospero's daughter. We, too, are a horrified audience with only a single thought:

> If by your art, my dearest father, you have
> Put the wild waters in this roar, allay them.

The sky, it seems, would pour down stinking pitch,
But that the sea, mounting to th' welkin's cheek,
Dashes the fire out. O, I have sufferèd
With those that I saw suffer! A brave vessel,
Who had, no doubt, some noble creature in her,
Dashed all to pieces! O, the cry did knock
Against my very heart! Poor souls, they perished.
Had I been any god of power, I would
Have sunk the ship within the earth, or ere
It should the good ship so have swallowed and
The fraughting souls within her.

1.2.1–13

"O, I have sufferèd / With those that I saw suffer!" Miranda, whose name comes from the Latin word *mirari,* "to wonder at," is the ideal spectator of tragedy and catharsis. Had *she* been any god of power, she would have intervened. But her father, Prospero, tells her—and us—that we are to have "[n]o more amazement," no more wonder: "There's no harm done." As for Miranda, "[T]hee, my daughter," he says, "[a]rt ignorant of what thou art." His remarks framed by this suggestively chiasmic sentence ("*art* ignorant of what thou *art*"), Prospero will "pluck [his] magic garment" from him, saying, "Lie there, my art," and will begin to tell his daughter that the storm is a fiction, that its victims are safe; and that the entire event is a function of his art. Thus, from the very beginning, *art* the noun, meaning "magic," and *art* the verb, the present indicative of "to be," establish a frame for both the sentence and the play. The question of whether art is linked primarily to ordinary being or to magical creation will lie, as we have already begun to sense, at the very heart of Shakespeare's play.

As the audience soon learns, this is not the first tempest to have touched the lives of Prospero and Miranda. The play is structured like a hall of mirrors, a palimpsest, or a mise en abyme. Twelve years ago, says Prospero, in a very similar storm, "i'th' dead of darkness, / The ministers" of Naples and Milan "hurried thence / Me and thy crying self." This tempest is thus a cyclical event, a repetition (like the performance of a play)—a wrought and invented storm, to answer and resolve the first storm, a dozen years earlier, when Miranda was "a cherubin," an angel, "that did preserve me." So Prospero, formerly powerless or overpowered, now returns to the storm as a "god of power," in Miranda's phrase—one who can look into the "dark backward and abyss of time" and can transform it into both present and future.

This scene of necessary exposition, explaining what has happened before the play begins, is beautifully and concisely handled. To Miranda the past is "rather like a dream than an assurance," and the figure of life as a dream, and the difficulty of telling dreaming from waking, will persist as a major theme. As her name implies, Miranda is the ideal audience, hanging on every word; the play begins at a key moment in her life, as well as in her father's, a moment when everything is about to change. Yet we may notice that there is something odd in the way Prospero tells his tale. Over and over again he asks her whether she is paying attention to his story. "I pray thee mark me." "Dost thou attend me?" "Thou attend'st not!" "Dost thou hear?" Why does he do this, when, as she protests, "Your tale, sir, would cure deafness," and when the audience in the theater, too, listens almost as if spellbound? Perhaps for that very reason. Prospero's repetition itself is a kind of charm or spell, hypnotizing his wondering daughter, so that finally, as he says, "Thou art inclined to sleep; 'tis a good dullness, / And give it way. I know thou canst not choose" (1.2.186–187).

The shape of the play is predicated on the general thesis—one omnipresent in Renaissance literature and drama, and given eloquent expression in Shakespeare's plays as early as Puck's Epilogue in *A Midsummer Night's Dream*—that life may all be an illusion, "[n]o more yielding but a dream," or, as Prospero will express it in an equally celebrated passage, that "our little life / Is rounded with a sleep." When Prospero enchants his beloved daughter, when Miranda sleeps, the audience is transported into the world of possibility that is also the world of theater and of art.

What does it mean to sleep in this play about dream and fantasy, about the seen and the unseen? For Miranda, it is the point of entry into a whole new world. For Prospero, it means that he can evoke his "tricksy spirit" Ariel, whom he has charged with overseeing the storm and its effects. Allied with imagination, invisible to everyone but Prospero—and the audience—Ariel seems to be the embodiment of music and sound. He plays on pipes and tabors throughout the action, and he sings a number of songs, the first two of which may be the most striking, though all of them are lovely. The play, like the isle, is full of music. These first two songs are both sung to Ferdinand in act 1, scene 2, when Ferdinand thinks of himself as the sole survivor of a shipwreck that has drowned his father and left him King of Naples.

In the first song we hear what is in essence a prediction of the action of the play to come—a song of plot, of forethought:

> Come unto these yellow sands,
>   And then take hands;
> Curtsied when you have and kissed—
>   The wild waves whist—
> Foot it featly here and there,
>   And, sweet sprites, bear
> The burden. Hark, hark.

1.2.378–384

This song is closely related to the riddles and prophecies that play such a large part in the other romances. Decoded, it is the whole story of the play. Ferdinand, Alonso's son, *has* come unto these yellow sands—landed on the isolated island that is the central romance locale. He will shortly take hands with Miranda, Prospero's daughter, and both "curtsy" and "kiss"—that is, both obey the rules of decorum and chastity—and express his love and plight his troth. Doing so will make the "wild waves whist," stilling the tempest, a tempest that has really been raging since Prospero and the infant Miranda were put out to sea, a tempest that is, as Prospero says (sounding much like King Lear), the counterpart of his "beating mind." Once the tempest or dissension is stilled, the play will move to a marriage dance ("Foot it featly here and there") performed by the masque of the nymphs and the mowers, both symbols of fertility. "And, sweet sprites, bear / The burden." The word "burden" here carries two meanings: the heavy task of bringing this plot about, and also the chorus of the song, since a "burden" in music is a refrain or chorus. As they bring about the desired marriage and reconciliation, the sweet sprites, and Ariel in particular, will accompany that transformation with music and song, bearing both burdens at once.

Ariel's second song to Ferdinand is even more celebrated, and makes a cameo appearance, as readers of modern poetry will recognize, in *The Waste Land* by T. S. Eliot. But where Eliot's poem centers on fragmentation and loss, in the Shakespearean context Ariel's song is one of metamorphosis and transformation, though it begins with a lie:

> Full fathom five thy father lies.
> Of his bones are coral made;
> Those are pearls that were his eyes;
> Nothing of him that doth fade
> But doth suffer a sea-change
> Into something rich and strange.
>
> *1.2.400–405*

Of course, Ferdinand's father is *not* dead. But for the son who does not yet know this, the terrifying aspects of human death are, in this song, entirely masked or transcended. Instead of decay or fear, we have metamorphosis: "Of his bones are coral made"; "Those are pearls that were his eyes." Coral and pearls are natural materials, transformed from minuscule sea creatures, from shells and sand. Metamorphosis here is not only fantasy; it is an aspect of nature and of change. Audiences and readers familiar with Shakespeare's language may call to mind the very similar, and yet very different, passage in *Richard III,* when Richard's brother Clarence dreams of death by drowning (1.4.21–33). As we saw in a consideration of that play, the similarity of the imagery in the two passages (gems in place of eyes; fish gnawing upon the bodies of the dead; gold, pearls, and jewels scattered on the sea floor) points up the radical difference in tone. Clarence's horrific vision of decay becomes Ariel's blithe assurance of eternal change. The concept of a "sea-change / Into something rich and strange" clearly goes beyond the local relevance of the song here—Ferdinand's mourning for his father—to comment upon the progress of the entire play. As in *Antony and Cleopatra,* in *Twelfth Night,* and elsewhere in Shakespeare, the sea is fertile and even eternizing. The formal structure of this song, with its patterns of chiasmus, or crossing, beautifully mirrors the pattern of metamorphosis here:

> *bones / coral* : *pearls / eyes*
> [body / jewel : jewel / body]
> *nothing / doth fade* : *doth suffer / something*
> [negation / change : change / affirmation]

For the audience, the summoning of Ariel signals a fundamental shift in perception. Throughout the play, as we will see, sleep and waking will be used as a measure of the imaginative capabilities of the dreamer. By this simple but powerful device the play splits the visual and imaginative field, allowing for parallel and distinct planes of awareness. We see what Prospero sees. Others, though, see less, see differently. Sleep and dream—as in a contemporary Renaissance play like Calderón's *La vida es sueño* (1635) or a modern play like Eugene O'Neill's *The Iceman Cometh* (1946)—are ways of entering and exiting the dramatic action, as well as indices of consciousness and conscience.

Thus the play is framed by the sleep of the mariners, who take no part in the action. Ariel has put them in safe harbor, as he explains to his master, Prospero: "all under hatches stowed, / Who, with a charm joined to their suffered labour, / I have left asleep" (1.2.231–233). At the close of the play, rubbing their eyes in a touchingly innocent ignorance, they will emerge from their temporary prison. The Boatswain speaks for them all as he explains his puzzlement:

> If I did think, sir, I were well awake
> I'd strive to tell you. We were dead of sleep,
> And—how we know not—all clapped under hatches,
> Where but even now, with strange and several noises
> . . . .
> We were awaked. . . .
>
> *5.1.232–238*

They find their ship magically restored to wholeness, their captain alive and "[c]ap'ring to eye her." The Boatswain concludes his explanation:

> On a trice, so please you,
> Even in a dream, were we divided from them,
> And were brought moping hither.
>
> *5.1.241–243*

In a sense, the whole play takes place during the mariners' dream, the dream of the uninformed, and the uninvolved.

But if sleep is a sign of innocence, wakefulness is—as often in Shakespearean tragedy—a sign of guilt. In act 2, scene 1, when one by one the courtiers fall asleep to the music of Ariel's pipe, the King, Alonso, remains awake, and wonders why: "What, all so soon asleep?" Although Alonso is guilty of complicity in the exile of Prospero, he is now also a figure of sympathy and pathos, since he is mourning the supposed death of his own son, Ferdinand, and he, too, soon falls asleep, leaving awake upon the stage only two men: Antonio, Prospero's brother, and Sebastian, the brother of Alonso—that is, the already usurping Duke of Milan and the potentially usurping King of Naples. Sleeplessness afflicts them as it afflicts other Shakespearean characters of uneasy conscience, and they speak to each other in the language of sleep and dream. When Antonio suggests that Sebastian might become king, Sebastian rejoins,

> What, art thou waking?
>
> . . . .
>
>   surely
> It is a sleepy language, and thou speak'st
> Out of thy sleep.
>
>   *2.1.205–209*

"[W]hat a sleep were this / For your advancement!" Antonio replies. Here "sleepy language," like the "sleepy drinks" mentioned at the beginning of *The Winter's Tale,* suggests a wish, a fantasy, a condition contrary to fact. The sleep of Alonso provides an opportunity for Sebastian to realize his dream of usurpation.

The sleep of the courtiers, like the raging of the storm, is one of Ariel's devices. Dressed by Prospero in a cloak of invisibility, and therefore unseen by anyone but his master and the audience, Ariel marks the borderline between visible and invisible, conscious and unconscious. He is fire, the element associated above all with transformation, but he is also the spirit of air—by which is meant both wind and breath, or "inspiration": "Now on the beak, / Now in the waste, the deck, in every cabin, / I flamed amazement" (1.2.197–199); "I come / To answer thy best pleasure. Be't to fly, / To swim, to dive into the fire, to ride / On the curled clouds" (190–193). As a wind god, he causes the tempest itself. Addressing the royal conspirators in act 3, scene 3, as "three men of sin," he will appear to them in a clap of thunder and a streak of lightning—air and fire—to accuse them of their past misdeeds against Prospero. "Methought," exclaims a horrified Alonso, "the billows spoke and told me of it, / The winds did sing it to me, and the thunder, / That deep and dreadful organ-pipe, pronounced / The name of Prosper" (3.3.96–99). In this scene, the stage direction indicates that Ariel appears "like a harpy"; the harpies were figures associated by ancient poets such as Homer and Hesiod with wind spirits, and with the souls of the dead.

It is significant, though, that for all of Ariel's capacity to describe and bring about metamorphosis, he himself remains under Prospero's control for almost the entire duration of the play. His persistent requests to be liberated from bondage are easy to miss if we focus on his apparent freedom: to fly, to sing, to remain invisible, to invent stratagems, to speak in many voices, to entrap the unwary conspirators. Yet Ariel's situation under Prospero's rule has many similarities with his situation under the sway of Caliban's mother, Sycorax, who imprisoned Ariel in a pine tree for twelve years—the same amount of time that Ariel has been serving his new master, Prospero. As with the cyclic and emblematic tempests, which take place a dozen years apart, the question of Ariel's freedom returns with new urgency as the play opens. Even Sycorax, who is described as a type of Circe, or female magician, is imaged as powerful and aversive, as a bent old hag who is also a walking sign of cyclical repetition, endlessly returning upon herself: "The foul witch Sycorax, who with age and envy / Was grown into a hoop" (1.2.259–260). Indeed, as we will see, the very pattern of *The Tempest*—a play that, unlike most by Shakespeare, obeys the three supposed classical "unities" of time, space, and action—is to repeat, with a difference, all the main events of the past (tempest, usurpation, bondage, rule of the island). As they are repeated, each is interrogated, reversed, and undone.

Compared to that of Caliban, though, Ariel's bondage looks a great deal like freedom. For Prospero's two servants are constantly, and directly, contrasted. In terms of the four elements, Caliban is clearly earth and water, spending his time in "bogs, fens, [and] flats," mistaken for a fish (and smelling like one), fond of fishing, and eagerly volunteering to dig sustenance in the form of pignuts out of the earth with his long fingernails.

Ariel was once imprisoned in the cloven pine, and Caliban now complains to Prospero that "I am all the subjects that you have, / Which first was mine own king, and here you sty me / In this hard rock" (1.2.344–346). Prospero keeps Caliban penned up in a cave, a naturalistic prison, but also the traditional allegorical place in which to restrain lustful desire. Yet he, too, once had a kind of innocence. There is pathos in his memory of Prospero and Miranda's arrival on the island, when they treated him with kindness, and he taught them what he knew:

> When thou cam'st first,
> Thou strok'st me and made much of me, wouldst give me
> Water with berries in't, and teach me how
> To name the bigger light, and how the less,
> That burn by day and night; and then I loved thee,
> And showed thee all the qualities o'th' isle,
> The fresh springs, brine pits, barren place and fertile—

> *1.2.335–341*

In one way, this seems like a classic version of the New World encounter, the guileless native inhabitant cunningly persuaded to lead the invaders to local treasure. But at the same time, rhetorically and tonally, the lines seem to be spoken in the remembered voice of a child, lacking language, or at least European language ("the bigger light . . . the less"). With elegant economy, Shakespeare's play enacts at once ontogeny and phylogeny, the history of the individual and the history of the species.

This sensory impression of Caliban as a child is made even stronger by his unexpectedly lovely praise of music, in a passage that rivals even Ariel's songs for its beauty:

> Be not afeard. The isle is full of noises,
> Sounds, and sweet airs, that give delight and hurt not.
> Sometimes a thousand twangling instruments
> Will hum about mine ears, and sometime voices
> That if I then had waked after long sleep
> Will make me sleep again; and then in dreaming
> The clouds methought would open, and show riches
> Ready to drop upon me, that when I waked
> I cried to dream again.
>
> *3.2.130–138*

Waking, sleeping, dreaming, crying to dream again—this, too, seems like the voice of a child. Like another aversive figure in the romances, *Cymbeline*'s Cloten, Caliban is associated with lovely music even as he also spits forth curses and the raw language of sexually explicit desire. But to be a child, even a child of nature, is not enough, as the play's persistent wordplay on the two senses of "natural" suggests. A "natural" in early modern English is a fool—" 'Lord,' quoth he. 'That a monster should be such a natural!' " exclaims Trinculo—and Caliban is presented here, in Prospero's resonant, dismissive phrase, as one upon whose nature nurture can never stick. The play requires civility and civilization.

The turning point comes with the awakening of sexual desire, the transformation of a child into a sexual rival, when Caliban, in Prospero's words, tried "to violate / The honour of my child" (1.2.350–351). "O ho, O ho!" Caliban retorts. "Would't had been done! / Thou didst prevent me; I had peopled else / This isle with Calibans" (352–354). Caliban's desire estranges him from his foster father, Prospero, and causes him to be imprisoned in the rock. When a more appropriate suitor appears in the person of Ferdinand, Prince of Naples, Prospero will be sure to stress the importance of chastity before marriage.

As if to provide contrast with the supposedly unregenerate nature of Caliban, the play presents a number of other indigenous islanders who are spirits of a different sort. In the banquet scene (3.3), the good-hearted counselor Gonzalo praises the "several strange shapes" who enter bringing food, observing that

> though they are of monstrous shape, yet note
> Their manners are more gentle-kind than of
> Our human generation you shall find
> Many, nay, almost any.
>
> 3.3.31–34

So these spirit "monsters" compare favorably in manners to human beings. In a similar moment, later in the play, the spirit Ariel will convince Prospero to show mercy rather than to exact revenge, and Prospero will praise him as a paradoxical model of exemplary *humanity.*

Even the endearingly human Miranda, who came to the island as an infant, herself might be regarded as a kind of "noble savage," although she has been "home-schooled," in our modern parlance, by her father and his library of learned and powerful books. Her famous—and often misapplied—observation, "O brave new world / That has such people in't!" (5.1.186–187), is quickly countered by Prospero in the most paternal of put-downs (" 'Tis new to thee"). But of course he is secretly delighted at her interest in humankind, and in the husband he has imported for her with such effort. Like other noble children raised outside the court in the romances—like Perdita in *The Winter's Tale,* or Guiderius and Arviragus in *Cymbeline*—she exhibits a "natural" nobility and generosity of spirit that are manifestly lacking in some of the supposedly civilized Europeans who are shipwrecked on the island's shores. Caliban alone stands out in the play as a manifest refutation of the romantic view of the "noble savage." Is Prospero right to call him "[a] devil, a born devil, on whose nature / Nurture can never stick" (4.1.188–189)? The play raises a question that may seem to modern readers very modern: What is the relation of nature to nurture, or—as we would say today—of heredity or genetics to environment?

If the figure of Caliban suggests one view of the situation of mankind in thrall to nature rather than nurture, the Neapolitan court party has a different view, as we have already seen. Gonzalo, who will be so impressed by the "several strange shapes" when they enter to bring a banquet, is also the one who offers a more extended philosophical view of "natural man" in his notion of an ideal commonwealth. In such a place there would be

> use of service, none; contract, succession,
> Bourn, bound of land, tilth, vineyard, none;
> No use of metal, corn, or wine, or oil;
> No occupation, all men idle, all;
> And women too—but innocent and pure;
> No sovereignty—
>
> . . . . . .
>
> All things in common nature should produce
> Without sweat or endeavour. Treason, felony,

> Sword, pike, knife, gun, or need of any engine,
> Would I not have; but nature should bring forth
> Of its own kind all foison, all abundance,
> To feed my innocent people.
>
> *2.1.151–156, 159–164*

This is an almost word-for-word transcription of a famous passage from Montaigne's "Of Cannibals," and it has, of course, one glaring fault in the context of Shakespeare's play. It refuses to acknowledge that human beings are prone to anarchy, rivalry, and strife—that they are all, in some sense, Calibans. "No occupation" may have been appropriate for an unfallen Adam and Eve, but not for the inhabitants of Gonzalo's lesser day. Gonzalo plans "[t]o feed my innocent people," but the fertile isle itself is not enough to certify the innocence of people formerly corrupt and fallen. His fellow courtiers mock him for wanting to be king, while he declares that there will be "[n]o sovereignty."

When Gonzalo compares his commonwealth to the Golden Age, we know that we have caught him in a primal error, though an error that is admirable and idealizing. The human society of Gonzalo's time—and that of any audience, in Shakespeare's time or our own—is not innocent or golden, and the play insists upon the importance of occupation, labor, and "service," whether it is dealing with the "high," or aristocratic, conspirators or the "low" conspiracy of servants and monsters (Stephano and Trinculo, Caliban). It is in the scene in which Gonzalo proposes his ideal commonwealth, to the disgust and disdain of his more corrupt companions, that we hear about another planned usurpation, in which Sebastian and Antonio plot to kill Alonso and seize the kingship of Naples, just as twelve years before Antonio had seized the dukedom of Milan from his brother Prospero. Once again a cycle seems about to repeat itself—a second storm, and a second usurpation. Shakespeare's craftsmanship in this play is superbly evocative and economical, so that such doublings and repetitions become an intrinsic, almost uncanny, part of the structure and effect of the play.

Thus, for example, we hear Alonso in this same scene bemoan what he believes to be the death of his son, Ferdinand (the son thinks the father is dead; the father believes the same about the son), "O thou mine heir / Of Naples and of Milan, what strange fish / Hath made his meal on thee?" (2.1.111–113). The "strange fish" might well remind Renaissance audiences of the biblical story of Jonah, as told in the Geneva Bible of 1560, which was Shakespeare's most likely text: "Now the Lord had prepared a great fish to swallow up Jonah: and Jonah was in the belly of the fish three days, and three nights" (Jonah 1:17).

From this description, it is easy to see why Christians of the period thought of Jonah as a type of Christ, another man who was reborn after three days and nights. Since Ferdinand explicitly associates himself with resurrection ("a second life"), this is very likely to be a shadow of meaning behind the image of the devouring "strange fish." But in act 2, scene 2, the strange fish comes to life, revealing itself to be Caliban, who has swallowed up his strange bedfellow, Trinculo. As with other Shakespearean comic low characters—Bottom in *A Midsummer Night's Dream* comes to mind—what is *figurative* or metaphorical in the "high" plot becomes *literal* or unmetaphored in the "low" one. Bottom, who behaves like an ass and is called one, acquires a literal ass's head and an appetite for hay. (Helena in the same play declares that she will be Lysander's "spaniel," but she does not turn into a dog.) So Caliban, who looks like a fish and smells like one, enacts the same scenario as in the Book of Jonah, first encompassing, then releasing, the hapless jester Trinculo. "What have we here, a man, or a fish?" Trinculo asks himself as he stumbles upon the "monster." Frightened by the storm, he decides to take refuge under Caliban's gaberdine (or cloak), and the audience is treated to a remarkable spectacle, four arms and four legs sticking out from under a tarpaulin. Trinculo/Caliban becomes a monster-of-a-man, with two heads and two voices.

We might recall that the basic situation in these two scenes in *The Tempest* is closely parallel: instead of "high," royal conspirators planning to seize Alonso's crown by murder, we have "low," comic conspirators planning to seize Prospero's isle by murder. Gonzalo is able to prevent the murder of Alonso because he is awakened by Ariel's song; and the drinking song of Stephano, Alonso's butler, pervades the atmosphere of the scenes that follow. "That's a brave god, and bears celestial liquor," Caliban declares once he has tasted from Stephano's bottle. "I will kneel to him" (2.2.109–110). In this scene Caliban sings ("Farewell, master, farewell, farewell!"), and by act 3, scene 2, they are all singing a drunken "catch," or round, with the ominous refrain, or "burden," "Thought is free." Similarly, Stephano is as astonished as Ferdinand to learn that an inhabitant of this island speaks Italian: "Where the devil should he learn our language?" Ferdinand's response is more genteel but equally surprised: "I am the best of them that speak this speech." Both speakers, incidentally, think they are addressing nonhuman creatures. Stephano calls Caliban a monster, while Ferdinand views Miranda as a goddess.

Caliban wants to people the isle with Calibans; Stephano—to whom Caliban proffers Miranda as a lure ("She will become thy bed . . . [a]nd bring thee forth brave brood" [3.2.99–100])—would people it with Stephanos ("His daughter and I will be king and queen" [3.2.101–102]). Ferdinand, the approved suitor, will, as his father and hers both wish, take Miranda back with him to Italy, to found a new European dynasty. "O heavens," cries Alonso, still believing that his son and Prospero's daughter have been "lost" to death rather than to love, "that they were living both in Naples, / The king and queen there!" (5.1.151–152).

For as much as the play seeks to compare and contrast Caliban with Ariel, so it also compares him continually with Ferdinand. Each is the son of a ruler. Each thinks of himself as destined and entitled to be king. The analogy is made explicit and telling by juxtaposing them, in language and in action in connection with the topic of labor—an important theme in *The Tempest*. We may recall that in his fantasy of an ideal commonwealth, Gonzalo proposed that all men could be idle, but recognized that the realities of both the island and the world beyond it continually emphasize the need for occupation and for work. Caliban, naturally enough, dreams of being free from Prospero's solicitude and tutelage, and free from his bondage—as well as being free *with* his daughter. By contrast, Ferdinand swiftly discovers the essential truth that a certain kind of freedom comes only through a certain kind of bondage. Again and again we hear him assert that it is in restraint that he has at last found liberty. Believing his father dead, and himself therefore King of Naples, Ferdinand encounters Miranda, is enchanted by her, and—drawing his sword—is charmed from moving by Prospero:

> Ferdinand   My spirits, as in a dream, are all bound up.
> My father's loss, the weakness which I feel,
> The wreck of all my friends, nor this man's threats
> To who I am subdued, are but light to me,
> Might I but through my prison once a day
> Behold this maid. All corners else o'th' earth
> Let liberty make use of; space enough
> Have I in such a prison.
>
> *1.2.490–497*

Ferdinand's description of his enchantment ("My spirits, as in a dream, are all bound up") returns the play to the pervasive theme of dream and waking, as well as to the cognate pair of freedom and bondage. And this question of the role of bondage and enslavement, whether willing or coerced, lies at the heart of much of the political criticism of *The Tempest*. Remembering Ariel's "sweet sprites, bear the burden," and Miranda's charmingly mistaken identification of Ferdinand as a "spirit" and a "thing divine" (1.2.413, 423) rather than a human being, we may see Ferdinand here as about to enter into the service of his beloved.

When Ferdinand is bound, Caliban is freed (though in his case by liquor rather than by love), as his own song suggests: " 'Ban, 'ban, Cacaliban / Has a new master. —Get a new man!" (2.2.175–176). As he wanders off unsteadily toward his so-called freedom and his fate, warbling the burden "Freedom, high-day! High-day, freedom!" this scene and those words are juxtaposed to the next, the beginning of act 3, where the stage direction tells us, "Enter Ferdinand, bearing a log." Ferdinand, indeed, is the "new man" Prospero has gotten, per-forming the same tasks as Caliban (fetching wood, for example) but in a very different mood. "The mistress which I serve quickens what's dead, / And makes my labours pleasures," he declares (3.1.6–7), and "The very instant that I saw you did / My heart fly to your service" (64–65). This language of servitude to a mistress is borrowed, in part, from the conventions of Petrarchism and courtly love. Service and bondage are freedom for Ferdinand, as the humble task of carrying logs, so hated by Caliban, becomes a useful and even a gratifying job. We may note that Prospero will later make a very similar argument to Ariel, emphasizing that freedom and bondage are properly linked:

> Shortly shall all my labours end, and thou
> Shalt have the air at freedom. For a little,
> Follow, and do me service.
>
> *4.1.260–263*

But if slavery is an issue that links the concerns of Shakespeare's time to those of our own, so is the question of gender and power. Why should the audience prefer Prospero the magician and his daughter Miranda over Sycorax the magician and her son Caliban? Both Sycorax and Prospero keep Ariel in a condition of bondage. What makes us choose Prospero over his predecessor? It is not entirely easy to glean the "true" story here, since, by Shakespeare's design, we only hear and see one side—Prospero's side. Sycorax is silenced by the simple and definitive fact that she never appears in the play. Although she is, in theory, the most powerful female figure in the *Tempest* story, she is presented only in memory, through the accounts of Caliban ("This island's mine, by Sycorax my mother") and Prospero ("The foul witch Sycorax, who with age and envy / Was grown into a hoop"). Her place of origin, Argiers, marks her as one of the several strong North African women in Shakespeare who are associated with magic powers (Cleopatra, to give the most obvious example, but also the "Egyptian charmer" who gave the magic handkerchief to Othello's mother).

Ferdinand's sister Claribel, another potentially powerful woman, first in line to inherit the Neapolitan throne, has also in effect been exiled from the playing-space. The Neapolitan courtiers are returning from her wedding in Tunis when they are shipwrecked. Antonio asks Sebastian after the storm, "Who's the next heir of Naples?"

Sebastian	Claribel.
Antonio	She that is Queen of Tunis; she that dwells Ten leagues beyond man's life; she that from Naples Can have no note—unless the sun were post— The man i'th' moon's too slow—till new-born chins Be rough and razorable. . . .
	. . . .
Sebastian	. . . 'Tis true my brother's daughter's Queen of Tunis; So is she heir of Naples; 'twixt which regions There is some space.
Antonio	A space whose every cubit

Seems to cry out "How shall that Claribel
Measure us back to Naples? ..."

2.1.241–255

Sebastian unwittingly echoes the sentiments of Desdemona's father, Brabantio, in his estimate of this exogamous marriage. "Sir," he says to the King, "you
may thank yourself for this great loss, / That would not bless our Europe with
your daughter, / But rather loose her to an African" (2.1.123–125). Claribel, he
insists, did not want to go: "the fair soul herself / Weighed between loathness
and obedience" (129–130). (His "fair" emphasizes the whiteness of the bride in
contrast to her husband.) But this is a dynastic marriage, arranged by the father
for political purposes. The daughter's choice is not her own. Her marriage is an
affair of state, not an affair of the heart.

Claribel is married to an African and lives half a world away—news of her
father's death might take a generation to get to her (infants born now will by
that time be grown men with beards). So Sycorax, the former ruler of the isle,
and Claribel, the first heir of Naples, are exiled from the play by its playwright,
leaving only a single woman, Miranda, the good daughter. Miranda, who is
cautioned to hang on her father's every word, who becomes the object of all
male fantasies (from Caliban's to Ferdinand's), is the attentive student who is
both schooled and put down by her pedagogue father. Miranda does not lack
either charm or spirit. She does, importantly, rebel against her father (just as
Juliet did) to choose a lover apparently against the paternal will. But this play is
a romance or tragicomedy, and the father is playacting his opposition, as King
Simonides, the father of Thaisa, did in *Pericles*.

Miranda's marriage to Ferdinand is set up as a love match, a delightful
instance of love at first sight in which each overestimates the other (he thinks
she is a goddess, she thinks he is a spirit). Indeed, Prospero finds it necessary to
correct her: "No, wench, it eats and sleeps, and hath such senses / As we have"
(1.2.416–417). But at base this, too, is a dynastic marriage, an "arranged marriage" in the most literal sense, since Prospero has caused the wreck in order to
bring this suitor to the island ("It goes on, I see, / As my soul prompts it," he
remarks approvingly, aside to the audience, when the lovers are immediately
attracted [422–423]). Both fathers see immediate political advantage in the
match, and the magnificent climactic tableau in the fifth act, signaled by the
stage direction "Here Prospero discovers [i.e., reveals] Ferdinand and Miranda
playing at chess," draws upon the fact that chess is a "royal" game, in which the
pieces are kings and queens, bishops, knights, and pawns. Each piece moves by
particular rules that govern it, and some are "checked," or brought to a stand-
still in the course of the action, just as Ferdinand and the court party are,
"bound up" (1.2.491) "charmed from moving" (stage direction, 1.2.470), unable
to "budge" till Prospero releases them (5.1.11). The chess-playing lovers, reenact-
ing a scene common in stories of courtly love, are also exhibiting a mise en

abyme (a version of the familiar "play-within-the-play"), in which a model of the entire action is recapitulated *within* the action. Thus the lovers are in a sense *already* ruling the Europe that is represented in the alternating squares of their game board.

The term "checkmate," which comes from an Arabic phrase meaning "the King is dead," is the ritual exclamation of a chess player who is about to win a game. The term was in common use long before Shakespeare's day, and would have been understood as the key word of the game in question, even if not actually uttered. Indeed, the double and antithetical sense of "mate" here (to kill or rival; to marry) marks the transition at the center of the play's action, for instead of killing King Alonso, Prospero has contrived a marriage between the King's son and Prospero's daughter. Moreover, *The Tempest* itself could be regarded as a mise en abyme in this sense, since Prospero deliberately restages the events of the past in order to reverse their outcome for the future.

Three levels of language chart a hierarchy in the play: the "excellent dumb discourse" of the spirits, who do not need to speak in order to communicate; the language spoken by all the human characters in the play (fictively Italian, but actually, of course, Shakespeare's English); and the curses and expletives of Caliban ("When thou didst not, savage, / Know thy own meaning," Miranda says to him, "but wouldst gabble like / A thing most brutish, I endowed thy purposes / With words that made them known," and Caliban retorts, "You taught me language, and my profit on't / Is I know how to curse" [1.2.358–361, 366–367]). Thus again we have high, middle, and low, or suprahuman, human, and subhuman. Prospero, who can speak to any and all of these populations, apparently possesses—through his magic books—a fourth language as well, a language of spell and incantation.

But the play is also careful to situate him between and among the denizens of human society. Generations of critics have identified him as a playwright, reading the play as a metadrama about Shakespeare the maker and the fictional creatures he has under his sway. Viewed in this way, Prospero becomes the end point in a series of other "playwright figures," from Prince Hal to Hamlet to the Duke in *Measure for Measure,* who cast roles and play them as a way of reordering their worlds. The "playwright" reading has often also been linked to the popular notion that *The Tempest* is Shakespeare's farewell to the stage, and Prospero's Epilogue Shakespeare's final gesture of aesthetic relinquishment, before he retires to Stratford, as Prospero does to Milan, "where / Every third thought shall be my grave" (5.1.313–314). But in point of historical fact, *The Tempest* was not Shakespeare's last play, and the romantic notion of a "farewell to the stage" serves the Shakespeare myth better than the Shakespeare reality; it is we, not the playwright, who seem to need a ceremonial occasion to say good-bye.

Clearly, though, Prospero's power does come from his knowledge, and specifically from his books. As Caliban counsels the unheeding Stephano and Trinculo,

> Remember
> First to possess his books, for without them
> He's but a sot as I am, nor hath not
> One spirit to command. . . .
>
> *3.2.86–89*

The longer passage of which this is a part seems to recall the scenario of the murder of Hamlet's father, beginning, as it does, "Why, . . . 'tis a custom with him / I'th' afternoon to sleep. There thou mayst brain him, / Having first seized his books" (84–86). Caliban is insistent on the source of his master's power: "Burn but his books" (90). When at the close of the play Prospero himself declares, "I'll drown my book" (5.1.57), he voluntarily renounces the magic powers, spells, and alchemy that have come to him through his "secret studies" in magical lore.

Two things should be borne in mind here. First, that magic was not at this historical moment fully differentiated from what today we would call "science"; the latter word meant something more like general knowledge or "learning" in Shakespeare's day, and did not emerge fully as a term denoting either theoretical truths or practical experimentation until later in the seventeenth century. And second, that books were relatively rare possessions in this period. Although the governing classes in England in the sixteenth and early seventeenth centuries were being urged to read and to acquire books, the number of books they actually owned was very small. Prospero's possession of books is itself a sign of distinction. At the same time, as his failure to govern effectively in Milan seems to have demonstrated, it is also a sign of his turning away from the public and political world.

That Prospero proposes to "drown" his empowering book of magic may seem at first a less violent action than the book burning proposed by Caliban, but both methods have disturbing histories. Books deemed heretical were burned, as were heretics. But drowning was a test for suspected witches. To drown a book is a convenient mode of disposal if one lives, like Prospero, surrounded by water, but for a Renaissance audience, this plan to drown a book would have also evoked unmistakable and dangerous associations with witchcraft. If it is ever possible in the play to distinguish Prospero's "white," or beneficent, magic from the more dangerous practice of "black magic," his own explicit phrase of disavowal, "this rough magic / I here abjure" (5.1.50–51), sets magic on one side, and what the spirit Ariel calls the "human" on the other.

The Tempest starts out, as we have noted, as a kind of "revenge play," and then turns away from that mode toward forgiveness at a crucial moment. Prospero, despite his intellectual inclinations and his paternal instincts, is as obsessed with retribution as any other English Renaissance stage revenger. And Prospero's conversion from vengeance to "virtue" comes—with a gesture typical of the late Shakespeare—through the agency of an unlikely figure. The agent of conversion is not a human being, but is instead the spirit Ariel, whose wistful observation intervenes on the side of mercy for the hapless Neapolitan conspirators—the King and his followers—immobilized by Prospero's spell:

> Ariel   Your charm so strongly works 'em
> That if you now beheld them your affections
> Would become tender.
> Prospero   Dost thou think so, spirit?
> Ariel   Mine would, sir, were I human.
> Prospero   And mine shall.
> Hast thou, which art but air, a touch, a feeling
> Of their afflictions, and shall not myself,
> One of their kind, that relish all as sharply
> Passion as they, be kindlier moved than thou art?
> Though with their high wrongs I am struck to th' quick,
> Yet with my nobler reason 'gainst my fury
> Do I take part. The rarer action is
> In virtue than in vengeance. . . .
> . . . .
>   Go, release them, Ariel.
> My charms I'll break, their senses I'll restore,
> And they shall be themselves.
>
> *5.1.17–32*

As if this last phrase were itself a magic commandment ("And they shall be themselves"), Prospero now begins the series of divestments and restorations that will return him to his former identity, as man rather than mage, Duke rather than island ruler—and, ultimately, actor rather than dramatic character.

The Tempest is a play that could be said to end, in fact, three different times, each time with a gesture profoundly moving and rhetorically powerful. The first of these endings comes during the masque of Ceres that Prospero and his spirits have provided for the entertainment of the betrothed couple, Miranda and Ferdinand. The masque commemorates the ideal values of marriage—fidelity, fertility, progeny—and Ferdinand is enchanted: "So rare a wondered father and a wise / Makes this place paradise" (4.1.123–124). But no invocation of a timeless paradise can remain unchallenged in a Shakespearean world. Suddenly reminded of the plot against his life, and thus of the fallenness of man, Prospero abruptly breaks off the masque and speaks the lines that seem to resonate across the centuries:

> Our revels now are ended. These our actors,
> As I foretold you, were all spirits, and
> Are melted into air, into thin air;
> And like the baseless fabric of this vision,

> The cloud-capped towers, the gorgeous palaces,
> The solemn temples, the great globe itself,
> Yea, all which it inherit, shall dissolve;
> And, like this insubstantial pageant faded,
> Leave not a rack behind. We are such stuff
> As dreams are made on, and our little life
> Is rounded with a sleep. . . .

4.1.148–158

The "revels" of which he speaks are a formal part of the court masque, the moment when the noble actors dance with the audience, so that these lines prefigure the liminal encounter at the end of the play, when Prospero delivers his Epilogue. Although *The Tempest* was performed in a private theater and not in the company's more public playhouse, the Globe, the reference here to "the great globe itself" seems imbued with an unmistakable double significance. Prospero is "vexed," his "beating mind" remembers, just in time, the threat against him. The masque is thus abruptly sundered. Disappearing spectacles were a commonplace of the masque tradition, as much an aspect of the entertainment as the songs and dances themselves, and the extradramatic authority that postromantic readings have given to this magnificent passage derives, in part, from the tendency to quote it out of context as "Shakespeare's farewell." Almost invariably, though, in the modern theater, a hush attends the declamation of these lines, which have taken on a life, and an itinerary, of their own.

The play's second ending occurs immediately after the affecting scene with Ariel in the fifth act, in which Prospero affirms his own "nobler reason" and "rarer action" in offering mercy rather than seeking vengeance. No sooner does Ariel depart than Prospero, tracing a magic circle on the stage, invokes "Ye elves, of hills, brooks, standing lakes and groves," and the other spirits with whose aid he has dimmed the sun, called forth the winds, summoned the lightning and the thunder. His speech, a paraphrase of the incantation of the witch Medea in Ovid's *Metamorphoses* (book 7, lines 263–289), underscores the powers he is about to relinquish:

> [G]raves at my command
> Have waked their sleepers, oped, and let 'em forth
> By my so potent art. But this rough magic
> I here abjure. And when I have required
> Some heavenly music—which even now I do—
> To work mine end upon their senses that
> This airy charm is for, I'll break my staff,
> Bury it certain fathoms in the earth,
> And deeper than did ever plummet sound
> I'll drown my book.

5.1.48–57

The third and final ending is the play's famous Epilogue, in which Prospero addresses himself directly to the audience, putting himself in our hands and asking of us—as various characters in the play had sought from *him*—freedom from bondage and confinement. Requesting the "good hands" (applause) and "[g]entle breath" (praise) of the audience in the theater, he puts himself in the position in which he had previously put those who conspired against his life, asking for mercy and forgiveness. Again he emphasizes his powerlessness:

> Now I want
> Spirits to enforce, art to enchant;
> And my ending is despair
> Unless I be relieved by prayer,
> Which pierces so, that it assaults
> Mercy itself, and frees all faults.
> As you from crimes would pardoned be,
> Let your indulgence set me free.
>
> *Epilogue 13–20*

Prospero's loss of power has been demonstrated effectively in some recent productions by a modern stage device: a sudden shift, at the beginning of the Epilogue, from an amplified to a nonamplified voice, seeming to diminish and "humanize" the actor. As with some other Shakespearean epilogues we have encountered (Puck's in *A Midsummer Night's Dream,* and especially Rosalind's in *As You Like It*), this direct address to the audience—a common device in performances of the period—emphasizes both the fictive nature of the play and the human identity of the actor/performer/speaker. Puck, a spirit, and Rosalind, who calls herself a magician, have much in common with Prospero. But Prospero's dramatic persona, not only a magician but also a political figure and a mortal and suddenly aging man ("Every third thought shall be my grave"), renders the tonality of this Epilogue somber rather than playful, reaching across the boundaries of stage and audience, from actor to spectator, from age to age, and from mortality to the dream of eternity and art.

Henry VIII (All Is True)

DRAMATIS PERSONAE

Prologue
King Henry the Eighth
Duke of Buckingham
Lord Abergavenny, *Buckingham's son-in-law*
Earl of Surrey, *Buckingham's son-in-law*
Duke of Norfolk
Duke of Suffolk
Lord Chamberlain
Lord Chancellor
Lord Sands (Sir William Sands)
Sir Thomas Lovell
Sir Anthony Denny
Sir Henry Guildford
Cardinal Wolsey
Two Secretaries
Buckingham's Surveyor
Cardinal Campeius
Gardiner, *the King's new secretary, later Bishop of Winchester*

His Page
Thomas Cromwell
Cranmer, *Archbishop of Canterbury*
Queen Katherine, *later Katherine, Princess Dowager*
Griffith, *her gentleman usher*
Patience, *her waiting-woman*
Other Women
Six spirits, *who dance before Katherine in a vision*
A Messenger
Lord Caputius
Anne Bullen
An Old Lady
Brandon, *who arrests Buckingham and Abergavenny*
Serjeant-at-arms, *who arrests Buckingham and Abergavenny*

AFTER BUCKINGHAM'S ARRAIGNMENT

Sir Nicholas Vaux
Tipstaves

Halberdiers
Common people

APPEARING AT THE LEGANTINE COURT

Two vergers
Two Scribes
Archbishop of Canterbury
Bishop of Lincoln
Bishop of Ely
Bishop of Rochester

Bishop of Saint Asaph
Two priests
Serjeant-at-arms
Two noblemen
A Crier

APPEARING IN THE CORONATION

Three Gentlemen	Marquis Dorset
Two judges	Four Barons of the Cinque Ports
Choristers	Stokesley, *Bishop of London*
Lord Mayor of London	Old Duchess of Norfolk
Garter King-of-Arms	Countesses

AT CRANMER'S TRIAL

A Doorkeeper	Pursuivants, pages, footboys,
Doctor Butts, *the King's physician*	grooms

AT THE CHRISTENING

A Porter	Six noblemen
His Man	Old Duchess of Norfolk,
Two aldermen	*godmother*
Lord Mayor of London	The child, Princess Elizabeth
Garter King-of-Arms	Marchioness Dorset, *godmother*

Epilogue
Ladies, gentlemen, a Servant,
   guards, attendants,
   trumpeters

VEN FOR THOSE who have never read or seen it, this play, initially entitled *All Is True*, enjoys a curious celebrity, since it was during its first performance at the Globe on June 29, 1613, that the theater caught fire and burned down. The best-known account of this catastrophe, an account characteristically leavened with urbane wit and shrewd political analysis, is that of the poet and diplomat Sir Henry Wotton. Wotton, credited with such pertinent observations as "An ambassador is an honest man sent to lie abroad for the commonwealth," "Tell the truth, and so puzzle and confound your adversaries," and "Critics are like brushers of noblemen's clothes," wrote a long letter to a friend that included a report of the fire as a kind of amusing afterthought to weightier matters of state:

> The King's players had a new play, called *All is True,* representing some principal pieces of the reign of Henry VIII, which was set forth with many extraordinary circumstances of Pomp and Majesty, even to the matting of the stage; the Knights of the Order, with their Georges and garters; the Guards with their embroidered coats, and the like: sufficient in truth within a while to make greatness very familiar, if not ridiculous. Now,

King Henry making a masque at the Cardinal Wolsey's house, and certain chambers being shot off at his entry, some of the paper, or other stuff, wherewith one of them was stopped, did light on the thatch, where being thought at first but an idle smoke, and their eyes more attentive to the show, it kindled inwardly, and ran round like a train, consuming within less than an hour the whole house to the very grounds.

This was the fatal period of that virtuous fabric; wherein yet nothing did perish but wood and straw, and a few forsaken cloaks; only one man had his breeches set on fire, that would perhaps have broiled him, if he had not by the benefit of a provident wit put it out with bottle ale.[1]

Early-twentieth-century critics took especial pleasure in the genre detail of the man with the burning trousers and his helpful neighbor dousing them with beer; more recent historicists have zeroed in on Wotton's phrase about making "greatness very familiar" and used it as a general jumping-off point for discussions of theater and power. "Greatness" here refers to persons of title and rank; to make greatness familiar is to take liberties, and indeed to risk, as Wotton goes on to note, the possibility of slipping into the realm of the comic or the derisive. His narrative, designed to charm rather than alarm, contains its own delightful hyperbole and elevated diction ("the fatal period," or catastrophic end, of wood and straw, the structural members and thatched roof of the structure in Bankside). A "fabric" is a building or edifice (as in Prospero's famous "baseless fabric of this vision," after the dissolution of the masque of Ceres—in his case the term also carries a sense of a contrivance or engine). "Virtuous," when applied to things rather than to persons, means "glorious," or "powerful, potent, and strong," or, most interestingly—but usually when applied to items like precious stones—"endowed with magical or supernatural power." But "virtuous fabric" is archly oblique as a description of the "house" of the King's Men, and the epithet is shortly (and masterfully) subjected to the lowering of style that reduces it to "wood and straw." At the other end of the social scale, "bottle ale" appears in *Henry IV Part 2* as a manifest insult; the whore Doll Tearsheet calls the posturing braggart Pistol a "bottle-ale rascal" (*2 Henry IV* 2.4.110), marking the consumers of this beverage as "low" rather than high. The lucky patron whose flaming breeches almost broiled him comes last in a descending sartorial sequence ("the Knights of the Order, with their Georges and garters" and "the Guards with their embroidered coats") and is as lively and robust as the court officials are formal and hieratic.

What is most striking in this account, though, is its tone of urbane distance, genial indulgence, and the lack of any anxiety, either about the critique of "greatness" or the threat to life and limb. The burning of the Globe theater is offered as an incidental anecdote, intended, as Wotton writes, to "entertain" his correspondent after a discussion of more serious matters of state. Its seriocomic events—a large-scale disaster happens, no one is injured, a man is saved by an inelegant but expeditious contrivance—could be said to mirror the typical events of tragicomedy and romance. But *Henry VIII* is a fascinating play in its own right.

Henry VIII was born in 1491, came to the throne in 1509, and died in 1547—sixty-six years and three monarchs prior to the date of the play that, in the Shakespeare First Folio, bears his name. By 1613 England was mourning the death of another Henry, the elder son of James I, who had died unexpectedly in 1612 at the age of eighteen. Coming as it does right after the unexpected death of Prince Henry, and at the time of Princess Elizabeth's marriage to Frederick, Elector Palatine, in 1613, this play, with its reminiscence of another royal Henry and another "maiden phoenix," Elizabeth, is full of topical relevance.

The events of the play span a series of "falls" of persons of high estate: in act 1 the fall of the Duke of Buckingham, whose servants have been suborned by his enemy, Cardinal Wolsey; in act 2 the fall of Queen Katherine, who has failed to provide the King with a male heir, and whose twenty-year marriage to Henry is now put aside in favor of a new marriage, to Anne Bullen; in act 3 the fall of Wolsey himself, a butcher's son risen to high eminence, brought low by his acquisitiveness and financial dealings as well as his political connivance; and in act 5 the attempt—foiled by the King—to bring down Thomas Cranmer, Archbishop of Canterbury. Since the play ends, triumphantly, with Cranmer's praise of the "chosen infant," Elizabeth, to her father the King, with the Queen decorously offstage, the unhappy fate of Anne Bullen, her own fall, is not directly accounted for (although her absence indeed hints at it). What ties these falls together, beyond their inevitability and remorseless dramatic succession (exacerbated by the play's severe truncation of historical events), is the word "divorce," which appears, like an uncanny specter, linking the tragical plot of "falls of greatness" to the romantic plot of masque, courtship, marriage, and birth. Thus Buckingham, foreseeing his own beheading ("[e]ven as the axe falls"), calls it a "long divorce of steel" (2.1.62, 77). Katherine, the center of the divorce narrative, appropriates the word to her own use, telling the Cardinals who come to try to persuade her that "[n]othing but death / Shall e'er divorce my dignities" (3.1.140–141). And Anne, commiserating with the Queen's plight in conversation with an Old Lady, says compassionately,

> Much better
> She ne'er had known pomp; though't be temporal,
> Yet if that quarrel, fortune, do divorce
> It from the bearer, 'tis a sufferance panging
> As soul and bodyies severing.
>
> Henry VIII *2.3.12–16*

This is a classic instance of what is sometimes called "discrepant awareness": the audience is aware, as Anne is not, of the violent "severing" of soul and body that will be her own fate, even though this speech is situated within a scene that is, in general tone, comic, bawdy, and joyful, and that ends in Anne's designation as Marchioness of Pembroke. ("Much better / She ne'r had known pomp" might be the audience's own choric commentary, looking into Anne's future, and history's past.)

Retitled when it was included among the history plays in the First Folio, *Henry VIII* is a play written at the end of Shakespeare's career that closes with the christening of Queen Elizabeth, and thus with the inauguration of the era that was to become so closely associated with his name.

Why is it that this play is, relatively speaking, so little discussed today, except by scholars of early modern drama—and by actors? *Henry VIII* was not always an afterthought or footnote, although it has come to be regarded (often by those who have not read it) as "lesser" or "minor" Shakespeare—itself a questionable designation, since the fortunes and estimations of the plays have varied so widely over the years. The play was extremely popular in the eighteenth and nineteenth centuries, providing a star vehicle for actresses in the role of Katherine. Sarah Siddons was considered a notable Katherine, as was the American actress Charlotte Cushman. The part of Cardinal Wolsey, too, was a star part, and the opportunity for elaborate "historical" staging and spectacle made *Henry VIII* a favorite of theater managers. But despite the fact that *The Famous History of the Life of King Henry the Eight* appears in the First Folio of William Shakespeare's plays, it is acknowledged to be a play written collaboratively, with many scenes not by Shakespeare but by John Fletcher, the author of *Bonduca* and *The Faithful Shepherdess,* a regular collaborator with Francis Beaumont (*Philaster, The Maid's Tragedy, A King and No King*), and Shakespeare's coauthor of *The Two Noble Kinsmen* and the lost play *Cardenio.* For some scholars the fact of collaborative authorship (a common practice in the period, much as it is in screenwriting today) devalued the play, since it rendered more difficult, indeed impossible, the identification of "Shakespeare's philosophy and beliefs" or "Shakespeare's intentions," challenging the notion that literary texts should put us in touch with the minds that made them.

Is the play a "Shakespeare play"? Yes, in the sense that it was printed in the First Folio, and that it seems clear that Shakespeare wrote many of its scenes and speeches. (The current scholarly consensus regards 1.1, 1.2, 2.3, 2.4, the first half of 3.2, and 5.1 as scenes "by Shakespeare.") But to subdivide the play into Shakespearean and Fletcherean sections (an earlier, less collaboration-friendly era would have said "Shakespearean" and "non-Shakespearean") for the purpose of an analysis of its dramaturgy, themes, and theatrical effect is to miss the point of collaborative authorship.

This play's motifs do have some affinities with other key moments in Shakespearean drama—notably with the late plays, and especially *The Winter's Tale,* but also with *Romeo and Juliet, Hamlet, Othello,* and even early works like *Love's Labour's Lost* and *Henry VI Part 1.* Thus, for example, the masque at York Place

(1.4), in which a disguised King Henry and others, "habited like shepherds," appear before Cardinal Wolsey and his guests, resembles both the masque of the "Muscovites" in *Love's Labour's Lost* and the scene in *Henry VI Part 1* in which Joan la Pucelle correctly identifies the disguised Dauphin. The masquers are said to "speak no English," like the supposed Muscovites, and to have come to pay their respects to the ladies' beauty; the Lord Chamberlain acts as translator, and Wolsey, archly guessing that there should be "one amongst 'em by his person / More worthy this place than myself" (1.4.81–82), unerringly picks out the King (though in the source in Holinshed he initially fails to do so). "More worthy this place than myself," though a standard compliment, acquires a belated tinge of irony when, by the middle of the play, we find that the King has broken with Wolsey and taken York Place as his own.

Likewise the engagingly bawdy scene between Anne Bullen and an Old Lady offers an exchange reminiscent of Juliet and her Nurse, or, even more closely, Emilia and Desdemona in *Othello*:

> Old Lady   You would not be a queen?
> Anne   No, not for all the riches under heaven.
> Old Lady   'Tis strange. A threepence bowed would hire me,
>   Old as I am, to queen it. . . .
>
>   2.3.34–37

Compare Desdemona's question to Emilia about sexual infidelity, "Wouldst thou do such a deed for all the world?" and Emilia's reply, "The world's a huge thing. It is a great price for a small vice" (*Othello* 4.3.67–68). By the end of the scene Anne has received word that Henry has made her Marchioness of Pembroke, with a thousand pounds a year.

The effect of *Henry VIII* as a stage vehicle or a literary text does not, however, depend upon those associations as "Shakespearean" credentials. Some of its finest dramatic and rhetorical moments come in scenes that have been firmly attributed to Fletcher, like Wolsey's farewell to greatness and the prophecy by Thomas Cranmer, Archbishop of Canterbury.

The design of *Henry VIII* depends upon an interweaving of three kinds of scenes: (1) the great speeches of regret, recrimination, defiance, and farewell that attend the fall of various principals; (2) a series of spectacles, masques, and state occasions; and (3) a number of scenes, many of them very dramatically effective and engaging, in which an onstage conversation among gentlemen or nobles reports on events that have taken place offstage.

Its spectacular stagings range from the masque at York Place (1.4), performed by the King and courtiers in disguise (the occasion on which Henry meets and dances with Anne Bullen), to Katherine's dream vision (4.2), also masquelike in its form, and sometimes performed as the pendant or reversal of the earlier masque; and from the scene at Blackfriars in which the King and Cardinals summon Katherine (2.4) to the elaborate scene of Anne's coronation procession (4.1) and the equally elaborate and formal christening of Elizabeth (5.4). The play is distinctive in its lengthy stage directions, which often pay meticulous attention to placement and to costumes and props, unlike the terser phrases that serve this purpose in other Shakespeare plays. The effect for the reader is one of a rich and sumptuous ceremony.

As for onstage/offstage reports, among the key scenes in this last category are the discussion by Norfolk and Buckingham of the (offstage) meeting of Henry VIII and Francis I of France at the Field of the Cloth of Gold (1.1); a comically dismissive account of the deleterious effects of French fashion at the English court, in which the sartorial style is discussed as a kind of heretical religion (returned travelers are imagined as "renouncing clean / The faith they have in tennis and tall stockings, / Short blistered breeches, and those types of travel" in order to "understand again like honest men" [1.3.29–32]); the conversation between two gentlemen in act 2, scene 1, in which they describe the dignified bearing of Buckingham when accused of high treason, and, later in the scene, after Buckingham has entered, spoken, and gone off to his death, the same gentlemen's court gossip about the impending divorce ("Did you not of late days hear / A buzzing of a separation / Between the King and Katherine?" [2.1.148–150]); and the remarkable description by the Third Gentleman, who has been to the Abbey to see Anne's coronation (4.1).

The discussion of the meeting between Henry VIII and Francis I of France at the Field of the Cloth of Gold is a particularly effective example of a Shakespearean "unscene," closely resembling the scene (5.2) in *The Winter's Tale* in which various gentlemen report the offstage "wonder" of Perdita's return, and also Enobarbus's account of the meeting of the lovers at the Cydnus in *Antony and Cleopatra* (2.2). In *The Winter's Tale* one gentleman asks, "Did you see the meeting of the two kings?" and, receiving a negative answer, launches into a panegyric: "Then have you lost a sight which was to be seen, cannot be spoken of. There might you have beheld one joy crown another" (*Winter's Tale* 5.2.36, 38–40). The rhetorical "inexpressibility topos" of narrative poetry (the idea that words cannot do justice to this event) here comes to life on the stage. The Duke of Norfolk in *Henry VIII* offers similar report—Buckingham has missed the events, kept home by an "untimely ague"—with the key difference that Norfolk's report of offstage marvels is deeply ironic:

Norfolk   Then you lost
                    The view of earthly glory. Men might say
                    Till this time pomp was single, but now married
                    To one above itself. Each following day
                    Became the next day's master, till the last
                    Made former wonder its. Today the French,
                    All clinquant all in gold, like heathen gods

> Shone down the English; and tomorrow they
> Made Britain India. Every man that stood
> Showed like a mine. Their dwarfish pages were
> As cherubim, all gilt; the *mesdames,* too,
> Not used to toil, did almost sweat to bear
> The pride upon them, that their very labour
> Was to them as a painting. . . .
>
> . . . .
>
>   The two kings
> Equal in lustre, were now best, now worst,
> As presence did present them. . . .
>   When these suns—
> For so they phrase 'em—by their heralds challenged
> The noble spirits to arms, they did perform
> Beyond thought's compass, that former fabulous story
> Being now seen possible enough, got credit
> That *Bevis* was believed.

Buckingham   O, you go far!

                                                   1.1.13–38

The similarities to Enobarbus's description of Cleopatra are worth noting. The gilt cherubim and almost-sweating ladies, whose "very labour / Was to them as a painting," are close relatives to Cleopatra and her Cupid-like fanning boys:

Enobarbus   The barge she sat in, like a burnished throne
             Burned on the water. The poop was beaten gold;
             Purple the sails, and so perfumèd that
             The winds were love-sick with them. The oars were silver,
             Which to the tune of flutes kept stroke, and made
             The water which they beat to follow faster,
             As amorous of their strokes. For her own person,
             It beggared all description. She did lie
             In her pavilion—cloth of gold, of tissue—
             O'er-picturing that Venus where we see
             The fancy outwork nature. On each side her
             Stood pretty dimpled boys, like smiling Cupids,
             With divers-coloured fans whose wind did seem
             To glow the delicate cheeks which they did cool,
             And what they undid did.

Agrippa   O, rare for Antony!
                                 Antony and Cleopatra 2.2.197–212

But even the skeptical Enobarbus was, for the moment, enraptured by the Egyptian queen. Norfolk is far less enchanted by the "masque" at the Field of

the Cloth of Gold, especially when it comes time to identify the master of ceremonies for these expensive entertainments, Henry's Lord Chancellor, Cardinal
Wolsey:

> Norfolk   All this was ordered by the good discretion
>   Of the right reverend Cardinal of York.
> Buckingham   The devil speed him! No man's pie is freed
>   From his ambitious finger.
>
> *Henry VIII 1.1.50–53*

Wolsey, the lowborn son of a butcher, is in Buckingham's view "a keech," or
lump of fat (1.1.55), and a "butcher's cur . . . venom-mouthed" (120). The Cardinal is his enemy, and "the private difference" between the two men will present
the first of the play's several one-on-one rivalries.

What is also established, very clearly, in this scene is Wolsey's profligacy, or
rather his willingness to spend others' money for political effect. The costs of
the French adventure have, for several noble families, "sickened their estates,"
and "many / Have broke their backs with laying manors on 'em" (1.1.82, 84–85).
The familiar metaphor of sickness in the state here afflicts the nobility. Shortly
King Henry will take up a version of the same theme for his own purposes,
blaming the absence of a male heir on his "incestuous" marriage to Katherine.

The cyclicality of structure offered by a play that ends with the birth of
Elizabeth is mirrored, as well, by the clever and knowing way that locales within
the play are tied to their contemporary (Jacobean) use. Thus York Place, the
sumptuous palace that was the home of Cardinal Wolsey, grander than any residence owned by Henry VIII, is taken over by Henry after Wolsey's fall, renamed
Whitehall, and chosen as the place for the celebration after Anne Bullen's coronation as queen. In act 4 the Second Gentleman says the coronation procession
"paced back again / To York Place, where the feast is held," and the First Gentleman corrects him:

>   Sir,
>   You must no more call it York Place—that's past,
>   For since the Cardinal fell, that title's lost.
>   'Tis now the King's, and called Whitehall.
>
> *4.1.95–98*

Whitehall was King James's palace at the time of the first performance of the
play; the audience would have registered the pertinence of this "doubling," as
they would, at the same time, have appreciated that " 'Tis now the King's" was
true in their time as in Henry VIII's.

Likewise in the play the divorce proceedings of King Henry against his first
wife, Katherine, take place at Blackfriars, which had been—before Henry's dissolution of the monasteries—a residence for Dominican friars (whose black

robes gave the building its name). "The most convenient place that I can think of / For such receipt of learning is Blackfriars," the King declares to the Cardinals Wolsey and Campeius, who are appointed by the Pope as supposedly "unpartial" judges in the divorce case (2.2.137–138). But by 1613—and, in fact, since 1608—Blackfriars was not a monastery but a private theater leased by Shakespeare's company, the King's Men. It is quite possible that *All Is True* (as the play would then have been known) was first staged there in 1613. So Henry's mention of Blackfriars, like the First Gentleman's mention of Whitehall, might well have produced for the Jacobean audience that sense of uncanny déjà vu that is one of the most unsettling and pleasurable sensations of drama.

Although the play begins with an account of Wolsey's venality and thus in some sense aims, dramatically, at his discomfiture and disgrace, the plight of Katherine is at the center of the action. Katherine herself appears early in the next scene to plead with the King on behalf of the ordinary people who suffer from unjust taxation. (Those afflicted, "clothiers all," including, in the Duke of Norfolk's summary, the "spinsters, carders, fullers, [and] weavers" who make up the domestic cloth trade [1.2.32, 34], contrast sharply, in their homely product, with the fancy and affected French fashions that will be deplored in the following scene.) This initial introduction to Katherine presents her as articulate, well-spoken, and passionate, and the King treats her as a partner ("You have half our power" [1.2.12]). His meeting with Anne, and their flirtation, arouses in him some belated qualms of "conscience":

Chamberlain	It seems the marriage with his brother's wife
	Has crept too near his conscience.
Suffolk	No, his conscience
	Has crept too near another lady.

2.2.15–17

Henry's official doubts derive from the fact that he has married his brother's widow. Katherine, the daughter of Ferdinand and Isabella of Spain, had wed Henry's older brother Arthur, then Prince of Wales, in 1501. Arthur's death a year later left Henry the heir to the throne, and he and Katherine were married shortly after he became King in 1509. As she reminds the King—and the audience—Katherine bore Henry many children, but only one lived, the future Mary I ("Bloody Mary," r. 1553–1558, succeeded by Elizabeth I), and Henry, whether disingenuously or not, takes this as a sign that the marriage was unlawful. (Various biblical injunctions proscribed the marriage of a brother's widow as a kind of incest.) His request for a papally sanctioned divorce led ultimately to his split with Rome and the founding of the Church of England.

The question of "incest," and especially Katherine's long and eloquent speech on her own behalf, invites comparison with the situation of Gertrude in *Hamlet,* who married her husband's brother. Hamlet calls the liaison "incestuous" (*Hamlet* 1.2.157), and the ghost of old Hamlet describes his brother as "that

incestuous, that adulterate beast" (*Hamlet* 1.5.42). In *Henry VIII,* Henry's description of Katherine as "[s]ometimes our brother's wife" (2.4.178) is close to the
play's source in Holinshed, but also, inevitably to modern ears, recalls Claudius's
"our sometime sister, now our queen" (*Hamlet* 1.2.8). Hermione in *The Winter's
Tale,* a play written in 1610, close to the time of *Henry VIII,* is another queen
accused in open court, and wrongly; her words of love and self-defense in act 3,
scene 2, of that play are often compared to Katherine's. Hermione is accused of
adultery with Polixenes, a man her husband once regarded as his "twinned"
brother. Hermione's defense, like Katherine's, is at once proud and loving, and
makes reference to her royal heritage ("The Emperor of Russia was my father").
Katherine's "We are a queen, or long have dreamed so" links her with both
Hermione and Hermione's daughter, Perdita. Critics have also noted another
historical affinity with a story that goes—quite understandably—unmentioned
in the play: the fact that Henry VIII had an affair with Anne Bullen's sister
Mary before he met Anne. Leviticus forbade marrying a brother's wife and was
equally firm about not "taking a wife to thy sister" (Leviticus 18:16, 18). Ultimately the King accused Anne of being both adulterous and incestuous. She
was sentenced to death together with her brother, with whom, it was claimed,
she had had an incestuous affair.

Katherine's refusal of Wolsey as her judge allows for a magnificent exit, as
she storms out of the consistory, to the admiration of the King, who is moved to
an expression of familiar affection: "Go thy ways, Kate" (2.4.130). Nowhere else
in the play does he use this affectionate nickname, and to this point the audience may not have associated the royal, and Spanish, Katherine with her Shakespearean English namesakes, from Kate in *The Taming of the Shrew* to Hotspur's
wife in *Henry IV Part 1,* nor to that French Princess Catherine whom an earlier
King Henry also suddenly called "Kate" (*Henry V* 5.2). The King's subsequent
speech in her praise ("That man i'th' world who shall report he has / A better
wife, let him in naught be trusted" [2.4.131–132]), however reluctantly delivered,
rings true.

Wolsey wants Henry to marry the sister of the King of France, not Anne
Bullen, whom he regards as too lowborn to be Queen of England:

> It shall be to the Duchess of Alençon,
> The French King's sister—he shall marry her.
> Anne Bullen? No, I'll no Anne Bullens for him:
> There's more in't than fair visage. Bullen?
> No, we'll no Bullens. Speedily I wish
> To hear from Rome. The Marchioness of Pembroke?
>
> *3.2.86–91*

The modern spelling, "Boleyn," Anne's own preference, emphasizes the French
element—she was educated at the French court—while the play's "Bullen" is
more flatly English, emphasizing Wolsey's point: for him she is a local upstart,

not a real Frenchwoman of title. As Norfolk and Suffolk watch, unobserved, from another part of the stage—for this is another of the play's superb onlooker scenes—Norfolk notes with splendid lack of emphasis, "He's discontented." In fact, Wolsey's fall will be directly linked to this preference for a liaison with the French throne. He is exposed, and ruined, by the discovery of a letter he has sent to the Pope asking him to delay granting the divorce so Wolsey can try to persuade Henry to marry the French princess. In this play, although not in the historical sources, Wolsey has inadvertently included in a letter to Henry an inventory of all his own wealth and possessions, another error that turns Henry against him. (Long before the heyday of the "Freudian slip," this seems, in the context of the drama of Wolsey's overreaching, to be the playwright's way of signifying the Cardinal's psychological self-betrayal.)

Although he is often an onlooker rather than an actor in the play, Henry has a few strong dramatic moments, notably his exposé of Wolsey's financial chicanery, nicely and pointedly expressed in a speech that underscores the materialism and materiality of this supposedly spiritual figure ("You are full of heavenly stuff, and bear the inventory / Of your best graces in your mind," Henry says. "You have scarce time / To steal from spiritual leisure a brief span / To keep your earthly audit" [3.2.138–139, 140–142]), and his clever ploy in giving Cranmer his ring to protect him against enemies at court.

Much later in the play, the new Queen, Anne Bullen, is described—though in a "Fletcher" scene—in what seems yet another reminiscence of Cleopatra. The scene is delightfully earthy and comic in spirit, as the Third Gentleman joins his friends, reporting that he has been

> Among the crowd i'th' Abbey, where a finger
> Could not be wedged in more. I am stifled
> With the mere rankness of their joy.

Second Gentleman	You saw the ceremony?
Third Gentleman	That I did.
First Gentleman	How was it?
Third Gentleman	Well worth the seeing.
Second Gentleman	Good sir, speak it to us.

4.1.58–63

This amusing—and audience-teasing—taciturnity soon turns into volubility, as the Gentleman comes to describe the Queen, who sat

> In a rich chair of state, opposing freely
> The beauty of her person to the people.
> Believe me, sir, she is the goodliest woman
> That ever lay by man; which when the people
> Had the full view of, such a noise arose

> As the shrouds make at sea in a stiff tempest,
> As loud and to as many tunes. Hats, cloaks—
> Doublets, I think—flew up, and had their faces
> Been loose, this day they had been lost. Such joy
> I never saw before. Great-bellied women,
> That had not half a week to go, like rams
> In the time of war, would shake the press,
> And make 'em reel before 'em. No man living
> Could say "This is my wife" there, all were woven
> So strangely in one piece.
>
> *4.1.69–83*

We may notice the attention in this passage to physicality: smell and sensuality, "rank" bodies (without rank—the same joke as in *Cymbeline*). (The historical Anne Bullen was pregnant at her coronation, though this is of course never mentioned in the play.) That no man could say "This is my wife" is innocently ominous, since this becomes Henry's problem all too soon. The image of the crowd all blended together into "one piece" also strangely recalls the opening description, also of a magnificent and indescribable offstage event, of the meeting of the two kings on the Field of the Cloth of Gold: "how they clung / In their embracement as they grew together" into "a compounded one" (1.1.9–12).

Henry VIII ends with a double epitaph on Cardinal Wolsey (Katherine's bitter estimate then revised and gentled by her gentleman usher Griffith), with Katherine's dream vision and her death, with Henry's gift of the ring to Archbishop Cranmer, and with the birth of Elizabeth. Katherine's dying petition to Henry on behalf of their daughter and her own faithful attendants ends with her request for a seemly burial, in tones that again recall the spirit of the romances and tragicomedies for which both Shakespeare and Fletcher were known:

> Strew me over
> With maiden flowers, that all the world may know
> I was a chaste wife to my grave. Embalm me,
> Then lay me forth. Although unqueened, yet like
> A queen and daughter to a king inter me.
>
> *4.2.169–173*

In the course of the next act the new Queen, Anne, is brought to bed with a daughter, the announcement made to the King by the Old Lady in an exchange that is more comic than sublime.

The play's last and climactic scene—probably not written by Shakespeare—presents the baptism of the infant Elizabeth and a stirring prophecy, by Cranmer, that predicts with exemplary accuracy Elizabeth's reign, her lifelong virginity, and the succession of King James, unnamed but clearly identifiable ("She shall

be, to the happiness of England, / An agèd princess"; "a virgin, / A most unspot-
ted lily shall she pass / To th' ground"; a "maiden phoenix," she will from her
ashes "new create another heir / As great in admiration as herself"; she will rise
"star-like," "great in fame," flourishing "like a mountain cedar," and "make new
nations" [5.4.56–57, 60–62, 40, 41–42, 46, 46, 53, 52]). Like all such prophecies
embedded in the history plays (the Bishop of Carlisle in *Richard II*; Queen
Margaret's curse in *Richard III*), this theatrical prediction has the benefit of perfect hindsight, since it is written and performed long after the historical events
it "foretells."

The Two Noble Kinsmen

DRAMATIS PERSONAE

Prologue
Theseus, *Duke of Athens*
Hippolyta, *Queen of the Amazons*
  later wife of Theseus
Emilia, *her sister*
Pirithous, *friend of Theseus*
Palamon, *noble kinsman, cousin of*
  Arcite, nephew of Creon, the
  King of Thebes
Arcite, *noble kinsman, cousin of*
  Palamon, nephew of Creon,
  the King of Thebes
Hymen, *god of marriage*
A Boy, *who sings*
Artesius, *an Athenian soldier*
Three Queens, *widows of kings*
  killed in the siege of Thebes
Valerius, *a Theban*
A Herald
Woman, *attending Emilia*
An Athenian Gentleman
Messengers

Six Knights, *three attending on*
  Arcite and three on Palamon
A Servant
A Jailer in charge of Theseus's
  prison
The Jailer's Daughter
The Jailer's Brother
The Wooer of the Jailer's
  daughter
Two Friends of the Jailer
A Doctor
Six Countrymen, *one dressed as*
  a babion, or baboon
Gerald, a Schoolmaster
Nell, *a country wench*
Four other country wenches:
  Friz, Madeline, Luce, and
  Barbara
Timothy, a Taborer
Epilogue
Nymphs, attendants, maids,
  executioner, guard

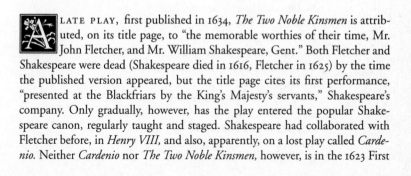 LATE PLAY, first published in 1634, *The Two Noble Kinsmen* is attributed, on its title page, to "the memorable worthies of their time, Mr. John Fletcher, and Mr. William Shakespeare, Gent." Both Fletcher and Shakespeare were dead (Shakespeare died in 1616, Fletcher in 1625) by the time the published version appeared, but the title page cites its first performance, "presented at the Blackfriars by the King's Majesty's servants," Shakespeare's company. Only gradually, however, has the play entered the popular Shakespeare canon, regularly taught and staged. Shakespeare had collaborated with Fletcher before, in *Henry VIII,* and also, apparently, on a lost play called *Cardenio.* Neither *Cardenio* nor *The Two Noble Kinsmen,* however, is in the 1623 First

Folio; the presence there of *Henry VIII* seems to indicate that collaboration was no bar to a claim of authorship, and in fact many stage plays of this period were to some extent collaborative works, with additions offered by other playwrights, and by players, and sometimes with improvised bits that became regular parts of the acting script.

The chief source of the play is Chaucer's "Knight's Tale," and the personae therefore have a certain commonality with Shakespeare's earlier comedy *A Midsummer Night's Dream,* which likewise opens with the expectation of the wedding of Theseus, Duke of Athens, and his Amazonian bride, Hippolyta. Unlike *Dream,* a true comedy in which all dangers are averted or contraverted and everything ends (relatively) happily, *The Two Noble Kinsmen* is a tragicomedy, so described by the publisher in the Stationers' Register. One of its noble heroes dies, tragically and somewhat unexpectedly (at least to those unfamiliar with the plot of Chaucer's tale). While the virtues and pleasures this play offers are very considerable—it is full of magnificent poetry, and also of the kind of theatrical spectacle that distinguishes *Henry VIII*—it will probably be most useful here to discuss patterns in *The Two Noble Kinsmen* that are both like and unlike better-known plays in the Shakespeare canon, not in order to assimilate and tame this play by suppressing all its interesting singularities, but rather to make it legible, so that its differences and special qualities are easier to discern and to appreciate.

The Two Noble Kinsmen begins with a Prologue and ends with an Epilogue, thus bracketing its ceremonial, romantic, and tragic events from a faraway past with gestures toward the present-day audience. The Prologue is jaunty, bawdy, and colloquial—a nice, and deliberate, contrast with the more formal, even hieratic scene that is to follow. The "breeder" to which the Prologue alludes is the author of the play's source:

> New plays and maidenheads are near akin:
> Much followed both, for both much money giv'n
> If they stand sound and well. And a good play,
> Whose modest scenes blush on his marriage day
> And shake to lose his honour, is like her
> That after holy tie and first night's stir
> Yet still is modesty, and still retains
> More of the maid to sight than husband's pains.
> We pray our play may be so, for I am sure
> It has a noble breeder and a pure,
> A learnèd, and a poet never went
> More famous yet 'twixt Po and silver Trent.
> Chaucer, of all admired, the story gives:
> There constant to eternity it lives.
> If we let fall the nobleness of this

> And the first sound this child hear be a hiss,
> How will it shake the bones of that good man . . . ?
> Two Noble Kinsmen *Prologue 1–17*

Instead of the "hiss" of a dissatisfied audience, the Prologue sues for applause (in a figure recognizable from Prospero's Epilogue in *The Tempest*): "Do but you hold out / Your helping hands and we shall tack about / And something do to save us" (Prologue 25–27). The play, he assures the audience, is "[w]orth two hours' travel," where "travel" is the same as "travail" (effort or labor). The phrase recalls the "two hours' traffic of our stage" from the Prologue to *Romeo and Juliet*. The result, at least for a modern audience, is to suture this play to the framing techniques of other, more familiar "Shakespeare" plays, and also to replace the narrator figure of Gower (in Shakespeare's earlier medieval romance, *Pericles*) with a free-standing actor, the Prologue, who will then disappear into the action.

The Epilogue, spoken by a different actor, and coming almost immediately after the onstage death of Arcite, one of the play's attractive eponymous "kinsmen," will be even more colloquial and flirtatious (Lois Potter in the Arden edition writes that "the most likely speaker is a boy actor dressed as a woman"),[1] more closely resembling Rosalind than Prospero:

> I would now ask ye how ye like the play,
> But, as it is with schoolboys, cannot say.
> I am cruel fearful. Pray yet stay awhile,
> And let me look upon ye. No man smile?
> Then it goes hard, I see. He that has
> Loved a young handsome wench, then, show his face—
> 'Tis strange if none be here—and if he will,
> Against his conscience let him hiss and kill
> Our market. . . .
> . . . .
>   If the tale we have told—
> For 'tis no other—any way content ye,
> For to that honest purpose it was meant ye,
> We have our end. . . .
>
> *Epilogue 1–15*

Prologues and epilogues of this kind are, of course, present in numerous early modern stage plays, and the evocation of the modes of address of Prospero, Rosalind, and the *Romeo and Juliet* Prologue here is meant to be indicative rather than exhaustive.

The play contained between these two audience-engaging parentheses begins with a broken ceremony. The stage direction to act 1, scene 1, like those in *Henry VIII*, is highly detailed, and both descriptive and prescriptive:

Music. Enter Hymen with a torch burning, a BOY *in a white robe before,
singing and strewing flowers. After Hymen, a nymph encompassed in her
tresses, bearing a wheaten garland. Then* THESEUS *between two other
nymphs with wheaten chaplets on their heads. Then* HIPPOLYTA, *the bride,
led by* [PIRITHOUS] *and another holding a garland over her head, her tresses
likewise hanging. After her,* EMILIA *holding up her train.*

The occasion is the marriage of Theseus and Hippolyta. Emilia (Chaucer's
"Emily," a character deriving from his source, a tale by Boccaccio) is Hippolyta's sister, and Pirithous a friend of Theseus. Hymen—also present in the wedding finale of *As You Like It*—is the classical god of marriage. But before
the ceremony can take place, it is interrupted by the arrival of three queens,
dressed in black, seeking Theseus's assistance in the war against "cruel Creon"
of Thebes, who has slain their husbands and refuses to yield up the bodies for
burial. Theseus at first declines to interrupt his marriage ceremony, and its
erotic aftermath, for this mission of mercy, but he is importuned by Hippolyta
and Emilia, and by the eloquent widowed queens. "O when /
Her twinning
cherries shall their sweetness fall / Upon thy tasteful lips, what wilt thou think /
Of rotten kings or blubbered queens?" (1.1.176–179), one of the queens demands of him with pathos and pertinence. Hippolyta lends the force of her own
persuasion, sounding, as she does so, rather like Portia sending Bassanio off to
rescue Antonio before he comes to her marriage bed—or like Othello post-
poning his own wedded pleasure in order to quell the Turks in Cyprus. Here is
Hippolyta:

> Though much unlike
> You should be so transported, as much sorry
> I should be such a suitor—yet I think
> Did I not by th'abstaining of my joy,
> Which breeds a deeper longing, cure their surfeit
> That craves a present medicine, I should pluck
> All ladies' scandal on me. [*Kneels*] Therefore, sir,
> As I shall here make trial of my prayers,
> Either presuming them to have some force,
> Or sentencing for aye their vigour dumb,
> Prorogue this businesss we are going about, and hang
> Your shield afore your heart—about that neck
> Which is my fee, and which I freely lend
> To do these poor queens service.
>
> *1.1.185–198*

Theseus charges Pirithous to "[k]eep the feast full," to go on with the festivities, and prepares to assist the queens: "As we are men, / Thus should we do;

being sensually subdued / We lose our human title" (1.1.230–232). This, too, echoes the *Othello* theme of the subjugation of private sensuality to public service.

The scene then shifts to Thebes, and the two "kinsmen," Palamon and Arcite, cousins and best friends, are introduced. They lament the "decays" of Thebes and the fallenness of the city, "where every evil / Hath a good colour; where every seeming good's / A certain evil" (1.2.38–40). Affectations of style, speech, and dress have overtaken the court of Creon, and the two young men are determined to "leave his court that we may nothing share /Of his loud infamy" (1.2.75–76). No sooner have they made this declaration, however, than the situation changes. The announcement of Theseus's approach turns the two men into patriots, who will fight for their city's honor rather than for its dishonorable tyrant: "Our services stand now for Thebes, not Creon" (1.2.99). Palamon and Arcite go to battle to defend Thebes against Athens, are injured, and are treated kindly by Theseus, who orders that they be tended back to health, and imprisoned. Described by a herald as "[m]en of great quality, . . . / sisters' children, nephews to the King" (1.4.15–17), they are taken to an Athenian jail and cared for by a jailer and his daughter. "[T]he prison itself is proud of 'em, and they have all the world in their chamber," rhapsodizes the Daughter, echoing a common theme of Renaissance lyric from Ralegh to Donne to Lovelace. "It is a holiday to look on them. Lord, the difference of men!" (2.1.22–24, 50–51). The stage is set for a move from pageantry to love comedy, and then, via the Daughter's unrequited love for Palamon, to madness.

In Athens, meanwhile, those left behind discuss male and female friendship, and articulate strong models of same-sex allegiance, akin to those articulated in other Shakespeare plays (Antonio and Bassanio; Hermia and Helena; Leontes and Polixenes; and so on). In our discussion of *The Merchant of Venice, A Midsummer Night's Dream,* and *The Winter's Tale,* we touched upon the Renaissance ideal of friendship and its Platonic and erotic associations. In *The Two Noble Kinsmen,* as in most—though not all—Shakespearean instances, these discussions locate the ideal model of friendship in the past, as something to be accommodated to the changed circumstances of marriage (in the case of Theseus and Pirithous) or as something lost and perhaps irreplaceable (in the case of Emilia and her friend Flavina, who died when she was eleven years old). It is worth examining the ways in which these two paradigmatic friendships are described, early in the play, since these models will have a bearing on the relationship between Palamon and Arcite, and the manner in which that "ideal friendship" will be breached, first by competitive love for the same woman, Emilia (a version of critic Réné Girard's concept of "mimetic desire"), and then by death. Shakespeare's plays use the pattern of mimetic desire over and over, as we have seen in the early comedies. In *The Two Noble Kinsmen* this triangular desire underwrites much of the action, coloring eroticism with rivalry—and rivalry with eroticism.

"How his longing / Follows his friend!" exclaims Emilia about Pirithous, whose mind seems divided between thinking of the absent Theseus and fulfilling his injunction to keep the festivities alight (1.3.26–27). Hippolyta is happy to agree: "Their knot of love, / Tied, weaved, entangled with so true, so long, / And with a finger of so deep a cunning, / May be outworn, never outdone" (41–44). This reflection reminds Emilia of her own loss, which she describes in one of those passages of exposition that are plainly for the audience's enlightenment. Hippolyta, though she listens with every evidence of close attention, makes it clear that she has heard this tale before:

> Emilia   I was acquainted
> Once with a time when I enjoyed a playfellow;
> You were at wars when she the grave enriched,
> Who made too proud the bed; took leave o'th' moon—
> Which then looked pale at parting—when our count
> Was each eleven.
> Hippolyta   'Twas Flavina.
> Emilia   Yes.
> You talk of Pirithous' and Theseus' love:
> Theirs has more ground, is more maturely seasoned,
> More buckled with strong judgement, and their needs
> The one of th'other may be said to water
> Their intertangled roots of love; but I
> And she I sigh and spoke of were things innocent,
> Loved for we did, and like the elements,
> That know not what, nor why, yet do effect
> Rare issues by their operance, our souls
> Did so to one another. What she liked
> Was then of me approved; what not, condemned—
> No more arraignment. The flower that I would pluck
> And put between my breasts—O then but beginning
> To swell about the blossom—she would long
> Till she had such another, and commit it
> To the like innocent cradle, where, phoenix-like,
> They died in perfume. On my head no toy
> But was her pattern. Her affections—pretty,
> Though happily her careless wear—I followed
> For my most serious decking. Had mine ear
> Stol'n some new air, or at adventure hummed one,
> From musical coinage, why, it was a note
> Whereon her spirits would sojourn—rather, dwell on—
> And sing it in her slumbers. . . .

1.3.49–78

In short, Emilia speculates, "true love 'tween maid and maid may be / More than in sex dividual" (1.3.81–82). Hippolyta intercedes to interpret, translating Emilia's thoughts: "[T]his high-speeded pace is but to say / That you shall never, like the maid Flavina, / Love any that's called man" (1.3.83–85). To which Emilia replies promptly and roundly, "I am sure I shall not" (86).

We might pause here to note the oddity of this conversation, in which Hippolyta, the Amazon Queen, maintains the view of heterosexual love and marriage, while her sister insists upon her "faith" in the fact that she will never love a man as she loved the dead Flavina. Hippolyta's peroration, in which she gently advises her sister that she will change her mind one day, may seem contrary in spirit to the idea of a Shakespeare imagined as limning powerful patterns of same-sex love—and, indeed, from that of a Fletcher memorably described as sharing a bed and a wench with his best friend and frequent collaborator Francis Beaumont[2]—but it is nonetheless quite in line with the usual plots and practices of Shakespeare's plays. Hermia and Helena in *A Midsummer Night's Dream*, Celia and Rosalind in *As You Like It*, are first twinned, then divided. Each chooses a husband, although that choice does not invalidate either the passion, or the eloquence, or their romantic friendship. In *Twelfth Night* Olivia's love for the cross-dressed Viola—whom she knows as the boy "Cesario"—is transmuted, by the machinations of the plot, into a marriage with Viola's twin, Sebastian, and the embrace of Viola herself as a "sister." *The Two Noble Kinsmen* revisits this classic Shakespearean scenario in which passionate childhood loves between persons of the same sex, while they may be rhetorically reconfirmed at the play's end, are also formally augmented or superseded by heterosexual marriage.

Hippolyta	Now alack, weak sister,
	I must no more believe thee in this point—
	Though in't I know thou dost believe thyself—
	Than I will trust a sickly appetite
	That loathes even as it longs. But sure, my sister,
	If I were ripe for your persuasion, you
	Have said enough to shake me from the arm
	Of the all-noble Theseus, for whose fortunes
	I will now in and kneel, with great assurance
	That we more than his Pirithous possess
	The high throne in his heart.

1.3.87–97

Hippolyta's "we" is the personal plural, what is sometimes called the "royal we." She is confident that she, and not his childhood friend Pirithous, is Theseus's chosen partner.

Perhaps it is enough that Shakespeare does allow the alternative view to stand, at least for the moment—"I am not / Against your faith, yet I continue mine," says Emilia—and the form that these philosophical conversations always take in the plays is dialogic, so that there is no "right" or "wrong" answer to such a debate. But "never" in such conversations serves almost always, especially in the comedies, as a kind of dare, waiting to be proved wrong ("That you shall never, like the maid Flavina, / Love any that's called man").

The "dead twin" theme is a familiar one in the plays (compare Juliet and the dead Susan in *Romeo and Juliet*—"Susan is with God" [*Romeo and Juliet* 1.3.21]; Viola/Cesario and her imaginary sister who pined away "like patience on a monument" in *Twelfth Night;* and the dead sister of the merry Catherine in *Love's Labour's Lost*). Empirical social history tells us that child mortality in this period was high, but we do not need recourse to the "real" to see that dramatically and poetically speaking the dead twin emblematizes a road not taken. Flavina dies at eleven, the partner and soul mate of her loving and beloved Emilia. But Emilia lives, and her life changes. Her definitive "I am sure I shall not" dangles as a tantalizing piece of plot bait, waiting for its reversal—and this would be true no matter *what* she averred to be unalterably true. The reversal, in other words, is theatrical, not merely narrative and psychological.

Part of the importance of this scene is the way it skillfully sets up a similar conversation between the imprisoned Palamon and Arcite in act 2, in which the noble kinsmen articulate the pattern of their friendship and the implications of their captivity. Palamon starts with the twin theme: "O never / Shall we two exercise, like twins of honour, / Our arms again" (2.2.17–19). Arcite sees the end of their hopes for a future, and for progeny:

> Here we are,
> And here the graces of our youths must wither,
> Like a too-timely spring. Here age must find us
> And, which is heaviest, Palamon, unmarried—
> The sweet embraces of a loving wife
> Loaden with kisses, armed with thousand Cupids,
> Shall never clasp our necks; no issue know us;
> No figures of ourselves shall we e'er see
> To glad our age. . . .
> . . . .
> This is all our world.
> We shall know nothing here but one another,
> Hear nothing but the clock that tells our woes.
>
> *2.2.26–42*

Still, there is some comfort in the fact that they are together. "Whilst Palamon is with me, let me perish / If I think this our prison," Arcite says, and Palamon replies in the same spirit: " 'Tis a main goodness, cousin, that our fortunes /

Were twined together" (2.2.61–62, 63–64). This leads Arcite to a further set of
speculations and escapist fantasies (in the same vein as John of Gaunt's counsel
to his exiled son Bolingbroke, to suppose "the singing birds musicians" in
Richard II):

> Let's think this prison holy sanctuary,
> To keep us from corruption of worse men.
> We are young, and yet desire the ways of honour
> That liberty and common conversation,
> The poison of pure spirits, might, like women,
> Woo us to wander from. What worthy blessing
> Can be, but our imaginations
> May make it ours? And here being thus together,
> We are an endless mine to one another:
> We are one another's wife, ever begetting
> New births of love; we are father, friends, acquaintance;
> We are in one another, families—
> I am your heir, and you are mine. . . .
>
> . . . .
>   Were we at liberty
> A wife might part us lawfully, or business;
> Quarrels consume us; envy of ill men
> Crave our acquaintance. I might sicken, cousin,
> Where you should never know it, and so perish
> Without your noble hand to close mine eyes,
> Or prayers to the gods. . . .
>
>   *2.2.71–94*

Palamon is overwhelmed with this vision: "You have made me— / I thank you,
cousin Arcite—almost wanton / With my captivity" (2.2.95–97). The conversation ends on a note of certainty:

Palamon	Is there record of any two that loved
	Better than we do, Arcite?
Arcite	Sure there cannot.
Palamon	I do not think it possible our friendship
	Should ever leave us.
Arcite	Till our deaths it cannot.

2.2.112–115

Like Emilia's "never," Palamon's "not . . . ever" invites a dramatic reversal, and
that is exactly, and immediately, what it gets. Having rhetorically claimed that
their captivity protects them from women who might seduce them away

from the path of honor, that "[W]e are one another's wife," and that "[a] wife might part us," Palamon and Arcite are about to become rivals for the love of a woman they behold from afar, as Emilia and her waiting-woman enter the garden below their prison window to admire the flowers that grow there, especially the one "called narcissus." (By this time Emilia has changed her views at least enough to critique the "fair boy" who was "a fool / To love himself," for "[W]ere there not maids enough?" [2.2.120–121].)

"Never till now was I in prison, Arcite," says Palamon (2.2.132), and shortly—having nothing better to do—these two noble kinsmen have both fallen in love:

Palamon	Might not a man well lose himself and love her?
Arcite	I cannot tell what you have done; I have,
	Beshrew mine eyes for't. Now I feel my shackles.
Palamon	You love her then?
Arcite	Who would not?
Palamon	And desire her?
Arcite	Before my liberty.
Palamon	I saw her first.
Arcite	That's nothing.
Palamon	But it shall be.
Arcite	I saw her too.
Palamon	Yes, but you must not love her.

2.2.156–164

And so on and on, putting their friendship, and their kinship, in jeopardy. "Why then would you deal so cunningly, / So strangely, so unlike a noble kinsman, / To love alone?" asks Arcite. "Speak truly. Do you think me / Unworthy of her sight?" (2.2.193–195). Like another eponymous duo, the two gentlemen of Verona in Shakespeare's play of that name, likewise sundered by their love for Silvia, Palamon and Arcite split apart over their "love" for Emilia, to whom neither has ever spoken. When, shortly, Theseus sends for Arcite, gives him his liberty, but banishes him from Athens, Arcite's first thought is that Palamon is far more fortunate, since he can look at Emilia every day from his prison window. "I will not leave the kingdom," Arcite resolves. "If I go he has her" (2.3.19, 21). Learning from some rustic countrymen that "games" are going forward and that Duke Theseus himself will be present, Arcite determines to put on a "poor disguise" and enter the competition, hoping, he says, that "happiness prefer me to a place / Where I may ever dwell in sight of her" (2.3.84–85). At the country sports, Arcite—like Pericles disguised in his play as "the mean knight"—distinguishes himself as the fastest runner and best wrestler, identifies himself as a "youngest" son (in the time-honored spirit of fairy tales), and is presented to Emilia—whose birthday has, it turns out, inspired these celebrations—as her courtly servant. Theseus admires both the man and his prowess, and urges

Emilia to supply Arcite with horses and to look upon him with favor, perhaps as a "master," or husband.

There is, however, another love story in the making, one with a less "noble" shape and—for a while at least—boding a far less happy ending. For the Jailer's Daughter has fallen in love with Palamon, just as Palamon has fallen in love with Emilia. Smitten, the Jailer's Daughter frees Palamon from prison. He encounters Arcite in the wood, where the two kinsmen determine to fight a duel for the right to claim Emilia as "my mistress" (3.1.29)—a duel that takes place in act 3, scene 6, and constitutes the second of this play's "broken," or interrupted, ceremonies.

As for the Daughter, she promptly goes mad, afflicted by melancholy or madness arising from passionate love. Her situation and her onstage response to it recall that of Ophelia, and she sings a similar song of unrequited passion and betrayal, with similar slips into sexual innuendo ("O for a prick now, like a nightingale, / To put my breast against" [3.4.25–26]). The Daughter will be recruited as a "dainty madwoman" into an antic dance being staged by a pedantic schoolmaster and his countrymen and "wenches" for the edification of the Duke (much in the spirit of the sheepshearing scene in *The Winter's Tale*, or the pageant of the "Nine Worthies" staged by the pedant Holofernes in *Love's Labour's Lost*). Madwomen—and madmen—were regarded in some quarters as figures of entertainment in this period. Webster's *Duchess of Malfi* features a dance of eight madmen (4.2). The Schoolmaster's long rhyming preface to his entertainment staged in act 3, scene 5, as a play-within-the-play with Theseus, Hippolyta, and Emilia in the onstage audience, features dubiously chiming couplets ("The body of our sport, of no small study, / I first appear, though rude and raw and muddy") and some fearsome alliteration ("dainty Duke, whose doughty dismal fame / From Dis to Daedalus"), and gives way to a morris dance, constituting a rustic spectacle in the middle of the play, between the "high" "comic," or romantic, movement, in which the noble kinsmen fall nobly in love with an unattainable woman, and the "tragic" movement, in which they fight for her to the death, and one of them actually dies.

But as for the Daughter, her plight is less hopeless than it may at first have appeared—the play is, after all, a tragicomedy, not a tragedy like *Hamlet*. In fact, she is recovered to her wits by a piece of extended role-playing undertaken by her faithful Wooer, who is advised by the Doctor,

> [T]ake upon you . . . the name of Palamon; say you come to eat with her and to commune of love. . . . Sing to her such green songs of love as she says Palamon hath sung in prison; come to her stuck in as sweet flowers. . . . Learn what maids have been her companions and play-feres, and let them repair to her, with Palamon in their mouths, and appear with tokens as if they suggested for him. It is a falsehood she is in, which is with falsehoods to be combated.
>
> *4.3.64–80*

Like the trope of entertaining a mad world with madmen, this strategy has a peculiarly "modern" feel. ("It is a falsehood she is in, which is with falsehoods to be combated.") The "cure" is effected in act 5, with the Doctor, the Jailer, the Wooer, and the Daughter all onstage, and the Doctor's down-home sexual advice to the Wooer ("Lie with her if she ask you. / . . . in the way of cure" [5.4.18–20]) comically resisted by the Jailer, who is as concerned for his daughter's "honesty" as for her sanity ("You fathers are fine fools," the Doctor comments caustically [5.4.27]). The "low" plot of the Jailer's Daughter and the faux Palamon offers a nice counterbalance to the "high" plot of Emilia and her two suitors, since Emilia has as little real cognizance of the individual qualities and natures of the courtly kinsmen Palamon and Arcite as the mad Daughter does of the difference between "Palamon" and Palamon.

As for the duel scene (3.6), it is structured, as we have already noted, as a second broken ceremony, paralleling the interrupted wedding in act 1, scene 1. Again the women will kneel and plead with Theseus, and again he will ultimately yield to their request. The scene has some strong elements of comedy, a little reminiscent of the threatened duel in *Twelfth Night* between Viola/Cesario and Sir Andrew Aguecheek, in which each for different reasons is terrified to fight the other. Palamon and Arcite have no such fear; they are defined, and they consistently define themselves, as soldiers (as Arcite says, "We were not bred to talk, man. When we are armed / And both upon our guards, then let our fury, / . . . fly strongly from us" [3.6.28–30]). But they find themselves caught in a courtly dilemma and rather wish there were an honorable way out. "Your person I am friends with," Arcite tells Palamon, as he gives him a choice of swords and armors. "And I could wish I had not said I loved her, / Though I had died; but loving such a lady, / And justifying my love, I must not fly from't" (3.6.39–42). And Palamon replies, "Arcite, thou art so brave an enemy / That no man but thy cousin's fit to kill thee" (43–44). As they outfit themselves and each other—putting on armor is not a task that is easy for a man to do for himself—they chat in a homely and intimate way that is the opposite of martial confrontation:

Palamon	Pray thee tell me, cousin,
	Where gott'st thou this good armour?
Arcite	'Tis the Duke's,
	And to say true, I stole it. Do I pinch you?

3.6.53–55

And:

Arcite	. . . use your gauntlets, though—those are o'th' least.
	Prithee take mine, good cousin.
Palamon	Thank you, Arcite.

> How do I look? Am I fall'n much away?
>
> Arcite   Faith, very little—love has used you kindly.
>
> 3.6.64–67

Such affectionate and even comical exchanges, born of long familiarity, give way to an awkward ceremonial: as the stage direction says, "They bow several ways, then advance and stand" before they commence their fight. "Once more farewell, my cousin," says Arcite, and Palamon replies in kind: "Farewell, Arcite." But no sooner have they begun to trade blows in earnest than they are interrupted—yet another interrupted ceremony—by the hunting horns of Theseus and the arrival of Theseus, Hippolyta, Emilia, Pirithous, and their train.

The scene here will resemble both the beginning of *A Midsummer Night's Dream,* when Theseus enforces the restrictive law of Athens, and the late scene in that same play when he and Hippolyta encounter the sleeping lovers in the woods. In *The Two Noble Kinsmen,* Theseus demands:

> What ignorant and mad malicious traitors
> Are you, that 'gainst the tenor of my laws
> Are making battle, thus like knights appointed,
> Without my leave and officers of arms?
> By Castor, both shall die.
>
> 3.6.132–136

Theseus has forbidden the kind of individual armed combat in which they were about to engage if it were not under his control. Palamon's reply is eloquent— as, indeed, is Arcite's—as both undertake to explain the code of love that has inspired their ritual enmity. "We are certainly both traitors," acknowledges Palamon,

>   both despisers
> Of thee and of thy goodness. I am Palamon,
> That cannot love thee, he that broke thy prison—
> Think well what that deserves. And this is Arcite;
> A bolder traitor never trod thy ground,
> A falser ne'er seemed friend. This is the man
> Was begged and banished; this is he contemns thee,
> And what thou dar'st do; and in this disguise,
> Against thine own edict, follows thy sister,
> That fortunate bright star, the fair Emilia,
> Whose servant—if there be a right in seeing
> And first bequeathing of the soul to—justly
> I am; and, which is more, dares think her his.
>
> 3.6.137–149

This is the "treachery" that Palamon would combat. As for Arcite, he embraces the title of traitor:

> Let me say thus much—if in love be treason,
> In service of so excellent a beauty,
> As I love most, and in that faith will perish,
> As I have brought my life here to confirm it,
> As I have served her truest, worthiest,
> As I dare kill this cousin that denies it,
> So let me be most traitor and ye please me.
> For scorning of thy edict, Duke, ask that lady
> Why she is fair, and why her eyes command me
> Stay here to love her, and if she say, "Traitor,"
> I am a villain fit to lie unburied.
>
> *3.6.161–171*

"Let's die together, at one instant, Duke," proposes Palamon (his line here echoes, probably unconsciously, another famous Shakespearean "twinning" passage, Celia's "We still have slept together, / Rose at an instant, learned, played, eat together" [*As You Like It* 1.3.67–68]). "Only a little let him fall before me, / That I may tell my soul, he shall not have her" (3.6.178–179).

Perhaps unsurprisingly, the Athenians—all but Theseus—are swept away by this idealistic rhetoric. "O heaven, / What more than man is this!" exclaims Pirithous when he hears Palamon. In a visual echo of the play's opening scene, the two women, Emilia and Hippolyta, fall to their knees in supplication, and they are joined by Pirithous. "These are strange conjurings," observes the disconcerted Theseus, but he is persuaded—as is the way with Shakespeare's overstrict law-enforcing Dukes—to seek a better solution. Asked how she would solve this problem, Emilia, the object of the noble kinsmen's adoration, modestly suggests that they should both be banished and have nothing further to do with her, a suggestion that enrages both smitten men ("forget I love her? / O all ye gods, despise me then" [3.6.257–258]) and makes the rest of the company admire them. ("These are men!" exclaims Pirithous [3.6.264]. Coming shortly after his "What more than man is this!" this delirious approbation may suggest to a director a moment risibly over-the-top.)

In any case, Theseus, forced to rethink his harsh edict and avoid Emilia's kindly meant but harsher one (as in *Romeo and Juliet,* the lovers' choices would have been death or banishment), ordains a new contest, under his own aegis, to replace the outlaw duel between the rival friends. In three months' time they are to reappear before him, each accompanied by three knights, and participate in a challenge, a kind of jousting contest. Whichever of the men can force the other "[b]y fair and knightly strength" to touch a pyramid installed by Theseus will win Emilia; the other will lose his head, as will his knightly friends.

One of the play's many pleasures is the way it juxtaposes the "high" courtly and triangulated romance of Palamon, Arcite, and Emilia with the "low" story of the Jailer's Daughter and her Wooer. The fact that these country characters have labels rather than names—not unusual in plays of the period—underscores their difference from the nobility. Yet the Jailer's Daughter, and indeed the Jailer himself, are in some ways far more vivid characters than their courtly counterparts. The Daughter falls in love with Palamon after at least slightly more acquaintance than the noble kinsmen have with Emilia, and Emilia, for her part, reenacts that scene of falling-in-love-from-afar in a comical replay in act 4, after she has told them both to forget her and then agreed to marry whichever wins the contest. "*Enter* EMILIA, *with two pictures,*" says the stage direction, and the lady proceeds to admire first one, then the other, then the first again. "What a sweet face has Arcite!" she rhapsodizes (4.2.7). "Palamon / is but his foil" (25–26). And then, "I have lied so lewdly / . . . On my knees / I ask thy pardon, Palamon, thou art alone / And only beautiful" (4.2.35–38). "Lie there, Arcite," she says, putting down his picture. "Thou art a changeling to him, a mere gypsy, / And this the noble body. I am sotted, / Utterly lost" (4.2.43–46). Ultimately she confesses to herself that she is unable to choose. "What a mere child is fancy, / That, having two fair gauds of equal sweetness, / Cannot distinguish, but must cry for both!" (4.2.52–54).

Emilia's dialogue with the two pictures (presumably miniatures, of the sort often given as love tokens) will remind a modern Shakespeare audience of the more famous scene in *Hamlet,* where Hamlet challenges his mother to see the *dis*similarity between her two husbands, old Hamlet and Claudius, who are also, technically, "noble kinsmen" ("Look here upon this picture, and on this, / The counterfeit presentment of two brothers" [*Hamlet* 3.4.52–53]). The stage echo of *Hamlet* is given more pertinence by the fact that in the previous scene (4.1) we hear of the madness of the Jailer's Daughter, presented, like that of Ophelia in *Hamlet,* in a long set piece, an "unscene" narrating events that have taken place offstage and out of our sight. The lovesick girl is described as singing songs—including Desdemona's "Willow, willow, willow"—unbinding her hair (loose hair was a classic stage sign of madness in women), plucking flowers, and speaking aimlessly of her father's death and burial. But the Daughter will live to marry her faithful Wooer (in his therapeutic disguise as "Palamon"), and the Jailer will not meet Polonius's ignominious end. Like many of the last plays in which Shakespeare had a hand, and especially his late romances, this play seems to cite, quote, and excerpt from key moments in earlier Shakespearean plays, especially those that were—and are—memorable onstage. And as was the case in those late other plays, the citation (for example, Leontes' jealousy of Hermione, compared with Othello's jealousy of Desdemona) is briefer, less motivated, and slightly more distanced from character and personality than its tragic original. It has, in short, become a trope, a figure in this case not so much "of speech" as "of stage," recognizable as a Shakespearean minigenre.

The battle that will be the play's denouement is also, curiously enough, an "unscene," only reported to us—and to Emilia—by a servant (5.5). While this denies the audience the full enjoyment of a pageant and a rousing fight, it increases the sense of random chance, and also of the untrustworthiness of report. (A good comparison here is the early "unscene" in *Julius Caesar,* in which Caesar is three times offered a crown—offstage—while the onstage characters try to guess at the tone and import of the events at one remove.) Emilia's excuse is that she cannot bear to watch either of these brave men die. Instead of following the hardier Theseus and Hippolyta, the audience is left behind with her, and gets its information from the servant and from periodic offstage shouts of "A Palamon" (i.e., the fight is going Palamon's way), "Arcite, Arcite!" and finally— or apparently finally—"Arcite, victory!" Emilia, like a sports fan listening to an event on the radio rather than watching it on television, is moved to supply her own mental pictures. One of these, of the two kinsmen merged into a single "composed" entity, is memorable in its own right and closely akin to a phrase in another play by Shakespeare and Fletcher, *Henry VIII,* describing another heroic offstage encounter. Here is Emilia:

> Were they metamorphosed
> Both into one! O why? There were no woman
> Worth so composed a man: their single share,
> Their nobleness peculiar to them, gives
> The prejudice of disparity, value's shortness,
> To any lady breathing—
>
> *5.5.84–89*

And here is the passage from *Henry VIII,* in which the Duke of Norfolk describes how the two kings of France and England met on the Field of the Cloth of Gold:

> I was then present, saw them salute on horseback,
> Beheld them when they lighted, how they clung
> In their embracement as they grew together,
> Which had they, what four throned ones could have weighed
> Such a compounded one?
>
> *Henry VIII 1.1.8–12*

Arcite is the victor, and Palamon must die. But once Arcite has claimed his garland and his bride, and has departed the stage to be replaced by the pinioned Palamon and his knights, the play presents its audience with yet another reversal. Palamon, onstage, is generous in the face of death, giving money to the Jailer as a dowry for his daughter—Palamon's knights following suit—and laying his head on the execution block, only to be rescued at the very last minute by Pirithous and a messenger, who run in, the messenger crying "Hold! Hold!" "What / Hath waked us from our dream?" asks Palamon, echoing a familiar Shakespearean theme that is also the theme of Calderón de la Barca's *La vida es sueño* (*Life Is a Dream*). The story is a tragic one, yet again recounted rather than shown: Arcite had been presented by his newly betrothed Emilia with a spirited black horse in honor of his victory. The horse, frightened by a spark, bucked and threw his noble rider to the "flinty pavement." The dying Arcite now requests to be brought to his cousin's side:

> Palamon O miserable end of our alliance!
> The gods are mighty. Arcite, if thy heart,
> Thy worthy manly heart, be yet unbroken,
> Give me thy last words. I am Palamon,
> One that yet loves thee dying.
> Arcite   Take Emilia,
> And with her all the world's joy. Reach thy hand—
> Farewell—I have told my last hour. I was false,
> Yet never treacherous. Forgive me, cousin—
> One kiss from fair Emilia—[*they kiss*] 'tis done.
> Take her; I die.
>
> 5.6.86–94

Those audience members familiar with Chaucer's "Knight's Tale" would perhaps recall that Palamon and Arcite are there distinguished by their differing allegiances to the classical gods. Palamon prays to Venus, the goddess of love, while Arcite swears fealty to Mars, the god of war. In the poetic logic of the tale, both of them "win": Arcite is the victor in the battle, Palamon gets the girl. In Shakespeare and Fletcher's dramatized version, some of the hieratic "appropriateness" of this division of spoils is inevitably lost, and the two kinsmen in this play have, if not more "personality" in the modern sense, at least more homely and confiding moments, suitable for sustained dramatic action. Palamon does see Emilia first, which may give him a prior claim, assuming that the lady has no opinion in the matter. So in this sense the play's ending not only echoes Chaucer's but is in some slim way "just."

But poetic justice is not, or not always, dramatic justice. After witnessing the mad affections of the Jailer's Daughter and Palamon's admirable and stoic deportment at the supposed moment of execution, we are vouchsafed a glimpse of Palamon through others' admiring eyes. And Theseus tries to shore up this sense in his closing words:

> Palamon,
> Your kinsman hath confessed the right o'th' lady
> Did lie in you, for you first saw her and

> Even then proclaimed your fancy. He restored her
> As your stol'n jewel, and desired your spirit
> To send him hence forgiven. The gods my justice
> Take from my hand, and they themselves become
> The executioners. Lead your lady off,
> And call your lovers from the stage of death,
> Whom I adopt my friends. . . .
>
> *5.6.115–124*

Palamon and his knights ("your lovers") are freed and rewarded, and Theseus will make the best of the situation, decreeing "[a] day or two" for the funeral of Arcite and then—shades of Gertrude and Claudius—moving right along to the marriage. His scene-clearing gesture, "Let's go off / And bear us like the time" (5.6.136–137), is a familiar gesture but also a somewhat unsettling one, since so much has happened so quickly, and one virtually identical suitor has been replaced by another. Emilia, we may recall, could not bring herself to choose between them, though she expressed to herself a strong preference first for the one, and then for the other. The final love tableau, though, remains a triad rather than a dyad. Arcite takes Palamon's hand, and Emilia's kiss, before giving them to each other.

This play, written by two authors, seems to have as its ideal the melting of two (kinsmen, authors) into one. This would eliminate friction and rivalry but at the price of a death. It is fitting that the final tableau displays both the triangle of rivalry and, in the end, the death that thus anchors union.

NOTES

INTRODUCTION

1. Thomas Carlyle, "The Hero as Poet: Dante; Shakespeare" [1841], in *On Heroes, Hero-Worship, and the Heroic in History*, ed. C. Niemeyer (Lincoln: University of Nebraska Press, 1966), pp. 108–9.

2. Thomas Coryate, *Coryate's Crudities* (London, 1611), p. 247.

3. Thomas Bodley to Thomas James, January 15, 1612, in *Letters of Sir Thomas Bodley to Thomas James, First Keeper of the Bodleian Library*, ed. G. W. Wheeler (Oxford: Clarendon Press, 1926), p. 222.

4. Samuel Johnson, "Preface to Shakespeare" [1765], in *Johnson on Shakespeare*, vols. 7–8 of *The Works of Samuel Johnson*, 2-vol. facsimile, ed. Arthur Sherbo (New Haven, Conn.: Yale University Press, 1968), pp. 94–95.

5. Ibid., pp. 105, 108, 109.

6. Fredson Bowers, *On Editing Shakespeare* (Charlottesville: University of Virginia Press, 1966), p. 116.

7. Samuel Johnson, "King Lear," in *Selections from Johnson on Shakespeare,* ed. B. H. Bronson with J. M. O'Meara (New Haven, Conn.: Yale University Press, 1986), p. 240.

8. Johnson, "Preface, 1765," in *Selections*, pp. 10–11.

9. Johnson, "Preface to Shakespeare," pp. 61–62.

10. Alexander Pope, Preface to *The Works of Mr. William Shakespear*, ed. Alexander Pope (1725; New York: AMS Press, 1969), 1:xxiii.

11. "From a Report by J. P. Collier of a Lecture Given by Coleridge, 1811–12," in Samuel Taylor Coleridge, *Writings on Shakespeare*, ed. T. Hawkes (New York: Capricorn Books, 1959), p. 86.

12. Samuel Taylor Coleridge, "From 'Essay on Method and Thought,' from *The Friend*, 1818," in *Writings on Shakespeare*, p. 81.

13. John Keats, "Letter to George and Georgiana Keats, February–May 1819," in *Selected Letters of John Keats*, ed. G. F. Scott, rev. ed. (Cambridge, Mass.: Harvard University Press, 2002), p. 261.

14. Keats, "Letter to George and Thomas Keats, 21, 27 (?) December 1817," in *Selected Letters of John Keats*, p. 60.

15. Keats, "Letter to Richard Woodhouse, 27 October 1818," in *Selected Letters of John Keats*, pp. 194–95.

16. William Hazlitt, in *The Times* (London), October 14, 1905.

17. Walter Savage Landor, cited in Ralph Waldo Emerson, "Quotation and Originality," in *Letters and Social Aims* (Boston: Houghton, Mifflin, 1884), p. 154.

18. John H. Stotsenburg, *An Impartial Study of the Shakespeare Title* (Louisville, Ky.: J. P. Morgan, 1904), p. 174.

19. Charles Dickens to William Sandys, June 13, 1847, in *Complete Writings of Charles Dickens*, ed. "by his sister-in-law" (Boston: Charles E. Lauriat, 1923), 37:206.

20. Matthew Arnold, "Shakespeare," in *The Poems of Matthew Arnold*, ed. K. Allott (London: Longmans, Green, 1965), pp. 48–50.

21. Elizabeth I, quoted in J. E. Neale, *Elizabeth I and Her Parliaments* (New York: St. Martin's Press, 1958), 2:119.

22. James I, *Basilicon Doron* [1599], ed. J. Craigie (London: William Blackwood & Sons Ltd., 1944), p. 163.

23. Adam Smith, *The Theory of Moral Sentiments* (1759; Indianapolis: Liberty Classics, 1976), p. 88.

24. Jane Austen, *Mansfield Park* (1821; New York: Doubleday, 1997), pp. 320–21.

25. Samuel Taylor Coleridge, "Shakespeare's Judgment Equal to His Genius," in *Coleridge's Essays and Lectures on Shakespeare* (New York: Everyman's Library/E. P. Dutton, 1907), pp. 42, 46.

26. Carlyle, "Hero as Poet," p. 141.

27. Henry W. Simon, *The Reading of Shakespeare in American Schools and Colleges: An Historical Survey* (New York: Simon & Schuster, 1932), pp. 7, 9.

28. Ralph Waldo Emerson, "April–May 1864," in *The Journals and Miscellaneous Notebooks,* sel. and ed. J. Porte (Cambridge, Mass.: Belknap Press of Harvard University Press, 1982), pp. 519–21.

29. Ralph Waldo Emerson, "Notes on Poetry," in *The Journals of Ralph Waldo Emerson,* ed. W. H. Gilman and A. R. Ferguson (Cambridge, Mass.: Belknap Press of Harvard University Press, 1963), 3:40.

30. Ralph Waldo Emerson, "Shakespeare; or, The Poet," in *Representative Men: Seven Lectures* (1850; Boston: Houghton, Mifflin, 1903), p. 204.

31. Sigmund Freud, "Some Character-Types Met with in Psycho-Analytic Work" [1915], in *The Standard Edition of the Complete Psychological Works of Sigmund Freud,* 24 vols., trans. from the German under the general editorship of J. Strachey in collaboration with A. Freud (London: Hogarth Press and the Institute of Psycho-Analysis, 1953–74), 14:31.

32. Marx writes: "[T]he use-value of a thing is realized without exchange . . . while, inversely, its value is realized only in exchange. . . . Who would not call to mind at this point the advice given by the good Dogberry to the night-watchman Seacoal?" Karl Marx, "The Fetishism of the Commodity and Its Secret," in *Capital,* vol. 1, *A Critique of Political Economy* [1867], trans. B. Fowkes (New York: Vintage Books, 1977), p. 177.

33. Marx, "The Value-Form, or Exchange-Value," in *Capital,* 1:138.

34. Marx, *The Eighteenth Brumaire of Louis Bonaparte* [1852], trans. E. & C. Paul (New York: International Publishers, 1926), p. 84.

35. Freud, "The Dream Work," in *The Interpretation of Dreams* (part 2), in *Standard Edition,* 5:462.

36. Eleanor Marx, "Letter 1858," in *The Portable Karl Marx,* ed. E. Kamenka (New York: Viking Press, 1983), p. 52.

37. Lawrence A. Cremin, *American Education: The Colonial Experience, 1607–1783* (New York: Harper & Row, 1970), p. 438. This passage is cited in Lawrence W. Levine, *Highbrow/Lowbrow: The Emergence of Cultural Hierarchy in America* (Cambridge, Mass.: Harvard University Press, 1988), p. 37.

38. Mark Twain, "Is Shakespeare Dead?" in *What Is Man? And Other Essays* (New York: Harper & Brothers, 1917), p. 300.

39. Graham Holderness, ed., *The Shakespeare Myth* (Manchester: Manchester University Press, 1988); Michael Dobson, *The Making of the National Poet: Shakespeare Adaptation and Authorship, 1660–1769* (Oxford: Clarendon Press, 1992).

40. Edmund Burke, "Letter III (1797)," in *Select Works,* vol. 3, *Four Letters on the Proposals for Peace with the Regicide Directory of France,* ed. and intro. E. J. Payne (Oxford: Clarendon Press, 1878), p. 163.

41. See Norman Augustine and Kenneth Adelman, *Shakespeare in Charge: The Bard's Guide to Leading and Succeeding on the Business Stage* (New York: Hyperion, 1999); Paul Corrigan, *Shakespeare on Management: Leadership Lessons for Today's Managers* (Dover, N.H.: Kogan Page, 1999); Jay M. Shafritz, *Shakespeare on Management: Wise Business Counsel from the Bard* (New York: HarperBusiness, 1999).

42. Andrew Carnegie, *The Gospel of Wealth and Other Timely Essays,* ed. E. C. Kirkland (Cambridge, Mass.: Belknap Press of Harvard University Press, 1962), pp. 91, 147, 22.

43. Senator Byron L. Dorgan of North Dakota, *Congressional Record,* September 12, 2001.

44. Representative Roscoe Bartlett of Maryland, *Congressional Record,* June 9, 2000.

45. Senator Jeff Bingaman of New Mexico, *Congressional Record,* May 14, 2001.

46. Representative T. Cass Ballenger of North Carolina, *Congressional Record,* March 15, 2000.

47. Representative Clifford B. Stearns of Florida, *Congressional Record,* October 24, 2000.

48. Representative Major Owens of New York, *Congressional Record,* December 15, 2000.

THE TWO GENTLEMEN OF VERONA

1. John Caius, *Of English Dogges*, in *The Works of John Caius, M.D.*, ed. E. S. Roberts (Cambridge: Cambridge University Press, 1912), pp. 17–18.

THE TAMING OF THE SHREW

1. George Gascoigne, *Supposes*, in F. S. Boas, ed., *Five Pre-Shakespearean Comedies* (London: Oxford University Press, 1934), p. 275.

2. James Joyce, *Ulysses* (New York: Vintage Books, 1990), p. 432.

TITUS ANDRONICUS

1. Cited in Jonathan Bate, ed., *Titus Andronicus*, Arden 3rd edition (New York: Routledge, 1995), p. 230.

HENRY VI PART I

1. Edward Hall, *Union of the Two Noble and Illustre Famelies of Lancastre and York* [1548], cited in *Narrative and Dramatic Sources of Shakespeare*, ed. G. Bullough (New York: Columbia University Press, 1960), 3:102, 105–6

2. Ibid., 3:73.

HENRY VI PART 2

1. Raphael Holinshed, *Chronicles of Englande, Scotlande, and Irelande* (London: John Harison, George Bishop, Rafe Newberie, Henrie Denham, and Thomas Woodcocke, 1587), 2:740.

HENRY VI PART 3

1. Raphael Holinshed, *Chronicles of Englande, Scotlande, and Irelande* (London: John Harison, George Bishop, Rafe Newberie, Henrie Denham, and Thomas Woodcocke, 1587), 3:659.

2. George Peele, *The Battle of Alcazar*, ed. J. Yoklavich, vol. 2 of *The Dramatic Works of George Peele*, ed. F. Scott Hook and J. Yoklavich (New Haven, Conn.: Yale University Press, 1961), p. 313.

RICHARD III

1. Sigmund Freud, "The Exceptions," in "Some Character-Types Met with in Psycho-Analytic Work" [1915], in *The Standard Edition of the Complete Psychological Works of Sigmund Freud*, 24 vols., trans. from the German under the general editorship of J. Strachey in collaboration with A. Freud (London: Hogarth Press and the Institute of Psycho-Analysis, 1953–74), 14:313, 315.

A MIDSUMMER NIGHT'S DREAM

1. Elizabeth I, Queen of England, quoted in J. E. Neale, *Elizabeth I and Her Parliaments, 1559–1581* (London and New York: Jonathan Cape in association with British Book Centre, 1953), p. 127.

RICHARD II

1. Edmund Plowden, *The Commentaries, or Reports of Edmund Plowden* [1548–1579] (London, 1816); cited in E. H. Kantorowicz, *The King's Two Bodies* (Princeton, N.J.: Princeton University Press, 1957), p. 7.

2. Ibid., p. 13.

3. Raphael Holinshed, "Henrie the Fourth," in *Chronicles of England, Scotland and Ireland* (1587; London: Brooke, Printer, Paternoster-Row, 1808), 3:14.

KING JOHN

1. Raphael Holinshed, *Chronicles of Englande, Scotlande, and Irelande* (London: John Harison, George Bishop, Rafe Newberie, Henrie Denham, and Thomas Woodcocke, 1587), 3:158.

THE MERCHANT OF VENICE

1. Freud's essay "The Theme of the Three Caskets" can be found in *The Standard Edition of the Complete Psychological Works of Sigmund Freud,* 24 vols., trans. from the German under the general editorship of J. Strachey in collaboration with A. Freud (London: Hogarth Press and the Institute of Psycho-Analysis, 1953–74), 12:291–301. See also my essay "Freud's Choice: 'The Theme of the Three Caskets,' " in *Shakespeare's Ghost Writers* (New York: Methuen, 1987), which subjects Freud himself to the same type of literary and cultural scrutiny that he applies in his interpretation of the three caskets.

2. S. L. Lee, "The Original of Shylock," *Gentleman's Magazine* 246 (1880): 185.

3. William Hazlitt, *"The Merchant of Venice,"* in *Characters of Shakespeare's Plays* (1817; New York: E. P. Dutton, 1906), p. 206.

4. Thomas Hobbes, *Leviathan* [1651], ed. E. Curley (Indianapolis: Hackett, 1994), p. 327.

HENRY IV PART 2

1. Virgil, *Aeneid,* trans. W. F. Jackson Knight (1956; Baltimore: Penguin, 1959), p. 102.

THE MERRY WIVES OF WINDSOR

1. Nicholas Rowe, "Some Account of the Life, &c of Mr. William Shakespear," in *The Works of Mr. William Shakespear,* ed. Nicholas Rowe (1709; London: Pickering & Chatto, 1999), 1:viii–ix.

JULIUS CAESAR

1. William Camden, *The History of the Most Renowned and Victorious Princess Elizabeth, Late Queen of England,* ed. and intro. W. T. MacCaffrey (1688; Chicago: University of Chicago Press, 1970), p. 138.

AS YOU LIKE IT

1. George Puttenham, *The Arte of English Poesie* (1589; London: A. Murry & Son, 1869), p. 53.

2. Erwin Panofsky's *"Et in Arcadia Ego:* Poussin and the Elegiac Tradition," in *Meaning in the Visual Arts* (Garden City, N.Y.: Anchor Books / Doubleday, 1955), pp. 295-320, offers a study of Poussin's work in which Panofsky argues against modern interpretations of the Latin phrase *Et in Arcadia ego* (I, too, was born, or lived, in Arcady) in favor of the traditional interpretation (Death is even in Arcadia).

HAMLET

1. Samuel Taylor Coleridge, *The Collected Works of Samuel Taylor Coleridge,* vol. 14, *Table Talk* [1836], ed. C. Woodring (Princeton, N.J.: Princeton University Press, 1990), p. 77 n. 22.

2. Friedrich Nietzsche, *The Use and Abuse of History* [1873], trans. A. Collins, 2nd rev. ed. (New York: Liberal Arts Press, 1957), p. 6.

3. Ibid., p. 8.

4. Ibid., p. 7.

5. Queen Elizabeth is quoted as saying, "God's death! My Lords, (for that was her oath even in anger,) I have been enforced this day to scour up my old Latin, that hath lain long in rusting"; quoted in "A Letter from Robert Cecil to the Earl of Essex" [1597], in *Narrative and Dramatic Sources of Shakespeare,* vol. 7, *Major Tragedies,* ed. G. Bullough (New York: Columbia University Press, 1973), p. 187.

6. Joan Landis, "Shakespeare's Poland," *Hamlet Studies* 6 (1984): 8–17.

7. Eleanor Prosser's *Hamlet and Revenge,* 2nd ed. (Stanford, Calif.: Stanford University Press, 1971), recounts the innumerable theological arguments surrounding the play. See also Stephen Greenblatt's more

accessible, more recent, new historicist study *Hamlet in Purgatory* (Princeton, N.J.: Princeton University Press, 2001).

8. 6 May 1562, 4 Elizabeth I (referring to the fourth year of Elizabeth's reign). See Maggie Secura, *Life in Elizabethan England: A Compendium of Common Knowledge, 1558–1603,* 7th ed., online edition.

9. Sir Francis Bacon, "Of Revenge," in *The Essayes or Counsels, Civill and Morall* [1597–1625], ed. M. Kiernan (Cambridge, Mass.: Harvard University Press, 1985), p. 16.

10. Giovanni Pico della Mirandola, *Oration on the Dignity of Man,* trans. A. Robert Caponigri (Washington, D.C.: Regnery Gateway, 1956), pp. 8–11.

11. T. S. Eliot, "Hamlet and His Problems," in *The Sacred Wood: Essays on Poetry and Literature,* 2nd ed. (London: Methuen, 1928), pp. 98, 100.

12. E. P. Vining, *The Mystery of Hamlet* (Philadelphia: J. B. Lippincott, 1881).

13. Ibid., p. 59.

14. Sigmund Freud, *The Interpretation of Dreams* [part 1], in *The Standard Edition of the Complete Works of Sigmund Freud,* 24 vols., trans. from the German under the general editorship of J. Strachey in collaboration with A. Freud (London: Hogarth Press and the Institute of Psycho-Analysis, 1953–74), 4:265.

15. Freud to Wilhelm Fliess, in *The Complete Letters of Sigmund Freud to Wilhelm Fliess, 1887–1904,* trans. and ed. J. M. Masson (Cambridge, Mass.: Belknap Press of Harvard University Press, 1985), pp. 272–73.

16. Freud, "Remembering, Repeating, and Working-Through" [1914], in *Standard Edition,* 12:150.

17. Marjorie Garber, "MacGuffin Shakespeare," in *Quotaion Marks* (New York: Routledge, 2002).

TWELFTH NIGHT

1. This is the conjecture of Leslie Hotson in *The First Night of "Twelfth Night"* (London: R. Hart-Davis, 1954), p. 166, as cited by J. M. Lothian and T. W. Craik in their 1974 second-series Arden edition of *Twelfth Night.*

2. Daniel J. Boorstin, *The Image: A Guide to Pseudo-Events in America* (New York: Atheneum, 1964), p. 45.

3. 15 June 1574, 16 Elizabeth I, in Maggie Secura, *Life in Elizabethan England: A Compendium of Common Knowledge, 1558–1603,* 7th ed., online edition.

TROILUS AND CRESSIDA

1. As per the Norton edition, the line here—providing the contrast to "Th'unworthiest"—may be lost.

MEASURE FOR MEASURE

1. Samuel Taylor Coleridge, *Specimens of the Table Talk of the Late Samuel Taylor Coleridge,* ed. H. N. Coleridge (New York: Harper & Brothers, 1836), p. 85.

2. *A Sermon preached at Westminster before the King and Queenes Maiesties at their Coronations . . . by the Lord Bishop of Winchester* (1603), sig. A6. Cited in the Arden edition of *Measure for Measure,* ed. J. W. Lever (Walton-on-Thames, Surrey: Thomas Nelson, 1997), p. lxiv.

3. Thomas Hobbes, "Of Persons, Authors, and Things Personated," in *Leviathan* [1651], ed. E. Curley (Indianapolis: Hackett, 1994), p. 101.

4. Sir Walter Ralegh, "On the Life of Man" [1612], in *Sir Walter Ralegh: Selected Writings,* ed. G. Hammond (Manchester: Carcanet Press, 1984), p. 55.

OTHELLO

1. Thomas Rymer, "Othello," in *A Short View of Tragedy* (1693; Yorkshire: Scholar Press, 1970), pp. 89, 139–40, 146.

2. Samuel Johnson, *Johnson on Shakespeare,* vols. 7–8 of *The Works of Samuel Johnson,* 2- vol. facsimile, ed. Arthur Sherbo (New Haven, Conn.: Yale University Press, 1968), p. 1045.

TIMON OF ATHENS

1. *Timon of Athens,* Arden 3rd edition, ed. H. J. Oliver (London: Methuen, 1963), pp. 116–17.

KING LEAR

1. Henry S. Turner, "King Lear Without: The Heath," *Renaissance Drama* 28 (1997): 161–93.

MACBETH

1. George Russell French, *Shakespeareana Genealogica* (London: Macmillan, 1869), p. 296; cited in the Arden edition of *Macbeth,* ed. Kenneth Muir (London: Methuen, 1951), p. 146.

ANTONY AND CLEOPATRA

1. John Knox, *Selected Writings of John Knox: Public Epistles, Treatises, and Expositions to the Year 1559,* ed. Kevin Reed (Dallas: Presbyterian Heritage Publications, 1995), pp. 14, 30.
2. Ibid., p. 59.

PERICLES

1. Sigmund Freud, "The Dream-Work," in *The Interpretation of Dreams,* trans. and ed. J. Strachey (New York: Avon Books, 1965), pp. 389–92.

CORIOLANUS

1. William Safire, "Swarmin' for Norman," *New York Times,* March 18, 1991, p. A14.
2. F. J. Furnivall, introduction to the *Leopold Shakspere* (London: Cassell, Better, & Galpin, 1877), p. lxxxiii.
3. Livy, *History of Rome,* trans. B. O. Foster (Cambridge, Mass.: Harvard University Press, 1967), 1:323–25.

CYMBELINE

1. *Edmund Spenser's Poetry,* 2nd ed., ed. H. Maclean (1968; New York: Norton, 1982), p. 7 n. 4, p. 7 n. 6.
2. Michel de Montaigne "Of Cannibals," in *The Essays of Michel de Montaigne,* trans. and ed. M. A. Screech (London: Allen Lane / Penguin Press, 1991), p. 236.
3. Algernon Charles Swinburne, *A Study of Shakespeare,* 3rd ed., rev. (1880; London: Chatto & Windus, 1895), p. 227.
4. William Camden, *Remains Concerning Britain* [1605], ed. R. D. Dunn (Toronto and Buffalo: University of Toronto Press, 1984), p. 139.

THE TEMPEST

1. Michel de Montaigne, "Of Cannibals," in *The Essays of Michel de Montaigne,* trans. and ed. M. A. Screech (London: Allen Lane/Penguin Press, 1991), p. 236.

HENRY VIII (ALL IS TRUE)

1. *The Life and Letters of Sir Henry Wotton,* ed. Logan Pearsall Smith (Oxford: Clarendon Press, 1907), 2:32–33.

THE TWO NOBLE KINSMEN

1. John Fletcher and William Shakespeare, *The Two Noble Kinsmen,* Arden 3rd ed., ed. L. Potter (Walton-on-Thames, Surrey: Thomas Nelson, 1997), p. 328.
2. John Aubrey, *Brief Lives,* ed. Andrew Clark (Oxford: Clarendon Press, 1898), 1:96.

SUGGESTIONS FOR FURTHER READING

This list of selected readings includes both articles and book chapters. In many bibliographies, only the title of a book is given, making it unclear where within that book the reader might find a specific treatment of one or another of Shakespeare's plays; as a result, some fine treatments of the plays are occasionally overlooked. The citations here are in part an attempt to make both books and articles more accessible to interested readers. In entries referring to an essay or chapter that has been reprinted in another volume, the original date and place of publication, as well as the more recent reprint, are indicated below. For many of the plays, a list of films has also been included.

ABBREVIATIONS

CD	*Comparative Drama*
CI	*Critical Inquiry*
CL	*Comparative Literature*
CQ	*Critical Quarterly*
ELH	*A Journal of English Literary History*
ELR	*English Literary Renaissance*
MLQ	*Modern Language Quarterly*
MLR	*Modern Language Review*
PMLA	*Publications of the Modern Language Association of America*
RD	*Renaissance Drama*
RQ	*Renaissance Quarterly*
SEL	*Studies in English Literature 1500–1900*
SQ	*Shakespeare Quarterly*
SS	*Shakespeare Survey*
SSt	*Shakespeare Studies*

SHAKESPEARE EDITIONS
MULTIVOLUME EDITIONS

The Arden Shakespeare, 3rd series, gen. eds. Richard Proudfoot, Anne Thompson, and David Scott Kastan. London: Arden Shakespeare.

The New Cambridge Shakespeare, gen. ed. Brian Gibbons, associate gen. ed. A. R. Braunmuller. Cambridge: Cambridge University Press.

The New Folger Library Shakespeare, ed. Barbara A. Mowat and Paul Werstine. New York: Simon & Schuster.

SINGLE-VOLUME EDITIONS

The Complete Works of Shakespeare, 5th ed., ed. David Bevington. New York: Longman, 2003.

The Complete Pelican Shakespeare, ed. Stephen Orgel and A. R. Braunmuller. New York: Penguin, 2002.

The Norton Shakespeare, gen. ed. Stephen J. Greenblatt, ed. Walter Cohen, Jean E. Howard, and Katharine Eisaman Maus. New York: Norton, 1997.

The Oxford Shakespeare, ed. Stanley Wells and Gary Taylor. Oxford: Clarendon Press, 1986.

The Riverside Shakespeare: The Complete Works, 2nd ed., ed. G. Blakemore Evans and J.J.M. Tobin. Boston: Houghton Mifflin, 1997.

THE TWO GENTLEMEN OF VERONA

Brooks, Harold F. "Two Clowns in a Comedy (to Say Nothing of the Dog): Speed, Launce (and Crab) in *The Two Gentlemen of Verona*." *Essays and Studies: Collected for the English Association* 16 (1963): 91–100.

Lindenbaum, Peter. "Education in *The Two Gentlemen of Verona*." *SEL* 15 (1975): 229–44.

Masten, Jeffrey. "Between Gentlemen: Homoeroticism, Collaboration, and the Discourse of Friendship." In *Textual Intercourse: Collaboration, Authorship, and Sexualities in Renaissance Drama*. Cambridge: Cambridge University Press, 1997.

Rossky, William. "*The Two Gentlemen of Verona* as Burlesque." *ELR* 12 (1982): 210–19.

Simmons, J. L. "Coming Out in Shakespeare's *The Two Gentlemen of Verona*." *ELR* 60 (1993): 857–77.

Skura, Meredith. "*Two Gentlemen of Verona*: Woman's Part, Dog's Part." In *Shakespeare the Actor and the Purposes of Playing*. Chicago: University of Chicago Press, 1993.

Smith, Bruce. "Combatants and Comrades." In *Homosexual Desire in Shakespeare's England: A Cultural Poetics*. Chicago: University of Chicago Press, 1991.

Weimann, Robert. "Laughing with the Audience: *The Two Gentlemen of Verona* and the Popular Tradition of Comedy." *SS* 22 (1969): 35–42.

THE TAMING OF THE SHREW

Boose, Lynda. "Scolding Brides and Bridling Scolds: Taming the Woman's Unruly Member." *SQ* 42.2 (1991): 179–213.

Fineman, Joel. "The Turn of the Shrew." In *Shakespeare and the Question of Theory*, ed. Patricia Parker and Geoffrey Hartman. New York: Methuen, 1985.

Freedman, Barbara. "Taming Difference in *The Taming of the Shrew*." In *Staging the Gaze: Postmodernism, Psychoanalysis, and Shakespearean Comedy*. Ithaca, N.Y.: Cornell University Press, 1991.

Haring-Smith, Tori. *From Farce to Metadrama: A Stage History of "The Taming of the Shrew," 1594–1983*. Westport, Conn.: Greenwood Press, 1985.

Marcus, Leah. "The Editor as Tamer: *A Shrew* and *The Shrew*." In *Unediting the Renaissance: Shakespeare, Marlowe, Milton*. New York: Routledge, 1996.

———. "The Shakespearean Editor as Shrew-Tamer." *ELR* 22 (1992): 177–200.

Newman, Karen. "Renaissance Family Politics and Shakespeare's *Taming of the Shrew*." In *Fashioning Femininity and English Renaissance Drama*. Chicago: University of Chicago Press, 1991.

Novy, Marianne L. "Patriarchy and Play in *The Taming of the Shrew*." In *Love's Argument: Gender Relations in Shakespeare*. Chapel Hill: University of North Carolina Press, 1984.

Roberts, Jeanne Addison. "Horses and Hermaphrodites: Metamorphoses in *The Taming of the Shrew*." *SQ* 34.2 (1983): 159–71.

Underdown, David. "The Taming of the Scold: The Enforcement of Patriarchal Authority in Early Modern England." In *Order and Disorder in Early Modern England*, ed. Anthony Fletcher and John Stevenson. Cambridge: Cambridge University Press, 1985.

FILMS AND FILM ADAPTATIONS

The Taming of the Shrew (Mary Pickford, Douglas Fairbanks), dir. Sam Taylor, 1929.
Kiss Me Kate (Kathryn Grayson, Howard Keel), dir. George Sidney, 1953.
The Taming of the Shrew (Elizabeth Taylor, Richard Burton), dir. Franco Zeffirelli, 1967.

TITUS ANDRONICUS

Barker, Francis. "A Wilderness of Tigers: *Titus Andronicus,* Anthropology, and the Occlusion of Violence." In *The Culture of Violence: Essays on Tragedy and History.* Chicago: University of Chicago Press, 1993.

Eaton, Sara. "A Woman of Letters: Lavinia in *Titus Andronicus.*" In *Shakespearean Tragedy and Gender,* ed. Shirley Nelson Garner and Madelon Sprengnether. Bloomington: Indiana University Press, 1996.

James, Heather. "Cultural Disintegration in *Titus Andronicus:* Mutilating Titus, Vergil, and Rome." In *Violence in Drama,* ed. James Redmond. Cambridge: Cambridge University Press, 1991.

Jones, Eldred. *Othello's Countrymen: The African in English Renaissance Drama.* London: Oxford University Press, 1965.

Kahn, Coppélia. "The Daughter's Seduction in *Titus Andronicus,* or, Writing Is the Best Revenge." In *Roman Shakespeare: Warriors, Wounds, and Women.* New York: Routledge, 1997.

Miola, Robert. *Shakespeare's Rome.* Cambridge: Cambridge University Press, 1983.

Noble, Louise. " 'And Make Two Pastries of Your Shameful Heads': Medicinal Cannibalism and Healing the Body Politic in *Titus Andronicus.*" *ELH* 70.3 (2003): 677–708.

Rowe, Katherine. "Dismembering and Forgetting in *Titus Andronicus.*" *SQ* 45.3 (1994): 279–303. Reprinted as " 'Effectless Use': Dismembering and Forgetting in *Titus Andronicus.*" In *Dead Hands: Fictions as Agency, Renaissance to Modern.* Stanford, Calif.: Stanford University Press, 1999.

Spivack, Bernard. *Shakespeare and the Allegory of Evil: The History of a Metaphor in Relation to His Major Villains.* New York: Columbia University Press, 1958.

Stamm, Rudolf. "The Alphabet of Speechless Complaint: A Study of the Mangled Daughter in Shakespeare's *Titus Andronicus.*" In *The Triple Bond: Plays, Mainly Shakespearean, in Performance,* ed. Joseph G. Price. University Park: Pennsylvania State University Press, 1975.

Stimpson, Catharine. "Shakespeare and the Soil of Rape." In *The Woman's Part: Feminist Criticism of Shakespeare,* ed. Carolyn Ruth Swift Lenz, Gayle Greene, and Carol Thomas Neely. Urbana: University of Illinois Press, 1980.

Waith, Eugene. "The Metamorphosis of Violence in *Titus Andronicus.*" *SS* 27 (1957): 39–59.

Willbern, David. "Rape and Revenge in *Titus Andronicus.*" *ELR* 8 (1978): 159–82.

Willis, Deborah. " 'The Gnawing Vulture': Revenge, Trauma Theory, and *Titus Andronicus.*" *SQ* 53.1 (2002): 21–52.

Wynne-Davies, Marion. " 'The Swallowing Womb': Consumed and Consuming Women in *Titus Andronicus.*" In *The Matter of Difference: Materialist Feminist Criticism of Shakespeare,* ed. Valerie Wayne and Catherine Belsey. Ithaca, N.Y.: Cornell University Press, 1993.

FILMS AND FILM ADAPTATIONS

Titus Andronicus (Candy K. Sweet, Lexton Raleigh), dir. Christopher Dunne, 1999.
Titus (Jessica Lange, Anthony Hopkins), dir. Julie Taymor, 1999.

HENRY VI PART I

Berman, Ronald. "Fathers and Sons in the *Henry VI* Plays." *SQ* 13.4 (1962): 487–97.

Burckhardt, Sigurd. " 'I Am But Shadow of Myself': Ceremony and Design in *1 Henry VI.*" *MLQ* 28 (1967): 139–58. Reprinted in *Shakespearean Meanings.* Princeton, N.J.: Princeton University Press, 1968.

Jackson, Gabriele Bernhard. "Topical Ideology: Witches, Amazons, and Shakespeare's Joan of Arc." *ELR* 18 (1988): 40–65.

Kurtz, Martha A. "Tears and Masculinity in the History Plays: Shakespeare's *Henry VI.*" In *Grief and Gender, 700–1700,* ed. Jennifer C. Vaught with Lynne Dickson Bruckner. New York: Palgrave Macmillan, 2003.

Lull, Janis. "Plantagenets, Lancastrians, Yorkists, and Tudors: *1–3 Henry VI, Richard III, Edward III*." In *The Cambridge Companion to Shakespeare's History Plays*, ed. Michael Hattaway. Cambridge: Cambridge University Press, 2002.

Marcus, Leah. "Elizabeth." In *Puzzling Shakespeare: Local Reading and Its Discontents*. Berkeley: University of California Press, 1988.

Rackin, Phyllis. "Patriarchal History and Female Subversion." In *Stages of History: Shakespeare's English Chronicles*. Ithaca, N.Y.: Cornell University Press, 1990.

Riggs, David. *Shakespeare's Heroical Histories: "Henry VI" and Its Literary Tradition*. Cambridge, Mass.: Harvard University Press, 1971.

Saccio, Peter. "Henry VI: The Loss of Empire." In *Shakespeare's English Kings: History, Chronicle, and Drama*. New York: Oxford University Press, 1977.

HENRY VI PART 2

Bernthal, Craig A. "Jack Cade's Legal Carnival." *SEL* 42 (2002): 259–74.

Berry, Edward. "*2 Henry VI:* Justice and Law." In *Patterns of Decay: Shakespeare's Early Histories*. Charlottesville: University Press of Virginia, 1975.

Cartelli, Thomas. "Jack Cade in the Garden: Class Consciousness and Class Conflict in *2 Henry VI*." In *Enclosure Acts: Sexuality, Property, and Culture in Early Modern England*, ed. Richard Burt and John Michael Archer. Ithaca, N.Y.: Cornell University Press, 1994.

Greenblatt, Stephen. "Murdering Peasants: Status, Genre, and the Representation of Rebellion." *Representations* 1 (1983): 1–30. Reprinted in *Learning to Curse: Essays in Early Modern Culture*. New York: Routledge, 1990.

Harvey, I.M.W. *Jack Cade's Rebellion of 1450*. Oxford: Clarendon Press; New York: Oxford University Press, 1991.

Helgerson, Richard. "Staging Exclusion." In *Forms of Nationhood: The Elizabethan Writing of England*. Chicago: University of Chicago Press, 1992.

Manley, Lawrence. "From Strange's Men to Pembroke's Men: *2 Henry VI* and *The First Part of the Contention*." *SQ* 54.3 (2003): 253–87.

Manning, Roger B. "Apprentice Riots in London." In *Village Revolts: Social Protest and Popular Disturbances in England, 1509–1640*. Oxford: Clarendon Press, 1988.

Patterson, Annabel. "The Peasant's Toe: Popular Culture and Popular Pressure." In *Shakespeare and the Popular Voice*. Cambridge, Mass.: Basil Blackwell, 1989.

Urkowitz, Steven. "'If I Mistake in These Foundations Which I Build Upon': Peter Alexander's Textual Analysis of *Henry VI Parts 2 and 3*." *ELR* 18 (1988): 230–56.

HENRY VI PART 3

Hodgdon, Barbara. "Enclosing Contention: *1, 2,* and *3 Henry VI*." In *The End Crowns All: Closure and Contradiction in Shakespeare's History*. Princeton, N.J.: Princeton University Press, 1991.

Kahn, Coppélia. "'The Shadow of the Male': Masculine Identity in the History Plays." In *Man's Estate: Masculine Identity in Shakespeare*. Berkeley: University of California Press, 1981.

Leggatt, Alexander. "*Henry VI.*" In *Shakespeare's Political Drama: The History Plays and the Roman Plays*. New York: Routledge, 1988.

Schwarz, Kathryn. "Fearful Simile: Stealing the Breech in Shakespeare's Chronicle Plays." *SQ* 49.2 (1998): 140–67. Reprinted in *Tough Love: Amazon Encounters in the English Renaissance*. Durham, N.C.: Duke University Press, 2000.

Tillyard, E.M.W. "The Third Part of Henry VI." In *Shakespeare's History Plays*, 1944. New York: Penguin, 1991.

Willis, Deborah. *Malevolent Nurture: Witch-hunting and Maternal Power in Early Modern England*. Ithaca, N.Y.: Cornell University Press, 1995.

RICHARD III

Burnett, Mark Thornton. " 'Monsters' and 'Molas': Body Politics in *Richard III.*" In *Constructing "Monsters" in Shakespearean Drama and Early Modern Culture.* New York: Palgrave Macmillan, 2002.

Carroll, William C. " 'The Form of Law': Ritual and Succession in *Richard III.*" In *True Rites and Maimed Rites: Ritual and Anti-Ritual in Shakespeare and His Age,* ed. Linda Woodbridge and Edward Berry. Urbana: University of Illinois Press, 1992.

Clemen, Wolfgang H. *A Commentary on Shakespeare's "Richard III."* London: Methuen, 1968.

Dubrow, Heather. " 'I Fear There Will a Worse Come in His Place': Surrogate Parents and Shakespeare's *Richard III.*" In *Maternal Measures: Figuring Caregiving in the Early Modern Period,* ed. Naomi J. Miller and Naomi Yavneh. Brookfield, Vt.: Ashgate, 2000.

Freud, Sigmund. "Some Character-Types Met With in Psycho-Analytic Work" (1916). In *Character and Culture,* ed. Philip Rieff. New York: Collier Books, 1961.

Garber, Marjorie. "Descanting on Deformity: Richard III and the Shape of History." In *Shakespeare's Ghost Writers: Literature as Uncanny Causality.* New York: Routledge, 1987.

Hunter, Robert G. *Shakespeare and the Mystery of God's Judgments.* Athens: University of Georgia Press, 1976.

Levin, Harry. "Two Tents on Bosworth Field: *Richard III,* V.iii, iv, v." *Canadian Review of Comparative Literature* 18.2–3 (1991): 199–216. Reprinted in *Reading the Renaissance: Culture, Poetics, and Drama,* ed. Jonathan Hart. New York: Garland, 1996.

Marche, Steven. "Mocking Dead Bones: Historical Memory and the Theater of the Dead in *Richard III.*" *CD* 37.1 (2003): 37–57.

Ornstein, Robert. *A Kingdom for a Stage: The Achievement of Shakespeare's History Plays,* esp. chaps. 1, 3, and 10. Cambridge, Mass.: Harvard University Press, 1972.

Rossiter, A. P. "Angel with Horns: The Unity of *Richard III.*" In *Angel with Horns and Other Shakespeare Lectures.* New York: Theater Arts Books, 1961.

Steible, Mary. "Jane Shore and the Politics of Cursing." *SEL* 43.1 (2003): 1–17.

Targoff, Ramie. " 'Dirty' Amens: Devotion, Applause, and Consent in *Richard III.*" *RD* 31 (2002): 61–84.

Tillyard, E.M.W. "Richard III." In *Shakespeare's History Plays,* 1944. New York: Penguin, 1991.

FILMS AND FILM ADAPTATIONS

Richard III (Robert Gemp, Frederick Warde), dir. André Calmettes and James Keane, 1912.

Richard III (Laurence Olivier, John Gielgud), dir. Laurence Olivier, 1955.

Richard III (Ian McKellen, Robert Downey Jr.), dir. Richard Loncraine, 1995.

Looking for Richard (Al Pacino, Kevin Spacey), dir. Al Pacino, 1996.

THE COMEDY OF ERRORS

Bishop, T. G. "Compounding *Errors.*" In *Shakespeare and the Theatre of Wonder.* Cambridge: Cambridge University Press, 1996.

Brooks, Harold F. "Themes and Structure in *The Comedy of Errors.*" In *Early Shakespeare,* ed. John R. Brown and Bernard Harris. New York: Schocken, 1966. Reprinted in *The Comedy of Errors: Critical Essays,* ed. Robert S. Miola. New York: Routledge, 1997.

Candido, Joseph. "Dining Out in Ephesus: Food in *The Comedy of Errors.*" *SEL* 30 (1990): 217–41.

Clubb, Louise G. "Italian Comedy and *The Comedy of Errors.*" *CL* 19 (1967): 240–51.

Freedman, Barbara. "Egeon's Debt: Self-Division and Self-Redemption in *The Comedy of Errors.*" *ELR* 10 (1980): 360–83.

Frye, Northrop. "The Argument of Comedy." In *English Institute Essays.* New York: AMS Press, 1948.

Girard, René. "Comedies of Errors: Plautus—Shakespeare—Molière." In *American Criticism in the Poststructuralist Age,* ed. Ira Konigsberg. Ann Arbor: University of Michigan Press, 1981.

Kehler, Dorothea. "Shakespeare's Emilias and the Politics of Celibacy." In *In Another Country: Feminist Perspectives on Renaissance Drama,* ed. Dorothea Kehler and Susan Baker. Metuchen, N.J.: Scarecrow Press, 1991.

Miola, Robert. *Shakespeare and Classical Comedy: The Influence of Plautus and Terence.* New York: Oxford University Press, 1994.

Salingar, Leo. *Shakespeare and the Traditions of Comedy.* Cambridge and New York: Cambridge University Press, 1974.

Shaw, Catherine. "The Conscious Art of *The Comedy of Errors.*" In *Shakespearean Comedy,* ed. Maurice Charney. New York: New York Literary Forum, 1980.

LOVE'S LABOUR'S LOST

Barber, C. L. "The Folly of Wit and Masquerade in *Love's Labour's Lost.*" In *Shakespeare's Festive Comedy: A Study of Dramatic Form and Its Relation to Social Custom.* Princeton, N.J.: Princeton University Press, 1959.

Breitenberg, Mark. "The Anatomy of Masculine Desire in *Love's Labour's Lost.*" SQ 43 (1992): 430–49.

Carroll, William C. *The Great Feast of Language in "Love's Labour's Lost."* Princeton, N.J.: Princeton University Press, 1976.

Colie, Rosalie. "Criticism and the Analysis of Craft: *Love's Labour's Lost* and the Sonnets." In *Shakespeare's Living Art.* Princeton, N.J.: Princeton University Press, 1974.

Corum, Richard. " 'The Catastrophe Is a Nuptial': *Love's Labour's Lost,* Tactics, Everyday Life." In *Renaissance Culture and the Everyday,* ed. Patricia Fumerton and Simon Hunt. Philadelphia: University of Pennsylvania Press, 1999.

Elam, Keir. *Shakespeare's Universe of Discourse: Language-Games in the Comedies.* Cambridge and New York: Cambridge University Press, 1984.

Ellis, Herbert. *Shakespeare's Lusty Punning in "Love's Labour's Lost."* The Hague: Mouton, 1973.

Evans, Malcolm. "The Converse of Breath." In *Signifying Nothing: Truth's True Contents in Shakespeare's Text.* Brighton, UK: Harvester, 1986.

Maus, Katherine Eisaman. "Transfer of Title in *Love's Labour's Lost:* Language, Individualism, Gender." In *Shakespeare Left and Right,* ed. Ivo Kamps. New York: Routledge, 1991.

Mazzio, Carla. "The Melancholy of Print: *Love's Labour's Lost.*" In *Historicism, Psychoanalysis, and Early Modern Culture,* ed. Carla Mazzio and Douglas Trevor. New York: Routledge, 2000.

Montrose, Louis Adrian. *"Curious-Knotted Garden": The Form, Themes, and Contexts of Shakespeare's "Love's Labour's Lost."* Salzburg: Institut für Englische Sprache und Literatur der Universität Salzburg, 1977.

Pater, Walter. "On *Love's Labour's Lost.*" In *Appreciations, with an Essay on Style,* 1924. Folcroft, Pa.: Folcroft Library Editions, 1978.

Skura, Meredith. "Armando and Costard in the French Academy: Player as Clown." In *Shakespeare the Actor and the Purposes of Playing.* Chicago: University of Chicago Press, 1993.

FILM AND FILM ADAPTATIONS

Love's Labour's Lost (Kenneth Branagh, Alicia Silverstone), dir. Kenneth Branagh, 2000.

ROMEO AND JULIET

Belsey, Catherine. "The Name of the Rose in *Romeo and Juliet.*" *Yearbook of English Studies* 23 (1993): 126–42. Reprinted in *Shakespeare's Tragedies,* ed. Susan Zimmerman. New York: St. Martin's Press, 1998.

Cartwright, Kent. "Theater and Narrative in *Romeo and Juliet.*" In *Shakespearean Tragedy and Its Double: The Rhythms of Audience Response.* University Park: Pennsylvania State University Press, 1991.

Coleridge, S. T. "Lecture VII." In *Shakespearean Criticism,* ed. Thomas Middleton Raysor. Cambridge, Mass.: Harvard University Press, 1930.

Garber, Marjorie. "Apparent Prodigies." In *Dream in Shakespeare: From Metaphor to Metamorphosis.* New Haven, Conn.: Yale University Press, 1974.

———. *Coming of Age in Shakespeare.* London: Methuen, 1981.

Kahn, Coppélia. "Coming of Age in Verona." In *The Woman's Part: Feminist Criticism of Shakespeare,* ed. Carolyn Ruth Swift Lenz, Gayle Green, and Carol Thomas Neely. Urbana: University of Illinois Press, 1983.

Kristeva, Julia. "*Romeo and Juliet:* Love-Hatred in the Couple." In *Tales of Love,* trans. Leon S. Roudiez. New York: Columbia University Press, 1987. Reprinted in *Shakespearean Tragedy,* ed. John Drakakis. London and New York: Longman, 1992.

Levenson, Jill L. "Editing *Romeo and Juliet:* 'A challenge[,] on my life.' " In *New Ways of Looking at Old Texts II,* ed. W. Speed Hill. Tempe, Ariz.: Medieval and Renaissance Texts and Studies in conjunction with Renaissance English Text Society, 1998.

Liebler, Naomi Conn. " 'There is no world without Verona walls': The City in *Romeo and Juliet.*" In *A Companion to Shakespeare's Works,* vol. I, ed. Richard Dutton and Jean E. Howard. Malden, Mass.: Blackwell Publishing, 2003.

Moisan, Thomas. " 'O Any Thing of Nothing, First Create!': Gender and Patriarchy and the Tragedy of *Romeo and Juliet.*" In *In Another Country: Feminist Perspectives on Renaissance Drama,* ed. Dorothea Kehler and Susan Baker. Metuchen, N.J.: Scarecrow Press, 1991.

Nevo, Ruth. "Tragic Form in *Romeo and Juliet.*" *SEL* 9 (1969): 241–58.

Pollard, Tanya. " 'A Thing Like Death': Sleeping Potions and Poisons in *Romeo and Juliet* and *Antony and Cleopatra.*" *RD* 32 (2003): 95–121.

Porter, Joseph. *Shakespeare's Mercutio: His History and Drama.* Chapel Hill: University of North Carolina Press, 1988.

Snow, Edward. "Language and Sexual Difference in *Romeo and Juliet.*" In *Shakespeare's "Rough Magic": Renaissance Essays in Honor of C. L. Barber,* ed. Peter Erickson and Coppélia Kahn. Newark: University of Delaware Press, 1985.

FILMS AND FILM ADAPTATIONS

Romeo and Juliet (Norma Shearer, Leslie Howard), dir. George Cukor, 1936.

Romeo and Juliet (Laurence Harvey, Susan Shentall, John Gielgud), dir. Renato Castellani, 1954.

Romeo and Juliet (Leonard Whiting, Olivia Hussey), dir. Franco Zeffirelli, 1968.

William Shakespeare's Romeo + Juliet (Leonardo DiCaprio, Claire Danes), dir. Baz Luhrman, 1996.

A MIDSUMMER NIGHT'S DREAM

Barber, C. L. "May Games and Metamorphoses on a Midsummer's Night." In *Shakespeare's Festive Comedy: A Study of Dramatic Form and Its Relation to Social Custom.* Princeton, N.J.: Princeton University Press, 1959.

Bate, Jonathan. *Shakespeare and Ovid.* Oxford: Clarendon Press, 1993.

Boehrer, Bruce. "Bestial Buggery in *A Midsummer Night's Dream.*" In *Shakespeare Among the Animals: Nature and Society in the Drama of Early Modern England.* New York: Palgrave, 2002.

Briggs, Katherine Mary. *The Anatomy of Puck.* London: Routledge and Kegan Paul, 1959.

Freedman, Barbara. "Dis/Figuring Power." In *Staging the Gaze: Postmodernism, Psychoanalysis, and Shakespearean Comedy.* Ithaca, N.Y.: Cornell University Press, 1991.

Garber, Marjorie. "Spirits of Another Sort." In *Dream in Shakespeare: From Metaphor to Metamorphosis.* New Haven, Conn.: Yale University Press, 1974.

Girard, René. "Myth and Ritual in Shakespeare: *A Midsummer Night's Dream.*" In *Textual Strategies: Perspectives in Post-Structuralist Criticism,* ed. Josué V. Harari. Ithaca, N.Y.: Cornell University Press, 1979.

Kott, Jan. "Titania and the Ass's Head." In *Shakespeare Our Contemporary,* 2nd ed., trans. Boleslaw Taborski. London: Methuen, 1967.

Marshall, David. "Exchanging Visions." *ELH* 49.3 (1982): 543–75.

Montrose, Louis Adrian. " 'Shaping Fantasies': Figurations of Gender and Power in Elizabethan Culture." *Representations* 2 (1983): 61–94. Reprinted in *The Purpose of Playing: Shakespeare and the Cultural Politics of the Elizabethan Theatre.* Chicago: University of Chicago Press, 1996.

Parker, Patricia. "(Peter) Quince: Love Potions, Carpenter's Coins, and Athenian Weddings." *SS* 56 (2003): 39–54.

———. "Rude Mechanicals." In *Subject and Object in Renaissance Culture,* ed. Margreta de Grazia, Maureen Quilligan, and Peter Stallybrass. Philadelphia: University of Pennsylvania Press, 1996.

Patterson, Annabel. "Bottom's UP: Festive Theory in *A Midsummer Night's Dream.*" *Renaissance Papers* (1988): 25–39. Reprinted as "Bottom's UP: Festive Theory," in *Shakespeare and the Popular Voice.* Cambridge, Mass.: Basil Blackwell, 1989.

Schwarz, Kathryn. "Tragical Mirth: Framing Shakespeare's Hippolyta." In *Tough Love: Amazon Encounters in the Renaissance.* Durham, N.C.: Duke University Press, 2000.

Young, David. *Something of Great Constancy: The Art of "A Midsummer Night's Dream."* New Haven, Conn.: Yale University Press, 1966.

FILMS AND FILM ADAPTATIONS

A Midsummer Night's Dream (Mickey Rooney, James Cagney), dir. Max Reinhardt and William Dieterle, 1935.

A Midsummer Night's Dream (Diana Rigg, Helen Mirren), dir. Peter Hall, 1968.

A Midsummer Night's Dream (Michelle Pfeiffer, Calista Flockhart), dir. Michael Hoffman, 1999.

RICHARD II

Berger, Harry, Jr. "*Richard II* 3.2: An Exercise in Imaginary Audition." *ELH* 55.4 (1988): 755–96. Reprinted in *Imaginary Audition: Shakespeare on Stage and Page* (Berkeley: University of California Press, 1989).

Bergeron, David. "*Richard II* and Carnival Politics." *SQ* 42.1 (1991): 33–43.

Calderwood, James L. "*Richard II* and the Fall of Speech." In *Shakespearean Metadrama: The Argument of the Play in "Titus Andronicus," "Love's Labour's Lost," "A Midsummer Night's Dream," and "Richard II."* Minneapolis: University of Minnesota Press, 1971.

Clegg, Cyndia Susan. " 'By the choise and inuitation of al the realme': *Richard II* and Elizabethan Press Censorship." *SQ* 48.4 (1997): 432–48.

Gaudet, Paul. "The 'Parasitical Counselors' in Shakespeare's *Richard II:* A Problem in Dramatic Interpretation." *SQ* 33.2 (1982): 142–54.

Goldberg, Jonathan. "Rebel Letters: Postal Effects from *Richard II* to *Henry IV.*" *RD* 19 (1988): 3–28. Reprinted in *Shakespeare's Hand.* Minneapolis: University of Minnesota Press, 2003.

Howard, Jean E., and Phyllis Rackin. "*Richard II.*" In *Engendering a Nation: A Feminist Account of Shakespeare's English Histories.* London and New York: Routledge, 1997.

Hutson, Lorna. "Not the King's Two Bodies: Reading the 'Body Politic' in Shakespeare's *Henry IV,* Parts 1 and 2." In *Rhetoric and Law in Early Modern Europe,* ed. Victoria Kahn and Lorna Hutson. New Haven, Conn.: Yale University Press, 2001.

Kantorowicz, Ernst Hartwig. *The King's Two Bodies: A Study in Medieval Political Theology.* Princeton, N.J.: Princeton University Press, 1957.

Kastan, David Scott. "Proud Majesty Made a Subject: Shakespeare and the Spectacle of Rule." *SQ* 37.4 (1986): 459–75. Reprinted in *Shakespeare After Theory.* New York: Routledge, 1999.

McDonald, Russ. "Uneasy Lies: Language and History in Shakespeare's Lancastrian Tetralogy." *SQ* 35.1 (1984): 22–39.

McMillin, Scott. "*Richard II:* Eyes of Sorrow, Eyes of Desire." *SQ* 35.1 (1984): 40–52.

Moore, Jeanie Grant. "Queen of Sorrow, King of Grief: Reflections and Perspectives in *Richard II.*" In *In Another Country: Feminist Perspectives on Renaissance Drama,* ed. Dorothea Kehler and Susan Baker. Metuchen, N.J.: Scarecrow Press, 1991.

Pye, Christopher. "The Betrayal of the Gaze: Theatricality and Power in Shakespeare's *Richard II.*" *ELH* 55.3 (1988): 575–98.

Saccio, Peter. "*Richard II:* The Fall of the King." In *Shakespeare's English Kings: History, Chronicle, and Drama.* Oxford: Oxford University Press, 1977.

Tillyard, E.M.W. "Richard II." In *Shakespeare's History Plays.* 1944; New York: Penguin, 1991.

Zitner, Sheldon. "Aumerle's Conspiracy." *SEL* 14.2 (1974): 239–57.

FILMS AND FILM ADAPTATIONS

Richard II (Derek Jacobi, John Gielgud), dir. David Giles, 1978.

King Richard II (David Birney, Paul Shenar), dir. William Woodman, 1982.

KING JOHN

Braunmuller, A. R. "*King John* and Historiography." *ELH* 55.2 (1988): 309–32.

Burckhardt, Sigurd. "King John: The Ordering of This Present Time." *ELH* 33.2 (1966): 133–53. Reprinted in *Shakespearean Meanings*. Princeton, N.J.: Princeton University Press, 1968.

Dusinberre, Juliet. "*King John* and Embarrassing Women." *SS* 42 (1989): 37–52.

Findlay, Alison. *Illegitimate Power: Bastards in Renaissance Drama*. Manchester, UK: Manchester University Press, 1994.

Hodgdon, Barbara. "Fashioning Obedience: *King John*'s 'True Inheritors.' " In *The End Crowns All: Closure and Contradiction in Shakespeare's History*. Princeton, N.J.: Princeton University Press, 1991.

Levine, Nina. "Refiguring a Nation: Mothers and Sons in *King John*." In *Women's Matters: Politics, Gender, and Nation in Shakespeare's Early History Plays*. Newark: University of Delaware Press, 1998.

Schwarz, Kathryn. "A Tragedy of Good Intentions: Maternal Agency in *3 Henry VI* and *King John*." *RD* 32 (2003): 69–93.

Tillyard, E.M.W. "King John." In *Shakespeare's History Plays*, 1944. New York: Penguin, 1991.

Waith, Eugene. "King John and the Drama of History." *SQ* 29.2 (1978): 192–211.

Weimann, Robert. "Figurenposition: The Correlation of Position and Expression." In *Shakespeare and the Popular Tradition in the Theater*. Baltimore: Johns Hopkins University Press, 1978.

THE MERCHANT OF VENICE

Adelman, Janet. "Her Father's Blood: Race, Conversion, and Nation in *The Merchant of Venice*." *Representations* 81 (2003): 4–30.

Auden, W. H. "Brothers and Others." In *The Dyer's Hand, and Other Essays*. London: Faber and Faber, 1975.

Barber, C. L. "The Merchants and the Jew of Venice: Wealth's Communion and an Intruder." In *Shakespeare's Festive Comedy: A Study of Dramatic Form and Its Relation to Social Custom*. Princeton, N.J.: Princeton University Press, 1959.

Belsey, Catherine. "Love in Venice." *SS* 44 (1992): 41–53.

Berger, Harry, Jr. "Marriage and Mercifixtion in *The Merchant of Venice*: The Casket Scene Revisited." *SQ* 32 (1981): 155–62. Reprinted in *Making Trifles of Terrors: Redistributing Complicities in Shakespeare*. Stanford, Calif.: Stanford University Press, 1997.

Boehrer, Bruce. "Shylock and the Rise of the Household Pet: Thinking Social Exclusion in *The Merchant of Venice*." *SQ* 50.2 (1999): 152–70.

Bulman, James C. "Shylock, Antonio, and the Politics of Performance." In *Shakespeare in Performance: A Collection of Essays*, ed. Frank Occhiogrosso. Newark: University of Delaware Press, 2003.

Burckhardt, Sigurd. "*The Merchant of Venice*: The Gentle Bond." *ELH* 29.3 (1962): 239–62. Reprinted in *Shakespearean Meanings*. Princeton, N.J.: Princeton University Press, 1968.

Cohen, Walter. "*The Merchant of Venice* and the Possibilities of Historical Criticism." *ELH* 49.4 (1982): 765–89.

Danson, Lawrence. *The Harmonies of "The Merchant of Venice."* New Haven, Conn.: Yale University Press, 1978.

Darcy, Robert F. "Freeing Daughters on Open Markets: The Incest Clause in *The Merchant of Venice*." In *Money and the Age of Shakespeare: Essays in New Economic Criticism*, ed. Linda Woodbridge. New York: Palgrave Macmillan, 2003.

Engle, Lars. "Money and Moral Luck in *The Merchant of Venice*." In *Shakespearean Pragmatism: Market of His Time*. Chicago: University of Chicago Press, 1993.

Fiedler, Leslie. "The Jew as Stranger: or 'These be the Christian husbands.' " In *The Stranger in Shakespeare*. New York: Stein and Day, 1972.

Freud, Sigmund. "The Theme of the Three Caskets." In *Character and Culture*, ed. Philip Rieff. New York: Collier Books, 1961.

Garber, Marjorie. "Freud's Choice: 'The Theme of the Three Caskets.' " In *Shakespeare's Ghost Writers: Literature as Uncanny Causality*. New York: Routledge, 1987.

Girard, René. " 'To Entrap the Wisest': A Reading of *The Merchant of Venice*." In *Literature and Society*, ed. E. W. Said. Baltimore: Johns Hopkins University Press, 1980. Reprinted as " 'To Entrap the Wisest': Sacrificial Ambivalence in *The Merchant of Venice* and *Richard III*." In *A Theater of Envy: William Shakespeare*. Oxford: Oxford University Press, 1991.

Goldberg, Jonathan. "Shakespearean Inscriptions: The Voicing of Power." In *Shakespeare and the Question of Theory*, ed. Patricia Parker and Geoffrey Hartman. London: Methuen, 1985.

Greenblatt, Stephen. "Marlowe, Marx, and Anti-Semitism." *CI* 5 (1978): 291–307. Reprinted in *Learning to Curse: Essays in Early Modern Culture*. New York: Routledge, 1990.

Gross, John. *Shylock: A Legend and Its Legacy*. New York: Simon & Schuster, 1992.

Hall, Kim. "Guess Who's Coming to Dinner? Colonization and Miscegenation in *The Merchant of Venice*." *RD* 23 (1992): 87–111.

Halpern, Richard. "The Jewish Question: Shakespeare and Anti-Semitism." In *Shakespeare Among the Moderns*. Ithaca, N.Y.: Cornell University Press, 1997.

Hutson, Lorna. *The Usurer's Daughter: Male Friendship and Fictions of Women in Sixteenth-Century England*. New York: Routledge, 1994.

Kahn, Coppélia. "The Cuckoo's Note: Male Friendship and Cuckoldry in *The Merchant of Venice*." In *Shakespeare's "Rough Magic": Renaissance Essays in Honor of C. L. Barber*, ed. Peter Erickson and Coppélia Kahn. Newark: University of Delaware Press, 1985.

Lewalski, Barbara K. "Biblical Allusion and Allegory in *The Merchant of Venice*." *SQ* 13.3 (1962): 327–43.

Newman, Karen. "Portia's Ring: Unruly Women and the Structure of Exchange in *The Merchant of Venice*." *SQ* 38.1 (1987): 19–33.

Shapiro, James. *Shakespeare and the Jews*. New York: Columbia University Press, 1996.

FILMS AND FILM ADAPTATIONS

The Merchant of Venice (Laurence Olivier, Joan Plowright), dir. John Sichel, 1973.

Merchant of Venice (Al Pacino, Joseph Fiennes), dir. Michael Radford, 2005.

HENRY IV PART I

Auden, W. H. "The Prince's Dog." In *The Dyer's Hand, and Other Essays*. London: Faber and Faber, 1975.

Barber, C. L. "Rule and Misrule in *Henry IV*." *Shakespeare's Festive Comedy: A Study of Dramatic Form and Its Relation to Social Custom*. Princeton, N.J.: Princeton University Press, 1959.

Bradley, A. C. "The Rejection of Falstaff." In *Oxford Lectures on Poetry*, 1909. London: Macmillan, 1963.

Bristol, Michael D. "The Festive Agon: The Politics of Carnival." In *Carnival and Theater: Plebeian Culture and the Structure of Authority in Renaissance England*. New York: Routledge, 1989.

Goldberg, Jonathan. "Desiring Hal." In *Sodometries: Renaissance Texts, Modern Sexualities*. Stanford, Calif.: Stanford University Press, 1992.

Greenblatt, Stephen. "Invisible Bullets." *Glyph* 8 (1981): 40–61. Reprinted in *Shakespearean Negotiations: The Circulation of Social Energy in Renaissance England*. Berkeley: University of California Press, 1988.

Hosley, Richard. *Shakespeare's Holinshed*. New York: Putnam, 1968.

Howard, Jean E., and Phyllis Rackin. "Gender and Nation: Anticipations of Modernity in the Second Tetralogy." In *Engendering a Nation: A Feminist Account of Shakespeare's English Histories*. New York: Routledge, 1997.

Kastan, David Scott. " 'The King Hath Many Marching in His Coats'; or, What Did You Do During the War, Daddy?" In *Shakespeare Left and Right*, ed. Ivo Kamps. New York: Routledge, 1991. Reprinted in *Shakespeare After Theory*. New York: Routledge, 1999.

Kris, Ernst. "Prince Hal's Conflict." In *The Design Within: Psychoanalytic Approaches to Shakespeare*, ed. M. D. Faber. New York: Science House, 1970.

Morgann, Maurice. *An Essay on the Dramatic Character of Sir John Falstaff*, 1777. New York: AMS Press, 1970.

Mullaney, Steven. "The Rehearsal of Cultures." In *The Place of the Stage: License, Play, and Power in Renaissance England*. Chicago: University of Chicago Press, 1988.

Poole, Kristen. "The Puritan in the Alehouse: Falstaff and the Drama of Marprelate." In *Radical Religion from Shakespeare to Milton: Figures of Nonconformity in Early Modern England*. Cambridge: Cambridge University Press, 2000.

Taylor, Gary. "The Fortunes of Oldcastle." *SS* 38 (1985): 85–100.

Tillyard, E.M.W. "Henry IV." In *Shakespeare's History Plays*, 1944. New York: Penguin 1991.

Traub, Valerie. "Prince Hal's Falstaff: Positioning Psychoanalysis and the Female Reproductive Body." *SQ* 40.4 (1989): 456–74. Reprinted in *Desire and Anxiety: Circulations of Sexuality in Shakespearean Drama*. New York: Routledge, 1992.

Wilson, John Dover. *The Fortunes of Falstaff*, 1943. Cambridge: Cambridge University Press, 1979.

FILMS AND FILM ADAPTATIONS

Chimes at Midnight (Falstaff) (Orson Welles, John Gielgud), dir. Orson Welles, 1965.

My Own Private Idaho (River Phoenix, Keanu Reeves), dir. Gus Van Sant, 1992.

HENRY IV PART 2

Barkan, Leonard. "The Human Body and the Commonwealth." In *Nature's Work of Art: The Human Body as Image of the World*. New Haven, Conn.: Yale University Press, 1975.

Berger, Harry, Jr. "On the Continuity of the Henriad." In *Shakespeare Left and Right*, ed. Ivo Kamps. New York: Routledge, 1991.

Bulman, James C. "Henry IV Parts One and Two." In *The Cambridge Companion to Shakespeare's History Plays*, ed. Michael Hattaway. Cambridge: Cambridge University Press, 2002.

Burckhardt, Sigurd. " 'Swoll'n with Some Other Grief': Shakespeare's Prince Hal Trilogy." In *Shakespearean Meanings*. Princeton, N.J.: Princeton University Press, 1968.

Calderwood, James. *Metadrama in Shakespeare's Henriad: "Richard II" to "Henry V."* Berkeley: University of California Press, 1979.

Hodgdon, Barbara. " 'Let the End Try the Man': *1 and 2 Henry IV*." In *The End Crowns All: Closure and Contradiction in Shakespeare's History*. Princeton, N.J.: Princeton University Press, 1991.

Jones, Robert. "What Perils Past, What Crosses to Ensue." In *The Valiant Dead: Renewing the Past in Shakespeare's Histories*. Iowa City: University of Iowa Press, 1991.

Knights, L. C. "Time's Subjects: The Sonnets and *King Henry IV, Part II*." In *Some Shakespearean Themes, and an Approach to "Hamlet."* London: Chatto & Windus, 1959.

MacDonald, Ronald R. "Uses of Diversity: Bakhtin's Theory of Utterance and Shakespeare's Second Tetralogy." In *"Henry IV Parts One and Two": Theory and Practice*, ed. Nigel Wood. Buckingham, UK: Open University Press, 1995.

Mullaney, Steven. "The Rehearsal of Cultures." In *The Place of the Stage: License, Play, and Power in Renaissance England*. Chicago: University of Chicago Press, 1988.

Rackin, Phyllis. "Historical Kings/Theatrical Clowns." In *Stages of History: Shakespeare's English Chronicles*. Ithaca, N.Y.: Cornell University Press, 1990.

Wiles, David. "Kemp's Jigs" and "Falstaff." In *Shakespeare's Clowns: Actor and Text in the Elizabethan Playhouse*. Cambridge: Cambridge University Press, 1987.

THE MERRY WIVES OF WINDSOR

Barton, Anne. "Falstaff and the Comic Community." In *Shakespeare's "Rough Magic": Renaissance Essays in Honor of C. L. Barber*, ed. Peter Erickson and Coppélia Kahn. Newark: University of Delaware Press, 1985.

Erickson, Peter. "The Order of the Garter, the Cult of Elizabeth, and Class-Gender Tension in *The Merry Wives of Windsor*." In *Shakespeare Reproduced: The Text in History and Ideology*, ed. Jean E. Howard and Marion F. O'Connor. New York: Methuen, 1987.

Helgerson, Richard. "The Buck Basket, the Witch, and the Queen of Fairies: The Women's World of Shakespeare's Windsor." In *Renaissance Culture and the Everyday*, ed. Pamela Fumerton and Simon Hunt. Philadelphia: University of Pennsylvania Press, 1999.

Hunter, George K. "Bourgeois Comedy: Shakespeare and Dekker." In *Shakespeare and His Contemporaries: Essays in Comparison*, ed. E.A.J. Honigmann. Manchester, UK: Manchester University Press, 1986.

Kahn, Coppélia. " 'The Savage Yoke': Cuckoldry and Marriage." In *Man's Estate: Masculine Identity in Shakespeare*. Berkeley: University of California Press, 1981.

Katz, Leslie S. "*The Merry Wives of Windsor:* Sharing the Queen's Holiday." *Representations* 51 (1995): 77–93.

Kegl, Rosemary. " 'The Adoption of Abominable Terms': Middle Classes, Merry Wives, and the Insults That Shape Windsor." In *The Rhetoric of Concealment: Figuring Gender and Class in Renaissance Literature.* Ithaca, N.Y.: Cornell University Press, 1994.

Neely, Carol Thomas. "Constructing Female Sexuality in the Renaissance." In *Feminism and Psychoanalysis,* ed. Richard Feldstein and Judith Roof. Ithaca, N.Y.: Cornell University Press, 1989.

Parker, Patricia. "*The Merry Wives of Windsor* and Shakespearean Translation." *MLQ* 52 (1991): 225–61.

Pittenger, Elizabeth. "Dispatch Quickly: The Mechanical Reproduction of Pages." *SQ* 42 (1991): 389–408.

Siegel, Paul. "Falstaff and His Social Milieu." *Shakespeare-Jahrbuch* 110 (1974): 139–45. Reprinted in *Weapons of Criticism: Marxism in America and the Literary Tradition,* ed. Norman Rudich. Palo Alto, Calif.: Ramparts Press, 1976.

Wall, Wendy. "*The Merry Wives of Windsor:* Unhusbanding Desires in Windsor." In *A Companion to Shakespeare's Works,* vol. 3, ed. Richard Dutton and Jean E. Howard. Malden, Mass.: Blackwell Publishers, 2003.

MUCH ADO ABOUT NOTHING

Berger, Harry, Jr. "Against the Sink-a-Pace: Sexual and Family Politics in *Much Ado About Nothing.*" *SQ* 33.3 (1982): 302–13. Reprinted in *Making Trifles of Terrors: Redistributing Complicities in Shakespeare.* Stanford, Calif.: Stanford University Press, 1997.

Berry, Ralph. "Problems of Knowing." In *Shakespeare's Comedies: Explorations in Form.* Princeton, N.J.: Princeton University Press, 1972.

Cook, Carol. " 'The Sign and Semblance of Her Honor': Reading Gender Difference in *Much Ado About Nothing.*" *PMLA* 101.2 (1986): 186–202. Reprinted in *Shakespeare and Gender: A History,* ed. Deborah Barker and Ivo Kamps. London and New York: Verso, 1995.

Everett, Barbara. "*Much Ado About Nothing:* The Unsociable Comedy." In *English Comedy,* ed. Michael Cordner et al. Cambridge: Cambridge University Press, 1994.

Gay, Penny. "*Much Ado About Nothing:* A King of Merry War." In *As She Likes It: Shakespeare's Unruly Women.* New York: Routledge, 1994.

Howard, Jean E. "Renaissance Antitheatricality and the Politics of Gender and Rank in *Much Ado About Nothing.*" In *Shakespeare Reproduced: The Text in History and Ideology,* ed. Jean E. Howard and Marion F. O'Connor. New York: Methuen, 1987.

Leggatt, Alexander. "*Much Ado About Nothing.*" In *Shakespeare's Comedy of Love.* London: Methuen, 1974.

Lewalski, B[arbara] K. "Love, Appearance, and Reality: Much Ado About Something." *SEL* 8 (1968): 235–51.

Mahood, M. M. "A World of Words." In *Shakespeare's Wordplay.* New York: Routledge, 1957.

Prouty, Charles T. *The Sources of "Much Ado About Nothing."* New Haven, Conn.: Yale University Press, 1950.

FILMS AND FILM ADAPTATIONS

Much Ado About Nothing (Kenneth Branagh, Emma Thompson), dir. Kenneth Branagh, 1993.

HENRY V

Barton, Anne. "The King Disguised: Shakespeare's *Henry V* and the Comical History." In *The Triple Bond: Plays, Mainly Shakespearean, in Performance,* ed. Joseph G. Price. University Park: Pennsylvania State University Press, 1975.

Danson, Lawrence. "*Henry V:* King, Chorus, and Critics." *SQ* 34.1 (1983): 27–43.

Dollimore, Jonathan, and Alan Sinfield. "History and Ideology, Masculinity and Miscegenation." In *Faultlines: Cultural Materialism and the Politics of Dissident Reading,* by Alan Sinfield. Oxford and New York: Clarendon Press, 1992.

Eggert, Katherine. "Nostalgia and the Not Yet Late Queen: Refusing Female Rule in *Henry V.*" *ELH* 61.3 (1994): 523–50.

Greenblatt, Stephen. "Invisible Bullets: Renaissance Authority and Its Subversion, *Henry IV* and

Henry V." *Glyph* 8 (1981): 40–61. Reprinted in *Shakespearean Negotiations: The Circulation of Social Energy in Renaissance England.* Berkeley: University of California Press, 1988.

Hosley, Richard. *Shakespeare's Holinshed.* New York: Putnam, 1968.

Mason, Pamela. "*King Henry V:* 'The quick forge and working house of thought.' " In *The Cambridge Companion to Shakespeare's History Plays,* ed. Michael Hattaway. Cambridge: Cambridge University Press, 2002.

Ornstein, Robert. *"Henry V."* In *A Kingdom for a Stage: The Achievement of Shakespeare's History Plays.* Cambridge, Mass.: Harvard University Press, 1972.

Patterson, Annabel. "Back by Popular Demand: The Two Versions of *Henry V.*" *RD* 19 (1988): 29–62. Reprinted in *Shakespeare and the Popular Voice.* Cambridge, Mass.: Basil Blackwell, 1989.

Rabkin, Norman. "Either/Or: Responding to *Henry V.*" In *Shakespeare and the Problem of Meaning.* Chicago: University of Chicago Press, 1981.

———. "Rabbits, Ducks, and *Henry V.*" *SQ* 28.3 (1977): 279–96.

Taylor, Gary. *Three Studies in the Text of "Henry V."* Oxford and New York: Clarendon Press, 1979.

Tillyard, E.M.W. "Henry V." In *Shakespeare's History Plays,* 1944. New York: Penguin, 1991.

Traversi, Derek. *Shakespeare from Richard II to Henry V.* Stanford, Calif.: Stanford University Press, 1957.

FILMS AND FILM ADAPTATIONS

Henry V (Laurence Olivier, Leslie Banks), dir. Laurence Olivier, 1944.

Henry V (Kenneth Branagh, Derek Jacobi), dir. Kenneth Branagh, 1989.

JULIUS CAESAR

Burckhardt, Sigurd. "How Not to Murder Caesar." *The Centennial Review* 11 (1967): 141–56. Reprinted in *Shakespearean Meanings.* Princeton, N.J.: Princeton University Press, 1968.

Burke, Kenneth. "Antony in Behalf of the Play." *Southern Review* 1 (1935): 308–19. Reprinted in *Perspectives by Incongruity,* ed. Stanley Edgar Hyman with Barbara Karmiller. Bloomington: Indiana University Press, 1964.

Garber, Marjorie. "Dream and Interpretation: *Julius Caesar.*" In *Dream in Shakespeare: From Metaphor to Metamorphosis.* New Haven, Conn.: Yale University Press, 1974.

———. "A Rome of One's Own." In *Shakespeare's Ghost Writers: Literature as Uncanny Causality.* New York: Routledge, 1987.

Granville-Barker, Harley. "Cassius the Egotist vs. Antony the Opportunist." In *Prefaces to Shakespeare.* London: Sidgwick & Jackson, 1927–30.

Halpern, Richard. "The Shakespearian Mob: Mass Culture and the Literary Public Sphere." In *Shakespeare Among the Moderns.* Ithaca, N.Y.: Cornell University Press, 1997. Esp. pp. 69–92.

Kahn, Coppélia. "Mettle and Melting Spirits in *Julius Caesar.*" In *Roman Shakespeare: Warriors, Wounds, and Women.* New York: Routledge, 1997.

Knight, G. W. "The Eroticism of *Julius Caesar.*" In *The Imperial Theme: Further Interpretations of Shakespeare's Tragedies Including the Roman Plays.* London: Oxford University Press, 1931.

Knights, L. C. "Personality and Politics in *Julius Caesar.*" In *Further Explorations.* Stanford, Calif.: Stanford University Press, 1965.

Marshall, Cynthia. "Portia's Wound, Calphurnia's Dream." *ELH* 24.2 (1994): 471–88.

Miles, Gary B. "How Roman Are Shakespeare's 'Romans'?" *SQ* 40.3 (1989): 257–83.

Miola, Robert S. "*Julius Caesar* and the Tyrannicide Debate." *RQ* 38.2 (1985): 271–89.

Paster, Gail Kern. "Laudable Blood: Bleeding, Difference, and Humoral Embarrassment." In *The Body Embarrassed: Drama and the Disciplines of Shame in Early Modern England.* Ithaca, N.Y.: Cornell University Press, 1993.

Rose, Mark. "Conjuring Caesar: Ceremony, History, and Authority in 1599." *ELH* 19.3 (1989): 291–304.

Taylor, Gary. "Bardicide." In *Shakespeare and Cultural Traditions,* ed. Tetsuo Kishi et al. Newark: University of Delaware Press, 1991.

Traversi, Derek. *"Julius Caesar."* In *Shakespeare: The Roman Plays.* Stanford, Calif.: Stanford University Press, 1963.

FILMS AND FILM ADAPTATIONS

William Shakespeare's Julius Caesar (Marlon Brando, John Gielgud), dir. Joseph L. Mankiewicz, 1953.
Julius Caesar (Charlton Heston, John Gielgud), dir. Stuart Burge, 1970.

AS YOU LIKE IT

Alpers, Paul. *What Is Pastoral?* Chicago: University of Chicago Press, 1996.

Barber, C. L. "The Alliance of Seriousness and Levity in *As You Like It.*" In *Shakespeare's Festive Comedy: A Study of Dramatic Form and Its Relationship to Social Custom.* Princeton, N.J.: Princeton University Press, 1959.

Bate, Jonathan. *Shakespeare and Ovid.* Oxford and New York: Clarendon Press, 1993.

Colie, Rosalie. "Perspectives on Pastoral: Romance, Comic and Tragic." In *Shakespeare's Living Art.* Princeton, N.J.: Princeton University Press, 1974.

Frye, Northrop. *A Natural Perspective: The Development of Shakespearean Comedy and Romance.* New York: Harcourt, Brace & World, 1965.

Elam, Keir. "As They Did in the Golden World: Romantic Rapture and Semantic Rapture in *As You Like It.*" *Canadian Review of Comparative Literature* 18.2–3 (1991): 217–32. Reprinted in *Reading the Renaissance: Culture, Poetics, and Drama,* ed. Jonathan Hart. New York: Garland, 1996.

Erickson, Peter. "Sexual Politics and Social Structures in *As You Like It.*" *Massachusetts Review* 23.1 (1982): 65–83. Reprinted in *Patriarchal Structures in Shakespeare's Drama.* Berkeley: University of California Press, 1985.

Garber, Marjorie. "Rosalind the Yeshiva Boy." In *Vested Interests: Cross-Dressing and Cultural Anxiety.* New York: Routledge, 1992.

———. "Separation and Individuation." In *Coming of Age in Shakespeare.* London and New York: Methuen, 1981.

Howard, Jean E. "Power and Eros: Crossdressing in Dramatic Representation and Theatrical Practice." In *The Stage and Social Struggle in Early Modern England.* New York: Routledge, 1994.

Masten, Jeffrey. "Textual Deviance: Ganymede's Hand in *As You Like It.*" In *Field Work: Sites in Literary and Cultural Studies,* ed. Marjorie Garber, Paul B. Franklin, and Rebecca L. Walkowitz. New York: Routledge, 1996.

Montrose, Louis. " 'The Place of a Brother' in *As You Like It:* Social Process and Comic Form." *SQ* 32.1 (1981): 28–54.

Orgel, Stephen. "Call Me Ganymede." In *Impersonations: The Performance of Gender in Shakespeare's England.* Cambridge: Cambridge University Press, 1996.

Panofsky, Erwin. "*Et in Arcadia Ego:* Poussin and the Elegiac Tradition." In *Meaning in the Visual Arts.* Garden City, N.Y.: Anchor Books / Doubleday, 1955.

Smith, Bruce R. "The Passionate Shepherd." In *Homosexual Desire in Shakespeare's England: A Cultural Poetics.* Chicago: University of Chicago Press, 1991.

Traub, Valerie. "The Homoerotics of Shakespearean Comedy." In *Desire and Anxiety: Circulations of Sexuality in Shakespearean Drama.* New York: Routledge, 1992.

Wilson, Richard. "Like the Old Robin Hood: *As You Like It* and the Enclosure Riots." *SQ* 43.1 (1992): 1–19. Reprinted in *Will Power: Essays on Shakespearean Authority.* New York and London: Harvester Wheatsheaf, 1993.

Wofford, Susanne L. " 'To You I Give Myself, For I Am Yours': Erotic Performance and Theatrical Performatives in *As You Like It.*" In *Shakespeare Reread: The Texts in New Contexts,* ed. Russ McDonald. Ithaca, N.Y.: Cornell University Press, 1994.

Young, David. "Earthly Things Made Even: *As You Like It.*" In *The Heart's Forest: A Study of Shakespeare's Pastoral Plays.* New Haven, Conn.: Yale University Press, 1972.

FILMS AND FILM ADAPTATIONS

As You Like It (Laurence Olivier, Elizabeth Bergner), dir. Paul Czinner, 1936.

HAMLET

Adelman, Janet. "Man and His Wife Is One Flesh: *Hamlet* and the Confrontation with the Maternal Body." In *Suffocating Mothers: Fantasies of Maternal Origin in Shakespeare's Plays, "Hamlet" to "The Tempest."* New York: Routledge, 1992.

Bohannan, Laura. "Shakespeare in the Bush." *Natural History* 75 (1966): 28–33. Reprinted in *Critical Essays on Shakespeare's "Hamlet,"* ed. David Scott Kastan. New York: G. K. Hall, 1995.

Booth, Stephen. "On the Value of *Hamlet.*" In *Reinterpretations of Elizabethan Drama: Selected Papers from the English Institute,* ed. Norman Rabkin. New York: Columbia University Press, 1969.

Bradley, A. C. "Lecture III: Shakespeare's Tragic Period—*Hamlet*" and "Lecture IV: *Hamlet.*" In *Shakespearean Tragedy: Lectures on "Hamlet," "Othello," "King Lear," "Macbeth,"* 2nd ed. London: Macmillan, 1905.

Bristol, Michael D. " 'Funeral-Bak'd Meats': Carnival and the Carnivalesque in *Hamlet.*" In *Hamlet,* ed. S. L. Wofford. New York: Bedford Books of St. Martin's Press, 1994.

Burke, Kenneth. "Psychology and Form." *The Dial* 79 (1925): 34–46. Reprinted in *Perspectives by Incongruity,* ed. Stanley Edgar Hyman with Barbara Karmiller. Bloomington: Indiana University Press, 1964.

Eliot, T. S. "Hamlet and His Problems." In *The Sacred Wood.* London: Methuen, 1920.

Fineman, Joel. "Fratricide and Cuckoldry: Shakespeare's Doubles." In *Representing Shakespeare: New Psychoanalytic Essays,* ed. Murray M. Schwartz and Coppélia Kahn. Baltimore: Johns Hopkins University Press, 1980.

Freud, Sigmund. *The Complete Letters of Sigmund Freud to Wilhelm Fliess, 1887–1904,* ed. and trans. Jeffrey M. Masson. Cambridge, Mass.: Harvard University Press, 1985; see particularly letters of 1897.

———. "The Material and Sources of Dreams." In *The Interpretation of Dreams.* New York: Avon Books, 1965.

Garber, Marjorie. "*Hamlet:* Giving Up the Ghost." In *Shakespeare's Ghost Writers: Literature as Uncanny Causality.* New York: Routledge, 1987.

———. "MacGuffin Shakespeare." In *Quotation Marks.* New York: Routledge, 2002.

Girard, René. "Hamlet's Dull Revenge." In *Stanford Literature Review* 1 (1984): 159–200. Reprinted in *A Theater of Envy: William Shakespeare.* Oxford: Oxford University Press, 1991.

Granville-Barker, Harley. *Preface to "Hamlet,"* 1936. Princeton, N.J.: Princeton University Press, 1965.

Greenblatt, Stephen. *Hamlet in Purgatory.* Princeton, N.J.: Princeton University Press, 2001.

Hillman, David. "Visceral Knowledge." In *The Body in Parts: Fantasies of Corporeality in Early Modern Europe,* ed. Carla Mazzio and David Hillman. New York: Routledge, 1997.

Jones, Ann Rosalind, and Peter Stallybrass. "Of Ghosts and Garments: The Materiality of Memory on the Renaissance Stage." In *Renaissance Clothing and the Materials of Memory.* Cambridge: Cambridge University Press, 2000.

Jones, Ernst. *Hamlet and Oedipus.* London: Gollancz, 1949.

Lacan, Jacques. "Desire and the Interpretation of Desire in *Hamlet.*" In *Literature and Psychoanalysis: The Question of Reading, Otherwise,* ed. Shoshana Felman. Baltimore: Johns Hopkins University Press, 1982.

Levao, Ronald. " 'King Lear of Infinite Space': Hamlet and His Fictions." In *Renaissance Minds and Their Fictions.* Berkeley: University of California Press, 1995.

Levin, Harry. *The Question of "Hamlet."* Oxford: Oxford University Press, 1959.

Lupton, Julia Reinhard, and Kenneth Reinhard. *After Oedipus: Shakespeare in Psychoanalysis.* Ithaca, N.Y.: Cornell University Press, 1993.

Maguire, Laurie. " 'Actions that a man might play': Mourning, Memory, Editing." *Performance Research* 7 (2002): 66–76.

Marcus, Leah. "Bad Taste and Bad *Hamlet.*" In *Unediting the Renaissance: Shakespeare, Marlowe, Milton.* New York: Routledge, 1996.

McGee, Arthur. *The Elizabethan Hamlet.* New Haven, Conn.: Yale University Press, 1987.

Rose, Jacqueline. "*Hamlet*—the 'Mona Lisa' of Literature." *CQ* 28.1–2 (1986): 35–49. Reprinted in *Sexuality in the Field of Vision.* New York: Verso, 1996.

———. "Sexuality in the Reading of Shakespeare: *Hamlet* and *Measure for Measure.*" In *Alternative Shakespeares,* ed. John Drakakis. London and New York: Methuen, 1985.

Showalter, Elaine. "Representing Ophelia: Women, Madness, and the Responsibilities of Feminist Criticism." In *Shakespeare and the Question of Theory,* ed. Patricia Parker and Geoffrey Hartman. New York: Routledge, 1985.

Weimann, Robert. "Hamlet and the Purposes of Playing." In *Author's Pen and Actor's Voice: Playing and Writing in Shakespeare's Theatre,* ed. Helen Higbee and William West. Cambridge: Cambridge University Press, 2000.

Wilson, John Dover. *What Happens in "Hamlet."* Cambridge: Cambridge University Press, 1935.

Young, Alan R. *Hamlet and the Visual Arts, 1709–1900.* Newark: University of Delaware Press, 2002.

FILMS AND FILM ADAPTATIONS

Hamlet (Astra Nielson, Mathilde Brandt), dir. Sven Gade and Heinz Schall, 1921.

Hamlet (Laurence Olivier, Basil Sydney), dir. Laurence Olivier, 1948.

Hamlet (Richard Burton, John Gielgud), dir. John Gielgud and Bill Colleran, 1964.

Hamlet (Mel Gibson, Glenn Close), dir. Franco Zeffirelli, 1990.

Hamlet (Kenneth Branagh, Kate Winslet), dir. Kenneth Branagh, 1996.

Hamlet (Ethan Hawke, Bill Murray), dir. Michael Almereyda, 2000.

TWELFTH NIGHT

Arlidge, Anthony. *Shakespeare and the Prince of Love: The Feast of Misrule in the Middle Temple.* London: Giles de la Mare, 2000.

Auden, W. H. "Music in Shakespeare." In *The Dyer's Hand, and Other Essays.* London: Faber and Faber, 1975.

Barber, C. L. "Testing Courtesy and Humanity in *Twelfth Night.*" In *Shakespeare's Festive Comedy: A Study of Its Dramatic Form and Relation to Social Custom.* Princeton, N.J.: Princeton University Press, 1959.

Belsey, Catherine. "Disrupting Sexual Difference: Meaning and Gender in the Comedies." In *Alternative Shakespeares,* ed. John Drakakis. London and New York: Methuen, 1985.

Booth, Stephen. "*Twelfth Night* 1.1: The Audience as Malvolio." In *Shakespeare's "Rough Magic": Essays in Honor of C. L. Barber,* ed. Peter Erickson and Coppélia Kahn. Newark: University of Delaware Press, 1985.

Carroll, William C. "The Ending of *Twelfth Night* and the Tradition of Metamorphosis." In *Shakespearean Comedy,* ed. Maurice Charney. New York: New York Literary Forum, 1981.

Fineman, Joel. "Fratricide and Cuckoldry: Shakespeare's Doubles." In *Representing Shakespeare: New Psychoanalytic Essays,* ed. Murray M. Schwartz and Coppélia Kahn. Baltimore: Johns Hopkins University Press, 1980.

Freedman, Barbara. "Naming Loss: Mourning and Representation in *Twelfth Night.*" In *Staging the Gaze: Postmodernism, Psychoanalysis, and Shakespearean Comedy.* Ithaca, N.Y.: Cornell University Press, 1991.

Garber, Marjorie. "Transvestite Shakespeare," parts 1 and 2. In *Vested Interests: Cross-Dressing and Cultural Anxiety.* New York: Routledge, 1992.

Gay, Penny. "*Twelfth Night:* Desire and Its Discontents." In *As She Likes It: Shakespeare's Unruly Women.* New York: Routledge, 1994.

Greenblatt, Stephen. "Fiction and Friction." In *Reconstructing Individualism: Autonomy, Individuality, and the Self in Western Thought,* ed. Thomas C. Heller et al. Stanford, Calif.: Stanford University Press, 1986. Reprinted in *Shakespearean Negotiations: The Circulation of Social Energy in Renaissance England.* Berkeley: University of California Press, 1988.

Hamilton, Donna. "*Twelfth Night:* The Errors of Exorcism." In *Shakespeare and the Politics of Protestant England.* Lexington: University Press of Kentucky, 1992.

Hartman, Geoffrey H. "Shakespeare's Poetical Character in *Twelfth Night.*" In *Shakespeare and the Question of Theory,* ed. Patricia Parker and Geoffrey Hartman. New York: Methuen, 1985.

Hotson, Leslie. *The First Night of "Twelfth Night."* London: R. Hart-Davis, 1954.

Jardine, Lisa. "Twins and Travesties: Gender, Dependency, and Sexual Availability in *Twelfth Night.*" In *Erotic Politics: Desire on the Renaissance Stage,* ed. S. Zimmerman. New York: Routledge, 1992. Reprinted in *Reading Shakespeare Historically.* New York: Routledge, 1996.

Orgel, Stephen. "Call Me Ganymede." In *Impersonations: The Performance of Gender in Shakespeare's England.* Cambridge: Cambridge University Press, 1996.

Rackin, Phyllis. "Androgyny, Mimesis, and the Marriage of the Boy Heroine on the English Renaissance Stage." *PMLA* 102.1 (1987): 29–41.

FILMS AND FILM ADAPTATIONS

Twelfth Night: Or What You Will (Helena Bonham Carter, Ben Kingsley), dir. Trevor Nunn, 1996.

TROILUS AND CRESSIDA

Adelman, Janet. "Is Thy Union Here?: Union and Its Discontents in *Troilus and Cressida* and *Othello.*" In *Suffocating Mothers: Fantasies of Maternal Origin in Shakespeare's Plays, "Hamlet" to "The Tempest."* New York: Routledge, 1992.

———. " 'This Is and Is Not Cressid': The Characterization of Cressida." In *The (M)other Tongue: Essays in Feminist Psychoanalytic Interpretation,* ed. Shirley Nelson Garner, Claire Kahane, and Madelon Sprengnether. Ithaca, N.Y.: Cornell University Press, 1985.

Asp, Carolyn. "In Defense of Cressida." *Studies in Philology* 74 (1977): 406–17.

Bowen, Barbara E. *Gender in the Theater of War: Shakespeare's Troilus and Cressida.* New York: Garland, 1993.

Bruster, Douglas. " 'The Alternation of Men': *Troilus and Cressida,* Troynovant, and Trade." In *Drama and the Market in the Age of Shakespeare.* Cambridge: Cambridge University Press, 1992.

Campbell, Oscar J. *"Comicall Satyre" and Shakespeare's "Troilus and Cressida."* San Marino, Calif.: Huntington Library Publications, 1938.

Cartelli, Thomas. "Ideology and Subversion in the Shakespearean Set Speech." *ELH* 53.1 (1986): 1–25.

Charnes, Linda. " 'So Unsecret to Ourselves': Notorious Identity and the Material Subject in Shakespeare's *Troilus and Cressida.*" *SQ* 40.4 (1989): 413–40.

Freund, Elizabeth. " 'Ariachne's broken woof': The Rhetoric of Citation in *Troilus and Cressida.*" In *Shakespeare and the Question of Theory,* ed. Patricia Parker and Geoffrey Hartman. New York: Methuen, 1985.

Girard, René. "The Politics of Desire in *Troilus and Cressida.*" In *Shakespeare and the Question of Theory,* ed. Patricia Parker and Geoffrey Hartman. New York: Methuen, 1985.

Greene, Gayle. "Shakespeare's Cressida: 'A Kind of Self.' " In *The Woman's Part: Feminist Criticism of Shakespeare,* ed. Carolyn Ruth Swift Lenz, Gayle Green, and Carol Thomas Neely. Urbana: University of Illinois Press, 1980.

Harris, Jonathan Gil. " 'The Enterprise of the Sick': Pathologies of Value and Transnationality in *Troilus and Cressida.*" *RD* 29 (1998): 3–37.

Helm, Lorraine. " 'Still Wars and Lechery': Shakespeare and the Last Trojan Woman." In *Arms and the Woman: War, Gender, and Literary Representation,* ed. Helen M. Cooper, Adrienne Auslander Munich, and Susan Merrill Squier. Chapel Hill: University of North Carolina Press, 1989.

Knight, G. W. "The Philosophy of *Troilus and Cressida.*" In *The Wheel of Fire: Interpretations of Shakespearean Tragedy,* 1930. London and New York: Routledge, 1998.

Knights, L. C. *Some Shakespearean Themes, and an Approach to "Hamlet."* Stanford, Calif.: Stanford University Press, 1966.

Maguire, Laurie. "Performing Anger: The Anatomy of Abuses(s) in *Troilus and Cressida.*" *RD* 31 (2002): 153–83.

Mallin, Eric S. "Emulous Factions and the Collapse of Chivalry: *Troilus and Cressida.*" *Representations* 29 (1990): 145–79.

Parker, Patricia. "Dilation and Inflation: Shakespearean Increase." In *Shakespeare from the Margins.* Chicago: University of Chicago Press, 1996.

Smith, Bruce. "Combatants and Comrades" and "Master and Minion." In *Homosexual Desire in Shakespeare's England.* Chicago: University of Chicago Press, 1991.

MEASURE FOR MEASURE

Adelman, Janet. "Bed Tricks: On Marriage as the End of Comedy in *All's Well That Ends Well* and *Measure for Measure*." In *Shakespeare's Personality,* ed. Norman N. Holland, Sidney Homan, and Bernard J. Paris. Berkeley: University of California Press, 1989.

Baines, Barbara. "Assaying the Power of Chastity in *Measure for Measure*." *SEL* 30 (1990): 284–98.

Bennett, Josephine Waters. *"Measure for Measure" as Royal Entertainment.* New York: Columbia University Press, 1966.

Dollimore, Jonathan. "Transgression and Surveillance in *Measure for Measure*." In *Political Shakespeare: New Essays in Cultural Materialism,* ed. Jonathan Dollimore and Alan Sinfield. Manchester, UK: Manchester University Press, 1985.

Frye, Northrop. *The Myth of Deliverance: Reflections on Shakespeare's Problem Comedies.* Toronto: University of Toronto Press, 1983.

Goddard, Harold. *"Measure for Measure."* In *The Meaning of Shakespeare.* Chicago: University of Chicago Press, 1951.

Kirsch, Arthur. "The Integrity of *Measure for Measure*." *SS* 28 (1975): 89–105.

Knight, G. W. *"Measure for Measure* and the Gospels." In *The Wheel of Fire: Interpretations of Shakespeare's Tragedies,* 1930. London and New York: Routledge, 1998.

Maus, Katherine Eisaman. "Sexual Secrecy in *Measure for Measure*." In *Inwardness and Theater in the English Renaissance.* Chicago: University of Chicago Press, 1995.

Pater, Walter. *"Measure for Measure."* In *Appreciations, with an Essay on Style,* 1889. Evanston, Ill.: Northwestern University Press, 1987.

Shell, Marc. *The End of Kinship: "Measure for Measure," Incest and the Ideal of Universal Siblinghood.* Stanford, Calif.: Stanford University Press, 1988.

Shuger, Debora Kuller. *Political Theologies in Shakespeare's England: The Sacred and the State in "Measure for Measure."* New York: Palgrave Macmillan, 2001.

Skura, Meredith. "New Interpretations for Interpretation in *Measure for Measure*." *Boundary 2* 7.2 (1979): 39–60.

Wheeler, Richard. "The Problem with Problem Comedies: *Measure for Measure*." In *Shakespeare's Development in the Problem Comedies: Turn and Counter-Turn.* Berkeley: University of California Press, 1981.

OTHELLO

Auden, W. H. "The Joker in the Pack." In *The Dyer's Hand, and Other Essays.* London: Faber and Faber, 1975.

Burke, Kenneth. *"Othello:* An Essay to Illustrate a Method." *The Hudson Review* 4 (1951): 165–203. Reprinted in *Perspectives by Incongruity,* ed. Stanley Edgar Hyman with Barbara Karmiller. Bloomington: Indiana University Press, 1964.

Callaghan, Dympna. "Looking Well to Linens: Women and Cultural Production in *Othello* and Shakespeare's England." In *Marxist Shakespeares,* ed. Jean E. Howard and Scott C. Shershow. New York: Routledge, 2001.

Cavell, Stanley. "Othello and the Stake of the Other." In *Disowning Knowledge in Six Plays of Shakespeare.* Cambridge: Cambridge University Press, 1987.

Coleridge, Samuel Taylor. "Othello." In *Coleridge's Writings on Shakespeare,* ed. Terence Hawkes. New York: G. P. Putnam and Sons, 1959.

Fiedler, Leslie. "The Moor as Stranger." In *The Stranger in Shakespeare.* New York: Stein and Day, 1972.

Greenblatt, Stephen. "The Improvisation of Power." In *Renaissance Self-Fashioning: From More to Shakespeare.* Chicago: University of Chicago Press, 1980.

Greene, Gayle. " 'This That You Call Love': Sexual and Social Tragedy in *Othello*." *Journal of Women's Studies in Literature* 1 (1979): 16–32. Reprinted in *Shakespeare and Gender: A History,* ed. Deborah Barker and Ivo Kamps. London and New York: Verso, 1995.

Heilman, Robert B. *Magic in the Web: Action and Language in "Othello."* Lexington: University of Kentucky Press, 1956.

Knight, G. W. "The Othello Music." In *The Wheel of Fire: Interpretations of Shakespeare's Tragedies,* 1930. New York: Routledge, 1998.

Loomba, Ania. " 'Delicious Traffick': Racial and Religious Difference on the Early Modern Stage." In *Shakespeare and Race,* ed. Catherine M. Alexander and Stanley Wells. Cambridge: Cambridge University Press, 2000.

———. "Sexuality and Racial Difference." In *Gender, Race, Renaissance Drama.* Manchester, UK: Manchester University Press, 1989.

Lupton, Julia R. "*Othello* Circumcised: Shakespeare and the Pauline Discourse of Nations." *Representations* 57 (1997): 73–89.

Maus, Katherine Eisaman. " 'And wash the Ethiop white': Femininity and the Monstrous in *Othello.*" In *Shakespeare Reproduced: The Text in History and Ideology,* ed. Jean E. Howard and Marion F. O'Connor. New York: Methuen, 1987. Reprinted in *Fashioning Femininity and English Renaissance Drama.* Chicago: University of Chicago Press, 1991.

Neely, Carol Thomas. "Circumscriptions and Unhousedness: *Othello* in the Borderlands." In *Shakespeare and Gender: A History,* ed. Deborah Barker and Ivo Kamps. New York: Verso, 1995.

Parker, Patricia. "Fantasies of 'Race' and 'Gender': Africa, *Othello,* and Bringing to Light." In *Women, "Race," and Writing in the Early Modern Period,* ed. Margo Hendricks and Patricia Parker. New York: Routledge, 1994.

———. "*Othello* and *Hamlet:* Dilation, Spying, and the 'Secret Place' of Woman." *Representations* 44 (1993): 60–95.

Snow, Edward. "Sexual Anxiety and the Male Order of Things in *Othello.*" *ELR* 10 (1980): 384–412.

Stallybrass, Peter. "Patriarchal Territories: The Body Enclosed." In *Rewriting the Renaissance: The Discourses of Sexual Difference in Early Modern Europe,* ed. Margaret W. Ferguson, Maureen Quilligan, and Nancy J. Vickers. Chicago: University of Chicago Press, 1986.

Vitkus, Daniel. *Turning Turk: English Theater and the Multicultural Mediterranean, 1570–1630.* New York: Palgrave Macmillan, 2003.

FILMS AND FILM ADAPTATIONS

The Tragedy of Othello: The Moor of Venice (Orson Welles, Suzanne Cloutier), dir. Orson Welles, 1952.
Othello (Laurence Olivier, Maggie Smith), dir. Stuart Burge, 1965.
Otello (Plácido Domingo, Katia Ricciarelli), dir. Franco Zeffirelli, 1986.
Othello (Laurence Fishburne, Kenneth Branagh), dir. Oliver Parker, 1995.
O (Mekhi Phifer, Julia Stiles), dir. Tim Blake Nelson, 2001.

ALL'S WELL THAT ENDS WELL

Cole, Howard C. *The "All's Well" Story from Boccaccio to Shakespeare.* Urbana: University of Illinois Press, 1981.

Frye, Northrop. *The Myth of Deliverance: Reflections on Shakespeare's Problem Comedies.* Toronto: University of Toronto Press, 1983.

Huston, J. Dennis. " 'Some Stain of Soldier': The Functions of Parolles in *All's Well That Ends Well.*" *SQ* 21.4 (1970): 431–38.

Jardine, Lisa. "Cultural Confusions in Shakespeare's Learned Heroines." *SQ* 38.1 (1987): 1–18.

Kastan, David Scott. "*All's Well That Ends Well* and the Limits of Comedy." *ELH* 52.3 (1985): 575–89.

McCandless, David. "Helena's Bed-Trick: Gender and Performance in *All's Well That Ends Well.*" *SQ* 45.4 (1994): 449–68. Reprinted in *Gender and Performance in Shakespeare's Problem Comedies.* Bloomington: Indiana University Press, 1997.

Parker, Patricia. "*All's Well That Ends Well:* Increase and Multiply." In *Creative Imitation: New Essays on Renaissance Literature in Honor of Thomas Greene,* ed. David Quint et al. Binghamton, N.Y.: Medieval and Renaissance Texts and Studies, 1992.

Roark, Christopher. "Lavatch and Service in *All's Well That Ends Well.*" *SEL* 28.2 (1988): 241–58.

Snyder, Susan. "Naming Names in *All's Well That Ends Well.*" *SQ* 43.1 (1992): 265–79.

Sullivan, Garrett A., Jr. " 'Be this sweet Helen's knell, and now forget her': Forgetting, Memory, and Identity in *All's Well That Ends Well.*" *SQ* 50.1 (1999): 51–69.

Thomas, Vivian. "Virtue and Honor in *All's Well That Ends Well.*" In *The Moral Universe of Shakespeare's Problem Plays.* London: Croom Helm, 1987.

Tillyard, E.M.W. *"All's Well That Ends Well."* In *Shakespeare's Problem Plays*, 1950. Toronto: University of Toronto Press, 1971.

Wheeler, Richard. "Imperial Love and the Dark House: *All's Well That Ends Well*." In *Shakespeare's Development and the Problem Comedies*. Berkeley: University of California Press, 1981.

TIMON OF ATHENS

Burke, Kenneth. "*Timon of Athens* and Misanthropic Gold." In *Language as Symbolic Action: Essays on Life, Literature and Method*. Berkeley: University of California Press, 1966.

Empson, William. "Timon's Dog." In *The Structure of Complex Words*. London: Chatto and Windus, 1951.

Kahn, Coppélia. " 'Magic of Bounty': *Timon of Athens*, Jacobean Patronage, and Maternal Power." *SQ* 38 (1987): 34–57.

Kiefer, Frederick. "A Dumb Show of the Senses in *Timon of Athens*." In *In the Company of Shakespeare: Essays on English Renaissance Literature in Honor of G. Blakemore Evans*, ed. Thomas Moisan and Douglas Bruster. Madison, N.J.: Fairleigh Dickinson University Press, 2002.

Knights, L. C. *"Timon of Athens."* In *The Morality of Art*, ed. D. W. Jefferson. London: Routledge and Kegan Paul, 1969.

Paster, Gail Kern. *The Idea of the City in the Age of Shakespeare*. Athens: University of Georgia Press, 1985.

Soellner, Rolf. *Timon of Athens: Shakespeare's Pessimistic Tragedy*. Columbus: Ohio State University Press, 1979.

KING LEAR

Booth, Stephen. "On the Greatness of *King Lear*," *"King Lear,"* and *"Macbeth."* In *Indefinition and Tragedy*. New Haven, Conn.: Yale University Press, 1983.

Cavell, Stanley. "The Avoidance of Love: A Reading of *King Lear*." In *Disowning Knowledge in Six Plays of Shakespeare*. Cambridge: Cambridge University Press, 1987.

Colie, Rosalie, and F. T. Flahiff, eds. *Some Facets of "King Lear": Essays in Prismatic Criticism*. London: Heinemann, 1974.

Danby, John F. *Shakespeare's Doctrine of Nature: A Study of "King Lear."* London: Faber & Faber, 1949.

de Grazia, Margreta. "The Ideology of Superfluous Things: *King Lear* as Period Piece." In *Subject and Object in Renaissance Culture*, ed. Margreta de Grazia, Maureen Quilligan, and Peter Stallybrass. Cambridge: Cambridge University Press, 1996.

Dollimore, Jonathan. *"King Lear* (c. 1605–6) and Essentialist Humanism." In *Shakespearean Tragedy*, ed. John Drakakis. London: Longman, 1992.

Elton, William. *"King Lear" and the Gods*. San Marino, Calif.: Huntington Library, 1966.

Evans, Malcolm. "Star Wars." In *Signifying Nothing: Truth's True Content in Shakespeare*. Athens: University of Georgia Press, 1986.

Greenblatt, Stephen. "Shakespeare and the Exorcists." In *After Strange Texts: The Role of Theory in the Study of Literature*, ed. Gregory S. Jay and David L. Miller. Tuscaloosa: University of Alabama Press, 1984. Reprinted in *Shakespeare Negotiations: The Circulation of Social Energy in Renaissance England*. Berkeley: University of California Press, 1988.

Holland, Peter, ed. *King Lear and Its Afterlife. SS* 55 (2002): 1–180.

Kahn, Coppélia. "The Absent Mother in *King Lear*." In *Rewriting the Renaissance: The Discourses of Sexual Difference in Early Modern Europe*, ed. Margaret W. Ferguson, Maureen Quilligan, and Nancy J. Vickers. Chicago: University of Chicago Press, 1986.

Kott, Jan. *"King Lear,* or Endgame." In *Shakespeare Our Contemporary*, 2nd ed., trans. Boleslaw Taborski. London: Methuen, 1967.

Mack, Maynard. *"King Lear" in Our Time*. Berkeley: University of California Press, 1966.

McCoy, Richard. " 'Look upon Me, Sir': Relationships in *King Lear*." *Representations* 81.1 (2003): 46–60.

Rosenberg, Marvin. *The Masks of "King Lear."* Newark: University of Delaware Press, 1972.

Taylor, Gary, and Michael Warren, eds. *The Division of Kingdoms: Shakespeare's Revision of "King Lear."* Oxford: Clarendon Press, 1983.

Turner, Henry S. "King Lear Without: The Heath." *RD* 28 (1997): 161–93.

Urkowitz, Steven. *Shakespeare's Revision of "King Lear."* Princeton, N.J.: Princeton University Press, 1980.

FILMS AND FILM ADAPTATIONS

Korol Lir (Regimantas Adomaitis, Donatas Banionis), dir. Grigori Kozintsev, 1969.

King Lear (Paul Scofield, Jack MacGowran), dir. Peter Brook, 1971.

Ran (Tatsuya Nakadai, Akira Terao), dir. Akira Kurosawa, 1985.

King Lear (Woody Allen, Norman Mailer), dir. Jean-Luc Godard, 1987.

MACBETH

Adelman, Janet. " 'Born of Woman': Fantasies of Maternal Power in *Macbeth.*" In *Cannibals, Witches, and Divorce: Estranging the Renaissance,* ed. Marjorie Garber. Baltimore: Johns Hopkins University Press, 1987.

Booth, Stephen. "*Macbeth,* Aristotle, Definition, and Tragedy," "*King Lear,*" and "*Macbeth,*" in *Indefinition and Tragedy.* New Haven, Conn.: Yale University Press, 1983.

Bradley, A. C. "Lecture IX: *Macbeth,*" and "Lecture X: *Macbeth.*" In *Shakespearean Tragedy: Lectures on "Hamlet," "Othello," "King Lear," "Macbeth."* London: Macmillan, 1905.

Brooks, Cleanth. "The Naked Babe and the Cloak of Manliness." In *The Well-Wrought Urn: Studies in the Structure of Poetry.* New York: Harcourt, Brace, 1947.

Calderwood, James L. *If It Were Done: "Macbeth" and Tragic Action.* Amherst: University of Massachusetts Press, 1986.

Freud, Sigmund. "Some Character-Types Met with in Psycho-Analytic Work" (1916). In *Character and Culture,* ed. Philip Rieff. New York: Collier Books, 1961.

Garber, Marjorie. "*Macbeth:* The Male Medusa." In *Shakespeare's Ghost Writers: Literature as Uncanny Causality.* New York: Routledge, 1987.

Greenblatt, Stephen. "Shakespeare Bewitched." In *New Historical Literary Study: Essays on Reproducing Texts, Representing History,* ed. Jeffrey N. Cox and Larry J. Reynolds. Princeton, N.J.: Princeton University Press, 1993.

Kastan, David Scott. "*Macbeth* and the 'Name of the King.' " In *Shakespeare After Theory.* New York: Routledge, 1999.

Knights, L. C. "How Many Children Had Lady Macbeth?" In *Explorations: Essays in Criticism Mainly on the Literature of the Seventeenth Century.* New York: New York University Press, 1964.

Mullaney, Steven. "Lying Like Truth: Riddle, Representation, and Treason in Renaissance England." *ELH* 47.1 (1980): 32–47. Reprinted as "Lying Like Truth: Riddle, Representation, and Treason." In *The Place of the Stage: License, Play, and Power in Renaissance England.* Chicago: University of Chicago Press, 1988.

Neely, Carol Thomas. " 'Documents in Madness': Reading Madness and Gender in Shakespeare's Tragedies and Early Modern Culture." *SQ* 42.3 (1991): 315–38. Reprinted in *Shakespearean Tragedy and Gender,* ed. Shirley Nelson Garner and Madelon Sprengnether. Bloomington: Indiana University Press, 1996.

Orgel, Stephen. "Macbeth and the Antic Round." In *The Authentic Shakespeare, and Other Problems of the Early Modern Stage.* New York: Routledge, 2002.

Rosenberg, Marvin. *The Masks of "Macbeth."* Berkeley: University of California Press, 1978.

Sinfield, Alan. "*Macbeth:* History, Ideology and Intellectuals." *CQ* 28 (1986): 63–77.

Stallybrass, Peter. "*Macbeth* and Witchcraft." In *Focus on "Macbeth,"* ed. John Russell Brown. London: Routledge and Kegan Paul, 1982.

Zimmerman, Susan. "Duncan's Corpse." In *A Feminist Companion to Shakespeare,* ed. Dympna Callaghan. Malden, Mass.: Blackwell Publishers, 2000.

FILMS AND FILM ADAPTATIONS

Macbeth (Orson Welles, Jeanette Nolan), dir. Orson Welles, 1948.

Throne of Blood (Toshirô Mifune, Isuzu Yamada), dir. Akira Kurosawa, 1957.

Macbeth (TV) (Maurice Evans, Judith Anderson), dir. George Schaefer, 1960.

The Tragedy of Macbeth (Jon Finch, Francesca Annis), dir. Roman Polanski, 1972.

Scotland, Pa. (Maura Tierney, Christopher Walken), dir. Billy Morrissette, 2001.

ANTONY AND CLEOPATRA

Adelman, Janet. *The Common Liar: An Essay on "Antony and Cleopatra."* New Haven, Conn.: Yale University Press, 1973.

——. "Making Defect Perfection: Imagining Male Bounty in *Timon of Athens* and *Antony and Cleopatra*." In *Suffocating Mothers: Fantasies of Maternal Origin in Shakespeare's Plays, "Hamlet" to "The Tempest."* New York: Routledge, 1992.

Barroll, J. Leeds. *Shakespearean Tragedy: Genre, Tradition, and Change in "Antony and Cleopatra."* Washington, D.C.: Folger Shakespeare Library, 1984.

Bradley, A. C. "Antony and Cleopatra." In *Oxford Lectures on Poetry.* London: Macmillan, 1909.

Bushman, Mary Ann. "Representing Cleopatra." In *In Another Country: Feminist Perspectives on Renaissance Drama,* ed. Dorothea Kehler and Susan Baker. Metuchen, N.J.: Scarecrow Press, 1991.

Cantor, Paul A. *Shakespeare's Rome: Republic and Empire.* Ithaca, N.Y.: Cornell University Press, 1976.

Dollimore, Jonathan. "*Antony and Cleopatra* (c. 1607): *Virtus* Under Erasure." In *Radical Tragedy: Religion, Ideology, and Power in the Drama of Shakespeare and His Contemporaries.* Brighton, UK: Harvester, 1984.

Fitz, L. T. [Linda Woodbridge]. "Egyptian Queens and Male Reviewers: Sexist Attitudes in *Antony and Cleopatra* Criticism." *SQ* 28.3 (1977): 297–316.

Flesch, William. *Generosity and the Limits of Authority: Shakespeare, Herbert, Milton.* Ithaca, N.Y.: Cornell University Press, 1992.

Garber, Marjorie. "Fatal Cleopatra." In *Quotation Marks.* New York: Routledge, 2002.

Hall, Kim F. " 'Commerce and Intercourse': Dramas of Alliance and Trade." In *Things of Darkness: Economies of Race and Gender in Early Modern England.* Ithaca, N.Y.: Cornell University Press, 1995.

Harris, Jonathan Gil. " 'Narcissus in thy face': Roman Desire and the Difference It Fakes in *Antony and Cleopatra*." *SQ* 45.4 (1994): 408–25.

Hazlitt, William. "Cleopatra." In *Characters of Shakespeare's Plays,* 1817. Oxford: Oxford University Press, 1971.

Hughes-Hallett, Lucy. *Cleopatra: Histories, Dreams, and Distortions.* London: Bloomsbury, 1990.

James, Heather. "To Earn a Place in the Story: Resisting the *Aeneid* in *Antony and Cleopatra*." In *Shakespeare's Troy: Drama, Politics, and the Translation of Empire.* Cambridge: Cambridge University Press, 1997.

Kahn, Coppélia. "Antony's Wound." In *Roman Shakespeare: Warriors, Wounds, and Women.* New York: Routledge, 1997.

Murry, John Middleton. "North's Plutarch." In *Countries of the Mind: Essays in Literary Criticism.* Oxford: Oxford University Press, 1931.

Sprengnether, Madelon. "The Boy Actor and Femininity in *Antony and Cleopatra*." In *Shakespeare's Personality,* ed. Norman Holland, Sidney Homan, and Bernard J. Paris. Berkeley: University of California Press, 1989.

Traversi, Derek. "Antony and Cleopatra." In *Shakespeare: The Roman Plays.* Stanford, Calif.: Stanford University Press, 1963.

FILMS AND FILM ADAPTATIONS

Cleopatra (Claudette Colbert, Warren William), dir. Cecil B. DeMille, 1934.

Cleopatra (Elizabeth Taylor, Richard Burton), dir. Joseph L. Mankiewicz, 1963.

Antony and Cleopatra (Janet Suzman, Richard Johnson), dir. Trevor Nunn, 1974.

PERICLES

Archibald, Elizabeth. *Apollonius of Tyre: Medieval and Renaissance Themes and Variations, Including the Text of the "Historia Apollonii Regis Tyri" with an English Translation.* Cambridge: D. S. Brewer, 1991.

Barber, C. L. " 'Thou that beget'st him that did thee beget': Transformation in *Pericles* and *The Winter's Tale*." *SS* 22 (1969): 59–67.

Dubrow, Heather. " 'This jewel holds his building on my arm': The Dynamics of Parental Loss in *Pericles*." In *In the Company of Shakespeare: Essays on English Renaissance Literature in Honor of G. Blake-*

more Evans, ed. Thomas Moisan and Douglas Bruster. Madison, N.J.: Fairleigh Dickinson University Press, 2002.

Felperin, Howard. "The Great Miracle: *Pericles*." In *Shakespearean Romance*. Princeton, N.J.: Princeton University Press, 1972.

Frye, Northrop. "The Mythos of Summer: Romance." In *Anatomy of Criticism*. Princeton, N.J.: Princeton University Press, 1957.

Halpern, Richard. "Modernist in the Middle: The Centrality of Northrop Frye." In *Shakespeare Among the Moderns*. Ithaca, N.Y.: Cornell University Press, 1997. Esp. pp. 140–58.

Hoeniger, F. David. "Gower and Shakespeare in *Pericles*." *SQ* 33 (1982): 461–79.

Kahn, Coppélia. "The Providential Tempest and the Shakespearean Family." In *Representing Shakespeare: New Psychoanalytic Essays*, ed. Murray Schwartz and Coppélia Kahn. Baltimore: Johns Hopkins University Press, 1980.

Knight, G. W. "The Writing of *Pericles*." In *The Crown of Life: Essays in Interpretation of Shakespeare's Final Plays*. Oxford: Oxford University Press, 1947.

Leggatt, Alexander. "The Shadow of Antioch." In *Parallel Lives: Spanish and English National Drama, 1580–1680*, ed. Louise and Peter Fothergill-Payne. Lewisburg, Pa.: Bucknell University Press, 1991.

Masten, Jeffrey. "Representing Authority: Patriarchalism, Absolutism, and the Author on Stage." In *Textual Intercourse*. Cambridge: Cambridge University Press, 1997.

Mullaney, Steven. " 'All That Monarchs Do': The Obscured Stages of Authority in *Pericles*." In *The Place of the Stage: License, Play, and Power in Renaissance England*. Chicago: University of Chicago Press, 1987.

Nevo, Ruth. "The Perils of Pericles." In *The Undiscover'd Country: New Essays on Psychoanalysis and Shakespeare*, ed. B. J. Sokol. London: Free Association Press, 1993.

CORIOLANUS

Adelman, Janet. " 'Anger's My Meat': Feeding, Dependency, and Aggression in *Coriolanus*." In *Shakespeare: Pattern of Excelling Nature*, ed. David Bevington and Jay L. Halio. Newark: University of Delaware Press, 1978. Reprinted in *Representing Shakespeare: New Psychoanalytic Essays*, ed. Murray Schwartz and Coppélia Kahn. Baltimore: Johns Hopkins University Press, 1980.

Barton, Anne. "Livy, Machiavelli, and Shakespeare's *Coriolanus*." *SS* 38 (1985): 115–29.

Brecht, Bertolt. "Study of the First Scene of Shakespeare's *Coriolanus*." In *Brecht on Theatre: The Development of an Aesthetic*, ed. and trans. John Willett. New York: Hill & Wang, 1964.

Burke, Kenneth. "*Coriolanus*—and the Delights of Faction," *The Hudson Review* 19.2 (1966): 185–202. Reprinted in *Language as Symbolic Action: Essays on Life, Literature, and Method*. Berkeley: University of California Press, 1966.

Calderwood, James L. "*Coriolanus*: Wordless Meanings and Meaningless Words." *SEL* 6 (1966): 211–24.

Cantor, Paul. "Part One: *Coriolanus*." In *Shakespeare's Rome: Republic and Empire*. Ithaca, N.Y.: Cornell University Press, 1976.

Cavell, Stanley. "Who Does the Wolf Love?" *Representations* 3 (1983): 1–20. Reprinted in *Disowning Knowledge in Six Plays by Shakespeare*. Cambridge: Cambridge University Press, 1976.

Fish, Stanley E. "How to Do Things with Austin and Searle: Speech Act Theory and Literary Criticism." In *Is There a Text in This Class?: The Authority of Interpretive Communities*. Cambridge, Mass.: Harvard University Press, 1980.

Kahn, Coppélia. "Mother of Battles: Volumnia and Her Son in *Coriolanus*." In *Roman Shakespeare*. New York: Routledge, 1997.

Patterson, Annabel. " 'Speak, speak!': The Popular Voice and the Jacobean State." In *Shakespeare and the Popular Voice*. Cambridge, Mass.: Basil Blackwell, 1989.

Rabkin, Norman. *Shakespeare and the Common Understanding*. New York: Free Press, 1967.

Traversi, Derek. "*Coriolanus*." In *Shakespeare: The Roman Plays*. London: Hollis & Carter, 1963.

Williamson, Marilyn. "Violence and Gender Ideology in *Coriolanus* and *Macbeth*." In *Shakespeare Left and Right*, ed. Ivo Kamps. New York: Routledge, 1991.

FILMS AND FILM ADAPTATIONS

Coriolanus (Morgan Freeman, Gloria Footer), dir. Wilford Leach, 1979.

CYMBELINE

Adelman, Janet. "Masculine Authority and the Maternal Body: The Return to Origins in the Romances." In *Suffocating Mothers: Fantasies of Maternal Origins in Shakespeare's Plays, from "Hamlet" to "The Tempest."* New York: Routledge, 1992.

Bergeron, David M. "Shakespeare's Romances." In *Shakespeare's Romances and the Royal Family.* Lawrence: University Press of Kansas, 1985.

Harris, Bernard. " 'What's past is prologue': *Cymbeline* and *Henry VIII.*" In *Later Shakespeare,* ed. John Russell Brown and Bernard Harris. London: Edward Arnold, 1966.

Knight, G. W. "Cymbeline." In *The Crown of Life: Essays in Interpretation of Shakespeare's Final Plays.* Oxford: Oxford University Press, 1947.

Marcus, Leah "James." In *Puzzling Shakespeare: Local Reading and Its Discontents.* Berkeley: University of California Press, 1988.

Mikalachki, Jodi. "The Masculine Romance of Roman Britain: *Cymbeline* and Early Modern Nationalism." *SQ* 46.3 (1995): 301–22. Reprinted in *The Legacy of Boadicea: Gender and Nation in Early Modern England.* New York: Routledge, 1998.

Parker, Patricia. "Romance and Empire: Anachronistic *Cymbeline.*" In *Unfolded Tales: Essays on Renaissance Romance,* ed. George M. Logan and Gordon Teskey. Ithaca, N.Y.: Cornell University Press, 1989.

Skura, Meredith. "Interpreting Posthumus' Dream from Above and Below: Families, Psychoanalysis, and Literary Critics." In *Representing Shakespeare: New Psychoanalytic Essays,* ed. Murray Schwartz and Coppélia Kahn. Baltimore: Johns Hopkins University Press, 1980.

Swinburne, Algernon Charles. Section III of *A Study of Shakespeare,* 1880. London: Heinemann, 1929.

Wayne, Valerie. "The Woman's Parts of *Cymbeline.*" In *Staged Properties in Early Modern English Drama,* ed. Jonathan Gil Harris and Natasha Korda. Cambridge: Cambridge University Press, 2002.

THE WINTER'S TALE

Adelman, Janet. "Masculine Authority and the Maternal Body: The Return to Origins in the Romances." In *Suffocating Mothers: Fantasies of Maternal Origins in Shakespeare's Plays, from "Hamlet" to "The Tempest."* New York: Routledge, 1992.

Bristol, Michael. "In Search of the Bear: Spatiotemporal Form and the Heterogeneity of Economies in *The Winter's Tale.*" *SQ* 42.2 (1991): 145–67.

Colie, Rosalie. "Perspectives on Pastoral: Romance, Comedy, and Tragedy." In *Shakespeare's Living Art.* Princeton, N.J.: Princeton University Press, 1974.

Dolan, Frances E. "Finding What Has Been 'Lost': Representations of Infanticide and *The Winter's Tale.*" In *Dangerous Familiars: Representations of Domestic Crime in England, 1550–1700.* Ithaca, N.Y.: Cornell University Press, 1994.

Egan, Robert. " 'The Art Itself Is Nature': *The Winter's Tale.*" In *Drama Within Drama: Shakespeare's Sense of His Art in "King Lear," "The Winter's Tale," and "The Tempest."* New York: Columbia University Press, 1975.

Enterline, Lynn. " 'You speak a language that I understand not': The Rhetoric of Animation in *The Winter's Tale.*" *SQ* 48.1 (1997): 17–44. Reprinted in *The Rhetoric of the Body: From Ovid to Shakespeare.* Cambridge: Cambridge University Press, 2000.

Erickson, Peter. "Patriarchal Structures in *The Winter's Tale.*" *PMLA* 97.5 (1982): 819–29. Reprinted as "The Limitations of Reformed Masculinity in *The Winter's Tale,*" in *Patriarchal Structures in Shakespeare's Drama.* Berkeley: University of California Press, 1985.

Felperin, Howard. " 'Tongue-tied, our queen?': The Deconstruction of Presence in *The Winter's Tale.*" In *Shakespeare and the Question of Theory,* ed. Patricia Parker and Geoffrey Hartman. New York: Methuen, 1985.

Frey, Charles. *Shakespeare's Vast Romance: A Study of "The Winter's Tale."* Columbia: University of Missouri Press, 1980.

Frye, Northrop. "The Triumph of Time." In *A Natural Perspective: The Development of Shakespearean Comedy and Romance.* New York: Columbia University Press, 1965.

Mowat, Barbara. "Rogues, Shepherds, and the Counterfeit Distressed: Texts and Infracontexts of *The Winter's Tale* 4.3." *SSt* 22 (1994): 58–76.

Orgel, Stephen. "The Pornographic Ideal." In *Imagining Shakespeare: A History of Texts and Visions.* New York: Palgrave Macmillan, 2003.

Paster, Gail Kern. "Quarreling with the Dug, or I Am Glad You Did Not Nurse Him." In *The Body Embarrassed: Drama and the Disciplines of Shame in Early Modern Europe.* Ithaca, N.Y.: Cornell University Press, 1993.

Stockholder, Kay. "From Matter to Magic: *The Winter's Tale.*" In *Dreamworks: Lovers and Families in Shakespeare's Plays.* Toronto: University of Toronto Press, 1987.

Traub, Valerie. "Jewels, Statues, and Corpses: Containment of Female Erotic Power." *SSt* 20 (1987): 215–38. Reprinted in *Desire and Anxiety: Circulations of Sexuality in Shakespearean Drama.* New York: Routledge, 1992.

Young, David. "The Argument of Time: *The Winter's Tale.*" In *The Heart's Forest.* New Haven, Conn.: Yale University Press, 1972.

FILMS AND FILM ADAPTATIONS

The Winter's Tale (Laurence Harvey, Jane Asher), dir. Frank Dunlop, 1968.

THE TEMPEST

Auden, W. H. *The Sea and the Mirror: A Commentary on Shakespeare's "The Tempest,"* ed. Arthur Kirsch. Princeton, N.J.: Princeton University Press, 2003.

Barker, Francis, and Peter Hulme. "Nymphs and Reapers Heavily Vanish: The Discursive Con-texts of *The Tempest.*" In *Alternative Shakespeares,* ed. John Drakakis. New York: Methuen, 1985.

Bate, Jonathan. "Caliban and Ariel Write Back." *SS* 48 (1995): 155–62.

Berger, Harry, Jr. "Miraculous Harp: A Reading of Shakespeare's *Tempest.*" *SSt* 5 (1969): 253–83.

Brown, Paul. " 'This Thing of Darkness I Acknowledge Mine': *The Tempest* and the Discourse of Colonialism." In *Political Shakespeare: New Essays in Cultural Materialism,* ed. Jonathan Dollimore and Alan Sinfield. Ithaca, N.Y.: Cornell University Press, 1985.

Demaray, John G. *Shakespeare and the Spectacle of Strangeness: "The Tempest" and the Transformation of Renaissance Theatrical Forms.* Pittsburgh: Duquesne University Press, 1998.

Fiedler, Leslie. "The New World Savage as Stranger; or, 'Tis new to thee.' " In *The Stranger in Shakespeare.* New York: Stein and Day, 1972.

Graff, Gerald, and James Phelan, eds. "Sources and Contexts" section. In *The Tempest: A Case Study in Critical Controversy.* New York: Bedford/St. Martin's Press, 2000.

Greenblatt, Stephen. "Marital Law in the Land of Cockaigne." In *Shakespearean Negotiations: The Circulation of Social Energy in Renaissance England.* Berkeley: University of California Press, 1988.

Hulme, Peter. "Prospero and Caliban." In *Colonial Encounters: Europe and the Native Caribbean, 1492–1797.* New York: Routledge, 1992.

Hulme, Peter, and William H. Sherman, eds. *"The Tempest" and Its Travels.* Philadelphia: University of Pennsylvania Press, 2000.

Loomba, Ania. "Seizing the Book." In *Gender, Race, Renaissance Drama.* Manchester, UK: Manchester University Press, 1989.

Nixon, Rob. "Caribbean and African Appropriations of *The Tempest.*" *CI* 13 (Spring 1987): 557–87. Reprinted in *Politics and Poetic Value,* ed. Robert von Hallberg. Chicago: University of Chicago Press, 1987.

Orgel, Stephen. "Prospero's Wife." *Representations* 8 (1984): 1–13. Reprinted in *The Authentic Shakespeare, and Other Problems of the Early Modern Stage.* New York: Routledge, 2002.

Skura, Meredith. "Discourse and the Individual: The Case of Colonialism in *The Tempest.*" *SQ* 40.1 (1989): 42–69.

Sundelson, David. "So Rare a Wonder'd Father: Prospero's *Tempest.*" In *Representing Shakespeare: New Psycho-*

analytic Essays, ed. Murray Schwartz and Coppélia Kahn. Baltimore: Johns Hopkins University Press, 1980.

Spencer, Theodore. *Shakespeare and the Nature of Man.* New York: Macmillan, 1942.

Vaughan, Alden T., and Virginia Mason Vaughan. *Shakespeare's Caliban: A Cultural History.* Cambridge: Cambridge University Press, 1991.

FILMS AND FILM ADAPTATIONS

Forbidden Planet (Leslie Nielsen, Walter Pidgeon), dir. Fred M. Wilcox, 1956.

The Tempest (Heathcote Williams, Peter Bull), dir. Derek Jarman, 1979.

Tempest (Susan Sarandon, John Cassavetes), dir. Paul Mazursky, 1982.

Prospero's Books (John Gielgud, Michael Clark), dir. Peter Greenaway, 1991.

HENRY VIII (ALL IS TRUE)

Bergeron, David. *"HVIII."* In *Shakespeare's Romances and the Royal Family.* Lawrence: University Press of Kansas, 1985.

Cespedes, Frank V. " 'We are one in fortunes': The Sense of History in *Henry VIII.*" *ELR* 10 (1980): 413–38.

Felperin, Howard. "Tragical-Comical-Historical-Pastoral: *Cymbeline* and *Henry VIII.*" In *Shakespearean Romance.* Princeton, N.J.: Princeton University Press, 1972.

Kermode, Frank. "What Is Shakespeare's *Henry VIII* About?" In *Shakespeare: The Histories,* ed. Eugene M. Waith. Englewood Cliffs, N.J.: Prentice-Hall, 1965.

Kezar, Daniel. "Law/Form/History: Shakespeare's Verdict in *All Is True.*" *MLQ* 63 (2002): 1–30.

Knight, G. W. "Henry VIII and the Poetry of Conversion." In *The Crown of Life: Essays in Interpretation of Shakespeare's Final Plays.* London: Oxford University Press, 1947.

Kurland, Stuart M. "*Henry VIII* and James I: Shakespeare and Jacobean Politics," *SSt* 19 (1987): 203–17.

Noling, Kim H. "Grubbing Up the Stock: Dramatizing Queens in *Henry VIII.*" *SQ* 39.3 (1988): 291–306.

Patterson, Annabel. " 'All Is True': Negotiating the Past in *Henry VIII.*" In *Elizabethan Essays in Honor of S. Schoenbaum,* ed. R. B. Parker and S. P. Zitner. Newark: University of Delaware Press, 1996.

Rudnytsky, Peter L. "*Henry VIII* and the Deconstruction of History." *SS* 43 (1991): 43–57.

THE TWO NOBLE KINSMEN

Abrams, Richard. "Gender Confusion and Sexual Politics in *The Two Noble Kinsmen.*" In *Drama, Sex, and Politics,* ed. James Redmond. Cambridge: Cambridge University Press, 1985.

Bachinger, K. "Maidenheads and Mayhem: Morris-Dance Reading of W. Shakespeare's and J. Fletcher's *The Two Noble Kinsmen.*" In *English Language and Literature: Positions and Dispositions,* ed. James Hogg, Karl Hubmayer, and Dorothea Steiner. Salzburg: Institut für Anglistik und Amerikanistik der Universität Salzburg, 1990.

Beadle, Richard. "Crab's Pedigree." In *English Comedy,* ed. Michael Cordner, Peter Holland, and John Kerrigan. Cambridge: Cambridge University Press, 1994.

Bertram, Paul. *Shakespeare and "The Two Noble Kinsmen."* New Brunswick, N.J.: Rutgers University Press, 1965.

Briggs, Julia. "Tears at the Wedding: Shakespeare's Last Phase." In *Shakespeare's Late Plays: New Readings,* ed. Jennifer Richards and James Knowles. Edinburgh: Edinburgh University Press, 1999.

Bruster, Douglas. "The Jailer's Daughter and the Politics of Madwomen's Language." *SQ* 46.3 (1995): 277–300.

Frey, Charles, ed. *Shakespeare, Fletcher, and "The Two Noble Kinsmen."* Columbia: University of Missouri Press, 1989.

Masten, Jeffrey. "Between Gentlemen: Homoeroticism, Collaboration, and the Discourse of Friendship." In *Textual Intercourse: Collaboration, Authorship, and Sexualities in Renaissance Drama.* Cambridge: Cambridge University Press, 1997.

Potter, Lois. "Topicality or Politics? *The Two Noble Kinsmen,* 1613–34." In *The Politics of Tragicomedy: Shakespeare and After,* ed. Gordon McMullan and Jonathan Hope. New York: Routledge, 1992.

Rose, Mary Beth. "Transforming Sexuality: Jacobean Tragicomedy and the Reconfiguration of Private Life." In *The Expense of Spirit: Love and Sexuality in English Renaissance Drama.* Ithaca, N.Y.: Cornell University Press, 1988.

Thompson, Ann. *Shakespeare's Chaucer: A Study in Literary Origins.* Liverpool, UK: Liverpool University Press, 1978.

Wickham, Glynne. "*The Two Noble Kinsmen* or *A Midsummer Night's Dream, Part II.*" In *The Elizabethan Theatre,* vol. 7, ed. G. R. Hibbard. Hamden, Conn.: Archon Books, 1980.

TUDOR AND STUART HISTORY

Brigden, Susan. *New Worlds, Lost Worlds: The Rule of the Tudors, 1485–1603.* New York: Penguin, 2002.

Collinson, Patrick. *The Elizabethan Puritan Movement.* Oxford: Oxford University Press, 1990.

———, ed. *The Sixteenth Century, 1483–1603.* Oxford: Oxford University Press, 2002.

Cressy, David. *Birth, Marriage, and Death: Ritual, Religion, and the Life-Cycle in Tudor and Stuart England.* Oxford: Oxford University Press, 1999.

Daniell, David. *The Bible in English: Its History and Influence.* New Haven, Conn.: Yale University Press, 2003.

Durston, Christopher. *James I.* New York: Routledge, 1993.

Guy, John. *Tudor England.* Oxford: Oxford University Press, 1990.

Hindle, Steve. *The State and Social Change in Early Modern England, 1550–1640.* Basingstoke, UK: Macmillan, 2002.

Kishlansky, Mark. *A Monarchy Transformed: Britain, 1603–1714.* New York: Penguin, 1996.

Lockyer, Roger. *James VI and I.* London: Longman, 1998.

MacCulloch, Diarmaid. *The Later Reformation in England, 1547–1603.* New York: Palgrave, 2001.

Peck, Linda Levy, ed. *The Mental World of the Jacobean Court.* Cambridge: Cambridge University Press, 1991.

Somerset, Anne. *Elizabeth I.* New York: Anchor, 2003.

Starkey, David. *Elizabeth: The Struggle for the Throne.* New York: HarperCollins, 2001.

Strachey, Lytton. *Elizabeth and Essex: A Tragic History,* 1928. New York: Vintage, 1975.

Wrightson, Keith. *English Society, 1580–1680.* New Brunswick, N.J.: Rutgers University Press, 1985.

ELIZABETHAN AND JACOBEAN THEATER

Bate, Jonathan, and Russell Jackson, eds. *Shakespeare: An Illustrated Stage History.* Oxford: Oxford University Press, 1996.

Bentley, G. E. *The Jacobean and Caroline Stage.* 7 vols. Oxford: Clarendon Press, 1941–68.

Bradbrook, M. C. *The Rise of the Common Player: A Study of Actor and Society in Shakespeare's England.* Cambridge, Mass.: Harvard University Press, 1962.

Brown, John Russell. *Shakespeare's Plays in Performance.* New York: Applause Books, 1993.

Chambers, E. K. *The Elizabethan Stage.* 4 vols. Oxford: Clarendon Press, 1923.

Dessen, Alan. *Elizabethan Stage Conventions.* Cambridge: Cambridge University Press, 1984.

———. *Recovering Shakespeare's Theatrical Vocabulary.* Cambridge: Cambridge University Press, 1995.

Foakes, R. A., and R. T. Rickert, eds. *Illustrations of the English Stage, 1580–1642.* Stanford, Calif.: Stanford University Press, 1985.

Grote, David. *The Best Actors in the World: Shakespeare and His Acting Company.* Westport, Conn.: Greenwood Press, 2002.

Gurr, Andrew. *Playgoing in Shakespeare's London.* Cambridge: Cambridge University Press, 1987.

———. *The Shakespearean Stage, 1574–1642.* Cambridge: Cambridge University Press, 1970.

———. *The Shakespearian Playing Companies.* Oxford: Oxford University Press, 1996.

Gurr, Andrew, and Mariko Ichikawa. *Staging in Shakespeare's Theatres.* Oxford: Oxford University Press, 2000.

Harbage, Alfred. *Shakespeare and the Rival Traditions.* New York: Macmillan, 1952.

———. *Shakespeare's Audience.* New York: Columbia University Press, 1941.

————. *Theatre for Shakespeare.* Toronto: University of Toronto Press, 1955.

Hodges, C. Walter. *Enter the Whole Army: A Pictorial Study of Shakespearean Staging, 1576–1616.* Cambridge: Cambridge University Press, 1999.

Ingram, William. *The Business of Playing: The Beginnings of the Adult Professional Theater in Elizabethan London.* Ithaca, N.Y.: Cornell University Press, 1992.

Kinney, Arthur. *Shakespeare by Stages: An Historical Introduction.* Malden, Mass.: Blackwell Publishers, 2003.

Leggatt, Alexander. *Jacobean Public Theatre.* New York: Routledge, 1992.

Orgel, Stephen. *The Illusion of Power: Political Theater in the English Renaissance.* Berkeley: University of California Press, 1976.

Shapiro, Michael. *Children of the Revels: The Boy Companies of Shakespeare's Time and Their Plays.* New York: Columbia University Press, 1977.

Smith, Irwin. *Shakespeare's Blackfriars Playhouse: Its History and Its Design.* New York: New York University Press, 1964.

Styan, J. L. *Shakespeare's Stagecraft.* Cambridge: Cambridge University Press, 1967.

Weimann, Robert. *Author's Pen and Actor's Voice: Playing and Writing in Shakespeare's Theatre,* ed. Helen Higbee and William West. Cambridge: Cambridge University Press, 2000.

SHAKESPEARE AND AUTHORSHIP

Appleton, Elizabeth. *Edward de Vere and the War of Words: A Dramatic Discovery in the Field of Sixteenth-Century Writings Raises Questions About Shakespeare's Authorship and Reveals Hitherto Unknown Motives and Political Values in the Age of Elizabeth I.* Toronto: Elizabethan Press, 1985.

Brame, Michael, and Galina Polova. *Shakespeare's Fingerprints.* Vashon Island, Wash.: Adonis Editions, 2002.

Clark, Eva Lee Turner. *Hidden Allusions in Shakespeare's Plays: A Study of the Oxford Theory Based on the Records of Early Court Revels and Personalities of the Times.* New York: W. F. Payson, 1931.

Dobson, Michael. *The Making of a National Poet: Shakespeare, Adaptation and Authorship, 1660–1769.* Oxford: Oxford University Press, 1992.

Friedman, William F., and Elizabeth Friedman. *The Shakespearean Ciphers Examined.* Cambridge: Cambridge University Press, 1957.

Garber, Marjorie. "Shakespeare's Ghost Writers." In *Shakespeare's Ghost Writers: Literature as Uncanny Causality.* New York: Routledge, 1987.

"The Ghost of Shakespeare—Discussion over Authorship of Shakespeare's Plays." *Harper's Magazine,* April 1999, pp. 39–62.

Looney, J. Thomas. *"Shakespeare" Identified in Edward De Vere, Seventeenth Earl of Oxford, and the Poems of Edward De Vere,* 3rd ed. Port Washington, N.Y.: Kennikat Press for Minos Pub. Co., 1975.

McManaway, James G. *The Authorship of Shakespeare.* Washington, D.C.: Folger Shakespeare Library, 1962.

Nolen, Stephanie, ed. *Shakespeare's Face.* Toronto: Knopf Canada, 2002.

Ogburn, Charlton. *The Mysterious William Shakespeare: The Myth and the Reality.* New York: Dodd, Mead, 1984.

————. *Shakespeare and the Man of Stratford.* New York: Shakespeare Oxford Society, 1964.

Ogburn, Charlton, and Dorothy Ogburn. *Shakes-peare: The Man Behind the Name.* New York: Morrow, 1962.

Schoenbaum, Samuel. *Shakespeare's Lives.* Oxford: Clarendon Press, 1970.

————. *William Shakespeare: A Documentary Life.* Oxford: Oxford University Press, 1975.

Sobran, Joseph. *Alias Shakespeare: Solving the Greatest Literary Mystery of All Time.* New York: Free Press, 1997.

Vickers, Brian. *"Counterfeiting" Shakespeare: Evidence, Authorship, and John Ford's Funerall Elegye.* Cambridge: Cambridge University Press, 2002.

Whalen, Richard F. *Shakespeare—Who Was He?: The Oxford Challenge to the Bard of Avon.* Westport, Conn.: Praeger, 1994.

BOOKS AND THE PRINTING PRESS

Andersen, Jennifer, and Elizabeth Sauer, eds. *Books and Readers in Early Modern England.* Philadelphia: University of Pennsylvania Press, 2002.

de Grazia, Margreta, and Peter Stallybrass. "The Materiality of the Shakespearean Text." *SQ* 44.3 (1993): 255–83.

Eisenstein, Elizabeth. *The Printing Press as an Agent of Change.* Cambridge: Cambridge University Press, 1979.

Febvre, Lucien, and Henri-Jean Martin. *The Coming of the Book: The Impact of Printing, 1450–1800,* trans. David Gerard, ed. Geoffrey Nowell-Smith and David Wootton. London: N.L.B., 1976.

Finkelstein, David, and Alistair McCleery, eds. *The Book History Reader.* New York: Routledge, 2002.

Johns, Adrian. *The Nature of the Book: Print and Knowledge in the Making.* Chicago: University of Chicago Press, 1998.

Kastan, David Scott. *Shakespeare and the Book.* Cambridge: Cambridge University Press, 2001.

Masten, Jeffrey. *Textual Intercourse: Collaboration, Authorship, and Sexualities in Renaissance Drama.* Cambridge: Cambridge University Press, 1997.

Peters, Julie Stone. *The Theatre of the Book, 1480–1880: Print, Text, and Performance in Europe.* Oxford: Oxford University Press, 2000.

Wells, Stanley, and Gary Taylor. *William Shakespeare: A Textual Companion.* Oxford: Clarendon Press, 1987.

ACKNOWLEDGMENTS

The process of writing this book began at least as early as the mid-1970s, when, as a young assistant professor, I was given the opportunity to teach the Shakespeare lecture course at Yale. I taught a version of that course at Haverford College, and, in 1981, when I came to Harvard, I began lecturing in Emerson Hall, Paine Hall, and, ultimately, Sanders Theater, teaching undergraduates, graduate students, and—to my great pleasure—many alumni and members of the general public who began to attend these open lectures regularly and to share with me their own love of Shakespeare. From that time to this I have benefited from the thoughts, questions, suggestions, and wise counsel of many generations of Shakespearean critics and scholars. Some who were undergraduates or graduate students when I started to lecture on Shakespeare are now tenured scholars. To list those to whom I am indebted for a lifetime of conversations about Shakespeare's plays would fill a volume comparable in bulk to this one. The Suggestions for Further Reading section recommends books and articles by many of these critics. One of the great satisfactions of academic life is the realization that you are part of a dialogue that goes back hundreds of years and forward to the next generation and beyond.

For their invaluable assistance in the conception and preparation of the present volume, I want to thank, especially, a few friends and colleagues who have devoted much time and care in order to help bring it about. Marcie Bianco has been the best editorial assistant: imaginable, energetic, resourceful, wise, unflappable, and meticulous. Sarah Wall-Randell read through the final draft and provided generous and thoughtful commentary. I am also grateful to Wendy Hyman, Holger Schott Syme, Giulio Pertile, and Gustavo Secchi for research and editorial suggestions. Mary Halpenny-Killip and Shannon Greaney in the Harvard Humanities Center were enormously helpful in facilitating the necessary back-and-forth involved in such a substantial project. Erroll McDonald has been a superbly supportive, intuitive, and visionary editor; his faith in the idea of this book has been crucial at every stage. My literary agent, Beth Vesel, who has worked with me on many books over the years, has, as always, been a mainstay as this one moved forward. My greatest debt, to Barbara Johnson, is recorded in the dedication to this book.

Shakespeare After All. After centuries of discussion, production, and analysis; after decades of new and exciting work in the latter part of the twentieth century; after the reading and rereading, by Shakespearean scholars and aficionados, of literary criticism, history, and theory; after all the vital, essential, and transformative discussion and debate, we return, always, to Shakespeare's plays. Critics come and critics go; so do literary movements and theories. But the rich world of the plays—plays approached, of necessity, differently in every generation—remains. As readers and audiences well know, it is both a delight and an education to spend an hour, a day, or a year with these works. To spend a lifetime with them has been a privilege, a pleasure, and a gift.

GENERAL INDEX

Page numbers in **bold type** refer to main discussions of plays.

945

CHARACTER INDEX

ALSO BY MARJORIE GARBER

*"Illuminating. . . . Garber upends, tilts and shakes the house
of our cultural imagination."* —Newsday

SEX AND REAL ESTATE
Why We Love Houses

"When you stop to think about it, buying and selling a
house is a lot like dating," says Marjorie Garber, "the same
quickening of the pulse, the lingering around the phone,
willing it to ring." In this witty and incisive study of how
we relate to the ideas of house and home, Garber makes a
host of ingenious parallels between house love and human
love: the house as mother (it loves you as you are); the
Cinderella house (a fixer-upper to be transformed with
love); the house as beloved (the dream date and the dream
mate). And at a time when we've never been so obsessed
with real estate, Garber pronounces it a new form of yup-
pie pornography. Brilliantly drawing on cultural references
such as Chaucer, Waugh, and Woolf, as well as movies and
shelter magazines, *Sex and Real Estate* is as provocative as
it is pleasurable, enriching our understanding of the homes
and houses we covet.

Cultural Studies/0-385-72039-4

ANCHOR BOOKS
Available at your local bookstore, or call toll-free to order:
1-800-793-2665 (credit cards only)